Progress in
Neural Information Processing

Springer

Berlin
Heidelberg
New York
Barcelona
Budapest
Hong Kong
London
Milan
Paris
Santa Clara
Singapore
Tokyo

Progress in
Neural Information Processing

Proceedings of the International Conference on Neural Information Processing
Hong Kong, September 24-27, 1996

Editors: Shun-ichi Amari, Lei Xu, Lai-Wan Chan, Irwin King and Kwong-Sak Leung

Volume 1

Springer

Editors

Shun-ichi Amari
RIEKN
Frontier Research Program
Wako-shi, Hirosawa 2-1
Saitama 351-01
Japan

Lei Xu, Lai-Wan Chan, Irwin King and
  Kwong-Sak Leung
Department of Computer Science & Engineering
The Chinese University of Hong Kong
Shatin, New Territories
Hong Kong

Co-sponsors of the conference:

Library of Congress Cataloging-in-Publication Data

International Conference on Neural Information Processing (3rd : 1996
  : Hong Kong)
    Progress in neural information processing : ICONIP'96 :
proceedings of the International Conference on Neural Information Processing,
Hong Kong, 24-27 September 1996 / Shun-ichi Ameri ... [et al.].
      p.   cm.
  "Third annual conference of the Asian Pacific Neural Network Assembly"--
  ISBN 9813083034 (vol. 1 - softcover)
        9813083042 (vol. 2 - softcover)
  1. Neural networks (Computer science)--Congresses. I. Amari, Shun'ichi.
II. Asian Pacific Neural Network Assembly. III. Title.
QA76.87.I573   1996
006.3--dc20   96–27442
                                                    CIP

ISBN 981-3083-03-4 (Volume 1)
ISBN 981 3083-05-0 (Set)

Cover designed by Dr. LOW Boon Toh

Typesetting: Camera-ready by authors
5 4 3 2 1 0

Foreword

The 1996 International Conference on Neural Information Processing is the third annual conference of the Asian Pacific Neural Network Assembly. For the first time, it is held in Hong Kong.

Hong Kong is known to the world as a bustling city where free enterprise is practiced to its extremes and competition goes almost uninhibited. It is a financial center, a communications center, and a shipping center in the Asian pacific region. It is becoming an information technology center as well.

To stay competitive, businesses and industries must adopt the latest technologies not only to make their operations more efficient and their staff more productive, but also to help their leaders make decisions based on predictive models constructed from information gathered over the world. Hong Kong businesses and industries are no exception. Indeed, Hong Kong is always among the first to acquire the newest computer, communication and information processing systems, and to use the most up-to-date technology, including neural network techniques, to improve a company's bottom line.

It is therefore most appropriate that the Asian Pacific Neural Network Assembly chose Hong Kong as the site of its 1996 annual conference. The subject matter will be of interest not only to academics and engineers but also to persons in the business and industrial sectors. More important, Hong Kong now has a broadly-based core of neural network enthusiasts among the universities, who constituted the organizing committee of the conference. We are also fortunate to have recruited a large number of supporters all over the world to serve on the various committees. It was their hard work, often over sleepless nights, that had brought about the conference. We want to take this opportunity to thank them all. Their names and affiliations are shown in the Conference Program.

We especially want to express our appreciation to the staff of the Chinese University of Hong Kong for their boundless contributions to the organization of this conference: Professor Lei Xu for his leadership of the Program Committee; Professor Lai-wan Chan and Professor K. S. Leung as co-chairs and Professor Irwin King as Secretary of the Organizing Committee.

Lastly, we want to invite you all to come to Hong Kong, to experience the energy and fervor that is Hong Kong, and to see for yourselves what is happening as she transforms herself from a Crown colony of United Kingdom to a Special Administrative Region of China.

Omar Wing   Shun-ichi Amari
General Co-chair   General Co-chair
Chinese University of Hong Kong   Tokyo University

Preface

The 1996 International Conference on Neural Information Processing (ICONIP'96) is organized by The Engineering Faculty of the Chinese University of Hong Kong, IEEE Computer Chapter (Hong Kong Section), Hong Kong Computer Society, ACM; and in cooperation with IEEE Neural Networks Council, International Neural Network Society, European Neural Network Society, Japanese Neural Network Society, China Neural Networks Council. On behave of the Organizing Committee of the we would like to thank their support to this conference. In addition, we acknowledge the distinguished sponsors of ICONIP'96; Silicon Graphics Ltd, Sun Microsystems, Automated Systems (HK) Ltd. Mr Fritz Chiu and Ms Mary Chan of the Hong Kong Productivity Council have provided their expertise in the management of the conference, which we like to acknowledge here.

We would like to specially thank the following people. The General Co-chairs of the conference, Professors Omar Wing and Shun-ichi Amari have been very supportive and have provided a lot of helpful advice to us from the early beginning. The Conference Program Co-chairs, Professors Lei Xu, Michael Jordan, Erkki Oja and Mitsuo Kawato, have been spent a lot of efforts to make this conference a qualitative one. Professor Lei Xu is also the source of the driving force to bring ICONIP'96 to Hong Kong. Professor Ke Chen gave us much help on the conference program and on the preparation of this book, whom we like to acknowledge.

Last but not the least, thanks should also be given to all members of the Organizing Committee, especially our secretary, Professor Irwin King. They, whom we like to give our special acknowledgement, have devoted many days of their precious time to this conference Without their voluntary help, ICONIP'96 would not be a success.

<table>
<tr><td>Kwong-Sak Leung
Organizing Co-chair
Chinese University of Hong Kong</td><td>Lai-Wan Chan
Organizing Co-chair
Chinese University of Hong Kong</td></tr>
</table>

A Message from the Program Committee

The goal of ICONIP'96 is to provide a forum for researchers and engineers from academia and industry to meet and to exchange ideas on the latest developments in neural information processing. The conference consists of one-day tutorial focusing on Financial Engineering by well known experts in the field and a three-day program with only four parallel sessions. The overall program covers the major topics in neural information processing and reflects the latest progress with a good balance between scientific studies and industrial applications, as well as featured neural information processing approaches on Financial Engineering.

The conference contains a high quality contributed program and a very strong invited program. For the contributed program, we received 314 submissions from 33 countries, including Asia-Pacific areas, Europe, North and South America. Each submitted paper has been sent to three experts in the related fields from all over the world for reviewing. With their rigorously and timely efforts, a high quality technical program has been achieved with around 60% overall acceptance rate (20% in oral presentation, 20% in spotlight presentations, 20% in poster presentation). The spotlight presentation is a poster presentation plus a 5 minutes oral presentation which highlights the contribution of the poster paper. For the invited program, we have 5 keynote speakers, 3 honored speakers, and 22 invited speakers by well known international neural information processing scientists and experts. The invited program is also featured by 8 special sessions on current interesting topics. Each special session organizer is invited by the Program Committee and the success of each special session is completely due to the hard efforts of each organizer.

Using this chance, we would like to specially thank our general chairs, Professors Omar Wing and Shun-ichi Amari, for their leadership and support. We also would like to specially thank our keynote speakers, Professors Shun-ichi Amari, Yaser Abu-Mostafa, Leo Breiman, Christoph von der Malsburg, Erkki Oja; our honored speakers, Professors Rolf Eckmiller, Mitsuo Kawato, Kunihiko Fukushima; our tutorial lecturers, Professors John Moody, A-P. N. Refenes, Halbert White, our 22 invited speakers and 8 special session organizers as well as all the advisory committee members, program committee members, and reviewers for their invaluable contributions and strong efforts to the ICONIP'96 program. Particularly, we would like to express our heartfelt gratitude to the organizing committee co-chairs, Professors Lai-wan Chan and K. S. Leung, and secretary, Professor Irwin King, for their great efforts on many laborious jobs.

Last but not least, we greatly appreciate all the authors, speakers, session chairs as well as all the members of the organizing committee–it is them who make the conference a success.

Lei Xu	Michael Jordan	Erkki Oja	Mitsuo Kawato
Program Co-chair	Program Co-chair	Program Co-chair	Program Co-chair
Chinese U. of HK	MIT	Helsinki U. of Tech.	ATR

General Co-Chairs

Omar Wing, CUHK
Shun-ichi Amari, Tokyo University

Advisory Committee

International

Yaser Abu-Mostafa, Caltech
Michael Arbib, University of Southern California
Leo Breiman, UC Berkeley
Jack Cowan, University of Chicago
Rolf Eckmiller, University Bonn
Jerome Friedman, Stanford University
Stephen Grossberg, Boston University
Robert Hecht-Nielsen, HNC
Geoffrey Hinton, University of Toronto
Anil Jain, Michigan State University
Teuvo Kohonen, Helsinki University of Tech.
Sun-Yuan Kung, Princeton University
Robert Marks, II, University of Washington
Thomas Poggio, MIT
Harold Szu, US Naval SWC
John Taylor, King's College London
David Touretzky, CMU
Christopher von der Malsburg, Ruhr-University of Bochum
David Willshaw, Edinburgh University
Lofti Zadeh, UC Berkeley

Asia-Pacific Region

Marcelo H. Ang Jr, NUS, Singapore
Sung-Yang Bang, POSTECH, Pohang
Hsin-Chia Fu, NCTU, Hsinchu
Toshio Fukuda, Nagoya University, Nagoya
Kunihiko Fukushima, Osaka University, Osaka
Zhenya He, Southeastern University, Nanjing
Marwan Jabri, University of Sydney, Sydney
Nikola Kasabov, University of Otago, Dunedin
Yousou Wu, Tsinghua University, Beijing

Hong Kong Region

N.V. Balasubramanian, CityU
Richard Chen, CityU
Paul Cheung, HKU
Francis Chin, HKU
Ernest Lam, HKBU
Agnes Mak, HKCS
Vincent Shen, HKUST

Wan Chi Siu, HKPU
Chak-Kuen Wong, CUHK
Kam Fai Wong, CUHK
Daniel Yeung, HKPU

Organizing Committee

L.W. Chan (Co-Chair), CUHK
K.S. Leung (Co-Chair), CUHK
D.Y. Yeung (Finance), HKUST
C.K. Ng (Publication), CityUHK
A. Wu (Publication), CityUHK
B.T. Low (Publicity), CUHK
M.W. Mak (Local Arr.), HKPU
C.S. Tong (Local Arr.), HKBU
T. Lee (Registration), CUHK
K.P. Chan (Tutorial), HKU
H.T. Tsui (Industry Liaison), CUHK
I. King (Secretary), CUHK

Program Committee

Co-Chairs
Lei Xu, CUHK
Michael Jordan, MIT
Erkki Oja, Helsinki University of Technology
Mitsuo Kawato, ATR

Members
Yoshua Bengio, University of Montreal
Jim Bezdek, University of West Florida
Chris Bishop, Aston University
Leon Bottou, Neuristique
Gail Carpenter, Boston University
Laiwan Chan, CUHK
Huishen Chi, Peking University
Peter Dayan, MIT
Kenji Doya, ATR
Scott Fahlman, CMU
Francoise Fogelman, SLIGOS
Lee Giles, NEC Research Institute
Michael Hasselmo, Harvard University
Kurt Hornik, Technical University of Wien
Yu Hen Hu, University of Wisconsin - Madison
Jeng-Neng Hwang, University of Washington
Nathan Intrator, Tel-Aviv University

Larry Jackel, AT&T Bell Lab
Adam Kowalczyk, Telecom Australia
Soo-Young Lee, KAIST
Todd Leen, Oregon Grad. Institute
Cheng-Yuan Liou, National Taiwan University
David MacKay, Cavendish Lab
Eric Mjolsness, UC San Diego
John Moody, Oregon Graduate Institute
Nelson Morgan, ICSI
Steven Nowlan, Synaptics
Michael Perrone, IBM Watson Lab
Ting-Chuen Pong, HKUST
Paul Refenes, London Business School
David Sanchez, University of Miami
Hava Siegelmann, Technion
Ah Chung Tsoi, University of Queensland
Benjamin Wah, University of Illinois
Andreas Weigend, Colorado University
Ronald Williams, Northeastern University
John Wyatt, MIT
Alan Yuille, Harvard University
Richard Zemel, CMU
Jacek Zurada, University of Louisville

List of Reviewers

Most of the 44 program committee members and the following additional reviewers:

Andreas Andreou	Oliver Mihatsch
Sung-Yang Bang	Itraru Nagayama
Ke Chen	Ralph Neuneier
Yizong Cheng	Klaus Obermayer
Richard Coggins	Dirk Ormoneit
Bernd Fritzke	Joel Ratsaby
Kunihiko Fukushima	Steve Rehfuss
Michael Haft	Jiong Ruan
Michael Herrmann	Matt Saffell
Lester Ingber	Juergen Schmidhuber
Masumi Ishikawa	Sara A. Solla
Marwan Jabri	Ah-Hwee Tan
Arun Jagota	Michiaki Taniguchi
Fan Jin	Chong Sze Tong
Nikola Kasabov	Hung Tat Tsui
Dmitri Kaznachey	Jun Wang
Irwin King	Chris Williams
Kai Pui Lam	Kam Fai Wong
Chi-Sing Leung	Lizhong Wu
Kwong Sak Leung	Youshou Wu
Tsungnan Lin	Yeung Yam
Boon Toh Low	Howard Hua Yang
Bao-Liang Lu	Dit-Yan Yeung
Jinwen Ma	Bai-ling Zhang
Jianchang Mao	David Dapeng Zhang
Ronny Meir	Jieyu Zhao
Igor Milosavlevich	Yi Xin Zhong

Contents, Volume 1

Speech and Signal Processing *(Oral Presentation)* 281

Recurrent Networks, Automata and Dynamics *(Poster Presentation)* . . 555

Associative Memory *(Oral Presentation)* 579

Contents, Volume 2

Hybrid Systems and Applications *(Poster Presentation)*

Learning Theories and Algorithms

(Oral Presentation)

Information Geometry of Neural Networks
— New Bayesian Duality Theory —

Shun-ichi Amari

RIKEN Frontier Research Program, RIKEN,
Wako-shi, Hirosawa 2-1, Saitama 351-01, Japan
amari@zoo.riken.go.jp

Abstract— **Information geometry is a method of analyzing the geometrical structure of a family of information systems. A family of neural networks forms a neuromanifold. It is important to study its geometrical structures for elucidating its capabilities of information processing. The present paper proposes a new mathematical theory of dynamic interactions of a lower and a higher neural systems by feedback and feedforward connections. Here, a new duality structure is introduced in the Bayesian framework from the point of view of information geometry.**

1 Introduction

Theoreticians have so far speculated some basic but primitive mechanisms of information processing in the brain. We can mention, among others, the autocorrelation associative memory model or the Boltzmann machine (its stochastic version), and the formation of topological maps by self-organization, and so on. However, it is believed that a fundamental role is played by a much more complex hierarchical structure: It is, for example, dynamic interactions of a lower and a higher systems connected by feedforward and feedback connections. Recent physiological findings by Miyashita's group (Miyashita [1988]) and by Tanaka's group (Ito et al. [1994]) also suggest importance of such a hierarchical structure. This was also emphasized theoretically by Kawato et al. [1991], by Mumford [1991, 1992], and by many others. On the ohter hand, there are new structured theoretical models such as the mixture of expert nets, Helmholtz machine (Dayan, Hinton and Neal [1995]) and Ying-Yang machine (Xu [1996]). These are proposed in relation to learning or self-organization, and we need to construct models resposible for dynamic interactions of activation.

The present paper is the first attempt towards the construction of a new theoretical framework accountable for such dynamic interactions of a lower and a higher systems. It is based on the Bayesian statistics and information geometry. To this end, a new dualistic framework is given to Bayesian statistics, and the *EM* or *em* type dynamical interactions are introduced in the manifold of neural activities. This is only a first step and a lot of works are necessary in future in this direction.

2 Bayesian Duality in Exponential Families

Let us consider an exponential family of probability distributions of a vector random variable $\boldsymbol{x} = (x_i)$ parameterized by the natural vector parameter $\boldsymbol{\theta} = (\theta^i)$:

$$p(\boldsymbol{x}|\boldsymbol{\theta}) = \exp\{\boldsymbol{\theta} \cdot \boldsymbol{x} - \tilde{k}(\boldsymbol{x}) - \psi(\boldsymbol{\theta})\}. \tag{1}$$

The set of all such distribution forms a manifold S which is equipped with the Riemannian metric $g_{ij}(\boldsymbol{\theta})$ given by the Fisher information matrix and moreover which is equipped with dually flat affine connections (Amari [1985, 1995], Amari et al. [1992]). There are two fundamental coordinate systems $\boldsymbol{\theta}$ and $\boldsymbol{\eta}$ in it. Here the natural parameter $\boldsymbol{\theta}$ is e-affine, and the expectation parameter

$$\boldsymbol{\eta} = E_{\boldsymbol{\theta}}[\boldsymbol{x}] \tag{2}$$

is m-affine, where $E_{\boldsymbol{\theta}}$ denotes the expectation with respect to $p(\boldsymbol{x}|\boldsymbol{\theta})$.

Bayesian statistics introduces a prior distribution $p(\boldsymbol{\theta})$ in the parameter space S, by considering $\boldsymbol{\theta}$ as a random variable chosen subject to $p(\boldsymbol{\theta})$. We can then consider a joint probability distribution

$$p(\boldsymbol{x}, \boldsymbol{\theta}) = \exp\{\boldsymbol{\theta} \cdot \boldsymbol{x} - \psi(\boldsymbol{\theta}) - \tilde{k}(\boldsymbol{x}) + \mu(\boldsymbol{\theta})\} \tag{3}$$

where $\mu(\boldsymbol{\theta}) = \log p(\boldsymbol{\theta})$. The previous $p(\boldsymbol{x}|\boldsymbol{\theta})$ is the conditional distribution therefrom. The marginal distribution of $\boldsymbol{x}$ is given by

$$p(\boldsymbol{x}) = \int p(\boldsymbol{x}, \boldsymbol{\theta}) d\boldsymbol{\theta}. \tag{4}$$

We then have the conditional distribution $p(\boldsymbol{\theta}|\boldsymbol{x})$ of $\boldsymbol{\theta}$ conditioned on observed $\boldsymbol{x}$ which is also called a posterior distribution. An abuse use of notations such as $p(\boldsymbol{x})$, $p(\boldsymbol{\theta})$, $p(\boldsymbol{\theta}|\boldsymbol{x})$ etc. will be taken in the paper where the meaning is clear from the notation of variables. The conditional distribution is

$$p(\boldsymbol{\theta}|\boldsymbol{x}) = \exp\{\boldsymbol{x} \cdot \boldsymbol{\theta} - k(\boldsymbol{\theta}) - \tilde{\psi}(\boldsymbol{x})\}, \tag{5}$$

where

$$k(\boldsymbol{\theta}) = \psi(\boldsymbol{\theta}) - \mu(\boldsymbol{\theta})$$

$$\tilde{\psi}(\boldsymbol{x}) = \tilde{k}(\boldsymbol{x}) + \tilde{\mu}(\boldsymbol{x}),$$
$$\tilde{\mu}(\boldsymbol{x}) = \log p(\boldsymbol{x}).$$

By considering $\boldsymbol{x}$ as a parameter vector to specify the distributions of $\boldsymbol{\theta}$, the set of conditional probabilities $\{p(\boldsymbol{\theta}|\boldsymbol{x})\}$ can be regarded again as an exponential family, where the natural parameter is given by $\tilde{\boldsymbol{\theta}} = \boldsymbol{x}$, and the expectation parameter is by

$$\tilde{\boldsymbol{\eta}} = E_{\boldsymbol{x}}[\boldsymbol{\theta}], \tag{6}$$

the conditional expectaion of $\boldsymbol{\theta}$ with respect to the posterior distribution corresponding to an observed $\boldsymbol{x}$. The set of such distributions forms another dually flat manifold $\tilde{S}$, provided $\boldsymbol{x}$ is a continuous vector variable.

It is our intuitive idea that $\boldsymbol{\theta}$ and $\boldsymbol{x}$ represent the neural acitivities of a higher-order system and a lower-order system, respectively. Hence, $p(\boldsymbol{x}|\boldsymbol{\theta})$ and $p(\boldsymbol{\theta}|\boldsymbol{x})$ represent, respectively, the dynamic interactions caused by feedback and feedforward connections.

Before explaining the idea in more detail, we give a duality between S and $\tilde{S}$. There is a natural bijective mapping between them that maps a point $\boldsymbol{\theta} = (\theta^i)$ in S to $\tilde{\boldsymbol{\theta}} = (\tilde{\theta}^i)$ in $\tilde{S}$ by $\tilde{\boldsymbol{\theta}} = \boldsymbol{\theta}$, or that maps $\boldsymbol{\eta} = (\eta_i)$ to $\boldsymbol{x} = (x_i)$ in $\tilde{S}$ by $\boldsymbol{x} = \boldsymbol{\eta}$. Here, it should be noted that the natural and expectation parameters are interchanged by the mapping. This implies that the e-geodesic (m-geodesic) is mapped to m-geodesic (e-geodesic).

We summarize the roles of e- and m-projections in S. Let us consider a subanifold M in S. It is written in the form

$$M = \{\boldsymbol{\theta}(\boldsymbol{u})\}$$

where $\boldsymbol{u}$ is the parameters (coordinates) inside M, whose dimensionality is maller than that of S. Given a point $\boldsymbol{\theta}$ in S, let $\hat{\boldsymbol{u}}$ be the point in M that minimizes the KL-divergence

$$D[\boldsymbol{\theta} : \boldsymbol{\theta}(\hat{\boldsymbol{u}})] = \min_{\boldsymbol{\theta}(\boldsymbol{u}) \in M} D[\boldsymbol{\theta} : \boldsymbol{\theta}(\boldsymbol{u})],$$

where

$$D[\boldsymbol{\theta} : \boldsymbol{\theta}'] = E_{\boldsymbol{\theta}} \left[\log \frac{p(\boldsymbol{x}|\boldsymbol{\theta})}{p(\boldsymbol{x}|\boldsymbol{\theta}')} \right]. \tag{7}$$

Then, the m-geodesic connecting $\boldsymbol{\theta}$ and $\boldsymbol{\theta}(\hat{\boldsymbol{u}})$ is orthogonal to M at $\boldsymbol{\theta}(\hat{\boldsymbol{u}})$. This implies that $\boldsymbol{\theta}(\hat{\boldsymbol{u}})$ is the m-geodesic projection of $\boldsymbol{\theta}$ to M. In terms of statistics, $\hat{\boldsymbol{u}}$ gives the maximum likelihood estimator when the observed data point is $\boldsymbol{\theta}$.

On the contrary, let D be another submanifold of S defined by $D = \{\boldsymbol{\eta}(\boldsymbol{v})\}$ in terms of the η-coordinates. Here, $\boldsymbol{v}$ is the inner coordinates in D. Given a point $\boldsymbol{\eta}$ in S, let $\hat{\boldsymbol{v}}$ be the point in D that minimizes $D[\boldsymbol{\eta}(\boldsymbol{v}) : \boldsymbol{\eta}]$, that is,

$$\min_{\boldsymbol{\eta}(\boldsymbol{v}) \in D} D[\boldsymbol{\eta}(\boldsymbol{v}) : \boldsymbol{\eta}] = D[\boldsymbol{\eta}(\hat{\boldsymbol{v}}) : \boldsymbol{\eta}].$$

Then, $\boldsymbol{\eta}(\hat{\boldsymbol{v}})$ is given by the conditional expectation of $\boldsymbol{x}$ with respect to $\boldsymbol{\eta}$

$$\boldsymbol{\eta}(\hat{\boldsymbol{v}}) = E_{\boldsymbol{\eta}}[\boldsymbol{x}|\boldsymbol{x} \in D]$$

under a certain condition (Amarı [1995]).

Similar discussions hold in $\tilde{S}$ where the roles of m and e are interchanged.

3   Dual structure in layered Boltzmann machines

Let us consider a Boltzmann machine consisting of mutually connected lower and higher networks. Let $\boldsymbol{x}$ be an activity pattern of the lower machine (sensory machine) and $\boldsymbol{y}$ be an activity pattern of the higher machine (concept machine). Here, the components x_i and y_i take on 0 and 1, but we consider their activation rates (or averages over the ensembles of neurons playing the same role) so that they take real values between 0 and 1. We first consider the Boltzmann machine of symmetric connections where matrix $W^X = (W_{ij}^X)$ denotes the connections between nerons i and j in the lower machine, $W^Y = (W_{ij}^Y)$ those in the higher machine, and $W^{XY} = (W_{ij}^{XY})$ those between the two machines. Then, the stationary distribution of activities in the machine is given by

$$p(\boldsymbol{x}, \boldsymbol{y}) = \exp\{\boldsymbol{y}'W^{XY}\boldsymbol{x} + W^X \cdot X + W^Y \cdot Y - \psi(W)\}, \tag{8}$$

where we used the notation

$$W^X \cdot X = \frac{1}{2}\boldsymbol{x}'W^X\boldsymbol{x} \tag{9}$$

and so on, $'$ being the transposition.

By putting $\boldsymbol{\theta}(\boldsymbol{y}) = (W^{XY}\boldsymbol{y})$, we define the joint probability of $\boldsymbol{x}$ and $\boldsymbol{\theta}(\boldsymbol{y})$ given by

$$p(\boldsymbol{x}, \boldsymbol{\theta}) = \exp\{\boldsymbol{\theta} \cdot \boldsymbol{x} - k(\boldsymbol{\theta}) - \tilde{k}(\boldsymbol{x})\}; \tag{10}$$

where

$$k(\boldsymbol{\theta}) = -W^Y \cdot Y + \frac{1}{2}\psi(W), \tag{11}$$

$$\tilde{k}(\boldsymbol{x}) = -W^X \cdot X + \frac{1}{2}\psi(W). \tag{12}$$

This distribution is derived from the Boltzmann machine. Moreover, this defines the two conditional distributions $p(\boldsymbol{x}|\boldsymbol{\theta})$ and $p(\boldsymbol{\theta}|\boldsymbol{x})$ of the exponential type. They represent the dynamic interactions of neural activities between the two systems.

Let us consider the case where the number of neurons is smaller in the higher-order system. Then, the set of $\boldsymbol{\theta}$ determined by the neural activities $\boldsymbol{y}$ of the higher system forms an e-flat submanifold M in S,

$$M = \{\boldsymbol{\theta}(\boldsymbol{y})| \; \boldsymbol{\theta}(\boldsymbol{y}) = W^{XY}\boldsymbol{y}\}. \tag{13}$$

The parameter $\boldsymbol{\theta}(\boldsymbol{y})$, which is the activations of the higher system, specifies the probabilities of activations of $\boldsymbol{x}$ by the conditional probability $p(\boldsymbol{x}|\boldsymbol{\theta})$. This represents the effects by the feedback connections.

The lower system receives sensory intputs (or inputs from a further lower system). Let $\boldsymbol{s}$ be the sensory input. The lower system analyzes it, but the sensory inputs are usually imperfect and ambiguous. Let us consider the set of all possible excitations $\boldsymbol{x}$ in the system compatible with $\boldsymbol{s}$. This is the data set $D_{\boldsymbol{s}}$ specified by $\boldsymbol{s}$,

$$D_{\boldsymbol{s}} = \{\boldsymbol{x}| \; \boldsymbol{x} \text{ is compatible with } \boldsymbol{s}\}. \tag{14}$$

$D_{\boldsymbol{s}}$ is a submanifold of S. Let $\boldsymbol{h}$ shows the activities of hidden neurons in the lower system which are not uniquely determined by $\boldsymbol{s}$. More precisely $\boldsymbol{s}$ and $\boldsymbol{h}$ can be any parameters to determine $\boldsymbol{x} = \boldsymbol{x}(\boldsymbol{s},\boldsymbol{h})$, where $\boldsymbol{s}$ is observable but $\boldsymbol{h}$ is hidden and is to be determined by dynamics.

When $\boldsymbol{s}$ is observed, dynamical interactions take place in the lower system to obtain plausible $\boldsymbol{x} \in D_{\boldsymbol{s}}$. On the other hand, the first candidate $\boldsymbol{x}$ stimulates the higher system by the stochastic dynamics $p\{\boldsymbol{\theta}(\boldsymbol{y})|\boldsymbol{x}\}$ to generate the higher-order interpretation of $\boldsymbol{s}$ giving a concept corresponding to it.

The higher-order system has its inner connections to form an associative memory system. There are a number of peaks of stationary probabilities in it, each corresponding to a concept or a memorized pattern. This is the stochastic version of the autoassociative memory model. The activities $\boldsymbol{y}$ thus aroused from $\boldsymbol{x}$ in turn stimulate the lower system from the higher-order point of view to give a new $\boldsymbol{x}$. Thus the dynamical interactions take place, where the feedforward flow generates quickly a hypothetical conceptual recognition and the feedback flow checks the concept thus recognized to complete the lower data. This is the interpretation given by many researchers (for example, Kawato and Inui, Mumford).

Now we give its mathematical formulation in terms of information geometry.

4 Dynamical procedures of e- and m-projections

A. feedforward estimation

Given a sensory information $\boldsymbol{s}$, the lower net generates the first rough pattern $\boldsymbol{x} \in D_{\boldsymbol{s}}$. From this, the first candidate $\boldsymbol{\theta}(\boldsymbol{y}) \in M$ should be searched for quickly. The maximum posterior estimate $\boldsymbol{\theta}(\hat{\boldsymbol{y}})$ is the one that maximizes the posterior distribution

$$p(\boldsymbol{\theta}|\boldsymbol{x}) = p(\boldsymbol{\theta})p(\boldsymbol{x}|\boldsymbol{\theta})/p(\boldsymbol{x}),$$

or equivalently the one that maximizes

$$\log p(\boldsymbol{\theta}) + \log p(\boldsymbol{x}|\boldsymbol{\theta}) \tag{15}$$

under the constraint $\boldsymbol{\theta} \in M$. The maximum likelihood estimator $\hat{\boldsymbol{y}}_{\mathrm{mle}}$ is the one that maximizes the second term, and is given by m-projecting $\boldsymbol{x}$ to M in the space S. The first term transforms $\hat{\boldsymbol{y}}_{\mathrm{mle}}$ further into the maximum posterior $\hat{\boldsymbol{y}}$ in M by using the dynamical flow $\nabla \log(\boldsymbol{y})$ in M. This second transformation depends only on $\hat{\boldsymbol{y}}_{\mathrm{mle}}$ in the case that M is e-flat. Since the concepts are highly stable equilibrium points, it is expected that $\hat{\boldsymbol{y}}$ has a sharp distribution. Hence, $\hat{\boldsymbol{y}}$ is very close to the conditional expectation of $\boldsymbol{y}$ with respected to the posterior $p(\boldsymbol{\theta}|\boldsymbol{x})$. This latter is given by e-projecting $\boldsymbol{x}$ to M in $\tilde{S}$.

B. Feedback estimation

Given a candidate $\boldsymbol{\theta}(\boldsymbol{y})$, $p\{\boldsymbol{x}|\boldsymbol{\theta}(\boldsymbol{y})\}$ is rather broadly distributed. Since there are many neurons playing similar roles in the lower system, it is natural to think that the conditional expectation

$$E_{\boldsymbol{\theta}(\boldsymbol{y})}[\boldsymbol{x}|\boldsymbol{x} \in D_{\boldsymbol{s}}] \tag{16}$$

is realized by the feedback interactions. This minimizes

$$\arg\min_{\boldsymbol{x} \in D_{\boldsymbol{s}}} D[\boldsymbol{x}|\boldsymbol{\theta}(\boldsymbol{y})], \tag{17}$$

and is given by e-projecting $\boldsymbol{\theta}(\boldsymbol{y})$ to $D_{\boldsymbol{s}}$.

This dynamical process of feedforward and feedback interactions is sketched in S as follows.

1) Given $\boldsymbol{s}$, generate one $\boldsymbol{x} \in D_{\boldsymbol{s}}$.

2) m-project $\boldsymbol{x}$ to S and make necessary corrections by the associative dynamics of the higher system to give $\boldsymbol{\theta}(\boldsymbol{y})$.

3) e-project this $\boldsymbol{\theta}(\boldsymbol{y})$ to $D_{\boldsymbol{s}}$ to give a new $\boldsymbol{x} \in D_{\boldsymbol{s}}$.

4) Repeat 2) and 3) until it converges.

The convergence of the process will be analyzed geometrically. We can prove that the above procedure minimizes the function

$$F(\boldsymbol{x}, \boldsymbol{\theta}) = D\{\boldsymbol{x}|\boldsymbol{\theta}(\boldsymbol{y})\} - \log p(\boldsymbol{\theta}) \tag{18}$$

under the condition that $\boldsymbol{x} \in D_{\boldsymbol{s}}$ and $\boldsymbol{\theta} \in M$.

5   Conclusions

A primitive but new promising idea is given to the dynamic interactions of lower and higher systems in terms of information geometry. The Boltzmann machine is used for defining the conditional probabilities $p(\boldsymbol{x}|\boldsymbol{\theta})$ and $p(\boldsymbol{\theta}|\boldsymbol{x})$ of their interactions. However, it is not plausible to assume symmetric connections $W_{ij}^{XY} = W_{ji}^{YX}$ between the lower and higher systems. It is possible to define two conditional distributions even when the symmetry does not hold. This gives a more realistic framework.

There remain many researches to be done along this line. One is to give more rigorous mathematial descriptions. Another is to show interesting properties of this system in more detail. It is important to apply the framework to give palusible models to physiological findings such as Miyashita's and Tanaka's.

References

[1] S. Amari. *Differential-Geometrical Methods in Statistics, Lecture Notes in Statistics*, vol.**28**, Springer, 1985.

[2] S. Amari. Information geometry of the EM and em algorithms for neural networks, *Neural Networks*, **8**, No.9, 1379–1408, 1995.

[3] S. Amari, K. Kurata, H. Nagaoka. Information geometry of Boltzmann machines, *IEEE Trans. on Neural Networks*, **3**, 260–271, 1992.

[4] P. Dayan, G. E. Hinton, R. M. Neal and R. S. Zemel. The Helmholtz machine, *Neural Computation*, **7**, 889–904, 1995.

[5] M. Ito, I. Fujita, H. Tamura, K. Tanaka. Processing of contrast polarity of visual images in inferotemporal cortex of the Macaque Monkey, *Cerebral Cortex*, **5**, 499–508, 1994.

[6] M. Kawato, T. Inui, S. Hongo and H. Hayakawa. Computational theory and neural network models of interaction between visual cortical areas, *ATR Technical Report*, **TR-A-0105**, ATR, Kyoto, 1991.

[7] Y. Miyashita. Neuronal correlate of visual associative long-term memory in the primate temporal cortex, *Nature*, **335**, 817–820, 1988.

[8] D. Mumford. On the computational architecture of the neocortex, I The role of the thalamo-cortical loop, *Biological Cybernetics*, **65**, 135–145, 1991.

[9] D. Mumford. On the computational architecture of the neocortex, II The role of cortico-cortical loops, *Biological Cybernetics*, **66**, 241–251, 1992.

[10] L. Xu. A unified learning scheme: Bayesian-Kullback Ying-Yang machine, *Advances in Neural Information Processing Systems*, **8**, eds., David S. Touretzky, Michael Mozer, Michael Hasselmo, MIT Press, Cambridge MA, 1996.

Blind Signal Separation by Neural Networks

Erkki Oja and Aapo Hyvärinen
Helsinki University of Technology, Laboratory of Computer and Information Science
Rakentajanaukio 2C, 02150 Espoo, Finland
email `first.second@hut.fi`

***Abstract*— Neural learning rules for the problem of Independent Component Analysis (ICA) and Blind Source Separation are reviewed. The rules are unsupervised and can be implemented in a multilayer ICA network. Special emphasis is on new algorithms by which the independent source signals are found one at a time. A new computationally efficient fixed-point rule is discussed.**

1   Introduction

Independent Component Analysis (ICA) [5, 13] is a signal processing technique whose goal is to express a set of random variables as linear combinations of statistically independent component variables. The main applications are in blind source separation and blind deconvolution. In the simplest form of ICA [5], we observe m scalar random variables $x(1), ..., x(m)$ which are assumed to be linear combinations of n unknown components $s(1), ...s(n)$ which are zero-mean and *mutually statistically independent*. In addition, we must assume $n \leq m$. Let us arrange the observed variables $x(i)$ into a vector $\mathbf{x} = (x(1), x(2), ..., x(m))^T$ and the component variables $s(i)$ into a vector $\mathbf{s}$, respectively; then the linear relationship is given by

$$\mathbf{x} = \mathbf{As} \tag{1}$$

Here, $\mathbf{A}$ is an unknown $m \times n$ matrix of full rank, called the mixing matrix. The basic problem of ICA is then to estimate the original components $s(i)$ using only the mixtures $x(j)$ or, equivalently, to estimate the mixing matrix $\mathbf{A}$. The fundamental restriction of the model is that we can only estimate non-Gaussian independent components (except if just one of the independent components is Gaussian). Moreover, neither the energies nor the signs of the independent components can be estimated, because any constant multiplying an independent component in eq. (1) could be cancelled by dividing the corresponding column of the mixing matrix $\mathbf{A}$ by the same constant. For mathematical convenience, we define here that the independent components $s(i)$ have unit variance. This makes the (non-Gaussian) independent components unique, up to their signs. Note that no order is defined between the independent components.

In *blind source separation* [3, 13], the observed values of $\mathbf{x}$ correspond to a realization of an m-dimensional discrete-time signal $\mathbf{x}_t$, $t = 1, 2, ...$ Then the components $s_t(i)$ are called *source signals*; in the following, we shall adopt this term. The source signals are usually original, uncorrupted signals or noise sources.

The problem of estimating the matrix $\mathbf{A}$ in eq. (1) can be somewhat simplified by performing a preliminary *sphering* or prewhitening of the data $\mathbf{x}$ [5]. The observed vector $\mathbf{x}$ is linearly transformed to a vector $\mathbf{v} = \mathbf{Ux}$ such that its elements $v(i)$ are mutually uncorrelated and all have unit variance. Thus the correlation matrix of $\mathbf{v}$ equals unity: $E\{\mathbf{vv}^T\} = \mathbf{I}$. This transformation is always possible and can be accomplished by classical Principal Component Analysis. At the same time, the dimensionality of the data should be reduced so that the dimension of the transformed data vector $\mathbf{v}$ equals n, the number of independent components. This also has the effect of reducing noise. After the transformation we have

$$\mathbf{v} = \mathbf{Ux} = \mathbf{UAs} = \mathbf{Bs} \tag{2}$$

where $\mathbf{B} = \mathbf{UA}$ is an *orthogonal* matrix due to our assumptions on the components $s(i)$: it holds $E\{\mathbf{vv}^T\} = \mathbf{B}E\{\mathbf{ss}^T\}\mathbf{B}^T = \mathbf{BB}^T = \mathbf{I}$. Thus we have reduced the problem of finding an arbitrary full-rank matrix $\mathbf{A}$ to the simpler problem of finding an orthogonal matrix $\mathbf{B}$, which then gives $\mathbf{s} = \mathbf{B}^T\mathbf{v}$. Because of this inverse relation, the matrix $\mathbf{B}$ is called the (orthogonal) *separating matrix*. If the i-th column of $\mathbf{B}$ is denoted $\mathbf{b}(i)$, then the i-th independent component or source signal can be computed from the observed and whitened signal vector $\mathbf{v}$ as $s(i) = \mathbf{b}(i)^T\mathbf{v}$.

The current algorithms for Independent Component Analysis in blind source separation and blind deconvolution can be roughly divided into two categories. The algorithms in the first category [3, 5] rely on batch computations minimizing or maximizing some relevant criterion function. Perhaps the most

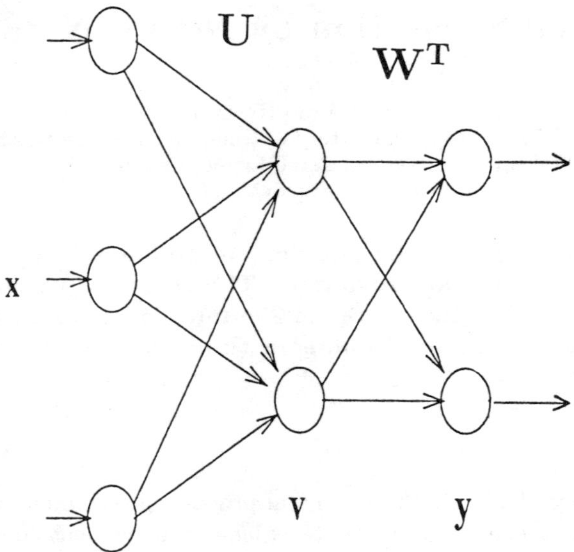

Figure 1: The ICA Neural Network

commonly used criterion function is based on the *kurtosis* which is defined for a zero-mean scalar random variable u as

$$\mathrm{kurt}(u) = E\{u^4\} - 3E^2\{u^2\}. \tag{3}$$

Note that this becomes $E\{u^4\} - 3$ if the variance of u equals 1. The problem with these batch algorithms is that they usually require quite complex matrix or tensorial operations. The second category contains adaptive algorithms often based on stochastic gradient methods, which may have implementations in neural networks [1, 2, 4, 6, 8, 9, 11, 12, 13, 17, 21]. In Section 2 we give a brief review of ICA separating algorithms, concentrating on the neural learning rules. Section 3 covers a set of recently introduced one-unit learning rules, which find the source signals one at a time and have the advantage that signals of both positive and negative kurtosis can be found using essentially the same learning rule. We also review a novel approach [10] for performing the computations needed in ICA using a very simple, yet highly efficient, fixed-point iteration scheme.

2   The ICA Neural Network and Learning Rules

2.1   The ICA Network

The network of Fig.1 is used in context with our ICA learning algorithms [14]. The two layers perform the two processing tasks required for ICA, whitening of the input signals and consequent separation. Both tasks can be performed using a number of alternative algorithms. The starting point is a sequence of mixture vectors $\mathbf{x}_t, t = 1, 2, \ldots$ obeying the model (1).

2.2   Whitening of the Input Data

Prior to inputting the data vectors $\mathbf{x}_t$ to the network, they are made zero-mean by subtracting the mean. This normalizes the data with respect to the first-order statistics. The effects of second-order statistics can be removed by whitening the data. This is done by applying the transformation $\mathbf{v}_t = \mathbf{U}\mathbf{x}_t$, where $\mathbf{U}$ is an $n \times m$ whitening matrix that simultaneously reduces the dimension of the data vectors from the number of mixtures m to the number of original source signals n if $m > n$.

PCA is often used for whitening, because one can then simultaneously compress information optimally in the mean-square error sense and filter possible Gaussian noise. The PCA whitening matrix is given by $\mathbf{U} = \mathbf{D}^{-1/2}\mathbf{E}^T$, where the $n \times n$ diagonal matrix $\mathbf{D} = \mathrm{diag}[\lambda(1), \ldots, \lambda(n)]$ and the $m \times n$ matrix $\mathbf{E} = [\mathbf{c}(1), \ldots, \mathbf{c}(n)]$ consist of the n first eigenvalues (in decreasing order) and the corresponding unit eigenvectors of the data covariance matrix $E\{\mathbf{x}_t\mathbf{x}_t^T\}$.

Alternatively, one can estimate the principal eigenvectors by a neural learning rule. For this purpose, many well-established algorithms are available [18]. An on-line algorithm for computing the eigenvalues was given in [20].

2.3 Learning the Separating Matrix

The most central task in ICA is learning the separating matrix $\mathbf{B}$. In [22], one of the authors proposed some nonlinear extensions of the PCA subspace learning rule that can be applied to learning the orthogonal separating matrix $\mathbf{B}$. Consider the *nonlinear subspace rule*:

$$\mathbf{W}_{t+1} = \mathbf{W}_t + \mu_t[\mathbf{v}_t - \mathbf{W}_t\mathbf{g}(\mathbf{y}_t)]\mathbf{g}(\mathbf{y}_t^T) \tag{4}$$

with

$$\mathbf{y}_t = \mathbf{W}_t^T\mathbf{v}_t, \quad \mathbf{g}(\mathbf{y}_t) = (g[y_t(1)], ..., g[y_t(n)])^T. \tag{5}$$

It has been analyzed in [19] how the weight matrix $\mathbf{W}_t$ in rule (4) converges to a (scaled) separating matrix $\mathbf{B}$, when the scalar function g in eq. (5) is a suitable nolinearity, e.g. the tanh function in the case when all the source signals have a negative kurtosis. Then the output vector $\mathbf{y}_t$ becomes the vector of sources $\mathbf{s}_t$.

Wang et al [24] developed another so-called *bigradient algorithm*:

$$\mathbf{W}_{t+1} = \mathbf{W}_t + \mu_t\mathbf{v}_t\mathbf{g}(\mathbf{y}_t^T) + \gamma_t\mathbf{W}_t(\mathbf{I} - \mathbf{W}_t^T\mathbf{W}_t). \tag{6}$$

Here γ_t is another gain parameter, usually about 0.5 or 1 in practice. The bigradient algorithm is a stochastic gradient algorithm for maximizing or minimizing the criterion $\sum_{j=1}^{n} \mathrm{E}\{G[y(j)]\}$, with $G' = g$, under the constraint that the weight matrix $\mathbf{W}$ must be orthogonal. The algorithm (6) is discussed in more detail in [24].

Other neural network alternatives for estimating the entire separating matrix are the seminal Jutten-Herault algorithm [13] and some more recently suggested algorithms e.g, by Cardoso and Laheld [16], Amari and Cichocki [1], and Bell and Sejnowski [2]. For more details and for the mathematical analysis on the algorithms, see [14].

3 One-Unit Learning Rules

Some of the learning rules for finding the separating matrix can also be used in the case when the number of neurons in the second layer of the ICA network of Fig. 1 is smaller than the number of sources n. Consider the nonlinear subspace rule (4). Figure 2, first row, shows a set of $n = 6$ images of natural scenes or objects that are now understood as 6 independent source signals. An image can be presented as a scalar signal $s_t(i), i = 1, ..., 6$ when the pixel gray levels are scanned row by row. Six mixtures were artificially made according to eq. (1) using a randomly chosen mixing matrix $\mathbf{A}$. These are shown on the second row of Fig. 2. These were now used as inputs in a set of ICA networks that have 6 units in the whitening layer but a varying number of output units. The number of output units varied from 6 to 1, and the outputs of a trained network are shown on the consequent rows of Fig. 2. The nonlinear function g in the learning rule (4) was the tanh function. It turned out that the result is a subset of the source signals, depending on the initial choice of the weight matrix.

The nonlinear subspace learning rule was analyzed in [19] in the case that there is only *one* column in the weight matrix, i.e., one output neuron with weight vector $\mathbf{w}$, in which case (4) becomes

$$\mathbf{w}_{t+1} = \mathbf{w}_t + \mu_t[\mathbf{v}_t g(\mathbf{w}_t^T\mathbf{v}_t) - \mathbf{w}_t g^2(\mathbf{w}_t^T\mathbf{v}_t)] \tag{7}$$

Assuming suitable nonlinear functions g, it was shown that the columns $\mathbf{b}(i)$ of the separating matrix, scaled by some scalar multipliers, are all locally asymptotically stable points of the related averaged differential equation. When the algorithm is started from the basin of attraction of one of the stable points, it will converge there.

However, the subspace learning rule may be unnecessarily complicated in the case of only one neuron, and so it is useful to search for simpler alternatives. Following [11, 12], these are reviewed here.

3.1 Separating One Source of Negative Kurtosis

Let us suppose, as above, that the observed signal $\mathbf{v}_t$ is sphered. Then we can separate one of the sources with *negative kurtosis* by using the following learning rule for the weight vector $\mathbf{w}$ of a neuron:

$$\mathbf{w}_{t+1} = \mathbf{w}_t + \mu_t[\mathbf{v}_t g(\mathbf{w}_t^T\mathbf{v}_t) - \mathbf{w}_t] \tag{8}$$

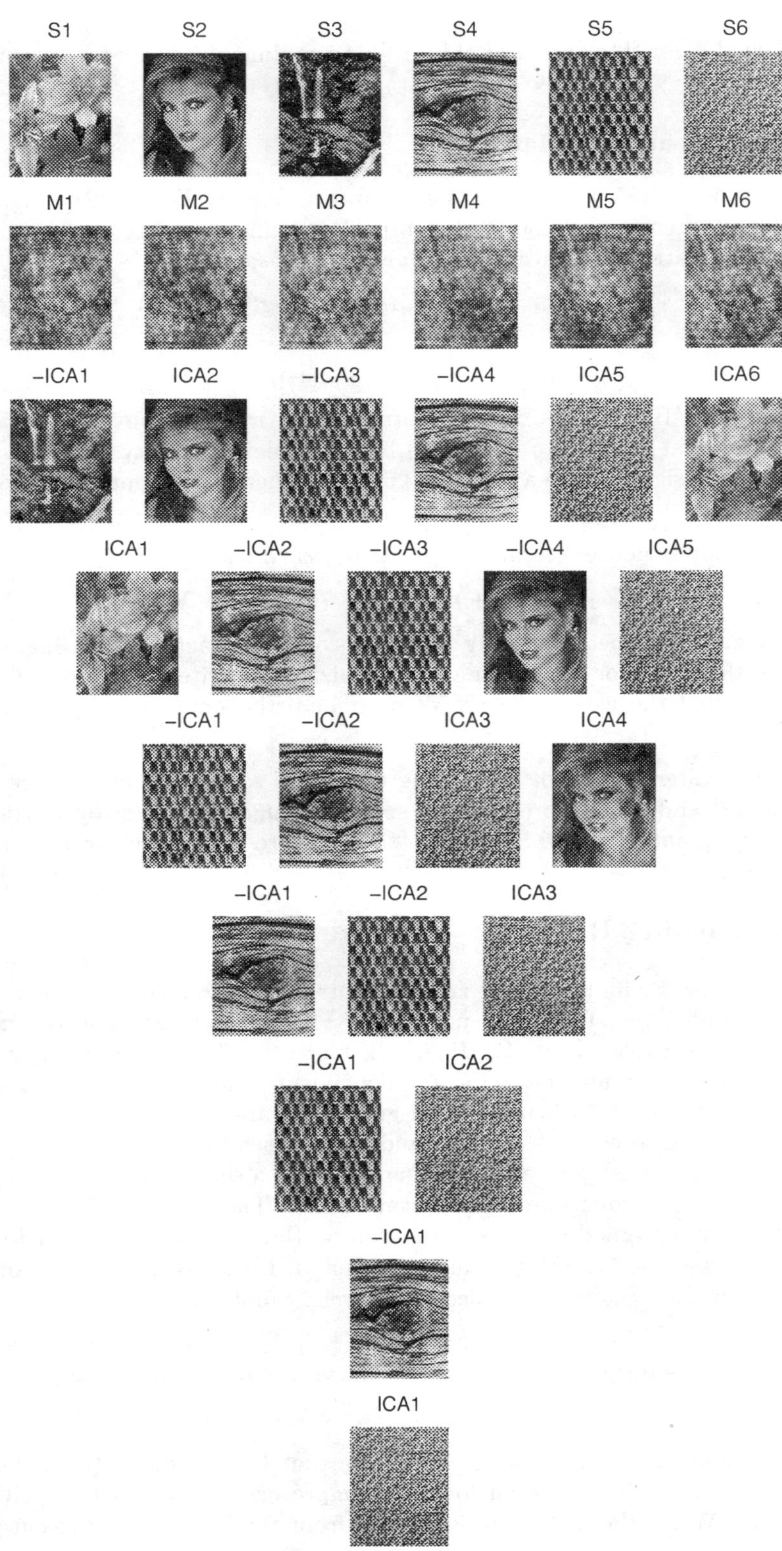

Figure 2: A signal separation experiment (see text). The separated source signals (independent components) have been re-scaled to the image gray level range, and in some cases the sign has been reversed

The function g is either the tanh function, or a polynomial that locally approximates a sigmoidal function, $g(t) = at - bt^3$ with $a > 1$ and $b > 0$. This is perhaps the simplest possible stable Hebbian learning rule for a nonlinear Perceptron.

Because of the simplicity of the learning rule (8), it can be analyzed in much more detail than most other ICA algorithms. It turns out that the weight vector $\mathbf{w}_t$ converges, up to a multiplicative constant, to one of the columns $\mathbf{b}(i)$ of the separating matrix [11, 12]. The convergence can be shown to be global. Thus, after convergence of the algorithm, we know one (randomly chosen) of the sources $s(i)$. The only condition for convergence is that one of the sources must have negative kurtosis; no other hypotheses on the distributions of $s(i)$ are needed.

The convergence of algorithm (8) is based on the fact that it can be interpreted as a stochastic gradient descent to minimize the function

$$J(\mathbf{w}) = -E\{G(\mathbf{w}^T\mathbf{v})\} - \frac{1}{2}\|\mathbf{w}\|^2$$

Where $G'(t) = g(t)$. Computing G for $g(t) = at - bt^3$, we get

$$J(\mathbf{w}) = \frac{b}{4}E\{(\mathbf{w}^T\mathbf{v})^4\} + \frac{1}{2}(1-a)\|\mathbf{w}\|^2 = \frac{b}{4}\,\mathrm{kurt}(\mathbf{w}^T\mathbf{v}) + [\frac{3b}{4}\|\mathbf{w}\|^4 + \frac{1}{2}(1-a)\|\mathbf{w}\|^2]. \tag{9}$$

It has been pointed out by several authors (see e.g. [5, 6, 17]) that minimization and maximization of kurtosis is closely related to separating components in ICA. This can easily be seen as follows. Denote again by $\mathbf{B}$ the (unknown) orthogonal separating matrix for which $\mathbf{s} = \mathbf{B}^T\mathbf{v}$. Denote $\mathbf{z} = \mathbf{B}^T\mathbf{w}$, whereby $\mathbf{w} = \mathbf{Bz}$. We have then

$$\mathrm{kurt}(\mathbf{w}^T\mathbf{v}) = \mathrm{kurt}(\mathbf{z}^T\mathbf{s}) = \sum z(i)^4\,\mathrm{kurt}[s(i)]. \tag{10}$$

If the norm of $\mathbf{w}$ is kept constant, the norm of $\mathbf{z}$ is also constant. Then it is rather obvious that the local minima of $\mathrm{kurt}(\mathbf{w}^T\mathbf{v})$ under the constraint $\|\mathbf{w}\| = \|\mathbf{z}\| = const$ are attained when $\mathbf{z} = \mathbf{e}(i)$, i.e. the i-th canonical base vector, where i is the index of one of the sources with negative kurtosis. But this corresponds to $\mathbf{w} = \mathbf{b}(i)$.

It is therefore not surprising that algorithm (8) works: it is in fact searching for a direction that minimizes the kurtosis of the scalar product $\mathbf{w}^T\mathbf{v}$. The second term in brackets in (9) only depends on the norm and is independent of the direction that $\mathbf{w}$ is pointing in. This implies that at a minimum of J, $\mathbf{w}$ points in a direction that minimizes the first term, which is the kurtosis of $\mathbf{w}^T\mathbf{v}$. The second term in (9) at the same time prevents $\mathbf{w}$ from becoming infinitely small (recall that $a > 1$). A rigorous mathematical analysis of the convergence of algorithm (8) has been presented in [12].

3.2 Separating One Source of Positive Kurtosis

To separate one of the sources with *positive kurtosis*, we can use the following simple learning rule [11]:

$$\mathbf{w}_{t+1} = \mathbf{w}_t + \mu_t[b\mathbf{v}_t(\mathbf{w}_t^T\mathbf{v}_t)^3 - \|\mathbf{w}_t\|^4\mathbf{w}_t] \tag{11}$$

where $b > 0$. This is the counterpart of algorithm (8) for sources with positive kurtosis. As above, the convergence of algorithm (11) is based on the fact that it can be interpreted as a stochastic gradient descent to *maximize* the function

$$J(\mathbf{w}) = \frac{b}{4}E\{(\mathbf{w}^T\mathbf{v})^4\} - \frac{1}{3}\|\mathbf{w}\|^6 \tag{12}$$

Thus, algorithm (11) works because of the same principles as algorithm (8). For details, see [12].

3.3 The General Case

The algorithms of the two preceding subsections can be unified to the general mathematical form

$$\mathbf{w}_{t+1} = \mathbf{w}_t + \mu_t[\sigma\mathbf{v}_tg(\mathbf{w}_t^T\mathbf{v}_t) - f(\|\mathbf{w}_t\|^2)\mathbf{w}_t] \tag{13}$$

where f is a scalar function, and $\sigma = \pm 1$ is a sign that determines whether we are minimizing or maximizing kurtosis. The function g is a polynomial $g(t) = at - bt^3$ with $a \geq 0$ and $b > 0$. Clearly, algorithms (8) and (11) are special cases of algorithm (13).

This algorithm is still a stochastic gradient descent. The function to be minimized is

$$J(\mathbf{w}) = \sigma[\frac{a}{2}\|\mathbf{w}\|^2 - \frac{b}{4}E\{(\mathbf{w}^T\mathbf{v})^4\}] - F(\|\mathbf{w}\|) \tag{14}$$

with $F'(t) = f(t)$.

For general a, b, and f, we have presented a theorem in [11], giving a set of conditions under which $\mathbf{w}_t$ in algorithm (13) will converge, up to a constant, to one of the columns $\mathbf{b}(i)$ of the separating matrix $\mathbf{B}$. No hypotheses on the distributions of $s(i)$ (in addition to the basic ones given in the Introduction) are needed, except that σ and f must be chosen according to the signs of the kurtoses of the source signals. Using the theorem, we can easily find other one-unit separation algorithms; see [11, 12].

3.4 Fixed-Point Learning Rules

The advantage of neural learning rules like (8) and (11) is that the inputs $\mathbf{v}_t$ can be used in the algorithm at once, without collecting a batch of input data. A resulting trade-off, however, is that the convergence is slow, and depends on a good choice of the learning rate sequence μ_t. A bad choice of the learning rate can, in practice, destroy convergence. Therefore, some ways to make the learning radically faster and more reliable may be needed. The *fixed-point iteration algorithms* are such an alternative. A fixed-point algorithm for ICA was proposed and analyzed by the authors in [10] as follows.

Consider the general neural learning rule (13) in which $\sigma = \pm 1$ and g and f are scalar functions. To illustrate the general idea of fixed point iterations, take $g(t) = t^3$. First, the fixed points $\mathbf{w}$ of the learning rule (13) are obtained by taking the expectations and equating the change in the weight to 0:

$$E\{\mathbf{v}(\mathbf{w}^T\mathbf{v})^3\} \pm f(\|\mathbf{w}\|^2)\mathbf{w} = 0 \tag{15}$$

The time index (subscript t) has been dropped. Let us now write (15) in the form

$$E\{\mathbf{v}(\mathbf{w}^T\mathbf{v})^3\} - 3\mathbf{w} + (3 \pm f(\|\mathbf{w}\|^2))\mathbf{w} = 0 \tag{16}$$

whose solutions must satisfy

$$\mathbf{w} = scalar \times (E\{\mathbf{v}(\mathbf{w}^T\mathbf{v})^3\} - 3\mathbf{w}) \tag{17}$$

Actually, because the norm of $\mathbf{w}$ is irrelevant, it is the direction of the right hand side that is important. Therefore the *scalar* in eq. (17) is not significant and its effect can be replaced by explicit normalization.

Assume that we have collected a sample of the sphered (or prewhitened) random vector $\mathbf{v}$. We have the following fixed-point algorithm for ICA:

1. Take a random initial vector $\mathbf{w}_0$ of norm 1. Let $k = 1$.

2. Let $\mathbf{w}_k = E\{\mathbf{v}(\mathbf{w}_{k-1}^T\mathbf{v})^3\} - 3\mathbf{w}_{k-1}$. The expectation can be estimated using a large sample of $\mathbf{v}$ vectors (say, 1,000 points).

3. Divide $\mathbf{w}_k$ by its norm.

4. If $\|\mathbf{w}_k - \mathbf{w}_{k-1}\|$ is not small enough, let $k = k + 1$ and go back to step 2. Otherwise, output the vector $\mathbf{w}_k$.

The final vector $\mathbf{w}^* = \lim_k \mathbf{w}_k$ given by the algorithm separates *one* of the non-Gaussian source signals in the sense that $\mathbf{w}^{*T}\mathbf{v}_t$, $t = 1, 2, ...$ equals one of the source signals $s_t(i)$. This is because asymptotically $\mathbf{w}_k$ equals one of the columns $\mathbf{b}(i)$ of the separating matrix $\mathbf{B}$. A remarkable property of our algorithm is that a very small number of iterations, usually 5-10, seems to be enough to obtain the maximal accuracy allowed by the sample data. This is due to the fact that the convergence of the fixed point algorithm is in fact *cubic*, as shown in [10].

To estimate n source signals, we run this algorithm n times. To ensure that we estimate each time a different source signal, we only need to add a simple projection inside the loop, that forces the solution vector $\mathbf{w}_k$ to be orthogonal to the previously found solutions. Recall that the columns of the separating matrix $\mathbf{B}$ are orthonormal because of the sphering.

This fixed-point algorithm has several advantages when compared to other suggested ICA methods. First, as shown in [10], the convergence of our algorithm is cubic. This means very fast convergence and is rather unique among the ICA algorithms. It is also in contrast to other similar fixed-point algorithms, like the power method, which often have only linear convergence. In fact, our algorithm can be considered a higher-order generalization of the power method for tensors. Second, contrary to gradient-based algorithms, there is no learning rate or other adjustable parameters in the algorithm, which makes it easy to use and more reliable. Third, sources of both positive and negative kurtosis can be directly estimated by the same fixed-point algorithm.

4 Discussion

We have presented here some neural network based solutions to the simplest form of the ICA or source separation problem. Both multi-unit and one-unit learning rules were reviewed, by which the entire separating matrix or one of its columns can be found in an on-line algorithm. A computationally attractive batch version of the one-unit algorithms, based on fixed-point iteration, was also reviewed.

The basic methods presented above admit several extensions:

- Blind deconvolution [7] can also be performed by the one-unit neural learning rules [9].

- The neural learning rules can be modified so that they can use directly the raw, non-whitened data, thus eliminating the need for the prewhitening layer [9].

- The issue of locality may be important in some applications and in the case of biologically inspired modelling. The rather non-local, but computationally simple feedback used above can be replaced by a purely local kind of feedback [8].

- Instead of the simple linear mixtures as in eq. (1), we can also consider more general, *non-linear mixtures*. In [23], the Self-Organizing Map [15] was used for non-linear blind source separation for sources of negative kurtosis.

- In the online algorithms above, it was assumed that we determine in advance the signs of the kurtoses of the source signals that we want to estimate. This is not necessary, because we can also estimate the kurtosis on-line by a supplementary unit, and then use this information in the learning rule [12, 9]. Note, however, that the fixed-point algorithm directly separates sources of any (nonzero) kurtosis.

Acknowledgement. We are grateful for Figure 2 to Mr. Ricardo Vigario.

References

[1] S. Amari, A. Cichocki, and H.H. Yang. A new learning algorithm for blind source separation. In *Advances in Neural Information Processing 8 (Proc. NIPS'95)*, Cambridge, MA, 1996. MIT Press.

[2] A.J. Bell and T.J. Sejnowski. An information-maximization approach to blind separation and blind deconvolution. *Neural Computation*, 7:1129–1159, 1995.

[3] J.-F. Cardoso. Eigen-structure of the fourth-order cumulant tensor with application to the blind source separation problem. In *Proc. IEEE Int. Conf. on Acoustics, Speech, and Signal Processing*, pages 2655–2658, Albuquerque, NM, USA, 1990.

[4] A. Cichocki and R. Unbehauen. Novel neural networks with on-line learning for blind identification and blind separation of sources. *Submitted to IEEE Trans. on Circuits and Systems*, 1994.

[5] P. Comon. Independent component analysis – a new concept? *Signal Processing*, 36:287–314, 1994.

[6] N. Delfosse and P. Loubaton. Adaptive blind separation of independent sources: A deflation approach. *Signal Processing*, 45:59–83, 1995.

[7] S. Haykin. *Adaptive Filter Theory*. Prentice-Hall International, 3rd edition, 1996.

[8] A. Hyvarinen. Purely local neural principal component and independent component learning. In *Proc. Int. Conf. on Artificial Neural Networks*, Bochum, Germany, July 17-19 1996.

[9] A. Hyvarinen. Simple one-unit neural algorithms for blind source separation and blind deconvolution. In *Proc. Int. Conf. on Neural Information Processing*, Hong Kong, Sep 25-27 1996.

[10] A. Hyvarinen and E. Oja. A fast fixed-point algorithm for independent component analysis. Submitted to a journal. 1996.

[11] A. Hyvarinen and E. Oja. A neuron that learns to separate one independent component from linear mixtures. In *Proc. IEEE Int. Conf. on Neural Networks*, Washington, D.C., June 3-6 1996.

[12] A. Hyvarinen and E. Oja. Simple neuron models for independent component analysis. Technical report, Helsinki University of Technology, Laboratory of Computer and Information Science. Submitted to a journal, 1996.

[13] C. Jutten and J. Herault. Blind separation of sources, part I: An adaptive algorithm based on neuromimetic architecture. *Signal Processing*, 24:1–10, 1991.

[14] J. Karhunen, E. Oja, L. Wang, R. Vigario, and J. Joutsensalo. A class of neural networks for independent component analysis. Technical Report A 28, Helsinki University of Technology, Laboratory of Computer and Information Science. Submitted to a journal, 1995.

[15] T. Kohonen. *Self-Organizing Maps*. Springer-Verlag, Berlin, Heidelberg, New York, 1995.

[16] B. Laheld and J-F. Cardoso. Adaptive source separation with uniform performance. In M. Holt et al., editor, *Signal Processing VII: Theories and Applications*. EURASIP, 1994.

[17] E. Moreau and O. Macchi. New self-adaptive algorithms for source separation based on contrast functions. In *Proc. IEEE Signal Processing Workshop on Higher Order Statistics*, pages 215–219, Lake Tahoe, USA, June 1993.

[18] E. Oja. Principal components, minor components, and linear neural networks. *Neural Networks*, 5:927–935, 1992.

[19] E. Oja. The nonlinear PCA learning rule and signal separation – mathematical analysis. Technical Report A 26, Helsinki University of Technology, Laboratory of Computer and Information Science. Submitted to a journal, 1995.

[20] E. Oja and J. Karhunen. On stochastic approximation of the eigenvectors and eigenvalues of the expectation of a random matrix. *Journal of Math. Analysis and Applications*, 106:69–84, 1985.

[21] E. Oja and J. Karhunen. Signal separation by nonlinear hebbian learning. In M. Palaniswami, Y. Attikiouzel, R. Marks, D. Fogel, and T. Fukuda, editors, *Computational Intelligence - a Dynamic System Perspective*, pages 83 – 97. IEEE Press, New York, 1995.

[22] E. Oja, H. Ogawa, and J. Wangviwattana. Learning in nonlinear constrained Hebbian networks. In T. Kohonen et al., editor, *Artificial Neural Networks, Proc. ICANN'91*, pages 385–390, Espoo, Finland, 1991. North-Holland, Amsterdam.

[23] P. Pajunen, A. Hyvarinen, and J. Karhunen. Nonlinear blind source separation by self-organizing maps. In *Proc. Int. Conf. on Neural Information Processing*, Hong Kong, Sep 25-27 1996.

[24] L. Wang, J. Karhunen, and E. Oja. A bigradient optimization approach for robust PCA, MCA, and source separation. In *Proc. IEEE Int. Conf on Neural Networks '95*, pages 1684–1689, Perth, Australia, Nov 27–Dec 1 1995.

Neural Network Model of Spatial Memory

Kunihiko Fukushima

Faculty of Engineering Science, Osaka University
Toyonaka, Osaka 560, Japan

Abstract—

This paper offers a neural network model that can memorize and recall spatial maps. When driving through a place we have been before, we can recall and imagine the scenery that we cannot see yet but will see soon. Triggered by the newly recalled image, we can also recall other scenery further ahead of us. The model emulate such a recalling process using a correlation matrix memory. A correlation matrix memory by itself, however, does not accept shifts in location of stimulus patterns. In order to place stimulus patterns accurately at the location of one of the memorized patterns, we propose using the cross-correlation between the stimulus pattern and the "piled pattern".

A map of Europe is divided into a number of overlapping segments, and these segments are memorized in the proposed model. A map around Scotland is input to the model as the initial image. Triggered by the initial image, the model recalls maps of other parts of Europe sequentially up to Italy, for example.

1 Introduction

How does the brain memorize and recall spatial information of the external world? How is the spatial information decoded and represented in the brain? Neurophysiological and psychological experiments suggest that the spatial information of the external world is represented in the brain in a form of a topologically ordered spatial pattern like a map with an ego-centric coordinate system.

For example, this is suggested from observation of patients with a lesion in one cerebral hemisphere [1],[2]. A patient with a large lesion in the right cerebral hemisphere was requested to imagine himself looking at a famous building in a very familiar square in the city where he lived for many years. He reported several elements (buildings, streets, etc.) on his right side but none or very few on his left side, which is contralateral to the damaged cortex. When requested to imagine himself turned on his heels and to describe the square from the opposite perspective, he reported more elements on the right side of his mental image, which had previously been the left side of his mental image. This suggests that, when we are imagining a spatial map around us, the map is represented as a spatial activity pattern of neurons in some area of the brain, keeping the topology of the geographical features of the external world.

Let us consider a situation in which we are driving through a place we have been before. Even if our memory is ambiguous and we cannot draw a map from memory, we often can find the correct way to a destination when we actually go there. We can recall and imagine the scenery or geographical features that we cannot see yet but will see soon. Triggered by the newly recalled image, we can also recall other scenery further ahead of us. We can thus imagine scenery of a wide area by a chain of recalling processes.

If the spatial information of the external world is represented in the brain as a topologically ordered spatial pattern like a map, the visual imagery recalled at one time with a certain resolution must be bounded in size because of the limited number of cells in the brain. Furthermore, spatial information memorized at one time is also limited because of the limited size of our visual field. However, we can combine two different scenes memorized at adjacent locations and create one unified image in our mind.

Even if we are brought to a place without being told where to go, a chain process of recalling spatial maps around us can start once we see a familiar scene. This suggests that the brain stores fragmentary maps without appending any information representing the locations of the maps.

This paper offers a neural network model of spatial memory of this type. The model stores spatial information in the form of fragmentary patterns like spatial maps. From the memory of fragmentary patterns, an image covering an infinitely wide area is retrieved by a continuous chain process of recalling.

2 Outline of the Model

In a computer simulation of the proposed model, a spatial pattern (or a line-drawing of a map) of a large area is divided into many pieces of fragmentary two-dimensional patterns overlapping each other. These fragmentary patterns are then memorized in an associative memory circuit.

The imagery layer, which represents the mental image in our mind, is somewhat larger than the memorized fragmentary patterns. The mental image generated in the imagery layer is always represented in the form of a spatial pattern with an ego-centric coordinate system. When one moves, the mental image shifts opposite to the direction of body movement, so as to keep the body always at the center of the imagery layer.

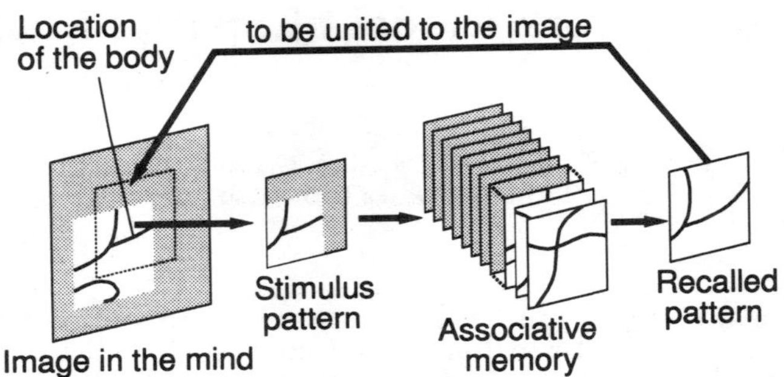

Figure 1: Process of finding a pattern that fills the vacancy in the imagery layer.

If the mental image, which has a finite size, shifts following the movement of the body, a vacant region appears in the imagery layer. In order to seamlessly fill the vacancy with a new pattern, the model searches the associative memory circuit for a pattern that tallies with the residual part of the mental image. If an appropriate pattern is found, it is united to the mental image to fill the vacancy in the imagery layer. Figure 1 illustrates this process of finding relevant patterns.

Since we do not have enough neurophysiological data to estimate what kind of associative memory circuit is actually used in the brain, we tentatively use in the proposed model an auto-associative correlation matrix memory to memorize and recall fragmentary patterns. In the recalling phase, the mental image with a vacant region is input to the correlation matrix as a stimulus pattern to retrieve a pattern that fills the missing part of the mental image. Since a correlation matrix memory by itself does not accept shifts in location of stimulus patterns, it becomes necessary to place stimulus patterns accurately at the location of one of the memorized patterns. We propose to adjust the location of the stimulus pattern using the cross-correlation between the stimulus pattern and the "piled pattern". The "piled pattern" is made by a pixelwise sum of all patterns memorized in the correlation matrix.

More specifically, the cross correlation function between the stimulus pattern and the piled pattern is calculated first, and the amount of shift that maximizes the cross correlation function is found. The stimulus pattern is then shifted by that amount. A new pattern is recalled from the correlation matrix memory by the sifted stimulus pattern. The computer simulation discussed later shows that, in most cases, appropriate patterns can be recalled by this recalling process.

Although this recalling process sometimes fails, it usually does no harm because the model contains a monitoring circuit that detects the failure. If a failure is detected, the recalled pattern is simply discarded, and the recalling process is repeated again after some period of time when the body has moved to another location.

3   Architecture and Behavior of the Model

Figure 2 illustrates the architecture of the proposed model. The model consists of a correlation matrix memory and many layers of cells as illustrated in the figure. Each layer is a two-dimensional array of cells. In the computer simulation discussed later, layers $\boldsymbol{S}$, $\boldsymbol{R}$ and $\boldsymbol{Z}$ have $N \times N$ cells, and layers $\boldsymbol{I}$ and $\boldsymbol{H}$ have $(2N-1) \times (2N-1)$ cells. The size of $\boldsymbol{C}$ depends on the range of cross-correlation, and is $N \times N$ in the simulation.

3.1   Correlation Matrix Memory

An auto-associative correlation matrix memory with recurrent connections is used in the model. As is well known, an auto-associative correlation matrix memory can recall a complete pattern from a portion of it, provided that a certain orthogonality condition among memorized patterns is satisfied.

Let $\boldsymbol{X}^{(k)}$ be the kth fragmentary (two-dimensional) pattern to be memorized, and $X^{(k)}(\boldsymbol{n})$ be the value (or brightness) of its pixel located at $\boldsymbol{n} \in P$. An upper bar, like $\bar{X}^{(k)}$, will be used to represent the average value of all pixels in a pattern.

Patterns are memorized in the correlation matrix memory in the form of the strengths of connections. If K patterns have been memorized, the strength of the connections, namely, the elements of the correlation matrix, take the following values:

$$\psi(\boldsymbol{n}, \boldsymbol{m}) = \sum_{k=1}^{K} \{X^{(k)}(\boldsymbol{n}) - \bar{X}^{(k)}\} \{X^{(k)}(\boldsymbol{m}) - \bar{X}^{(k)}\}. \tag{1}$$

Every time a pattern is memorized in the correlation matrix, the pattern is also stored in layer $\boldsymbol{Z}$ in a different way. Layer $\boldsymbol{Z}$ stores the piled pattern, which is a pixelwise sum of all patterns memorized in

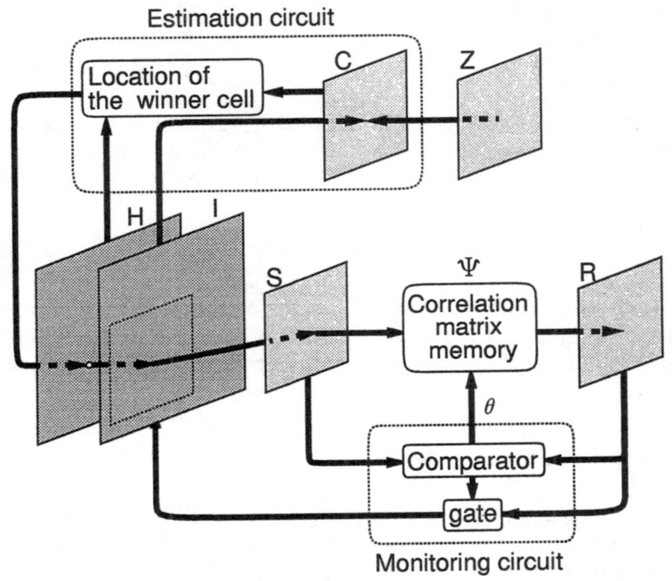

I: The imagery layer, which represents the image in our mind in an ego-centric coordinate system.

S: The stimulus pattern input to the correlation matrix memory Ψ.

Ψ: The auto-associative correlation matrix memory.

R: The recalled pattern from the correlation matrix memory Ψ.

Z: The piled pattern, which is a pixelwise sum of all patterns memorized in the correlation matrix Ψ.

C: Cross-correlation between I and Z.

H: History of the estimated locations, at which the center of the stimulus patterns had once been placed.

Figure 2: Architecture of the proposed model.

the correlation matrix Ψ. Mathematically,

$$Z(\boldsymbol{n}) = \sum_{k=1}^{K} X^{(k)}(\boldsymbol{n}) \,. \tag{2}$$

We will now consider the recalling phase of the correlation matrix memory. Let U_t be the response of the cells of the correlation matrix at discrete time t. The initial value U_0 is set equal to the stimulus pattern S input to this correlation matrix memory. Namely, $U_0(\boldsymbol{n}) = S(\boldsymbol{n})$.

The output of the correlation matrix at $t+1$ is given by

$$U_{t+1}(\boldsymbol{n}) = \mathbf{1}\left[\sum_{m \in P} \psi(\boldsymbol{n},\boldsymbol{m})\{U_t(\boldsymbol{m}) - \bar{U}_t\} - \theta_t\right], \tag{3}$$

using a threshold θ_t, where $\mathbf{1}[\ ]$ is a threshold function defined by

$$\mathbf{1}[x] = \left\{ \begin{array}{ll} 1 & \text{if } x > 0 \\ 0 & \text{if } x \leq 0 \,. \end{array} \right. \tag{4}$$

Threshold θ_t is set so as to minimize the error, which is defined from the number of erroneously recalled pixels (or Hamming distance) in the non-vacant region of S. Since the value of θ_t that minimizes the error usually has a wide range, θ_t is set at the middle of the upper and the lower bounds of this range.

The iterative calculation described by (3) is repeated until the response reaches a steady state, in which we have $U_{t+1} = U_t$. Notation U_∞ is used to represent the response at this steady state. U_∞ is the recalled output R from this auto-associative correlation matrix memory. Namely, $R = U_\infty$.

3.2 Behavior of the Model

The mental image that appears in the imagery layer I is always represented in the form of a spatial pattern with an ego-centric coordinate system. When one moves, the mental image shifts in the direction opposite to the direction of the body movement, so as to keep the body always at the center of the imagery layer. As a result of the mental image shift, a vacant region appears in the peripheral part of the imagery layer.

Now a new pattern that fills the vacancy in the mental image has to be recalled from the auto-associative correlation matrix memory Ψ. The new pattern to be recalled from the memory has to tally with the residual part of the mental image.

In the computer simulation, layer I has $(2N-1) \times (2N-1)$ pixels, and the patterns $X^{(k)}$ memorized in the correlation matrix memory have $N \times N$ pixels. I and $X^{(k)}$ are binary patterns, whose pixels take 1 or 0, but the values of the pixels in the vacant region in I are left undetermined. An area of $N \times N$ pixels, which has a vacant region, is cut out from I and is used as the stimulus S to the correlation matrix memory. Since this is a process of recalling a complete pattern from a portion of it, S has to be cut out from I in such a way that the non-vacant region of S coincides pixelwise with one of the memorized patterns. If there is a positional error between S and the memorized pattern to be recalled, a correct retrieval cannot be expected, because the correlation matrix memory does not accept shifts in location of the stimulus pattern.

Therefore, it becomes necessary to determine where in layer I the stimulus pattern S should be cut out from. The estimation circuit in Fig. 2 determines the location of the center of S in I. At first, the estimation circuit calculates the cross-correlation function $C(\nu)$ between the stimulus pattern S and the piled pattern Z:

$$C(\nu) = \frac{1}{|A|} \sum_{n \in A} \{I(n + \nu) - \bar{I}\} \{Z(n) - \bar{Z}\}. \tag{5}$$

A denotes the area where Z and I overlap and where I is not vacant. $|A|$ is the number of pixels in A. $\bar{I}$ and $\bar{Z}$ are the mean values of I and Z in A, respectively. Equation (5) can be interpreted as follows. Z is shifted by ν from the center of I and is laid down on I. The two patterns, from which mean values are subtracted, are multiplied pixelwise in area A and added up. The sum is $C(\nu)$.

The estimation circuit then searches for location ν_0 of the maximum output cell in layer C. This becomes the estimated location of the center of S in layer I, if it does not coincide with any of the estimated locations in the past, which are stored in layer H.

Incidentally, layer H stores the history of estimated locations, at which the centers of S have once been placed and recalling processes have been tried before. $H(\nu)$ takes value 0 or 1. We have $H(\nu) \equiv 0$ in the initial state, but if $\nu = \nu_0$ is selected as the estimated location of the center of S, the value of the cell at that location in layer H is replaced with 1. Namely, $H(\nu_0) = 1$. The response of layer H is made to shift in linkage with the shift of the mental image in layer I, and is always expressed in the ego-centric coordinate system. This prevents the recall of the same patterns twice and also prohibits the repeated use of erroneously estimated locations.

Once ν_0 is determined by the estimation circuit, the area of $N \times N$ whose center is at ν_0 is cut out from I and is used as S. S usually contains a missing region. The values of the pixels in this vacant region are replaced with the mean value of the pixels in the rest (non-vacant region) of S.

Stimulus pattern S is fed to the auto-associative correlation matrix memory Ψ, and the output of associative recall R is obtained as discussed in section 3.1.

The monitoring circuit compares R with S and measures the error rate ε, which is defined from the number of erroneously recalled pixels (or Hamming distance) in the non-vacant region of S. That is,

$$\varepsilon = \frac{1}{|B|} \sum_{n \in B} |R(n) - S(n)|, \tag{6}$$

where B denotes the area where S is not vacant, and $|B|$ is the number of pixels in B.

If R gives ε smaller than a certain criterion value (that is 0.05 in the simulation below), the monitoring circuit judges that the recall is successful, and the recalled pattern R is united to the mental image to fill the vacancy of the imagery layer I.

If error rate ε is larger than the criterion, the monitoring circuit judges that the recall has failed, and discards the recalled pattern R. On rare occasions, the iterative calculation represented by (3) does not reach a steady state. If condition $U_{t+1} = U_t$ has not been reached within a certain number of iteration ($t < 10$ in the simulation), the monitoring circuit also judges that the recall has failed. Although the recalling process at this location is terminated, it usually does no harm, because the recalling process is carried on again after some period of time when the body has moved to another location.

We can consider many different methods for determining the timing for starting each recalling process. In the computer simulation discussed below, the recalling process is started after every five pixels of movements of the body in the imagery layer I, provided that more than 10% of the central $N \times N$ area of layer I is vacant.

4   Computer Simulation

In the computer simulation of the proposed model, a map of Europe (Fig. 3(a)), which consists of 240×240 pixels, is divided into many fragmentary patterns ($N \times N$ in size, where $N = 39$) overlapping each other as shown in Fig. 3(b). Figure 3(c) displays these fragmentary patterns. They are binary patterns, whose pixels take 1 or 0. These fragmentary patterns are then memorized in the associative memory circuit. At the same time, the piled pattern Z, which is shown in Fig. 3(d), is created and stored. The imagery layer I is somewhat larger ($(2N - 1) \times (2N - 1)$) than the fragmentary patterns ($N \times N$) memorized.

We simulate a situation in which a person (or the model) catches a train at a city in Scotland and travels along a railway via Paris to Italy. A map, whose center is at the starting city, is first put at the central $N \times N$ area of the imagery layer I. We will show that, triggered by the initial image, maps of other parts of Europe are recalled sequentially up to the south end of Italy.

In the model, the mental image generated in the imagery layer is always represented in an ego-centric

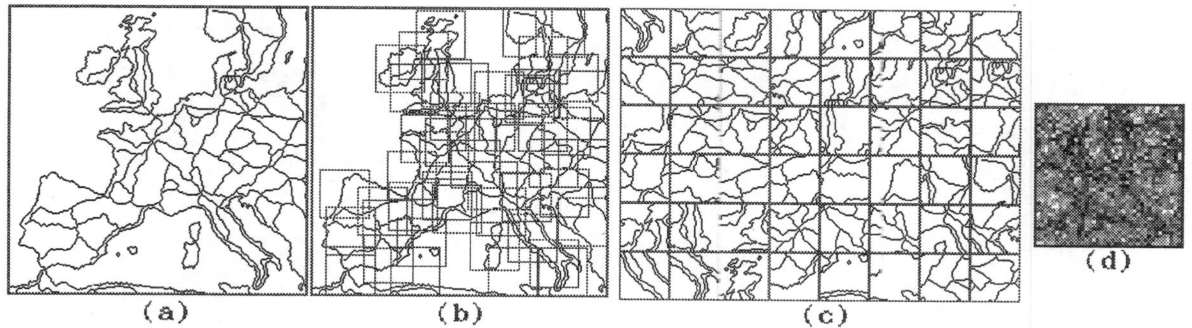

Figure 3: Patterns memorized in associative memory.

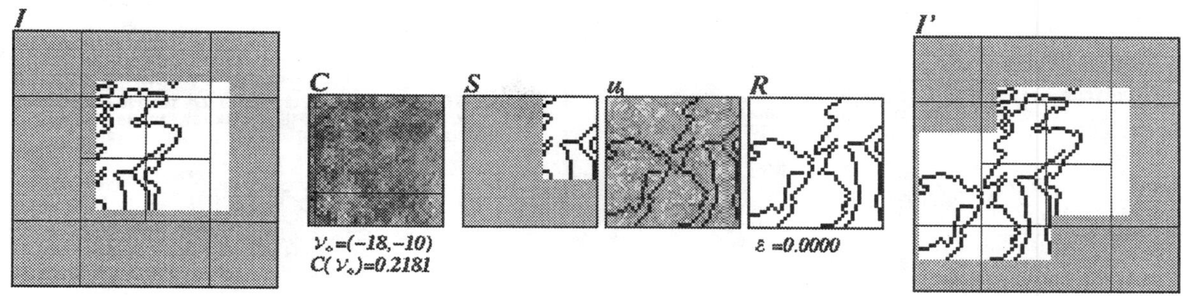

Figure 4: Example of the model response.

coordinate system. When one moves, the mental image shifts in the direction opposite to the direction of body movement, so as to keep the body always at the center of the imagery layer. Since the process of tracing the railway is not the problem of interest in this paper, we simply use an arbitrary technique of line tracing here.

It should be noted here that the centers of the patterns memorized in the correlation matrix are not necessarily located on the railway to be traced. If they are all distributed on the railway, the problem becomes too easy and trivial, because the stimulus pattern need not be shifted for a correct recalling.

Figure 4 shows an example of the response of the model. A map centered at the starting city is first presented in the central area of the imagery layer. After a short excursion along a railway, we had an egocentric image I as shown in the figure. Now the cross-correlation C between I and Z is obtained. The maximum output cell in C was located at $\nu_0 = (-18, -10)$. The $N \times N$ area centered at ν_0 was cut out from I, and S was produced. This stimulus S was input to the associative memory Ψ, and R was recalled. Error rate was $\varepsilon = 0.00$, and it was judged that the estimation of the location of the stimulus pattern S was correct. Therefore, R was shifted by ν_0 then united to I. Thus, we had a new image I' as shown in Fig. 4. Incidentally, u_1 in the figure represents U_1 before threshold operation, that is, the argument of the function in the right side of (3) after the first step of iterative calculation.

Figure 5 summarizes the patterns recalled during the trip from Scotland to Italy. Pattern $<00>$ in the figure shows the map at the starting point of the trip, and the others are the patterns recalled sequentially during the trip. Below each pattern are shown the coordinates of the center of the pattern in the original map of Europe; the estimated relative location ν_0 from the center of I; and the number of pixels erroneously recalled, i.e., the Hamming distance between R and the pattern actually memorized in the correlation matrix.

It can be seen from this figure that, triggered by the initial image of Scotland, maps of other parts of Europe were recalled sequentially up to Italy without interruption. No error occurred in any of the recalled patterns throughout this trip. Although failures of recalling fragmentary patterns occurred sometimes by estimation errors of the location of S, they were all detected by the monitoring circuit, and erroneous uniting of irrelevant patterns was successfully prevented.

Figure 6 shows another example of a sequence of patterns obtained by a chain process of recalling. In this case, the trip started from Oslo, Norway and continued via Paris to Lisbon, Portugal. This shows that many different recalling sequences can be correctly obtained from the same set of memorized patterns.

5   Discussions

This paper has offered a neural network model of spatial memory. The model stores spatial information in the form of fragmentary patterns like spatial maps. We have shown by computer simulation that an image covering an infinitely wide area is retrieved by a continuous chain process of recalling fragmentary patterns from the memory. Although it is an open question if the same process is actually used in the

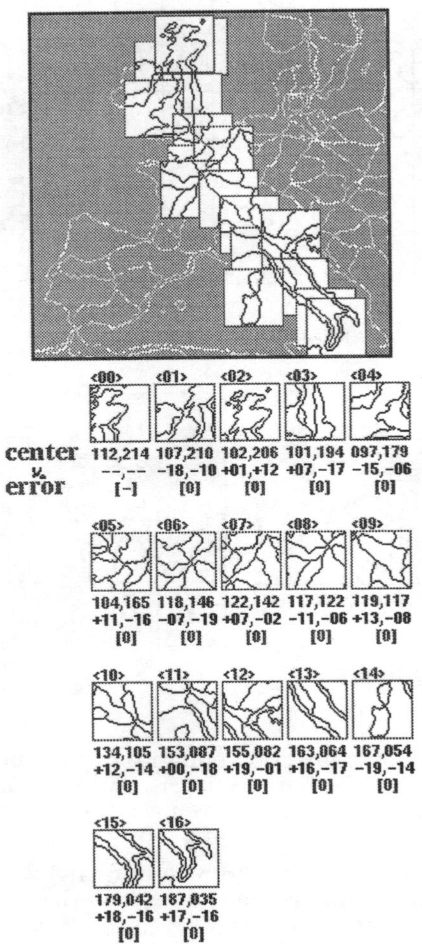

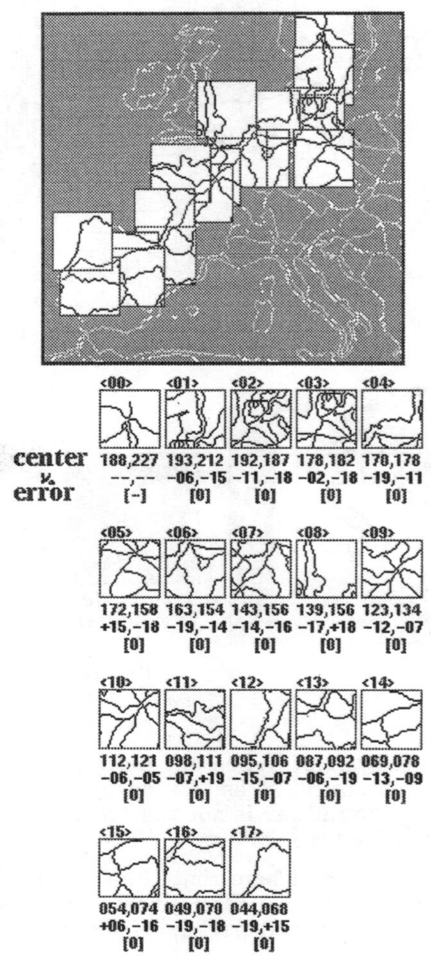

Figure 5: Sequence of patterns obtained by a chain process of recalling during the trip from Scotland via Paris to Italy.

Figure 6: Another example of a sequence of patterns obtained by a chain process of recalling. The trip is from Oslo via Paris to Lisbon.

biological brain as in our model, we believe that there is some fundamental principle in common between the two because our model can emulate some essential functions of associative recall of the brain. There are, however, still many problems left to be solved in the future. For example, our model has to be improved to cope with rotation, change in scale, and deformation of maps.

We can imagine that the performance of the model would be greatly improved if a feature extracting network like a "neocognitron" [3] is introduced in the model and input information is preprocessed before being fed to the associative memory. This might be one possible solution for endowing the network with an ability to accept deformation and change in size of the input patterns. We did not, however, introduce such a feature-extracting network in our present model, because the aim of this paper is to show that the associative recall of maps can be successfully performed even without having such feature-extracting network.

Acknowledgments: The author gratefully acknowledges his student, Yoshio Yamaguchi and his colleague, Masato Okada for their large contributions to this research. This work was supported in part by Grants-in-Aid #05267103 and #7408005 for Scientific Research from the Ministry of Education, Science, Sports and Culture of Japan; and by a grant for Frontier Research Projects in Telecommunications from the Ministry of Posts and Telecommunications of Japan.

References

[1] E. Bisiach, C. Luzzatti: "Unilateral neglect of representational space", *Cortex*, **14**, pp. 129–133 (1978).

[2] C. Guariglia, A. Padovani, P. Pantano, L. Pizzamiglio: "Unilateral neglect restricted to visual imagery", *Nature*, **364**[6434], pp. 235–237 (July 1993).

[3] K. Fukushima: "Neocognitron: A hierarchical neural network capable of visual pattern recognition", *Neural Networks*, **1**[2], pp. 119–130 (1988).

Concerning the development of retina implants with neural nets *

Rolf E. Eckmiller

Department of Computer Science VI, Division of Neuroinformatics, University of Bonn
Römerstr. 164, D-53117 Bonn, F.R. Germany
Tel.: ++49-228-550-422, FAX: ++49-228-550-425
email: eckmiller@nero.uni-bonn.de
URL: http://www.nero.uni-bonn.de

Abstract — The development of retina implants for blind humans suffering from various retinal degenerative diseases to regain a moderate amount of vision is the ambitious goal of several interdisciplinary research consortia worldwide. A retina encoder (RE) outside the eye has to replace the information processing of the retina. A retina stimulator (RS), implanted adjacent to the retinal ganglion cell layer at the retinal 'output', has to contact a sufficient number of retinal ganglion cells/fibers for electrical stimulation. A wireless signal- and energy transmission system (SE) has to provide the communication between RE and RS. This paper outlines the retina implant concept of our consortium of 14 expert groups and describes first results on the adaptive retina encoder RE. RE maps visual patterns onto impulse sequences for a number of contacted ganglion cells by means of adaptive dynamic spatial filters. These spatial filters as biology-inspired neural networks can be 'tuned' to various spatial and temporal receptive field properties of ganglion cells in the primate retina during a learning phase. RE adaptation will require a dialog between the implant-carrying subject and the corresponding RE.

1　Introduction

A significant number of visually impaired human subjects suffers from retinal degenerative defects (especially: retinitis pigmentosa, RP and macular degeneration, MD), which in many cases of RP begins with night blindness (loss of rod photoreceptors), deteriorates into tunnel vision, and finally leads to total blindness (additional loss of cone photoreceptors, even within the fovea) [6] [8] [31] [41]. However, a significant number of retinal ganglion cells forming the optic nerve at the 'retinal output' as well as subsequent parts of the central visual system often remain intact [44]. In a recent study by de Juan and his group [15] [16] it could be demonstrated that local electrical stimulation of the retinal ganglion cell layer in blind RP-patients yielded useful, localized visual sensations such as small dots or lines at defined locations in the visual space. Thus in principle it seems possible to bypass the defective retina under the following conditions:

a) development of a soft microcontact foil as retina stimulator (RS) with a sufficient number of contacts for stimulation of individual ganglion cells/fibers for long-term implantation adjacent to the ganglion cell layer;

b) development of a retina encoder (RE) for functional simulation of the defective 5-layered retina by mapping visual patterns onto spike trains by means of spatial filters with receptive field properties, and

c) development of a wireless signal- and energy transmission system (SE) for signal transmission from RE outside the eye to the individually addressable, microcontacts inside the eye.

Several groups in the USA [15] [16] [30] [37] [50] and Germany [10] [11] [40] are currently developing components for such retina implants. It is hoped to complete the development of entire retina implant prototypes and experimental tests in animals within the next 3 to 5 years and to apply this technology to humans within the next 10 years.

Alternative developments towards implantable photodiode arrays in the region of the degenerated photoreceptor cells are also in progress both in the USA and Germany.

---

* Supported by Federal Ministry for Education, Science, Research, and Technology (BMBF).

2   Approach

We have recently started the development and animal test of an 'intelligent' retina implant in a consortium of 14 expert groups funded by the research ministry, BMBF with 10 Mill. DM over four years. Our retina implant consortium (the three coordinators are underlined) with about 40 scientists comprises expertise in:

biomaterials science (C. Mittermayer / Aachen), **microelectronics** (B. Hosticka / Duisburg), **microsystems technology & biomedical engineering** (J.-U. Meyer / St. Ingbert, W. Mokwa / Duisburg, U. Schnakenberg / Berlin), **neural computation** (R. Eckmiller / Bonn), **optoelectronics** (D. Jäger /Duisburg), **retinal cell biology** (M. Eckmiller / Düsseldorf), **vitreoretinal surgery** (R. Effert / Essen, H. Gerding / Münster, K. Heimann / Köln, L. Hesse / Marburg, P. Wiedemann / Leipzig), and **visual neurophysiology** (R.Eckhorn / Marburg).

The considerable challenge of forging an interdisciplinary partnership for this mission-oriented project is met by a number of novel organizational measures, including:

3) **specification of a net plan with research topics**: retina encoder-RE, signal & energy transmission-SE, retina stimulator-RS, implantation & wound healing-IH, material compatibility & tissue reaction-MT, and systems integration & test-ST;

4) **assignment of working packages & mile stones** for the different partners and sub-teams with a tight time schedule in order to successfully develop a prototype of the retina implant system and test its function over an extended period of time in different animal species within four years;

5) **communication with visually impaired humans** throughout the implant development in order to properly consider various related ethical and acceptance questions of the possible future recipient group for these visual prostheses.

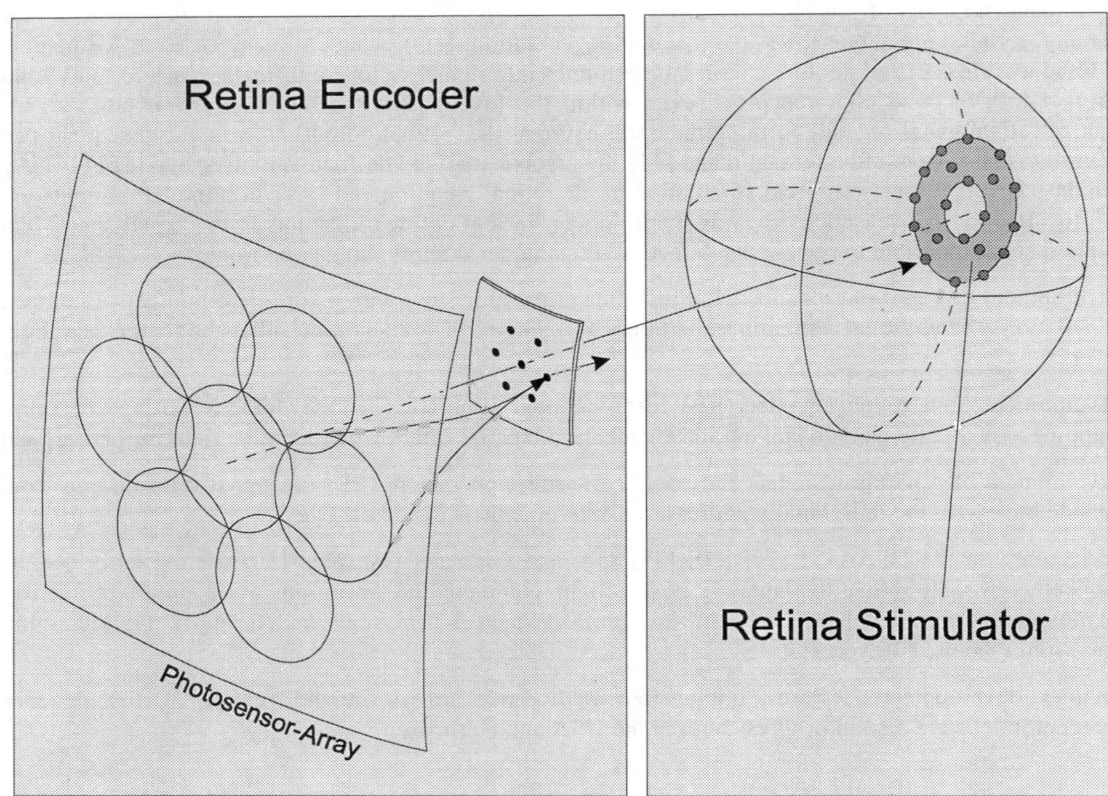

Figure 1:   Schema of the retina implant with a retina encoder outside the eye and an implanted retina stimulator adjacent to the ganglion cell layer. Circle and arrow structures in the retina encoder depict the individual adaptive spatial filters with receptive field properties of the primate retina.

Figure 1 depicts the retina implant schematically. The retina encoder (RE), which will be located outside the eye initially in a frame of glasses and later imbedded in a contact lens, has a photosensor array with about 10.000 to 100.000 smart pixels at the input and about 100 to 1.000 technical ganglion cell (G-cell) outputs generating impulse sequences for elicitation of spike trains. Information processing within RE simulates the receptive field type filter operations for each G-cell individually. The G-cell output is subsequently encoded and transmitted via an electromagnetic and/or optoelectronic wireless transmission channel (SE) to the implanted retina stimulator (RS). RS will be implanted adjacent to the retinal ganglion cell layer and consists of an array of 100 to 5.000 microcontacts for localized, bi-phasic electrical stimulation of ganglion cells/fibers as well as a receiver and signal distributor.

3 Concept of adaptive retina encoder

The retina encoder (RE) will consist of about 100 to 1.000 adaptive dynamic spatial filters. Each filter simulates the spatial and temporal receptive field properties of typical primate retinal ganglion cells as depicted in Figure 2. Each filter receives its light input via a selectable set of about 100 to 1.000 adjacent photosensor elements and generates a corresponding asynchronous impulse sequence at the G-cell output.

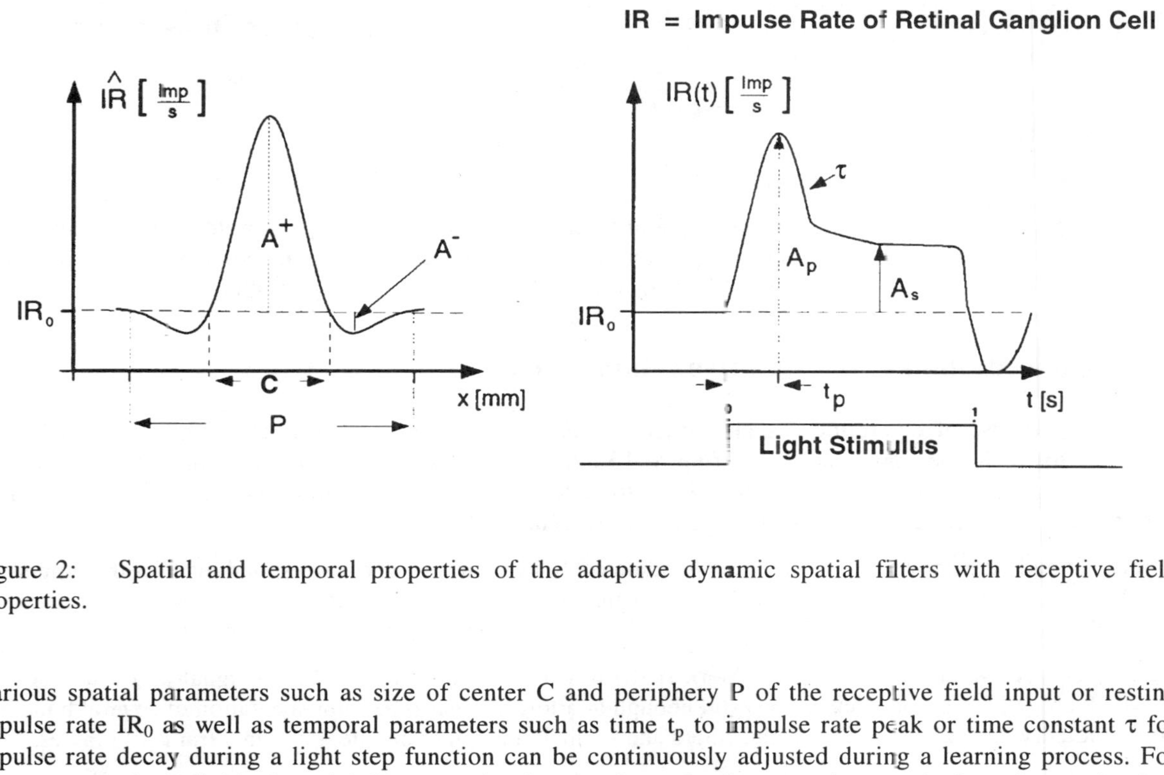

Figure 2: Spatial and temporal properties of the adaptive dynamic spatial filters with receptive field properties.

Various spatial parameters such as size of center C and periphery P of the receptive field input or resting impulse rate IR_0 as well as temporal parameters such as time t_p to impulse rate peak or time constant τ for impulse rate decay during a light step function can be continuously adjusted during a learning process. For this purpose, the individual spatial filters are implemented as adaptive neural networks in order to simulate various receptive field characteristics of the primate retina [18] [33] [46].

The implementation of the retinal information processing by a number of adaptive dynamic spatial filters emphasizes the input-output features of the retina and considers only a small portion of the large body of anatomical [3] [4] [17] [20] [26] [38] [39] [42] [47] and physiological data on intra-retinal structure and function. Rather, the adaptive spatial filters have to be flexible enough to be tunable in a multi-dimensional parameter space to the typical M-cell or P-cell receptive field properties of G-cells within the primate retina [14] [23] [24] [25] [45] [52].

As indicated schematically in Figure 3, a typical functional module of the retina encoder (RE) as adaptive dynamic spatial filter [2] [5] [9] [11] [12] [13] [14] [19] [21] [22] [27] [28] [29] [36] [43] [48] [49] [51] has an array of neighboring photosensors at the input and one G-cell output to map spatiotemporal events onto an asynchronous train of stimulation pulses for one-to-one elicitation of neural action potentials (spikes) at a given contacted retinal ganglion cell/fiber. The information processing of the spatial filter is flexible enough to assign a selectable set of photosensors to the excitatory (+) or inhibitory (-) receptive field center and another selectable set of adjacent photosensors to the corresponding inhibitory (-) or excitatory (+) receptive field periphery of a typical antagonistic On-Center or Off-Center receptive field. The receptive fields of different spatial filters can widely overlap as already indicated in Figure 1. Although their shape will typically be concentric circular, the receptive fields can also be changed to other shapes such as ellipses for example [39] in a pre-defined set or a learning process. In principle, the adaptive RE system can also be tuned to spatiotemporal receptive field properties of neurons in the central visual system (e.g.: in the LGN of the thalamus or in area V1 of the visual cortex, [1] [7] [14] [33].

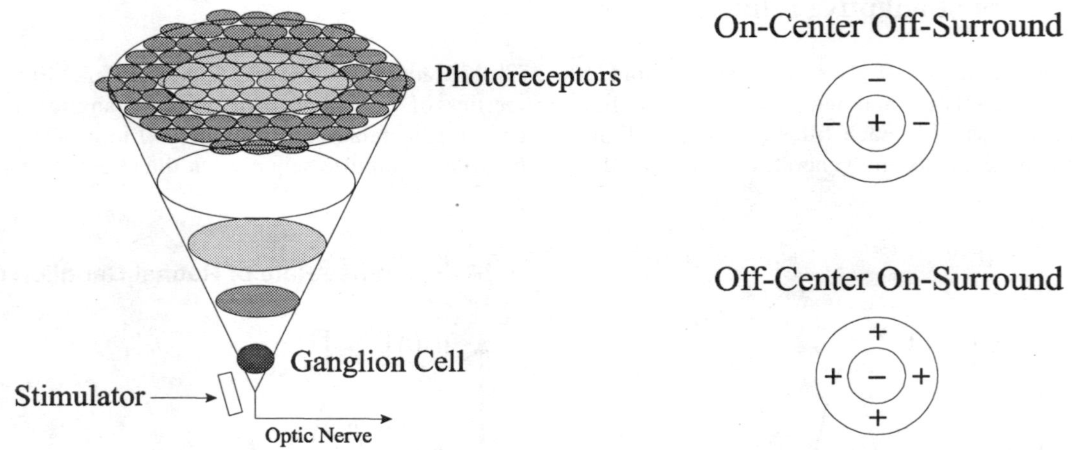

Figure 3. Scheme for an adaptive dynamic spatial filter with antagonistic receptive field properties similar to those of retinal ganglion cells in the primate retina. Filter properties can be tuned to various spatial and temporal characteristics for example of M-cells or P-cells with On-centers or Off-centers.

4   Implementation of the adaptive retina encoder

For the first phase of our retina implant project we have developed a Mark I retina encoder as hardware simulator for real-time implementation of up to 16 adaptive spatial filters attached to an array of discrete photosensors. The mixed analog and digital electronic circuits on several circuit boards are integrated in a portable system, which can be controlled and monitored via a PC.

Typical stimuli are moving or temporally modulated light patterns. The corresponding G-cell outputs are membrane potential time courses, which lead to impulse trains for simulation of a P-cell, as indicated in Figure 4. The Mark I RE as portable system may also be valuable for collaborations with other labs.

Simultaneously, we are developing the Mark II RE based on state-of-the-art digital signal processors (DSP). The DSP chip (TI, C80) is already powerful enough to allow the real-time implementation of several hundreds of individually adaptive dynamic spatial filters and is small enough to be integrated in a frame of glasses.

Several alternative learning algorithms for supervised vs. unsupervised learning and a dialog between the prospective implant carrying subject and the corresponding RE are currently under development. Since the implantation of RS will yield an unpredictable set of contacted ganglion cells/fibers, each corresponding spatial filter of the RE has to be tuned during a learning dialog as schematically indicated in Figure 5. The human visual system in this model is represented by five parallel visual channels w1 to w5 (e.g. for movement, color, form, etc.) , which map the retina output onto a putative perception vector [1] [7] [14] [33].

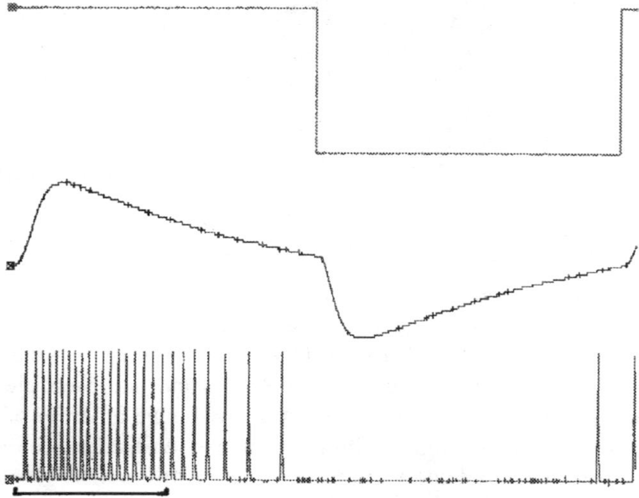

Figure 4: Typical recording from a Mark I RE spatial filter. Top trace: light spot time course centered on the On-center of the receptive field. Middle trace: membrane potential time course of the technical retina ganglion cell with a given setting of spatial and temporal filter parameters. Bottom trace: corresponding spike train at the ganglion cell output for stimulation of a contacted ganglion cell/fiber. Time scale: 100ms.

In the 4-years phase we aim to also complete the development of the Mark III RE with an integrated custom-designed smart photosensor array (Hosticka/Duisburg) [40]. Mark III RE will be able to adapt to different scotopic, mesopic, or photopic luminance levels [14] [22] [43] [52] within a range of at least six decades.

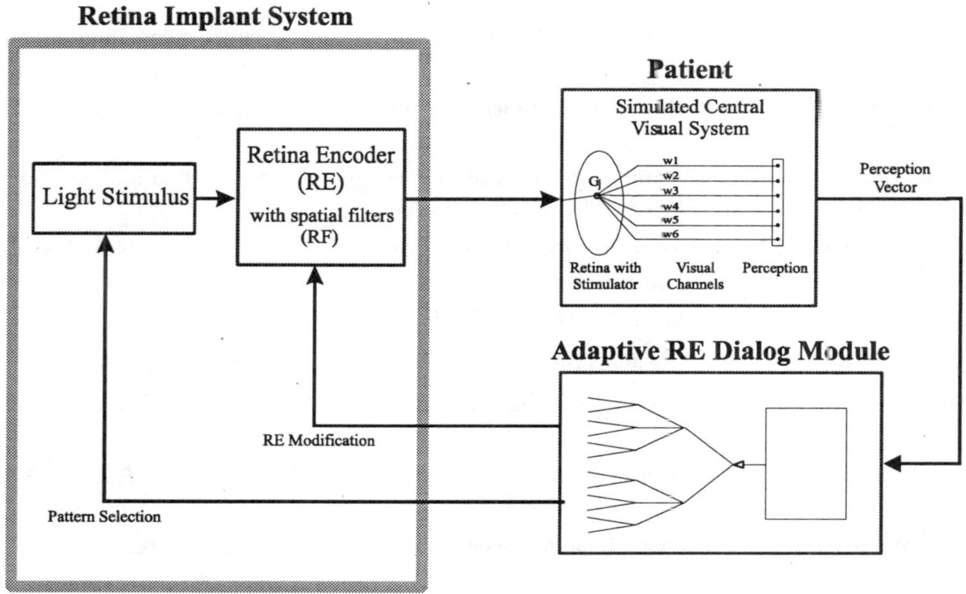

Figure 5. Concept of bi-directional communication between retina encoder (RE) and a given patient. The depicted Adaptive RE Dialog Module, closes the communication loop by decoding the patients perception reports, generating corresponding adjustment-signals for the various RE filter parameters via alternative neural network algorithms, and by selecting light stimulus patterns.

5   Future Developments

<u>a- Synchronization of the spike activity of different ganglion cells</u>

A growing body of recent neurophysiological data suggests the temporary coupling of the neural impulse activity of different retinal ganglion cells [32] [34] [35]. This may be an important information processing property caused by intra-retinal (e.g. spike activity of amacrine cells or coupling between neighboring ganglion cells) or extra-retinal (e.g. signal interaction between extra-thin unmyelinated ganglion cell fibers within the eye or even efferent neural input [42]) events. The currently developed adaptive retina encoder (RE) offers the temporary coupling (synchronization) of the impulse sequences of a given set of G-cells. During adaptation of the RE properties in a dialog with a given human subject, this temporary and selective spike synchronization will be considered.

<u>b- Information processing of color signals</u>

The primate retina uses cone photoreceptors with three different absorption spectra in the photopic and mesopic range and maps color patterns onto different types of color-opponent ganglion cell output signals (e.g. yellow-blue or red-green P-cells) [3] [7] [23] [24]. One has to assume that the central visual system of humans with RP still 'expects' color information from most P-cells and interprets electrically induced signals accordingly [16]. The retina encoder (RE) in an advanced stage will have an array of photosensors with three different absorption spectra in the visual range as input layer and will allow for the simulation of color-opponent cells with the characteristic spatial and temporal properties of P-cells.

<u>c- Selection of microcontact pairs or clusters for enhancement of localized ganglion cell/fiber stimulation</u>

The exactly localized implantation of microcontacts relative to pre-selected retinal ganglion cells or fibers will not be possible in the near future. Furthermore, the ability to selectively stimulate a single cell or fiber will depend on a combination of parameters such as pulse form, field distribution and anatomy. It may prove useful to use several microcontacts as clusters to improve localized cell or fiber stimulation. The spatio-temporal stimulation pattern of a given cluster could also be used to gradually 'scan' the adjacent ganglion cell/fiber area by means of phase modulation, thus stimulating several cells or fibers selectively by the same microcontact cluster.

References

[1] J. Bullier, L.G. Nowak, "Parallel versus serial processing: New vistas on the distributed organization of the visual system," Curr. Opin. Neurobiol. 5: 497-503, 1995

[2] D.P. Casasent, L.M. Neiberg, "Classifier and shift-invariant automatic target recognition neural networks," Neural Networks 8: 1117-1129, 1995.

[3] C.A. Curcio, K.R. Sloan, R.E. Kalina, A.E. Hendrickson, "Human photoreceptor topography," J. Comp. Neurol. 292: 497-523, 1990.

[4] D.M. Dacey, M.R. Peterson, "Dendritic field size and morphology of midget and parasol ganglion cells of the human retina," Proc. Natl. Acad. Sci. 89: 9666-9670, 1992.

[5] T. Delbrück, "Silicon retina with correlation-based velocity-tuned pixels," IEEE Trans. Neural Networks 4: 529-541, 1993.

[6] D.J. D'Amico, "Diseases of the retina," New England J. Med. 331: 95-106, 1994.

[7] R.L. De Valois, K.K. De Valois, "Spatial Vision," Oxford University Press, New York, 1988.

[8] T.P. Dryja, E.L. Berson, "Retinitis pigmentosa and allied diseases," Invest. Ophthal. & Vis. Sci. 36: 1197-1200, 1995.

[9] R. Eckmiller, "Electronic simulation of the vertebrate retina," IEEE Trans. Biomed. Eng. BME-22: 305-311, 1975.

[10] R. Eckmiller, et al., Neurotechnologie-Report, Bundesministerium f. Forschung u. Technologie, Bonn, April, 1994

[11] R. Eckmiller, "Towards retina implants for improvement of vision in humans with retinitis pigmentosa - Challenges and first results." Proc. WCNN'95, Washington, INNS-Press, Lawrence Earlbaum Assoc. Hillsdale, 1995, vol. I, pp.228-233.

[12] K. Fukushima, "Neural networks for visual pattern recognition," IEICE Trans. E 74: 179-190, 1991.

[13] P. Gaudiano, " Toward a unified theory of spatiotemporal processing in the retina," In: Neural Networks for Vision and Image Processing, G. Carpenter, S.Grossberg, eds., MIT Press, Cambridge,MA, 1992, pp.195-220.

[14] M.M. Gupta, G.K. Knopf, eds., "Neuro-Vision Systems," IEEE Press, Piscataway, NJ, 1994.

[15] M.S. Humayun, R.H. Propst, E. de Juan, K. McCormick, D. Hickingbotham, "Bipolar surface electrical stimulation of the vertebrate retina," Arch. Ophthal. 112: 110-116, 1994.

[16] M.S. Humayun, E. de Juan, G. Dagnelie, R. Greenberg, R. Propst, "Artificial vision," Invest. Ophthal. & Vis. Sci. 37: S451, 1996

[17] J.B. Jonas, U. Schneider, O.H. Naumann, "Count and density of human retinal photoreceptors," Graefes Arch. Clin. Exp. Ophthal. 230: 505-510, 1992.

[18] E. Kaplan, B.B. Lee, R.M. Shapley, "New views of primate retinal function," Prog. Retina Res. 9: 273-336, 1990.

[19] C. Koch, H. Li, eds. "Vision Chips: Implementing Vision Algorithms with Analog VLSI Circuits," IEEE Comp. Soc. Press, Los Alamitos, CA, 1995.

[20] H. Kolb, "The architecture of functional neural circuits in the vertebrate retina," Invest. Ophthal. & Vis. Sci. 35: 2385-2404, 1994.

[21] H. Kobayashi, T. Matsumoto, T. Yagi, T. Shimmi, "Image processing regularization filters and layered architecture," Neural Networks 6: 327-350, 1993.

[22] H. Kobayashi, T. Matsumoto, T. Yagi, K. Tanaka, "Light-adaptive architectures for regularization vision chips," Neural Networks 8: 87-101, 1995.

[23] J. Kremers, B.B. Lee, P.K. Kaiser, "Sensitivity of macaque retinal ganglion cells and human observers to combined luminance and chromatic temporal modulation," J. Opt. Soc. Am. 9: 1477-1485, 1992.

[24] B.B. Lee, P.R. Martin, A. Valberg, J. Kremers, "Physiological mechanisms underlying psychophysical sensitivity to combined luminance and chromatic modulation," J. Opt. Soc. Am. 10: 1403-1412, 1993.

[25] B.B. Lee, J. Pokorny, V.C. Smith, J. Kremers, "Responses to pulses and sinusoids in macaque ganglion cells," Vision Res. 34: 3081-3096, 1994.

[26] A.G. Leventhal, K.G. Thompson, D. Liu, "Retinal ganglion cells within the foveola of new world (Saimiri sciureus) and old world (Macaca fascicularis) monkeys," J. Comp. Neurol. 338: 242-254, 1993.

[27] J.S. Lim, "Two-dimensional Signal and Image Processing," Prentice Hall, Englewood Cliffs, NJ, 1990.

[28] R. Linsker, "Deriving receptive fields using an optimal encoding criterion," In: Adv. in Neural Information Processing Systems 5, S.J. Hanson, J.D. Cowan, C.L. Giles, eds., Morgan Kaufmann, San Mateo, CA, 1993, pp. 953-960.

[29] P.J.G. Lisboa, "Image classification using Gabor representations with a neural net," In: Neural Networks for Vision, Speech, and Natural Language, R. Linggard, D.J. Meyers, C. Nightingale, eds., Chapman & Hall, 1992, pp. 112-127.

[30] J. Mann, D. Edell, J.F. Rizzo, J. Raffel, J.L. Wyatt, "Development of a silicon retinal implant: Microelectronic system for wireless transmission of signal and power," Invest. Ophthal. & Vis. Sci. 35: S1380, 1994.

[31] R.W. Massof, D. Finkelstein, "A two-stage hypothesis for the natural course of retinitis pigmentosa," In: Adv. in the Biosciences, Pergamon Press, vol. 62, 1987, pp. 29-58.

[32] M. Meister, L. Lagnado, D.A. Baylor, "Concerted signaling by retinal ganglion cells," Science 270: 1207-1210, 1995.

[33] W.H. Merigan, J.H.R. Maunsell, "How parallel are the primate visual pathways?," Ann. Rev. Neurosci. 16: 369-402, 1993

[34] S. Neuenschwander, W. Singer, "Long-range synchronization of oscillatory light responses in the cat retina and lateral geniculate nucleus" Nature 379: 728-733, 1996.

[35] A.A. Penn, R.O.L. Wong, C.J. Shatz, "Neuronal coupling in the developing mammalian retina," J. Neurosci. 14: 3805-3815, 1994.

[36] P.A. Regalia, "Adaptive IIR Filtering in Signal Processing and Control," Marcel Dekker, New York, 1995.

[37] J.F. Rizzo, S. Miller, T. Denison, T. Herndon, J.L. Wyatt, "Electrically evoked cortical potentials from stimulation of rabbit retina with a microfabricated electrode array," Invest. Ophthal. & Vis. Sci. 37: S707, 1996.

[38] R.W. Rodieck, M. Watanabe, "Survey of the morphology of macaque retinal ganglion cells that project to the pretectum, superior colliculus, and parvicellular laminae of the lateral geniculate nucleus," J. Comp. Neurol. 338: 289-303, 1993.

[39] J.D. Schall, V.H. Perry, A.G. Leventhal. "Retinal ganglion cell dendritic fields of old-world monkeys are oriented radially," Brain Res. 368: 18-23, 1986.

[40] M. Schwarz, B.J. Hosticka, M. Scholles, R. Eckmiller, "Concept of a retina implant for ganglion cell stimulation applicable for patients suffering from retinitis pigmentosa," Proc. 5th Int. Workshop on Functional Electrostimulation, Vienna August 1995, pp.413-416.

[41] J. Sebag, "Anatomy and pathology of the vitreo-retinal interface," Eye 6: 541-552, 1992.

[42] M. Schütte, "Centrifugal innervation of the rat retina," Visual Neurosci. 12: 1083-1092, 1995.

[43] J. Skrzypek, "Lightness constancy: Connectionist architecture for controlling sensitivity," IEEE Trans. Systems, Man, Cybernetics SMC-20: 957-968, 1990.

[44] J.L. Stone, W.E. Barlow, M.S. Humayun, E. de Juan, A.H. Milam, "Morphometric analysis of macular photoreceptors and ganglion cells in retinas with retinitis pigmentosa," Arch. Ophthalmol. 110: 1634-1639, 1992.

[45] J.B. Troy, B.B. Lee, "Steady discharges of macaque retinal ganglion cells," Visual Neurosci. 11: 111-118, 1994.

[46] T. Wachtler, C. Wehrhahn, B.B. Lee, "A simple model of human foveal ganglion cell responses to hyperacuity stimuli," J. Comp. Neurosci. 3: 1-10, 1996.

[47] M. Watanabe, R.W. Rodieck, "Parasol and midget ganglion cells of the primate retina," J. Comp. Neurol. 289: 434-454, 1989.

[48] M.V. Wickerhauser, "Adapted Wavelet Analysis: From Theory to Software," A.K. Peters, Ltd., 1993; Adaptive Wavelet-Analysis, Theorie und Software, Vieweg, Braunschweig, 1996.

[49] M.J. Wright, "Training and testing of neural net window operators on spatiotemporal image sequences," In: Neural Networks for Vision, Speech, and Natural Language, R. Linggard, D.J. Meyers, C. Nightingale, eds., Chapman & Hall, 1992, pp. 93-111.

[50] J.L. Wyatt, J.F. Rizzo, A. Grumet: "Development of a silicon retinal implant: Epiretinal stimulation of retinal ganglion cells in the rabbit," Invest. Ophthal. & Vis. Sci. 35: S1380, 1994.

[51] J. Yang, A. Reeves, "Bottom-up visual image processing probed with weigthed hermite polynomials," Neural Networks 8: 669-691, 1995.

[52] T. Yeh, B.B. Lee, J. Kremers, "The time course of adaptation in macaque retinal ganglion cells," Vision. Res. 36: 913-931, 1996.

Neuronal Goals: Efficient Coding and Coincidence Detection

Nathan Intrator*
School of Mathematical Sciences
Tel Aviv University
nin@cns.brown.edu

Abstract— **Barlow's seminal work on minimal entropy codes and unsupervised learning is reiterated. In particular, the need to transmit the probability of events is put in a practical neuronal framework for detecting suspicious events. A variant of the BCM learning rule [15] is presented together with some mathematical results suggesting optimal minimal entropy coding.**

Key words: Sparse coding, Non-Gaussian distributions, BCM Theory, Minimal Entropy

1 Introduction

There is no doubt that much of what we do is determined by what has happened in the past. In particular, our ability to understand speech in noisy environment, understand under contextual constraints, or drive a car, is a manifestation of our ability to predict the next phoneme/word in a sentence, predict the next required control movement, or at least adjust our expectations according to the past context. Clearly, this is a fundamental concept without which the system would not function at all, or would be severely degraded.

It is largely assumed that if the role of sensory neurons is to detect features in their input representation, then they should transmit the probability of occurrence of the features they learn to detect. While this sounds very natural and simple, we argue that such coding is not optimal and in fact neurons can and should transmit additional information.

Following Barlow's seminal work on minimal entropy codes and unsupervised learning, we attempt to address some fundamental problems concerning neuronal coding, neuronal goals for learning, feature detection and information transmission. In particular, the need to transmit the probability of events is put in a practical neuronal framework for detecting suspicious events. We derive these assertions from basic principles of information theory, from energy conservation considerations, and from some assumptions about neuronal goals.

Several other researchers have been interested in these questions. Atick [1] studied information coding patterns in flys and mammalians retinal coding and supports the notion of redundancy reduction through effective information coding. Field et al. [10, 21] inferred about the goal of visual sensory coding from properties of the statistics of natural images. Their main conclusions are the need to extract higher order statistics (i.e., more than linear and pairwise) and the need for sparse coding as a mean to achieve efficient information relay.

In this paper we present a unifying theory that combines the need for efficient feature detection with the need for efficient information transmission and a fundamental neuronal goal for suspicious coincidence detection. We start with a review of Barlow's work on coincidence detection, continue with a review of a BCM neuron in terms of its feature detection ability and information coding properties, and later discuss some regularization properties of these neurons in terms of the probability of events they can become selective to and outlier avoidance. We conclude with a motivation from the principle of maximum entropy to the optimality of the code.

2 Neuronal goal: Suspicious coincidences detection

Barlow has been arguing for a long time that *suspicious coincidences* is the basic type of event to which the cerebral cortex must attune itself [2, 3, 6, 7]. Assuming that a major task of the brain is to form a statistical model of the world, Barlow asked what kind of events would be worth noting and keeping a record of. Clearly, neither isolated events (the falling of a stone) nor repeated occurrences of events (the ticking of a clock) deserve paying too much attention to. In contrast, a co-occurrence of two events may call for investigation or may justify remembering, but only if this co-occurrence is *surprising* (i.e., unlikely), given prior knowledge regarding the occurrence of the individual events. Coincidence detection is also a key idea in the *Compositional Machine* framework presented by Geman and Bienenstock [13].

Consider the statistical problem of learning which tries to determine whether a compound event such as C followed by U is a random co-occurrence or a significant association. If it is the latter then C is a conditional stimulus to U, can be useful in predicting it, and in some cases can be useful in detecting the event U out of several concurrently occurring events. Clearly, we can not determine anything about the combination of C and U before becoming independently selective to each of the events, and having

---

*Current address: Institute for Brain and Neural Systems, Box 1843, Brown University, Providence, RI 02912

estimated their prior probabilities. Hence, Barlow hypothesises that the perception of an event, not only should signal its occurrence, but must also indicate the prior probability of what has been signaled.

2.1 Selfridge's Pandemonium and Barlow's Probabilistic Pandemonium

The probabilistic line of reasoning suggests that sensory coding is "... the process of preparing a representation of the current sensory scene in a form that enables subsequent learning mechanisms to be versatile and reliable" [6]. Specifically, a representation is useful for learning if it includes records of recurring and co-occurring events. As noted by Barlow, a convenient substrate for such a representation is provided by Selfridge's Pandemonium [23]. In Barlow's Probabilistic Pandemonium, the response strength of a feature-detector demon would be proportional to $-\log P$, where P is the probability of occurrence of the feature the demon detects.   These signals are then propagated to an association network which receives *unconditional* inputs as well – inputs that follow and are assumed to be related to the *conditional* input. The main innovation in this setup, is the argument that each demon (feature detector) propagates information inversely proportional to the likelihood of the feature that is detected. This is sharply different than more conventional feature detectors, such as say Principal Components, in which the output is proportional to the degree of similarity between the input and the feature (when extracting PC from the correlation of inputs matrix), or the amount of variance explained by that feature (when extracting PC from the covariance matrix).

In the next section we present the feature extraction properties of a BCM neuron and emphasize its coding properties and relevance to coincidence detection.

3   The BCM feature extraction and coding

The feature extraction method briefly described below achieves dimensionality reduction by seeking features that would best distinguish among the members of the set.   The potential importance of these features is related to their invariance properties, or their ability to generalize. Invariance properties of features extracted by this method have been demonstrated previously in various recognition tasks [14, 16, 17].

From a mathematical viewpoint, extracting features from gray level images is related to dimensionality reduction in a high dimensional vector space, in which an $n \times k$ pixel image is considered to be a vector of length $n \times k$. The dimensionality reduction is achieved by replacing each image (or its high dimensional equivalent vector) by a low dimensional vector in which each element represents a projection of the image onto a vector of synaptic weights.

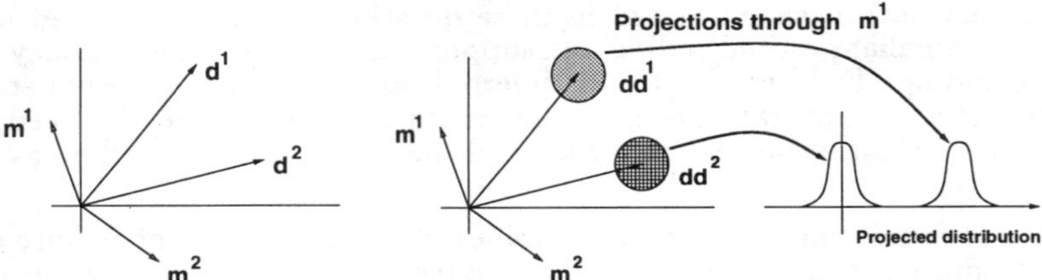

Figure 1: The stable solutions for a two dimensional two input problem are m_1 and m_2 (left) and similarly with a two-cluster data (right).

The BCM feature extraction [8, 15] seeks multi-modality in the projected distribution of these high dimensional vectors. A simple example is illustrated in Figure 1. For a two-input problem in two dimensions, the stable solutions (projection directions) are m_1 and m_2, each has the property of being orthogonal to one of the inputs. In a higher dimensional space, for n linearly independent inputs, a stable solution is one that is orthogonal to all but one of the inputs. In case of noisy but clustered inputs, a stable solution will be orthogonal to all but one of the cluster centers. As is seen in Figure 1 (right), this leads to a bimodal, or, in general, multi-modal, projected distribution.

The mathematical results concerning the type of feature detection and coding is given in [15]. One of the results roughly says:

Theorem With n clusters in an n-dimensional space, the only stable solutions are projections which are orthogonal to all but one of the clusters. There are at most n such solutions and each such solution occurs with probability P_i (the probability of cluster i). Moreover, the neuronal activity of a neuron that becomes tuned to cluster i (in the linear case) is $1/P_i$.

This result makes the BCM neuron a good candidate for efficiently coding events. By adding a monotone truncated log function on top of the neuronal activity, we get the desired -log probability of events (see the the discussion of the optimality of this code below). The truncation at zero is required as neuronal activity is expected to be non-negative.

While the activity of a neuron becomes close to the inverse of the probability of the event this is not always the case. If the event is only partially detected, namely, the probability that the event appears in the input at a certain time is not close to one, then the activity of the neuron is degraded accordingly.

3.1 Interplay between suspicious coincidence and avoiding outliers

The above results points at a potential weakness of the BCM neuron: sensitivity to outliers. Clearly, if a neuron becomes tuned to an event with vanishing probability (although the probability of such case is going to zero as well) its activity may grow unbounded. This fact had motivated us in the past to apply a saturating sigmoidal transfer function to the neuronal activity [15]. Such saturation function should have an upper bound that is larger than 1, and in fact the upper bound will determine the smallest probability of events that the neuron can become tuned to. The ability to control the probability of events the neuron can become tuned to is very important; It is likely that when detailed low-level features are required, the neuron should be able to detect events with very low probability, but when a high degree of generalization is needed, the neuron should not become tuned to events with very low probability.

Once avoidance of outliers is assured, we can add the monotone log function on top of the neuronal activity for efficient information relay.

4　A Coincidence detection network

In this section, we present a simple architecture that can serve as a coincidence detection network (CDN) and is based on the BCM neurons described above. The first layer of neurons (Figure 2) is composed of feature detectors of events A_i in the input representation. Without loss of generality, we assume that when the dynamic process of learning has stabilized, neuron i becomes selective to event A_i such that the maximal activity of the neuron is around $-\log(P_i)$, where P_i is the probability of event A_i. The second

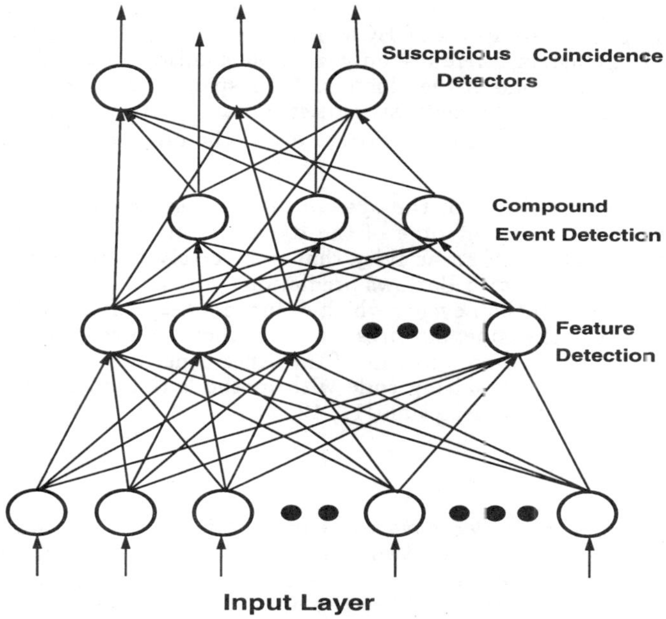

Figure 2: A suspicious coincidence detection network.

layer of neurons receives input from the previous layer, or from other sensory maps, and thus it can only detect events which have been found interesting by earlier feature detectors. Thus, the inputs to the second layer are much more quiet than the inputs to the previous layer, as the events are now sparsely coded, and compound events are more likely to be found. The second layer of BCM neurons again looks for multi-modal projected distribution, which indicate clusters in the activity of the first layer.

With additional sensory input (possibly from other modalities), events A_i and A_j may become correlated and can be detected by the second layer of neurons (e.g. red apple), then emerging projections in the second layer will generate cell activity that is of the form

$$-\sum_j w_j \log P(A_j) = -\log[\Pi_j P(A_j)^{w_j}],$$

such that the resulting neuronal activity represents $-\log P(B)$, where B denotes the compound event. The BCM rule for synaptic weight modification effectively seeks such projections along which the probability density deviates maximally from a Gaussian distribution.[1] The receptive fields of units trained

---

[1] Due to the central limit theorem, most projections are Gaussian, and thus can be described completely by their

with the BCM rule are thus tuned to the detection of interesting low-dimensional structure in the high-dimensional input space.

5   Minimum entropy coding

Barlow considered the question of "what properties should a representation have in order to make it suitable for use by subsequent learning mechanisms". He argues that not every complete representation would do, and in particular, a model based on Hebbian synapses can only access some of the information needed, but not all. There is an apparent contradiction between the desire to have redundant coding which is related to the simplicity of the code and the need for redundancy reduction as a mean for efficient transmission. Barlow stresses that a completely non redundant stimuli is indistinguishable from random noise [5], thus, requiring a highly sophisticated scheme (probably complex and slow) to decode the signal. Since neuronal code seems highly structured, one can infer that its encoding is highly redundant.

Minimal entropy codes satisfy the need to know the prior probability of events described by the code, and thus, if the variables of the sensory representation occur independently of each other, it is then possible to derive the prior probability of any logical function of these variables from prior probabilities of the individual variables. Therefore, such a representation allows a simple search for suspicious coincidence of events. More specifically, suppose we have a set of neurons tuned to bars at all orientations. A priori, one can assume that the different orientations are independent, but for a specific image, say the character 'A', we create a model by noting that several orientations are highly probable at certain locations of that object. Barlow goes on to describing a *minimum entropy coding* which should satisfy two constraints, it has to be reversible, namely reconstruction of the original input should be possible, and in addition the code should have minimal entropy. The essence of minimal entropy coding, is to form a factorial code, i.e., to find a set of symbols such that each of them occurs independently of the others, so that their joint probability is a multiplication of their individual ones. In the BCM network factorial coding of events, namely the independence of features detected by different neurons is achieved by the lateral inhibition architecture and reduced space of solutions of BCM neurons. The reduced space of solutions is due to the fact that for data with n clusters, there are only n stable solutions, each characterized by a synaptic vector being orthogonal to all but one of the clusters. This space of solutions is minimal and sufficient for distinguishing between n clusters. In contrast, a discriminant analysis method for separation between n clusters [22, for review], has $\binom{n}{2}$ possible solutions, i.e., on the order of n^2, and is thus, more likely to find correlated solutions.

Sparse coding, in which different states of the system are represented by neuronal activity with only a small number of active units, is an outcome of the dynamics of the BCM learning. This is because each BCM neuron conveys events with an activity that is inversely proportional to their probability of occurrence [15]. Thus, in accordance with Barlows predictions [4], events that occur with high probability are conveyed by a less active neuron than events which occur less frequently. Such events will be conveyed by a neuron that is quiet most of the time, but fires strongly when the event is detected. It follows that in the BCM coding case, sparse coding is an outcome of the other constraints and not a direct goal by itself. It will be interesting to compare the resulting code with methods that maximize sparsity or kurtosis as a goal for neuronal coding and feature detection [11, 12, 21].

6   Optimal neuronal code

When seeking optimal neuronal code, we have to bear in mind that the code should preserve spatial relations between the inputs. In particular, two events that are close to one another in measurement space, e.g. two views of the same person, should have an internal representation that preserves this correspondence [9, 25]. This requirement nullifies the use of classical coding theory, since we no longer can use a look-up table that translates the code into symbols to be conveyed from layer to layer, as the symbol representation does not preserve the metric of the original space. One can assume that the additional continuity constraint will limit the optimality and information capacity of codes generated by such a map.

We are now in the following situation: There is a measurement space (X, P) of vectors in R^k. We seek a continuous function on a compact domain in R^k,

$$fC^k :\mapsto R^+,$$

that conveys as much information about the measurement space as possible. The function f is found by learning from a set of observations $\{x_1, \ldots, x_N\}$ sampled from X with probability P. We assume that the activity of a cell is a function of its vector of synaptic weights and the inputs. This defines a distribution over the possible values of cell activity. We discretize those values to a given accuracy and thus are assuming that the collection of cell activity values is given by f_i, $i = 1, \ldots, n$, with corresponding probabilities p_i, $i = 1, \ldots, n$. The mean cell activity is given by

$$\bar{f} = \sum_{i=1}^{n} p_i f_i, \quad \sum_i p_i = 1, \tag{1}$$

---

covariance matrix (second-order statistics).

We ask the following question: what is the distribution that maximizes the information capacity of neurons subject to the constraint of a fixed average activity. We assume that the energy dissipated by the neuron is linearly related to the neuronal activity, and thus would like to study the information capacity of neuronal codes with a fixed average activity. We additionally assume that cell activity is non negative, so an inactive cell which dissipates the least amount of energy has zero activity. It turns out that the *principle of maximum entropy* [18, 19, For discussion], is directly applicable in this case. It gives an explicit relation between neuronal activity (possibly firing rate) and the corresponding probability for this activity level, so as to maximize information capacity subject to a fixed mean activity.

At a first glance, it is not intuitive at all that there is any such connection. We often study the information entropy of distribution which is given by

$$H(p_1, \ldots, p_n) = -K \sum_i p_i \ln p_i, \tag{2}$$

where K is a positive constant. However, this case is only applicable when the actual events to be relayed can be just a set of labels that has to be converted via a look up table at the receiving end to the actual event transmitted.

The maximum entropy principle implies that for maximal code capacity, the relation between the probability of activity and its value is given by

$$p_i = \frac{exp(-\mu f_i)}{\sum_j exp(-\mu f_j)}, \tag{3}$$

where μ is interpreted as temperature in statistical mechanics formulation. Under these probabilities, the entropy of that specific code is given by

$$H_f = -\mu \sum_i p_i f_i - Z, \tag{4}$$

where Z is the partition function. If instead of using the optimal probability distribution given by (3), we use a suboptimal distribution given by q_i's, then the entropy of the new code is less or equal that given in (4), more precisely [24]

$$H_q = -\mu \sum_i q_i f_i + \sum_i q_i \log(q_i/p_i), \tag{5}$$

namely the two entropies differ by the Kullback-Leibler divergence [20] between the given distribution q and the optimal one p. The latter term is non-negative and is zero if and only if $q \equiv p$. Thus, better distributions will have a small K-L divergence and smaller differences between the distributions are more desirable.

This formulation lets us compare between different coding schemes which have the same mean activity. It can be extended to networks of neurons, and it follows that a network of BCM neurons as described in [15] maximizes entropy under the additional (independent) constraint of sparse coding.

7 Summary

Motivated by Barlow's seminal work, we have presented a theory that includes feature detection and efficient feature coding. One possible application is a fundamental neuronal task of suspicious coincidence detection. In addition, we have shown a mechanism for probability regularization for the feature detectors, so that they do not become tuned to events occurring with too small probability. The principle of maximum entropy was used to demonstrate the optimality of such neuronal code.

Acknowledgements

Fruitful discussions with Shimon Edelman, Ömer Artun and other members of the Institute for Brain and Neural Systems at Brown University are greatfully acknowledged. This work was partially supported by the Office of Naval Research.

References

[1] J. J. Atick. Could information theory provide an ecological theory of sensory processing? *Network*, 3:213–251, 1992.

[2] H. B. Barlow. Possible principles underlying the transfomations of sensory messages. In W. Rosenblith, editor, *Sensory Communication*, pages 217–234. MIT Press, Cambridge, MA, 1961.

[3] H. B. Barlow. Cerebral cortex as model builder. In D. Rose and V. G. Dobson, editors, *Models of the visual cortex*, pages 37–46. Wiley, New York, 1985.

[4] H. B. Barlow. Single units and sensation. *Perception*, 1:371–394, 1989.

[5] H. B. Barlow. Unsupervised learning. *Neural Computation*, 1(3):295–311, 1989.

[6] H. B. Barlow. Conditions for versatile learning, helmholtz's unconscious inference, and the task of perception. *Vision Research*, 30:1561–1571, 1990.

[7] H. B. Barlow. What is the computational goal of the neocortex. In C. Koch and J. L. Davis, editors, *Large Scale Neuronal Theories of the Brain*. MIT Press, 1994.

[8] E. L. Bienenstock, L. N Cooper, and P. W. Munro. Theory for the development of neuron selectivity: orientation specificity and binocular interaction in visual cortex. *Journal Neuroscience*, 2:32–48, 1982.

[9] S. Edelman. Class similarity and viewpoint invariance in the recognition of 3D objects. CS-TR 92-17, Weizmann Institute of Science, 1992.

[10] D. J. Field. What is the goal of sensory coding. *Neural Computation*, 6:559–601, 1994.

[11] P. Földiák. Forming sparse representations by local anti-Hebbian learning. *Biological Cybernetics*, 64:165–170, 1990.

[12] C. Fyfe and R. Baddeley. Finding compact and sparse-distributed representations of visual images. *Network*, 6:333–344, 1995.

[13] S. Geman and E. Bienenstock. Compositional vision, 1995. Talk given at the Object Features for Visual Shape Representation workshop, NIPS.

[14] N. Intrator. Feature extraction using an unsupervised neural network. *Neural Computation*, 4:98–107, 1992.

[15] N. Intrator and L. N Cooper. Objective function formulation of the BCM theory of visual cortical plasticity: Statistical connections, stability conditions. *Neural Networks*, 5:3–17, 1992.

[16] N. Intrator and J. I. Gold. Three-dimensional object recognition of gray level images: The usefulness of distinguishing features. *Neural Computation*, 5:61–74, 1993.

[17] N. Intrator, D. Reisfeld, and Y. Yeshurun. Face recognition using a hybrid supervised/unsupervised neural network. *Pattern Recognition Letters*, 17:67–76, 1996.

[18] E. T. Jaynes. Information theory and statistical mechanics I. *Phys. Rev.*, 106:620–530, 1957.

[19] E. T. Jaynes. On the rationale of maximum entropy methods. *Proc. IEEE*, 70:939–952, 1982.

[20] S. Kullback. *Information Theory and Statistics*. John Wiley, New York, 1959.

[21] B. A. Olshausen and D. J. Field. Natural image statistics and efficient coding. *Network (to appear)*, 1996.

[22] G. Sebestyen. *Decision Making Processes in Pattern Recognition*. Macmillan, New York, 1962.

[23] O. G. Selfridge. Pandemonium: a paradigm for learning. In *The mechanisation of thought processes*. H.M.S.O., London, 1959.

[24] C. J. Thompson. *Classical Equilibrium Statistical Mechanics*. Clarendon Press, Oxford, 1988.

[25] Y. Weiss and S. Edelman. Representation of similarity as a goal of early visual processing. *Network*, 6:19–41, 1995.

Time Series Prediction Using Mixtures of Experts

R. Meir†, A.J. Zeevi‡, R.J. Adler♮

† Department of Electrical Engineering
Technion, Haifa 32000, Israel
‡ Department of Industrial Engineering
Technion, Haifa 32000, Israel
♮ Department of Industrial Engineering
Technion, Haifa 32000, Israel

Abstract— We consider a novel non-linear model for time series analysis. The study of this model emphasizes both theoretical aspects as well as practical applicability to a number of test cases. The architecture of the model is demonstrated to be sufficiently rich, in the sense of approximating unknown functional forms, yet, it retains some of the simple and intuitive characteristics of linear models. A comparison to some more established non-linear models will be emphasized, and theoretical issues are backed by prediction results for benchmark time series, as well as computer generated data sets. Efficient estimation algorithms are seen to be applicable, made possible by the mixture based structure of the model.

1 Introduction

In this work we pursue a new family of models substantially extending, but strongly related to and based on the classic linear autoregressive moving average (ARMA) family. We wish to exploit the linear autoregressive technique in a manner that will enable a substantial increase in modeling power, in a framework which is non-linear and yet mathematically tractable. The novel model, whose building blocks are essentially linear, deviates from linearity in the integration process, that is, the way these blocks are combined. This model was first formulated in the context of a regression problem, and an extension to a hierarchical structure was also given [4]. It was termed the mixture of experts model (MEM). Variants of this model have recently been used in prediction problems both in economics and engineering (see fo instance the work in [8] on acoustic vector prediction and speech coding).

Recently, some theoretical aspects of the MEM , in the context of non-linear regression, were studied by Zeevi *et al.* [9], and an equivalence to a class of neural network models has been established, in the sense of the function approximation capability and degree of approximation results. The MEM allows a fairly intuitive evaluation both of the final parameter set, as well as the modeling process itself, resulting in straightforward inference possibilities as to the data structure. Although conceptually simple to understand and manipulate, as a combination of linear models, successful analysis of a wide scope of data sets is seen to be possible.

The purpose of this paper is to extend the previous work regarding the MEM in the context of a regression problem to time series, and present some numerical results. This goal is pursued by developing theoretical foundations, examining algorithmic aspects, and finally observing the actual performance in applications through test cases. We shall demonstrate that the MEM is a generalization of several existing, state of the art, statistical non-linear models encompassing Tong's TAR (threshold autoregressive) model [7], and a certain version of Priestley's [6] state dependent models (SDM). The main significance of the preliminary results, both theoretical and applied, is the actual development of a powerful, yet easily interpretable tool for the study of time-series, applicable to the fields of statistics, economics, and signal processing.

2 Model Description and Relation to other Models

In this section we present the MEM as a non-linear model for time series analysis, and compare it with the TAR and SDM models.

2.1 Model Structure

We follow Jordan and Jacobs [4], defining an architecture involving a set of function approximators - 'expert networks' - that are combined by a 'gating network'. These networks are trained simultaneously so as to split the input space into regions where particular 'experts' can specialize.

The MEM is an architecture composed of n *expert networks*, each of which solves a density estimation problem over a local region of the input space. The experts are combined by a *gating* network, which partitions the input space accordingly. Considering a scalar time series $\{x_t\}$, we associate with each expert a probabilistic model (density function) relating input vectors $\mathbf{x} = (x_{t-1}, x_{t-2}, \ldots, x_{t-d})^T \in \mathbb{R}^d$ to an output scalar $x_t \in \mathbb{R}$ and denote these probabilistic models by $p(x_t|\, \mathbf{x}_{t-d}^{t-1}; \theta_j, \sigma_j)\ j = 1, 2, \ldots, n$ where (θ_j, σ_j) is the expert parameter vector, taking values in a compact subset of $\mathbb{R}^{d+1}$. This probabilistic model, utilizes an auxiliary function $h_j(\mathbf{x}; \boldsymbol{\theta}_j) : \mathbb{R}^d \to \mathbb{R}$, which will be defined below.

Letting the parameters of each expert network be denoted by $(\boldsymbol{\theta}_j, \sigma_j)$, $j = 1, 2, \ldots, n$, those of the gating network by $\boldsymbol{\theta}_g$ and letting $\Theta = (\{\boldsymbol{\theta}_j, \sigma_j\}_{j=1}^n, \boldsymbol{\theta}_g)$ represent the complete set of parameters specifying the model, we may express the conditional distribution of the model, $p(x_t|\mathbf{x}_{t-d}^{t-1}, \Theta)$, as

$$p(x_t|\mathbf{x}_{t-d}^{t-1}; \Theta) = \sum_{j=1}^{n} g_j(\mathbf{x}_{t-d}^{t-1}; \boldsymbol{\theta}_g)p(x_t|\mathbf{x}_{t-d}^{t-1}; \boldsymbol{\theta}_j, \sigma_j), \tag{1}$$

together with the constraint that $\sum_{j=1}^n g_j(\mathbf{x}_{t-d}^{t-1}; \boldsymbol{\theta}_g) = 1$ and $g_j(\mathbf{x}_{t-d}^{t-1}; \boldsymbol{\theta}_g) \geq 0 \ \ \forall \mathbf{x}_{t-d}^{t-1}$.

We assume that the parameter vector $\Theta \in \Omega$, a compact subset of $\mathbb{R}^{2n(d+1)}$. Following the work of Jordan and Jacobs [4] we take the probability density functions to be Gaussian with mean $\boldsymbol{\theta}_j^T \mathbf{x}_{t-d}^{t-1} + \theta_{j,0}$ and variance σ_j (representative of the underlying, *local* AR model). The function $g_j(\mathbf{x}; \boldsymbol{\theta}_g) \equiv \exp\{\boldsymbol{\theta}_{g_j}^T \mathbf{x} + \theta_{g_j,0}\}/(\sum_{i=1}^n \exp\{\boldsymbol{\theta}_{g_i}^T \mathbf{x} + \theta_{g_i,0}\}$, thus implementing a multiple output logistic regression function.

The underlying non-linear mapping (i.e., the conditional expectation) characterizing the MEM, is described in the following equation

$$f_n(X_{t-d}^{t-1}; \Theta) = \mathrm{E}[X_t|\mathcal{F}_{t-d}^{t-1}; \mathcal{M}] = \sum_{j=1}^{n} g_j(X_{t-d}^{t-1}; \boldsymbol{\theta}_g)[\boldsymbol{\theta}_j^T X_{t-d}^{t-1} + \theta_{j,0}] \tag{2}$$

where $\mathcal{M}$ denotes the MEM model and $\mathcal{F}_{t-d}^{t-1} = \sigma(X_{t-1}, X_{t-2}, \ldots, X_{t-d})$ is the sigma-algebra generated by the random variables $X_{t-1}, X_{t-2}, \ldots, X_{t-d}$. Here the subscript n stands for the number of experts. Thus, we have $\hat{X}_t = f_n(X_{t-d}^{t-1}; \Theta)$ where $f_n : \mathbb{R}^d \times \Omega \to \mathbb{R}$, and $\hat{X}_t$ denotes the projection of X_t on the 'relevant past', given the model. We will use the notation $\mathrm{MEM}(n; d)$ where n is the number of experts in the model (proportional to the complexity, or number of parameters in the model), and d the lag size (i.e., the effective memory of the process).

2.2 Comparison

Two alternatives to standard linear techniques have been pointed out in the introductory section. These are Tong's TAR (threshold autoregressive) model [7], and the more general SDM (state dependent models) introduced by Priestley. The latter models can be reduced to a TAR model by imposing a more restrictive structure (for further details see [6]) . We shall now take a closer look at the structure of these two models, followed by a comparison to the MEM based on the formulation and properties of the TAR and SDM.

The main idea underlying the TAR model is the assumption that the true process may be described as follows

$$X(t) = \varphi(X_{t-1}, X_{t-2}, \ldots, X_{t-d}) + \varepsilon_t \qquad t = 1, 2, \ldots \tag{3}$$

where the functional relation $\varphi(\cdot)$ can be a simple linear mapping, or a more general, complex, non-linear one. Assuming that $\varphi(\cdot)$ is a piecewise continuous function, it follows that a piecewise linear approximation can come close to $\varphi(\cdot)$ to any arbitrary accuracy in a given metric (e.g., based on a Weirstrass approximation theorem). This fact motivates the following formulation of the TAR model

$$x_t = [a^{(i)}]^T \mathbf{x}_{t-d}^{t-1} + \varepsilon_t^{(i)} \qquad \mathbf{x}_{t-d}^{t-1} \in \mathcal{R}^{(i)} \tag{4}$$

where $\mathcal{R}^{(i)}$ is a d dimensional subset of $\mathbb{R}^d$, and $i = 1, 2, \ldots, n$. This model will be denoted $\mathrm{TAR}(n; d_1, d_2, \ldots, d_n)$, where d_i is the lag size allocated to the ith region. Here n denotes the number of linear regions utilized by the model. The vectors $a^{(i)}$ are the coefficients corresponding to the local linear approximation of φ by the TAR model. The following discussion will establish the generality of the MEM w.r.t. the class of SDM models (see Proposition 2.1). This result implies the generality of the MEM also w.r.t. TAR models since they are a restricted case of the SDM. Further results in this context are given in Section 3.3.

Priestley [6] introduced a class termed state dependent models (SDM), applying local linearization, by means of a first order Taylor series expansion of the non-linear process $\{X(t)\}$, given in 3, and a state space representation, to construct the approximating model. Thus, if the relation between past and present of the process $\{X(t)\}$ is given by $X_t = \varphi(X_{t-d}^{t-1}) + \varepsilon_t$ then by local linearization (i.e., a first order Taylor series expansion) we obtain

$$X_t = \phi_0(X_{t-d}^{t-1}) + \sum_{i=1}^{d} \phi_i(X_{t-d}^{t-1})X_{t-i} \tag{5}$$

where $\phi_i(\cdot)$ are partial derivatives of φ. Obviously, the SDM includes the linear ARMA models, bilinear models, and the TAR model as restricted cases (see Priestley's monograph [6] for a more elaborate discussion).

Comparison of the SDM (5) with the MEM (2) reveals the similar structure of both models. An easy algebraic manipulation demonstrates the relation between the coefficients $\{\phi_i\}$ of the SDM and the gating and expert functions of the MEM, yielding

$$\phi_0(X_{t-d}^{t-1};\Theta) = \sum_{j=1}^{n} g_j(X_{t-d}^{t-1};\boldsymbol{\theta}_g)\theta_{j,0} \quad ; \quad \phi_i(X_{t-d}^{t-1};\Theta) = \sum_{j=1}^{n} g_j(X_{t-d}^{t-1};\boldsymbol{\theta}_g)\theta_{j,i} \, . \tag{6}$$

From this equivalence one may conclude that the MEM is a specific form of the SDM with ϕ_i specified as in (6).

In fact, the following proposition, proved in [9] for compact spaces and extended in [10] (in a slightly weaker form) to non-compact spaces, ensures that the MEM is indeed equivalent to the most general formulation of the SDM, for functions $\varphi(\cdot)$ in the Sobolev space W_p^r of functions with r continuous derivatives in L_p.

Proposition 2.1 *Let $\phi_0(\mathbf{x},\theta) = \sum_{j=1}^{n} g_j(\mathbf{x},\boldsymbol{\theta}_g)\theta_{j,0}$. Then, for any function φ belonging to the Sobolev class W_p^r we have under very mild conditions on $g_j(\mathbf{x},\boldsymbol{\theta}_g)$, that for any $\varepsilon > 0$*

$$\sup_{\varphi \in W_p^r} \inf_{\Theta \in \Omega} \|\varphi(\cdot) - \phi_0(\cdot;\Theta)\| \leq \frac{c(\varepsilon)}{r^{r/d}} + \varepsilon$$

where n is the number of experts, d the lag size and $c(\varepsilon)$ is finite for any non-zero ε. The norm implicit in the above equation is taken with respect to an integrable measure $\nu(\cdot)$ over $\mathbb{R}^d$.

Since ε can be arbitrarily small and n can be made as large as we need, this result establishes the universality of the MEM, w.r.t. an unknown mapping $\varphi(\cdot)$ assumed to belong to the Sobolev class. Set $\phi_i \equiv 0 \;\; \forall i \geq 1$, then by Proposition 2.1 we have established the approximation power of the MEM and described the convergence rate. Obviously, this statement is stronger than the local linearization claims, given in the context of the SDM and TAR models. Moreover, the actual manipulation of the SDM requires further linearization, resulting in substantial loss of generality.

3 Main Results

3.1 Background

This section will address the issue of statistical inference from an observed data set, i.e., how can the parameters of the MEM be estimated, and what claims can be made regarding the estimator's performance. We shall utilize the method of maximum likelihood (ML), and give results w.r.t. a *misspecified* scenario (i.e., when the data is generated according to another probabilistic law, that differs from the probabilistic structure of the MEM). Results for the well-specified case are straightforwardly obtained from standard martingale convergence theorems (for an example of the above see [7] w.r.t. the TAR model). In what follows it will be useful to make the following assumption regarding the the stochastic process generating the data.

Assumption 3.1 *The stochastic process $\{X_t : t = 0,1,\ldots\}$ is a stationary and ergodic Markov process, satisfying a known finite memory requirement of length d. The homogeneous transition kernel is absolutely continuous, thus the transition density function obeys*

$$p(X_t \mid X_{t-1}, X_{t-2},\ldots) = p(X_t \mid X_{t-1}, X_{t-2}\ldots,X_{t-d}) \quad \forall t \geq d$$

3.2 Parameter Estimation Results

Assume we are given a realization of $\{X_t\}$ in the form of a data set $\mathcal{D}_N = \{x_t\}_{t=1}^{N}$. Our goal is to use the MEM model, i.e., the transition function given in eq. (1), to learn the structure of underlying stochastic process. In the specific case where the data set $\mathcal{D}_N$ is a realization of a Markov chain, with the transition kernel of the MEM, we can be assured that the underlying structure is captured, in the limit of sufficiently large N. This is the *well specified* case.

In the more general *misspecified* scenario, the realization is governed by a transition function which differs in functional form from the transition kernel of the MEM. Although this will hamper our hopes of learning the underlying structure, we will still be able to obtain results concerning the estimator's characteristic behavior, i.e., asymptotic normality and consistency, w.r.t. a certain parameter value, which is 'best', in a sense that it minimizes the risk function. Assume now that the data generating mechanism (i.e., the stochastic process) is subject to Assumption 3.1 and is not necessarily endowed with a transition kernel of the MEM form. That is, the process is still a stationary ergodic Markov chain, though the functional form of the transition kernel is different. The main implications of the results of Domowitz and White (1982) are that, under the appropriate regularity conditions, the ML estimator exists, is unique and is asymptotically normal. It is easy to show then (see [9][10]), that the order of convergence of the error in this case is $O(1/N)$.

As a non-linear model, it is not clear whether efficient and robust procedures exist for estimating the parameters of the MEM via the maximum likelihood (ML) method. It turns out that a very efficient estimation procedure exists, the so-called Expectation-Maximization (EM) algorithm (Dempster *et al.* [2]). The algorithm was given in [4] in the context of a regression problem (for i.i.d. data), using the MEM as a parametric estimator. In [5], theoretical convergence results were obtained. These preliminary, yet fundamental, results may be readily extended to the time series scenario, where the observations are dependent.

Having settled the question of the estimator's performance in the face of misspecification, we may still inquire as to the specification error, i.e., 'how bad are we doing' in maximizing a risk function (log-likelihood) w.r.t. a model which is not adapted to the actual laws underlying the process. In other words, how far is the 'best' member of our family of parametric models, from the 'true' member of a larger class, generating the data. This question will be partially answered in the following section, where the approximation error (due to misspecification) is analyzed and bounded, yielding an overall upper bound on the error, induced by the MEM estimator. We note that this analysis is in terms of the regression function, i.e., the MEM is used to learn the structure of the 'true', underlying regression function.

3.3 Representational Power

In this section we pursue the question of representational power in the context of approximating the underlying non-linear mapping, or conditional expectation function

$$f_n(X_{t-d}^{t-1}; \Theta) = \mathrm{E}[X_t | \mathcal{F}_{t-d}^{t-1}; \mathcal{M}] = \sum_{j=1}^{n} g_j(X_{t-d}^{t-1}; \theta_g)[\theta_j^T X_{t-d}^{t-1}) + \theta_{j,0}] \tag{7}$$

where $\mathcal{M}$ denotes the MEM model and $\mathcal{F}_{t-d}^{t-1} = \sigma(X_{t-1}, X_{t-2}, \ldots, X_{t-d})$. That is, we use the MEM as a non-linear functional estimator, and attempt to reconstruct the conditional expectation of X_t, projected on its relevant past.

We will determine upper bounds on the expected mean squared error (MSE) between the MEM estimator and the unknown mapping $f(\cdot)$. We note that use of the L_2 norm in the context of functional estimation is quite common practice, and is in accordance with the derivations in Zeevi *et al.* [9] that will serve as the basis for the analysis herein. The total error is decomposed into a stochastic term which is due to the sample set $\mathcal{D}_N$, and a deterministic component which is due to the misspecification of the model w.r.t. the true mapping. In the process we give a result concerning the equivalence of the MEM and a class of non-linear function approximants known as *neural networks*. The analysis of the stochastic (estimation) error is pursued on the basis of mixing assumptions w.r.t. the stochastic process $\{X_t\}$. Denote by $\hat{f}_{n,N}$ the LS estimator of the conditional expectation function f, w.r.t. the MEM parameteric models.

The following Theorem summarizes the main theoretical contribution of this work. The complete proof is given in the full paper.

Theorem 3.1 (Upper bounds on the mean squared error)
Suppose the markov process generating the data is of order d, and that f, the conditional expectation function is in the Sobolev class W_p^r. Then, given some technical assumptions, and for N sufficiently large we have the following upper bound which holds for any $\varepsilon > 0$

$$\mathrm{E}\|f - \hat{f}_{n,N}\|_2^2 \leq \frac{c}{n^{2r/d}} + \frac{m^*}{2N} + \varepsilon + o\left(\frac{1}{N}\right), \tag{8}$$

where $c(\varepsilon)$ is a finite number independent of n, the complexity index (i.e., the number of experts in the architecture). The parameter r is the number of continuous derivatives in L_p that f is assumed to possess and d is the dimensonality of the input. Here, $m^* = \mathrm{Tr}\{B^*(A^*)^{-1}\}$ and the matrices A^* and B^* are related to the Fisher information in the case of misspecified estimation. N is the size of the data set $\mathcal{D}_N$. The random variable $\hat{\theta}_{n,N}$ is the LS estimator of the parameter vector of the MEM. The expectation here is taken w.r.t. the the d fold probability measure of the stochastic process $\{X_t\}$.

3.4 Numerical Results

The following examples focus on the feasibility and applicability of the MEM by examining its performance on certain test cases. We have compared the prediction quality of the MEM to ARMA and TAR models for two well known benchmark problems; the Canadian lynx data series and the solar activity (Wölfer sunspot numbers) time series. For the latter, a comparison with neural networks is also provided. Two artificially generated computer data sets have also been analyzed. A chirp (linear FM signal), and data generated by a TAR model are considered. We will utilize one-step prediction to assess the quality of the MEM. The average relative variance (arv) of a set $\mathcal{S}$, $arv(\mathcal{S}) = \frac{\sum_{k \in \mathcal{S}} (x_k - \hat{x}_k)^2}{\sum_{k \in \mathcal{S}} (x_k - \bar{x}_{\mathcal{S}})^2}$ is used as a measure of misfit, for the one step prediction results.

Analysis of the Canadian lynx is summarized in Figure 1. A variance stabilizing transformation (log) was applied to the data, prior to the analysis by the different models. Observations from the period of $1821 - 1920$ constituted the learning set, while $1921 - 1934$ was used as the prediction set. The best results were obtained (following the method of gradually increasing the number of experts) using an MEM(3; 6) that utilizes three experts, each an AR(6) model.

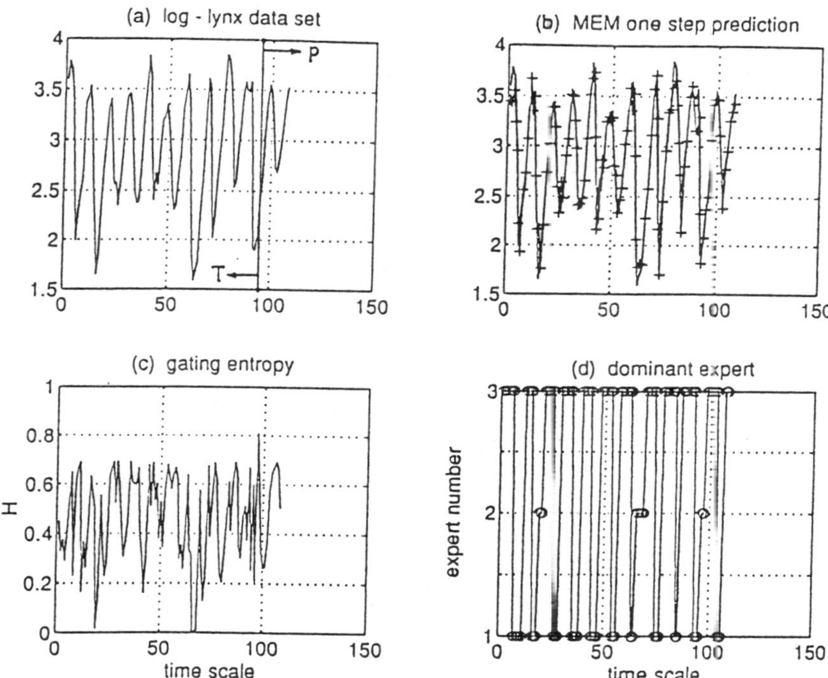

Figure 1: Analysis of the log transformed Canadian lynx time series (1821-1934). (a) The log lynx time series. (b) One step prediction of the MEM for the learning set (1821-1921) and prediction set (1921-1934), superimposed on the original data series. (c) Entropy of the discrete probability distribution induced by the gating network. (d) Most probable expert (largest value of the gating network output).

Training set (1821-1920) results	Prediction set (1921-1934) results
AR(7) - 0.1976	AR(7) - 0.07
TAR(2; 8, 3) - 0.132	TAR(2; 8, 3) - 0.045
MEM(3; 6) - 0.1214	MEM(3; 6) - 0.03

A similar deviation from linearity is exhibited by the Wölfer sunspot number, solar activity time series. We have compared the one-step prediction results for the MEM(3; 12) and the TAR, neural network model and best linear (ARMA) model, using the $arv(\cdot)$ measure. The results demonstrate that the MEM, TAR and neural network model behave similarly, while the best linear model, an AR(12), yields substantially less favorable results. A detailed analysis of the MEM's one step prediction performance demonstrates the allocation of different patterns in the time series to different experts, allowing a solid intuitive understanding of the non-linearity.

Moving to computer generated data sets, consider first a signal constructed from two linear regions as follows:

$$X_t = \begin{cases} 0.8X_{t-1} + 1 + \varepsilon_t & X_{t-1} < 0 \\ -0.5X_{t-1} - 0.6 + \varepsilon_t & X_{t-1} > 0 \end{cases}$$

where $\varepsilon_t \sim \mathcal{N}(0, \sigma^2)$ with $\sigma = 0.2$. This is an example of a first order TAR model with the same noise level at each region. We have simulated 100 data points from this model, and used them as a training set for an MEM(2; 1), that is a non-linear model composed of two AR(1) models. Figure 2 summarizes the performance results of the MEM(2; 1). The autoregressive structure is clearly seen in the phase plane, Figure 2(b) for this one-dimensional case. Pooling the experts, i.e., partitioning the input space and successfully combining the local models results in the overall fit shown in Figure 2(a).

As a second test case we considered a chirp (linear FM) signal of the form $x_t = \sin(\omega t^2)$ which can be interpreted as a time-varying frequency signal. Using the measure of average relative variance to summarize these results, and comparing the MEM and the best AR model, we have

$$MEM(5; 3) - 0.16 \quad ; \quad AR(3) - 0.85$$

Notice that the arv value for the one-step prediction fit of the AR(3) is close to unity, i.e., close to the fit that would have been obtained using the mean of the set as the predictor.

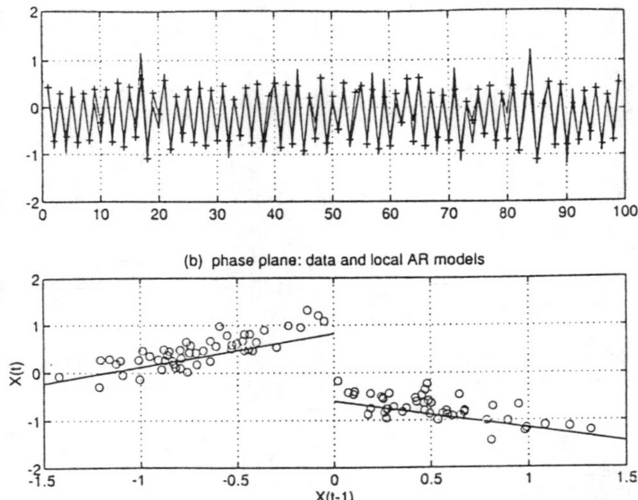

Figure 2: Analysis of TAR generated data. (a) One step prediction results for the MEM model superimposed on the original data set. (b) Data and local AR models fitted by the MEM, observed in the phase plane.

4 Discussion

In this work we have pursued a novel non-linear model for time series analysis. The mixture of experts model, termed MEM, has been demonstrated to be a promising non-linear model, endowed with a sound theoretical basis. An efficient learning algorithm, and parsimony with respect to other non-linear models are some points which are emphasized from a theoretical standpoint, and backed by numerical results. Overall, the performance of the MEM, w.r.t. a one step prediction criterion, has been promising, and in general favorable compared to other models.

All these numerical results are obtained on a 'first shot' basis, as no model selection or regularization criteria are employed. Moreover, we believe that just as in many other applications in engineering and statistics, the accumulated experience, combined with more sophisticated model selection criteria, will lead to greater success prospects.

References

[1] Brockwell, P.J. and Davis, R.A. *Time Series: Theory and Methods*, Second Edition, Springer Verlag, New York, 1991.

[2] Dempster, A.P. Laird, N.M. and Rubin, D.B. "Maximum Likelihood from Incomplete Data via the EM Algorithm", *J. Roy. Statis. Soc.*, vol. B39, pp. 1-38, 1977.

[3] Domowitz, I. and White, H. "Misspecified Models with Dependent Observations", *Journal of Econometrics*, vol. 20: 35-58, 1982.

[4] Jordan, M. and Jacobs, R. "Hierarchical Mixtures of Experts and the EM Algorithm", *Neural Computation*, vol. 6, pp. 181-214, 1994.

[5] Jordan, M.I. and Xu, L. "Convergence Results for the EM Approach to Mixtures of Experts Architectures", *Neural Networks*, to appear.

[6] Priestley M.B. *Non-linear and Non-stationary Time Series Analysis*, Academic Press, New York, 1988.

[7] Tong, H. *Threshold Models in Non-linear Time Series Analysis*, Springer Verlag, New York, 1983.

[8] Waterhouse, S.R. and Robinson, A.J. "Non-linear Prediction of Accoustic Vectors Using Hierarchical Mixtures of Experts", in *Neural Information Processing Systems 7*, Morgan Kaufmann, 1994.

[9] Zeevi, A.J., Meir, R. and Maiorov, V. "Error Bounds for Functional Approximation and Estimation Using Mixtures of Experts", submitted to *IEEE Transactions on Information Theory*, also in EE Pub. CC-132., Electrical Engineering Department, Technion, 1995.

[10] Zeevi, A.J., Meir, R. and Adler, R.J. "Non-linear Models for Time Series Using Mixtures of Experts", in preparation.

Data Manifolds, Natural Coordinates, Replicator Neural Networks, and Optimal Source Coding

Robert Hecht-Nielsen
HNC Software Inc.
5930 Cornerstone Court
San Diego, CA 92121
and
Department of Electrical and Computer Engineering and Institute for Neural Computation
University of California, San Diego
La Jolla, CA 92093

Abstract — Beginning 200 years ago with Gauss' concept of ellipsoidal statistical clouds of data points, many models for general data sources have been constructed. In this paper a new universal model of statistical data sources is proposed — the *data manifold*. Data manifolds are differentiable manifolds with a smooth probability density function which are diffeomorphic to an n-dimensional cube with uniform probability density. All real-world sources of data (i.e., sources defined by a regular a priori probability measure) can be approximated to arbitrary accuracy by data manifolds. *Natural coordinates* are the rectilinear cube coordinates of points in the data manifold. For a data manifold, natural coordinates are unique up to a set of uninteresting transformations. *Replicator* neural networks self-organize by using their inputs as desired outputs — they internally form a compressed representation for the input data. A new result presented here shows that three-hidden-layer multilayer perceptron replicator networks can, through the minimization of mean squared reconstruction error — e.g., by training on raw data examples drawn at random from a data manifold — develop a system of natural coordinates for that data manifold. Such networks, when their natural coordinates are uniformly quantized, also carry out Shannon-optimal source coding for data from the data manifold upon which they were trained. These new data manifold / natural coordinate / replicator neural network constructs may be the key to opening a vast new technological territory in real-world data representation, analysis, and compression. The cerebral cortex may utilize approximate versions of these constructs for the universal interoperable representation and association of sensory, motor, and cognitive information.

1 Introduction

My interest in the matters discussed here began in 1986 as a result of hearing an inspiring talk by David Zipser, Garrison Cottrell, and Paul Munro at UCSD [3]. They discussed the fact that multilayer perceptrons with one hidden layer could carry out image compression by self-organization training on image blocks drawn at random from a statistical class of images (i.e., by using a *replicator neural network* architecture which attempts to replicate its input as its output). Their work was a considerable extension of the original pioneering work of Kohonen [8, 9, 10, 12] (who originally invented the replicator neural network idea) and of the stimulating work of Sejnowski, Hinton, and Ackley [1]. Over the past 10 years I have been exploring this topic of replicator neural networks. A summary of the first results of this study was published last year in *Science* [6]. This paper discusses these results further.

2 Data Sources and Replicator Neural Networks

Consider Figures 1 and 2. A real-world statistical source of data vectors $\mathbf{x}$ in $\Re^m$ (defined by an a priori regular probability measure μ) is given. Vectors $\mathbf{x}$ from this source are chosen at random with respect to μ and used to train a multilayer perceptron replicator neural network with three hidden layers, the middle one of which has n units each equipped with an activation function with output values limited to the range [0,1] (as shown in Figure 1). The value of n is fixed (and usually much smaller than m – the dimension of the data source vectors), but we allow the first and third hidden layer sizes to be varied (these two layers have activation function *tanh* and the output layer activations are the identity).

Let us assume that we configure and train this neural network to get within a small value ε of the minimum possible mean squared error (e.g., by using backpropagation learning with some architecture adjustment scheme for the first and third hidden layers). Then each input vector $\mathbf{x}$ ends up being represented at the output of the middle hidden layer by the n unit output values u_1, u_2, ... , u_n each lying between 0 and 1. This representation vector $\mathbf{u} = (u_1, u_2,..., u_n)$, which belongs to the cube $[0,1]^n$ is then transformed by the top half of the network into an output vector $\mathbf{x}'$ which is as close as possible to the original input vector $\mathbf{x}$.

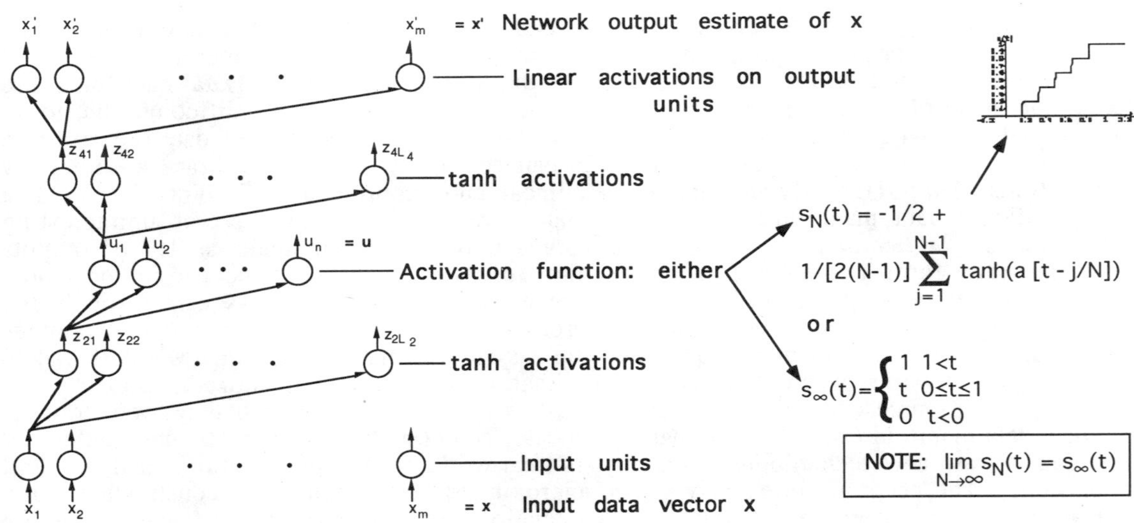

Figure 1.   The three hidden layer class of multilayer perceptron replicator neural network architectures discussed in this paper. Note that there are two possible middle hidden layer activation functions — a stairstep with a total of N steps and a ramp (which, for theoretical reasons, needs to be microscopically smoothed by rounding its corners at 0 and 1).

Thus, in effect, this neural network creates two mappings (as shown in the left side of Figure 2). The first mapping, called f, is from the data source region (the effective support of the a priori probability measure μ in $\Re^m$) to the n-dimensional unit cube $[0,1]^n$ (since each input vector $\mathbf{x}$ is mapped to a vector $\mathbf{u}$ lying in this unit cube). The second mapping, called g, is from a point $\mathbf{u}$ in the unit cube $[0,1]^n$ to a point $\mathbf{x}'$ in $\Re^m$. This second mapping tries to invert the first mapping.

This situation is universal. Given any real-world data source and any fixed n and $\varepsilon>0$ we could, presumably by training on $\mathbf{x}$ examples chosen at random in accordance with the source's a priori probability measure, build a replicator neural network with n middle hidden layer units having mean squared reconstruction error (i.e., $E[|\mathbf{x}-\mathbf{x}'|^2]$) within epsilon of minimum possible. We would then have a mapping between the data source region in $\Re^m$ and the cube (as well as the approximate inverse of this mapping).

In this discussion we are assuming use of the smoothed ramp activation function in the middle hidden layer of the replicator network (see Figure 1). Since the replicator neural network units therefore all have smooth activation functions, both the mapping f and the mapping g are automatically smooth.

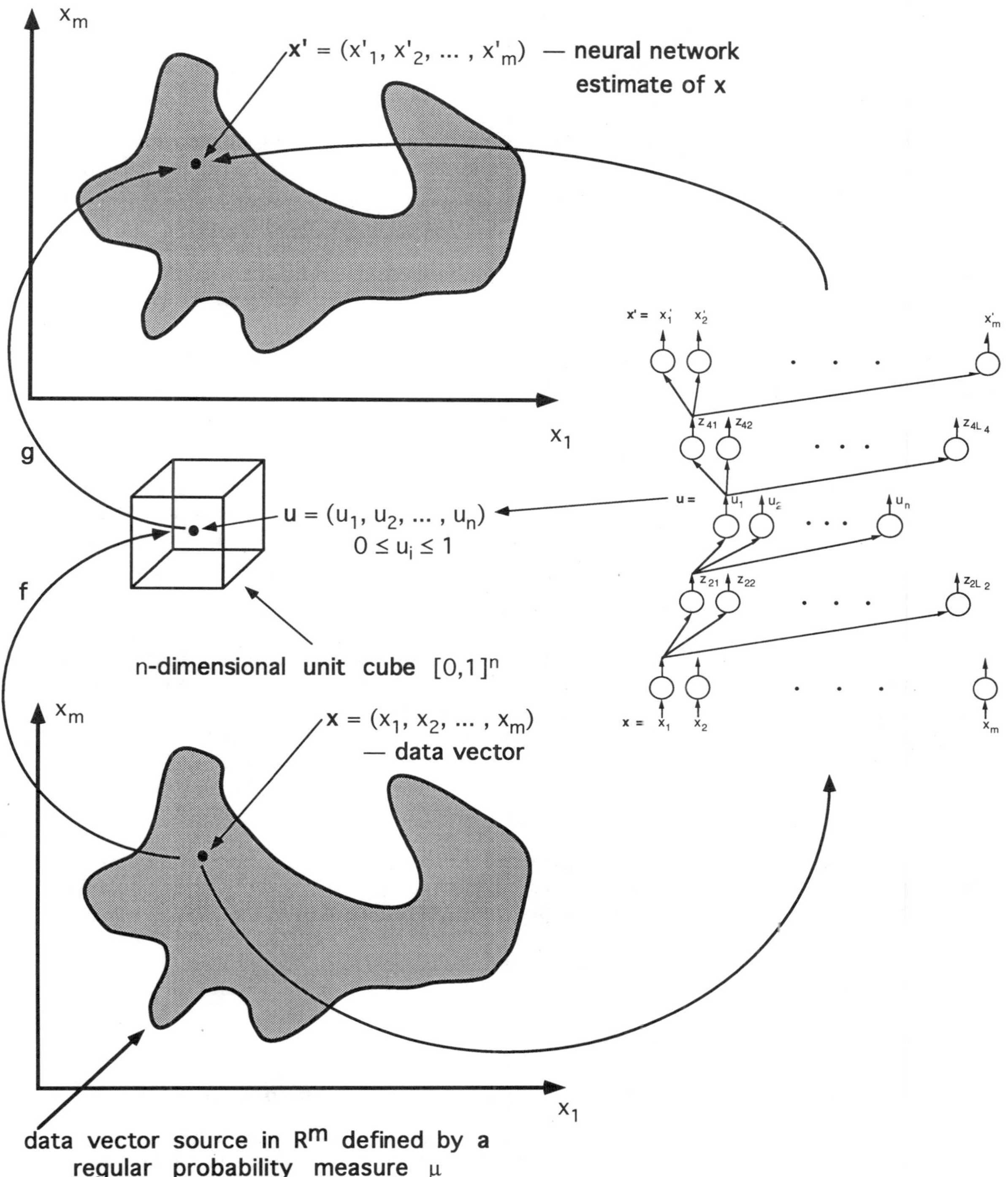

Figure 2. The three hidden layer replicator neural network trained to within ε of minimum possible mean squared error of replication induces mappings f (from the source region in $\Re^m$ defined by the source a priori probability measure μ to the unit n-dimensional cube $[0,1]^n$) and g (from $[0,1]^n$ to $\Re^m$). In the limit as ε approaches 0, these mappings automatically acquire several interesting and valuable properties; as described in the text.

3 Data Manifolds and their Relationship with Replicator Neural Networks

After years of study of this picture it has become clear that the fundamental part of this replicator neural network construction is the smooth mapping g between the cube and the data source region (and its inverse, which f approaches). Amazingly, it is possible to show that, in essence, (in the limit when ε approaches 0), the composition of f and μ yields the uniform probability distribution on the cube $[0,1]^n$. Conversely, the composition of g and the uniform density on the cube yields essentially a mollified version of μ. The smooth mappings f and g also become one-to-one and onto (and thus diffeomorphisms). These properties are automatic and inevitable! Thus, these features should be part of a general definition of a natural data source representation.

Combining and expanding these observations and results leads to an idea for a natural and general data source representation — the *data manifold* (defined to be a data set with a probability structure which is the diffeomorphic image of the unit cube $[0,1]^n$ with uniform probability density). Because of its origin, this structure is universal and intimately connected with replicator neural networks.

Besides its simplicity, the data manifold representation scheme has several compelling properties which recommend it as a universal tool for data source representation. First, it can be shown that if we quantize each cube coordinate (middle hidden layer unit output) to N evenly spaced values between 0 and 1 (see Figure 1), then the **u** representation vectors are a Shannon-optimal source code for the data vectors **x**. *Shannon-optimal* means that if we take any other representational scheme with $M=n^N$ codes (i.e., the same number as the number of possible **u** vectors after quantization), then the mean squared error of reconstruction $E[|\mathbf{x}-\mathbf{x'}|^2]$ of that other method will be greater than or equal to that of this method. This is a particularly important result because the known practical source coding schemes for complex data such as imagery and speech are probably at least two orders of magnitude from optimal (in terms of mean squared error for M codes). If we can find ways of training them to low mean squared errors, replicator networks may well be the first approach to source coding which is both mathematically optimal and practical (all of the other known optimal methods are not practical). Notice that replicator neural networks function as a kind of combinatorial vector quantizer [19]; in the sense that the **u** code vectors consist of n independent values each taking on one of N possible values.

Another nice property of the data manifold construct is that we can view the components of the cube vector **u** associated with a data vector **x** as a set of *natural coordinates* for x. In fact, except for a set of uninteresting transformations, these coordinates turn out to be unique. Further, if we think of natural coordinates as a set of parameterized coordinate curves in the data source region, these curves have the nice properties that the density of coordinate volumes is proportional to the mollified source vector probability density at each point. Also, the n natural coordinate curvilinear coordinate values (the components of **u**) are locally statistically independent at each point of the data source set.

4 Natural Coordinates — The Correct Generalization of Principal Components

Recently, many researchers [e.g., 2, 4, 5, 7, 11, 13, 14, 15, 16, 17, 18] have focused on self-organizing neural networks which generalize principal components analysis and/or have information-preserving properties. While these results are certainly interesting, conditions such as local statistical independence of coordinate systems and maximum information preservation in a limited class of architectures (e.g., the class of linear networks) are inadequate, by themselves, to uniquely define a representational scheme (there are an infinitude of very different coordinate systems which have such properties). Natural coordinates, on the other hand, are automatically locally statistically independent and, when uniformly individually quantized, provide absolute minimum information loss (in comparison with *all* other systems) and have the additional compelling properties of being: proportional in density to source probability and unique modulo an uninteresting set of transformations. These properties, which are not shared by any of the other general representations which have been proposed, make natural coordinates the compelling candidate for adoption as *the* proper curvilinear generalization of Gauss' principal component coordinates to general data sources.

References

1. D. H. Ackley, G. E. Hinton, T. J. Sejnowski (1985) "A learning algorithm for Boltzmann machines" *Cognitive Sci.* **9**, 147–169.

2. P. Baldi, K. Hornik (1989) "Neural networks and principal component analysis: Learning from examples without local minima" *Neural Networks* **2**, 53–58.

3. G. W. Cottrell, P. Munro, D. Zipser, in: *Proc. Ninth Annual Conference, Cognitive Science Society* (Seattle, Erlbaum, Hillsdale NJ, 1987).

4. K. Doya, A. I. Selverston (1994) "Dimension reduction of biological neuron models by artificial neural networks" *Neural Computation* **6**, 695–717.

5. T. Hastie, W. Stuetzle (1989) "Principal curves" *J. Am. Stat. Assoc.* **84**, 502–516.

6. R. Hecht-Nielsen (1995) "Replicator neural networks for universal optimal source coding" *Science* **269**, 1860-1863.

7. G. E. Hinton, P. Dayan, B. J. Frey, R. M. Neal, *Science* **267**, 1158 (1995).

8. T. Kohonen, et al. (1976) "A principle of neural associative memory", *Neuroscience (IBRO)* **2**, 1065–1076.

9. T. Kohonen, E. Oja, P. Lehtiö (1981) "Storage and processing of information in distributed associative memory systems" in: *Parallel Models of Associative Memory*, G. E. Hinton and J. A. Anderson, Eds. (Lawrence Erlbaum, Hillsdale NJ).

10. T. Kohonen (1995) *Self-Organizing Maps* (Springer-Verlag, Berlin).

11. M. A. Kramer (1991) "Nonlinear principal component analysis using autoassociative neural networks" *J. Amer. Inst. Chem. Eng.* **37**, 233–243.

12. P. Lehtiö and T. Kohonen (1978) "Associative memory and pattern recognition" *Medical Biology* **52**, 110–116.

13. R. Linsker (1992) "Local synaptic learning rules suffice to maximize mutual information in a linear network" *Neural Computation* **4**, 691–702.

14. E. Oja (1991) "Data compression, feature extraction, and autoassociation in feedforward neural networks" in: Kohonen, T., et al [Eds.] *Artificial Neural Networks*, pp 737–745 (Elsevier, Amsterdam).

15. E. Oja (1992) "Principal components, minor components, and linear neural networks" *Neural Networks* **5**, 927–935.

16. E. Oja (1994) "Beyond PCA: Statistical expansions by nonlinear neural networks" in: Marinaro, M., and Morasso, P. G. [Eds.], *ICANN'94. Proceedings of the international conference on artificial neural network*, 1049–1054 (Springer-Verlag, London).

17. L. Parra, G. Deco, S. Miesbach (1996) "Statistical independence and novelty detection with information preserving nonlinear maps" *Neural Computation* **8**, 260–269.

18. L. Xu, E. Oja, C. Y. Suen (1992) "Modified Hebbian learning for curve and surface fitting" *Neural Networks* **5**, 441–457.

19. P. Zador (1963) "Development and evaluation of procedures for quantizing multivariate distributions" Ph.D. Dissertation, Stanford University,

Comparing Adaptive and Non-Adaptive
Connection Pruning With Pure Early Stopping

Lutz Prechelt (prechelt@ira.uka.de)
Fakultät für Informatik
Universität Karlsruhe
D-76128 Karlsruhe, Germany

Abstract—Neural network pruning methods on the level of individual network parameters (e.g. connection weights) can improve generalization, as is shown in this empirical study. However, an open problem in the pruning methods known today (OBD, OBS, autoprune, epsiprune) is the selection of the number of parameters to be removed in each pruning step (pruning strength). This work presents a pruning method *lprune* that automatically adapts the pruning strength to the evolution of weights and loss of generalization during training. The method requires no algorithm parameter adjustment by the user. Results of statistical significance tests comparing autoprune, lprune, and static networks with early stopping are given, based on extensive experimentation with 14 different problems. The results indicate that training with pruning is often significantly better and rarely significantly worse than training with early stopping without pruning. Furthermore, lprune is often superior to autoprune (which is superior to OBD) on diagnosis tasks unless severe pruning early in the training process is required.

1   Pruning and Generalization

The principal idea of pruning is to reduce the number of free parameters in the network by removing dispensable ones. Pruning methods usually either remove complete input or hidden nodes along with all their associated parameters or remove individual connections, each of which carries one free parameter (the *weight*). This latter approach is very fine-grained and makes pruning particularly powerful. If applied properly, pruning often reduces overfitting and improves generalization. At the same time it produces a smaller network. Interestingly, most papers on pruning algorithms do show empirically that smaller networks can be obtained without loss of generalization, but do not show that generalization will often be *improved* compared to reasonable static-network training methods. The present paper makes up for that.

1.1   Related Work: Some Known Pruning Methods

The key to pruning is a method to calculate the approximate importance of each parameter. Several such methods have been suggested. The simplest one — with obvious flaws [3] — is to assume the importance to be proportional to the magnitude of a weight. More sophisticated approaches are the well-known *optimal brain damage* (OBD) and *optimal brain surgeon* (OBS) methods. OBD [1] uses an approximation to the second derivative of the error with respect to each weight to determine the *saliency* of the removal of that weight. Low saliency means low importance of a weight. OBS [5] avoids the drawbacks of the approximation by computing the second derivatives (almost) exactly, but is computationally very expensive.

Both methods have the disadvantage of requiring training to the error minimum before pruning may occur. For many problems, this introduces massive overfitting which often cannot be repaired by subsequent pruning. The *autoprune* method [3] avoids this problem. Its weight importance coefficients are defined by a test statistic T for the assumption that a weight becomes zero during the training process:

$$T(w_i) = \log \left(\frac{\left| \sum_p w_i - \eta \, (\partial E/\partial w_i)_p \right|}{\eta \sqrt{\sum_p ((\partial E/\partial w_i)_p - \overline{(\partial E/\partial w_i)})^2}} \right)$$

In contrast to OBD and OBS, this measure does not assume an error minimum has been reached; it can be computed at any time during training. In the above formula, sums are over all examples p of the training set, η is the learning rate, and the overline means arithmetic mean over the examples. A large value of T indicates high importance of the connection with weight w_i. Connections with small T can be pruned. [3] have convincingly shown autoprune to be superior to OBD.

Note that many more pruning methods than discussed here have been proposed in the literature. In particular, Bayesian methods can unify the notions of regularization and pruning [11].

1.2   An Open Problem: How Much To Prune?

Given the importance T of each weight at any time during training, two questions remain to be answered:

1. When should we prune?
2. How many connections should be removed in the next pruning step?

The first question is simple to answer: For OBD and OBS, pruning occurs when minimum training set error has been reached. For autoprune, pruning occurs when overfitting begins (here: when the validation set error increased twice during training; see below).

The second question, however, has not yet been answered satisfactorily. The authors of OBD suggest to delete *"some"* parameters. The authors of autoprune at least suggest a concrete pruning schedule: remove 35% of all parameters in the first pruning step and 10% in each following step. Such rules of thumb, however, are not satisfying, because obviously they cannot always be optimal. The following section presents a pruning method, called *lprune*, based on autoprune that tries to solve the problem. It computes the pruning schedule dynamically during training, adapting to the evolution of the weights and to the amount of overfitting observed.

2 Adaptive Pruning Schedules: The lprune Method

2.1 Observations

The lprune method is not based on a theory of weight development, because no such theory is currently available. Instead, it builds on a number of observations made for the distribution of the T coefficients during training:

1. The distribution of the values is roughly normal.
2. During training, both the mean μ_T and the variance σ_T of the distribution tend to increase.
3. When pruning occurs, the variance suddenly drops and the mean suddenly rises.
4. Afterwards, the variance increases again and the mean decreases again. After a while, normal development continues as in (2) above.

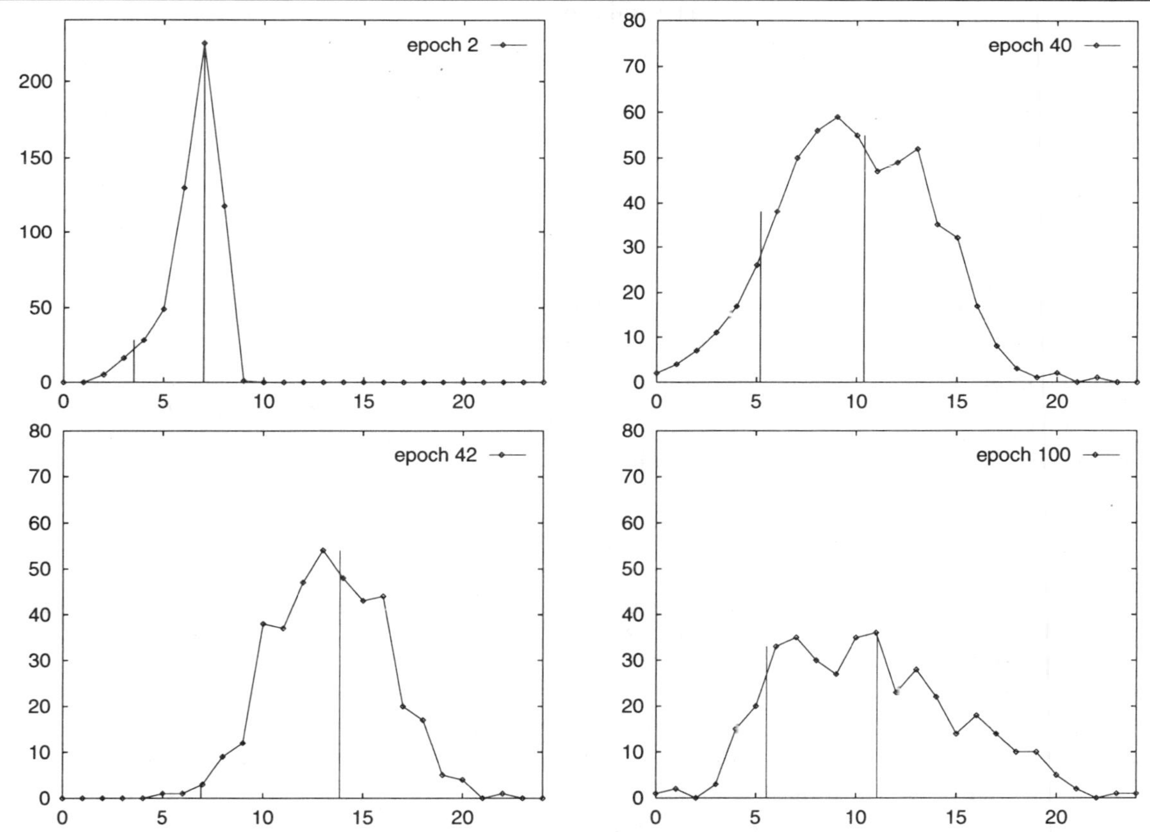

Figure 1: Four pruning coefficient histograms from the same training run (*glass1* problem with standard architecture) in epochs 2, 40, 42, and 100. Horizontal axis: coefficient size, grouped in classes of width 1. Vertical axis: absolute frequency of weights with this coefficient size. The right vertical line is the arithmetic mean of the coefficient sizes, the left vertical line is 0.5 times that. The area under the curve left of the left line thus indicates what would be pruned at that point for $\lambda = 0.5$ when a pruning step would occur. In the run shown, pruning occurred in epoch 41.

See Figure 1 for an example of this behavior. The observations suggest that a certain fraction of the mean of the coefficient distribution can be used as a threshold for pruning. Early during training the fraction of these connections is rather small, because the variance is small. Once the weights have evolved and differentiated, the variance is larger and it is safe to prune a larger fraction of the connections. After a pruning step, immediate further pruning should remove only a few connections, if any, since the remaining weights have to differentiate again before the important ones can confidently be distinguished from the less important ones. This reduction of pruning strength is ensured by the reduced variance after pruning and is further pronounced immediately after pruning due to the larger mean of the distribution (see epoch 42 vs. 40 in Figure 1).

2.2   Adaptation Approach

From these observations, the following rule seems reasonable for determining how many connections to prune:

At each pruning step, prune all those connections i whose weights w_i satisfy
$T(w_i) < \lambda \, \mu_T \quad$ *for some* $\quad \lambda \in [0 \ldots 1]$

However, no fixed value of λ results in good adaptation of pruning strength; we have to choose λ dynamically as well. The higher the overfitting, the more should be pruned, and the higher λ must be.

2.3   Definitions

To formalize this notion we define "overfitting" quantitatively, as well as some other concepts that can be used to express criteria for stopping or triggering pruning.

Let E be the error function of the training algorithm. Then $E_{tr}(t)$ is the average error per example over the training set, measured after epoch t. $E_{va}(t)$ is the error on the validation set and is used to determine overfitting. $E_{te}(t)$ is the error on the test set; it is not known to the training algorithm but characterizes the quality of the network resulting from training.

The value $E_{opt}(t)$ is defined to be the lowest validation set error obtained in epochs up to t:

$$E_{opt}(t) := \min_{t' \le t} E_{va}(t')$$

Now we define the *generalization loss* at epoch t to be the relative increase of the validation error over the minimum-so-far (in percent):

$$GL := GL(t) := 100 \cdot \left(\frac{E_{va}(t)}{E_{opt}(t)} - 1 \right)$$

The generalization loss directly characterizes the amount of overfitting.

A high generalization loss is one candidate reason to stop training or to perform a pruning step: stop or prune as soon as the generalization loss exceeds a certain threshold. We define the class GL_α as

$$GL_\alpha : \text{ satisfied after first epoch } t \text{ with } GL(t) > \alpha$$

However, we might want to suppress stopping or pruning if the training is still progressing very rapidly. When the training error still drops quickly, generalization losses may have a higher chance to be "repaired". To formalize this notion we define a *training strip of length k* to be a sequence of k epochs numbered $n+1 \ldots n+k$ where n is divisible by k. The training *progress* (in per thousand) measured after such a training strip is then

$$P_k(t) = 1000 \cdot \left(\frac{\sum_{t'=t-k+1}^{t} E_{tr}(t')}{k \cdot \min_{t'=t-k+1}^{t} E_{tr}(t')} - 1 \right)$$

that is, "how much was the average training error during the strip larger than the minimum training error during the strip?" In the following we will always assume strips of length 5 (i.e., $k = 5$) and measure the cross validation error only at the end of each strip.

Another class of triggering criteria relies only on the sign of the changes in the generalization error: stop or prune when the generalization error increased in s successive strips.

$$UP_s : \text{ satisfied after epoch } t \text{ iff } UP_{s-1} \text{ was satisfied after epoch } t - k \text{ and } E_{va}(t) > E_{va}(t - k)$$

$$UP_1 : \text{ satisfied after first end-of-strip epoch } t \text{ with } E_{va}(t) > E_{va}(t - k)$$

This class of criteria is independent of E_{opt}, which is required for triggering pruning steps, because in the short term pruning always makes GL higher.

2.4   Algorithm

Initial experiments showed that an appropriate way to adapt λ is to increase it with growing GL, saturating at some maximum value. This leads to the following adaptation rule for λ:

$$\lambda := \lambda(GL) := \lambda_{max}\left(1 - \frac{1}{1 + \frac{GL}{\alpha}}\right) \qquad \begin{aligned} \lambda_{max} &:= 2/3 \\ \alpha &:= 2 \end{aligned}$$

The given values of λ_{max} and α were found by a small number of experiments with 4 of the 42 example problems used below. These parameters are only moderately critical and the values given here are certainly not exactly optimal.

The complete *lprune* algorithm ('lambda-prune') can now be formulated as

```
REPEAT
    Train network for one epoch;
    IF epoch number MOD k = 0 THEN
        Compute Eva, Eopt, and GL using the validation set;
    END;
UNTIL GL > 5; (* i.e., apply normal early stopping *)
Reset network to the state that exhibited Eopt;
(* Now begin training with pruning: *)
REPEAT
    Train network for one epoch and compute T(wi) values;
    IF epoch number MOD k = 0 THEN
        Compute Eva, Eopt, and GL using the validation set;
        IF UP2(t) satisfied AND no pruning k epochs ago THEN
            Prune all connections i whose weights wi satisfy   T(wi) < λ(GL) μT;
        END;
    END;
UNTIL t > 5000 OR P5(t) < 0.1 OR
        (At Least 25 Epochs trained since last pruning AND GL > 100 AND P5(t) < 0.4)
```

The constants 5000, 0.1, 25, 100, and 0.4 are not critical and make a conservative stopping criterion for the whole process. The result of the training is the network that exhibited the lowest validation error E_{opt}.

3   Results And Discussion

3.1   Experiment Setup

Extensive benchmark comparisons were made between autoprune, lprune, and static backpropagation with early stopping. 14 different problems were used, all from the PROBEN1 benchmark set [7], a collection of diagnosis problems[1]. The problems have between 8 and 120 inputs, between 1 and 19 outputs, and between 214 and 7200 examples. 9 of the problems are classification tasks (*cancer, card, diabetes, gene, glass, heart, heartc, horse, soybean,* and *thyroid*), 4 are approximation tasks (*building, flare, hearta,* and *heartac*); all problems are real datasets from realistic application domains.

All runs were done using the RPROP weight update rule [9], squared error function, and the RPROP parameters $\eta^+ = 1.2$, $\eta^- = 0.5$, $\Delta_0 \in [0.05\ldots0.2]$ randomly per weight, $\Delta_{max} = 50$, $\Delta_{min} = 0$, initial weights from [-0.1...0.1] randomly. RPROP is a fast backpropagation variant that is about as fast as quickprop [2] but more robust in the choice of parameters. Note that RPROP requires a modification in the way the $T(w_i)$ are computed, because the weight change is not proportional to $\partial E/\partial w_i$.

In three different random ways, the examples of each problem were partitioned into training set (50%), validation set (25%), and test set (25% of examples), resulting in 42 datasets (*cancer1, cancer2, cancer3, card1, card2, card3* etc.). Each of these datasets was trained with two different initial topologies. The first is the dataset's *standard architecture* network topology (see [7]; in that reference, the standard architectures are called *pivot architectures.*), which can be considered a "reasonable" topology for the dataset. These topologies have between 2 and 32 hidden nodes, either one or two hidden layers, and contain all possible feedforward connections, not only those from one layer to the next. The second is the *noshortcut standard architecture*, which is derived from the standard architecture by excluding all connections that do not go from one layer to the *immediately* following layer. For each of the 42 datasets and each of the two network topologies for each dataset, 30 runs were made with autoprune, 30 with lprune, and 30 with backpropagation with early stopping using the GL_5 stopping criterion; more than 7500 runs overall.

After each of these runs, the error E_{te} of the resulting network was measured.[2] For each dataset, the autoprune sample of 30 such test set errors was compared to the corresponding lprune sample and the backprop sample using the t-test (with removing 2 percent outlier datapoints, using a log-normal distribution and applying the Cochran/Cox correction for the unequal variances case). The results of the tests are shown in Tables 1 to 4.

3.2   Qualitative Behavior

Each significant pruning step leads to a large sudden increase of GL, followed by a rapid decrease. Whether the decrease leads to a lower or higher GL than before pruning depends on whether the pruning occurred at the right time and in the right strength. To employ the UP_2 triggering criterion means to accept the view that pruning should occur whenever a substantial deterioration of generalization

---

[1] You can fetch the data at http://wwwipd.ira.uka.de/~prechelt/NIPS_bench.html

[2] Caveat: In the experiments, the data of the validation set was never used for actual gradient training. In a real application, one would not want to waste valuable data points in this manner.

behavior (as measured noisily by the validation set error) begins. It would probably be better in some cases to wait longer before pruning, because during certain phases in training overfitting occurs but vanishes automatically later. It is not at all clear, however, how such a situation should be detected at its beginning. Therefore, UP_2 seems to be a reasonable way to determine *when* to prune. The pruning strength of autoprune, however, is often not appropriate.

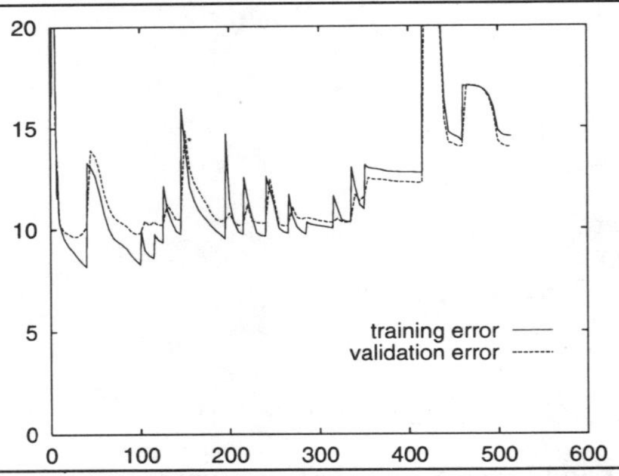

Figure 2: Development of training and validation set error over time for the same run of autoprune from which the figures above were derived. Horizontal axis: number of epoch; vertical axis: error. There are 15 pruning steps after which 15% of the initial connections remain. In this example pruning is not successful: no lower validation set error occurs than before the first pruning step. This is not a rare case.

Since early stopping is performed as the first phase of the pruning algorithm (for both autoprune and lprune), these training methods take significantly, but not prohibitively longer than training with static networks and early stopping. In the setup chosen, typically three to five times as many epochs are trained. However, epochs after pruning consume less time, since the network is smaller and the total number of epochs could be reduced by using a faster stopping criterion than the extremely conservative one chosen in the given setup.

In the example autoprune run shown in Figure 2, the network tolerates the 35% pruning of the first pruning step, yet is ruined by the second pruning step many epochs later, which removes only 10% of the weights. Towards the end of the training run, the network is always overpruned, since such a conservative stopping criterion is used.

For lprune, the situation is a bit different. As long as overfitting is only moderate, the pruning strength is usually small. The same is true when the weights have not yet sufficiently evolved since the last pruning step or since the beginning of training. On the other hand, when overfitting is large, pruning can be quite severe in lprune.

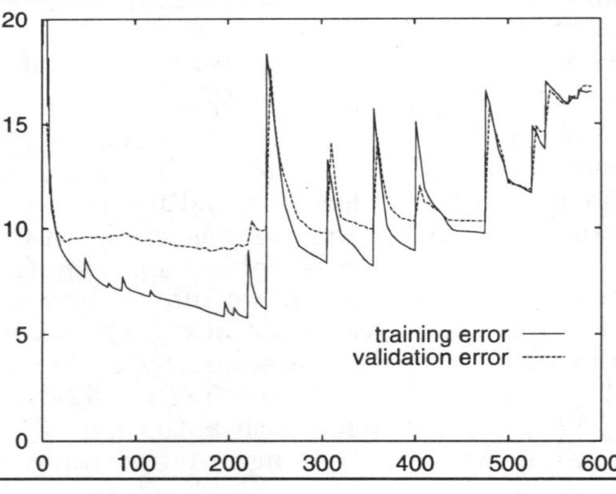

Figure 3: The corresponding curves for lprune. There are 21 pruning steps, initially removing only few connections, later removing more in each step. Finally, only 0.5% of the initial connections remain. Pruning is successful: after 7 pruning steps (in epoch 180) a lower validation set error is reached than before the first pruning step.

In the example lprune run shown in Figure 3, this behavior leads to several small pruning steps (the first four remove 2%, 3%, 3%, and 5% of the connections, respectively) that manage to keep overfitting low over a longer training period and finally reduce the validation error. In this example, lprune is superior to autoprune.

The behavior observed in this example is not prototypical, though. Very different error curves and pruning sequences occur as well. However, one observation prevails: pruning with a non-adaptive schedule sometimes destroys the generalization ability of the network unnecessarily. In the case of the schedule used in autoprune this is usually because of too heavy or too fast pruning. Significantly lower pruning strengths could avoid this, but would exhibit another problem: namely that overfitting cannot be reduced as fast as it builds up. Therefore, pruning with very small pruning strength and fixed schedule would probably be similar to OBD, which has been shown inferior to autoprune by [3]. Adaptive pruning schedules are clearly necessary.

3.3 Quantitative Results

standard architectures				noshortcut standard architectures			
Problem	1	2	3	Problem	1	2	3
building	L 0.0	—	—	building	L 0.3	—	L 3.7
cancer	—	—	—	cancer	—	A 0.9	—
card	—	—	—	card	—	—	—
diabetes	—	A 2.5	L 0.9	diabetes	—	A 4.3	—
flare	—	A 7.3	—	flare	A 0.8	A 1.0	A 0.0
gene	A 0.0	A 0.0	A 0.0	gene	A 5.4	L 6.6	A 1.7
glass	—	L 2.3	L 1.8	glass	A 7.6	—	—
heart	A 5.5	A 0.4	—	heart	—	A 3.3	—
hearta	—	A 0.1	—	hearta	—	—	—
heartac	—	—	—	heartac	—	—	—
heartc	—	—	A 2.5	heartc	—	—	—
horse	—	—	A 3.4	horse	—	—	A 1.5
soybean	—	—	—	soybean	L 7.0	—	—
thyroid	—	L 6.2	L 0.3	thyroid	—	—	L 0.0

Tables 1 and 2: Comparison of autoprune ("A") to lprune ("L") using the standard architectures and noshortcut standard architectures, respectively. Compares test set errors E_{te} for variants 1, 2, 3 of each problem. The entries show differences (in samples of 30 runs each) that are statistically significant on a 10% level and the corresponding p-values (in percent). Low p-values indicate high significance. The letter indicates which algorithm is better; a dash means that no significant difference was found.

Table 1 (standard architectures): 26 times no significant difference, 10 times A better, 6 times L better.

Table 2 (noshortcut standard architectures): 27 times no significant difference, 10 times A better, 5 times L better.

As we see in Tables 1 and 2, lprune is better in some cases and autoprune is better in others. For 2 of the 14 problems, there is never a significant difference. How *often* autoprune is better than lprune and vice versa, depends on the particular selection of datasets and should thus not be overemphasized. However, there is a pattern in the results: autoprune tends to be better for problems that have overly large networks, for instance the gene problems that have 120 input units — and the difference is larger with shortcut connections than without. On the other hand, lprune is often better when pruning is delicate, for instance for the *building, glass,* and *thyroid* problems that have only 14, 9, and 21 inputs, respectively.

An explanation of this effect is that lprune is unable to perform heavy pruning very early during training when overfitting is only small. However, such heavy pruning is what would be needed to perform well on e.g. the *gene* problems and it is what autoprune does. On the other hand, the fixed pruning schedule of autoprune is too rigid. It prunes too much in situations where waiting for further weight differentiation is required despite the fact that overfitting has begun. Such situations are recognized by lprune and its pruning removes only very few weights, sometimes even none at all. Thus, lprune solves a part of the pruning schedule problem, namely adapting pruning strength to the stage of development of the weights. The rest of the problem is still unsolved, namely determining the absolute number of weights that should be pruned.

In a second series of benchmarks, pruning was compared to training a static network with early stopping without pruning, using the same setup as before. The results are shown in Tables 3 and 4. We see that pruning indeed usually does improve generalization significantly; a fact that is often not properly recognized. Therefore, pruning algorithms are preferable over static networks, at least in applications where small improvements of generalization do matter. This is particularly true if one uses networks with very many parameters (as is often recommended for the early stopping method): without shortcut connections, backprop is significantly better than pruning in eight of the cases (Table 4), whereas with the shortcut connections this value drops to just two (Table 2).

4 Conclusion

Extensive benchmarking compared adaptive and non-adaptive pruning and backprop without pruning. For the former, a method for adaptive calculation of pruning strength for connection pruning algorithms was described. It represents a partial solution to an open problem in network pruning, determining pruning strength. The following conclusions apply to the class of learning tasks covered by the experiments:

1. Training with pruning very often results in better networks than training with early stopping without pruning, but rarely results in worse networks. Thus, pruning methods should be used more often than they are used today.
2. The automatic pruning strength adaptation of the lprune method can result in better networks than pruning with non-adaptive (fixed) pruning schedules. This is true in particular for small networks.
3. However, the lprune solution to the pruning strength problem is only partial, because lprune is unable to execute severe pruning in early training stages as it is sometimes needed, in particular for networks with overly many inputs.

standard architectures				noshortcut standard architectures			
Problem	1	2	3	Problem	1	2	3
building	(A 0.0)	—	—	building	(A 0.0)	—	B 7.9
cancer	—	B 3.1	B 9.9	cancer	—	—	B 0.1
card	—	A 0.0	A 2.2	card	—	A 0.0	A 7.1
diabetes	—	A 4.0	—	diabetes	—	A 6.1	—
flare	A 0.0	A 0.0	A 0.0	flare	—	A 0.0	A 0.3
gene	A 0.0	(A 0.0)	(A 0.0)	gene	A 1.1	—	(A 0.4)
glass	A 8.6	A 2.3	A 0.1	glass	—	—	—
heart	—	—	—	heart	B 0.2	—	—
hearta	—	A 2.0	—	hearta	B 2.4	A 3.4	A 0.5
heartac	—	—	—	heartac	—	B 9.2	(A 5.4)
heartc	—	—	A 0.0	heartc	—	B 2.4	A 1.3
horse	—	A 0.4	A 0.1	horse	B 4.7	—	B 8.6
soybean	—	—	—	soybean	—	(A 1.7)	—
thyroid	A 0.4	—	—	thyroid	A 0.0	A 0.1	A 2.2

Tables 3 and 4: Comparison of autoprune ("A") to backprop with early stopping ("B"). Analogous to Tables 1 and 2 above.

Table 3 (standard architectures): 22 times no significant difference, 18 times A better (3 times slightly dubious due to non-normal backprop samples), 2 times B better.

Table 4 (noshortcut standard architectures): 18 times no significant difference, 16 times A better (4 times slightly dubious), 8 times B better.

4. As the very different results for the various problems and even for the dataset permutations show, benchmarking has to be extensive and careful in order to yield significant and correct results — this is in sharp contrast to the state of the practice as described in [8].

References

[1] Yann Le Cun, John S. Denker, and Sara A. Solla. Optimal brain damage. In *[10]*, pages 598–605, 1990.

[2] Scott E. Fahlman. An empirical study of learning speed in back-propagation networks. Technical Report CMU-CS-88-162, School of Computer Science, Carnegie Mellon University, Pittsburgh, PA, September 1988.

[3] William Finnoff, Ferdinand Hergert, and Hans Georg Zimmermann. Improving model selection by nonconvergent methods. *Neural Networks*, 6:771–783, 1993.

[4] Stephen J. Hanson, Jack D. Cowan, and C. Lee Giles, editors. *Advances in Neural Information Processing Systems 5*, San Mateo, CA, 1993. Morgan Kaufman Publishers Inc.

[5] Babak Hassibi and David G. Stork. Second order derivatives for network pruning: Optimal brain surgeon. In *[4]*, pages 164–171, 1993.

[6] Richard P. Lippmann, John E. Moody, and David S. Touretzky, editors. *Advances in Neural Information Processing Systems 3*, San Mateo, CA, 1991. Morgan Kaufman Publishers Inc.

[7] Lutz Prechelt. PROBEN1 — A set of benchmarks and benchmarking rules for neural network training algorithms. Technical Report 21/94, Fakultät für Informatik, Universität Karlsruhe, Germany, September 1994. Anonymous FTP: /pub/papers/techreports/1994/1994-21.ps.gz on ftp.ira.uka.de.

[8] Lutz Prechelt. A study of experimental evaluations of neural network learning algorithms: Current research practice. Technical Report 19/94, Fakultät für Informatik, Universität Karlsruhe, Germany, August 1994. Anonymous FTP: /pub/papers/techreports/1994/1994-19.ps.gz on ftp.ira.uka.de.

[9] Martin Riedmiller and Heinrich Braun. A direct adaptive method for faster backpropagation learning: The RPROP algorithm. In *Proc. of the IEEE Intl. Conf. on Neural Networks*, pages 586–591, San Francisco, CA, April 1993.

[10] David S. Touretzky, editor. *Advances in Neural Information Processing Systems 2*, San Mateo, CA, 1990. Morgan Kaufman Publishers Inc.

[11] Peter M. Williams. Bayesian regularization and pruning using a Laplace prior. Technical Report CSRP-312, School of Cognitive and Computing Sciences, University of Sussex, Brighton, England, February 1994. ftp://ftp.cogs.susx.ac.uk/pub/reports/csrp/csrp312.ps.Z.

A Hierarchical CMAC Architecture
for Context Dependent Function Approximation

Chen-Khong Tham

Department of Electrical Engineering
National University of Singapore
Singapore
E-mail: eletck@nus.sg

Abstract— A hierarchical Cerebellar Model Articulation Controller (CMAC) architecture suitable for context-dependent function approximation is proposed. The objective is to approximate several distinct non-linear functions, one for each of several contexts. The active context is determined from the values of context variables, and smooth interpolation between different contexts is possible. The learning algorithms used can be similar to those of the Hierarchical Mixtures of Experts (HME) as CMAC networks are linear in parameters. The proposed architecture converges quickly and has very low computational requirements when first order learning algorithms are used. The effectiveness of the architecture is demonstrated on a composite non-linear regression task involving three Gaussian functions.

1   Introduction

In many application areas such as control, signal processing and pattern recognition, a single function approximator or neural network may not be sufficient to handle different modes of behaviour. An obvious approach is to use several neural networks, one for each mode of behaviour or context, with each neural network being trained separately. After this has been done, ad-hoc methods are commonly applied to select the relevant network in each context, with little consideration on how to interpolate smoothly between different contexts.

Modular neural networks [3] can be used for context-dependent learning. In this approach, each neural network specialising in a particular context, called an 'expert network', is not trained on its own. Instead, several expert networks and a 'gating network' which performs the switching and interpolation function, are trained together to model the data in a maximum likelihood sense.

In later work, Jordan & Jacobs [5] extended this idea and proposed the Hierarchical Mixtures of Experts (HME) architecture. The key features of the HME are that linear approximators, rather than multi-layer perceptron (MLP) networks, are used for expert and gating networks, with the 'softmax' non-linearity [2] being used at the output of the gating network. This simplicity enabled fast learning algorithms such as iteratively reweighted least squares (IRLS), least squares (LS) and recursive least squares (RLS) to be used for training the HME. However, the dependence on linear approximators means that a deep tree-like architecture is required to model complicated non-linear functions.

In this paper, a hierarchical Cerebellar Model Articulation Controller (CMAC) architecture (H-CMAC) in which CMAC networks are used to implement the expert and gating networks is proposed. With H-CMAC, a single-level tree-like architecture is sufficient to model a mixture of several non-linear functions. CMAC networks are commonly used for real-time non-linear function approximation [6, 7] because of their low computation and storage requirements. These networks also have the advantage of their output being linear in parameters - hence, the fast learning algorithms proposed by Jordan & Jacobs can still be applied.[1]

2   Cerebellar Model Articulation Controller (CMAC) networks

2.1   Overview

The CMAC was proposed by Albus [1] as a model of the information processing activities within the cerebellum. It is a coarse-coding structure where each point in input space excites a set of locally-tuned, overlapping and offset receptive fields in each dimension of the input vector. These receptive fields are defined by quantizing functions which operate on the input values. When the excited receptive fields of corresponding quantizing functions in all input dimensions are combined, a hypercube in the multi-dimensional input space is defined. This hypercube will correspond to one component of the output value. Since there are several quantizing functions in each input dimension, several hypercubes in input space will be affected in this way, with the point of interest being in the overlapping region of these hypercubes. The output value is the sum of the contributions from these active components.

---

[1]Radial basis function (RBF) networks are also linear in parameters and can be used in place of CMAC networks, but RBF networks have been shown to be significantly more computation intensive to train compared to CMAC networks of similar complexity [9].

2.2   Mappings within a CMAC network

Two mappings take place within a CMAC network each time an input vector is presented. The first mapping transforms a real-valued input vector **s** into a binary-valued vector **x** with a higher dimensionality using a fixed non-linear mapping function[2], written as $\phi(\cdot)$, i.e. $\mathbf{x} = \phi(\mathbf{s})$. The second mapping, which is linear, uses **x** and multiplies it with the current values of the weights **w** in order to produce the scalar output y

$$y = \mathbf{w}^{\mathrm{T}}\mathbf{x} \tag{1}$$

where **w** and **x** are column vectors. Vector **x** has zeros in all its elements except the $index_l$ positions corresponding to active weights, which have the value one.

Since **w** and **x** have many elements and most of the elements in **x** are zero, performing the vector multiplication of Equation 1 is computationally wasteful. It is more efficient to access the active weights directly and sum their contributions

$$y = \sum_{l=0}^{K-1} w[index_l] \tag{2}$$

where K is the number of quantizing functions.

This mathematical formulation can be easily extended to the case where the output is a vector and not a scalar. Each component of the output vector **y**, y_k, is independently produced by a CMAC network having the form described above. Equation 1 is now written as

$$\mathbf{y} = \mathbf{W}\mathbf{x} \tag{3}$$

where **W** is a matrix whose rows are $\mathbf{w}_k^{\mathrm{T}}$.

3   Hierarchical architectures for context-dependent function approximation

A detailed description of the Hierarchical Mixtures of Experts (HME) architecture on which the H-CMAC architecture is based can be found in Jordan & Jacobs [5]. The H-CMAC architecture is obtained by using CMAC networks in place of linear approximators for the gating and expert networks in the HME architecture. A one-level H-CMAC architecture is shown in Figure 1.

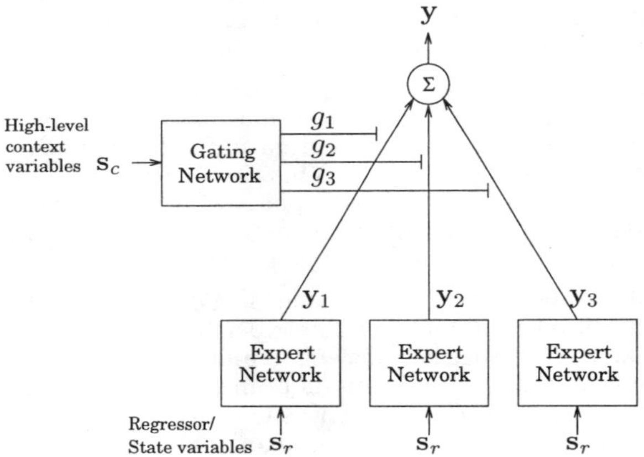

Figure 1: Context-dependent learning using the H-CMAC architecture.

This architecture is designed to take advantage of the ability of CMAC networks for fast learning of complex non-linear functions. The non-linear mapping $\mathbf{s} \rightarrow \mathbf{x}$ in a CMAC network transforms the real-valued input vector **s** to the high-dimensional binary-valued vector **x**. Subsequently, the output of a CMAC network is linear in parameters, with the form $y = \mathbf{w}^{\mathrm{T}}\mathbf{x}$ as expressed in Equation 1. In the case of first order algorithms, weight updates simply affect elements in the weight vector corresponding to non-zero elements in the input vector **x**.

In the formulation presented in [5], the gating network sees the same input vector as the expert networks. However, there are situations in which the variables which determine how the problem can be sub-divided are distinct from those for which the target function is to be approximated. An example of this is when different functions need to be learnt in different contexts. The former shall be referred to as *context variables* $\mathbf{s}_c$ and the latter, as *regressor variables* $\mathbf{s}_r$.

Instead of including context variables as additional dimensions of the input space seen by all networks, they can be used as input variables to the gating network, while regressor variables are used as input variables to expert networks. This method of dividing the input variables can be seen in Figure 1. The

---

[2]The function $\phi(\cdot)$ does not change over time, so the vector **x** obtained for a given **s** is always the same.

function approximation task is simplified considerably, resulting in more accurate predictions, less storage required, and a shorter learning process.

The non-linear mapping in the CMAC network transforms the real-valued vector $\mathbf{s}_r$ into a binary-valued vector $\mathbf{x}_r$ for expert networks. Likewise, $\mathbf{s}_c$ is transformed into $\mathbf{x}_c$ for the gating network. For the remainder of this section, we shall treat the H-CMAC architecture as being linear in parameters with respect to input vectors $\mathbf{x}_c$ and $\mathbf{x}_r$.

The gating network receives the input vector $\mathbf{x}_c$ and produces a scalar output g_i for the ith branch of its sub-tree. Expert networks are located at the leaves of the tree, each of them producing an output vector $\mathbf{y}_i$ for the input vector $\mathbf{x}_r$. These outputs are multiplied by the outputs of the gating network g_i as they proceed up the tree, producing the output vector $\mathbf{y}$ at the top.

Expert network i produces output $\mathbf{y}_i$ as a linear function of the input $\mathbf{x}_r$

$$\mathbf{y}_i = \mathbf{W}_i \mathbf{x}_r$$

where $\mathbf{W}_i$ is a weight matrix for expert i. The gating network produces intermediate variables ξ_i also as linear functions of the input vector $\mathbf{x}_c$

$$\xi_i = \mathbf{v}_i^{\text{T}} \mathbf{x}_c$$

where $\mathbf{v}_i$ is a weight vector associated with each gating network output. Subsequently, the ith output of the gating network is produced by the 'softmax' activation function [2]

$$g_i = \frac{e^{\xi_i}}{\sum_j e^{\xi_j}}$$

where the g_i values are positive and sum to one for each $\mathbf{x}_c$. The output at the top level of the tree is simply

$$\mathbf{y} = \sum_i g_i \mathbf{y}_i$$

3.1 A probability model and posterior probabilities

The HME and H-CMAC architectures can be considered as statistical models of the observed data. From this perspective, they are hierarchical mixture models [8] with mixture coefficients determined by the gating network and mixture components produced by the expert networks.

The probabilistic component at expert network i is taken to be the Gaussian probability density, written here as $P_i(\mathbf{y}^*) = P(\mathbf{y}^*|\mathbf{x}_r, \boldsymbol{\theta}_i)$, where $\mathbf{y}^*$ is the target output and $\boldsymbol{\theta}_i$ are the current values of the parameters in expert network i. The probability g_i is the *prior* probability that the probabilistic component i generated $\mathbf{y}^*$ - it is obtained based only on the input vector $\mathbf{x}_c$ without knowledge of the corresponding target output $\mathbf{y}^*$. The *posterior* probability can be evaluated using Bayes' rule once both the input and target output are known

$$h_i = \frac{g_i P_i(\mathbf{y}^*)}{\sum_j g_j P_j(\mathbf{y}^*)}$$

where the subscript have the same meaning as that of the prior probability. The posterior probability indicates the probability that expert network i generated the observed data based on the knowledge of both the input and target output.

3.2 Likelihood and a gradient ascent algorithm

The log likelihood of the data set $\mathcal{X} = \{(\mathbf{x}_c^{(t)}, \mathbf{x}_r^{(t)}, \mathbf{y}^{*(t)})\}_1^N$ is given by

$$l(\boldsymbol{\theta}; \mathcal{X}) = \sum_t \ln \sum_i g_i^{(t)} P_i(\mathbf{y}^{*(t)}) \tag{4}$$

where $\boldsymbol{\theta}$ are the unknown parameters of the whole model. The learning problem can now be treated as a maximum likelihood estimation problem. A gradient ascent algorithm was proposed in [4] for finding the values of the parameters $\boldsymbol{\theta}$ in expert and gating networks in order to maximize this expression. When this algorithm is used, weight updates are determined from the derivatives of $l(\boldsymbol{\theta}; \mathcal{X})$ with respect to the parameters.

For the expert networks, the weight matrix $\mathbf{W}_i$ is updated according to

$$\Delta \mathbf{W}_i = \rho_e \sum_t h_i^{(t)} (\mathbf{y}^{*(t)} - \mathbf{y}^{(t)}) \mathbf{x}_r^{(t)\text{T}} \tag{5}$$

and for the gating network, the ith weight vector is updated as follows

$$\Delta \mathbf{v}_i = \rho_g \sum_t (h_i^{(t)} - g_i^{(t)}) \mathbf{x}_c^{(t)} \tag{6}$$

where ρ_e and ρ_g are learning rates for the respective networks.

For a batch algorithm, the weight changes in Equations 5 and 6 are accumulated over a complete pass through the data set before weights are actually updated. Weights can also be updated after the presentation of every input-output pair, i.e. an on-line update algorithm is obtained by dropping the summation over t in the equations above.

The algorithm presented above is a first order gradient ascent algorithm. A variety of second order algorithms such as IRLS, LS and RLS described in [5] for the HME architecture can also be used in the H-CMAC architecture.

4   Solving a composite non-linear regression problem

Consider a four-dimensional regression problem where the real-valued input vector is $\mathbf{s} = [s_1, s_2, s_3, s_4]$ and y^* is the target value. Let the regressor variables be $\mathbf{s}_r = [s_1, s_2]$ and the context variables be $\mathbf{s}_c = [s_3, s_4]$. In the underlying process, data is generated according to the two-dimensional Gaussian function

$$g_n(\mathbf{s}_r, \boldsymbol{\mu}_i, \sigma) = C \times \frac{1}{2\pi\sigma^2}\, e^{-\frac{1}{2\sigma^2}(\mathbf{s}_r - \boldsymbol{\mu}_i)^{\mathrm{T}}(\mathbf{s}_r - \boldsymbol{\mu}_i)} + n(\sigma_N) \tag{7}$$

where $\boldsymbol{\mu}_i$ is the centre of the function, $C = 100$, $\sigma = 2.5$ and $n(\sigma_N)$ is additive Gaussian noise with zero mean and standard deviation $\sigma_N = 0.25$. There are 10,000 exemplars in the training set and 1,000 exemplars in the test set. The context variables $\mathbf{s}_c = [s_3, s_4]$ determine which data generation process i is in operation. Each process is characterized by a different value of $\boldsymbol{\mu}_i$, specified in the following way by the values of $\mathbf{s}_c$

$$\begin{array}{rclcrcrclcl}
-10 &<& s_3 &<& 0 & \text{and} & 0 &<& s_4 &<& 10 & \Rightarrow \text{Process 1 with } \boldsymbol{\mu}_1 = [-5, 5] \\
0 &<& s_3 &<& 10 & \text{and} & 0 &<& s_4 &<& 10 & \Rightarrow \text{Process 2 with } \boldsymbol{\mu}_2 = [5, 5] \\
-10 &<& s_3 &<& 10 & \text{and} & -10 &<& s_4 &<& 0 & \Rightarrow \text{Process 3 with } \boldsymbol{\mu}_3 = [0, -5]
\end{array}$$

The aim is to model this composite process using the H-CMAC architecture. Since $g_n(\mathbf{s}_r, \boldsymbol{\mu}_i, \sigma)$ is a non-linear function of the regressor variables $\mathbf{s}_r$, non-linear expert networks are needed to model the data. The decision boundary for selecting different expert networks in the space of the context variables $\mathbf{s}_c$ is also non-linear. Therefore, a non-linear gating network is also required.

It should be possible to model this process using a one-level H-CMAC architecture with one gating network and three expert networks. Each expert network comprises a single CMAC network with two inputs and produces the scalar output value y_i. The gating network contains three CMAC networks, each with two inputs, which produce the values of the intermediate variables ξ_i. These values are passed through the 'softmax' activation function in order to obtain the mixing proportions g_i.

In the implementation considered here, the non-linear mapping in the CMAC networks transforms the real-valued two-dimensional vectors $\mathbf{s}_c$ and $\mathbf{s}_r$ into 576-dimensional binary-valued vectors $\mathbf{x}_r$ for expert networks and $\mathbf{x}_c$ for the gating network. The weight vector $\mathbf{w}$ has the same size as $\mathbf{x}$ in each case.

4.1   Storage requirements

For a CMAC network with K quantizing functions, the number of storage locations required N_w is given by

$$N_w = K \prod_{i=1}^{N} Q_i \tag{8}$$

where N is the number of dimensions in $\mathbf{s}$ and Q_i is the number of resolution elements in dimension i.

In our implementation, each CMAC network had $N = 2, K = 4, Q_1 = 12$ and $Q_2 = 12$, so $N_w = 576$. There were six CMAC networks in the H-CMAC architecture - three expert networks and three networks providing the independent outputs in the gating network - leading to a total of $3,456$ weights. In contrast, a monolithic CMAC network with a four-dimensional input would require $4 \times 12^4 = 82,944$ weights.

5   Results

The on-line version of the learning algorithms in Equations 5 and 6 were used for training the H-CMAC architecture. The minimum test set root mean square error (RMSE) of 0.2869 was obtained only after 50 epochs of training.

The solutions learnt by each of the gating and expert networks in the H-CMAC architecture are shown in the mesh-plots in Figures 2 and 3. Each expert network models one of the three processes in the space of the regressor variables $\mathbf{s}_r = [s_1, s_2]$. The gating network partitions the space of the context variables $\mathbf{s}_c = [s_3, s_4]$ and selects the appropriate expert network in a given situation.

6   Conclusion

A hierarchical CMAC architecture based on the HME architecture was described in this paper. This architecture allows non-linear functions to be approximated by expert networks and non-linear decision

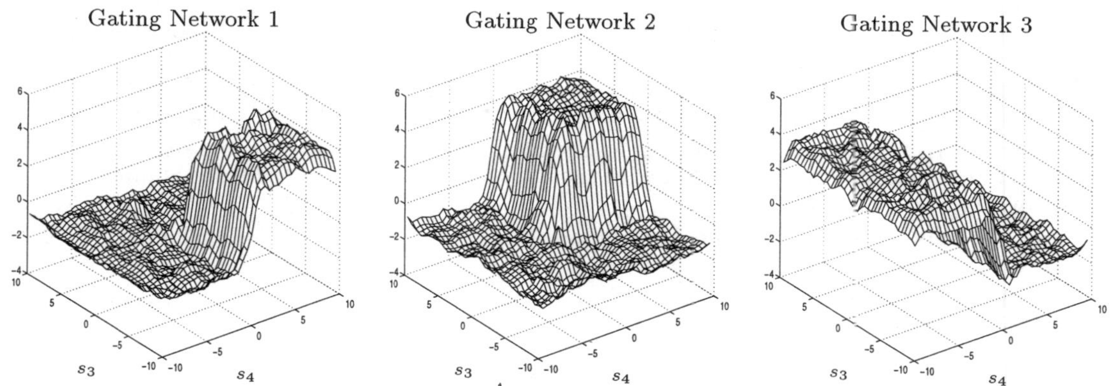

Figure 2: Outputs of the gating network for each expert network in the H-CMAC architecture. The input space consists of the context variables $s_c = [s_3, s_4]$.

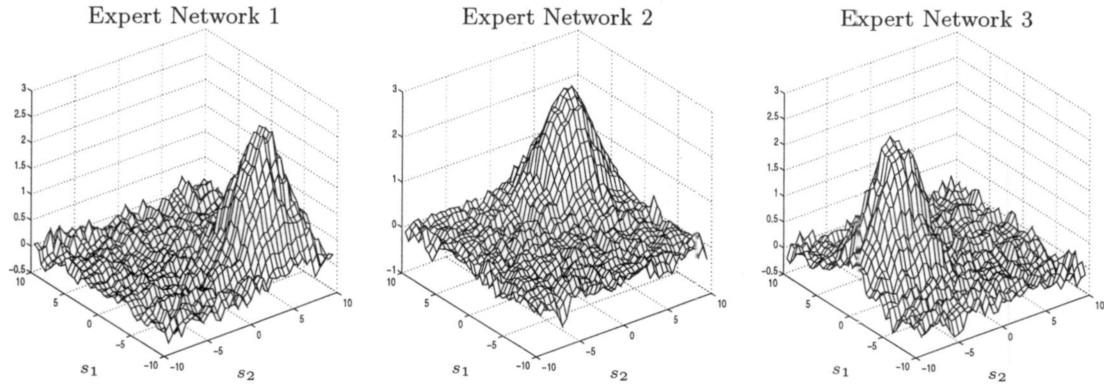

Figure 3: Output of expert networks in the H-CMAC architecture. The input space consists of the regressor variables $s_r = [s_1, s_2]$.

boundaries in the gating network. The utility of the approach in which the gating network sees context variables and expert networks see regressor variables was illustrated in a composite non-linear regression example consisting of a mixture of three non-linear processes. This approach leads to faster learning at lower computational cost and storage requirements compared to a monolithic approach.

In this paper, only results obtained using an on-line first order algorithm were presented. Second order algorithms such as IRLS, LS and RLS described in [5] involve linear matrix operations and can be performed in the H-CMAC architecture as well. Due to the high dimensionality of the binary-valued input vector x, these second order algorithms, which require matrix operations such as inversion, are significantly more computationally expensive than the first order method described in this paper. However, simplifications are possible as a result of the binary-valued nature of the x vector.

The H-CMAC architecture has been used in a reinforcement learning problem involving task decomposition for a robot manipulator arm [9]. A separate set of CMAC networks stores the evaluation function and policy for each sub-task which together represent the 'skill' of performing that sub-task. Complex behaviour consisting of a sequence of simpler sub-tasks can then be achieved by activating the appropriate sets of CMAC networks in different contexts.

References

[1] J.S. Albus. Data storage in the Cerebellar Model Articulation Controller (CMAC). *Journal of Dynamic Systems, Measurement and Control*, 97(3):228–233, Sept 1975.

[2] J.S. Bridle. Probabilistic interpretation of feedforward classification network outputs, with relationships to statistical pattern recognition. In F.F. Soulié and J. Hérault, editors, *Neurocomputing: Algorithms, Architectures and Applications*, volume 1 of *NATO ASI Series*, pages 227–236. Springer-Verlag, 1989.

[3] R.A. Jacobs, M.I. Jordan, S.J. Nowlan, and G.E. Hinton. Adaptive mixtures of local experts. *Neural Computation*, 3:79–87, 1991.

[4] M.I. Jordan and R.A. Jacobs. Hierarchies of adaptive experts. In J. Moody, S. Hanson, and R. Lippmann, editors, *Advances in Neural Information Processing Systems 4*, pages 985–993. Morgan Kaufmann, 1992.

[5] M.I. Jordan and R.A. Jacobs. Hierarchical Mixtures of Experts and the EM algorithm. Technical Report 9301, MIT Computational Cognitive Science, April 1993.

[6] W.T. Miller. Real-time application of neural networks for sensor-based control of robots with vision. *IEEE Transactions on Systems, Man, and Cybernetics*, 19(4):825–831, July/August 1989.

[7] W.T. Miller, F.H. Glanz, and L.G. Kraft. Application of a general learning algorithm to the control of robotic manipulators. *International Journal of Robotics Research*, 6(2):84–98, Summer 1987.

[8] S.J. Nowlan. *Soft Competitive Adaptation: Neural Network Learning Algorithms based on Fitting Statistical Mixtures*. PhD thesis, School of Computer Science, Carnegie Mellon University, Pittsburgh, PA 15213, USA, April 1991.

[9] C.K. Tham. *Modular On-Line Function Approximation for Scaling Up Reinforcement Learning*. PhD thesis, University of Cambridge Department of Engineering, Cambridge, U.K., October 1994.

Bayesian-Kullback Ying-Yang Machine: Reviews and New Results *

Lei Xu
1. Dept. of Computer Science, The Chinese University of Hong Kong
Shatin, Hong Kong (the correspondence address)
2. Information Science Center, Peking University, Beijing, China

***Abstract*—** After briefly reviewing the Bayesian-Kullback YING-YANG learning and its related achievements, this paper systematically summarizes my recent published results and unpublished new results on theories and algorithms for learning and model selection that are related to the Bayesian-Kullback YING-YANG learning, particularly focusing on (1) a general model number selection theory, its related criteria with EM algorithm and variants, as well as RPCL-type fast learning algorithms for finite mixtures (e.g, Gaussian mixture), mean square error clustering, multisets modeling learning, mixture of expert model as well as radial basis function and its extension; (2) a subspace dimension selection theory for principal component analysis; (3) the Bayesian-Kullback YING-YANG learning as a new scheme for hyperparameter decision and model selection.

1 Review on YING-YANG Machine and Its Achievements

The Bayesian-Kullback YING-YANG learning has been proposed recently for estimating the joint distribution of the input and representation space in two complement but equivalent Bayesian representations matched via the Kullback divergence (Xu, 1995a&96a). It acts as a general learning scheme which not only unifies several existing major unsupervised and supervised learning schemes, but also provides many new learning schemes as well as guides us to solve several classical hard open problems.

What is Bayesian-Kullback YING-YANG Machine ? As shown in Xu (1995a & 96a), both the supervised and unsupervised learning problems are summarized into the problem of estimating joint density $P(x, y)$ of patterns in the input space X and the representation space Y as shown in Fig.1 on the next page. Under Bayesian framework, we have two representations for $P(x, y)$. One is $P_{M_1}(x, y) = P_{M_1}(y|x)P_{M_1}(x)$, implemented by a model M_1 called *YANG/*(male) part since it performs the task of transferring a pattern/(a real body) into a code/(a seed). The other is $P_{M_2}(x, y) = P_{M_2}(x|y)P_{M_2}(y)$, implemented by a model M_2 called *YING* part since it performs the task of generating a pattern/(a real body) from a code/(a seed). They are complement to each other and together implement an entire circle $x \rightarrow y \rightarrow x$. This compliments to the ancient Chinese YING-YANG philosophy.

Here we have four components $P_{M_1}(x)$, $P_{M_1}(y|x)$, $P_{M_2}(x|y)$ and $P_{M_2}(y)$. Any combination of the different choices on the four components forms a potential YING-YANG pair belonging one of four types of marital status[1]: (a) *marry*, i.e., YING and YANG match each other; (b) *divorce*, i.e., YING and YANG go away from each other; (c) YING chases YANG, YANG escapes; (d) YANG chases YING, but YING escapes. The four types can be described by a combination of minimization (chasing) and maximization (escaping) the following Kullback divergence :

$$KL(M_1, M_2) = \int_{x,y} P_{M_1}(y|x)P_{M_1}(x) \log \frac{P_{M_1}(y|x)P_{M_1}(x)}{P_{M_2}(x|y)P_{M_2}(y)} dx dy, \tag{1}$$

or its variant $KL(M_2, M_1)$ by switching the position of $P_{M_1}(y|x)P_{M_1}(x)$ and $P_{M_2}(x|y)P_{M_2}(y)$. The minimization (maximization) can be implemented by the *Alternative* procedure which alternatively minimizes (maximizes) one model with the other temporarily fixed (Xu, 1995a, 1996a).

The four types of marital status together with the fact that each of $P_{M_1}(y|x)$, $P_{M_2}(x|y)$ and $P_{M_2}(y)$ can have several choices provide a large number of potential YING-YANG pairings. Although not all of them provide sensible learning models, a quite number of them indeed lead us to useful learning models. Since this scheme bases on the two complement YING and YANG Bayesian representations and their Kullback divergence for their marital status, we call it *Bayesian-Kullback YING-YANG* learning scheme. Furthermore, under this scheme we call each such obtained pair that is sensible for learning purpose as a *Bayesian-Kullback YING-YANG Machine* or *YING-YANG* machine shortly.

One large class of important YING-YANG Machines is obtained by fixing $P_{M_1}(x)$ at some Parzen window density estimate $P_{M_1}(x) = \frac{1}{Nh^d} \sum_{i=1}^{N} K(\frac{x-x_i}{h})$ on input data $D = \{x_i\}_{i=1}^{N}$ with $x_i \in R^d$. Putting it into eq.(1), as $h \rightarrow 0$ and $N \rightarrow \infty$ such that $Nh^d \rightarrow D$ (D is a constant irrelevant to M_1, M_2), we can have $KL(M_1, M_2) = D + \lim_{N\to\infty} K(M_1, M_2)$ with

$$K(M_1, M_2) = \frac{1}{N} \sum_i \{ \int_y P_{M_1}(y|x_i) \log P_{M_1}(y|x_i)dy - \int_y P_{M_1}(y|x_i) \log P_{M_2}(y)dy - \int_y P_{M_1}(y|x_i) \log P_{M_2}(x_i|y)dy \} \tag{2a}$$

$$K(M_1, M_2) = \frac{1}{N} \sum_{i,y} P_{M_1}(y|x_i) \log P_{M_1}(y|x_i) - \frac{1}{N} \sum_{i,y} P_{M_1}(y|x_i) \log P_{M_2}(y) - \frac{1}{N} \sum_{i,y} P_{M_1}(y|x_i) \log P_{M_2}(x_i|y), \tag{2b}$$

when N is large enough, we can directly consider the above $K(M_1, M_2)$ for learning.

Unifying existing major unsupervised learning schemes. Considering eq.(2b) and different choices

---

*This project was supported by the HK RGC Earmarked Grants CUHK250/94E and CUHK484/95E.

[1] Currently, only the status *marry* and *divorce* have been studied in detail (Xu, 1996a).

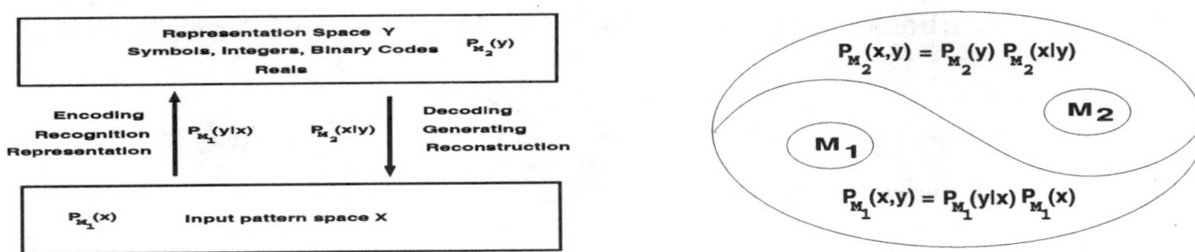

Figure 1   The joint spaces X, Y and the YING-YANG Machine

for components $P_{M_1}(y|x)$, $P_{M_2}(x|y)$ and $P_{M_2}(y)$. Under the *divorce* state, we can show that one special case of the YING-YANG machine reduces to maximum information preservation learning (Linsker, 1989; Atick & Redlich, 1990; Bell & Sejnowski, 1995). While under the *marry* state, the YING-YANG machine includes several major unsupervised learning schemes as special cases. As shown in Xu(1995a&96a), one special case of the YING-YANG Machine reduces to Maximum likelihood learning on finite mixture model with the EM algorithm proposed by Dempster et al(1977), to a cost function for mixture Gaussian by Hathaway (1986) and Neal & Hinton (1993), to the *Information Geometry* theory and the *em* algorithm (Amari, 1995a&b; Byrne, 1992; Csiszar, 1975&84), to MDL autoencoder with a "bits-back" argument by Hinton & Zemel (1994) and the autoencoder of minimizing the bits of uncoded residual errors and the unused bits in the transmission channel's capacity (Xu, 1995c). The special case can also reduce to multisets modeling learning (Xu, 1995e)–a unified learning framework for clustering, PCA-type learnings and self-organizing map. One other special case reduces to the recent proposed Helmholtz machine (Dayan et al, 1995; Hinton et al, 1995) with new understandings (e.g., when the gap between Helmholtz machine learning and Maximum likelihood learning can disappear ?).

Unifiyiny existing major supervised learning schemes. The YING-YANG machine includes also maximum likelihood learning, or least square learning in particular. Moreover, it has been further shown in (Xu, 1996c) to be able to include the popular mixture of expert model (Jacobs, Jordan, Nowlan, & Hinton, 1991) and its alternative model (Xu, Jordan & Hinton, 1994, 1995) as special cases.

Extended to temporal patterns and signal modeling. The YING-YANG machine has been extended to temporal processing with a number of new models for signal modeling, cognition, prediction and segmentation. Some of them can be regarded as the extensions of Helmholtz machine or maximum information preservation learning to temporal processing. Some of them include and extend the existing Hidden Markov Model (HMM), AMAR and AR models (Xu, 1995b).

Providing new learning models. As shown in (Xu, 1996a), through other different choices for components $P_{M_1}(x)$, $P_{M_1}(y|x)$, $P_{M_2}(x|y)$ and $P_{M_2}(y)$, as well as using $KL(M_2, M_1)$ instead of $KL(M_1, M_2)$, a number of new unsupervised and supervised learning models can be obtained. There remains many further efforts to be made on investigating these new models.

Providing a general Independent Component Analysis (ICA) framework. As shown in Xu & Amari(1996), it unifies the information maximization (INFORMAX) approach (Bell and Sejnowski, 1995) and the minimum mutual information (MMI) approach (Amari, Cichocki, and Yang, 1996). Moreover, an interesting constrained ICA probelm is studied with a theorem given.

Providing a general number selection theory for solving several classical hard open problems on multiple-model based supervised and unsupervised learning. Based on this theory, criteria have been developed for the problem of selecting numbers of Gaussians in a mixture density estimation as well as for the classical hard open problem of selecting number of clusters in least square clustering analysis (1995a, 1996b). Also, a criterion has been obtained for determining the dimension of subspace by the *principal component analysis (PCA)* related approaches. Moreover, a criterion has also been obtained (Xu, 1996c) for selecting an appropriate number of experts in the mixture of expert models (Jacobs, Jordan, Nowlan, & Hinton, 1991).

The following sections will systematically summarize my recent published results and unpublished new results on theories and algorithms for learning and model selection. In Sec.2, a general number selection theory is given with a new supporting theorem proved for finite mixture, and then it is applied to Gaussian mixture with a selection criterion in help of the EM algorithm. Next, the theory and criterion are further applied to clustering analysis via an induced Hard-cut finite mixture, particularly the hard-cut Gaussian mixture in help of the hard-cut EM algorithm, and from which we further obtain a cluster number selection criterion for the classical mean square error (MSE) clustering. In Sec. 3, Multi-sets modeling is formulated as a special case of finite mixture and solved by the EM algorithm. The theory and criterion given in Sec.2 are adopted to multi-sets modeling, with several problems given in Xu(1994&95d) introduced. In Sec.4, a general number selection theory is obtained for both the original mixture of experts model (Jacobs, Jordan, Nowlan, & Hinton, 1991) and its alternative model (Xu, Jordan & Hinton, 1994) with corresponding selection criteria provided. Furthermore, regarded as the special case of the alternative model for mixture of experts, the radial basis function and its extension can be learned under the guidance of this number selection theory and the EM algorithm, which can solve the difficulties encountered in the existing RBF net learnings. In Sec.5, the original RPCL and its general form are introduced and suggested for finite model learning, particularly for clustering, multiset modeling, mxiture of experts as well as RBF net with automatic number selection. Furthermore, Sec. 6 introduces a subspace dimension selection theory for principal component analysis with a new selection criterion. Sec. 7 proposed a Bayesian-Kullback YING-YANG learning based new scheme for hyperparameter decision and model selection. Finally, we give conclusions in Sec.7.

2 Learning and Model Selection on Finite Mixture Models

A general number selection theory for finite mixture with $\Theta = \{\alpha_y, \theta_y\}_{y=1}^k$

$$P(x, \Theta(k)) = \sum_{y=1}^k \alpha_y P_y(x, \theta_y), \ \alpha_y > 0, \qquad \sum_{y=1}^k \alpha_y = 1, \tag{3}$$

we consider a special design of the YING-YANG pair: (i) $P_{M_2}(y) = \alpha_y \geq 0$, M_2 consists of $P_{M_2}(x|y) = P_y(x, \theta_y), y = 1, \cdots, k$; (ii) $P_{M_1}(y|x) = p(y|x)$ is free, i.e., it can take any density in the form $P(y|x)$. Putting them into eq.(2b), the mimization of $K(M_1, M_2)$ will become

$$J(\Theta(k)) = K(M_1, M_2) = \frac{1}{N} \sum_{i,y} P(y|x_i) \log P(y|x_i) - \sum_y \alpha_y \log \alpha_y - \frac{1}{N} \sum_{i,y} P(y|x_i) \log P_y(x, \theta_y), \tag{4}$$

subject to
$$P(y|x_i) = \alpha_y P_y(x, \theta_y)/P(x, \Theta(k)),$$

By alternatively fixing $M_1(\{P(y|x_i)\})$, $M_2(\{\alpha_y, \theta_y\})$, the minimization of $K(M_1, M_2)$ will lead us to:

E-step: $P^{(t+1)}(y|x_i) = \frac{\alpha_y^{(t)} P_y(x, \theta_y^{(t)})}{P(x, \Theta^{(t)}(k))}$, (5a)

M-step : $\alpha_y^{(t+1)} = \frac{1}{N} \sum_{i=1}^N P^{(t+1)}(y|x_i)$, $\theta_y^{(t+1)} = \max_{\theta_y} J_y(\theta_y)$, $J_y(\theta_y) = \frac{1}{N} \sum_i P^{(t+1)}(y|x_i) \log P_y(x, \theta_y)$, (5b)

This is exactly the EM algorithm for the maximum likelihood learning on the finite mixture eq.(3). Actually, as shown in Xu(1995a&96a), via $\min_{\{M_1\}} K(M_1, M_2)$ we get $K(M_1, M_2) = -\frac{1}{N} \sum_i \log \sum_{y=1}^k \alpha_y P_y(x, \theta_y)$. In other word, $\min_{\{M_1, M_2\}} K(M_1, M_2)$ is equivalent to maximum likelihood learning on the finite mixture.

Theorem 1 Let Θ^* to be the true parameter of the finite mixture $P(x, \Theta^*(k^*))$ from which the data set $\{x_i\}_1^N$ comes from, where $\theta_r^* \neq \theta_q^*$ for $r \neq q$ and $P(x, \Theta^*(k^*))$ is uniquely defined by its parameter $\Theta^*(k^*)$ except of permutations on indices. Assume that there is no another finite mixture $P(x, \Theta(k))$ given by eq.(3) with $k \neq k^*$ but $P(x, \Theta(k)) = P(x, \Theta^*(k^*))$, then for $J(\Theta(k))$ given by eq.(4) and for any Θ, we have $J(\Theta(k)) < J(\Theta^*(k^*))$ as $N \to \infty$, as long as $k \neq k^*$.

Proof: As $h \to 0$ and $N \to \infty$, a Parzen window estimate $P_{M_1}(x)$ will tend to its true distribution $P(x, \Theta^*(k^*))$, and $J(\Theta(k))$ given by eq.(4) will tend to

$$J(\Theta(k)) = \int_{x,z} P(z|x_i) P(x, \Theta^*(k^*)) \log \frac{P(z|x_i) P(x, \Theta^*(k^*))}{P(z) P_y(x, \theta_y)} dx dz \geq 0,$$

with
$$P(z) = \int \sum_{y=1}^k P(y)\delta(z - y) dz \text{ and } P(z|x_i) = P(z) P_y(x, \theta_y)/P(x, \Theta(k)),$$

The equality holds if and only if

$P(z|x_i) P(x, \Theta^*(k^*)) = P(z) P_y(x, \theta_y)$ or $P(x, \Theta^*(k^*)) P(z) P_y(x, \theta_y)/P(x, \Theta(k)) = P(z) P_y(x, \theta_y)$, which is equivalent to $P(x, \Theta^*(k^*))/P(x, \Theta(k)) = 1$. That is, $P(x, \Theta^*(k^*)) = P(x, \Theta(k))$.

We get $J(\Theta(k)) < J(\Theta^*(k^*))$ since we assume that there is no another finite mixture $P(x, \Theta(k))$ given by eq.(3) with $k \neq k^*$ but $P(x, \Theta(k)) = P(x, \Theta^*(k^*))$. **Q.E.D.**

This theorem immediately suggests a theory for selecting the number of models in a finite mixture. This number is given by $k^* = arg \min_{\{k, \Theta\}} J(\Theta(k)) = arg \min_k J(\Theta'(k))$ with $\Theta'(k) = \{\min_\Theta J(\Theta(k))\}$ for a fixed k. $\Theta'(k)$ can be approximately obtained by the EM algorithm or some other algorithms.

The number selection criterion for Gaussian mixture. As a special case, for a gaussian $P_y(x, \theta_y) = G(x, m_y, \Sigma_y)$, from eq.(4) we can use a particular criterion

$$J(\Theta(k)) = \frac{1}{2} \sum_{y=1}^k \alpha_y tr(S_y \Sigma_y^{-1}) + J_G(\Theta(k)), \ S_y = \frac{1}{\alpha_y N} \sum_{i=1}^N P(y|x_i)(x_i - m_y)(x_i - m_y)^T$$

$$J_G(\Theta(k)) = \frac{1}{2N} \sum_{i=1}^N \sum_{y=1}^k P(y|x_i) \log P(y|x_i) + \sum_{y=1}^k \alpha_y \log (\sqrt{|\Sigma_y|}/\alpha_y), \tag{6a}$$

This criterion can be used for selecting the number of gaussians together with a learning algorithm for $\min_\Theta J(\Theta(k))$. Moreover, the M-step of the EM algorithm eq.(5) can be explicitly given as follows:

M-step : $\alpha_y^{(t+1)} = \frac{1}{N} \sum_{i=1}^N P^{(t+1)}(y|x_i)$, $m_y^{(t+1)} = \frac{1}{\alpha_y N} \sum_{i=1}^N P^{(t+1)}(y|x_i)x_i$,

$$\Sigma_y^{(t+1)} = \frac{1}{\alpha_y N} \sum_{i=1}^N P^{(t+1)}(y|x_i)(x_i - m_y^{(t+1)})(x_i - m_y^{(t+1)})^T \tag{6b}$$

In this case, its always satisfies $\Sigma_y = S_y$ and the first term of $J(\Theta(k))$ in eq.(6a) can be neglected. Therefore, we simply need $J_G(\Theta(k))$ only for selecting k^*.

Induced Hard-cut finite mixture and the number selection criterion for clustering analysis. The purpose of clustering analysis is to partition a data set into nonoverlap regions $R_y, y = 1, \cdots, k$. It is equivalent to assume that the data comes from a mixture of $P_y(x, \theta_y)$ with a priori $\alpha_y, y = 1, \cdots, k$ on the nonoverlap supports $R_y \subset R^d, y = 1, \cdots, k$ such that $P_y(x, \theta_y) = 0$ if x is not in R_y, and then we can classify $x \in R_y$ because $P(y|x) = 1$ and $P(j|x) = 0$ for $j \neq y$. Thus, a criterion for selecting the number of clusters can be obtained by simplifying eq.(4) into

$$J_h(\Theta(k)) = -\frac{1}{N}\sum_y \sum_{x \in R_y} P(y|x_i)\log P_y(x,\theta_y) - \sum_y \alpha_y \log \alpha_y, \tag{7}$$

Under the same condition as Theorem 1, we have $J_h(\Theta(k)) < J_h(\Theta^*(k^*))$ as $N \to \infty$ as long as $k \neq k^*$.

In practice, most of $P_y(x,\theta_y)$ are supported on overlapped regions. We often assign an x_i into one of not overlap regions by Bayesian Decision $y = arg\ max_y\ P(y|x_i)$. This is equivalent to hard-cut or forcely quantize $P(y|x_i)$ into

$$I(y|x_i) = 1,\ \text{if}\ y = arg\ max_y \alpha_y P_y(x,\theta_y);\qquad I(y|x_i) = 0,\ \text{otherwise} \tag{8a}$$

which partitions the whole domain R into $R_y, y = 1, \cdots, k$ nonoverlap regions such that each region R_y supports a hardcut-induced density from $P(x,\Theta(k))$ given by eq.(3):

$$q(x,R_y,\Theta(k)) = \frac{P(x,\Theta(k))}{\alpha'_y},\ \text{if}\ x \in R_y,\ q(x,R_y,\Theta(k)) = 0,\ \text{otherwise},\quad \text{where}\quad \alpha'_y = \int_{x \in R_y} P(x,\Theta(k))dx \tag{8b}$$

where α'_y is just the a priori of $q(x,R_y,\Theta(k))$. As a result, we have an induced finite mixture expression for $P(x,\Theta(k))$

$$P(x,\Theta(k)) = \sum_{y=1}^k \alpha'_y q(x,R_y,\Theta(k)) \tag{8c}$$

Noticing $\alpha'_y q(x,R_y,\Theta(k)) = P(x,\Theta(k))$ for $x \in R_y$, the criterion for selecting number of clusters is

$$J_h(\Theta(k)) = -\frac{1}{N}\sum_y \sum_{x \in R_y} I(y|x_i)\log P(x,\Theta(k)),\quad subject\ to\ eq.(8a) \tag{9}$$

The hard-cut EM algorithm, cluster number selection, and MSE clustering. If the overlaps between the distributions in the original finite mixture eq.(3) can be neglected, then we can approximately have $P(x,\Theta(k)) = P_y(x,\theta_y)\alpha_y$ for $x \in R_y$ and eq.(9) becomes

$$J_h(\Theta(k)) = -\sum_y \alpha_y \log \alpha_y - \frac{1}{N}\sum_y \sum_{x \in R_y} I(y|x_i)\log P_y(x,\theta_y),\ \alpha_y^{(t+1)} = \frac{1}{N}\sum_{i=1}^N I(y|x_i),\ subject\ to\ eq.(8a) \tag{10}$$

together with a hard-cut variant EM algorithm as already presented in (Xu, 1995b, 96a&b). In particular, for the case of gaussian mixtures with equal $\alpha_y = 1/k$ and equal ball shape variance $\Sigma_y = \sigma^2 I$, eq.(8a) is simplified into

$$I(y|x_i) = 1,\ \text{if}\ y = arg\min_y \|x_i - m_y\|^2;\qquad I(y|x_i) = 0,\ \text{otherwise}. \tag{11a}$$

and the Hardcut-EM becomes simply the classical batch-way K-means algorithm for the classical MSE clustering. Moreover, from eq.(11a) we get the number selection criterion :

$$J_G^h(k) = \log k + 0.5d\log \sigma^2,\quad \sigma^2 = \frac{E^2}{dN},\quad E^2 = \sum_{i=1}^N I(y|x_i)\|x_i - m_y\|^2, \tag{11b}$$

Moreover, for the cases that $\Sigma_y \neq \sigma^2 I$, the problem is just the so called Weighted MSE clustering based on Mahalanobis distance, which are still studied in the literature recently. Here we see that this problem can be solved by the hardcut EM with the cluster number selected by eq.(10).

3   Multisets Modeling Leanring and Finite Mixture

As proposed in Xu (1994&1995d), we can use a parmetric set $C_y(\theta_y)$ to represent a model, and the error or distortion of using this model to represent a sample x_i can be defined as the shortest distance between the set and x_i, denoted by $\varepsilon(x_i,\phi_y) \geq 0$. Furthermore, we can use multiple such sets $C_y(\phi_y), y = 1, \cdots, k$ to model a comlpicated data. Interestingly, the multisets learning can naturely include the conventional mean square clustering analysis as the special case that $C_y(\phi_y)$ is a point, we have $\phi_y = \{m_y\}$ and

$$\varepsilon(x_i,\phi_y) = \|x_i - m_y\|^2, \tag{12a}$$

Moreover, when $C_y(\phi_y)$ is a line passing through m_y, we have $\phi_y = \{m_y, w_y\}$ and

$$\varepsilon(x_i,\phi_y) = \|(x_i - m_y) - (w_j - m_y)(w_j - m_y)^T(x_i - m_y)\|^2,$$

$$\text{or}\qquad \varepsilon(x_i,\phi_y) = \|x_i - m_y\|^2 - \frac{[(w_y - m_y)^T(x_i - m_y)]^2}{\|w_y - m_y\|^2}. \tag{12b}$$

As shown in Xu (1994& 95d), $E\varepsilon(x_i,\phi_y)$ is minimized when $m_y,\ w_y - m_y$ are the mean and principal component of cluster C_y. That is, it does principal components analysis (PCA) for each of cluster located at different points, we call it localized PCA, which is a more general form of clustering that includes the conventional MSE clustering as a special case $w_j - m_y = 0$. Also, by discarding the first term in eq.(12b) and changing its following '-' sign into '+' sign, we encounter the case that $C_y(\phi_y)$ is a superplane passing through m_y, which performs PCA's complement varaint– minor components analysis (MCA).

More complicatedly, let $C_y(\phi_y)$ to be a subspace located at m_y and spanned by $W_y = [w_y^{(1)} - m_y, \cdots w_y^{(r)} - m_y]$, we have $\phi_y = \{m_y, W_y\}$ and

$$\varepsilon(x_i,\phi_y) = \|(I - P)(x_i - m_y)\|^2,\ P = W_y(W_y^t W_y)^{-1}W_y^t,\ \text{or}\ P = W_y W_y^t,\ (W_y^t W_y) = I, \tag{12c}$$

$$\text{or}\qquad \varepsilon(x_i,\phi_y) = \|x_i - m_y\|^2 - \|P(x_i - m_y)\|^2,\ P = (W_y^t W_y)^{-\frac{1}{2}}W_y^t,\ \text{or}\ P = W_y^t,\ (W_y^t W_y) = I, \tag{12d}$$

As shown in Xu (1994& 95d), $E\varepsilon(x_i,\phi_y)$ is minimized when m_y is the mean of the cluster C_y and W_y either consists of or spans the same subspace by the first r principal components of cluster C_y. That is, it does principal subspace analysis (PSA) for each of cluster located at different points, we call it localized PSA, which is an even more general form for clustering which includes the localized PCA.

Now we show that Multisets Modeling Leanring can be modeled into the problem of finite mixture. Since x is a random vector, its transformation $\varepsilon(x, \phi_y)$ is also a positive random variable, we use $\varepsilon = \varepsilon(x_i, \phi_y)$ to denote a value of its realization and assume that ε is from the following exponential distribution

$$P_y(\varepsilon, \theta_y) = \lambda_y^{-1} e^{-\lambda_y^{-1} \varepsilon(x_i, \phi_y)}, \quad \theta_y = \{\phi_y, \lambda_y\} \tag{13a}$$

Then we can get a finite mixture model for ε

$$P(\varepsilon, \Theta(k)) = \sum_{y=1}^{k} \alpha_y P_y(\varepsilon, \theta_y), \ \alpha_y > 0, \qquad \sum_{y=1}^{k} \alpha_y = 1, \tag{13b}$$

Its general number selection criteria can be directly obtained from eq.(4)

$$J(\Theta(k)) = \frac{1}{N} \sum_{i,y} P(y|x_i) \log P(y|x_i) - \sum_y \alpha_y \log \alpha_y + \sum_y \alpha_y \log \lambda_y + \frac{1}{N} \sum_{i,y} P(y|x_i)\varepsilon(x_i, \phi_y), \tag{14a}$$

and its EM algorithm from eq.(5) by changing its updating for $\theta_y^{(t+1)}$ into a more specific form

$$\phi_y^{(t+1)} = \max_{\phi_y} J_y(\phi_y), \quad J_y(\phi_y) = \frac{1}{N} \sum_i P^{(t+1)}(y|x_i)\varepsilon(x_i, \phi_y), \quad \lambda_y^{(t+1)} = \frac{1}{N} \sum_i P^{(t+1)}(y|x_i)\varepsilon(x_i, \phi_y^{(t+1)}), \tag{14b}$$

Similarly, we can get the hardcut form for eq.(14a)

$$J(\Theta(k)) = -\sum_y \alpha_y \log \alpha_y + \sum_y \alpha_y \log \lambda_y + \frac{1}{N} \sum_{i,y} I(y|x_i)\varepsilon(x_i, \phi_y), \ \alpha_y^{(t+1)} = \frac{1}{N} \sum_{i=1}^{N} I(y|x_i) \tag{15}$$

and its EM algorithm obtained simply by replacing $P^{(t+1)}(y|x_i)$ by $I(y|x_i)$ in eq.(14b).

4   Learning and Selection on Mixture of Experts and RBF Nets

The number selection theory and criteria for mixture of experts. For supervised learning that performs a mapping $x \to z$, we consider $P_{M_1}(z, y|x) = P_{M_1}(y|x, z)P_{M_1}(z|x)$ as YANG part and $P_{M_2}(z, y|x) = P_{M_2}(z|x, y)P_{M_2}(y|x)$ as YING part. Putting it into eq.(1), we have

$$KL(M_1, M_2|x) = \int_{y,z} P_{M_1}(y|x, z)P_{M_1}(z|x) \log \frac{P_{M_1}(y|x,z) P_{M_1}(z|x)}{P_{M_2}(z|x,y) P_{M_2}(y|x)} dzdy,$$

$$KL(M_1, M_2) = \int_x KL(M_1, M_2|x)p(x)dx, \tag{16}$$

where $KL(M_1, M_2|x)$ is conditioned on x and thus should be averaged over $p(x)$.

We consider the minimization of this $KL(M_1, M_2)$. Given a training set $\{x_i, z_i\}_{i=1}^{N}$. Let us make such a design: (i) $p(x)$ is given by a parzen window estimate; (ii) $P_{M_1}(z|x_i) = \delta(z - z_i)$, and $P_{M_1}(y|x) = P(y|x)$ is free; (iii), $P_{M_2}(y|x) = P(y|x, \psi)$, $P_{M_2}(z|x, y) = P_{M_2}(z|x, y, \theta_y)$; (iv) y is discrete $y = 1, \cdots, k$. Putting it into eq.(16), as $h \to 0$ and $N \to \infty$ such that $Nh^d \to D$, we can have $KL(M_1, M_2) = J(\Theta(k)) + \lim_{N \to \infty} K(M_1, M_2)$ with

$$J(\Theta(k)) = \frac{1}{N} \sum_{i=1}^{N} \sum_{y=1}^{k} P(y|x_i)\{log\ P(y|x_i) - logP(z_i|x_i, y, \theta_y)P(y|x_i, \psi)\}, \ \Theta(k) = \{\psi, \theta_y, y = 1, \cdots, k\} \tag{17a}$$

For the minimization of $J(\Theta(k))$ by alternatively fixing $P(y|x_i)$s' and $\Theta(k)$, as shown in Xu(1996c), we get exactly the EM algorithm for maximum likelihood learning on the original model of mixture of experts (Jacobs, Jordan, Nowlan & Hinton, 1991; Jordan & Jacobs, 1994)

$$P(z|x, \Theta(k)) = \sum_{y=1}^{k} P(y|x, \psi)P(z|x, y, \theta_y). \tag{17b}$$

That is, it is a special case of Bayesian-Kullback YING-YANG learning scheme. Moremore, let

$$P(y|x_i, \psi) = P(x|y, \psi_y)\alpha_y / \sum_{y=1}^{k} P(x|y, \psi_y)\alpha_y \tag{17b}$$

we can actually get the alternative gating net proposed in (Xu, Jordan, & Hinton, 1994, 1995) with its corresponding EM algorithm.

Theorem 2   Let Θ^* to be the true parameter of the mixture-of-experts $P(z|x, \Theta^*(k^*))$ given in eq.(17b) from which the data set $\{x_i, z_i\}_{i=1}^{N}$ comes from, where $\theta_r^* \neq \theta_q^*$ for $r \neq q$ and $P(z|x, \Theta^*(k^*))$ is uniquely defined by its parameter $\Theta^*(k^*)$ except of permutations on indices. Assume that there is no another the mixture-of-experts $P(z|x, \Theta(k))$ given by eq.(17b) with $k \neq k^*$ but $P(z|x, \Theta(k)) = P(z|x, \Theta^*(k^*))$, then for any Θ, we have $J(\Theta(k)) < J(\Theta^*(k^*))$ as $N \to \infty$, as long as $k \neq k^*$.

Proof: It is similar to the proof of Theorem 1.

As $N \to \infty$, $J(\Theta(k))$ given by eq.(17a) will tend to

$$J(\Theta(k)) = \frac{1}{N} \sum_{i=1}^{N} \int_{s,z} P_{M_1}(s|x_i, z)P(z|x_i, \Theta^*(k^*)) \log \frac{P_{M_1}(s|x_i, z) P(z|x_i, \Theta^*(k^*))}{P(z|x_i, s, \theta_y) P(s|x_i, \psi)} dzds \geq 0,$$

$$P(s|x_i, \psi) = \int \sum_{y=1}^{k} P(y|x_i, \psi)\delta(s - y)ds, \quad P_{M_1}(s|x_i, z) = P(s|x_i, \psi)P(z_i|x_i, s, \theta_y)/P(z_i|x_i, \Theta(k)) \tag{17d}$$

The equality holds if and only if $P_{M_1}(s|x_i, z)P(z|x_i, \Theta^*(k^*)) = P(z|x_i, s, \theta_y)P(s|x_i, \psi)$ and from eq.(17d) it becomes $P(z|x_i, \Theta^*(k^*)) = P(z|x_i, \Theta(k))$. We proved the theorem when there is no another finite mixture $P(z|x, \Theta(k))$ with $k \neq k^*$ but $P(z|x_i, \Theta(k)) = P(z|x_i, \Theta^*(k^*))$ for any set $\{x_i\}_{i=1}^{N}$.   **Q.E.D.**

Similar to the case of finite mixture in Sec.2, we can select the number of experts by $k^* = arg\min_k \{\min_\Theta J(\Theta(k))\}$. Practically, again it can be approximately implemented by using the the EM algorithm for $\min_\Theta J(\Theta(k))$.

For the special case that the regression error of each expert is gaussian, i.e., $P(z|x, y, \theta_y) = G(z, f(x, W_y), \Sigma_y)$, we can get the following particular criterion for the original model of mixture of experts (Jacobs, Jordan, Nowlan & Hinton, 1991; Jordan & Jacobs, 1994)

$$J(\Theta(k)) = \tfrac{1}{2}\sum_{y=1}^{k} \alpha_y tr(S_y\Sigma_y^{-1}) + J_G(\Theta(k)), \quad \Sigma_y = \tfrac{1}{\alpha_y N}\sum_{i=1}^{N} P(y|x_i)[z_i - f(x_i,W_y)][z_i - f(x_i,W_y)]^T,$$

$$\alpha_y = \tfrac{1}{N}\sum_{i=1}^{N} h(y|x_i), \quad J_G(\Theta(k)) = \tfrac{1}{2}\sum_{y=1}^{k}\alpha_y log|\Sigma_y| + \tfrac{1}{N}\sum_{i=1}^{N}\sum_{y=1}^{k} P(y|x_i)log\frac{P(y|x_i)}{P(y|x_i,\psi)}, \tag{18a}$$

Moreover, when the EM algorithm is used for $\min_\Theta J(\Theta(k))$, it always satisfies $\Sigma_y = S_y$. As a result, we can simply use $J_G(\Theta(k))$ only for selecting k^* in this case.

For the alternative gating net eq.(17c) with its corresponding EM algorithm(Xu, Jordan, & Hinton, 1994, 1995), the criterion eq.(18a) further becomes

$$J_G(\Theta(k)) = \tfrac{1}{2}\sum_{y=1}^{k}\alpha_y log|\Sigma_y| + \tfrac{1}{N}\sum_{i,y} P(y|x_i)log\, P(y|x_i) - \tfrac{1}{N}\sum_{i,y} P(y|x_i)\log P(x|y,\psi_y) - \sum_{y=1}^{k}\alpha_y log\alpha_y. \tag{18b}$$

Learning and selection on Radial Basis Function (RBF) nets. we consider the special cases of eq.(17b) that

$$\text{(i)}\; P(z|x,y,\theta_y) = G(z,c_y,\sigma^2), \qquad \text{(ii)}\; P(z|x,y,\theta_y) = G(z,\theta_y^t x + c_y,\sigma^2) \tag{19a}$$

$$P(y|x_i,\psi) = \frac{exp[-0.5(x-m_y)\Sigma^{-1}(x-m_y)]}{\sum_{y=1}^{k} exp[-0.5(x-m_y)\Sigma^{-1}(x-m_y)]}. \tag{19b}$$

By taking expectation on the both sides of eq.(17b) over z, we get

$$out(x) = E(z|x,\Theta(k)) = \sum_{y=1}^{k} c_y \frac{exp[-0.5(x-m_y)\Sigma^{-1}(x-m_y)]}{\sum_{y=1}^{k} exp[-0.5(x-m_y)\Sigma^{-1}(x-m_y)]}. \tag{20a}$$

$$out(x) = E(z|x,\Theta(k)) = \sum_{y=1}^{k} (\theta_y^t x + c_y)\frac{exp[-0.5(x-m_y)\Sigma^{-1}(x-m_y)]}{\sum_{y=1}^{k} exp[-0.5(x-m_y)\Sigma^{-1}(x-m_y)]}. \tag{20b}$$

We can easily find that eq.(20a) is just a normalized RBF nets with k hidden units and eq.(20b) is an extended RBF net, both of which have been widely studied in the literature. Also, the training on RBF networks is based on the least square learning, which is a special case of Maximum likelihood learning. Therefore, the alternative model for mixture of experts (Xu, Jordan, & Hinton, 1994, 1995) with maximum likelihhod learning actually includes RBF networks as special cases that each expert is either a constant value c_y or a linear regression, while the gatting net has equal α_y and gaussians $P(x|y,\psi_y) = G(x,m_y,\Sigma)$ being with equal variance matrices.

The existing learning methods on RBF networks have at least three problems. One is that the number of hidden units is decided heuristically. The second is that Σ is heuritically prespecified and is usually chosen as I. Third, the training on the output layer and on the center $m_y, y = 1,\cdots,k$ is separatedly made. That is, the centers are obtained directly from input data by some clustering approaches without considering to get a better regression relation between $out(x), x$. Here, all the problems can be solved via the above bridge between RBF nets and the mixture of experts.

First, the maximum likelihood learning on RBF nets can be made directly by the EM algorithm proposed in (Xu, Jordan, & Hinton, 1994, 1995) to get all the parameters Σ, m_y, c_y, θ_y, σ such that a globally more optimal solution is obtained. If fact, the EM algorithm for RBF nets can be simplified considerably. Taking the case of the standard normalized RBF nets by eq.(20a) with one output variable as an example, we have the following iterative EM algorithm

$$\textbf{E-step:}\; P^{(t+1)}(y|x_i) = \frac{G(x,m_y,\Sigma)G(z,c_y,\sigma^2)}{\sum_{y=1}^{k} G(x,m_y,\Sigma)G(z,c_y,\sigma^2)} \tag{21a}$$

$$\textbf{M-step}: \; c_y^{(t+1)} = \tfrac{k}{N}\sum_{i=1}^{N} P^{(t+1)}(y|x_i)out(x_i), \quad {}^{(t+1)}\sigma^2 = \tfrac{1}{N}\sum_{y=1}^{k}\sum_{i=1}^{N} P^{(t+1)}(y|x_i)[out(x_i) - c_y^{(t+1)}]^2$$

$$m_y^{(t+1)} = \tfrac{k}{N}\sum_{i=1}^{N} P^{(t+1)}(y|x_i)x_i, \quad \Sigma^{(t+1)} = \tfrac{1}{N}\sum_{y=1}^{k}\sum_{i=1}^{N} P^{(t+1)}(y|x_i)(x_i - m_y^{(t+1)})(x_i - m_y^{(t+1)})^T \tag{21b}$$

Second, the number k can be selection by inserting eqs.(19a&b) into eq.(18b). This can also be simplified. Again, taking eq.(20a) as an example we have

$$J_G(\Theta(k)) = \log\sigma + \tfrac{1}{N}\sum_{i,y} P(y|x_i)log\, P(y|x_i) + 0.5\log|\Sigma| + logk. \tag{21c}$$

with the above σ,Σ and $P(y|x_i)$ given by the converged value of eqs.(21a&b).

5   RPCL Learning and Automatic Model Number Selection

Rival Penalized Competitive Learning (RPCL) is a heuristic competitive learning algorithm proposed for clustering with a very favorable feature that it can drive away extra neurons during learning with automatic number selection (Xu, Krzyzak, and Oja, 1993). The key idea of RPCL is that for each input x_i not only the winner is learned to approach x, but also the second winner (rival) is de-learned away from x_i for a bit. That is,

$$m_c^{(t+1)} = m_c^{(t)} + \gamma_c(x_i - m_c) \;\text{ for } c = arg\; min_j\, f_j\|x_i - m_y\|^2,$$

$$m_r^{(t+1)} = m_r^{(t)} - \gamma_r(x_i - m_r) \;\text{ for } r = arg\; min_{j\neq c}\, f_j\|x_i - m_y\|^2$$

$$m_y^{(t+1)} = m_y^{(t)}, \quad y \neq c,\; y \neq r, \tag{22}$$

with $\gamma_c > \gamma_r$ and f_j being the frequency that m_j wins the competition up to now. Many experiments have shown that RPCL works well although there is no theoretical justification. In Xu(1995a), via an incremental EM algorithm, we have justified the RPCL's heuristic use of de-learning together with learning.

The general forms of RPCL. We start at considering two types of competitions:

Competition Type A: $\quad c = arg\ max_y \alpha_y P_y(x, \theta_y), \quad r = arg\ max_{y \neq c} \alpha_y P_y(x, \theta_y)$ $\qquad$ (23a)

Competition Type B: $\quad c = arg\ max_y \alpha_y \ln P_y(x, \theta_y), \quad r = arg\ max_{y \neq c} \alpha_y \ln P_y(x, \theta_y);$ $\qquad$ (23b)

Type A is equivalent to $c = arg\ max_y\ P(y|x)$ because $P(y|x) = \alpha_y P_y(x, \theta_y)/P(x)$, which is usually called Baysian or Maximum Posterior Decision. Also, $\alpha_c P_c(x, \theta_c)$ is the largest component in the mixture denisty $P(x) = \sum_{y=1}^{k} \alpha_y P_y(x, \theta_y)$, which represents the average likelihood. For Type B, $\alpha_c \ln P_y(x, \theta_c)$ is the largest component in the mixture log-likelihhod function, which represents the average log-likelihood. The two types become the same when α_y is equal for each y. They are different in accouting the effect of α_y, which can be simply approximated by f_y–the frequency that m_y wins the competition up to now. For a smaller α_y, the neuron's competitive ability becomes weaker in Type A, but strong in Type B. In the other word, Type B is more conscience.

Based on either of the two types of competition, we give the following general form for RPCL, that is, for each input x we update parameters by

$$\theta_c^{(t+1)} = \theta_c^{(t)} + \gamma_c \frac{\partial \log P(x, \theta_c)}{\partial \theta_c^{(t)}}, \quad \theta_r^{(t+1)} = \theta_y^{(t)} - \gamma_r \frac{\partial \log P(x, \theta_r)}{\partial \theta_r^{(t)}}; \quad \theta_y^{(t+1)} = \theta_y^{(t)}, \quad y \neq c,\ y \neq r, \qquad (23c)$$

The idea of this RPCL is to further enforce the winner component in the mixture while weaken its rival component in responsible to the current input x. As a result, input data set will be divided into groups according the above two types of decision.

RPCL Algorithms for gaussian components. When $P_y(x, \theta_y)$ is a gaussian $G(x, m_y, \Sigma_y)$, the above eqs.(22a&b) become

Type A: $\quad c = arg\ min_y d_y, \quad r = arg\ max_{y \neq c} d_y, \quad d_y = (x - m_y)\Sigma_y^{-1}(x - m_y) + \log |\Sigma_y| - 2\log \alpha_y;$ $\qquad$ (24a)

Type B: $\quad c = arg\ min_y d_y, \quad r = arg\ max_{y \neq c} d_y, \quad d_y = \alpha_y[(x - m_y)\Sigma_y^{-1}(x - m_y) + \log |\Sigma_y|],$ $\qquad$ (24b)

and from eq.(23c) the updation on parameters on m_y becomes

$$m_c^{(t+1)} = m_c^{(t)} + \gamma_c(x - m_c^{(t)}), \quad m_r^{(t+1)} = m_r^{(t)} - \gamma_r(x - m_r^{(t)}); \quad m_y^{(t+1)} = m_y^{(t)}, \quad y \neq c,\ y \neq r, \qquad (24c)$$

This is an adaptive equation. In order to run the competition adaptively, we also need updating formula for α_y, which can be simply approximated by f_y–the frequency that m_y wins the competition up to now, and for Σ_y, which is not easy. One way to deal with this is the batch why, that is, to use updated m_y, α_y with the old Σ_y into eq.(24a) or eq.(24b) to divid the whole data set into groups $C_y, y = 1, \cdots, k$, and then compute

$$\Sigma_y^{(t+1)} = \frac{1}{\#C_y} \sum_{i=1}^{N} (x_i - m_y^{(t+1)})(x_i - m_y^{(t+1)})^T \qquad (24d)$$

This actually distroys the on-line property of the algorithm and becomes the bottle-neck of computing time complexity. One solution for this is to update eq.(24d) not for every inupt but after a certain period.

It is deserve to mention that when $\Sigma_y = I$, Type B competition eq.(24b) with eq.(24c) becomes the same as the original equation eq.(22).

RPCL Algorithms for multisets modeling. Putting eq.(13a) into eqs.(23a,b&c), we can directly apply RPCL learning to multisets modeling. Similar to the above case for gaussians, the updating formula can be simplified from case to case. For example, for the line set eq.(12b) we can use eq.(24c) and the following combined Oja rule (1982) and its anti-hebbian variant to replace eq.(23c):

$$y_c = (x_i - m_c^{(t+1)})^T (w_c^{(t)} - m_c^{(t+1)}), \quad w_c^{(t+1)} = w_c^{(t)} + \gamma_c y_c[(x_i - m_c^{(t+1)}) - y_c(w_c^{(t)} - m_c^{(t+1)})], \qquad (25a)$$

$$y_r = (x_i - m_r^{(t+1)})^T (w_r^{(t)} - m_r^{(t+1)}), \quad w_r^{(t+1)} = w_r^{(t)} - \gamma^r y_r[(x_i - m_r^{(t+1)}) - y_r(w_r^{(t)} - m_r^{(t+1)})], \qquad (25b)$$

Similarly, for the subspace set eq.(12c) we can use eq.(24c) and the following combined Oja subspace rule (1989) and its anti-Hebbian variant to replace eq.(23c)

$$y_c = (W_c(t) - m_c^{(t+1)}[1, \cdots, 1])^T (x_i - m_c^{(t+1)}),$$

$$W_c^{(t+1)} = W_c^{(t)} + \gamma_c[(x_i - m_c^{(t+1)}) - (W_c^{(t)} - m_c^{(t+1)}[1, \cdots, 1])y_c]y_c^T, \qquad (26a)$$

$$y_r = (W_r^{(t)} - m_r^{(t+1)}[1, \cdots, 1])^T (x_i - m_r^{(t+1)}),$$

$$W_r^{(t+1)} = W_r^{(t)} - \gamma^r[(x_i - m_r^{(t+1)}) - (W_r^{(t)} - m_r^{(t+1)}[1, \cdots, 1])y_r]y_r^T, \qquad (26b)$$

RPCL algorithms for mixture of expters and RBF nets. For the model of mixture expert eq.(17b) with the original gate net (Jacobs, Jordan, Nowlan & Hinton, 1991; Jordan & Jacobs, 1994), the general RPCL learning consists of training and testing phases. On the training phase, for each given pair (x, z), the competition is made via

$$c = arg\ max_y P(y|x, \psi)P(z|x, y, \theta_y), \quad r = arg\ max_{y \neq c} P(y|x, \psi)P(z|x, y, \theta_y); \qquad (27a)$$

and then we update the gatting net and expert nets according to

$$\psi^{(t+1)} = \psi^{(t)} + \gamma_c \frac{\partial \log P(c|x, \psi)}{\partial \psi^{(t)}} - \gamma_r \frac{\partial \log P(r|x, \psi)}{\partial \psi^{(t)}} \qquad (27b)$$

$$\theta_c^{(t+1)} = \theta_c^{(t)} + \gamma_c \frac{\partial \log P(z|x, y, \theta_c)}{\partial \theta_c^{(t)}}, \quad \theta_r^{(t+1)} = \theta_r^{(t)} - \gamma_r \frac{\partial \log P(z|x, y, \theta_r)}{\partial \theta_r^{(t)}}; \quad \theta_y^{(t+1)} = \theta_y^{(t)}, \quad y \neq c,\ y \neq r, \qquad (27c)$$

On the testing phase, the competition is made by the gatting net only $c = arg\ max_y P(y|x, \psi)$, and then the output is given by $out(x) = E(z|x, c, \theta_c)$.

For the model with the alternative gating net eq.(17c), eq.(27a) become

Type A: $\quad c = arg\ max_y \alpha_y P(x|y, \psi_y) P(z|x, y, \theta_y), \quad r = arg\ max_{y \neq c} \alpha_y P(x|y, \psi_y P(z|x, y, \theta_y);$ $\quad$ (27a)

Type B: $c = arg\ max_y \alpha_y \log[P(x|y, \psi_y) P(z|x, y, \theta_y)], \quad r = arg\ max_{y \neq c} \alpha_y \log[P(x|y, \psi_y) P(z|x, y, \theta_y)];$ (28a)

and the updating equation eq.(27b) becomes the following eq.(28b), but with eq.(27c) unchanged

$$\psi_c^{(t+1)} = \psi_c^{(t)} + \gamma_c \frac{\partial \log P(x|c, \psi_c)}{\partial \psi_c^{(t)}}, \quad \psi_r^{(t+1)} = \psi_r^{(t)} - \gamma_r \frac{\partial \log P(x|c, \psi_r)}{\partial \psi_r^{(t)}}; \quad \psi_y^{(t+1)} = \psi_y^{(t)}, \quad y \neq c,\ y \neq r, \quad (28b)$$

with α_y estimated by the winning frequecy. On the testing phase, the competition is made by $c = arg\ max_y \alpha_y P(x|y, \psi_y)$, and then the output is given by $out(x) = E(z|x, c, \theta_c)$.

Several examples of RPCL algorithms and variants for particular gates and experts are given in Xu (1996c). The above RPCL learning can also be used for the RBF nets eqs.(20a&b). Taking the normalized RBF net eq.(20a) as an example, we have that eq.(28a) is simplified into

Type A: $\quad c = arg\ min_y d_y, \quad r = arg\ max_{y \neq c} d_y, \quad d_y = (x - m_y)\Sigma^{-1}(x - m_y) + (z - c_y)^2/\sigma^2 - 2\log \alpha_y;$

Type B: $\quad c = arg\ min_y d_y, \quad r = arg\ max_{y \neq c} d_y, \quad d_y = \alpha_y[(x - m_y)\Sigma^{-1}(x - m_y) + (z - c_y)^2/\sigma^2];$ $\quad$ (29a)

eq.(28b) is simplified into eq.(24c) and eq.(27c) becomes simply

$$c_c^{(t+1)} = c_c^{(t)} + \gamma_c(z - c_c^{(t)}), \quad c_r^{(t+1)} = c_r^{(t)} - \gamma_r(z - c_r^{(t)}); \quad c_y^{(t+1)} = c_y^{(t)}, \quad y \neq c,\ y \neq r, \quad (29b)$$

6   A Criterion for Selection Subspace Dimension for PCA Learning

Assume that $y \in R^{k^*}$ comes from gaussian with $\Sigma_y = diag[\lambda_1, \cdots, \lambda_k^*]$ with $\lambda_1 > \cdots > \lambda_k^* > 0$, and $x \in R^n$ is generated from x by an orthogonal mixtrix W^* via the YING model $x = W^{*t}y + e_x$ disturbed by gaussian noise e_x with variance $\sigma^2 I$, then we have a Yang model $y = W^* x + e_y$ to decorrelate $x - e_x$ back to y with $e_y = -W^* e_x$ which is gaussian with variance $e_y = W^* \sigma^2 I W^{*t} = \sigma^2 I$. Therefore, we have joint gaussian density for (x, y).

Consider the following components for the Ying-Yang pair in eq.(2a):

$$P_{M_2}(y) = G(y, 0, \Sigma_y), \quad P_{M_2}(x|y) = N(e_x, W^t y, \sigma^2 I), \quad P_{M_1}(y|x) = N(e_y, Wx, \sigma^2 I), \quad s.t.\ WW^t = I \quad (30)$$

Then the true W^* with the true dimension k^* should provide the best match between the Ying and Yang parts, and thus minimize $K(M_1, M_2)$ given in eq.(2a).

From the eq.(10) given in Xu(1995e), with eq.(30) we have eq.(2a) simplified into $K(M_1, M_2) = J(W, k) + const$ and

$$J(W, k) = \tfrac{1}{2} \ln \{|\Sigma_y| \sigma^{2(n-k)}\} + \sigma^{-2} \tfrac{1}{2}(E_2 + k\sigma^2), \quad E_2 = \tfrac{1}{N} \sum_{i=1}^{N} \|x_i - W^t W x_i\|^2. \quad (31a)$$

For a fixed k, we see that min $_W J(W, k)$ is equivalent to min $_W E_2$, which is the LMSER self-organization (Xu, 1991& 1993) with its solution W indeed satisfies $WW^t = I$ and span the same subspace spanned by the k principal components of input data x. Since $x_i - W^t W x_i = x_i - W^t y_i = e_x$, $E_2 \approx tr(\Sigma_{x|y}) = n\sigma^2$, eq.(31a) can be further simplified into

$$J(k) = J(W^*, k) = \ln |\Sigma_y| + (n - k)\log \tfrac{E_2}{n} + k, \quad (31b)$$

which should reach the minimum when k is the true one k^*. Therefore, we can use eq.(31a) as the criterion for selecting the dimension of subspace in the PCA related subspace analyses.

7   Bayesian-Kullback Scheme for Hyper-parameters and Model Selection

Considering to replace y in eq.(2a) by θ–the parameters of $P_{M_2}(x_i|\theta)$ model, we can get

$$K(M_1, M_2) = \tfrac{1}{N} \sum_i \{ \int_\theta P_{M_1}(\theta|x_i) \log P_{M_1}(\theta|x_i) d\theta - \int_\theta P_{M_1}(\theta|x_i) \log P_{M_2}(\theta) d\theta - \int_\theta P_{M_1}(\theta|x_i) \log P_{M_2}(x_i|\theta) d\theta \} \quad (32a)$$

Let $P_{M_1}(\theta|x_i)$ free and $P_{M_2}(\theta)$ to be some a priori distribution, e.g., gaussian $G(\theta, m_\theta, \Sigma_\theta)$ with m_θ, Σ_θ usually called as hyper-parameters, we can get

$$P_{M_1}(\theta|x_i) = P_{M_2}(x_i|\theta) P_{M_2}(\theta) / \int_\theta P_{M_2}(x_i|\theta) P_{M_2}(\theta) d\theta \quad (32b)$$

Instering it into eq.(3a), after integration over θ we can see that $K(M_1, M_2) = J(M_2, m_\theta, \Sigma_\theta)$ becomes a function of the model M_2, which is to be selected among a number of different possible ones, and of the hyper-paramters m_θ, Σ_θ with a priori density. *As a result, to minimize $J(M_2, m_\theta, \Sigma_\theta)$ with respect $M_2, m_\theta, \Sigma_\theta$ can guide us to decide the best choice of model M_2 and hyper-parameters of m_θ, Σ_θ that matches a given data set $D = \{x_i\}_{i=1}^N$.*

That is, the Bayesian-Kullback Ying-Yang learning can provide us a new scheme for choosing hyper-parameters and selecting models for learning. This scheme is different from the Bayesian evidence and other related approaches in the literature (Ruanaidh & Fitzgerald, 1996; Mackey, 1992), where such work is made by maximizing the evidence $P(D|M_2, m_\theta, \Sigma_\theta) = \int_\theta P_{M_2}(x_i|\theta) P_{M_2}(\theta) d\theta$ to get m_θ, Σ_θ and then further integrating out m_θ, Σ_θ to maximize the evidence $P(D|M_2) = \int_\theta P(D|M_2, m_\theta, \Sigma_\theta) P(m_\theta, \Sigma_\theta) dm_\theta d\Sigma_\theta$

to select M_2, which needs to assume the distribution of $P(m_\theta, \Sigma_\theta)$ again.

The computation of eq.(32a) and eq.(32b) involve integrand operations, which is usually difficult to implement, unless both $P_{M_2}(x_i|\theta)$ and $P_{M_2}(\theta)$ are gaussians. When $P_{M_2}(x_i|\theta)$ and $P_{M_2}(\theta)$ are not gaussians, we can approximate them by gaussians via Talyor expansion on their log-likelihood functions. For example, we can use

$$P_{M_2}(\theta) = P_{M_2}(\hat{\theta})exp[\tfrac{1}{2}(\theta - \hat{\theta})^T H(\hat{\theta})(\theta - \hat{\theta})], \tag{32b}$$

where $H(\theta)$ is the Hessian of $\log P_{M_2}(\theta)$. With the gaussians approximations, we can find that the $J(M_2, m_\theta, \Sigma_\theta) = K(M_1, M_2)$ obatined from eq.(32a) will relates to the input data $D = \{x_i\}_{i=1}^N$, the dimension of the parameter θ and x, the eigenvalues of Hessian $H(\hat{\theta})$.

8   Concluding Remarks

The results on theories and algorithms for learning and model selection that are related to the Bayesian-Kullback YING-YANG learning have been systematically reviewed or proposed, focusing on a general model number selection theory, its related criteria with EM algorithm and variants, as well as RPCL-type fast learning algorithms for finite mixtures (e.g., Gaussian mixture), mean square error clustering, multisets modeling learning, mixture of expert model as well as radial basis function and its extension. In addition, a cirterion is also given for a subspace dimension selection based PCA analysis, and the Bayesian-Kullback YING-YANG learning is proposed as a new scheme for hyperparameter decision and model selection.

References

Amari, S(1995a), *Neural Networks 8*, No.9, 1379-1408.
Amari, S(1995b), *Neural Computation 7*, pp13-18.
Atick, J.J. & Redlich, A.N. (1990), *Neural Computation* Vol.2, No.3, pp308-320.
Bell A. J. & Sejnowski, T. J.(1995), *Neural Computation* Vol.7, No.6, 1129-1159.
Byrne, W. (1992), *IEEE Trans. Neural Networks 3*, pp612-620.
Csiszar, I., (1975), *Annals of Probability 3*, pp146-158.
Dayan, P., Hinton, G. E., & Neal, R. N. (1995), *Neural Computation* Vol.7, No.5, 889-904.
Dempster, A.P., Laird, N.M., & Rubin, D.B. (1977), *J. Royal Statist. Society, B39*, 1-38.
Hathaway, R.J.(1986), *Statistics & Probability Letters 4*, pp53-56.
Hinton, G. E., et al, (1995), *Science 268*, pp1158-1160.
Hinton, G. E. & Zemel, R.S. (1994), *Advances in NIPS 6*, pp3-10.
Linsker, R. (1989), *Advances in NIPS 1*, pp186-194.
Jacobs, R.A., Jordan, M.I., Nowlan, S.J., & Hinton, G.E., (1991), *Neural Computation, 3*, pp 79-87.
Jordan, M.I.& Jacobs, R.A. (1994), *Neural Computation 6*, 181-214
Mackey, D.J.C. (1992), *Neural Computation 4*, pp415-472.
Ruanaidh, J.J.K.O & Fitzgerald, W.J. (1996), *Numerical Bayesian Methods Applied to Signal Processing*, Springer-Verlag
Xu, L. (1996a), "A Unified Learning Scheme: Bayesian-Kullback YING-YANG Machine", to appear on *Advances in Neural Information Processing Systems 8*, eds., David S. Touretzky, et al, MIT Press, Cambridge MA, 1996.
Xu, L. (1996b), "How Many Clusters ? : A YING-YANG Machine Based Theory For A Classical Open Problem In Pattern Recognition", to appear on *Proc. IEEE ICNN96*.
Xu, L. (1996c), "Bayesian-Kullback Cooperated YING-YANG Machines for Supervised Learning", Invited Talk, to appear on Proc. WCNN96, San Diego, CA, Sept. 15-18, 1996
Xu, L. and Amari, S (1996), 'A General Independent Component Analysis (ICA) Framework Based on Bayesian-Kullback Ying-Yang Learning', to appear on Proc of 1996 Intl Conf. on Neural Information Processing (ICONIP96).
Xu, L. (1995a), "YING-YANG Machine: a Bayesian-Kullback scheme for unified learnings and new results on vector quantization", Keynote talk, Proc. Intl Conf. Neural Information Processing (ICONIP95), pp977-988.
Xu, L.(1995b), "YING-YANG Machine for Temporal Signals", Keynote talk, Proc IEEE intl Conf. Neural Networks & Signal Processing, Vol.I, pp644-651, Nanjing, 10-13, 1995.
Xu, L. (1995c), "Cluster Number Selection, Adaptive EM Algorithms and Competitive Learnings", Invited paper, Proc. 1995 IEEE Intl Conf. on Neural Networks and Signal Processing, Nanjing, Vol.II, pp1499-1502, Dec. 10-13.
Xu, L. (1995d), " A Unified Learning Framework: Multisets Modeling Learning" Invited paper, Proc. World Congress On Neural Networks, July 17-21, 1995, Washington, DC, Vol.I, pp35-42.
Xu, L. (1995e), "New Advances on The YING-YANG Machine", Proceedings of 1995 International Symposium on Artificial Neural Networks, ppIS07-12, Dec. 18-20, Taiwan.
Xu, L., Jordan, M.I., & Hinton, G. E. (1995), " An Alternative Model for Mixtures of Experts", *Advances in Neural Information Processing Systems 7*, eds., Cowan, J.D. et al, MIT Press, pp633-640.
Xu, L. (1994), "Multisets Modeling Learning: An Unified Theory for Supervised and Unsupervised Learning", Invited paper, Proc. 1994 IEEE Intl Conf. on Neural Networks, June 26-July 2, Orlando, FL, Vol.I, pp315-320.
Xu, L., Krzyzak, A. & Oja, E.(1993), *IEEE Tr. Neural Networks*, Vol.4, No.4, pp636-649.

Constructive Learning Algorithm of Multilayer Neural Network Using Linear Least Square Technique

C. K. NG, Peng Wen, and Angus K. M. Wu
EDA Laboratory, Dept. of Electronic Engineering,
City University of Hong Kong, HONG KONG

Abstract: The paper presented a new method for determining the optimal architecture of multilayer feed-forward neural networks using linear least square technique. The constructive learning approach considers the network as a nonlinear mapping defined in the linear space., and transform the nonlinear optimal problem of the training process into a linear optimal one with the inverse activation function. In this paper, both learning algorithm and the initial network size determination are studied. The results shows that both network size and convergent time are optimized.

1. Introduction

Multilayer feedforward neural networks are capable of approximating any continuous multivariate function. However, it is very difficult to determine the required number of hidden neurons. In [1,2,3,4,5] Error Back-Propagation (BP) has been used as a standard training process for optimizing the network size. However, both training speed and generalization of BP are affected to a large extend by network architecture and size[2,3,4]. Furthermore, if the initial network size is badly chosen, the training process will never converge or generalization performance of the trained networks will be very poor[3]. Some theoretical works bounds the network size for learning a class of problems. However, most of these studies are worst case analysis based on one or more unrealistic assumptions, hence, not practical. To optimize the size of the hidden layer, it is desirable to have a fast and accurate training algorithm that assesses the network performance easily. Hence, Linear Least Squares Method can be used.

2. Theory

2.1 Linear Space Description of Multilayer Networks

Architecture of a three layers network is shown in Figure 1. X and Y are the input and out put respectively. The network can be represented by a series of transformations and a diagonal nonlinear operator G with identical sigmoidal elements. In other words, each layer of the network is regarded as the composition of transformations with a nonlinear mapping:

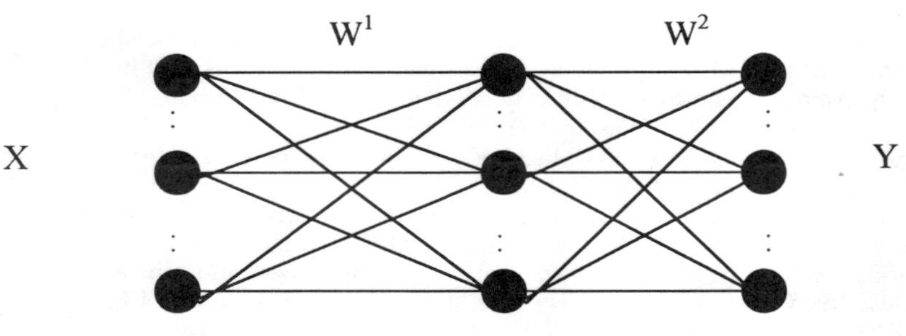

Figure 1   Three Layers Networks

$$I = N_{input}(X) = GW(X), \qquad Y = N_{output}(I) = GW(I)$$

Architecture of the three layers neural network is defined by $S(W^1, W^2)$.

Let $A_l = (a_l^1, a_l^2, \ldots, a_l^M)$ with $\leq l \leq L$, be a data sequence. The training data set of L observations has associated with each variable a $A^m = (a_1^m, a_2^m, \ldots a_N^m)$, where $\leq m \leq M$, $A^m \in R^L$. Then the data space A is defined as an L-dimensional space form a MxL matrix A. Matrix A can be regarded as an array of L vectors (training data set) in a M dimensional space (network inputs). Now the input training data space X is an L-dimensional space in which the input data sequence X_m ($\leq m \leq M$)lies if M is the number of input neurons and L is the length of training data set. Similarly, the target data sequence Y is an L-dimensional space within which the target data sequence Y ($\leq k \leq N$) lies, with N being the number of output neurons. In practice, the number of input nodes and the number of neurons in the output layer are fixed by the number of inputs and outputs of the system being considered. However, the numbers and states of the neurons in the hidden layer are uncertain. They are not only determined the structure of the network but also the approximation ability of the network. This can be state as the following: Let X and Y be any finite date spaces corresponding to the finite dimensional compact manifolds, and let f be any continuous function that maps X to Y. Within the three layer feedforward neural network, shown in Figure 1, there exists a unique approximated best approximation to f, if the number of neurons in hidden layers match the dimension of the subspace of the decomposition of f.

The above gives the sufficient and necessary condition for the existence of a decomposition approximation of any continuous function by a neural network. These conditions are that the input space I and the output space O must be the maximum subspace of X and Y respectively. If the number of neurons is larger than the dimensions of the subspace in the decomposition of f, the network can still be the best approximation of f. if the number of neurons is underspecified, the best approximation can be unique but not necessarily optimal. This therefore explains why excessive or insufficient neurons could, in practice, lead to poor approximations.

2.2 Linear Least Square Algorithm

Sometimes, it is desirable to modify network architecture during training process. Modification is needed when training process does not converge or output errors is outside the desirable range. To asses the network efficiently, Least Square method is used instead of error back-propagation. It is because BP is both time consuming and easy to be trapped by local minima. As the result suggested, Least Square method converge very fast, within 3 to 5 iterations.

Referring to the network shown in Figure 1, the connection weights between the k-th layer and the (k+1)-th layer form a matrix W^k of real number,

$$W^k = \begin{bmatrix} w_{00}^k \cdots w_{0p}^k \\ \cdots\cdots\cdots \\ w_{M0}^k \cdots w_{Mp}^k \end{bmatrix}$$

Element w_{ij}^i connects i-th neuron in the k-th layer with the j-th neuron in the (k+1)-th layer. The input layer is specified with k=0. Sigmoidal function, $Q(x)$ is used as the activation function of the neurons.

$$Q(x) = \frac{1}{1 + e^{-x}} \tag{1}$$

Therefore, by multiplying the input matrix with the weights matrix between layers and applying the activation function to the resultant matrix, we have

$$A^1 = [0.5|Q(A*W^i) \tag{2}$$
$$A^2 = [0.5|Q(A^1*W^o)] \tag{3}$$

where A^1 and A^2 are the outputs of the hidden layer and output layer respectively. If T is the target value, A^2 will be forced to equal to [0.5|T] during training.

Define the inverse of the activation function.

$$S=Q^{-1}(T) \tag{4}$$

Hence, the training process can be done inversely. W^2 can be adjusted so that S is as close as possible to A^1*W^2. In general, the reversed process can b described as a linear least problem:

$$\text{minimize}\|AW\text{-}S\|_2 \tag{5}$$

A linear least squares problem can be solved either directly by employing Housseholderm transformations and a QR decomposition or iteratively . Having computed an optimal set W of weights, we could determine a required output matrix R of hidden layer which is as close as possible to A and fulfills

$$\|RW\text{-}S\|_2=\text{minimal} \tag{6}$$

Again, this is for given matrix W and S, a linear least square problem. Equivalently, one can find the minimal norm solution of ΔR in

$$\|\Delta RW\text{-}(S\text{-}AW)\|_2=\text{minimal} \tag{7}$$

and determine R as $R=A+\Delta R$

Since the output of the bias node is constant 0.5, we require the first column of ΔR to vanish. Hence, we have to reformulate equation (7) to take care of this constraint. Let T and ΔT be the matrixes containing all columns of R and ΔR except the first and V be the matrix containing all rows of W except the first. We then have to solve the linear least squares problem.

$$\|\Delta TV\text{-}(S\text{-}AW)\|_2=\text{minimal} \tag{8}$$
$$R=[0.5|T]=A+[0.0|\Delta T] \tag{9}$$

We could now try to adjust the weights between input layer and hidden layer to reach R as output in hidden layer. But since the activation function (1) can only produce values between 0 and 1 this is only feasible if all elements of R are in this range. In order to transform R to a matrix with elements between 0 and 1, we construct a matrix C with p rows and columns such that

$$R_{\text{trans}}=RC^{-1} \text{ and } W_{\text{trans}}=CW \tag{10}$$

The minimal condition (8) is then still valid for the new matrices.

2.3 Feasibility to Add Neurons During a Training

According to above analysis, the key problem of least square algorithm is the solution to the problem AW=S. It is well known that the solvability condition requires that S lies in the linear subspace spanned by the column vector of A. In the case of $n \geq L$, which is generally of no practical significance, any setting of the weights W which generates linear independent column of A satisfies the solvability condition, i.e., accurate learning is always possible given a sufficiently large number of hidden neurons. On the other hand, however, when applied in practice, backpropagation algorithm shows poorer convergence behavior if there is an excessive number of hidden neurons, or are getting caught up in local minima.

In the case of n<L, we have to set the weight W in such a way that linear subspace spanned by the column of A includes the right-hand side. This is certainly the case if already the first column of A can be aligned parallel (or antiparallel) to S. As a general rule, however, it will only be possible to ensure that the first column is aligned "optimally". Let a_j denote the j-th column vector of A. Since the j-th column a_j only depends on w^i_{kj} (k=1,....m), the first column is optimal for those w^i_{kl} maximizing the normalized scalar product:

$$\frac{\langle a_1, S \rangle}{\|a\|_2} \qquad (11)$$

We now set w^o_1 in such a way that $w_1 a_1$ is identical to the projection vector of s into the direction of a_1, that is :

$$w_1 = \frac{\langle a_1, S \rangle}{\|a\|_2} \qquad (12)$$

For networks with one internal neuron, this is the optimal solution. In other cases, using

$$c_j = S - \sum_{k=1,..j-1} w_k a_k \qquad (13)$$

We now determine w^i_{kj} for j=2,...n such that the following expression is maximized:

$$\frac{\langle a_1, c_j \rangle}{\|a_j\|_2} \qquad (14)$$

and, on similar lines to equation (20), establish w_j using

$$w_j = \frac{\langle a_1, c_j \rangle}{\|a_j\|_2} \qquad (15)$$

Working down the columns, the error $\|S - AW\|$ can be reduced.

In general, in the case of n<L, at least a strict descent condition applies to the process, i. e. , the error decreases strictly monotonically. Furthermore, it is immediately apparent that convergence increases with the number of hidden neurons. Since the algorithm processes the hidden neurons cyclically, it is no problem to add further neurons at any time.

For efficient system identification, it is well known that the input sequence must excite all the modes of the system[5]. A necessary condition is that the length of the data is compared to the order of the system. If we assume that each weights in the network is a parameter of a system, therefore, it is better to let each training pair has a respect parameter Many experiments have support above assumption. So, we let the initial number of hidden neurons satisfies (M+N)P=L, that is every training sample has a trainable weight in the networks at the very beginning, then the number of hidden neurons should be P=L/(M+N). Here, M is the number of input neurons; N is the number of output neurons and L is the number of training pairs.

2.4 Constructive Learning Algorithm

In addition to the normal updating and learning rules of neural networks, a constructive learning scheme must also address how to architecturally (or topological) change the network.

In general, the changing of the network's structure would most likely change the error surface dramatically. For efficient learning, we should solve the following questions:

A. When to change the network structure
Comparing to classical backpropagation algorithm, the least square algorithm converges very fast (refer to [6] and the following experimental result). In general, it can reach its steady error within 3--5 iterations. So, the learning error will be directly taken as the criteria to change the structure of network.

B. How to connect the newly created neurons to the existing network
As we have mentioned , the least square algorithm processes the hidden neurons cyclically, it is no problem to add further neurons at any time. When a new neuron is added, the added neuron connects the original inputs and outputs neurons. The initial values of the added weights are assigned the number within 0 to 1 randomly.

3. Experiment

A multi-input multi-output (MIMO) nonlinear mapping example is used to test the proposed constructive learning algorithm. The network is used to map the following equations:

$$y_1=(x_1x_2+x_3x_4+x_5x_6+x_7x_8)/4$$
$$y_2=(x_1+x_2+x_3+x_4+x_5+x_6+x_7+x_8)/8 \tag{16}$$
$$y_3=(1-y_1)^2$$

which are defined within the range of 0 and 1.

The initial number of the hidden neurons is defined by the training set. In this experiment, training set with 100, 150 and 200 training samples are used. Thus three networks with different initial number of hidden neurons are formed. The initial number of hidden neurons, $P=L/(N+M)=[100\ 150\ 200]/(8+3)=[9\ 14\ 18]$. The initial structures of the network are 8-9-3, 8-14-3 and 8-18-3, the initial values for the weights of the networks have also been determined between 0 and 1 using a random number generator.

Starting with the initial structure, an additional neuron is added to the hidden layer should the networks failed to converge to the desired accuracy. The whole procedure will be repeated until the set error is achieved. The following tables show the progress of the learning process with different initial number of hidden neuron. All simulations are performed on a IBM-PC486 by using MATLAB for Windows. The error reported is the average absolute error on this learning set example and output node. The desired error is set to 0.0150.

Table 1 Learning Process for 100 Pares

Structures	8--9--3	8--10--3
Errors	0.0155	0.0148
Iterations	4	3

Table 2 Learning Process for 150 Pairs

Structures	8--14--3	8--15--3	8--16--3
Errors	0.0153	0.0151	0.0150
Iterations	3	4	3

Table 3 Learning Process for 200 Pairs

Structures	8--18--3	8--19--3	8--20--3	8—21--3
Errors	0.0153	0.0151	0.0151	0.0147
Iterations	4	4	4	3

Conclusions

Referring to the results, a stable output error can be obtained quickly, within the order of ten iterations, by using linear least square method. Comparing to Bp, this provide a convenient way to assess the network for the necessity of additional hidden neuron(s). Convergent time has been shorten by considering the learning process as a linear space point and optimizing the weights of the network layer by layer. In addition, the method also takes the initial size of the network into account, which is often omitted by near all of the known constructive algorithms. In contract to conventional constructive learning procedure, the initial number of hidden neurons is selected according to the complexity of the training set. This prevent the training from wasting time on evaluating network with too few number of hidden neurons.

References

[1] C. Lee Giles, Dong Chen, Gao-Zheng Sun etc., Constructive Learning of recurrent Neural Networks: Limitations of Recurrent Casade Correlation and a Simple Solution, IEEE Transaction on Neural Networks, Vol.6, No.4, July 1995, pp829--835

[2] Justin Fletcher & Zoran Obradovic, Constructively Learning a Near-Minimal Neural Network Architecture, IEEE International Conference on Neural Networks. IEEE World Congress on Computational Intelligence, pp204--208, 27 June--2 July 1994, Orlando, FL, USA

[3] Byoung-Tak Zhang, An Incremental Learning Algorithm That optimizes Network Size and Sample Size in One Trial, IEEE International Conference on Neural Networks. IEEE World Congress on Computational Intelligence, pp215--220, 27 June----2 July 1994, Orlando, FL, USA

[4] J. Fletcher, Z. Obradovic, Parallel and Distributed Systems for Constructive Neural Network Learning, Proceedings the 2nd International Symposium on High Performance Distributed Computing, pp174--178, July 1993, Spokane, WA, USA

[5] Zhenni Wang, Christine Di Massimo, Ming T. Tham and A. Julian Morris, A Procedure for Determining the Topology of Multilayer Feedforward Neural Networks, Neural Networks Vol.7, No.2, pp291--300, 1994

[6] Friedrich Biegler-Konig & Frank Barmann, A Learning Algorithm for Multilayered Neural Networks Based on Linear Least Squares Problems. Neural Networks, Vol.6, pp127--131, 1993

Using Ancillary Statistics in On-Line Learning Algorithms

Huaiyu Zhu and Richard Rohwer
Dept of Computer Science and Applied Mathematics
Aston University, Birmingham B4 7ET, UK
Email: H.Zhu@aston.ac.uk, R.J.Rohwer@aston.ac.uk

Abstract— Neural networks are usually curved statistical models. They do not have finite dimensional sufficient statistics, so on-line learning on the model itself inevitably loses information. In this paper we propose a new scheme for training curved models, inspired by the ideas of ancillary statistics and adaptive critics. At each point estimate an auxiliary flat model (exponential family) is built to locally accommodate both the usual statistic (tangent to the model) and an ancillary statistic (normal to the model). The auxiliary model plays a role in determining credit assignment analogous to that played by an adaptive critic in solving temporal problems. The method is illustrated with the Cauchy model and the algorithm is proved to be asymptotically efficient.

1 Introduction

Neural network (NN) training algorithms are essentially statistical estimators since they map random samples to some general rules or distributions underlying these samples. The main difference between NN models and classical statistical models is that NN models are in general non-linear, which in statistical terms means non-exponential family models. We shall call them curved models. This creates two problems, local minima and loss of information. The former is well known in NN community and will not be addressed here. The latter is less well known and often confused with the former. This is the issue considered here.

For a deterministic optimisation problem, including a stochastic problem in batch learning mode, the optimal choice of steplength is determined by the Hessian. For a flat statistical model, the optimal choice of steplength is determined by the variance, or equivalently by the sample size. Here we deal with on-line stochastic training of a curved model, so we must take into account the interplay between these two effects.

We have previously shown [14, 13, 12] that any statistical inference problem can be decomposed, at least in theory, into two problems: computing an ideal estimate in a flat model and projecting it onto the curved model. The first step does not involve curvature, while the second step is deterministic. The trouble is that the ideal estimate is usually infinite dimensional, so computing it is tantamount to retaining the whole data set.

It was an old idea of R. A. Fisher [5] that by keeping a finite dimensional ancillary statistic we ought to be able to construct an asymptotically efficient algorithm. This amounts to locally expanding the model to a flat model of higher dimension, spanned by the tangents and normals of the original model. The estimate in the tangent direction corresponds to the usual statistics, while that in the normal direction is called an ancillary statistic. The estimate is projected onto the model so a new auxiliary model can be constructed. The process is iterated until convergence. Fisher showed that if one starts from a consistent estimator, a single extra step will give an efficient estimator. This is still not an on-line method.

One of the best known on-line learning algorithms is the adaptive critic algorithm for learning in temporal problems. It can be explained as an auxiliary statistical model, although this is generally not recognised due to the special form of the curved model, composed of iterated conditional distributions in a Markov chain. The "moving target" method [10] can be interpreted as an adaptive critic method for structural credit assignment. The moving targets correspond to the point estimate in the auxiliary model, which unfortunately has to be infinite dimensional since the auxiliary model is fixed.

In this paper we combine all these ideas together to construct a method which is on-line, finite dimensional and asymptotically efficient, even when applied to models without a finite dimensional sufficient statistic. As far as we are aware, this is the first example of this kind in either the statistical literature or the neural network literature. The basic idea is to let the finite dimensional auxiliary model move with the current estimate, thus forming a moving frame along the model [7], and to transfer the moving target from one frame to its successor without projecting onto the main model.

In this paper we shall illustrate this method on the Cauchy model, a one dimensional model whose minimum sufficient statistic is infinite dimensional. This makes it a relatively simple model for illustrating the non-trivial aspects of more general NN models.

2 Statistical background and outline of the algorithm

Consider a sample space X and the space of probability distributions $\mathcal{P}$ on X. If X is of infinite size $\mathcal{P}$ forms an infinite-dimensional manifold. A statistical model is a finite dimensional submanifold $\mathcal{Q} \subseteq \mathcal{P}$. We shall also consider the space $\tilde{\mathcal{P}}$ of finite measures on X. It is also an infinite dimensional manifold, containing $\mathcal{P}$ as a smooth submanifold. See [4, 1, 2, 6, 14, 12].

It has been shown [14, 12] that in general a statistical inference problem can be specified by a prior $P(p)$ on $\mathcal{P}$, the information divergence $D_\delta(p, q)$. $\delta \in [0, 1]$, and the model $\mathcal{Q}$. For a given sample x, there exists a unique ideal estimate, called the δ-estimate, $\hat{p} \in \tilde{\mathcal{P}}$, given by $\hat{p}^\delta = \int_p P(p|x)p^\delta$. The optimal estimate in the model, $\hat{q} \in \mathcal{Q}$, is given by the δ-projection of $\hat{p}$ onto $\mathcal{Q}$, which minimises $D_\delta(\hat{p}, q)$. It is important to note that this only works if we allow $\hat{p} \in \tilde{\mathcal{P}}$ to be unnormalised.

Here we shall only consider maximum likelihood estimates (MLE), which are equivalent to 1-estimates with a 0-uniform prior. In this case the ideal estimate $\hat{p}$ is simply the empirical distribution, and the optimal estimate $\hat{q} \in \mathcal{Q}$ is solution to $\text{Min}_{q \in \mathcal{Q}} K(\hat{p}, q)$, where the generalised KL-divergence is given by $D_1(p, q) = K(p, q) := \int \left(q - p + p \log \frac{p}{q} \right)$. If both p, q are normalised, ie., if $\int p = \int q = 1$, then we get the usual $K(p, q) = \int p \log(p/q)$.

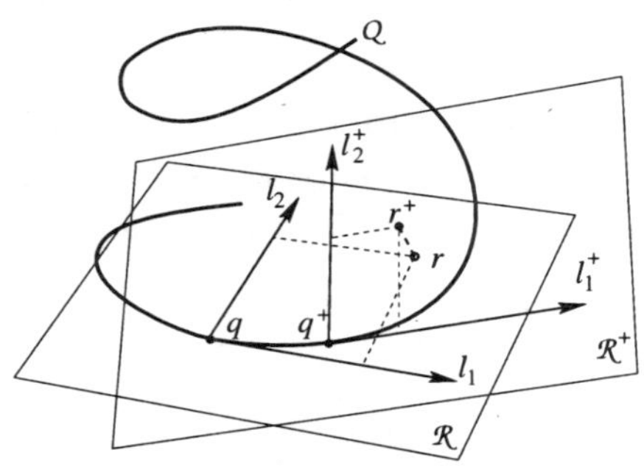

$q \in \mathcal{Q}$ is the current estimate. l_1 and l_2 are the tangent and normal of $\mathcal{Q}$ at q. $r \in \mathcal{R}$ is the current auxiliary estimate. The entities with superscript $+$ correspond to the updated version.

Figure 1: Schematic illustration of the adaptive critic method

To avoid complicated notation, in this paper we shall only consider one-dimensional models $\mathcal{Q}$, ie. smooth curves $\mathcal{Q} \in \tilde{\mathcal{P}}$. As observed by Fisher [5], the reason behind the information loss of curved models is the turning of the tangent in the log-likelihood space when the estimate moves. To hold all the information in the sample relevant for statistical estimation on model $\mathcal{Q}$, we need a flat model $\mathcal{R} \subseteq \tilde{\mathcal{P}}$ spanned by $\mathcal{Q}$. If the smallest such $\mathcal{R}$ is infinite dimensional, then it is impossible to do so exactly without keeping an increasing amount of data. This is the case for the Cauchy distribution model. Locally, however, a curve only turns in the direction of its normal. The basic idea of our proposed algorithm is to construct an $\mathcal{R}$ to hold information both in the tangent and normal directions of the model. This guards against the information loss caused by the turning of tangent within the osculating plane. The residual information loss is due to non-zero torsion, the fact that the osculating space itself is also turning. We shall show that this only gives a higher order term so the algorithm is asymptotically efficient. The outline of the algorithm is as follows (cf. Figure 1).

1. Find an estimate $q \in \mathcal{Q}$ parameterised by μ.

2. Construct tangent $l_1 := \partial_\mu \log q$ and normal $l_2 := \partial_\mu^2 \log q$ of the model $\mathcal{Q}$ at point q. Define the auxiliary model as the exponential family (not normalised) spanned by $[l_1, l_2]$,

$$\mathcal{R} := \left\{ r : r = q \exp(\theta_1 l_1 + \theta_2 l_2),\ \theta \in \mathbb{R}^2 \right\}, \tag{2.1}$$

3. Update the MLE $r \in \mathcal{R}$ parameterised by $[\theta_1, \theta_2]$, in light of new data.

4. Compute new estimate $q^+ \in \mathcal{Q}$ by projecting r onto $\mathcal{Q}$. Compute the new frame $[l_1^+, l_2^+]$. Project r onto $r^+ \in \mathcal{R}^+$, the new auxiliary model spanned by $[l_1^+, l_2^+]$. This is accomplished by computing $[\theta_1^+, \theta_2^+]$.

5. Transfer statistics from $\mathcal{R}$ to $\mathcal{R}^+$, and calculate the effective sample size.

6. Go back to step 3.

3   Details

The relevant geometry for a statistical model in IID training is the exponential geometry, a special case of information geometry [4, 1, 2, 6]. Roughly speaking, it is defined by the Fisher information metric, which specifies an inner product on the tangent space, and the exponential affine connection, which specifies that exponential families are to be considered flat submanifolds. Note that as we are considering geometry for the whole $\widetilde{\mathcal{P}}$, exponential families are not normalised, and the metric is defined by the correlation $\langle uv \rangle_q$, instead of the covariance $\langle u, v \rangle_q$. [12]

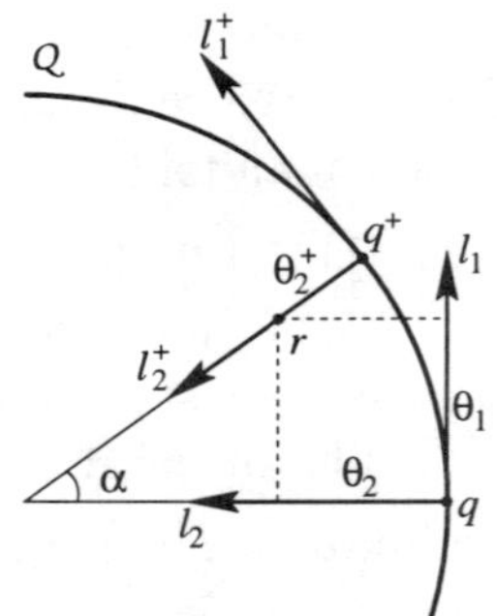

$q \in \mathcal{Q}$ is the current estimate, with tangent l_1 and normal l_2. $r \in \mathcal{R}$ is the current auxiliary point, with auxiliary coordinates θ_1 and θ_2. The new estimate on $\mathcal{Q}$ is q^+, with tangent l_1^+ and normal l_2^+. The auxiliary point r is unchanged and is represented in the new auxiliary coordinates as θ_1^+ and θ_2^+, where $\theta_1^+ = 0$.

Figure 2: Change of coordinates caused by curvature

Locally, a curve looks like a helix up to third order approximation. It is characterised by its metric κ_1^2, curvature κ_2 and torsion κ_3. For the Cauchy model, it can be calculated that $\kappa_1^2 = 1/2$, $\kappa_2^2 = 7/2$, $\kappa_3^2 = 20/7$. The value of κ_2 is the absolute curvature in $\widetilde{\mathcal{P}}$. The relative curvature in $\mathcal{P}$ was calculated by [5, 4] as $\kappa_2'^2 = 5/2$, using covariance in place of correlation. The difference $\kappa_2^2 - \kappa_2'^2$ is the square of normal curvature of $\mathcal{P}$ in $\widetilde{\mathcal{P}}$, which is unity for any direction in $\mathcal{P}$ [11]. The calculation of torsion for the Cauchy model appears to be original.

Doing statistics on the exponential family $\mathcal{R}$ can be easily accomplished by projecting $\widehat{p}$ to $r \in \mathcal{R}$ with Newton's method (denoting $\partial_i := \partial/\partial_{\theta_i}$)

$$[\Delta \theta_i] = -\left[\partial_i \partial_j K(\widehat{p}, r)\right]^{-1} \left[\partial_j K(\widehat{p}, r)\right] = \left[\int r l_i l_j\right]^{-1} \left[\int \widehat{p} l_j - \int r l_j\right], \tag{3.1}$$

where $\int r l_i l_j$ and $\int r l_j$ are functions of θ and can be computed without knowing the sample, and $\int \widehat{p} l_j$ is simply the sample mean of l_j which can be accumulated easily.

Up to second order approximation, $\mathcal{Q}$ can be locally identified with the osculating circle, and $\mathcal{R}$ with the osculating plane. The new estimate q^+ and auxiliary estimate r^+ can be calculated by projecting r onto them (Figure 2).

$$\Delta \mu = \frac{\alpha}{K} = \frac{1}{K} \operatorname{atan} \left(\frac{\theta_1 K}{1 - \theta_2 K^2} \right), \tag{3.2}$$

$$\theta_1^+ = 0, \qquad \theta_2^+ = \frac{1}{K^2} \left(1 - \sqrt{(\theta_1 K)^2 + (1 - \theta_2 K^2)^2} \right), \tag{3.3}$$

where $K := \kappa_1 \kappa_2$ is the rate the tangent turns relative to the parameter μ.

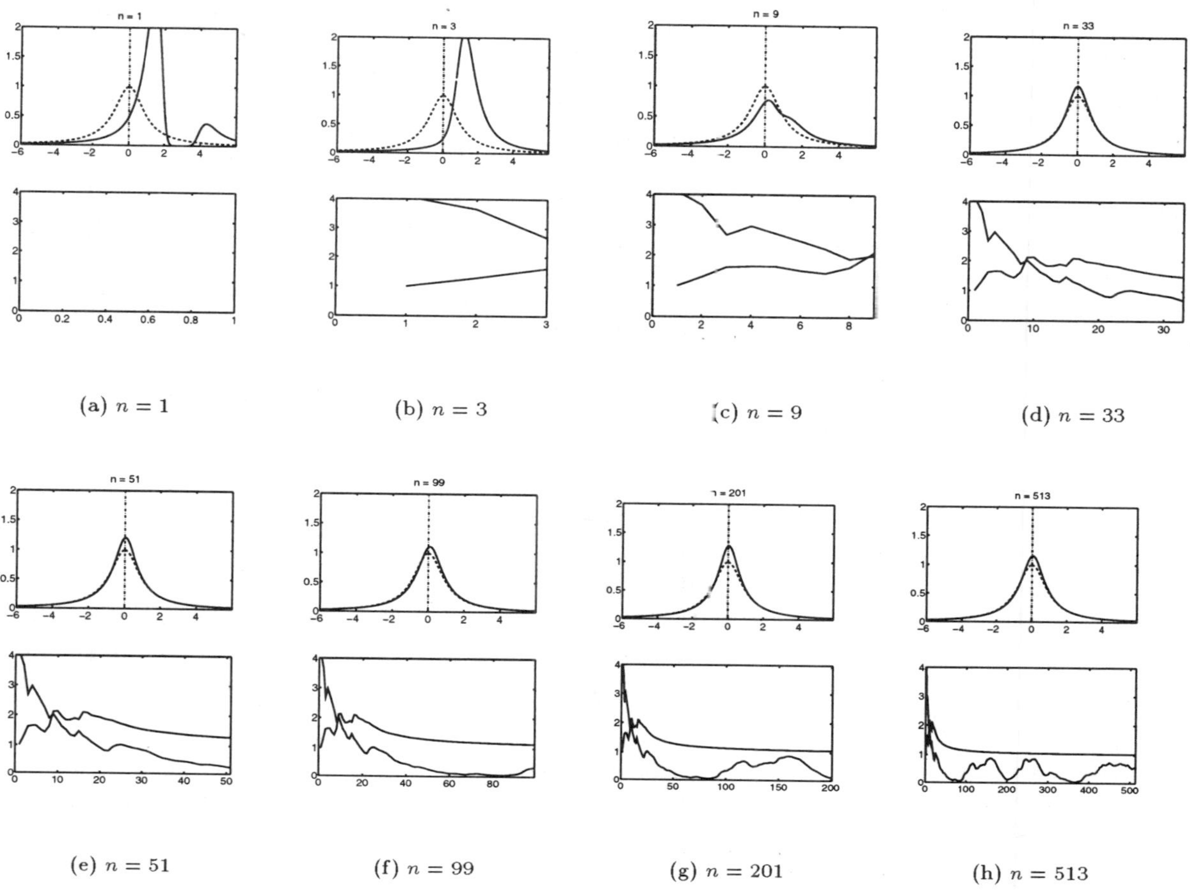

(a) $n = 1$ (b) $n = 3$ (c) $n = 9$ (d) $n = 33$

(e) $n = 51$ (f) $n = 99$ (g) $n = 201$ (h) $n = 513$

The upper part of each sub-plot depicts p (dashed line) and r (solid line). The lower part of each sub-plot depicts the expected squared error (smoother line) and the true squared error (rougher line), both multiplied by the sample size.

Figure 3: A typical run of the algorithm

The crucial point of this algorithm is using $\int r l_j^+$ in place of $\int \hat{p} l_j^+$ for the new auxiliary model. That is, the previous information as summarised by $r \in \mathcal{R}$ is projected onto $r^+ \in \mathcal{R}^+$, so that the algorithm is on-line. Because the osculating plane is also turning, there is inevitable information loss as r is replaced by r^+. This is determined by the angle by which the osculating plane turned, $\alpha = T \Delta \mu$, where $T := \kappa_1 \kappa_3$ is the rate of direction change of the osculating plane in the μ coordinate. It can be shown that, asymptotically, the one-step efficiency ϵ, the proportion of information retained, is at least $\cos^2 \alpha$. Since the direction change of the osculating plane is orthogonal to the model, the actual information loss is even less. Numerical experiments show that $\epsilon = \cos \alpha$ is more accurate. This is used to update $r^+ \in \mathcal{R}^+$. In any case the exact rate is irrelevant asymptotically, since all these reduce to $\epsilon = 1 - a \Delta s^2$, where a is a constant and s is the arc-length parameter. The overall information loss after n samples can be shown to be $a \log n + O(1)$, even if we have used $\epsilon = 1 - b \Delta s$, with $b \neq a$. The asymptotic efficiency of the algorithm is therefore

$$e_n = 1 - \frac{a \log n}{n} - O\left(\frac{1}{n}\right) \to 1, \qquad (n \to \infty). \tag{3.4}$$

The initial estimate can be obtained by using a good classical estimator on a small sample, such as the optimal L-estimator [8]. We find that a sample of size five is good enough in our case.

4   Experiments and Discussion

One typical run of the algorithm is shown in Figure 3. Note that r is markedly non-Cauchy initially. The bimodal shape is caused by the tangent and the normal. The normalised expected squared error $\frac{n}{\kappa_1^2}(\mu - \mu_0)^2$ approaches 1 as $n \to \infty$ since the algorithm is asymptotically efficient. The actual squared error is χ_1^2 distributed (of which this figure only gives one sample), since the Cauchy distribution is locally one dimensional.

The expected and actual loss of information are plotted in Figure 4, showing that our calculation of asymptotic information loss is correct. It should be pointed out that there is an additional loss of a small sample used for the initial estimate.

The novelty of this algorithm is that the auxiliary information is retained and transferred at each step. Intuitively speaking, this means that "If you don't know which unimodal model to estimate, then use a multi-modal model". By allowing r to be outside $\mathcal{Q}$, or even outside $\mathcal{P}$, we are able to represent whatever information as simply the point r, which need not be outside $\tilde{\mathcal{P}}$. Furthermore, locally or asymptotically, it is enough for r to be in a two dimensional exponential $\mathcal{R}$.

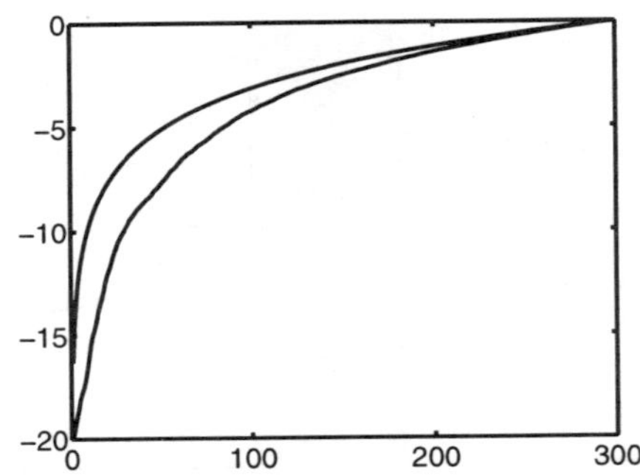

The upper line is the expected loss of information $\kappa_3^2 \log n$; the lower line is the observed loss averaged over 20 runs. They are shifted and superimposed to show the asymptotic equivalence.

Figure 4: Expected and actual loss of information

Recently Leen and Orr [9] proposed a stochastic search method to avoid inverting the stochastically updated Hessian. It appears that their method is intuitively equivalent to using (compare with (3.2))

$$\Delta\mu \approx \theta_1(1 + (\theta_2 K^2) + (\theta_2 K^2)^2 + \dots), \tag{4.1}$$

Since in our method the "denominator" is maintained this problem does not occur. It would be interesting to see how their method performs on the Cauchy model.

Most of the interesting curved models, including the Cauchy model and most tanh-type NNs such as the MLP, BM and Hopfield net, are mixture-of-exponential models. The best known method for such models is the EM algorithm, which has recently been given an information-geometric interpretation [3]. It would also be interesting to elucidate the relation between our method and the EM method. Our current understanding is that EM is more like Fisher's original algorithm which is not on-line.

For multilayer networks with an m-dimensional weight space, the tangent space is m-dimensional, but the normal space becomes m^2-dimensional. The method described here can still be applied, with more complicated differential-geometric notation. This will appear elsewhere. In many interesting cases using the diagonal of the normal tensor would be reasonably good so the algorithm requires keeping a $2m$-dimensional statistic. At present we do not know the asymptotic efficiency of such a diagonal approximation.

5   Conclusion

We have proposed and analysed an on-line training algorithm for curved models. It is asymptotically efficient even for models without finite dimensional sufficient statistics. This removes the need for any *ad hoc* adjustable parameters in training algorithms, such as a momentum term and step-length. The idea and performance of the algorithm is illustrated with the Cauchy model. It is expected that this method will have a significant impact in the area of on-line training of non-linear models. This also shows the importance of rigorous statistical theory, especially information geometry, in this active area.

Acknowledgement

We would like to thank people in the Aston NCRG for a discussion on asymptotic information loss, especially D. Saad, C. Williams and D. Barber for their comments. This work was supported by EPSRC grant GR/J17814.

References

[1] S. Amari. Differential geometry of curved exponential families—curvature and information loss. *Ann. Statist.*, 10(2):357–385, 1982.

[2] S. Amari. *Differential-Geometrical Methods in Statistics*, volume 28 of *Springer Lecture Notes in Statistics*. Springer-Verlag, New York, 1985.

[3] S. Amari. Information geometry of the EM and em algorithms for neural networks. Technical Report METR94-4, Univ. Tokyo, 1994. `ftp://archive.cis.ohio-state.edu/pub/neuroprose/amari.geometryofem.tar.Z`.

[4] B. Efron. Defining the curvature of a statistical problem (with applications to second order efficiency) (with discussion). *Ann. Statist.*, 3:1189–1242, 1975.

[5] R. A. Fisher. Theory of statistical estimation. *Proc. Camb. Phi. Soc.*, 122:700–725, 1925.

[6] R. E. Kass. The geometry of asymptotic inference (with discussion). *Statist. Sci.*, 4(3):188–234, 1989.

[7] W. Klingenberg. *A Course in Differential Geometry*. Graduate Texts in Mathematics, 51. Springer-Verlag, New York, 1978. Translated by David Hoffman.

[8] E. L. Lehmann. *Theory of Point Estimation*. J. Wiley, New York, 1983.

[9] G. B. Orr and T. K. Leen. Using curvature information for fast stochastic search. Manuscript, Oregan Grad. Inst. Sci. Tech. (Presened at post-NIPS'95 Workship), 1995.

[10] R. Rohwer. The "moving targets" training algorithm. In D. S. Touretzky, editor, *Advances in Neural Information Processing Systems*, volume 2, pages 558–565, San Mateo, CA, 1990. Morgan Kaufmann.

[11] H. Zhu. On the curvatures of information manifold. Manuscript, 1996.

[12] H. Zhu and R. Rohwer. A Bayesian geometric theory of statistical inference. Submitted to *Ann. Statist.*

[13] H. Zhu and R. Rohwer. Bayesian invariant measurements of generalisation. *Neural Proc. Lett.*, 2(6):28–31, 1995.

[14] H. Zhu and R. Rohwer. Information geometric measurements of generalisation. Technical Report NCRG/4350, Aston University, 1995. `ftp://cs.aston.ac.uk/neural/zhuh/generalisation.ps.Z`.

An Equidistortion Principle Constrained SOM for Vector Quantisation

Hujun Yin and Nigel M. Allinson

Department of Electrical Engineering and Electronics
UMIST
PO Box 88, Manchester M60 1QD, UK
(Email: *mchp5yin@afs.mcc.ac.uk; allinson@fs5.ee.umist.ac.uk*)

Abstract — **A constrained SOM based on an equal-distortion principle is proposed for producing globally optimal, or near-optimal, vector quantisation. The principle is applied indirectly to control the width of the neighbourhood of the SOM. Little extra computation costs are introduced but improved performance, both in lower distortion and in stable and fast convergence, is achieved.**

1 Introduction

The self-organising map (SOM) [1] has been widely used in vector quantisation (VQ), data clustering, and pattern recognition. It has been shown that the SOM is potentially optimal to VQ and related data compression, since it will eventually satisfy the two necessary conditions for optimal VQ [2]. The LBG [3] and competitive learning (CL) are popular algorithms for VQs. They can provide reasonable good results together with fast convergence. However, they rely heavily on the initial references, and may suffer from "under-utilisation" and/or "over-utilisation" problems. There are also some constrained versions of the CL algorithm, such as *frequency-sensitive competitive learning* [4], which applies "conscience" learning to the algorithm, so that less-fired neurons are encouraged while over-fired neurons are restricted in order to avoid under-utilisation problems. It is intend to produce (but cannot guarantee) an approximately equal firing frequency for all neurons. This will results in a maximum entropy, instead of minimum mean-square-error (MSE), criterion.

The SOM's neighbourhood can provide a solution to the under-utilisation problem. Since the neighbourhood size or radius is very large at the beginning of the training, this will enable all references to respond to the input samples. This is a nature "conscience" learning. A large neighbourhood results in a large cluster of references; and similar references, in an input space distance sense, will be close together in the output space. While a small neighbourhood results in a spreading of references. When the neighbourhood size contracts properly, the input space will be well covered and quantised by all of the references. Such a role also gives the SOM algorithm a distinct ability in escaping local minima, as updating in a neighbourhood can disturb the minimum state. Although it can not be guaranteed that the SOM will yield a global minimum, the algorithm can provide a better local minimum. The problem is that the emergence, the frequency, and the quality of such local minima are unpredictable, i.e. the reliability of the algorithm is not high. The results depend on the algorithm's parameters and training procedures. An improved version of the algorithm is proposed here, which makes the algorithm more robust in finding the global or, at least, a better local minimum.

2 An equidistortion constrained SOM towards the (global) optimal VQ

VQ algorithms are optimisation methods which use a very limited number of references to approximate the input space. A general principle for these methods is to minimise the MSE distortion. Most existing algorithms can not guarantee to reach the globally minimum distortion. The local minimum problem has become a very challenging issue in VQ design. Some algorithms, which combine the LBG or CL learning with combinatorial optimisation methods from statistical physics (e.g. stochastic relaxation), have been proposed for escaping local minima [5]. Theoretically such relaxation schemes will converge to the global minimal energy configuration, if a slow enough annealing schedule is followed [6]. However this schedule is too slow for practical applications. Even when using a fixed temperature, the convergence of the process is still very slow. The relaxation methods are passive and blind at avoiding local optima.

More recently, more active searching strategies have been proposed in VQ designs for escaping local minima. Ueda and Nakano [7] have proposed a so-called *competitive and selective learning* VQ algorithm based on CL, genetic selection mechanism, and an equal-distortion or *equidistortion* principle, This principle states that *for a smooth underlying probability density and large number of the code vectors, all regions in an optimal Voronoi partition have the same within-region variances* [8]. Another interesting method, termed the optimal adaptive k-means algorithm which also applies the equidistortion principle, has been proposed by Chinrungrueng and Sequin [9]. This algorithm adaptively weights the distance measure and adjusts the learning rate of competitive learning VQs according to the variances of subsets. Both methods apply this asymptotical equidistortion property of optimal VQs. These two new approaches are CL based with randomly arranged codebooks.

Since the SOM algorithm updates not only the winner but also its neighbouring references, this may result in better quantisation. Another great advantage of the SOM algorithm is that its codebook is ordered, which can inherently increase the tolerance to encoding and/or transmission channel noise. To ensure that the SOM algorithm converges to a global or near-global minimum, its learning procedure has to be monitored and properly guided. In the following, an equidistortion constrained SOM (ECSOM) is proposed. The ECSOM algorithm differs from the above two methods in that the asymptotical equidistortion principle is indirectly applied. The above two methods require two asymptotical conditions, i.e. a very large number of code vectors and a smooth input density, so that the resulting partitions have exactly the same variance. This may not be true in many practical applications. In the ECSOM, the constraints are indirect and soft, because they are applied through controlling the radii of the neighbourhood function. Updating in a neighbourhood, rather than just the winner, will result in the neighbouring references closer to the winner, therefore the winner will have lower variance. Using this function of the neighbourhood, an estimated variance of each reference in its partition is employed to control the width of the neighbourhood function of that neuron. The variances can be easily estimated on-line through the distance measures used in the SOM algorithm, that is at no extra computational costs.

Equidistortion Constrained SOM (ECSOM) VQ algorithm:

The most parts of the algorithm are identical to the SOM in its initial state selection and winning rule. The neighbourhood function shrinks with time, but is multiplied by a factor, which is controlled by the variance of the subset that the appropriate neuron covers, and is defined as

$$F_v = \frac{\sqrt{\sigma_v^2(n)P_v}}{average\{\sqrt{\sigma_v^2(n)P_v}\}} \tag{1}$$

The updating within such a constrained neighbourhood at each iteration is given by

$$\mathbf{w}_c(n+1) = \mathbf{w}_c(n) + \alpha(n)[\mathbf{x}(n) - \mathbf{w}_c(n)], \qquad if\ c \in \aleph_v(n)F_v(n) \tag{2}$$

where $\{\mathbf{w}_c\}$ are the neuron weights, $\aleph_v(n)$ is the width of the SOM neighbourhood function[1], and $\sigma_v^2(n)$ is the variance of the winning set, which can be updated on-line from distances $\{d(\bullet)\}$,

$$\sigma_v^2(n+1) = \sigma_v^2(n) + \alpha(n)\{\min d^2[\mathbf{w}_c(n) - \mathbf{x}(n)] - \sigma_v^2(n)\} \tag{3}$$

P_v is the winning probability of neuron v, which is updated by: $P_v = P_v + 1$.

As we can see, in the ECSOM algorithm, when a winning neuron has a large variance, its neighbourhood size is also large – so more of its neighbouring neurons will be updated towards to it. This will tend to make its variance smaller. This kind of constraint is not strict, so there is no need to require that the final partitions have the same variance. However, this constraint will bring the variances of all partitions as close as possible. This is the general principle for more practical applications, where the input probability density is not smooth and/or the number of code references is not large.

This constraint principle can be also applied through the learning rate instead of the neighbourhood (or both), so that large variance partitions have large learning gains. Here we only demonstrate the effects of constraints on the neighbourhood. Two typical examples are given below.

3 Experiment and Results

Example 1 *– A Lloyd's example: Using two scalar references, $\{w_1, w_2\}$, to quantise the input space $[0, 1]$ with the probability density function as shown in Fig. 1(a), in which p_1 and p_2 represents the probability density for the first and second half of input space respectively, where $p_1 \geq 0$, $p_2 \geq 0$, and $(p_1 + p_2)/2 = 1$.*

---

[1] Such control on the width can be also applied to the width of exponential neighbourhood functions if they are used.

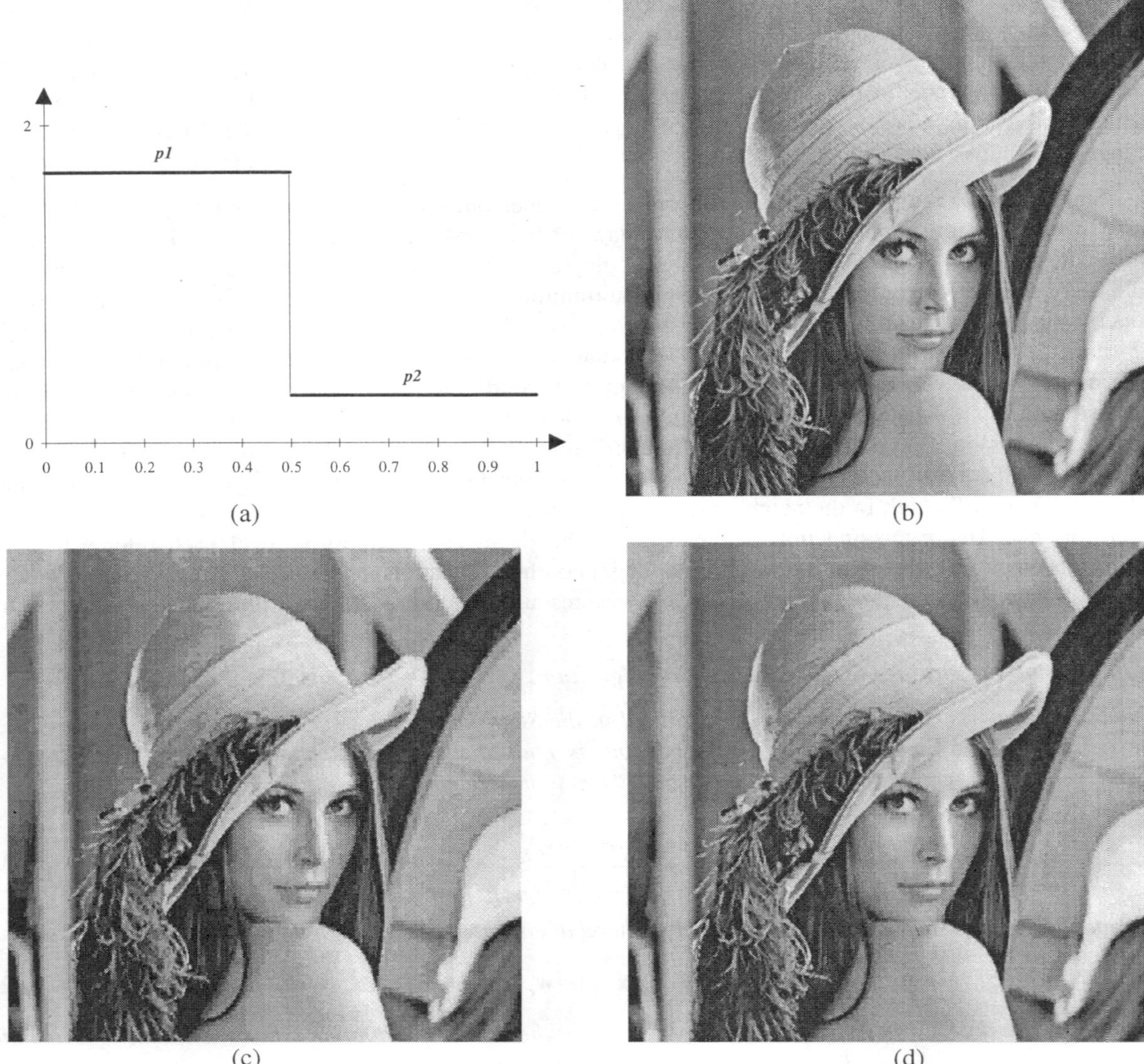

Figure 1: (a) The input density function in a Llyod's example; (b) Original Lena image;
(c) ECSOM-VQ of Lena at 0.375 bpp; (d) ECSOM-VQ of Lena at 0.5 bpp.

The strict mathematical calculation shows that when the ratio $p_1/p_2 \leq 3$, there is only one minimum in the MSE distortion at $\{w_1, w_2\} = \{0.25, 0.75\}$. However, when the ratio $p_1/p_2 > 3$, there are two minima: the local minimum is always at $\{w_1, w_2\} = \{0.25, 0.75\}$, while the global minimum depends on the ratio. For example, when $p_1/p_2 = 4$, the global minimum is at $\{w_1^*, w_2^*\} = \{0.21875, 0.65625\}$. When there are two minima, most VQ algorithms (e.g. LBG, CL) will usually converge to the local one unless the initial references are chosen very close to the global optimum points. The SOM algorithm does not depend greatly on the initial states and is better in finding the global or a good local optimum. However the SOM cannot ensure convergence to the global one. When constraints are applied, the ECSOM algorithm will indeed converge to the global optimum as verified in our intensive simulations. At the global minimum, the variances of two partitions are not the same, but have a smaller difference than that at the local one. This example shows that non-equidistortion optimal partitions exist in many practical cases where the number of reference vectors is not large and the probability density is not smooth. The effort of this constraint is to reduce the differences between variances of partitions to be as small as possible, but not necessary to be exactly the same.

Example 2– *Image compression ("Lena" image):*

The test image is the well-known "Lena" image (512×512, 8 bit) and is encoded using 64 4×4 references (i.e. at 0.375 bpp) and 256 4×4 references (0.5 bpp) by the ECSOM-VQ algorithm. Results are shown in Fig. 1

(c) and (d). Visually SOM- and ECSOM-VQ results are almost identical at this degree of quantisation. When comparing their distortion performances, as shown in Fig. 2, some difference can then be seen.

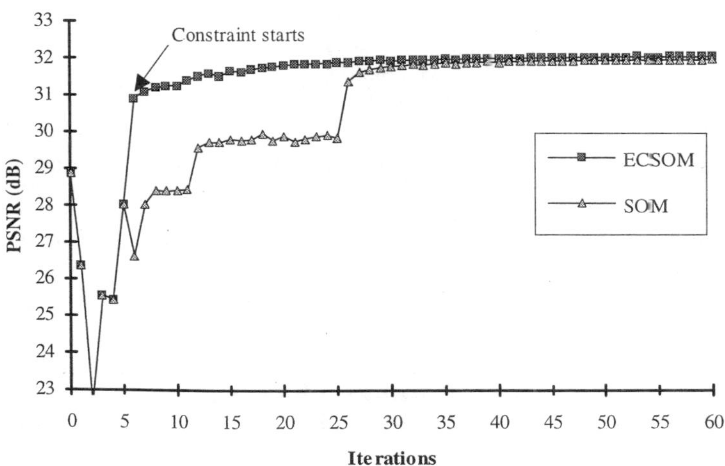

Figure 2: PSNR performance comparison of SOM-VQ and ECSOM-VQ, at 0.5 bpp.

For high dimensional data and/or many reference vectors, the global or local minima cannot easily be observed. In practical applications, it is impossible to apply an algorithm repeatedly to verify the results for the global or a good local optimum, thus an algorithm which can generally produce good quantisation and has less demands on parameter setting is more desirable in practice. The proposed ECSOM-VQ is a more generalised SOM algorithm. It has normally yielded even lower total distortion than the SOM-VQ during our extensive experiments. It can also be seen that when the constraints are applied, the distortion reduces faster. This means that the constrained processes converge faster than the original ones. These two advantages will be very useful in practical applications.

4   Conclusions

A method of applying the equidistortion principle to tangible problems has been proposed for the SOM and related algorithms. The aim of this constraint is to cause the local variances to be as close as possible, when the exactly equal variances do not exist. Some examples have been given to support this suggestion. The explicit role of the neighbourhood in the SOM algorithm is worth further investigation.

5   References

[1]   Kohonen, T., 1984, *Self-Organization and Associative Memory*, Berlin: Springer-Verlag.

[2]   Yin, H. and Allinson, N.M., 1995, "On the distribution and convergence of feature space in self-organising maps," *Neural Computation*, vol. 7, pp. 1178-1187.

[3]   Linde, Y., Buzo, A., and Gray, R.M., 1980, "An algorithm for vector quantizer design," *IEEE Trans. Communications*, vol. 28, no. 1, pp. 84-95.

[4]   Ahalt, S.C., Krishnamurthy, A.K., Chen, P., and Melton, D.E., 1990, "Competitive learning algorithms for vector quantization," *Neural Networks*, vol. 3, pp. 277-290.

[5]   Zeger, K., Vaisey, J. and Gersho, A., 1992, "Globally optimal vector quantizer design by stochastic relaxation, " *IEEE Trans. Signal Processing*, vol. 40, no. 2, pp. 310-322.

[6]   Geman, S. and Geman, D., 1984, "Stochastic relaxation, Gibbs distributions, and the Bayesian restoration of images," *IEEE Trans. Patt. Anal. and Machine Intell.*, vol. 6, pp. 721-741.

[7]   Ueda, N. and Nakano, R., 1994, "A new competitive learning approach based on an equidistortion principle for designing optimal vector quantizers," *Neural Networks*, vol. 7, no. 8, pp. 1211-1227.

[8]   Gersho, A., 1979, "Asymptotically optimal block quantization," *IEEE Trans. Inform. Theory*, vol. 25, pp. 373-380.

[9]   Chinrungrueng, C. and Sequin, C.H., 1995, "Optimal adaptive k-means algorithm with dynamic adjustment of learning rate," *IEEE Trans. Neural Networks*, vol. 6, no. 1, pp. 157-169.

Classifying Seismic Signals by Integrating Ensembles of Neural Networks

Yair Shimshoni and Nathan Intrator
School of Mathematical Sciences, Tel-Aviv University
Tel Aviv 69978, Israel
`shimsh@math.tau.ac.il`

Abstract— **This paper proposes a classification scheme based on integration of multiple Ensembles of ANNs. It is demonstrated on a classification problem, in which seismic signals of *Natural* Earthquakes must be distinguished from seismic signals of *Artificial* Explosions. A Redundant Classification Environment consists of several Ensembles of Neural Networks is created and trained on Bootstrap Sample Sets, using various data representations and architectures. The ANNs within the Ensembles are aggregated (as in Bagging) while the Ensembles are integrated non-linearly, in a *signal adaptive* manner, using a posterior confidence measure based on the agreement (variance) within the Ensembles. The proposed *Integrated Classification Machine* achieved 92.1% correct classifications on the seismic test data. Cross Validation evaluations and comparisons indicate that such integration of a collection of ANN's Ensembles is a robust way for handling high dimensional problems with a complex non-stationary signal space as in the current Seismic Classification problem.**

1   Introduction

The lack of a-priori knowledge about the true underlying model of the data in many real-life problems, leads the practitioner to examine various sub-optimal estimators. Different estimators can exploit various types and sets of features, hence combining multiple estimators might yield better performance than the best single candidate.

In this paper we propose a classification scheme based on integration of multiple Ensembles of Artificial Neural Networks (ANN). It will be demonstrated it on a two class classification problem, in which Seismic recordings of *Natural* Earthquakes must be distinguished from the recordings of *Artificial* Explosions. Although being implemented here on a Seismic Classification problem, the presented scheme is general purpose and can be applied directly on any two class classification, while problems with more than two classes require only slight changes. We will first give some background on Seismic Classification and elaborate on the subject of Combining Multiple Estimators. Next, we will present the framework of our approach and formulate the Integrated Classification Machine (ICM). A posterior classification confidence measure will be discussed and a method for integrating the Ensembles of ANNs will be suggested. Then will follow the implementation details, namely, the pre-process of the seismic signals, the training and evaluation scheme and the results.

Seismic Signal Classification

In the recent years researchers have addressed the problems of Seismic Classification using various disciplines other than classic seismologic methods including Artificial Neural Networks [3, 4]. The vast majority of the recorded seismicity in most countries is artificial (i.e., man-made events like quarry blasts, mine explosions, etc.). The amount of recorded events have grown rapidly in the last decade (especially for weak events) due to the improvements of the seismometers, thus the work load in the seismic observatories have grown accordingly. As natural events are much more important for the analysis of the regional seismicity and for seismic hazard assessment, constructing a reliable automatic method for selecting the signals of the natural events is crucial for efficient seismic research.

Most of the works done so far on this classification problem concern with regional events vs. nuclear tests, rather than local events vs. conventional explosions at near distances. Many of the methods appear in the literature are based on geophysical parametric models [4] which need explicit information to be extracted or estimated by the analyst, thus are very difficult to be fully automated. The signal space formed by the seismic waveforms is very high dimensional and when dealing with weak local events, one has to face also a low Signal-to-Noise ratio due to the weak signal energy. The non-homogeneous earth crust and the various source mechanisms of the seismic events cause the signal space to have a considerable complexity and variability, while the waveforms' distribution is usually non-stationary.

This work presents a model which can be applied to automated classification of seismic signals, including weak local events. The model is data-driven and does not require prior information or any intervention of a human analyst. It is designed to handle the non-stationary nature of the data and uses the frequency spectrum of the waveform recorded by a single seismometer to produce the class label of a *Natural* or *Artificial* event.

Combining Multiple Estimators

In the statistical and machine learning literature there are several methods for combining estimators and the questions involved with this topic mainly *what* types of estimators to combine and *how* to combine them, are recently getting considerable attention.

Mixture models like Adaptive Mixture of Experts [10] and Hierarchical Mixture of Experts [11], are based on the *divide and conquer* approach in which a mixture of experts compete to gain responsibility in modeling the output in a given input region. The system's output is obtained as a linear combination of the experts' output, where the weights are computed as a parametric function of the input. The underlying probabilistic model is based on the assumption of mutual exclusivity, i.e., a single expert is responsible for each data point. Usually in such models, the different experts are trained on a single data set simultaneously by minimizing a combined cost function and the final combination of the experts is determined by a gating module which is constructed in the same training session as well.

A more general framework for combining multiple estimators is "Stacked Generalization" [19, 1], where each estimator is trained with different sub-set of the data and the optimal combination is estimated using cross validation methods. It was shown that in order for the combination of experts to be optimal, the experts should be made as independent as possible [12, 9, 14] and the optimal combination of the experts should be estimated in a robust way i.e., by averaging or cross validation techniques rather than by parametric estimation based on the same training data [13]. Combining multiple classifiers can eliminate the need to regularize over-fitted models as it reduces the variance of the combined estimator [12].

A new method which produces an aggregated estimator using Bootstrap replicas of the training data is known as Bagging [2]. It is reported to be useful whenever the estimator is un-stable i.e., when perturbing the training set can cause significant changes in the constructed classifier.

A Redundant Classification Environment

Since the search for an optimal classifier is strongly bound with the search for a suitable data representation. It is advisable to examine (and possibly use) more than a single representation, especially when there is no solid assumption about a unique underlying model.

As the desire is to maximize the information extracted from the data, we suggest to construct a Redundant Classification Environment, which allows for different data representations to supply a wide coverage of the effective feature space, using several modeling architectures. For example, when the input signals are waveforms, one can represent the data by multiple Time-Frequency or Atomic Dictionary decompositions, apply various smoothening methods, as well as use several estimating methods.

In the hierarchical scheme we will propose shortly, the Experts are Ensembles of ANNs, where each Ensemble is associated with a specific setting of data representation and network architecture. The ANNs in an Ensemble have the same number of hidden units and use one specific data representation from the Classification Environment. In order to enhance the collective contribution of the Ensembles, the ANNs are trained on different sub-sets of the data, yielding relatively independent realizations, that are aggregated to give the Ensemble's opinion. Finally, all the Ensembles are integrated to produce a robust prediction of the whole Classification Environment. This scheme will be now formulated, followed by a suggested method to implement the integration.

2 The Integrated Classification Machine

The *Integrated Classification Machine* (ICM) is constructed of a hierarchy of classifiers shown in Figure 1. It's smallest building block is a Neural Network (Feed-Forward MLP with Sigmoidal units) which are trained to predict the class label of the given signals. The input dimension (N) of the ANNs is according to the input representation used and the hidden layer can contain various numbers (H), of sigmoidal units. The desired output of the ANNs is {1,0} or {0,1} according to the class membership, thus the output layer contains two sigmoidal units as follows:

$$O^l = \sigma(\sum_{i=1}^{H} W_{li} \ \sigma(\sum_{j=1}^{N} w_{ij} x_j + w_{i0}) + W_{l0}) \quad l = 1, 2. \tag{1}$$

Let us define the *prediction-value* of an ANN as the difference of its two output units: $y(x) = (O^1 - O^2)$. As we use sigmoidal outputs, $y \in [-1, 1]$, the predicted class label is given by thresholding y at zero.

Each ANN can be trained on T repeated trials, changing only the initial random weights. Hence, the *prediction-value* of the Network components in the ICM is the average *prediction-value* $y(x)$ over the T training trials: $y^{\mathrm{NET}}(x) = \frac{1}{T} \sum_{t=1}^{T} y_t(x)$.

Each Ensemble is a collection of B Networks, where every Network is trained on one of B Bootstrap Sample Sets [6], re-sampled from the original data: $D_r^b \quad b = 1, \ldots, B$ (for some data representation r). All the Networks in an Ensemble share the same data representation and the same architecture. The Ensemble's *prediction-value* is defined as the average *prediction-values* over all the participating Networks, as in 'Bagging' [2]:

$$y^{\text{ENS}}(x|D_r) = \frac{1}{B} \sum_{b=1}^{B} y_b^{\text{NET}}(x|D_r^b) \tag{2}$$

A collection of Ensembles ($\mathcal{K}$), which use different input representations and architectures, form the *Integrated Classification Machine* (ICM). The integrated *prediction-value* is defined as follows:

$$y^{\star}(x) = \sum_{k \in \mathcal{K}} \alpha_k \, \beta_k(x) \, y_k^{\text{ENS}}(x) \tag{3}$$

Where α_k is a prior reliability measure of the k'th Ensemble, which can be determined from the training data or assumed using prior knowledge (otherwise, $\alpha_k = \frac{1}{K}$). The second value, $\beta_k(x)$ is a posterior classification confidence measure (specific to each signal), on which we discuss in the next section. Both measures are normalized and determine together the strength of the vote of Ensemble k in the Classification Committee of signal x.

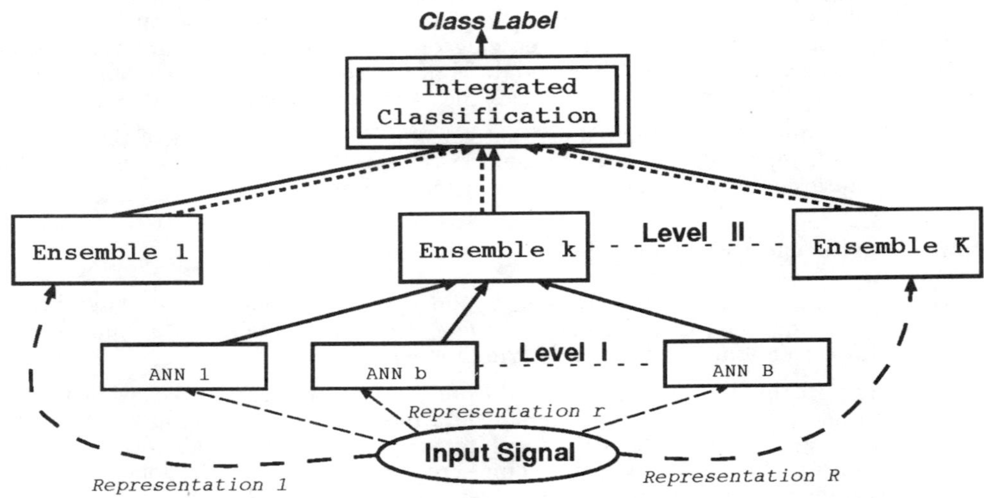

Figure 1: The Integrated Classification Machine (ICM). Several representations of the input signals are fed into different Ensembles in level I, while the integration of those Ensembles is made in level II. (The regular arrows are *prediction values* and the dotted arrows are confidence values).

Measuring the Classification Confidence

High dimensional signals from different classes are often separated along the input space in a very unsmooth manner. The difficulty in classifying a given signal can be measured by its distance from the decision boundaries. However, in high dimensional, non-linear input spaces, it is not realistic to estimate these boundaries explicitly. In order to detect signals with an ambiguous class membership and monitor the classification accuracy, we have constructed a confidence measure for classification of signal x by Ensemble k. This posterior confidence is based on the variance of the Networks' *prediction-value* which represents the amount of 'agreement' among all the participating Networks in the Ensemble [8, 12].

$$CONF^{\text{ENS}}(x) = [\text{VAR}(y^{\text{NET}}(x))]^{-1} \tag{4}$$

3 Combining the Hierarchy of Classifiers

The ICM shown in Figure 1, is a hierarchy of classifiers which are combined in two levels. In Level I, for every Ensemble, B Networks are combined using simple averaging to construct an aggregated ('bagged') Ensemble classification. These Networks are in fact multiple realizations of the same classifier trained on different Bootstrap samples. In the second level the Ensembles are integrated into the final classification (3). When integrating the Ensembles, decision must be made regarding the strength of the 'vote' of each Ensemble in the classification of a given signal x. In this level (II), it is less likely that a fixed weighting will produce better classification than *all* single Ensembles. Considering our 'pluralistic' classification environment, there might be some Ensembles which use inferior data representations or less suitable model architectures, which will have a disturbing effect on a fixed weighted result as well as on a non-fixed linear weighted result.

Given a low signal-to-noise ratio and the non-stationarity of the signal space, along with a shortage of training data, it is furthermore desirable not to decide upon the integration coefficients based on the characteristics of the current available data set. Therefore, we suggest using the signal x in order to find the optimal integration of its 'own' Classification Committee. Assuming our confidence measure $CONF^{ENS}(x)$ is effective (i.e., that the bias of the classifier is small enough), we have implemented a non-linear weighting, which is an adaptive version of *'Winner Takes All'* strategy, namely, for *each* signal x, one optimal Ensemble is chosen. The algorithm that is presented in the next section, finds this optimal Ensemble for each signal x separately, using the classification confidence $CONF^{ENS}(x)$. This approach is different from the *linear* non-fixed weighting that was suggested by [18] for combining ANNs, where all modules participate in the Classification Committee, with weights inversely proportional to the variance (which is similar to the $CONF$ values used here, but estimated in a different way as they use single ANN modules rather than Ensembles of ANNs).

Competing Rejection Algorithm (CRA)

A signal is said to be rejected by a classifier if some measure representing the quality of classification, does not exceed a pre-defined threshold. Obviously, the higher is the threshold, the more signals will be rejected thus the smaller will be the miss classification rate over the remaining un-rejected signals. We present an algorithm which performs a sequence of classifications by polling the group of K classifiers w.r.t. the signal at hand. Each classifier (Ensemble) in turn, can either classify or reject the signal. The main motivation is based on the observation that some classifiers perform globally better than others. Nevertheless, classifiers can outperform 'superior' classifiers on a local basis, thus should be given the opportunity to compete and possibly 'steal' a classification whenever the signal was rejected by those 'superior' classifiers. To implement this idea, a prior ranking of the classifiers has to be set and a rejection criterion has to be defined. The rejection is done by thresholding the confidence measure $CONF^{ENS}(x)$, while the algorithm is set to reject a classification when it's confidence value is lower than the *Reject-Threshold* θ_k, $k \in \mathcal{K}$. Each Ensemble k has its own threshold θ_k depending on it's accuracy, that fixes the minimum level of confidence 'allowed' for it's classifications. The θ_k's are calculated from un-labeled data, as a function of the classifier's variability: $\theta_k = \text{percentile}\{CONF^k(x), \varphi_k\}$. The *Reject-Rate* (φ_k) of a classifier, represents its global credibility. One can determine the φ_k's from the performance on training data or by using subjective information. Otherwise, all Ensembles are considered to have the same credibility and a uniform *Reject-Rate* is set. When all classifiers reject a signal, it can be either 'globally rejected' or classified by one of the classifiers which was pre-defined by the user as the *Ultimate Classifier*.

Notice that the ICM is easily scalable and no re-training is required when new Ensembles are added. It is also flexible in the sense that it is straight forward to incorporate other types of Experts (including human ones) as long as they produce suitable *prediction-value* and $CONF$ value.

4   Pre-Processing the Seismic Signals

To test the above classification scheme on the seismic classification problem, we have collected a comprehensive seismic data set[1] which consists of 380 events that occurred from January 1990 to June 1993 at a restricted area of 22500 km². The events were band-pass filtered to frequency band (0.2-12.5 Hz) and digitized with sampling rate of 50 Hz, using 12 bits A/D converter. All events have magnitude $M_L < 2.7$, 77% of them are below 2.0 and the mean magnitude is 1.53. A given recorded event, includes 8000 samples on average, about half of which consist the actual seismic event, while the rest are recorded before and after the event for synchronization with other seismometers (see Figure 2). We have detected (automatically) the signals' on-set and extracted a fixed size window of $\sim$ 2000 samples, starting at the on-set. This window is about 45 seconds of recording [17].

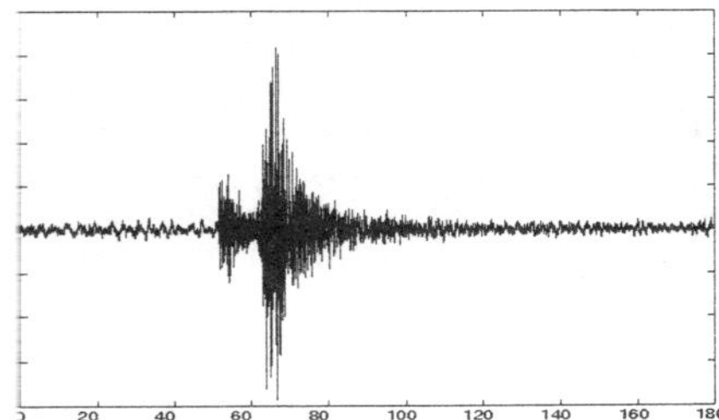 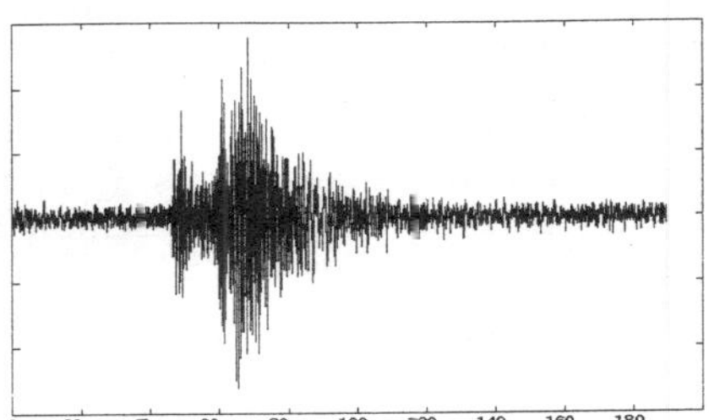

Figure 2: Examples of Seismic Waveforms. Left: Natural Earthquake, Right: Artificial Explosion. (The horizontal axis is recording time in seconds, the Sampling Rate is $50H_z$).

We have used three spectral decompositions of the waveforms as our basic input representations (denoted: W1,W3,W10). The first decomposition is made of one window of 2048 samples. The second is based on three windows of 1024 samples each, with 384 overlapping samples. For the third representation we used

---

[1]`ftp.math.tau.ac.il/pub/shimsh/seismic-data/`

ten windows of 256 samples and 32 overlapping. The size of those windows and their overlapping define the *Time-Frequency* Resolution of the representation.

After the *FFT* was applied on a window of samples, it consists of frequency coefficients representing the amplitudes of the respective frequency components in this specific window. For the W3 and W10 representations, the transformed windows were concatenated after scaling to form the final input representation. As the seismic power spectra show a fast decay of energy, it was more appropriate to use a Logarithmic scale, which has also a smoothening effect. The signals after the Log scaling were standardized making each dimension (frequency coefficient) zero-meaned with variance equal one unit.

The pre-processed signals contain more than 1000 dimensions, and are hardly smooth. Before training any classifier on it, we smoothened by taking the averages of a sliding window (thus also reducing its dimension). We applied four levels of smoothening, to achieve the final dimensionalities of: $333, 127, 50, 31$.

Constructing the Bootstrap Sample Sets

Eight input representations were selected from the combinations of the three T-F resolutions and the four smoothening levels. For each one we have constructed a data set $D_r, r = 1, \ldots, 8$, containing 191 *Earthquakes* and 189 *Explosions*. We followed the *"Bootstrap Pairs"* technique [13], by which every data set D_r was pseudo replicated $B = 30$ times by sampling uniformly with repetitions from the two sets of signals respectively (to preserve the class probability in the resulting replicated samples).

The result is 30 different TRAIN-SETs of 380 signals, each set does *not* contain about 36% of the signals on average. The remaining (un-sampled) signals form 30 corresponding TEST-SETs. These sets are *not* used in any part of the training process, they are used only to evaluate the generalization performance of the model as described in the next section. In conclusion, for each input representation, we have the data sets D_r replicated into 30 couples of disjoint sets such that, $D_r^b = \text{TRAIN}_r^b \cup \text{TEST}_r^b \ \ b = 1, \ldots, 30 \ ; \ r = 1, \ldots, 8$.

5   Training and Evaluating the Ensembles

All the Networks were trained on 5 trials using Back-Propagation (MATLAB'S TRAINBP), with a fixed learning rate $\eta = 0.001$, initial weights $\in U[-0.1, 0.1]$ and 1000 epochs. The performance estimates we used for comparison and evaluation of the classifiers, were based on Cross-Validation techniques [6].

A single Network's performance (averaged over 5 trials) is estimated via the misclassification rate (MCR) over the TEST-SET corresponds to the TRAIN-SET on which it was trained. The performance of an Ensemble could have been evaluated by averaging the performance of it's 30 Networks and the final integrated classification could have been evaluated accordingly by averaging over the Ensembles. However, this simple bottom-up evaluation does not take into consideration the *combined* classification [2, 15], thus yields a pessimistic performance estimate.

In order to present a more realistic cross validated error estimation, we classify every signal x, by combining only a subset of the Ensemble, namely only those Networks that were trained on data sets which did *not* contain the signal x. Denote this subset of Networks as the *Cross-Validated Subset $CV(x)$* corresponding to signal x. It consists of $B^\star < B$ Networks (each signal was excluded from 11 TRAIN-SETs on average). Hence, for all signals, we have produced a combined classification which can be cross-validated, based on approximately 11 Networks in the corresponding subset $CV(x)$ as follows:

$$\hat{y}^{\text{ENS}}(x) = \frac{1}{B^\star} \sum_{b \in CV(x)} y_b^{\text{NET}}(x) \tag{5}$$

This estimate is similar to the ϵ_0 in [6], where it is used in a weighted combination with the Apparent error (calculated over the original data set) to construct the .632 estimator: $Err_{.632} = 0.632 \, \epsilon_0 + 0.368 \, \text{Err}_{app}$. We think that in the framework of trained Neural Networks the .632 estimator is still quite optimistic, therefore we have used the pure ϵ_0. Notice that in a later work the .632 was refined to enable more freedom in choosing the above weights as a function of the *relative overfitting rate* [5]. As we combine only one third of the Networks in each Ensemble and use possibly pessimistic estimate ϵ_0, we suggest to consider our evaluation of the Ensembles' performance, thus of the whole ICM, as a lower bound of it's true performance.

6   Results

The ICM model we presented in this work, was tested on a comprehensive seismic data set consists of 380 events. Fifteen Ensembles of 30 Networks each, were trained 5 trials, on 8 different input representation with various numbers of hidden units (2250 ANNs in total). The data set along with the complete results are available by `ftp` [16]. Table 1 shows the performance of the ANN classifiers, along with two other classical classifiers for comparison, *LDA* and *k-NN* (applied on the same Bootstrap Sample Sets, under the exact scheme of aggregating multiple classifiers of the ICM). The table shows the Miss Classification Rates (MCR) for single and aggregated (30 realizations) classifiers. The results for *ANN* and *k-NN* are for the best among several values of H and k respectively.

Representation		Single Classifier			Aggregated Classifier		
T-F	DIM	k-NN	LDA	ANN	k-NN	LDA	ANN
W1	333	0.141	0.462	0.099	0.116	0.437	0.082
W1	127	0.137	0.215	0.100	0.116	0.174	0.087
W1	50	0.129	0.132	0.102	0.113	0.121	0.089
W1	31	0.142	0.117	0.110	0.118	0.105	0.095
W3	375	0.156	0.467	0.104	0.137	0.392	0.097
W3	75	0.155	0.149	0.111	0.134	0.139	0.103
W10	300	0.191	0.484	0.125	0.176	0.471	0.111
W10	120	0.213	0.238	0.134	0.168	0.195	0.113

Table 1: Miss Classification Rates (MCR) of single and aggregated classifiers, for eight different representations.

The results show that the most relevant factor is the data representation, namely, the Time-Frequency resolution and also the smoothening level. For all three T-F resolutions, the larger models (higher input dimensionalities) yielded better results than models with more smoothened data. This have probably occurred because of the lower bias of the large models due to their greater capacity [7]. The exact Bias-Variance calculation which appear in the complete results, showed that the massive averaging decreases the variance of the classifiers, thus eliminating the need for regularization. It was also evident that there was hardly any influence of the number of hidden units within the tested range of 3 to 12. The preferred model is of the single spectral window (W1) using the higher input dimensionality (dim=333). Comparing the ANN with the classical methods showed that the ANN were preferable addressing the problem at hand, than *LDA* or *k-NN*, for single as well as for aggregated classification.

To test level II of the ICM, we have grouped together the large models of the three T-F representations, providing a wide Time-Frequency coverage. The Ensembles were ordered [W1,W3,W10] (for the rejection algorithm) and the *Ultimate Classifier* was set to be W1. The Rejection Rate was set to 20% for all three Ensembles and the *Rejection Thresholds* θ_k, were extracted from the unlabeled data as defined earlier.

Table 2 shows MCR of the ICM, using three (level II) integration methods: (i) the Competing Rejection Algorithm; (ii) non-fixed, linear weighting based on the variance; (iii) uniform averaging. The table summarizes the MCR for the different levels in the ICM, starting from a single ANN (right), until the full integrated machine (left). All models were trained on the same data and were evaluated as we have described in the previous section.

Integrated Machine			Ensemble	Network
CRA	VAR	AVG	(W1-333)	
0.079	0.095	0.095	0.082	0.099

Table 2: Integrated and non-integrated Miss Classification Rates. The 1st column corresponds to non-linear integration with the Competing Rejection Algorithm, the 2nd column shows the result with linear integration based on variance. The 3rd column refers to fixed uniform averaging. The last two columns show the best MCR for un-integrated Ensemble and un-aggregated ANN.

The results show that the best Ensemble's MCR (based on W1, dim=333) was further improved by the integration with the other two Ensembles of the three & ten spectral windows (W3,W10) only when the *CRA* was used. It is also shown that the result of the best single Network is improved by the Ensemble (level I), proving the benefit of averaging multiple ANNs. On average the combined Ensemble classification results, improved the single Network classification by 10-20%.

7   Conclusions

An Integrated Classification Machine, based on Ensembles of ANNs, was presented and used to address the problem of Seismic Signal Classification. We have created a Redundant Classification Environment that consists of over 2000 ANNs of several architectures, trained with different input representations. By integrating such a large number of classifiers we tried to achieve a robust classification for the noisy and non-stationary seismic waveforms.

Since the massive averaging of the ICM reduces the classification variance, it is advisable in such aggregated models, to use classifiers with larger capacity thus greater ability to handle high-dimensional signals with lower bias, and then apply an efficient combination methods, in order to achieve better generalization.

Examining the classification results corresponding to the different input representations, it appears that there was no gain in using more than a single spectral window (W1), unless using the Competing Rejection Algorithm, which succeeded in extracting a complementary contribution to the final integrated classification. The algorithm, chooses the optimal Ensemble per signal, using the posterior classification confidence, which is based on the classification variance of the Ensemble. By applying such method, we aim to exploit both the robustness of the aggregated classification (level I) and the adaptiveness of the integration strategy (level II). The integrated classification by this method outperformed the non-integrated models as well as other integration methods like linear non-fixed weighting (also based on the variance) and uniform averaging of the Ensembles.

Achieving a result of 92.1% correct classifications on the testing data, while using waveform recordings from a single monitoring station only, motivates an implementation of the proposed method for classification of seismic events, a task generally done by humans.

References

[1] L. Breiman. Stacked regression, 1992. Technical report TR-367, Univ. of Cal, Berkely.

[2] L. Breiman. Bagging predictors, 1994. Technical report TR-421, Univ. of Cal, Berkeley.

[3] F. U. Dowla, S.R. Taylor, and R.W. Anderson. Seismic discrimination with artificial neural networks: Preliminary results with regional spectral data. *Bull. of the Seis. Soc. of Am.*, 80:1346–1373, 1990.

[4] P. S. Dysart and J.J. Pulli. Regional seismic event classification at the NORESS array: Seismological measurements and the use of trained neural networks. *Bull. of the Seis. Soc. of Am.*, 80:1910–1933, 1990.

[5] B. Efron and R. Tibshirani. Cross-validation and the bootstrap: Estimating the error rate of a prediction rule. 1995. Technical Report (TR-477), Dept. of Statistics, Stanford University.

[6] B. Efron and R. J. Tibshirani. *An Introduction to the Bootstrap.* Chapman And Hall, New York, 1993.

[7] S. Geman, E. Bienenstock, and R. Doursat. Neural networks and the bias-variance dilemma. *Neural Computation*, 4:1–58, 1992.

[8] L. K. Hansen and P. Salamon. Neural networks ensembles. *IEEE Transactions on Pattern Analysis and Machine Intelligence*, 12:993–1001, 1990.

[9] R. A. Jacobs. Methods for combining experts' probability assessments. *Neural Computation*, 7:867–888, 1995.

[10] R. A. Jacobs, M. I. Jordan, S. J. Nowlan, and G. E. Hinton. Adaptive mixtures of local experts. *Neural Computation*, 3(1):79–87, 1991.

[11] M. I. Jordan and R. A. Jacobs. Hierarchical mixtures of experts and the EM algorithm. *Neural Computation*, 6:181–214, 1994.

[12] A. Krogh and J. Vedelsby. Neural network ensembles, cross validation, and active learning. *Advances in Neural Information Processing Systems 7*, 1995.

[13] M. LeBlanc and R. Tibshirani. Combining estimates in regression and classification. *NeuroProse*, 1993.

[14] R. Meir. Bias, variance and the combination of estimators: The case of linear least squares, 1994. Technical report TR-922, Dept of Electrical Eng., Technion, Haifa, Israel.

[15] M. P. Perrone. *Improving Regression Estimation: Averaging Methods for Variance Reduction with Extensions to General Convex Measure Optimization.* PhD thesis, Brown University, 1993.

[16] Y. Shimshoni. Classification of seismic signals using ensembles of neural networks - results appendix, 1995. (`ftp.math.tau.ac.il/pub/shimsh/results.ps.Z`).

[17] Y. Shimshoni and N. Intrator. Automatic discrimination between local earthquakes and quarry blasts by integrating ensembles of neural networks. 1995. Proc. of the 2'nd Workshop for AI in Seismology, Lxembourg 1995.

[18] V. Tresp and M. Taniguchi. Combining estimators using non-constant weighting functions. *Advances in Neural Information Processing Systems 7*, 1995.

[19] D. H. Wolpert. Stacked generalization. *Neural Networks*, 5(2):241–259, 1992.

A Framework for Extending the Noise Sensitivity Signature Method for Model Complexity Selection

Michael P. Perrone

IBM T.J. Watson Research Center

and

Brown University Institute for Brain and Neural Systems

mpp@watson.ibm.com

Abstract— The Noise Sensitivity Signature (NSS) [3] has been proposed as an alternative to cross-validation for selecting network complexity. Recently NSS has been extended to the regression estimation [11] and shown to provide better estimates of optimal complexity for sparse data than Generalized Cross-Validation (GCV) [15]. This paper presents a general framework for extending NSS which provides insight as well as a wide assortment of new tools for selecting optimal complexity. This paper also presents a synthesis of NSS and GCV which improves both.

1 Introduction

In order to avoid overfitting to finite noisy training data and the corresponding negative effects on generalization performance, one typically employs some form of smoothing or regularization. A strict interpretation of regularization [5] dictates that one minimizes a cost, C, given by

$$C(f, \mathcal{D}, \lambda) = E(f, \mathcal{D}) + \lambda R(f) \tag{1}$$

where $E(f)$ measures how well a function, f, fits a data set, $\mathcal{D}$; the regularizer, $R(f)$, measures some property of f independent of the data; and λ is a nonnegative "tuning parameter" which sets the relative importance between fitting the data and minimizing the regularizer. The fit to the data is generally measured by the mean squared error, entropy, mutual information, or similar measure while the regularizer can correspond to a Bayesian prior [7] like Weight Decay [16], the Minimum Description Length complexity [12], the number of effective parameters [9], splining [15] or other common measure of function complexity. Heuristic methods for implementing regularization include adding noise during training [8] which is asymptotically equivalent to Tihkonov regularization in the small noise level limit [1]; averaging [10] which smooths over noisy estimates; cross-validation stopping rules [13] which prevent parameters from becoming too large; weight pruning techniques [6, 4] and others. These heuristic methods, though typically easier to implement, are more difficult to analyze mathematically.

One problem which is common to all of these regularization techniques, though not as obviously in the heuristic methods, is the need to select a value for the tuning parameter, λ. The standard solution to this problem is to use cross-validation. Recently an alternative to cross-validation has been proposed in the form of the Noise Sensitivity Signature (NSS) [3] a variant of which has been shown [11] to select the optimal tuning parameter better than Generalized Cross-Validation (GCV) [15].

The goal of this paper is to present a more principled examination of how NSS can be generalized; to explore the implications of these generalizations; and to show how NSS can be hybridized with cross-validation. The next section reviews NSS for both regression and classification. The third section presents a general approach to extending and implementing the NSS method. Experimental results are presented in the fourth section which is followed by a discussion section.

2 NSS Review

The basic idea behind NSS is to generate a "noisy" data set, $\mathcal{N}$, by adding artificial noise to a given data set, $\mathcal{D}$, and to use $\mathcal{N}$ to train a network. The performance of the network optimized on $\mathcal{N}$ is then tested using the original data set, $\mathcal{D}$. If the training error is lower than the testing error, then the network has overfit to the artificially added noise and therefore the network has more than sufficient complexity to model the data. If on the other hand, the testing error is lower than the training error, then the network has insufficient complexity. Ideally, one would choose the network complexity such that the average training and testing performance are equal.

Grossman and Lapedes (1993) implemented this selection process for a binary classification problem in the following way: Define $Q_n(p)$ as the percent correct classification from a neural network trained on noisy data for which a fraction, $p \in [0, 1]$, of the total data set is randomly selected and has had noise added. For classification data, noise is added by flipping the class label of the input point. Define $Q_f(p)$ as the percent correct classification of the same network tested on the noise free data. The $Q_n(p)$ and $Q_f(p)$ are random variables that depend on the finite training set and the choice of noise added. For each p in a range of p, one then trains several networks of varying complexities and plots Q_n and Q_f vs. p for each network. The NSS criterion is to select the network complexity for which the plots of Q_n and Q_f vs. p are most similar. Once a complexity is selected, training is performed on all of the noise free data.

For regression, this process has been extended and made more precise in the following way [11]: Define an artificial noise process which takes $\mathcal{D}$ to $\mathcal{D}+\delta$ such that each $(x,y) \in \mathcal{D}$ becomes $(x+\delta_x, y+\delta_y)$ where δ_x and δ_y are zero mean random variables; x is the input variable; and y is the regression variable. The amount of noise is regulated by its variance. Q_n and Q_f are now given by

$$Q_n(f) = C(f, \mathcal{D} + \delta, \lambda) \tag{2}$$

and

$$Q_f(f) = C(f, \mathcal{D}, \lambda). \tag{3}$$

Training with noise is equivalent to selecting

$$f_\lambda^* = \arg\min_f Q_n(f). \tag{4}$$

The original NSS criterion assumed that

$$Q_f(f_\lambda^*) > Q_n(f_\lambda^*) \tag{5}$$

indicates complexity should be increased while

$$Q_f(f_\lambda^*) < Q_n(f_\lambda^*) \tag{6}$$

indicates complexity should be decreased; or in other words, the Q_f and Q_n will be almost equal at the optimal complexity. To capture this behavior, λ is chosen to minimize

$$\lambda_{\text{NSS}} = \arg\min_\lambda \mathrm{E}_\delta \left[\left(Q_f(f_\lambda^*) - Q_n(f_\lambda^*) \right)^2 \right] \tag{7}$$

where $\mathrm{E}_\delta[\cdot]$ is the expected value over the artificial noise model for δ. Here the variance of the artificial noise plays the same role as p in the classification version of NSS. Once λ_{NSS} is found using Eqn. 7, the optimal regression function is given by

$$f_{\text{NSS}} = \arg\min_f C(f, \mathcal{D}, \lambda_{\text{NSS}}). \tag{8}$$

3 Extending the NSS Framework

Motivated by the success of the two NSS implementations reviewed in the previous section, we now develop a taxonomy of possible alternate implementations. As we shall see, the NSS approach can be quite general. In order to see how NSS might be extended, we look to the basic structure of this approach. NSS at its most basic level has three components: the training cost; the use of a "signature"; and an optimization criterion for the signature. Each of these components will be consider in turn.

Regarding the training cost, first note that the choice of error function, regularizer and training method are not essential to the development of an extended NSS framework; although these choices will determine the final form of the selection criterion used. However, we will consider as distinct the special case of no regularization (i.e. $R(f) = 0$.); since this choice allows us to train wit or withiut regularization and to test with the opposite. Another seemingly essential aspect of the NSS training cost is the use of artificial noise added to the training data. Here, motivated by the fact that training with noise is equivalent to a particular form of regularization in the infinitesimal noise limit [1], we instead treat the addition of noise as a special case. This relaxation of NSS allows for the development of a class of NSS criteria which are much easier to analyze and implement because of the absence of artificial noise; but which still incorporate the ability to select an optimal λ. Thus our taxonomy begins with four possible forms of training cost: with and without noise, and with and without regularization; or equivalently $C(f, \mathcal{D}, 0)$, $C(f, \mathcal{D}+\delta, 0)$, $C(f, \mathcal{D}, \lambda)$, and $C(f, \mathcal{D}+\delta, \lambda)$.

The next component, the "signature", by which we mean the measurement of the system on which NSS criterion will be based, is a comparison of two different measures of the system. In the original NSS, these two measures were the training cost with noise, Q_n, and the testing cost without noise, Q_f. However, this view is unnecessarily restrictive. Here, we allow the two measures to be any of the four possible training costs and we restrict the signature of the two measures to be simply their difference. One could imagine much more complicated comparison methods; but we will not pursue that direction here. Since the two measures selected must be different, there are 6 different choices. This leads to 4 distinct signatures: $E(f^*, \mathcal{D}+\delta) - E(f^*, \mathcal{D})$, $\lambda R(f^*)$, $E(f^*, \mathcal{D}+\delta) - E(f^*, \mathcal{D}) + \lambda R(f^*)$, and $E(f^*, \mathcal{D}+\delta) - E(f^*, \mathcal{D}) - \lambda R(f^*)$. f^* is used to emphasize that we use the f found by training. The first of these signatures has previously been investigated [3, 11] while the second will be compared to the first in Section 4. The other two signatures will not be pursued here.

The final component, the optimization criterion, makes explicit the procedure for selecting complexity. Driven by a desire to select simple interpretable, criterions, we consider three different criterions. For convenience let Q_1 and Q_2 correspond to one of the four costs in this framework. The original NSS criterion, which may be written as

$$\mathrm{E}_\delta[Q_1(f_{\lambda_{\text{NSS}}}^*)] = \mathrm{E}_\delta[Q_2(f_{\lambda_{\text{NSS}}}^*)], \tag{9}$$

is motivated by a desire to find a balance between the complexity when fit to noise and tested without noise. This criterion has since been shown to have limited utility in linear regression since it neglects potentially large anticorrelated variations which are ignored by the mean behavior. The criterion proposed for regression,

$$\lambda_{\text{NSS}} = \arg\min_\lambda \mathrm{E}_\delta \left[(Q_1(f_\lambda^*) - Q_2(f_\lambda^*))^2 \right] \tag{10}$$

can be motivated by a maximum likelihood argument (See Sec. 3.1). And a new criterion given by

$$\lambda_{\text{NSS}} = \arg\max_{\lambda} E_\delta \left[Q_1(f_\lambda^*) - Q_2(f_\lambda^*) \right] \tag{11}$$

which is motivated by the desire to find the complexity which minimizes the testing cost while maximizing the training cost.

This analysis leads to a total of 48 different NSS model selection methods. Based on the type of problem being solved, the type of model being used and the ease of implementation; one can select an appropriate NSS configuration. Note however, that some of these have trivial solutions (i.e. either they set $\lambda = 0$ or $\lambda = \infty$) and can be discarded. Further, some of these do not refer to λ at all. This is not a problem however as in all the preceding, it is assumed that one could also optimize over additional degrees of complexity (e.g. the number of parameters in a model, the number of hidden units in a neural net, etc.) without having to change any of the NSS framework.

The last issue to address is that of the choice of an appropriate artificial noise model for evaluating the expected values over δ. This has been purposefully left open to be selected according to particular problems domains. However, a reasonable choice is to set the artificial noise model to match the true noise in the data as closely as possible. This has the added advantage that no noise is added when the training data is known to be noise free.

3.1 A Maximum Likelihood Interpretation for NSS

It is possible to interpret the NSS choice of λ as a maximum likelihood procedure in the following sense. Assuming the training data is i.i.d., the Central Limit Theorem implies that the distribution of $Q_1 - Q_2$ converges to a normal distribution as the number of data points increases. This holds for any signature which can be written as a sum over the training data[1]. Since each instance of artificial noise, δ, is i.i.d., $Q_1 - Q_2$ is also i.i.d.; therefore the negative log-likelihood of observing $Q_1 - Q_2$ for various instances of artificial noise, δ_i, is given by

$$\sum_i (Q_1(f_{\lambda i}^*) - Q_2(f_{\lambda i}^*))^2 \tag{12}$$

In the infinite limit, Eqn. (12) becomes

$$E_\delta[(Q_1(f_{\lambda i}^*) - Q_2(f_{\lambda i}^*))^2]. \tag{13}$$

Minimizing Eqn. (13) over λ is equivalent to finding the maximum likelihood estimate of λ over the artificial noise. This interpretation emphasizes the connection between the optimal λ and the choice of artificial noise model for δ, It also motivates choosing the artificial noise model to match the the intrinsic noise model of the real data, $\mathcal{D}$. One problem is that the accuracy of this approximation improves as the size of $\mathcal{D}$ increases while experiments suggest that this selection method works best for sparse data sets.

3.2 Ridge Regression NSS

In the case of linear regression, the NSS criterion may be stated explicitly. For ridge regression [14] the cost function is given by

$$C(\beta, \mathcal{D}, \lambda) = (Y - X^t\beta)^t(Y - X^t\beta) + \lambda\beta^t\beta. \tag{14}$$

where β is the d dimensional parameter vector to be estimated; Y is the N dimensional vector of y_i; X as the matrix of d dimensional vectors x_i; and N as the number of data points in $\mathcal{D}$.

In order to derive a Q_f qnd Q_n from C, we must specify the type of artificial noise used. It is reasonable that the form of the artificial noise match that of the noise in the data. Therefore, chose $\delta_y \sim \mathcal{N}(0, \sigma^2)$ and $\delta_x = 0$; and define δ as the N dimensional vector of δ_y's. With this choice, Q_n becomes

$$Q_n(\beta) = (Y + \delta - X^t\beta)^t(Y + \delta - X^t\beta) + \lambda\beta^t\beta. \tag{15}$$

Minimizing Q_n gives

$$\beta_\lambda^* = (XX^t + \lambda)^{-1}X(Y + \delta). \tag{16}$$

We can now use Eqn. 16 to write the expected value from Eqn. 10 as

$$E_\delta[(Q_n(\beta_\lambda^*) - Q_f(\beta_\lambda^*))^2] = \sigma^4\left[tr^2(1 - 2A) + 2tr(1 - 2A)^2\right] + \sigma^2 Y^t(1 - A)^2 Y \tag{17}$$

where $A \equiv X^t(XX^t + \lambda)^{-1}X$. One should note two things about Eqn. 17. First, it is reassuring to note that as the noise variance approaches zero, we recover the usual ridge regression term; and second, unless either $tr^2(1 - 2A) + 2tr(1 - 2A)^2 = 0$ or $Y^t(1 - A)^2 Y = 0$, which is not true in general, we must choose a value for σ^2. If we proceed by analogy to classification NSS, we should optimize this signature over all values of σ^2. This leads to an undefined integral over all σ^2 which must be handled either by renormalization or by assuming a distribution over σ^2. Renormalization leads to setting $\sigma^2 = \infty$ (i.e. neglecting the second term in Eqn. 17.) Here we choose σ^2 equal to the noise in the real data. Surprisingly, these two approaches lead to very similar experiments results. λ_{NSS} is then given by combining Eqns. 17 and 10. This criterion is used to generate our experimental results. (See Section 4.)

---

[1] In general, this does not apply for signatures which explicitly depend on a regularizer.

3.3   Combined NSS/GCV Criterion

NSS was proposed as an alternative to cross-validation; however it is possible to use these methods in conjunction. Below we propose two possible methods to combine NSS with GCV in the linear ridge regression context.

The GCV criterion for selecting λ can be stated as

$$\lambda_{\text{GCV}} = \arg\min_{\lambda} \frac{Y^t(1-A)^2 Y}{tr^2(1-A)}. \tag{18}$$

Comparing this criterion to Eqn. 17, we see that GCV implements a multiplicative modification to the usual MSE while the Eqn. 17 implements an additive modification. Combining these two modifications gives

$$\lambda_{\text{NSS/GCV-Post}} = \arg\min_{\lambda} \left[\sigma^2 \frac{tr^2(1-2A)}{tr^2(1-A)} + 2\sigma^2 \frac{tr(1-2A)^2}{tr^2(1-A)} + \frac{Y^t(1-A)^2 Y}{tr^2(1-A)}\right]. \tag{19}$$

This can be interpreted as applying the GCV correction *after* finding the expected value over the noise. This can be reversed such that we apply CV *before* evaluating the expected value by adding artificial noise directly to the ordinary leave-one-out cross-validation criterion given by

$$\lambda_{\text{OCV}} = \arg\min_{\lambda} \sum_i (y_i - \beta_{-i}^t x_i)^2 \tag{20}$$

where β_{-i} is the β found when training without the i-th data point. This leads to the following criterion

$$\lambda_{\text{NSS/GCV-Pre}} = \arg\min_{\lambda} \left[8\sigma^2 \frac{tr(1-A)^2}{tr^2(1-A)} + \frac{Y^t(1-A)^2 Y}{tr^2(1-A)}\right]. \tag{21}$$

GCV may similarly be combined with other NSS extensions proposed in this paper.

4   Experimental Results

In order to test the NSS complexity selection criterions described in Section 3, a series of linear ridge regression simulations in 10 and 20 dimensions were performed. In each case, the MSE was calculated between the true solution and the estimate found using NSS with regularization and noise (Eqn. 10); NSS with regularization and no noise (Eqn. 11); NSS with GCV after the expected value (Eqn. 19); NSS with OCV before the expected value (Eqn. 21); GCV (Eqn. 18); the optimal λ (i.e. best possible λ using ridge regression[2]); and $\lambda = 0$ (i.e. linear regression without NSS or GCV or regularization.)

Following Breiman (1992), we begin by selecting two normalized D-dimensional β's: β^{flat} has all elements equal and β^{ramp} has "ramped" elements such that each element is proportional to its index. We define $x \sim \mathcal{N}(0, I_D)$ where I_D is a $D\text{x}D$ identity matrix. Using this distribution, we generate X_i which is the ith instance of a $D\text{x}N$ matrix of N x vectors. Using X_i, β^{flat}, β^{ramp}, the relation $Y = X^t\beta + n$ and $n \sim \mathcal{N}(0, \sigma_n^2 I_N)$, we generate the D-dimensional vector Y_i^{flat} and Y_i^{ramp}. The X_i, Y_i^{flat} and Y_i^{ramp} are then treated as training data to calculate the λ and corresponding MSE of each of the criterions[3]. Thus, D, N, σ_n^2 and β can be varied to compare the relative performances of each criterion.

This comparison is shown in Fig. 1 for the MSE estimates averaged over 2000 different runs. The figure contains six graphs: one for each of two dimensions and each of three values of σ_n^2. Each graph shows the average MSE calculated relative to to the β^{ramp} as a function of the number of data points in the training set. All of the graphs are for β^{ramp} because the corresponding graphs for β^{flat} are qualitatively the same. Similarly, graphs corresponding to Eqn. (10) with artificial noise variance matched to the variance of the noise in the data because, surprisingly, they are quantitatively very similar to those of Eqn. (10) with infinite artificial noise. The results for linear regression are not shown because they are consistently and dramatically worse than any of the other estimates. This behavior was expected since $D < N < 2D$ for these experiments giving an average of 1.5 data points per parameter to be estimated.

The most important feature to note from the graphs is that one or more of the criterions proposed in this paper always perform better than standard GCV. This fact combined with the observation that the graphs for "Pre" and "Post" typically do well in high noise situations while the graphs for "NSS" and "Anti" typically do well in low noise situations suggests that one can consistently do better that GCV if one knows which regime one is in. Furthermore, almost always, all of the NSS based criterion perform as well or better than GCV for small data sets suggesting that NSS is particularly desirable technique for sparse data.

A cusp can be see in the "NSS" and "Anti" graphs for the experiments in 10 dimensions. These also exist for the 20D experiments but are not in the range of the plots. These cusps occur as the criterion begins to consistently select $\lambda = 0$. In these regimes, the criterions are under-regularizing (i.e. allowing too much complexity) which appears to be a general property of some of the NSS criterion.

---

[2] The optimal MSE is not available in practice but is included here to indicate the best possible average performance.

[3] In the simulations presented, the input variables for each dimension are zero mean, independent and identical unit variance; therefore the expected MSE is given by $\text{E[MSE]} = ||\beta - \hat{\beta}||^2$

One final note: The overall behavior is fairly independent of dimensionality suggesting that the results here may scale well.

5   Discussion

This work has presented a framework for generalizing the NSS model selection criterion which provides a wide array of criterions which are flexible enough to be tailored to particular estimation problems. This new framework includes methods which dramatically simplify the process of model selection as compared to the original NSS. The framework adds rigor to the original NSS criterion by making explicit the the complexity selection rule and by allowing for detailed mathematical analysis of the resulting equations. One disadvantage of the original NSS was that its selection rule was subjective. The approach presented here removes this problem.

Further, a realization of this framework for the case of linear regression has been presented which removes the computational burden of explicitly adding artificial noise to the data set. Computer simulations of linear ridge regression have been presented which indicate that through judicicus selection of NSS criterion on can generate estimates which consistently perform better than GCV.

Acknowledgements

This paper is dedicated to the memory of Tal Grossman.

References

[1] BISHOP, C. M. Training woth noise is equivalent to Tihkonov regularization. *Complex Systems 7*, 1 (1995), 108–116.

[2] BREIMAN, L. Stacked regression. Technical Report TR-367, Department of Statistics, University of California, Berkeley, August 1992.

[3] GROSSMAN, T., AND LAPEDES, A. Use of bad training data for better predictions. In *Advances in Neural Information Processing Systems 6* (1993), J. D. Cowan, G. Tesauro, and J. Alspector, Eds., Morgan Kaufmann, pp. 342–350.

[4] HASSIBI, B., AND STORK, D. Second order derivatives for network pruning: Optimal brain surgeon. In *Advances in Neural Information Processing Systems 5* (1993), S. J. Hanson, J. D. Cowan, and C. L. Giles, Eds., pp. 164–171.

[5] HAYKIN, S. *Neural Networks: A Comprehsive Foundation.* Macmillan, New York, 1994.

[6] LE CUN, Y., DENKER, J. S., AND SOLLA, S. Optimal brain damage. In *Advances in Neural Information Processing Systems 2* (1990), D. S. Touretzky, Ed., pp. 598–605.

[7] MACKAY, D. J. C. Bayesian interpolation. *Neural Computation 4*, 3 (1992), 415–447.

[8] MATSUOKA, K. Noise injection into inputs in back-propagation training. *IEEE Trans. on Systems, Man and Cybernetics 22* (1992), 436–440.

[9] MOODY, J. E. The effective number of parameters, an analysis of generalization and regularization in nonlinear learning system. In *Advances in Neural Information Processing Systems 4* (1992), J. E. Moody, S. J. Hanson, and R. P. Lippmann, Eds., Morgan Kaufmann Publication, pp. 847–854.

[10] PERRONE, M. P. *Improving Regression Estimation: Averaging Methods for Variance Reduction with Extensions to General Convex Measure Optimization.* PhD thesis, Brown University, Institute for Brain and Neural Systems; Dr. Leon N Cooper, Thesis Supervisor, May 1993.

[11] PERRONE, M. P., AND BLAIS, B. S. Regression NSS: An alternative to cross validation. In *COLT'95: Proceedings of the Eighth Annual Conference cn Computational Learning Theory* (1995), ACM.

[12] RISSANEN, J. Stochastic complexity and modeling. *Annals of Statistics 14*, 3 (1986), 1080–1100.

[13] STONE, M. Cross-validatory choice and assessment of statistical predictions (with discussion). *Journal of the Royal Statistical Society, Series B 36* (1974), 111–147.

[14] VINOD, H. D., AND ULLAH, A. *Recent Advances in Regression Methods.* Marcel Dekker, Inc., 1981.

[15] WAHBA, G. *Spline Models for Observational Data.* SIAM, Philadelphia, 1990.

[16] WEIGEND, A. S., RUMELHART, D. E., AND HUBERMAN, B. A. Generalization of weight elimination with applicationto forecasting. In *Advances in Neural Information Processing Systems 3* (1991), R. P. Lippmann, J. E. Moody, and D. S. Touretzky, Eds., Morgan Kaufmann, pp. 875–882.

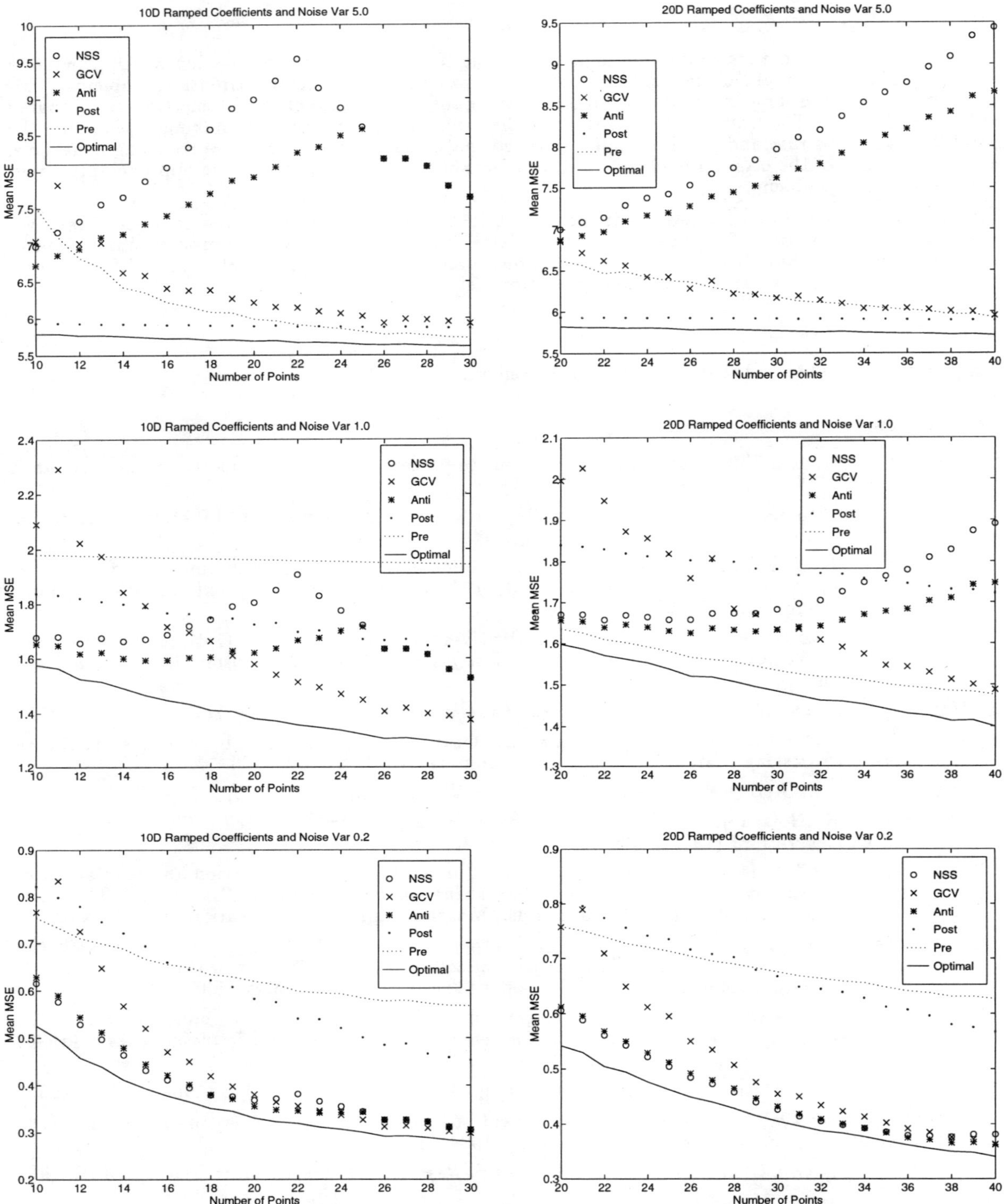

Figure 1: β^{ramp} Experiments: Graphs of the Average Mean Squared Error for various criterions as a function of the number of points in the training set for each of three noise variances and each of two dimensions. The signal to noise ratio for the top, middle and lower graphs are 1:5, 1:1 and 5:1, respectively. In the legends, NSS corresponds to Eqn. (10); Anti corresponds to Eqn. (11); Post corresponds to Eqn. (19); Pre corresponds to Eqn. (21); and GCV corresponds to Eqn. (18).

Finding Cluster Directions by Nonlinear Hebbian Learning

Aapo Hyvärinen
Helsinki University of Technology
Laboratory of Computer and Information Science
Rakentajanaukio 2 C, FIN-02150 Espoo, Finland
Email: `aapo.hyvarinen@hut.fi`

Abstract— We introduce a nonlinear Hebbian neural network that finds directions (i.e. 1-D linear subspaces) around which input data is clustered. The convergence of the algorithm is analytically proven in the framework of an utterly simplified model for clustered data. It is claimed that because of its robustness properties, the algorithm may be expected to find cluster directions even with real-life data. In contrast to most other clustering algorithms, our algorithm finds the cluster directions sequentially (one by one), and requires thus no a priori knowledge of the number of cluster directions. The algorithm can also be used for projection pursuit.

1   Introduction

Nonlinear PCA type networks, or more generally, nonlinear Hebbian networks, have received increasing attention quite recently [5, 6, 2, 7, 3, 4]. This is for the most part due to discovery of new applications, especially independent component analysis and projection pursuit. In this paper, we present a new kind of application, which is (automatic) clustering.

Our nonlinear Hebbian algorithm finds directions, i.e. one-dimensional linear subspaces, around which input data is clustered. The output of the algorithm is simply a set of unit vectors, each of which points in one of the cluster directions. Note that in contrast to some other nonlinear Hebbian algorithms, which help in clustering by performing a certain kind of projection pursuit [7], our algorithm finds the clusters automatically, without need for visual inspection of the projections. The algorithm can, however, be used for finding directions or 2-D planes that allow a clearer visualization of the data. Therefore, the algorithm can also be considered a projection pursuit algorithm [1, 2].

Moreover, our algorithm finds the cluster directions one-by-one, beginning with those cluster directions that contain most data. Thus, our algorithm requires no a priori assumptions on the number of cluster directions. This is in contrast to most other algorithms for automatic clustering, which require fixing the number of clusters in advance.

2   A Simplified Data Model

To be able to analyze mathematically the convergence of our algorithm, we introduce an utterly simplified mathematical model of clustered data. In this model, the *input data is assumed to be completely contained in a finite number of one-dimensional linear subspaces* (i.e. directions), which correspond to cluster directions in real data.

Suppose we have m such cluster directions in an n-dimensional space. Let $\mathbf{a}_i$, $i = 1...m$ be unit vectors, each of which points in one cluster direction. We must assume that the $\mathbf{a}_i$ are linearly independent. In applications related to, e.g., signal processing, we usually have $m << n$, in which case this assumption is quite realistic. Furthermore, let u_i, where $i = 1...m$, be random variables describing the distribution of the data in the i-th cluster direction, i.e. the i-th cluster follows the distribution of $u_i\mathbf{a}_i$. In this paper, no assumptions on the distributions of the u_i are made.

Sampling the data, we get n-dimensional vectors $\mathbf{y}$ which belong to one of the cluster directions. Denoting by I the random index of the $\mathbf{a}_i$ that spans the cluster direction of $\mathbf{y}$, we can write the following data model:

$$\mathbf{y} = \mathbf{a}_I u_I \tag{1}$$

where the index I follows a multinomial distribution, i.e. $P(I = i) = p_i$, $i = 1...m$. The index I depends on the sampling procedure, and is thus independent of the u_i.

To be able to use standard methods of linear algebra, we prefer to reformulate model (1) in matrix notation. Let us define

$$\tilde{u}_i = \begin{cases} u_i, & \text{if } I = i \\ 0 & \text{otherwise} \end{cases} \tag{2}$$

Then, model (1) becomes

$$\mathbf{y} = \mathbf{A}\tilde{\mathbf{u}} \tag{3}$$

where $\mathbf{A}$ is an $(n \times m)$-matrix whose columns are the vectors $\mathbf{a}_i$, and $\tilde{\mathbf{u}} = (\tilde{u}_1, \tilde{u}_2, ..., \tilde{u}_m)^T$.

3   The Necessity for Robustness

It is easy enough to develop methods that find the cluster directions if the data is ideally clustered according to model (3). Most such methods, however, will never work on real-life data. This is because real data can follow model (3) only very approximately; therefore a practical algorithm must work even when model (3) is true only approximately. In other words, the algorithm must be very robust.

In the sections that follow, we develop an algorithm for finding cluster directions using data model (3). To make sure that the algorithm will also work in practice, we shall require the algorithm to have the following two properties:

1. The algorithm must converge exactly to one of the vectors $\mathbf{a}_i$ in the theoretical model given by (3)

2. The convergence (in the theoretical model) must be *robust* in the following sense:

   - The convergence must not depend on unknown parameters whose admissible values are functions of the distances (or the angles) between the points $\mathbf{a}_i$.
   - The probability that the algorithm converges to the vector $\mathbf{a}_i$ must depend on the probability p_i (i.e. the importance of the cluster) in such a way that for a very small p_i, the probability of convergence to $\mathbf{a}_i$ must be very small, regardless of the distribution of u_i.

The first of these requirements is self-evident. If the algorithm does not converge even in the ideal situation of model (3), it cannot be expected to converge in real-life situations.

The first part of the robustness requirement is necessary because inter-point distances change completely when noise is added to model (3). The second part means that the algorithm searches primarily for cluster directions that contain a large number of observations. This helps the algorithm to be insensitive to such violations of the theoretical model as the existence of noise or outliers, because such additional points correspond to directions with a small probability p_i.

In this way, we take the lack of realism of model (3) into account by requiring the algorithm to be robust in the sense defined above. The two conditions mentioned above are, of course, necessary but not sufficient for the convergence of an algorithm with real data. However, it seems that in the context of nonlinear Hebbian learning, these conditions are almost sufficient. Thus, we claim that our algorithm can be used for approximating cluster directions even in real data, because it has both above-mentioned properties. Simulations (see, e.g., Section 7) seem to confirm this claim.

4   First Stage: Linear PCA

The first processing stage of the algorithm consists of ordinary PCA sphering of the data. Note that centering would be senseless as we are considering directions instead of data points. PCA sphering means that we calculate an $m \times n$ matrix $\mathbf{M}$ such that the linear transform $\mathbf{x} = \mathbf{M}\mathbf{y}$ is sphered, i.e.

$$E\{\mathbf{x}\mathbf{x}^T\} = \mathbf{I}_m$$

and the maximal amount of variance is preserved in the transformation.

Then, we have a transformed data model

$$\mathbf{x} = \mathbf{M}\mathbf{A}\tilde{\mathbf{u}} = \mathbf{B}\tilde{\mathbf{u}} \tag{4}$$

where we have defined $\mathbf{B} = \mathbf{M}\mathbf{A}$. The usefulness of sphering resides in the fact that we get

$$E\{\mathbf{x}\mathbf{x}^T\} = \mathbf{B}E\{\tilde{\mathbf{u}}\tilde{\mathbf{u}}^T\}\mathbf{B}^T = \mathbf{B}\mathbf{D}\mathbf{B}^T = \mathbf{I}_m \tag{5}$$

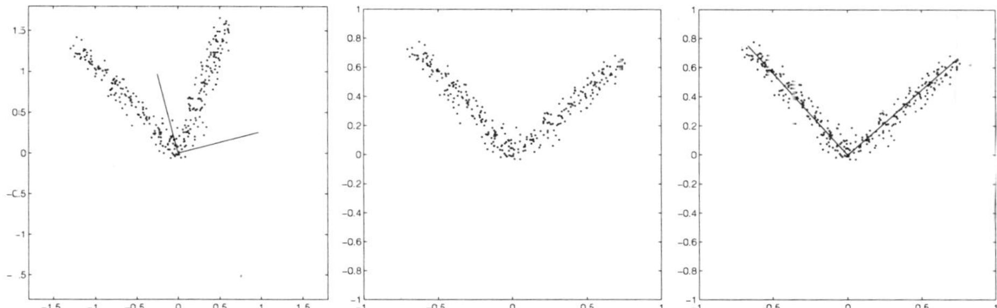

Figure 1: On the left, a 2-D data set with two cluster directions is depicted. The principal components are given by solid lines. Note that the principal components are not aligned with the clusters. In the middle, the same data is shown after sphering. The cluster directions are now orthogonal. On the right, output of our algorithm is given by solid lines. The algorithm finds the cluster directions.

where $\mathbf{D} = \mathrm{diag}(E\{\tilde{u}_i^2\})$. This implies that the columns of $\mathbf{B}$ (which we denote by $\mathbf{b}_i$) are orthogonal to each other, i.e. *the cluster directions become orthogonal* after sphering. This property is most important: it means that, in a certain sense, linear PCA separates the clusters from one another, but fails to find any of them. Indeed, principal components usually point in directions that are half-way between any two cluster directions. This is a direct consequence of the basic idea of linear PCA: presenting as much variance as possible by a single 1-D subspace. See Figure 1.

5   Second Stage: Nonlinear Hebbian Learning

After sphering the data with linear PCA, we locate the cluster directions with nonlinear Hebbian learning. We formulate an error function whose local minima correspond to the unit vectors pointing in the cluster directions. This optimization can easily be implemented as stochastic gradient descent in a neural network, where each neuron finds one cluster direction. A feedback term can be introduced to prevent several neurons from finding the same direction.

5.1   A Non-quadratic Error Function

Consider minimizing the following error function on the unit circle:

$$\min_{\|\mathbf{w}\|=1} E\|\mathbf{x} - (\mathbf{w}^T\mathbf{x})\mathbf{w}\| \tag{6}$$

Here, $\mathbf{w}$ is an m-dimensional vector, perhaps the weight vector of a neuron which tries to find one cluster direction in the sphered data $\mathbf{x}$.

Note that if we had taken the square of the norm in (6), this problem would be equivalent to ordinary linear PCA. It is this use of a non-quadratic error function that leads to a non-linear algorithm.

In the next section, we prove that the *solutions of (6) correspond exactly to the cluster directions*, i.e. the local minima of the error function under the given constraint are obtained when $\mathbf{w} = \mathbf{b}_i/\|\mathbf{b}_i\|$ for some $i = 1...m$. The theoretical data model (3) is assumed to hold. In addition, the algorithm is proven to be robust in the sense defined in Section 3.

Indeed, the error function in (6) has a simple *intuitive interpretation*. First, we measure how well the 1-D subspace (line) spanned by $\mathbf{w}$ describes a given data point $\mathbf{x}$. This measure is usually given by the square of the distance between the point and its projection $\|\mathbf{x} - \mathbf{w}(\mathbf{w}^T\mathbf{x})\|^2$. Here, however, we use the distance itself. This has the consequence that far-away points do not have much influence on the limit of convergence (cf. the use of absolute error in regression), and thus $\mathbf{w}$ converges to a direction that *locally* approximates the distribution of the data with minimum error. But this means finding the cluster directions.

5.2   Neural Network Implementation

Let us assume that we observe $(\mathbf{x}_k)$, $k = 1, 2, ...$, a sequence of samples from the (sphered) data $\mathbf{x}$. The minimization in (6) can then easily be done using stochastic gradient descent. To take the constraint

$\|\mathbf{w}\| = 1$ into account 'neurally', we can use a bigradient type [8] normalization term $M_k(1 - \|\mathbf{w}_k\|^2)\mathbf{w}_k$, where $M_k \to \infty$. This forces $\|\mathbf{w}_k\|$ to converge to 1.

Thus, we get the stochastic gradient *learning rule*

$$\mathbf{w}_{k+1} = \mathbf{w}_k + \mu_k[\frac{\mathbf{x}_k(\mathbf{w}_k^T\mathbf{x}_k)}{e_k} + M_k(1 - \|\mathbf{w}_k\|^2)\mathbf{w}_k] \tag{7}$$

where μ_k is a learning rate sequence that fulfils the usual conditions in stochastic approximation, and $e_k = \|\mathbf{x}_k - (\mathbf{w}_k^T\mathbf{x}_k)\mathbf{w}_k\|$ is the error in the approximation of $\mathbf{x}_k$ by its projection on the 1-D subspace spanned by $\mathbf{w}_k$. Note that the linear Hebbian term $\mathbf{x}_k(\mathbf{w}_k^T\mathbf{x}_k)$ is divided by the approximation error. Thus, points far away from the subspace have relatively less significance that in linear PCA learning.

5.3   Introducing Feedback

If we simply minimize $\mathbf{w}$ to find a solution of the problem in (6), there is no way to choose which cluster direction $\mathbf{w}$ converges to. However, if we have already found N cluster directions (say $\mathbf{v}_i, i = 1...N$), we need to modify the algorithm so that it will find a cluster direction *different* from the previously found ones.

To achieve this 'neurally', we introduce a linear projective *feedback* in the learning rule (7), and obtain

$$\mathbf{w}_{k+1} = \mathbf{w}_k + \mu_k[\frac{\mathbf{x}_k(\mathbf{w}_k^T\mathbf{x}_k)}{e_k} + M_k(1 - \|\mathbf{w}\|^2)\mathbf{w} - d\sum_{i=1}^{N} \mathbf{v}_i(\mathbf{w}_k^T\mathbf{v}_i)] \tag{8}$$

where d is a moderately large positive constant (e.g. $d = 10$). Now, $\mathbf{w}_k$ converges (very probably) to a unit vector that points in a cluster direction different from the directions of the $\mathbf{v}_i$. Note that the addition of feedback does not necessarily prevent $\mathbf{w}$ from converging to one of the vectors $\mathbf{v}_i$, but it makes the probability of this happening very small. A mathematical analysis of the feedback is given in the next section.

6   Proof of the Minimality Property

In this section we present an analytical proof of the properties announced in the previous section.

First note that by (5) and (4), we have $\tilde{\mathbf{u}} = \mathbf{DB}^T\mathbf{x}$. Let us denote the error function in (6) by G. Using the theorem of Pythagoras, and making the change of variables $\mathbf{z} = \mathbf{D}^{1/2}\mathbf{B}^T\mathbf{w}$ (which preserves the norm because of (5)), we get

$$G(\mathbf{z}) = E\sqrt{\tilde{\mathbf{u}}^T\mathbf{D}^{-1}\tilde{\mathbf{u}} - (\mathbf{z}^T\mathbf{D}^{-1/2}\tilde{\mathbf{u}})^2}.$$

Next, by the independence of I from $\mathbf{u}$, we obtain $\mathbf{D}_{ii} = E\tilde{u}_i^2 = p_iEu_i^2$. Taking the expectation first in respect to I, and then in respect to u_i, we get

$$G(\mathbf{z}) = \sum_{i=1}^{m} p_iE\sqrt{\frac{u_i^2 - z_i^2u_i^2}{p_iEu_i^2}} = \sum_{i=1}^{m} C_i\sqrt{p_i}\sqrt{1 - z_i^2}$$

where $C_i = E|u_i|/\sqrt{Eu_i^2}$.

Now, it is rather obvious that G is minimized under the constraint $\|\mathbf{z}\| = 1$ when one of the components of $\mathbf{z}$ is equal to one and the other components are zero. But in such a point $\mathbf{w} = \mathbf{b}_i/\|\mathbf{b}_i\|$, which proves that the minima of G correspond to the cluster directions.

To prove this fact rigorously, make another change of variables: $q_i = z_i^2$. Then the optimization problem (6) becomes:

$$\min_{q_i \geq 0, \sum q_i = 1} \sum_i C_i\sqrt{p_i}\sqrt{1 - q_i}$$

Now, the error function is strictly concave as a function of $\mathbf{q} = (q_1, ..., q_m)^T$, and the domain of $\mathbf{q}$ is a convex polygon. This implies that the minima are attained in the corners of the polygon, which correspond to points where one of the components of $\mathbf{q}$ is 1 and the others 0.

Moreover, it is easy to see that the algorithm is robust in the sense defined in Section 2. The term corresponding to a given cluster direction is weighted by the square root of its probability p_i when

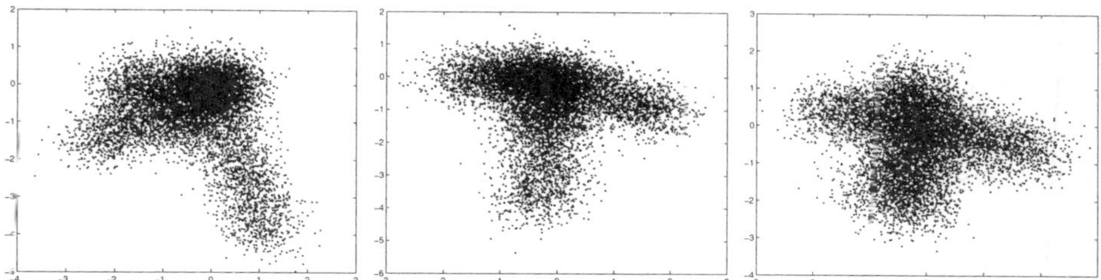

Figure 2: The projections of the data set on the 3 planes spanned by all couples formed by the first 3 principal components. The principal components are not aligned with the cluster directions. The clustered structure of the data is not clearly visible.

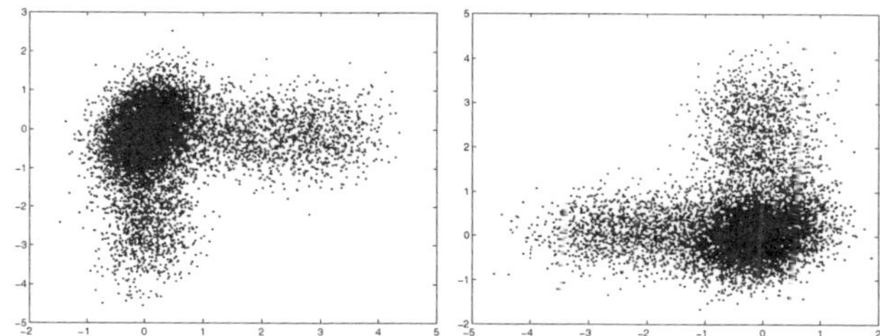

Figure 3: Projections of the same data set as in Figure 2 on two planes spanned by vectors given by our algorithm. Clearly, the algorithm found the the cluster directions. The visual representation of the data is also improved. The projections on other vectors given by the algorithm look all similar.

calculating the error function. Thus, the algorithm searches primarily for cluster directions with a large p_i. Note that the constant C_i, $(0 < C_i < 1)$ does not depend on the dispersion of u_i; it only depends on the shape of the distribution of u_i. On the other hand, G contains no free parameters that could depend on inter-point distances. This means that the algorithm based on the minimization of G is robust against deviations from the theoretical model.

Introducing *feedback* in the learning rule means that we add a *penalty* term $d/2 \sum_{i=1}^{N} (\mathbf{w}^T \mathbf{v}_i)^2$ in G. It is clear enough that this reduces the basin of attraction of the cluster directions that have already been found.

7   Simulation Results

The algorithm was applied on input data that consisted of five cluster directions in a 10-dimensional space. Five (non-normalized) vectors, whose components were independently drawn from a standard normal distribution, defined the cluster directions. To generate one sample of input data, one of these vectors was randomly chosen, and multiplied by a random variable whose distribution was uniform on the interval [0,1]. Finally noise, whose energy was half of the signal energy, was added to the data vectors.

Figure 2 shows the different possible projections of the data on the 3 first principal components. The principal components do not give the cluster directions. Moreover, projections on the principal components give a poor visual representation.

The result of applying our algorithm on the data are shown in Figure 3. As can be seen, the algorithm found the cluster directions, typically to an accuracy of 5 degrees. This accuracy, of course, depends on the noise level; with no noise the results are (practically) exact. This shows that the algorithm is applicable even when the ideal model (3) is not correct.

Figure 3 also shows how our algorithm can be used for projection pursuit. Projections on planes spanned by two vectors found by the algorithm show clearly the clustered structure of the data.

8 Conclusions

Our nonlinear Hebbian algorithm is able to find cluster directions, i.e. directions that locally approximate input data optimally.

The algorithm consists of two stages. The first stage performs (PCA) sphering, thus equalizing second order moments in all directions. In the second stage, we can then use higher-order cumulants of the data to find cluster directions.

Instead of explicitly minimizing or maximizing higher-order cumulants, we use them implicitly by minimizing the square root of the usual quadratic reconstruction error. We do this because of robustness considerations: higher-order moments tend to put much weight on outliers, especially after sphering.

Indeed, as real data is never ideally clustered, a practical algorithm must necessarily be a very robust one. Thus we must require two things from our clustering algorithm: Firstly, the algorithm must find cluster directions in ideally clustered data exactly, and secondly, it must be robust in a relevant sense.

Though our algorithm is primarily conceived for automatic clustering, it can also be used for projection pursuit. It should also be noted that the algorithm requires no a priori knowledge of the cluster structure.

References

[1] J.H. Friedman. Exploratory projection pursuit. *J. of the American Statistical Association*, 82(397):249–266, 1987.

[2] C. Fyfe and R. Baddeley. Non-linear data structure extraction using simple Hebbian networks. *Biological Cybernetics*, 72:533–541, 1995.

[3] A. Hyvärinen and E. Oja. Simple neuron models for independent component analysis. Technical report, Helsinki University of Technology, Laboratory of Computer and Information Science. Submitted to a journal, 1996.

[4] J. Karhunen and J. Joutsensalo. Generalizations of principal component analysis, optimization problems, and neural networks. *Neural Networks*, 8(4):549–562, 1995.

[5] J. Karhunen, L. Wang, and R. Vigario. Nonlinear PCA type approaches for source separation and independent component analysis. In *Proc. IEEE Int. Conf. Neural Networks '95*, pages 995–1000, Perth, Australia, Nov 27–Dec 1 1995.

[6] E. Oja. The nonlinear PCA learning rule and signal separation – mathematical analysis. Technical Report A 26, Helsinki University of Technology, Laboratory of Computer and Information Science. Submitted to a journal, 1995.

[7] A. Sudjianto and M.H. Hassoun. Statistical basis of nonlinear Hebbian learning and application to clustering. *Neural Networks*, 8(5):707–715, 1995.

[8] L. Wang, J. Karhunen, and E. Oja. A bigradient optimization approach for robust PCA, MCA, and source separation. In *Proc. IEEE Int. Conf on Neural Networks '95*, pages 1684–1689, Perth, Australia, Nov 27–Dec 1 1995.

A self-supervised learning system for category detection by sensory integration

Koichiro YAMAUCHI†, Mikiya OOTA†, Naohiro ISHII†
† Department of Intelligence and Computer Science,
Nagoya Institute of Technology,
Gokiso-cho, Showa-ku, Nagoya 466, Japan
E-mail yamauchi@egg.ics.nitech.ac.jp

Abstract— Artificial neural network is a useful tool for pattern recognition because the network can realize nonlinear mapping between input and output spaces. This ability is tuned by supervised learning methods such as back-propagation. In the supervised learning methods, desired outputs of the neural network are needed. However, the desired outputs are usually unknown in unpredictable environments. To solve this problem, this paper presents a self-supervised learning system for category detection. This system learns categories of objects and boundaries between them automatically by integrating information from several sensors. We assume that these sensory inputs are always ambiguous patterns which include some noises according to deformation of the objects. After the learning, the system recognizes objects with controlling a priority of each sensor according to the deformation of the sensory input pattern.

1 Introduction

Multi-layered neural network is a useful tool for pattern recognition because it can realize nonlinear mapping between input and output spaces. The nonlinear mapping is very useful for representing complex boundaries between categories. This ability is tuned by a supervised learning method such as 'back-propagation.' In the supervised learning method, desired outputs of the neural network are needed. However, in the real world, the desired outputs are usually unknown.

On the other hand, in unsupervised learning methods, a neural network can learn clusters of input patterns without referring desired outputs. However, it is difficult to make a neural network learn nonlinear mappings exactly using unsupervised leaning methods. This brings up a question on how can biological systems learn nonlinear mappings without a teacher.

There is an interesting answer to the question. It is well known that owls can detect the location of a target only by hearing the sound of the target at night. They do it by detecting the time or intensity difference between the right ear and the left ear to catch the sound of the target. The time and intensity differences are called interaural time difference (ITD) and interaural intensity difference (IID), respectively. Eric l. Knudsen, et al [1] showed that the owls cannot locate the sound source when moving upside or downside if their eyelids are sutures to close in their early life. They also showed that the relation between the IID and the direction of the sound source placed upside or downside is nonlinear. This finding suggests that vision plays an important role for learning of the nonlinear mapping during owls' early life. Therefore, it seems that owls predict the desired output using visual inputs. From this observation, we believe that mammalian neural systems acquire knowledge by integrating several sensory inputs.

To accomplish the integration, we propose the system as shown in Figure. 1. The system is constructed by several neural networks each of which receives inputs from corresponding sensor. The center of the system integrates all outputs of neural networks by averaging outputs of all networks. In the learning phase, each network adjusts its parameters so as to make its output pattern close to the pattern of the center. In the recognition phase, the system recognizes objects by controlling a priority of each sensor according to the deformation of the each sensory input.

A similar system which is based on LVQ technique has been presented [2]. The system consists of an output layer and several sets of learning vector quantizers (LVQs) each of which is connected to the corresponding sensor. The output layer yields a labeled class by integrating the outputs of the LVQs. During the learning phase, the system adjusts the code book vectors of each LVQ so as to minimize disagreements between outputs of the LVQs. Before the learning process, the code book vectors have to be initially chosen randomly from the data patterns and to be given an initial label. However, it is difficult to determine the initial label in an unpredictable environment.

On the other hand, the new system can acquire the labels only by observing the patterns without initial labels.

2 An Outline of the System

The structure of the system is illustrated in Figure 1(a). This system consists of several sets of multi-

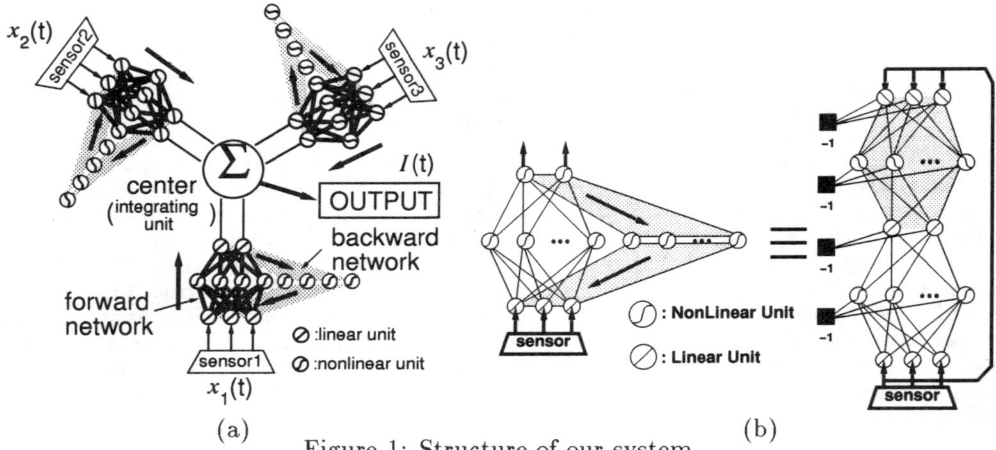

Figure 1: Structure of our system

layered neural networks and sensors. We assume that all sensors always observe a same object simultaneously. However all sensory inputs always include some noises according to the deformation of the object. Each neural network consists of a forward network and a backward network. The forward network receives inputs from the corresponding sensor, while the backward network receives inputs from the forward network.

The outputs of all forward networks are sent to an integrating unit. The unit integrates all the outputs by calculating the weighted sum (or average) of the outputs. The integrated output is the final output of the system. Let $I(t)$ be the output vector of the integrating unit at time t, then,

$$I(t) = \sum_s \sigma_s(t) f^f[\theta_s^f(t), x_s(t)] \tag{1}$$

where $f^f[\theta_s^f(t), x_s(t)]$ is the output vector of the s-th forward network to the sensory input vector: $x_s(t)$, $\theta_s^f(t)$ denotes a vector of parameters of the forward network, and $\sigma_s(t)$ (< 1) denotes a priority of the s-th sensor which satisfies $\sum_s \sigma_s(t) = 1$. The priorities are fixed to certain values in the learning phase but they are controlled according to the confidence in the output of each neural network in the recognition phase. The control strategy will be explained in section 4 in detail.

During a learning phase, each forward network fundamentally adjust its parameters so as to make its output $f^f[\theta_s^f(t), x_s(t)]$ close to that of the integrating unit $I(t)$. In the early step of the learning, outputs of each forward network are usually affected by the noises of its sensory inputs. However, the variance of the integrated output $I(t)$ caused by the noises is less than that of each forward network because $I(t)$ is the averaged output vector of the forward networks. As the result, after the learning, each forward network can produce outputs which are not affected by the noises of the sensory inputs.

The above learning strategy, however, is not power enough to learn categories of objects. The problem comes from that this forward network can only adjusts its parameters to ignore any changes of sensory inputs. It cannot discover categories of input patterns. To solve this problem, the system adjusts the parameters of the forward network by using the backward network.

The forward network with the backward network is similar to the 5 layered network for data compression proposed in Ref [3] (see Figure 1(b)).

An output vector of the backward network is described as $f^b\left[\theta_s^b(t), f^f[\theta_s^f(t), x_s(t)]\right]$ where $\theta_s^b(t)$ denotes a parameter vector of the backward network. During the learning phase, the whole network adjusts its parameters not only to make the output of the backward network $f^b[\theta_s^b(t), f^f[\theta_s^f(t), x_s(t)]]$ close to its sensory input $x_s(t)$ but also to make the output of the forward network $f^f[\theta_s^f(t), x_s(t)]$ close to that of the integrating unit $I(t)$. Note that error signals through the backward network also affect the modification of parameters of the forward network. As the result, the forward network tries to represent the varieties of sensory inputs but yield outputs which are not affected by the noises. Therefore, the forward network can represent the categories of the sensory inputs. Ultimately, the integrating unit yields an output vector that describes the category of the object.

3 Learning Algorithm

During the learning phase, the priorities of the sensors σ_s are fixed to some certain values.

Each forward network learns sensory inputs so as to minimize the following two estimators. The first estimator represents differences between the integrated output vector and the output vector of each forward network. The second estimator denotes differences between the sensory input and output vector of the backward network.

$$E_s^{(1)}(t) = \left\| \, \boldsymbol{I}(t) - \boldsymbol{f}^f[\boldsymbol{\theta}_s^f(t), \boldsymbol{x}_s(t)] \, \right\|^2, \qquad E_s^{(2)}(t) = \left\| \, \boldsymbol{x}_s(t) - \boldsymbol{f}^b\left[\boldsymbol{\theta}_s^b(t), \boldsymbol{f}^f[\boldsymbol{\theta}_s^f(t), \boldsymbol{x}_s(t)]\right] \, \right\|^2. \qquad (2)$$

Therefore, the change in parameters of the forward network is

$$\frac{d\boldsymbol{\theta}_s^f(t)}{dt} = -\varepsilon \frac{\partial\{(1 - k_s)E_s^{(1)}(t) + k_s E_s^{(2)}(t)\}}{\partial \boldsymbol{\theta}_s^f(t)}, \qquad (3)$$

where k_s (< 1) is a parameter denoting the ratio of the effect of the second estimator:$E_s^{(2)}(t)$. In the computer simulation described later, k_s was set to 0.5 for all s. ε is a parameter denoting the speed of the learning.

The change in parameters of the backward network is

$$\frac{d\theta_{si}^b(t)}{dt} = -\varepsilon(M^2 - \{\theta_{si}^b(t)\}^2)\frac{\partial E_s^{(2)}(t)}{\partial \theta_{si}^b(t)}, \qquad (4)$$

where $\theta_{si}^b(t)$ is the i-th element of the vector $\boldsymbol{\theta}_s^b(t)$. The term $(M^2 - \{\theta_{si}^b(t)\}^2)$ is for bounding the changes in parameters. This term restricts the interval of each parameter to $-M < \theta_{si}^b(t) < M$ $(M > 0)$. So, the initial value of $\theta_{si}^b(t)$ should be set to a value in the interval as above. This restriction is for making each forward network represent categories of sensory inputs clearly [1].

Thresholds, which are the weights of connections come from black box in Figure 1(b), are updated without the restriction as below.

$$\frac{d\theta_{sT}^b(t)}{dt} = -\varepsilon\frac{\partial E_s^{(2)}(t)}{\partial \theta_{sT}^b(t)}, \qquad (5)$$

where $\theta_{sT}^b(t)$ denotes the threshold.

4 Recognition

In the recognition phase, this system recognizes objects by integrating information of all sensors as described in Eq (1). The output vector of the integrating unit $\boldsymbol{I}(t)$ is the final recognition result of the system. $\boldsymbol{I}(t)$ represents the category of the current object in a distributed manner. $\boldsymbol{I}(t)$ can be the input to other independent systems. To use $\boldsymbol{I}(t)$ as the input, the systems have to collect and memorize $\boldsymbol{I}(t)$s for the matching process. Therefore, it will be a useful input for the reinforcement learning system of a mobile robot such as the system proposed in [4].

To have the new system work successfully, it is desirable that all sensors are always available. However, there is no guarantee that such the condition is always kept. To solve this problem, during the recognition phase, this system controls the priorities σ_s according to the confidence in the output of each forward network. The confidence of it is measured by the procedure as follows. If there are a large difference between the output vector of the backward network $\boldsymbol{f}^b[\boldsymbol{\theta}_s^b(t), \boldsymbol{f}^f[\boldsymbol{\theta}_s^f(t), \boldsymbol{x}_s(t)]]$ and the sensory input vector $\boldsymbol{x}_s(t)$, the confidence in the forward output $\boldsymbol{f}^f[\boldsymbol{\theta}_s^f(t), \boldsymbol{x}_s(t)]$ is low. In this case the system make

---

[1] Without the restriction, there are cases that each backward network learns a relation between a large change of sensory inputs and a small difference of the output vector of the forward network completely. In such cases, the error signals through the backward network become too small to modify parameters of the forward network. This means that the learning reaches an equilibrium even if the forward network does not represent varieties of sensory inputs well. In this the case, a small change of the forward output represents a large change of its sensory input.

On the other hand, each forward network adjusts its parameters so as to make its output vector close to that of the integrating unit. However, after the learning phase, small gaps between the forward output and that of integrating unit usually remain. The small gaps correspond to large differences of sensory inputs in this case. As the result, the output vector of the integrating unit eventually does not represent the categories of objects correctly.

To solve this problem, this system restricts the parameters of the backward network. With the restriction, the forward network becomes to represent categories of objects clearly.

the corresponding priority small. To the opposite, if the difference is small, this system makes the priority close to the value which is set in the learning phase. Mathematically,

$$\sigma_s(t) = \frac{\frac{p_s}{G_s(t)+\epsilon}}{\sum_{s'}\frac{p_{s'}}{G_{s'}(t)+\epsilon}}, \quad G_s(t) = \frac{\left\| x_s(t) - f^b\left[\theta_s^b(t), f^f[\theta_s^f(t), x_s(t)]\right]\right\|^2}{D_s}, \tag{6}$$

where $\epsilon \ll 1$ is a positive constant, p_s is a value of the priority used in the learning phase, and D_s is the number of the dimension of the s th sensory input x_s. $G_s(t)$ denotes the difference between $f^b[\theta_s^b(t), f^f[\theta_s^f(t), x_s(t)]]$ and $x_s(t)$ normalized by the number of dimension. Therefore, $1/\{G_s(t) + \epsilon\}$ denotes the confidence in the output of corresponding forward network. In the learning phase, $G_s(t)$ is fixed to 0.

5 Computer Simulation

This section shows two computer simulations. In the first simulation, one or two dimensional patterns are presented to the system to show the ability of the system clearly. After the learning phase, representations of the integrating unit are examined. In the second simulation, we apply this system to a character recognition task. In the both simulations, three sets of neural networks and sensors are used. The neural networks are multi layered perceptrons whose nonlinear output function is a sigmoid function.

5.1 Simulation1

The number of cells of each forward network and priorities are listed in the right tabular. In this simulation, each priority is fixed to the listed values.
Note that the number of middle units and output units

S	σ_s	1st layer	2nd layer	3rd layer
1	0.4	2	12	1
2	0.4	2	12	1
3	0.2	1	10	1

of each backward network are the same as the number of middle and input units of corresponding forward network respectively. Input units and output units are linear unit but middle units are nonlinear unit. The nonlinear units are characterized by the sigmoid function: $f(x) = 1/\{1+\exp(-5x)\}$. ε in Eq(3)(4) is set to 0.01. M in Eq(3) is set to 0.25. The value of each element in weight vectors θ_s^b and θ_s^f is initialized to a random value in a range of [-0.05, 0.05].

In this simulation, we use artificial sensory input patterns below instead of actual sensory input patterns.

$$x_s(t) = \overline{x_s}[C(t)] + \delta_s(t) \quad (\text{for } s = 1, 2, 3), \tag{7}$$

where $C(t)$ denotes a category at time t, $\overline{x_s}[C(t)]$ denotes the averaged pattern of the s-th sensory input of category $C(t)$, and $\delta_s(t)$ denotes Gauss noise at time t. $C(t)$ specifies the categories at random sequences. The total number of categories are 5. The learning process is repeated from t=0 to 100000.

Figure 2 shows the outputs of integrating unit. The top stage of the figure shows 500 sets of sensory input patterns. The labels (1) $\sim$ (5) specify categories. Particularly, the 3rd set of sensory input patterns, which are one dimensional patterns, are illustrated with curves representing distribution of the patterns. Note that the distributions of (1) and (2) are same and the boundary between (4) and (5) is ambiguous.

The middle and lower stage of Figure 2 show the output values of the integrating unit before and after the learning process, respectively. We can see from this figure that the integrating unit before the learning yields almost the same output values and does not detect categories of the input patterns. On the opposite, after the learning, the integrating unit yields the output values which depend on the categories of the input. Moreover, the output value is not affected by the variance of x-axe of the input patterns caused by the noises. This means that the system can detect the categories without being affected by the noises. In the left lower side of the figure, the responses are re-plotted in order that its x-axe corresponds to that of the 3rd set of sensory inputs. We can see that the system detects the categories (1) and (2) even if the 3rd one has the same distribution. More over, the system discriminates (4) and (5) even if the boundary between (4) and (5) is ambiguous.

As an example, the responses of the 3rd forward network are also shown in Figure. 2. We can see that the curves of responses to each category are flat shapes. The responses to the patterns between (4) and (5) are constricted. This means that the 3rd forward network tries to represent the boundary between (4) and (5) continuously. The responses corresponding to (1) and (2) are an average value of the responses of the integrating unit.

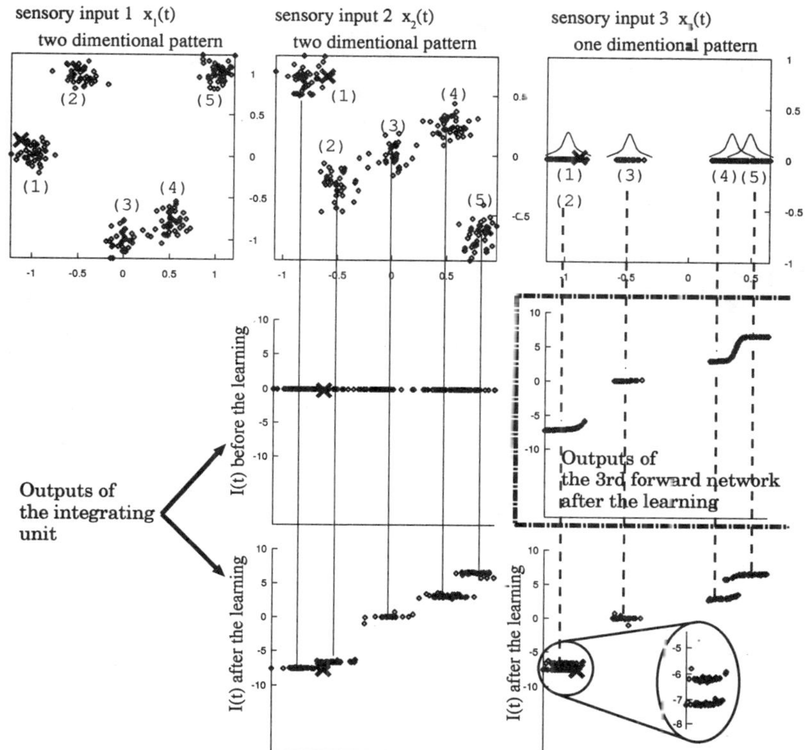

Figure 2: Sensory inputs and responses of the integrating unit. The top stage plots 3 sensory inputs. Labels (1) ~ (5) specify same categories. The responses of the integrating unit are shown in the middle and lower stages whose x-axe corresponds to that of the 2nd set of sensory input patterns: x_2. The middle and lower stages show the responses before and after the learning, respectively. For example, if the sensory inputs of category (1) which are specified by '×' s in the figure are presented, the corresponding response becomes the value specified '×' in the middle or lower stage. For reference, in the right lower side of this figure, the responses are re-plotted in order that its x-axe corresponds to that of the 3rd set of sensory inputs. For reference, the outputs of the 3rd forward network after the learning are also shown.

5.2 Simulation2

The system is implemented for a character recognition. Four sets of characters of 5×5 patterns whose elements consist of 1 or 0 are used. The character sets are shown in the right tabular.

x_s	C1	C2	C3	C4
x_1	'A'	'B'	'C'	'D'
x_2	'a'	'b'	'c'	'd'
x_3	'α'	'β'	'χ'	'δ'

These character patterns always include noises. Each pixel of the pattern is tuned over in a certain probability. In this experiment, the probability is set to 5 %. The number of cells and p_s in Eq(6) are set as the below tabular.

The nonlinear output function of the network is $f(x) = 1/1 + \exp(-x)$. ε and M are set to 0.01 and 0.8 respectively. The initial value of each element of weight vectors are assigned to a random value in a

S	p_s	1st layer	2nd layer	3rd layer
1	0.33	25	12	2
2	0.33	25	12	2
3	0.33	25	12	2

range of $[-0.05, 0.05]$. The learning process is repeated from $t = 0$ to 60000.

Figure 3 shows an example of the responses of the integrating unit to input patterns after the learning. Each input pattern is one of training patterns. In this figure, the outputs of backward networks to the integrated output vector are also shown for examining what the network recognizes. In the recognition phase, the priority of each sensor is controlled using Eq (6) which value is shown in the figure. We can see from this figure that the output patterns of backward networks are complete patterns even if the input patterns are distorted. This means that the system can recognize them correctly.

The next Figure 4 show the responses of the system when one of the sensors is not available. The priority of each sensor is controlled according to the difference between the sensory input $x_s(t)$ and the output of corresponding backward network $f^b[\theta_s^b(t), f^f[\theta_s^f(t), x_s(t)]]$ (see Eq (5)). The parameter ϵ in Eq (6) is set to 0.0001. The priority of the 1st sensor becomes small because there are large difference between

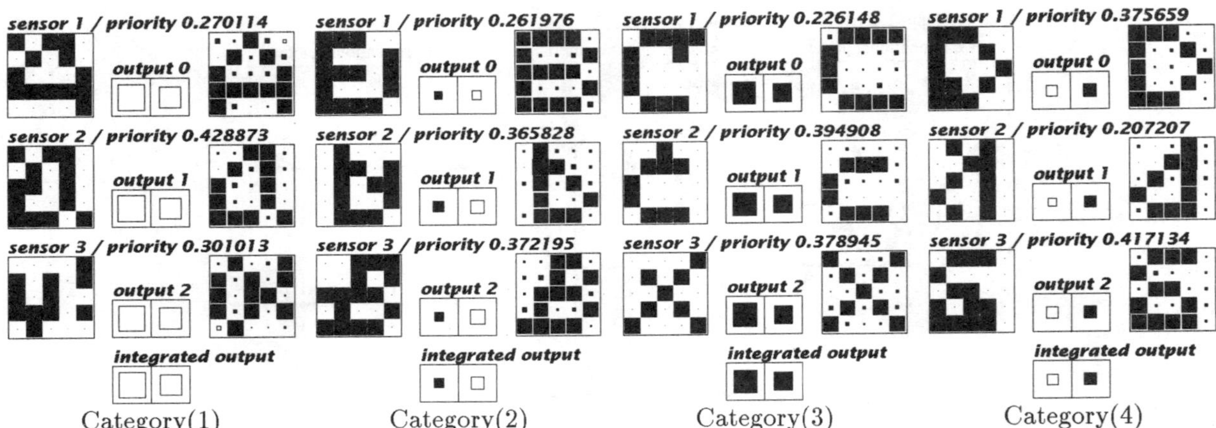

Category(1)   Category(2)   Category(3)   Category(4)

Figure 3: Responses of the system to training patterns. Black and white boxes denote positive and negative value, respectively. The size of the box represents the absolute value. In each figure, the left and right part show sensory inputs and outputs of the backward networks to the integrated output , respectively. The center part shows outputs of the forward networks and the integrating unit.

x_1 and $f^b[\theta_1^b(t), f^f[\theta_1^f(t), x_1(t)]]$ is large. As the result, the abnormal output of the 1st forward network does not affect the integrated output so that the outputs of backward networks to the integrated output represent reconstructed input patterns correctly. These results support that the system can recognize objects even if some sensors are not available.

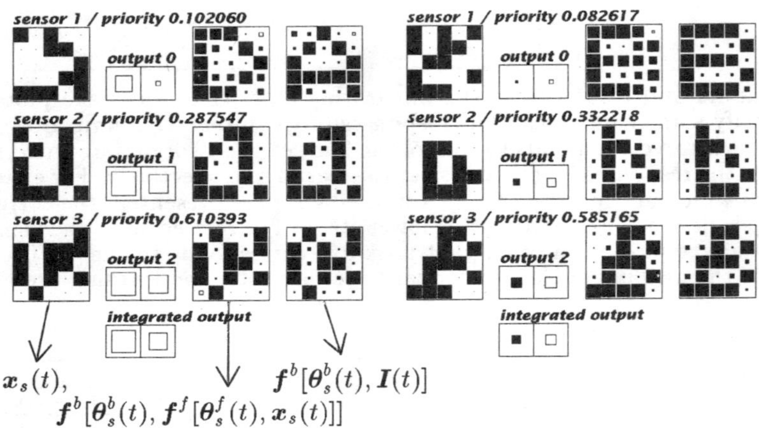

$x_s(t),$ $f^b[\theta_s^b(t), I(t)]$

$f^b[\theta_s^b(t), f^f[\theta_s^f(t), x_s(t)]]$

Figure 4: Responses of the system when the 1st sensor is not available

6   Conclusion and Discussion

This paper presents a self-supervised learning system for category detection by integrating information of several sensors. The simulation result suggests that the system can acquire knowledge about the categories and the boundaries between the categories only by observing noisy input patterns. Moreover, the system yields flexible recognition ability even if some sensors are not available. The proposed system probably will be a useful tool for robots that work in unpredictable environments.

One of our future research is the construction of techniques to send the acquired knowledge to other systems. In the techniques, the system probably needs to create a language for the communication.

References

[1] L. Knudsen Eric, Steven D. Esterly, and Sascha du Lac. Stretched and upside-doen maps of auditory space in the optic tectum of blind reared owels. *The Journal of Neuroscience*, 11(6):1727–1747, June 1991.

[2] Virginia R. de Sa. Learning classification with unlabeled data. In Jack D. Cowan, Gerald Tesauro, and Joshua Alspector, editors, *Advances in Neural Information Processing Systems 6*, pages 112–119. Morgan Kaufmann Publishers, Inc., 1994.

[3] B. Irie and S. Miyake. Capabilities of three-layered perceptrons. *Proc. ICNN88*, 1:641–648, 1988.

[4] Kazushige Saga, Tamami Sugasaka, and Minoru Sekiguchi. Self-supervised learning model. *FUJITSU Scientific and Technical Journal*, 29(3):209–216, September 1993.

Reference Priors for Neural Networks:
Laplace versus Gaussian

Tin-Yau Kwok (jamesk@cs.ust.hk),   Dit-Yan Yeung (dyyeung@cs.ust.hk)
Department of Computer Science
Hong Kong University of Science and Technology
Clear Water Bay, Kowloon
Hong Kong

Abstract— **Motivated by the principle of maximum entropy, the Laplace prior has been introduced in the Bayesian inference approach to training feedforward neural networks as the prior distribution for network weights. In this paper, we examine in detail the arguments supporting the Laplace prior and argue that network weights, being continuous quantities with no obvious upper bound, complicate the application of the maximum entropy principle. On the other hand, we motivate the use of the Gaussian prior as reference prior in neural networks, basing on the assumptions of exchangeability and spherical symmetry.**

1 Introduction

The Bayesian approach [1, 2, 3] is attractive in being logically consistent, simple and flexible. Recently, various researchers [4, 5, 6, 7] have incorporated Bayesian methods into the learning of feedforward neural networks. Compared with the traditional approach, it provides a rigorous framework and enables objective comparison between solutions using alternative network architectures and objective stopping rules for network pruning and growing procedures. However, as for Bayesian inference in general, a central controversy is in determining the prior. Critics often find arbitrariness in the choice of prior an overwhelming difficulty. For linear models, there have been efforts in eliciting personal priors from the user [8]. However, extension to neural networks, which are highly nonlinear, seems difficult. MacKay [5, 9] argued that this controversy may be alleviated by trying as many priors as desired by the user, and then comparing them in the light of the data. While we support this attitude and agree that there is no single prior that is "correct" under all circumstances [4], we also caution that abuse of the above freedom may lead to *ad hoc* priors and sidestep the need for a good one [10]. Hence, it is always important to understand the underlying rationales in obtaining each prior and check if they can be applied in the specific problem domain.

In the context of neural networks, the priors include priors on network architecture[1] and network weights. In this paper, we will concentrate on the latter. Priors on network weights are related to the penalty terms in pruning algorithms. In particular, weight decay [11] corresponds to the use of a Gaussian prior:

$$p(\mathbf{w}) \propto \exp(-\frac{\alpha}{2} \sum_{j=1}^{N} w_j^2),$$

where $\mathbf{w} = (w_1, w_2, \ldots, w_N)$ is the network weight vector, N is the number of weights, and $\alpha \geq 0$ is a regularization parameter. Despite the popularity of Gaussian prior in the context of neural networks [5], little theoretical justification has so far been given. Extension to the form of a Gaussian mixture has also been proposed [12].

Recently, Williams [13], inspired by the principle of maximum entropy from Jaynes' paper [14], introduced the Laplace prior:

$$p(\mathbf{w}) \propto \exp(-\alpha \sum_{j=1}^{N} |w_j|).$$

It has the added advantage that automatic pruning can be incorporated into the framework.

Obviously, when more precise prior information is available, one will be able to define other functional forms for the prior. In this paper, however, we consider the case when little such knowledge is available. We call such priors *reference priors*[2], in line with [3, 16], in denoting priors that are convenient to be used as a standard. A reference prior is similar to a default option in a computer package. When prior knowledge is not available, the users may feel that the reference prior is a good approximation to any reasonable subjective prior for that problem. When prior knowledge is available, reference prior can be used to make baseline comparisons with other priors that incorporate various prior knowledge.

---

[1]The prior on network architecture is useful in, for example, the level three inference in the evidence framework [9]. Usually a flat prior is taken.

[2]Note that we have avoided using the term *non-informative prior* common in the Bayesian literature, as the word "non-informative" tends to be misleading. "Put bluntly, data cannot ever speak entirely for themselves; every prior specification has *some* informative posterior or predictive implications. [...deleted...] There is no *objective* prior that represents ignorance." [2]. Moreover, readers are cautioned not to confuse with the *reference priors* proposed by Bernardo [15], which is one particular way to the construction of prior.

The rest of this paper is organized as follows. In Section 2, the arguments put forward by Williams for the use of the Laplace prior as reference prior in neural network models are examined in detail. We found that these arguments are problematic. In Section 3, we motivate the use of the Gaussian prior basing on arguments of exchangeability and spherical symmetry. Conclusion and future research directions are given in the last section.

2 Laplace Prior

2.1 Arguments for the Use of the Laplace Prior

For completeness, we quoted in the following reasons advocated by Williams that the Laplace prior is especially suitable for neural network models.

> For any feedforward network in which there are no direct connections between input and output units, there is a functionally equivalent network in which the weight on a given connection has the same size but opposite sign. This is also true if there are direct connections, except for the direct connections. This is evident if the transfer function is odd, [...deleted...] Consistency then demands that the prior for a given weight w_j should be a function of $|w_j|$ alone.
>
> If it is assumed that all that is known about $|w_j|$ is its scale, and that the scale of a positive quantity is determined by its mean rather than some higher order moment, the most noncommittal distribution for $|w_j|$ according to the principle of maximum entropy is the exponential distribution, since this is the maximum entropy distribution for a positive quantity constrained to have a given mean [17]. It would follow that the signed weight w_i has the two-sided exponential or Laplace density.

2.2 Background Concepts

As Williams' arguments are based on the concepts of consistency and maximum entropy, hence, for completeness, we state the two concepts below.

Consistency principle [14]: In two problems where we have the same prior information, we should assign the same prior probabilities.

Principle of maximum entropy [1]: The principle states that we should choose the prior distribution which maximizes entropy[3] among all those distributions which satisfy the given set of restrictions (i.e. given prior information). Since the entropy of a distribution is a measure of its uncertainty, increase in information about the distribution results in decrease in entropy. Hence, intuitively, this should result in a prior that incorporates the available *a priori* information but is maximally noncommittal with regard to the missing information.

2.3 Discussions on Williams' Arguments

The major problem in Williams' arguments is in the application of the principle of maximum entropy, in that the weights in neural networks are typically continuous quantities and there is then no completely natural definition of entropy. But, first, let us consider the simpler case for a discrete random variable θ, taking on values from the finite set $\Theta = \{a_1, \ldots, a_m\}$ with the corresponding probabilities of occurrence given by $(p_1, \ldots, p_m)$. The entropy of its probability density p is defined as [18]

$$H(p) \stackrel{\text{def}}{=} -\sum_{i=1}^{m} p_i \log p_i, \tag{1}$$

where the logarithm may be taken to base e or to base 2. It is well-known that this definition enjoys the properties as a measure of "uncertainty" or "randomness" of a random phenomenon.

When θ becomes a d-dimensional continuous random variable, with probability density function $p(\theta)$ taking on values from $\Theta \subset \Re^d$, definition for its entropy becomes more problematic. One can define the *entropy* [18] (also called *continuous entropy* or *differential entropy*) of p, in an analogous form with (1), as

$$h(p) \stackrel{\text{def}}{=} -\int_{\Theta} p(\theta) \log p(\theta) d\theta. \tag{2}$$

However, (2) is not the correct information measure for a continuous distribution [14]. Contrary to (1) for discrete random variables, the entropy defined in (2) can be negative and is not invariant under a coordinate transformation. Also, it is not the limiting case of the entropy of a discrete random variable[4] [18].

---

[3] A more detailed discussion on the definitions of entropy will be presented in Section 2.3.

[4] As an illustration, consider the uniform distribution over the range $[a, b]$, $a < b$. Then we have

$$p(x) = \begin{cases} \frac{1}{b-a} & a \leq x \leq b, \\ 0 & \text{otherwise.} \end{cases}$$

Therefore, $h(p) = \log(b - a)$. Now partition the range $[a, b]$ in k equal subintervals to obtain the discrete distribution $q = (\frac{1}{k}, \ldots, \frac{1}{k})$ whose entropy is $H_k(q) = \log k$. As a result, one has $\lim_{k \to \infty} H_k(q)$ goes to infinity, which is not $\log(b - a)$.

To remedy these problems, Jaynes [14] advocated the use of the *relative entropy* (also called *Kullback-Leibler information number, information divergence, information for discrimination, information gain, or cross entropy*):

$$H(p, m) \stackrel{\text{def}}{=} - \int_\Theta p(\theta) \log(p(\theta)/m(\theta)) d\theta, \tag{3}$$

where $m(\theta)$ is some base "non-informative" prior to measure against. Ihara [18] showed that in the special case when $|\Theta|$ has a finite volume and m is the uniform distribution U on Θ,

$$H(p, U) = -h(p) + \log|\Theta|. \tag{4}$$

Thus, the continuous entropy coincides with the relative entropy with respect to the uniform distribution, except for the additive constant $\log|\Theta|$ and the multiplicative constant -1. In general situations, Jaynes [14] suggested the construction of base measures $m(\theta)$ based on invariance arguments. However, having to choose a base measure is no different than having to choose a prior so that this maximum entropy solution is rather circular [16].

If we settle on the use of (3) as a proper definition of entropy, then when the prior information is of the form

$$E[g_k(\theta)] = \int_\Theta g_k(\theta)p(\theta)d\theta = \mu_k, \qquad k = 1, \ldots, m, \tag{5}$$

the (proper) prior density satisfying these restrictions which maximizes the entropy given in (3) is given (provided it exists) by [1] as:

$$p(\theta) = \frac{m(\theta) \exp[\sum_{k=1}^m c_k g_k(\theta)]}{\int_\Theta m(\theta) \exp[\sum_{k=1}^m c_k g_k(\theta)] d\theta}, \tag{6}$$

where the c_k's are constants to be determined from the constraints in (5)

Returning back to Williams' argument on the use of the Laplace prior, he used the result in Tribus [17], saying that the exponential distribution is the maximum entropy distribution for a positive quantity constrained to have a given mean. Unfortunately, in Tribus [17], this result follows only when the entropy for distributions of a continuous random variable is defined as in (2). If one adopts the entropy definition in (3) and is willing to take m to be the uniform distribution, then some support for the Laplace prior can be found as (4) shows that maximizing (2) is equivalent to minimizing the relative entropy when the probability distribution of the network weight vanishes outside a domain Θ with finite volume, i.e. there is an upper limit on the magnitude of the weight. However, such an upper bound is most often not obvious.

Nevertheless, we can still proceed with the principle of maximum entropy. In Williams' argument, it is assumed, without providing justification, that the expected magnitude of network weights is the only constraint to be satisfied in the maximum entropy problem. Note that different sets of constraints may lead to different maximum entropy distributions. Jaynes [14] took a more open-minded approach on the construction of the constraint set by comparing experimental data against predictions from the maximum entropy analysis. If the experiment fails to confirm the maximum entropy prediction, then additional constraints are explored and taken into account in the maximum entropy calculation. This is not the approach taken by Williams however. Anyway, in his case, (5) can then be simplified to:

$$E[\theta] = \mu, \tag{7}$$

for some $\mu \in \Re$. Again, using the uniform distribution as m, (6) shows that the maximum entropy prior must then be of the form

$$p(\theta) = \frac{\exp\{c_1\theta\}}{\int_0^\infty \exp\{c_1\theta\} d\theta}. \tag{8}$$

Using a negative value for c_1 such that (8) satisfies the constraint (7), the Laplace prior is finally obtained.

In summary, if we are to determine the maximum entropy prior for the network weights, we are left with the following three options:

1. Use the incorrectly defined entropy in (2) and arrive at the Laplace prior.

2. Use the relative entropy defined in (3) with respect to the uniform distribution. Then, either one puts an upper bound on the magnitude of the weights or assumes that the expected magnitude of network weights is the only constraint to be satisfied. Again, the Laplace prior will be arrived. However, the choices of using the uniform distribution, of determining an upper bound and of constructing the constraint set cannot be easily justified.

3. Use the entropy as defined in (3), and use other forms of base measure for m. Priors, other than the Laplace prior, may be derived depending on the exact form of m. However, this method is sort of circular argument.

There are other theoretical arguments against the use of maximum entropy prior in general. For example, there is a conflict between using the principle of maximum entropy and Bayesian updating when new constraints are added [19]. But such details will not be further pursued here.

Moreover, $h(p)$ is negative when $(b - a)$ is sufficiently small.

To conclude, we find the arguments for justifying the use of the Laplace prior in neural network models are not sound enough.

3   Gaussian Prior

Williams [13] argued that the Gaussian prior would be obtained if constraints were placed on the first two moments of the distribution of the signed weights. But this, of course, is only required if derivation of the prior using the principle of maximum entropy is followed. In the following, we motivate the use of Gaussian prior in neural networks basing on concepts of exchangeability and spherical symmetry.

3.1   Background Concepts

In this section, we give a brief introduction to the concepts of exchangeability and spherical symmetry. Details can be found in [2].

Definition: The random quantities $x_1, \ldots, x_n$ are said to be judged *(finitely) exchangeable* under a joint distribution P if

$$P(x_1, \ldots, x_n) = P(x_{\pi(1)}, \ldots, x_{\pi(n)}),$$

for all permutations π defined on the index set $\{1, \ldots, n\}$.

Intuitively, this means that there is a complete symmetry in $x_1, \ldots, x_n$: all the marginal distributions for the individual random quantities are judged as identical, and similarly for all the marginal joint distributions for all possible pairs, triples, etc. of the random quantities. Additional structure may be imposed on the random quantities to further simplify the problem.

Definition: A sequence of random quantities $x_1, \ldots, x_n$ is said to have *spherical symmetry* under P if P defines the distributions of $\mathbf{x} = (x_1, \ldots, x_n)$ and $\mathbf{Ax}$ to be identical, for any orthogonal $n \times n$ matrix $\mathbf{A}$.

This definition encapsulates a judgment of rotational symmetry, in the sense that, although measurements happened to have been expressed in terms of a particular coordinate system (yielding $x_1, \ldots, x_n$), our quantitative beliefs would not change even if they had been expressed in a rotated coordinate system. Moreover, note that exchangeability is a special case of spherical symmetry, as permutation is a special case of orthogonal transformation. Besides, spherical symmetry places a strict limitation on the family of P. In particular, we have the following representation theorem:

Theorem 1 *If $x_1, x_2, \ldots$ is an infinite sequence of real-valued random quantities, and if, for any n, $x_1, \ldots, x_n$ have spherical symmetry, there exists a distribution function Q on $\Re^+$ such that the joint distribution function of $x_1, \ldots, x_n$ has the form*

$$P(x_1, \ldots, x_n) = \int_{\Re^+} \prod_{i=1}^{n} \Phi(\lambda^{1/2} x_i) dQ(\lambda),$$

where Φ is the standard normal distribution function and

$$Q(\lambda) = \lim_{n \to \infty} P(s_n^{-2} \leq \lambda),$$

with $s_n^2 = n^{-1}(x_1^2 + \cdots + x_n^2)$, and $\lambda^{-1} = \lim_{n \to \infty} s_n^2$.

Interpretation of this representation theorem is therefore as if

1. the observations $x_1, \ldots, x_n$ are conditionally independent normal random quantities, given the random quantity λ;

2. λ is itself assigned a distribution Q, with Q being interpreted as "beliefs about the reciprocal of the limiting mean sum of squares of the observations".

3.2   Motivating the Use of the Gaussian Prior

In this section, we use the concepts discussed in the previous section to motivate the use of the Gaussian prior in the context of neural networks. We consider feedforward networks in which the net inputs to the hidden units are linear combinations of the incoming inputs, i.e. each hidden unit produces a function of the form

$$f(\mathbf{x}) = g(\mathbf{w}^T \mathbf{x} + w_0), \tag{9}$$

where $\mathbf{w}$ is the weight vector (excluding the bias w_0), $\mathbf{x}$ is the incoming input vector, and T denotes the transpose. Consider first a hidden unit connected to the input. If an orthogonal transformation $\mathbf{A}$ is performed on the input $\mathbf{x}$, the hidden unit implements

$$f(\mathbf{x}) = g(\mathbf{w}'^T \mathbf{Ax} + w_0'), \tag{10}$$

where $\mathbf{w}'$ is the new weight vector, w_0' is the new bias. Obviously, (9) and (10) can implement the same function if $\mathbf{w}' = \mathbf{Aw}$ and $w_0 = w_0'$. Moreover, it is reasonable to assume that the hidden unit has gained no extra information on the distribution of its weights following this transformation. Thus, from the consistency principle, we would expect the old and new weight vectors to share the same prior distribution, i.e., the probability distributions of $\mathbf{w}$ and $\mathbf{Aw}$ are the same. In other words, there is a spherical symmetry in the components of $\mathbf{w}$. From a Bayesian point of view, these components are random variables, and may be identified as the random quantities $x_1, x_2 \ldots$ in Theorem 1. Assuming that this particular hidden unit has infinitely many incoming connections, Theorem 1 allows one to view the weights leading into a particular hidden unit as all following the normal distribution determined by a hyperparameter λ, or, in other words, they all take a Gaussian prior. One can easily extend this argument to all hidden units in the same layer. In particular, if we judge all the weights from all hidden units in the same layer as exchangeable, then a suitable prior is a Gaussian prior with a common hyperparameter. Otherwise, if there are reasons to judge that weights from different groups of hidden units are not exchangeable (this is called *partial exchangeability* [2]), different hyperparameters may be assigned to different groups. Note that the Gaussian prior is also in line with the consistency argument in Williams [13] that the prior should be independent of the sign of the weight (Section 2.1).

The next step is to consider hidden units whose input connections are from other hidden units. First, we make the reasonable belief that the prior distribution for the network weights is independent of the training algorithm. Then consider algorithms that train the weights in a layer-by-layer manner, as in [20, 21]. To be more specific, weights connecting the input layer and the lowest[5] hidden layer are first trained, with the weights in all the other layers fixed. Afterwards, this layer of weights is fixed and the next higher layer of weights is trained, and so on. The whole process iterates until there is no further significant improvement. At any instant, there is then only one layer of weights to be trained. Hidden units in all lower layers perform different transformations on the inputs, and the particular layer of hidden units currently being trained operates on the transformed variables combining these different transformations. These variables play the same role as the input units in the previous paragraph, and hence, by the same reasoning, the use of the Gaussian prior is also justified.

Note that the above argument naturally considers the network weights in a layer-by-layer manner. Across layers, the network weights are expected to be independent but not exchangeable. This justifies the use of distinct hyperparameters for different layers of weights, as is employed in the works by MacKay [5].

We mentioned earlier that exchangeability is a special case of spherical symmetry. As in linear models, it is usually more reasonable to assume exchangeability of the components of $\mathbf{w}$ when the incoming inputs share the same mean and variance [22, 23]. A common procedure is then to have each component of $\mathbf{x}$ to have zero mean and unit variance. For the input units, such standardization can be performed before training commences. For the hidden units, note that

$$w_i x_i = (w_i \sigma_{x_i})((x_i - \bar{x}_i)/\sigma_{x_i}) + c,$$

where $\bar{x}_i$ and σ_{x_i} are the mean and standard deviation, respectively, of the incoming input x_i averaged over all training patterns, while c can be included into the bias. Thus, standardization of x_i can be equivalently obtained by using $w_i \sigma_{x_i}$, instead of w_i, when computing the penalty due to w_i. Note that this procedure implies that updating of the weights has to be performed in a per-epoch manner, rather than in a per-pattern manner, for calculation of σ_{x_i} to be possible.

4   Conclusion

In this paper, we examine in detail the arguments for the use of the Laplace prior as reference prior in neural networks, as proposed by Williams [13]. We argue that the weights, being continuous quantities, complicate the issue of properly defining an entropy that measures the amount of uncertainty. The arguments by Williams implicitly assume bounded network weights and the use of a uniform prior as a base density to compare against. Moreover, using the expected magnitude of the network weights as the only constraint in the maximum entropy argument needs to be further justified. On the other hand, we support the commonly used Gaussian prior based on arguments of exchangeability and spherical symmetry. By making these underlying assumptions in the Gaussian prior explicit, practitioners can then assess the validity of these assumptions in their specific problem domain before adopting it.

The arguments in this paper only represent one of the formal ways to construct reference prior. A future direction is to explore other formal rules as described in [16]. Robustness of different priors will also be investigated.

Acknowledgments

This research has been partially supported by the Hong Kong Research Grants Council (RGC) Competitive Earmarked Research Grants (RGC/HKUST 15/91 and RGC/HKUST 614/94E).

References

[1] J.O. Berger. *Statistical Decision Theory and Bayesian Analysis.* Springer Series in Statistics. Springer-Verlag, New York, 2nd edition, 1985.

[2] J.M. Bernardo and A.F.M. Smith. *Bayesian Theory.* Wiley, 1994.

---

[5] In the following, we call the hidden layer closest to the input layer the *lowest* hidden layer, while those that are closer to the output layer the *higher* layers.

[3] G.E.P. Box and G.C. Tiao. *Bayesian Inference in Statistical Analysis.* Addison-Wesley, 1973.

[4] W.L. Buntine and A.S. Weigend. Bayesian back-propagation. *Complex Systems*, 5:603–643, 1991.

[5] D.J.C. MacKay. A practical Bayesian framework for backpropagation networks. *Neural Computation*, 4(3):448–472, May 1992.

[6] R.M. Neal. *Bayesian Learning for Neural Networks.* PhD thesis, Graduate Department of Computer Science, University of Toronto, 1995.

[7] H. H. Thodberg. A review of Bayesian neural networks with an application to near infrared spectroscopy. *IEEE Transactions on Neural Networks*, 7(1):56–72, 1996.

[8] J.B. Kadane, J.M. Dickey, R.L. Winkler, W.S. Smith, and S.C. Peters. Interactive elicitation of opinion for a normal linear model. *Journal of the American Statistical Association*, 75(372):845–854, December 1980.

[9] D.J.C. MacKay. Bayesian interpolation. *Neural Computation*, 4(3):415–447, May 1992.

[10] D.H. Wolpert. On the use of evidence in neural networks. In S.J. Hanson, J.D. Cowan, and C.L. Giles, editors, *Advances in Neural Information Processing Systems 5*, pages 539–546. Morgan Kaufmann, San Mateo, CA, 1993.

[11] D.C. Plaut, S.J. Nowlan, and G.E. Hinton. Experiments on learning by back propagation. Technical Report CMU-CS-86-126, Carnegie Mellon University, 1986.

[12] S.J. Nowlan and G.E. Hinton. Simplifying neural networks by soft weight-sharing. *Neural Computation*, 4:473–493, 1992.

[13] P.M. Williams. Bayesian regularization and pruning using a Laplace prior. *Neural Computation*, 7:117–143, 1995.

[14] E.T. Jaynes. Prior probabilities. *IEEE Transactions on Systems Science and Cybernetics*, SSC-4:227–241, 1968.

[15] J.M. Bernardo. Reference posterior distributions for Bayesian inference (with discussion). *Journal of the Royal Statistical Society Series B*, 41:113–147, 1979.

[16] R.E. Kass and L. Wasserman. Formal rules for selecting prior distributions: A review and annotated bibliography. Technical Report 583, Department of Statistics, Carnegie Mellon University, 1994.

[17] M. Tribus. *Rational Descriptions, Decisions and Designs.* Pergamon Press, Oxford, 1969.

[18] S. Ihara. *Information Theory for Continuous Systems.* World Scientific, Singapore, 1993.

[19] T. Seidenfeld. Entropy and uncertainty. In I.B. MacNeill and G.J. Umphrey, editors, *Foundations of Statistical Inference*, pages 259–287. D. Reidel Publishing Company, 1987.

[20] S.E. Fahlman and C. Lebiere. The cascade-correlation learning architecture. In D.S. Touretzky, editor, *Advances in Neural Information Processing Systems 2*, pages 524–532. Morgan Kaufmann, Los Altos CA, 1990.

[21] J.N. Hwang, S.R. Lay, M. Maechler, D. Martin, and J. Schimert. Regression modeling in back-propagation and projection pursuit learning. *IEEE Transactions on Neural Networks*, 5(3):342–353, May 1994.

[22] D.V. Lindley and A.F.M. Smith. Bayes estimates for the linear model (with discussion). *Journal of the Royal Statistical Society Series B*, 34:1–41, 1972.

[23] S.D. Oman. Shrinking towards subspaces in multiple linear regression. *Technometrics*, 24(4):307–311, 1982.

The Dynamics of On-Line Learning

Sara A. Solla
AT&T Research Labs
Holmdel, NJ 07733, USA

Abstract— We present an analytic solution to the problem of on-line gradient-descent learning for two-layer neural networks with an arbitrary number of hidden units in both teacher and student networks. The approach results in dynamical equations for the evolution of the overlaps among the various hidden units and allows for a computation of the generalization error.

1 Introduction

Learning in layered neural networks refers to the modification of internal parameters $\{\mathbf{J}\}$ which specify the strength of the interneuron couplings, so as to bring the map $f_{\mathbf{J}}$ implemented by the network as close as possible to a desired map $\tilde{f}$. The degree of success is monitored through the *generalization error*, a measure of the dissimilarity between $f_{\mathbf{J}}$ and $\tilde{f}$.

The functional capabilities of a neural network are described through the class $\{f_{\mathbf{J}}\}$ of implementable functions as determined by its architecture. Although neural networks including several layers of hidden units have at times been considered for specific applications, it is known that two-layer networks (involving two levels of processing and a single layer of hidden units) are sufficient for the exact implementation of Boolean maps [1] and the approximation of continuous maps with any desired degree of accuracy [2].

Here we consider continuous maps from an N-dimensional input space $\boldsymbol{\xi}$ onto a scalar ζ as arise in the formulation of classification and regression tasks, for which two-layer networks with an arbitrary number of hidden units have been shown to be universal approximators [2]. We therefore focus on the training of a *student* network with N input units, K sigmoidal hidden units, and a single linear output unit.

Information about the desired map $\tilde{f}$ is provided through independent *training examples* $(\boldsymbol{\xi}^{\mu}, \zeta^{\mu})$, with $\zeta^{\mu} = \tilde{f}(\boldsymbol{\xi}^{\mu})$ for all μ. The target map $\tilde{f}$ is defined through a *teacher* network of similar architecture, except that its number M of hidden units is not necessarily equal to K.

We investigate the emergence of generalization ability in an *on-line* learning scenario [3], in which the couplings are modified after the presentation of each example so as to minimize the corresponding error. The resulting changes in $\{\mathbf{J}\}$ are described as a dynamical evolution, with the number of examples playing the role of time. The average that accounts for the disorder introduced by the independent random selection of an example at each time step can be performed directly. The result is expressed in the form of dynamical equations for *order parameters* which describe correlations among the various nodes in the trained network as well as their degree of specialization towards the implementation of the desired task.

Here we obtain *analytic* equations of motion for the order parameters in a general two-layer scenario that allows us to investigate the dynamics of the learning process and the emergence of generalization ability in realizable ($K = M$), overrealizable ($K > M$), and unrealizable ($K < M$) learning scenarios.

2 Dynamical Equations

In this paper we limit our discussion to the case of the soft-committee machine [3], in which all the hidden units are connected to the output unit with positive couplings of unit strength, and only the input-to-hidden couplings are adaptive. Consider the student network: hidden unit i receives information from input unit r through the weight J_{ir}, and its activation under presentation of an input pattern $\boldsymbol{\xi} = (\xi_1, \ldots, \xi_N)$ is $x_i = \mathbf{J}_i \cdot \boldsymbol{\xi}$, with $\mathbf{J}_i = (J_{i1}, \ldots, J_{iN})$ defined as the vector of incoming weights onto the i-th hidden unit. The output of the student network is $\sigma(\mathbf{J}, \boldsymbol{\xi}) = \sum_{i=1}^{K} g\,(\mathbf{J}_i \cdot \boldsymbol{\xi})$, where g is the sigmoidal activation function of the hidden units, taken here to be the error function $g(x) \equiv \mathrm{erf}(x/\sqrt{2})$, and $\mathbf{J} \equiv \{\mathbf{J}_i\}_{1 \le i \le K}$ is the set of input-to-hidden adaptive weights.

Training examples are of the form $(\boldsymbol{\xi}^{\mu}, \zeta^{\mu})$. The components of the independently drawn input vectors $\boldsymbol{\xi}^{\mu}$ are uncorrelated random variables with zero mean and unit variance. The corresponding output ζ^{μ} is given by a deterministic teacher whose internal structure is that of a network similar to the student except for a possible difference in the number M of hidden units. Hidden unit n in the teacher network receives input information through the weight vector $\mathbf{B}_n = (B_{n1}, \ldots, B_{nN})$, and its activation under presentation of the input pattern $\boldsymbol{\xi}^{\mu}$ is $y_n^{\mu} = \mathbf{B}_n \cdot \boldsymbol{\xi}^{\mu}$. The corresponding output is $\zeta^{\mu} = \sum_{n=1}^{M} g\,(\mathbf{B}_n \cdot \boldsymbol{\xi}^{\mu})$. We will use indices $i, j, k, l, \ldots$ to refer to units in the student network and $n, m, \ldots$ for units in the teacher network.

The error made by a student with weights $\mathbf{J}$ on a given input $\boldsymbol{\xi}$ is given by the quadratic deviation

$$\epsilon(\mathbf{J},\boldsymbol{\xi}) \equiv \frac{1}{2}\left[\,\sigma(\mathbf{J},\boldsymbol{\xi}) - \zeta\,\right]^2 = \frac{1}{2}\left[\sum_{i=1}^{K} g(x_i) - \sum_{n=1}^{M} g(y_n)\right]^2 . \tag{1}$$

Performance on a typical input defines the generalization error $\epsilon_g(\mathbf{J}) \equiv\, <\epsilon(\mathbf{J},\boldsymbol{\xi})>_{\{\boldsymbol{\xi}\}}$ through an average over all possible input vectors $\boldsymbol{\xi}$, to be performed implicitly through averages over the activations $\mathbf{x} = (x_1,\ldots,x_K)$ and $\mathbf{y} = (y_1,\ldots,y_M)$. Note that both $< x_i > = < y_n > = 0$, while the components of the covariance matrix $\mathcal{C}$ are given by overlaps among the weight vectors associated with the various hidden units: $< x_i\, x_k > = \mathbf{J}_i \cdot \mathbf{J}_k \equiv Q_{ik}$, $< x_i\, y_n > = \mathbf{J}_i \cdot \mathbf{B}_n \equiv R_{in}$, and $< y_n\, y_m > = \mathbf{B}_n \cdot \mathbf{B}_m \equiv T_{nm}$. The averages over $\mathbf{x}$ and $\mathbf{y}$ are performed using a joint probability distribution given by the multivariate Gaussian:

$$\mathcal{P}(\mathbf{x},\mathbf{y}) = \frac{1}{\sqrt{(2\pi)^{K+M}|\mathcal{C}|}}\,\exp\left\{-\frac{1}{2}(\mathbf{x},\mathbf{y})^T \mathcal{C}^{-1}(\mathbf{x},\mathbf{y})\right\} , \text{ with } \mathcal{C} = \left[\begin{array}{cc} Q & R \\ R^T & T \end{array}\right] . \tag{2}$$

The averaging yields an expression for the generalization error in terms of the order parameters Q_{ik}, R_{in}, and T_{nm}. For $g(x) \equiv \mathrm{erf}(x/\sqrt{2})$ the result is:

$$\begin{aligned}
\epsilon_g(\mathbf{J}) \;=\; & \frac{1}{\pi}\left\{\sum_{ik}\arcsin\frac{Q_{ik}}{\sqrt{1+Q_{ii}}\,\sqrt{1+Q_{kk}}} + \sum_{nm}\arcsin\frac{T_{nm}}{\sqrt{1+T_{nn}}\,\sqrt{1+T_{mm}}}\right. \\
& \left. -2\sum_{in}\arcsin\frac{R_{in}}{\sqrt{1+Q_{ii}}\,\sqrt{1+T_{nn}}}\right\} .
\end{aligned} \tag{3}$$

The parameters T_{nm} are characteristic of the task to be learned and remain fixed, while the overlaps Q_{ik} and R_{in} are determined by the student weights $\mathbf{J}$ and evolve during training.

A gradient descent rule for the update of the student weights results in $\mathbf{J}_i^{\mu+1} = \mathbf{J}_i^{\mu} + \frac{\eta}{N}\,\delta_i^{\mu}\,\boldsymbol{\xi}^{\mu}$, where the learning rate η has been scaled with the input size N, and

$$\delta_i^{\mu} \equiv g'(x_i^{\mu})\left[\sum_{n=1}^{M} g(y_n^{\mu}) - \sum_{j=1}^{K} g(x_j^{\mu})\right] \tag{4}$$

is defined in terms of both the activation function g and its derivative g'.

The time evolution of the overlaps R_{in} and Q_{ik} can be explicitly written in terms of similar difference equations. The dependence on the current input $\boldsymbol{\xi}^{\mu}$ is only through the activations $\mathbf{x}$ and $\mathbf{y}$, and the corresponding averages can be performed using the joint probability distribution (2). In the thermodynamic limit $N \to \infty$ the normalized example number $\alpha = \mu/N$ can be interpreted as a continuous time variable, leading to the equations of motion:

$$\frac{dR_{in}}{d\alpha} \;=\; \eta\left\{\sum_{m} I_3(i,n,m) - \sum_{j} I_3(i,n,j)\right\} ,$$

$$\frac{dQ_{ik}}{d\alpha} \;=\; \eta\left\{\sum_{m} I_3(i,k,m) - \sum_{j} I_3(i,k,j)\right\} + \eta\left\{\sum_{m} I_3(k,i,m) - \sum_{j} I_3(k,i,j)\right\} +$$

$$\eta^2\left\{\sum_{n,m} I_4(i,k,n,m) - 2\sum_{j,n} I_4(i,k,j,n) + \sum_{j,l} I_4(i,k,j,l)\right\} . \tag{5}$$

The multivariate Gaussian integrals: $I_3 \equiv\, < g'(u)\,v\,g(w) >$ and $I_4 \equiv\, < g'(u)\,g'(v)\,g(w)\,g(z) >$ represent averages over the probability distribution (2). The averages can be performed analytically for the choice $g(x) = \mathrm{erf}(x/\sqrt{2})$. Arguments assigned to I_3 and I_4 are to be interpreted following our convention to distinguish student from teacher activations. For example, $I_3(i,n,j) \equiv\, < g'(x_i)\,y_n\,g(x_j) >$, and the average is performed using the three-dimensional covariance matrix $\mathcal{C}_3$ which results from projecting the full covariance matrix $\mathcal{C}$ of Eq. (2) onto the relevant subspace. For $I_3(i,n,j)$ the corresponding matrix is:

$$\mathcal{C}_3 = \left(\begin{array}{ccc} Q_{ii} & R_{in} & Q_{ij} \\ R_{in} & T_{nn} & R_{jn} \\ Q_{ij} & R_{jn} & Q_{jj} \end{array}\right) .$$

I_3 is given in terms of the components of the $\mathcal{C}_3$ covariance matrix by

$$I_3 = \frac{2}{\pi}\,\frac{1}{\sqrt{\Lambda_3}}\,\frac{C_{23}(1+C_{11}) - C_{12}C_{13}}{1+C_{11}} , \tag{6}$$

with $\Lambda_3 = (1+C_{11})(1+C_{33}) - C_{13}^2$. The expression for I_4 in terms of the components of the corresponding C_4 covariance matrix is

$$I_4 = \frac{4}{\pi^2} \frac{1}{\sqrt{\Lambda_4}} \arcsin\left(\frac{\Lambda_0}{\sqrt{\Lambda_1}\sqrt{\Lambda_2}}\right), \tag{7}$$

where $\Lambda_4 = (1 + C_{11})(1 + C_{22}) - C_{12}^2$, and

$$
\begin{aligned}
\Lambda_0 &= \Lambda_4 C_{34} - C_{23}C_{24}(1 + C_{11}) - C_{13}C_{14}(1 + C_{22}) + C_{12}C_{13}C_{24} + C_{12}C_{14}C_{23} , \\
\Lambda_1 &= \Lambda_4(1 + C_{33}) - C_{23}^2(1 + C_{11}) - C_{13}^2(1 + C_{22}) + 2C_{12}C_{13}C_{23} , \\
\Lambda_2 &= \Lambda_4(1 + C_{44}) - C_{24}^2(1 + C_{11}) - C_{14}^2(1 + C_{22}) + 2C_{12}C_{14}C_{24} .
\end{aligned}
$$

These dynamical equations are the main result of our paper, and provide a novel tool for analyzing the learning process for a general soft-committee machine with an arbitrary number K of hidden units, trained to perform a task defined by a soft-committee teacher with M hidden units. This set of coupled first-order differential equations can be easily integrated numerically, even for large values of K and M, providing valuable insight into the process of learning in multilayer networks, and allowing for the calculation of the time evolution of the generalization error [4]. The equations of motion (5) are easily extended to the case where the hidden-to-output teacher weights are not restricted to be positive and of unit strength, and are adaptive in the student network. The requirement of linear output units can be relaxed to allow for continuous activation functions at the output level [5].

In what follows we apply the tools developed in this section to the analysis of a variety of learning scenarios. The tasks to be learned are characterized by the number M of teacher hidden units and the matrix $T_{nm} = \mathbf{B}_n \cdot \mathbf{B}_m$. We consider uncorrelated teacher vectors, with $T_{nm} = T_n \delta_{nm}$. Two cases are of interest: i) All teacher hidden nodes are equally relevant to the implementation of the target task, as described by an isotropic teacher with $T_n = T$. The actual value of T is of no importance as long as it does not depend on n; we have used $T = 1$ in the analysis and simulations to be presented here. ii) An anisotropic teacher with uncorrelated but graded weight vectors which can be ordered according to their relevance in determining the output: $T_{n_1} \leq T_{n_2}$ for $n_1 < n_2$. As a special case of such a graded teacher we consider $T_n = n$.

The time evolution of the order parameters R_{in} and Q_{ik} follows from integrating the equations of motion (5) from initial conditions determined by a random initialization of the student vectors $\{\mathbf{J}_i\}_{1 \leq i \leq K}$. This initialization results in random norms Q_{ii} for the student weight vectors, represented here through the independent initialization of each Q_{ii} from a uniform distribution in the $[0, 0.5]$ interval, $U[0, 0.5]$. Overlaps Q_{ik} between independently chosen student vectors $\mathbf{J}_i$ and $\mathbf{J}_k$ are of order $1/\sqrt{N}$ and vanishingly small in the regime $N \gg K$. Initial values for Q_{ik}, $i \neq k$, are independently drawn from a uniform distribution $U[0, Q_o]$, with $Q_o \ll 1$. The overlaps R_{in} between a randomly initialized student vector $\mathbf{J}_i$ and an unknown teacher $\mathbf{B}_n$ are also small numbers of order $1/\sqrt{N}$ for $N \gg K$ and $N \gg M$. Initial values for each R_{in} are independently drawn from a uniform distribution $U[0, R_o]$, with $R_o \ll 1$. The numerical results shown in this paper for $Q_o = R_o = 10^{-12}$ are indistinguishable from those obtained with $Q_o = 0$. No differences arise from setting $R_o = 0$ for graded teachers, but it is necessary to keep a nonzero R_o in order to break the symmetry among teacher nodes and achieve specialization in the case of isotropic teachers.

3   Unrealizable and Overrealizable Scenarios

In this section we consider two simple examples which demonstrate the power of the approach developed here when applied to the analysis of overrealizable ($K > M$) and unrealizable ($K < M$) learning scenarios. We focus on a graded teacher with $T_{nm} = n \, \delta_{nm}$ for all $1 \leq n, m \leq M$.

The first example demonstrates that the learning process prunes unnecessary nodes when the student network has excessive resources. A teacher with $M = 2$ hidden units is to be learned by a student with $K = 3$ hidden units. The time evolution of the various order parameters is shown in Fig. 1a-c for $\eta = 1$. The picture that emerges is one of specialization with increasing α; asymptotically the first student node imitates the first teacher node ($R_{11} \to T_{11}$) while ignoring the second one ($R_{12} \to 0$), the second student node imitates the second teacher node ($R_{22} \to T_{22}$) while ignoring the first one ($R_{21} \to 0$), and the third student node gets eliminated. The evolution of the student norms shown in Fig. 1a demonstrates $Q_{11} \to T_{11} = 1$, $Q_{22} \to T_{22} = 2$, and $Q_{33} \to 0$ as $\alpha \to \infty$. The off-diagonal components Q_{ik} shown in Fig. 1b reveal an intermediate regime in which both surviving student nodes are anticorrelated while correlated with the node to be pruned. The two surviving student vectors become increasingly uncorrelated as overlaps involving the third student node decay to zero with Q_{33}. The overlap between student and teacher hidden nodes shown in Fig. 1c displays a small α behavior dominated by an undifferentiated symmetric solution, followed by a transition onto the specialization required to obtain perfect generalization. The corresponding evolution of the generalization error is shown in Fig. 1d.

The second example reveals the learning strategy in an unrealizable scenario, in which the student does not have enough resources to implement the task and cannot achieve perfect generalization as $\alpha \to \infty$. Numerical results are shown in Fig. 2 for $K = 3$, $M = 4$, and $\eta = 0.6$. Examination

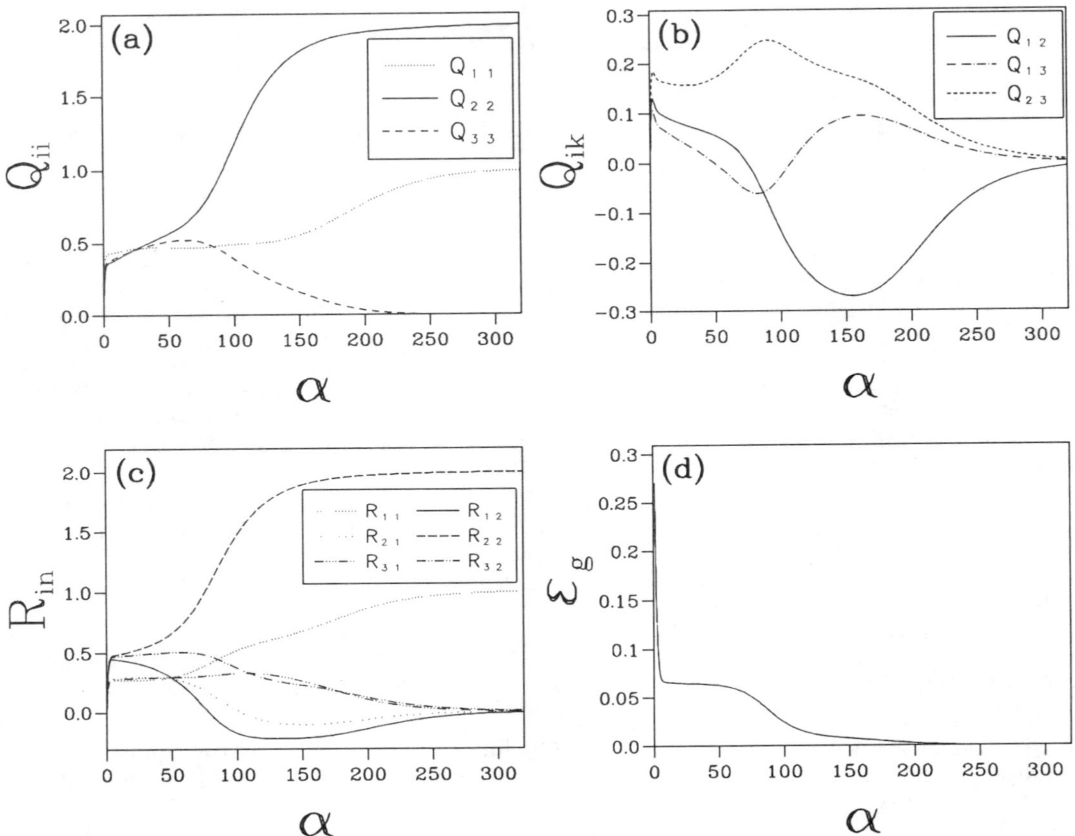

Figure 1: Dependence of the overlaps and the generalization error on the normalized number of examples α, for a three-node student learning a two-node teacher: (a) the lengths of student vectors, (b) the correlation between student vectors, (c) the overlap between various student and teacher vectors, and (d) the generalization error.

of the time evolution of the order parameters reveals an initial behavior dominated by a symmetric solution in which all three student nodes have the same overlap with any given teacher node and the only differentiation is due to the graded norm $T_{nn} = n$ of the teacher weight vectors. Trapping in the symmetric subspace is followed by a process in which each student unit specializes to one of the three dominant teacher nodes . The specialization of student node i to teacher node n results in $R_{in}^2 \to Q_{ii}T_{nn}$, so that $R_{in} \to T_{nn}$ as $Q_{ii} \to T_{nn}$. The evolution of the norm of the student vectors shown in Fig. 2a demonstrates $Q_{11} \to T_{22} = 2$, $Q_{22} \to T_{44} = 4$, and $Q_{33} \to T_{33} = 3$ as $\alpha \to \infty$. The student-teacher overlaps shown in Fig. 2c indicate that as each student node imitates one of the dominant teacher nodes, it ignores the other two dominant nodes ($R_{12} \to T_{22}$ while R_{13} and $R_{14} \to 0$, $R_{24} \to T_{44}$ while R_{22} and $R_{23} \to 0$, and $R_{33} \to T_{33}$ while R_{32} and $R_{34} \to 0$), but all three student nodes retain some overlap with the less dominant teacher node $n = 1$ (note the residual asymptotic value of R_{11}, R_{21}, and R_{31}). Such nonvanishing overlaps result in persistent correlations among the three student vectors, as shown in Fig. 2b. Note that the specialization of the student nodes does not occur simultaneously, but is ordered according to the relevance of the corresponding teacher nodes, resulting in a cascade of specialization transitions. The evolution of the generalization error shown in Fig. 2d reveals this structure: a plateau characteristic of trapping in the symmetric subspace is followed by a monotonic decrease where two observable inflection points correspond to the specialization of $i = 2$ onto $n = 4$ followed by that of $i = 3$ onto $n = 3$. An nonvanishing asymptotic error is the signature of unrealizable learning.

These examples illustrate the first step in a systematic application of the equations of motion (5) to the analysis of a given learning scenario: numerical studies of small networks that reveal the essential features are followed by studies of increasingly large networks to capture trends and regularities, which are then quantified through analytic investigation of the relevant fixed points and their stability. A detailed analysis of the unrealizable case is currently under preparation [6]; we have conducted a detailed analysis of the realizable case [7] as summarized in the following section, and extended the method to include the effect of noise at both input and output level, as well as regularization through weight decay [8].

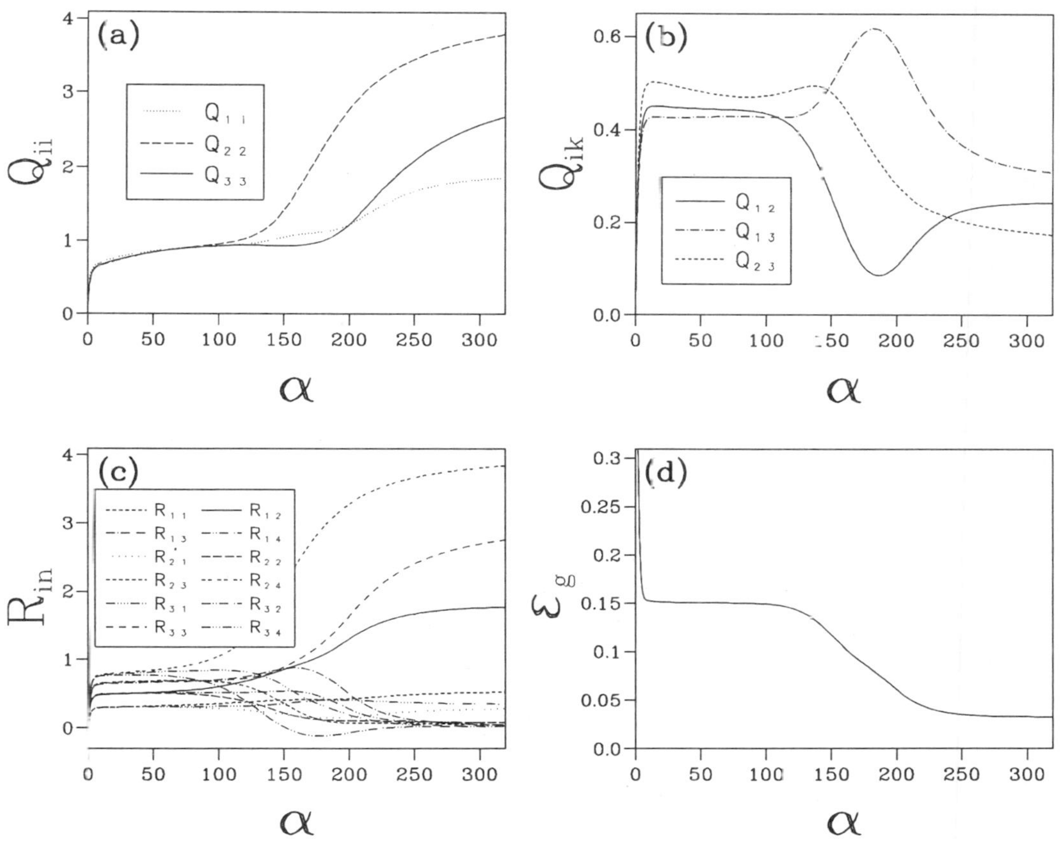

Figure 2: Dependence of the overlaps and the generalization error on the normalized number of examples α, for a three-node student learning a four-node teacher: (a) the lengths of student vectors, (b) the correlation between student vectors, (c) the overlap between various student and teacher vectors, and (d) the generalization error.

4   Realizable Scenarios

We now focus on the dynamics of learning in a realizable scenario, with $M = K$. The task to be learned is defined through uncorrelated teacher vectors of unit length, $T_{nm} = \delta_{nm}$.

We show in Fig. 3a-c the resulting evolution of the overlaps and generalization error for $M = K = 3$ and $\eta = 0.1$. This example illustrates the successive regimes of the learning process [7]. The system quickly evolves into a symmetric subspace controlled by an unstable suboptimal solution which exhibits no differentiation among the various student hidden units. Trapping in the symmetric subspace prevents the specialization needed to achieve the optimal solution, and the generalization error remains finite, as shown by the plateau in Fig. 3c. The symmetric solution is unstable, and the perturbation introduced through the random initialization of the overlaps R_{in} eventually takes over: the student units become specialized and the matrix R of student-teacher overlaps tends towards the matrix T, except for a permutational symmetry associated with the arbitrary labeling of the student hidden units. The generalization error plateau is followed by a monotonic decrease towards zero once the specialization begins and the system evolves towards the optimal solution.

Curves for the time evolution of the generalization error for different values of η shown in Fig. 3d for $K = 3$ identify trapping in the symmetric subspace as a small η phenomenon. We therefore consider the equations of motion (5) in the small η regime. The term proportional to η^2 is neglected and the resulting truncated equations of motion are used to investigate a phase characterized by students of similar norms: $Q_{ii} = Q$ for all $1 \leq i \leq K$, similar correlations among themselves: $Q_{ik} = C$ for all $i \neq k$, and similar correlations with the teacher vectors: $R_{in} = R$ for all $1 \leq i, n \leq K$. The resulting dynamical equations exhibit a fixed point solution at

$$Q^* = C^* = \frac{1}{2K - 1} \quad \text{and} \quad R^* = \sqrt{\frac{Q^*}{K}} = \frac{1}{\sqrt{K(2K - 1)}} . \tag{8}$$

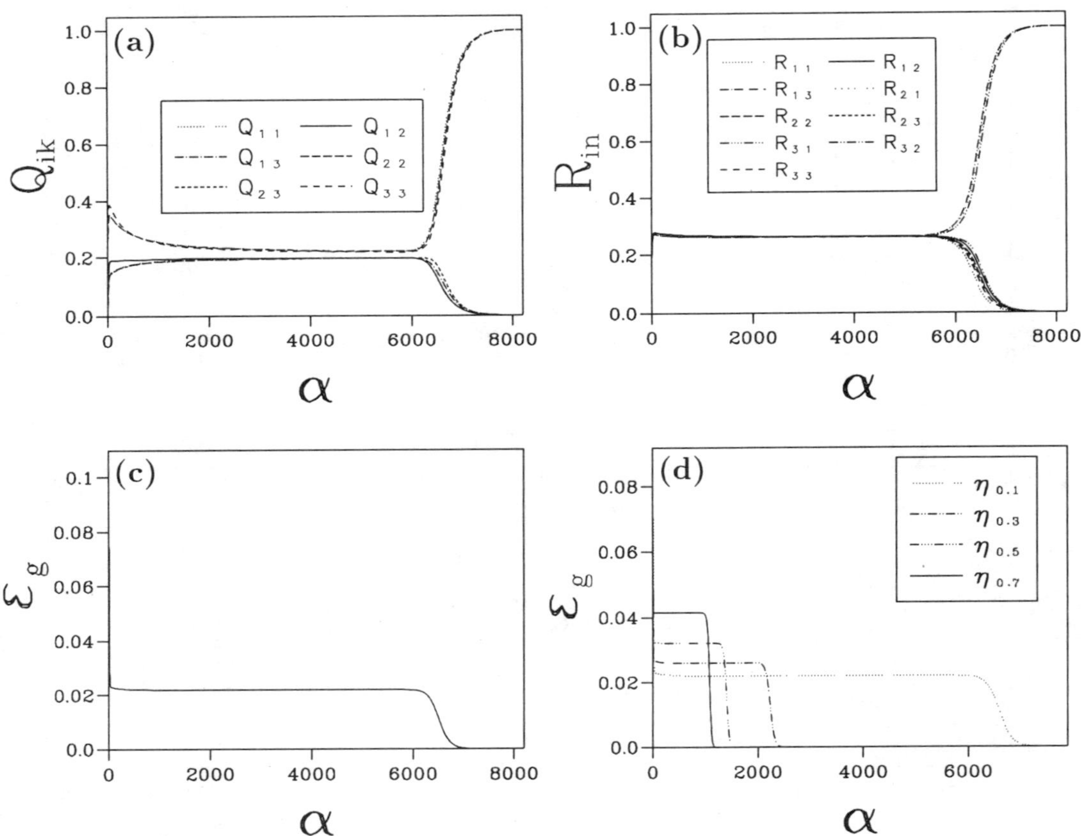

Figure 3: Dependence of the overlaps and the generalization error on the normalized number of examples α for a three-node student learning a three-node teacher characterized by $T_{nm} = \delta_{nm}$. Results for $\eta = 0.1$ are shown for (a) student-student overlaps Q_{ik} and (b) student-teacher overlaps R_{in}. The generalization error is shown in (c), and again in (d) for different values of the learning rate η.

The corresponding generalization error is given by

$$\epsilon_g^* = \frac{K}{\pi} \left\{ \frac{\pi}{6} - K \arcsin\left(\frac{1}{2K}\right) \right\} . \tag{9}$$

A simple geometrical picture explains the relation $Q^* = C^* = K(R^*)^2$ at the symmetric fixed point. The learning process confines the student vectors $\{\mathbf{J}_i\}$ to the subspace $\mathcal{S}_B$ spanned by the set of teacher vectors $\{\mathbf{B}_n\}$. For $T_{nm} = \delta_{nm}$ the teacher vectors form an orthonormal set: $\mathbf{B}_n = \mathbf{e}_n$, with $\mathbf{e}_n \cdot \mathbf{e}_m = \delta_{nm}$ for $1 \leq n, m \leq K$, and provide an expansion for the weight vectors of the trained student: $\mathbf{J}_i^* = \sum_n R_{in}\mathbf{e}_n$. The student-teacher overlaps R_{in} are independent of i in the symmetric phase and independent of n for an isotropic teacher: $R_{in} = R^*$ for all $1 \leq i, n \leq K$. The expansion $\mathbf{J}_i^* = R^* \sum_n \mathbf{e}_n$ results in $Q^* = C^* = K(R^*)^2$.

The length of the symmetric plateau is controlled by the degree of asymmetry in the initial conditions [3] and by the learning rate η. The small η analysis predicts trapping times inversely proportional to η, in quantitative agreement with the shrinking plateau of Fig. 3d. The increase in the height of the plateau with increasing η is a second order effect, as the truncated equations of motion predict a unique value of $\epsilon_g^* = 0.0203$ at $K = 3$. The mechanism for the second order effect is revealed by an examination of Fig. 3a: the student-student overlaps do agree with the prediction $C^* = 0.2$ of the small η analysis for $K = 3$, but the norms of the student vectors remain larger, at $Q = Q^* + \Delta$. The gap Δ between diagonal and off-diagonal elements is observed numerically to increase with increasing η, and is responsible for the excess generalization error. A first order expansion in Δ at $R = R^*$, $C = C^*$, and $Q = Q^* + \Delta$ yields

$$\epsilon_g = \frac{K}{\pi} \left\{ \frac{\pi}{6} - K \arcsin\left(\frac{1}{2K}\right) + \sqrt{\frac{2K-1}{2K+1}}\, \Delta \right\} , \tag{10}$$

in agreement with the trend observed in Fig. 3d.

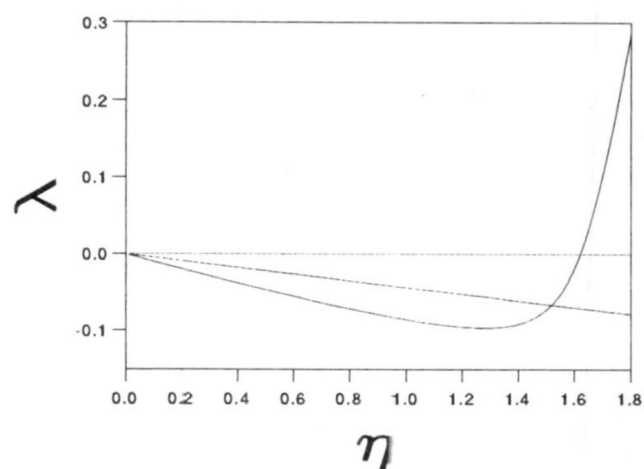

Figure 4: Dependence of the two leading decay eigenvalues on the learning rate η in the realizable case: λ_1 (curved line) and λ_2 (straight line) are shown for $M = K = 3$.

The excess norm Δ of the student vectors corresponds to a residual component in $\mathbf{J}_i$ not confined to the subspace $\mathcal{S}_B$. The weight vectors of the trained student can be written as $\mathbf{J}_i = R^* \sum_n \mathbf{e}_n + \mathbf{J}_i^\perp$, with $\mathbf{J}_i^\perp \cdot \mathbf{e}_n = 0$ for all $1 \leq n \leq K$. Student weight vectors are not constrained to be identical; they differ through orthogonal components $\mathbf{J}_i^\perp$ which are typically uncorrelated: $\mathbf{J}_i^\perp \cdot \mathbf{J}_k^\perp = 0$ for $i \neq k$. Correlations $Q_{ik} = C$ do satisfy $C = C^* = K(R^*)^2$, but norms $Q_{ii} = Q$ are given by $Q = Q^* + \Delta$, with $\Delta = \| \mathbf{J}^\perp \|^2$. Learning at very small η tends to eliminate $\mathbf{J}^\perp$ and confine the student vectors to $\mathcal{S}_B$.

Escape from the symmetric subspace signals the onset of hidden unit specialization. As shown in Fig. 3b, the process is driven by a breaking of the uniformity of the student-teacher correlations: each student node becomes increasingly specialized to a specific teacher node, while its overlap with the remaining teacher nodes decreases and eventually decays to zero. The matrix of student-teacher overlaps can no longer be characterized by a unique parameter, as we need to distinguish between a dominant overlap R between a given student node and the teacher node it begins to imitate, and secondary overlaps S between the same student node and the remaining teacher nodes. The student nodes can be relabeled so as to bring the matrix of student-teacher overlaps to the form $R_{in} = R\delta_{in} + S(1 - \delta_{in})$. The emerging differentiation among student vectors results in a decrease of the overlaps $Q_{ik} = C$ for $i \neq k$, while their norms $Q_{ii} = Q$ increase. The matrix of student-student overlaps takes the form $Q_{ik} = Q\delta_{ik} + C(1 - \delta_{ik})$.

In order to describe the incipient specialization as the student network escapes from the symmetric subspace we extend the small η analysis to allow for $S \neq R$. The resulting dynamical equations are linearized around the fixed point solution at $Q^* = C^* = 1/(2K - 1)$ and $R^* = S^* = 1/\sqrt{K(2K - 1)}$, and the generalization error is expanded around its fixed point value (9) to first order in the deviations q, c, r, and s. The analysis identifies a relevant perturbation with $q = c = 0$ and $s = -r/(K-1)$, which leaves the generalization error unchanged and explains the behavior illustrated in Fig. 3a-b. It is the differentiation between R and S which signals the escape from the symmetric subspace; the differentiation between Q and C occurs for larger values of α. The relevant perturbation corresponds to an enhancement of the overlap $R = R^* + r$ between a given student node and the teacher node it is learning to imitate, while the overlap $S = S^* + s$ between the same student node and the remaining teacher nodes is weakened. The time constant associated with this mode is $\tau = (\pi/2K)(2K - 1)^{1/2}(2K + 1)^{3/2}$, with $\tau \sim 2\pi K$ in the large K limit. Trapping times are inversely proportional to η and directly proportional to τ.

As the specialization continues, the dominant overlaps R grow, and the secondary overlaps S decay to zero. Further specialization involves the decay to zero of the student-student correlations C and the growth of the norms Q of the student vectors. To investigate the convergence to the optimal solution we linearize the equations of motion around the asymptotic fixed point at $S^* = C^* = 0$, $R^* = Q^* = 1$, with $\epsilon_g^* = 0$. We describe convergence to the optimal solution by applying the full equations of motion (5) to a phase characterized by $R_{in} = R\delta_{in} + S(1 - \delta_{in})$ and $Q_{ik} = Q\delta_{ik} + C(1 - \delta_{in})$.

Linearization of the full equations of motion around the asymptotic fixed point results in four eigenvalues; the dependence of the two largest eigenvalues on η is shown in Fig. 4 for $M = K = 3$. An initially slow mode corresponds to the eigenvalue λ_2 (straight line), which remains negative for all values of η, while the eigenvalue λ_1 (curved line) for the initially fast mode becomes positive as η exceeds η_{max}, given by

$$\eta_{max} = \frac{\pi}{K} \frac{75 - 42\sqrt{3}}{25\sqrt{3} - 42} \tag{11}$$

to first order in $1/K$. The optimal solution with $\epsilon_g^* = 0$ is not accessible for $\eta > \eta_{max}$. Exponential convergence of R, S, C, and Q to their optimal values is guaranteed for all learning rates in the range $(0, \eta_{max})$; in this regime the generalization error decays exponentially to $\epsilon_g^* = 0$, with a rate controlled by the slowest decay mode. An expansion of ϵ_g in terms of $r = 1 - R$, s, c, and $q = 1 - Q$ reveals that of the leading modes whose eigenvalues are shown in Fig. 4 only the mode associated with λ_1 contributes to the decay of the linear term, while the decay of the second order term is controlled by the mode associated with λ_2 and dominates the convergence if $2|\lambda_2| < |\lambda_1|$. The learning rate η_{opt} which guarantees fastest asymptotic decay for the generalization error follows from the condition $\lambda_1(\eta_{opt}) = 2\lambda_2(\eta_{opt})$. The ratio

η_{opt}/η_{max} is a monotonically decreasing function of K and takes values within the relatively narrow range $(0.52, 0.55)$. This result provides analytic support to the heuristic practice of chossing $\eta_{opt} \approx (1/2)\eta_{max}$.

Specialization as described here and illustrated in Fig. 3 is a simultaneous process in which each student node acquires a strong correlation with a specific teacher node while becoming decorrelated from the remaining teacher nodes. Such synchronous escape from the symmetric phase is characteristic of learning scenarios where the target task is defined through an isotropic teacher. In the case of a graded teacher characterized by $T_{nm} = n\,\delta_{nm}$ we find that specialization occurs through a sequence of escapes from the symmetric subspace ordered according to the relevance of the corresponding teacher nodes, as shown in the preceding section.

Acknowledgment The work reported here has been done in collaboration with David Saad; I thank him for a most enjoyable interaction.

References

[1] J. S. Denker, D. B. Schwartz, B. Wittner, S. A. Solla, R. E. Howard, L. D. Jackel, and J. J. Hopfield, 'Automatic learning, rule extraction, and generalization,' *Complex Systems*, vol. 1, 877 (1987).

[2] G. Cybenko, 'Approximations by superpositions of a sigmoidal function,' *Math. Control Signals and Systems*, vol. 2, 303 (1989).

[3] M. Biehl and H. Schwarze, 'Learning by online gradient descent,' *J. Phys. A*, vol. 28, 643 (1995).

[4] D. Saad and S. A. Solla, 'Exact solution for on-line learning in multilayer neural networks,' *Phys. Rev. Lett.* , vol. 74, 4337 (1995).

[5] P. Riegler and M. Biehl, 'On-line backpropagation in two-layered neural networks,' *J. Phys. A*, vol. 28, L507 (1995).

[6] D. Saad and S. A. Solla, 'On-line learning of unlearnable tasks,' in preparation (1996).

[7] D. Saad and S. A. Solla, 'On-line learning in soft committee machines,' *Phys. Rev. E*, vol. 52, 4225 (1995).

[8] D. Saad and S. A. Solla, 'Learning from corrupted examples in multilayer neural networks,' in preparation (1996).

Monotonicity Hints for Credit Screening

Joseph Sill[†], Yaser Abu-Mostafa[‡]
† Computation and Neural Systems program, California Institute of Technology
Pasadena, CA
‡ Departments of Electrical Engineering and Computer Science, California Institute of Technology
Pasadena, CA

Abstract— **A hint is any piece of side information about the target function to be learned. We describe an application of monotonicity hints to a real world problem. The task considered is the screening of credit card applicants. A measure of the monotonicity error of a candidate function is defined and an objective function for the enforcement of monotonicity is derived from Bayesian principles. We report experimental results which show that using monotonicity hints leads to a statistically significant improvement in performance on the credit screening problem.**

1 Introduction

Designing a machine learning model involves balancing two conflicting concerns [1]. The model used should be powerful enough to implement the details of the unknown target function f, but simple enough that the optimal parameters for doing so may be estimated accurately from the available data.

The use of hints [2] in the learning process allows us to satisfy the second requirement better without compromising the first. A hint is any piece of information known about f beyond the available input-output examples. For instance, f may be known to be invariant or symmetric with respect to some transformation of the input. The constraint imposed by a hint results in a model which is effectively simpler and has fewer degrees of freedom [3]. However, no loss in the ability to implement f is incurred[1], since f is known to satisfy the constraint. Invariances in character recognition [4] and symmetries in financial market forecasting [5] are some of the instances of hints which have proved beneficial to learning systems applied to real-world problems.

Monotonicity is another hint which suggests itself in many applications. In screening credit card applicants, for instance, one might expect that the probability of default decreases monotonically with the applicant's salary. This paper describes the incorporation of monotonicity hints into a learning system applied to a noisy real-world classification task concerned with credit card applications. Artificial neural networks are the learning models used here, although the method may be used with other models as well.

Section II derives, from Bayesian principles, an appropriate objective function for simultaneously enforcing monotonicity and fitting the data. Section III discusses the rationale behind the assertion of monotonicity for the credit card application and describes the details and results of the experiments. Section IV analyzes the results and considers possible future directions.

2 Bayesian Interpretation of Objective Function

Let $\mathbf{x}$ be a vector drawn from the input distribution and $\mathbf{x}'$ be such that

$$\forall j \neq i, x'_j = x_j \tag{1}$$

$$x'_i > x_i \tag{2}$$

The statement that f is monotonically increasing in input variable x_i means that for all such $\mathbf{x}, \mathbf{x}'$ defined as above

$$f(\mathbf{x}') \geq f(\mathbf{x}) \tag{3}$$

Decreasing monotonicity is defined similarly.

---

[1]This is true assuming the model can implement f exactly. If this is not the case, satisfying a hint may lead to some loss in approximation ability, but is usually still beneficial on the balance.

Suppose we believe the target function f to be monotonic in all input variables- monotonically increasing in some and monotonically decreasing in others. We wish to define a single scalar measure of the degree to which a particular candidate function y violates this set of monotonicities.

One such natural measure, the one used in the experiments in Section IV, is defined in the following way: Let $\mathbf{x}$ be an input vector drawn from the input distribution. Let one input variable be chosen randomly from a uniform distribution over the set of input variables. Define a perturbation distribution, e.g., U[0,1], and draw δx_i from this distribution, where the subscript i indicates the input variable chosen. Define $\mathbf{x}'$ such that

$$\forall j \neq i, x'_j = x_j \tag{4}$$

$$x'_i = x_i + sgn(i) * \delta x_i \tag{5}$$

where $sgn(i) = 1$ or -1 depending on whether f is monotonically increasing or decreasing in variable i. We will call E_h the *monotonicity error* of y on the input pair $(\mathbf{x}, \mathbf{x}')$.

$$E_h = \begin{cases} 0 & y(\mathbf{x}') \geq y(\mathbf{x}) \\ (y(\mathbf{x}) - y(\mathbf{x}'))^2 & y(\mathbf{x}') < y(\mathbf{x}) \end{cases} \tag{6}$$

Our measure of y's violation of f's set of monotonicities is $E[E_h]$, where the expectation is taken with respect to random variables $\mathbf{x}$, i, and δx_i.

We believe that the best possible approximation to f given the architecture used is probably approximately monotonic. This belief may be quantified in a prior distribution over the candidate functions implementable by the architecture:

$$Pr(y) \propto e^{-\lambda E[E_h]} \tag{7}$$

This distribution represents the *a priori* probability density, or likelihood, assigned to a candidate function with a given level of monotonicity error. The normalization constant is unimportant and is neglected here. The probability that a function is the best possible approximation to f decreases exponentially with the increase in monotonicity error. λ is a positive constant which indicates how strong our bias is towards monotonic functions.

In addition to obeying prior information, the model should fit the data well. The two possible classes are denoted by 0 and 1, respectively. We take the network output y to represent the probability of class 1 conditioned on the observation of the input vector. Under this interpretation, the log likelihood of observing the data (normalized by the number of examples M) assuming that the network is the correct model is given by

$$\frac{1}{M} \sum_{m=1}^{M} c_m log(y_m) + (1 - c_m)log(1 - y_m) \tag{8}$$

where m is an index over the examples, c_m represents the class of example m, and y_m represents the network output on example m. We wish to pick the most probable model given the data. Equivalently, we may choose to maximize $log(P(model|data))$. Using Bayes' Theorem,

$$log(P(model|data)) \propto log(P(data|model) + log(P(model)) \tag{9}$$

$$= \frac{1}{M} \sum_{m=1}^{M} c_m log(y_m) + (1 - c_m)log(1 - y_m) - \lambda E[E_h] \tag{10}$$

The Bayesian prior leads to a familiar form of objective function, with the first term reflecting the desire to fit the data and a second term penalizing deviation from monotonicity.

3   Experimental Results

The credit card database was obtained via FTP from the machine learning database repository maintained by UC-Irvine [2]. The task is to predict whether or not an applicant will default. For each of 690 applicant case histories, the database contains 15 features describing the applicant plus the class label indicating whether or not a default ultimately occurred. The meaning of the features is confidential for proprietary reasons. Only the 6 continuous features were used in the experiments reported here. 24 of the case histories had at least one feature missing. These examples were omitted, leaving 666 which were used in the experiments. The two class labels occur with nearly equal frequency; the split is 55%-45%.

Intuition suggests that the classification should be monotonic in the features. Although the specific meanings of the continuous features are not known, we assume here that they represent various quantities such as salary, assets, debt, number of years at current job, etc. Common sense dictates that the higher the salary or the lower the debt, the less likely a default is, all else being equal. Monotonicity in all features was therefore asserted.

In all experiments, batch-mode backpropagation with a simple adaptive learning rate scheme was used [3]. Several methods were tested. The performance of a linear perceptron was observed for benchmark purposes. For the experiments using nonlinear methods, a single hidden layer neural network with 6 hidden units and direct input-output connections was used. The most basic method tested was simply to train the network on all the training data for the full 5000 iterations. Another technique tried was to use a validation set to avoid overfitting. Training for all of these models was performed by maximizing (8). Finally, training the networks with the monotonicity constraints was performed, using an approximation to (10).

The linear perceptrons were trained for 300 batch mode iterations each, while the nonlinear networks were trained for 5000 batch mode iterations. These amounts of training more than sufficed for the networks to approach regions near minima where the decrease in training error had become very slow.

A leave-k-out procedure was used in order to get statistically significant comparisons of the difference in performance. For each method, the data was randomly partitioned 200 different ways into 550 training examples and 116 test examples. The results shown in Table 1 are averages over the 200 different partitions.

In the early stopping experiments, the training set was further subdivided into 450 examples used for direct training and 100 validation examples. The classification error on the validation set was monitored over the course of the 5000 iterations, and the values of the network weights at the point of lowest validation error were chosen as the final values.

The process of training the networks with the monotonicity hints was divided into two stages. Since the meanings of the features were unaccessible, the directions of monotonicity were not known *a priori*. These directions were determined by training a linear perceptron on the training data for 300 iterations and observing the resulting weights. A positive weight was taken to imply increasing monotonicity, while a negative weight meant decreasing monotonicity.

Once the directions of monotonicity were determined, a two-layer network with 6 hidden units was trained by maximizing an approximation to the theoretical objective function (10) derived in the previous section:

$$\frac{1}{M} \sum_{m=1}^{M} c_m log(y_m) + (1 - c_m)log(1 - y_m) - \frac{\lambda}{N} \sum_{n=1}^{N} E_{h,n} \qquad (11)$$

$E_{h,n}$ represents the network's monotonicity error on a particular pair of input vectors $\mathbf{x}, \mathbf{x}'$. Each pair was generated according to the method described in Section II. The input distribution was modelled as a joint gaussian with a covariance matrix estimated from the training data. The input variables were normalized to have zero mean and unit variance.

For each input variable, 500 pairs of vectors representing monotonicity in that variable were generated. This yielded a total of N=3000 hint example pairs. λ was chosen to be 5000. No optimization of λ was attempted; 5000 was chosen somewhat arbitrarily as simply a high value which would greatly penalize

---

[2] The database may be obtained as follows: ftp ics.uci.edu. cd pub/machine-learning-databases/credit-screening.
[3] If the previous iteration resulted in a increase in likelihood, the learning rate was increased by 3%. If the likelihood decreased, the learning rate was cut in half

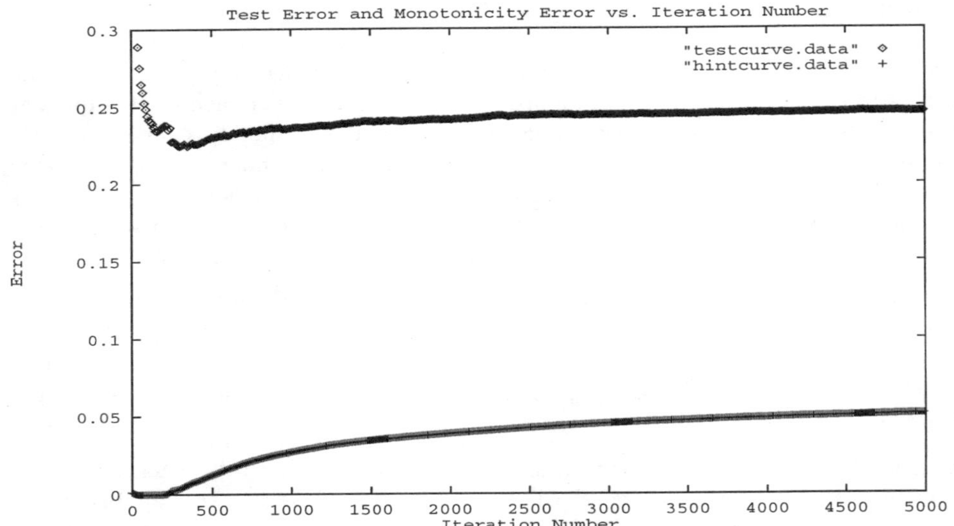

Figure 1: The violation of monotonicity tracks the overfitting occurring during training

non-monotonicity. Hint generalization, i.e. monotonicity test error, was measured by using 100 pairs of vectors for each variable which were not trained on but whose monotonicity error was calculated. For contrast, monotonicity test error was also monitored for the two-layer networks trained only on the input-output examples. Figure 1 is a plot of out-of-sample classification rate (test error) and of monotonicity error vs. training time for the networks trained only on (8), averaged over the 200 different data splits. The monotonicity error is multiplied by a factor of 10 in the figure to make it more easily visible. The figure indicates a substantial correlation between overfitting and monotonicity error during the course of training.

Method	training error	test error	hint test error
Linear	$22.7\% \pm 0.1\%$	$23.7\% \pm 0.2\%$	-
6-6-1 net	$15.2\% \pm 0.1\%$	$24.6\% \pm 0.3\%$	.005115
6-6-1 net, w/val.	$18.8\% \pm 0.2\%$	$23.4\% \pm 0.3\%$	-
6-6-1 net, w/hint	$18.7\% \pm 0.1\%$	$21.8\% \pm 0.2\%$	.000020

Table 1: Performance of methods tested

The performance of each method is shown in table 1. Without early stopping, the two-layer network overfits and performs worse than a linear model. Even with early stopping, the performance of the linear model and the two-layer network are almost the same; the difference is not statistically significant. This similarity in performance is consistent with the thesis of a monotonic target function. A monotonic classifier may be thought of as a mildly nonlinear generalization of a linear classifier. The two-layer network does have the advantage of being able to implement some of this nonlinearity. However, this advantage is cancelled out (and in other cases could be outweighed) by the overfitting resulting from excessive and unnecessary degrees of freedom. When monotonicity hints are introduced, much of this unnecessary freedom is eliminated, although the network is still allowed to implement monotonic nonlinearities. Accordingly, a modest but clearly statistically significant improvement (nearly 2%) results from the introduction of monotonicity hints. Such an improvement could translate into a substantial increase in profit for a bank.

4   Conclusion

This paper has shown that monotonicity hints can significantly improve the performance of a neural network on a noisy binary classification task. It is worthwhile to note that the beneficial effect of imposing monotonicity does not necessarily imply that the target function is entirely monotonic. If there exist some non-monotonicities in the target function, then monotonicity hints may result in some decrease in the model's ability to implement this function. It may be, though, that this penalty is outweighed by the improved estimation of model parameters due to the decrease in model complexity. Therefore, the use of monotonicity hints probably should be considered in cases where the target function is thought to be at least roughly monotonic and the training examples are limited in number and noisy.

The reverse of the above point is also true: the target function may be strictly monotonic, and yet it may be best in some cases to enforce monotonicity in a model only approximately. Normally, it is not known whether the model being used has sufficient power to implement the target function exactly. Suppose the model does not have enough resources (e.g. not enough hidden units). Then there will be some discrepancy between the model's best possible approximation y^* and the target function f. From the monotonicity of f, it does not necessarily follow that y^* is *strictly* monotonic. The model may need to violate monotonicity slightly in order to do the best it can in approximating f. Enforcing monotonicity in the way presented here (i.e., "softly", with a penalty term) allows the model this freedom.

Future work may include the application of monotonicity hints to other real world problems and further investigations into the experimental details of enforcing the hints. An interesting theoretical question also arises: what is the capacity of the class of monotonic functions? The answer would provide a bound on the capacity of any particular model where monotonicity hints are enforced.

References

[1] S. Geman, E. Bienenstock & R. Doursat. "Neural Networks and the bias/variance dilemma" *Neural Computation*, vol. 4, pp. 1-58, 1992.

[2] Y. Abu-Mostafa. "Hints" *Neural Computation*, vol. 7, pp. 639-671, 1995.

[3] Y. Abu-Mostafa. "Hints and the VC Dimension" *Neural Computation*, vol. 4, pp. 278-288, 1993.

[4] P. Simard, Y. LeCun & J Denker. "Efficient Pattern Recognition Using a New Transformation Distance" *NIPS5*, pp. 50-58.

[5] Y. Abu-Mostafa. "Financial Market Applications of Learning from Hints" *Neural Networks in the Capital Markets*, A. Refenes, ed., pp. 221-232. Wiley, London, UK.

Supervised Competitive Learning with Adaptive Similarity

Kosei Demura, Yuichiro Anzai
Department of Computer Science, Keio University
Yokohama, 223 Japan
email:demura@aa.cs.keio.ac.jp

Abstract— The generalization ability of supervised competitive learning algorithms is determined by their similarity measures. However conventional competitive learning algorithms use the euclidean distance, the direction cosines, the inner product and so on. Therefore, the generalization ability is not desirable when the data structure is not based on those similarity measures. To improve the generalization, we introduce the adaptive similarity that adapts the similarity during the course of training. The basic idea of the adaptive similarity is to minimize the distance of data that belongs to the same category and to maximize the distance of data that belongs to different categories on a similarity space. To compute the adaptive similarity, we use the gradient decent method with a modular network that is composed of two subnetworks. Each subnetwork computes the similarity and an output of the modular network is an average of those networks. The adaptive similarity improves the generalization ability of supervised competitive learning algorithms significantly.

1 Introduction

Competitive learning(CL) algorithms adaptively quantize weight vectors according to the nearest neighbor rule. Self-organizing feature map(SOFM)[1] by Kohonen, adaptive resonance theory[3], Hamming networks[4], Counter-propagation[5], etc. are based on the principle of CL algorithms. It is widely used in applications such as pattern recognition, speech recognition, robot control, image coding and compression, and other tasks.

Some of those applications showed good results, however those results are not satisfactory compared to other methods in solving general problems.

The reason why the generalization ability is not desirable is that CL algorithms use the euclidean distance or the direction cosines for the similarity measure to determine the winner unit. Those similarity measures are independent from the structure of a data set. That is, a computation of the similarity never changes. The similarity is made by those similarity measures, does not correspond with the similarity of the training set. Therefore, conventional supervised competitive learning(SCL) algorithms do not have the good generalization ability.

To improve the generalization power, we introduce the adaptive similarity for CL algorithms that adapts the similarity measure according to the training set.

We present comparative results for a classification problem, showing a drastic performance improvement over the conventional SCL algorithms.

2 Supervised Competitive Learning

Supervised competitive learning[1, 2] starts the training as follows. A network calculates similarities between an input datum $\mathbf{x(t)}$ and weights vectors $\mathbf{w}_i(t)(i = 0, 1, \cdots, N)$, and selects the winner that is the highest value of its similarities. The winner unit changes weights as

$$\mathbf{w}_i(t + 1) = \mathbf{w}_i(t) + \alpha(t)[\mathbf{x(t)} - \mathbf{w}_i(t)] \tag{1}$$

if $\mathbf{x}$ is classified correctly,

$$\mathbf{w}_i(t + 1) = \mathbf{w}_i(t) - \alpha(t)[\mathbf{x(t)} - \mathbf{w}_i(t)] \tag{2}$$

if $\mathbf{x}$ is not classified correctly

where $0 \leq \alpha(t) \leq 1$ and $\alpha(t)$ defines a function that decreases slowly.

This algorithm shows that SCL algorithms determine the class borders according to the nearest neighbor algorithm.

3 Adaptive Similarity

3.1 Definition

Input data $\mathbf{x}_p (p = 1, 2, \cdots, P)$ are N dimensional row vectors as follows

$$\mathbf{x}_p = (x_{p1}, \cdots, x_{pi}, \cdots, x_{pN}), \tag{3}$$

where $0 \le x_{pi} \le 1$ $(i = 1, 2, \cdots, N)$, N and P are the number of attributes of $\mathbf{x}_p$ and training data, respectively.

3.2 Adaptive Similarity

Conventional SCL algorithms use the euclidean distance, the direction cosines, the inner product and others for the similarity measure. In the case of the supervised learning, those similarity measures do not present the similarity between training data properly. Because those similarity measures do not use the information of the supervisor. In this paper, we introduce the adaptive similarity that uses the information of the supervisor and adjusts the similarity based on the training set.

Let us first describe an axiom of the similarity $s(\mathbf{x}_p, \mathbf{x}_q)$ between $\mathbf{x}_p$ and $\mathbf{x}_q$.

$$i)\ s(\mathbf{x}_p, \mathbf{x}_p) \ =\ 1 \tag{4}$$

$$ii)\ s(\mathbf{x}_p, \mathbf{x}_q) \ =\ s(\mathbf{x}_q, \mathbf{x}_p) \tag{5}$$

$$iii)\ s(\mathbf{x}_p, \mathbf{x}_r) \ <\ s(\mathbf{x}_q, \mathbf{x}_r); \mathbf{x}_p \in C_i, \mathbf{x}_q \in C_j, \mathbf{x}_r \in C_j (i \ne j) \tag{6}$$

where C_i is a category i.

We want to make the adaptive similarity that is defined by the training set and satisfies the above axiom. The basic idea of the adaptive similarity is to minimize the distance of data that belongs to the same category and to maximize the distance of data that belongs to the different category.

The adaptive similarity $s_a(\mathbf{x}_p, \mathbf{x}_q)$ is defined as follows

$$s_a(\mathbf{x}_p, \mathbf{x}_q) \ =\ \frac{f(\sum_j v_j y_j + \phi) + f(\sum_j v'_j y'_j + \phi')}{2} \tag{7}$$

$$y_j \ =\ f(\sum_i w1_{ji} x_{pi} + \sum_i w2_{ji} x_{qi} + \theta_j) \tag{8}$$

$$y'_j \ =\ f(\sum_i w1'_{ji} x_{qi} + \sum_i w2'_{ji} x_{pi} + \theta'_j) \tag{9}$$

$$f(x) \ =\ 1/(1 + exp(-x)) \tag{10}$$

where $v_j, v'_j, w1_{ji}, w2_{ji}, w1'_{ji}, w2'_{ji}, \phi, \phi', \theta_j, \theta'_j$ are parameters.

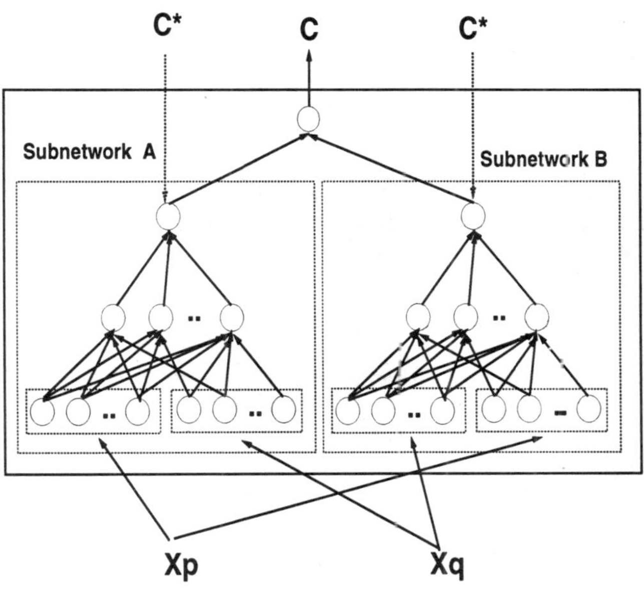

Fig. 1: Adaptive Similarity Network

3.3   Algorithm

To compute the adaptive similarity, we use a modular network architecture as shown in Fig.1, that is composed of two subnetworks and each subnetwork is a three-layer feedforward network with an input layer, a hidden layer and an output layer. The reason why a modular network has two subnetwork is to satisfy Equation (5). Each subnetwork computes the similarity and an output of the modular network is an average of outputs of subnetworks.

To determine the parameters of the adaptive similarity, we define the cost function E such as

$$E \;=\; \sum_{p}\sum_{q}(c^* - s_a(\mathbf{x}_p, \mathbf{x}_q))^2 \tag{11}$$

$$c^* \;=\; 1 \;\; if \;\; \mathbf{x}_p, \mathbf{x}_q \in C_k \tag{12}$$

$$c^* \;=\; 0 \;\; if \;\; \mathbf{x}_p \in C_j, \mathbf{x}_q \in C_k (j \neq k) \tag{13}$$

The parameters Δw_{ij} of the adaptive similarity are adjusted based on the simple gradient descent rule

$$\Delta w_{ij} = -\eta \, \frac{\partial E}{\partial w_{ij}} \tag{14}$$

4   Simulation Results

We examine the generalization ability of BP, Supervised competitive learning (SCL) and Competitive learning with the adaptive similarity(CLAS) with respect to a five-input logic function $g = (X1 \bigvee X2) \bigwedge (X4 \bigvee X5)$ which is non-linearly separable. TABLE 1 shows the training set. Each instance of the training set belongs to either a positive instance(a value of the function g is 1) or a negative instance(a value of g is 0).

Fig.4 shows the simulation result of BP, SCL and CLAS. The horizontal axis gives the number of training data. As there are 5 input units, the maximum number of training data is 32. If the number of training data is 5, we use 27 unknown data for the test of generalization. The vertical axis gives the accuracy of the classification for unknown data. We generate 50 random data for the simulation.

The network structure of BP is a 5-2-1 feedforward network, set a learning rate η to 1.0 and a momentum term α to 0.2. Each subnetwork of CLAS is a 10-4-1 feedforward network and parameters is the same as BP.

The accuracy of SCL is not above than about 70 %. On the other hand, the accuracy of CLAS increases as the number of training examples increase and shows the best generalization ability. Fig.2 and Fig.3 show the reason why the generalization ability is so different. Fig.2 represents a distribution of the training set on the similarity plane of which the horizontal axis and the vertical axis represent the averaged similarity over all positive instances and negative instances, respectively. Each plot in Fig.2 and Fig.3 represents a training example. For example, the training example $\mathbf{p}_1$ is mapped in the similarity plane as follows. The value of the horizontal axis is the averaged similarity between $\mathbf{p}_1$ and the positive instances($\mathbf{p}_2, \mathbf{p}_3, \cdots, \mathbf{p}_{31}$). The value of the vertical axis is the averaged similarity between $\mathbf{p}_1$ and the negative instances($\mathbf{p}_4, \cdots, \mathbf{p}_{30}, \mathbf{p}_{32}$). The other plots are computed in a similar way. Therefore, there are 32 plots in Fig.2 and Fig.3. The distribution is computed based on the direction cosines, and the distribution of Fig.3 is computed based on the adaptive similarity network which was trained for 100 epochs.

It is difficult to determine the border which separates two instances in Fig.2. On the other hand, it is very easy to determine the border in Fig.3. Therefore, the acurracy of CLAS increases as the number of training examples increases and shows the best generalization ability. This simulation results indicate that the adaptive similarity improves the generalization ability of CL algorithms significantly.

5   Conclusion

We have described the adaptive similarity that adapts the similarity measure on the course of training and improves the generalization ability of SCL algorithms significantly.

The conventional similarity measures such as the euclidean distance, the inner product, the humming distance, etc. are not suitable for SCL algorithms. Therefore we introduced the adaptive similarity for SCL algorithms. The adaptive similarity is constructed by the training set and it does not use any a priori knowledges except the axiom of the similarity.

However, the adaptive similarity network needs N^2 training examples for learning where N is the number of the original training data, thus it requires the high computational cost. To reduce the computational cost is the prime topic of our future works.

6 Acknowledgements

This work has been supported by the Japan Society for the Promotion of Science.

References

[1] Kohonen,T.: "Self-Organization Maps", Springer-Verlag, 1994

[2] Kosko,B.: "Stochastic Competitive Learning", IEEE Trans. Neural Networks, Vol.2, No.5, pp.522-529, 1991

[3] Carpenter, G.A. and S. Grossberg:"The ART of Adaptive pattern Recognition by a Self-Organizing Neural Network" , IEEE Computer,pp.77-88,1988

[4] Yang, X. and Yu, F.T.S.:"Optical implementation of the hamming net", Applied Optics, Vol.31. pp.3999-4003,1992

[5] Hecht-Nielsen, R.:"Counterpropagation networks", Applied Optics, Vol.26, pp.4979-4984,1987

TABLE 1

$$g = (X1 \lor X2) \land (X4 \lor X5)$$

	$X1$	$X2$	$X3$	$X4$	$X5$	g
p_1	1	1	1	1	1	1
p_2	1	1	1	1	0	1
p_3	1	1	1	0	1	1
p_4	1	1	1	0	0	0
...	...	...	...	...	...	...
p_{30}	0	0	0	0	1	0
p_{31}	0	0	0	0	0	1
p_{32}	0	0	0	0	0	0

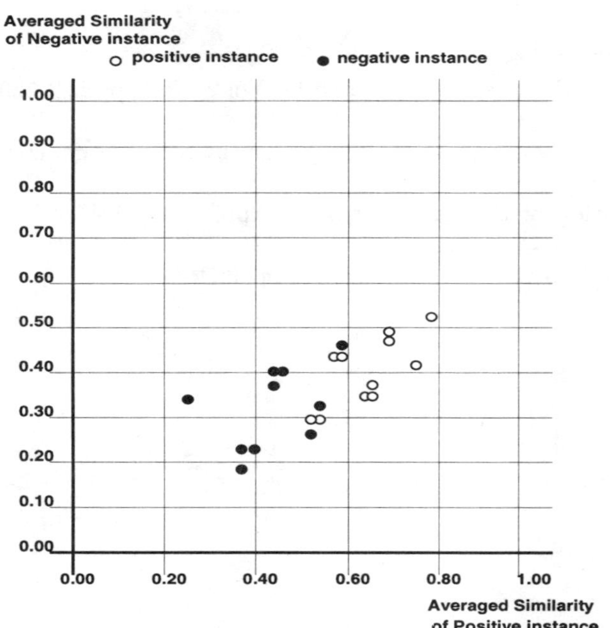

Fig. 2: Direction Cosines

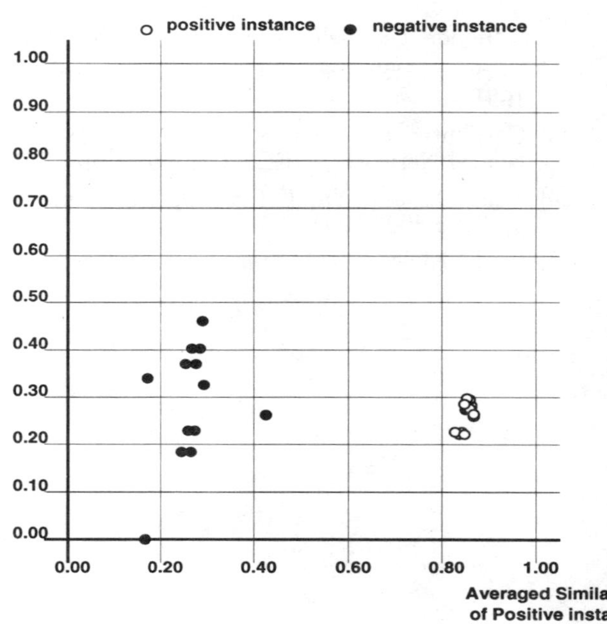

Fig. 3: Adaptive Similarity

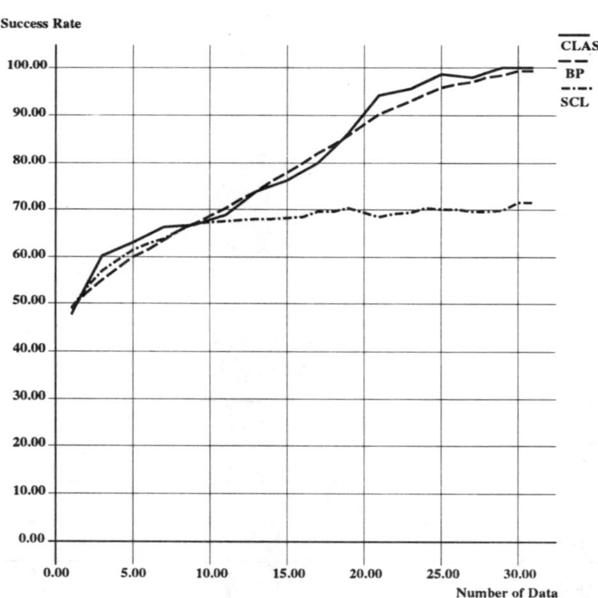

Fig. 4: $f = (X1 \bigvee X2) \bigwedge (X4 \bigvee X5)$

DISTRIBUTION BASED TREES ARE MORE ACCURATE

Nong Shang   Leo Breiman
School of Public Health   Statistics Department
University of California   University of California
shang@stat.berkeley.edu   leo@stat.berkeley.edu

ABSTRACT

Classification trees are attractive in that they present a simple and easily understandable structure. But on many data sets their accuracy is far from optimal. Much of this lack of accuracy is due to their instability--small changes in the data can lead to large changes in the resulting tree. This instability is the reason that combining many trees by voting can lead to dramatic decreases in test set error (Breiman[1995]). But combining trees loses the simple structure. To keep the simple structure and improve accuracy, a way must be found to reduce the instability in the construction. If we knew the true probability distribution of the inputs and outputs, then the splits in the tree could be based on this distribution and give more accuracy then the splits based on a finite data set. So we turn the tree procedure around--instead of basing the splits on the data, the data is used to estimate the input-output probability distribution and the splits are then based on this estimate. We give the details of this construction. The experimental results on a number of well-know data sets indicate that this procedure has potential for producing much more accurate trees.

1. **Introduction**

Classification and regression trees ala CART and C4.5 are sensitive to small changes in the data. A small change may result in a substantially altered tree. Because of this, tree predictors have high variance (Breiman [1995], [1996]) which results in inflated test set error rates.   Tree construction proceeds by recursively splitting the data. Thus the sample size available for determining the splits decreases rapidly with the depth of the tree. The result is increasingly noisy and poorly determined splits.

Denote the output, numerical or a class label, by Y and the multivariate inputs by **X.** If we knew the joint probability distribution of Y,**X** then we could determine the optimal splits at each node using this distribution. We would have, essentially, infinite sample size to use in tree construction. This suggests the following possibility--

Instead of using the given data set to determine the splits, use the data set to estimate the Y,X distribution and then use this estimate to determine the splits.

This idea works and gives some dramatic decreases in test set error as compared with the standard method of tree construction. In this paper, we focus on classification trees, but the same methods (actually simplified) hold for regression. In classification, we construct a separate density estimate for each class using a kernel density estimate of the Y,**X** distribution. Then optimal splits are found in each node by using the estimated distributions to compute the Gini criterion for a grid of splits points on each variable. We will refer to this procedure as DB-CART where DB stands for distribution based.

Note that because we are using the estimated probability and not the data points to split with, that when a parent is split, the influence of a single data point may be divided between the two children nodes. Thus, the splits in the lower nodes may be influenced by probability contributions from many data points.

Tree construction, consisting of the determination of node splits and node class probabilities is based on the estimated probabilities. The rest of the procedure is standard. Using the estimates a large tree is grown and a sequence of pruned subtrees determined. To select one of these subtrees, either a test set or 10-fold cross-validation is used. If a large enough test set is available, it is run down the sequence of pruned trees and the tree with lowest test set error selected. If not, 10% of the data is deleted, a tree grown on the other 90% using estimated probabilities, and the 10% run down it to give test set error estimates. Then a different 10% is let out, and so on.

The layout for this paper is as follows: Section 2 has experimental results concerning error rates of DB-CART compared to CART on a number of well-known data sets. In Section 3 we review how splits and node class probabilities would be determined if we knew the Y,$\mathbf{X}$ distribution. Section 4 gives the details of the probability estimates and Section 5 has comments.

2. Experimental Results for DB-CART Compared to CART

DB-CART was compared to CART on some well-known data sets summarized in table 1.

Table 1 Summary of Data Sets

Data Set	#Classes	#Predictors	#training	#test
Waveform	3	21	300	3000
Vowel	11	10	990	
Ionosphere	2	33	351	
Sonar	2	60	208	
Diabetes	2	8	786	
Glass	6	9	214	
Breast Cancer	2	30	569	

All of these data sets are in the UCI repository and are documented there. Waveform is artificial data.   Test set errors were computed as follows: for the waveform data a 300 case training set and 3000 case test set were independently generated 10 times. The test set error rate was computed as the average over the 10 runs.   In the other data sets the data was divided at random in 90%-10%. The tree was grown and pruned on the 90%, and the 10% then used to measure test set error. This was repeated 50 times and the test set errors averaged. The results are given in Table 2.

Table 2   Test Set Error(%) for CART and DB-CART

Data Set	CART Error	DB-CART Error	Decrease
Waveform	28.4	24.7	13%
Vowel	21.8	10.0	54%
Ionosphere	11.1	8.7	22%
Sonar	32.1	18.2	43%
Diabetes	26.3	25.6	3%
Glass	28.6	29.4	-3%
Breast Cancer	6.5	3.8	42%

Using the estimated distribution to construct trees can produce surprisingly large decreases in error rates. But in two of the data set, glass and diabetes, there is no significant difference. We are studying these two to try and understand the problem. Because using the estimated distribution emulates a larger sample size, the trees grown by DB-CART are generally larger than those grown by CART. The comparison of sizes is in Table 5.

<u>Table 5 Number of Terminal Nodes in Trees Constructed by CART and DB-CART</u>

Data Set	CART	DB-CART
Waveform*	15	49
Vowel	107	244
Ionosphere	6	16
Sonar	6	41
Diabetes	11	33
Glass	11	26
Breast Cancer	7	40

3. <u>Using the Distribution to Construct the Tree</u>

Suppose we know the joint distribution of the random vector Y,X where Y is the class label and X is a vector of M predictor variables, i.e. $\mathbf{X} = (X_1, \ldots, X_M)$. That is, suppose we know $P(Y=j, \mathbf{X} \in dx)$. Let $P(j)=P(Y=j)$. A node t of the tree corresponds to $\mathbf{X} \in I$ where I is a multidimensional rectangle.

Suppose we want to split I by a split of the form $X_m \leq c$. Let

$$P_L = P(X_m \leq c | \mathbf{X} \in \mathbf{I}) \qquad P_R = P(X_m > c | \mathbf{X} \in \mathbf{I})$$
$$q_{jL} = P(j | X_m \leq c, \mathbf{X} \in \mathbf{I}) \qquad q_{jR} = P(j | X_m > c, \mathbf{X} \in \mathbf{I})$$

The optimal split is defined to be the one minimizing the Gini criterion (see Breiman et. al [1984]). This is equivalent to maximizing

$$G = P_L \sum_j q_{jL}^2 + P_R \sum_j q_{jR}^2 \tag{3.1}$$

Look at the first term

$$P(X_m \leq c | \mathbf{X} \in \mathbf{I}) \sum_j P^2(j | X_m \leq c, \mathbf{X} \in \mathbf{I})$$

This equals

$$[\sum_j P^2(X_m \leq c, \mathbf{X} \in \mathbf{I} | j) P^2(j)] / P(\mathbf{I}) P(X_m \leq c, \mathbf{X} \in \mathbf{I}) \tag{3.2}$$

Note that

$$P(X_m \leq c, \mathbf{X} \in \mathbf{I}) = \sum_j P(X_m \leq c, \mathbf{X} \in \mathbf{I} | j) P(j)$$

The second term in (2.1) has an expression similar to (2.2) but uses $X_m > c$. A search is made over all m,c to find the values that maximize (21.). Call these m*,c*. Now the new left and right nodes become

$$t_L = \mathbf{I}\,\mathrm{I}\{X_{m*} \le c*\} \qquad t_R = \mathbf{I}\,\mathrm{I}\{X_{m*} > c*\}$$

and the process is iterated.

Using the probability distribution to construct the tree is equivalent to having an infinite number of samples available from the **Y,X** distribution. By known consistency proofs (see Breiman et.al [1984]), trees constructed this way converge toward the minimal obtainable error rate as they are grown larger.

4. **Estimating the Distribution.**

But given a finite training data set T, the distribution isn't known.   However, it can be estimated.   Let T $=\{(j_n, \mathbf{x}_n),\ n = 1,\ \dots\ ,N\}$, L_j the set of all indices n such that $j_n{=}j$, and N_j the number of instances in class j.   We will estimate the density of $P(d\mathbf{x}\,|\,j)$ by a kernel density estimate:

$$\hat{f}_j(\mathbf{x}) = \frac{1}{N_j}\sum_{n\in L_j} K(\mathbf{x} - \mathbf{x}_n)$$

4.1 <u>Numerical Variables</u>

To begin with, normalize all numerical variables to have range 0 to 1. Let f(x) be a Gaussian density with mean zero and standard deviation h > 0, and define

$$K(\mathbf{x}) = \prod_m f(x_m) \tag{4.1}$$

where the product is over all numerical variables. Thus, the cumulative distribution function $F_j(\mathbf{x})$ of the estimated density is

$$F_j(\mathbf{x}) = \frac{1}{N_j}\sum_{n\in L_j}\prod_m F((x_m - x_{m,n})/h)$$

where F is the standard N(0,1) cumulative distribution function. For any interval I = [a,b], let F(I)=F(a)-F(b). If $\mathbf{I} = I_1 \otimes I_2 \otimes \dots \otimes I_M$ then

$$P_j(\mathbf{I}) = \frac{1}{N_j}\sum_{n\in L_j}\prod_m F((I_m - x_{m,n})/h) \tag{4.2}$$

Define

$$q(n,\mathbf{I}) = \prod_m F((I_m - x_{m,n})/h)$$

Now using these estimated probabilities, we want to evaluate the Gini (3.1) for splits of the form $\{X_m \leq c\}$ Denote by I(m,c) the interval $\{x_m \leq c\}$, and let $R_n(m,c)$ be the ratio

$$R_n(m,c) = F((I_m \amalg I(m,c) - x_{m,n}) / h)) / F((I_m - x_{m,n}) / h)$$

Then

$$P_j(\mathbf{I} \amalg I(m,c)) = \frac{1}{N_j} \sum_{n \in L_j} q(n,\mathbf{I}) R_n(m,c) \tag{4.3}$$

Putting P(j)=Nj/N and using the (4.3) estimate in (3.2) gives the first term in the Gini. The second term is gotten by using the complement of I(m,c) in the expression for $R_n(m,c)$.

3.2 Non-numeric Variables

Suppose x takes on non-numerical values we label as 1,2, ..., I. The density $f(x,x_n)$ that appears in the product (4.1) is then a probability distribution on these values. This distribution is defined in the following way: let the proportion of categories 1,2, ... ,I for instances in class j be given by p(i,j). Suppose x_n is in class j and $x_n = i0$. Then , for $0<q<1$, set

$$f(x,x_n) = \begin{cases} (1-q)+q \cdot p(i0,j), & \text{if } x = i0 \\ q \cdot p(i,j) & , \text{if } x = i \neq i0 \end{cases}$$

4.3 Maximization search

If the variable x has many distinct values, then the search over splits of the form $\{x \leq c\}$ is confined to a grid of 100 equally spaced c values. If x has only a few distinct values, then the search is confined to splits for which c is at the midpoint between two x-values.

4.4 Setting parameter values.

For numerical variables, the value of h needs to be selected, and for non-numerical, the value of q. This is done by cross-validation. Our current procedure is to search over a small grid of h and q values values to find those giving the lowest cross-validation error rates. This is expensive computationally since for each grid point examined, a tree is grown and its error rate estimated using 10-fold cross-validation. One current research priority is to find a faster method for locating optimal parameter values.

5. Comments

Given the training data $T = \{(j_n,x_n), n= 1, ... ,N\}$, if we estimate the Y,X distribution by the empirical distribution that puts weight 1/N at each of the points (j_n,x_n), then using this estimate gets us back to CART. If an oversmoothed estimate is used, then it's too far away from the "true" distribution and the accuracy drops. Density estimates in high dimensional spaces are known to be quite noisy. In particular, kernel density estimates do not perform well. But the evidence seems to be that the accuracy of CART is significantly enhanced by using an estimated distribution.

We believe that the reason is that the relevant estimates needed are low dimensional. CART splits are univariate. So what is needed are fairly good univariate density estimates together with rough estimates of interactions. Kernel density estimation does this well enough to produce increased test set accuracy. We are encouraged by these preliminary results and will explore further along this direction. Our distribution estimate is admittedly a first approximation and we plan to see if it can be improved. Its possible, for instance, that variable kernel estimates will provide better accuracy. But the results to date are encouraging in that they shown that accuracy can be improved without loss in simplicity and interpretability.

References

Breiman, L., Friedman, J.,Olshen, R., and Stone, C. [1984] Classification and Regression Trees, Wadsworth

Breiman, L.[1995] Bagging Predictors, in press, Machine Learning

Breiman, L.[1996] Bias, Variance, and Arcing Classifiers, submitted to Annals of Statistics, ftp ftp.stat.berkeley.edu   pub/breiman/arcall.ps

Levenberg-Marquardt Learning and Regularization

Lai-Wan CHAN
Computer Science and Engineering Department
The Chinese University of Hong Kong, Shatin, HONG KONG
Email : lwchan@cs.cuhk.hk

Abstract— **Levenberg-Marquardt Learning was first introduced to the feedforward networks to improve the speed of the training. This method is an improved Guass-Newton method which has an extra term to prevent the cases of ill-conditions. Interestingly, if we regard the learning as a constrained least square method, that extra term becomes a regularization term to deal with the additive noise in the training samples. In this paper, we look at the Levenberg-Marquardt Learning from the viewpoint of regularization. We show that the Levenberg-Marquardt learning allows other forms of regularization operators by some simple modifications. In addition, with the inclusion of test for validation error, the regularization parameter can be chosen in such a way that both the training error and validation error decrease. Thus, it prevents the occurrence of over-training.**

1 Introduction

Levenberg-Marquardt Learning had been introduced to feedforward networks for a number of years [HM94]. The primary objective of this learning algorithm is to speed up the learning process. Generalized delta-rule, the original learning algorithm of multi-layered feedforward networks, is based on gradient descent which is usually slow and the convergence is of linear order [RHW85]. In addition, the speed usually depends on some parameters, for example, the step size. Alternatively, various second order learning methods had been proposed [Bat92]. Among these second order methods, Levenberg-Marquardt method, a modification to the Gauss-Newton method, is one of the popular and effective methods. One characteristic of this method is that it incorporates an extra term to stabilize the system and to deal with the small residual problems in the learning.

In the past, the discussion of the Levenberg-Marquardt method was mainly related to the speed and convergence issue. This paper looks at the regularization aspect of the Levenberg-Marquardt Learning, on top of the convergence issue. By deriving the Levenberg-Marquardt Learning from the constrained least square method, we relate the extra term in the Levenberg-Marquardt Learning to the addition of a regularization term in the cost function. Unlike other papers on generalization and regularization, we are not trying to propose optimal or novel regularization methods. Instead, we are aiming at exploring the advantages of the Levenberg-Marquardt or related learning method.

2 The Single Layer Feedforward Network

Before going to the non-linear case of multi-layer feedforward network, we first consider the linear one where only one layer of neurons is concerned. As long as the activation function is a monotonic function, we can always rewrite the output of that layer as $y = xw$, where x is the input, and w is the weight vector. Using the ridge regression to solve the above equation gives

$$w_K = (x^T x + K)^{-1} y$$

When $K = \gamma I$, I being the identity matrix, $\gamma > 0$, and $\gamma \in \mathcal{R}$. $w_K = w_\gamma = (x^T x + \gamma I)^{-1} y$. This gives the ordinary ridge estimator. When K is a diagonal matrix of biasing factors γ_i (*i.e.* $K = diag(\gamma_i)$), it becomes the generalized ridge estimator. In either case, the estimators are the minima of the form

$$C(w) = (y - xw)^T (y - xw) + \frac{1}{2} w^T K w \tag{1}$$

Equation (1) is indeed a mean square error term together with a weight decaying term. Previous result shows that $E(w_k - w^*)^T (w_k - w^*) < E(w_0 - w^*)^T (w_0 - w^*)$ for some $0 < k < k_{max}$. w^* and w_0 are optimal weight vector and the solution of the ordinary least square method respectively [VU81]. k_{max} has been estimated as $\frac{2\sigma^2}{w^{*T} w^*}$ or $\frac{2}{[-\min(0,\zeta)]}$ and ζ is the minimum eigenvalue of $(x^T x)^{-1} - (w^* w^{*T}/\sigma^2)$. Thus, the ridge regression solution gives a small variance in the weight vector.

3 The Multi-layer Feedforward Network

In contrast to the single layer network, iterative updating is often used in a non-linear multi-layer feedforward networks. Let $y = f(x, w)$ be the function modeled by the network, with x and y as the input and output variables respectively. Using Taylor's series expansion of f, we have

$$f(x, w + \Delta w) = f(x, w) + J \Delta w \tag{2}$$

where J is the Jacobian matrix. Equating $f(x, w + \Delta w)$ to t, the expected output of the training samples, and let $e = t - y$, Equation 2 becomes

$$J\Delta w = e \tag{3}$$

The Levenberg-Marquardt learning gives $\Delta w = (J^T J + \gamma I)^{-1} Je$ as the solution of the above equation, with γ being a regularization parameter to prevent the ill-condition of the matrix $J^J J$. However, relating the Levenberg-Marquardt Learning to the constrained least square solution reveals that this learning method is indeed equivalent to the minimum square error of a cost function with some regularization.

Let w^* be the optimal weight vector and we assume that the training set, $\{\tilde{t}, x\}$, contains zero-mean additive noise, i.e. $\tilde{t} = f(x, w^*) + \eta$, where η has a variance of σ^2.

If $\tilde{e}$ denotes the difference between the target output of the training data and the model output, we have $\tilde{e} = \tilde{t} - y = e + \eta$. Thus,

$$E[\|\tilde{e} - J\Delta w\|^2] = N\sigma^2$$

with N being the dimension of $\tilde{e}$. Following the "Occam's razor", a less complex model is preferred. Thus, our object turns to the minimization of the model complexity subjected to the above constraint. Assuming that the initial weights are small in magnitude, we define the model complexity as $\|Q\Delta w\|^2$ and Q is a regularization operator on Δw. The expectation in the constraint term is estimated from the sum square error of the training data.

Use Lagrange multipliers,

$$C(\Delta w) = \|Q\Delta w\|^2 + \mu(\|\tilde{e} - J\Delta w\|^2 - N\sigma^2) \tag{4}$$

Now, suppose Q is linear. The minimization of equation (4) yields

$$\Delta w = (J^T J + \gamma Q^T Q)^{-1} J^T \tilde{e} \tag{5}$$

where $\gamma = 1/\mu$.

4   The Regularizer

We see that equation (4) is in the form of a sum square error term with a regularizer. When regularization is concerned, it is not an easy task to evaluate the optimal form of the regularizers and the optimal value of the regularization parameter. The regularizer, based on some prior information, constrains the search space of the weight vector. For example, it controls the smoothness of the network output. This smoothness consequently affects the generalization performance of the network.

Different forms of regularizers have been proposed, for examples, the weight decaying [PNH86], the weight elimination [WRH91], the smoothing regularizers [WM95]. The regularizer that we are referring to in this paper differs from theirs in the way that the regularization is imposed on Δw instead of w. Instead of constraining the magnitude of the weight vector, as in the cases of the single layer network or the weight decaying, it constrains the magnitude of the changes of the weight vector. Since only the weight update is constrained, thus a prior requirement is that the magnitude of the initial weight vector has to be small. Comparing with the regularizer in the form of $\|w - w^*\|^2$ discussed in [SL94], this regularization uses the weight vector at the current iteration as a nominal guess of w^*.

In equation (5), which is the constrained least square solution of equation (3), we permit any form of linear regularizers, Q. A specific example is the case when $Q = I$, equation (5) becomes

$$\Delta w = (J^T J + \gamma I)^{-1} J^T \tilde{e}$$

If we choose γ according to the Marquardt strategy (we discuss it again in Section 4), it becomes the Levenberg-Marquardt Learning Algorithm [HM94].

Apart from $Q = I$, another example of Q is the finite difference matrix.

$$Q = \begin{pmatrix} -2 & 1 & & & & \\ 1 & -2 & 1 & & & \\ 0 & 1 & -2 & & 0 & \\ & & & \ddots & \ddots & \\ & 0 & & 1 & -2 & 1 \\ & & & & 1 & -2 \end{pmatrix}$$

It guarantees that the estimation Δw does not oscillate wildly in the constrained solution by minimizing higher-order differences.

In addition to the regularization operator, the optimal choice of the regularization parameter is another interesting topic to study. Many research papers have shown the effects of varying the regulation parameters and have discussed the evaluation of the optimal value of the regularization factor [Wah94]. For examples, if the noise variance is known, λ can be estimated by the minimization of the Total Predicted Mean Square Error, $TPMSE(\gamma) = \|(I - K(\gamma))J\tilde{e}\|^2 + \sigma^2 tr\{K(\gamma)\}^2, K(\gamma) = J(J^T J + \gamma Q^T Q)^{-1} J^T$. If the noise variance is unknown, we can estimate the parameter from the generalized cross validation function, $GCV(\gamma) = RSS(\gamma)/tr\{I - K(\gamma)\}^2$ [TBKT91]. Alternatively, γ can be estimated from the equivalent degrees of freedom method, in which γ satisfies $RRS(\gamma) = \sigma^2\{n - trK(\gamma)\}$ [TBKT91]. Weigend [WRH91] assigned different values of the regularization parameter before and after overfitting. Rögnvaldsson estimated the parameter based on the early stopping points [Rög96]. Hansen [HRSL94] adapted the regularization parameter by using a gradient descent in the estimated generalization error and showed that the regularization parameter decreases as pruning proceeds.

The above methods choose the regularization parameter mainly based on the final generalization performance. On the other hand, this parameter affects the stability and convergence of the training. As we can see from the constrained least square solution, the estimated SSE after a weight updating is

$$\hat{e} = J\Delta w \tag{6}$$

$$= J(J^T J + \gamma Q^T Q)^{-1} J^T \tilde{e}$$

$$\hat{e} - \tilde{e} = (I - J(J^T J + \gamma Q^T Q)^{-1} J^T)\tilde{e}$$

If $Q = I$,

$$\hat{e} - \tilde{e} = (I - (I - (I + \frac{JJ^T}{\gamma})^{-1}))\tilde{e}$$

$$= (I + \frac{JJ^T}{\gamma})^{-1}\tilde{e}$$

The eigenvalues of $(I + \frac{JJ^T}{\gamma})^{-1}$ are $\frac{\gamma}{\gamma + \lambda_i}$, where λ_i's are the eigenvalues of JJ^T. Since all eigenvalues of $(I + \frac{J^T J}{\gamma})^{-1}$ are smaller than 1, $\|t - y\|$ is decreasing, and γ is a crucial factor to determine the rate of convergence.

From the view point of convergence, there are numerous ways to adapt this parameter, for examples, the Levenberg method, the Marquardt method and the Fletcher methods [Sca85], the Kollias and Anastassiou method [KA89]. Among them, the Marquardt strategy, is a popular method used in the training of feedforward networks.

In Levenberg-Marquardt Learning [HM94], the regularization parameter is adaptive as follows.

Step 1	Compute $SSE_{train}(w)$
Step 2	while $SSE_{train}(w) >$ threshold and gradient_vector > min_gradient do
Step 3	decrement γ
Step 4	compute Δw according to equation (5).
Step 5	compute $SSE_{train}(w + \Delta w)$
Step 6	if $SSE_{train}(w + \Delta w) > SSE_{train}(w)$ then
Step 7	increment γ
	else
Step 8	$w \leftarrow w + \Delta w$
	end
	done

Note that this algorithm adapts the regularization parameter based on the criteria that there is a reduction in the training error (SSE_{train}). Considering that there are noises in the training samples, we prefer the reduction of the validation error ($SSE_{validation}$) to the reduction of the training error. In this respect, we modify the Levenberg-Marquardt Learning Algorithm by replacing the condition in Step 6 of the above with

Step 5	if $SSE_{validation}(w + \Delta w) > SSE_{validation}(w)$ then

Thus γ is adjusted to ensure the decrease in the validation error. At the same time, the training error usually decreases as long as the condition of $\gamma < \gamma_{max}$ (for some γ_{max}) is satisfied. It has to pointed out that the algorithm terminates when there is no further reduction on the validation error. In that case, γ continues to increase until the gradient vector diminishes below the threshold value.

5 Experimental Results

We illustrate the effects of the above strategy by an example. We generated 40 training data points from the equation

$$y = \frac{1}{2}sin(2x) + \frac{1}{2} + \eta \qquad\qquad -2 < x \leq 2 \tag{7}$$

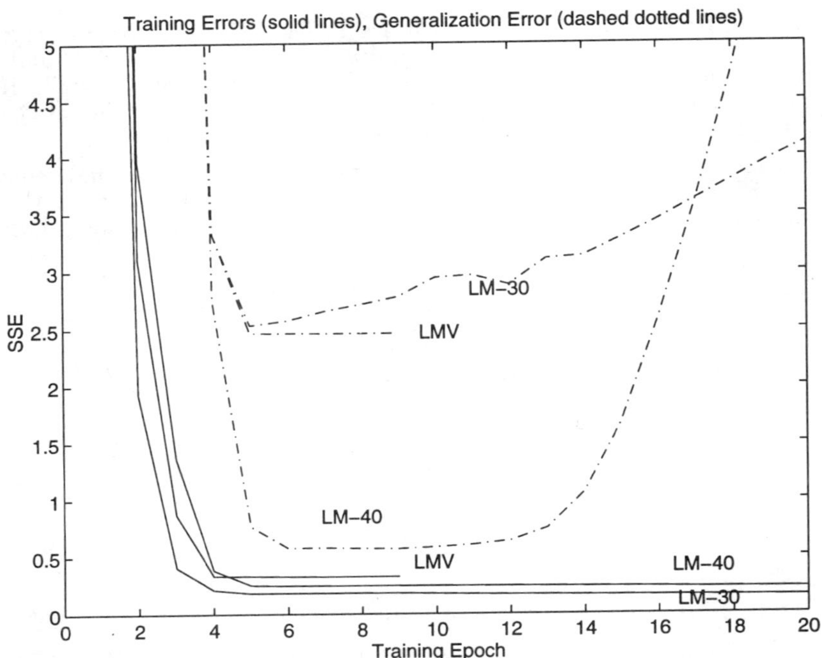

Figure 1: The training (solid lines) and generalization (dashed dotted lines) error during the training.

with $\eta = \mathcal{N}(0, 0.01)$. A one-hidden-layer feedforward network with 50 hidden nodes was trained using two different learning schemes; Levenberg-Marquardt Learning (LM) and the Levenberg-Marquardt with validation method (LMV). The weights were initialized with random numbers between [-1,+1]. LMV was trained with 30 data samples and the rest were put in the validation set. As a comparison, we trained LM with all data points (LM-40) and with only the 30 data points as in LMV (LM-30). Generalization error was measured by the sum square error (SSE) of 400 evenly distributed points in the same range. Figure 1 shows the SSE of the training set and the generalization error. The training error of LM and LMV were very close to each other. The training SSE of LMV stopped decreasing at around 0.25 but the training SSE of LM continued to decrease slowly. Figure 1 also shows that the generalization error of LM dropped to a minimum and then increased again, showing that the network is over-trained. The minimum of the generalization curve of LM-40 is quite flat, and this could be due to the effect of the regularization. When we look at the number of training iterations, about 5 iterations were required to reduce both training and generalization error to the minima and the generalization error maintained at similar level for another 8 iterations, which is about 1.5 the training time. For LMV, the generalization error converged to about 2.5 and did not increase further. Note that the generalization error of LMV and LM-30 is higher than that of LM-40. This is explained by the difference in the number of training data. LMV and LM-30 contained only 75% of the training data as in LM. The final network output is shown in Figure 2. It is obvious that the LM over-trained the system.

6   Conclusion and Discussion

Levenberg-Marquardt Learning Algorithm has a number of advantages over the gradient descent learning. Apart from the widely-known fact that it has a fast convergency, it has regularization effect. It provides regularization to stabilize the ill-condition cases during training. This regularization can also be regarded as a constraint to the amount of weight updating in each iteration. In addition, it can be generalized to cater for other linear regularizers. It provides a framework which has flexibility for the implementation of different types of regularization operators. Finally, the regularization parameter in Levenberg-Marquardt Learning was selected adaptively so as to reduce the training error. As generalization performance is concerned, this can be modified to form the Levenberg-Marquardt with validation Learning Algorithm. This method selects the regularization parameter based on the cross validation set so that it guarantees the decrease of both the training error and validation error. A major advantage of LMV is that it does not require any *a priori* knowledge of the data, such as the noise variance etc. In conclusion, Levenberg-Marquardt Learning provides an efficient and flexible learning method for feedforward network, in terms of training speed and the feasibility in the amalgamation with regularizers and cross-validation tests.

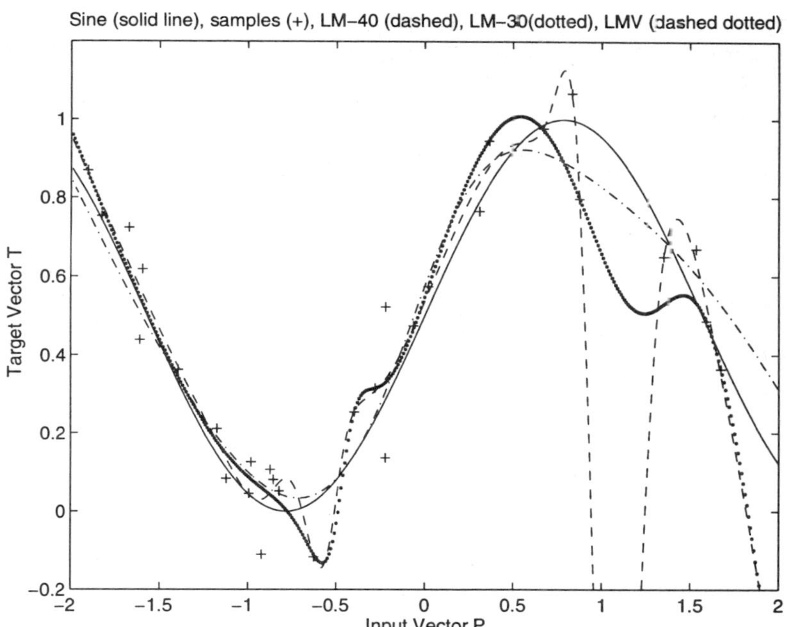

Figure 2: The training data (the crosses), the sin curve (solid line) and the prediction made by LM (dashed line) and the LMV (dashed dotted line).

Acknowledgement

The author would like to thank the RGC research grant for the financial support of this project. She would also like to thank the following people for valuable discussion during the preparation of the manuscript; C. P. Kwong, John Moody, John Sum, Z.B. Xu and members of the Neural Computing and Engineering Laboratory in the Computer Science and Engineering Department of The Chinese University of HongKong

References

[Bat92]   R. Battiti. First and second-order methods for learning : Between steepest descent and newton's method. *Neural Computation*, 4(2):141–166, 1992.

[HM94]   M. T. Hagan and M. B. Menhaj. Training feedforward networks with the Marquardt algorith. *IEEE Transactions on Neural Networks*, 5(6):989–993, November 1994.

[HRSL94]   L. K. Hanson, C. E. Rasmussen, C. Svarer, and J. Larsen. Adaptive regularization. In *Proc. of the 4th IEEE workshop on Neural Networks for signal processing, Greece*, 1994.

[KA89]   S. Kollias and D. Anastassiou. An adaptive least squares algorithm for the efficient training of artificial neural networks. *IEEE Transactions on Systems, Man and Cybernetics*, 36(8):1092–1101, 1989.

[PNH86]   D. C. Plaut, S. J. Nowlan, and Geoffrey E. Hinton. Experiments on learning by back-propagation. Technical Report CMU-CS-86-126, Carnegie Mellon University, Pittsburgh PA 15213, June 1986.

[RHW85]   D.E. Rumelhart, G.E. Hinton, and R.J. Williams. Learning internal representations by error propagation. In *Parallel Distributed Processing: Explorations in the Microstruct ure of Cognition. Vol. 1: Foundations.* Cambridge, MA: Bradford Books, MIT Press, David E. Rumelhart. Institute for Cognitive Science, C-015; University of California, San Diego; La Jolla, CA 92093, September 1985.

[Rög96]   T. S. Rögnvaldsson. A simple method for estimating the weight decaying parameter. Department of Computer Science and Engineering, Oregon Graduate Institute, Technical Report CSE 96-003, 1996.

[Sca85]   L. E. Scales. *Introduction to Non-Linear Optimization*. MacMillian, 1985.

[SL94]   J. Sjöberg and L. Ljung. Overtraining, regularization, and searching for minimum with application to neural networks. Department of Electrical Engineering, Linköping University, LiTH-ISY-R-1567, 1994.

[TBKT91] A. M. Thompson, J. C. Brown, J. W. Kay, and D. M Titterington. A study of methods of choosing the smoothing parameter in image restoration by regularization. *IEEE Transactions on Pattern Analysis and Machine Intelligence*, 13(4):326–338, 1991.

[VU81]   H. D. Vinod and A. Ullah. *Recent Advances in Regression Methods*. Marcel Dekker, Inc, 1981.

[Wah94]   G. Wahba. Generalization and regularization in nonlinear learning systems. Technical Report Technical Report : 921, Department of Statistics, University of Wisconsin, 1994.

[WM95]   L. Wu and J.E. Moody. A smoothing regularizer for feedforward and recurrent neural networks. *Neural Computation*, 8(3):463–491, 1995.

[WRH91]   A. S. Weigend, D. E. Rumelhart, and B. A. Huberman. Generalization by weight-elimination with application to forecasting. In Richard P. Lippmann, John E. Moody, and David S. Touretzky, editors, *Advances in Neural Information Processing Systems 3*, pages 875–882. Morgan Kaufmann, 1991.

Interpreting Internal Representation by Information Maximization

Ryotaro Kamimura† and **Shohachiro Nakanishi**‡
† Information Science Laboratory
‡ Department of Electrical Engineering
Tokai University
1117 Kitakaname Hiratsuka Kanagawa 259-12, Japan

Abstract— In this paper, we propose a method to maximize the information contained in the hidden units. The information maximization aims to interpret the mechanisms of network behaviors explicitly by generating simpler networks and by specializing hidden units. The information is defined by the decrease of the uncertainty of hidden units with respect to input patterns. By maximizing the information, a small number of hidden units are eventually turned on, whose effect consists in the compressing of the information into a small number of hidden units. In addition, the information maximization can specialize the roles of hidden units explicitly if a constraint is introduced by utilizing the tendency of distributed representation inherent to the neural learning. Thus, by the information maximization, hidden units can easily be interpreted by making networks simpler and by specializing hidden units. Our method was applied to the acquisition of rules for past tense forms of an artificial language. It was observed that the simple and constrained information maximization can produce different but reasonable models for the rules respectively.

1 Information Maximization

The information maximization in this paper is a method to simplify networks and to specialize hidden units for the better interpretation of hidden units. We explain briefly two properties of our information maximization method, that is, simplification and specialization,

In the first place, the information maximization is concerned with the simplification of networks, because our information maximization has an effect to condense the information into a small number of hidden units in easily interpretable ways. The information is defined as the decrease of the uncertainty of hidden units. The uncertainty is measured by using the entropy for hidden units. If we increase the information for hidden units, a hidden unit tends eventually to be turned on, while all the other hidden units are off. The information on input patterns is condensed into one hidden unit, as shown in Figure 1-(a). In addition, as can be seen in Figure 1-(b), the information maximization has an effect to turn all the hidden completely off. The number of hidden units can significantly be reduced and eventually the network is simplified and easily interpretable. Obtained hidden units represent explicitly features of input patterns or rules of input patterns. Concerning this property of the information maximization, many attempts have been made, aiming to obtain networks with a suitable or optimal network size by the sensitivity analysis, the node pruning and the introduction of the complexity penalty term. Our approach is an information theoretical formulation of the network size reduction. In other words, all these approaches can be incorporated in our framework of the information method.

In the simple information maximization, the information is maximized to simplify networks as much as possible. The constrained information maximization is introduced not mainly to reduce the network size but to make a function of each hidden unit more explicit. In this method, a constraint that the sum of all the hidden unit activities is unity is introduced. Thus, by the constrained information maximization, only one hidden unit is always on for any input pattern, as shown in Figure 1-(a). Then by the effect of the neural learning, having a tendency to distribute the information over many hidden units, each hidden unit turned on respond only to a specific input pattern. In this case, the roles of all the units composed of a network can completely be determined, though the simplification is slightly weak. This enables us to interpret the network behaviors more explicitly.

2 Information Maximization Method

Let us define an information function and rules for updating to maximize the information [1] [2]. Suppose that a network is composed of three layers: input, hidden and output layers. See Figure 2. The jth hidden unit activity is denoted by v_j^s and the kth input unit by ξ_k^s. Then, a connections from the kth input unit to the jth hidden unit is denoted by w_{jk} and connections from the jth hidden unit to the ith output unit is denoted by W_{ij}. The jth hidden unit produces an output

$$v_j^s = f(u_j^s), \tag{1}$$

where

$$u_j^s = \sum_k^L w_{jk}\xi_k^s. \tag{2}$$

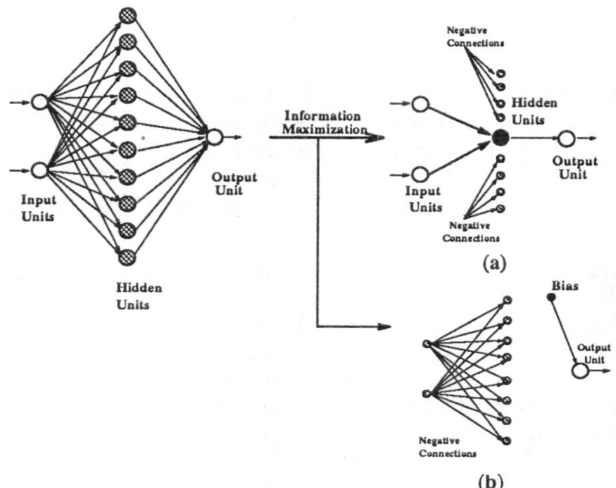

Figure 1: Information maximization to reduce the number of hidden units and to simplify networks for the explicit interpretation.

where ξ_k^s is the kth element of an input pattern, L is the number of elements in the pattern and f is the sigmoid activation function defined by

$$f(u_j^s) = \frac{1}{1 + \exp(-u_j^s)}. \tag{3}$$

An entropy function, given the sth input pattern, on the hidden layer has been defined by

$$H^s = -\sum_j^M p_j^s \log p_j^s, \tag{4}$$

where

$$p_j^s = \frac{v_j^s}{\sum_r^M v_r^s}, \tag{5}$$

and M is the number of hidden units. Summing this function over all the input patterns, we have total entropy:

$$H = -\sum_s^S \left(\sum_j^M p_j^s \log p_j^s \right), \tag{6}$$

where S is the number of input patterns. The information can be defined by the decrease of the entropy from the maximum entropy at the initial stage. Thus, the information is

$$I = S \log M + \sum_s^S \left(\sum_j^M p_j^s \log p_j^s \right). \tag{7}$$

The information maximization is completely equivalent to the entropy minimization in our framework. Thus, differentiating the entropy function with respect to input-hidden connections: w_{jk}, we can obtain rules for updating:

$$-\frac{\partial H}{\partial w_{jk}} = \sum_s^S \left(\log p_j^s - \sum_m p_m^s \log p_m^s \right) p_j^s (1 - v_j^s) \xi_k^s. \tag{8}$$

The information is naturally maximized under the condition that the errors between targets and outputs are sufficiently small. We incorporate the cross entropy minimization in the formulation of the information maximization. The cross entropy functions is defined by

$$G = \sum_s^S \left[\sum_i^N \left\{ \zeta_i^s \log \frac{\zeta_i^s}{O_i^s} + (1 - \zeta_i^s) \log \frac{1 - \zeta_i^s}{1 - O_i^s} \right\} \right], \tag{9}$$

where ζ_i^s is a target for the ith output unit O_i^s and the summation is over all the output units (N units) and all the input patterns (S patterns). If the difference between targets and outputs is smaller, the cross

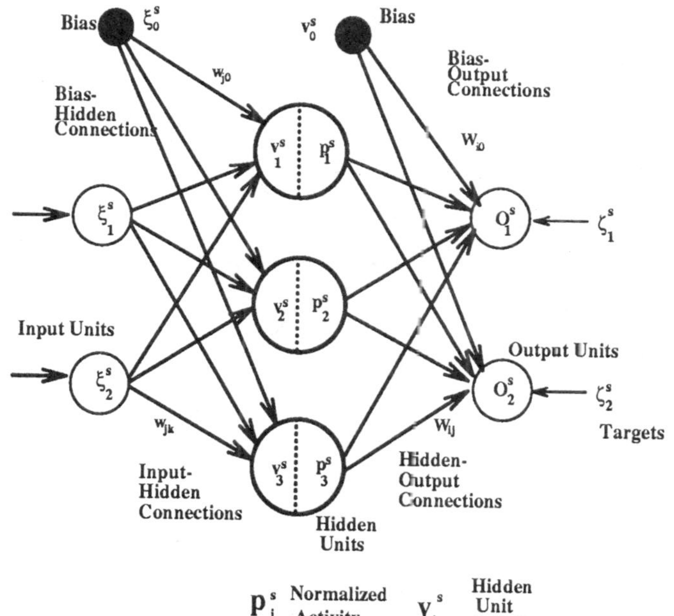

Figure 2: Network architecture for defining the hidden entropy and information.

entropy function is decreased. For hidden-output connections, we have rules for updating:

$$\Delta W_{ij} = -\eta \frac{\partial G}{\partial W_{ij}}$$

$$= \eta \sum_s^S (\zeta_i^s - O_i^s) v_j^s. \tag{10}$$

For input-hidden connections, we must maximize the information as well as the error minimization. Thus, rules for updating are

$$\Delta w_{jk} = -\beta \frac{\partial H}{\partial w_{jk}} - \eta \frac{\partial G}{\partial w_{jk}}$$

$$= \beta \sum_s^S \left(\log p_j^s - \sum_m p_m^s \log p_m^s \right) p_j^s (1 - v_j^s)\xi_k^s$$

$$+ \eta \sum_s^S \left\{ \sum_i^N (\zeta_i^s - O_i^s) W_{ij} \right\} v_j^s (1 - v_j^s)\xi_k^s. \tag{11}$$

3   Constrained Information Maximization Method

In the previous section, we have been concerned with the so-called *unconstrained* information maximization. This means that the information function is simply maximized. This simple information maximization is used to simplify networks, that is, to reduce the number of hidden units. Our objective in this section is to maximize this information function (I^s) subject to a constraint that the sum of all the activities is a constant θ, that is,

$$\sum_r^M v_r^s = \theta. \tag{12}$$

Constraints are necessary for controlling a process of the information maximization and minimization. If constraints are different, we can obtain different states of the information minimization or maximization. Figure 3 shows different states of the maximum information. If the constraint parameter θ is 1 and the information is maximized, only one hidden unit is completely turned on, while all the other hidden units are off. See Figure 3-(a). If the constraint θ is decreased to 0.5, the activity of one hidden unit to be turned on, is decreased from 1 to 0.5 (b). If the constraint is further decreased to 0.1, the hidden unit activity is also decreased to 0.1 (c). In the case of the simple information maximization, some hidden units tend to be turned off completely, leading to the reduction of necessary hidden units.

In the case of the unconstrained information maximization, all the hidden units happen to be turned off

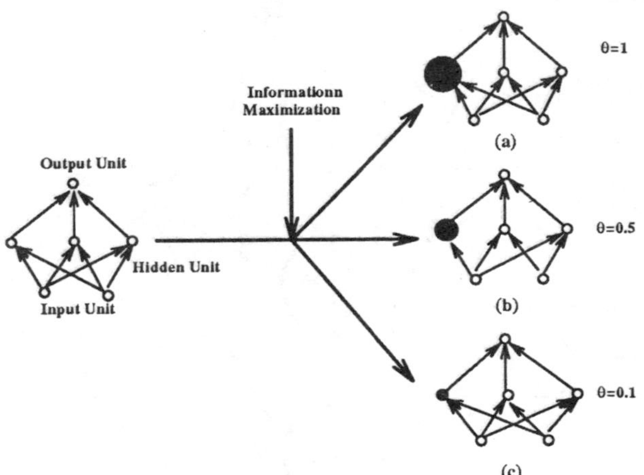

Figure 3: Different hidden unit activity patterns with different constraints obtained by the information maximization.

for input patterns. By this effect, the number of hidden units can be reduced. What is an appropriate value of the parameter for the constrained information maximization? As the parameter θ is smaller, it becomes more difficult to see characteristics of hidden unit activity patterns. Thus, the parameter θ should be one. This means that at least one hidden unit is always turned on. We have observed that the usual neural learning tends to produce distributed hidden unit activity patterns, meaning that input patterns are represented over many hidden units. By utilizing this tendency of distribution, each hidden unit strongly activated tends to respond to a specific input pattern.

We have discussed a concept of the constraint in the information maximization. Then, we formulate rules for updating for the constrained information maximization [1]. We must maximize the information function under a constraint that the total hidden unit activity is θ, that is, $\sum_m v_m^s = \theta$. The constraint can be incorporated by the following equation:

$$B = \frac{1}{2} \sum_s^S \left(\sum_j^M v_j^s - \theta \right)^2 . \tag{13}$$

Thus, total function to be minimized is

$$U = \beta H + \gamma B + \eta G,$$

$$= -\beta \sum_s^S \left(\sum_j^M p_j^s \log p_j^s \right) + \frac{\gamma}{2} \sum_s^S \left(\sum_j^M v_s^s - \theta \right)^2$$

$$+ \eta \sum_s^S \left[\sum_i^N \left\{ \zeta_i^s \log \frac{\zeta_i^s}{O_i^s} + (1 - \zeta_i^s) \log \frac{1 - \zeta_i^s}{1 - O_i^s} \right\} \right], \tag{14}$$

where β, η and γ are parameters. Differentiating this function with respect to input-hidden connections, we have

$$\Delta w_{jk} = -\frac{\partial U}{\partial w_{jk}},$$

$$= \beta \sum_s^S \left(\log p_j^s - \sum_r p_r^s \log p_r^s \right) p_j^s (1 - v_j^s) \xi_k^s$$

$$- \gamma \sum_s^S \left(\sum_m^M v_m^s - \theta \right) v_j^s (1 - v_j^s) \xi_k^s$$

$$+ \eta \sum_s^S \left\{ \sum_i^N (\zeta_i^s - O_i^s) W_{ij} \right\} v_j^s (1 - v_j^s) \xi_k^s . \tag{15}$$

4   Rule Acquisition for Past Tense Forms

In this section, the simple and constrained information maximization are applied to the language acquisition problem, that is, the rule acquisition for past tense forms. It is shown that the simple information

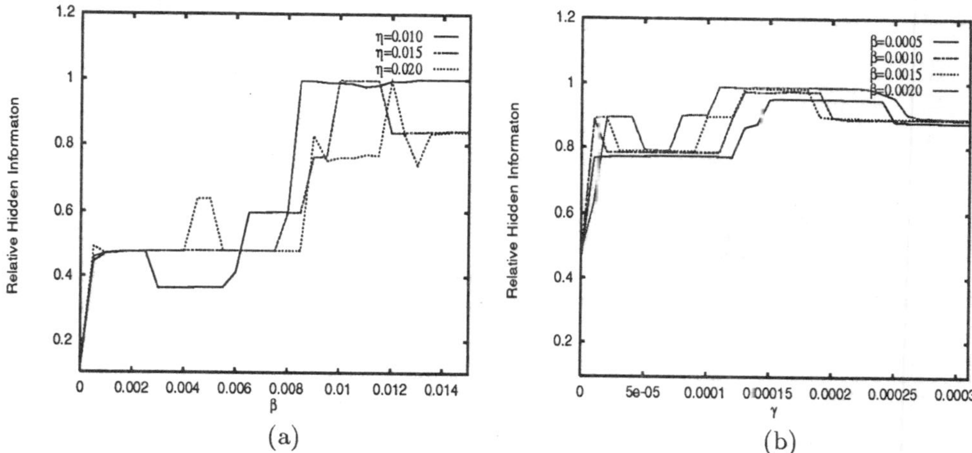

(a)　　　　　　　　　　　　(b)

Figure 4: Relative information by the unconstrained (a) and the constrained (b) information maximization.

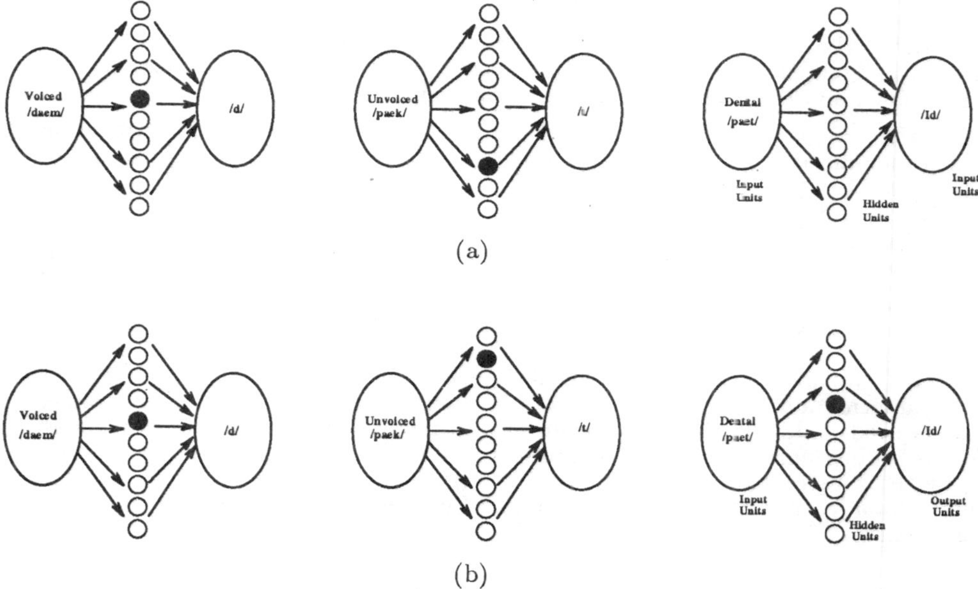

(a)

(b)

Figure 5: Activity patterns of the hidden units by the unconstrained maximization (a) and by the constrained maximization (b).

maximization and the constrained information maximization can produce rules, corresponding to our intuition of the rules for the past tense forms.

A past tense form acquisition is a very important problem for demonstrating the performance of neural networks, which has extensively been discussed in the cognitive sciences [3]. For our experiments, only three rules were incorporated to make training and testing patterns for the simplicity of the explanation. The first rule is that if a word ends in dental consonants like $/d/$ and $/t/$, where $//$ means a letter or word inside this symbol is a phoneme, the past tense form is $/Id/$. If a word $/pæt/$ is given, the past tense form is $/Id/$, that is, $/pætId/$. If another word $/pæd/$ is given, the past tense form is also $/Id/$, that is, $/pædId/$. If a word ends in a voiced consonant except dental consonants, the past tense form is $/d/$. A voiced $/d/$ is the past tense form, if a word ends in a voiced consonant $/dæm/$. If a word ends in a voiceless consonant except dental consonants, the past tense form is $/t/$. A past tense form $/t/$ is given to the network, if a word end in a voiceless consonant $/pæk/$. Words in our artificial language were composed of a word type of CVC, where C is a consonant and V is a vowel. The number of total words was 5290 words. Some of the words did not correspond to words in English. Words in our artificial language were represented in the phonological representation. In an actual network architecture, the number of input, hidden units, and output units was 48, 10, 16 respectively. Training and testing words were randomly chosen from a set of words. The number of training words and testing words was 60 and 100 words.

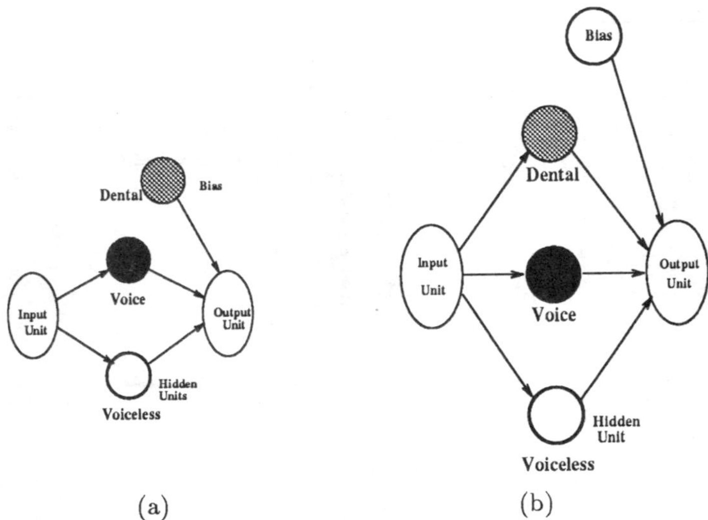

Figure 6: Hidden and bias to output units obtained by the unconstrained (a) and the constrained information maximization (b).

Figure 4 shows the relative information by the unconstrained (a) and the constrained (b) information maximization. The figure shows that the relative information is increased and close to a maximum value by the unconstrained and the constrained information maximization.

Figure 5 shows the activity patterns of the hidden units by the unconstrained maximization (b) and by the constrained maximization (c). The parameters were chosen so as to give the maximum information. As shown in Figure 5-(a), by using the unconstrained information maximization, only one hidden unit is turned on for the voiced and voiceless consonants. However, for the dental consonants such as $/d/$ and $/t/$, all the hidden units are completely turned off. Figure 5-(b) shows the activity patterns by the constrained information maximization. In this case, to three different kinds of consonants, correspond three different hidden units.

Compared with internal representations obtained networks by the standard back-propagation, networks by the unconstrained and constrained maximization are easily interpreted. Figure 6 shows a fundamental mechanism of the two hidden units and the bias to output units by the unconstrained (a) and the constrained (b) information maximization. As can be seen in the figure, if the unconstrained information maximization is used, hidden units are specialized into two different special units, that is, a *voice* and *voiceless* feature hidden unit. The bias to output units is transformed into a *dental* feature unit. On the other hand, by the constrained information maximization, three different special units, that is, a *voice*, *voiceless* and *dental* feature hidden unit, are turned on. Thus, our information maximization method can produce two kinds of interpretation for the past tense form formation, corresponding to the linguistic interpretation.

References

[1] R. Kamimura and S. Nakanishi, "Hidden information maximization for feature detection and rule discovery," *Network: Computation in Neural Systems*, Vol.6, pp.577-602, 1995.

[2] R. Kamimura, and S. Nakanishi, "Feature detectors by autoencoders: decomposition of input patterns into atomic features by neural networks," *Neural Processing Letters*, Vol.2, No.6, pp.1-6, 1995.

[3] K. Plunkett, V. Marchman, and S. L. Knudsen, "From Rote Learning to System Building: Acquiring Verb Morphology in Children and Connectionist Nets," in *Connectionist Models: Proceedings of the 1990 Summer School*, D. S. Touretzky, J. L. Elman and G. E. Hinton, Eds, Morgan Kaufmann Publishers, Inc, San Mateo: California, pp.201-219, 1990.

A Context-Sensitive Generalization of ICA

Barak A. Pearlmutter†   Lucas C. Parra‡
†Dept. of Cog. Sci., UCSD, La Jolla, California, USA, barak.pearlmutter@alumni.cs.cmu.edu
‡Siemens Corporate Research, Princeton, New Jersey, USA, lucas@scr.siemens.com

Abstract— **Source separation arises in a surprising number of signal processing applications, from speech recognition to EEG analysis. In the square linear blind source separation problem without time delays, one must find an unmixing matrix which can detangle the result of mixing n unknown independent sources through an unknown $n \times n$ mixing matrix. The recently introduced ICA blind source separation algorithm (Baram and Roth 1994; Bell and Sejnowski 1995) is a powerful and surprisingly simple technique for solving this problem. ICA is all the more remarkable for performing so well despite making absolutely no use of the temporal structure of its input! This paper presents a new algorithm, contextual ICA, which derives from a maximum likelihood density estimation formulation of the problem. cICA can incorporate arbitrarily complex adaptive history-sensitive source models, and thereby make use of the temporal structure of its input. This allows it to separate in a number of situations where standard ICA cannot, including sources with low kurtosis, colored gaussian sources, and sources which have gaussian histograms. Since ICA is a special case of cICA, the MLE derivation provides as a corollary a rigorous derivation of classic ICA.**

1   The ICA algorithm

In the blind source separation problem, one is given the output of a number of microphones, each of which records a mixture of a number of sources. The task is to recover the sources. In the blind linear square case, there are the same number of microphones as sources, and the mixing is linear. In the absence of time delays or echos, the mixing is characterized by an $n \times n$ matrix $\mathbf{A}$, so if $\mathbf{s}(t)$ is a vector of the sources at time t then $\mathbf{x}(t) = \mathbf{A}\mathbf{s}(t)$ is a vector of the signals received by the microphones at time t. Naturally we will assume that $\mathbf{A}$ is full rank.

In the absence of noise, which is the case we consider, the solution to this problem is to find a full rank $n \times n$ matrix $\mathbf{W}$ which has the property that $\mathbf{W}\mathbf{A}$ has exactly one nonzero element in each row and each column. We denote the result of the unmixing process as $\mathbf{y}(t)$, and note that $\mathbf{y}(t) = \mathbf{W}\mathbf{x}(t) = \mathbf{W}\mathbf{A}\mathbf{s}(t)$. If we have found an appropriate $\mathbf{W}$ then the product $\mathbf{W}\mathbf{A}$ will be equal to the product of a diagonal matrix with a permutation matrix, and the elements of $\mathbf{y}(t)$ will be the same as the elements of $\mathbf{s}(t)$, but shuffled and scaled.

With no prior information about $\mathbf{A}$ or the source signals $s_i(t)$, the problem might sound impossible. However, for non-gaussian distributions, it is not. An algorithm called *independent components analysis* was introduced by Comon (1994). This version of the algorithm approximates some distributions by their first few moments, which is both approximate and computationally burdensome. Single coordinate higher order cumulants are used in a somewhat simpler algorithm by Obradovic and Deco (1995). A surprisingly simple, but inexpensive and exact, variant of the Comon (1994) algorithm was recently introduced (Baram and Roth 1994; Bell and Sejnowski 1995). In a now standard abuse of notation, this new algorithm will be refered to as ICA. This simpler ICA algorithm takes each component of the vector $\mathbf{y}(t)$ and passes it though a saturating monotonic nonlinearity, giving a vector $\mathbf{z}(t)$. Gradient descent is used to modify the components of the matrix $\mathbf{W}$ and the bias terms of the nonlinearities in order to increase the entropy of the distribution of $\mathbf{z}(t)$ induced by the input distribution. ICA was motivated by considerations of biological optimality, which flow from experiments showing that, when presented with natural stimuli, many neurons appear to make good use of their available axonal channel capacity (Bialek *et al.* 1991).

The ICA algorithm, in various configurations, has been applied to a surprising number of problems, from separation of digitally mixed speech signals (Bell and Sejnowski 1995), to separating the componenets of electroencephalographic data (Makeig *et al.* 1996), to blind deconvolution (Bell and Sejnowski 1995), to finding the higher-order structure of a natural sound (Bell and Sejnowski 1996b), and even to financial forecasting (Baram and Roth 1995) and image processing (Bell and Sejnowski 1996a). There have been attempts to generalize the algorithm, the most notable being extensions to tolerate time delays and echos introduced by Torkkola (1996a, 1996b).

The usual intuition for why ICA tends to separate sources runs roughly as follows: if the output entropy is maximized, then the components of the output vector must be statistically independent. If so, then the signals must also be statistically independent prior to the nonlinearity. That being the case, the sources must be separated.

However, there are problematic cases which ICA cannot separate. For instance, a mixture of two uniform distributions, or more generally two low-kurtosis distributions, is not properly separated. (Although separation in this case might be achieved by using a special nonlinearity chosen for the problem.) Since a two-dimensional gaussian distribution is rotationally symmetric, a mixture of white gaussian sources is inherently impossible to separate. Any

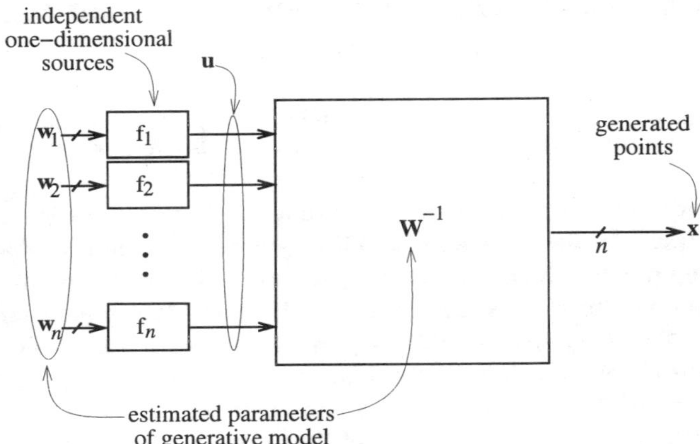

Figure 1: The ICA algorithm fits this parameterized generative model to data.

algorithm that makes no use of the temporal structure of its inputs can by definition make use of only the cumulative histograms of its inputs. If these histograms are gaussian, then such an algorithm will be in principle unable to separate. Since ICA makes no use of the temporal structure of its inputs, it is in principle unable to separate sources whose histograms are gaussian. This includes, for example, colored gaussian sources, speech or music which happen to have gaussian histograms, etc. It is sometimes speculated that any mixture of sources with high-kurtosis histograms is separable by ICA—but there is as yet no proof of this.

We shall now proceed to derive an ICA-like algorithm that can make use of temporal context. We do this by reformulating the blind source separation problem in a maximum likelihood framework.

2   Source separation and maximum likelihood density estimation

Consider the abstract problem of density estimation from samples. One desires to estimate some true distribution $p(\mathbf{x})$ over a space $\mathcal{R}^n$ from which samples $\mathbf{x}_1, \mathbf{x}_2, \ldots$ have been drawn. The maximum likelihood approach (Mendel and Burrus 1990) is to use a density estimator of some parametric form, say $\hat{p}(\mathbf{x}; \mathbf{w})$. Given a setting of the parameter vector $\mathbf{w}$, this will constitute the estimated probability density. In order to set $\mathbf{w}$ appropriately, we find a value for it that minimizes a measure of the difference between $p(\mathbf{x})$ and $\hat{p}(\mathbf{x}; \mathbf{w})$. An appropriate difference measure is the asymmetric divergence

$$G[p, \hat{p}] = \int p(\mathbf{x}) \, \log \frac{p(\mathbf{x})}{\hat{p}(\mathbf{x}; \mathbf{w})} \, d\mathbf{x} = H[p] - \int p(\mathbf{x}) \, \log \hat{p}(\mathbf{x}; \mathbf{w}) \, d\mathbf{x} \tag{1}$$

This is the entropy of the (fixed) input distribution p minus the likelihood of p given $\hat{p}$, and the $\mathbf{w}$ which minimizes this maximizes the likelihood; hence the term. (In a full Bayesian treatment, a prior distribution over $\hat{p}$ would have to be specified. This term would manifest itself here as an extra term giving the description length of the model $\hat{p}$.)

Although G itself is not available to us, an unbiased estimate of it can be obtained by taking a sample $\mathbf{x}$ from p,

$$\widehat{G} = H[p] - \log \hat{p}(\mathbf{x}; \mathbf{w}) \tag{2}$$

In order to apply a stochastic gradient optimization method, we wish to find an unbiased estimate of $dG/d\mathbf{w}$ (Robbins and Monro 1951). Due to the linearity of differentiation, $d\widehat{G}/d\mathbf{w} = -(d/d\mathbf{w}) \log \hat{p}(\mathbf{x}; \mathbf{w})$ is such an estimate.

For blind source separation, we consider the parametric form for $\hat{p}(\mathbf{x}; \mathbf{w})$ shown in figure 1. Let $\mathbf{u}$ be an n-dimensional vector whose components u_j are drawn from n independent parameterized one-dimensional density functions $f_j(u_j; \mathbf{w}_j)$. Now let $\mathbf{W}$ be an $n \times n$ matrix, and let $\mathbf{x} = \mathbf{W}^{-1}\mathbf{u}$. The consequent density on $\mathbf{x}$ is denoted $\hat{p}(\mathbf{x}; \mathbf{w})$, where the parameter vector $\mathbf{w}$ is a concatenation of the elements of $\mathbf{W}$ with the parameters $\mathbf{w}_1, \ldots, \mathbf{w}_n$ of the densities $f_1, \ldots, f_n$. The components of $\mathbf{u}$ represent the n independent sources which we would like to recover from the observed linear mix $\mathbf{x}$, and $\mathbf{W}$ represents the appropriate unmixing matrix.

To calculate $d\widehat{G}/d\mathbf{w}$ we expand $\log \hat{p}(\mathbf{x}; \mathbf{w}) = \log |\mathbf{W}| + \sum_j \log f_j(u_j; \mathbf{w}_j)$ where $\mathbf{u} = \mathbf{W}\mathbf{x}$. We then obtain

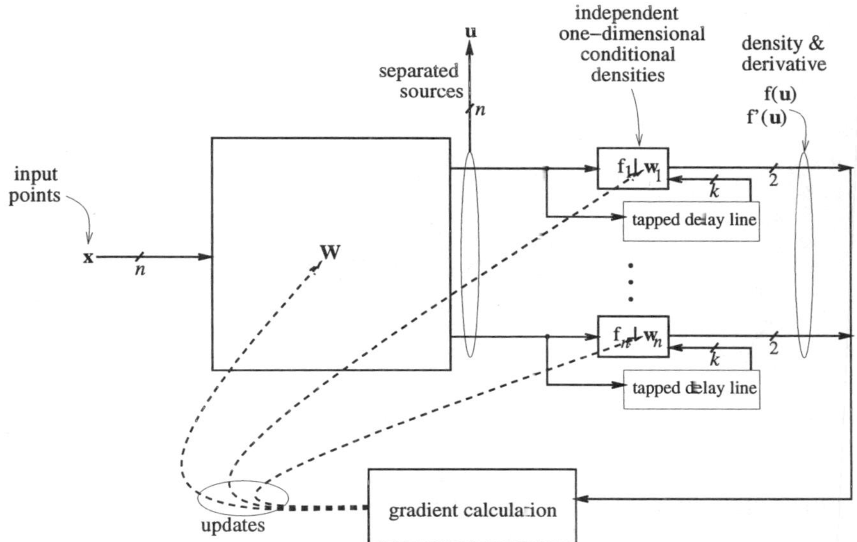

Figure 2: The contextual ICA (cICA) algorithm uses conditional densities which are not memoryless.

formulas for the two different sorts of parameters involved,

$$\frac{d\widehat{G}}{d\mathbf{W}} = -\mathbf{W}^{-T} - \left(\frac{f_j'(u_j; \mathbf{w}_j)}{f_j(u_j; \mathbf{w}_j)}\right)_j \mathbf{x}^T \tag{3}$$

$$\frac{d\widehat{G}}{d\mathbf{w}_j} = -\frac{df_j(u_j; \mathbf{w}_j)/d\mathbf{w}_j}{f_j(u_j; \mathbf{w}_j)} \tag{4}$$

where $(expr(j))_j$ denotes the column vector whose elements are $expr(1), \ldots, expr(n)$.

This is precisely the ICA algorithm, where our $f_j(u_j; \mathbf{w}_j)$ is the derivative of the Bell and Sejnowski (1995) saturating monotonic nonlinearity $g(u_j)$, and our parameter vector $\mathbf{w}_j$ holds the jth component of their $\mathbf{w}_0$ vector of bias terms, $f_j(u_j; \mathbf{w}_j) = g'(u_j + (\mathbf{w}_0)_j)$. In our formulation no squashing nonlinearity is ever calculated, except perhaps as a common subexpression in the computation of the derivatives of the densities. However, the output of the squashing nonlinearity is never actually used for anything in classic ICA.

3   Generalizing ICA

Under this MLE formulation of source separation, there is no restriction on the form of the distributions f_j. The density function $f_j(u_j)$ can have complex structure, and can be conditioned on other information—such as its recent history (as shown in figure 2), or even information from other modalities. All that is required is that the components of $\mathbf{u}$ be *conditionally* independent. In general, f_j can be of the form

$$f_j(u_j(t)|\mathbf{u}(t-1), \mathbf{u}(t-2), \ldots, \text{other information}, \ldots; \mathbf{w}_j)$$

We call this algorithm *contextual ICA* or cICA. To give a vivid example, if the sources were different people speaking, then the "other information" might be lip position measured using a visual modality, and $u_j(t)$ would be primarily conditioned on the recent history of that source itself, $u_j(t-1), u_j(t-2), \ldots$, but there might also be some small influence from other speakers. Although f_j can in principle be made arbitrarily complex, there is no practical reason to make it more complex than is necessary to permit proper separation of the sources.

Of course we must still calculate $df_j(u_j; \mathbf{w}_j)/d\mathbf{w}_j$ as per equation 4. In doing so, the history $u_j(t-1), u_j(t-2), \ldots$ of source j is treated as constant with respect to changes in $\mathbf{w}_j$. This is correct, because the unmixing depends only on the matrix $\mathbf{W}$ and not the parameters $\mathbf{w}_j$ of the individual source distributions. On the other hand, changing $\mathbf{W}$ changes the estimated recent history of source u_j, which in turn has an influence on f_j. However we use equation 3 without adding these extra terms. The approximation of dropping these cross terms is ubiquitous in time series analysis, and in this case the successful results of our simulations leads us to believe that it is benign.

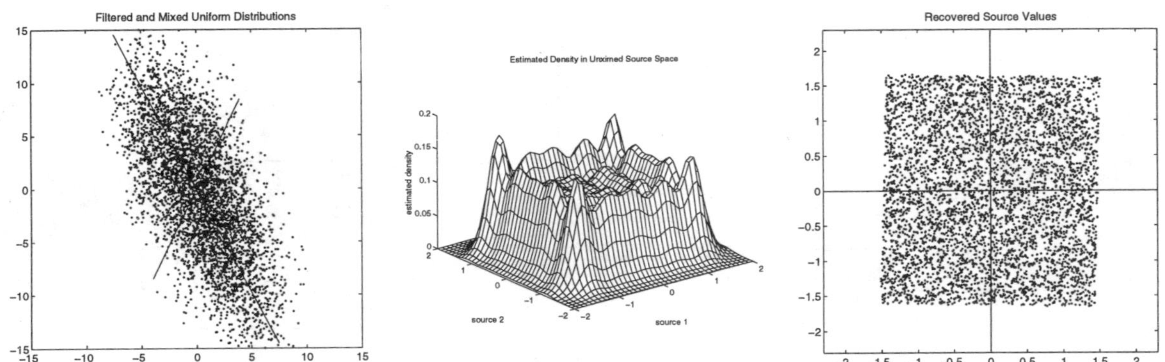

Figure 3: cICA using a history of one time step and a mixture of five logistic densities for each source was applied to 5,000 samples of a mixture of two one-dimensional uniform distributions each filtered by convolution with a decaying exponential of time constant of 99.5. Shown is a scatterplot of the data input to the algorithm, along with the true source axes (left), the estimated residual probability density (center), and a scatterplot of the residuals of the data transformed into the estimated source space coordinates (right). The product of the true mixing matrix and the estimated unmixing matrix deviates from a scaling and permutation matrix by about 3%.

4   Experiments

In our simulations we chose to make f_j a weighted sum of logistic density functions[1] with variable means and scales, and make these means linear functions of the recent history of source j. This allowed us to revert to classic ICA by setting the amount of temporal context to zero and the number of logistic densities in the sum to one. This density estimator, and the corresponding derivatives, are described in detail in appendix A.

Here we experiment with two distributions that conventional ICA is unable to separate. The first is an extremely simple two-dimensional distribution with no temporal context: both x_1 and x_2 are chosen iid from a uniform distribution. Conventional ICA incorrectly rotates the distribution 45 degrees, for reasons explained very well by Bell and Sejnowski (1995) in their discussion of this problematic case. The cICA algorithm successfully separates the sources. To make the problem more challenging, we then filtered each source through low-pass filter. The resulting time series has very gaussian histograms, but as shown in figure 3, cICA again correctly separates the sources.

The second experiment is somewhat more involved. Ten acoustic sources, which include the six used by Bell and Sejnowski (1995), were obtained, courtesty of Dr. Tony Bell. As shown in figure 4, the cumulative density of each source was measured and used to construct a monotonically increasing normalizer which, when applied to each sample from a source, gave the time series a gaussian histogram. These preprocessed time series were mixed using a random matrix. As shown in figures 5 and 6, ICA was unable to separate the resulting babble, but cICA separates properly, even when using only a very small amount of temporal context.

5   Discussion

In deriving cICA we have seen that ICA can regarded as a gradient method for performing maximum likelihood density estimation using a linear historyless factorial model and rigid source densities. The resulting error measure is naturally the same as in the Bell and Sejnowski (1995) derivation, but taking an MLE viewpoint allows a number of generalizations, which allow cICA to to separate a wider variety of sources.

A weakness this method shares with other blind source separation techniques is that it not robust to modulation of the dimensionality. In other words, it is not designed for a non-square mixing matrix. If $\mathbf{x} = \mathbf{As}$ and $\mathbf{x}$ is n-dimensional but $\mathbf{s}$ is m-dimensional, then in the case that $n > m$ the algorithm presented here can make no good use of the extra information but to imagine that a few extra Gaussian sources were mixed into the signal. This may perhaps be solved by using a $\mathbf{W}$ matrix of a special form. In the case that $n < m$ no linear unmixing can separate the sources, and it seems that a strong prior will be necessary to distinguish a single complex one-dimensional source from the one-dimensional sum of two simple independent one-dimensional sources, and a nonlinear unmixing process will be necessary to separate them.

---

[1] If $g(t)$ is the fraction of the susceptible population already infected, then the Verhulst (1844) epidemic equation, $dg/dt = g(t)(1 - g(t))$, expresses a random-contact homogeneous-population model of growth. This results in a logistic cumulative distribution function $g(t) = 1/(1+ \exp -t)$. The logistic density function is $h(t) = dg/dt$, the corresponding probability density of contracting the disease at time t.

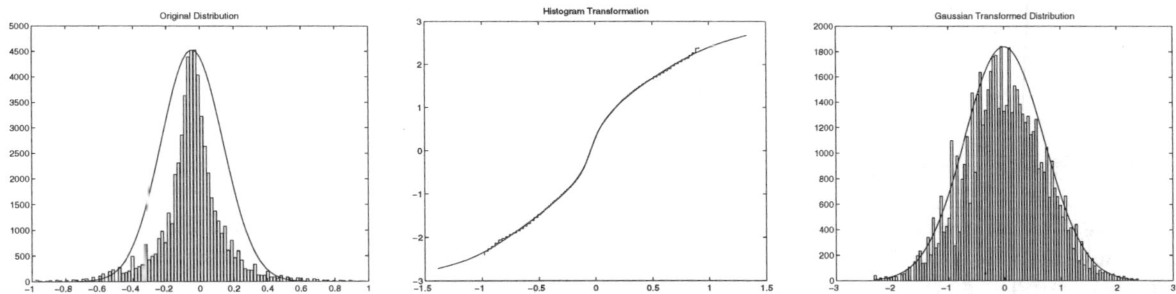

Figure 4: Histogram of samples from one of the acoustic sources used in the mixture below (left), nonlinear transformation applied to the data (center), histogram of transformed data (right).

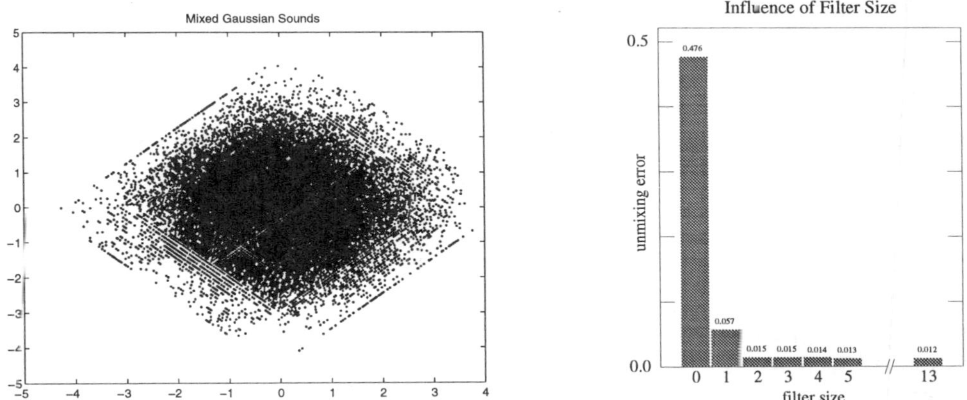

Figure 5: Scatterplot of linear mixture of two gaussianified acoustic sources (left), and unmixing error of cICA (using linear predictive sources with a single logistic) as a function of the length of the history used in the predictive filter (right). The zero history case corresponds to classic ICA, which fail to separate due to the gaussian histograms. (The parallelogram-shaped boundary and the stripes in the scatterplot on the left are artifacts of the signal quantization and the digital mixing.)

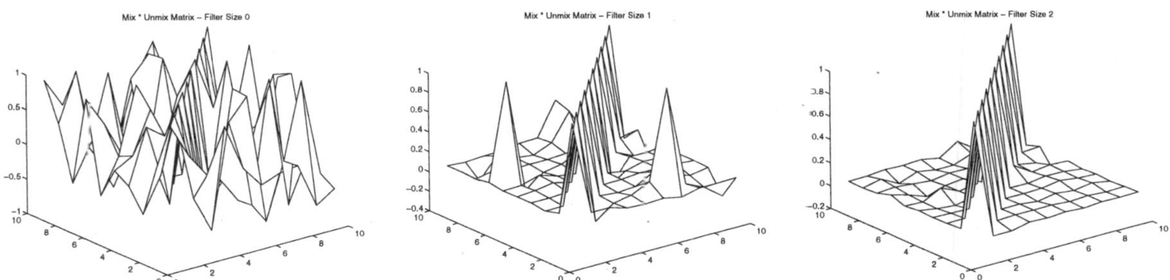

Figure 6: Plot of the elements of the product of the true mixing matrix and the estimated unmixing matrix, with each row normalized to make the largest element equal to one, and the rows permuted to place large elements along the diagonal. If the unmixing is perfect, the result will be a ridge along the diagonal with all off-diagonal elements equal to zero. The ten sources mixed are acoustic sources (courtesy of Tony Bell) which have had a monotonic nonlinearity applied to them to make their histograms exhibit gaussian statistics (see figure 4.) These are mixed using a random mixing matrix, and cICA with linear predictive sources and a single logistic density is used to estimate the unmixing matrix. The length of the history used is varied from zero, which corresponds to conventional ICA (left), to one (center), to two (right).

Finally, we would like to compare ICA with PCA. The principal components algorithm (Hotelling 1933) fits a linear mixture of one-dimensional Gaussian sources of minimal variance to samples from a high-dimensional distribution. ICA performs a similar action, but instead uses a linear mixture of potentially non-Gaussian distributions. As such, ICA might be viewed as a linear but non-Gaussian generalization of PCA—except that without PCA's minimum variance constraint, if Gaussian distributions are used for the f_j distributions of ICA, the unmixing matrix W has a great deal of freedom. It need not be orthogonal, and the coordinate system it embodies need have no special status. A challenge that remains with us is to find a sensible nonlinear analogue of PCA. One algorithm was proposed for this purpose by Parra, Deco, and Miesbach (1995), who replaced the orthogonal linear mixture of PCA by a symplectic mixing function while retaining PCA's minimal variance Gaussian source model. Unfortunately the symplectic map has a great deal of undesired freedom, so again the coordinate system it produces need have no special status.

6 Future work

Our current work concentrates on combining source separation with deconvolution, to enable the system to both tolerate and cancel the effects of echos and time delays between the sources and the microphones. An inherent ambiguity is introduced, which amounts to a freedom of one filter per source. We hope to resolve this ambiguity in a more symmetric fashion than in Torkkola (1996a), where identity filters are placed along the diagonal of the matrix of deconvolution filters. We are also exploring the incorporation of microphone nonlinearities, and microphone noise of known distribution, into the model.

Acknowledgments

Thanks are due to Dr. Tony Bell for provocative discussions and for generously sharing his data. Portions of this work were performed while BAP was visiting the Sloan Center for Theoretical Neurobiology at the Salk Institute.

References

Amari, S., Cichocki, A., and Yang, H. H. (1996). A new learning algorithm for blind signal separation.. In NIPS*95 (1996). In press.

Baram, Y. and Roth, Z. (1994). Density Shaping by Neural Networks with Application to Classification, Estimation and Forecasting. Tech. rep. CIS-94-20, Center for Intelligent Systems, Technion, Israel Institute for Technology, Haifa.

Baram, Y. and Roth, Z. (1995). Forecasting by Density Shaping Using Neural Networks. In *Computational Intelligence for Financial Engineering* New York City. IEEE Press.

Bell, A. J. and Sejnowski, T. J. (1995). An Information-Maximization Approach to Blind Separation and Blind Deconvolution. *Neural Computation*, 7(6), 1129–1159.

Bell, A. J. and Sejnowski, T. J. (1996a). The Independent Components of Natural Scenes. *Vision Research*. Submitted.

Bell, A. J. and Sejnowski, T. J. (1996b). Learning the higher-order structure of a natural sound. *Network*. In press.

Bialek, W., Rieke, F., de Ruyter van Stevenick, R. R., and Warland, D. (1991). Reading a Neural Code. *Science*, 252, 1854–1857.

Comon, P. (1994). Independent component analysis: A new concept. *Signal Processing*, 36, 287–314.

Hotelling, H. (1933). Analysis of a complex of statistical variables into principal components. *Journal of Educational Psychology*, 24, 417–441, 498–520.

Makeig, S., Bell, A. J., Jung, T.-P., and Sejnowski, T. J. (1996). Independent component analysis of Electroencephalographic data.. In NIPS*95 (1996). In press.

Mendel, J. M. and Burrus, C. S. (1990). *Maximum-likelihood deconvolution: a journey into model-based signal processing*. Springer-Verlag.

NIPS*95 (1996). *Advances in Neural Information Processing Systems 8*. MIT Press. In press.

Nowlan, S. J. and Hinton, G. E. (1992). Adaptive Soft Weight Tying using Gaussian Mixtures. In *Advances in Neural Information Processing Systems 4*, pp. 993–1000. Morgan Kaufmann.

Obradovic, D. and Deco, G. (1995). Linear Feature Extraction in non-Gaussian Networks. In *World Congress on Neural Networks*, Vol. 1, pp. 523–526 Washington.

Parra, L. C., Deco, G., and Miesbach, S. (1995). Redundancy reduction with information-preserving maps. *Network: Computation in Neural Systems*, 6, 61–72.

Pearlmutter, B. A. (1992). Temporally Continuous vs. Clocked Networks. In *Neural Networks in Robotics*, pp. 237–252. Kluwer Academic Publishers.

Robbins, H. and Monro, S. (1951). A Stochastic Approximation Method. *Annals of Mathematical Statistics*, 22, 400–407.

Torkkola, K. (1996a). Blind separation of convolved sources based on information maximization. In *Neural Networks for Signal Processing VI* Kyoto, Japan. IEEE Press. In press.

Torkkola, K. (1996b). Blind separation of delayed sources based on information maximization. In *Proceedings of the IEEE International Conference on Acoustics, Speech and Signal Processing* Atlanta, GA. In press.

Verhulst, P. F. (1844) *Nouveaux memoires de l'Academie royale des sciences et belles-lettres de Bruxelles, 18*, 1. Also 1846, *20*, 1.

A   Linear predictive source distributions

In the simulations of section 4 the $f_j(u_j; \mathbf{w}_j)$ distribution used is a mixture of logistic densities,

$$f_j(u_j(t)|u_j(t-1), u_j(t-2), \ldots; \mathbf{w}_j) = \sum_k m_{jk}\, h((u_j(t) - \bar{u}_{jk})/\sigma_{jk})/\sigma_{jk} \tag{5}$$

where σ_{jk} is a scale parameter for logistic density k of source j and is an element of $\mathbf{w}_j$, and the mixing coefficients m_{jk} are elements of $\mathbf{w}_j$ and are constrained by $\sum_k m_{jk} = 1$. The component means $\bar{u}_{jk}$ are taken to be linear functions of the recent values of that source,

$$\bar{u}_{jk} = \sum_{\tau=1} a_{jk}(\tau)\, u_j(t - \tau) + b_{jk} \tag{6}$$

where the linear prediction coefficients $a_{jk}(\tau)$ and bias b_{jk} are elements of $\mathbf{w}_j$.

To perform stochastic gradient descent it is necessary to calculate the derivative $df_j(u_j; \mathbf{w}_j)/d\mathbf{w}_j$. We accomplish this using the following equations. For conciseness, when we below refer to f_j, h_{jk}, and their simple derivatives f_j', h_{jk}', we leave off the arguments, which are the same as the corresponding arguments above. The h logistic density function and its cumulative distribution function g are as in footnote 1.

$$\frac{d\widehat{G}}{dm_{jk}} = -\frac{h_{jk}}{\sigma_{jk}\, f_j} \tag{7}$$

$$h_{jk}' = h_{jk}(1 - 2g) \tag{8}$$

$$\frac{d\widehat{G}}{d\sigma_{jk}} = \frac{(h_{jk}\, \sigma_{jk} + (u_j - \bar{u}_{jk})h_{jk}')m_{jk}}{\sigma_{jk}^3\, f_j} \tag{9}$$

$$\frac{d\widehat{G}}{da_{jk}(\tau)} = \frac{m_{jk}\, h_{jk}'\, u_j(t - \tau)}{\sigma_{jk}^2\, f_j} \tag{10}$$

$$\frac{d\widehat{G}}{db_{jk}} = \frac{m_{jk}\, h_{jk}'}{\sigma_{jk}^2\, f_j} \tag{11}$$

$$f_j' = \sum_k \frac{m_{jk}\, h_{jk}'}{\sigma_{jk}^2} \tag{12}$$

After each weight update the mixing coefficients must be normalized, $m_{jk} \leftarrow m_{jk}/\sum_{k'} m_{jk'}$.

B   Stochastic gradient descent

In the above experiments a number of techniques were used to improve the efficiency and robustness of the stochastic gradient descent procedure as applied to cICA.

First, rather than performing gradient descent directly on the scale parameters σ_{jk} and mixing parameters m_{jk}, we performed gradient descent upon their logarithms. Using such log scale parameters automatically guarantees $\sigma_{jk} > 0$. In addition, the stability and robustness of the gradient descent process are improved (Nowlan and Hinton 1992; Pearlmutter 1992).

Second, an important contribution to the computational efficiency of our experiments is due to Amari, Cichocki, and Yang (1996), who post-multiply their ICA-like gradient by $\mathbf{W}^T\mathbf{W}$. Since this is a positive-definite matrix it does not effect the stochastic gradient convergence criteria, and the resulting quantity

$$\Delta\mathbf{W} \propto -\frac{d\widehat{G}}{d\mathbf{W}}\mathbf{W}^T\mathbf{W} = \mathbf{W} - \left(\frac{f_j'(u_j; \mathbf{w}_j)}{f_j(u_j; \mathbf{w}_j)}\right)_j \mathbf{u}^T\mathbf{W} \tag{13}$$

is therefore an admissible pseudo-gradient. This post-multiplication neatly eliminates the matrix inversion, and makes the algorithm scale-invariant to the true mixing matrix $\mathbf{A}$.

Neural Mechanics

Robert L. Fry

The Johns Hopkins University/Applied Physics Laboratory
Laurel, MD USA 20723-6099
robert_fry@jhuapl.edu

Abstract — Elements of classical, statistical, and even quantum mechanics can be found in the described neural model through analogous constructs of position, momentum, Gibbs distributions, partition functions, and perhaps most importantly, observability. Such analogies suggest that the subject model represents a type of *neural mechanics* that is distinguished from other mechanical formulations of physics in two important regards. First, physical constants are not constant, but rather represent Lagrange factors that vary over time in response to learning. Secondly, neural systems attempt to optimize the very information-theoretic objective functions upon which their structure is founded. This paper provides an overview of an approach to neural modeling and understanding and highlights correspondences between this model, mechanical formulations of physics, and computational neurophysiology.

1. Overview

It is posited that information theory, as it stands, is an incomplete theory and that a dual theory exists that characterizes the transduction of information within physical devices as opposed to the transmission of information between physical devices which is the main emphasis of traditional information theory. Traditional information theory, together with its dual theory, may provide a succinct logical explanation of the physical theories of quantum, statistical, and even classical mechanics. However, the scope of this paper is more limited in that it highlights some basic properties of such a dual theory of information as they relate to the analysis of neural computation. A surprising result is that many known computational properties of cortical neurons can be deduced from the developed theory independent of biological assumptions. These properties include action potentials, Hebbian learning, nonlinear synaptic conductances, and other known computational properties of neurons which are described. The proposed model predicts other biologically-plausible properties as well which may validate the proposed model through focused physiological studies.

One can conceive that physics, as we know it, arises as a natural and logical consequence of a set of information laws that have been only partially formalized. In particular, consider the information and physics hierarchies shown in Figure 1. The left side of Figure 1 shows an information hierarchy which has the concept of distinguishability at the root and complexity at the highest level. The right side represents a hierarchy of mechanical formulations in physics; again with distinguishability at its root. Each intervening layer in both hierarchies arise through logical necessity from underlying and more fundamental layers. For example, Spencer-Brown [1] developed a mathematics of distinguishability with Boolean logic arising as one of its many consequences. Cox [2],[3] uses functional analysis to show that probability is the only logically consistent measure which generalizes to degrees of truthfulness or falseness on Boolean propositions or distinctions. Both Cox [3] and Jaynes [4] use a similar functional argument to show that entropy is the only logically consistent measure of degree of uncertainty on the part of an observer regarding which proposition of a set is the "true" state of nature.

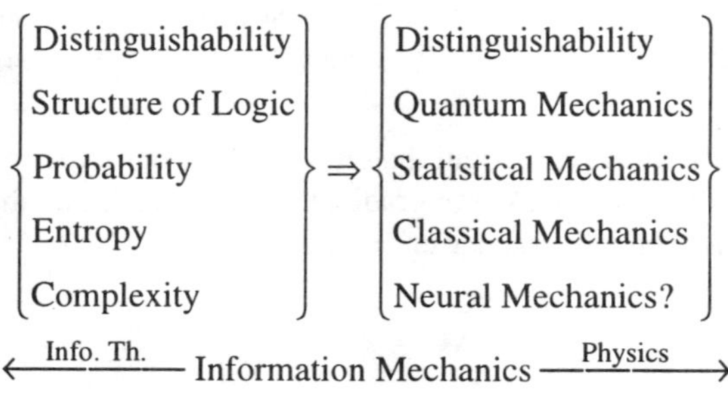

Figure 1

Finally, Rissanen [5] and Feder [6] show that the minimum descriptor length criterion generalizes formulations where maximized entropy would otherwise be used in the formation of a model by an observer of the observed information, e.g., an observer should form the model that has minimal complexity, yet is consistent with all observed information.

Distinguishability may also provide the basis for physical laws as suggested on the right side of Figure 1. More fundamentally, though, one can posit that basic information laws, perhaps realized through some type of *information mechanics*, dictates the essential details of both hierarchies shown in Figure 1 where both ultimately arise from a common notion of distinguishability. The idea that distinguishability and information furnish the basis of physics is not new and has been quantified to a large extent by Kantor [7], suggested by Wheeler [8], and discussed by many other physicists. Distinguishability is also a profound and persistent theme in Chinese philosophy being recognized as far back as 600 B.C. as found in the teachings of Lao Tsu [9] and also embodies the notion of the Yin and the Yang, i.e., that ultimately, concepts in its various forms arise in mutual relation to one another.

Distinguishability may then necessarily provide an information-theoretic basis for understanding neural computation. Neurons manifest distinguishability in two important regards that define their intrinsic nature as an observer and an assertor. First, neurons observe spatiotemporal patterns of input synaptic activity. These activity patterns induce the neuron to learn where learning is tantamount to symmetry breaking on the part of the neuron. That is, the neuron is driven to distinguish between patterns that generate action potentials and patterns that do not. These two classes of patterns of course only exist in mutual relation to one another. An action potential may be deemed an outward manifestation of a neural decision-making process. Regarding the second type of neural distinguishability, there is mounting evidence that neurons distinguish input potentials in a similar manner. That is, if a pre-synaptic potential is of sufficient magnitude, then a post-synaptic dendritic potential is generated which can then influence the somatic potential and which in turn affects the decision-making process of the same neuron. Even these two manifestations of distinguishability are complementary to one another in that one manifestation dictates what the neuron will assert (answer) while the other dictates what the neuron will inquire (asked). This duality is ubiquitous to many quantitative information-theoretic aspects of neural function which are summarized later in this paper.

Justification of the observed computational properties of biological neurons from an information-theoretic perspective has largely remained an elusive goal. One can speculate that perhaps information theory, as a mathematical tool, is somehow incomplete. That is, essential aspects of a more complete theory of information may exist that are important to understanding neural computation and which have not been formalized. In his original development of information theory, Shannon [10] provides modest clues regarding the nature of this incompleteness. In fact, Shannon explicitly obviates in both [10] and [11] an important aspect of information theory that is not considered in his seminal work. This aspect consists of that of the *meaning* of information and in fact in [11], Weaver develops the idea that the concept of meaning can be quantified using the same information measures developed by Shannon for the transmission of information.

Shannon dealt primarily with the transmission of information between a source and a receiver. However, the objective consideration of meaning requires the analysis of the transduction of information by a physical device in that meaning represents a continuous-valued assignment to observed information on the part of a measurement device (as noted by Weaver [11]). Both transmission and transduction are of intrinsic importance to the analytic treatment of processes of information flow *between and within* physical systems. This paper highlights the fact that neurological systems epitomize this perspective. In particular, interneural information exchange is accomplished through the use of action potentials which represent discrete events in both time and space. Alternatively, intraneural information transduction occurs through a sequential process of: (*i*) *Observation*; (*ii*) *Assimilation*; (*iii*) *Conclusion*; and ultimately, (*iv*) *Decision*. This paper summarizes how interneural transmission can be treated in a more or less classical manner, while intraneural transduction requires the acknowledgment of a complementary aspect of information theory that specifically addresses semantic aspects of information theory in an objective manner. This complementary aspect of information theory is the primary focus of this paper and is thought to give rise to the many relationships between the described neural model and traditional mechanical formulations in physics.

2. Highlights of the Described Neural Model

Although there is insufficient time to exhaustively cover every detail and ramification of the subject model, the essential approach and the primary results are delineated. Neural processing in space and time are both briefly covered under the aegis of distinguishability. Spatial domain processing is seen to have a statistical mechanics formulation including Gibbs' distributions, partition functions, and temperature-like construct. Alternatively, time domain processing requires the consideration of position and momentum constructs by way of analogy to classical mechanics. Neural observability is seen to be a key issue in both time and space processing and hence lends itself to a quantum-mechanical interpretation.

It is posited that individual neurons are rational in that they use probability (or a monotonic function thereof in the form of somatic energy), in their rational decision making. Action potential can be viewed as a logical decision arising as a consequence of a rational and structured decision-making process on the part of the neuron, or equivalently, an assertion in response to observed spatiotemporal activity regarding a posed question that is intrinsic to the neuron. From this perspective, a neuron functions as a passive observer or measurement device that awaits observable information upon which it will subsequently (*i′*) *Measure*, (*ii′*) *Process*, (*iii′*) *Infer*, and then outwardly (*iv′*) *Decide*. Decisions take the form of an action potential or the lack thereof. The methodology by which the neuron derives its intrinsic question and decision rule must formally correspond to learning. For the sake of conciseness in the following discussions, denote the subject model neuron by q.

The following questions can be asked of the conceptual neural model described so far.

(1) How does the propositional question intrinsic to q become defined? This question is synonymous with the question of how a neuron, which functions as a measurement device, is driven to determine what it will measure.

(2) Assuming that the interrogative proposition has been formed, how then does q draw conclusions and generate rational decisions to this intrinsic question given that particular patterns of spatiotemporal activity are observed?

(3) Finally, how should neural behavior vary over time in response to statistical changes to its external or environmental input? Moreover, in acknowledgment of the eventual loss or denial of information on which decisions are made, how should q maintain function which is somehow useful to the organism in the long-term?

If one precisely delineates the information observable to q, then it has been shown [12]-[15] that a maximum entropy (ME) formulation dictates the architectural structure of q which formally corresponds to a Hopfield [16] neuron paradigm for specified neural measurement functions. The set of measurements which the neuron can perform are specified by the vector $f = (\, x_1 y,\ x_2 y,\ x_3 y\ ,...,\ x_n y,\ y\,)^{\mathrm{T}}$, where $x_j y$ denotes the Boolean conjunction of input x_j and the output decision y. The presence of the output y alone in the vector f signifies neural observability of its own output. Note that each component of f must be interpreted as a neural measurement in both space and time since the conjunctive operator will sometimes evaluate *true* and sometimes *false*.

A simple Gibbs distribution and corresponding partition function arise from this formulation which are described by

$$P(x, y) = \frac{\exp[-\lambda^{\mathrm{T}} xy + \mu y]}{Z} \tag{1}$$

and

$$Z = \sum_{x' \in X} \sum_{y' \in Y} \exp[-\lambda^{\mathrm{T}} x' y' + \mu y'] \quad , \tag{2}$$

respectively. However, there are several problems with this approach that include: (*i*) the under constrained nature of the problem due to the lack of the supervised specification of moments required for an ME formulation; (*ii*) its biological implausibility due to mathematical intractability in solving the nonlinear ME problem; and (iii) the lack of a clear and meaningful objective function for obtaining values for the Lagrange factors which formally correspond to the synaptic efficacies and decision threshold, respectively. References [12] and [13] show that a maximized mutual information (MMI) criterion eliminates all these problems and yields a simple computational modality that is in close agreement with physiological models and measurements. Some areas of agreement are listed in Table I and will be highlighted during the paper presentation. The resulting adaptation equations and neural structure describe neural function in space.

Neural processing in time can be addressed in a similar fashion using the same MMI objective function used for ascertaining the neural architecture just described. The most important consequence of this analysis is the prediction of a set of adaptable parameters τ which are conjugate to the synaptic efficacies λ, where both sets of parameters are modified through a common Hebbian adaptation mechanism. Whereas λ serves to effect neural MMI in space, the adaptation of τ serves to effect MMI in time through the temporal equalization of *meaningful* synaptic inputs relative to the soma, where the term *meaningful* here denotes those inputs which have been successfully encoded by q and play a direct role in its decision-making process. Table II highlights some important results regarding neural temporal adaptation which requires the consideration of a construct analogous to momentum where mass corresponds to the synaptic efficacy, velocity corresponds to the time-derivative of the input potential, and the neural output $y(t)$ enables measurement of the momentum by q. Another important result regarding neural processing in time, is the derived requirement for a stochastic mechanism that is necessary to effect the discussed spatial and temporal adaptation mechanisms and which is consistent with integrate-and-fire dynamical neural models. This stochastic mechanism may functionally arise through inputs that are *non-meaningful* to the neuron where the term non-meaningful denotes the uncoded synaptic inputs that are complementary to the meaningful inputs and which ultimately give rise to a Wiener process at the soma.

Spatial and temporal MMI considerations describe the transduction of information *within* the model neuron. In addition, a further consideration of this transduction process indicates how transmission of information occurs *between* neurons. The entirety of information flow between neurons can be understood through the following four exhaustive information exchange cases.

(1) An action potential is sent and then measured by another neuron waiting to see it.
(2) An action potential is sent, but the other neuron is not waiting to measure it.
(3) No action potential is sent, but the other neuron waits to measure it anyway.
(4) No action potential is sent and the other neuron is not waiting to measure it anyway.

Those familiar with coding theory can recognize the above as being realizable through a pulse-code modulation scheme or PCM. There are many advantages of such a coding scheme [17] in a neural setting including efficient use of the average neural transmit power, simplicity of signal modulation and demodulation, optimality over virtually all other modulation schemes, precise signal regeneration, almost optimal performance for low average signal-to-noise ratios, and minimal intersymbol interference from other proximal transmission lines such as in a dense neural environment. Perhaps most importantly, the information capacity C in units of bits/s of each interneural channel must abide by the Shannon [10] limit

$$ C = B \log_2 \left(1 + \frac{P_{avg}}{N} \right) \ , \tag{3} $$

where the channel has bandwidth B and white Gaussian noise with in-band noise power N is added to the transmitted action potential subject to an average neural transmit power constraint P_{avg}. Equation (3) holds regardless of the type of modulation scheme used to transmit information through the channel. Table III suggests biological correspondence of various aspects of neural function with computational functions derived within the framework of the subject neural model, including the implementation of PCM through nonlinear postsynaptic activations in response to input action potentials.

3. Summary

This paper describes how many neural properties can be derived and described in terms of a type of neural mechanics by way of analogy to other mechanical formulations in physics. The subject model is easily extended to networks of connected neurons which is then described by a composite Gibbs distribution and a corresponding energy function which is the sum of the energies of the component neurons. The neural significance and interpretation of *meaning* in the present model is clear. Meaning corresponds to the continuous-valued somatic evidence $\zeta(x) = \lambda^T x - \mu$ computed by the neuron in response to observed information and used by the neuron in rational decision making.

References

[1] G. Spencer-Brown, *The Laws of Form*. New York: E. P. Dutton, 1979.

[2] R. T. Cox, "Probability, frequency, and reasonable expectation," *Am. J. Physics* Vol. 14, pp. 1-13, 1946.

[3] R. T. Cox, *The Algebra of Probable Inference*. Baltimore: The Johns Hopkins Press, 1961.

[4] E. T. Jaynes, "Prior probabilities," IEEE Trans. on Sys. Sci. and Cyber, vol. 4, pp. 227-241, 1968.

[5] J. Rissanen, "Modeling by shortest data description," *Automatics*, vol. 14, pp. 465-471, 1978.

[6] Feder M, "Maximum entropy as a special case of the minimum descriptor length criterion," *IEEE Trans. Info.Th*, vol. 32, pp. 847-849, 1986.

[7] F. Kantor, *Information Mechanics*. New York: John Wiley and Sons, 1977.

[8] J. A. Wheeler, "Information, physics, quantum: The search for links," in *Complexity, Entropy, and the Physics of Information*, pp. 3-28, Addison-Wesley, 1990.

[9] L. Tsu, *Tao Te Ching*. A contemporary translation by Gia-Fu Feng and Jane English, New York: Random House, 1972. Originally dated to around the sixth century B.C.

[10] C. E. Shannon, "A mathematical theory of communication," *Bell Sys. Tech. J*, vol. 27, pp. 379-423, 623-656, 1948.

[11] C. E. Shannon and W. Weaver, *The mathematical theory of communication*. Urbana, IL: The University of Illinois Press, 1949.

[12] R. L. Fry, "Neural processing of information," *Proc.1994 IEEE international symposium on information theory*, Norway, 1994.

[13] R. L. Fry, "Observer-participant models of neural processing," *IEEE Trans. Neural Networks*, vol. 6, pp. 918-928, 1995.

[14] R. L. Fry, "Rational neural models based on information theory," *Proc. 1995 workshop on maximum entropy and Bayesian methods*. Sante Fe, NM, 1995.

[15] R. L. Fry, "Rational neural models based on information theory," *Proc. 1995 neural information processing systems - Natural and synthetic*. Denver, CO, 1995.

[16] J. J. Hopfield and D. W. Tank, "Neural computations of decisions in optimization problems," *Biological Cybernetics*, vol. 52, pp. 141-152, 1985.

[17] B. Oliver, J. R. Pierce, and C. E. Shannon, "The philosophy of PCM," *Proc. IRE*, vol. 36, pp. 1324-1332, 1948.

λ	Lagrange multiplier vector corresponding to synaptic efficacies and describing the question intrinsic to the neuron in generating its answers.
μ	Lagrange multiplier corresponding to the decision threshold. It describes how answers are generated by the subject neuron in response to measured information and in turn serves to modify the intrinsic neural question.
$\lambda^T x(t)$	Time-varying somatic potential induced by dendritic inputs which can be coded by the subject neuron.
$I(X;Y)$	Maximized mutual information of the neuron realized through the simultaneous maximization of $H(Y)$ and minimization of $H(Y\|X)$.
$H(Y)$	Maximized through the adaptation of the decision threshold μ, and serves to optimize neural transmission of information.
$H(Y\|X)$	Minimized through the adaptation of λ and conditionalized principal components analysis; important to neural reception of information.
$\zeta(x)$	(*i*) Formally corresponds to *statistical evidence* as defined by the log of the odds function and mathematically described by $\log \Pr\{Firing\,x\}/\Pr\{No\,Firing\|x\}$. (*ii*) A *sufficient statistic* for firing; i.e., it contains all the information necessary for the neuron to make a decision. (*iii*) Provides a maximum-likelihood decision rule in the limit as $T \to 0$. (*iv*) Provides the optimum nonlinear minimum mean-squared-error estimator for y. (*v*) $E_q = -\zeta(x)y$ is the neural energy function. (*vi*) The potential $\zeta(x)$ must be computed at some point within the soma.
$P(y{=}1\|x)$	The probability of action potential as conditionalized on the current input x. This is a sigmoidally shaped function of the evidence $\zeta(x)$ and the auxiliary time-varying temperature parameter T.

Table I: Key results of the analysis of neural function in space along with some noteworthy properties of the evidence function $\zeta(x) = \lambda^T x - \mu$.

Condition:	Output: $y(t)$	Efficacy: λ_i	Derivative: $\partial x(t-\tau_i^d)/\partial t$	Explanation
1	O	O	O	No adaptation due to lack of output
2	O	O	●	No adaptation due to lack of output
3	O	●	O	No adaptation due to lack of output
4	O	●	●	No adaptation due to lack of output
5	●	O	O	No or little adaptation due to minimal
6	●	O	●	or nonexistent synaptic efficacy
7	●	●	O	No input or equilibrated adaptation
8	●	●	+/−	Temporal adaptation occurs

Table II: Summary of the eight conditions under which the input momentum as defined by $p_i = \lambda_i\, x_i(t-\tau_i)y(t)$ is zero. The symbol O denotes zero; ● denotes non-zero. The notation +/− denotes the positive or negative derivative, respectively, of the input action potential. Temporal adaptation only occurs in case 8.

Neural Function and Association	Speculated Computational Importance
Modified Oja's equation	A means of implementing the optimal conditionalized learning rule: $$\lambda(t + \Delta t) = \lambda(t) + \pi\zeta(x)[x(t) - \gamma^2\zeta(x)\lambda(t)]$$
Hebbian paradigm	Provides for feedback for maximized mutual information through spatiotemporal adaptation. This allows the minimization of conditional entropy $H(Y|X)$ and temporal equalization of coded inputs.
Decision threshold	Provides for optimal decision making to maximize the output entropy denoted by $H(Y)$. Adaptation is driven by the rule: $\mu(t + \Delta t) = \alpha\mu(t) + (1-\alpha)\zeta(x)$
Synaptic efficacies	Correspond to the Lagrange multipliers for microcanonical neural distributions.
Temporal delay parameters	Are the temporal equivalent to the synaptic efficacies. They serve to equalize arrival times of potentials at the soma. Temporal adaptation driven by $\dfrac{d\tau_i^d}{dt} = y(t)\lambda_i \dfrac{dx_i(t - \tau_i^d)}{dt}$
Nonlinear postsynaptic conductance	Implements quantization of induced somatic charge as measured by the subject synaptic efficacy and provides for PCM reception.
Sigmoidal activation function	Implements optimal inference and learning through stochastic adaptation and neural decision making.
Action potential	Represents the simplest decision/indicational form for transmission of neural "decision" and also represents a very energy-efficient way of transmitting information between neurons through PCM.
Distal coincidence detection	Provides for temporal adaptation at sites providing the best temporal resolution and sensitivity.
Dendritic spines	Provide substrate for channel group delay and advance modification and are the temporal analog to efficacy modification. In fact, spines may implement both functions.
Hopfield neuron model	Is a by-product of theoretical model.
Background synaptic activity	Implements the stochastic adaptation rule for λ and μ.

Table III: Speculated computational correspondence of various aspects of neural function with computational functions derived within the framework of the developed neural model.

A Statistical Mechanics Study of Weight Decay

Siegfried Bös
Lab for Information Representation, RIKEN
Hirosawa 2–1, Wako–shi, Saitama, 351–01, Japan
Tel: +81–48-, phone: -467–9625, fax: -462–9881
email: boes@zoo.riken.go.jp

***Abstract*— Weight decay was proposed to reduce overfitting as it often appears in the learning tasks of artificial neural networks. In this paper weight decay is applied to a well defined model system based on a single layer perceptron, which exhibits strong overfitting. Since the optimal non-overfitting solution is known for this system, we can compare the effect of the weight decay with this solution. A strategy to find the optimal weight decay strength is proposed, which leads to the optimal solution for any number of examples.**

1 The Model

Overfitting is a problem in neural network learning which can reduce the performance drastically. Simply defined, overfitting means that the networks learns too many details from the examples and neglects its generalization ability. In this paper we study how weight decay, see [3], can help to avoid overfitting.

In previous works [1] and [2], we have established a model system, which can be handled analytically, but shows already many of the characteristics of general feedforward learning. The system is based on a continuous single–layer perceptron, which has one layer of N variable weights W_i between its input units and the output unit. To compute the output z, a continuous function g is applied on the weighted sum h of the inputs x_i, i.e.

$$z = g(h), \qquad \text{with} \qquad h = \frac{1}{\sqrt{N}} \sum_{i=1}^{N} W_i\, x_i. \tag{1}$$

Learning is done in a *supervised* fashion. That means one uses example inputs $\vec{x}^\mu$ (with $\mu = 1, \ldots, P$) from the input space I, for which the correct outputs z_*^μ are known. For theoretical purposes we assume that the learning task is provided by another network, which we call *teacher network*.

The mean squared error is used to measure the difference between the outputs of the teacher and student. Training tries to minimize the *training error* E_T, which is the mean error over the set of examples, and the performance is measured by the *generalization error* E_G, which is averaged over all possible inputs, i.e.

$$E_\mathrm{T} := \frac{1}{2P} \sum_{\mu=1}^{P} [z_*^\mu(\vec{x}^\mu) - z^\mu(\vec{x}^\mu)]^2, \qquad E_\mathrm{G} := \frac{1}{2} < [z_*(\vec{x}) - z(\vec{x})]^2 >_{\{\vec{x} \in I\}}. \tag{2}$$

The concept of the teacher network allows an efficient monitoring of the training process. Suitable quantities for the monitoring of the training process are the normalized *order parameters*,

$$q := \sqrt{\frac{1}{N} \sum_{i=1}^{N} (W_i)^2} = ||\vec{W}||, \qquad r := \frac{1}{||\vec{W}||} \frac{1}{N} \sum_{i=1}^{N} W_i^* W_i, \tag{3}$$

in which the '*' denotes the variables belonging to the teacher net. Both have obvious meanings, q is the norm of the student's weights and r is the cosine of the angle between the two weight vectors of teacher and student.

In this paper we will study how weight decay can help to reduce overfitting, which appears usually in unrealizable learning tasks. We implement the unrealizability simply by different choices of the output function for teacher and student, i.e. $g_*(h) = \tanh(\gamma h)$ and $g(h) = h$. We can assume $||\vec{W}^*|| = 1$, another norm can be taken into account by a change of the gain γ.

The generalization error (2) can be expressed in terms of these order parameters. We assume uniformally distributed random inputs $\vec{x}$, with $<x_i> = 0$ and $<(x_i)^2> = 1$. Then the weighted sums h_* and h are correlated Gaussians. The average over the inputs $\vec{x}$ can be transformed in a Gaussian integral, with the uncorrelated variables $\tilde{h}_*$ and $\tilde{h}$,

$$E_\mathrm{G}(r, q) = \frac{1}{2} < \left\{ g_* \left[\gamma \tilde{h}_* \right] - g \left[q(r \tilde{h}_* + \sqrt{1 - r^2}\, \tilde{h}) \right] \right\}^2 >_{\tilde{h}_*, \tilde{h}}, \tag{4}$$

where $< \ldots >_{\tilde{h}}$ denotes the following integral,

$$< F(\tilde{h}) >_{\tilde{h}} := \int_{-\infty}^{\infty} \frac{d\tilde{h}}{\sqrt{2\pi}} \exp\left(-\frac{\tilde{h}^2}{2} \right) F(\tilde{h}).$$

The two constants, $G(\gamma)$ and $H(\gamma)$,

$$G(\gamma) := <g_*^2(\gamma \tilde{h}_*)>_{\tilde{h}_*}, \qquad H(\gamma) := <g_*(\gamma \tilde{h}_*)\tilde{h}_*>_{\tilde{h}_*}, \tag{5}$$

summarize the dependence on the teacher. They can also be used to describe other learning tasks with a linear student network. Therefore our theory is not restricted to this special task, but can be applied to other tasks, like the noisy teacher (affects only G and H).

We start with a recapitulation of the results without weight decay, see [1]. Later we will see that these results are very important for the comprehension of the case with weight decay.

2   Without Weight Decay

Now we briefly discuss the results of the case without weight decay. The learning is done by gradient descent, $\Delta W_i = -\eta \frac{\partial E_T}{\partial W_i}$.

A good theoretical description can be achieved by methods from *statistical mechanics*. This implies the thermodynamic limit, i.e. the number of weights $N \to \infty$. We assume that the number of examples P becomes also infinite, but the fraction $\alpha = \frac{P}{N}$ remains finite. Already systems of quite moderate size, such as $N \geq 100$, are well described by this theory. A general introduction to the calculation of the free energy with the *replica method* can be found [3]. For more details especially about this problem consult [1].

The free energy f describes the behavior of the system. In the case of the linear student network the free energy can be expressed analytically as $f(r, q, Q)$. The stationarity conditions, $\frac{\partial f}{\partial r} = 0$ and $\frac{\partial f}{\partial q} = 0$, define the values of the order parameters, i.e. $r(\alpha, a)$ and $q(\alpha, a)$. They depend on the parameters G and H, which describe the learning task, and a parameter,

$$a := 1 + \frac{1}{\beta(Q^2 - q^2)}, \tag{6}$$

which expresses the temperature dependence, since $\beta = T^{-1}$.

Both errors E_G and E_T are fully determined by the values of α and a. The parameter a relates the quality of the training, measured by $E_T(\alpha, a)$, to the generalization performance of the system $E_G(\alpha, a)$. *Exhaustive training* corresponds to the absolute minimum of the training error. In the thermodynamic theory this is the zero–temperature limit. The resulting generalization error shows strong overfitting around $\alpha = 1$ (see upper solid line in Fig. 1). Asymptotically, i.e. for $\alpha \gg 1$, it shows the optimal convergence rate,

$$E_G^{\text{exh}}(\alpha > 1) = \frac{G - H^2}{2} \frac{\alpha}{\alpha - 1}, \qquad E_T^{\text{exh}}(\alpha > 1) = \frac{G - H^2}{2} \frac{\alpha - 1}{\alpha}. \tag{7}$$

But in the intermediate regime better solutions can be found. In [1] it was shown that a certain finite training error can have positive effects on the generalization ability. The parameter a can be optimized leading to

$$E_G^{\text{opt}}(\alpha) = \frac{1}{2}\left(G - \frac{\alpha}{a^{\text{opt}}(\alpha)}H^2\right), \tag{8}$$

with

$$a^{\text{opt}}(\alpha) := c + \sqrt{c^2 - \alpha}, \quad \text{and} \quad c = \frac{1}{2}\left(\alpha + \frac{G}{H^2}\right). \tag{9}$$

The resulting curve for the generalization error is shown in Fig. 1 as the lower solid line and exhibits no overfitting.

3   With Weight Decay

Now we want to examine whether weight decay can help to reach the optimal generalization for all values of α. Weight decay can be expressed by a penalty term in the training energy, i.e.

$$E_T = E_T + \frac{\lambda}{2N} \sum_{i=1}^{N}(W_i)^2, \tag{10}$$

where the parameter λ determines the relative strength of the weight decay. This changes the gradient descent learning in such a way that the additional term decreases the amount of the weights.

Now we have to recapitulate the statistical mechanics approach from the last section with the additional weight decay term. The calculation follows the same guidelines as without weight decay. As result we find that only one term is added to the free energy,

$$-\beta \tilde{f}(r, q, Q) = -\beta f(r, q, Q) - \frac{\alpha \beta \lambda Q^2}{2}. \tag{11}$$

Since this additional term is independent of q and r, the corresponding order parameter equations remain unchanged. Only the equation for Q is affected. This has serious implications because it means, that a system with weight decay can be transformed in an equivalent system without weight decay at another temperature.

The determination of Q, by $\frac{\partial f}{\partial Q} = 0$, leads to the following relation between a and λ,

$$b^2 \alpha\lambda + b(\alpha\lambda + \alpha - 1) - 1 = 0\,, \quad \text{with} \quad b := \beta(Q^2 - q^2) = (a-1)^{-1}\,. \tag{12}$$

The problem is now already more or less solved. We can directly use the solution of the case without weight decay, if we rescale the temperature.

First, we will assume that the weight decay strength is fixed. This resembles the situation, when no further knowledge about the system is available and one has to make a more or less well educated guess about the weight decay strength.

We resolve the equation (12) to receive a as a function of λ,

$$a(\lambda) = \frac{1}{b_{1,2}(\lambda)} + 1\,, \qquad b_{1,2}(\lambda) = \frac{1 - \alpha - \alpha\lambda \pm \sqrt{(1 - \alpha - \alpha\lambda)^2 + 4\alpha\lambda}}{2\alpha\lambda}\,. \tag{13}$$

Only the solution with the 'plus'–sign, i.e. b_1, is a relevant solution. Then we insert $a(\lambda)$, G, and H in the order parameter equations for r and q, which yields the behavior of the errors E_{G} and E_{T}.

Fig. 1 shows the generalization error as a function of the loading rate $\alpha = P/N$ for different fixed values of λ. The curves are the theoretical predictions and the points are simulated results. We can see that the overfitting is already reasonably reduced, but the optimal curve is reached only once for each choice of λ, see also [4]. So the weight decay strength should be chosen more accurately.

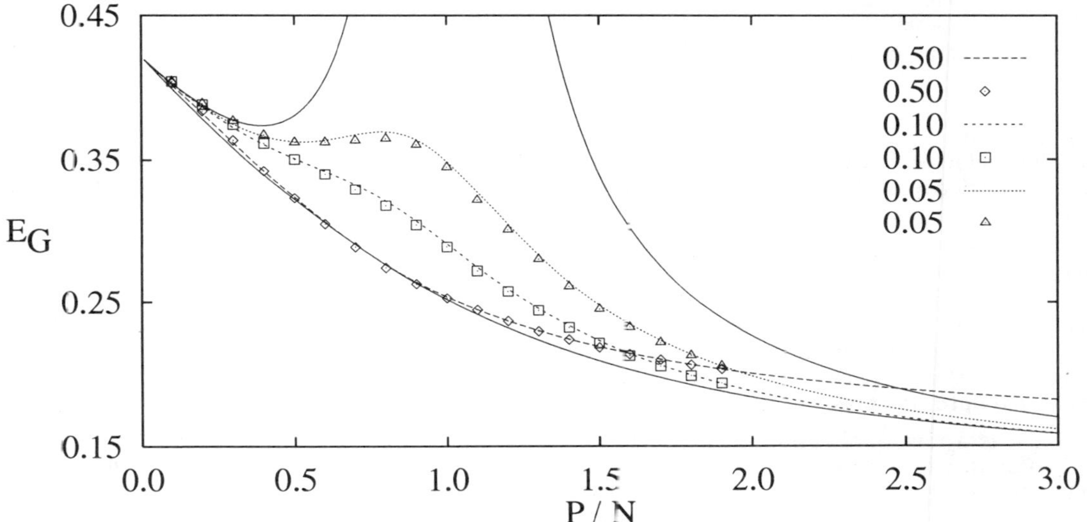

Figure 1: The generalization error as a function of the loading rate $\alpha = P/N$ for different weight decay factors $\lambda = 0.5$, 0.1, and 0.05. Lines are calculated by the theory and points are simulation results ($N = 200$, 100 independent runs, gain $\gamma = 5$).

Now we want to determine the optimal value for the weight decay strength for each α. As a starting point we look at the generalization error as a function of λ for different choices of α, see Fig. 2. Again it can be seen that there is always one optimal choice for λ. If the number of examples becomes large the weight decay becomes less and less important, i.e. $\lambda^{\mathrm{opt}}(\alpha \to \infty) = 0$.

To find the optimal value for the weight decay strength, we use the relation (12) between a and λ, and get λ as a function of a,

$$\lambda(a) = \frac{1 + (1 - \alpha)b}{\alpha b(b + 1)} = \frac{1}{\alpha}\frac{a - 1}{a}(a - \alpha)\,. \tag{14}$$

If we insert $a^{\mathrm{opt}}(\alpha)$ from eq. (9) we receive $\lambda^{\mathrm{opt}}(\alpha)$. It is surprising that the expression can be simplified extremely. After applying some algebra we find

$$\lambda^{\mathrm{opt}}(\alpha) = \left(\frac{G}{H^2} - 1\right)\frac{1}{\alpha}\,. \tag{15}$$

This simple dependence of the optimal weight decay strength on α allows a practical training strategy, which should reach the optimal curve for all values of α. Only the constant prefactor has to be determined. From a theoretical point of view the equations above can be exploited. The initial learning error, i.e.

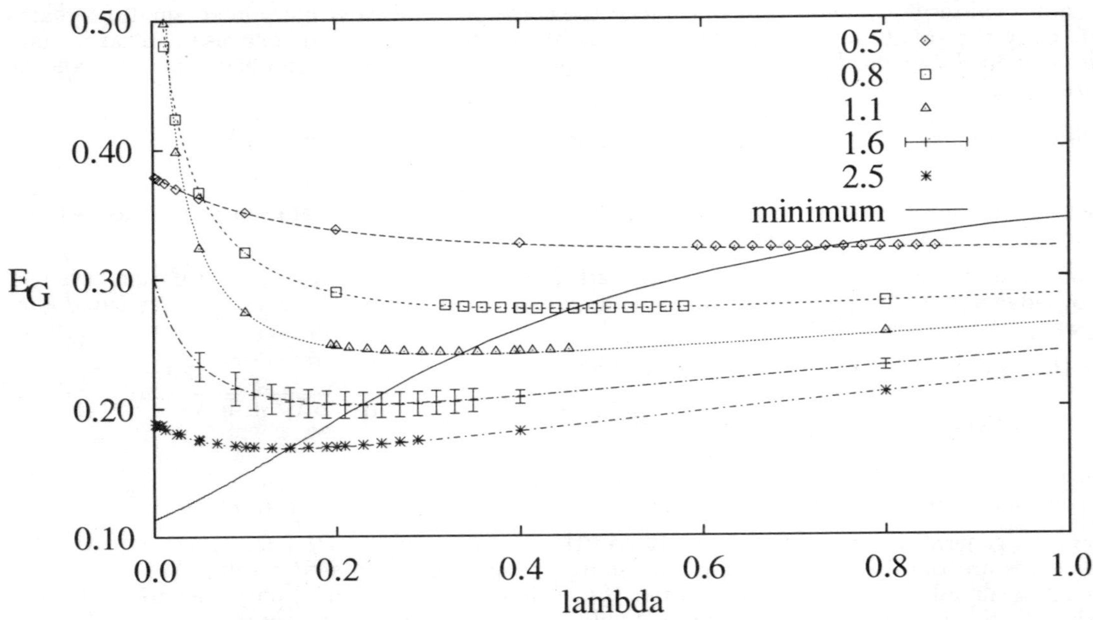

Figure 2: The generalization error as a function of the weight decay strength λ for different $\alpha = 0.5$, 0.8, 1.1, 1.6, 2.5. Lines are calculated by the theory and points are simulation results ($N = 200$, $\gamma = 5$). For each α there is exactly one optimal weight decay strength $\lambda^{\mathrm{opt}}(\alpha)$, indicated by the solid line.

$E_G(0) = G/2$, yields G. The value of H can be calculated from $E_T^{\mathrm{exh}}(\alpha)$, if we use expression (7). More practically the prefactor can be determined for a smaller system by the use of a cross–validation scheme. Based on the knowledge of the prefactor the optimal weight decay strength $\lambda^{\mathrm{opt}}(\alpha)$ is given for arbitrary system sizes.

4   Summary

In this paper we have studied the influence of weight decay on the generalization ability of a single–layer perceptron. A task with strong overfitting was investigated carefully. We could show that an optimally chosen weight decay strength can avoid the overfitting totally. A possible strategy to find this optimal weight decay strength has been proposed also.

Furthermore, it is a nice application of the theory of learning with errors, which was introduced in [1]. In [2] we had shown how this theory can be applied to nonlinear systems. It would be interesting to extend it to more practical learning tasks. A different approach to study the same problem exactly is in progress.

Acknowledgment: We thank Xiao Yan SU and Herbert WIKLICKY for comments on the manuscript.

References

[1] S. Bös (1995), 'Avoiding overfitting by finite temperature learning and cross–validation', in *International Conference on Artificial Neural Networks 95 (ICANN'95)*, edited by EC2 & Cie, Vol.2, p.111–116.

[2] S. Bös (1996), 'A realizable learning task which exhibits overfitting', in *Advances in Neural Information Processing Systems 8 (NIPS*95)*, editors D. Touretzky, M. Mozer, and M. Hasselmo, MIT Press, Cambridge MA, in press.

[3] J. Hertz, A. Krogh, and R.G. Palmer (1991), *Introduction to the Theory of Neural Computation*, Addison–Wesley, Reading.

[4] A. Krogh, and J. Hertz (1992), 'A simple weight decay can improve generalization', in *Advances in Neural Information Processing Systems 4*, editors J.E. Moody, S.J. Hanson and R.J. Lippmann, Kaufmann, San Mateo CA, p.950–957.

Bin Model for Neural Networks

Yaser Abu-Mostafa†, Xubo Song‡
† Dept. of Electrical Engineering and Dept. of Computer Science
California Institute of Technology
Pasedena, CA 91125 USA
‡ Dept. of Electrical Engineering
California Institute of Technology
Pasedena, CA 91125 USA

Abstract— **We propose a theoretical framework for the modeling of learning machines, such as neural networks, which we call the *bin model*, in which we consider a function as a Bernoulli distribution. Using this model, we study the issues related to generalization, such as the expected test error given a certain training error, and the expected test error given the *best* training error. Noise in the data is also captured by the bin model, and the effect of noise on generalization is quantified.**

1 Introduction

In learning, what we have is a finite and often noisy data set. To approximate the target function embodied in the data set, we choose a class of functions, e.g., the functions that can be implemented by a feed-forward neural network with certain architecture, as our candidates. Each candidate function approximates the target function to certain precision. From the candidate functions, we will choose the one that fits the data well according to some criterion. We have only access to training error. How well does the training error indicate the test error? How is this effected when there is noise in the data? To attack these questions, we introduce the Bin Model.

Let $f : X \rightarrow \{0, 1\}$ be the target function. A bin represents a candidate function $g : X \rightarrow \{0, 1\}$. Each bin is characterized by a parameter π, which is the probability that $g(x)$ disagrees with $f(x)$ on a point x picked from X according to the possibly unknown input distribution $\Omega(x)$.

$$\pi = P\{g \neq f\}$$

$$= \int [g(x) - f(x)]^2 \Omega(x)dx$$

A bin can be visualized as containing red and green marbles. The probability of picking a red marble is π. When we draw i.i.d. examples from the input space and test them on function g, we are virtually drawing marbles from a bin and checking their colors. We can consider each example as a Bernoulli trial with probability π of error and probability $1 - \pi$ of success. When we have N examples, we have N independent, identically distributed Bernoulli trials. Let n be the number of errors, and let $\nu = n/N$ be the frequency of error. The Law of Large Numbers tells us that as $N \rightarrow \infty$, the random variable ν approaches its mean π. That is to say, the frequency will be a very good estimate of the probability for large sample size N.

In reality, instead of one candidate function, we are actually looking at a set G of candidate functions, such as a given neural network with free weights. Each single function has its probability of error π. A set of functions give us an array of $\pi_1, \pi_2, ..., \pi_M$, which we call the π distribution. The π distribution indicates the suitability of a function class G for approximating the target function. The smaller the probability of error π and the more the functions that have small π, the better suited this function class is for the approximation of f. Furthermore, we assume that this function class can implement M different functions, i.e. there are M elements in G. In the case of an infinite function class, we approximate it by a finite one by means of discretization. How M, as a measure of model complexity, relates to other measures such as VC dimension [1] and Effective Number of Parameters P_{eff} [2], needs to be pursued. Figure 1 is an example of a π distribution, in which we have some "good" functions with error probability around 0.2, some "bad" ones around 0.8, and a lot of mediocre ones that lie in between. The π's are ordered in an increasing way for convenience. This does not change the results to be discussed later.

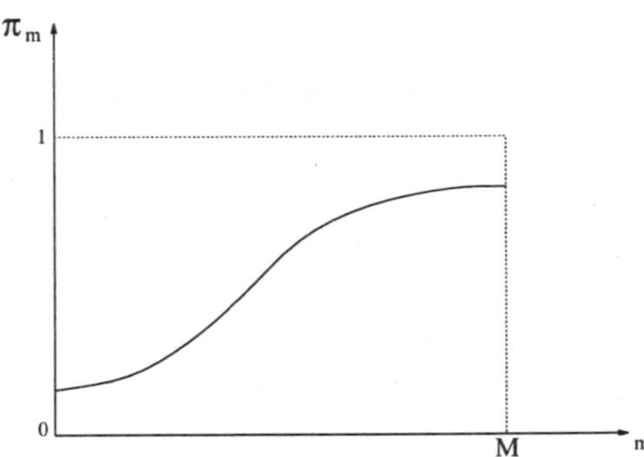

Figure 1: An Example of a π Distribution.

The learning algorithm picks a candidate function g from G based on its performance on the examples. We again define a random variable n (the number of errors made on the examples by g) and the frequency of error $\nu = n/N$. Quantities can be defined in different ways with respect to ν. They will be discussed later.

It is worth noticing that the π distribution and M are all the information that we need to specify a bin model. We do not need the information about the specific forms that the candidate functions assume. Neither do we need to know anything about the inputs and input distribution. All that we do is to draw marbles (equivalent to i.i.d. inputs) from the bins characterized by the π distribution and M. This makes it possible to model learning machines in the simplest way without loss of generality.

2   Modeling of Expected Test Error Given Training Error

The game of interest here is the following. We have M candidate functions at hand, each one has its probability of error π. We have N examples. One candidate is randomly picked and tested on the examples. This is equivalent to saying we pick a sample of size N from this bin. An error frequency ν is obtained, which we call the training error. If we are happy with this training error, we keep this function as our approximation to the target function f, otherwise we put it back. This reminds us of what we do in learning – we stop at a fairly small training error, and keep the function that achieves this training error as the winner. Besides, to make sure, we usually do another test on this function – we pick another sample, not necessarily of the same size, from the corresponding bin and see what the error frequency is this time. This is usually referred to as the test error on the test set. It is clear that the expectation of test error over all possible test sets is the error probability π of that function. We want to know how well the training error indicates the test error on average. Denote the random variables training error and test error by $\nu^{'}$ and $\nu^{''}$ respectively.

This question can be formalized by the expected test error given training error is ν, i.e., $E(\nu^{''}|\nu^{'} = \nu)$.

In the case of picking one bin, it can be shown that

$$E(\nu^{''} \mid \nu^{'} = \nu) \approx \frac{\sum_{m=1}^{M} M^{-\lambda H(\nu, \pi_m)} \pi_m}{\sum_{m=1}^{M} M^{-\lambda H(\nu, \pi_m)}}$$

where

$$H(\nu, \pi_m) = -\nu \log \frac{\nu}{\pi_m} - (1 - \nu) \log \frac{(1 - \nu)}{(1 - \pi_m)}$$

is the relative entropy between two Bernoulli distributions ν and π_m and λ is defined as

$$\lambda = \frac{N}{\log M}$$

which is normalized sample size.

Figure 2(b) is an illustration of $E(\nu^{''}|\nu^{'} = \nu)$ for the π distribution given in 2(a). From it we can see that if we stop at training error, say, $\nu = 0.1$, the expected test error is actually 0.2, which means we would be over optimistic, if we used the training error as an indication of the test error. The $y = x$ diagonal line is perfect generalization since on this line the training error indicates the test error exactly. Not surprisingly, bigger sample size gives better generalization, by which we mean the training error is a better estimator of test error, as we can see from 2(c).

The monotonicity of $E(\nu^{''}|\nu^{'} = \nu)$ with respect to ν implies that we can always benefit from getting smaller training error. This does not contradict overfitting since in this case we assume both sample size and M are fixed whereas in the case of overfitting the ratio of information versus complexity decreases as training error gets smaller due to that we are exploring more and more functions in the weight space.

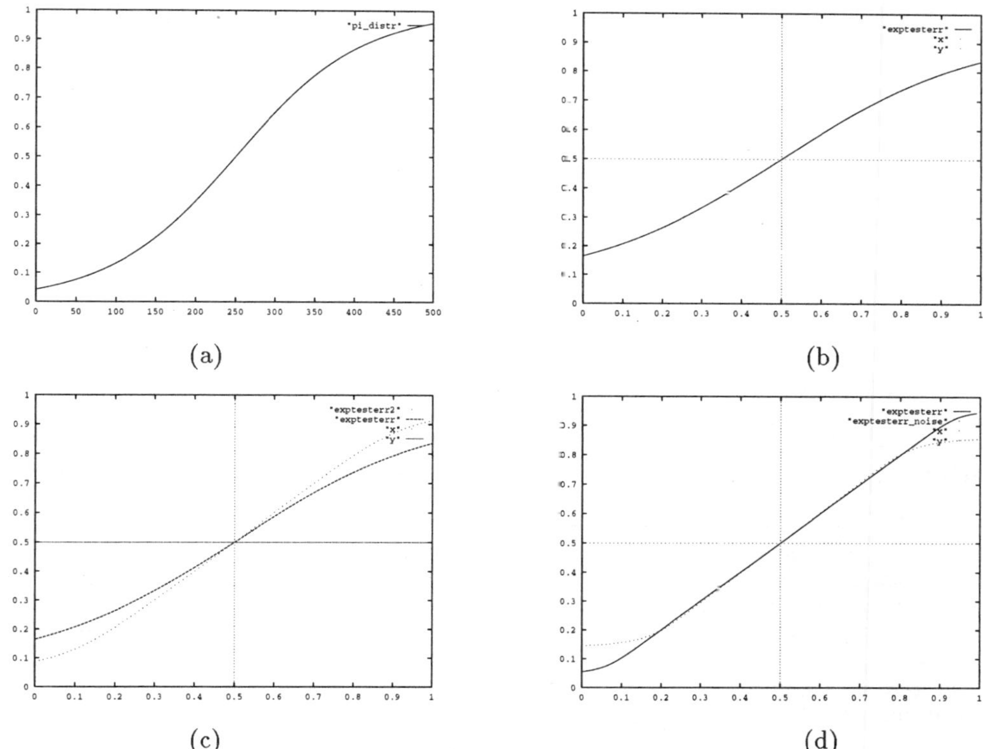

Figure 2: A demonstration of expected test error given certain training error.(a)is a π distribution for $M = 500$ bins. The x axis is the index for bins, and y axis is π. In (b), (c) and (d), the x axis is ν, and y axis $E(\nu''|\nu' = \nu)$. The curve in (b) is for $\lambda = 0.5$. The solid curve in (c) is for $\lambda = 0.5$, and the dotted one for $\lambda = 4.0$. The solid curve in (d) is for $\lambda = 10$ without noise and the dotted one for same λ but with noise level $\varepsilon = 0.1$.

3 Modeling of Noise

When we draw a sample from a bin and obtain error frequency ν, it generally deviates from the mean π. We define the discrepancy between ν and π as noise. At a closer look, we find that noises come from two sources. One is *Bernoulli noise*, which is the discrepancy between Bernoulli frequency and the mean due to finite sample size. The other is *data noise* which corresponds to the physical noise in real world. We formalize the latter source of noise by flipping the samples with certain probability ε. It is equivalent to putting the sample through a binary symmetric channel(BSC) with cross probability ε [3]. We are not able to tell the noise source when we draw a sample and observe discrepancy. However, they are intrinsicly different. Bernoulli noise can be overcome by taking large sample size, whereas data noise can not. Let $\nu_{Bernoulli}$ denote the error frequency effected only by Bernoulli noise, and ν_{BSC} be that effected also by data noise. It can be shown that for Bernoulli noise,

$$E(\nu_{Bernoulli}) = \pi$$
$$Var(\nu_{Bernoulli}) = \frac{\pi(1 - \pi)}{N}$$

whereas for data noise,

$$E(\nu_{BSC}) = (1 - 2\varepsilon)\pi + \varepsilon$$
$$Var(\nu_{BSC}) = \frac{(1 - 2\varepsilon)^2 \pi(1 - \pi) + \varepsilon(1 - \varepsilon)}{N}$$

It can also be shown that introducing data noise with noise level ε is equivalent to replacing the original error probability π by a diluted version $(1 - 2\varepsilon)\pi + \varepsilon$. π is pushed closer to a random function which has $\pi = 0.5$, as we can see from Fig 3. This leads us to the important conclusion that data noise gives rise to intrinsic generalization error (the deviation of test error from training error) [Fig 2(d)], and it can not be cured by taking large sample size.

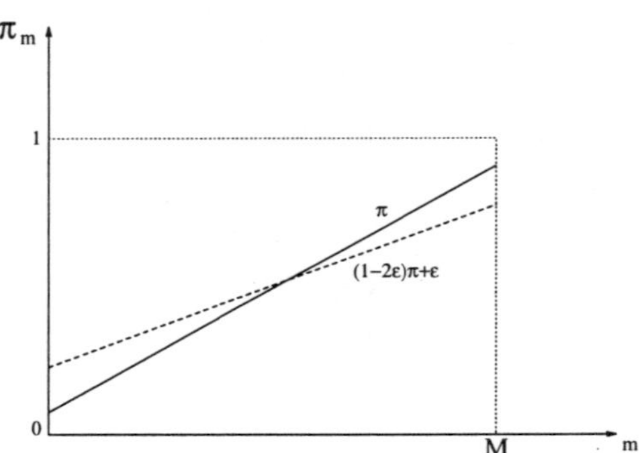

Figure 3: Effect of Noise – the original π is pushed closer to random function.

4   Modeling of Expected Test Error Given the Best Training Error

Instead of setting *a priori* a threshold for training error that we are content with, as discussed in section 2, now we use a different strategy. Given M candidate functions, we take i.i.d. samples from input space and test them on each function, i.e. we draw marbles from corresponding bins and obtain an error frequency for each bin. The error frequencies are ordered. The bin that gives the *smallest* error is then picked as the winner. This means we pick the function that does the best on the training set. A similar question is asked: Does it mean by doing this we always pick the best candidate function? This question can be answered by studying the quantity $E(\nu'' \mid \nu_{min} = \nu)$, where random variable ν_{min} denotes the smallest training error.

For the following calculation, we assume the M candidate functions are statistically independent. In reality, the neural network hypotheses are usually dependent. For instance, by slightly tuning a weight in a neural network, we can get another function whose behavior is, not surprisingly, very similar to the first one. In a later paper, we will investigate the equivalence between independent and dependent cases by defining a quantity *effective number of bins* M_{eff}.

Under the independence assumption, we can show that

$$E(\nu'' \mid \nu_{min} = \nu) = \frac{\sum_{m=1}^{M} \pi_m P(\text{ the } m^{th} \text{ bin achieves min error } \nu)}{P\{\nu_{min} = \nu\}}$$

$$= \frac{\sum_{m=1}^{m} \pi_m \prod_{i=1}^{m-1} P(\nu_i > \nu) P(\nu_m = \nu) \prod_{i=m+1}^{M} P(\nu_i \geq \nu)}{\prod_{i=1}^{M} P(\nu_i \geq \nu) - \prod_{i=1}^{M} P(\nu_i > \nu)}$$

where

$$P(\nu_m = \nu) = \binom{N}{N\nu} \pi_m^{N\nu} (1 - \pi_m)^{N-N\nu}$$

$$P(\nu_m > \nu) = \sum_{v=\nu+\frac{1}{N}}^{1} P(\nu_m = v)$$

$$P(\nu_m \geq \nu) = \sum_{v=\nu}^{1} P(\nu_m = v)$$

The derivation is based on the convention that if a tie appears, i.e., if more than one bin achieves the minimum, we pick the bin that achieves it first. The property of $E(\nu'' \mid \nu_{min} = \nu)$ seems to be numerically sensitive to the convention of breaking the tie. Now we are working on an approach that gets rid of the dependence on the convention.

5   Summary

In this paper we have introduced the bin model which is intended to model learning machines. One merit of the bin model is that it captures the essence of learning machines such as neural networks without going into the details of the candidate functions. Using the bin model, we have addressed issues that are related to generalization using various strategies. We also discussed the effect of the number of examples and noise on generalization. Future work may include finding the *effective number of bins* which captures the dependence among the bins (such as neural network functions) and equates a case of dependent bins with a corresponding case of independent bins. Mapping real learning models to the appropriate bin model is another possible future direction.

References

[1] Yaser Abu-Mostafa, "The Vapnik-Chervonenkis Dimension: Information versus Complexity in Learning," *Neural Computation*, vol. 1, pp. 312-317, 1989.

[2] John Moody, "The *Effective* Number of Parameters: An Analysis of Generalization and Regularization in Nonlinear Learning Systems," *Advances in Neural Information Processing Systems*, vol.4, pp. 847-854, 1991.

[3] Thomas Cover and Joy Thomas, *Elements of Information Theory*, John Wiley and Sons, Inc. 1991.

A NEW WORST-CASE TRAINING ALGORITHM FOR RBF NEURAL NETWORKS

Shaohua Tan[†], A. C. Tsoi[‡], Andrew Back[‡] and Ann-Kai Chan[†]

[†] Department of Electrical Engineering
National University of Singapore
10 Kent Ridge Crescent, Singapore 0511

[‡] Department of Electrical and Computer Engineering
The University of Queensland
St Lucia, Queensland 4072, Australia

Abstract—

A novel worst-case learning scheme is developed in this paper for training radial-basis-function (RBF) neural networks. It minimizes the maximum error rather than the average error as in the case of conventional least-squares learning. This scheme is applicable to a variety of practical situations where the nature of the applications demands a worst-case modeling solution. The scheme will be presented along with an illustrative example.

1   Introduction

The training of radial-basis-function (RBF) neural networks has so far been developed by minimizing the *quadratic cost function* [5] [7] [8]. Our objective in this paper is to develop a RBF neural network training algorithm which minimizes the worst-case error. There are two underlying motivations for our work. Firstly, there are many applications that require the RBF model to guarantee a worst-case error to be within certain bound. Such applications range from the adaptive control to detection and protection problems. Secondly, which is more fundamental, even the well-known universal approximation property of neural networks is formulated and proved under the worst case cost function. It is of considerable theoretical interest to find a RBF model constructively which gives rise to a worst case error function.

Our contribution in the present paper is to develop a general, systematic, and convergent scheme for training a RBF neural network to achieve a worst case error function. We will illustrate the scheme using a simple example.

The structure of the paper is as follows: in section 2 we will give a description of hte problem formulation. In section 3, we will describe the learning algorithm, and in section 4 we will give an illustrative example.

2   Problem formulation

Structure of a radial basis function network   We begin with a brief description of the general structure of RBF neural networks [4, 1]. This neural network is a special type of the more general multilayer perceptron architecture [3], in that it has only two layers *, one hidden layer and one output. The first layer (hidden layer) consists of neurons with nonlinear activation functions and the second layer (output layer) of linear neurons. The inputs to such a neural network are directly connected to the neurons in the first layer. The outputs of these neurons are then connected to the linear neurons in the second layer through weighted links. The activation function of the ith hidden layer neuron is of the form

$$z_i(x) = r\left(\frac{\|x - p_i\|}{\sigma_i}\right);\tag{1}$$

where $z_i(x)$ is the output of the ith neuron in the first layer; $i = 1, 2, \ldots, n$; x is the ℓ-dimensional input vector of the form $x = [x_1\, x_2 \cdots x_\ell]^T$; $r(\cdot)$ is a radial basis function (RBF) [6]; and $p_i \in \mathcal{R}^\ell$ and $\sigma_i \in \mathcal{R}$ are the center and width of the ith RBF neuron respectively, which may be different for each neuron.

For the sake of definiteness, we will choose the function $r(\cdot)$ to be the Gaussian function [6]:

$$z_i(x) = e^{-\frac{\|x - p_i\|^2}{\sigma_i^2}}\tag{2}$$

The function form for the ith linear neuron is simply

---

*Note that in this paper, we will follow the convention that the input layer is not counted towards the number of layers.

$$y_i = \sum_{j=1}^{n} w_{ij} z_j(x), \qquad (3)$$

where y_i is the output of the ith neuron in the second layer; $i = 1, 2, \ldots, m$; w_{ij} is the weight from the jth neuron in the first layer to the ith linear neuron in the second layer; and n is the number of neurons in the first layer. We can write the equation for the entire neural network more conveniently in the following matrix form

$$y = W^T z(x), \qquad (4)$$

where $y = [y_1 \, y_2 \cdots y_m]^T$, $z(x) = [z_1(x) \, z_2(x) \cdots z_n(x)]^T$, $x = [x_1 \, x_2 \cdots x_\ell]^T$, and W, an $n \times m$ matrix, commonly known as the weight matrix, with ijth entry w_{ij}. It is convenient to denote the i th column of W as w_i $(i = 1, 2, \ldots, m)$. It is observed that the RBF neural network has a *linear-in-the-parameter* type of structure (4).

The RBF neural network has been shown to be a universal approxiamtor [5], in that it can approximate, to an arbitrary degree of accuracy, a nonlinear static mapping, satisfying some generic properties, between the input x, and the output y, provided a sufficient number of hidden layer neurons is used.

Radial basis function network as a model of nonlinear dynamical system   Consider a discrete-time multi-channel signal $\{y^t\} \in \mathcal{R}^m$ is generated by an unknown discrete-time dynamic system of the following form:

$$y^{t+1} = f(x^t) = f(y^t, y^{t-1}, \cdots, y^{t-k+1}; u^t, u^{t-1}, \cdots, u^{t-p+1}), \qquad (5)$$

where $u^t \in \mathcal{R}^q$ is the excitation at time t; $f(\cdot) : \mathcal{R}^\ell \to \mathcal{R}^m$ where $\ell = mk + pq$; k and p are two positive integers relating the current sample to k previous samples and p previous excitation samples.

We use the RBF neural network (4) as the general model structure for the nonlinear function $f(\cdot)$. In other words, the given signal $\{y^t\}$ is modeled as

$$y^{t+1} = W^T z(x^t),$$

where W and $z(x)$ are defined in (2), (3) and (4); $x^t = [y^t, y^{t-1}, \cdots, y^{t-k+1}; u^t, u^{t-1}, \cdots, u^{t-p+1}]$.

Decomposition of the modelling problem using radial basis function networks   The modeling problem can now be broken into two separate subtasks of determining the structural parameters n, p_i and σ_i involved in $z(x)$ and the weight matrix W. Note that the emphasis of this paper is placed on developing a novel worst-case learning algorithm to find W. However, in order to make the discussion complete, we briefly explain the procedure in setting up the RBF neural network structure as described in [8] †.

First, $\{x^t\}$ is used to determine a compact set $S \in R^\ell$, the region of operation for the underlying system. Then a uniformly spaced grid in S is formed, which is preferably symmetrical about the origin. The distance between two neighbouring grid points, denoted by Δ, can be adjusted to change the size of the grid. Once the grid is set up, the number of RBF neurons n is simply the number of grid points, and their centers p_i's are the coordinates of the grid points. Generally, we set $\Delta \leq \epsilon)_{max}$, ϵ_{max} is the maximum modeling error. However, we must also bear in mind that a smaller Δ will mean more neurons and hence more weights, which increases the computational load. Finally, the width of the RBF neurons σ_i should be chosen [8] to be in the region $[\frac{2}{3}\Delta, \Delta]$. For simplicity, we assume σ_i to be constant for all i.

This procedure determines the unknown center p_i and the unknown width σ_i, $i1 =, 2, \ldots, m$. Once these parameters are determined, the estimation of the unknown weight matrix W is a linear estimation problem.

The worst case learning problem   We proceed to formulate the worst-case learning problem. Assume a set of sample data $\{(x^t, y^t)\}$ $(t = 1, 2, \cdots, N)$ of the unknown system be given. Our objective is to develop a *recursive* algorithm to find the weights of the RBF neural network (4) by minimizing the following cost function:

$$J_{max}(W) = \max_{1 \leq i \leq m} J^t_{max}(w_i) \qquad (6)$$

where

---

† There are a number of methods for setting up a RBF network, see e.g., [1, 4].

$$J^i_{max}(w_i) = \frac{1}{2} \max_{1 \le t \le N} e^2_{i,t} = \frac{1}{2} \max_{1 \le t \le N} (y^t_i - w^T_i z(x^t))^2 \tag{7}$$

in which

$$e_{i,t} \triangleq y^t_i - w^T_i z(x_t) \tag{8}$$

is the modeling error of the ith output when the tth training data (x^t, y^t) is presented.

Equation (7), which is called the worst-case cost function, measures the maximum error or the infinity norm of the error vector of each output after the N training data is presented. As such, any learning algorithm that minimizes J_{max} is called the worst-case or the L_∞ learning.

Unlike the familiar quadratic cost function [2], however, J_{max} is not a differentiable function. This creates considerable difficulties in developing an effective L_∞ learning algorithm. Indeed, simple least-squares and gradient descent ideas are no long applicable in this context, and a different methodology will have to be followed. In the next section, we will describe such a learning algorithm.

3   The worst-case learning algorithm

To simplify the description, we will consider the MISO (multi-input single-output) version of (4). It easily extends to the multi input multi output case. As the MISO version limits m to 1, the cost function (6) reduces to

$$J_{max}(w) = \frac{1}{2} \max_{1 \le t \le N} e^2_t = \frac{1}{2} \max_{1 \le t \le N} (y^t - w^T z(x_t))^2 \tag{9}$$

where the index i can be dropped, and $W \in \mathcal{R}^{n \times m}$ becomes a weight vector $w \in \mathcal{R}^n$.

Alternatively, J_{max} can be written as follows:

$$J_{max}(w) = \frac{1}{2} \sum_{t=1}^N \lambda_t e^2_t \tag{10}$$

where

$$\lambda_t = \begin{cases} 1 & \text{if } t = t_{max} \\ 0 & \text{if } t \ne t_{max} \end{cases} \tag{11}$$

where t_{max} denotes the index where the error is a maximum. If the maximum error occurs at more than one index, t_{max} can be chosen to be any of these indices.

Using (10) and (11), $J_{max}(w)$ can further be formulated in the following matrix form:

$$J_{max}(w) = \frac{1}{2} e^T(w) \Lambda(w) e(w) \tag{12}$$

where $e(w) = [e_1, e_2, \cdots, e_N]^T$, and $\Lambda(w) = \text{diag}\{\lambda_1, \lambda_2, \cdots, \lambda_N\}$. Noting $e(w) = Y_N - Z_N w$, where $Y_N = [y^1, y^2, \ldots, y^N]^T \in \mathcal{R}^N$, $Z_N = [z(x^1), z(x^2), \ldots, z(x^N)]^T \in \mathcal{R}^{N \times n}$, we have

$$\begin{aligned} J_{max}(w) &= \frac{1}{2}(Y_N - Z_N w)^T \Lambda(w)(Y_N - Z_N w) \\ &= \frac{1}{2} w^T Z^T_N \Lambda(w) Z_N w - w^T Z^T_N \Lambda(w) Y_N + \frac{1}{2} Y^T_N \Lambda(w) Y_N \\ &= \frac{1}{2} w^T P_N w - w^T q_N + \frac{1}{2} r_N \end{aligned} \tag{13}$$

where

$$\begin{aligned} P_N &= Z^T_N \Lambda(w) Z_N = \sum_{t=1}^N \lambda_t z(x^t) z^T(x^t) = \max_{1 \le t \le N} z(x^t) z^T(x^t), \\ Q_N &= Z^T_N \Lambda(w) Y_N = \sum_{t=1}^N \lambda_t y^t z(x^t) = \max_{1 \le t \le N} y^t z(x^t), \\ r_N &= Y^T_N \Lambda(w) Y_N = \sum_{t=1}^N \lambda_t (y^t)^2 = \max_{1 \le t \le N} (y^t)^2. \end{aligned} \tag{14}$$

The max operations are performed elementwise. The preceding equations also allow us to construct these quantities at arbitrary time instants. For instance, P_k can simply be constructed by finding the maximum entries among the first k matrices $z(x^t)z^T(x^t)$, $t = 1, 2, \ldots, k$.

Let us assume that there exists a parameter vector w^* such that J_{max} is minimized, *i.e.*,

$$J_{max}(w^*) = \frac{1}{2}(e^*)^T \Lambda^* e^* = \frac{1}{2}\inf_w\{e^T(w)\Lambda(w)e(w)\} \triangleq \frac{1}{2}\delta^2 \tag{15}$$

where $e^* = [e_1^*, \cdots, e_N^*]^T$ is the residual vector obtained at $w = w^*$, $\Lambda^* = \Lambda(w^*)$, and $\delta \geq 0$ is a real number. If this δ is known, then a sequence of positive integers $\{\tau_t, t = 1, 2, \ldots, N\}$ can be found [‡] such that

$$\frac{8\delta^2}{(4 - \frac{1}{2^{\tau_{t-1}}})^2} > J_{max,t} \geq \frac{8\delta^2}{(4 - \frac{1}{2^{\tau_t}})^2}.$$

With this sequence, we can build the following nonlinear dynamical system that will assume w^* as the global convergent point. It can be proved rigorously that it will converge to w^*, therefore pushing the cost function to the global minimum $\frac{1}{2}\delta^2$.

The Worst-case Learning Algorithm:

$$w_t = w_{t-1} + \frac{\alpha_t J_{max,t} \Gamma}{\beta + (q_t - P_t w_{t-1})^T \Gamma (q_t - P_t w_{t-1})}(q_t - P_t w_{t-1}) \tag{16}$$

where $\beta > 0$, $t = 1, 2, \cdots$, Γ is any constant positive definite matrix, and $\alpha_t = \frac{1}{2^{\tau_t+1}}$.

The following theorem asserts that the learning algorithm (16) brings the worst-case cost function J_t to its global minimum.

Theorem 1 *The learning algorithm (16) has the following properties:*

(1) $\quad 0 \leq J_t - \dfrac{\delta^2}{2} \leq \kappa_3 V_{t-1}$ $\hspace{5cm}$ (17)

$\quad$ *where κ_3 is a positive number, and V_{t-1} is a monotonically decreasing sequence.*

(2) $\quad \lim\limits_{t\to\infty} J_t = \dfrac{\delta^2}{2}$ $\hspace{6cm}$ (18)

The proof of the results requires a detailed analysis which, while being an extension of the quadratic cost function case [2], is too long to be presented in this short paper. The full convergence proof as well as other properties will be shown elsewhere.

We will summarize the key steps of the new worst-case training algorithm for the RBF neural networks as follows:

1. Set up the appropriate RBF network structure as described in section 2.

2. Select suitable values for α, β, Γ of (16) and w_0, the initial weight estimate.

3. When the tth sample data $\{(x^t, y^t)\}$ is present, form $Y_t = [Y_{t-1}^T, y^t]^T$ and $Z_t = [Z_{t-1}^T, z(x^t)]^T$.

4. Next, compute the error vector $e(w_{t-1}) = Y_t - Z_t w_{t-1}$. Use it to compute $J_{max,t}$, P_t and Q_t given in (14). Then update the weights using (16).

5. Repeat steps 3 and 4 until t reaches the prescribed number of recursions or when the modeling error becomes less than the prescribed error bound.

4 Illustrative examples

A simple example is presented in this section to demonstrate the effectiveness of the proposed algorithm for the RBF neural network training.

Example
A time series $\{y_t\}$ is generated by driving the following nonlinear dynamic system

$$y_{t+1} = \frac{y_t}{1 + y_t^2} + u_t^3, \tag{19}$$

with a random discrete-time sequence $\{u_k\}$ uniformly distributed in $[-1.1, 1.1]$. We use the algorithm 16 to build a RBF neural network model for the signal.

[‡] The proof of this bound can be obtained by an extension of the usual treatment in quadratic cost function case [2].

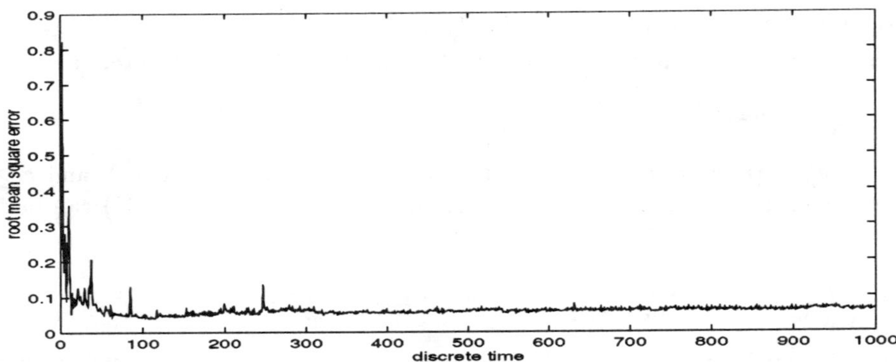

Figure 1: Convergence of root-mean-square error during learning

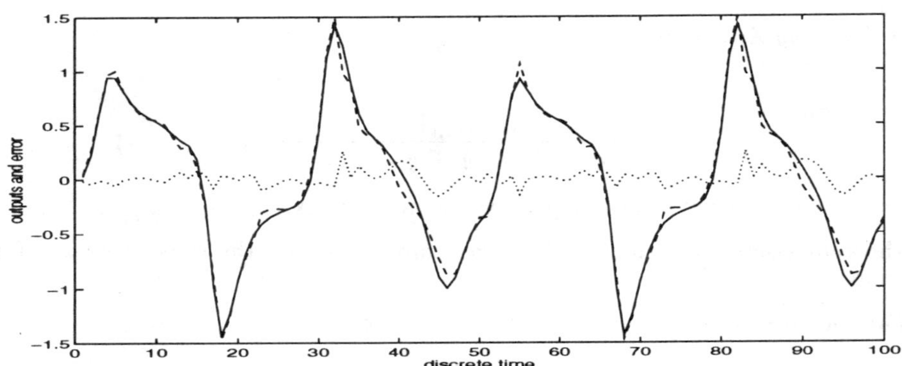

Figure 2: The results of the RBF modeling

The first step of the modeling scheme is to determine the compact region of operation S for the system. By exciting the system with the random excitation sequence given above, we can easily verify the range of y_k to be $[-1.8, 1.8]$. This, along with the input range of $[-1.1, 1.1]$, defines S. Note that S in this case is a rectangle in the 2-D space.

Following the structure of the RBF network chosen for the same problem in [8], δ is set to be 0.31. Once δ is known, a grid can be evenly laid inside the rectangular S with the grid points giving the number of neurons and their centers. There will be a total of 96 neurons associated with this structure, therefore a total of 96 weights to be learned. The radius of the neurons, σ is chosen to be $\frac{2}{3}\delta = 0.21$. With the centers and radii fixed, the RBF network can now be trained using the L_∞ weight updating algorithm. Other parameters are chosen as $\alpha = 2$, $\beta = 1$, and $\Gamma = 40I$ in the weight update algorithm.

After about 1000 weights updates, the root-mean square error converges to about 0.06 as shown in Fig. 1.

To test the constructed RBF model, we excite both the real system and the RBF neural network model with the following periodic time-series

$$u_t = 0.8\sin(2\pi t/25) + 0.2\sin(2\pi t/10).$$

Note that u_t is bounded within $[-1.1, 1, 1]$. Fig. 2 shows the real signal (solid line), the signal generated by the model (dashed line), and the modeling error (dotted line), using the weights obtained at the end of 1000 updates. It is noted that the error between the constructed model and the system never exceeds 0.31.

5   Conclusions

A novel worst-case learning algorithm is described and applied to RBF neural network training. We will provide a detailed analytical development in the full version of the paper.

References

[1] D. Broomhead, D. Lowe, "Multivariable functional interpolation and adaptive networks". *Complex Systems*. Vol 2, 321 - 355, 1988.

[2] G Goodwin, K S Sin, *Adaptive Filtering, Prediction and Control*. Eaglewood Cliffs: Prentice Hall, 1984.

[3] S. Haykin, *Neural Networks*. New York: McMillian, 1994.

[4] J. Moody, C. Darken, "Fast learning in networks of locally tuned processing units". *Neural Computation*. Vol 1, 281 - 294, 1989.

[5] T.Poggio and F.Girosi, "Networks for approximation and learning," *Proc. IEEE*, Vol. 78, pp. 1481-1497, 1990.

[6] M. Powell, "Radial basis functions for multivariable interpolation: a review". *IMA Conf on Algorithms for the Approximation of Functions and Data*. Royal Military College of Sciences, Shrivenham, pp 143 - 167, 1985.

[7] R.M.Sanner and J.E.Slotine, "Gaussian Networks for Direct Adaptive Control," *IEEE Trans. Neural Net.*, Vol. 3, pp. 837-863, 1992.

[8] S.Tan, J.Hao, J.Vandewalle, "Stable and Efficient Neural Network Modeling of Discrete Multi-Channel Signals," *IEEE Trans. Circ. and Syst.*, Vol. 41, pp. 829-840, 1994.

Models of generalization error in learning systems with training error selection

A. Kowalczyk

Telstra Research Laboratories & Institute of Chemical and Physical Research (RIKEN)
770 Blackburn Road,   Frontier Research Program
Clayton, Vic. 3168, Australia   Brain Information Processing Group
(a.kowalczyk@trl.oz.au)   2-1 Hirosawa
                                     Wako-shi, Saitama 351-01, Japan

Abstract— The paper presents general models of average generalization error in the case of selection of random binary valued classifiers with training error below a predefined threshold. The emphasis is on a model for very large learning systems. To that end we present rigorous calculations of thermodynamic limit and its essential dependence on "entropy distribution of error levels", although the proof is only outlined. The formal results are illustrated on examples of Ising perceptron and homogeneous perceptron compared against popular universal VC-bounds. Dramatic differences in scaled learning curves in these two examples allow us to conclude that at least some statistical properties of the learning system have to be taken into account if tight models of generalization at low training sample sizes are desired.

1   Introduction

One of the most challenging tasks for the theory of learning is to provide tractable models and rigorous explanations for the dependence between the size of a (random) training sample and the generalization error of classifiers trained (selected) according to it. Although a number of attempts in this direction have been undertaken and a number of remarkable results achieved, the problem is still far from been resolved. The mainstream research in this area can be roughly divided into two categories which differ in terms of techniques used: the bounds on the worst case error and the estimates of average error.

The bulk of results for the worst case error bounds are based on pioneer research of V. Vapnik and D. Chervonenkis in the early seventies in statistics (c.f. [16, 17] for an account and later extensions); the so called PAC-learning [15] and computational learning theory [5] are more recent modifications or extensions of this formalism, c.f. [4, 5, 9] and references therein. We shall refer to these estimates collectively as VC-bounds, and specifically we shall refer here to a part of this theory as presented in [5] or [4].

Models of average generalization error were initially researched by statistical physicists who were utilizing formal similarities between models of generalization in learning systems and some models of statistical physics such as Ising model of ferromagnetism (c.f. [14, 18] and references therein). An alternative approach to this issue can be found also in more recent works of S. Amari and his co-workers [1, 2, 3].

The main results of this paper are placed somewhere in between the VC-formalism and statistical theory of learning and have roots in the work [8] which presented a statistical physics motivated approach to modeling of the worst case learning curve for a finite space of hypothesis. In this paper we concentrate on estimates for average error, which is the statistical physics approach, but our model uses the learning threshold selection criteria rather than Gibbs statistics making the backbone of the statistical physics formalism. We estimate the sample complexity, which is the concept introduced in PAC-learning, but for learning with errors and with a subtly different meaning, with the aim of finding its thermodynamic limit which is a concept inspired by statistical physics. In our theory a key role is played by the distribution of "error levels". Using examples of the homogeneous perceptron and the Ising perceptron we shall demonstrate that this distribution can significantly influence the average error indicators at low training sample sizes, while VC-bounds are unchanged. This will lead us to the final conclusion that at least some statistics of error distribution have to be taken into account if tight bounds on generalization are required for small training samples, i.e. of order of the number of synaptic weights.

2   Formal Results

On a sample space X we consider a class H of binary functions $h : X \rightarrow \{0, 1\}$ which we shall call *a hypothesis space*. A simple prototype here is a set of all mappings form an input space to the binary output space which can be implemented by a fixed feedforward neural network architecture for all possible combinations of synaptic weights. Further we assume that there are given a probability distribution μ_X on X, a probability distribution μ_H on H and a *target concept* $t \in H$. The quintuple $\mathcal{L} = (X, \mu_X, H, \mu_H, t)$ will be called *a learning system*.

We define the *generalization error* of a hypothesis $h \in H$

$$\epsilon_h \stackrel{def}{=} \mathbf{E}_X\big[|t(x) - h(x)|\big], \tag{1}$$

and *the training error* (or *sample error*) on a *training m-sample* $\vec{x} = (x_1, ..., x_m) \in X^m$

$$\epsilon_{h,\vec{x}} \stackrel{def}{=} \frac{1}{m}\sum_{i=1}^{m} |t(x_i) - h(x_i)|. \tag{2}$$

Given a number $0 \leq \lambda \leq 1$ called *the learning threshold*. We shall consider the *annealed learning curve*[1] defined as the average generalization error for all pairs (m-sample, hypothesis) with an acceptable training error ($\leq \lambda$):

$$\epsilon_\lambda^{an}(m) \overset{def}{=} \mathbf{E}_{X^m \times H}[\epsilon_h \mid \epsilon_{h,\vec{x}} \leq \lambda] \tag{3}$$

and *the annealed sample complexity*, denoted by $m_\lambda^{an}(\epsilon, \delta)$, which is defined as

$$m_\lambda^{an}(\epsilon, \delta) \overset{def}{=} \min\{m \,;\, \mathbf{P}_{X^m \times H}[\epsilon_h \leq \epsilon \mid \epsilon_{h,\vec{x}} \leq \lambda] \geq 1 - \delta\}, \tag{4}$$

and gives the smallest size of the random sample such that for a randomly chosen hypothesis its generalization error is $\leq \epsilon$ with confidence $1 - \delta$ if the sample error is $\leq \lambda$.

2.1 The thermodynamic limit

Following the methodology of statistical physics [8] we introduce now the concept of the thermodynamic limit which is necessary to precisely state and simplify the results for very large learning systems.

Let us consider *a sequence of learning systems*, $\mathcal{L}_N = (X_N, \mu_{X_N}, H_N, \mu_{H_N}, t_N)$, $N = 1, 2, ...$ and *a scaling* $N \mapsto \tau_N \in \mathbf{R}^+$, with the property $\tau_N \to \infty$; the scaling can be thought of as a measure of the size (complexity) of a learning system. Some examples will be given in Section 3.

Now we extend definitions of the previous section. *The thermodynamic limit of the annealed learning curves* is defined for $\alpha > 0$ as follows [2]

$$\epsilon_{\lambda\infty}^{an}(\alpha) \overset{def}{=} \limsup_{N \to \infty} \epsilon_{\lambda N}^{an}(\lfloor \alpha \tau_N \rfloor). \tag{5}$$

Here, and below, the additional subscript N refers to the N-th learning system. *The thermodynamic limit of the annealed sample complexity*, $\alpha_{\lambda\infty}^{an}(\epsilon, \delta)$, is the smallest $\alpha > 0$ such that

$$\limsup_{N \to \infty} \mathbf{P}_{X^{\lfloor \alpha \tau_N \rfloor} \times H}[\epsilon_h \leq \epsilon \mid \epsilon_{h,\vec{x}} \leq \lambda] \geq 1 - \delta.$$

In other words, $\alpha_{\lambda\infty}^{an}(\epsilon, \delta)$, is the smallest coefficient α such that in the limit as the size of the learning system goes to infinity, if the training error on on a random sample of $\geq \alpha \tau_N$ examples is $\leq \lambda$ then the generalization error is $\leq \epsilon$ with the confidence $\geq 1 - \delta$. Note that

$$\alpha_{\lambda\infty}^{an}(\epsilon, \delta) \leq \limsup_{N \to \infty} \frac{m_{\lambda,N}^{an}(\epsilon, \delta)}{\tau_N}.$$

2.2 Main results

It is convenient to associate with any function $S : [0, 1] \to \mathbf{R}$ the following two families of functions defined for $\alpha > 0$ and $0 \leq \lambda, \epsilon \leq 1$:

$$\Phi_{S\alpha}(\epsilon, \lambda) \overset{def}{=} S(\epsilon) + \alpha\left(\mathcal{H}(\lambda) + \lambda \ln \epsilon + (1 - \lambda)\ln(1 - \epsilon)\right), \tag{6}$$

$$\Phi_{S\alpha\lambda}^*(\epsilon) \overset{def}{=} \Phi_{S\alpha}(\epsilon, \min(\epsilon, \lambda)), \tag{7}$$

where $\mathcal{H}(y) \overset{def}{=} -y \ln y - (1 - y)\ln(1 - y)$ for $0 < y < 1$ and $\mathcal{H}(y) \overset{def}{=} 0$ for $y = 0, 1$ denotes the (information) entropy function [6]. In terms of this family we define now two additional functions

$$\epsilon_{S\lambda}^{max}(\alpha) \overset{def}{=} \arg \max_{\epsilon \in [0,1]} \Phi_{S\alpha\lambda}^*(\epsilon), \tag{8}$$

$$\epsilon_{S\lambda}^+(\alpha) \overset{def}{=} \max\{\epsilon \in [0, 1] \,;\, \Phi_{S\alpha\lambda}^*(\epsilon) > 0\}.. \tag{9}$$

In a particular case when $\lambda = 0$ (so called *consistent learning case*) the above definitions simplify significantly and allow nice geometrical interpretations, similar to those in [8]:

$$\epsilon_{S0}^{max}(\alpha) \overset{def}{=} \arg \max_{\epsilon \in [0,1]} \left(S(\epsilon) + \alpha \ln(1 - \epsilon)\right), \tag{10}$$

$$\epsilon_{S0}^+(\alpha) \overset{def}{=} \max\{\epsilon \in [0, 1] \,;\, S(\epsilon) + \alpha \ln(1 - \epsilon) > 0\}. \tag{11}$$

Now we can state our main formal result.

Theorem 2.1 *Given a sequence of learning systems* $\mathcal{L}_N = (X_N, \mu_{X_N}, H_N, \mu_{H_N}, t_N)$ *with a scaling* τ_N *and a function* $S(\epsilon)$. *We assume that*

---

[1] The name is inspired by statistical physics of learning [8]; the discussion of the relation to the annealed approximation of the quenched learning curve studied there to our definitions is beyond the scope of this paper.

[2] We recall that $\lfloor x \rfloor$ denotes the smallest integer $\geq x$ and $\limsup_{N \to \infty} x_N$ is defined as $\lim_{N \to \infty}$ of the monotonic sequence $N \mapsto \max\{x_1, x_2, ..., x_N\}$. Note that in contrast to the ordinary limit, $\limsup$ always exists.

1. *All random variables $h \in H_N \mapsto \epsilon_{t_N}(h)$ have discrete distributions or all of them have continuous distributions. In the discrete case we assume additionally that the union of error levels $\bigcup_{N=1}^{\infty}\{\epsilon_{Nh} \; ; \; h \in H_N\}$ is dense in $[0,1]$;*

2. *There exists a sequence $K_N > 0$ such that if $P_{H_N}[\epsilon_{t_N}(h) = \epsilon] \neq 0$, then*
$$P_{H_N}[\epsilon_{t_N}(h) = \epsilon] = K_N e^{\tau_N S(\epsilon) + o(\tau_N)}. \tag{12}$$
   for any $\epsilon \in [0,1]$.

3. *The function $\Phi^*_{S\alpha\lambda}(\epsilon)$ has a "proper" maximum at $\epsilon^{\max}_{S\lambda}(\alpha)$, e.g. it is twice differentiable and $\frac{\partial^2}{\partial \epsilon^2}\Phi^*_{S\alpha\lambda}(\epsilon^{\max}_{S\lambda}(\alpha)) < 0$.*

Then
$$\epsilon^{an}_{\lambda\infty}(\alpha) = \epsilon^{\max}_{S\lambda}(\alpha), \tag{13}$$
$$\alpha^{an}_{\lambda\infty}(\epsilon,\delta) = \min\{\alpha \; ; \; \epsilon^{\max}_{S\lambda}(\alpha) \leq \epsilon\}. \tag{14}$$

A function $S(\epsilon)$ satisfying the Assumption 2 of the above theorem will be called *an entropy distribution* of the learning sequence $\mathcal{L}_N$ with respect to the scaling τ_N; note that an additive constant in entropy distribution does not change its properties in terms of estimates (13) or (14).

This result is an extension of [11, Theorem 2.ii] towards the inclusion of the continuous distributions case. The proof will be outlined in the Appendix.

The main advantage of the above results is that the investigation of the learning curves is reduced to the properties of the function $\Phi^*_{S\alpha\lambda}(\epsilon)$ defined by (6) and (7).

2.3   The worst case version

For completeness the worst case analogue of the Theorem 2.1 will be stated now. It is a reformulation of [11, Theorem 2.i] and is given in this paper without a proof.

Following [11] we introduce the thermodynamic limits of *the worst case learning curve* and *the worst case sample complexity* as follows

$$\epsilon^{wc}_{\lambda\infty}(\alpha) \stackrel{def}{=} \limsup_{N\to\infty} \frac{\mathbf{E}_{X\lfloor\alpha\tau_N\rfloor}[\max_{h\in H}\{\epsilon_h \; ; \; \epsilon_{h,\vec{x}} \leq \lambda\}]}{\lfloor\alpha\tau_N\rfloor}, \tag{15}$$

$$\alpha^{an}_{\lambda\infty}(\epsilon,\delta) \leq \min\left\{\alpha \; ; \; \limsup_{N\to\infty}\mathbf{P}_{X\lfloor\alpha\tau_N\rfloor}[\max_{h\in H}\{\epsilon_h \; ; \; \epsilon_{h,\vec{x}} \leq \lambda\} \leq \epsilon] \geq 1-\delta.\right\}. \tag{16}$$

Theorem 2.2 *Given a sequence of learning systems $\mathcal{L}_N = (X_N, \mu_{X_N}, H_N, \mu_{H_N}, t_N)$ with a scaling τ_N and a function $S(\epsilon)$. We assume that*

1. *For each N, the random variable $h \in H_N \mapsto \epsilon_{t_N}(h)$ has discrete distribution and takes $r_N = o(\tau_N)$ values (error levels).*

2. *The occupancy of error level has the following bound:*
$$\#\{h \in H_N \; ; \; \epsilon_{t_N}(h) = \epsilon\} \leq e^{\tau_N S(\epsilon) + o(\tau_N)}. \tag{17}$$

Then
$$\epsilon^{wc}_{\lambda\infty}(\alpha) \leq \epsilon^{+}_{S\lambda}(\alpha), \tag{18}$$
$$\alpha^{wc}_{\lambda\infty}(\epsilon,\delta) \leq \min\{\alpha \; ; \; \epsilon^{+}_{S\lambda}(\alpha) \leq \epsilon\}. \tag{19}$$

The function $S(\epsilon)$ satisfying (9) will be called *an entropy bound* with respect to the scaling τ_N after terminology used in [8].

We recall [11] that in the case of consistent learning, i.e. $\lambda = 0$, for a learning sequence scaled by VC-dimension[3] (i.e. with the scaling $\tau_N = d_{VC}(H_N)$) the VC-formalism provides the following universal estimates

$$\epsilon^{wc}_{0\infty}(\alpha) \leq \min\left(1, \frac{2\log_2(2e\alpha)}{\alpha}\right), \tag{20}$$

$$\alpha^{wc}_{0\infty}(\epsilon,\delta) \leq \frac{4}{\epsilon}\log_2\frac{12}{\epsilon}. \tag{21}$$

The first of these bounds is compared against some bounds from Theorem 2.1 in Figure 2.

Remark 2.1 *Note that the sample complexity estimates in the above theorems are virtually given by the inverse functions of estimates for learning curves (since the latter are monotonically decreasing; c.f. Figures 2 and 3).*

Remark 2.2 *The function $S(\epsilon)$ satisfying (9) has been called [8] the entropy bound with respect to the scaling τ_N.*

---

[3]VC-dimension of the N-th hypothesis space, denoted $d_{VC}(H_N)$, means a combinatorial parameter called *the Vapnik-Chervonenkis dimension* [4, 11, 16]. It is defined as the largest dimension m such that there exists an $\vec{x} \in X^m$ for which hypothesis in H can implement all 2^m of its possible partitions.

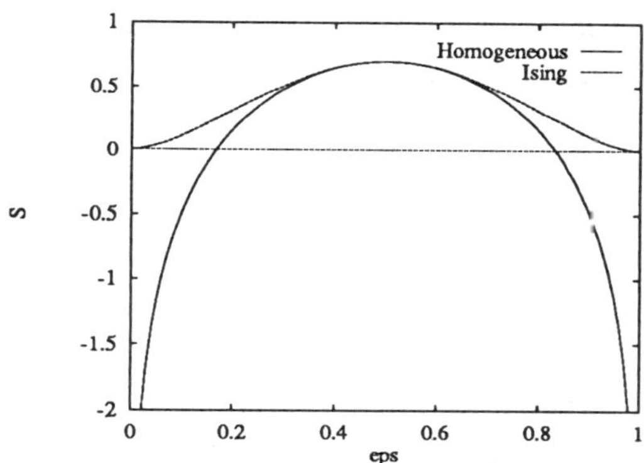

Figure 1: Plots of entropy distributions for the homogeneous perceptron, $S = \ln(\sin(\epsilon)) + \ln 2$, and Ising perceptron, $S = \mathcal{H}(\sin^2(\pi\epsilon/2))$; c.f. Section 3. The latter curve is also the entropy bound.

3 Example Applications

In this section we illustrate our formal results on two examples: the homogeneous perceptron with the continuous distribution and the Ising perceptron with discrete distribution of error levels.

If $h \in H$ has generalization error $\epsilon = \epsilon_h$, then the probability that for a random m-sample $\vec{x} \in X^m$ there are exactly j errors is $\binom{m}{j}\epsilon^i(1-\epsilon)^{m-j}$. Thus if we assume that the random variable ϵ_h has a continuous distribution $C\phi(\epsilon)d\epsilon$, where $C > 0$ is a constant, then

$$\mathbf{P}_{H\times X^m}[\epsilon_h \leq \lambda] = C \int_0^1 \sum_{j=0}^{\lfloor \lambda m \rfloor} \binom{m}{j}\epsilon^j(1-\epsilon)^{m-j}\phi(\epsilon)\,d\epsilon,$$

and the annealed learning curve can be expressed as follows

$$\epsilon_\lambda^{an}(m) = \frac{\int_0^1 \sum_{j=0}^{\lfloor \lambda m \rfloor} \binom{m}{j}\epsilon^{j+1}(1-\epsilon)^{m-j}\phi(\epsilon)\,d\epsilon}{\int_0^1 \sum_{j=0}^{\lfloor \lambda m \rfloor} \binom{m}{j}\epsilon^j(1-\epsilon)^{m-j}\phi(\epsilon)\,d\epsilon}. \tag{22}$$

Analogously the annealed sample complexity (4) takes the form:

$$m_\lambda^{an}(\epsilon, \delta) = \min\left\{ m \; ; \; \frac{\int_0^\epsilon \sum_{j=0}^{\lfloor \lambda m \rfloor} \binom{m}{j}\epsilon^j(1-\epsilon)^{m-j}\phi(\epsilon)\,d\epsilon}{\int_0^1 \sum_{j=0}^{\lfloor \lambda m \rfloor} \binom{m}{j}\epsilon^j(1-\epsilon)^{m-j}\phi(\epsilon)\,d\epsilon} \geq 1 - \delta \right\}. \tag{23}$$

These direct expressions illustrate the technical difficulties one encounters here: the sums and integrals are hard to evaluate directly when m is large, say of order hundreds or thousands. The asymptotic analysis in the form of thermodynamic limit presented above has been specifically designed to cope with such issues.

3.1 Homogeneous perceptron

We consider a learning sequence $\mathcal{L}_N = (X_N, \mu_{X_N}, H_N, \mu_{H_N}, t_N)$ where H_N is a family of all ordinary N-dimensional homogeneous perceptrons

$$h(x_1, ..., x_N) \overset{def}{=} \Theta(\mathbf{w}\cdot\mathbf{x}) = \Theta(\sum w_i x_i) \in \{0, 1\} \qquad (\forall \vec{x} = (x_1, ..., x_N) \in \mathbf{R}^N)$$

with the synaptic vector weights $\mathbf{w} = (w_1, w_2, ..., w_N) \in \mathbf{R}^N$; here Θ denotes *the Heaviside function*. We identify H_N with $\mathbf{R}^N$ and assume that μ_{X_N} and μ_{H_N} are two spherically symmetric probability distributions on $\mathbf{R}^N$. Further we assume that t_N is any element of $\mathbf{R}^N$ and consider the scaling $\tau_N \overset{def}{=} N$.

For a spherically symmetric distribution μ_N, the probability of disagreement between two perceptrons is proportional to the angle between their weight vectors. Thus it is easy to see that the distribution of ϵ_h is given by

$$\phi(\epsilon) \overset{def}{=} C \sin^{N-2}(\pi\epsilon)\,d\epsilon,$$

where C equals the surface area of $N-2$ dimensional unit sphere. The explicit expressions for annealed error curve and sample complexity can be derived for (22) and (23). Further, setting $K_N \overset{def}{=} C$ we get

$$\mathbf{P}_H[\epsilon_{t_N}(h) = \epsilon] = K_N e^{\tau_N \ln(\sin(\pi\epsilon)) + o(\tau_N)} \tag{24}$$

thus

$$S(\epsilon) \overset{def}{=} \ln(\sin(\pi\epsilon)) \tag{25}$$

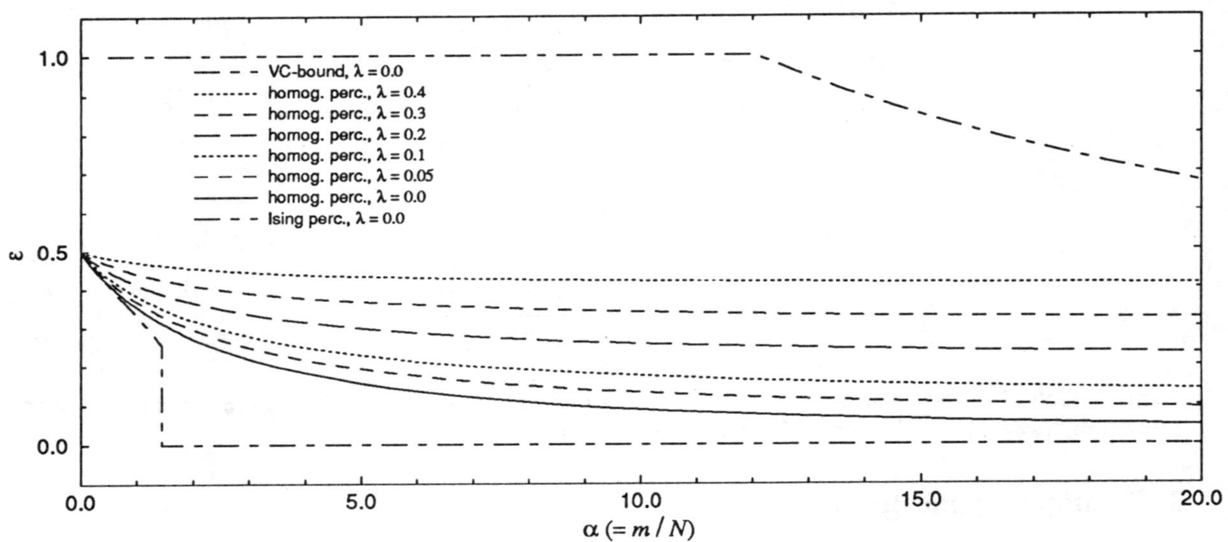

Figure 2: Plots of thermodynamic limit for annealed learning curves implied by Theorem 2.1, $\epsilon_\lambda^{an}(\alpha) = \epsilon_\lambda^{max}(\alpha)$, for homogeneous perceptron and selected values of learning threshold λ. For comparison, in chain lines we also plot: (*i*) the universal VC-bound (20) on the worst case learning curve $\epsilon_{S0}^{wc}(\alpha)$ for consistent learning case ($\lambda = 0$) and (*ii*) the analogous bound for the Ising perceptron given by Theorem 2.2 for the entropy bound (26).

is an entropy distribution for this learning system sequence, i.e. Assumption 2 of Theorem 2.1 is satisfied. We plot function (25) in Figure 1. Examples of annealed learning curves implied by Theorem 2.1 for this entropy distribution are shown in Figure 2 along with the VC-bound (20) on the worst case learning curve.

3.2 Ising perceptron

We consider the learning sequence $\mathcal{L}_N$ and the scaling as for the homogeneous perceptron (the previous Subsection) but with two differences: with the finite family H_N consisting of all perceptrons

$$h(x_1, ..., x_N) \stackrel{def}{=} \Theta(\mathbf{w}\cdot\mathbf{x}) = \Theta(\sum w_i x_i) \in \{0, 1\}$$

with bi-valued weights $\mathbf{w} = (w_1, w_2, ..., w_N) \in \{\pm 1\}^N$, and with the uniform distribution μ_{H_N} on H_N.

As before the probability of disagreement between two perceptrons is proportional to the angle between their weight vectors. Thus if $\mathbf{w}_{t_N}$ is the vector of the target hypothesis $t_N \in H_N$, then

$$\epsilon_h = \frac{1}{\pi} \cos^{-1} \frac{\mathbf{w}_{t_N}\cdot\mathbf{w}_N}{N} = \frac{1}{\pi} \cos^{-1} \left(1 - \frac{2d_H(\mathbf{w}_{t_N}, \mathbf{w}_N)}{N}\right),$$

where d_H denotes the Hamming distance. The Hamming distance layers H_N like an onion into $N + 1$ error shells surrounding the target at the center. The number of perceptrons at the Hamming distance j from the target, i.e. in the j-th error shell, is

$$Q_j^N = \binom{N}{j} = e^{N\mathcal{H}(j/N)+o(N)},$$

(c.f. [6]) and they all have generalization error $\epsilon_{N,j} = (\frac{1}{\pi}) \cos^{-1}(1 - 2j/N)$ for $j = 0, 1, ..., N$. Hence

$$S(\epsilon) \stackrel{def}{=} \mathcal{H}\left(\sin^2(\pi\epsilon/2)\right) \tag{26}$$

satisfies Assumption 2 in both Theorems 2.1 and 2.2 with respect to the scaling $\tau_N \stackrel{def}{=} N$, i.e. it serves as both an entropy bound and an entropy approximation for this learning sequence of Ising perceptrons. The other assumption of these theorems are also satisfied in this case as $r(N) = \#Q_j^N = N = o(e^N)$ and the set of all error levels, $\epsilon_{N,j}, N = 1, 2, ...$ and $0 \leq j \leq N$, is obviously dense in $[0, 1]$ in the sense of Assumption 2 in Theorem 2.1. In particular the function (6) takes the following form

$$\Phi_{S\alpha}(\epsilon, \lambda) = \mathcal{H}\left(\sin^2(\pi\epsilon/2)\right) + \alpha\left(\mathcal{H}(\lambda) + \lambda\ln\epsilon + (1 - \lambda)\ln(1 - \epsilon)\right).$$

In Figure 3A we plot the thermodynamic limit of the annealed learning curve $\epsilon_\lambda^{an}(\alpha) = \epsilon_{S\lambda}^{max}(\alpha)$ given by Theorem 2.2 for $S(\epsilon)$ as in (26). In Figure 3B we plot the upper bound $\epsilon_{S\lambda}^{max}(\alpha)$ on the worst case learning curve $\epsilon_{0\infty}^{wc}(\alpha)$ for the entropy bound (26).

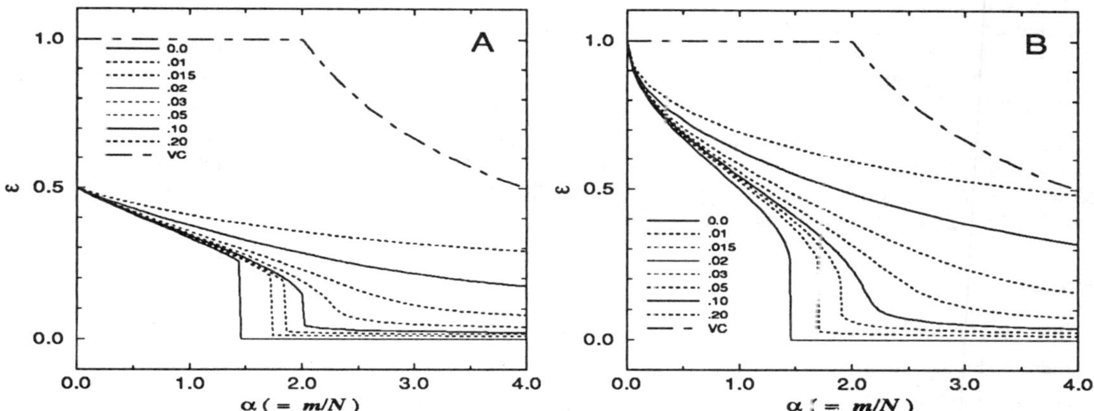

Figure 3: (A) Plots of the thermodynamic limit of annealed learning curves $\epsilon_\lambda^{an}(\alpha) = \epsilon_{S\lambda}^{max}(\alpha)$ for the Ising perceptron for selected learning thresholds $\lambda = 0.0, 0.01, 0.017, 0.02, 0.05, 0.1, 0.2$ (the bottom up order). These curves viewed as relations parameterized by ϵ provide the thermodynamic limits of annealed sample complexity curves $\epsilon \mapsto \alpha_{\lambda\infty}^{an}(\epsilon, \delta)$ for any $0 < \delta < 1$.

(B) Plots of the upper bounds $\epsilon_{S\lambda}^+(\alpha)$ on the worst case learning curves $\alpha \mapsto \epsilon_{\lambda\infty}^{wc}(\alpha)$ for the Ising perceptron, for training thresholds λ selected as above; these bounds are implied by Theorem 2.2 with the entropy bound (26). These curves viewed as functions of ϵ provide an upper bound on the sample complexity $\epsilon \mapsto \alpha_{\lambda\infty}^{wc}(\epsilon, \delta)$ for any $0 < \delta \leq 1$ (c.f. Section 3).

As a reference, in the chain line we have plotted also a modified VC-bound to suit the particular case of Ising perceptron (c.f. bounds 27 and 28). The corresponding universal VC-bound on learning curve given by (20) is trivial ($\equiv 1$) in the range $0 < \alpha \leq 12$ and is not plotted here (c.f. Figure 2).

A slight modification of the VC-formalism provides for the Ising perceptron a much tighter bound than the universal bound given by (20) or (21). In this case there are 2^N hypotheses in H_N in total, so we can use in the fundamental theorem of computational learning [4] the tighter upper bound, on the growth function, namely $2^{d_N} = 2^N$, rather than $(2em/N)^N$. Consequently we get the following bounds [11]:

$$\epsilon_{0\infty}^{wc}(\alpha) \leq \min(1, 2/\alpha), \tag{27}$$
$$\alpha_{0\infty}^{wc}(\epsilon, \delta) \leq 2/\epsilon. \tag{28}$$

The first of these bounds is plotted in chain lines in Figure 3.

4 Discussion and conclusions

From Theorems 2.1 and 2.2 it follows that in the thermodynamic limit the sample complexity curves are inverses of learning curves. Geometrically these curve can be obtained by reflection in the 45° line in the α-ϵ-plane.

Note that a relatively rough information on entropy distribution or entropy bound is necessary in order to determine the thermodynamic limits of learning curves as any polynomial factor in τ_N on the R.H.S. of either (12) or (17) can be absorbed into the term $o(\tau_N)$ in the exponent.

In Figure 2 we have plotted universal VC-bound and in Figure 3 a VC-type bound modified specifically for Ising perceptron (c.f. upper chain lines in these Figures). The latter bound is the best possible bound based on the growth function [4, 17] (since the bound 2^{dvc} used to derive it is the lower bound on the growth function for any learning system). From Figures 2 and 3 it is clear that these bounds are much looser in the small training sample range than the bounds from Theorems 1 and 2 obtained with some statistical properties of the learning systems taken into account. The obvious conclusion is that model specific information other than VC-dimension or the growth function has to be taken into account if the modelling of generalization in the small training sample range is an objective. This is further strengthened by dramatic differences between annealed learning curves for Ising and homogeneous perceptrons, which are linked to differences in their entropy distributions (c.f. Figure 1).

Note that in this paper we did not present any model specific bound for the worst case learning curve for the homogeneous perceptron since applicability of Theorem 2 is restricted to finite learning systems. However, some results in this direction are presented in [12, 13, 10]. The examples of learning systems considered there show again that inclusion of some model specific information is vital for modelling of generalization in the small training sample range ($\alpha < 12$), where VC-bounds are trivial.

Theorem 1 shows that in the thermodynamic limit the learning curves are fully determined by the shape of the entropy distribution. This leads to the following paradox. The ultimate aim of the consistent learning ($\lambda = 0$) is to select a perfect classifier (i.e. the target) on the basis of the labelled training samples. To that end, if the target is relatively isolated, one may expect the task to be easier, since there are fewer classifiers which correctly classify the training sample to choose from. Figure 1 shows clearly that there are relatively fewer perceptrons near the target in the homogeneous case compared to Ising. In spite of this, the corresponding annealed learning curves in Figure 2 (the lower chain line and the solid line), show that selecting the perfect classifier for Ising perceptron is much easier! Thus the "common sense" does not provide the right intuition and a more subtle formal analysis is required here. (Note that the fact that in the Ising case there is a finite number of classifiers is irrelevant here.)

Note that *the upper bound* on phase transition to the perfect generalization at $\alpha = 1.448$ for the worst case learning curve found originally in [8] for Ising perceptron coincides with "the exact" value for such a phase transition for annealed learning curve as defined in this paper. This result is still to be reconciled with the prediction of phases transition at $\alpha = 1.245$ from some "inexact" replica models, e.g. [7, 14].

References

[1] S. Amari. A universal theorem on learning curves. *Neural Networks*, 6:161–166, 1993.

[2] S. Amari, N. Fujita, and S. Shinomoto. Four types of learning curves. *Neural Computation*, 4(4):605–618, 1992.

[3] S. Amari and N. Murata. Statistical theory of learning curves under entropic loss criterion. *Neural Computation*, 5:140–153, 1993.

[4] M. Anthony and N. Biggs. *Computational Learning Theory*. Cambridge University Press, 1992.

[5] A. Blumer, A. Ehrenfeucht, D. Haussler, and M.K. Warmuth. Learnability and the Vapnik-Chervonenkis dimensions. *Journal of the ACM*, 36:929–965, (Oct. 1989).

[6] T.M. Cover and J.A. Thomas. *Elements of Information Theory*. Wiley, New York, 1991.

[7] G. Gyorgyi. First order phase transition to perfect generalisation in a neural network with binary synapses. *Phys. rev.*, A41:7097–7100, 1990.

[8] D. Haussler, M. Kearns, H.S. Seung, and N. Tishby. Rigorous learning curve bounds from statistical mechanics. In *Proc. 7th Annual ACM Conf. on Computational Learning Theory*, pages 76–87, 1994.

[9] M.J. Kearns and U.V. Vazirani. *Introduction to Computational Learning Theory*. The MIT Press, 1994.

[10] A. Kowalczyk. An asymptotic version of EPD-bounds on generalisation in learning systems. 1996. submitted.

[11] A. Kowalczyk. Entropy bounds on learning curves and sample complexity. In *Proceedings of the Seventh Australian Conference on Neural Networks, ACNN'96*, 1996. To appear.

[12] A. Kowalczyk, J. Szymański, P.L. Bartlett, and R.C. Williamson. Examples of learning curves from a modified VC-formalism. Proc. NIPS 8, the MIT Press (to appear), 1996.

[13] A. Kowalczyk, J. Szymanski, and R.C. Williamson. Learning curves from a modified VC-formalism: a case study. In *Proceedings of ICNN'95, Perth (CD-ROM)*, VI: 2939–2943, 1995. IEEE/Causal Production.

[14] H. Sompolinsky, H.S. Seung, and N. Tishby. Statistical mechanics of learning curves. *Physical Reviews*, A45:6056–6091, 1992.

[15] L.G. Valiant. A theory of the learnable. *Communications of the ACM*, 27 (11):1134–1142, 1984).

[16] V. Vapnik. *Estimation of Dependences Based on Empirical Data*. Springer-Verlag, 1982.

[17] V. Vapnik. *The Nature of Statistical Learning Theory*. Springer-Verlag, 1995.

[18] L.H. Watkin, A. Rau, and M. Biehl. The statistical mechanics of learning rule. *Rev. Mod. Phys.*, 65:499–556, 1993.

5   Appendix: outline of the proof of Theorem 2.1

We concentrate here on the case when ϵ_h has continuous distribution (an outline of the proof for the discrete case can be found in [11]). First we explain the idea.

Let us fix $\alpha > 0, 0 \le \lambda \le 0$ and set $m = \lfloor \alpha \tau_N \rfloor$. For the N-th learning system we introduce the notation

$$\psi_N(\epsilon) \stackrel{def}{=} \sum_{i=0}^{\lfloor \lambda m \rfloor} \binom{m}{j} \epsilon^j (1 - \epsilon)^{m-j} \phi_N(\epsilon)$$

assuming that ϕ_N is such that $K_N \phi_N(\epsilon)$ is the density of the random variable $h \mapsto \epsilon_h$ for $h \in H_N$. Then

$$\rho_N(\epsilon) \stackrel{def}{=} \frac{\psi_N(\epsilon)}{\int_0^1 \psi_N(\epsilon) d\epsilon}$$

is a continuous probability density on $[0, 1]$. The crux of the proof is to show that under the assumption of the theorem this distribution is "concentrated" for large N near $\epsilon_{S\lambda}^{\max}(\alpha)$ defined by (6). In other words, we need to show that $\rho_N(\epsilon) d\epsilon$ approaches the singular distribution given by Dirac's delta, $\delta_{\epsilon_{S\lambda}^{\max}(\alpha)}(\epsilon)$:

$$\lim_{N \to \infty} \int_0^1 f(\epsilon) \rho_N(\epsilon) d\epsilon = \int_0^1 f(\epsilon) \, \delta_{\epsilon_{S\lambda}^{\max}(\alpha)}(\epsilon) \, d\epsilon = f(\epsilon_{S\lambda}^{\max}(\alpha)) \tag{29}$$

for any continuous function f on $[0,1]$. Having done this, we find analogously as in (22) and (23) that

$$\epsilon^{an}_{\lambda,N}(\lfloor \alpha \tau_N \rfloor) = \int_0^1 \epsilon \rho_N(\epsilon) d\epsilon \longrightarrow_{N \to \infty} \epsilon^{max}_{S\lambda}(\alpha)$$

and

$$\mathbf{P}_{X \lfloor \alpha \tau_N \rfloor \times H}[\epsilon_h \le \epsilon \mid \epsilon_{h,\vec{x}} \le \lambda] = \int_0^\epsilon \rho_N(x) dx \longrightarrow_{N \to \infty} \int_0^\epsilon \delta_{\epsilon^{max}_{S\lambda}(\alpha)}(z) dx = \Theta(\epsilon - \epsilon^{max}_{S\lambda}(\alpha)).$$

The last relation implies that

$$\left(\limsup_{N \to \infty} \mathbf{P}_{X \lfloor \alpha \tau_N \rfloor \times H}[\epsilon_h \le \epsilon \mid \epsilon_{h,\vec{x}} \le \lambda] \ge 1 - \delta \right) \Longleftrightarrow \left(\epsilon \le \epsilon^{max}_{S\lambda}(\alpha) \right)$$

for any $0 < \delta < 1$, which gives (14).

To complete the proof it remains to show (29). Our first step is to express $\psi_N(\epsilon)$ in terms of $\Phi^*_{S\alpha\lambda}(\epsilon)$. As $\binom{m}{i} = e^{m\mathcal{H}(\frac{i}{m}) + o(\tau_N)}$ (c.f. [6]) we get immediately from the equation (12)

$$\psi_N(\epsilon) = K_N \sum_{j=0}^{\lfloor \lambda m \rfloor} e^{\tau_N \left[S(\epsilon) + \frac{m}{\tau_N}\left(\mathcal{H}(\frac{i}{m}) + \frac{i}{m}\ln \epsilon + (1 - \frac{i}{m})\ln(1-\epsilon)\right)\right] + o(\tau_N)} = K_N \sum_{j=0}^{\lfloor \lambda m \rfloor} e^{\tau_N \Phi_S \frac{m}{\tau_N}(\epsilon, \frac{i}{m}) + o(\tau_N)}.$$

The last sum of $\lfloor \lambda m \rfloor + 1 = e^{\ln(\lfloor \lambda m \rfloor + 1)} = e^{o(\tau_N)}$ positive terms is equal to its maximal term up to a factor $e^{o(\tau_N)}$. Thus

$$\psi_N(\epsilon) = K_N e^{\tau_N \max_{0 \le j \le \lfloor \lambda m \rfloor} \Phi_S \frac{m}{\tau_N}(\epsilon, \frac{i}{m}) + o(\tau_N)}$$

$$= K_N e^{\tau_N \max_{0 \le y \le \lambda} \Phi_{S\alpha}(\epsilon, y) + o(\tau_N)}.$$

The last equality is justified by continuity of $\Phi_{S\alpha}(\epsilon, \lambda)$ in both α and λ (c.f. Eqn. 6). Let us notice that

$$\mathrm{sgn}\left(\frac{\partial}{\partial y} \Phi_{S\alpha}(x, y) \right) = \mathrm{sgn}\left(\alpha \ln \frac{y^{-1} - 1}{x^{-1} - 1} \right) = \mathrm{sgn}(x - y) \tag{30}$$

hence

$$\max_{0 \le y \le \lambda} \Phi_{S\alpha}(x, y) = \Phi_{S\alpha}\left(x, \min(x, \lambda) \right) = \Phi^*_{S\alpha\lambda}(x).$$

Thus we get

$$\psi_N(\epsilon) = K_N e^{\tau_N \Phi^*_{S\alpha\lambda}(\epsilon) + o(\tau_N)}. \tag{31}$$

Now let us denote for convenience $\epsilon^{max}_{S\lambda}(\alpha)$ by ϵ_o and by $\Phi^*_o \stackrel{def}{=} \Phi^*_{S\alpha\lambda}(\epsilon_o)$ the maximal value of $\Phi^*_{S\alpha\lambda}$ on $[0,1]$. By virtue of Assumption 4 of the theorem, the function $\Phi^*_{S\alpha\lambda}$ has a proper maximum at ϵ_o, i.e. for every $\kappa > 0$ there exist $\delta_1 = \delta_1(\kappa)$ and $\delta_2 = \delta_2(\kappa)$ such that

$$\Phi^*_{S\alpha\lambda}(\epsilon) \ge \Phi^*_o - \kappa \quad (\forall \epsilon \text{ s.t. } |\epsilon - \epsilon_o| < \delta_1),$$
$$\Phi^*_{S\alpha\lambda}(\epsilon) \le \Phi^*_o - 2\kappa \quad (\forall \epsilon \text{ s.t. } |\epsilon - \epsilon_o| > \delta_2)$$

and $\lim_{\kappa \to 0} \delta_i = 0$ for $i = 1, 2$.

Let us fix $\kappa > 0$ and corresponding δ_1 and δ_2 with properties as above. We can write

$$\int_0^1 f \rho_N d\epsilon = \int_{\epsilon_o - \delta_2}^{\epsilon_o + \delta_2} f \rho_N d\epsilon + I_N(f) \tag{32}$$

where

$$I_N(f) \stackrel{def}{=} \int_0^{\epsilon_o - \delta_2} f \rho_N d\epsilon + \int_{\epsilon_o + \delta_2}^1 f \rho_N \, d\epsilon.$$

Using (31) we obtain the estimate

$$I_N(f) \le \int_0^1 \max_{[0,1]}(f) \frac{K_N e^{\tau_N(\Phi^*_o - 2\kappa) + o(\tau_N)}}{K_N \int_{\epsilon_o - \delta_1}^{\epsilon_o + \delta_1} e^{\tau_N(\Phi^*_o - \kappa) + o(\tau_N)} d\epsilon} d\epsilon = \max_{[0,1]}(f) \frac{\int_0^1 e^{-\tau_N \kappa + o(\tau_N)} d\epsilon}{\int_{\epsilon_o - \delta_1}^{\epsilon_o + \delta_1} e^{o(\tau_N)} d\epsilon} \le \max_{[0,1]}(f) \frac{e^{-\tau_N \kappa + o(\tau_N)}}{2\delta_1 e^{o(\tau_N)}}.$$

Hence $\lim_{N \to \infty} I_N(f) = 0$ for any continuous function f on $[0,1]$. On application of this observation to the function $\epsilon \mapsto f(\epsilon) - f(\epsilon_o)$ we obtain the bound

$$|f(\epsilon_o) - \int_0^1 f \rho_N d\epsilon| \le \int_0^1 |f(\epsilon_o) - f| \rho_N d\epsilon = \int_{\epsilon_o - \delta_2}^{\epsilon_o + \delta_2} |f(\epsilon_o) - f| \rho_N d\epsilon + I_N(|f - f(\epsilon_o)|)$$

$$\le \max_{|\epsilon - \epsilon_o| \le \delta_2} |f(\epsilon_o) - f(\epsilon)| + I_N(|f(\epsilon_o) - f|) \longrightarrow_{N \to \infty} \max_{|\epsilon - \epsilon_o| \le \delta_2} |f(\epsilon_o) - f(\epsilon)|.$$

Since this holds for any κ, and $\delta_2 = \delta(\kappa) \longrightarrow_{\kappa \to 0} 0$ and the function f is continuous, we can make the last expression as small as desired. Hence we have shown that

$$f(\epsilon_o) - \int_0^1 f \rho_N \, d\epsilon \longrightarrow_{N \to \infty} 0,$$

which completes our proof. Q.E.D.

The Statistical Behavior of Bidirectional Associative Memory under Forgetting Learning

Chi-sing LEUNG, Lai-wan CHAN and John SUM

Department of Computer Science and Engineering, The Chinese University of Hong Kong

Shatin, N.T., Hong Kong

Abstract— Forgetting learning is an incremental learning rule in associative memories. With it, the recent learning items can be encoded and the old learning items will be forgotten. In this paper, the storage behavior of bidirectional associative memory (BAM) under the forgetting learning is first analyzed. That is, "Can the most recent k learning item be stored as a fixed point ?". We then discuss the way to choose the forgetting constant in the forgetting learning such that BAM can correctly store the most recent learning items as many as possible. The magnitude of the weights under the forgetting learning is also discussed. Lastly, we investigate the error correction capability of BAM under forgetting learning. Simulations are provided to verify the theoretical analysis.

I Introduction

Associative memory is a major class of neural networks with a wide range of applications such as in content addressable memory and pattern recognition [6]. As its name indicates, an important feature of associative memory is its associative nature, that is, the ability to recall the stored item based on partial or noisy information. One form of associative memories is bivalent additive Bidirectional Associative Memory (BAM) [7]. BAM is used to store bipolar library pairs (X_h, Y_h), where $X_h = (x_{1h}, \ldots, x_{nh})^T$, $Y_h = (y_{1h}, \ldots, y_{ph})^T$, $h = 1, \cdots, m$, and m is the number of library pairs. There are two layers in BAM, namely F_X and F_Y with n and p neurons respectively. The connection matrix W, proposed by Kosko, is

$$W = \sum_{h=1}^{m} Y_h X_h^T \, . \tag{1}$$

The retrieval process is an iterative feedback process that starts with a stimulus vector $X^{(0)}$ in F_X:

$$Y^{(v+1)} = \text{sgn}\left[W X^{(v)} \right], \quad \text{and} \quad X^{(v+1)} = \text{sgn}\left[W^T Y^{(v+1)} \right], \tag{2}$$

$$\text{where} \quad \text{sgn}(x) = \begin{cases} +1 & x > 0 \\ -1 & x < 0 \\ \text{state unchanged} & x = 0 \end{cases} \, .$$

Kosko proved that one of the fixed points (X_f, Y_f) can be obtained from this iterative process. Apparently, such a fixed point is desired to be one of the library pairs. A fixed point has the following properties: $X_f = \text{sgn}(W Y_f)$ and $Y_f = \text{sgn}(W^T X_f)$. Hence, a library pair can be retrieved only if it is a fixed point. With the iterative process, BAM can achieve both heteroassociative and autoassociative data recollections. The final state in F_X represents the autoassociative recall. The final state in F_Y represents the heteroassociative recall.

The storage behavior of BAM under Kosko's encoding method and its variants have been studied by various researchers [2, 9, 8, 10]. Sometimes it is expected that BAM can operate under an adaptive environment. That is, it can extract the recent information from the environment. One advantage of using Kosko's encoding method is the ability of incremental learning. That is, encoding new library pairs to the model is based on the current connection matrix only. However, with Kosko's encoding method, BAM can only correctly store up to $\frac{\min(n,p)}{2\log\min(n,p)}$ library pairs. When the number of library pairs exceeds that value, all library pairs, including the old and new items, may not be stored as fixed points. To avoid this matter, it is required that BAM should have the ability of *forgetting*, i.e., the model should be able to create space for the new library pairs . In modeling the forgetting behavior, we would like to have the following physiological requirements, (**1**)locality and being incremental, (**2**)the magnitude of the weights should be bounded. To achieve these requirements, we can introduce a decay factor $\alpha_f \in (0, 1)$, called forgetting constant, in the original Kosko's encoding method

$$W_{(t)} = \alpha_f W_{(t-1)} + Y_t X_t^T \tag{3}$$

where $W_{(0)}$ is a zero matrix and (X_t, Y_t) is the new library pair. According to the decay factor, the forgetting learning can encode the recent library pairs as fixed points with high chance and can delete some old stored library pairs. Moreover, the magnitude of the weights is upper bounded by $O(\frac{n}{\log n})$ in the worst case and is upper bounded by $O(\sqrt{n})$ in the probabilistic sense (see Section III).

The storage behavior of Hopfield network under *other forgetting rules* has already been studied numerically or theoretically [5, 11, 3]. The 'learning within bounds' [5] was proposed for Hopfield network and studied numerically by [11]. Its updating rule is

$$W_{(t)} = \phi\left(W_{(t-1)} + X_t X_t^T\right) \tag{4}$$

where $\phi(x) = x$ for $|x| < A\sqrt{n}$, otherwise $\phi(x) = \text{sgn}(x)A\sqrt{n}$. Using the *nonrigorous replica method*, [3] showed that with a suitable value of A the recent $0.04n$ previous library patterns can be kept in the memory when a small number of errors are allowed in the retrieval items. As mentioned in [1], one should be noticed that the replica method for averaging over the disorder in the system due to the different possible realizations of nominal patterns, is only strictly valid for temperature $T' > 0$. In fact, $T' = 0$ in [3] violates this criterion.

Instead of using the classical nonrigorous replica method and allowing error in the retrieval pattern, the main goal of this paper is to **study the storage behavior of BAM under the simple forgetting rule (i.e., equation (3)) when error is not allowed in the retrieval pair**. Also, we will discuss the role to choose the forgetting constant α_f. Under some assumptions, we will prove the following theorem in the next section.

Theorem 1 *Under the forgetting learning (equation (4)), if a BAM is trained with t library pairs and k is less than*

$$\frac{\log \frac{(1-\alpha_f^2)\min(n,p)}{2\log\min(n,p)}}{2\log\frac{1}{\alpha_f}} \tag{5}$$

then the probability of the $(t-k)$-th library pair (X_{t-k}, Y_{t-k}) being a fixed point tends to 1, as $n \to \infty$, $p \to \infty$.

By Theorem 1, given a α_f, we can determine the number of the most recent library pairs that the BAM can correctly store.

In the next section, we will first analyze the storage behavior of BAM under forgetting learning and then we will discuss how to choose the forgetting constant such that the BAM can correctly store the most recent library pairs as many as possible. Section III addresses the magnitude of the weights in deterministic and probabilistic senses. Section IV presents the error correction capability of BAM under forgetting learning. Lastly, a brief conclusion is drawn in Section V.

II Capacity of Forgetting Learning

The following assumptions and notations are used.

- The dimensions, n and p, are large. Also, $p = rn$, where r is a positive constant.

- Each component of the library pairs (X_h, Y_h) is a ± 1 equiprobable independent random variable.

- $EU_{j,t-k}$ is the event that the j-th component of $\text{sgn}(W^{(t)} X_{t-k})$ is equal to the j-th component of Y_{t-k}. Also, $\overline{EU}_{j,t-k}$ is the complement event of $EU_{j,t-k}$.

- $EV_{i,t-k}$ is the event that the i-th component of $\text{sgn}(W^{(t)^T} Y_{t-k})$ is equal to the i-th component of X_{t-k}. $\overline{EV}_{i,t-k}$ is the complement event of $EV_{i,t-k}$.

Lemma 1 *Chebyshev's inequality* : *For any random variable χ and $u \geq 0$, $Prob(\chi \geq u) \leq \inf_{\tau \geq 0} e^{-\tau u} E(e^{\tau \chi})$.*

Lemma 2 *Let $v_1, v_2, \ldots, v_N$ be independent ± 1 equiprobable random variables, $S_N = \sum_{i=1}^{N} v_i$, and β is a real number,*

$$E\left[\exp\left\{\tau\beta\frac{S_N}{\sqrt{N}}\right\}\right] \leq \exp\left\{\frac{\beta^2\tau^2}{2}\right\}$$

for $\tau > 0$.

From Lemma 1 and Lemma 2, we can get the following two lemmas.

Lemma 3 *For $j = 1, \ldots, p$, the probability $Prob(\overline{EU}_{j,t-k})$ is less than $\exp\left\{-\frac{(1-\alpha_f^2)\alpha_f^{2k}n}{2}\right\}$.*

Lemma 4 *For $i = 1, \cdots, n$, the probability $Prob(\overline{EV}_{i,t-k})$ is less than $\exp\left\{-\frac{(1-\alpha_f^2)\alpha_f^{2k}p}{2}\right\}$.*

With Lemma 3 and 4, Theorem 1 can be proven in the following way. We denote the probability that (X_{t-k}, Y_{t-k}) is a fixed point as P_*. Then,

$$\begin{aligned}
P_* &= \text{Prob}\left(EU_{1,t-k} \cap \cdots \cap EU_{p,t-k} \cap EV_{1,t-k} \cap \cdots \cap EV_{n,t-k}\right) \\
&\geq 1 - p\text{Prob}\left(\overline{EU}_{1,t-k}\right) - n\text{Prob}\left(\overline{EV}_{1,t-k}\right) .
\end{aligned} \tag{6}$$

With Lemma 3 and 4, it is easy to show that in the following condition the right-hand side of equation (6) tends one, as n tends to ∞.

$$k < \min\left(\frac{\log\frac{(1-\alpha_f^2)n}{2\log n}}{2\log\frac{1}{\alpha_f}}, \frac{\log\frac{(1-\alpha_f^2)p}{2\log p}}{2\log\frac{1}{\alpha_f}}\right) = \frac{\log\frac{(1-\alpha_f^2)\min(n,p)}{2\log\min(n,p)}}{2\log\frac{1}{\alpha_f}} = f(\alpha_f) .$$

Thus, Theorem 1 is obtained. From Theorem 1, the most recent k library pair, (X_{t-k}, Y_{t-k}), can be stored as a fixed point with high probability if $k < f(\alpha_f)$. The most interesting point is how to choose the value of $\alpha_f \in (0,1)$ such that $f(\alpha_f)$ is maximal. We denote the value of α_f, with which $f(\alpha_f)$ being maximal, as $\alpha_{f,max}$.

Clearly, $f(\alpha_f)$ is a continuous function of $\alpha_f \in (0,1)$. Also,

$$\frac{d f(\alpha_f)}{d \alpha_f}\Big|_{\alpha_f=0+} > 0, \quad \text{and} \quad \frac{d f(\alpha_f)}{d \alpha_f}\Big|_{\alpha_f=1-} < 0 .$$

Hence, $f(\alpha)$ has at least one local maximum when $0 < \alpha_f < 1$. Using simple numerical method, we obtain Table 1 which summarizes the values of $\alpha_{f,max}$ at different values of $\min(n,p)$. From the table, as $\min(n,p)$ increases, $\alpha_{f,max}$ tends to one. Based on this phenomenon, we can further derive the close-form-solution of $\alpha_{f,max}$ for a large $\min(n,p)$:

$$\alpha_{f,max} \approx \sqrt{1 - \exp\left\{-\log\frac{\min(n,p)}{2\log\min(n,p)} + 1\right\}} \tag{7}$$

The above equation gives us a guideline to choose the value of α_f. Table 1 also shows $\alpha_{f,max}$ at different values of $\min(n,p)$ based on equation (7). From Table 1, equation (7) is a good approximation of $\alpha_{f,max}$ when $\min(n,p)$ is large. Substituting equation (7) into Theorem 1, we can obtain the following corollary.

Corollary 1 *Under the forgetting learning with*

$$\alpha_{f,max} \approx \sqrt{1 - \exp\left\{-\log\frac{\min(n,p)}{2\log\min(n,p)} + 1\right\}},$$

if a BAM is trained with t library pairs and k is less than

$$\frac{\min(n,p)}{2e\log\min(n,p)} , \tag{8}$$

then the probability of the $(t-k)$-th stored pair (X_{t-k}, Y_{t-k}) being a fixed point tends to one, as $n, p \to \infty$.

From Corollary 1, the storage ability of the forgetting learning is similar to that of Kosko's encoding method. With Kosko's encoding method, BAM can only encode up to $\frac{\min(n,p)}{2\log\min(n,p)}$ library pairs. Further encoding the new library pairs will damage the whole system. On the other hand, the forgetting learning can encode any number of library pairs and always keep the most recent $\frac{\min(n,p)}{2e\log\min(n,p)}$ library pairs in the model. **Hence, BAM with the forgetting learning is similar to an adaptive memory, which always extract the most recent information from the environment.**

We have carried out a simulation to verify equation (7) and Corollary 1. The dimensions are 512. We randomly generate the library pairs and use the forgetting rule to encode them with different constants. Figure 1 shows the percentage of the most recent library pairs being stored as fixed points.

Suppose that we use 90 % as the threshold. From the figure, if α_f is too large (such as 0.990), all library pairs (including the old and new items) may not be stored as fixed points. When we use a very small α_f (say 0.940), the percentage of the most recent items being stored as fixed points is very small. In general, the case of $\alpha_f = 0.9663$, which is based on Table 1, is better than other cases. Also, there is a sharply decreasing change for $k > 14$ ($\alpha_f = 0.9663$). This is consistent with our theoretical work presented in Table 1.

Table 1 Summary of $\alpha_{f,max}$ and $f(\alpha_{f,max})$.

$\min(n,p)$	from numerical method		from the equation (7)	
	$\alpha_{f,max}$	$f(\alpha_{f,max})$	$\alpha_{f,max}$	$f(\alpha_{f,max})$
16	0.613	0.6012	0.2407	0.35
32	0.742	1.223	0.6412	1.13
64	0.837	2.3453	0.8042	2.29
128	0.902	4.3611	0.9810	4.33
256	0.943	7.9967	0.9393	7.98
512	0.9675	14.599	0.9663	14.59
1024	0.982	26.673	0.9814	26.67

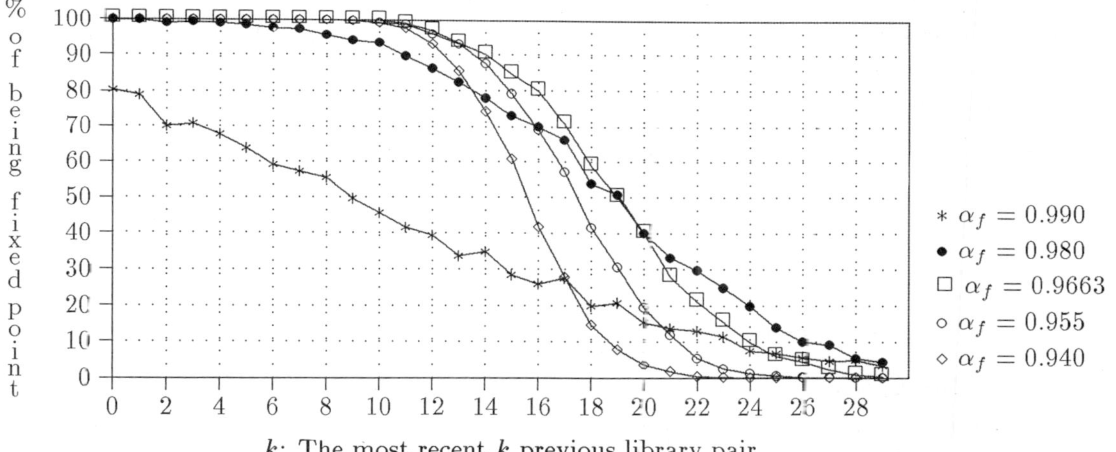

k: The most recent k previous library pair

Figure 1 The percentage of the most recent k previous library pairs being stored as a fixed point where $n = p = 512$ and $\alpha_f = 0.940, 0.955, 0.9663, 0.980, 0.990$. Note that $\alpha_{f,max} = 0.9663$.

III   Magnitude of the Weights

A. The Worst Case Bound

Let $w_{t,ji}$ be the weight between the jth neuron in F_Y and the ith neuron in F_X. After t library pairs have been encoded using equation (3), $w_{t,ji} = \sum_{h=1}^{t} \alpha_f^{t-h} x_{h,i} y_{h,j}$. In the worst case, $x_{h,i} = y_{h,j}$ for all h (or $x_{h,i} = -y_{h,j}$ for all h), $|w_{t,ji}| = \sum_{h=1}^{t} \alpha_f^{t-h} \leq \frac{1}{1-\alpha_f}$. Clearly, when α_f is a constant, the magnitude of $w_{t,ji}$ **is upper bounded** by $O(1)$. If α_f is selected based on equation (7), then

$$|w_{t,ji}| \leq \frac{1}{1 - \sqrt{1 - \exp\left\{-\log \frac{\min(n,p)}{2\log\min(n,p)} + \cdot\right\}}} \tag{9}$$

$$= \frac{1}{\frac{1}{2}\frac{2e \log \min(n,p)}{\min(n,p)} + \frac{1}{8}(\frac{2e \log \min(n,p)}{\min(n,p})^2 + \text{high order terms}} . \tag{10}$$

Hence, for large n and p (note that $p = rn$), $|w_{t,ji}|$ **is upper bounded** by $\leq O(\frac{n}{\log n})$.

B. The Probabilistic Bound Now, if $x_{h,i}$ and $y_{h,j}$ are ± 1 equiprobable independent random variables, $w_{t,ji} = \sum_{h=1}^{t} \alpha_f^{t-h} z_h$ where z_h's are ± 1 equiprobable independent random variables. Let η be a standard normal random variable with variance one. It is not difficult to show that $E(\exp\{\tau z_h\}) < E(\exp\{\tau \eta\})$. With Lemma 1,

$$\text{Prob}\left\{|w_{t,ji}| > A\sqrt{\min(n,p)}\right\} \quad \leq \quad 2 \inf_{\tau \geq 0} \exp\left\{-\tau A \sqrt{\min(n,p)}\right\} \exp\left\{\frac{\sum_{h=1}^{t} \alpha_f^{2t-2h} \tau^2}{2}\right\}$$

$$\leq \quad 2 \inf_{\tau \geq 0} \exp\left\{-\tau A \sqrt{\min(n,p)}\right\} \exp\left\{\frac{\tau^2}{2(1 - \alpha_f^2)}\right\} ,$$

where A is a positive constant. The right-hand side becomes minimum when $\tau = A\sqrt{\min(n,p)}(1 - \alpha_f^2)$. With such a value of τ, $\text{Prob}\left\{|w_{t,ji}| > A\sqrt{\min(n,p)}\right\} \leq 2\exp\left\{-\frac{(1-\alpha_f^2)A^2 \min(n,p)}{2}\right\}$. **When α_f is a constant, it exponentially tends to zero as $n \to \infty$. If α_f is selected based on equation (7),** $\text{Prob}\left\{|w_{t,ji}|) > A\sqrt{\min(n,p)}\right\} \leq 2\exp\left\{-eA^2 \log \min(n,p)\right\}$. It also tends to zero as $n \to \infty$. Hence, the magnitude of the weight under the forgetting learning is upper bounded by $O(\sqrt{\min(n,p)}) = O(\sqrt{n})$ in the probabilistic sense.

IV   Error Correction Capability

So far, we have not yet mentioned the error correction capability of BAM under the forgetting learning. In this section, we first estimate the probability P_t that the most recent k previous library pair (X_{t-k}, Y_{t-k}) can be correctly recalled within two–shots, given a noisy input X_{noise} of X_{t-k} with ρn errors. *Two–shots* means that the noisy input is first presented in F_X and the state of F_Y is then obtained; this state of F_Y is feedback to F_X and then a new state of F_X is obtained.

Corollary 2 *Under the forgetting learning with*

$$\alpha_{f,max} \approx \sqrt{1 - \exp\left\{-\log \frac{\min(n,p)}{2\log \min(n,p)} + 1\right\}}$$

and large n and p, if a BAM is trained with t library pairs and k is less than

$$\min\left(\frac{(1 + \log((1 - 2\rho)^2))n}{2e \log n}, \frac{p}{2e \log p}\right) , \tag{11}$$

then the probability that the $(t - k)$-th library pair (X_{t-k}, Y_{t-k}) can be correctly recalled with high probability, given a noisy input X_{noise} of X_{t-k} with ρn errors .

We have carried out a simulation to verify Corollary 2. The dimensions are 512. We feed the noisy input into the BAM and then we record the percentage of correct recall within two shots. The noisy levels in the initial input are: $\rho = \frac{16}{512}, \frac{32}{512}$, and $\frac{64}{512}$.

Figure 2 shows the percentage of the most recent previous library pairs being correctly recalled within two shots. From the figure, if k is less than 12.70 (for $\rho = \frac{16}{512}$); 10.69 (for $\rho = \frac{32}{512}$); 6.20 (for $\rho = \frac{64}{512}$), then the percentage of correct recall is more than 90 %. It should be noticed that from Corollary 2 if k is less than 12.70 (for $\rho = \frac{16}{512}$); 10.69 (for $\rho = \frac{32}{512}$); 6.20 (for $\rho = \frac{64}{512}$), then the desired library pair can be correctly recalled with high probability within two shots. To sum up, the result of this simulation result quite matches the theoretical result from Corollary 2.

V   Conclusion

We have estimated the number of the recent library pairs can be stored as fixed points in BAM when the forgetting learning is used. Also, we have derived a formula for choosing the forgetting constant. This is, $\alpha_{f,max} \approx \sqrt{1 - \exp\left\{-\log\frac{\min(n,p)}{2\log\min(n,p)} + 1\right\}}$. The forgetting learning rule can encode any number of library pairs and always keep the recent $\frac{\min(n,p)}{2e\log\min(n,p)}$ library pairs. The magnitude of the weights under the forgetting learning is upper bounded by $O(\sqrt{n})$ in the probabilistic sense and is upper bounded by $O(\frac{n}{\log n})$ in the worst case. Moreover, we have examined the error correction capability of BAM under the forgetting learning. An initial noisy input of the most recent k previous library pair with ρn errors can correctly recall the desired library pair within two shots if the inequality

$$k < \min\left(\frac{(1 + \log((1-2\rho)^2))n}{2e\log n}, \frac{p}{2e\log p}\right)$$

is satisfied. Computer simulations have been done to verify the theoretical results.

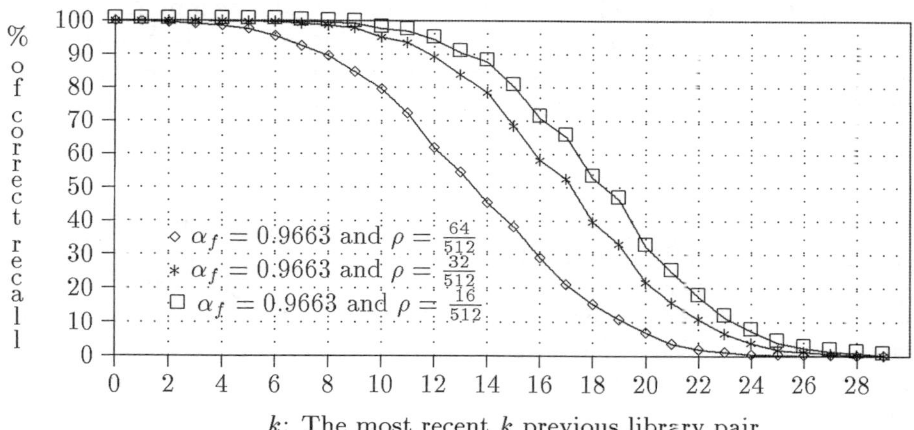

Figure 2 The percentage of the most recent previous library pair being correctly recall within two shots where $n = p = 512$ and $\alpha_f = 0.9663$.

References

[1] B.M. Forrest B.M. and D.J. Wallace, "Storage Capacity and Learning in Ising-Spin Neural Networks," *Models of Neural Networks*, Springer-Verlag, 1991.

[2] K. Haines and R.H. Nielsen, "A BAM with Increased Information Storage Capacity," *Proc. of the 1988 IEEE Int. Conf. on Neural Networks*, pp.181–190, 1988.

[3] J.L. Hemmen, G. Keller, and R. Kuhn, "Forgetful Memories," *Europhys. Lett.*, vol. 5, pp. 663-668, 1988.

[4] J.L. Hemmen, and R. Kuhn, "Collective Phenomena in Neural Networks," *Models of Neural Networks*, Springer-Verlag, 1991.

[5] J.J. Hopfield, "Neural networks and physical systems with emergent collective computational abilities," *Proc. Natl. Acad. Sci.*, vol. 79, pp.2554–2558 1982.

[6] T. Kohonen, "Correlation Matrix Memories," *IEEE Trans. Comput.*, vol. 21, pp.353–359, 1972.

[7] B. Kosko, "Bidirectional Associative Memories," *IEEE Trans. on Syst., Man., and Cybern.*, vol. 18, no.1, pp.49–60, 1988.

[8] C.S. Leung, "Encoding Method for Bidirectional Associative Memory using Projection on Convex Sets," *IEEE Trans. on Neural Networks*, vol 4, no. 5, pp.879–871, 1993.

[9] C.S. Leung, L.W. Chan, and E. Lai, "Stability, Capacity and Statistical Dynamics of Second Order Bidirectional Associative Memory," *IEEE Trans. on Syst., Man, and Cybern.*, vol 25 no. 10., pp. 1414–1424, 1995.

[10] Y.F. Wang, J.B. Cruz, and J.H. Mulligan, "Two Coding Strategies for Bidirectional Associative Memory," *IEEE Trans. on Neural Networks*, vol. 1, no.1, pp.81–92, 1990.

[11] G. Parisi, "A memory which forgets," *J. Phys. A:Math. Gen.*, vol. 19, pp.L617–L620, 1986.

The Neural Heat Exchanger

Jürgen Schmidhuber
IDSIA, Corso Elvezia 36
6900 Lugano, Switzerland
juergen@idsia.ch
http://www.idsia.ch/~juergen

Abstract— The "Neural Heat Exchanger" is an alternative, supervised learning method
for multi-layer neural nets. It is inspired by the physical heat exchanger. Unlike backprop,
it is entirely local. This makes its parallel implementation trivial. It was first presented
during occasional talks since 1990, and is closely related to Hinton *et. al.*'s recent Helmholtz
Machine (1995). For the first time, this paper presents the basic ideas in written form. To
fully understand the Neural Heat Exchanger's advantages and limitations, however, much
theoretical and empirical work remains to be done.

1   Introduction

Most conventional supervised algorithms for multi-layer neural nets are not local in space and time. Backprop, for instance, requires a global control mechanism that first propagates activation signals through all
successive layers, then waits until the error signals come back, then changes the weights. Many suspect,
however, that the brain *does* use an entirely local algorithm. One advantage of truly local algorithms is
that their parallel implementation is trivial. The method to be described below is designed to be entirely
local while still being able to deal with hidden units and non-linearities [5]. See [4] for another local
alternative.

2   The Neural Heat Exchanger

First consider a conventional, physical heat exchanger. See Figure 1 (C). There are two touching water
pipes with opposite flow direction. Cold water enters the first pipe. Hot water enters the second pipe. But
hot water exits the first pipe, and cold water exits the second pipe! At any given point where both pipes
touch, their temperatures are the same (provided the water speed is low enough to allow for sufficient
temperature exchange). Entirely local interaction can lead to a complete reversal of global, macroscopic
properties such as temperature. Physical heat exchangers are common in technical applications (e.g.,
nuclear power plants) and animals, e.g., rodents (Geoff Hinton, personal communication, 1994).

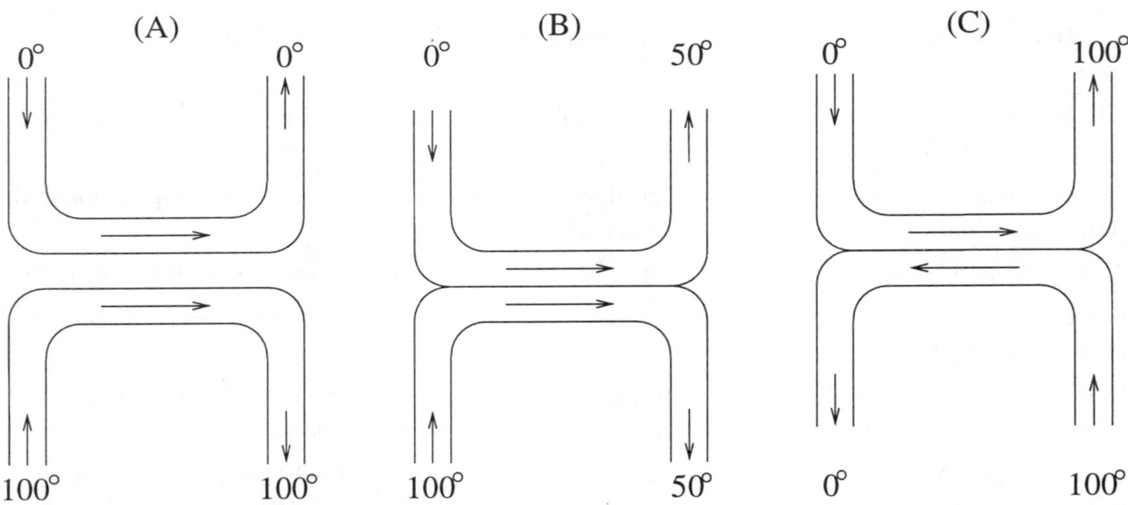

Figure 1: *(A) shows two water pipes that don't touch. Cold water enters and exits the first pipe. Hot
water enters and exits the second pipe. (B) shows two touching water pipes with equal flow direction.
Cold water enters the first pipe. Hot water enters the second pipe. Lukewarm water exits both. (C) shows
two touching water pipes with opposite flow direction (a heat exchanger). Cold water enters the first pipe
to become hot water. Hot water enters the second pipe to become cold water.*

Basic idea. In analogy to the physical heat exchanger, I build a "Neural Heat Exchanger". There are two multi-layer feedforward networks with opposite flow direction. They correspond to the pipes. Both nets have the same number of layers. They are aligned such that each net's input layer is "next" to the other net's output layer, and each hidden layer in the first net is "next" to exactly one hidden layer in the other net. Input patterns enter the first net and are propagated "up". Desired outputs (targets) enter the "opposite" net and are propagated "down". Using the local, simple delta rule, each layer in each net tries to be similar (in information content) to the preceding layer *and* to the corresponding layer in the other net. The input entering the first net slowly "heats up" to become the target. The target entering the opposite net slowly "cools down" to become the input. No global control mechanism is required. See Figure 2 and details below.

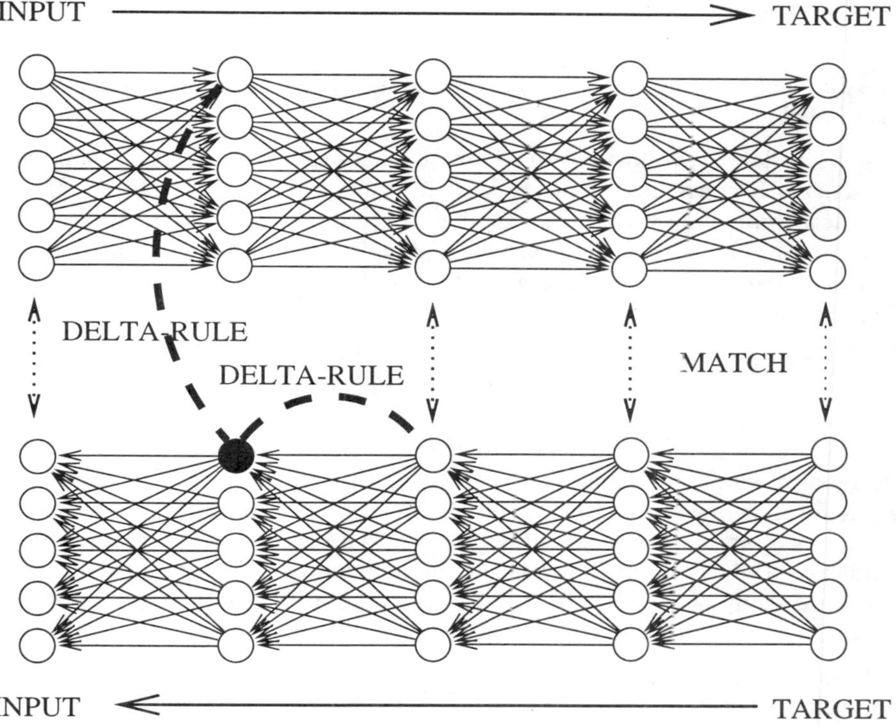

Figure 2: *The Neural Heat Exchanger requires two multi-layer feedforward nets with opposite flow direction. Each net's input layer is next to the other net's output layer. Each hidden layer in the upper net is next to exactly one hidden layer in the lower net. Input patterns enter the upper net and are propagated to the right. Desired outputs (targets) enter the lower net and are propagated to the left. Each layer in each net tries to be similar to the preceding layer and to the corresponding layer in the other net. For example, consider the black unit: two dotted lines connect the black unit to those two units it tries to match using the simple delta rule. Inputs entering the upper net slowly "heat up" to become like the targets. Targets entering the lower net slowly "cool down" to become like the inputs. No global control mechanism is required.*

Architecture. See Figure 2. The first pipe corresponds to a feedforward network F with n layers F_1, F_2, ..., F_n. Each unit in F_i has directed connections to each unit in F_{i+1}, $i \in \{1, 2, \ldots, n-1\}$. The second pipe corresponds to a feedforward network B with n layers B_1, B_2, ..., B_n. Each unit in B_{i+1} has directed connections to each unit in B_i, $i \in \{1, 2, \ldots, n-1\}$. For simplicity, let all layers have m units. The k-th unit in F_i is denoted F_i^k. The k-th unit in B_i is denoted B_i^-. The randomly initialized weight on the connection from some unit l to some unit k is denoted w_{kl}.

Dynamics (example). See Figure 2. Input patterns enter F at F_1. Output patterns exit F at F_n. The goal is to make the output patterns like the targets. B's flow direction is opposite to F's. Targets (desired outputs) enter B at B_n. Output patterns exit B at B_1. The goal is to make the output patterns like F's inputs. Input units are those in F_1 and B_n. At any given discrete time step, their activations are set by the environment, according to the current task. Furthermore, at any given time, each noninput unit i updates its variable activation o_i (initialized with 0.0) as follows: with probability $f(\sum_k w_{ik} o_k)$, set $o_i \leftarrow 1.0$; with probability $1 - f(\sum_k w_{ik}o_k)$, set $o_i \leftarrow 0.0$; where $f(x) = \frac{1}{1+e^{-x}}$, for instance.

Learning. At any given discrete time step, using the simple delta rule (no backprop), weights are adjusted such that each noninput unit F_i^k reduces its current (expected) distance to the corresponding unit B_i^k. Symmetrically: each noninput unit B_i^k reduces its current distance to the corresponding unit F_i^k. Why? Because each layer should be similar to ("have the same temperature as") the corresponding layer in the net with opposite flow direction.

Furthermore, at any given time step, using the simple delta rule (no backprop), weights are adjusted such that each noninput unit F_i^k reduces its distance to unit F_{i-1}^k. Symmetrically: each noninput unit B_i^k reduces its distance to B_{i+1}^k. Why? Because this tends to make successive units similar — just like neighboring parts of a physical heat exchanger have similar temperature. The target entering B slowly "cools down" to become the input. Likewise, the input entering F slowly "heats up" to become the target.

Clearly, each weight gets error signals from two different local minimization processes. Simply add them up to change the weights.

Variants. The discussion above focused on the case where each layer has the same number of units. This makes it particularly convenient to define what it means for one layer to be similar to the preceding one: each unit's activation simply has to be similar to the one of the unit at the same position in the previous layer. *Varying* numbers of units per layer require us to refine our notion of layer similarity. For instance, layer similarity can be defined by measuring mutual information between successive layers. Non-probabilistic variants of the Neural Heat Exchanger may sometimes be appropriate as well.

Experiments. Three ETHZ undergrad students, Alberto Salerno, Thomas Fasciania, and Giorgio Pazmandi, recently reimplemented the Neural Heat Exchanger. They report that it was able to solve XOR more quickly than backprop. For larger scale parity problems, however, their system did not work as well as backprop. Sepp Hochreiter (personal communication) also implemented variants of the Neural Heat Exchanger. He learned simple functions such as AND with 5 and more hidden layers. He reports that the system prefers local coding in deep hidden layers. He also successfully tried variants where each layer has different numbers of units, and where either local auto-association or mutual information is used to define layer similarity. Unfortunately, however, at the moment of this writing, there has not yet been a detailed experimental study of the Neural Heat Exchanger. My own, very limited 1990 toy experiments also do not qualify as a systematic analysis. Much remains to be done.

Relation to recent work. According to Peter Dayan (personal communication, 1994), the Neural Heat Exchanger is essentially a supervised variant of the recent Helmholtz Machine [3, 2]. Or, depending on the point of view, the Helmholtz Machine is an unsupervised variant of the Neural Heat Exchanger.

According to Peter Dayan and Geoff Hinton [1], a trouble with the Neural Heat Exchanger is that in non-deterministic domains, there is no reason why B's output should match F's input. Dayan and Hinton's algorithm overcomes this problem by using completely separate learning phases for top-down and bottom-up weights. This, however, makes their algorithm non-local in time: a global mechanism is required to separate the learning phases.

An alternative way to overcome the problem above may be to force part of F's output to reconstruct a unique representation of F's input, and to feed this representation also into B, together with the target.

3 Conclusion

The Neural Heat Exchanger is an entirely local method for training multi-layer nets. It is inspired by principles of conventional, physical heat exchangers. It was first presented in 1990, and is very similar to the 1995 Helmholtz Machine. It can solve certain non-linear tasks. To fully understand its advantages and limitations, however, much theoretical and empirical work remains to be done.

4   Acknowledgments

Thanks to Sepp Hochreiter, Alberto Salerno, Thomas Fasciania, and Giorgio Pazmandi, for sharing their preliminary results with implementations of the Neural Heat Exchanger. Thanks for comments to Peter Dayan, Marco Wiering, Rafal Salustowicz, and Jieyu Zhao (supported by SNF grant 21-43'417.95 "Incremental Self-Improvement").

References

[1] P. Dayan and G. E. Hinton. Varieties of Helmholtz machine. *Neural Networks, in press*, 1996.

[2] P. Dayan, G. E. Hinton, R. M. Neal, and R. S. Zemel. The Helmholtz machine. *Neural Computation*, 7:889–904, 1995.

[3] G. E. Hinton, P. Dayan, B. J. Frey, and R. M. Neal. The wake-sleep algorithm for unsupervised neural networks. *Science*, 268:1158–1160, 1995.

[4] J. H. Schmidhuber. The Neural Bucket Brigade: A local learning algorithm for dynamic feedforward and recurrent networks. *Connection Science*, 1(4):403–412, 1989.

[5] J. H. Schmidhuber. The Neural Heat Exchanger, 1990. Talk presented at Technische Universität München. The same talk was given at University of Colorado at Boulder (1992), at various other institutions, and at Zhaoping Li's NIPS*94 workshop on unsupervised learning.

Discretizing Continuous Neural Networks Using a Polarization Learning Rule

Lifeng Wang, Heng-Da Cheng
Department of Computer Science, Utah State University
Logan, Utah, USA
cheng@hengda.cs.usu.edu

Abstract— **Neural networks using continuous activation functions develop representations in a continuous space, which is not desirable for certain applications dealing only with discrete values. Common problems faced by researchers are: unstable, infinite internal representations (states) are developed in continuous space while finite, discrete states are desired. This paper presents a polarization learning rule, which forces the activation values of neurons to the two poles of the activation function. The polarization learning rule can be combined with traditional error back-propagation learning without compromising the theoretical foundation of gradient descent algorithm. Using the proposed polarization learning rule, several experiments are conducted. One particular application is in grammatical inference using second-order recurrent network. By using the polarization learning rule, no clustering algorithms are needed, and the FSAs developed during training are, most of the time, the ideal FSAs for the grammars being inferred.**

1   Introduction

Neural networks using discrete activation functions can be applied to a variety of applications, e.g., pattern classifiers, associative memories, etc. One advantage of discrete neural networks is their simplicity – no complicated calculations are required to compute the activation value of a neuron. More importantly, since a neuron can take only discrete values, usually 0 or 1, the activation space of a discrete neural network is discrete and finite. Therefore, it is easy to interpret the behavior of such networks. One factor severely limiting the application of discrete networks is that for a multilayered network, no known training method exists.

On the other hand, continuous neural networks have more expressive power than discrete ones. Error back-propagation (BP) network is a typical continuous network with gradient-descent learning rule. In a BP network, activation function has to be continuous because the derivative of the activation function needs to be calculated. During training of a BP network, the internal representations developed in the hidden layers are in a continuous space. For certain applications, especially the ones in which only discrete values are involved, e.g., grammatical inference, data compression, and language learning, the internal representations in a continuous space are not preferred.

The dilemma presented to us is: we need to use continuous activation function in order to effectively train a neural network, meanwhile, we want the neural network to behave as a discrete network. Several approaches to address this problem have been studied. These efforts center around using recurrent neural networks to solve grammatical inference problem. Giles *et al* used a second-order recurrent network to learn regular language [2]. After training, the hidden states are clustered and FSA is constructed. Zeng *et al* introduced a rigid discretization during training [6]. As pointed out in [3], clustering after training is arbitrary and the sensitivity-to-initial-conditions nature of recurrent systems may cause clustering methods to fail. Zeng's work used pseudo-gradient descent and lacks theoretical justification. Das and Mozer built a clustering mechanism inside the training procedure[1]. Their dynamic on-line clustering and state extraction (DOLCE) architecture facilitates the forming of more distinguishable clusters during training. But these clusters are still in a continuous space and extra effort is needed to extracted FSA from the trained network.

In this paper, we present a polarization learning rule to discretize continuous networks. This learning rule can be combined with existing neural network training algorithms. When the polarization learning rule is applied to the grammatical inference problems, the solution is discrete and stable, and the task of extracting FSA becomes straightforward. The experimental results are superior to the existing approaches mentioned above.

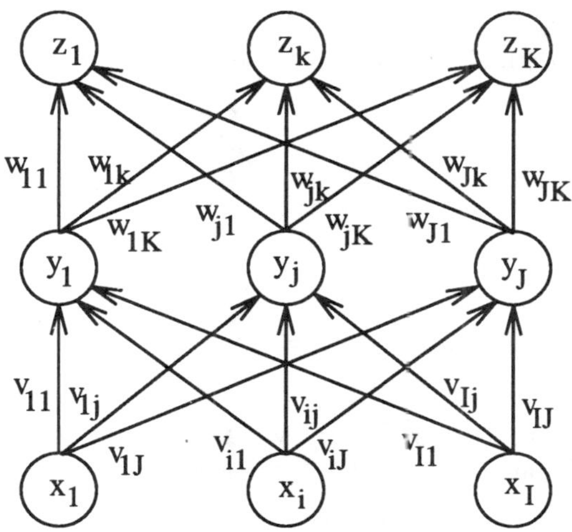

Figure 1: Back-propagation network architecture with one hidden layer

2 The General Polarization Learning Rule

Without loss of generality, the following bipolar sigmoid activation function is used through out this paper:

$$f(x) = \frac{2}{1 + e^{-x}} - 1 \tag{1}$$

Neuron n receives inputs from several other neurons. The activation of n can be computed by applying the activation function on the weighted sum of its inputs. Neuron m, one of the input neurons of n, is connected to n with a weight w. If at a certain time, the activation values of neurons m and n are x and y, respectively, then by the polarization rule, the weight w should be adjusted by:

$$\Delta w = \beta xy(1 - y^2)^2 \tag{2}$$

where $\beta \geq 0$ is the polarization learning rate.

The meaning of this learning rule can be interpreted as following. If the current activation value of an output neuron is larger than 0, then the weights from its input neurons are adjusted in such a way that next time the activation of the output neuron is closer to 1, and vice versa. The term $(1 - y^2)^2$ limits the change of w to avoid saturation when the activation of n is already close to one of the two poles.

3 The Polarization Learning Rule in Error Back-propagation Networks

The architecture of an error back-propagation network with single hidden layer is shown in Figure 1 [7]. The error function is defined in (3).

$$E = \frac{1}{2} \sum_{k=1}^{K} (d_k - z_k)^2 \tag{3}$$

The objective of training a BP network is to minimize the above error function by adjusting the connection weights. Using gradient descent, the weight adjustment rule can be derived as follows:

$$\Delta w_{jk} = -\eta \frac{\partial E}{\partial w_{jk}} = \eta \delta_k y_j \tag{4}$$

$$\Delta v_{ij} = -\alpha \frac{\partial E}{\partial v_{ij}} = \frac{1}{2}\alpha(1 - y_j^2)x_i \sum_{k=1}^{K}[\delta_k w_{jk}] \tag{5}$$

where η is the learning rate for the output layer neurons, α is the learning rate for the hidden layer neurons and δ_k is defined as follows:

$$\delta_k = \frac{1}{2}(d_k - z_k)(1 - z_k^2) \tag{6}$$

To apply the polarization learning rule, we add the following error term (*polarization error*) to the traditional error function (the original error term will be called *performance error*).

$$E_{polarization} = \frac{1}{2} \sum_{j=1}^{J} (1 - y_j^2)^2 \tag{7}$$

Now the modified error function becomes:

$$E = A \times E_{performance} + B \times E_{polarization} = A \times \frac{1}{2} \sum_{k=1}^{K} (d_k - z_k)^2 + B \times \frac{1}{2} \sum_{j=1}^{J} (1 - y_j^2)^2 \tag{8}$$

where A and B are non-negative real numbers, which are used to control the relative weights of $E_{performance}$ and $E_{polarization}$ contributing to the total error function.

The weight adjustment rule for the output layer neurons remains the same. The weight adjustment rule for the hidden layer neurons becomes:

$$\Delta v_{ij} = \frac{1}{2}\alpha(1 - y_j^2)x_i \sum_{k=1}^{K} [\delta_k w_{jk}] + \frac{1}{2}\beta \sum_{j=1}^{J} [x_i y_j (1 - y_j^2)^2] \tag{9}$$

where α is the traditional learning rate and β is the polarization learning rate. Notice that the second term in equation (9) is in the form of polarization learning rule in equation (2).

The above learning rule can be generalized to BP networks with more than one hidden layers. The polarization learning rule can be used on any or all hidden layers. Another generalization is that the activation of a neuron can be pulled towards arbitrary attractors instead of two poles (1 and -1). If we want the activation value to use one of the following values: $a_1, a_2, \cdots, a_N$ where $-1 \leq a_n \leq 1$ for all $1 \leq n \leq N$, then the following error function can be used:

$$E = A \times \frac{1}{2} \sum_{k=1}^{K} (d_k - z_k)^2 + B \times \frac{1}{2} \sum_{j=1}^{J} \prod_{n=1}^{N} (y_j - a_n)^2 \tag{10}$$

Let us look at a special case where two attractors 1 and -1 are used. In this case, we have $a_1 = 1, a_2 = -1$. From equiation (10), we have:

$$\begin{aligned} E &= A \times \frac{1}{2} \sum_{k=1}^{K} (d_k - z_k)^2 + B \times \frac{1}{2} \sum_{j=1}^{J} (y_j - 1)^2 (y_j - (-1))^2 \\ &= A \times \frac{1}{2} \sum_{k=1}^{K} (d_k - z_k)^2 + B \times \frac{1}{2} \sum_{j=1}^{J} (1 - y_j^2)^2 \end{aligned} \tag{11}$$

Notice this equation is the same as equation (8), thus we prove that equation (8) is a special case of equiation (10).

4   The Polarization Learning Rule in Second-order Recurrent Networks

There are several approaches using first-order and second-order recurrent network architectures to solve grammatical inference problems. The recurrent architecture lends itself very well in emulating a Finite State Automaton (FSA). Compared with the first-order recurrent network, the second-order recurrent network is more powerful in learning a grammar. A second-order recurrent network [2] has N recurrent hidden neurons labeled S_j, L non-recurrent input neurons labeled I_i and $N^2 \times L$ weights labeled W_{ijk}, where $i = 1, \cdots, L, j = 1, \cdots, N$ and $k = 1, \cdots, N$. W_{ijk} is the weight between the product of hidden neuron S_j and input neuron I_i to the hidden neuron S_k. The dynamics of the net is described by the following equation:

$$S_k(t+1) = f(\sum_{i,j}^{L,N} W_{ijk} S_j(t) I_i(t)) \tag{12}$$

The training process of such a network usually uses a gradient descent learning procedure with error back-propagation through time. The characters in a training string are presented to the network one at a time. At the end of the string, the output of the net is compared with the desired output and the error is back-propagated to adjust the weights. The error function is defined as:

$$E = \frac{1}{2}(Target - S_0(T))^2 \tag{13}$$

where $S_0(T)$ is the output neuron value when the final character is presented and the *Target* is the desired value of (-1, 1) for (negative, positive) examples. Using gradient descent learning, the weight adjustment is:

$$\Delta W_{lmn} = -\alpha \nabla E = \alpha(Target - S_0(T))\frac{\partial S_0(T)}{\partial W_{lmn}} \tag{14}$$

The derivative of $S_0(T)$ can be calculated using the following recursive equation:

$$\frac{\partial S_k(t+1)}{\partial W_{lmn}} = f' \cdot [\delta_{nk} S_m(t) I_l(t) + \sum_{i,j}^{L,N} W_{ijk} I_i(t)\frac{\partial S_j(t)}{\partial W_{lmn}}] \tag{15}$$

where f' is the derivative of the activation function $f(net)$. This equation is derived from equation (12). At time step 0, $\partial S(0)/\partial W_{lmn} = 0$.

Similar to what we did for the BP networks, we add a polarization error term in the error function. Now the new error function is:

$$E = A \times \frac{1}{2}(Target - S_0(T))^2 + B \times \frac{1}{2}\sum_{t}^{T}\sum_{k}^{N}(1 - S_k(t)^2)^2 \tag{16}$$

and the weight update rule becomes:

$$\Delta W_{lmn} = \alpha(Target - S_0(T))\frac{\partial S_0(T)}{\partial W_{lmn}} + \beta \sum_{t}^{T}\sum_{k}^{N} S_k(t)(1 - S_k(t)^2)\frac{\partial S_k(t)}{\partial W_{lmn}} \tag{17}$$

where $\partial S_0(T)/\partial W_{lmn}$ and $\partial S_k(t)/\partial W_{lmn}$ can be calculated from equation (15).

5 Experimental Results

5.1 Encoder-decoder problem using bp network

An encoder problem was studied in [4]. There are N orthogonal input patterns each paired with one of N orthogonal output patterns. Only $log_2 N$ hidden units are used. The problem is to train the net to encode N bit input pattern to a $log_2 N$ bit pattern and then to decode this $log_2 N$ bit pattern into a N bit output pattern.

Using the traditional BP algorithm, the hidden layer values are real values. Therefore, the internal representations formed on the hidden layer are not the most efficient. Table 1 is one soultion for 8-3-8 encoder using traditional BP algorithm [4].

We applied the polarization learning rule to the encoder problem using the same network architecture. The output layer learning rate is 0.2. The hidden layer learning rate is 0.4. The polarization learning rate is 0.002. Table 2 shows a solution for the 8-3-8 encoder problem. We also solved the 4-2-4 and 16-4-16 encoder problems using the polarization learning rule. As shown in Table 2, after the network is trained, the hidden unit values are all binary values.

5.2 Grammatical inference using second-order recurrent networks

Tomita proposed a set of regular grammars using only 0's and 1's [5]. These grammars are: 1) 1*; 2) (10)*; 3) no odd number of consecutive of 1's is directly followed by an odd number of consecutive 0's; 4) any string not containing "000" as substring; 5) even number of 0's and even number of 1's; 6) (number of 1's - number of 0's) mod 3 = 0; 7) 0*1*0*1*. Tomita grammars are used to train a second-order recurrent network with polarization learning rule.

Table 1: Solution found for 8-3-8 encoder problem using traditional BP algorithm

INPUT PATTERNS	HIDDEN PATTERNS	OUTPUT PATTERNS
10000000	.5 0 0	10000000
01000000	0 1 0	01000000
00100000	1 1 0	00100000
00010000	1 1 1	00010000
00001000	0 1 1	00001000
00000100	.5 0 1	00000100
00000010	1 0 .5	00000010
00000001	0 0 .5	00000001

Table 2: Solution found for 8-3-8 encoder problem using polarization learning rule

INPUT PATTERNS	HIDDEN PATTERNS	OUTPUT PATTERNS
10000000	100	10000000
01000000	111	01000000
00100000	001	00100000
00010000	101	00010000
00001000	000	00001000
00000100	011	00000100
00000010	110	00000010
00000001	010	00000001

The network architecture for each grammar has one input neuron, 3 state neurons for grammar 1, grammar 2, grammar 4 and grammar 6, and 4 state neurons for grammar 3, grammar 5 and grammar 7. The training set for each grammar contains about a hundred strings randomly selected from all binary strings with length less than 9. A null string is always considered as a positive string.

The connection weights of the network are initialized to small real values in the range of (-0.25, 0.25). The traditional learning rate α is 0.1. Initially, the polarization learning rate β is set to 0. During training, each string is presented one character at a time. Weight update occurs at the end of a string. After the training converges, which is indicated by the accumulated $E_{performance}$ over all training strings is less than a threshold $\varepsilon = 0.1$, β is set to 0.001 and training continues. After the training converges again, β is doubled. The value of β is gradually increased this way until the state neurons have only -1 and 1 as activation values. If the training does not converge, the weights are reinitialized and training is restarted. After a network is trained, the transition of states can be directly mapped to a FSA.

Five successful trainings were performed for each grammar. For grammar 1, 2, 4, 5 and 6, all five trainings produced FSAs that are identical to the ideal FSA of the corresponding grammars. For grammar 7 and grammar 3, the extracted FSAs sometime contain garbage states. But this does not affect the network's ability to classify all strings correctly. Compared with the existing approaches, these results are more stable and do not require clustering technique after training.

6 Discussion

6.1 Contributions

This paper proposed two novel ideas for the purpose of discretizing continuous neural networks.

1. The polarization learning rule. This learning rule is based on the assumption that there is a mechanism which pulls the activation of a neuron towards one of its poles. The polarization learning rule allows us to train a continuous network and as a result of successful training, the network will behave as a discrete network.

2. The addition of the polarization error term to the traditional error function of BP networks. The modified error function unifies the polarization learning rule with the gradient descent learning algorithm of

BP networks. Using this error function, continuous networks can be discretized without compromising the foundation of the gradient descent algorithm.

There are several advantages realized by using the polarization rule to train a network as compared to using traditional BP algorithm.

1. Discrete and finite internal representations can be formed in hidden layers. The interpretability of the internal representations is increased.

2. After training, continuous neurons can be replaced by discrete neurons without downgrading the performance of the network. For networks which are put to practical use after training, the amount of calculation needed will be greatly reduced.

3. Stable internal states can be reached during training of recurrent networks and there is no need to cluster internal representations and extract states for grammatical inference. The problems of extracting FSA from recurrent networks pointed out in [3] are avoided.

6.2   Future work

Some future work can be done along the following directions.

1. Experiment with networks containing more than one hidden layer.

2. Design a methodology to choose the proper polarization learning rate. A network with the modified error function and the polarization learning rule is more difficult to train. The selection of polarization learning rate is critical to successful training. Therefore, an efficient learning scheme needs to be designed. A general strategy is to choose a relative by small polarization learning rate at first, then gradually increase it.

3. Apply the polarization learning rule to other network architectures and other applications. For instance, the polarization learning rule can also be used in first-order recurrent networks, with either full or truncated gradient descent learning.

References

[1] S. Das and M. C. Mozer, "A unified gradient-descent / clustering architecture for finite state machine induction," In J. D. Cowan *et al* (ed.), *Advances in Neural Information Processing Systems 6*, pp. 19-26. San Francisco, CA: Morgan Kaufmann, 1994.

[2] C. L. Giles, C. B. Miller, D. Chen, H. H. Chen, G. Z. Sun and Y. C. Lee, "Learning and extracting finite state automata with second-order neural networks," *Neural Computation* **4**(3), pp. 393-405, 1992.

[3] J. F. Kole, "Fool's Gold: Extracting finite state machines from recurrent network dynamics," In J. D. Cowan *et al* (ed.), *Advances in Neural Information Processing Systems 6*, pp. 501-508, San Francisco, CA: Morgan Kaufmann, 1994.

[4] D. E. Rumelhart, J. L. McClelland, and the PDP Research Group. *Parallel Distributed Processing.* pp. 318-362, Cambridge, MA: The MIT Press, 1986.

[5] M. Tomita, "Dynamic construction of finite-state automata from examples using hill-climbing," *Proceedings of the Fourth Annual Cognitive Science Conference*, pp. 105-108, 1982.

[6] Z. Zeng, R. Goodman, and P. Smyth, "Learning finite state machines with self-clustering recurrent networks," *Neural Computation* **5**(6), pp. 976-990, 1993.

[7] J. M. Zurada, *Introduction to Artificial Neural Systems.* 175-190. West Publishing Company, 1992.

Fusion Of Neural Network Experts

Chan Khue Hiang, Patrick
Institute of System Science, National University of Singapore, Singapore 119597
pchan@iss.nus.sg

Sevki S. Erdogan and Ng Geok See
School of Applied Science, Nanyang Technological University, Singapore 639798
aserdogan@ntuvax.ntu.ac.sg and asgsng@ntuvax.ntu.ac.sg

Abstract- Large variations in writing styles and various kinds of noise make off-line handwritten character recognition a complicated problem. Recently, a new trend has emerged to tackle this problem through the use of multiple classifiers. This method combines classifiers to derive final decisions. In this paper, a neural network classifier is used as a gating expert for the fusion of multiple neural network classifiers. The effect of the fusion of similar domain knowledge experts and different knowledge domain experts are explored and discussed. The experimental results show that fusion of similar domain knowledge domain experts are beneficial only in simple problems whereas fusion of cross-domain knowledge experts are advantageous in more complex classification problems.

1 Introduction

Handwritten character recognition research has been evolving in the last 30 years and had since then produced many different methods to solve the problem. Ultimately, the aim is to achieve an algorithm with the highest recognition rate and near zero error rate. However, many existing difficulties like unconstrained shape variations, different writing styles, broken characters , and various kinds of noise complicate the advancement in Optical Character Recognition (OCR) technology. In spite of these problems, research work can be expanded into viable system if stable and reliable rejection of non-recognizable characters can be achieved.

Many researchers recently attempted to solve the classification problem using a multiple expert approach to improve the recognition performance. Many claimed an increase in recognition performance compared to the use of one classifier [1-5]. Cho and Kim[1] used fuzzy logic fusion method to combine different classifiers and benchmark their results on the on-line handwritten alphanumeric characters. The major contribution of their methodology is that not only the classification results are combined but also the relative importance of the different networks are highlighted. Hashem and Schmeiser [2] proposed an Optimal Linear Combinations (OLCs) of multiple neural network classifiers and claimed an improvement in the performance accuracy in the area of time-series modeling. Teow and Tan [3] used a modified fuzzy art network to combine multiple Supervised Clustering and Matching (SCM) networks and had an improvement in accuracy in their 4-circles-in-the-square classification problem. Jordan and Jacobs [4] also proposed ways to hierarchically combine experts to give a better performance. Huang, Ke Liu and Suen [5] proposed several data transformation functions for the multiple classifier output to be combined. A neural network is used to combine the resulting normalized output of the experts. The neural network approach is compared to different classifiers combination approaches like using Borda count [6] , Polynomial Classification [7] and Linear Confidence Aggregation [8]. The experimental results show that neural network serves as a better gating expert than other methods in terms of both speed and recognition accuracy.

In this paper, the fusion of different neural network classifiers are analysed. The approach is similar to that of Huang, Liu and Suen [5] in that a neural network is used to combine expert modules. Two approaches are proposed. The first approach combines different domain knowledge neural network experts and the second approach uses similar domain knowledge neural network experts with different features. The emphasis is to compare the two approaches. In particular a neural network trained with a combination of features and a neural network serving as a combined expert of individual neural networks trained with individual features are examined.

2 Proposed Method

2.1 Features

The main difficulty in pattern recognition is to extract the primitive features of the iconic characters. Features should be invariant to translation, rotation and distortion. Different features are usually combined to achieve a higher level of recognition performance. Features can be divided into two groups : local and global. The features are local if the calculation of these features are restricted to a local domain in the image. The features are global if the calculation are performed with respect to the entire domain of the image.

In the proposed experiments, five features named Feature A - E are used.

Feature A is Stroke Count feature [9] which is commonly used in the Chinese character recognition community.

Feature B is Grey Scale feature which is a useful global feature that helps to increase error tolerance.

Feature C is Cellular feature which is used by Oka [10]. This global feature is used to extract different orientation from the character image contour and edges. Tao and Zhou [11] used this feature and a Kohonen network to achieve good performance on their handwritten character database.

Feature D is Contour Directional feature. Mohiuddin and Mao [12] used this feature on the character image which was divided into different directional zones. This feature served as a part of the feature space to their hybrid classifier .

Feature E is Density Projection feature. In the Chinese character recognition community [9], stroke count and density projection features are useful local features. Images are scanned in 2 directions, basically vertical and horizontal and their stroke intersections are recorded to form the stroke count features while their pixels aggregated in each scan line to form the projection density features.

2.2 Classifiers

Neural networks are useful function mapper which have the following characteristics:
a) Inference mechanism from subtle, unknown relationships from data.
b) Generalization from learning data samples provided the learning samples are sufficient.
c) Nonlinear mapping capabilities which can be used in solving complex classification domain.

Back-propagation neural network is proposed and used in the experiments. Its use in handwriting classification is most adequate since the data domain is wide and complex. Distortion and noisy images causes classification to be hard. Its ability to train on these data and to do a better job than other classifiers such as LVQ, SOM and Neocognitron is the reason for its usage both as an individual expert as well as a gating expert in our paper. A fixed number of sigmoidal neurons is used in our application with the number of output dependent on the classification domain.

3 Experimental Results

The first experiment investigates the performance of the fusion of similar domain knowledge experts trained with different features (see Figure 1). The domain is the handwritten NIST SD3 DIGIT. A database of 30000 x10 digits is used for the training while 5500x10 is used for testing. It can be seen from Table 1 that the performance of the NN Expert 4 and NN Expert 5 are very similar. There is an improvement of at 0.6% over the other experts.

	Inputs to NN Expert	Accuracy
NN Expert 1	Feature B	95.88%
NN Expert 2	Feature C	96.96%
NN Expert 3	Feature D	94.47%
NN Expert 4	Features B, C, D	97.53%
NN Expert 5	Outputs of NN Experts 1,2 3	97.52%

Table 1: Results of the first experiment using NIST SD3 DIGIT.

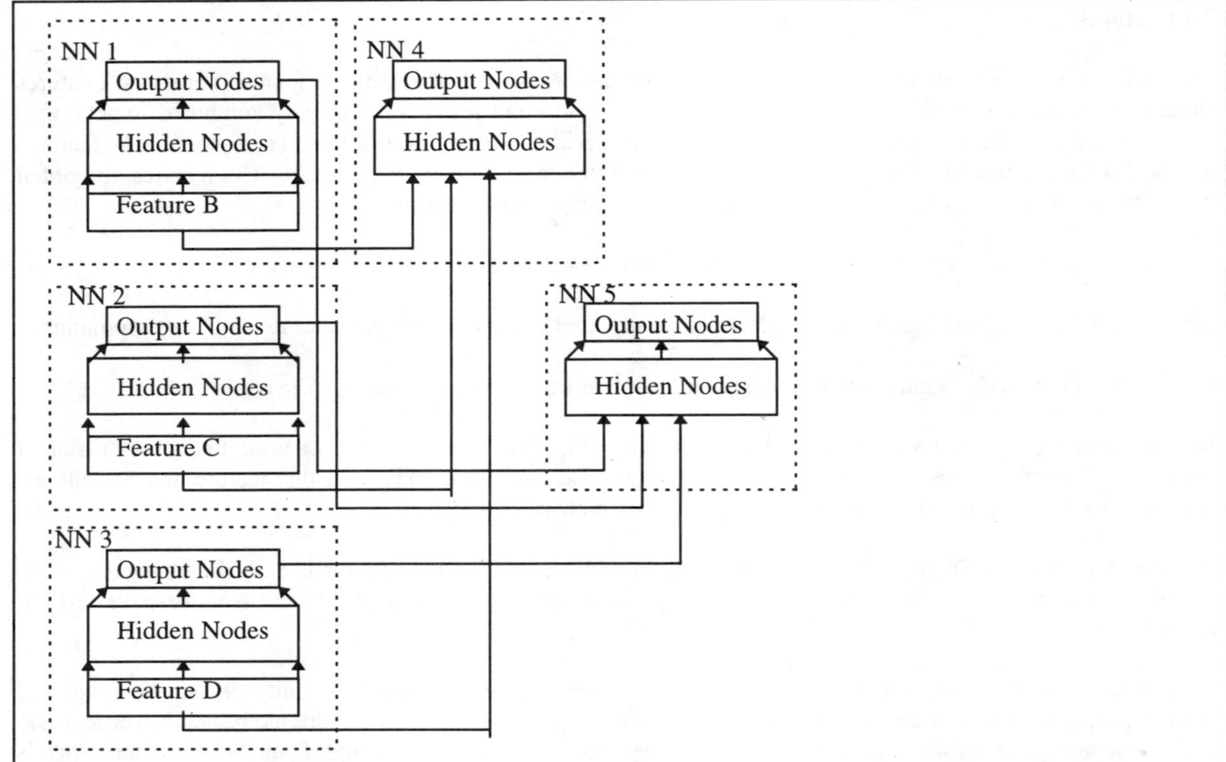

Figure 1 : Fusion of similar domain knowledge experts trained with different features (DIGITS).

The second experiment uses a more complex domain, namely the handwritten NIST SD3 UPPERCASE ALPHABET (see Figure 2). A database of 30000x26 characters is used for training while 360x26 is used for testing. Table 2 shows that NN Expert 6 is weaker than NN Expert 5. Such phenomenon can be attributed to the complexity of the classification domain. The ALPHABET classification is a more complex task compared to the DIGIT classification task.

	Inputs to NN Expert	**Accuracy**
NN Expert 1	Feature A	71.05%
NN Expert 2	Feature B	91.60%
NN Expert 3	Feature D	92.07%
NN Expert 4	Feature E	75.96%
NN Expert 5	Features A,B,D,E	95.74%
NN Expert 6	Outputs of NN Expert 1,2,3,4	94.54%

Table 2 : Results of the second experiment using NIST SD3 UPPERCASE ALPHABET.

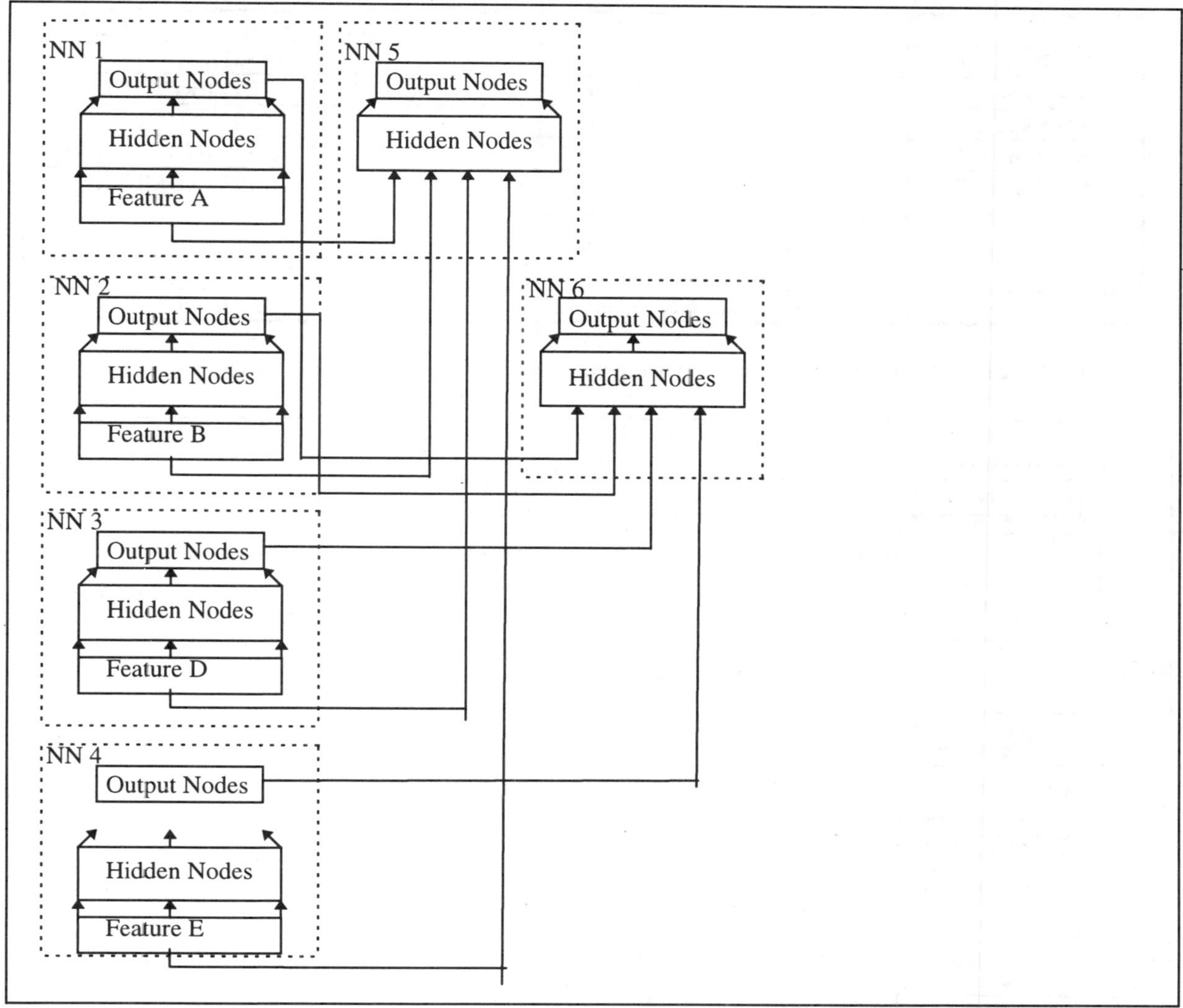

Figure 2 : Fusion of similar domain knowledge experts trained with different features
(UPPERCASE ALPHABET).

The third experiment investigates the effect of cross domain knowledge expert fusion. The domain is the NIST SD3 UPPERCASE ALPHABET and DIGIT. The database in the first two experiments are mixed and the testing samples are restricted to 360x36. Note that the pairs 1 and I, 0 and O are treated as correct classifications.

Table 3 shows that the fusion of the output of different subspace domain knowledge classifier namely, NN Expert 1 and NN Expert 2 which are trained on DIGIT and UPPERCASE respectively leads to a poorer result of 87.39% in the ALPHANUMERIC domain. However, by also feeding the hidden node activation values of the subspace domain knowledge NN classifiers (see Figure 3), a significant boost in performance from 87.39% to 92.07% can be obtained. Furthermore, if subspace domain knowledge classifiers are combined with the whole domain knowledge classifiers, the accuracy is increased to 92.71%.

	Inputs to NN Expert	Performance on test data
NN Expert 1	Features A,B,D,E	97.03% (DIGITS)
NN Expert 2	Features A,B,D,E	95.74% (UPPERCASE)
NN Expert 3	Features A,B,D,E	91.82% (ALPHANUMERIC)
NN Expert 4	Outputs of NN Expert 1,2	87.39% (ALPHANUMERIC)
NN Expert 5	Outputs of NN Expert 1, Hidden Activation Values of NN Expert 1, Outputs of NN Expert 2, Hidden Activation Values of NN Expert 2.	92.07% (ALPHANUMERIC)
NN Expert 6	Outputs of NN Expert 1,2,3	92.71% (ALPHANUMERIC)

Table 3 : Results of the third experiment using NIST SD3 UPPERCASE ALPHABET and DIGIT.

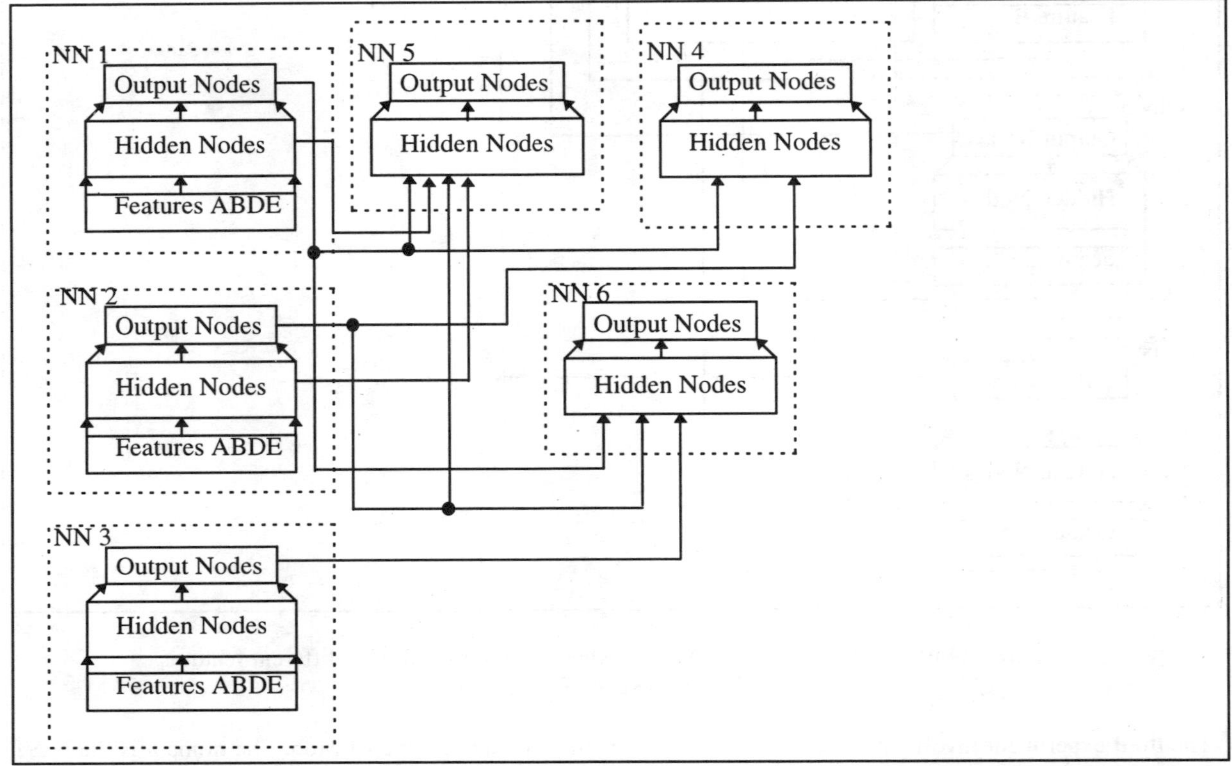

Figure 3 : Fusion of similar domain knowledge experts trained with different features
(UPPERCASE ALPHABET and DIGIT).

4 Conclusion

Fusion of neural network experts are explored both in the context of similar and different domain knowledge experts. By appropriate combination, the accuracy in complex classification problem like the handwritten alphanumeric classification can be improved. The input-level combination of features to a neural network can perform equally well if not better than the multiple combination of single feature-trained neural networks through a gating neural network on the DIGIT and UPPERCASE classification problems. If features can be combined at the input level, it should be done so. As for cross domain knowledge classifier fusion, an appropriate partitioning of the domain into simpler domains and then fusion of these domains together via a neural network can improve the accuracy of the final classification. This approach enhances the flexibility of the local domain learner and allows the data to influence the choice between local and global representations, resulting in a higher recognition result.

References

[1] S. B. Cho and H. J. Kim, "Multiple Network Fusion using Fuzzy Logic," *IEEE Transactions on Neural Networks*, Vol. 6, No. 2, pp. 497-501, March 1995.

[2] S. Hashem and B. Schmeiser, "Improving Model Accuracy using Optimal Linear Combinations of Trained Neural Networks," *Technical Report SMS 92-16, School of Industrial Engineering*, Purdue University.

[3] L. N. Teow and A. H. Tan, "Adaptive Integration of Multiple Experts," *Proc. ICNN'95*, Perth, Western Australia, 22 November-1 December, 1995, Vol. 3, pp. 1215-1219.

[4] R. A. Jacobs, M. I. Jordan, S. J. Nowlan and G. E. Hinton, "Adaptive Mixtures of Local Experts," *Neural Computation*, 3, pp. 79-87, 1991.

[5] Y. S. Huang, K. Liu and C. Y. Suen, "The Combination of Multiple Classifiers by a Neural Network Approach," *International Journal of Pattern Recognition and Artificial Intelligence*, Vol. 9, No. 3, pp. 579-597, 1995.

[6] J. C. Borda, "Memoire sur les elections au scrutin, *Hist. Acad. Royale Sci*", *1781*, translated with commentory, de Grazia, 1953.

[7] J. Franke, "Statistical Combination of Multiple Classifiers Adapted on Image Parts," *Proc. 1st European Conference Dedicated to Postal Technologies*, JET POSTE 93, Nantes, 1993, pp. 566-572.

[8] Y. S. Huang and C. Y. Suen, "Combination of Multiple Classifiers with Measurement Values", *Proc. 2nd Int. Conf. on Document Analysis and Recognition*, Tsukuba, Japan, 1993, pp. 598-601.

[9] W. K. Leow, "Research in Chinese Character Recognition," *Chinese Computing Seminar 1987, ISS*, pp. 81-100.

[10] R. Oka, "Handwritten Chinese-Japanese characters recognition using Cellular Feature," *Proc. 1982 Int. Conf. Chinese Language Comput. Soc.*, Washington, DC, September 1982, pp. 399-410.

[11] H. Tao and J. C. Zhou, "A Neural Network Approach to Character Recognition by using Cellular Feature," *Proc. IJCNN*, Beijing, China, Nov 3-6, 1992.

[12] K. M. Mohiddin and J. C. Mao, "A comparative study of different classifiers for Handprinted Character Recognition", *Pattern Recognition in Practice IV*, E. S. Gelsema and L. N. Kanal, pp. 437-448, 1994.

Fuzzy Function Approximation and the Shape of Fuzzy Sets

Sanya Mitaim and Bart Kosko

Signal and Image Processing Institute
Department of Electrical Engineering — Systems
University of Southern California
Los Angeles, California 90089-2564, U.S.A.

Abstract— **The choice of fuzzy set functions affects how well fuzzy systems approximate functions. The most common fuzzy sets are triangles, trapezoids, and Gaussian bell curves. We compared these sets with many others on a wide range of approximand functions. Supervised learning tuned the if-part set functions and the centroids and volumes of the then-part sets. We compared the set functions based on how closely the adaptive fuzzy system converged to the approximand. The sinc function $\sin(x)/x$ performed best or nearly best in most cases.**

1   Fuzzy Sets and Function Approximation

A fuzzy system $F : R^n \to R^p$ stores m if-then rules and can uniformly approximate continuous and bounded measurable functions on compact domains [5]. This approximation theorem allows any choice of if-part fuzzy sets $A_j \subset R^n$. It also allows any choice of the then-part fuzzy sets $B_j \subset R^p$ because the system uses only the centroid c_j and volume V_j of B_j to compute the output $F(x)$ from the vector input $x \in R^n$.

The theorem does not say how to pick the if-part sets A_j. Each shape affects how well F approximates a given approximand f and how quickly an adaptive fuzzy system F approximates f when learning tunes the parameters of A_j. We tested a wide range of set candidates and compared them with the popular choices of triangles, trapezoids, and Gaussian bell curves. The sinc function $\sin(x)/x$ gave the best and fastest function approximation in most cases even though it can take on negative values in its lesser lobes. We found no formal reason for this result. It suggests that an engineer should check whether a sinc choice can improve a given fuzzy system.

2   Function Approximation with the Standard Additive Model

We used the *standard additive model* (SAM) [4, 7, 8] for the fuzzy function approximator:

$$F(x) \;=\; Centroid(\sum_{j=1}^{m} w_j a_j(x) B_j) \;=\; \frac{\sum_{j=1}^{m} w_j a_j(x) V_j c_j}{\sum_{j=1}^{m} w_j a_j(x) V_j} \;=\; \sum_{j=1}^{m} p_j(x) c_j \tag{1}$$

The fuzzy system $F : R^n \to R^p$ covers the graph of an approximand f with m fuzzy rule patches of the form $A_j \times B_j \subset R^n \times R^p$ or of the word form "If $X = A_j$ then $Y = B_j$." If-part set $A_j \subset R^n$ has joint [3] set function $a_j : R^n \to [0,1]$ that factors: $a_j(x) = a_j^1(x_1) \cdots a_j^n(x_n)$. Then-part fuzzy set $B_j \subset R^p$ has set function $b_j : R^p \to [0,1]$ and volume (or area) $V_j = \int_{R^p} b_j(y)\,dy$ and centroid $c_j = (\int_{R^p} y\,b_j(y)\,dy)/V_j$. The convex weights $p_j(x) = (w_j a_j(x) V_j)/(\sum_{i=1}^{m} w_i a_i(x) V_i)$ give the SAM output $F(x)$ as a convex sum of then-part set centroids. We can ignore the rule weights w_j if we put $w_1 = \cdots = w_m > 0$. The SAM centroidal structure (1) implies that $F(x) = E[Y|X = x]$ for conditional probability density $p(y|x) = \int_{R^p} b(x,y)\,dy$ even though $b > 1$ may hold [5, 8].

Figure 1 shows the parallel structure of the additive system and its state-space graph cover. The graph cover leads to an exponential rule explosion. A fuzzy system needs on the order of k^{n+p-1} rules to approximate a function $f : R^n \to R^p$ on a compact domain. Optimal rules cover extrema [6] and can help allocate a scarce rule budget in high dimensions [6]. Learning tends to move the rule patches toward the extrema or "bumps" and fill in with rule patches between the bumps. Supervised learning [7] tuned the parameters of the many if-part set functions we tried [7]. It also tuned the then-part volumes and centroids.

3   Fuzzy Set Functions

A joint set function $a_j : R^n \to [0,1]$ measures the degree to which input $x \in R^n$ belong to the fuzzy or multivalued set A_j: $a_j(x) = Degree(x \in A_j)$. Most fuzzy systems use unimodal set functions and even these differ enough to affect the system output [1]. The sinc function we tried was multimodal and could take on negative values. We viewed these negative values as low degrees of set membership. Most fuzzy systems also factor the joint set function though some use distance to maintain the joint structure and

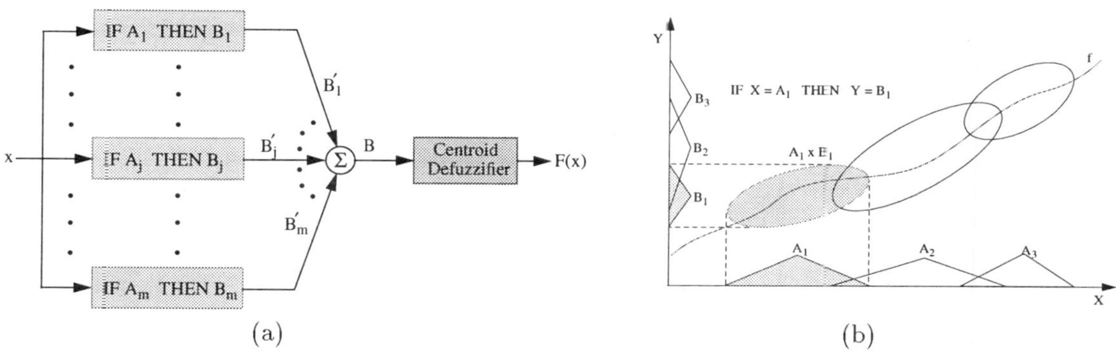

(a)   (b)

Figure 1: (a) The parallel structure of the additive fuzzy system. Each input $x \in R^n$ fires each fuzzy rule to some degree to give a convex sum as the output: $F(x) = Centroid(\sum_{j=1}^{m} w_j a_j(x) B_j)$. (b) Fuzzy rules define patches in the input-output space and cover the graph of the approximand f. This leads to exponential rule explosion in high dimensions. Optimal lone rules cover the extrema of the approximand.

thus to maintain the correlation among input components [3]. Product combined the scalar factored set functions: $a_j(x) = a_j^1(x_1) \cdots a_j^n(x_n)$.

We tested a wide range of if-part set functions. Below we list the scalar form of some of these set functions. Again product formed the joint or multidimensional set functions from these scalar set functions. Figure 2 plots the scalar set functions for sample choices of parameters.

- **Triangle set function.** We define the triangle set function as a 3-tuple (l_j, m_j, r_j) where $l_j > 0$ and $r_j > 0$. $m_j \in R$ denotes the location of a peak of the triangle:

$$a_j(x) = \begin{cases} 1 - \frac{m_j - x}{l_j} & \text{if } m_j - l_j \leq x \leq m_j \\ 1 - \frac{x - m_j}{r_j} & \text{if } m_j < x \leq m_j + r_j \\ 0 & \text{else} \end{cases} \tag{2}$$

- **Trapezoid set function.** We define the trapezoid set function as a 4-tuple (l_j, ml_j, mr_j, r_j) where $ml_j \leq mr_j \in R$. $l_j > 0$ and $r_j > 0$ denote the distance of the support of a function to the left and right of ml_j and mr_j. We can view the *center* as $m_j = \frac{1}{2}(ml_j + mr_j)$:

$$a_j(x) = \begin{cases} 1 - \frac{ml_j - x}{l_j} & \text{if } ml_j - l_j \leq x \leq ml_j \\ 1 & \text{if } ml_j \leq x \leq mr_j \\ 1 - \frac{x - mr_j}{r_j} & \text{if } mr_j < x \leq mr_j + r_j \\ 0 & \text{else} \end{cases} \tag{3}$$

- **Gaussian set function.** The Gaussian set function depends on the mean m_j and standard deviation d_j:

$$a_j(x) = \exp\{-(\frac{x - m_j}{d_j})^2\} \tag{4}$$

- **Cauchy set function.** The Cauchy set function is a bell curve with thicker tails than the Gaussian bell curve and with infinite variance in its statistics [3]:

$$a_j(x) = \left(1 + (\frac{x - m_j}{d_j})^2\right)^{-1} \tag{5}$$

- **Sinc set function.** We define the sinc set function centered at m_j and *width* $d_j > 0$ as

$$a_j(x) = \sin\left(\frac{x - m_j}{d_j}\right) \bigg/ \left(\frac{x - m_j}{d_j}\right) \tag{6}$$

The sinc set function is a map $a_j : R \to [-0.217, 1]$. So the denominator of a sinc SAM in (1) can in theory become zero or negative. We never observed a zero or negative denominator in millions of trials. One can also set a logic flag to check if the denominator is positive.

- **Laplace set function.** The Laplace set function is an exponential curve:

$$a_j(x) = \exp\{-\left|\frac{x - m_j}{d_j}\right|\} \tag{7}$$

m_j is the center and $|d_j| > 0$ picks the decay rate of the curve.

- **Logistic set function.** The logistic or sigmoid function with *steepness* $\alpha_j > 0$ has the form of $S_j(x) = 1/(1 + \exp\{-\alpha_j x\})$. We define a symmetric logistic set function centered at m_j with *width*

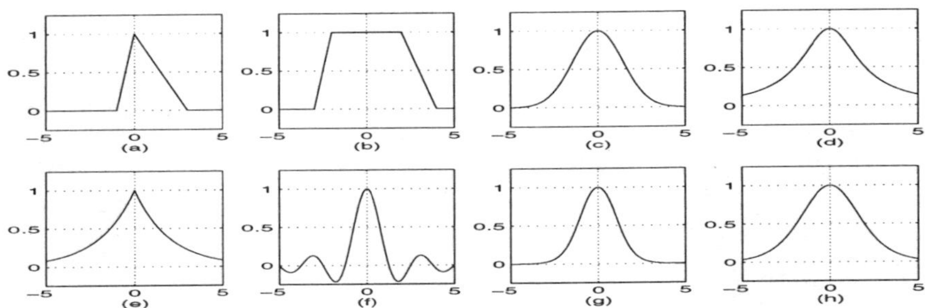

Figure 2: Set functions centered at $m = 0$. (a) Triangle: $l = 1$ and $r = 3$. (b) Trapezoid: $l = 1$, $ml = -2$, $mr = 2$, and $r = 2$. (c) Gaussian: $d = 2$. (d) Cauchy: $d = 2$. (e) Laplace: $d = 2$. (f) Sinc: $d = 0.4$. (g) Logistic: $\alpha = 2$ and $l = 1$. and (h) Hyperbolic Tangent: $d = 2$ and $l = 1$.

$l_j > 0$ as

$$a_j(x) \;=\; \frac{1}{D_j}\left[S_j(x - m_j + l_j) - S_j(x - m_j - l_j)\right] \tag{8}$$

The normalizer $D_j = S_j(l_j) - S_j(-l_j)$ ensures that $\max_{x \in X} a_j(x) = 1$.

- **Hyperbolic tangent set function**. This set function has the difference form

$$a_j(x) \;=\; \frac{1}{D_j}\left[\tanh\left(\frac{x - m_j + l_j}{d_j}\right) - \tanh\left(\frac{x - m_j - l_j}{d_j}\right)\right] \tag{9}$$

The term $l_j > 0$ defines the *width* of the function and $D_j = 2\tanh(l_j/d_j)$ gives the normalization factor.

4   Supervised Learning in SAMs

Supervised gradient descent can tune all the parameters in the SAM model (1) [7, 8]. Below we derive the supervised learning laws for the 8 if-part set functions in Figure 2. A gradient descent learning law for a SAM parameter ξ has the form

$$\xi(t + 1) \;=\; \xi(t) - \mu_t \frac{\partial E}{\partial \xi} \tag{10}$$

where μ_t is a learning rate at iteration t. We seek to minimize the squared error $E(x) = 1/2\,(f(x) - F(x))^2$ of the function approximation. Let ξ_j^k denote the kth parameter in the set function a_j. Then the chain rule gives the gradient of the error function with respect to ξ_j^k, with respect to the then-part set centroid c_j, and with respect to the then-part set volume V_j:

$$\frac{\partial E}{\partial \xi_j^k} = \frac{\partial E}{\partial F}\frac{\partial F}{\partial a_j}\frac{\partial a_j}{\partial \xi_j^k}, \qquad \frac{\partial E}{\partial c_j} = \frac{\partial E}{\partial F}\frac{\partial F}{\partial c_j}, \qquad \text{and} \qquad \frac{\partial E}{\partial V_j} = \frac{\partial E}{\partial F}\frac{\partial F}{\partial V_j} \tag{11}$$

where

$$\frac{\partial E}{\partial F} \;=\; -(f(x) - F(x)) \;=\; -\varepsilon(x) \tag{12}$$

$$\frac{\partial F}{\partial a_j} \;=\; \frac{\left(\sum_{i=1}^m a_i(x)\,V_i\right)(V_j\,c_j) - V_j\left(\sum_{i=1}^m a_i(x)\,V_i\,c_i\right)}{\left(\sum_{i=1}^m a_i(x)\,V_i\right)^2} \;=\; \frac{[c_j - F(x)]\,V_j}{\sum_{i=1}^m a_i(x)\,V_i} \;=\; [c_j - F(x)]\frac{p_j(x)}{a_j(x)} \tag{13}$$

The SAM ratios (1) gives [7]

$$\frac{\partial F}{\partial c_j} \;=\; \frac{a_j(x)\,V_j}{\sum_{i=1}^m a_i(x)\,V_i} \;=\; p_j(x) \quad \text{and} \quad \frac{\partial F}{\partial V_j} \;=\; \frac{a_j(x)\,[c_j - F(x)]}{\sum_{i=1}^m a_i(x)\,V_i} \;=\; [c_j - F(x)]\frac{p_j(x)}{V_j} \tag{14}$$

Then the learning laws have the final form

$$c_j(t+1) \;=\; c_j(t) + \mu_t\,\varepsilon(x)\,p_j(x) \qquad \text{and} \qquad V_j(t+1) \;=\; V_j(t) + \mu_t\,\varepsilon(x)\,[c_j - F(x)]\frac{p_j(x)}{V_j} \tag{15}$$

- **Triangle set function.**

$$m_j(t+1) \;=\; \begin{cases} m_j(t) - \mu_t\varepsilon(x)\,[c_j - F(x)]\frac{p_j(x)}{a_j(x)}\frac{1}{l_j} & \text{if } m_j - l_j \le x \le m_j \\[2mm] m_j(t) + \mu_t\varepsilon(x)\,[c_j - F(x)]\frac{p_j(x)}{a_j(x)}\frac{1}{r_j} & \text{if } m_j < x \le m_j + r_j \\[2mm] m_j(t) & \text{else} \end{cases} \tag{16}$$

$$l_j(t+1) \;=\; \begin{cases} l_j(t) + \mu_t \varepsilon(x)\,[c_j - F(x)]\frac{p_j(x)}{a_j(x)}\frac{m_j-x}{l_j^2} & \text{if } m_j - l_j \le x \le m_j \\ l_j(t) & \text{else} \end{cases} \tag{17}$$

$$r_j(t+1) \;=\; \begin{cases} r_j(t) + \mu_t \varepsilon(x)\,[c_j - F(x)]\frac{p_j(x)}{a_j(x)}\frac{x-m_j}{r_j^2} & \text{if } m_j < x \le m_j + r_j \\ r_j(t) & \text{else} \end{cases} \tag{18}$$

- Trapezoid set function.

$$ml_j(t+1) \;=\; \begin{cases} ml_j(t) - \mu_t \varepsilon(x)\,[c_j - F(x)]\frac{p_j(x)}{a_j(x)}\frac{1}{l_j} & \text{if } ml_j - l_j \le x \le ml_j \\ ml_j(t) & \text{else} \end{cases} \tag{19}$$

$$mr_j(t+1) \;=\; \begin{cases} mr_j(t) + \mu_t \varepsilon(x)\,[c_j - F(x)]\frac{p_j(x)}{a_j(x)}\frac{1}{r_j} & \text{if } mr_j < x \le mr_j + r_j \\ mr_j(t) & \text{else} \end{cases} \tag{20}$$

$$l_j(t+1) \;=\; \begin{cases} l_j(t) + \mu_t \varepsilon(x)\,[c_j - F(x)]\frac{p_j(x)}{a_j(x)}\frac{ml_j-x}{l_j^2} & \text{if } ml_j - l_j \le x \le ml_j \\ l_j(t) & \text{else} \end{cases} \tag{21}$$

$$r_j(t+1) \;=\; \begin{cases} r_j(t) + \mu_t \varepsilon(x)\,[c_j - F(x)]\frac{p_j(x)}{a_j(x)}\frac{x-mr_j}{r_j^2} & \text{if } mr_j < x \le mr_j + r_j \\ r_j(t) & \text{else} \end{cases} \tag{22}$$

- Gaussian set function.

$$m_j(t+1) \;=\; m_j(t) + 2\mu_t \varepsilon(x)\,p_j(x)[c_j - F(x)]\frac{x-m_j}{d_j^2} \tag{23}$$

$$d_j(t+1) \;=\; d_j(t) + 2\mu_t \varepsilon(x)\,p_j(x)[c_j - F(x)]\frac{(x-m_j)^2}{d_j^3} \tag{24}$$

- Cauchy set function.

$$m_j(t+1) \;=\; m_j(t) + 2\mu_t \varepsilon(x)\,p_j(x)[c_j - F(x)]\frac{x-m_j}{d_j^2}\,a_j(x) \tag{25}$$

$$d_j(t+1) \;=\; d_j(t) + 2\mu_t \varepsilon(x)\,p_j(x)[c_j - F(x)]\frac{(x-m_j)^2}{a_j^3}\,a_j(x) \tag{26}$$

- Sinc set function.

$$m_j(t+1) \;=\; m_j(t) + \mu_t\, \varepsilon(x)\,[c_j - F(x)]\frac{p_j(x)}{a_j(x)}\left(a_j(x) - \cos(\frac{x-m_j}{d_j})\right)\frac{1}{x-m_j} \tag{27}$$

$$d_j(t+1) \;=\; d_j(t) + \mu_t\, \varepsilon(x)\,[c_j - F(x)]\frac{p_j(x)}{a_j(x)}\left(a_j(x) - \cos(\frac{x-m_j}{d_j})\right)\frac{1}{d_j} \tag{28}$$

- Laplace set function.

$$m_j(t+1) \;=\; m_j(t) + \mu_t \varepsilon(x)\,[c_j - F(x)]\,p_j(x)\,\text{sign}(x - m_j)\frac{1}{|d_j|} \tag{29}$$

$$d_j(t+1) \;=\; d_j(t) + \mu_t \varepsilon(x)\,[c_j - F(x)]\,p_j(x)\,\text{sign}(d_j)\frac{|x-m_j|}{d_j^2} \tag{30}$$

- Logistic set function.

$$m_j(t+1) \;=\; m_j(t) + \mu_t\, \varepsilon(x)p_j(x)[c_j - F(x)]\alpha_j[1 - S_j(x - m_j + l_j) - S_j(x - m_j - l_j)] \tag{31}$$

$$\alpha_j(t+1) \;=\; \alpha_j(t) + \mu_t\varepsilon(x)[c_j - F(x)]\frac{p_j(x)}{a_j(x)}\frac{1}{D_j}\{[x - m_j + l_j]S_j(x - m_j + l_j) \times$$

$$[1 - S_j(x - m_j + l_j)] - [x - m_j - l_j]S_j(x - m_j - l_j)[1 - S_j(x - m_j - l_j)]$$
$$- l_j a_j(x)\,(S_j(l_j)[1 - S_j(l_j)] + S_j(-l_j)[1 - S_j(-l_j)])\} \tag{32}$$

$$l_j(t+1) \;=\; l_j(t) + \mu_t\, \varepsilon(x)\,[c_j - F(x)]\frac{p_j(x)}{a_j(x)}\frac{\alpha_j}{D_j}\{S_j(x - m_j + l_j)\,[1 - S_j(x - m_j + l_j)]$$

$$+ S_j(x - m_j - l_j)[1 - S_j(x - m_j - l_j)] - a_j(x)\,(S_j(l_j)[1 - S_j(l_j)] + S_j(-l_j)[1 - S_j(-l_j)])\} \tag{33}$$

- Hyperbolic tangent set function.

$$m_j(t+1) \;=\; m_j(t) + \mu_t\varepsilon(x)p_j(x)\frac{c_j - F(x)}{d_j}[\tanh(\frac{x-m_j+l_j}{d_j}) + \tanh(\frac{x-m_j-l_j}{d_j})] \tag{34}$$

$$d_j(t+1) \;=\; d_j(t) + \mu_t\varepsilon(x)\,[c_j - F(x)]\frac{p_j(x)}{a_j(x)}\frac{1}{D_j d_j}\left(\frac{x-m_j+l_j}{d_j}\tanh^2(\frac{x-m_j+l_j}{d_j})\right.$$

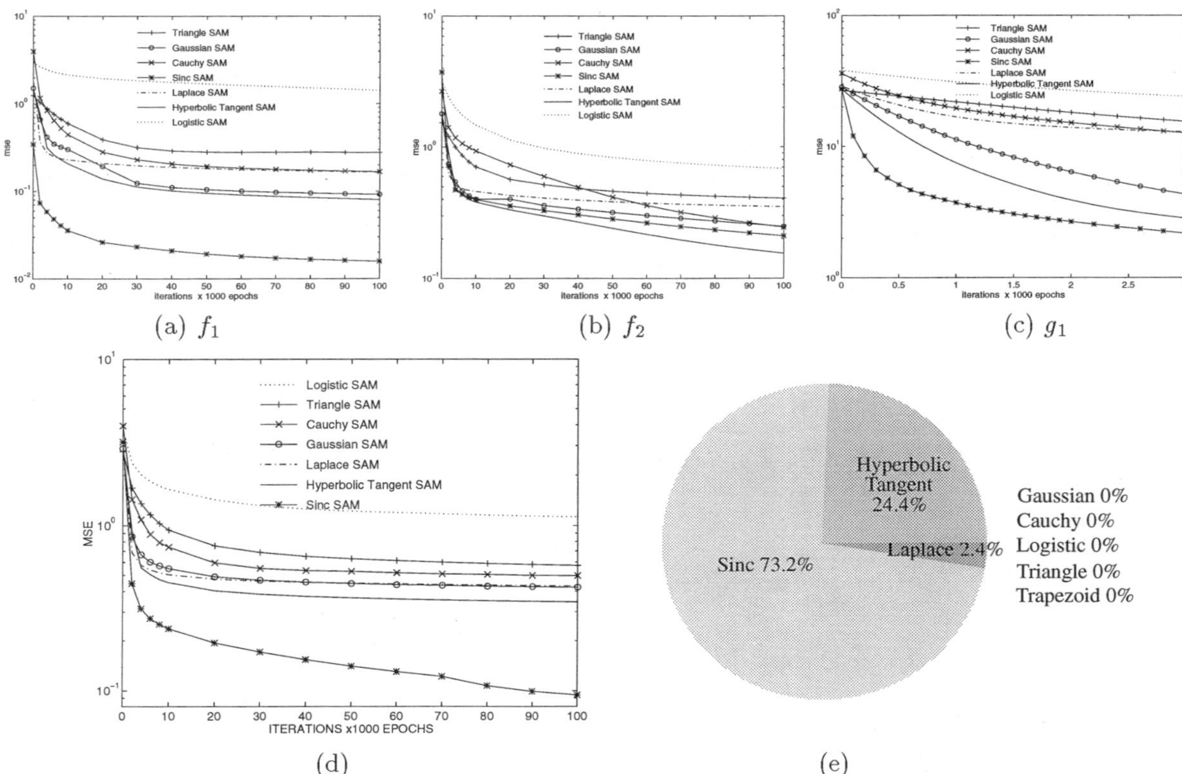

(a) f_1 (b) f_2 (c) g_1

(d)   (e)

Figure 3: Mean-squared approximation error. (a) and (b): 1-D cases. Sinc set function performed the best in case (a) while hyperbolic tangent set function performed the best in case (b). (c): 2-D case. (d) Average MSEs over all 1-D test functions. (e) Proportion of test cases where each function performed best.

$$- \frac{x - m_j - l_j}{d_j} \tanh^2\left(\frac{x - m_j - l_j}{d_j}\right) - \frac{2l_j}{d_j} + 2\frac{l_j}{d_j}a_j(x)[1 - \tanh^2(\frac{l_j}{d_j})] \right) \quad (35)$$

$$l_j(t+1) = l_j(t) + \mu_t\varepsilon(x)\left[c_j - F(x)\right]\frac{p_j(x)}{a_j(x)}\frac{1}{D_jd_j}\left(2 - \tanh^2(\frac{x - m_j + l_j}{d_j})\right.$$

$$\left. - \tanh^2(\frac{x - m_j - l_j}{d_j}) - 2a_j(x)[1 - \tanh^2(\frac{l_j}{d_j})]\right) \quad (36)$$

We also can approximate the learning laws for the triangle and trapezoid set functions with Gaussian learning laws. Like results hold for the learning laws of n-D set functions. A factored set function $a_j(x) = a_j^1(x_1)\cdots a_j^n(x_n)$ leads to a new form for the error gradient. The gradient with respect to the parameter m_j^k of the jth set function a_j has the form

$$\frac{\partial E}{\partial m_j^k} = \frac{\partial E}{\partial F}\frac{\partial F}{\partial a_j}\frac{\partial a_j}{\partial a_j^k}\frac{\partial a_j^k}{\partial m_j^k} \qquad \text{where} \qquad \frac{\partial a_j}{\partial a_j^k} = \prod_{i\neq k}^{n} a_j^i(x_i) = \frac{a_j(x)}{a_j^k(x_k)} \quad (37)$$

5   Simulation Results

We trained the SAMs with different set functions to approximate different functions. We scored each test in terms of the mean-squared error (MSE) of the function approximation and the convergence time for a fixed learning rate μ. We tested the adaptive set functions on more than 40 approximands. Many set functions such as the trapezoid, exponential, and clipped parabola did not perform well. Their learning curves were not stable and so we often did not have their MSE results. We have reported only the functions that performed well.

The 1-D SAMs used 12 rules and the 2-D SAMs used 64 rules. The learning rate was small because each learning law is highly nonlinear. Else the learning might not have converged. We picked the constant $\mu = 10^{-8}$ for all learning laws. We sampled 200 points of the function in the 1-D case and $30 \times 30 = 900$ samples in the 2-D case to give a training set. One epoch passed all 200 or 900 samples through the SAM to train it.

Different initializations led to convergence to different local minima of the MSE surface. There are no formal ways to find the initial conditions that lead to the global minimum and so we had to guess at them. We spread rule patches uniformly along the input space. So we spread the if-part set centers m_j uniformly along the x-axis. We picked the then-part set centroids c_j as the values of the sampled approximand f at m_j: $c_j = f(m_j)$. We set the then-part volumes (areas) to unity at first: $V_1 = \cdots = V_m = 1$. Then supervised learning tuned each SAM parameter. Below are some sample test functions we used as approximands:

$$g(x_1, x_2) = 10\tan^{-1}(\frac{10(x_1 - 0.2)(x_1 - 0.7)(x_1 + 0.8)}{x_1 + 1.4}) \times$$

$$\tan^{-1}(\frac{10(x_2 - 0.2)(x_2 + 0.8)(x_2 - 0.7)(x_2 + 0.2)(x_2 - 1.5)}{(x_2 + 1.4)(x_2 - 1.1)x_2(x_2 + 0.3) + 0.7}) \quad -1 \le x_1, x_2 \le 1 \quad (38)$$

$$f_1(x) = 10\tan^{-1}(10(x + 0.8)(x + 0.3)(x - 0.4)(2x - 0.7)) \quad -1 \le x \le 1 \quad (39)$$

$$f_2(x) = 3x(x - 1)(x - 1.9)(x - 0.7)(x + 1.8) \quad -2 \le x \le 2 \quad (40)$$

Figure 3 (a)-(c) plots the MSEs against the number of learning cycles and (d) shows the average MSE of our tests. The simulation results show that the sinc set function often converged faster and more accurately than did the other set functions. The 2-D cases with factored set functions showed the same pattern. The pie chart in Figure 3 (e) shows the frequency with which each set function performed best in the 1-D test cases.

6   Conclusions

The sinc function emerged as the if-part set function most likely to give a quick and accurate function approximation. Its negative values require us to view it as a generalized set function [8]. Fuzzy set functions need map only into a totally ordered range of values. We cannot explain so easily the many lobes in the sinc function. The sinc lobes act as interpolation artifacts in SAMs just as they do in the reconstruction theorem of band-limited functions in signal processing. The lobes may have no linguistic meaning.

Sinc set functions failed to perform best in some cases even though they almost always converged fastest. Hyperbolic tangent set functions won in the 1-D cases where the sinc set functions lost. The 2-D tests gave like results. But the Cauchy set functions tied with sinc set functions in the 3-D tests.

These results suggest that engineers should consider sinc set functions when they model unknown approximand. It may help to first use triangles or bell curves to pick the set centers and widths. Then the same values can pick the first set of sinc functions as learning or hand tuning begins.

The results raise a key question: Why does sinc work so well? We did not answer this question. Chance alone cannot explain the results. Sinc won too often and across too many test cases. Future research may find approximation bounds that let us compare the set functions in a formal sense. Other research may explore how optimal learning rates [9] affect the function approximation. Meanwhile the sinc function may well remain a contender in future run-offs among set functions.

References

[1] A. K. Dhingra, S. S. Rao, and V. Kumar, "Nonlinear Membership Functions in Multiobjective Fuzzy Optimization of Mechanical and Structural Systems," *AIAA Journal*, Vol. 30, No. 1, 251-260, January 1992.

[2] J. A. Dickerson and B. Kosko, "Fuzzy Function Approximation with Supervised Ellipsoidal Learning," *Proceedings of the World Congress on Neural Networks (WCNN-93)*, Vol. 2, 9-17, July 1993.

[3] H. M. Kim and B. Kosko, "Fuzzy Prediction and Filtering in Impulsive Noise," *Fuzzy Sets and Systems*, Vol. 77, No. 1, 15-33, 15 January 1996.

[4] B. Kosko, *Neural Networks and Fuzzy Systems: A Dynamical Systems Approach to Machine Intelligence*, Prentice Hall, 1991.

[5] B. Kosko, "Fuzzy Systems as Universal Approximators," *IEEE Transactions on Computers*, Vol. 43, No. 11, 1329-33, November 1994; an earlier version appears in the *Proceedings of the 1st IEEE International Conference on Fuzzy Systems (IEEE FUZZ-92)*, 1153-1162, March 1992.

[6] B. Kosko, "Optimal Fuzzy Rules Cover Extrema," *International Journal of Intelligent Systems*, Vol. 10, No. 2, 249-255, February 1995.

[7] B. Kosko, "Combining Fuzzy Systems," *Proceedings of the IEEE International Conference on Fuzzy Systems (IEEE FUZZ-95)*, Vol. IV, 1855-1863, March 1995.

[8] B. Kosko, *Fuzzy Engineering*, Prentice Hall, 1996.

[9] D. G. Luenberger, *Linear and Nonlinear Programming*, second edition, Addison Wesley, 1984.

Least Mean Square Error Reconstruction Learning in Lateral Inhibitory Network for Multiple Cause Model

Bai-ling Zhang [1] and   Lei Xu [2]
[1] Department of Electrical and Computer Engineering
The University of Newcastle,Callaghan, NSW 2308, Australia
[2] Department of Computer Science
The Chinese University of Hong Kong, Shatin, N.T. Hong Kong

Abstract— *In this paper we apply the Least Mean Square Error Reconstruction (LMSER) learning principle to a lateral inhibitory nonlinear network. Such a combination of LMSER learning and anti-Hebbian mechanism is a straightforward realization of discovering multiple causal relations among the input data, which is quite efficient and reliable. LMSER learning can also be directly applied to hierarchical decorrelation network with qualitatively similar results, which was confirmed by experiments.*

1   Introduction

The objective of unsupervised learning is to discover features reflecting regularities in data. Many theories, models and applications related to an important unsupervised learning principle, redundancy reduction, which was first formulated by Barlow[3], have been proposed in recent years. This kind of learning is also called factorial learning, because zero redundancy means that joint probability distribution can be expressed as the product of component probability distribution.

While factorial learning aiming at finding distributed, independent representation, a lately proposed multiple causes model (MCM) further addressed the importance of causal relationship between input and such a representation or hidden causes. From an explanative viewpoint, MCM aims at discovering a set of independent causes or generators such that each input can be completely described by the cooperative action of a few of these possible generators. In this aspect, a multiple cause model is different from some single cause models such as the well-known mixture of experts [6], in which one expert or generator is only responsible for a single example. Recently, several papers have addressed the multiple causes model in the literature.

Földiák was the first to suggest a multiple cause model [5]. In the sparse code realized by anti-Hebbian learning, input patterns can be represented combinatorially by a relatively small number of the available units. However, the success of Földiák strategy strongly depends on a prior constraints on the activity patterns at the encoding layer, which is inappropriate when the generating probability for input component is not available.

Saund considered a form of autoencoder network, with the conventional sigmoidal function at the output layer being replaced by a noisy-or activation function [7]. Here, such a scheme has a severe problem of local minimum [8]. Recently, Dayan started from the viewpoint of learning a set of priors and conditional priors to minimize the description length of a set of examples drawn from the input distribution [8]. Specifically, an autoencoder network is trained to reconstruct the input on its output units with the goal of learning the underlying distributions. This scheme is a special case of the general stochastic learning framework Helmholtz machine [15], *i.e.*, learning the distribution for hidden units in the recognition model is simplified by a fixed independent prior distribution and the parameter of the generative model is simply taken as interpreting probability from hidden causes.

Multiple cause model is a typical example that involve a balance between cooperation and competition. The statistical inference based learning framework such as the Helmholtz machine[15] can offer an explicit explanation of the learning mechanism. Here, we study the MCM issue from the viewpoint of best reconstruction of input via extracted features. This principle was formulated as LMSER in [1,2], which has a nonlinear decorrelation property in a nonlinear feedforward network, *i.e.*, a set of nodes in the network can selectively respond to inputs. However, the selectivity provided by the original LMSER learning is generally not sufficient. In order to meet some further requirements, for example, making the nodes' output decorrelated up to higher order or independent, we proposed to apply the LMSER principle to a lateral inhib! itory network for solving more gen eral feature extraction problems. Our learning scheme realizes redundancy reduction and multiple cause model. Preliminary experimental results are given to demonstrate the potentials of the algorithm. Relations with other relevent works are discussed.

2   Combination of the LMSER and anti-Hebbian mechanism

We consider a feedforward nonlinear networks, which have L inputs, x_j, $j = 1, \cdots, L$, and M representation units, y_i, $i = 1, \cdots, M$, with output units recurrently connected. Such an architecture has been studied by Földiák [4,5] , in which Hebbian and anti-Hebbian rule was respectively applied to the feedforward weight and feedback inhibitory weight. The network dynamics can be describted by

$$\frac{dy_i}{dt} = f(\sum_{j=1}^{L} W_{ij} x_j + \sum_{j=1}^{M} V_{ij} y_j) - y_i \tag{1}$$

where W_{ij} is the connection weight from x_j to y_i, V_{ij} is the connection between units y_i and y_j and the nonlinearity of the units is represented by a sigmoidal function, e.g., $f(t) = 0.5(tanh(t) + 1)$.

Under the attainment of steady-state condition, eqn (1) can be replaced by the following algebria equation

$$y_i = f(\sum_{j=1}^{L} W_{ij} x_j + \sum_{k=1}^{M} V_{ik} y_k) \tag{2}$$

Upon presentation of a new learning pattern, the feedforward connections are modified according to the LMSER principle. Specifically, denote $\hat{\mathbf{x}} = \mathbf{W}\mathbf{y}$, representing a reconstruction vector of the input data $\mathbf{x}$ from the network output $\mathbf{y}$, then learning of $\mathbf{W}$ is based on the following optimization criterion:

$$J(\mathbf{W}) = E\{\|\mathbf{x} - \hat{\mathbf{x}}\|^2\} = E\{\|\mathbf{x} - \mathbf{W}\mathbf{y}\|^2\} \tag{3}$$

Using stochastic approximation with gradient descent, a learning algorithm in matrix form is obtained [1,2] :

$$\mathbf{W}_{k+1} = \mathbf{W}_k + \mu_k[\mathbf{x}_k \mathbf{e}_k^{\mathrm{T}} \mathbf{W}_k \mathbf{y}_k' + \mathbf{e}_k \mathbf{y}_k^{\mathrm{T}}] \tag{4}$$

where k denoting a time scale, $\mathbf{e}_k = \mathbf{x}_k - \hat{\mathbf{x}}_k$ is the reconstruction error vector, $\mathbf{y}'$ is derivatives of $\mathbf{y}$. μ_k is a learning rate.

If we consider a weight vector associated with each output neuron as a featue or cause extracted from input space, a general assumption is that these features cr causes should be independent. In this aspect, nonlinear anti-Hebbian learning provides the most straightforward way for enforcing independency. Specifically, on each learning trial, after the output has been calculated by eqn (2) and feedforward weights updated according to eqn (4), the lateral connections are then modified via following anti-Hebbian rule

$$\mathbf{V}_{k+1} = \mathbf{V}_k - \alpha_k \, offdicg(\mathbf{y}_k \mathbf{y}_k^{\mathrm{T}}) \tag{5}$$

where *offdiag* operator sets all diagonal entries to zero. α_k is a learning rate.

Anti-Hebbain learning was previously set up on an intuitive idea of decorrelating outputs of a linear network, i.e., whenever two units in a layer are active simultaneously, the connection between them becomes more inhibitory, so that the joint activity is discouraged in the future and their correlation is decreased. In linear network, anti-Hebbian decorrelation combined with Hebbian learning for transfering information result in a principal subspace solution. Here the anti-Hebbian rule is applied to the nonlinear output $\mathbf{y} = f(net) = tanh(net)$, net means the net input vector to nonlinear output units. If we expand $f(t)$ in Taylor series, e.g., $tanh(t) = t - t^3/3 + 2t^5/15 \cdots$, (for $|t| < \frac{\pi}{2}$), we can see that decorrelation of $y_i (i = 1, \cdots, M)$ is equivalent to setting some higher-order moments cf net_i to zeros, $i = 1, \cdots, M$.

3   Discussions

Our algorithm discussed above for the symmetrical network is different from Földiák's nonlinear anti-Hebbian model [5]. First, in Földiák's model, neuron's selectivity is jointly decided by an artifically designed threshold and anti-Hebbian rule, for which a sparness assumption was incorporated by taking form as pressure for few output units to become active at one time. Such a prior cause generating probability is not assumed in our model. Second, the Hebbian learning rule in Földiák s learning scheme had to contain a weight decay term in order to keep the feedforward weight vectors bounded, which is unnecessary in our algorithm as weights developed under the LMSER principle will be automatically scaled.

In the literature, another type of anti-Hebbian learning in a hierarchical network is also well known, which was proposed by Rubner and Tavan [9]. A linear hierarchical network with anti-Hebbian decorrelation combined wiht Hebbian learning for transfering information result in PCA. Such a scheme has been further studied for adaptive principal components extraction [12]. In ncnlinear case, the activity of each

file=gau2.ps

Figure 1: Learned responses of a pair of nodes trained on randomly placed Gaussian spots.
file=gau3.ps

Figure 2: Learned responses of three output nodes trained on randomly placed Gaussian spots.
file=L.ps

Figure 3: Multiple causes representation for 2000 randomly generated data points discovered by the LMSER learning in lateral inhibitory networks

output is determined by the sum of the signals it receives,

$$y_i = f(\sum_{j=1}^{L} \mathbf{W}_{ij} x_j + \sum_{k<i}^{M} \mathbf{V}_{ik} y_k) \tag{6}$$

Similarly, the LMSER learning rule eqn (4) can be applied to such a nonlinear asymmetrical network and the lateral weights are updated according to a hierarchical anti-Hebbian rule:

$$\mathbf{V}_{k+1} = \mathbf{V}_k - \alpha_k \, subdiag(\mathbf{y}_k \mathbf{y}_k^T) \tag{7}$$

where *offdiag* operator sets all entries which are on or above the main diagonal to zero.

A nonlinear extension of Rubner & Tavans' work was proposed in [10], in which bistable neurons were characterized by a threshold and a transition width. If these two parameters are suitably adjusted, the network will sort input patterns into classes. Parameters characterizing output nonlinearities can also been adapted via LMSER principle and we'll not discuss it in this paper. Another nonlinear generalization of the hierarchical decorrelation learning was also studied in [13] for nonlinear projections from the viewpoint of best reconstruction of input. As we know, in linear networks, anti-Hebbian learning performs quite different in symmetrical and asymmetrical (hierarchical) structures, with PSA resulted from the first and PCA the second. In nonlinear networks, hierarchy is not so important because nonlinearities break the complete symmetry during learning process. This has been pointed out in [2,14] and is further confirmed by our expe! riments in the following.

4   Simulations

As a first demonstration of the learning algorithm, we take the problem of learning to respond to randomly placed Gausian-shaped spots, which has been frequently adopted in the literature for studying the formation of certain type of spatial feature detectors. In the experiments, each input vector was a randomly located Gaussian spot, with its center at arbitary position except that there must be two input units away from the nearest edge in the input array.

We have compared the LMSER learning algorithm together with eqns (5) & (7), with nonlinear function $f(t) = 0.5(tanh(t) + 1)$, for the two lateral inhibitory networks. The results were quanlitatively similar. 100 input units with 10×10 square array were tested. The average brightness of 1000 Gaussian spots was calculated beforehand and then substracted from each random Gaussian spot during training. Initial weights were set to small random values. Figure 1 and Figure 2 illustrated typical results of two-nodes and three-nodes cases, respectively, demonstrating that the nodes have developed strong responses in minimally overlaped different regions of the input space. The localized masks equivalent to cluster centers which descriptive scopes have been narrowed to only certain subspaces of the data space. The receptive field of distinct units share their responsibility in accounting for each observed data.

Our learning scheme can be applied to binary data without modification. Here we take the multiple causes model as an example. A multiple causes model aims at discovering a bank of independent causes or generators in order for each input being totally explained by the cooperative action of a few of these possible causes. A representative example that embody the model is the extraction of independent horizontal and vertical lines in an input pixel grid. Following Földiák's experiment scheme, the training data set consists of random horizontal and vertical lines on an 8×8 grid. Each of the 16 possible lines are drawn with a fixed probability, for example, $\frac{1}{8}$, independently from all the others. Pixels that are part of a drawn line have the value 0, all others are 1. The network has 16 representation units. An extra node is introduced to account for the average brightness. The sigmoidal nonlinearity is taken as $f(x) = 0.5(tanh(x) + 1)$.! With the symmetrical and hierarch ical lateral networks, we've tested with a generating probability $\frac{1}{8}$. Figure 3 shows a typical result of the learned weights, which clearly reveal the generative model they embody. Then we changed the generating probability to $\frac{2}{8}$ and $\frac{3}{8}$, respectively, yielding the same results. The success of our algorithms in seperating causes suggests that sigmoidal nonlinear function with appropriate learning scheme is capable of capturing separate features or causes.

5 Conclusions

The perspective of best reconstructing input via features (causes) is significant to many learning tasks. In this aspect, we further studied the LMSER principle for learning multiple causes and more general redundancy redunction. In nonlinear feedforward networks with lateral connections, anti-Hebbian learning can be incorporated for improving the selectivity. Being different from linear networks, hierarchy does not play an important role as symmetry-breaking is strengthened by output nonlinearities.

References

[1] L.Xu, "Least MSE reconstruction for self-organization: (I) Multi-layer neural nets and (II) further theoretical and experimental studies on one layer nets," In *Proceedings of the International Joint Conference on Neural Networks* (Singapore,1991), 2363-2373.

[2] L.Xu, "Least mean square error reconstruction principle for self-organizing neural-nets," *Neural Networks* 6 (1993), 627-648.

[3] H.Barlow, "Unsupervised learning," *Neural Computation* 1(1989), 295-311.

[4] P.Földiak "Adaptive network for optimal linear feature extraction," in *Proceedings of the IEEE International Conference on Neural Networks, Washington D.C.* (1989), 401-405.

[5] P.Földiak "Forming sparse representationsby local anti-Hebbian learning," *Biological Cybernetics* 64(1990), 165-170.

[6] S.J.Nowlan, "Competing experts: An experimental investigation of associative mixture models " *Tech. Rep. CRG-TR-90-5, Department of Computer Science, University of Toronto, Canada* .

[7] E.Saund "A multiple causes mixture model for unsupervised learning," *Neural Computation* 7(1995), 51-71.

[8] P.Dayan and R.S.Zemel, " Competition and multiple cause model," *Neural Computation* 7(1995), 565-579.

[9] J.Rubner, and P.Tavan, "A self-organizing network for principal-component analysis," *Europhysics Letters* 10(1989), 693-698.

[10] A Carlson, "Anti-Hebbian learning in a non-linear neural network," *Biological Cybernetics,* 64(1990), 171-176.

[11] B.L.Zhang, L.Xu and M.Y.Fu, "Learning Multiple Causes by Competition Enhanced Least Mean Square Error Reconstruction ," accepted for publication in *Intl.J. Neural Systems*.

[12] S.Y.Kung and K.I.Diamantaras, "Adaptive Principal Component EXtraction (APEX) and applications, " *IEEE Tran. Signal Processing* 42(5) (1994) 1202-1217.

[13] F.Palmieri "Linear self-association for universal memory and approximation," in *Proc. WCNN'93-Portland* (1993), vol.II, 339-343.

[14] J. Karhunen and J.J.Joutsensalo, "Generalizations of principal component analysis, optimization problems, and neural networks," *Neural Networks* 8(4) (1995) 549-562.

[15] P.Dayan, G.E.Hinton, R.M.Neal and R.S.Zemel, "The Helmholtz machine," *Neural Computation* 7(1995), 889-904.

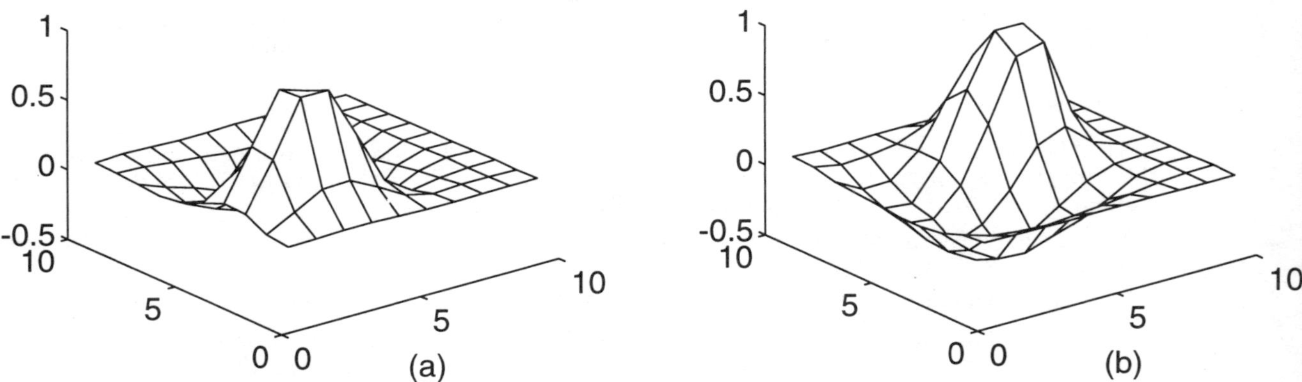

Figure 1: Learned responses of a pair of nodes trained on randomly placed Gaussian spots.

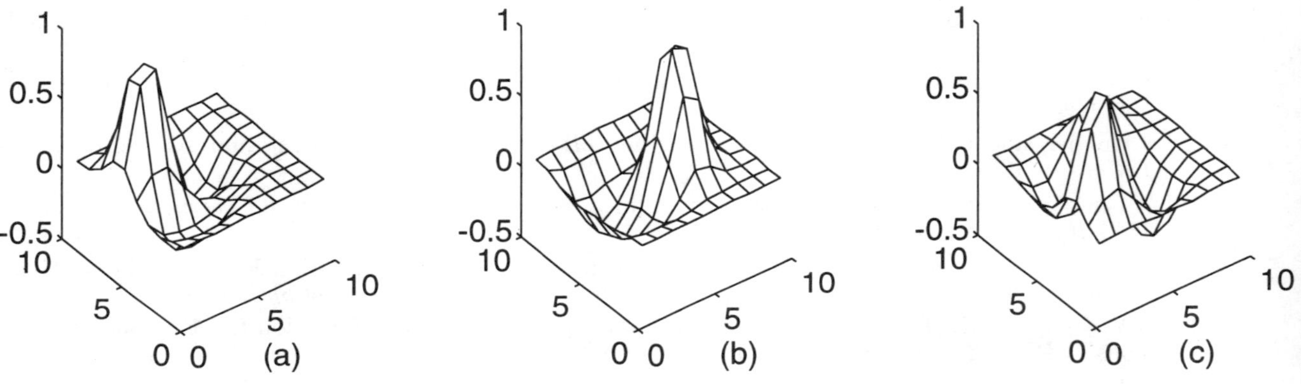

Figure 2: Learned responses of three output nodes trained on randomly placed Gaussian spots.

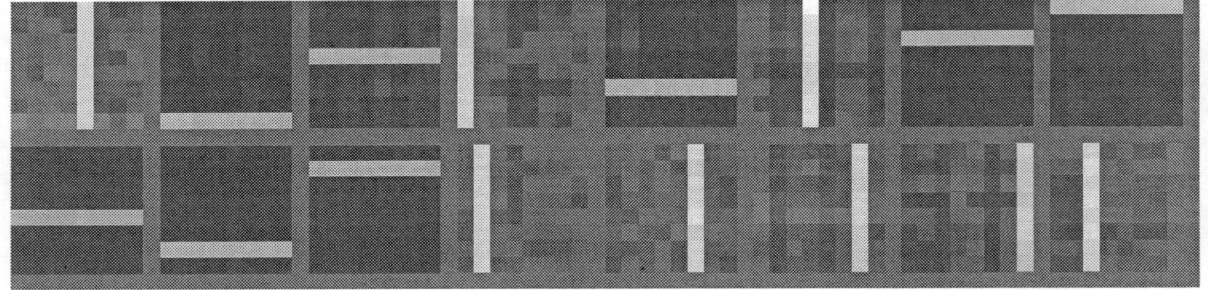

Figure 3: Multiple causes representation for 2000 randomly generated data points discovered by the LMSER learning in lateral inhibitory networks

Learning Belief Networks from Realistic Data:
A Comparative Study

Hyunsuk Kim and Sungzoon Cho
Department of Computer Science and Engineering
POSTECH Information Research Laboratories (PIRL)
Pohang University of Science and Technology (POSTECH)
San 31 Hyojadong, Pohang, 790–784, Korea
hskim@albireo.postech.ac.kr and zoon@vision.postech.ac.kr

Yun Peng
Department of Computer Science
University of Maryland, Baltimore County
Baltimore, MD21228, USA
ypeng@cs.umbc.edu

Abstract— Recently, several belief network learning algorithms have been proposed to learn both the network structures and probabilities from the case data. Although most of these methods (e.g., Cooper's K2 algorithm) are based on traditional machine learning techniques, some of them, e.g., Neal's Boltzmann machine method and Peng's extended Hebbian method take neural network learning approaches. In this paper, we compare the performance of the Cooper's, Neal's and Peng's learning algorithms with more realistic data sets, particularly data without null patterns and data contaminated by noise. Formulae that convert the original probability distribution to the distribution of all non-null patterns are derived. Systematic computer simulations with a bipartite noisy-or belief network using both data without null patterns and data with noise are conducted. Simulation results show that Cooper's and Peng's algorithms are superior to Neal's in average error for learning probabilities, and Peng's algorithm performed better in learning structures from noisy data.

1 Introduction

A belief network, also known as Bayesian network, causal network, or influence diagram, has the structure of a directed acyclic graph (DAG) where a node corresponds to a variable in a problem domain and an arc corresponds to a direct cause-effect or influence association between variables. Attached to each node is a conditional probability distribution for the corresponding variable, given all of its parents. This representation rigorously describes relationships between variables and has formal probability-theoretic semantics, making it suitable for various statistical manipulation [3]. We can, in principle, compute the joint probability of any combination of nodes of interest using a belief network.

To reduce the number of conditional probabilities required for a network, a class of simplified belief networks, called networks of disjunctive interaction or noisy-or gates, was developed [2, 5, 7]. In such a network, instead of conditional probability distributions, the probabilistic aspect of the causal relation is represented by a single probability value, called *causal strength*, associated with each causal link which measures the strength the parent node is to cause the child node. Among all noisy-or networks, the ones with *bipartite* structures are of particular interest in this paper.

According to [7], a bipartite binary noisy-or network consists of a layer of cause nodes D and a layer of effect node M. In diagnostic settings, these nodes are called *disorders* and *manifestations*, respectively. A node can take the value of either one or zero, indicating its presence or absence. A causal link exists between $d_i \in D$ and $m_j \in M$ if and only if d_i can cause m_j. Each disorder d_i is attached with its prior probability $p_i = P(d_i)$, and each causal link with causal strength $c_{ij} = P(m_j : d_i \mid d_i)$. Here the symbol "$m_j : d_i$" denotes a probabilistic event called *causation*, meaning that "the presence of disorder d_i is actually causing the presence of manifestation m_j". When there does not exist a causal link from d_i to m_j, then causal strength c_{ij} is set to 0. Therefore, the network structure can be completely depicted by the causal strengths of all disorder-manifestation pairs, if the partitioning of all nodes into D and M is known. While conjunctive event "$m_j \wedge d_i$" can be observed in statistical data, causation event "$m_j : d_i$" must be inferred or guessed. In situations where multiple disorders can occur simultaneously, an input confirming both d_i and m_j does not give any direct indication on if m_j is actually been caused by d_i.

Although belief networks have been applied to some real-world problems, including diagnosis, forecasting, automated vision, etc., their applications are restricted by the lack of effective methods to acquire needed causal knowledge, including both the network structures and the probability distributions. Recently, several learning methods have been proposed to learn causal knowledge from a large amount of case data [2, 4, 6, 8]. Some of these methods take more traditional machine learning approaches, while others explore the structural similarity between belief networks and neural networks and adapt different neural network learning models such as Boltzmann machine and Hebbian rule to learning belief networks.

These learning methods are empirically tested in various environments, however, thus their performance results were anecdotal and not compared systematically with each other. Moreover, almost all of these tests use artificial case data randomly generated from some given underlying belief networks. Such test data are different from real-world case data in several ways. In particular, these test data contain null patterns and they are noise-free.

Null patterns are defined as those patterns where there are no manifestations or no disorders. In many real-world applications such patterns never become part of the data set. Taking medical diagnosis as an example, one with no symptoms will not visit a doctor, thus null manifestation patterns will not enter the case records. Also, the case of someone with a few symptoms but no diagnosed disease will usually not become part of the data set, either. Thus, in a more realistic experiment setting, we need to exclude those null patterns. Data sets without null patterns are called *normalized* data. The exclusion of null patterns from learning data changes the priors of disorders p_i and causal strengths c_{ij} for the remaining patterns. We derive analytically the formulae to convert p_i and c_{ij} to $\hat{p}_i$ and $\hat{c}_{ij}$, their changed, or normalized versions under the condition that null patterns are not present. These normalized probabilities are then used to compare with the learned values in the experiments.

Many real-world data sets contain noise. Due to many reasons, noise can be introduced at any step from the source data collection all the way before they are presented to the learning process. To compare the noise resistance capability of these learning algorithms, we test them with randomly generated non-null patterns, corrupted by different levels of noise.

With these more realistic data sets, we compare three belief network learning algorithms, Cooper and Herskovits's K2 algorithm based on Bayesian theory, Neal's Boltzmann machine learning algorithm, and Peng's Hebbian learning algorithm. The main ideas of these algorithms are briefly presented in the next section. Section 3 describes the formulae to compute the normalized $\hat{p}_i$ and $\hat{c}_{ij}$ from the original p_i and c_{ij}. Experiments to validate these formulae using Peng's Hebbian learning algorithm are also presented there. Section 4 shows experiment results of performance comparison of the three algorithms. Finally, we conclude the results and discuss implications and further research in Section 5.

2   K2, Boltzmann Machine, and Hebbian Learning Algorithms

In this section, we describe briefly the three learning algorithms which we compare.

Cooper and Herskovits took an Bayesian approach to learning belief networks [2]. Basically, K2 is a greedy-search algorithm which heuristically finds the approximately most probable network structure based on a formula that evaluates the posterior probability of a structure, given the learning data. K2 algorithm begins by making the assumption that a node has no parents, and then incrementally adds as its parent a node whose addition increases the probability of the resulting structure the most. This method is mathematically well founded and general in that it works for both general belief networks as well as noisy-or networks. Also, this method is robust in that the learning is not affected by operational parameters such as learning rate used in Neal's and Peng's algorithm. On the other hand, this method is non-incremental, and thus can only work with a fixed database.

Neal proposed Boltzmann machine algorithm [4], which allows a number of hidden nodes in the learning network for a better fit of the data. This approach applies gradient ascent method similar to Boltzmann machines to maximize the log-likelihood function L below,

$$L \;=\; \ln \prod_{v \in \gamma} P(\tilde{V} = v),$$

where $\tilde{V}$ is an instantiation of, V, the visible units in the state vector, and v is a case input vector from the training data set γ (which also involves only visible nodes). With some manipulation, $P(\tilde{V} = v)$ can be expressed in terms of the inter-node connection weights s_{ij} which is related to the causal strengths by $exp(-s_{ij}) = 1 - c_{ij}$. Learning takes place by updating the inter-node connection strength s_{ij} by an amount proportional to the partial derivative $\partial L/\partial s_{ij}$ with each case input. As a result, the network is trained to have its probability distribution very close (in the sense of local maximum) to that of the training data set. One problem with this method is that the learning takes a long time to complete. Also, the learning network may get stuck at local but not global maximum of the likelihood. Simulated annealing may be used to cope with this problem, but the time required for learning would be further increased significantly.

Peng developed Hebbian-like learning rules for both prior probabilities of nodes and inter-node causal strengths [6, 8]. The latter rule also learns the structures of networks because non-zero causal strengths indicate the existence of causal links. Learning is done by updating the variables of the respective probabilities whenever a case description is applied, and thus is incremental. However, like the Neal's method, this method cannot be applied to general belief networks, only to noisy-or cases. Let e_i denote the event of occurrence of d_i, and $e_i(n) = 1$ if the nth input confirms the occurrence of d_i, and $e_i(n) = 0$, otherwise. Also let e_{ij} denote the conjunctive event $d_i \wedge m_j$. Three quantities $x_i(n)$, $w_{ij}(n)$, and $q_{ij}(n)$ are computed iteratively as follows.

$$x_i(n) \;=\; x_i(n-1) + \alpha(e_i(n) - x_i(n-1)), n > 0 \tag{1}$$

$$w_{ij}(n) \;=\; w_{ij}(n-1) + \alpha(q_{ij}(n)e_{ij}(n) - w_{ij}(n-1)), \tag{2}$$

$$q_{ij}(n) \;=\; \frac{w_{ij}(n)/x_i(n)}{1 - \prod_{d_k = 1\,in\,D}(1 - w_{kj}(n)/x_k(n))} \tag{3}$$

Here x_i is to be trained to p_i and w_{ij} to $P(m_j : d_i)$. Consequently, $y_{ij} = w_{ij}/x_i$ will be trained to $c_{ij} = P(m_j : d_i)/p_i$. Note that Eq. 2 is essentially a Hebbian rule in which w_{ij} increases when both d_i and m_j are 1 (i.e., $e_{ij} = 1$) and decreases otherwise, except that when $e_{ij} = 1$, the amount of increase in w_{ij} is controlled by the quantity q_{ij}. That is, when $m_j = 1$ in a given case, all disorders $d_k = 1$ in that case are competing to increase their w_{kj}, with q_{kj} are their normalized competing factor.

In their previous reports, all three learning methods can learn well both the structures and probabilities from perfect data sets. However, Peng's method converged one and two orders of magnitude faster than Cooper's and Neal's, respectively [8].

3   Handling of Null Patterns

Since we train the network with normalized data set, we need to compute the normalized probabilities, $\hat{p}_i$ and $\hat{c}_{ij}$ from the original p_i and c_{ij} in a given belief network. Let $\bar{D}_\phi$ and $\bar{M}_\phi$ denote the negations of the null disorder pattern $(d_i = 0, \forall i)$ and the null manifestation pattern $(m_j = 0, \forall j)$, respectively, we then have

$$\hat{p}_i \;=\; P(d_i \mid \bar{D}_\phi, \bar{M}_\phi)$$
$$=\; \frac{p_i\{1 - \prod_{m_j \in M}(1 - c_{ij})[\sum_{D_I \in \mathcal{P}(D - \{d_i\})} \prod_{d_k \in D_I}(p_k \prod_{m_j \in M}(1 - c_{kj})) \prod_{d_l \notin D_I, l \neq i}(1 - p_l)]\}}{(1 - \prod_{d_k \in D}(1 - p_k))[1 - \frac{\sum_{D_I \in \mathcal{P}(D) - \phi} \prod_{e_k \in D_I}(p_k \prod_{m_j \in M}(1 - c_{kj})) \prod_{d_l \notin D_I}(1 - p_l)}{1 - \prod_{d_k \in D}(1 - p_k)}]}, \tag{4}$$

$$\hat{c}_{ij} \;=\; P(m_j : d_i \mid d_i, \bar{M}_\phi)$$
$$=\; \frac{c_{ij}}{1 - \prod_{m_j \in M}(1 - c_{ij})[\sum_{D_I \in \mathcal{P}(D - \{d_i\})} \prod_{d_k \in D_I}(p_k \prod_{m_j \in M}(1 - c_{kj})) \prod_{d_l \notin D_I, l \neq i}(1 - p_l)]}. \tag{5}$$

The actual derivation is given in the appendix. A computer experiment using Peng's Hebbian learning rules (Eqs. 1 ~ 3) was conducted to test the validity of the derivation. We used a randomly generated bipartite network consisting of 10 disorders, 10 manifestations, and 35 causal links, together with prior probabilities for all disorders (ranging from 0.003 to 0.098) and causal strengths for all causal links (ranging from 0.11 to 0.96) (see Table 1). The quantities x_i and w_{ij} in the learning network were initialized as 0.0001 and 0.00001, respectively, reflecting the ignorance of the causal knowledge before learning was started. We randomly generated a database of 2,000 normalized patterns and also calculated normal-

Table 1: original network/normalized network

dis.(i) #	manif.(j) # $c_{ij}/\hat{c_{ij}}$										$p_i/\hat{p_i}$
	1	2	3	4	5	6	7	8	9	10	
1		.31/.32		.85/.89			.3/.32				.026/.074
2							.5/.75				.014/.030
3		.29/.29		.64/.65	.15/.15	.11/.11		.72/.73	.62/.63		.054/.160
4			.88/.94					.27/.29			.06/.17
5	.72/.72	.92/.92		.12/.12	.47/.47				.73/.73	.96/.96	.003/.009
6						.32/.48	.26/.39				.023/.045
7	.69/.69	.8/.8		.73/.73				.58/.58			.048/.140
8		.89/.90		.26/.26		.23/.23	.69/.69			.51/.51	.079/.230
9		.12/.12					.95/.96			.67/.68	.098/.290
10				.43/.60	.18/.25	.11/.15					.027/.058

ized probabilities, $\hat{p_i}$ and $\hat{c_{ij}}$ using Eq. 4 and 5. The generated patterns were presented to the network and the quantities x_i and w_{ij} were computed with learning rate $\alpha = 0.0002$. We compared whether the quantities x_i and y_{ij} converge to original probabilities p_i and c_{ij} or normalized probabilities $\hat{p_i}$ and $\hat{c_{ij}}$. The mean squared error (MSE) between x_i and p_i is smaller than that of x_i and $\hat{p_i}$ at first since x_i was initialized to a very small number while all p_i's are relatively small (see Table 1's rightmost column), but increases continuously to become 0.00944, while MSE between x_i and $\hat{p_i}$ gets smaller and smaller to become 0.00012 after 10 epochs. MSE between y_{ij} and $\hat{c_{ij}}$ becomes smaller than that of y_{ij} and c_{ij} as the network learns. Fig. 1 shows they both converge to normalized probabilities.

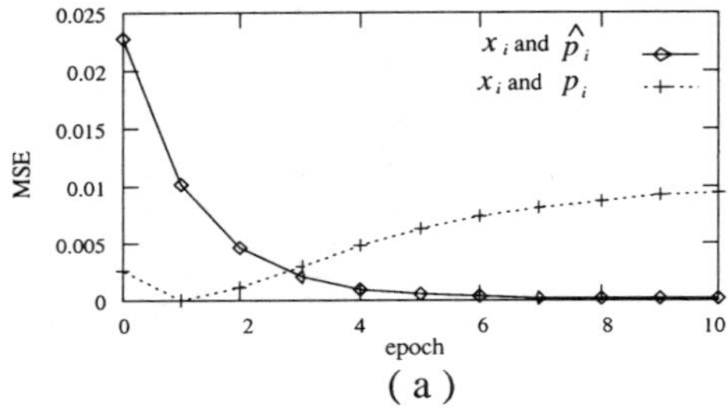

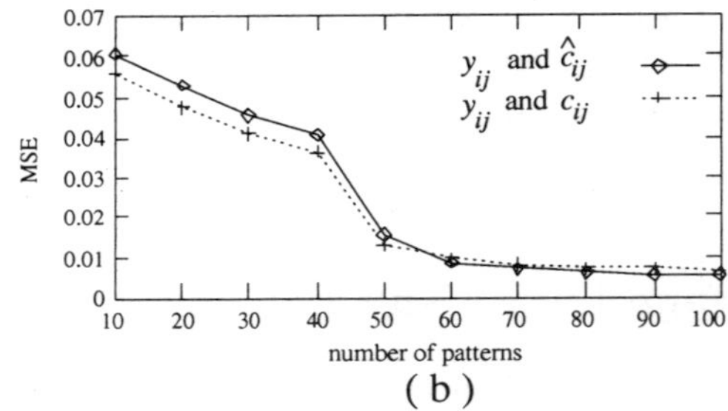

Figure 1: (a) MSE between x_i and $\hat{p_i}$, and between x_i and p_i (b) MSE between y_{ij} and $\hat{c_{ij}}$, and between y_{ij} and c_{ij}

4   Experiments and Comparison

The following procedure was used to generate normalized and noisy data in the experiments. First, we generated a set of 2,000 non-null patterns from the same network as in section 3. Then, noise was added randomly by reversing certain bits of the case data at the levels of 2%, 4%, 6%, 8% and 10% of the total bits in the data set. To add 2% of noise to the data set, we randomly reversed 2,000 patterns × (10 bits in input + 10 bits in output) × 2% = 800 bits. For each noise level, ten noisy data sets were generated, thus we had 51 data sets in total (one noise-free data set included). Each of these 51 data sets was presented to the three learning algorithms, and their learning results were averaged over the ten databases at each noise level.

Four performance measures were used to evaluate the algorithm's performance. Two of them are for numerical probability values, in comparison to $\hat{p_i}$ and $\hat{c_{ij}}$. They are AAE_p, the averaged absolute error of prior probabilities over all ten disorders, and AAE_c, that of causal strengths over all 100 potential causal links. Note that many of those which do not correspond to causal links in the underlying network will have their strengths reduced to a very small value. The other two measures are for the learned network structures. They are the number of *missing* links and the number of *extra* links. For any pair of d_i and m_j, Cooper's algorithm gives a categorical answer to whether there is a causal link between them. Such answers are compared with the underlying network to determine these two counts. Neal's and Peng's algorithms, on the other hand, start with a fully connected bipartite network, and whether there should be a link between d_i and m_j depends on if the learned causal strength y_{ij} is above or below a small threshold value ϵ. In the experiments, ϵ was chosen as 0.1.

In Fig. 2(a), AAE_p's of three methods are nearly the same at the same noise level. AAE_p's of Cooper's and Neal's methods are actually the same since they are computed by the frequencies of their occurrences in the learning case data. In Fig. 2(b), Neal's method shows large AAE_c while those of Cooper's and Peng's methods are small. The reason that Cooper's method results in small AAE_c is that we use a kind of frequency method to compute them after the structure is learned. Fig. 2(c) and (d) shows the number of *missing* and *extra* links for the three methods. When there is no noise, i.e., noise level 0%, Cooper's and Peng's methods resulted in no missing and extra links while Neal's method resulted in 6 missing and 11 extra links. When noise is introduced, i.e., noise level 2% ~ 10%, Peng's method clearly outperformed the other two at all noise levels. We suspect that the competition of w's through the denominator of Eq. 3 suppresses unwanted spurious causal associations caused by random noise.

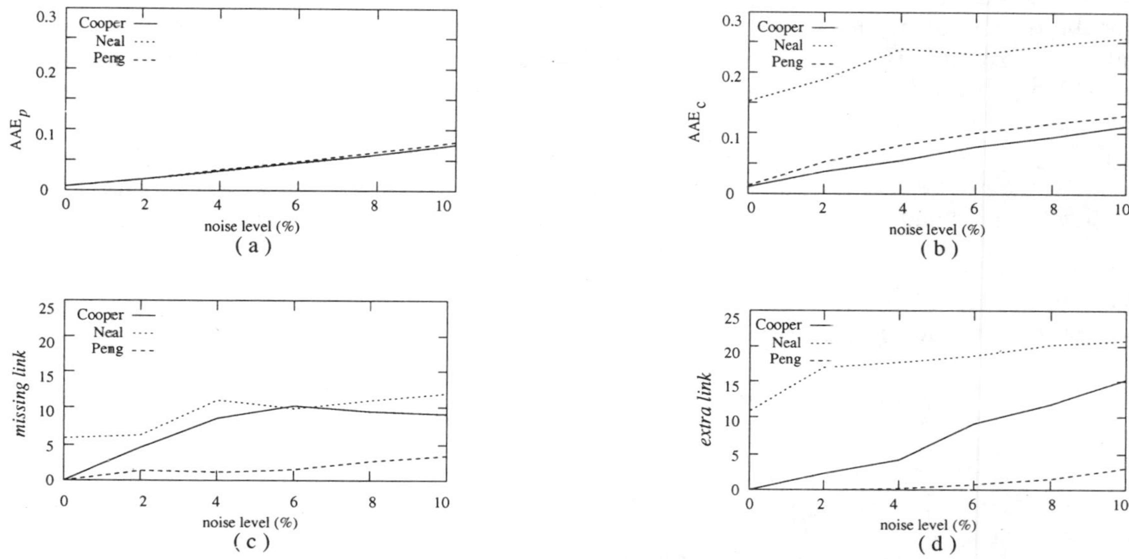

Figure 2: performance comparisons of three methods, (a) AAE_p, (b) AAE_c, (c) *missing* link, and (d) *extra* link

5 Conclusions

Three representative belief network learning algorithms were systematically compared using a large number of more realistic case data which exclude null patterns and contain different levels of noise. Experiment results show that Neal's algorithm performed most poorly and tends to take much longer learning time. Both Cooper's algorithm and Peng's algorithm learned numerical probabilities relatively well. But Peng's algorithm outperform Cooper's with respect to learning structures of the network when noise is present. This may be due to the competition process used in the Peng's algorithm. Competition in neural networks has been found to guard against small perturbations [1].

Certain issues merit further investigation.. Currently, the formulae to compute normalized priors and causal strengths are applicable only to bipartite networks. It is desirable to extend these formulae for more general non-bipartite networks. This will enable us to extend the comparative study to belief networks of general structures. Also many real case data do not have their variables fully instantiated. How to handle data with missing bits has become an area of intense research recently. Incorporating missing bits into the test data and applying already proposed techniques will make the comparison environment even more realistic. Finally, a huge number of artificially generated networks can be used to test to compare the various learning algorithms. This paper just presents a first step toward that direction.

Acknowledgements

The work reported here was supported by POSTECH PIRL Grant B94918 and KOSEF Grant 941-0900-031-02 to Sungzoon Cho, and by USA NSF Grant IRI-9309136 to Yun Peng.

Appendix

1. *Derivation of Eq. 4*

Normalized prior probability $\hat{p}_i$ is defined as $P(d_i \mid \bar{D}_\phi, \bar{M}_\phi)$. Applying Bayes' theorem and the fact that d_i implies $\bar{D}_\phi$, we get $\hat{p}_i = p_i(1 - P(M_\phi \mid d_i))/[(1 - P(D_\phi))(1 - \frac{P(M_\phi, \bar{D}_\phi)}{1 - P(D_\phi)})]$. Term $P(M_\phi \mid d_i) = P(\bigwedge_{m_j \in M} \bar{m}_j \mid d_i)$ in the numerator can be computed as

$$\prod_{m_j \in M}(1 - c_{ij})\Big[\sum_{D_I \in \mathcal{P}(D - \{d_i\})} \prod_{d_k \in D_I}(p_k \prod_{m_j \in M}(1 - c_{kj})) \prod_{d_l \notin D_I, l \neq i}(1 - p_l)\Big], \tag{6}$$

where the first term products the probabilities that each m_j which has causal link with d_i doesn't appear and the second term sums, for each element of power set of disorders excluding d_i, the products of the probabilities that d_k in the disorder set occur while m_j's which have causal link with d_k do not appear and the probabilities that d_l not present in disorder set doesn't occur. Term $P(D_\phi)$ in the denominator can be computed as $\prod_{d_k \in D}(1 - p_k)$, which products the probabilities that each d_k in disorder set doesn't occur. Term $P(M_\phi, \bar{D}_\phi)$ in the denominator can be computed as $\sum_{D_I \in \mathcal{P}(D) - \phi} \prod_{d_k \in D_I}(p_k \prod_{m_j \in M}(1 - c_{kj})) \prod_{d_l \notin D_I}(1 - p_l)$, where the term sums, for each element of power set of disorders excluding null patterns, the products of probabilities that d_k in the set occur while m_j's which have causal link with d_k do not appear and probabilities that d_l not in disorder set doesn't occur.

2. *Derivation of Eq. 5*

Normalized causation probability $\hat{c}_{ij}$ is defined as $P(m_j : d_i \mid d_i, \bar{M}_\phi)$. Applying Bayes' theorem, we get

$$
\begin{aligned}
\hat{c}_{ij} &= \frac{P(m_j : d_i \mid d_i)P(\bar{M}_\phi \mid \{m_j : d_i \mid d_i\})}{P(\bar{M}_\phi \mid d_i)} \\
&= \frac{P(m_j : d_i \mid d_i)}{P(\bar{M}_\phi \mid d_i)} \quad \text{using the fact that } P(\bar{M}_\phi \mid \{m_j : d_i \mid d_i\}) = 1, \text{ we have} \\
&= \frac{c_{ij}}{1 - P(M_\phi \mid d_i)} \quad \text{by property of probability of mutually exclusive events.}
\end{aligned}
$$

Term $P(M_\phi \mid d_i)$ in the denominator is in Eq. 6.

References

[1] S. Cho and J. Reggia, "Learning Competition and Cooperation," *Neural Computation*, vol. 5, pp. 242-259, 1993.

[2] G. Cooper and E. Herskovits, "A Bayesian Method for the Induction of Probabilistic Networks from Data," *Machine Learning*, vol. 9, pp. 309–347, 1992.

[3] D. Heckerman and M. Wellman, "Bayesian Networks," *Communications of the ACM*, vol. 38, pp. 25–30, 1995.

[4] R. Neal, "Connectionist Learning of Belief Networks," *Artificial Intelligence*, pp. 71–113, 1992.

[5] J. Pearl, *Probabilistic Reasoning in Intelligent Systems.* Calif: Morgan Kaufmann, 1988.

[6] Y. Peng and N. Jiang, "A Learning Method for Belief Networks," in *International Workshop on Principle of Diagnosis*, (Washington DC), Oct. 1994.

[7] Y. Peng and J. Reggia, *Abductive Inference Methods for Diagnostic Problem-Solving.* New York: Springer-Verlag, 1990.

[8] Y. Peng and Z. Zhou, "A Neural Network Learning Method for Belief Networks," submitted to *International Journal of Intelligent Systems.*

Supervised Feedforward Neural Networks are Provably Secure

Andrew J. Blumberg

MIT Artificial Intelligence Laboratory
Room 701
Cambridge, MA 02138

Harvard University Mathematics Department
Cambridge, MA 02138

blumberg@ai.mit.edu

Abstract—

Recent work has demonstrated that the problem of training neural networks is NP-complete. It has been shown that even approximate training is NP-complete. Furthermore, work in computational learning theory suggests that training neural networks is as hard as inverting certain cryptographically secure mappings. Although these results suggest difficulties in applying neural networks to practical problems of nontrivial size, in this paper we demonstrate a new result which turns this property of neural networks into an advantage. Specifically, in this paper it is shown that the problem of sabotaging neural networks is also NP-hard; given a feed-forward supervised neural network and the ability to arbitrarily change the weights on the connections in the network, we prove it that it is intractable to determine which connections to change to produce the greatest output error.

1 Introduction

In recent years, there have been a spate of theoretical results demonstrating the intrinsic difficulties of training neural networks. Blum and Rivest [1] and Judd [2,3] have shown that the problem of training feed-forward supervised neural networks is NP-complete. Wiklicky [4] extended these results to hold for recurrent supervised neural networks. Blumberg [5] showed that the unsupervised case was also NP-hard and that generating approximate solutions in either case was NP-hard. The work of Reif [6] demonstrated that the existence of an algorithm for training neural networks in the PAC sense (an algorithm such that with probability $1 - \delta$ a solution correct to $1 - \epsilon$ is returned in time polynomial in ϵ^{-1} and δ^{-1}) would imply the existence of a polynomial algorithm for factoring integers. In summary, training neural network models is intrinsically difficult.

Intuitively, these results suggest that the problem of credit assignment in neural networks is difficult; it is computationally hard to tell which weights are responsible for which changes in output (when the problem is considered over all the class of all inputs). In turn, this suggests that the problem of sabotaging neural networks might also be difficult; it is likely to be difficult for an adversary to decide which connections of the neural network to adjust to defeat the network. In the next sections we will prove results to the effect that this is indeed the case; in some sense, neural networks are an optimally secure form of information storage from the perspective of tolerance to sabotage.

2 Sabotaging Neural Networks

The sabotage problem asks an adversary to optimally damage a neural network. Specifically, given a fixed network and the ability to arbitrarily modify the weights in the network, adjust the weights to maximally change the output of the network. Phrased in style of Garey and Johnson [7], we have the problem of ρ-sabotaging a neural network.

Instance : A neural architecture T, consisting of a weighted directed graph G (with weights W) and a set of tasks for the neural network (for which the weights are a successful instantiation) X, and a number $0 \leq \rho \leq 1$.

Question : Is there a new assignment for the weights, W', such that the output of the neural network over the tasks in X has an error rate (in terms of absolute output errors) greater than ρ?

3 The Problem of Sabotaging Boolean Expressions

Conveniently, it turns out that there is a polynomial time identification between the class of CNF formulae and a subset of the class of neural networks; that is, for every CNF formula there is a corresponding neural network, and the identification can be computed efficiently [2,3]. Essentially, each clause of the formula represents a single member of the set of tasks for the network. Thus, the neural network problems we expressed above can be characterized in terms of problems involving CNF formula. The recharacterized problem is the problem of ρ-sabotaging CNF formula.

Instance : A CNF expression f, a satisfying assignment of variables c, and a number $0 \leq \rho \leq 1$.

Question : Is there a new assignment for the variables such that at most a fraction $1 - \rho$ of the clauses of the CNF expression are satisfied?

Here, we have :

Theorem 1 *The 1-sabotage problem for CNF formula is NP-hard.*

The proof of this is a straightforward construction that would allow a polynomial solution to the 1-sabotage problem to be employed to solve satisfiability, thereby generating a contradiction. So assume we had a polynomial time algorithm for the 1-sabotage problem. Consider an arbitrary CNF formula f. f has the form $f_1 \wedge f_2 \wedge f_3 \ldots$, where each f_i is a finite disjunction of variables. Now, transform this into f', where f' is of the form $\lambda \wedge (\bar{f}_1 \vee \lambda) \wedge (\bar{f}_2 \vee \lambda) \ldots$. Clearly, the assignment which makes λ true and all other variables false satisfies f'. So now run the algorithm for solving 1-sabotage. There exists a 1-sabotaging expression if and only if there exists an expression which does not satisfy $\bar{f}_1$ and does not satisfy $\bar{f}_2$ and so on. But such an expression would necessarily satisfy f_1 and f_2 and in fact all f_i - such an expression satisfies f. Thus, we can decide whether f is satisfiable. Since f was an arbitrary CNF formula, we have developed a polynomial time algorithm for satisfiability. This is a contradiction, and so the theorem follows (also note that checking sabotage is a polynomial time operation and so 1-sabotage is in NP).

Now, this result is somewhat too constrained to be useful (as it only applies to total disruption of the output of the network). However, building on the earlier work on approximation [5], we immediately have the following corollary.

Corollary 1 *The ρ-sabotage problem for CNF formula is NP-hard.*

This follows almost immediately from the identification shown above between sabotage and satisfiability. Specifically, a polynomial time solution to the ρ-sabotage problem would imply the existence of a polynomial time solution to the ρ-satisfiability problem (which requires the determination of an assignment satisfying at least a fraction ρ of the clauses in the formula). But it has been shown [5,7] that the ρ-satisfiability problem is NP-complete. Thus we have the stated result.

This allows us to finally claim

Corollary 2 *The ρ-sabotage problem for feed-forward neural networks is NP-hard*

This follows directly from the above corollary and the aforementioned identification of neural networks with CNF formula; a polynomial solution to this problem would imply the existence of a polynomial solution to the ρ-sabotage problem for CNF formula, which we now know to be NP-hard.

4   Conclusions

Thus, in this paper we've shown that it is intrinsically difficult to sabotage functions embodied as neural networks. Therefore, although it is also intractable to encode information as a neural network, once encoded that information is secure against direct adversarial attack (as long as the adversary is polynomially bounded). Furthermore, note that this is a result that is stronger than redundancy; the adversary is permitted to attack all of the weights. Further work on the expected difficulty of sabotaging the neural networks that actually arise in practice will be necessary to evaluate the applicability of these results.

References

[1] A. Blum and R. L. Rivest, "Training a 3-node Neural Net is NP-Complete," in *Advances in Neural Information Processing 1*, pp. 494-501, 1989.

[2] J. S. Judd, *Neural Network Design and the Complexity of Learning*. Cambridge: MIT Press, 1990.

[3] J. S. Judd, "How Loading Complexity is Affected by Node Function Sets," in *Computational Learning Theory and Natural Learning Systems*, pp. 49-64, Cambridge: MIT Press, 1994.

[4] H. Wiklicky, "On the Non-Existence of a Universal Learning Algorithm for Recurrent Neural Networks," in *Advances in Neural Information Processing 6*, pp. 431-436, 1994.

[5] A. J. Blumberg, "Intractability Results for Feed-Forward Neural Networks," in *Proceedings of the World Conference on Neural Networks*, pp. 64-67, 1995.

[6] J. Reif, "On Threshold Circuits and Polynomial Computations," in *Proceedings of the 2nd Conference on Structure in Complexity Theory*, pp. 118-125, 1987.

[7] M. R. Garey and D. S. Johnson, *Computers and Intractability - A Guide to the Theory of NP-Completeness*. New York: W.H. Freeman, 1979.

Learning Theories and Algorithms

(Poster Presentation)

A MODIFIED LEARNING ALGORITHM FOR IMPROVING THE FAULT TOLERANCE OF BP NETWORKS

Naihong Wei, Shiyuan Yang and Shibai Tong

Department of Automation, Tsinghua University
Beijing 100084, P.R.CHINA

Abstract—The conventional back-propagation (BP) algorithm is not suitable for building fault tolerant networks, since it usually develops non-uniform weights. In this paper, a learning method to improve the fault tolerance in classification is therefore presented and a metric is devised to evaluate the performance. The new method is based on the BP algorithm. During the training, the magnitude of each weight is restrained from over-increasing. This modification enforces that the information be distributed across weights more evenly. Simulation results demonstrate that the modified algorithm leads to significant enhancement in the network's ability to cope with internal hardware failures.

1   Introduction

In recent years, BP networks have played an important role in various problems such as pattern recognition and classification. For use in applications requiring high reliability, BP networks should possess a high degree of fault tolerance to its internal hardware failures BP networks are distributed parallel processing elements, with each node contributing to the final output response. This characteristic makes the networks have potential fault tolerant ability. A simple and necessary way to enhance such potential ability is through redundancy. Nevertheless, the traditional BP learning algorithm can not guarantee more fault tolerance by adding more hidden nodes. This is because BP algorithm develops non-uniform weights with a few that are critical and many others that are insignificant. If the critical weights are damaged, the outputs of network will change greatly, which reveals the BP algorithm may not be suited for fault tolerance. Therefore, merely providing extra hidden nodes is insufficient and the fault tolerance behavior must be activated by an appropriate learning scheme.

Neti *et al.* proposed a method to generate a maximally fault tolerant neural network by solving a nonlinear constrained optimization problem[1], yet more experiments are needed to draw any general conclusions. Clay *et al.* introduced a procedure for achieving fault tolerance[2]: every type of failures that one might expect to occur during operation are randomly added to components of the network during training. This type of training yields a more fault tolerant net, but it may not converge unless the number of faulty units is small. Phataket *et al.*[3] and Emmerson *et al.*[4] found that replicating the hidden units can achieve good fault tolerance. However, the fault tolerance of the augmented network is inevitably determined by the algorithm used to train the original network. Jou *et al.* pointed out that constraining the magnitude of each weight below small bound during the training process can improve fault tolerance[5], but selecting an adequate bound is very difficult. The network may not converge if the bound is too low. On the other hand, it is not advantage to fully promote the fault tolerance if the bound is too high.

In view of limitations of above methods, this paper presented a modified BP learning algorithm. The new algorithm enforces that the magnitude of each weight be as small as possible and the information be distributed across weights more evenly.

The rest of this paper is organized as follows: In section 2, the BP networks and the BP algorithm are introduced. Then the modified algorithm for training fault tolerant network is proposed in section 3. In section 4, a metric to quantify the fault tolerance of BP networks is devised and illustrative examples showing results of the novel algorithm are studied. Conclusions are given in section 5.

2   The BP Networks and BP Algorithm

A standard BP network consists of one input layer, one output layer and one or more hidden layers. Each layer contains a number of nodes. Connections exist only between the nodes of two successive layers. The functions animating the network are the same for all hidden layers and output layer:

$$o_{pi}^{(k)} = f(I_{pi}^{(k)}) = 1/(1+\exp(-I_{pi}^{(k)}))-1/2 \tag{1}$$

$$I_{pi}^{(k)} = \sum_{j=1}^{n_{k-1}} (W_{ij}^{(k)} \cdot o_{pj}^{(k-1)}) + bias_i^{(k)} \tag{2}$$

where $o_{pi}^{(k)}$ is the output of node i in layer k, the subscript p denotes the order of arrangement of the training patterns used in the training phase, $W_{ij}^{(k)}$ is the corresponding weight between the node j in layer k-1 and the node i in layer k, $bias_i^{(k)}$ is the bias for the node i in layer k, and n_{k-1} is the number of nodes in layer k-1. The output value of each node ranges over -0.5 to 0.5. BP networks are usually trained by following delta rule with a momentum term[6]:

$$\Delta W_{ij}^{(k)}(n) = -\frac{1}{P} \cdot \eta_{ij}^{(k)}(n) \cdot \sum_{p=1}^{P} \frac{\partial E_p(n)}{\partial W_{ij}^{(k)}} + \beta \cdot \Delta W_{ij}^{(k)}(n-1) \tag{3}$$

$$\Delta bias_i^{(k)}(n) = -\frac{1}{P} \cdot \eta_i^{(k)}(n) \cdot \sum_{p=1}^{P} \frac{\partial E_p(n)}{\partial bias_i^{(k)}} + \beta \cdot \Delta bias_i^{(k)}(n-1) \tag{4}$$

where $E_p(n)$ is the square error function of the pattern p after n-th iteration and P is the number of training patterns. At $(n+1)$th iteration during training, the update of connection weight $\Delta W_{ij}^{(k)}$ is based on two components. The first component is a function of the error gradient. The second component is proportional to the amount of weight change in the previous iteration. β is the momentum factor which helps prevent the oscillation problem near the solution point. η denotes the learning rate which can be modified in each training epoch as follows:

$$\text{If} \quad \sum_{p=1}^{P} \frac{\partial E_p(n)}{\partial W_{ij}^{(k)}} \cdot \sum_{p=1}^{P} \frac{\partial E_p(n-1)}{\partial W_{ij}^{(k)}} \geq 0 \qquad \text{then} \quad \eta_{ij}^{(k)}(n) = \eta^+ \cdot \eta_{ij}^{(k)}(n-1) \tag{5}$$

$$\text{If} \quad \sum_{p=1}^{P} \frac{\partial E_p(n)}{\partial W_{ij}^{(k)}} \cdot \sum_{p=1}^{P} \frac{\partial E_p(n-1)}{\partial W_{ij}^{(k)}} < 0 \qquad \text{then} \quad \eta_{ij}^{(k)}(n) = \eta^- \cdot \eta_{ij}^{(k)}(n-1) \tag{6}$$

where η^+ and η^- are positive constants for which the values are slightly higher than or lower than 1 respectively[7]. The adjustment rule of $\eta_i^{(k)}$ is similar to that of $\eta_{ij}^{(k)}$. The adaptive modification of learning rate can considerably speed up the training. Essentially, the learning algorithm described above is a kind of conventional BP algorithm.

3   The Modified Training Algorithm

The faults might occur in BP networks are versatile and it is very difficult to modeling them precisely. There are two fault types usually used to measure the fault tolerance of BP networks. One fault type is node fault of stuck-at node's extreme values. Another fault type is connection fault. Setting the relevant weight to zero is chosen as a physically plausible type of connection damage[2-4][8].

Fault tolerance of BP network is the capacity that the network remains in its normal operation if substantial network is damaged. In this paper, we concentrate only on classification tasks. Thus, the normal operation means the value of output nodes remains larger than zero for the high state and remains smaller than zero for the low state.

To make a redundant net more fault tolerant, a modified training algorithm is addressed in this section. The novel method restrains the magnitude of each weight from over-increasing during the training process, which strives to distribute the information across the weights as evenly as possible.

As some layers are perhaps intrinsically more important than others, it is inadequate to require that every weight in a network contain the same quantity of information. Therefore, we have defined two types of influence degrees only to judge if information is evenly distributed across the weights which are between the same pair of successive layers. During the training, it is necessary to check the influence degree of each weight from epoch to epoch. Among weights between the same pair of layers, if a weight has relatively high influence degree, its magnitude should be constrained not to rise temporarily. Trained by this strategy, each weight and node contribute to the final output response, but the contributions are relatively small and uniform. As a result, the network is not easy to produce a classification error under damage conditions.

3.1 The thresholds of weights

Restraining the magnitudes of weights from increasing is not necessary for small magnitude weights and may degrade the convergent speed. Thus, we should assign each weight a threshold. A weight is constrained in the new algorithm only when its magnitude is greater than its corresponding threshold. Considering that the average input magnitude of one input node might differ from that of another input node, a positive constant M should be selected to calculate the threshold $\sigma_{ij}^{(1)}$ of each weight between input layer and the first hidden layer:

$$\sigma_{ij}^{(1)} = \frac{M}{\sqrt{\sum_{p=1}^{P}(o_{p\cdot}^{(0)})^2}} \tag{7}$$

For the other weights, ones fed to the same layer may have the same thresholds We should first train a network by using conventional BP algorithm, then determine the values of M and σ from the weights of the trained network as follows:

$$M \le \frac{1}{3} \cdot \frac{1}{n_0 \cdot n_1} \sum_{i=1}^{n_1} \sum_{j=1}^{n_0} \left(|W_{ij}^{(1)}| \cdot \sqrt{\sum_{p=1}^{P}(o_{pj}^{(0)})^2} \right) \tag{8}$$

$$\sigma^{(k)} \le \frac{1}{3} \cdot \frac{1}{n_{k-1} \cdot n_k} \sum_{i=1}^{n_k} \sum_{j=1}^{n_{k-1}} |W_{ij}^{(k)}| \tag{9}$$

3.2 The influence degree

Let $n_i^{(k)}$ denote the node i in layer k, $\Delta I_i^{(k)}$ denote the increment of $I_i^{(k)}$ If the connection between $n_j^{(k-1)}$ and $n_i^{(k)}$ is damaged, i.e. $W_{ij}^{(k)}=0$, $|\Delta I_i^{(k)}|=|W_{ij}^{(k)}|\cdot|o_j^{(k-1)}|$. If $n_j^{(k-1)}$ is damaged, i.e. $o_j^{(k-1)}=\pm0.5$, $|\Delta I_i^{(k)}|=|W_{ij}^{(k)}|\cdot|\pm0.5-o_j^{(k-1)}|$. $|\Delta I_i^{(k)}|$ is proportional to $|W_{ij}^{(k)}|$. Therefore the magnitude of the weight $|W_{ij}^{(k)}|$ has direct influence upon $I_i^{(k)}$ when its corresponding connection or $n_j^{(k-1)}$ is damaged. This influence eventually affects the final response of BP network. For simplicity, here we only consider the influence of $|W_{ij}^{(k)}|$ upon $I_i^{(k)}$.

Definition 1: For a weight $W_{ij}^{(k)}$, its influence degree $\rho_{ij}^{(k)}$ is computed as below:

$$\rho_{ij}^{(k)}(n) = \begin{cases} \sqrt{\sum_{p=1}^{P}(o_{pj}^{(k-1)}(n) \cdot W_{ij}^{(k)}(n))^2} & \text{if } k=1 \\[2ex] \sqrt{\sum_{p=1}^{P}((0.5+|o_{pj}^{(k-1)}(n)|) \cdot W_{ij}^{(k)}(n))^2} & \text{otherwise} \end{cases} \tag{10}$$

$\rho_{ij}^{(k)}$ reflects the possible maximum influence of $|W_{ij}^{(k)}|$ on $I_i^{(k)}$ for all training patterns. For the weights between the same pair of layers, their influences upon network can be approximately compared each other according to ρ.

Definition 2: The standard influence degree of the weights between layer k-1 and layer k is

$$\rho_s^{(k)}(n) = \gamma^{(k)} \cdot \sqrt{\sum_{i=1}^{n_k} \sum_{j=1}^{n_{k-1}} (\rho_{ij}^{(k)}(n))^2 / (n_{k-1} \cdot n_k)} \tag{11}$$

where $\gamma^{(k)}$ is equal to or greater than 1. $\rho_s^{(k)}$ is a standard to judge whether the influence degree of each $W_{ij}^{(k)}$ is too high or not. To train a network using the modified algorithm, in general, the higher the redundancy degree of the network, the smaller the γ, hence the more strict the constraints applied to weights. For the output layer, γ should be relatively small.

3.3 The modified learning algorithm

The modified algorithm is based on the conventional one introduced in previous section, with Eqs. (1) through (6) still used. For a weight $W_{ij}^{(k)}$, at $(n+1)$th iteration during training, $W_{ij}^{(k)}(n+1)$ is first determined from Eq. (3) in the new algorithm. Then the weight might be modified if it's magnitude increases, i.e.,

$$|W_{ij}^{(k)}(n+1)| > |W_{ij}^{(k)}(n)| \tag{12}$$

Under such necessary condition, the specific modifications are listed below:

(a) When $|W_{ij}^{(k)}(n)| < \sigma_{ij}^{(k)}$

$$\text{if } W_{ij}^{(k)}(n+1) > \sigma_{ij}^{(k)} \qquad \text{then} \quad W_{ij}^{(k)}(n+1) = \sigma_{ij}^{(k)} \tag{13}$$

$$\text{if } W_{ij}^{(k)}(n+1) < -\sigma_{ij}^{(k)} \qquad \text{then} \quad W_{ij}^{(k)}(n+1) = -\sigma_{ij}^{(k)} \tag{14}$$

(b) When $|W_{ij}^{(k)}(n)| \ge \sigma_{ij}^{(k)}$

$$\text{if } \rho_{ij}^{(k)}(n) \ge \rho_s^{(k)}(n) \qquad \text{then} \quad \eta_{ij}^{(k)}(n+1) = \eta_{ij}^{(k)}(n)$$

$$W_{ij}^{(k)}(n+1) = W_{ij}^{(k)}(n) \tag{15}$$

In each training epoch, if a weight has relatively high influence degree, its magnitude should be constrained not to increase.

If $\rho_{ij}^{(k)}(n) < \rho_s^{(k)}(n)$ and $|W_{ij}^{(k)}(n+1)| \geq (1 + f_{ij}^{(k)}(n)) \cdot |W_{ij}^{(k)}(n)|$

then $W_{ij}^{(k)}(n+1) = (1 + f_{ij}^{(k)}(n)) \cdot W_{ij}^{(k)}(n) \tag{16}$

where $f_{ij}^{(k)}(n)$ is the maximum gain factor of $W_{ij}^{(k)}$. If a weight has relatively low influence degree, its magnitude is permitted to increase, but $f_{ij}^{(k)}(n)$ must be small lest the weight jumps up to be one with over-high magnitude. $f_{ij}^{(k)}(n)$ can be calculated as below:

$$f_{ij}^{(k)}(n) = \alpha^{(k)} + (\rho_s^{(k)}(n) / \rho_{ij}^{(k)}(n) - 1)^2 \cdot \zeta^{(k)} \tag{17}$$

where $\alpha^{(k)}$ and $\xi^{(k)}$ are small positive constants. $f_{ij}^{(k)}$ decreases as the weight $W_{ij}^{(k)}$ becomes more important, i.e., the ratio between $\rho_s^{(k)}$ and $\rho_{ij}^{(k)}$ becomes greater.

Under the conditions not mentioned above, $W_{ij}^{(k)}(n+1)$ remains unchanged.

4   Simulation

Two particular applications studied in this section are XOR problem and a fault diagnosis problem. For all the following BP networks, the initial weights varied randomly between -0.1 and 0.1, and the initial learning rate $\eta = 1$, $\eta^+ = 1.02$, $\eta^- = 0.9$, $\beta = 0.9$. However, the exact settings of these coefficients were uncritical.

4.1 A metric to quantify the fault tolerance of BP networks

Let P_f denote the probability of connection fault or hidden node fault, f_n denote the fraction of misclassifications, where n is the number of connection faults or hidden node faults in the network. When P_f is definite, the number of connection faults or node faults increases as net size becomes larger. Therefore, to estimate the fault tolerant ability of BP networks according to f_n [3] is unreasonable.

We suggest that the probability of misclassification $P_{misclass}$ should be chosen as the performance metric for assessing fault tolerance. When P_f is definite, the smaller the $P_{misclass}$, the higher the degree of fault tolerance.

For small nets, f_n is obtained through an exhaustive testing of all possible n-faults. Then $P_{misclass}$ is calculated as follows:

$$P_{misclass} = \sum_{n=1}^{n_{max}} \left(C_{n_{max}}^n \cdot p_f^n \cdot (1 - p_f)^{n_{max} - n} \cdot f_n \right) \tag{18}$$

where n_{max} denote the total number of connections or hidden nodes in the network.

For large nets, exhaustive testing of all possible faults is prohibitive. Therefore, for a certain damage level P_f, $P_{misclass}$ is calculated as follows: In the connection weight testing, each weight is set at 0 with probability P_f. In the hidden node testing, the output of each hidden node is set at +05 or -0.5 with probability $P_f/2$ respectively. All the training patterns are tested and all the outputs that go wrong are counted. The above procedures should be repeated thousands of times in order to achieve acceptable fault coverage.

$$P_{misclass} = n_f / (n_{out} \cdot n_p \cdot n_{rep}) \tag{19}$$

where n_f is the total number of outputs that go wrong, n_{out} is the number of output nodes, n_p is the number of training patterns, n_{rep} is the number of repetitions.

4.2 The XOR problem

Some papers[5][9] have used the XOR problem to explain the fault tolerance of neural networks. In order to make the problem more general, we change its input magnitudes. Table 1 lists all the training sample pairs.

Table 1   Training Sample Pairs

input	(0.1,0.5)	(-0.15,-0.35)	(0.1,-0.5)	(-0.15,0.35)
output	0.5	0.5	-0.5	-0.5

Three groups of networks were generated to perform this classification task.

Group 1: $2 \times 2 \times 1$ networks, trained by the conventional BP algorithm described in section 2. Learning was employed until the mean squared error ε dropped below 10^{-25} for the entire training set.

Group 2: $2 \times 6 \times 1$ networks, trained by the conventional BP algorithm, the mean squared error $\varepsilon \leq 10^{-25}$.

Group 3: $2 \times 6 \times 1$ networks, trained by the modified algorithm, the mean squared error $\varepsilon \leq 10^{-8}$, $M=2$, $\sigma^{(2)}=4$, $\gamma^{(1)}=1.02$, $\gamma^{(2)}=1$, $\xi^{(1)}=\xi^{(2)}=0.03$, $\alpha^{(1)}=\alpha^{(2)}=0.0001$.

As the initial weights influence heavily upon the property of BP networks, each group contained 20 nets. All nets were tested under damage conditions. Three nets were chosen as the representatives in terms of fault tolerance. Net 1 and net 2 were the best networks in group 1 and group 2, respectively. However, net 3 was the medium one in group 3. The three nets required 1500, 1500 and 8988 training epochs, respectively. Table 2 shows the parameters of net 3.

Table 2   Parameters of Net 3

Hidden Nodes #	Weights of Hidden Nodes		Biases of Hidden Nodes	Weights of Output Nodes	Bias of Output Node
1	41.610142	-12.290730	-4.564821	-6.255763	
2	41.610153	12.290729	6.585641	-6.306289	
3	41.610153	-12.290731	-4.566183	-6.255565	-3.137727
4	41.610134	12.290734	-4.543042	6.255797	
5	41.610146	12.290732	-6.562265	-6.306049	
6	41.610149	-12.290729	6.562169	6.305992	

For above 3 nets, exhaustive testing was feasible to calculate f_n and $P_{misclass}$. Some f_n are shown in table 3. When n is definite, the fraction of misclassifications of net 3 is the lowest, that of net 1 is the highest. As the net size of net 1 is smaller than those of net 2 and net 3, the fault tolerance of the three nets can not be compared according to f_n.

Table 3   Fraction of misclassifications

		# Connection Faults						# Hidden Node Faults	
		1	2	3	4	5	6	1	2
Fraction of	Net 1	33.333	45.000	50.000	50.000	50.000	50.000	37.500	50.500
Misclassifications	Net 2	4.167	12.581	20.986	27.941	33.248	37.292	12.500	25.833
f_n (%)	Net 3	0	0.163	5.423	13.211	20.780	27.627	0	13.333

Table 4   Probability of Misclassification

| Fault Probability P_f | Probability of Misclassification $P_{misclass}$ | | | | | |
	Connection faults			Hidden node faults		
	Net 1	Net 2	Net 3	Net 1	Net 2	Net 3
0.001	1.997×10^{-3}	7.565×10^{-4}	2.900×10^{-7}	7.498×10^{-4}	7.501×10^{-4}	1.997×10^{-6}
0.002	3.987×10^{-3}	1.526×10^{-3}	1.318×10^{-6}	1.499×10^{-3}	1.500×10^{-3}	7.975×10^{-6}
0.005	9.919×10^{-3}	3.908×10^{-3}	1.113×10^{-5}	3.744×10^{-3}	3.753×10^{-3}	4.961×10^{-5}
0.010	1.968×10^{-2}	8.116×10^{-3}	6.302×10^{-5}	7.475×10^{-3}	7.512×10^{-3}	1.969×10^{-4}
0.050	9.224×10^{-2}	4.991×10^{-2}	4.406×10^{-3}	3.688×10^{-2}	3.770×10^{-2}	4.624×10^{-3}
0.100	1.703×10^{-1}	1.127×10^{-1}	2.523×10^{-2}	7.250×10^{-2}	7.539×10^{-2}	1.711×10^{-2}
0.900	4.999×10^{-1}	5.008×10^{-1}	4.986×10^{-1}	4.725×10^{-1}	4.739×10^{-1}	4.521×10^{-1}

Table 4 shows $P_{misclass}$ under some damage levels. It is seen from the table that the fault tolerance of net 2 is only slightly higher than that of net 1. This implies that the conventional BP training fails to effectively exploit redundancy in terms of improving fault tolerance. If P_f is quite small (<2%), net 3 is clearly superior to the other nets, providing at least an order-of-magnitude enhancement in fault tolerance. However, $P_{misclass}$ of each network gradually approaches 0.5 as P_f increases toward 1. Generally speaking, P_f is small in practice. Hence the modified training algorithm is effective in promoting the fault tolerance of BP networks.

4.3 A fault diagnosis problem

Three groups of BP networks were generated to diagnose faults in a video amplifier circuit[10]. Totally 20 single faults of 9 components (5 triodes, 4 Zenar diodes) were considered. In order for fault components to be isolated, 5 test nodes and 2 stimuli were required. Hence there were 10 test voltages obtained, but only 6 of them were needed to perform the above diagnosis task. The 6 test voltage deviations from the nominal values were then calculated and composed the 6-dimensional input vector. Each BP network had 6 input nodes, one for each element of the input vector, and 9 output nodes, one for each component under test. The desired output corresponding to the faulty component was -0.5. The others were 0.5.

Group 1: $6 \times 4 \times 9$ networks, trained by the conventional BP algorithm, $\varepsilon \leq 10^{-12}$.

Group 2: $6 \times 12 \times 9$ networks, trained by the conventional BP algorithm, $\varepsilon \leq 10^{-12}$.

Group 3: $6 \times 12 \times 9$ networks, trained by the modified algorithm, $\varepsilon \leq 10^{-12}$, $M=4$, $\sigma^{(2)}=8$, $\gamma^{(1)}=1.5$, $\gamma^{(2)}=1.1$, $\xi^{(1)}=\xi^{(2)}=0.1$, $\alpha^{(1)}=\alpha^{(2)}=0.001$.

Three representative nets were correspondingly selected from above three groups. Net 1, net 2 and net 3 required 3000, 2601 and 3270 training epochs, respectively. In this example, $P_{misclass}$ were determined from Eq. (19). Some $P_{misclass}$ are shown in table 5. Clearly, net 2 is more fault tolerant than net 1, but less fault tolerant than net 3. Although merely increasing the size of the hidden layer sometimes could enhance fault tolerance of BP network, the enhancement is limited. The experimental results once again demonstrate that the modified learning algorithm is highly suitable for improving the fault tolerance of BP networks.

Table 5   Probability of Misclassification

Fault Probability p_f	Probability of Misclassification $P_{misclass}$					
	Connection Faults			Hidden Node Faults		
	Net 1	Net 2	Net 3	Net 1	Net 2	Net 3
0.001	1.103×10^{-3}	1.626×10^{-4}	4.678×10^{-6}	7.485×10^{-4}	1.637×10^{-4}	0
0.002	2.526×10^{-3}	2.971×10^{-4}	2.339×10^{-5}	1.351×10^{-3}	3.520×10^{-4}	3.509×10^{-6}
0.005	6.181×10^{-3}	8.070×10^{-4}	1.708×10^{-4}	3.228×10^{-3}	1.037×10^{-3}	4.678×10^{-5}
0.010	1.208×10^{-2}	1.697×10^{-3}	7.006×10^{-4}	6.531×10^{-3}	2.034×10^{-3}	2.596×10^{-4}
0.050	5.324×10^{-2}	1.519×10^{-2}	1.273×10^{-2}	3.200×10^{-2}	1.257×10^{-2}	5.487×10^{-3}
0.100	9.197×10^{-2}	3.806×10^{-2}	3.769×10^{-2}	6.163×10^{-2}	2.831×10^{-2}	1.849×10^{-2}
0.900	1.368×10^{-1}	1.111×10^{-1}	1.069×10^{-1}	2.826×10^{-1}	2.280×10^{-1}	1.711×10^{-1}

5   Conclusions

Fault tolerance is a particularly important property when neural networks are implemented in hardware. Traditional BP training does not make best use of any redundancy in the network. This paper therefore proposes a modified algorithm that can bring the BP network's potential fault tolerant capability into full play. Nevertheless, the new algorithm needs more training epochs. Moreover, during each training epoch, additional computations are required to determine the influence degree of each weight. Thus the modified algorithm is time consuming. Since the network needs only be constructed once, this should be an acceptable tradeoff.

Acknowledgment

The work reported in this paper is sponsored by National Natural Science Foundation of China.

References

[1]   C.Neti *et al.*, "Maximally fault tolerant neural networks," *IEEE Trans. on Neural Networks*, Vol.3, No.1, pp. 14-23, 1992.

[2]   R.D.Clay *et al.*, "Fault tolerance training improves generalization and robustness," *Proc. IJCNN'92*, Baltimore, 1992, pp. 769-774.

[3]   D.S.Phataket *et al.*, "Complete and partial fault tolerance of feedforward neural nets," *IEEE Trans. on Neural Networks*, Vol.6, No.2, pp.446-456, 1995.

[4]   M.D.Emmerson *et al.*, "Determining and improving the fault tolerance of multilayer perceptrons in a pattern-recognition application,". *IEEE Trans. on Neural Networks*, Vol.4, No.5, pp.788-793,1993.

[5]   I.C.Jou *et al.*, "Analysis of hidden nodes for multi-layer perceptron neural networks," *Pattern Recognition*, Vol.27, No.6, pp.859-864, 1994.

[6]   D.E.Rumelhart *et al.*, Parallel Distributed Processing. MIT Press, 1986.

[7]   Sixin Xu *et al.*, "A fast learning method and application for the neural toward-networks," *Control and Decision*, Vol.8, No.4, pp.284-288,1993.

[8]   A.F.Murray *et al.*, "Synaptic weight noise during multilayer perceptron training: fault tolerance and training improvements," *IEEE Trans. on Neural Networks*, Vol.4, No.4, pp.722-725,1993.

[9]   T.R.Damarla *et al.*, "Fault tolerance of neural networks," *Proc. Southeastcon*, New York, 1991, pp. 328-331.

[10]   W.Hochwald *et al.*, "A DC approach for analog fault dictionary determination," *IEEE Trans. on Circuits and System*. Vol.26, No.7, pp.523-529, 1979.

A study of the effectiveness of Meta Neural Networks in RPROP parameter adaptation

Colin McCormack

Dept. of Computer Science,
University College Cork,
Cork, Ireland.
`colin@odyssey.ucc.ie`

Abstract

This paper proposes an application independent method of automating learning rule parameter selection using a form of supervisor neural network, known as a Meta Neural Network, to alter the value of a learning rule parameter during training. The Meta Neural Network is trained using data generated by observing the training of a neural network and recording the effects of the selection of various values for the η^- parameter of the RPROP learning rule. Experiments are undertaken to see how this method performs by using it to adapt this global parameter of the RPROP learning rule and comparing the results with more conventional methods.

1 Introduction

Despite the development of more efficient learning rules it remains necessary to manually select appropriate learning rule parameter values in order to achieve an acceptable solution. Two of the major problems associated with the selection of suitable parameters are the erratic nature of the quality of the solution (where quality can be defined as the speed of convergence and the accuracy of the resultant network) and the waste of resources used to train an inappropriately initialised network.

The goal of this paper is to contribute towards a learning method which requires as little intervention or initialisation as possible. The method presented in this paper reduces the amount of information needed to use a learning rule without reducing the quality of the solution.

This paper investigates a method of parameter adaptation which involves the use of a separate neural network (called a Meta Neural Network) to select appropriate values for the η^- parameter of the RPROP learning rule. We look at the results obtained when a standard RPROP rule and a set of Meta Neural Networks are applied to four benchmark problems.

1.1 RPROP

Resilient Backpropagation (RPROP) [1] is a local adaptive learning scheme. In it the size of the derivative is taken to indicate the direction of the weight update. The size of the weight update, $\Delta w_{ij}^{(t)}$, is determined by a weight update value $\Delta_{ij}^{(t)}$, where t is the current epoch and i, j are the nodes adjoining the weight being updated. The weight update value is adjusted as training is carried out. The initial value of all Δ_{ij} is 0.1.

The adaptation rules for the RPROP algorithm are:

$$\Delta w_{ij}^{(t)} = \begin{cases} -\Delta_{ij}^{(t)}, & if\ \dfrac{\delta E^{(t)}}{\delta w_{ij}} > 0 \\[2mm] +\Delta_{ij}^{(t)}, & if\ \dfrac{\delta E^{(t)}}{\delta w_{ij}} < 0 \\[2mm] 0, & else \end{cases} \quad where \quad \Delta_{ij}^{(t)} = \begin{cases} \eta^+ * \Delta_{ij}^{(t-1)}, & if\ \dfrac{\delta E^{(t-1)}}{\delta w_{ij}} * \dfrac{\delta E^{(t)}}{\delta w_{ij}} > 0 \\[2mm] \eta^- * \Delta_{ij}^{(t-1)}, & if\ \dfrac{\delta E^{(t-1)}}{\delta w_{ij}} * \dfrac{\delta E^{(t)}}{\delta w_{ij}} < 0 \\[2mm] \Delta_{ij}^{(t-1)}, & else \end{cases}$$

Where $\dfrac{\delta E^{(t)}}{\delta w_{ij}}$ denotes the summed gradient information (slope) over all patterns in the training set and $0 < \eta^- < 1 < \eta^+$. The value of η^- is usually 0.5 and η^+ is set to 1.2.

Currently RPROP appears to be the most effective supervised learning rule [2],[7]. This paper shows that the performance of RPROP can be improved further by adding a supervisor network to make suggestions for parameter values.

2 Experimental Description

The experiments performed investigate the effectiveness of using a Meta Neural Network to adapt the η^- parameter of RPROP. A Meta Neural Network (MNN) is a form of supervisor neural network which makes suggestions to a conventional learning rule for the values of various parameters. The earliest work on MNN's [3] proposed a system which made suggestions for weight and parameter values, previous work in the area of parameter selection used a MNN to adjust the ε parameter for the Quickpropagation [4] learning rule [5]. In this paper four different MNN's are evaluated, one which uses its experience of learning on the same problem domain as the network it is aiding and three which use experience of learning on a different problem domain.

2.1 MNN Methodology

The scheme for creating a MNN to aid a conventional neural network is composed of three stages. In the first stage data for training the MNN is created, in the second stage the MNN is trained and in the third stage the MNN is used to guide a conventional learning rule.

In stage 1 a backtracking system was set up which allowed a learning algorithm to see the results of the selection of the next η value. Backtracking allows the learning rule to backtrack from a parameter value choice that does not lead to a short term decrease in error value. At each epoch potential η values are evaluated with the η value leading to the greatest reduction in error in the training set being retained and the training process continued. The value of η is limited to six values (in the range 0.3 to 0.8) and at each epoch η is allowed to increase or decrease by 0.1 or remain at the current value, these three η values are then evaluated. After the evaluation the results are used to augment a set S with the current network slope, the previous network slope and the action (increment/maintain/decrement) which produced the best value of η (i.e. the value of η which caused the largest reduction in error).

In stage 2 the set S is used as a training set for a MNN, where the inputs are: current network slope, previous network slope and the output is a single value which indicated whether the value of η increased, decreased or remained the same. The learning rule used to train the MNN was RPROP, as described above.

In stage 3 at each epoch the RPROP learning rule passes the value of the current network slope and the previous network slope to the MNN which suggests an increase/decrease or no change in the value of η. The upper and lower bounds for η are 0.3 and 0.8.

3 Evaluation of the Meta Neural Networks

3.1 Benchmark problem description

Four benchmark problems, the Thyroid problem, the Building problem, the Soybean problem and the Heart problem are used to evaluate the effectiveness of MNN's. These problems are also used to produce data for the MNN's which are in turn trained and evaluated. The problems are taken from a comprehensive study of neural network benchmarks [6] and have seen wide use in AI and Neural Network literature. The problems are referred to in [6] as 'Thyroid a', 'Building a', 'Soybean a' and 'Heart a'. A description of each problems attributes and the structure of the network used with this problem is given in Table 1. All the networks used had full feed forward connections.

Problem	Nr. of Inputs	Nr. of Outputs	Nr. of Examples	Network Used
Thyroid	21	3	7200	21-7-3
Building	14	3	4208	14-16-3
Soybean	82	19	683	82-32-19
Heart	35	2	920	35-7-2

Table 1: Benchmark problem description

3.2 Result Evaluation

The set of available examples is divided into three sets: a training set is used to train the network, a validation set is used to evaluate the quality of the network during training and to measure overfitting, finally a test set is used at the end of training to evaluate the resultant network. In the series of experiments undertaken 50% of the problems total available examples are allocated for the training set, 25% for the validation set and 25% for the test set.

The error measure, E, used was the squared error percentage [6], this was derived from the normalisation of the mean squared error to reduce its dependence on the number of coefficients in the problem representation and on the range of output values used.

$$E = 100.\frac{o_{max} - o_{min}}{N.P} \sum_{p=1}^{P} \sum_{i=1}^{N} (o_{pi} - tr_{pi})^2 \quad \text{where } o_{min} \text{ and } o_{max} \text{ are the minimum and maximum values of the}$$

output coefficients used in the problem, N is the number of output nodes of the network, P is the number of patterns in the data set, o is the network output and tr is the target value.

Training progress P [6] is measured after a training strip of length k, which is a sequence of k epochs numbered n+1,...,n+k where n is divisible by k:

$$P_k(t) = 1000. \left(\frac{\sum_{t' \in t-k+1...t} E_{tr}(t')}{k.\min_{t' \in t-k+1...t} E_{tr}(t')} - 1 \right), \text{ where } E_{tr} \text{ is the training set error. In the experiments detailed in this}$$

paper k=5. The training progress gives the extent of the difference between the average training set error in the strip and the minimum training set error and is used to determine when the network has reached a point where no further training is effectively taking place. In the experiments performed in this paper training is halted when the progress P drops below 0.1.

Since the goal of this work is to contribute towards a method whereby neural networks can be used with little or no initialisation or intervention the errors reported are those obtained at the cessation of training as opposed to the minimum error obtained during training.

4 Experiments

Each MNN is trained using a set S derived from backtracking on a particular problem. The networks trained using these MNN to suggest parameter values are known as 'Thyroid MNN' (i.e. the MNN was trained using results obtained from training on the Thyroid problem), 'Building MNN', 'Soybean MNN' and 'Heart MNN'.

In the experiments ten networks were trained using: the normal RPROP parameter ($\eta^- = 0.5$), RPROP using the best η^- values obtained from a previous set of experiments which evaluated the result of each of the η^- values in the range 0.3 to 0.8 (this meant that the best η^- value was found by trial and error) and four MNN each of which was trained using a set S from each problem. The η^- values which resulted in the most accurate results obtained by trial and error were: $\eta^- = 0.3$ for the Thyroid problem, 0.5 for the Building problem, 0.7 for the Soybean problem and 0.5 for the Heart problem, these are listed in the results under the key 'Optimal Rprop'. For the Building and Heart problems the 'optimal' values were equivalent to the parameter value for normal Rprop ($\eta^- = 0.5$) so no additional 'optimal' results exist for these problems. The use of the word 'optimal' in this paper implies the best result from a set of pre-tested training's as opposed to a best possible result. This trial and error approach is one of the most popular means of ascertaining the correct learning rule parameters and was undertaken to get an accurate reflection of how well the MNN would perform in realistic circumstances.

All initial learning rule and network architecture parameters were fixed apart from the initial weight set which was random for each network. The average of the results for the training set (Train), validation set (Valid) and the test set (Test) are presented in figures 1-4. The standard deviation for the validation set is illustrated in the form of an error bar. This particular standard deviation was chosen because it was usually the most significant and gave a good idea of the consistency of the learning rule used. The average number of epochs taken to reach cessation of the training process is included in the figures as a column.

5 Results

5.1 Analysis

Results are evaluated with the best network being judged to be the one which produced the lowest training, validation and test set errors although the average number of epochs taken to reach cessation is also deemed relevant.

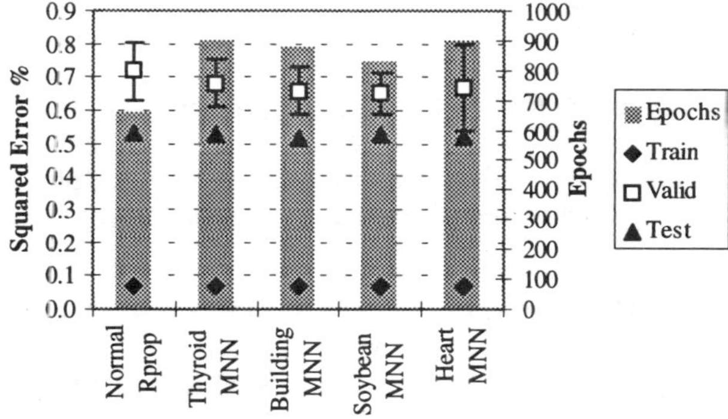

Figure 1: Results for the Building problem.

Figure 1 (left) illustrates the results for the Building problem. It shows that the different methods of training do not make a significant difference to the results. Indeed the use of the normal parameters values seems to produce the lowest average epochs taken to reach cessation. For the errors however the learning rule using the Building MNN is the best training method followed by the rule using the Soybean MNN.

The standard deviations indicate that using a MNN is usually as consistent or more consistent than using the normal η^- parameter value. This however is not the case with the Heart MNN which returns a credible performance as regards average error values but which has a high standard deviation indicating it is the most inconsistent method of training for this problem.

Figure 2 (right) shows the results for the Thyroid problem. These results show that all the learning rules using MNN significantly outperform both the normal η^- parameter values and the 'optimal' η^- value chosen by trial and error. The number of epochs taken for the MNN are at least half those taken for the normal Rprop and at least 20% lower than those for the 'optimal' η^- value.

Standard deviations for the MNNs are also substantially lower than those obtained for normal or optimal Rprop.

The best performer is the Thyroid MNN but the other MNNs are not significantly worse. The Building MNN and Heart MNN do

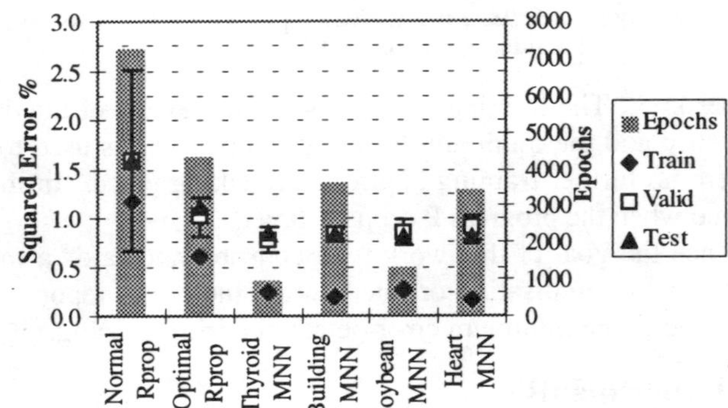

Figure 2: Results for the Thyroid problem.

however take almost three times as long as the Thyroid MNN to reach approximately the same accuracy.

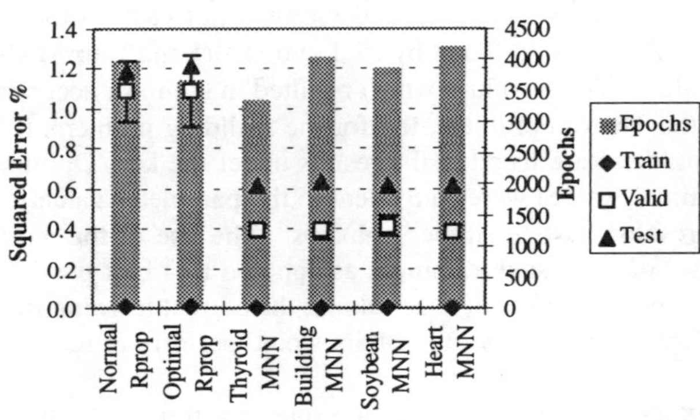

Figure 3: Results for the Soybean problem.

Figure 3 (left) shows the results for the Soybean problem. The learning rules using the MNNs have obtained a performance 50% better than using normal or 'optimal' parameter values. For this problem in fact the 'optimal' values yield a worse performance than the normal values.

Standard deviation for the MNNs is also dramatically lower than that for the normal and 'optimal' parameters.

The best performer is the learning rule using the Heart MNN, but this is beaten by the Thyroid MNN if the amount of epochs is taken into account.

Figure 4 (right) illustrates the results for the Heart problem. The best result is obtained using a Thyroid MNN with the Soybean MNN coming second. The Building MNN doesn't fare so well being marginally outperformed in the test set error by the normal Rprop, it is however returning a lower average training/ validation set error and standard deviation.

The standard deviations for the MNNs are lower than that for the Normal Rprop.

The results for the Heart MNN are however a major disappointment. Not only is it outperformed by the normal Rprop but it also takes on average over twice as long to reach cessation. This result

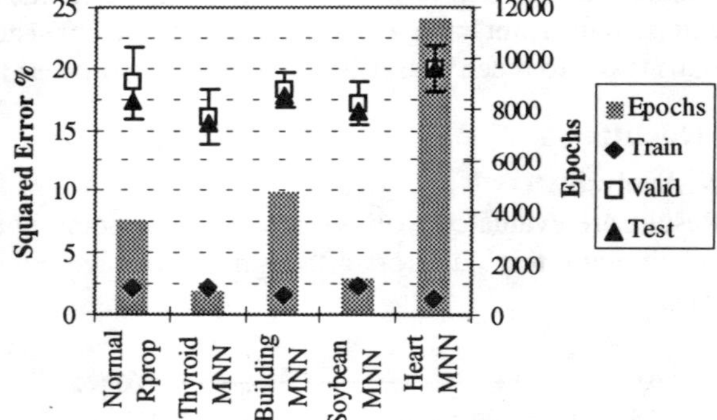

Figure 4: Results for the Heart problem.

represents the only time out of sixteen uses of a MNN that using a MNN is a disadvantage. On the plus side the test and validation set errors for the Heart MNN are only about 10% worse than the Normal Rprop result.

5.2 Result summary

In every case except one (the Heart MNN applied to the Heart problem) the performance of a MNN exceeds that of a normal Rprop parameter value or an 'optimal' parameter chosen using trial and error.

The standard deviation for all but one of the MNNs (again the Heart MNN this time applied to the Building problem) are equal to or lower than those obtained using a normal method of training, this indicates that a MNN will give a consistent performance and can be relied on to produce better results than a normal training procedure.

For the experimental results detailed above the Thyroid MNN is the best overall performer, it may be that some MNN are better than others (but all the MNN we have seen offer an improvement over normal methods) but it is more likely that the Thyroid MNN is better because its training set contained more examples than the ones used to train the other MNNs.

6 Conclusion

A Meta Neural Network is a way of acquiring and using information about the learning mechanism of a neural network. In this paper we have seen that a MNN trained using knowledge derived from an unrelated problem domain can be used to outperform a learning rule which has had the optimal parameter values for that problem domain preselected by trial and error. The advantage of a MNN scheme is that a MNN's effectiveness on a problem is independent of the MNN's original training problem and its associated architecture. MNN's can thus be trained once and used successfully on different problem domains. While a MNN may not always outperform a conventional learning method the use of a 'bad' MNN does not result in a significant degradation in performance and when a MNN does perform well the benefits are significant. This approach compares favourably with the more usual approaches of developing more general learning rules (which may not be optimal for every type of problem), developing specialised learning rules which are only suitable for specific types of problem and using ad-hoc methods of tuning parameter values in that it makes an improvement to an existing general learning rule while reducing the amount of parameters needed for that rule.

This paper shows a successful approach to adaptation of the η^- parameter of the RPROP learning rule. To improve the capabilities of neural networks it may be worthwhile considering the incorporation of parameter adapting MNN's into learning rules so they can be more flexible, more generally applicable, produce a better quality solution and require less intervention

References

[1] Riedmiller, M. and Braun, H. A direct adaptive method for faster Backpropagation learning: The RPROP algorithm. *Procs of the IEEE International Conference on Neural Networks, San Francisco.* 586-591. (1993)

[2] Riedmiller, M. Advanced supervised learning in multi-layered perceptrons: From Backpropagation to adaptive learning algorithms. *Computer Standards and Interfaces.* vol 16 part 3. 265-278. (1994)

[3] Naik, D.K. Meta-Neural Networks that learn by learning. *IJCNN '90.* I 437-442. (1990)

[4] Fahlman, S. Faster-Learning variations on Back-Propagation: An Empirical Study. *Proceedings of the 1988 Connectionist Models Summer School.* Morgan Kaufmann. (1988)

[5] McCormack, C. Parameter Adaptation using a Meta Neural Network. *Proceedings of the World Conference on Neural Networks, Washington D.C.* Vol 3, 147-150. (1995)

[6] Prechelt, L. PROBEN1: A set of neural network benchmark problems and benchmarking rules. *Technical Report 21/94, Dept. of Informatics, University of Karlsruhe, Germany.* ftp://ftp.ira.uka.de/pub/neuron/proben1.tar.gz. (1994)

[7] Schiffmann, W. Optimisation of the Backpropagation Algorithm for training multilayer perceptrons. *Technical report, Dept of Physics, University of Kobelnz Germany.* ftp://archive.cis.ohio-state.edu/pub/neuroprose/schiff.bp_speedup.ps.Z (1993)

Neural Network Classification of Non-Uniform Data

K. Y. Michael Wong and H. C. Lau
Department of Physics, The Hong Kong University of Science and Technology,
Clear Water Bay, Kowloon, Hong Kong.
E-mail addresses: phkywong@usthk.ust.hk, phhclau@usthk.ust.hk

Abstract— **We consider a model of non-uniform data, which resembles typical data for system faults in diagnostic classification tasks. Phase diagrams illustrate the role reversal of the informators and background as parameters change. With no prior knowledge about the non-uniformity, the Bayesian classifier may perform worse than other neural network classifiers for few examples.**

1   Introduction

Neural networks have been widely applied in general classification tasks such as the diagnosis of system faults or medical illnesses [1, 2]. They have the advantages of being tolerant to noisy and incomplete data. While noises are rather uniform in many recognition tasks, they are much less uniform and highly correlated in many diagnostic tasks. Some symptoms are more essential to a given fault, and are therefore more informative than the others, and some group of symptoms have a high correlation in their occurrence.

In this paper we consider a model of non-uniform data, which resembles typical data for system faults in diagnostic classification tasks, and study the generalization performance of neural network classifiers for this model, presenting both analytic and simulation results. The model is characterized by the presence of a minority of informative bits (or the "informators") among a background of less informative ones. Phase diagrams for generalization performances will be found in log-log plots of background error rates and training set size, and they exhibit a rich behaviour when the informator strength and frequency varies. While it is not surprising that the informative bits help classification, it is interesting to see that the Bayesian estimator is not always the best when examples are few. Implications to the choice of classifiers will be discussed.

2   The Informator Model of Data

We consider a data model with N input bits, which model the symptoms, and K output classes, which model the possible faults to be diagnosed. For an output class k, the ith input bit S_{ki} may either be 1, indicating that a symptom has occurred, or 0, indicating that the symptom is absent. The probability of symptom p_{ki} for an ith bit belonging to the kth class is assumed to be independent of each other. For each class k, there are C randomly chosen "informators", whose probability of occurrence p_{ki} has a typical magnitude of the order p_c, and $C \ll N$. All the other $N - C$ bits have a low probability of occurrence, i.e. $p_{ki} \sim p_0 \ll p_c$ and can be considered as background.

For convenience we assume that the prior probabilities for all output classes are the same; for the background bits, $p_{ki} = (1 \pm 1/2)p_0$ with probability $1/2$ respectively, whereas for the informators, $p_{ki} = p_0^\epsilon$ with $0 \leq \epsilon < 1$. So there are three types of symptoms: informators, strong and weak backgrounds. All bits contain information about the output class, but the informators are more informative than the background bits. Below, p_0 lies in the range $1/N \leq p_0 < 1$ and will be referred to as the *error rate*, $\bar{\epsilon} \equiv 1 - \epsilon$ as the *informator strength*, and $\gamma \equiv \ln C / \ln N$ as the *informator frequency*.

An example generated by the data model consists of the N input bits and the associated output class. To build a classifier, a set of P training examples per output class is provided. To test the performance of the resultant classifier, an example is drawn randomly from the data model, independent of the training set. The averaged probability that the example is classified correctly is the *generalization performance*.

3   The Classification Rules

(a) **The Optimal Classifier:** First we argue that the optimal classifier can be implemented by a single-layer winner-take-all network. Suppose that the details of the above data model are known, namely that the error probability for input bit of type α is p_α, and that the fraction of type α error per example is f_α. From the training set one observes that there are n_{ki} errors for the ith bit out of the P examples of class k. As shown in Appendix A, the most probable output class $F(\mathbf{S})$ is

$$F(\mathbf{S}) = \arg \max_k [\sum_i \ln P(S_i|k)] = \arg \max_k (h_k), \tag{1}$$

where $h_k \equiv \sum_i J_{ki}S_i + J_{k0}$ is the local field for output class k, and $J_{ki} = \ln[\sum_\alpha f_\alpha p_\alpha^{n_{ki}+1}(1-p_\alpha)^{P-n_{ki}}] - \ln[\sum_\alpha f_\alpha p_\alpha^{n_{ki}}(1-p_\alpha)^{P-n_{ki}+1}]$, $J_{k0} = \sum_i \{\ln[\sum_\alpha f_\alpha p_\alpha^{n_{ki}}(1-p_\alpha)^{P-n_{ki}+1}] - \ln[\sum_\alpha f_\alpha p_\alpha^{n_{ki}}(1-p_\alpha)^{P-n_{ki}}]\}$, which can be implemented by a single-layer winner-take-all network with weights J_{ki}.

(b) **The Bayesian Classifier:** Of course, the data model is seldom known *a priori*. We will thus consider a Bayesian approach with no prior knowledge, which would use the bit frequencies for the estimated probabilities, resulting in the weights $J_{ki} = \ln(n_{ki}/P) - \ln(1 - n_{ki}/P)$ and $J_{k0} = \sum_i \ln(1 - n_{ki}/P)$ [3]. Zero values of n_{ki}/P or $1 - n_{ki}/P$ are replaced by a small number δ. In the limit of many examples, its behaviour will approach the optimal classifier.

(c) **The Hebb Classifier:** It is equivalent to the maximum likelihood estimation [4] prescribed by

$$J_{ki} = \frac{1}{P} \sum_{\mu_k} \xi_i^{\mu_k} = \frac{n_{ki}}{P}, \tag{2}$$

where $\xi_i^{\mu_k}$ is the ith input of the μ_kth example belonging to class k.

(d) **The Perceptron Classifier:** It learns the examples iteratively [5]. If during a learning step, the local field for the desired class of the presented example cannot exceed other outputs by a learning threshold τ, update of weights take place:

$$\Delta J_{ki} = \begin{cases} n\eta S_i & \text{if } k \text{ is the desired output, and } n = \text{number of outputs exceeding } h_k - \tau, \\ -\eta S_i & \text{if } h_k + \tau \text{ exceeds the desired output field}, \\ 0 & \text{otherwise.} \end{cases} \tag{3}$$

Here η is the learning rate. The learning threshold is introduced to increase the stability of the network. Learning proceeds until a satisfactory percentage of examples are classified correctly.

4   The Theory

The generalization performance f_g for output class 1 of the winner-take-all classifier is given by

$$f_g = \langle \prod_{k>1} \Theta(h_1 - h_k) \rangle_{\mathbf{S}}, \tag{4}$$

where Θ is the step function, and the averaging is performed over input states $\mathbf{S}$ randomly generated from class 1. In the large N limit, the phase diagram is conveniently studied in terms of the error rate exponent $x \equiv \ln p_0 / \ln N$ and the training set size exponent $y \equiv \ln P / \ln N$. Generalization is determined by the exponent of the signal-to-noise ratio, $E \equiv 2 \ln \mathrm{SNR} / \ln N$; results for the Bayesian and Hebb rules are outlined in Appendix B. If $E > 0$, the classifier generalizes perfectly, i.e. $f_g = 1$; if $E < 0$, the classifier generalizes randomly, i.e. $f_g = 1/K$. At the boundary separating the two phases, $E = 0$ and f_g rises steeply in the large N limit, i.e. the generalization undergoes a phase transition.

Three regimes can be identified in the phase diagram. (1) The white regime: for few examples, namely $P \ll p_0^{-\epsilon}$ (or $y < -\epsilon x$), all except a few n_{ki} are 0, and the informators and backgrounds are not distinguishable. (2) The grey regime: when $p_0^{-\epsilon} \ll P \ll p_0^{-1}$ (or $-\epsilon x < y < -x$), n_{ki} for the background bits remain dominated by zeros but for the informators, $n_{ki} \gg 1$. Classification relies heavily on the informators. (3) The black regime: for sufficient examples, namely $P \gg p_0^{-1}$ (or $y > -x$), $n_{ki} \gg 1$ for all bits. Both the informators and backgrounds contribute to classification, and the Bayesian probabilities can be estimated accurately.

Fig. 1 shows the rich behaviour in the phase diagrams for the Bayesian classifier when the informator strength $\bar{\epsilon}$ varies at a given informator frequency γ. We observe the following trends:

(a) **Classification eases with error rate:** For a given error rate exponent x there is a critical training set size, with exponent y, necessary for perfect generalization, which yields the phase lines. When the error rate p_0 (or its exponent x) increases, the input background bits are more and more populous, carrying more and more information. Hence the critical training set size exponent y decreases. When x is sufficiently large, classification is easy and the critical y reaches 0. A small training set size $\sim N^0$ is already sufficient for generalization.

(b) **Classification eases with informator strength:** When the informator strength is below $(1 - \gamma)/(1 + \gamma)$, the random generalization phase is maximally bounded by the phase line $2x + y + 1 = 0$. When the informator strength increases, classification becomes easier and the random generalization phase narrows. For informator strengths $\bar{\epsilon}$ above $1 - \gamma/2$, the entire space has perfect generalization.

(c) **Backgrounds may interfere or assist classification:** This effect is most observable in the case of certainty informators ($\bar{\epsilon} = 1$). This case has to be analyzed separately, because those terms such as the first one in (8) vanish, while they contribute for $\bar{\epsilon} = 1^-$ in the large N limit. In other words, there is a discontinuity in behaviour at $\bar{\epsilon} = 1$. In the grey regime at very low values of P, almost all background weights are set to the very negative value $\ln \delta$, and classification is done with the information extracted from the informators. When P increases, the probability for the occurrence of a symptom bit in the training set is of the order Pp_0, hence the contribution to the local field of an output class is of the order $Pp_0^2 N$. When this contribution is comparable to that due to the informators, which is of the order $p_0^\epsilon C$, generalization is *interfered*. However, on further increase in P, the background bits become numerous enough, so that their information traces accumulate to *assist* the classification. A drop in generalization is thus expected around the line $(2 - \epsilon)x + y + 1 - \gamma = 0$. Indeed one finds that although the SNR exponent E is positive in the entire space, it *decreases* with training at error rates below $(\gamma - 1)/2$, reaching a minimum value of γ at intermediate training set sizes. As we will see, this leads to a performance depression for finite values of N.

(d) Weak informators may misinform: This is observed in the Hebb classifier, where generalization may become impossible if the error rates are too low, even for infinitely large training sets. This threshold error rate exists at intermediate informator strengths, namely for $(1 - \gamma)/3 < \bar{\epsilon} < 1 - \gamma$. This is because the informators help classification when they are strong, and are irrelevant when they are weak. When their strength is intermediate, they are relevant but may misinform the classifier. We may say that $1 - \gamma < \bar{\epsilon} < 1$, is the *true informator phase*, $(1 - \gamma)/3 < \bar{\epsilon} < 1 - \gamma$ the *misinformator phase*, and $0 < \bar{\epsilon} < (1 - \gamma)/3$ the *non-informator phase*. On the other hand, generalization in the Bayesian classifier is always possible for sufficiently large training sets, irrespective of the informator strength.

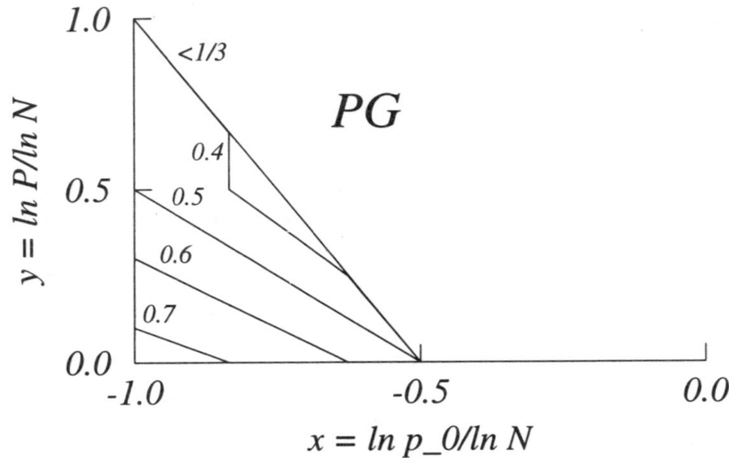

Figure 1: Phase diagram for the Bayesian classifier at informator frequency $\gamma = 0.5$ for several values of informator strength $\bar{\epsilon}$. PG represents the perfect generalization phase above the lines.

5   Simulations

To study deviations from the large N limit, we perform Monte Carlo simulations of the classifiers using an input dimension of $N = 100$ and $K = 4$ output classes. For comparison we first consider the predictions of the large N theory for the Bayesian and Hebb classifiers. With no informators ($C = 0$ or $\gamma \rightarrow -\infty$), E of both classifiers becomes $2x + y + 1$ in the white and grey regimes, and $x + 1$ in the black regime. Both have perfect generalization above the line $2x + y + 1 = 0$, except that $x = -1$ is a singular line in the black regime, where f_g tends to 0.39 at $x = -1$, but 1 elsewhere.

As shown in Fig. 2(a) for the case of no informators ($C = 0$) using the Hebb classifier, the region of poor generalization decreases with p_0, agreeing with the theory. The asymptotic generalization drops as x tends to -1, in agreement with the large N prediction that $x = -1$ is a singular line.

For one informator ($C = 1$ or $\gamma = 0$) with certainty ($\bar{\epsilon} = 1$), the generalization of the Bayesian classifier is perfect in the entire space, but marginal along the singular line $2x + y + 1 = 0$, where f_g tends to 0.55, but to 1 elsewhere. This is a consequence of the role reversal between the informators and backgrounds explained in (c) above. By comparison, marginal generalization in the Hebb classifier only exists at the singular point $(x, y) = (-1/2, 0)$, where f_g tends to 0.55, but to 1 elsewhere.

Fig. 2(b) shows the case with one informator ($C = 1$) classified by the Hebb classifier. Comparing with Fig. 2(a), the region of poor generalization is much reduced. This confirms that the informators provides a significant assistance to the classification task. The initial generalization drops near $x = -0.5$, reflecting the large N prediction that it is a singular point. Fig. 2(c) shows the same case using the perceptron classifier. The generalization performance is similar to the Hebb classifier.

Fig. 2(d) shows the case with one informator using the Bayesian classifier. Comparing with Figs. 2(b-c), generalization is poorer for intermediate training set sizes in the present case, in agreement with the line of marginal generalization predicted by the large N theory.

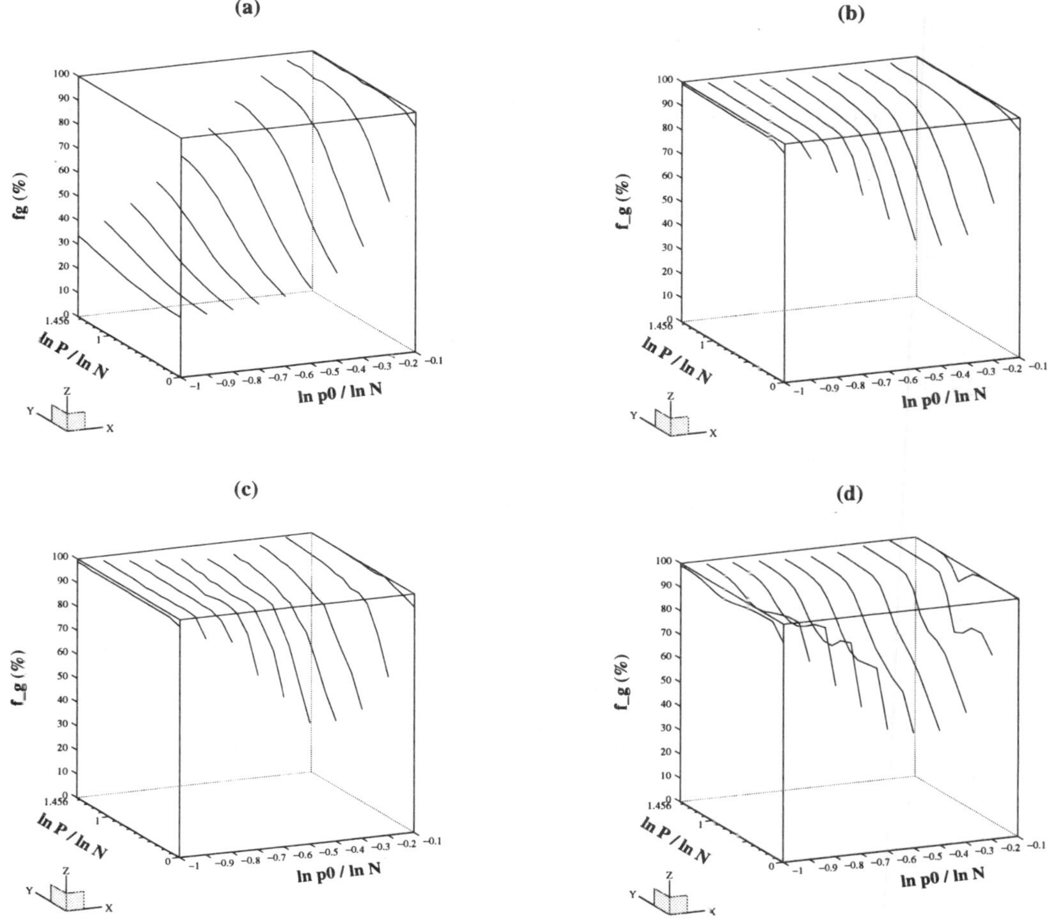

Figure 2: Simulation of the generalization performance with no informators for (a) the Hebb classifier, and with one informator for (b) the Hebb classifier, (c) the perceptron classifier, (d) the Bayesian classifier.

6   Discussions

We have studied a model of non-uniform data, in which some input bits are more informative about the output than the others. By studying the phase diagram in the space of background error rate and training set size we have demonstrated, both analytically and simulationally, that the presence of informators makes the classification task easier. When the informators are not too strong, the data is relatively uniform. Hence the Bayesian classifier performs better than other classifiers such as Hebb, as illustrated by the absence of the misinformator phase therein. However, the Bayesian classifier is not always optimal, as shown in both the theory in the large N limit, and simulations for finite size networks. When the training examples are not sufficient, the Bayesian probabilities are not estimated accurately. This is especially valid in diagnostic models such as ours, in which the probability of occurrence differs largely between the informators and backgrounds. A Bayesian approach with no prior knowledge of the non-uniformity performs poorly. On the other hand, a Hebb or a perceptron classifier is preferable in extracting the informator features with relatively few examples, though they are not necessarily optimal in the asymptotic limit of numerous examples. The complementary dependence on the informator strength implies that a combination of both classifiers may be useful in a wider range of applications.

We have tried other classifiers and using alternative representations. Using an Ising representation, i.e. healthy and erroneous bits are ± 1 respectively, the random generalization regions are widened, showing that the Ising representation is not optimal for a low error rate model such as ours. We have also found that for the resultant Hebb rule, the critical training set size increases with p_0 at low error rate, but decreases with p_0 at higher error rate, and can be explained again by the role reversal of the informators and backgrounds.

Recently, a number of hybrid expert systems for diagnosis of system faults were proposed [6, 1, 2]. In such applications the input data are very likely non-uniform. These classifiers extract features from the input data by matching them with a set of rules obtained by rule-based techniques such as CART [7]. The transformed inputs are then measures of the probabilities that these rules are matched, and are subsequently fed into a neural network for classification. Motivated by these approaches, we have used CART to preprocess the data for a perceptron, but the generalization rate is lower than without preprocessing in our model, though the perceptron always improves the CART generalization [8]. Further study on this issue is needed.

This work is supported by the Hong Kong Telecom Institute of Information Technology, HKUST.

Appendix A: The Optimal Classifer

The Bayesian probability given the examples ξ is

$$P(p_{ki} = p_\alpha | \xi) = \frac{f_\alpha p_\alpha^{n_{ki}} (1 - p_\alpha)^{P - n_{ki}}}{\sum_\alpha f_\alpha p_\alpha^{n_{ki}} (1 - p_\alpha)^{P - n_{ki}}}. \tag{5}$$

For an arbitrary input vector $\mathbf{S}$, the Bayesian probabilities for output class k are:

$$P(k|\mathbf{S}) = \prod_i P(k|S_i) = \prod_i \frac{P(S_i|k)P(k)}{P(S_i)} = \prod_i \frac{P(S_i|k)P(k)}{\sum_l P(S_i|l)P(l)} = \prod_i \frac{P(S_i|k)}{\sum_l P(S_i|l)}. \tag{6}$$

$P(S_i|k) = \sum_\alpha p_\alpha^{S_i} (1 - p_\alpha)^{1 - S_i} P(p_{ki} = p_\alpha | \xi)$, which for $S_i = 0$ and 1 reduces to $[\sum_\alpha p_\alpha P(p_{ki} = p_\alpha | \xi)]^{S_i} [\sum_\alpha (1 - p_\alpha) P(p_{ki} = p_\alpha | \xi)]^{1 - S_i}$. This yields the result of (1).

Appendix B: The Signal-to-Noise Ratios

For our proposed data model we introduce the Gaussian approximation that the local fields become Gaussian distributed in the large N limit. Their means and covariances correspond to the signals and noises. Using the permutation symmetry of the classes, only six parameters are involved: $M_1 = \langle h_1 \rangle$, $M_2 = \langle h_k \rangle$ for $k \neq 1$, $Q_1 = \langle h_1^2 \rangle - \langle h_1 \rangle^2$, $Q_2 = \langle h_k^2 \rangle - \langle h_k \rangle^2$ for $k \neq 1$, $R_1 = \langle h_1 h_k \rangle - \langle h_1 \rangle \langle h_k \rangle$ for $k \neq 1$, and $R_2 = \langle h_k h_l \rangle - \langle h_k \rangle^2$ for $k \neq l \neq 1$. The generalization performance is determined by the signal-to-noise ratio $\mathrm{SNR} \equiv \sqrt{N}(M_1 - M_2)/\sqrt{(Q_1 - 2R_1 + R_2) + (Q_2 - R_2)}$. In the white regime for the Bayesian rule, for example,

$$M_1 - M_2 \approx |\ln(P\delta)| \left(\frac{C}{N} P p_0^{2\epsilon} + \frac{1}{4} P p_0^2 \right), \tag{7}$$

$$Q_1 - 2R_1 + R_2 \approx |\ln(P\delta)|^2 \left(\frac{C}{N} P p_0^{2\epsilon}(1 - p_0^\epsilon) + \frac{5}{4} P p_0^2 \right), \tag{8}$$

$$Q_2 - R_2 \approx |\ln(P\delta)|^2 \left(\frac{C}{N} P p_0^{1+\epsilon} + P p_0^2 \right). \tag{9}$$

The SNR exponent E becomes $\max[2\epsilon x + y + \gamma, 2x + y + 1]$ in the white regime. Similarly, E becomes $\max[\epsilon x + \gamma, 2x + y + 1]$ in the grey regime, and $\max[\epsilon x + \gamma, x + 1]$ in the black regime. For the Hebb rule, the SNR exponent E becomes $\max[2\epsilon x + y + \gamma, 2x + y + 1]$ in the white regime, $2\max[2\epsilon x + y + \gamma, 2x + y + 1] - \max[3\epsilon x + 2y + \gamma, 2x + y + 1]$ in the grey regime, and $2\max[2\epsilon x + y + \gamma, 2x + y + 1] - \max[3\epsilon x + 2y + \gamma, 3x + 2y + 1]$ in the black regime.

References

[1] A. Holst and A. Lansner, "Diagnosis of Technical Equipment Using a Bayesian Neural Network", *Proceedings of the International Workshop on Applications of Neural Networks to Telecommunications*, ed. by J. Alspector, R. Goodman and T. X. Brown, Hillsdale, NJ: Lawrence Erlbaum, pp. 147-153, 1993.

[2] H. C. Lau, K. Y. Szeto, K. Y. M. Wong and D. Y. Yeung, "A Hybrid Expert System for Error Message Classification", *Proceedings of the International Workshop on Applications of Neural Networks to Telecommunications 2*, ed. by J. Alspector, R. Goodman and T. X. Brown, Hillsdale, NJ: Lawrence Erlbaum, pp. 339-346, 1995.

[3] A. Lansner and Ö. Ekeberg, "A one-layer feedback, artificial neural network with a Bayesian learning rule", *Int. J. Neural Systems*, vol. 1, pp. 77-88, 1989.

[4] R. O. Duda and P. E. Hart, *Pattern Classification and Scene Analysis* New York: Wiley, 1973.

[5] J. Sklansky and G.N. Wassel, *Pattern Classifiers and Trainable Machines*, New York: Springer-Verlag, 1981.

[6] R. M. Goodman, C. M. Higgins, J. W. Miller and P. Smyth, "Rule-Based Neural Networks for Classification and Probability Estimation", *Neural Computation*, vol. 4, pp. 781-804, 1992.

[7] L. Breiman, J. H. Friedman, R. A. Olshen and C. J. Stone, *Classification and Regression Trees*, Belmont, CA: Wadsworth, 1984.

[8] H. C. Lau, *Neural Network Classification Techniques for Diagnostic Problems*, MPhil Thesis, HKUST, 1995.

An Extension of the Back-propagation Algorithm to Quaternions

Tohru Nitta

Electrotechnical Laboratory,
1-1-4 Umezono, Tsukuba Science City Ibaraki, 305 Japan
Email: tnitta@etl.go.jp

Abstract— **A quaternary version of the back-propagation algorithm is proposed for multi-layered neural networks whose weights, threshold values, input and output signals are all quaternions. This new algorithm can be used to learn patterns consisted of quaternions in a natural way. An example was used to successfully test the new formulation.**

1   Introduction

Recently several neural network models with two- (complex-valued) or three-dimensional parameters have been proposed [4, 6, 7, 8, 9] and demonstrated to have the inherent properties such as the abilities to learn 2D or 3D affine transformations [6, 8, 10, 11, 12], and particularly the Complex-BP [6, 8] and the 3DV-BP [7] have been successfully applied to computer vision [5, 14].

This paper presents a quaternary (four-dimensional) version of the back-propagation algorithm (called *Quaternary-BP*), which can be applied to multi-layered neural networks whose weights, threshold values, input and output signals are all *quaternions*, where a quaternion is a four-dimensional number and was invented by W. R. Hamilton in 1843 [2]. We expect that Quaternary-BP can be effectively used in the fields such as robotics and computer vision in which quaternions have been found useful [1, 3]. This new algorithm was applied to a simulated example on quaternary patterns Results suggest that the new method is superior to standard BP [13].

Section 2 presents the new Quaternary-BP algorithm. The rest of the paper presents experimental results.

2   The Quaternary-BP Algorithm

2.1   A Quaternary Neuron

There appear to be several approaches for extending the standard neural networks to higher dimensions. One approach is to extend the number field, i.e. from real numbers x (1 dimension), to complex numbers $z = x + yi$ (2 dimensions; [4, 6, 8]), to quaternions $q = a + bi + cj + dk$ (4 dimensions), to octaves (8 dimensions), to sedenions (16 dimensions), $\cdots$. Another approach is to extend the dimensionality of the weights and threshold values from 1 dimension to n dimensions using n-dimensinal real valued vectors. Moreover, the latter approach has two varieties : (a) weights are n-dimensional matrices [7], (b) weights are n-dimensional vectors [9]. In this paper we use quaternions in the former approach to extend neural networks to 4 dimensions.

A model neuron used in the Quaternary-BP algorithm is as follows. The input signals, weights, thresholds and output signals are all quaternions. The activity A_n (analogous to the real activity in the standard BP) of neuron n is defined to be :

$$A_n = \sum_m S_m W_{nm} + T_n, \qquad (1)$$

where S_m is the quaternary input signal coming from the output of neuron m, W_{nm} is the quaternary weight connecting neuron m and n, T_n is the quaternary threshold value of neuron n. To obtain the quaternary output signal, convert the activity value A_n into its four parts as follows.

$$A_n = x_1 + x_2 i + x_3 j + x_4 k = x, \qquad (2)$$

where $i^2 = j^2 = k^2 = -1$, $ij = -ji = k$, $jk = -kj = i$, $ki = -ik = j$.
The output signal $f_4(x)$ is defined to be

$$f_4(x) = f(x_1) + f(x_2)i + f(x_3)j + f(x_4)k, \qquad \text{where} \quad f(x_l) = \frac{1}{1 + \exp(-x_l)}. \qquad (3)$$

The multiplication $S_m W_{nm}$ in eqn (1) should be carefully treated, because the equation $S_m W_{nm} = W_{nm} S_m$ does not hold (the non-commutative property of quternions on multiplication), which produces two kinds of quaternary neurons: one is called *normal quaternary neuron* which calculates $A_n = \sum_m S_m W_{nm} + T_n$, the other is called *inverse quaternary neuron* which calculates $A_n = \sum_m W_{nm} S_m + T_n$.

2.2   A Quaternary Neural Network

In this section, we introduce the network used in the Quaternary-BP algorithm. It has 3 layers and consists of only *normal quaternary neurons*, for the sake of simplicity.

We use $w_{ml} = w_{ml}^a + w_{ml}^b i + w_{ml}^c j + w_{ml}^d k \in \boldsymbol{H}$ for the weight between the input neuron l and the hidden neuron m (where $\boldsymbol{H}$ denotes the set of quaternions), $v_{nm} = v_{nm}^a + v_{nm}^b i + v_{nm}^c j + v_{nm}^d k \in \boldsymbol{H}$ for the weight between the hidden neuron m and the output neuron n, $\theta_m = \theta_m^a + \theta_m^b i + \theta_m^c j + \theta_m^d k \in \boldsymbol{H}$ for the threshold of the hidden neuron m, $\gamma_n = \gamma_n^a + \gamma_n^b i + \gamma_n^c j + \gamma_n^d k \in \boldsymbol{H}$ for the threshold of the output neuron n. Let $I_l = I_l^a + I_l^b i + I_l^c j + I_l^d k \in \boldsymbol{H}$ denote the input signal to the input neuron l, and let $H_m = H_m^a + H_m^b i + H_m^c j + H_m^d k \in \boldsymbol{H}$ and $O_n = O_n^a + O_n^b i + O_n^c j + O_n^d k \in \boldsymbol{H}$ denote the output signals of the hidden neuron m, and the output neuron n, respectively. Let $\Delta_n = \Delta_n^a + \Delta_n^b i + \Delta_n^c j + \Delta_n^d k = T_n - O_n \in \boldsymbol{H}$ denote the error between O_n and the target output signal $T_n = T_n^a + T_n^b i + T_n^c j + T_n^d k \in \boldsymbol{H}$ of the pattern to be learned for the output neuron n. We define the square error for the pattern p as $E_p = (1/2) \sum_{n=1}^{N} |T_n - O_n|^2$, where N is the number of output neurons,

$$|x| \stackrel{\text{def}}{=} \sqrt{x_1^2 + x_2^2 + x_3^2 + x_4^2}, \quad x = x_1 + x_2 i + x_3 j + x_4 k \in \boldsymbol{H}.$$

2.3   The Learning Algorithm

Next, we define a learning rule for the Quaternary-BP model described above. For a sufficiently small learning constant $\varepsilon > 0$, and using a steepest descent method, we can show that the weights and the thresholds should be modified according to the following equations.

$$
\begin{aligned}
\Delta v_{nm} &\stackrel{\text{def}}{=} \Delta v_{nm}^a + \Delta v_{nm}^b i + \Delta v_{nm}^c j + \Delta v_{nm}^d k \\
&= -\varepsilon \left(\frac{\partial E_p}{\partial v_{nm}^a} + \frac{\partial E_p}{\partial v_{nm}^b} i + \frac{\partial E_p}{\partial v_{nm}^c} j + \frac{\partial E_p}{\partial v_{nm}^d} k \right),
\end{aligned}
\tag{4}
$$

$$
\begin{aligned}
\Delta \gamma_n &\stackrel{\text{def}}{=} \Delta \gamma_n^a + \Delta \gamma_n^b i + \Delta \gamma_n^c j + \Delta \gamma_n^d k \\
&= -\varepsilon \left(\frac{\partial E_p}{\partial \gamma_n^a} + \frac{\partial E_p}{\partial \gamma_n^b} i + \frac{\partial E_p}{\partial \gamma_n^c} j + \frac{\partial E_p}{\partial \gamma_n^d} k \right),
\end{aligned}
\tag{5}
$$

$$
\begin{aligned}
\Delta w_{ml} &\stackrel{\text{def}}{=} \Delta w_{ml}^a + \Delta w_{ml}^b i + \Delta w_{ml}^c j + \Delta w_{ml}^d k \\
&= -\varepsilon \left(\frac{\partial E_p}{\partial w_{ml}^a} + \frac{\partial E_p}{\partial w_{ml}^b} i + \frac{\partial E_p}{\partial w_{ml}^c} j + \frac{\partial E_p}{\partial w_{ml}^d} k \right),
\end{aligned}
\tag{6}
$$

$$
\begin{aligned}
\Delta \theta_m &\stackrel{\text{def}}{=} \Delta \theta_m^a + \Delta \theta_m^b i + \Delta \theta_m^c j + \Delta \theta_m^d k \\
&= -\varepsilon \left(\frac{\partial E_p}{\partial \theta_m^a} + \frac{\partial E_p}{\partial \theta_m^b} i + \frac{\partial E_p}{\partial \theta_m^c} j + \frac{\partial E_p}{\partial \theta_m^d} k \right),
\end{aligned}
\tag{7}
$$

where Δx denotes the amount of the correction of a parameter x. The above equations (4) – (7) can be expressed as:

$$\Delta v_{nm} = \overline{H}_m \Delta \gamma_n, \tag{8}$$

$$\Delta \gamma_n = \varepsilon \left[\Delta_n^a (1 - O_n^a) O_n^a + \Delta_n^b (1 - O_n^b) O_n^b i + \Delta_n^c (1 - O_n^c) O_n^c j + \Delta_n^d (1 - O_n^d) O_n^d k \right], \tag{9}$$

$$\Delta w_{ml} = \overline{I}_l \Delta \theta_m, \tag{10}$$

$$
\begin{aligned}
\Delta \theta_m = {} & (1 - H_m^a) H_m^a \cdot Re\left[\sum_n (\Delta \gamma_n \overline{v}_{nm}) \right] + (1 - H_m^b) H_m^b \cdot Im^i\left[\sum_n (\Delta \gamma_n \overline{v}_{nm}) \right] i \\
& + (1 - H_m^c) H_m^c \cdot Im^j\left[\sum_n (\Delta \gamma_n \overline{v}_{nm}) \right] j + (1 - H_m^d) H_m^d \cdot Im^k\left[\sum_n (\Delta \gamma_n \overline{v}_{nm}) \right] k,
\end{aligned}
$$

$$\tag{11}$$

where $\overline{x} \stackrel{\text{def}}{=} x_1 - x_2 i - x_3 j - x_4 k$, $Re[x] \stackrel{\text{def}}{=} x_1$, $Im^i[x] \stackrel{\text{def}}{=} x_2$, $Im^j[x] \stackrel{\text{def}}{=} x_3$ and $Im^k[x] \stackrel{\text{def}}{=} x_4$ for a quaternion $x = x_1 + x_2 i + x_3 j + x_4 k \in \boldsymbol{H}$.

3   Simulation

An example on quaternary patterns was used to compare the performance of the new Quaternary-BP algorithm with the standard back-propagation algorithm.

We used a 1-2-1 three-layered network for the Quaternary-BP, and a 4-9-4 three-layered network for the standard BP. Table 1 shows that their *time complexities* per learning cycle are almost equal. The learning constant used in the experiment was 0.5. The initial first, second, third and fourth parts of the weights and the thresholds were chosen to be random real numbers between -0.3 and $+0.3$. The input data were presented in sequence, together with the desired output, to the net as shown in Table 2.

The results of the simulation are plotted in Fig.1. The new algorithm converged in 400 iterations, whereas the original algorithm required 600. Furthermore, the *space complexity* (i.e. the number of parameters) is almost one-third of that of the standard BP, as seen in Table 1.

Network	Time complexity			Space complexity		
	$\times$ and $\div$	$+$ and $-$	Sum	Weights	Thresholds	Sum
Quaternary-BP 1-2-1	185	152	337	16	12	28
Standard BP 4-9-4	210	116	326	72	13	85

Table 1 :   The Computational Complexity of the Quaternary-BP and the Standard BP. Time complexity means the sum of the four operations performed per learning cycle. Space complexity means the sum of the parameters (weights and thresholds).

Input	Output
$1 + i + j + k$	1
$1 + 2i + j + 2k$	i
$2 + i + 2j + k$	j
$2 + 2i + 2j + 2k$	k

Table 2 :   The Input Patterns and the Corresponding Desired Output Patterns for the Simulation. The first component of a quaternion is given to the first component of the input/output neuron 1, the second is the second component, the third is the third component, and the fourth is the fourth component in the Quaternary-BP network. The first component of a quaternion is given to the input/output neuron 1, the second is the neuron 2, the third is the neuron 3, and the fourth is the neuron 4 in the standard BP network.

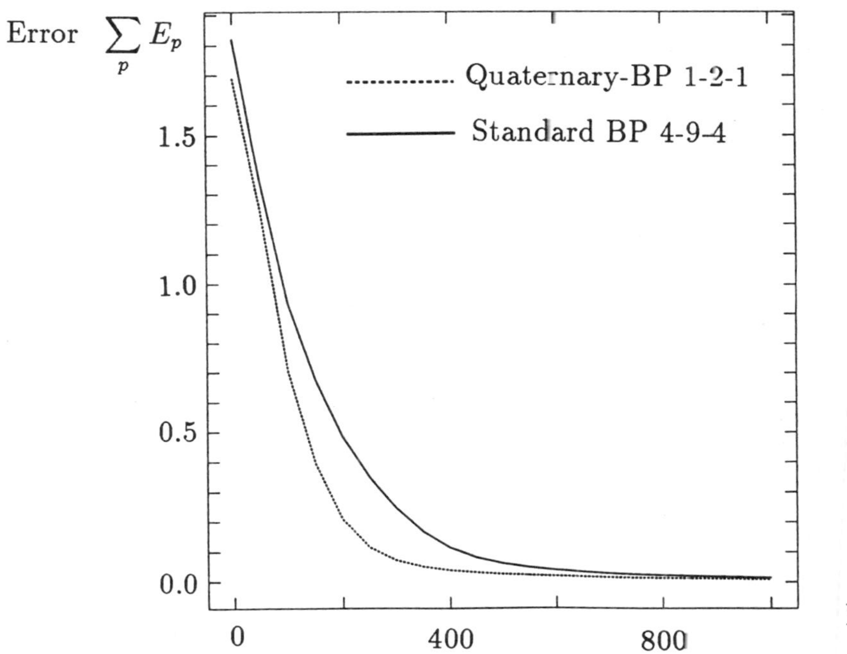

Figure 1 :   Learning Curves for the Simulation.

4   Conclusions

We have proposed a quaternary version of the back-propagation learning algorithm, where the input signals, weights, thresholds, and output signals are all quaternions. An simple example was used to test the presented method and it showed excellent performance. We expect that this new algorithm has the improved generalization ability and the inherent properties such as the abilities of the Complex-BP to learn *2D affine transformation* [6, 8] and the 3DV-BP *3D affine transformation*[12], and will demonstrate its real ability in the areas dealing with quaternions. The extension of the Quaternary-BP algorithm to fully connected neural networks will be presented in a future paper.

Acknowledgements

The author expresses his thanks to Dr.K.Ohta, Director of the Computer Science Division, and Dr.T.Higuchi, Chief of the Computational Models Section, for having an opportunity to do this study and their continual encouragement.

References

[1] Canny, J. F. (1988). *The Complexity of Robot Motion Planning*, MIT Press.

[2] Ebbinghaus, H.-D. etl al. (Eds.). (1988). *Zahlen*, Springer-Verlag Berlin Heidelderg (in German).

[3] Faugeras, O. (1993). *Three-Dimensional Computer Vision*, MIT Press.

[4] Kim, M. S. and Guest, C. C. (1990). Modification of Backpropagation Networks for Complex-valued Signal Processing in Frequency Domain. *Proc. IEEE/INNS International Joint Conference on Neural Networks*, IJCNN'90-SanDiego, June, Vol.3, pp.27–31.

[5] Miyauchi, M., Seki, M., Watanabe, A. and Miyauchi, A. (1993). Interpretation of Optical Flow through Complex Neural Network. *Proc. International Workshop on Artificial Neural Networks*, IWANN'93-Barcelona, Lecture Notes in Computer Science, Vol.686, Springer-Verlag, pp.645–650.

[6] Nitta, T. and Furuya, T. (1991). A Complex Back-propagation Learning. *Transactions of Information Processing Society of Japan*, Vol. 32, No. 10, pp.1319–1329 (in Japanese).

[7] Nitta, T. and deGaris, H. (1992). A 3D Vector Version of the Back-propagation Algorithm. *Proc. IEEE/INNS International Joint Conference on Neural Networks*, IJCNN'92-Beijing, Nov.3-6, Vol.2, pp.511–516.

[8] Nitta, T. (1993). A Complex Numbered Version of the Back-propagation Algorithm. *Proc. INNS World Congress on Neural Networks*, WCNN'93-Portland, Vol. 3, pp. 576–579.

[9] Nitta, T. (1993). A Back-propagation Algorithm for Neural Networks Based on 3D Vector Product. *Proc. IEEE/INNS International Joint Conference on Neural Networks*, IJCNN'93-Nagoya, Oct. 25–29, Vol.1, pp.589–592.

[10] Nitta, T. (1994). Structure of Learning in the Complex Numbered Back-propagation Network. *Proc. IEEE International Conference on Neural Networks*, ICNN'94-Orlando, June 28-July 2, Vol.1, pp.269–274.

[11] Nitta, T. (1994). An Analysis on Decision Boundaries in the Complex Back-propagation Network. *Proc. IEEE International Conference on Neural Networks*, ICNN'94-Orlando, June 28-July 2, Vol.2, pp.934–939.

[12] Nitta, T. (1994). Generalization Ability of the Three-dimensional Back-propagation Network. *Proc. IEEE International Conference on Neural Networks*, ICNN'94-Orlando, June 28-July 2, Vol.5, pp.2895–2900.

[13] Rumelhart, D. E. et al. (1986). *Parallel Distributed Processing*, Vol. 1, MIT press.

[14] Watanabe, A., Yazawa, N., Miyauchi, A. and Miyauchi, M. (1994). A Method to Interpret 3D Motions Using Neural Networks. *IEICE Transactions on Fundamentals of Electronics, Communications and Computer Sciences*, Vol.E77-A, No.8, pp.1363–1370.

Nonlinear Mappings and Classification of Interval Vectors Using Neural Networks

Lei Huang

Department of Automation
South China University of Technology
Guangzhou 510641, P.R.China
email:ecwqzh@scut.edu.cn

Abstract

In this paper, we present a neural network based approach for nonlinear mappings and classifications of interval vectors. Our proposed network model can be viewed as a simplified interval neural network. For nonlinear mappings of interval vectors, our proposed method can not only satisfiy the desirable properties of interval mappings, i.e., continuity and inclusion monotonicity, but have good fitting and generalization ability. In addition, it can achieve perfect classification of interval vectors.

1   Introduction

In real-world applications, available information is often uncertain and uncomplete. One of the most intuitive and most realistic ways for representing the uncertain and uncomplete information is the interval representation[4]. An uncertain value can be symbolized by the range of its possible value, that is, by its upper and lower bounds. In addition, we are often faced with handle of "don't care attributes" where "don't care" means "whatever the value of" this attribute[2]. For example, in a neural expert system for the diagnostics of hereditary muscular disease designed by Šima[9], the inputs correspond to the outcomes of various examinations, and the outputs are diagnoses or medications recommended by a doctor. In the particular case, most of the inputs are irrelevant for the determination of output diagnosis. A scheme for solving this coding problem is to encode the irrelevent or even unknown value of an expert input or output using the full interval neuron state [-1,1][9]. In short, it is significant to develop the learning algorithms of neural networks that can handle the intervals as input values and/or target values.

Three neural network based approaches for nonlinear mappings of interval vectors have been proposed[2,3,4]. In Approach One[3], the interval data are converted the numerical data by the preprocessor, and then these numerical data are handled by the classical back-propagation (BP) algorithm[8]. Approach Two can be view as a directive generalization of the BP algorithm to interval data[2,3,6], which has been successfully applied to the classification of interval patterns[1,2,6]. As for Approach Three, it employs an interval neural network with interval weights and interval biases to realize the nonlinear mappings of interval vectors[3,4]. In addition to Approach One, other methods satisfiy the desirable properties of interval mappings, i.e., continuity and inclusion monotonicity[3].

In this paper, we advance a neural network model and its learning algorithm for nonlinear mappings and classifications of interval vectors using neural networks, which can be viewed as a simplified interval neural network (SINN). Simulation results show the proposed approach can achieve perfectly nonlinear mappings and classifications of interval vectors.

2   Network Architecture of The SINN

In the SINN, the weights and the biases to hidden units are restricted to real numbers and only the weights and the biases to output units are intervals. A similar structure has been employed to construct nonlinear fuzzy regression model from the input-output patterns[5], which is different from the SINN in that it only includes one output unit and it is limited to handle crisp input vectors.

The network architecture of the SINN is shown in Figure 1. We denote the input-output relation of the SINN with n_I input units, n_H hidden units and n_O output units by interval arithmetic[7] for the interval input vector $X_P = (X_{P1}, X_{P2}, \cdots, X_{Pn_I})$ as followed:

$$\text{Input units: } O_{Pi} = X_{Pi} \quad i = 1,2,\cdots,n_I \tag{1}$$

$$\text{Hidden units: } O_{Pj} = f(Net_{Pj}) \tag{2}$$

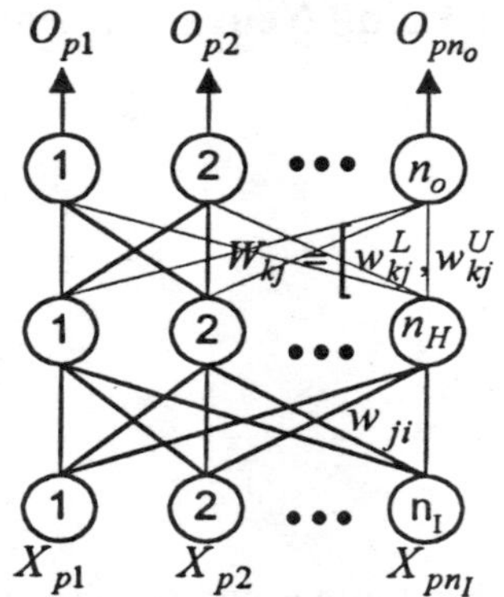

Fig.1 Network Architecture of
The SINN

$$Net_{Pj} = \sum_{i=1}^{n_I} w_{ji} O_{Pi} + \theta_j \quad j = 1, 2, \cdots, n_H \quad (3)$$

Output units: $O_{Pk} = f(Net_{Pk})$ $\qquad (4)$

$$Net_{Pk} = \sum_{j=1}^{n_H} W_{kj} O_{Pj} + \Theta_k \quad k = 1, 2, \cdots, n_O \quad (5)$$

where the weight W_{kj} and the bias Θ_k are intervals, w_{ji} and θ_j are real numbers. In the above input-output relation, the uppercase and lowercase letters represent intervals and real numbers, respectively.

For the simplicit of calculation, we assume that the interval inputs $X_{pi} = [x_{pi}^L, x_{pi}^U]$, $i = 1, 2, \cdots, n_I$ are non-negative, that is,

$$0 \le x_{pi}^L \le x_{pi}^U, \quad p=1,2,\cdots,m; \ i=1,2,\cdots,n_I \quad (6)$$

From the interval operation, the input-output relation of each unit of the SINN can be explicitly calculated as follows:

Input units: $O_{Pi} = [o_{pi}^L, o_{pi}^U] = [x_{pi}^L, x_{pi}^U]$ $\qquad (7)$

$$O_{Pj} = [o_{pj}^L, o_{pj}^U] = [f(net_{pj}^L), f(net_{pj}^U)] \qquad (8)$$

Hidden units: $net_{PJ}^L = \sum_{\substack{i=1 \\ w_{ji} \ge 0}}^{n_I} w_{ji} o_{pi}^L + \sum_{\substack{i=1 \\ w_{ji} < 0}}^{n_I} w_{ji} o_{pi}^U + \theta_j$ $\qquad (9)$

$$net_{PJ}^U = \sum_{\substack{i=1 \\ w_{ji} \ge 0}}^{n_I} w_{ji} o_{pi}^U + \sum_{\substack{i=1 \\ w_{ji} < 0}}^{n_I} w_{ji} o_{pi}^L + \theta_j \qquad (10)$$

Output units: $O_{Pk} = [o_{pk}^L, o_{pk}^U] = [f(net_{pk}^L), f(net_{pk}^U)]$ $\qquad (11)$

$$net_{Pk}^L = \sum_{\substack{i=1 \\ w_{kj}^L \ge 0}}^{n_H} w_{kj}^L o_{pj}^L + \sum_{\substack{i=1 \\ w_{kj}^L < 0}}^{n_H} w_{kj}^L o_{pj}^U + \theta_k^L \qquad (12)$$

$$net_{Pk}^U = \sum_{\substack{i=1 \\ w_{kj}^U \ge 0}}^{n_H} w_{kj}^U o_{pj}^U + \sum_{\substack{i=1 \\ w_{kj}^U < 0}}^{n_H} w_{kj}^U o_{pj}^L + \theta_k^U \qquad (13)$$

Since the input-output relation of each unit in (7)-(13) is calculated by interval arithmetic, characteristic features of interval arithmetic, such as continuity and inclusion monotonicity, are also valid for the SINN.

3   The Learning of The SINN

In order to train the SINN, a cost function must be defined. We denote the cost function as follows:

$$e_p = \sum_{k=1}^{n_O} e_{pk} = \sum_{k=1}^{n_O} \left(e_{pk}^L + e_{pk}^U \right) \qquad (14)$$

where e_{pk}^L and e_{pk}^U are the squared errors of the lower and upper bounds, respectively.

$$e_{pk}^L = \left(o_{pk}^L - t_{pk}^L \right) \big/ 2 \qquad (15)$$

$$e_{pk}^U = \left(o_{pk}^U - t_{pk}^U \right) \big/ 2 \qquad (16)$$

The learning of the SINN is to adjust the weights W_{kj}, w_{ji} and the biases Θ_k, θ_k so as to minimize the cost function (14). Since the biases Θ_k and θ_k are changed in the same fashion as the weights W_{kj} and w_{ji}, we only show the update rules for the weights W_{kj} and w_{ji} as follows.

$$\Delta w_{ji}(t+1) = \eta(-\partial e_p / \partial w_{ji}) + \alpha \Delta w_{ji}(t) \qquad (17)$$

$$\Delta w_{kj}^L(t+1) = \eta(-\partial e_p / \partial w_{kj}^L) + \alpha \Delta w_{kj}^L(t) \qquad (18)$$

$$\Delta w_{kj}^U(t+1) = \eta(-\partial e_p / \partial w_{kj}^U) + \alpha \Delta w_{kj}^U(t) \qquad (19)$$

where t indexes the number of presentations of the patterns, η is the learning constant, and α is the momentum constant. The derivatives in (17)-(19) can be calculated from the cost function (14) by means of the explicit input-output relation (7)-(13) of the SINN(For explicit derivation, see Appendix).

Since the lower and upper limits of the interval weights W_{kj} are independently changed according to the update rules (17)-(19), it is possible that the lower limits of the interval weights W_{kj} exceed the corresponding upper limits. To handle the undesirable situation, we set the interval weights W_{kj} as follows.

$$W_{kj} = [\min\{w_{kj}^L(t+1), w_{kj}^U(t+1)\}, \max\{w_{kj}^L(t+1), w_{kj}^U(t+1)\}] \tag{20}$$

It should be noted that when the porposed algorithm is used to classify the interval patterns, what we need do is to set the target output of the corresponding output unit to be one, and set those of other output units to be zeros.

4 Simulation

As an application to the nonlinear mappings of interval vectors, we apply the proposed method to a numerical example[3,4]. To enhance the graphical explanation, let us consider a single input and single output interval mapping. There exist four pairs of interval input-output training patterns represented by the rectangles in Figure 2 . Using these training data, we trained the SINN with a single input unit, six hidden units and single output unit. The learning rate η and the momentum constant α in (17)-(19) were specified as 0.5 and 0.9, respectively. All the initial values of the weights and the biases were selected randomly in the closed interval [-1,1]. Interval outputs from the trained SINN after 10000 iterations is demonstrated in Figure 3. In Figure 3, we depicted the interval outputs corresponding to ten interval inputs. From the comparison between Figure 2 and Figure 3, we can see the actual outputs in corresponding to the interval inputs in the training data are almost the same as the interval targets. We can conclude the proposed method have good fitting and generalization ability.

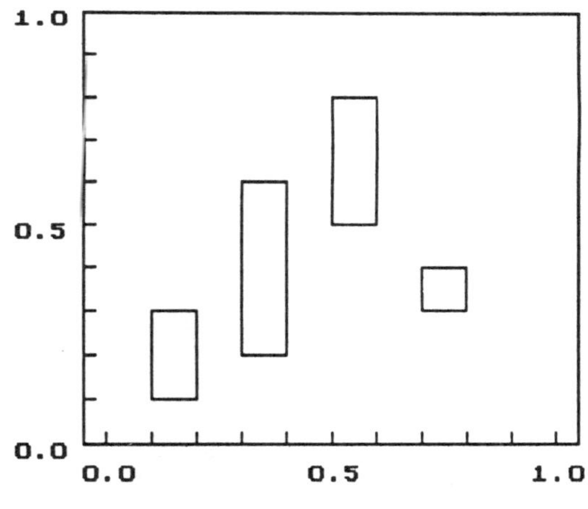
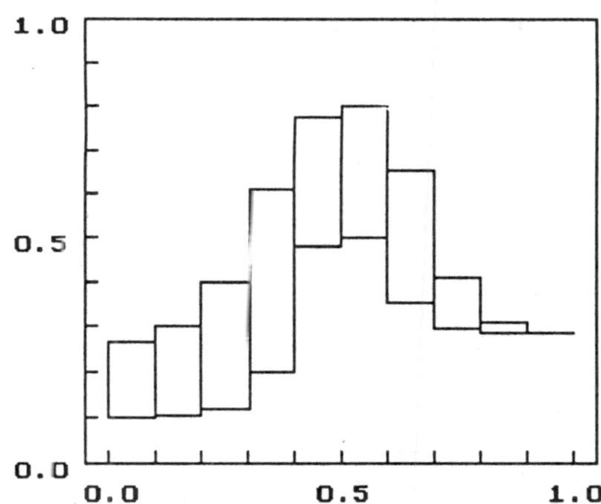

Fig.2 Training data   Fig.3 The actual output form the trained SINN

To illustrate the inclusion monotonicity, we presented the following eight interval inputs to the trained SINN.

$$X_1 = [0.1, 0.2], X_2 = [0.3, 0.4], X_3 = [0.5, 0.6], X_4 = [0.6, 0.7],$$
$$X_5 = [0.05, 0.25], X_6 = [0.25, 0.45], X_7 = [045, 065], X_8 = [0.65, 0.85]$$

The inclusion relation between interval inputs is shown as follows

$$X_n \subset X_{n+4}, \quad n=1,2,3,4$$

The eight interval outputs from the trained SINN corresponding to these interval inputs are shown in Figure 4. From Figure 4, we can see that the inclusion relation between interval input vectors have been transferred correctly to the interval output vectors.

We presented three bidimensional examples[2] to illustrate the classification ability of the proposed method. Example One in Figure 5 corresponds to a mixture of real and interval vectors in the training set, the real vectors are codified as the closed interval vectors with only one point inside each intervals. The training data of Example Two contain only interval vectors represented as the rectangles in Figure 6. The input set of

Example Three is the same as that of the example two, but the calssification classes are different. The solid lines in Figure 4, 5 and 6 represent the threshold 0.5 of each output units, i.e., the achieved classification. Example One correspond to a SINN with 2 input units, 5 hidden units and2 output units. In Example Two, we employ a SINN with 2 input units, 8 hidden units and 3 output units. The SINN used in Example Three contains 2 input units, 9 hidden units and 5 output units. It is achieved a perfect classification of the training data in all three examples.

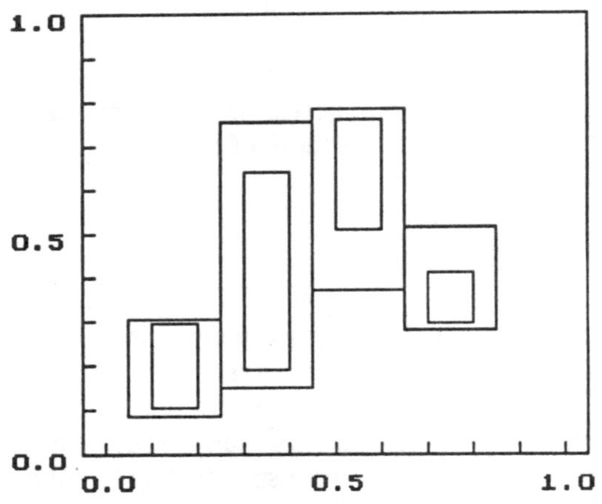

Fig.4 The actual outputs from the trained SINN

Fig.5 Example One, Classification

5 Conclusion

In this paper, we proposed a neural network related approach for nonlinear mappings and classifications of interval vectors. For nonlinear mappings of interval vectors, our proposed method can not only satisfiy the characteristic features of interval mappings, that is, continuity and inclusion monotonicity, but also have good fitting and generalization ability. In addition, it can achieve perfect classification of interval vectors. It should be pointed out that if the expert's knowledge is a set of the interval if-then rules[2], it is very easy to achieve the integration of expert's knowledge and sample data using the proposed method.

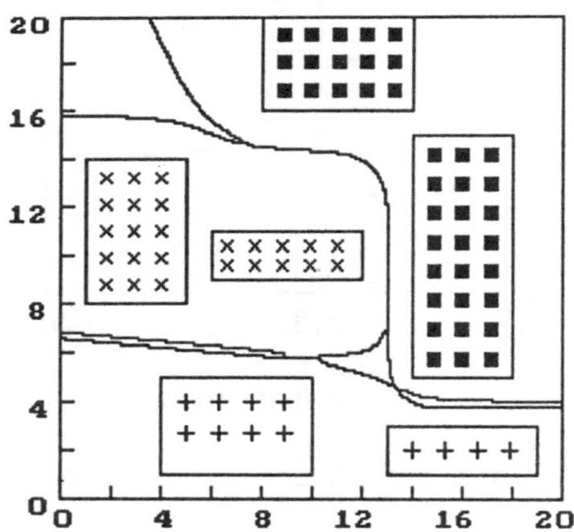

Fig.6 Example Two , Classification

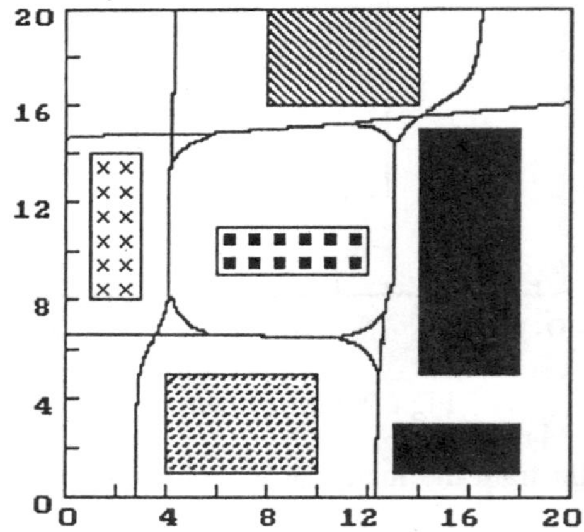

Fig.7 Example Three, Classification

References

[1] H.Ishibuchi and H.Tanaka, "An extension of the BP algorithm to interval input vectors," Proc. IJCNN'91, Singapore, pp.1588~1593.

[2] C.A.Hernández et al., "Interval arithmetic backpropagation,"Proc.IJCNN'93, Nagoya, Japan, pp. 375~378.

[3] K.Kwon et al., "Nonlinear mapping of interval vectors by neural networks," Proc. IJCNN'93, Nagoya, Japan, pp. 758~761.

[4] K.Kwon et al., "Neural networks with interval weights for nonlinear mappings of interval vectors," IEICE Trans. INF.& SYST., vol.4, pp. 409~417, 1994.

[5] H.Ishibuchi et al., "An architecture of neural networks with interval weights and its applications to fuzzy regression analysis," Fuzzy Sets and Systems, vol. 57, pp. 27~39, 1993.

[6] H.Ishibuchi et al., "Learning from incomplete training data with missing values and medical application," Proc. IJCNN'93, Nagoya, Japan, pp. 1871~1874.

[7] G.Alefeld and J.Herzberger, "Introduction to Interval Computations," New York:Academic Press, 1983.

[8] D.E.Rumelhart et al., "Parallel Distributed Processing," Cambridge: MIT Press, 1986.

[9] J.Šima, "Neural expert systems," Neural networks, vol. 8, pp. 261~271, 1995.

Appendix :Explicit Derivation of The Learning Algorithm

(1) $\partial e_p / \partial w_{kj}^L$

(i) if $w_{kj}^L \geq 0$

$$\frac{\partial e_p}{\partial w_{kj}^L} = \frac{\partial e_{pk}^L}{\partial w_{kj}^L} = \frac{\partial}{\partial o_{pk}^L}\left\{\left(t_{pk}^L - o_{pk}^L\right)^2 / 2\right\}\frac{\partial o_{pk}^L}{\partial net_{pk}^L}\frac{\partial net_{pk}^L}{\partial w_{kj}^L}$$

$$= -\,\delta_{pk}^L o_{pj}^L$$

$$\delta_{pk}^L = (t_{pk}^L - o_{pk}^L)\,o_{pk}^L\,(1 - o_{pk}^L)$$

(ii) if $w_{kj}^L < 0$

$$\frac{\partial e_p}{\partial w_{kj}^L} = \frac{\partial e_{pk}^L}{\partial w_{kj}^L} = -\,\delta_{pk}^L o_{pj}^U$$

(2) $\partial e_p / \partial w_{kj}^U$

(i) if $w_{kj}^U \geq 0$

$$\frac{\partial e_p}{\partial w_{kj}^U} = \frac{\partial e_{pk}^U}{\partial w_{kj}^U} = \frac{\partial}{\partial o_{pk}^U}\left\{\left(t_{pk}^U - o_{pk}^U\right)^2 / 2\right\}\frac{\partial o_{pk}^U}{\partial net_{pk}^U}\frac{\partial net_{pk}^U}{\partial w_{kj}^U}$$

$$= -\,\delta_{pk}^U o_{pj}^U$$

$$\delta_{pk}^U = (t_{pk}^U - o_{pk}^U)\,o_{pk}^U\,(1 - o_{pk}^U)$$

(ii) if $w_{kj}^U < 0$

$$\frac{\partial e_p}{\partial w_{kj}^U} = \frac{\partial e_{pk}^U}{\partial w_{kj}^U} = -\,\delta_{pk}^U o_{pj}^L$$

(3) $\partial e_p / \partial w_{ji}$

(i) if $w_{ji} \geq 0$

$$\frac{\partial e_p}{\partial w_{ji}} = \partial\sum_{k=1}^{n_O}\left(e_{pk}^L + e_{pk}^U\right)\Big/ \partial w_{ji}$$

$$= -\delta_{pj}^L o_{pi}^L \;\; \delta_{pj}^U o_{pi}^U$$

$$\delta_{pj}^L = \left(\sum_{\substack{k=1 \\ w_{kj}^L \geq 0}}^{n_O}\left(\delta_{kj}^L w_{kj}^L\right) + \sum_{\substack{k=1 \\ w_{kj}^U < 0}}^{n_O}\left(\delta_{kj}^U w_{kj}^U\right)\right) o_{pj}^l\,(1 - o_{pj}^L)$$

$$\delta_{pj}^U = \left(\sum_{\substack{k=1 \\ w_{kj}^L < 0}}^{n_O}\left(\delta_{kj}^L w_{kj}^L\right) + \sum_{\substack{k=1 \\ w_{kj}^U \geq 0}}^{n_O}\left(\delta_{kj}^U w_{kj}^U\right)\right) o_{pj}^U\,(1 - o_{pj}^U)$$

(ii) if $w_{ji} < 0$

$$\frac{\partial e_p}{\partial w_{ji}} = \partial\sum_{k=1}^{n_O}\left(e_{pk}^L + e_{pk}^U\right)\Big/ \partial w_{ji}$$

$$= -\delta_{pj}^L o_{pi}^U \;\; \delta_{pj}^U o_{pi}^L$$

An Information-based Distance Metric
for Instanced-based Learning

W.Z. Liu

Department of Information Science
University of Portsmouth
Locksway Road
Milton
Hampshire PO4 8JF
United Kingdom

Email: liuw@sis.port.ac.uk

Abstract — In this paper, problems with the instance-based learning method are discussed. Earlier remedial attempts have been reviewed. A novel approach of using an association measure as a distance metric is proposed. Initial empirical results showed considerable promise for further work in this direction.

1   Introduction

The fundamental problem of learning to classify objects has been tackled from many different angles, by researchers in statistics, artificial intelligence and other fields. One such classification method is the instance-based learning approach [1]. Sometimes it is also called nearest neighbour method. The basic principle of instance-based learning algorithms is to store a set of training instances and classify a new case according to its nearest stored instances. The set of stored instances is usually called the *training set*. Each instance in the training set is called an *exemplar*. All the cases in the problem domain consist of a class indicator and values on a number of attributes. The machine learning task is to classify new cases (with unknown class membership), according to the information provided in the training set.

In order to measure the distance between instances, some distance metric needs to be used. The conventional method treats examples as points in feature spaces and uses Euclidean distance as the distance metric. For a numeric attribute, the value difference between two values is simply an arithmetic difference. (In order to avoid attributes with large variance dominate the distance computation, the original real-valued attributes are standardised). For nominal attributes, the 'overlap' metric (or Hamming distance) is usually used. This method simply gives a zero value difference if the two symbolic values match, and gives one otherwise. To handle classification tasks that have mixed types of attributes, the two *different* metrics are simply combined.

2   Problems of the Conventional Distance Metrics

There are a few problems working with this conventional approach. The first problem arises from the fact that the Euclidean distance between two instances is calculated from all the attributes indiscriminately, i.e. the technique really involves conditioning on *all* the available variables. Recently, Liu and White [2] made a comparison between nearest neighbour and tree-based classification techniques and showed that the nearest neighbour method can suffer from overfitting which, in turn, renders sub-optimal performances in domains where the number of variables is large or the variables are of unequal importance in discriminating between the classes. It is not difficult to see that the worst case would be the situation when a lot of attributes are present and some of these attributes are irrelevant to the discrimination task. In order to overcome this problem, attributes really need to be *weighted* (either explicitly or implicitly) in the calculation of the overall distance between two cases.

The second problem is that using the simple 'overlap' metric to measure the difference between two values of a nominal attribute can often fail to capture the complexity and subtlety of the problem domain and, as a result, may yield poor classification performance [3].

3   Recent Remedial Attempts

One approach attempts to overcome these problems reported by Lee [4] is to incorporate a weight term in the calculation of the distance between two instances. Thus, for two instances X and Y, the distance between them, $D(X, Y)$, is defined as:

$$D(X, Y) = \sum_{i=1}^{k} w_i d(x_i, y_i) \tag{1}$$

where k is the number of attributes for each case in the training set; x_i and y_i ($i = 1, 2, \ldots, k$) are the values of the i-th attribute for X and Y; w_i is the weight of attribute A_i and $d(x_i, y_i)$ denotes the distance between values x_i and y_i.

The idea adopted by Lee [4] for calculating the weight of each attribute is based on the information theoretic approach. That is, the more information an attribute gives to the target attribute, the more weight the attribute is to have. In defining the distance between two attribute values, the simple 'overlap' metric (or the Hamming distance) is used for binary attributes and an information theoretic definition is used for categorical variables. For numeric values, the standardised arithmetic difference is used.

It is not difficult to see that this approach mitigates the problems mentioned in Section 2, because the explicit incorporation of weight term in the distance definition partically reduces the contributions of noisy attributes to the overall distance computation. However, according to the arguments presented earlier, it is still sub-optimal to use the Hamming distance for binary attributes and the *superficial* arithmetic difference for real-valued attributes. In order to completely eliminate the bias of noisy attributes in the calculation of the overall distance, some other distance metric needs to be used.

Another different method proposed by Stanfill and Waltz [5] is to use the Value Difference Metric (VDM) for measuring the distance between values of symbolic features. This measure was later adapted by Cost and Salzberg [3] to produce the Modified Value Difference Metric (MVDM). This measure takes into account the overall similarity of classification of all cases, in the training set, for each possible value of each feature. This means that a matrix defining the distance between all values of an attribute can be derived statistically, based on the information provided by the examples in the training set. Empirical results have shown that, although these metrics do not define weights for attributes explicitly, attribute importance is taken care of by the metric itself [3, 6, 7, 8, 9, 10].

Careful study of the VDM reveals the fact that the VDM is really a measure of association between class and an attribute value pair. Once this is appreciated, the field is widely open for other more conventional statistical measures of association to be used in a similar way. In this paper, we propose the novel idea of using the well-known transmitted information [11, 12, 13], H_T (also known as information gain), as a distance measure in instance-based learning.

4   Algorithm and Experimental Results

Our instance-based learning algorithm works in a similar way as PEBLS [3]. In our system, the association measure H_T is used as a distance measure. In calculating the

distance between two discrete values, these two values are cross-tabulated against class
and the information about class membership conveyed by the two values is calculated
and regarded as the distance between them. Real-valued attributes are discretised
first and then distance calculated in the same way as discrete attributes. The overall
distance between two instances is the summation of the information values on all
dimensions.

The discretisation procedure used considers all possible cutting points (between
ordered values appear in the training set) and selects the cutting point that gives the
greatest value on a particular measure such as the information gain [11] or the chi-
square test [13]. The method is recursively re-applied to the subsets of the previous
split until a stopping criterion is satisfied. The most commonly used stopping criteria
are based on the chi-square significance test [12] or the minimum description length
principle [14]. In our system, the chi-square test is used for these purposes.

When a case is classified, the distances (as defined above), between this test case
and all cases in the training set, are calculated and its closest instances are used to
determine the class of this case.

The system is tested using a large data set from British Steel, in attempting to
detect surface defects in flat steel products using machine learning techniques. The
whole data set consisted of 2461 records of images, each of which contained 121
attributes in addition to the classification label. The classification label was obtained
by the surface inspector in the plant and was cross-checked by other experts in the
field. For the purpose of the present study, the classifications are grouped into two
classes. Class 1 (the defect steel group) consisted of those images which belong to
any of about 30 different defect types. A total of 1626 cases fell into the defect group.
Class 2 (the good steel group) comprised the remaining 835 cases with no significant
defect.

Using cross-validation, the classification accuracy for 1-NN (1 Nearest Neighbour),
3-NN, 5-NN are 81.6%, 82.8% and 82.6% respectively. For the 3-NN, the cross-
validated classification matrix is shown in Table 1. As can be worked out easily, the

Predicted Class

		1	2
Actual Class	1	1488	138
	2	286	549

Table 1: Cross-validated classification matrix for surface defect detection of flat steel
products using 3-NN. Class 1 represents cases with defects and class 2 represents good
steel.

odds ratio for this cross-validated classification matrix is (1488*549)/(138*286)=20.7,
which is much higher than 1.0 (the odds ratio for random discrimination).

At this stage, because of the continuing developments of the system, the results
should be regarded as illustrative of the techniques, rather than accurately descriptive
of their discriminative power. With 121 attributes in the data set, it is almost certain
that there are many noisy variables. In such a situation, one would naturally expect
the conventional nearest neighbour approach to perform poorly, according to the
arguments presented earlier. Nevertheless, by using our novel idea of defining an
association measure as a distance metric, the results obtained are both interesting
and encouraging.

Perhaps it should be mentioned that there is no weighing scheme incorporated in
our system for more reliable instances, as is done in the systems designed by Cost and
Salzberg [3] and Lee [4]. This improvement is planned in the near future. Another
general criticism to instance-based learning algorithms that interactions between attributes can not detected by them also applies to our system. Further research should

also include a thorough comparison between our system and other well-known learning algorithms such as ID3 [11], CN2 [15] and PEBLS [3]. One point which can be concluded is that, in order for instance-based learning algorithms to work well, the concept (i.e. the association between class and attributes) must be taken into account by the distance measure.

References

[1] D. Aha, D. Kibler and M. Albert, "Instance-based learning algorithms", *Machine Learning*, **6**, pp. 37-66, 1991.

[2] W.Z. Liu and A.P. White, "A comparison of nearest neighbour and tree-based discriminant analysis", *Journal of Statistical and Computational Simulation*, **53**, pp. 41-50, 1995.

[3] S. Cost and S. Salzberg, "A weighted nearest neighbour algorithm for learning with symbolic features", *Machine Learning*, **10**, pp. 57-78, 1993.

[4] C. Lee, "An instance-based learning method for databases an information thecretic approach", *Machine Learning: ECML-94*, edited by F. Bergadano and L. De Raedt, Springer-Verlag, Berlin, 1994, pp. 387-390.

[5] C. Stanfill and D. Waltz, "Towards memory-based reasoning", *Communications of the ACM*, **29 (12)**, pp. 1213-1228, 1986.

[6] K.M. Ting, "Discretisation of continuous-valued attributes and instance-based learning", *Technical Report*, **491**, Basser Department of Computer Science, University of Sydney, 1994.

[7] K.M. Ting, "Towards using a single uniform metric in instance-based learning", *Case-Based Reasoning Research and Development: Proceedings of the First International Conference, ICCBR-95*, Sesimbra, Portugal, October 1995, pp. 559-568.

[8] K.M. Ting, "Discretisation in lazy learning algorithms", *Artificial Intelligence Review*, to appear.

[9] J. Rachlin, S. Kasif, S. Salzberg and D. Aha, "Towards a better understanding of memory-based and Bayesian classifiers", *Proceedings of the Eleventh International Conference on Machine Learning*, New Brunswick, NJ, 1994, pp. 242–250,

[10] F. Ricci and P. Avesani, "Learning a local similarity metric for case-based reasoning" *Case-Based Reasoning Research and Development: Proceedings of the First International Conference, ICCBR-95*, Sesimbra, Portugal, October 1995, pp. 301–312.

[11] J.R. Quinlan, "Induction of decision trees", *Machine Learning*, **1**, pp. 81-106.

[12] W.Z. Liu and A.P. White, "The importance of attribute selection measures in decision tree induction", *Machine Learning*, **15**, pp. 25-41, 1994.

[13] A.P. White and W.Z. Liu, "Bias in information-based measures in decision tree induction", *Machine Learning*, **15**, pp. 321-329.

[14] J.R. Quinlan and R.L. Rivest, "Inferring decision trees using the minimum description length principle", *Information and Computation*, **80**, pp. 227-248, 1989.

[15] P. Clark and T. Niblett, "The CN2 induction algorithm", *Machine Learning*, **3**, pp. 261-283, 1989.

A Learning Algorithm For Fuzzy Neural Networks Based on Fuzzy Number Operations

Zhenquan Li, Yanchun Zhang , Masahiro Nishikawa† , Akira Ichikawa‡

Dept. of Mathematics & Computing,University of Southern Queensland
Toowoomba Q 4350, Australia
†Graduate School of Electronic Science and Technology, Shizuoka University
Hamamatsu 432, Japan
‡Department of Electrical and Electronic Engineering, Shizuoka University
Hamamatsu 432, Japan

Abstract— **In this paper, firstly we will give some theorems and their proofs for computing addition, subtraction, multiplication and division of fuzzy numbers, then present some arithmetic results of triangular fuzzy numbers, propose and simulate a learning algorithm for fuzzy neural network based on fuzzy number operations.**

1   Introduction

Recently significant advances have been made in both fuzzy logic and computational neural network. The fuzzy logic provides a mathematical framework to capture the uncertainties associated with human congitive processes. On the other hand, the computational neural networks have evolved in the process of understanding the incredible learning and adaptive features of neuronal mechanisms inherent in certain biological species. The fuzzy neural networks have the potential to capture the benefits of fuzzy logic and computational neural networks.

Usually the inference rules in fuzzy logic can be written as follow:

$$\text{If } X_1 \text{ is } A_1^1 \text{ and ... and } X_I \text{ is } A_1^I \text{ then } Y \text{ is } B_1.$$
$$\text{If } X_1 \text{ is } A_2^1 \text{ and ... and } X_I \text{ is } A_2^I \text{ then } Y \text{ is } B_2.$$
$$\cdots\cdots\cdots\cdots\cdots\cdots\cdots\cdots\cdots\cdots\cdots\cdots$$
$$\text{If } X_1 \text{ is } A_J^1 \text{ and ... and } X_I \text{ is } A_J^I \text{ then } Y \text{ is } B_J.$$

where A and B are fuzzy numbers. How a fuzzy neural network realizes fuzzy logic is the main problem we should solve. Recently various approaches to fuzzy neural network have been proposed. Most approaches are to extend real inputs and real targets in conventional neural network architectures to fuzzy numbers. Ishibuchi et al.[2] gave an architecture of multi-layer feedforward neural networks for fuzzy input vectors, and the architecture was applied to the implementation of fuzzy if-then rules in [3,4]. Hayashi et al.[5] fuzzified connection weights of multi-layer feedforward neural networks. Ishibuchi et al.[6] and [8] discussed a multi-input and single-output fuzzy neural network for real input vectors and a multi-input and multi-output fuzzy neural network with triangular fuzzy weights for fuzzy input vectors, respectively. These approaches could not give arbitrary fuzzy outputs that approximate the results of fuzzy logic very well. To realize how fuzzy neural network can give a better description of fuzzy logic, we here propose a different approach to fuzzy neural network based on fuzzy number operations and the shape of membership function of targets, which has been shown superior to the other approaches mentioned above through simulation.

The operations of fuzzy numbers are one of bases in fuzzy theory and its application. Increasing theoretic and applied problems deal with fuzzy arithmetic, such as fuzzy neural network. In general, the weights and biases of fuzzy neural network were restricted to triangular fuzzy number, although we didn't know what output result fuzzy neural network was. It is convenient if we know the shapes of membership functions of output according to the inputs and weights (we want to select) of fuzzy neural network before selecting the weights.

This paper gives a learning algorithm of fuzzy neural networks that select the shape of membership function of weights first, then calculate the parameters of each weight. In Section 2, we give some theorems on arithmetic of fuzzy numbers. Section 3 presents operation results of triangular fuzzy numbers. Section 4 proposes a learning algorithm for fuzzy neural networks. Section 5 give a simulation of proposed learning algorithm and Section 6 is a brief summary.

2   Operations of fuzzy numbers

Let us now give some basic notation that will be used in this paper. We will place a bar over a symbol if it represents a fuzzy set. So $\bar{A}$, $\bar{B}$, $\cdots$ are fuzzy sets. All our fuzzy sets will be fuzzy subsets of the real numbers. The membership function for a fuzzy set $\bar{A}$, evaluated at x, will be written as $\bar{A}(x)$. So $\bar{A}(x)$ is in $[0,1]$ for all x. $\bar{A}[0]$ is the support of $\bar{A}$. Let $\bar{A}[0] = [a.b]$, a (b) is called the left value (right value) of $\bar{A}$. c is called the mean value of $\bar{A}$, if $\bar{A}(c) = 1$. A strictly positive fuzzy number $\bar{A}$ means $\bar{A}(x) = 0$, $\forall x \leq 0$, a strictly negative fuzzy number $\bar{B}$ means $\bar{B}(y) = 0$, $\forall y \geq 0$. The triangular fuzzy number $\bar{A}$ that satisfy $\bar{A}(0) = 1$ is denoted by $\bar{0}$.

Let $\bar{A}$, $\bar{B}$ be two fuzzy numbers, $\bar{P} = \bar{A} \oplus \bar{B}$, $\bar{T} = \bar{A} \otimes \bar{B}$, $\bar{M} = \bar{A} \ominus \bar{B}$ and $\bar{S} = \bar{A} \oslash \bar{B}$, respectively. These are defined as following

$$\bar{P}(z) = \vee_{z=x+y}(\bar{A}(x) \wedge \bar{B}(y)), \qquad \bar{T}(z) = \vee_{z=xy}(\bar{A}(x) \wedge \bar{B}(y)),$$
$$\bar{M}(z) = \vee_{z=x-y}(\bar{A}(x) \wedge \bar{B}(y)), \qquad \bar{S}(z) = \vee_{z=\frac{x}{y}}(\bar{A}(x) \wedge \bar{B}(y)). \tag{1}$$

Let mean values of $\bar{A}$ and $\bar{B}$ be a_2 and b_2, then the mean values of $\bar{P}$, $\bar{T}$, $\bar{M}$ and $\bar{S}$ are $a_2 + b_2$, $a_2 b_2$, $a_2 - b_2$ and a_2/b_2 $(b_2 \neq 0)$, respectively. Let $\bar{A}[0] = [a_1, a_3]$, $\bar{B}[0] = [b_1, b_3]$ then

$$\bar{P}[0] = [a_1 + b_1, a_3 + b_3]. \tag{2}$$

In this section, that x and y situate in the same sides of mean value of $\bar{A}$ and $\bar{B}$ means that x is smaller than the mean value a_2 of $\bar{A}$ and y is also smaller than the mean value b_2 of $\bar{B}$ or x is bigger than the mean value a_2 of $\bar{A}$ and y is also bigger than the mean value b_2 of $\bar{B}$. That x and y situate in the different sides of mean value of $\bar{A}$ and $\bar{B}$ means if that x is smaller than the mean value a_2 of $\bar{A}$ then y is bigger than the mean value b_2 of $\bar{B}$ and vice versa.

Theorem 1 $\bar{P}(z) = \bar{A}(x_0)$ where $z = x_0 + y_0$ and $\bar{A}(x_0) = \bar{B}(y_0)$, x_0, y_0, and z situate in the same sides of mean value of $\bar{A}$, $\bar{B}$ and $\bar{P}$.

Proof: 1. $z \leq a_2 + b_2$. If $z \leq a_1 + b_1$, then $\bar{P}(z) = 0$. Let $z = x + y$, if $x \leq x_0$, then $\bar{P}(z) = \bar{A}(x_0) \geq \bar{A}(x) \geq \bar{A}(x) \wedge \bar{B}(y)$, otherwise if $x > x_0$, then $y < y_0 \leq b_2$, $\bar{P}(z) = \bar{B}(y_0) \geq \bar{B}(y) \geq \bar{A}(x) \wedge \bar{B}(y)$.

    2. $z > a_2 + b_2$. Let $z = x + y$, if $x \geq a_2$ and $y \geq b_2$, it can be proved by the same method as 1. If $x \leq a_2$, then $y > b_2$ and $y \geq y_0$, $\bar{P}(z) = \bar{B}(y_0) \geq \bar{B}(y) \geq \bar{A}(x) \wedge \bar{B}(y)$. If $x > a_2$ and $y \leq b_2$, then $x \geq x_0$, $\bar{P}(z) = \bar{A}(x_0) \geq \bar{A}(x) \geq \bar{A}(x) \wedge \bar{B}(y)$.

For $\bar{A}[0] = [a_1, a_3]$, $\bar{B}[0] = [b_1, b_3]$, then

$$\bar{M}[0] = [a_1 - b_3, a_3 - b_1]. \tag{3}$$

Theorem 2 $\bar{M}(z) = \bar{A}(x_0)$ where $z = x_0 - y_0$ and $\bar{A}(x_0) = \bar{B}(y_0)$, x_0, y_0 situate in the different sides of mean value of $\bar{A}$, $\bar{B}$ and x_0 and z situate in the same sides of mean value of $\bar{A}$ and $\bar{M}$.

Proof: 1. $z \leq a_2 - b_2$.

    (a) if $z \leq a_1 - b_3$, then $\bar{M}(z) = 0$.

    (b) if $z > a_1 - b_3$ then $x_0 \leq a_2$ and $y_0 \geq b_2$, for each pair (x, y), $z = x - y$, if $x \geq x_0$ then $y \geq y_0$ and $\bar{M}(z) = \bar{B}(y_0) \geq \bar{B}(y) \geq \bar{A}(x) \wedge \bar{B}(y)$, otherwise if $x < x_0$ then $\bar{M}(z) = \bar{A}(x_0) \geq \bar{A}(x) \geq \bar{A}(x) \wedge \bar{B}(y)$.

    2. $z > a_2 - b_2$.

    (a) if $z \leq a_3 - b_1$, then $\bar{M}(z) = 0$.

    (b) if $z > a_3 - b_1$ then $x_0 > a_2$ and $y_0 \leq b_2$, for each pair (x, y), $z = x - y$, if $x \geq x_0$ then $\bar{M}(z) = \bar{A}(x_0) \geq \bar{A}(x) \geq \bar{A}(x) \wedge \bar{B}(y)$, otherwise if $x < x_0$ then $y \leq y_0$ and $\bar{M}(z) = \bar{B}(y_0) \geq \bar{B}(y) \geq \bar{A}(x) \wedge \bar{B}(y)$.

For $\bar{A}[0] = [a_1, a_3]$, $\bar{B}[0] = [b_1, b_3]$, suppose $\bar{A}$ and $\bar{B}$ are strictly positive or negative fuzzy number, then

$$\bar{T}[0] = \begin{cases} [a_1 b_1, a_3 b_3] & a_1 \geq 0, b_1 \geq 0 & \text{(4a)} \\ [a_1 b_3, a_3 b_1] & a_3 \leq 0, b_1 \geq 0 & \text{(4b)} \\ [a_3 b_1, a_1 b_3] & a_1 \geq 0, b_3 \leq 0 & \text{(4c)} \\ [a_3 b_3, a_1 b_1] & a_3 \leq 0, b_3 \leq 0 & \text{(4d)} \end{cases}$$

Theorem 3 $\bar{T}(z) = \bar{A}(x_0)$ *where* $z = x_0 y_0$ *and* $\bar{A}(x_0) = \bar{B}(y_0)$. *For* (4a), x_0, y_0 *and* z *situate in the same sides of mean value of* $\bar{A}$, $\bar{B}$ *and* $\bar{T}$. *For* (4b), x_0 *and* z *situate in the same sides of mean value of* $\bar{A}$ *and* $\bar{T}$, y_0 *situates in the different sides of mean value of* $\bar{B}$. *For* (4c), y_0 *and* z *situate in the same sides of mean value of* $\bar{B}$ *and* $\bar{T}$, x_0 *situates in the different sides of mean value of* $\bar{A}$. *For* (4d), x_0 *and* y_0 *situate in the same sides of mean value of* $\bar{A}$ *and* $\bar{B}$, z *situates in the different sides of mean value of* $\bar{T}$.

Proof: For (4a), it is similar to Theorem 1.

For (4b), i.e., $\bar{A}$ is negative, $\bar{B}$ is positive. Let $z = xy$ and $z \leq a_2 b_2$. If $z \leq a_1 b_3$, then $\bar{T}(z) = 0$. If $z > a_1 b_3$ and $x \leq x_0$, then $x \leq a_2$ and $\bar{T}(z) = \bar{A}(x_0) \geq \bar{A}(x) \geq \bar{A}(x) \wedge \bar{B}(y)$, otherwise, If $x > x_0$, then $y > y_0$ (since $x_0 \leq a_2$, then $y_0 \geq b_2$) and $\bar{T}(z) = \bar{B}(y_0) \geq \bar{B}(y) \geq \bar{A}(x) \wedge \bar{B}(y)$. Let $z = xy$ and $z \geq a_2 b_2$. If $z \geq a_3 b_1$, then $\bar{T}(z) = 0$. If $z < a_3 b_1$ and $x \geq x_0$, then $\bar{T}(z) = \bar{A}(x_0) \geq \bar{A}(x) \geq \bar{A}(x) \wedge \bar{B}(y)$, otherwise, If $x < x_0$, then $y < y_0$ and $\bar{T}(z) = \bar{B}(y_0) \geq \bar{B}(y) \geq \bar{A}(x) \wedge \bar{B}(y)$.

For (4c), it can be proved similarly to (4b).

The proof of (4d) is similar to that of Theorem 1.

Suppose $\bar{A}$ and $\bar{B}$ are both strictly positive fuzzy numbers or $\bar{A}$ and $\bar{B}$ are both strictly negative fuzzy numbers.

For $\bar{A}[0] = [a_1, a_3]$, $\bar{B}[0] = [b_1, b_3]$, then

$$
\bar{S}[0] = \begin{cases} [a_1/b_3, a_3/b_1] & a_1 > 0, b_1 > 0 \qquad\qquad\qquad (5a)\\ [a_3/b_1, a_1/b_3] & a_3 < 0, b_3 < 0 \qquad\qquad\qquad (5b) \end{cases}
$$

Theorem 4 $\bar{S}(z) = \bar{A}(x_0)$ *where* $z = x_0/y_0$ *and* $\bar{A}(x_0) = \bar{B}(y_0)$. *For* (5a), x_0 *and* z *situate in the same sides of mean value of* $\bar{A}$ *and* $\bar{S}$, y_0 *situate in the different sides of mean value of* $\bar{B}$. *For* (5b), y_0 *and* z *situate in the same sides of mean value of* $\bar{B}$ *and* $\bar{S}$, x_0 *situates in the different sides of mean value of* $\bar{A}$.

Proof: Here only give the proof of (5a), the proof of (5b) is similar to (5a). Let $z = x/y$.

1. $z \leq a_2/b_2$. If $z \leq a_1/b_3$, then $\bar{S}(z) = 0$. If $z > a_1/b_3$ and $x \leq x_0$, then $\bar{S}(z) = \bar{A}(x_0) \geq \bar{A}(x) \geq \bar{A}(x) \wedge \bar{B}(y)$, otherwise, if $x > x_0$, then $y > y_0$ and $\bar{S}(z) = \bar{B}(y_0) \geq \bar{B}(y) \geq \bar{A}(x) \wedge \bar{B}(y)$ (since $y_0 > b_2$).

2. $z > a_2/b_2$. If $z \geq a_3/b_1$, then $\bar{S}(z) = 0$. If $z < a_3/b_1$ and $y \leq y_0$, then $\bar{S}(z) = \bar{B}(y_0) \geq \bar{B}(y) \geq \bar{A}(x) \wedge \bar{B}(y)$, otherwise, if $y > y_0$, then $x > x_0$ and $\bar{S}(z) = \bar{A}(x_0) \geq \bar{A}(x) \geq \bar{A}(x) \wedge \bar{B}(y)$ (since $x_0 > a_2$).

3 Operations of triangular fuzzy numbers

Operations of triangular fuzzy numbers can be computed according to theorem 1, 2 and 3. Here we give some results for positive fuzzy numbers.

Let

$$
\bar{A}(x) = \begin{cases} \dfrac{1}{a_2 - a_1}(x - a_1) & a_1 \leq x \leq a_2 \\[2mm] \dfrac{1}{a_2 - a_3}(x - a_3) & a_2 \leq x \leq a_3 \\[2mm] 0 & \text{otherwise} \end{cases} \qquad\qquad (6)
$$

$$
\bar{B}(y) = \begin{cases} \dfrac{1}{b_2 - b_1}(y - b_1) & b_1 \leq y \leq b_2 \\[2mm] \dfrac{1}{b_2 - b_3}(y - b_3) & b_2 \leq y \leq b_3 \\[2mm] 0 & \text{otherwise} \end{cases} \qquad\qquad (7)
$$

then

$$\bar{P}(z) = \begin{cases} \dfrac{z}{p_1} - \dfrac{a_1 + b_1}{p_1} & a_1 + b_1 \leq z \leq a_2 + b_2 \\[2mm] \dfrac{z}{p_2} - \dfrac{a_3 + b_3}{p_2} & a_2 + b_2 \leq z \leq a_3 - b_3 \\[2mm] 0 & \text{otherwise} \end{cases} \tag{8}$$

where $p_1 = (a_2 - a_1) + (b_2 - b_1)$, $p_2 = (a_2 - a_3) + (b_2 - b_3)$

$$\bar{T}(z) = \begin{cases} \dfrac{1}{a_2 - a_1}\sqrt{t_1 z + u_1} - w_1 & a_1 b_1 \leq z \leq a_2 b_2 \\[2mm] \dfrac{1}{a_2 - a_3}\sqrt{t_2 z + u_2} - w_2 & a_2 b_2 \leq z \leq a_3 b_3 \\[2mm] 0 & \text{otherwise} \end{cases} \tag{9}$$

where $\quad t_1 = \dfrac{a_2 - a_1}{b_2 - b_1}, \quad u_1 = \dfrac{1}{4}\left(\dfrac{a_1 b_2 - a_2 b_1}{b_2 - b_1}\right)^2, \quad w_1 = \dfrac{b_1}{2(b_2 - b_1)},$

$\qquad\quad t_2 = \dfrac{a_2 - a_3}{b_2 - b_3}, \quad u_2 = \dfrac{1}{4}\left(\dfrac{a_2 b_3 - a_3 b_2}{b_2 - b_3}\right)^2, \quad w_2 = \dfrac{b_3}{2(b_2 - b_3)}.$

$$\bar{M}(z) = \begin{cases} \dfrac{z}{m_1} - \dfrac{a_1 - b_3}{m_1} & a_1 - b_3 \leq z \leq a_2 - b_2 \\[2mm] \dfrac{z}{m_2} - \dfrac{a_3 - b_1}{m_2} & a_2 - b_2 \leq z \leq a_3 - b_1 \\[2mm] 0 & \text{otherwise} \end{cases} \tag{10}$$

where $m_1 = (a_2 - a_1) - (b_2 - b_3)$, $m_2 = (a_2 - a_3) - (b_2 - b_1)$.

From further computing, following results can be obtained:

1. Addition and subtraction of triangular fuzzy nubers are triangular fuzzy numbers.

2. Multiplication of two triangular fuzzy numbers is a fuzzy number of LR-type, $L(z)$ and $R(z)$ are both expression with order $\dfrac{1}{2}$ (for example, $\sqrt{tz + u} + w$, $\sqrt{tz - \sqrt{\alpha z^2 + \beta z + \gamma}} + w$, $\cdots$). In general, multiplication of n triangular fuzzy numbers is also a fuzzy number of LR-type, but $L(z)$ and $R(z)$ are both expression with order $\dfrac{1}{n}$.

3. Addition and subtraction of fuzzy numbers of LR-type with order $\dfrac{1}{n}$ are fuzzy numbers of LR-type with order $\dfrac{1}{n}$.

4 A Learning algorithm

Let us derive a learning algorithm for the fuzzy neural network from operations of fuzzy numbers. At first, We select the shape of membership function of fuzzy weights and fuzzy biases according to the shape of membership function of inputs and operations of fuzzy numbers so that the shape of membership function of actual output is the most probably similar to that of the target corresponding to the same inputs. Then adjust each one of the three parameters (left value, right value and mean value) of each fuzzy weight and biases by crisp learning algorithem respectively.

Let us assume that m input-output pairs (X_p, T_p), $p = 1, 2, \cdots, m$, of fuzzy vectors are given as training set.

Learning algorithm

Step 1 : Initialize the fuzzy weights and the fuzzy biases with the shape we selected.

Step 2 : Repeat the following procedures for $p = 1, 2, \cdots, m$.

(1)   **Forward calculation :** calculate the left value, right value and mean value of the fuzzy output vector O_p corresponding to the fuzzy input vector X_p.

(2)   **Back-propagation :** adjust the left value, right value and mean value of fuzzy weights and fuzzy biases using the crisp learning algorithm.

Step 3 : If a prespecified stopping condition is not satisfied, go to Step 2.

5   Simulation result

In this section, we discuss a simulation result of the above learning algorithm. We assume that the fuzzy numbers in training data are strictly positive triangular and the trained fuzzy neural network is a three-layer feedforward with two input, three hidden and one output units and the all activation functions are identities and there is not any bias.(see Fig.1)

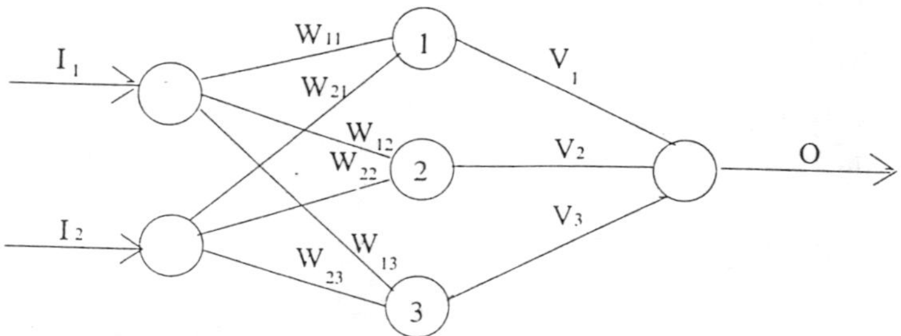

Figure 1: three-layer feedforward neural network model.

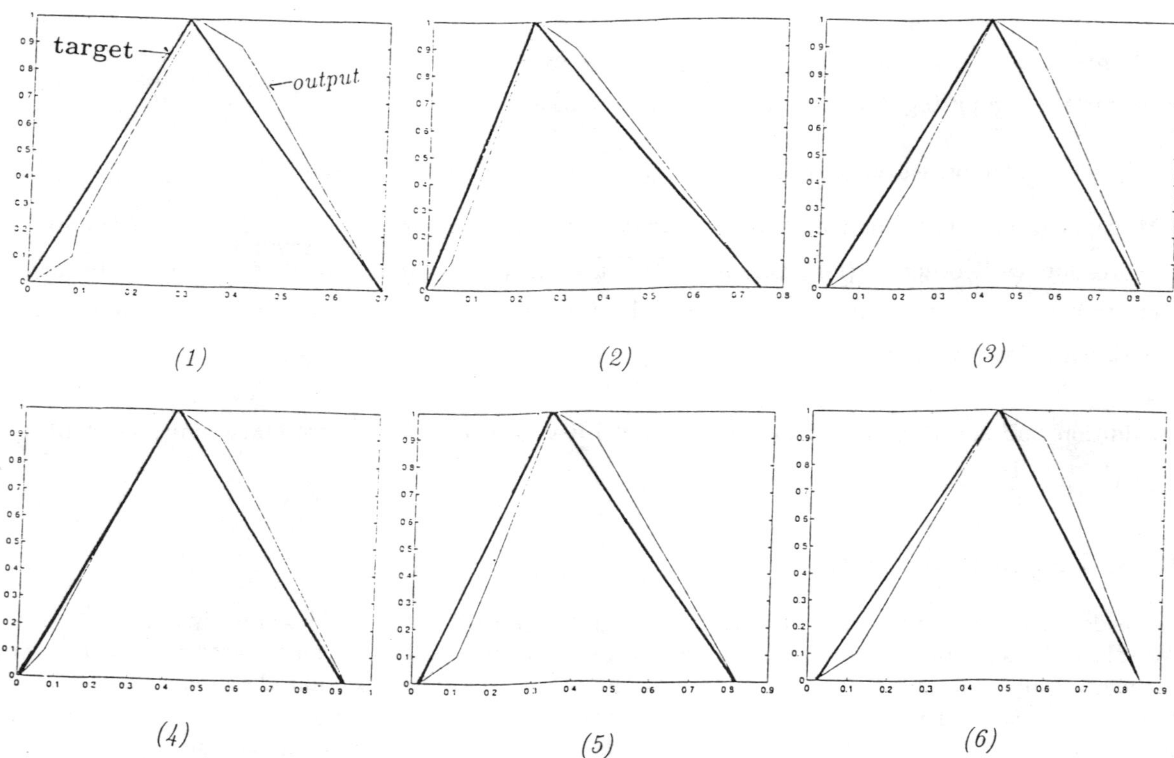

Figure 2: demonstration of differences between targets and practical outputs.

To find better approximation of targets, we have selected 6 as the order of weights, then the order of practical output is 3/4. In fact, the higher the order of weights, the more precise the approximation of targets is. We denoted triangular fuzzy numbers by (a,m,b) where a, m and b are left, mean and right values of the fuzzy number, respectively. Let us assume that both the input space and the output space are the unit interval [0, 1]. The training data we used in the simulation is:

$$[(0.1,0.4,0.6),(0.1,0.4,0.8),(0,0.3,0.7)]\ [(0,0.3,0.8),(0.2,0.3,0.6),(0,0.23,0.75)]$$

$$[(0.2,0.5,0.8),(0.2,0.6,0.8),(0.02,0.42,0.82)]\ [(0.1,0.5,0.9),(0.1,0.6,0.9),(0.01,0.42,0.93)]$$

$$[(0.2,0.4,0.8),(0.2,0.5,0.8),(0.02,0.34,0.82)]\ [(0.2,0.6,0.9),(0.2,0.6,0\ 7),(0.02,0.47,0.85)]$$

where the order in the square brackets is the first input, the second input, and the target corresponding to the first and second inputs. For computing simplicity, we only use the theorems in Section 2 at point $x=\{x|A(x)=h:h=0.1,0.2,...,0.9\}$. From following figures, we can find the differences between targets and practical outputs. If we use the center of gravity(COG)method that is the most widely used defuzzification strategy to do defuzzification of the outputs of neural networks, the results between targets and practical outputs are almost same.(see fig.2)

6 Conclusion

In this paper, we derived a learning algorithm for fuzzy neural network with fuzzy inputs, fuzzy weights and fuzzy targets. After selecting the architecture of fuzzy neural network, we can choose the order of fuzzy weights of the neural network according to the theorems in Section 2, so that we can get a better approximation of targets. The effectiveness of the derived learning algorithm was demonstrated by computer simulation. This paper is one of the first attempts to derive learning algorithms for fuzzy neural networks with fuzzy inputs, fuzzy targets and fuzzy weights that are not triangular. In the future work, we will further investigate its applications.

References

[1] H. J. Zimmermamm, *Fuzzy set theory and its application (second edition)*. Kluwer Academic Publishers, 1991.

[2] H. Ishibuchi, R.Fujioka and H. Tanaka, "An architecture of neural network for input vectors of fuzzy numbers," *Proc. FUZZ-IEEE'92*, San Diego, Mar. 8-12, 1992, pp. 643-650.

[3] H. Ishibuchi, R. Fujioka and H. Tanaka, "Neural networks that learn from fuzzy if-then rules," *IEEE Trans.Fuzzy System*, vol. 1(2), pp. 85-97, 1993.

[4] H. Ishibuchi, H. Okada and H. Tanaka, "Interpolation of fuzzy if-then rules by neural networks," *Internat. J. Approx. Reason*, vol. 10(1), pp. 3-27, 1994.

[5] Y. Hayashi, J.J. Buckley and E. Czogala, "Fuzzy neural network with fuzzy signals and weights", *Internat. J. Intelligent Systems*, vol. 8, pp. 527-537, 1994.

[6] H. Ishibuchi, H. Okada and H. Tanaka, "Fuzzy neural networks with fuzzy weights and fuzzy biases", *Proc. ICNN'93*, San Francisco, Mar. 28- Apr.1, 1993, pp. 1650-1655.

[7] J.J. Buckley and Y. Hayashi, "Fuzzy neural network: a survey", *Fuzzy Sets and Systems*, vol. 66, pp. 1-13, 1994.

[8] H. Ishibuchi, K. Kwon, H. Tanaka, "A learning algotithm of fuzzy neural networks with triangular fuzzy weights", *Fuzzy sets and systems*, vol. 71, pp. 277-293, 1995.

[9] J. J. Buckley and Y. Hayashi, "Neural nets for fuzzy systems", *Fuzzy sets and systems*, vol. 71, pp. 265-276, 1995.

[10] J. J. Buckley and Y. Hayashi, "Fuzzy neural nets and applications", *Fuzzy systems and AI*, vol. 3, pp. 11-14, 1992.

More on Overfitting in Learning Discrete Patterns

Extended version of "Overfitting and generalization in learning discrete patterns", *Neurocomputing: An International Journal*, 8: 341–347. 1995.

Charles X. Ling

Department of Computer Science, University of Hong Kong, Pokfulan Road, Hong Kong
(On leave from University of Western Ontario, Ontario, Canada)
E-mail: ling@cs.hku.hk

Abstract— Understanding and preventing overfitting is a very important issue in artificial neural network design, implementation, and application. Weigend (1994) reports that the presence and absence of overfitting in neural networks depends on how the testing error is measured, and that there is no overfitting in terms of the classification error (symbolic-level errors). In this paper, we show that, in terms of the classification error, overfitting does occur for certain representation used to encode the discrete attributes. We design simple Boolean functions with clear rationale, and present experimental results to support our claims. In addition, we report some interesting results on the best generalization ability of networks in terms of their sizes.

1   Introduction

The problem of overfitting has drawn significant attention recently (cf. (Weigend, 1994; Wang, Venkatesh, & Judd, 1994; Grossman, 1994)). The operational definition of overfitting is that the error on the testing sample increases if training goes on for too long. Therefore, training should be stopped at an appropriate point, rather than allowing to proceed until the training error is as small as possible (e.g. near-zero). Contradictory results, however, are reported even about the mere presence and absence of the overfitting effect. Weigend (1994) discovered that in a text-to-phoneme mapping learning, whether overfitting occurs depends on how the testing error is measured. He shows that with the cross-entropy error[1] overfitting is very evident, but that no overfitting is observed with the sum squared error and the sum absolute error. Since his problem concerns with a symbolic mapping, the error that defines overfitting should be at symbolic level; however, the three error measurements he uses are based on the numerical difference between the network outputs and the target output patterns.

We study the general problem of overfitting in learning symbolic patterns in this paper. Many applications of neural networks concern symbolic pattern learning (such as text-to-speech mapping (Sejnowski & Rosenberg, 1987), or verb past-tense learning (Rumelhart & McClelland, 1986; MacWhinney & Leinbach, 1991; Ling & Marinov, 1993)). Since we are learning discrete (symbolic) patterns, the error we really *care about* is the *symbolic-level error*, or the *classification error* of discrete patterns. Therefore, unless otherwise indicated, we use the term *error* in the rest of the paper as the classification error, and *overfitting* as an increase in the classification error on the testing sample.

2   Overfitting and Generalization on Boolean Functions

Due to the space limitation, the results of this section are omitted here, but they can be found in "Overfitting and generalization in learning discrete patterns", *Neurocomputing: An International Journal*, 8: 341–347, 1995; or from URL: http://www.cs.hku.hk/~ling.

3   A Brief Analysis of Overfitting

A sensible explanation for overfitting is that, if the representation is allowed to capture a primary regularity and a secondary regularity, then a network with a proper size and proper training would, at a certain point, capture most of the primary regularity before picking up the secondary one. This network would have the best predictive accuracy for the primary regularity in the testing examples. Excessive training causes the network to fit the secondary regularity as well, which in turn interferes with and *worsens* the prediction of the primary regularity in the testing examples. The result of these is an increase in the testing errors — the overfitting phenomenon. This is schematically illustrated in Figure 1.   Our

---

[1] The error for each pattern is chosen to be the logarithm of the activation value of the output unit that corresponds to the target class (Weigend, 1994).

analyses have been clearly verified in the Boolean functions with and without the overfitting effect in the previous sections.

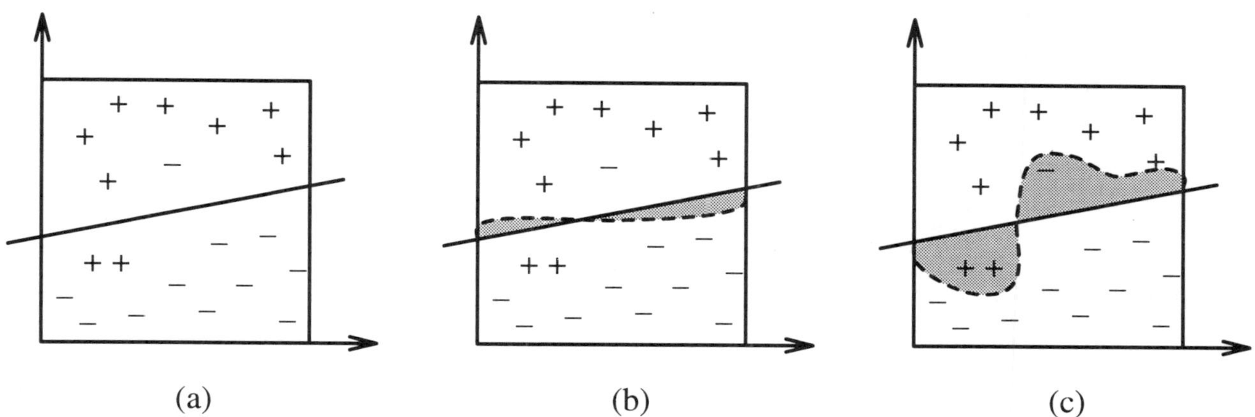

(a)   (b)   (c)

Figure 1: A schematic illustration of overfitting.

Figure (a) shows an instance space with a primary regularity (a linear separator with positive above and negative below), and a secondary regularity (a few exceptional instances in the space). Figure (b) shows a network that learns mostly the primary regularity. The shaded area is the error where testing examples will be incorrectly predicted. Figure (c) shows a network that is trained to zero classification errors. Overfitting occurs since the prediction of the primary regularity is worsened, as the shaded area in (c) is much larger for the primary regularity than in (b).

With the distributed representation but no flipped values (e.g., g), or with the one-per-value representation, there is no secondary regularity in the target function. Therefore, there is no overfitting problem. The disadvantage of one-per-value representation is that it does not capture any regularity, and thus results in very high testing errors. A good distributed representation uses a small number of bits to capture micro-features among attribute values for the primary regularity, and thus has better generalization accuracy (Hinton, McClelland, & Rumelhart, 1986). The trade-off introduced is that it may suffer from overfitting since these micro-features may inevitably cast unwanted secondary regularity (noise). A good strategy of avoiding overfitting is to stop training appropriately. The common practice is to use the cross-validation technique — monitoring the predictive error on an independent validation set of examples, and stop training when the minimal validation error is reached.

4   Learning the Past Tense of English Verbs

In this section, we confirm our findings of the last section in a more complex, "real-world" task of learning the past tense of English verbs. Past-tense acquisition has become a benchmark for the adequacy of cognitive modeling of language acquisition and processing. In 1986, Rumelhart and McClelland (1986) designed and implemented a connectionist system for the modeling of past-tense acquisition. Claims were made that such connectionist models, while requiring no symbol processing, grammatical rules, or explicit representation, as in the traditional grammatical theories, would be better models for the past-tense acquisition. Over the years a number of criticisms of connectionist modeling appeared (Pinker & Prince, 1988; Lachter & Bever, 1988; Prasada & Pinker, 1993), and there has been a heated debate over the symbolic and connectionist modeling of the task. Several subsequent attempts at improving the original results with new connectionist models have been made (Plunkett & Marchman, 1991; Cottrell & Plunkett, 1991; MacWhinney & Leinbach, 1991; Daugherty & Seidenberg, 1993). Most notably, MacWhinney and Leinbach (1991) constructed a multilayer neural network trained with the backpropagation algorithm. A challenge for a better symbolic model was posed (MacWhinney & Leinbach, 1991). Ling and Marinov (1993), Ling (1994) constructed a purely symbolic pattern associator (SPA) and showed that SPA outperforms neural networks on the generalization ability by a wide margin.

To make the experiment computationally feasible (since we need to make many runs), we take only English verbs that have at most 4 phoneme letters[2]. To make the learning even easier, we train networks only for the mapping from the verb stems to the third phoneme letter in the past tense. (One can build

---

[2]Phoneme representation is used to model spoken English. Here, a special phoneme representation, called UNIBET (MacWhinney, 1990; MacWhinney & Leinbach, 1991), is used. It uses 36 alphabet letters and numbers to represent 36 different phonemes.

several such nets to predict other phoneme letters in the past tense.) Clearly, if overfitting happens on the third letter, it would be observed in the whole past tense as well, since we count a classification error if any phoneme letter in the past tense is incorrectly predicted.

The verb source in our experiment came from MacWhinney and Leinbach (1991), which contains 600 verbs that have at most 4 phoneme letters. The set of 600 verbs is randomly split into two equally-sized sets of training and testing examples without overlap. Table 1 lists some typical examples of the verbs we used (note that "_" indicates the blank phoneme).

Table 1: Some examples of English verbs and their past tenses.

```
Verb Stem                                 Past Tense
Spelling   Reg/Irreg   UNIBET    UNIBET     3rd    Rules

allot      R           6lat      6latId     a      copy 3rd
base       R           bes_      best__     s      copy 3rd
ease       R           iz__      izd___     d      reg. suffix
ache       R           ek__      ekt___     t      reg. suffix
aid        R           ed__      edId__     I      reg. suffix
bend       I           bEnd      bEnt__     n      copy 3rd
blow       I           blo_      blu___     u      irreg. phoneme change
grow       I           gro_      gru___     u      irreg. phoneme change
go         I           go__      went__     n      irreg. phoneme change
```

Clearly, predicting the third phoneme letter in the past tense depends heavily on the third phoneme letter in the verb stem — in most cases, they are the same (examples 1, 2 and 6 above), or regular suffixation (examples 3,4, and 5), and occasionally, irregular phoneme changes (examples 7, 8, and 9). There are in fact three rules for the regular suffix adding: suffixing Id if the verb stem ends with t or d (in UNIBET), suffixing t if the verb stem ends with a unvoiced consonant, and suffixing d if the verb stem ends with a voiced consonant or vowel. Irregular phoneme changes are only *partially* predictable (e.g., examples 7 and 8 above) (cf. (Ling, 1994)), and therefore can be regarded as a secondary regularity existing among the more regular, primary regularities (i.e., the identity relation and the regular suffix-adding) — just like those flipped function values among more "regular" ones governed by the linear equations described in the last section. There are about 20 such irregular phoneme changes in each of the training and testing sets. Therefore, the training is considered to be converged if the training error is reduced below or equal to 20 in our experiments.

Error backpropagation (with the initial weights set within $[0.01, -0.01]$ and the learning rate set to 0.01) is used for small networks, while the conjugate gradient (CG) method for the larger ones (see table). (In this Section we mainly concern the overfitting effect rather than networks and training algorithms that produce the lowest testing errors.) In order to observe when exactly overfitting starts and how primary and secondary regularities are learned and overfitted, we report the results of 5 individual runs with different random seeds (instead of only the averages) in Table 2. In addition, each entry is in the form of the sum of errors for regular and irregular verbs respectively.

For the distributed representation we take the one from (MacWhinney & Leinbach, 1991; MacWhinney, 1993), which uses a specific set of (binary) phonetic features to encode each UNIBET phoneme letter. Each vowel and consonant is encoded by a total of 14 phonetic features (bits)[3]. Therefore, the networks have 56 (4×14) input units and 14 output units. Networks with 20 hidden units (an adequate number, by experiments) and 100 hidden units (overly large) are tested. Clearly, because the three rules for the regular suffix adding as well as some irregular phoneme changes use micro-features (such as voiced or unvoiced) of the phonemes, the distributed representation is likely to have a better generalization than the one-per-value. In the one-per-value representation, each phoneme letter is encoded by 37 bits (36 UNIBET phoneme letters plus the blank phoneme). The networks thus have 148 (37×4) input units and 37 output units. Networks with 60 and 120 hidden units are tested. Everything else (including the training and testing sets) is the same. Not to our surprise, overfitting never occurs in any run in this representation. See Table 2.

---

[3] Since in the original distributed representation the feature lists of vowels and consonants are disjoint, We have to add extra bits to distinguish the vowels from the consonants.

Table 2: Summary of the overfitting in learning past tenses of English verbs.

Distributed Representation, 56-to-14 mappings					
# of h.u.	converged or not	min testing error	training error at that point	overfit when converged	training error at that point
20 (BP)	yes	18+19	3+11	10+1	2+4
	yes	15+19	4+13	17+1	2+5
	yes	20+17	5+14	8+0	2+2
	yes	16+18	3+12	14 + (−1)	2+4
	yes	17+18	3+11	15+1	2+4
100 (CG)	yes	15+17	5+14	18+1	1+3
	yes	26+19	1+17	8+1	0+5
	yes	17+18	4+14	17+1	2+4
	yes	22+17	4+15	10+0	2+4
	yes	13+16	4+14	21+1	1+1
one-per-value Representation, 148-to-37 mappings					
# of h.u.	converged or not	min testing error	training error at that point	overfit when converged	training error at that point
60 (CG)	yes	32+15	16+4	NO	16+4
	yes	27+16	1+3	NO	1+3
	yes	26+17	2+1	NO	2+1
	no	N/A	N/A	NO	N/A
	yes	27+17	2+1	NO	2+1
120 (CG)	yes	29+16	4+6	NO	4+6
	yes	35+19	13+0	NO	13+0
	no	N/A	N/A	NO	N/A
	yes	30+18	6+5	NO	6+5
	no	N/A	N/A	NO	N/A

The results are in the form of the sum of errors for regular and irregular verbs respectively.

We can draw the following conclusions about overfitting:

- Overfitting occurs in every run with the distributed representation. While training errors continue to drop, testing errors drop and reach to a minimum and then increase. For example, in the first row of the table, the testing error drops to a minimum of 18+19 (18 errors for regular verbs and 19 errors for irregular verbs), and then increases to 28 (18+10) for regulars and 20 (19+1) for irregulars.

- The training errors at the point when the testing errors are minimum range from 14 to 19. It is clear that, at that point, most of the training errors for the regular verbs have been eliminated (only 1 to 5 are left), but not for the irregulars (11 to 17 are left). That is, overfitting starts to occur when the primary regularity, but not the secondary regularity, has mostly been learned. This confirms again our analyses in Section 3.

- When overfitting does occur, the testing errors for regular verbs increase much more (8 to 21) than the testing errors of the irregular verbs (−1, a drop, to 1). That is, overfitting occurs for *regular verbs only*. This confirms our analyses in Section 3 that overfitting occurs when the fitting of the secondary regularity interferes with and worsens the prediction of the primary regularity.

- With the one-per-value representation, the micro-features in the phoneme letters become implicit. The networks cannot capture the secondary regularity governed by the phonetic features (such as voiced consonants) in the partially productive irregular verbs and suffix-adding regular verbs. Therefore, there is no overfitting. Weigend (1994) used one-per-value representation in his phoneme mapping task, and probably for the same reason, he did not observe overfitting in learning. In addition, one-per-class representation results in higher minimum testing errors than the distributed representation.

5 Conclusions

We design simple experiments on Boolean functions with clear rationale and show that the degree of overfitting at symbolic level depends on the representation. If the representation allows the networks to capture *both* a primary regularity and one or more secondary regularities, overfitting occurs after learning the primary regularity. The fitting of the secondary regularities interferes with and thus worsens the prediction of the primary regularity in the testing set. We also observed in series of experiments that no matter what training algorithms are used, the networks that are just large enough (just enough hidden units for near-zero training error), or overly large (e.g., roughly four times larger than just enough) have better and more stable generalization than networks of the size in between.

Reference

Cottrell, G., & Plunkett, K. (1991). Using a recurrent net to learn the past tense. In *Proceedings of the Cognitive Science Society Conference*.

Daugherty, K., & Seidenberg, M. (1993). Beyond rules and exceptions: A connectionist modeling approach to inflectional morphology. In Lima, S. (Ed.), *The Reality of Linguistic Rules*. John Benjamins.

Grossman, T. (1994). Use of bad training data for better predictions. In Cowan, J. D., Tesauro, G., & Alspector, J. (Eds.), *Advances in Neural Information Processing Systems — 6 (NIPS*93)*.

Hinton, G., McClelland, J., & Rumelhart, D. (1986). Distributed representation. In Rumelhart, D., McClelland, J., & the PDP Research Group (Eds.), *Parallel Distributed Processing Vol 1*, pp. 77 – 109. Cambridge, MA: MIT Press.

Lachter, J., & Bever, T. (1988). The relation between linguistic structure and associative theories of language learning – a constructive critique of some connectionist learning models. In Pinker, S., & Mehler, J. (Eds.), *Connections and Symbols*, pp. 195 – 247. Cambridge, MA: MIT Press.

Ling, C. X. (1994). Learning the past tense of English verbs: the Symbolic Pattern Associator vs. connectionist models. *Journal of Artificial Intelligence Research, 1*, 209 – 229.

Ling, C. X., & Marinov, M. (1993). Answering the connectionist challenge: a symbolic model of learning the past tense of English verbs. *Cognition, 49*(3), 235–290.

Ling, C. X. (1994). Predicting irregular past tenses. In *Proceedings of The Sixteenth Annual Conference of the Cognitive Science Society*, pp. 577 – 582.

MacWhinney, B. (1990). *The CHILDES Project: Tools for Analyzing Talk*. Hillsdale, NJ: Erlbaum.

MacWhinney, B. (1993). Connections and symbols: closing the gap. *Cognition, 49*(3), 291–296.

MacWhinney, B., & Leinbach, J. (1991). Implementations are not conceptualizations: Revising the verb model. *Cognition, 40*, 121 – 157.

Pinker, S., & Prince, A. (1988). On language and connectionism: Analysis of a parallel distributed processing model of language acquisition. In Pinker, S., & Mehler, J. (Eds.), *Connections and Symbols*, pp. 73 – 193. Cambridge, MA: MIT Press.

Plunkett, K., & Marchman, V. (1991). U-shaped learning and frequency effects in a multilayered perceptron: Implications for child language acquisition. *Cognition, 38*, 43 – 102.

Prasada, S., & Pinker, S. (1993). Generalization of regular and irregular morphological patterns. *Language and Cognitive Processes, 8*(1), 1 – 56.

Rumelhart, D., & McClelland, J. (1986). On learning the past tenses of English verbs. In Rumelhart, D., McClelland, J., & the PDP Research Group (Eds.), *Parallel Distributed Processing, Vol. 2*, pp. 216 – 271. Cambridge, MA: MIT Press.

Sejnowski, T., & Rosenberg, C. (1987). Parallel networks that learn to pronounce English text. *Complex Systems, 1*, 145 – 168.

Wang, C., Venkatesh, S. S., & Judd, J. S. (1994). Optimal stopping and effective machine complexity in learning. In Cowan, J. D., Tesauro, G., & Alspector, J. (Eds.), *Advances in Neural Information Processing Systems — 6 (NIPS*93)*.

Weigend, A. S. (1994). On overfitting and the effective number of hidden units. In Mozer, M. C., Smolensky, P., Touretzky, D., Elman, J. L., & Weigend, A. S. (Eds.), *Proceedings of the 1993 Connectionist Models Summer School*, pp. 335 – 342. Erbaum Associates.

Optimal Radial Basis Function Nets with Applications to Nonlinear Function Learning and Classification *

Adam Krzyżak†, Lei Xu‡

†Dept. of Computer Science, Concordia University
Montreal, Canada
krzyzak@cs.concordia.ca
‡Dept. of Computer Science, Chinese University of Hong Kong
Shatin, Hong Kong
lxu@cs.cuhk.hk

Abstract— Single layer radial basis function (RBF) networks in nonlinear functional estimation and classification are considered. Analytical expressions the optimal radial functions are given and the optimal rates of convergence in the class of smooth functions are derived.

1 Introduction

Recently many authors investigated universal approximation properties and rates of convergence of sigmoidal nets Cybenko [1], Hornik et al. [2], Barron [3], McCafrey and Gallant [4] and RBF nets Poggio and Girosi [5], Girosi et al [6], Specht [7], Park and Sandberg [8, 9], Xu et al [10] and Krzyżak et al [11]. Xu et al [10] pointed out the connections between RBF nets and KRE and exploited these connections to obtain the rates of convergence for RBF nets in terms of the number of hidden units for fixed radial functions satisfying some tail conditions. In the present paper we will further these results by allowing the radial functions themselves to vary with the number of hidden units and we will find the optimal radial functions in terms of the Fourier transform of estimated mappings.

In the general setting a neural network uncovers the relationship between an input vector x and a scalar output y. In classification problem the network is trained on the learning sequence containing feature vectors and their correct labels in order to achieve a correct classification on a unlabeled pattern x. In functional approximation the network forecasts the variable y based on the observed vector x relating input x to its target y. Statistical model describing the relationship between x and y is the regression function

$$Y = f(X) + \epsilon$$

where $f : R^d \to R$ is an unknown mapping and ϵ is a random error. Single hidden layer RBF networks are represented by

$$f_n(x) = \sum_{i=1}^{n} w_i \phi([xx - c_i]^t \Sigma^{-1}[x - c_i]) \tag{1}$$

where ϕ is a radial basis function or kernel, and parameters of the network $w_i \in R$, $c_i \in R^d$, $i = 1, \ldots, n$ and $\Sigma \in R^d x R^d$ are the weights, the centers and the positive definite receptive field matrix, respectively. Denote by Θ the vector of network parameters. Networks of type (1) have been considered by Poggio and Girosi [5], Hornik et al [2], Krzyżak et al [11] and others. Moody and Darken [12], and Xu et al [10] considered the normalized version of (1):

$$f_n(x) = \frac{\sum_{i=1}^{n} w_i \phi([x - c_i]^t \Sigma^{-1}[x - c_i])}{\sum_{i=1}^{n} \phi([x - c_i]^t \Sigma^{-1}[x - c_i])}. \tag{2}$$

The problem of determining a specific value $\hat{\Theta}$ for Θ using sample set $\mathcal{D}_N = \{X_i, Y_i\}_1^N$ is called *learning* or *training*. Usually, a value $\hat{\Theta}$ (and thus an $\hat{f}_{n,N}(x)$, which depends on $\mathcal{D}_N$) is obtained by minimizing the empirical error:

$$\varepsilon_{RBF}^2(\mathcal{D}_N, \hat{f}_{n,N}) = \min_{\{f_{n,N} \in \mathcal{F}_n\}} \varepsilon_{RBF}^2(\mathcal{D}_N, f_{n,N}) = \min_{\Theta} \varepsilon_{RBF}^2(\mathcal{D}_N, f_{n,N}(x, \Theta)),$$

$$\varepsilon_{RBF}^2(\mathcal{D}_N, f_{n,N}(x, \Theta)) = \frac{1}{N} \sum_{i=1}^{N} |Y_i - f_{n,N}(X_i, \Theta)|^2. \tag{3}$$

This minimization is a hard nonlinear problem and the resulting net with parameters learned by (3) is difficult to analize. Using VC theory Krzyżak et al [11] proved consistency of net (1) trained by (3). Xu et al [10] found the connection between net (2) and the KRE defined below and proved consistency properties and rates for the normalized RBF net via kernel regression analysis. In the present paper we will study the optimal shape and the optimal rate of convergence of net (1) trained by assigning c_i to X_i and w_i to Y_i. By exploiting the connection between RBF nets and KRE we will also study the optimal rates of convergence of RBF net (2) trained as in (3).

---

*The research of the first author was supported by the grant from Natural Sciences and Engineering Research Council of Canada and by the Alexander von Humboldt Foundation of Germany.
Address for correspondence: A. Krzyżak, Department of Computer Science LB921-1, Concordia University, 1450 De Maisonneuve Blvd. West, Montreal, Que., Canada H3G 1M8, phone: (514) 848 3007, fax: (514) 848 2830, email: krzyzak@cs.concordia.ca.

2 MISE Optimal RBF Nets and Optimal Rates of Convergence

In this section we consider RBF nets in nonlinar functional estimation problem and nonparametric classification. We analitically derive the optimal radial functions in RBF networks and corresponding optimal MISE rates of convergence. The results obtained in this section are motivated by the celebrated study of the optimal kernel in density estimation by Watson and Leadbetter [13] specialized to a class of Parzen kernels by Davis [14].

Let (X, Y) be a random vector and let density of X be known and denoted by $f(x)$. Let $E\{Y|X = x\} = R(x)$ be regression function of Y given X and $EY^2 < \infty$. We focus our attention on recovering from the training sequence $\mathcal{D}_n = \{X_i, Y_i\}_1^n$ a nonlinear mapping $G(x) = R(x)f(x) = ER(X)$ using RBF network,

$$G_n(x) = \sum_{i=1}^{n} Y_i K_n(||x - X_i||) \tag{4}$$

which is equivalent to network 1 with parameters Θ trained by setting $w_i = Y_i$, $c_i = X_i$, and

$$K_n(||x||) = \frac{1}{n}\phi(x^t \Sigma^{-1} x). \tag{5}$$

and $||x|| = x^t \Sigma^{-1} x$. For the estimate of We derive analitically the optimal form of radial kernel K and obtain the exact expression for the best MISE rate of convergence of network 4. Estimation of G plays the important role in the following problems:

- nonlinear function approximation

  Consider the problem of recovering nonlinear input-otput map in the following model $Y = R(X) + Z$, where Z is a zero mean noise and R is an unknown map. It is obvious that R is regression function $E(Y|X = x)$. In order to estimate R we generate a sequence of i.i.d. random variables $X_i, i = 1, \ldots, n$ from a given density f and observe $Y_i, i = 1, \ldots, n$. Our estimate G_n enables us to recover $G(x) = R(x)f(x)$. Hence the estimate of R is naturally given by $G_n(x)/f(x)$.

- nonparametric classification

  In two-class decision problem, based upon the observation of a random vector $X \in R^d$, one has to guess the value of a class label Y corresponding to the observation of a random feature vector $X \in R^d$, where Y is a random variable taking values from $\{-1, 1\}$. The decision is a function $g : R^d \to \{-1, 1\}$, whose goodness is measured by the *error probability* $L(g) = P\{g(X) \neq Y\}$. It is well known that the decision function that minimizes the error probability is given by

$$g^*(x) = \begin{cases} -1 & \text{if } m(x) \leq 0 \\ 1 & \text{otherwise,} \end{cases}$$

  where $m(x) = E(Y|X = x)$, g^* is called the *Bayes decision*, and its error probability $L^* = P\{g^*(X) \neq Y\}$ is the *Bayes risk*.

  When the joint distribution of (X, Y) is unknown, a good decision has to be learned from a training sequence $\mathcal{D}_n$, which consists of n independent copies of the $R^d \times \{-1, 1\}$-valued pair (X, Y). Then formally, a decision rule g_n is a function, whose error probability is given by $L(g_n) = P\{g_n(X, D_n) \neq Y|D_n\}$. It is intuitively clear that pattern recognition is closely related to regression function estimation. This is seen by observing that the function m defining the optimal decision g^* is just the regression function $E(Y|X = x)$. Thus, having a good estimate $f_n(x)$ of the regression function m, we expect a good performance of the decision rule

$$g_n(x) = \begin{cases} -1 & \text{if } f_n(x) \leq 0 \\ 1 & \text{otherwise.} \end{cases} \tag{6}$$

  Indeed, we have the well-known inequality (see e.g. Devroye et al. [15]),

$$P\{g_n(X) \neq Y|X = x, D_n\} - P\{g^*(X) \neq Y|X = x\} \leq |f_n(x) - m(x)| \tag{7}$$

  and in particular,

$$P\{g_n(X) \neq Y|D_n\} - P\{g^*(X) \neq Y\} \leq \left(E\left((f_n(X) - m(X))^2\big| D_n\right)\right)^{1/2}.$$

  Therefore, any consistent estimate f_n of the regression function m leads to a consistent classification rule g_n. For example, if f_n is an RBF-estimate of m based on minimizing the empirical L_2 error $J_n(f_\theta)$, then g_n is universally consistent classification rule [11]. The optimal classification rule is obtained by assigning a given feature vector X to a class with a highest *aposteriori* probability, i.e. to a class i, if $P_i(x) = \max_j P_j(x)$, where $P_i(x) = EI_{(\theta=i, X=x)} = ER_i(X)$, θ is a class label, $R_i(x) = E(I_{(\theta=i)}|X = x)$ and I_A is indicator of set A. Therefore it is sufficient to estimate G to obtain a good classification rule.

Let us now derive the optimal K_n^* radial function K_n in network (4). where $K_n(||x||)$ is some square integrable kernel. Consider MISE of $G_n(x)$

$$Q = E \int \left(G(x) - G_n(x)\right)^2 dx. \tag{8}$$

Denote by $\Phi(g)$ Fourier transform of g, i.e.

$$\Phi(g) = \int g(x)e^{itx}dx$$

and

$$g(x) = \frac{1}{2\pi}\int \Phi(t)e^{-itx}dt.$$

The following theorem gives Fourier transform of the optimal MISE radial function for network (4).

Theorem 1 *Suppose that $G \in L_2$. The optimal kernel K_n^* minimizing (8) is defined by the equation*

$$\Phi(K_n^*) = \frac{n|\Phi(G)|^2}{EY^2 + (n-1)|\Phi(G)|^2}. \tag{9}$$

The optimal rate of MISE corresponding to the optimal kernel (9) is given by

$$Q^* = \frac{1}{2\pi}\int \frac{\left(EY^2 - |\Phi(G)|^2\right)|\Phi(G)|^2}{EY^2 + (n-1)|\Phi(G)|^2}dt. \tag{10}$$

Notice that for bandlimited R and f with the rate of MISE convergence with the kernel (9) is

$$nQ^* \to \frac{1}{2\pi}\int_{-T}^{T}\left(EY^2 - |\Phi(G)|^2\right)dt$$

as $n \to \infty$, where T is the maximum of bands of R and f. Therefore $Q^* = O(1/n)$. For other classes of R and f we will get optimal kernels and rates dependent on these classes. Currently we are studying specific classes nonlinearities and densities for which we derive exact rates of convergence. These classes include polynomial and exponential classes that is classes of R and f with tails of $\Phi(R)$ and $\Phi(f)$ decreasing either polynomially or exponentially.

The problem with formula (9) is that the optimal kernel depends on the unknown regression G and it also varies with n. We can consider a sublass of networks (1) in which $\phi(x^t\Sigma^{-1}x) = nh^{-1}K_n(||x||/h)$, $\Sigma = \mathrm{diag}(h, \ldots, h)$ and $||x|| = x^tx$. It can be shown that for bandlimited regressions and input densities the optimal rate $O(1/n)$ is achieved for $K(||x||) = sin(||x||)/||x||$ or the sinc kernel. The same kernel is also optimal for polynomial and exponential classes of R and f.

3   MISE Optimal Normalized RBF Nets and Optimal Rates of Convergence

In this section we will derive the optimaRBF nets and the optimal rate of convergence in case when the f is estimated from $(X_1, Y_1), \cdots, (X_n, Y_n)$. We consider normalized networks given by (2). If the network parameters Θ are trained in the similar fashion as in the previous section we obtain the following network

$$R_n(x) = \frac{G_n(x)}{f_n(x)} = \frac{\frac{1}{n}\sum_{i=1}^{n}Y_iK_n(||x - X_i||)}{\frac{1}{n}\sum_{i=1}^{n}K_n(||x - X_i||)} \tag{11}$$

with radial function K given by (5). The MISE of R_n is given by

$$Q = E\int |R_n(x) - R(x)|^2f(x)dx. \tag{12}$$

It is difficult to work with MISE directly. Instead we will use the relationship between expectation and probability of deviation

$$EX \le \epsilon + (M - \epsilon)P\{X > \epsilon\} \tag{13}$$

which is valid for bounded random variables, i.e. $X \le M$. Let $|Y| \le M < \infty$ a.s. and $f(x) \le T < \infty$. We use (13) to obtain the following upper bound on $\overline{Q}$ optimal bound on Q,

$$\epsilon + (M - \epsilon)\frac{1}{2\pi}\int\left[\epsilon_m(A_3|\Phi(K)|^2 - B_3\overline{\Phi(K)} - \overline{B_3}\Phi(K) + B_3)\right]dt \tag{14}$$

where $A_2 = \frac{1-|\Phi(f)|^2}{n} + |\Phi(f)|^2$, $B_2 = |\Phi(f)|^2$, $A_3 = A_1 + A_2$, $B_3 = B_1 + B_2$, $\epsilon_m = \max(\epsilon_1^{-1}, \epsilon_2^{-1})$, $\epsilon_1 = \epsilon^2/2^{16}M^2T$, $\epsilon_2 = \epsilon^3/2^9M^4T(2^7M^2 + \epsilon)$ and ϵ is an arbitrary positive number. Minimizing the above bound with respect to kernel K we get

Theorem 2 *The optimal kernel K_n^* minimizing (14) is defined by the equation*

$$\Phi(K_n^*) = \frac{n[|\Phi(f)|^2 + |\Phi(G)|^2]}{(1 + EY^2) + (n-1)[|\Phi(f)|^2 + |\Phi(G)|^2]}. \tag{15}$$

The optimal rate of MISE corresponding to the optimal kernel (15) is given by

$$Q^* = \frac{1}{2\pi}\int \frac{\left(EY^2 - [|\Phi(f)|^2 + |\Phi(G)|^2]\right)|\Phi(G)|^2}{(1 + EY^2) + (n-1)[|\Phi(f)|^2 + |\Phi(G)|^2]}dt. \tag{16}$$

The discussion given after the proof of Theorem 1 also applies to Theorem 2. Using the connection between RBF nets and kernel regression estimates pointed out by Xu et al. [10, Lemma 1] Theorem 2 provides the upper bound on performance of the normalized net (2) learned by minimizing the empirical MISE error

$$\varepsilon_{RBF}^2(\mathcal{D}_n, g_n) = \frac{1}{n} \sum_{i=1}^{n} |Y_i - f_n(X_i)|^2 \tag{17}$$

with respect to parameter vector Θ and tested on the learning sequence.

References

[1] G. Cybenko, "Approximations by superpositions of sigmoidal functions," *Math. Control, Signals, Systems*, vol. 2, pp. 303–314, 1989.

[2] K. Hornik, M. Stinchcombe, and H. White, "Multi-layer feedforward networks are universal approximators," *Neural Networks*, vol. 2, pp. 359–366, 1989.

[3] A. R. Barron, "Universal approximation bounds for superpositions of a sigmoidal function," *IEEE Transactions on Information Theory*, vol. 39, pp. 930–944, 1993.

[4] D. F. McCaffrey and A. R. Gallant, "Convergence rates for single hiddden layer feedforward networks," *Neural Networks*, vol. 7, no. 1, pp. 147–158, 1994.

[5] T. Poggio and F. Girosi, "A theory of networks for approximation and learning," *Proceedings of IEEE*, vol. 78, pp. 1481–1497, 1990.

[6] F. Girosi, M. Jones, and T. Poggio, "Regularization theory and neural network architectures," *Neural Computation*, vol. 7, pp. 219–267, 1995.

[7] D. F. Specht, "Probabilistic neural networks," *Neural Networks*, vol. 3, pp. 109–118, 1990.

[8] J. Park and I. W. Sandberg, "Universal approximation using radial-basis-function networks," *Neural Computation*, vol. 3, pp. 246–257, 1991.

[9] J. Park and I. W. Sandberg, "Approximation and radial-basis-function networks," *Neural Computation*, vol. 5, pp. 305–316, 1993.

[10] L. Xu, A. Krzyżak, and A. Yuille, "On radial basis function nets and kernel regression: approximation ability, convergence rate and receptive field size," *Neural Networks*, vol. 7, pp. 609–628, 1994.

[11] A. Krzyżak, T. Linder, and G. Lugosi, "Nonparametric estimation and classification using radial basis function nets and empirical risk minimization," *IEEE Transactions on Neural Networks*, vol. 7, pp. 475–487, March 1996.

[12] J. Moody and J. Darken, "Fast learning in networks of locally-tuned processing units," *Neural Computation*, vol. 1, pp. 281–294, 1989.

[13] G. Watson and M. Leadbetter, "On the estimation of the probability density, I,," *Annals of Mathematical Statistics*, vol. 34, pp. 480–491, 1963.

[14] K. Davis, "Mean integrated error properties of density estimates," *Annals of Statistics*, vol. 5, pp. 530–535, 1977.

[15] L. Devroye, L. Györfi, and G. Lugosi, *A Probabilistic Theory of Pattern Recognition*. New York: Springer-Verlag, 1996.

Extended Cauchy Machines

S. Cuchet‡, E. Fiesler†

† IDIAP, C.P. 592, CH-1920 Martigny, Switzerland
‡ Steria Informatique SA, rue Bains 35, CH-1205 Geneva, Switzerland

Abstract— The Cauchy machine is a stochastic neural network related to the Boltzmann machine that uses fast simulated annealing instead of classical simulated annealing. Both these machines have the advantage that they enable a global minimum search of the error function. The main drawback of these machines is the slow training process and, like with other multilayer neural networks, the lack of knowledge for choosing the number of hidden neurons. If higher order connections are employed, a smaller number of training cycles can be expected and hidden neurons can be avoided. Hence, high order extensions of the Cauchy machine has been developed and are presented here.

The problem with fully connected higher order neural networks is that the number of possible connections increases exponentially with the order. To overcome this problem, three ontogenic methods, a pruning, a growing, and an hybrid growing-pruning method have been developed to produce a sparsely connected network topology during the training process, thereby further extending the Cauchy machine. The performance of these extended Cauchy machines is evaluated by means of four benchmark data sets.

1 Introduction

The Cauchy machine is a recurrent neural network with symmetric connections. Its interconnection weights are modified in order to store prototypes of patterns in dynamically stable configurations of the neural network.

Recurrent neural networks have been investigated by many researchers during the 60's and 70's. It was in Hopfield's paper [1] that the principle of storing information in a dynamically stable network was formulated in precise terms for the first time.

Hinton, Sejnowski, and Ackley have proposed a generalization of the Hopfield neural network, that uses stochastic neurons, symmetric connections updated by a statistical version of the Hebbian rule, hidden neurons like multilayer feedforward neural networks, and simulated annealing [2] [3]. They have given the name Boltzmann machine to this neural network, in honor of Boltzmann who discovered in 1872 that the random motion of the molecules of a gas has an energy related to the temperature of the gas.

Simulated annealing is an optimization method that, contrary to gradient descent, allows hill-climbing which enables it to escape from local minima in the energy landscape. Simulated annealing finds a global minimum with high probability, and thus, overcomes the drawback of gradient descent of getting trapped in local minima. However, simulated annealing is a relatively slow process since the learning requires the calculation of co-occurrences of neurons during the simulated annealing processes performed repeatedly on all patterns.

Sejnowski has proposed a generalized Boltzmann machine, that uses high order connections[1] with the aim of speeding up the learning [5]. He does not however give solutions of how to handle the large number of possible connections that grows exponential with the order, which is likely to overrule the advantage in speed.

Szu has proposed the use of a faster cooling schedule that is inversely linear in time [6]. Hence, the function that generates the states as well as the acceptance function has to be modified to reach optimal states faster. A multi-dimensional Cauchy probability is used instead of the Boltzmann probability, which facilitates the generation of distant states. Szu has therefore

---

[1]For definitions of high order connections and high order neural networks, see [4].

called this machine *Cauchy machine*. The shape of the Cauchy acceptance function remains the same, although it accepts more likely changes that increase the energy, because of the new cooling schedule.

Jong and Park have given a lower bound for the Cauchy machine annealing schedule that shows that the cooling schedule can be inversely proportional to a power of time [7].

2   Higher order Cauchy machines

Cauchy machines have symmetric connections that have the same weight when used in either direction. The proposed extended Cauchy machines have a high order topology. Multiplication is used as the splicing function[2] in the experiments performed.

In order to extend the Cauchy machine for handling high order connections, some alterations to its learning rule have to be made. The high order energy function is the sum over all orders of the energy due to connections of each order:

$$E = \Sigma_{\omega=1}^{\Omega} \left(\frac{1}{\omega+1} \Sigma_{n_1} \Sigma_{n_2} \cdots \Sigma_{n_{\omega+1}} \mathrm{w}_{n_1 n_2 \cdots n_{\omega+1}} \cdot a_{n_1} \cdots a_{n_{\omega+1}} \right) \tag{1}$$

where $\mathrm{w}_{n_1 n_2 \cdots n_{\omega+1}}$ is the weight tensor and a_{n_i} a neuron activation value. The variation in energy actually used in the Cauchy machine learning rule is therefore:

$$\Delta E_{n_{\omega+1}} = \Sigma_{\omega=1}^{\Omega} \left(\Sigma_{n_1} \Sigma_{n_2} \cdots \Sigma_{n_\omega} w_{n_1 n_2 \cdots n_{\omega+1}} \cdot a_{n_1} \cdots a_{n_\omega} \right) \tag{2}$$

Moreover, it is necessary to consider co-occurrences, or correlations of ω-tuples of neurons, instead of considering only pairs of neurons, and weights are updated according to the equation:

$$\Delta \mathrm{w}_{n_1 n_2 \cdots n_{\omega+1}} = \eta \left(p^+_{n_1 n_2 \cdots n_{\omega+1}} - p^-_{n_1 n_2 \cdots n_{\omega+1}} \right), \tag{3}$$

where η is the learning rate and $p^+_{n_1 n_2 \cdots n_{\omega+1}}$ and $p^-_{n_1 n_2 \cdots n_{\omega+1}}$ are the co-occurrences of neurons n_1 to $n_{\omega+1}$ when the visible neurons are clamped and unclamped respectively.

The Cauchy machine extensions presented here uses multiplication as the splicing function. To introduce other splicing functions in the learning rule, the energy function has to be modified by applying the other splicing function to the outputs of neurons, instead of multiplying them. With the product splicing function, the energy is increased/decreased by setting the output of the current neuron to 1, if and only if all other neurons are ON. With the exclusive-or splicing function for example, the energy is increased/decreased if the current neuron is set to 1 and the result of the XOR on other linked neurons is 0, or if the current neuron is set to 0, and the result of the XOR on other linked neurons is 1. In the same way, when using other splicing functions, one should not compute the co-occurrences of neurons, but the number of times that the splicing function applied on all linked neurons gives a positive result.

The extension of the Cauchy machine to higher order architectures implies a higher storage capacity and usually allows it to learn a task in less iterations. Note that higher order connections do not necessarily speed up the learning process, because the number of connections in a fully connected network can be very large. The second element of extending the Cauchy machine tries to circumvent this drawback by ontogenically modifying the architecture of the neural network during the learning to obtain a sparsely connected topology.

3   Three Ontogenic methods

Ontogenic methods automatically adapt the topology of a neural network to the task to be solved, thereby relieving the neural network designer from the notorious problem of finding

---

[2]The *splicing function* is the function that operates on the information available to a connection.

an optimized topology, which is typically done by trial-and-error. Among the advantages of ontogenic neural networks [8] are also the reduced training time and memory required to implement the neural network, due to the smaller topology.

3.1   A connection pruning method

The output of a neuron in the Cauchy machine changes easily from 0 to 1, or from 1 to 0, if the activation value is close to its threshold. When the activation is much greater or much smaller than the threshold value, the output does not depend on a small variation of the activation. The activation is the sum of the weights of the connections that link a neuron to its activated predecessors. Hence, if the absolute value if one of these weights is small in comparison to the other weights of the incoming connections, it could be removed without modifying the output of that neuron. At each training iteration, one could remove the connections with small weight values. Care should be taken not to remove potentially important connections that temporarily have a small value. A small variation of a weight over time would mean that it is stabilizing at a small value, whereas a great variation would indicate that they are in the process of changing. Consequently, weights could be removed if both their value and variation are small.

The proposed pruning method has therefore three parameters: the minimal weight change, the minimal absolute weight value, and a number of *suspicion* iterations. Connections are *suspected* if their absolute value and their variation are smaller than the values specified by the parameters. The method consists in removing the weights if a connection is suspected during more successive iterations than specified by the third parameter. This last parameter has been added since long oscillating periods were observed at the end of the learning. It should allow for more flexibility in choosing the first two parameters since the suspected behavior of a connection is now monitored over a period of time.

3.2   A connection growing method

When a first order Cauchy machine without hidden neurons is able to solve the task that it should learn, ontogenic methods can be employed to speed up the training process. On the other hand, when a problem is unsolvable with a first order neural network, high order connections can be added by a growing method to increase the power of the network. Two indicators of a first order network falling short are when the error does not decrease as fast as expected, and when some weights are expected to grow due to some patterns and at the same time expected to diminish due to others.

The growing method described here adds new connections when at least one output neuron produces a wrong answer and some of its incoming connections would not be able to modify their weights in the right direction because some patterns demand a weight change in the other direction. The new connection added should be a higher order connection that solves the conflict.

An output neuron of a Cauchy machine can have only two errors: either it produces a 1 instead of a 0, or a 0 instead of a 1. A connection encounters conflicts between patterns if, and only if, all the source neurons are ON. If one source neuron is OFF, the connection is not used to compute the activation of the target neuron. Conflicts therefore appear in two situations[3]: to have $1 \rightarrow 0$ instead of a desired $1 \rightarrow 1$, or to have $1 \rightarrow 1$ instead of $1 \rightarrow 0$. In the former case, a weight increase is invoked by the pattern which is responsible for the error; in the latter, a decrease.

A necessary condition for a conflict at the connection between neurons j and i is $p^+ > 0$ and $\Theta^+ - p^+ > 0$, which means that the two states $1 \rightarrow 0$ and $1 \rightarrow 1$ exist among the patterns. Θ^+ is the probability that the source neurons are ON simultaneously when all patterns are presented. A Cauchy machine can learn a task even though the condition above is true, if some other inputs clearly distinguish the patterns. The method suggests to add a connection

---

[3] $1 \rightarrow 0$ means that all source neurons are ON and the target neuron is OFF, and $1 \rightarrow 1$ means that all source neurons are ON and the target neuron is ON.

only if $\Theta^+ - p^+ > p^+$ when the target is 0, and only if $\Theta^+ - p^+ < p^+$ when the target is 1, and if the weight has the wrong sign. This additional condition enables the addition of a connection only if the conflicting connection does not tend toward the correct value due to other input neurons. The first condition is comprised in the second one.

The connection to be added has an order higher than that of the connection with the conflict. The new connection will bind the target neuron, the current source neurons, and one or more other input neurons. Some of these other neurons should have different outputs for each conflicting pattern, otherwise they would conserve the conflict. It is not necessary to consider other patterns, since the conflicts will still be recognized even if the order of the connections grows.

However, some neurons are better candidates. Those that are OFF, risk to be OFF for all patterns and those that have a small threshold value, risk to be always ON. The best candidates are those neurons that are ON and have the greatest threshold value.

If ω is the order of the connection where a conflict has been detected, $\omega + 1$ is the order of the connection to be added. If the new source neuron does not solve the problem, because it also is in conflict with the same pattern, another connection of order $\omega + 1$ or a connection of higher order can be added at the next iteration.

An initial weight of zero would enable the pruning method to perform faster if it is used simultaneously with the growing method (compare section 3.3). However, it is necessary to wait at least one iteration to see if the new connection is able to diminish the number of conflicts. Otherwise, many other connections would be added, even if they are not useful.

The initial weight of the new connection is therefore chosen to be the opposite of that of the conflicting connection.

3.3 A hybrid connection growing-and-pruning method

This method is a combination of the two methods where the pruning and growing algorithms are both active at the same time. This enables the addition of high order connections as well as the removal of unimportant links in general.

4 Results

Four benchmark data sets (two artificial and two real world applications) have been selected for our simulations: exclusive OR, *letters* (included in the SNNS simulator and explained in its documentation [9]), *digits* (a subset of the NIST handwritten digit database [10], scaled down to 16 by 16 pixels), and *sonar*; see [11]. Due to space limitation only the results for *letters* and *digits* are shown; see [12] for an extended version of this paper including all the results.

For the results presented in this section the following default parameter settings were used: a learning rate of one, for the three ontogenic parameters: 0.01, 0.3, and 5, and a fully first order connected initial topology. The results are shown in tabular form, where 'basic Cauchy' stands for the standard fully first order connected Cauchy machine and '2nd order Cauchy' for a fully second order connected one. The percentages in brackets indicate what percentage of all possible connections have been created randomly as an (initial) partially connected topology. The next four columns contain the number of training iterations needed (I), the number of connections of the initial topology (W_{init}), the number of connections in the final topology (W_{final}), and the order of the highest order connection in the final topology (Ω_{final}). The last three columns for the digits result tables show the generalization performance as percentage correct, percentage incorrect, and percentage unknown patterns.

4.1 Letters

The temperature schedule for the letters benchmark [9] was kept at zero since the letters benchmark could not be learned with a non-zero temperature schedule, which is likely due to large similarities among the patterns.

learning rule	I	W_{init}	W_{final}	Ω_{final}
basic Cauchy	69	3660	3660	1
basic (50%)	200	1830	1830	1
2nd order Cauchy	21	117242	117242	2
pruning	66	3660	1591	1
growing	42	3660	4618	4
hybrid	56	3660	3046	4
hybrid (75%)	78	2745	1057	6

Table 1: Results for the letters benchmark.

The results, as summarized in table 1, show that the number of training iterations for a fully second order Cauchy machine are considerably less that those necessary for a first order one, but at the cost of a 32-fold in connectivity. The ontogenic methods present a solution where the number of iterations is comparable or lower than those for the first order machine, while reducing the connectivity in case of the pruning and hybrid method. The growing method adds 26% more connections but converges in 39% less iterations. Also presented are the results for two partially connected networks. A 50 percent connectivity for the non-ontogenic basic Cauchy machine required three times the number of iterations. A 75% initial connectivity for the hybrid method, on the other hand, resulted in a small network which learned in a number of iterations comparable to the basic machine.

4.2 Digits

A cooling schedule starting at temperature five and cooling until zero was used for the digits application.

learning rule	I	W_{init}	W_{final}	Ω_{final}	% right	% wrong	% unknown
basic Cauchy	19	35245	35245	1	35.0	47.8	17.2
pruning	19	35245	26987	1	34.4	54.8	10.8
growing	17	35245	35622	3	33.4	49.6	17.0
hybrid	20	35245	27217	4	34.6	56.0	9.4

Table 2: Results for the digits benchmark.

The results for the digits application, as shown in table 2, are similar to those of the letters. The main difference is due to the small number of required training iterations, which also implies a smaller variance. The reduction in connectivity is still considerable for both the pruning and the hybrid method, and only a very small amount of high order connections (1%) is added by the growing method, while gaining two training iterations. The generalization, which is poor as expected for only ten training patters, is only slightly affected by the ontogenic methods.

5 Conclusions

The number of iterations necessary to train a high order Cauchy machine is shown to be much smaller than for a first order one. The associated exponential explosion of the number of high order connections in a fully connected Cauchy machine can be successfully avoided by using the proposed ontogenic methods which produce very sparsely connected topologies. In specific, the pruning method typically produces a significantly smaller topology in less iterations as compared to the basic Cauchy machine, while the growing method shows a more significant reduction in the number of training iterations. The overall performance of the hybrid method, which is a combination of the growing and the pruning method, is good.

The combined results show that higher order Cauchy machines are worth further studying. A future study could include more experiments for obtaining results with statistical 'confidence', more applications, especially since the letters, digits, and sonar are solvable by a first order Cauchy machine, and perhaps trying other splicing functions, or combinations thereof.

The principles of the extended Cauchy machines can also be applied directly to the Boltzmann machine and related neural networks.

References

[1] John J. Hopfield, Neural Networks and physical systems with emergent collective computational abilities, *Proceedings of the National Academy of Science of the U.S.A.*, 79 (April 1982) 2554-2558.

[2] Geoffrey E. Hinton, Terrence J. Sejnowski, and David H. Ackley Boltzmann Machines : Constraint Satisfaction Networks that Learn, Technical Report CMU-CS-84-119, School of Computer Science, Carnegie-Mellon University, Pittsburg, PA, 1984.

[3] David H. Ackley, Geoffrey E. Hinton, and Terrence J. Sejnowski, A Learning Algorithm for Boltzmann Machines, *Cognitive Science* 9 (1985) 147–169.

[4] E. Fiesler, Neural Network Classification and Formalization, *Computer Standards & Interfaces* 16 (3) John Fulcher, ed., special issue on Neural Network Standards, (June, 1994) 231–239.

[5] Terrence Sejnowski, Higher-Order Boltzmann Machines, in: John S. Denker, ed., *Neural Networks for Computing* (Snowbird, Utah, U.S.A., April 13-16, 1986), AIP Conference Proceedings number 151 (American Institute of Physics, New York, New York, 1986) 398–403.

[6] Harold Szu, Fast Simulated Annealing, in: John S. Denker, ed., *Neural Networks for Computing* (Snowbird, Utah, U.S.A., April 13-16, 1986), AIP Conference Proceedings number 151 (American Institute of Physics, New York, New York, 1986) 420–425.

[7] Hong Jeong and Jeong Ho Park, Lower Bounds of Annealing Schedule for Boltzmann and Cauchy Machines, in: Proceedings of the International Joint Conference on Neural Networks (IJCNN) (Washington D.C., June 18–22, 1989) I (SOS Printing, San Diego, California, 1989) 581–586.

[8] E. Fiesler, Comparative Bibliography of Ontogenic Neural Networks, in: Maria Marinaro and Pietro G. Morasso, editors, *Proceedings of the International Conference on Artificial Neural Networks (ICANN 94)* (Springer-Verlag, London, U.K., 1994) 1 793–796. ISBN 3-540-19887-3.

[9] SNNS User Manual; available by anonymous FTP: ftp.informatik.uni-stuttgart.de /pub/SNNS/SNNSv3.2.Manual.ps.Z.

[10] M. D. Garris and R. A. Wilkinson, NIST Special Database 3, National Institute of Standards and Technology, Advanced System Division, Image Recognition Group, (February 1992).

[11] R. P. Gorman and T. J. Sejnowsky, Analysis of Hidden Units in a Layered Network Trained to Classify Sonar Targets, *Neural Networks* 1 (1) (1988) 75–89.

[12] S. Cuche and E. Fiesler, "Generalized Cauchy Machines." Submitted to the special issue of *Neurocomputing* on 'Recurrent Networks'.

Speech and Signal Processing

(Oral Presentation)

Voice Command : A Digital Neuro-Chip for Robust Speech Recognition in Real-World Noisy Environments

Soo-Young Lee, Ki-Hwan Ahn, Doh-Suk Kim, Jung Wook Cho, Jae-Hoon Jeong,
Ja-Weon Kim, and Sung-Oh Kwon
Computation and Neural Systems Laboratory, Department of Electrical Engineering

Rhee-Man Kil
Department of Basic Science

Korea Advanced Institute of Science and Technology
373-1 Kusong-dong, Yusong-gu, Taejon 305-701, Korea
Fax: +82-42-869-3431 / E-mail: sylee@ee.kaist.ac.kr

Abstract - **A digital neuro-chip is developed for speech recognition in noisy environments. The "Voice Command" chip was designed to accomplish 3 goals, i.e., high recognition rates in noisy environments, simple system interfaces for consumer electronics applications, and the flexibility to accommodate different word sets in a single chip. A simplified auditory model, i.e., zero-crossing with peak amplitude, is implemented for the noise robust feature extraction at the pre-processing stage. Local feature extraction with the fuzzy data abstraction is also incorporated in front of the multilayer Perceptron classifier. The neuro-chip receives A/D converted speech signals as inputs, and generates binary-coded word index as the output. The synaptic weights are stored at external ROMs, of which values may be trained for any 50 word set at workstations.**

1. Introduction

Although speech recognition has been studied for years, it has been successful for restricted domain only. Especially, current speech recognition systems show poor performance in noisy signals, which prevents the speech recognition technology from popularity in real world noisy environments. Also, there exist many stand-alone applications for consumer and car electronics, which do not use high-performance CPU or digital signal processors. Therefore, it is strongly encouraged to develop ASICs (Application Specific Integrated Circuits) for noise-robust speech recognition.

The robustness in noise may be achieved by 2 different approaches, i.e., noise-robust feature extraction and insensitive classifiers to input disturbances. Human auditory systems hear well even in very noisy environments, and it is natural to learn from the mother nature. Although several auditory models demonstrated their usefulness in invariant feature extraction in noisy environments, they usually require excessive computational efforts and tedious parameter adjustments.[1-3] On the other hand artificial neural network has been developed as an universal pattern classifier and demonstrated good performances for classification of speech signals.[4,5] However, it is still required to improve robustness of the neural network classifiers for input disturbances.[6] Also, several hardwares have been developed to take advantages of massive parallelism of neural networks[7], but only a few has been designed for specific real-world problems.[8] The better performance is required, the more computational powers are in demand. And the hardware need be optimized for the specific problem and algorithm.

In this paper we report a digital neuro-chip "Voice Command" for speech recognition in noisy environments. Special emphasis was given to make trade-offs between high recognition rates in noisy environments and hardware implementability. A new auditory model has been developed for noise-robust feature extraction, and a new neural network model has been developed for robust classifications with input disturbances. Both the auditory and neural networks models have been developed for easy hardware implementations, and the digital chip is under fabrication.

2. Architecture of the "Voice Command" Neuro-Chip

The architecture of the "Voice Command" speech recognition neuro-chip is shown in Fig.1. It receives speech signals from a microphone through an A/D converter, and generates a binary-coded word index. The sampled speech signal always goes to the "word boundary detection" module, which determines word boundaries based on energy and zero-crossing rates during 20 msec time frames. When a word starting point is detected, the pre-processing modules, i.e., "filter bank" and "ZCPA (Zero Crossing with Peak Amplitude)" modules, generate abstracted speech features and send to the "SOFFA (Self-Organized Features with Fuzzy Abstraction)" neural classifier module.   The SOFFA module uses external ROMs to store synaptic weights, which are trained for a specific word set.   Therefore, by simply changing the ROMs, a "Voice Command" chip may be used for many different word sets.

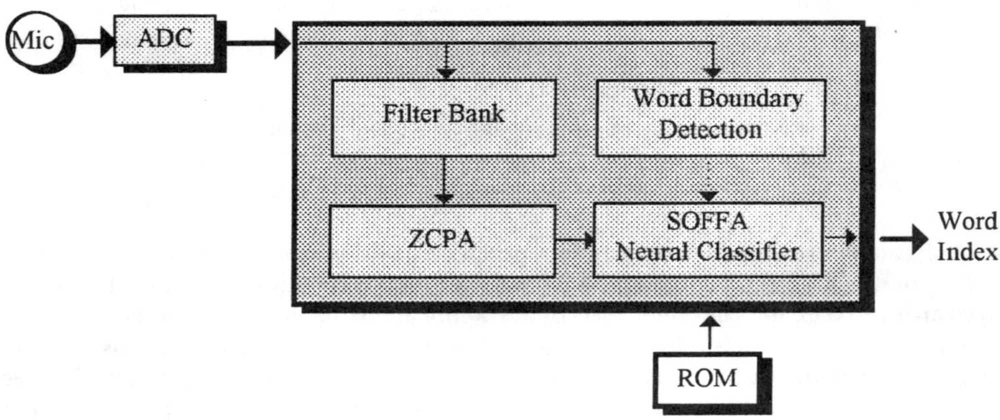

Fig.1 Architecture of the "Voice Command" neuro-chip

3. Noise Robust Feature Extraction based on an Auditory Model

Many auditory models consist of a bank of bandpass cochlea filters and an array of nonlinear processors at the output of each cochlea filter.   The former models frequency selectivity at various points along a basilar membrane in a cochlea, and the latter models the ensemble of nerve fibers innervating inner hair cells.   As shown in Fig.2, a simple but efficient nonlinear processor, i.e., ZCPA (Zero-Crossing with Peak Amplitude)[9], is implemented in the "Voice Command" neuro-chip. The filterbank used is a cochlea filter with 16 bands, of which center frequencies are distributed from 200 to 5000 Hz according to a logarithm-like frequency-position relationship.[10] The frequency response is asymmetric to show longer tail on the low frequency side. Also, higher frequency filters have sharper resonance than lower ones. Each bandpass filter is implemented as an FIR (Finite Impulse Response) digital filter in the "Voice Command.".

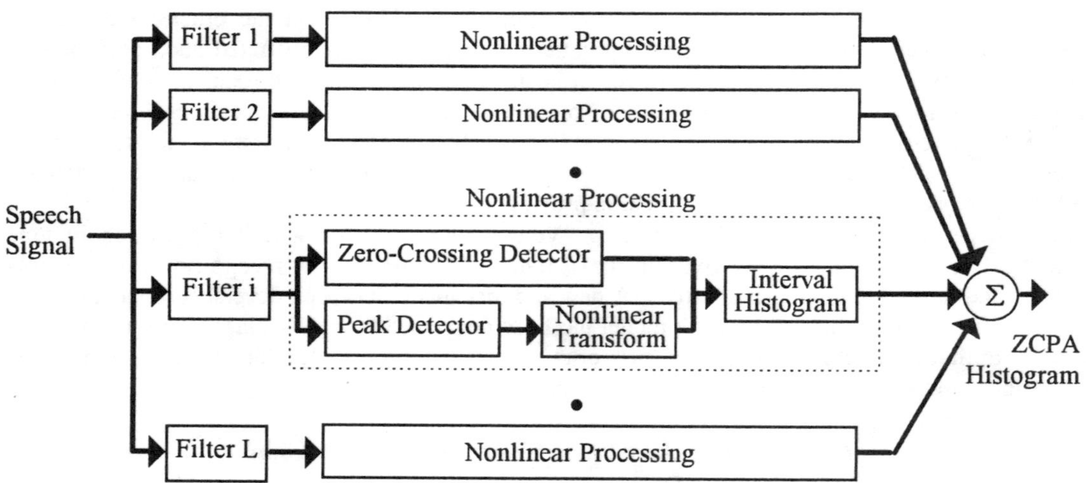

Fig.2 Block diagram of the ZCPA auditory model

The nonlinear processor at the end of each bandpass filter extracts frequency and intensity information of the speech signal.   Inverse of time intervals between two adjacent zero-crossings is coded as a frequency histogram, and the histograms for all the filter channels are combined together to represent outputs of the auditory model. To obtain intensity information Ghitza utilized multiple level-crossing detectors.[3] However, proper determination of the number of levels and the level values is very important to the performance, and there is no theory available to determine those values.   We had shown that the higher level values result in higher sensitivity of the interval histogram on additive noise, and developed a new feature extraction method based on zero-crossings only for noise robustness.[9] The intensity information is incorporated by the peak detection, which may be done by cilia attached to inner hair cells. When two zero-crossing times and a peak intensity between them are found, the value of the corresponding frequency bin is increased by a nonlinear transform of the peak intensity. In connection with human auditory system, a log function is used for the nonlinear transforms.   In experiments the ZCPA model successfully extracts invariant features from speech data with additive noises.

4. SOFFA Neural Network Classifier

Although the ZCPA auditory model provides noise-robust speech features, it is inevitable to get disturbances from noises.   Also, for the speaker-independent speech recognition, it is impossible to collect speech data from all users for the training.   Therefore, to make the "Voice Command" work in real world applications, the classifier itself need be insensitive to input perturbations and maintain good generalization capability.   It is well known that more training data are required for better generalization performance.   To improve generalization capability of neural network classifiers with small training datasets, we had developed a new hybrid Hebbian/EBP learning algorithm which successfully reduced sensitivity of the classifier outputs over the input perturbations.[7,11]   On the other hand the local feature extraction based on windowed convolutions showed good performance in character recognition[8,12] and speech recognition[13] problems.   Since the local features are less subject to size and translational-shift of the patterns, they usually showed reasonable size and shift-invariance and better recognition rates in real world problems.   By combining the local feature extraction and multi-layer Perceptron neural classifiers a new neural network classifier model, SOFFA (Self-Organized features with Fuzzy Abstraction)[14], is implemented at the "Voice Command" neuro-chip.

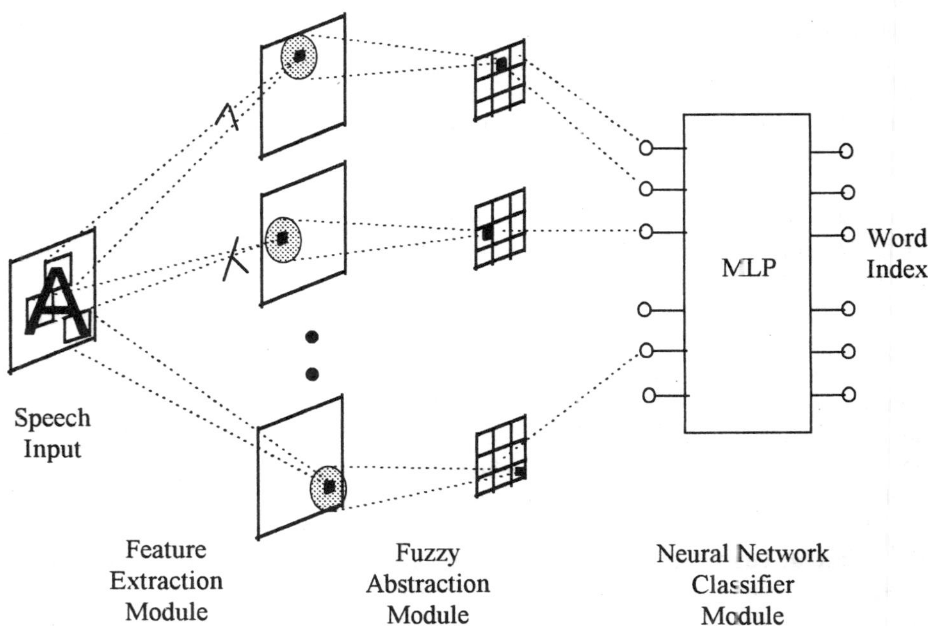

Fig.3 Architecture of the SOFFA Neural Network Model

As shown in Fig.3, the SOFFA model consists of 3 modules, i.e. feature extraction, fuzzy abstraction, and classification modules. The first and second modules are similar to one double-layer module in the Neocognitron model.[12] The first feature extraction module is basically identical to the S-cell layer of the Neocognitron, and extracts local features by moving-window convolutions. Each feature plane in the first layer has a small number of synapses, i.e., windows size, which may be set up by intuition or trained by competitive learning. Although local features may be quite distinctive and very useful for the robust recognition of complex patterns, several feature planes are usually required and the number of signal variables becomes much larger in the first module. Unlike the C-cell layer of the Neocognitron, we try to reduce the number of signal variables at the second module while maintaining enough information for classifications. The number of output neurons at the second module is much smaller than that of input neurons. Provided that the output of the second module consisted of 3x3 neurons for each feature plane, the output neuron will represent the existence of the specific local feature at (Upper-Middle-Lower, Left-Center-Right) position. We adopted the Gaussian function for the input-output mapping at the second module, and denote as "fuzzy abstraction". It is also beneficial to provide slight shift-invariance during this abstraction stage. These abstracted local features become inputs of the last multi-layer Perceptron classifier module for the final word recognition.

There exist two approaches to train the SOFFA model. At the module-based sequential learning approach the local feature extraction module is first set by intuition or trained by competitive learning, and the width of the Gaussian membership is chosen later. Then the last stage multilayer Perceptron is trained. The error back-propagation approach trains the whole network simultaneously. However, the non-monotonic Gaussian function in the second "fuzzy abstraction" module may make very complicated surface contour of the output cost function, and good initial condition is extremely important in this approach. In practice one may start with the sequential learning approach first, and fine tune the convolution feature filters and synaptic weights later by error back-propagation. Experimental results show better recognition rates for the latter than that of the sequential approach.

5. Implementation of the "Voice Command" Chip

The "Voice Command" neuro-chip is designed for the recognition of 50 Korean words in noisy environments. The input speech signal is sampled at 11.06 kHz sampling rate. The "word boundary detection" module and the 2 pre-processing modules calculate speech features at every 10 msec with 20 msec moving windows. The recognized word index is expected to come out within 0.3 second after the completion of the word utterance.

The filterbank is similar to the cochlea filterbank in Ref. 10. However, numbers with power-of-two are convenient for digital implementations, and 16 is chosen for the number of the bandpass filters. Depending upon the center frequency, the number of taps for the FIR digital filter varies from 24 to 100. Although more efficient digital implementations may exist, currently the 16 FIR filters are implemented separately.

Since we use a time-frequency joint representation of the speech signal and classify it as a pattern, the time axis should be properly normalized to have same length for all the training and test patterns. Especially the number of syllables varies from 1 to 4 within the selected 50 word set, and time normalization is very important. Although the DTW (Dynamic Time Warping) algorithm may be incorporated for this time normalization, the much simpler "trace" algorithm is implemented for easy hardware implementation. Experimental results show that this simple time-normalization method degrades the recognition performance slightly, but still is acceptable for the "Voice Command" chip.

Although the speech signal is initially sampled in 12 bit resolution, it is calculated with 8 to 16 bit resolutions in the chip. At first we designed the whole system with floating point arithmetics, and optimized the system parameters. Number of the feature planes and size of the local features at the first module, and size of the fuzzy-abstracted features are the main system parameters. Then, we came up with an integer version. Careful consideration was made to determine the resolution at each stage of the calculations. Trade-offs are made between the system performance and hardware complexity. The chip consists of about 80,000 gates, and the first version of the chip is now under fabrication in FPGAs.

6. Conclusion

A new "Voice Command" neuro-chip is reported for the robust speech recognition in noisy environments. Special auditory model is developed for the noise-robust feature extraction of speech signals with digital hardwares. Also, it consists of the SOFFA neural network model for classifier, which utilizes the local feature extraction and fuzzy data abstraction for robust recognition. The first version is now under fabrication, and the second version will come with better recognition rate and additional functions such as speaker adaptation.

Acknowledgment: This research was supported by LG Electronics Research Center, Korea. The SOFFA model had been developed for character recognition during the sabbatical leave of S.Y.Lee at University of Erlangen, Germany. Prof. Gerd Hausler and Mr. Xavier Labourex co-develeoped the SOFFA neural network model.

References

[1] R. Meddis, "Simulation of mechanical to neural transduction in the auditory receptor," J. Accoust. Soc. Am., vol. 79, no. 3, pp. 702-711, 1986.

[2] S. Seneff, "A joint synchrony/mean-rate model of auditory processing," J. Phonetics, vol. 16, no. 1, pp. 55-76, 1988.

[3] O. Ghitza, "Auditory models and human performances in tasks related to speech coding and speech recognition," IEEE Trans. Speech and Audio Processing, vol. 2, no. 1, part II, pp. 115-132, 1994.

[4] R. Lippmann, "Review of neural networks for speech recognition," Neural Computation, vol. 1, pp. 1-38, 1989.

[5] D.S. Kim and S.Y. Lee, "Intelligent judge neural network for speech recognition," Neural Processing Letters, vol. 1, no. 1, pp. 17-20, 1994.

[6] Y.K. Choi and S.Y. Lee, "Subthreshold MOS implementation of neural networks with on-chip error back-propagation learning," Proc. Inter. Joint Conf. on Neural Networks, Nagoya, Japan, Oct. 1993.

[7] S.Y. Lee and D.G. Jeong, "Error minimization, generalization, and hardware implementability of supervised learning," World Congress Neural Networks, San Diego, USA, June 1994.

[8] Y. LeCun, B. Boser, J.S. Denker, D. Henderson, R.E. Howard, W. Hubbard, and L.D. Jackel, "Backpropagation applied to handwritten zip code recognition," Neural Computation, vol. 1, no. 4, pp. 541-551, 1989.

[9] D.S. Kim, J.H. Jeong, J.W. Kim, and S.Y. Lee, "Feature Extraction Based on Zero-Crossings with Peak Amplitudes for Robust Speech Recognition in Noisy Environments," Proc. International Conf. on Acoustics, Speech, and Signal Processing, Atlanta, USA, May 7-10, 1996.

[10] J.M. Kates, "A time-domain digital cochlea model," IEEE Trans. Signal Processing, vol. 39, no. 12, pp. 2573-2592, 1991.

[11] D.G. Jeong and S.Y. Lee, "   ", Neural Networks (accepted).

[12] K. Fukushima, "Neocognitron: a self-organizing neuralnetwork model for a mechanism of pattern recognition unaffected by shift in position," Biol. Cybernetics, vol. 36, pp. 193-202, 1980.

[13] A. Waibel, T. Hanazawa, G. Hinton, K. Shikano, and K. Lang, "IEEE Trans. Acoustics, Speech, and Signal Processing, vol. 38, pp. 328-339, 1988.

[14] J.W. Kim, *Isolated Word Recognition using SOFFA Neural Network*, MS Thesis, Department of Electrical Engineering, Korea Advanced Institute of Science and Technology, Feb. 1996.

Is Word Recognition a Linearly Separable Problem!

M(Sasheei) Saseetharran, Fac of Engineering, UWS Nepean, PO Box 10, K'wood, NSW 2747, AUSTRALIA
Email: msaseeth@nepean.uws.edu.au

Abstract

Kammerer and Kupper [4] demonstrated that preprocessing of speech utterances of Texas Instruments Isolated Word Database (TI-20) using Mel-Frequency Cepstral Coefficients (MFCCs), reduces the word recognition problem to become linearly separable.

Single-Layer Perceptron (SLP) and 2-Layer Perceptron (2LP) that comprise the proposed modified neural model [11, 12] were trained using Delta Rule (DR) and Generalised-Delta Rule (GDR) respectively. PARCOR parameters and MFCCs were computed from isolated words taken from TI-20 database and ISOLET database. They were time normalised and used as the input to the SLP and 2LP. Word recognition experiments on an SLP and 2LP analyse the effect of preprocessing on linear separability.

1   Introduction

Interest in Artificial Neural Networks (ANNs) applied to speech recognition has had a recent resurgence following the development of the Generalised Delta Rule (GDR) [9]. Parallel processing computational advantages of ANN have strengthened this interest.

Peeling and Moore [6] showed that an excessive increase in the number of units in a Multi-Layer Perceptron (MLP) can cause these units to become specialised to the training data and, therefore, generalise poorly. Kammerer and Kupper [4] demonstrated that preprocessing of speech utterances of Texas Instruments Sixteen Speaker Isolated Word Database (TI-20) using Mel-Frequency Cepstral Coefficients (MFCCs), reduces the word recognition problem to become linearly separable. Kammerer and Kupper, using a fully interconnected Single-Layer Perceptron (SLP) of 20 units, achieved a best recognition rate of 100% for Speaker-Dependent (SD) cases using MFCCs as features. These experiments used the TI-20 database [4] with additional time warped training data to compensate for temporal distortion.

The issues involved in training such as saturation, scaling, generalisation and optimum number of units in a perceptron were not addressed by Rumelhart et al. [9], when the GDR was developed. An earlier publication demonstrated the effectiveness of a modified neural model applied to a 3-layer perceptron [11]. A recent publication [12] demonstrated the effectiveness of the modified neural model to perceptrons. This paper uses this modified neural model with an Hyperbolic Tangent Function (HTF) on an SLP and on a 2-Layer Perceptron (2LP), and trained by Delta Rule (DR) and Generalised-Delta Rule (GDR) respectively. The recognition experiments are conducted using MFCC and PARCOR parameters using TI-20 database and then extended using the ISOLET spoken letter database to verify the effect of preprocessing on isolated word recognition problem.

2   A Modified Neural Model

Earlier publications [11, 12] proposed a modified neural model with a scaling factor, ß(N), (equation (1)) which eliminate saturation and network paralysis at initialization and while training is in progress. ß(N) is chosen to be equal or greater than 1, so that units are not saturated at initialization and while training is in progress (experiments in Section 4.2.1 investigates this further and make recommendations on suitable ß(N) values).

$$y = \tanh\left[\frac{NET}{2}\right] \quad \text{where} \quad NET = \frac{1}{\text{ß}(N)}\left(\sum_{i=1}^{N} w_i\, x_i - \theta\right) \quad \text{and} \quad \text{ß}(N) \geq 1 \tag{1}$$

3   Preprocessing

Preprocessing utilised PARCOR parameters [10] and MFCC features [3] in order to facilitate investigation of linear separability and to make comparison with that of Kammerer and Kupper [4].

A supervised energy-based end point detection algorithm was developed based on Rabiner and Sambur [7], to detect the end points of the isolated words and to verify. Tenth and twelfth order LPC analysis [8] and tenth order MFCC analysis [3] was conducted on Hamming windowed 256 samples at an overlapping rate of 50%. An earlier algorithm [5] is extended to perceptron which is an architecture of ANN classifier to facilitate fixed frame length representation of input features to give a total of 25, 30, 35 and 40 frames for each isolated word.

For word recognition experiments, the end point detection algorithm, based on Rabiner and Sambur [7], was modified to the supervised algorithm to detect the end points of the isolated words since a major error source in word recognition is due to errors in end point detection.

4   Simulation Results
4.1 Pilot Experiments

An SLP and 2LP, fully interconnected with 20 output units and HTF as transducer function, was simulated in C programming language. Each of the 20 output units in the output layer represents one word of the 20 words. The 2LP consist of 40 units in the first layer which are connected to the input features. The training vectors to the perceptrons are PARCOR and MFCC features computed from the training set of the TI-20 database.

As training is sensitive to the randomly chosen initial set of weighting coefficients, it was repeated with 20 different randomly chosen sets of initial weighting coefficients. A learning rate of 0.1 and a gain for the momentum term of 0.4 were chosen. Application of each of the 20 training vectors to the perceptron and subsequent modifications of the weighting coefficient is defined as an epoch. In all experiments, the convergence criterion was set to attain classification of all the training patterns. Empirical observation revealed that this occurs for an average squared error over the training patterns of the DR and GDR of 0.04 or less.

Some experiments were conducted to decide on the number of frames needed to represent isolated words. While it is expected that the larger the frame length, the better the recognition rate; it is not attractive to have a large number of feature representations because they do not lead to an efficient implementation as features extracted from adjacent frames of a vowel are very similar. In addition, a large number of features would result in a large fan-in to the units of the perceptron likely to be causing difficulties in training through the saturation of units and consequent network paralysis. Therefore, for the ALK speaker, epochs for convergence were estimated for different ranges of initial weights and for frame lengths of 25 to 40 in steps of 5 for PARCOR features using the HTF() transducer function (Figure 2). Thirty frames performed better than 25 frames, when initial weight range was smaller than [-1/5, 1/5]. 30 frames performed better 35 and 40 frames for all initial weight ranges. Experiments were extended to another speaker and based on these results, 30 frames of features were chosen.

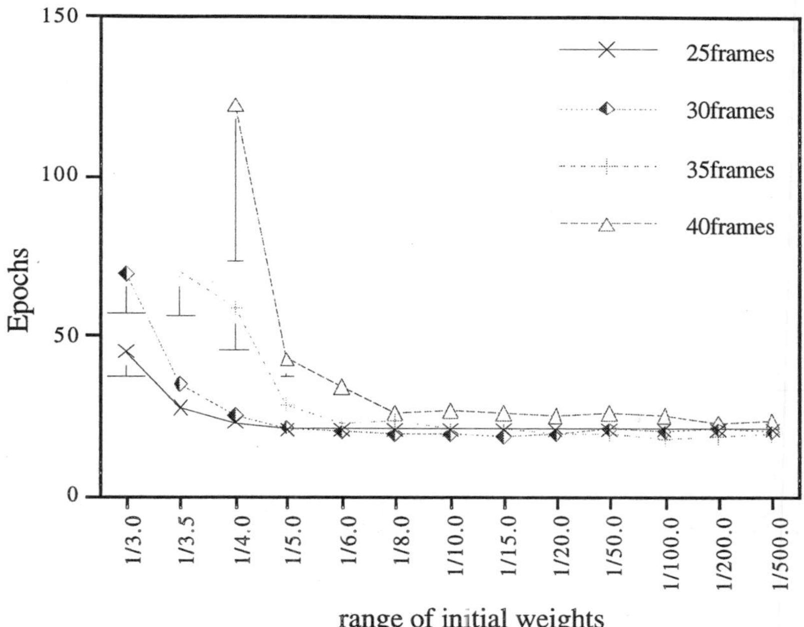

Figure 1: Comparison of Number of Frames;
Speaker initials "ALK"; PARCOR Features.

All pole modelling is an approximation in LPC speech processing. It seems likely that the error term in the processing of speech does not contribute to the recognition rate. Therefore, initial experiments were conducted for verification on one speaker from the TI-20 database. An SLP was trained using 30 frames of preprocessed features, 10 repetitions of the 20 isolated words, taken from the TI-20 database, and the epochs for convergence were estimated by varying ß(N). At convergence, preprocessed 16 repetitions of the same 20 words taken from the testing directory of the TI-20 database, were presented and the recognition rate was evaluated and plotted in Figure 2 and marked as "<xx>rate", where "xx" is the number of features per frame.

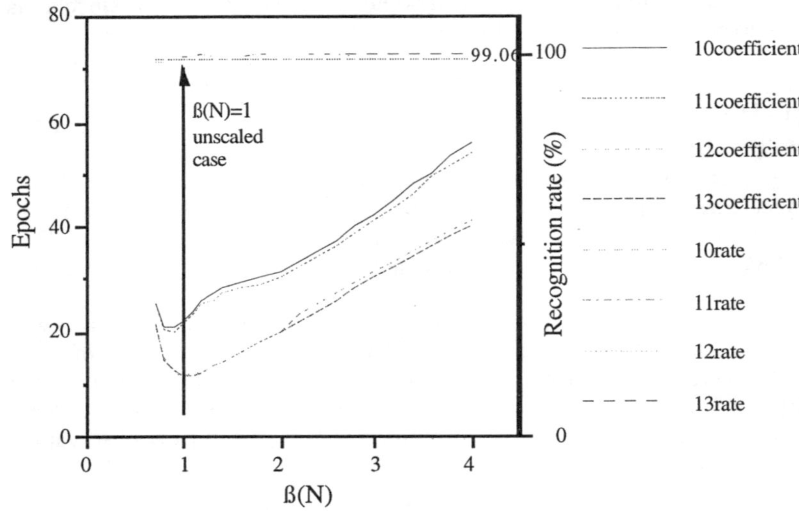

Figure 2: Variation of Epochs with ß(N) for PARCOR; Speaker initials "MSW".

It can be seen clearly that the presence of the error term has not made significant difference to either the epochs or the recognition rate as expected. Further, the 12th order filter takes considerably less training time, epochs, than that of the 10th order filter. Therefore, it was decided to use 12th order filter for the future experiments. The figure also includes the best recognition rate that was obtained.

4.2 Recognition Experiments
4.2.1 TI-20 Database

SPEAKERS'	RECOGNITION SCORE (tested on 320 words)				
INITIALS	MFCC	MFCC		PARCOR	
& GENDER	[Kammerer & Kupper, '90]	SLP	2LP	SLP	2LP
GRD (m)	318	310	309 †	300	299
KAB (m)	319	319	318	304	308
MSW (m)	320	320	317	315	315
RLD (m)	313	311	312	306	310
REH (m)	320	316	314	316	316
ALK (f)	320	315 †	312	302	299
CJP (f)	315	317	318	311	315
DFG (f)	315	309	309	316	313
GNL (f)	319	315 †	311	316	315
HNJ (f)	320	316 †	318	312	315
JWS (f)	319	319 †	317 †	318	318
Average Rate (%)	99.4	98.5	98.2	97.0	97.2
Average Epochs	60	22.2	35.7	14.1	37.7

Table 1: Comparison of SD recognition score;
m - male speaker and f - female speaker; † ß(N) > 1.

The simulation experiments for SD mode used 10 repetitions of 20 isolated words from the TI-20 Database that comprise 10 digits and 10 control words. As mentioned before learning rate of 0.1 and a gain for the momentum term of 0.4 were chosen. Experiments are conducted on a fully interconnected SLP and 2LP with ß(N) = 1. Testing for a recognition score used the sixteen repetitions of the same twenty words. As can be seen in the Table 1, for five cases, training was never achieved for ß(N) = 1, or took a long time (epochs) for convergence. Such difficulties were overcome, with the use of ß(N) > 1. The details are furnished in the Table 2.

EPOCHS	Speaker Initials	GRD (2LP)	GNL (SLP)	HNJ (SLP)	JWS (SLP)	JWS (2LP)
(MFCC	ß(N) = 1	190	57			1046
Features)	ß(N) > 1	84	23	69	43	143

Table 2: Comparison of epochs for convergence.

Based on these results of Tables 1 and 2, which further demonstrate the effectiveness of the proposed modified neural model, a training strategy was developed:

(a) For small word recognition problem training is initially attempted with ß(N) set to 1. If convergence takes long time or not achieved at all, then ß(N) is given a value greater than 1 (different initial weight configuration is not recommended since the use of small initial weights considerably reduces the standard error which is a measure of sensitivity due to the initial weight configuration).

(b) For large word recognition problem, ß(N) is ALWAYS given a value greater than 1 (typically ß(N) = 2).

In the Speaker-Independent (SI) case all 26 repetitions of the utterances spoken by ten speakers were used for training. All 26 repetitions of the 20 utterances (ie 520) of the last remaining speaker were used for testing. All the utterances used for training were randomly ordered. In the SI mode, it was not possible to attain a 100% recognition rate using the extracted features of MFCC and PARCOR. Therefore, the convergence criterion was altered to attain an average squared error over the training patterns to be equal to or less than 0.05 and 0.10 for MFCC features and PARCOR parameters respectively. The experiments were conducted using an SLP of 20 units and the recognition scores are tabulated in Table 3 below.

SPEAKERS	RECOGNITION SCORE (tested on 520 words)		
INITIALS & GENDER	MFCC [Kammerer & Kupper,1990]	MFCC	PARCOR
GRD (m)	509	463	388
KAB (m)	514	503	423
MSW (m)	504	510	459
RLD (m)	498	501	476
REH (m)	516	509	461
ALK (f)	498	485	435
CJP (f)	497	472	338
DFG (f)	493	501	430
GNL (f)	507	472	451
HNJ (f)	515	484	461
JWS (f)	514	502	486
Average (%)	97.3	94.4	84.1

Table 3: Comparison of SI recognition score;
m - male speaker, f - female speaker

Kammerer and Kupper demonstrated [4] that preprocessing TI-20 database using MFCCs, reduces the word recognition problem to become linearly separable. Kammerer and Kupper also said that it must not be concluded that the word recognition problem of TI-20 database is linearly separable. Word recognition experiments were extended to use a database similar to but larger than the TI-20 database, called the ISOLET spoken letter database [2]. Recognition of spoken alphabets has been one of the most difficult and challenging tasks in the field of computer speech recognition due to the acoustic similarity of many of the letters.

4.2.2 ISOLET Database

The ISOLET spoken letter database comprise the 26 English language alphabets, from *a* to *z* spoken by 150 speakers. The database is organized into five directories. Each directory consist of two repetitions of 15 male and 15 female speaker's utterances. The database consist of a total of 7800 utterances and sampled at 16kHz.

First set of utterances of every speaker from the first 4 directories are used for training. The second set of utterances of every speaker from the first 4 directories are used for multi-speaker (MS) experiments. For the Speaker Independent (SI) experiment all the utterances of the fifth directory was chosen. Thirty frames of features were extracted as described in Section 3.

From Table 4, it can be seen that 2LP perform better than SLP in all cases, confirming that the preprocessing used in this work does not reduce the problem of recogniton of ISOLET database to become linearly separable. In addition, it is noticeable that MFCC performed better than PARCOR in all cases.

MODE	MFCC [Cole et al., 1990] (2LP)	RECOGNITION RATE (%)			
		MFCC		PARCOR	
		SLP	2LP	SLP	2LP
Training [3120 words]		95.0	96.8	65.1	92.3
MS [3120 words]	96	82.2	87.4	63.1	73.4
SI [1560 words]	95	80.9	83.9	55.6	69.0

Table 4: Recognition rate using ISOLET database;
MS-multi speaker, SI-speaker independent.

5 Conclusion

Perceptron consisting of the proposed modified neural model [11, 12], with a scaling factor, ß(N), using a Hyperbolic Tangent Transducer Function, was used to analyse the effect of preprocessing on linear separability.

MFCCs and PARCOR parameters were used as features to an SLP and 2LP for word recognition of TI-20 database and compared with the earlier work [4]. The SD recognition rate achieved when using the PARCOR parameters (97.0% for SLP and 97.2% for 2LP) compare well with the recognition rate achieved using the MFCCs (98.5% for SLP and 98.2% for 2LP) on the TI-20 database.

In the SD experiments using the TI-20 database, an SLP performed measurably better than a 2LP with MFCC preprocessing of the speech utterances and an SLP performed measurably better than a 2LP with PARCOR preprocessing of the speech utterances. This confirms that the SD recognition of the 20 words of the TI-20 database is a non linearly separable problem. The high recognition rate (> 97%) confirms that the MFCC and the PARCOR preprocessing reduce the nature of the SD recognition task involving the 20 words of the TI-20 database to a linearly separable problem.

The performance of the proposed system using an SLP compares well with that of Kammerer and Kupper [4], but does not require compressing features non-linearly, time-align, nor enlarged training data. This demonstrates the suitability of the proposed method for small vocabulary isolated word SD recognition.

For SI experiments ß(N) > 1 was always used. The SI recognition score for MFCCs is lower than that of Kammerer and Kupper [1990]. The coarse time alignment and lack of expansion of the training material probably contributed to the error in this SI case which has a larger number of training and testing sets than the SD case. Further, the use of PARCOR parameters produced a much lower recognition rate (84.1%) than the use of MFCC features (94.4%). This demonstrates that MFCC representation of speech utterances simplifies the classification problem of an SLP more effectively than does the use of PARCOR parameters and that SI word recognition of the words in the TI-20 database is not a linearly separable problem in the absence of preprocessing.

During experimentation on the ISOLET database (ß(N) > 1), it was found that a 2LP performed better than an SLP in all cases, confirming that the preprocessing used in this work does not reduce the problem of recognition of the ISOLET database to a linearly separable problem.

Further, the performance achieved when using the MFCC features was better than that achieved when using the PARCOR parameters in all cases, confirming that the MFCC representation simplifies the classification of the TI-20 database and the ISOLET database more effectively than the use of PARCOR parameters. This is thought to be due to the fact that processing of MFCC features is nonlinear as in human auditory perception [1], whereas PARCOR is not.

The recognition rate achieved by Cole et al. [2] on the ISOLET database is higher than the reported results in this paper. This encourages further investigations to confirm whether careful selection of preprocessing techniques and features may reduce any word/speech recognition problem to become linearly separable.

6   Acknowledgments

I wish to acknowledge the help and support received from my principal supervisor Prof M P Moody, School of Electrical & Electronic Eng, QUT, Brisbane who has now become inaccessible to collaborate on this paper. I also wish to thank Dr Jim Franklin, School of Mathematics, UNSW, Sydney and Prof J G Lucas, Fac of Engineering, UWS Nepean, Kingswood for a number of valuable discussions.

7   References

[1]   Bladon, A. "Acoustic phonetics, auditory phonetics, speaker sex, and speech recognition: A thread", *Computer speech processing*, pp. 29, Englewood Cliffs; Prentice-Hall, 1985.

[2]   Cole, R., Fanty, M., Muthusamy, Y. et al. "Speaker-Independent recognition of spoken English letters", In Proceedings of the *IEEE Joint International Conference on Neural Networks*, Vol. 2, pp. 45-51, 1990.

[3]   Davis, S., B. and Mermelstein, P. "Comparison of Parametric Representations for Monosyllabic Word Recognition in Continuously Spoken Sentences", *IEEE Transactions on Acoustics, Speech and Signal Processing*, ASSP-28(4), pp. 357-366, 1980.

[4]   Kammerer, B. and Kupper, W. "Experiments for Isolated-Word Recognition with Single and Multi-Layer Perceptrons", *Neural Networks*, vol. 3(6), pp. 693-706, 1990.

[5]   Myers, C., Rabiner, L., R. and Rosenberg, A., E. "Performance Tradeoffs in Dynamic Time Warping Algorithms for Isolated Word Recognition", *IEEE Transactions on Acoustics, Speech, and Signal Processing*, ASSP-28(6), Dec 1980.

[6]   Peeling, S., M. and Moore, R., K. *Experiments in Isolated Digit Recognition Using the Multi-Layer Perceptron*, Technical Report 4073, Royal Speech and Radar Establishment, Malvern, Worcs., Great Britain, 1987.

[7]   Rabiner, L., R. and Sambur, M., R. "An Algorithm for Determining the Endpoints of Isolated Utterances", *The Bell System Technical Journal*, 54(2), pp. 297-315, 1975, USA.

[8]   Roux, Le J., Gueguen, C. "A Fixed Point Computation of Partial Correlation Coefficients", *IEEE Transactions on Acoustics, Speech and Signal Processing*, pp. 257-259, 1977.

[9]   Rumelhart, D., E., Hinton, G., E. and Williams, R. J. *Parallel Distributed Processing*, 1, MIT Press, pp 318-362, 1986.

[10]   Saseetharan, M. and Forward, K., E. "PARCOR Parameters as Features Applied to an Artificial Neural Network Word Recognizer", In *Proceedings of the Third Australian Conference on Speech Science and Technology*, pp 10-15, Melbourne, Australia, November 1990.

[11]   Saseetharan, M. and Moody, M., P. "A Modified Neuron Model that Scales and Resolves Network Paralysis", In *Proceedings of the Network: Computation in Neural Systems*, 3(2), pp. 101-104, IOP Publishing, Bristol, England, May 1992.

[12]   Saseetharran, M. and Moody, M., P. "Experiments that reveal the limitations of the small initial weights and the importance of the modified neural model", In *Proceedings of the ICNN*, USA, June 1996.

Text-Dependent Speaker Identification Based on The Modular Tree: An Empirical Study

Ke Chen, Xiang Yu and Huisheng Chi
National Lab of Machine Perception and Center for Information Science
Peking University, Beijing 100871, China
Email: chen@cis.pku.edu.cn

***Abstract*—** Recently, a novel self-architecture modular neural network model called Modular Tree was proposed based upon the principle of divide-and-conquer [1][2]. In this paper, we apply the modular neural network architecture to text-dependent speaker identification. Based upon the experimental results, we demonstrate that the performance of the system using the Modular Tree is satisfactory. Moreover, the use of the Modular Tree yields fast training and updating in the system.

1 Introduction

Speaker identification is to classify an unlabeled voice token as belonging to one of a set of N reference speakers. For speaker identification, moreover, the systems can be either text-dependent or text-independent. In this paper, we only pay attention to the text-dependent problem in which the text in both training and test is same or known. The speaker's voice often changes in time, which results in that speaker identification becomes a very hard problem [3]. There have been extensive researches in this field based upon conventional techniques of speech signal processing [4]. Recently, neural computing techniques were successfully applied to the problem [5][6][7]. As a result, the performance of systems has been improved by means of neural computing techniques. Unfortunately, the training of such systems often suffers from a high computational burden. In addition, due to the variation of speaker's voice in time, it is necessary to periodically update data for the robustness of systems. As a result, the speed of both training and updating in such systems is a crucial problem in practice. However, many earlier methods had to spend much time in updating due to the catastrophic interference which refers to the phenomenon that later training disrupts results of previous training.

The principle of divide-and-conquer is often used to attack a complex problem by dividing it into smaller and simpler problems whose solutions can be combined to yield final solution to the complex problem. Based upon the principle, a self-architecture modular neural network model called *Modular Tree* has been proposed [1][2] and turned to be useful to some benchmark problems. Using such an architecture, a modular neural network with tree structure could be automatically generated for a given task and a fast training is also available. Thanks to the principle of divide-and-conquer, the catastrophic interference could be alleviated to a great extent in the Modular Tree, which often yields fast updating. As a result, we have applied the Modular Tree to text-dependent speaker identification for yielding fast training and updating. Experimental results demonstrate that the system based upon the Modular Tree could achieve satisfactory performance and yield fast training and updating.

The rest of the paper is organized as follows. Section 2 reviews the architecture of the Modular Tree. Section 3 presents the system overview and results. Conclusions are drawn in the final section.

2 Review of The Modular Tree Architecture

Basically, the proposed architecture is a binary tree structure which is automatically generated through the use of constructive learning by partitioning a given input space recursively. In general, the tree consists of two kinds of nodes called *non-terminal* and *terminal* nodes, respectively. The non-terminal node is prepared for a hyperplane which partitions a data set $\mathcal{S}$ into two data subsets $\mathcal{S}_l$ and $\mathcal{S}_r$ where $\mathcal{S} = \mathcal{S}_l \bigcup \mathcal{S}_r$ and $\mathcal{S}_1 \bigcap \mathcal{S}_r \neq \phi$ (ϕ is the null set). The terminal node sits at a leaf of the tree and is prepared for a feedforward neural network also called a *component net* in the Modular Tree. In such an architecture, the hyperplane in a non-terminal node plays the 'divide' role in the the principle of divide-and-conquer which may partition a large training set into two smaller or simpler training sets with overlapping. Accordingly, the feedforward neural network in a terminal node plays the 'conquer' role in the principle of divide-and-conquer which can solve a supervised learning problem in a smaller or simpler training set. For a classification task, a Modular Tree can be automatically generated with the elaborate *growing algorithm* described in the sequel. During test, an unknown pattern is first fed to the root node then it is located by hyperplanes with top-down style in several terminal nodes due to the aforementioned overlapping. In each specified terminal node, the feedforward neural network works for the unknown input pattern and produces a result. Then, both an elaborate *credit-assignment algorithm* and a combining mechanism are used to achieve the final result by combining those results produced in different terminal nodes.

In the phase of training, the growing algorithm is used to automatically generated a classifier with the binary tree structure. It is summarized as follows,

Growing Algorithm:

---

1. Choose a feedforward neural network architecture and an existed learning algorithm accordingly. Set a maximal iteration number I_{max} and a mean square error threshold E_T. For a classification task, input the training set. Create a *terminal* node and put the feedforward neural network in it.

2. Initialize the feedforward neural network.

3. Let I and E_I denote the iteration number and the mean square error at time I. Train the feedforward neural network(s) by using the chosen learning algorithm and the current training set until one of the following conditions[1] is satisfied: (1) $I > I_{max}$ and $E_I > E_T$, (2) $I \leq I_{max}$ and $E_I \leq E_T$.

4. If condition (1) is satisfied, save the weight matrix of the trained component net as W_{old} and replace the *terminal* node with a *non-terminal* node. Accordingly, generate a hyperplane according to a partitioning strategy and put it in the node. Using the hyperplane, partition the current training set S into two training subsets S_l and S_r. Then create two *terminal* nodes for the *non-terminal* node and put two new feedforward neural networks (whose architectures have been chosen in step 1) in them for training on S_l and S_r, respectively. Initialize the new component nets with the randomly perturbing version of W_{old}. Go to step 3.

5. Repeat from step 2 to step 4 until condition (2) is satisfied for those feedforward networks in all created *terminal* nodes.

In order to support the above algorithm, a heuristic criterion is defined to determine a hyperplane in the partitioning strategy. Let us denote the training data set with N patterns and K classes as $\{\{\vec{p}_{ij}\}_1^{N_i}, \omega_i\}_1^K$ where ω_i is the label of class i, $\vec{p}_{ij}$ is the jth input pattern in class i and N_i is the number of patterns in class i, $\sum_{i=1}^K N_i = N$. For class i, its centroid can be achieved by $\vec{p}_{i,c} = \frac{1}{N_i} \sum_{j=1}^{N_i} \vec{p}_{ij}$. For all K classes, moreover, two special centroids $\vec{p}_{i_0,c}$ and $\vec{p}_{i_1,c}$ can be found as follows,

$$d(\vec{p}_{i_0,c}, \vec{p}_{i_1,c}) = \max_{1 \leq i,j \leq K} d(\vec{p}_{i,c}, \vec{p}_{j,c}) \tag{1}$$

where $d(\cdot, \cdot)$ is the Euclidean distance metric. Let $\vec{p}_c$ be $\frac{1}{2}(\vec{p}_{i_0,c} + \vec{p}_{i_1,c})$ which represents the central point of the line segment between point $\vec{p}_{i_0,c}$ and point $\vec{p}_{i_1,c}$. If $d(\vec{p}_{i_0,c}, \vec{p}_{i_1,c}) \neq 0$, the hyperplane is defined as the one through the point $\vec{p}_c$ and orthogonal to the vector $\vec{p}_{i_0,c} - \vec{p}_{i_1,c}$, that is,

$$l(\vec{x}) = (\vec{p}_{i_0,c} - \vec{p}_{i_1,c})^T (\vec{x} - \vec{p}_c) = 0 \tag{2}$$

For the special case of $\vec{p}_{i_0,c} = \vec{p}_{i_1,c}$, the hyperplane may be determined according to another criterion. In the criterion, the centroid of all input patterns in the current training set, $\vec{p}_c$, is first computed as

$$\vec{p}_c = \frac{1}{N} \sum_{i=1}^K \sum_{j=1}^{N_i} \vec{p}_{ij}.$$

Then, the hyperplane is defined as follows,

$$l(\vec{x}) = \vec{p}_c^T (\vec{x} - \vec{p}_c) = 0 \quad \text{if } \vec{p}_c \neq \vec{0} \quad or \quad l(\vec{x}) = \vec{p}_r^T \vec{x} = 0 \quad \text{if } \vec{p}_c = \vec{0}, \vec{p}_r \neq \vec{0} \tag{3}$$

where $\vec{p}_r$ is chosen at random from one of N input patterns. Based upon the obtained hyperplane on the training set S, for $\vec{x_i} \in S$, the partitioning strategy is defined as follows,

$$\text{If } l(\vec{x_i}) \leq D \text{ , } \vec{x_i} \text{ belongs to the subset } S_l; \quad \text{If } l(\vec{x_i}) \geq -D, \vec{x_i} \text{ belongs to the subset } S_r. \tag{4}$$

where $D = \eta D_{\max}, 0 \leq \eta < 1$. $D_{\max}$ is $d_{\max}(\vec{p}_{i_0,c}, \vec{p}_{i_1,c})$ if the hyperplane is determined with Eq.(2) or the maximal distance from all points in the training set to the hyperplane if the hyperplane is determined with Eq.(3). The value of η determines the size of an overlapping region between two adjacent training subsets. Currently, it is determined by trial and error for an appropriate size of the overlapping.

Using the growing algorithm, a Modular Tree is automatically generated for a given task after training. During test, however, there is a problem how to draw the final result by using results produced in multiple terminal nodes since several terminal networks may have contributions to the final result due to the overlapping between two adjacent training subsets. To solve the problem, we develop a *credit-assignment* algorithm. First two functions are defined to serve the algorithm. That is,

$$C_l(x) = \begin{cases} 1 & x < -D \\ -\frac{1}{2}(x-1) & -D \leq x \leq D \\ 0 & x > D \end{cases} \qquad C_r(x) = \begin{cases} 0 & x < -D \\ \frac{1}{2}(x+1) & -D \leq x \leq D \\ 1 & x > D \end{cases} \tag{5}$$

For Eq.(5), it is easy to show that $C_l(x) + C_r(x) = 1$.

---

[1] We may enhance condition (1) by incorporating more complicated constraints for escaping a possible local minima so as to terminate the current training in a more appropriate point.

Credit-Assignment Algorithm

---

1. **Initialization. Let $\vec{x}_s$ denote an unknown input pattern during test. $W \longleftarrow 1$ and pointer $\longleftarrow$ root. $l(\vec{x}) = 0$ is the hyperplane put in the non-terminal node pointed by the pointer.**

2. **If $\vec{x}_s$ is put to S_l according to the hyperplane in the node pointed by pointer and Eq.(4), do $W \longleftarrow W \times C_l(l(\vec{x}_s))$ and pointer $\longleftarrow$ pointer→leftchild.**

3. **If $\vec{x}_s$ is put to S_r according to the hyperplane in the node pointed by pointer and Eq.(4), do $W \longleftarrow W \times C_r(l(\vec{x}_s))$ and pointer $\longleftarrow$ pointer→rightchild.**

4. **Repeat step 2 and step 3 until pointer $=$ NULL.**

Using the credit-assignment algorithm, we may assign a credit factor W to each terminal node in which the input pattern $\vec{x}_s$ may be located. Thus, the combining mechanism is defined as follows,

$$O(\vec{x}_s) = \sum_i W_i(\vec{x}_s) \times O_i(\vec{x}_s) \tag{6}$$

where $O(\vec{x}_s)$ is the final output result for $\vec{x}_s$. $W_i(\vec{x}_s)$ and $O_i(\vec{x}_s)$ are the credit factor and output of the ith terminal node, respectively.

3   System Overview and Results

We have developed a text-dependent speaker identification system based upon the Modular Tree in a Sun Sparc II workstation. The scheme of the system is illustrated in Fig. 1.

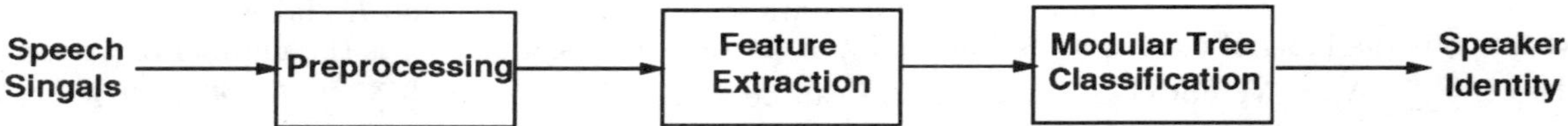

Fig. 1. The scheme of speaker identification system based on the Modular Tree.

The *preprocessing* of the acoustic data includes several steps. First, an utterance is sampled with 11.025 KHz simpling frequency and 16 bits digitization. Then the processed acoustic data is pre-emphasized by $H(z) = 1 - 0.95z^{-1}$. In the system, we use the power spectrum based on the Linear Predictive(LP) analysis as the features. In the phase of *feature extraction*, the length of the Hamming analysis window is 25.6 ms with 12.8 ms overlapping. A 16-order LP analysis is performed for each speech frame and LP based power spectrum is computed using a 256 points FFT for each frame. Moreover, a critical bandwidth filter is employed for processing the LP based power spectrum further. For this purpose, the power spectrum is divided from low frequency to high one (0-5.512 KHz) into 24 channels [8]. In each channel, the energy is accumulated and denoted as E_i, $(i = 1, 2, \cdots, 24)$. Finally, an entropy is also defined over each channel for producing a 24-order feature vector for each frame as follows [9],

$$I_i = -P_i \log P_i, \qquad P_i = \frac{E_i}{\sum_{j=1}^{24} E_j}; \quad i = 1, 2, \cdots, 24. \tag{7}$$

In the current system, we choose 10 isolated digits from '0' to '9' as the fixed text. Depending upon the chosen text, accordingly, 10 Modular Tree neural nets will be established as classifiers which correspond to 10 digits, respectively.

We have created a database for the system. The database consists of 10 isolated digits from '0' to '9' uttered in Chinese. Currently, 10 male speakers ($N = 10$) are registered in it. We recorded the utterances in three different sessions. In each session, each digit was uttered 10 times by a speaker. We chose the first 5 utterances of each digit recorded in the first session as the training data and all utterances recorded in the additional two sessions as testing data. Indeed, we may use last 5 utterances of each digit recorded in the first session as testing data and identifying accuracies could be close to 100% accordingly. However, it does not indicate that the system is robust since there is little variation of speakers' voice in both time and the environment in the same recording session. As a result, the performance of a speaker identification system should be evaluated by testing data recorded in those sessions with the exception of sessions used for training. After preprocessing and feature extraction, we achieved three sets of feature vectors corresponding to the training and testing data, called Set-1 (training), Set-2 (test) and Set-3 (test), respectively. As a result, TABLE I lists numbers of feature vectors in all sets.

TABLE I

Numbers of feature vectors in each set of the database

Text	'0'	'1'	'2'	'3'	'4'	'5'	'6'	'7'	'8'	'9'
Set-1	1162	1163	1159	1125	1141	1174	1204	1173	1171	1198
Set-2	2399	2379	2335	2215	2164	2424	2403	2261	2318	2408
Set-3	2204	2175	2210	2149	2192	2348	2270	2148	2194	2298

We used the data in Set-1 for training, and used data in Set-2 and Set-3 for test, respectively. In the current system, we chose a three-layered MLP with 24-6-10 as the architecture of component net in the Modular Tree and the Levenberg-Marquat algorithm [10] as the learning algorithm. For sequence recognition, it has been justified in our earlier work [2] that the overlapping between two training subsets generated by a hyperplane is quite useful for improving the performance and speeding up training since it could balance numbers of patterns belonging to different classes in a training set and make the layout of the training set more appropriate for classification. During training, we chose appropriate η values using trail and error in the partitioning strategy to determine the overlapping. According to Eq.(4), values of all η used in the current system are listed in TABLE II.

TABLE II

The values of η for determining overlapping in the partitioning strategy

Modular Tree	'0'	'1'	'2'	'3'	'4'	'5'	'6'	'7'	'8'	'9'
η	0.15	0.10	0.15	0.10	0.18	0.15	0.10	0.15	0.10	0.15

As a result, 10 Modular Tree classifiers have been automatically generated. Accordingly, the 10 generated structures are illustrated in Fig. 2. In order to evaluate the performance of the system, we adopted two testing methods, i.e. *digit-based test* and *sequence-based test*. The digit-based test refers to identifying a speaker merely by the utterance of a digit. As a result, TABLE III shows the identifying accuracies where Test-1 and Test-2 refer to results that the data in Set-1 and Set-2 are used for test, respectively.

TABLE III

The identifying accuracies(%) of the Modular Tree in the digit-based test

Text	'0'	'1'	'2'	'3'	'4'	'5'	'6'	'7'	'8'	'9'	mean
Test-1	88.0	85.0	88.0	80.0	87.0	88.0	94.0	85.0	83.0	88.0	86.6
Test-2	93.0	98.0	90.0	90.0	87.0	89.0	84.0	87.0	81.0	89.0	88.8

In comparison with the MLP, we also employed 10 three-layered MLPs with 24-20-10 as the classifiers and the Levenberg-Marquat algorithm was used for training. Such an MLP architecture was achieved by means of the 2-fold cross-validation technique. Accordingly, the identifying accuracies of MLP is shown in TABLE IV. It is worth pointing out that the training of the Modular Tree is significantly faster than one of the MLP (about 1.2 hours vs. 4.5 hours).

TABLE IV

The identifying accuracies(%) of the MLP in the digit-based test

Text	'0'	'1'	'2'	'3'	'4'	'5'	'6'	'7'	'8'	'9'	mean
Test-1	85.0	81.0	87.0	79.0	85.0	77.0	88.0	90.0	77.0	88.0	83.7
Test-2	88.0	90.0	87.0	85.0	82.0	83.0	84.0	83.0	77.0	89.0	84.8

To investigate the robustness of the system, moreover, we also adopted sequence-based method to test the system. In the method, we first produced a sequence with the length of 5 digits at random (it may be considered a password), then asked a speaker to utter digits in the sequence one by one. Obviously, for each digit in the sequence there was an identified result using the digit-based method. Based upon those separate results, the system tolls a vote with the *principle of majority* that a speaker can be identified only if there are at least three same identification results for the speaker; otherwise, the system refuses to identify the unknown speaker. Using the method, the identifying accuracy of the system is 99.85% with 0.0% rejection rate over 2000 tests.

During updating, the system may distribute all new data to some corresponding terminal nodes also using the partitioning strategy adopted during training. Thus, the new data incorporated the original data in the training sets of the component nets into new training sets, respectively. In the current system, we have added some new data to each Modular Tree classifier illustrated in Fig. 2. The growing algorithm was still employed in each terminal node whose training set has been updated during updating. We chose the first utterance of each digit in Set-2 as the new data, called Set-Add. Accordingly, we used both the other nine utterances of each digit in Set-2, called Set-2', and all utterances in Set-3 as testing data, respectively. Numbers of feature vectors in Set-2' and Set-Add are listed in TABLE V and identifying accuracies of system is shown in TABLE VI after updating, where Test-1' means results that the data in Set-2' is used for test. During updating, moreover, the averaging training time was only about 40 minutes, while in the aforementioned MLP the averaging training time was more than 3.5 hours for the same updating.

TABLE V

Numbers of feature vectors in Set-2' and Set-Add

Text	'0'	'1'	'2'	'3'	'4'	'5'	'6'	'7'	'8'	'9'
Set-2'	2159	2135	2094	1994	1942	2182	2170	2022	2084	2168
Set-Add	240	244	241	221	222	242	233	239	234	240

TABLE VI

The identifying accuracies(%) of the Modular Tree after updating

Text	'0'	'1'	'2'	'3'	'4'	'5'	'6'	'7'	'8'	'9'	Averaging
Test-1'	92.2	96.7	93.3	86.7	92.2	92.2	95.6	86.7	88.9	90.0	92.1
Test-2	98.0	99.0	91.0	91.0	87.0	92.0	86.0	88.0	82.0	93.0	90.7

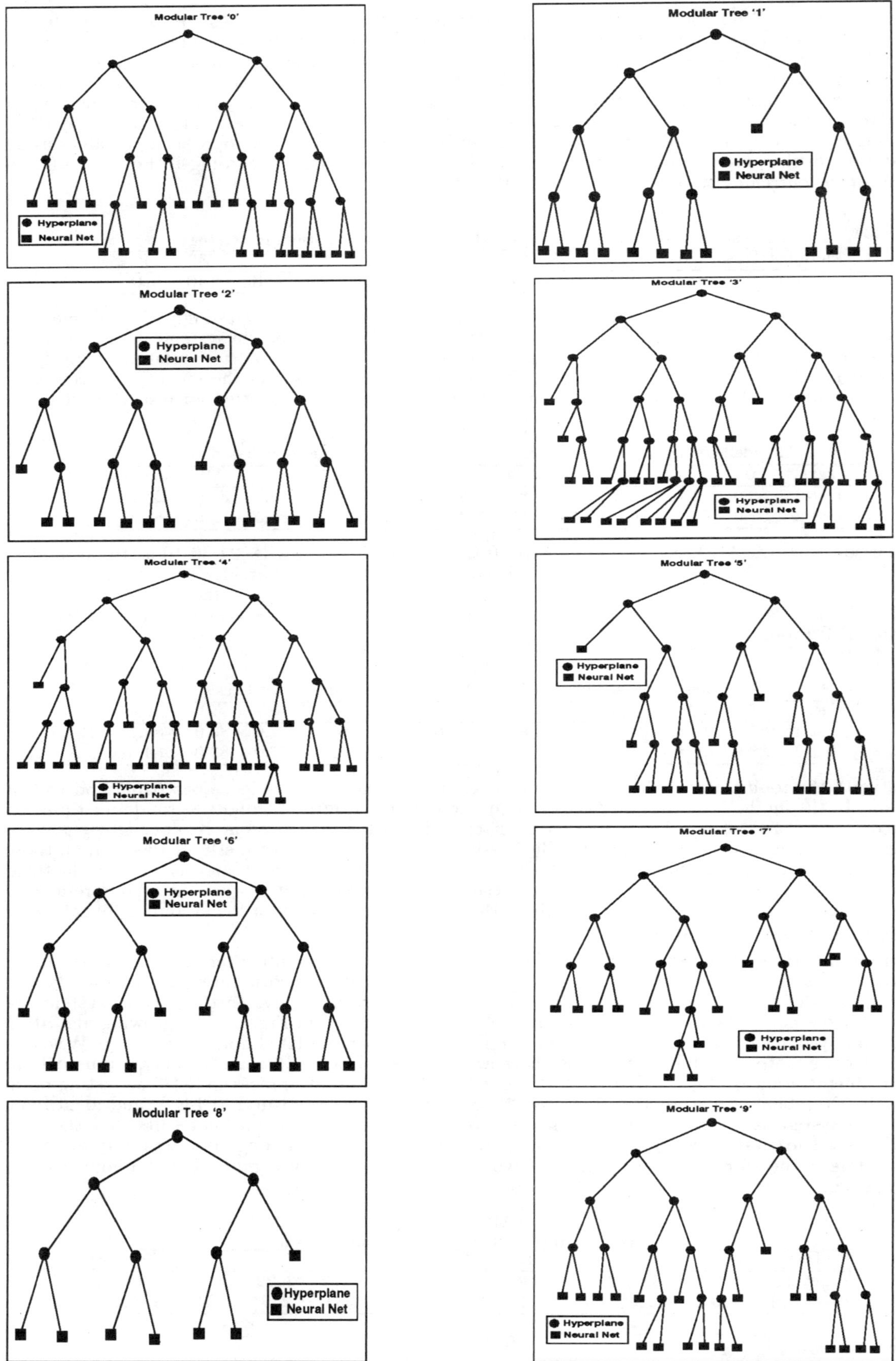

Fig. 2. Structures of 10 automatically generated Modular Tree nets.

In addition, using the sequence-based test, the identifying accuracy of the system reaches 100% with 0.0% rejection rate over another 2000 tests.

4   Conclusions

We have already described the application of the Modular Tree, a self-architecture modular neural network model, to text-dependent speaker identification. Accordingly, a text-dependent speaker identification system has been developed by means of the Modular Tree. Based upon experimental results, we have demonstrated that the system based upon the Modular Tree yields better performance and significantly faster training than the system based on a three-layered MLP. In particular, the merit of divide-and-conquer underlying the Modular Tree has been shown in the real-world problem, which results in fast training and updating.

Acknowledgements

Authors would like to thank Dr. Liping Yang for helpful discussions and supplying the program of the Levenberg-Marquat algorithm. This work was partially supported by National Science Foundation of China with Grants 69571002 and 69475007 as well as the Climbing Program – National Key Project for Fundamental Research in China with Grant NSC 92097.

References

[1] K Chen, L. Yang, X. Yu and H. Chi, "A self-architecture modular neural network," *Proc. ICONIP'95*, Beijing, pp. pp. 821-824, Nov. 1995.

[2] K Chen, X. Yu, H. Chi and L. Yang, "Modular-Tree: a self-architecture modular neural network architecture," *Acta Scientiarum Naturalium, Universitatis Pekinensis*, Vol. 32, No. 1, pp. 113-122, 1996

[3] G.R. Doddington, " Speaker recognition–identifying people by their voices," *Proceedings of IEEE*, Vol. 73, pp.1651-1664, 1986.

[4] T. Matsui and S. Furui, " Speaker recognition technology," *NTT Review*, Vol.7, No.2, pp. 40-48, 1995.

[5] Y. Bennani and P. Gallinari, "Connectionist approaches for automatic speaker recognition," *Proc. ESCA Workshop on Automatic Speaker Recognition*, pp. 95-102, 1994.

[6] J. Oglesby and J. S. Mason, "Optimization of neural models for speaker identification," *"Proc. Int. Conf. Acoust., Speech, Signal Processing*, pp. 261–264, 1990.

[7] J. Oglesby and J. S. Mason, "Radial basis function networks for speaker recognition," *Proc. Int. Conf. Acoust., Speech, Signal Processing*, pp. 393-396, 1991.

[8] K. Zwicker, "Subdivision of the audible frequency range into critical bands," *J. Acoust. Soc. Amer.*, 35(2), pp. 248-252, 1961.

[9] X. Jiang, "Speaker Identification Using Feedforward Neural Networks," *Master Thesis*, Center for Information Science, Peking University, 1994. (in Chinese)

[10] R. Fletcher, *Practical methods of optimization*, John Wiley&Sons, New York, 1987.

Arabic Vowel Classification via QR Factorization

M. F. Abu-El Yazeed

Dept. of Physics
United Arab Emirates University
Al-Ain, U.A.E.
mofaabbr@nyx.uaeu.ac.ae

M. A. El-Gamal

Dept. of Math. & Computer Science
United Arab Emirates University
Al-Ain, U.A.E.
mgamal@nyx.uaeu.ac.ae

Abstract

The generalization ability of a neural network is influenced by the size and efficiency of the training set. As a result, a key factor in any neural network application is the training set selection. In this paper, a new algorithm for optimizing this selection is proposed. The algorithm, based on the QR factorization of the training patterns, provides a systematic selection of an optimum training set. Consequently, the computational effort in the training phase of a neural network is significantly reduced and yet a satisfactory level of generalization is maintained. The potential of the algorithm is demonstrated on the problem of Arabic vowel classification.

1 Introduction

Neural networks have been successfully applied in many areas of pattern recognition and speech processing [1-3]. The high ability of neural networks to perform accurate classification is well suited to be employed in different speech segmentation problems. This ability is best exploited in hierarchical recognition systems where a high classification rate is essential. In such a system, a segmentation process is performed hierarchically in a tree structure down to the phoneme level. However, a misclassification error at any level of the system would produce more errors at the following levels. Therefore, at each level, a large number of training data is needed. This in turn leads to a drastic increase in the computational effort.

The central issue in any neural network-based approach is the selection of the training set of features that adequately characterize the speech recognition problem. This selection is crucial in order to achieve a successful learning and at the same time allowing the network to perform the desired generalization. On the other hand, a network that learns too many specific input-output relation may memorize the training data and therefore be less able to generalize between similar input-output patterns. Moreover, the size of the network is increased as well as the training time.

A common method for evaluating the generalization performance is known as cross-validation [4]. In this method, data is divided randomly into a training set and a test set. The network is trained on the training set and its performance is evaluated on the test set. Different data partitions are tried until a satisfactory generalization is achieved. A clear disadvantage of cross-validation is the lengthy time it takes.

In this paper, a systematic procedure for optimizing the size of the training set without affecting the level of generalization is proposed. The QR factorization (QRF) process [5] is utilized to select an optimum set of training patterns. These patterns are used in the training phase of a neural network to approximate the desired input-output mapping. In particular, Self-Organizing Maps (SOM) followed by learning vector quantizers (LVQ) [6] are trained to classify Arabic vowels. The classification is performed in two levels. In the first level, a vowels/consonant classification is achieved while a complete vowel classification is carried out in the second level.

The paper is organized as follows. In section 2, data collection, feature selection and training set design are described. The training phase is briefly presented in section 3. Results are demonstrated in section 4. Finally, conclusions are drawn in section 5.

The authors are on leave from the faculty of Engineering, Cairo University, Giza, Egypt.

2. Problem Formulation

A major source of difficulty in speech recognition problems is the size of the vocabulary. The vocabulary size varies in an inverse manner with the system accuracy and efficiency. In this section, an efficient selection of the training date out of a large speech vocabulary is introduced. The basic steps for such selection are outlined below.

2.1 Data Collection

Arabic language has 34 phonemes, namely, 28 consonants, 3 short vowels and 3 corresponding long vowels. The short vowels are the "Fatha /فتحة/", the "Kasra /كسرة/" and the "Damma /ضمة/" which are denoted, in the present work, by A, E and O respectively. The corresponding long vowels are the "Alef Madd /ألف مد/", the "Yaa Madd /ياء مـد/"   and the "Waw Madd /واو مـد/" which will be denoted by AA, EE and OO respectively

Arabic language has five types of syllables, namely, CV, CVV, CVC, CVVC and CVCC where C refers to a consonant and V to a vowel. A common feature in Arabic language is that a vowel is always the second phoneme in all syllables. As a result, vowel/consonant classification reveals the syllabic structure of any Arabic word. Consequently, this classification is an important step in a hierarchical Arabic speech recognition system. This step followed by a vowel classification completes one branch in such a system.

In this research, the speech data base includes 568 syllables. Those syllables are extracted from natural Arabic isolated words. Syllables are selected since they have the advantage of including different coarticulation effects. This bank of syllables was successfully used in an Arabic text-to-speech system [7,8]. Syllables are manually segmented into phonemes. The frames of each phoneme are then labeled as one class.

The original speech material is recorded by a male speaker at 8 kHz sampling frequency with 12 bits per sample. Features   are then calculated   at a frame basis with a frame length of 12.5 msec. As such, each frame is represented by   10 cepstral coefficients. Cepstral coefficients are selected since they are proved to have a high performance in different speech applications [9].

2.2 Feature Selection and Training Set Design

Frames of each   phoneme are grouped in different clusters. The number of clusters for each phoneme is determined by an appropriate unsupervised learning algorithm [10]. For each cluster, a training matrix T is constructed. The columns of this matrix are the cluster frames while the rows are the input features of each frame (cepstral coefficients). Due to the large number of possible frames which can be used as training patterns, there is an absolute need for a criterion to select those patterns that contain the necessary information required to adequately describe the speech recognition problem. To this end, the QRF method is employed to select and order the training patterns.

2.2.1 Selection of Training Patterns via the QRF Algorithm

The QRF process factors a matrix into a product QR, where Q is orthogonal and R is upper-triangular. This is accomplished, by performing a series of Householder transformations on the matrix [5].

The QRF process with pivoting is often applied to a matrix in order to select a robust set of linearly independent column vectors which span the matrix [11,12]. This selection is performed in subsequent steps. First, the column of the largest norm is selected and all remaining columns are orthognalized to it. In the second step, the column of the largest norm of those remaining is selected and orthogonalization is repeated. The process continues until the norms of all the remaining columns are less than a specified threshold.

Formally, the QRF of a matrix T is denoted as :

$$T*E = Q*R \tag{1}$$

where, E is the permutation matrix which reorders the columns of T such that the diagonal of R is monotonically decreasing. This permutation puts these columns in   their order of importance. The first L columns of T span approximately the same space as T. In this work, L is selected to be equal to the number of input features.

For a certain phoneme, the QRF process is applied to the training matrix T of each cluster. The selected frames (columns) are grouped to constitute the input training patterns for this phoneme. This process is repeated for all phonemes. As a result, the training patterns of all phonemes are grouped in a global training set. A standard one out of N output coding is used for the outputs. A flow diagram that describes the above procedure is depicted in Fig. 1.

3 Training Phase

Training is performed in two steps. In the first step, frames of each phoneme are clustered using an unsupervised learning algorithm that implement a ""follow the leader approach". Frames (input patterns) are partitioned into clusters by discovering their similarities. These similarities are measured by the Euclidean metric function and a threshold called the vigilance parameter. The algorithm does not require an initial guess of the number of clusters. Details of the algorithm are given in [10]. Accordingly, the number of clusters of each phoneme is determined.

In the second step, the classification of frames of different phonemes is performed by a learning vector quantization neural network model. The LVQ is a classification network which assigns patterns to one of several classes. It contains an input layer, Kohonen layer and an output layer. The input layer contains one node for each input parameter while the output layer has one node for each class. The Kohonen layer contains an equal number of nodes for each class. Every set of nodes in the Kohonen layer is only connected to their corresponding output class node. The input layer is fully connected to the Kohonen layer.

Denote the input vector by $x = [x_1, x_2, ... x_n]^T$ and the weight vector of node j in the Kohonen layer by $m_j = [m_1, m_2, ... m_n]^T$. The LVQ learning algorithm can be summarized as follows:

Step 1   Initialize weights to small random values.

Step 2   Compute the distance between the input vector x and each of the vectors m_j. Select the best matching node c with minimum distance.

$$\| x(t)-m_c(t)\| = \min_j \{\|x(t)-m_j(t)\|\} \tag{2}$$

Step 3   Modify the weights of the selected node and its neighboring nodes by:

$$m_j(t+1) = m_j(t) + \alpha(t)(x(t)-m_j(t)) \qquad j \in N_c(t)$$
$$= m_j(t) \qquad\qquad \forall j \notin N_c(t) \tag{3}$$

where t is the iteration number, $\alpha(t)$ is monotonically decreasing function of time and $N_c(t)$ is an Euclidean distance neighborhood around the selected vector node m_c.

Step 4 Repeat steps 2 and 3 until a stable cluster information occurs. This concludes the unsupervised learning part of the algorithm. Classification is improved by applying the following steps.

Step 5 Compute the Euclidean distance between every training vector x and each node vector m_j. The closest node vector m_c is updated as follows:

$$m_c(t+1) = m_c(t) + \alpha(t)(x(t)-m_c(t)) \qquad \text{if x is classified correctly.}$$
$$= m_c(t) - \alpha(t)(x(t)-m_c(t)) \qquad \text{if x is not classified correctly.}$$
$$m_i(t+1) = m_i(t) \qquad\qquad \text{for } i \neq c. \tag{4}$$

Step 6 Repeat step 5 for a specified number of iterations or until the desired classification rate is achieved.

4 Results

The procedure outlined in section 2 is applied to achieve a complete Arabic vowel classification. The classification is carried out in two levels. In the first level, vowel/consonant classification is performed. In the second level, different vowels are recognized.

4-1 Vowel/Consonant Classification

In this level, each frame is represented by 11 features. The first 10 features are the cepstral coefficients while the 11th feature is the short time energy function. The energy function is added to the feature vector since vowels are known to have higher energy than consonants.

The hand segmented data consists of 5082 frames representing the 28 Arabic consonants and 4810 frames representing the six Arabic vowels. The procedure described in section 2 is applied for training pattern selection. As a result, consonants are represented by only 979 frames while vowels are represented by 374 frames.

Training using different LVQ network architecture is carried out. In each experiment the performance of 2 networks is compared.   Network 1 is trained by all patterns and network 2 is trained with the QRF selected patterns (less than 14% of the total patterns). The reported results are obtained using an LVQ network of three layers: 11   input nodes, 2 output nodes (representing the two classes) and 150 nodes in the Kohonen layer. These results are given in Table 1. It is remarkable to note that the classification accuracy of network 2 is fully comparable with that of network 1.

Figure 2 compares the performance of the two networks at different number of training iterations. Moreover, the performance using a variable number of nodes in the Kohonen layer is shown in Fig. 3. In both figures, the potential of the proposed pattern selection algorithm is demonstrated.

4-2 Vowel Classification

In   this level, each short vowel and its corresponding long vowel are labeled as one class. Accordingly, the vowels are classified in 3   classes. In particular, frames representing the vowels A and AA are labeled as class 1. On the other hand, E and EE frames are labeled as class 2 while O and OO are labeled as class 3. The reported results are obtained using an LVQ network of three layers: 11   input nodes, 3 output nodes (representing the three classes) and 99 nodes in the Kohonen layer. The number of frames of each class is shown in Table 2. Network A   is trained with all patterns and network B is trained with the QRF selected patterns (less than 8% of the total patterns). Results are given Table 2. Once more, the classification accuracy of the two networks is comparable.

5 Conclusions

The size of a training set is an important parameter in real problems. Thus, the generalization a neural network makes, based on a limited training set, is highly desirable. A new algorithm for an optimum selection of a training set is presented. In the proposed algorithm, patterns are clustered. For each cluster, a set of patterns is selected using   the QRF   process. The selected patterns are grouped to form a global training set. Using this approach, two training sets, out of a large Arabic speech vocabulary, are constructed. The first set is designed for vowel/consonant classification while the second set is designed for vowel classification. In both cases, an LVQ network is trained to perform the desired classification. The generalization ability and the high classification accuracy of the two networks demonstrate the effectiveness of the algorithm.

References

[1]   K. Lang, A. Waibel and G.   Hinton, " A Time-Delay Neural Network Architecture for Isolated Word Recognition," Neural Networks, vol. 3, pp. 23-43, 1990.

[2]   M . Hanes,   S. Ahalt and A. Krishnamurthy, " Acoustic -to -Phonetic Mapping Using Recurrent Neural Networks," IEEE Trans. Neural Networks, vol. 5, pp. 659-662, 1994.

[3]   P. Boda, " Robust Voiced/Unvoiced Speech Classification with Self-Organizing Maps," Proc. IEEE Int. Symp. Circuit and Systems, Seattle, Washington, pp. 1516-1519 , 1995.

[4]   C. Bishop, " Novelty Detection and Neural Network Validation," IEE Proc. Visual Image Signal Process., vol. 141, pp. 217-222, 1994.

[5]   S. Leon, Linear Algebra with Applications, Macmillan Publishing Co., New York, 1980.

[6]   T. Kohonen, " The Self-Organizing Map," Proc. of IEEE, vol. 78, pp. 1464-1480, 1990.

[7]   H. A. Fathi,   M. F. Abu-El Yazeed,   S. A. Mashali and M. R. El-Ghonemy, " A Real- Time Arabic Text-to-Speech   System Based on Parallel Processing", Journal of the King Saud University, Computer and Information Sciences, vol. 7, pp. 49-67,   1995.

[8]   M. F. Abu-El Yazeed, An Arabic Text-to- Speech System , Ph.D. Dissertation, Cairo University, 1990.

[9]   S. Furui   and   M. M. Sondhi, Advances in Speech Signal Processing, Marcel Dekker Inc., New York, 1992.

[10] Y. Pao, Adaptive Pattern Recognition and Neural Networks, Addison-Wesley, 1989.

[11] M. A. El-Gamal, Fault Location and Parameter Identification in Analog Circuits, Ph. D. Dissertation, Ohio University, Athens, Ohio, 1990.

[12] G. Stenbakken and T. Souders, " Developing Linear Error Models for Analog Devices," IEEE Trans. Instrum. Meas., vol. 43, pp. 157-163, 1994.

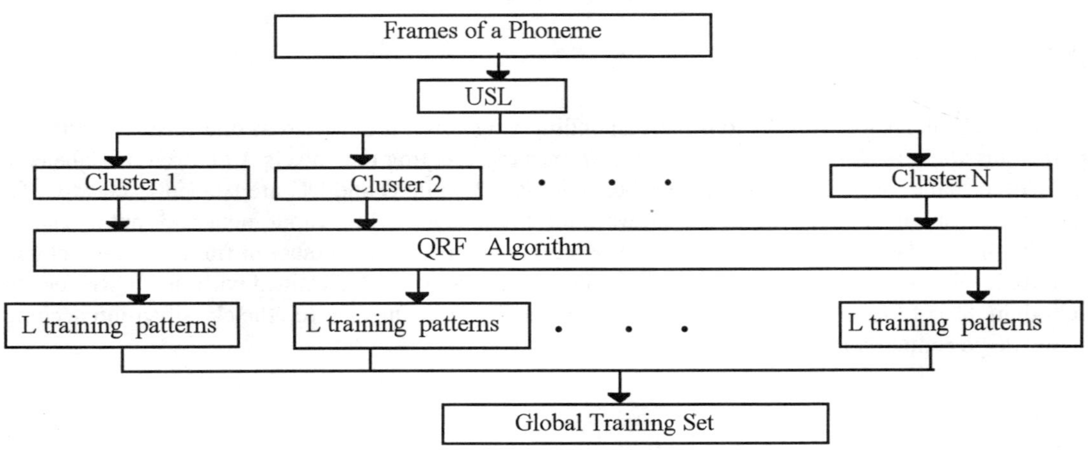

Fig. 1 Training Set Design for a phoneme; USL : Unsupervised Learning.

	Network 1		Network 2	
	Vowels	Consonants	Vowels	Consonants
No. of training patterns	4815	5082	374	979
No. of testing patterns	4815	5082	4815	5082
Training classification rate (%)	98.6	97.9	98.7	98.1
Testing classification rate (%)	98.6	97.9	95.6	97.8
No. of iterations	445000		75000	

Table 1 Vowel / Consonant Classification Performance of Network 1 and Network 2.

	Network A			Network B		
	Class 1	Class 2	Class 3	Class 1	Class 2	Class 3
No. of training patterns	1670	1681	1464	132	110	132
No. of testing patterns	1670	1681	1464	1670	1681	1464
Training classification rate (%)	95.6	94.1	95.8	93.9	92.7	97
Testing classification rate (%)	95.6	94.1	95.8	89.6	91.7	92.7
No. of iterations	100000			7000		

Table 2 Vowel Classification Performance of Network A and Network B.

Fig.2 Generalization performance of network 1 & network 2 for the testing set as a function of the number of iterations.

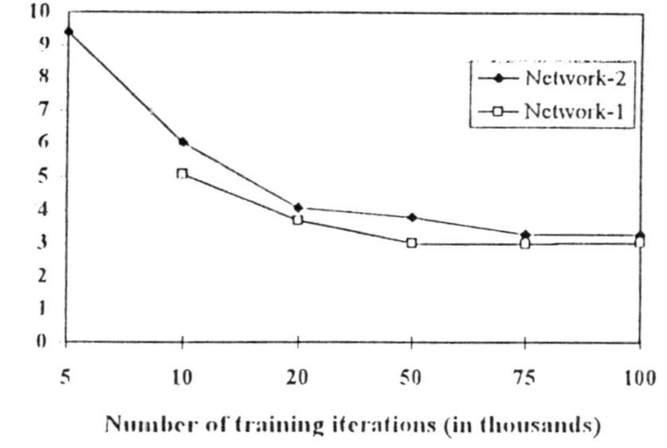

Fig.3 Generalization performance for the testing set as a function of the number of nodes in the Kohonen layer.

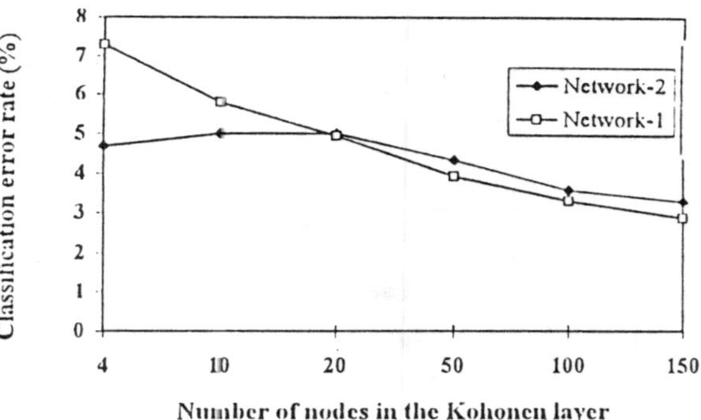

A Three-Stage Model of Speech Processing and Recognition in the Auditory System

T. Wesarg, B. Brückner, C. Schauer
Informatics, Federal Institute for Neurobiology
P.O.Box 1860, 39008 Magdeburg, Germany
e-mail:brueckner@ifn-magdeburg.de

Abstract— One approach to the construction of an engineered system for hearing and efficient speech recognition is the modeling of the human auditory system. We applied this approach to our speech recognition tasks using a coupled modeling concept (Fig. 1) which should reproduce this system in a plausible way (Brückner et al. [1]). Starting with a model of signal processing by the cochlea (Kates [4]), our coupled modeling concept contains a lateral inhibitory neural network (LIN) system (Shamma [2]) performing filter operations by spatial processing of the speech evoked activity in the auditory nerve, and a structured formal neural network (Brückner et al. [3]) for learning and recognition of the spectral representations of the speech stimuli provided by the LIN.

1   Introduction

The first stage of our model is a digital time-domain model of the human cochlea which is mainly based on the cochlear model of Kates [4]. Digitalized speech signals obtained by recording the analogue waveform of speech with a condensor microphone and a following 48-kHz ADC conversion, form the input (tympanic membrane pressure) to the middle-ear front-end of the cochlear model. The model output consists of the instantaneous firing rates and spike patterns in the auditory nerve.

The aim of the second stage of the complete model is to find and highlight characteristic properties like peaks and edges in the complex structure of the firing rate patterns in the auditory nerve. For this purpose one of the fundamental neural network topologies, the lateral inhibition based on the LIN model of Shamma [2], is used. A nonrecurrent network is responsible for the detection of spectral peaks in the spatio-temporal pattern of firing rates, and a network with recurrent inhibition is utilized for further sharpening of the averaged firing rate profiles. The extracted features depend on the spectral content and sound intensity of speech stimuli and enable the segmentation of the LIN output.

The third stage is a structured multi-layer formal neural network realized as a modification of the Hypermap Architecture (Brückner et al. [3]). The modified Hypermap network is trained with segmented LIN output of speech signals. Each segment of the LIN output time sequence which represents the properties of a whole syllable or a part of a syllable, is related to one layer in the input vector. The whole time sequence represents the input vector for one complete speech component, i.e. a word or a part of a sentence. After training the network is able to classify untrained speech signals, i.e. can recognize several words spoken by different subjects.

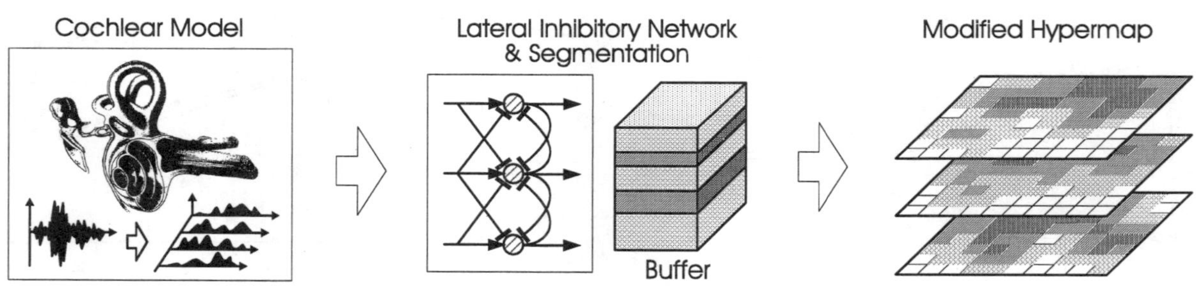

Figure 1: Overall structure of the three-stage speech processing and recognition model

2   Cochlear Model

A digital time-domain model of the human cochlea similar to the cochlear model of Kates [4] is utilized for modeling the processing of sound in the auditory periphery.

Natural sound processing in the cochlea is realized by the conversion of the sound pressure waveform into neural excitation patterns in the auditory nerve at many different places along the cochlear length dimension. The place-domain continuous cochlea is modeled as 112 discrete sections covering a frequency range of 100 Hz to 16 kHz. Each section consists of the following main structural and functional components:

- the mechanical motion of the cochlea,

- the mechanical-to-neural signal transduction and

- the dynamic range compression concerning cochlear input/output relationships and the adaptive adjustment of the mechanical filter behaviour.

A block diagram for one section of the complete model is shown in Fig.2.

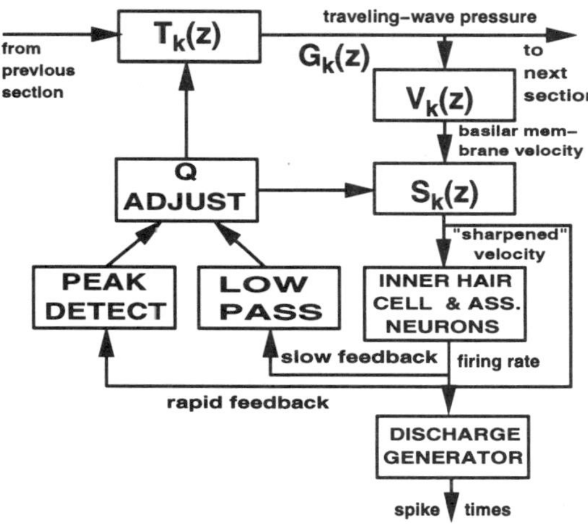

Figure 2: Block diagram of the k. section of the complete cochlear model.

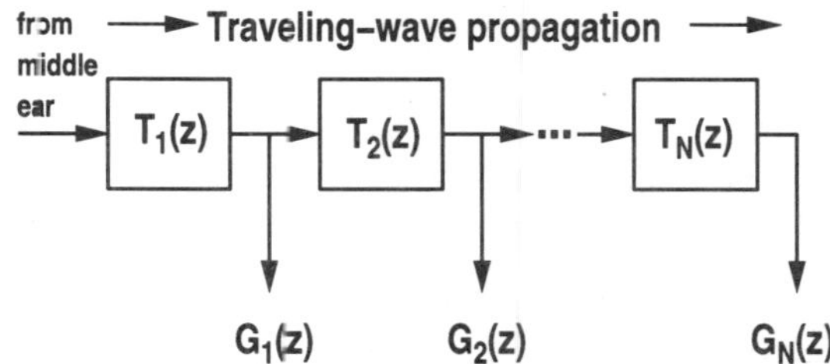

Figure 3: Traveling-wave propagation in the overall cochlear model realized as a cascade of digital resonant filter sections $T_k(z)$.

There are three aspects of the **mechanical motion** in the cochlear model (Kates [4]):

- the propagation of sound pressure traveling-waves on the cochlear partition (see Fig. 3) being represented as a cascade of discrete resonant filter sections $T_k(z)$,

- the transformation of the traveling-wave pressure to basilar membrane velocity at a particular cochlear location by the high pass velocity transformation filters $V_k(z)$ and

- the additional mechanical filtering of the velocity output at a particular location in the cochlea by the second filters $S_k(z)$.

The **mechanical-to-neural signal transduction system** at a particular cochlear location whose input is the velocity output from the second filter, is realized by a complex of an inner hair cell and four attached neurons and their fibres. This complex converts the cochlear partition's motion into a neural firing rate. A nonhomogeneous Poisson process based discharge generator is used for the determination of spike times from the neural firing rate.

There is a **dynamic range compression** with a ratio of 2.5:1 concerning the cochlear input/output relationships under steady-state conditions integrated into the model. The dynamic range compression mechanism is combined with a **feedback system** which consists of a rapid and a slow feedback path.

3   Spatial and Temporal Processing of the Cochlear Model Response

An important function of the auditory system is to discriminate and recognize complex sounds based on their spectral composition (Shamma [2]). Because of its complex structure, a speech evoked response pattern of the cochlear model is little suitable as a direct input for learning and classification algorithms. A preprocessing with neural filter networks is required to detect and highlight characteristic properties like peaks and edges in the spatio-temporal signal. For this purpose we implemented the LIN model of Shamma [2] using one of the fundamental neural network topologies, the lateral inhibition. This topology is assumed to be involved in auditory sensory reception performed by various nuclei, e.g. the cochlear nucleus. Two types of lateral inhibitory networks are distinguished: a nonrecurrent network with a simple feed-forward architecture (LIN.I), and a network with recurrent inhibition (LIN.II). Fig.4. illustrates the typical inhibitory and excitatory interconnections of the model.

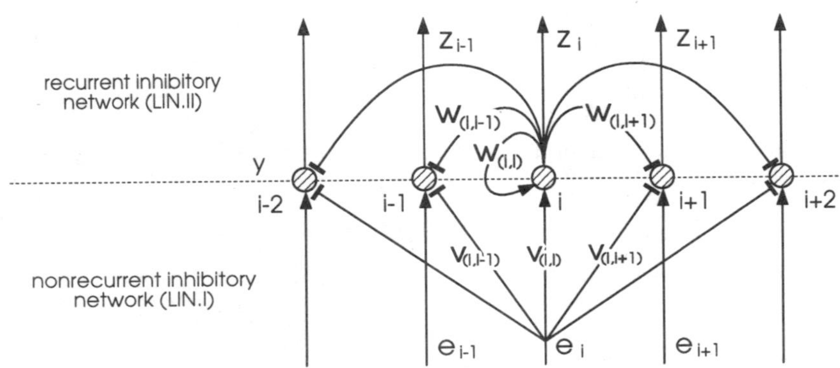

Figure 4: Schematic of a lateral inhibitory network

The intracellular potentials in the neurons of the networks are given by

$$y_i = e_i - \sum_{j=0}^{N} v_{ij} e_j \tag{1}$$

for the nonrecurrent (LIN.I), and

$$y_i = \sum_{j=0}^{N} v_{ij} e_j - \sum_{j=0}^{N} w_{ij} g(y_j) \tag{2}$$

for the recurrent case (LIN.II), where **e** represents the input vector, **v** and **w** are the vectors, containing the inhibitory weights and $g(y_i)$ is a sigmoidal transfer function of the neurons. The mean firing rate at the output of the neurons, generated by $g(y_i)$ is

$$z_i = g(y_i(t)) = \frac{z_{\max}}{1 + e^{-b(y_i(t) - y_0)}} \tag{3}$$

Both networks are simulated as separate filter stages whose inhibitory weights cause a typical high pass behaviour. The LIN.I filter already detects spectral peaks which represent perceptually significant features of the stimuli such as formants of voiced speech. The recurrent network is used for further sharpening of these features.

a) LIN.I-Output pattern

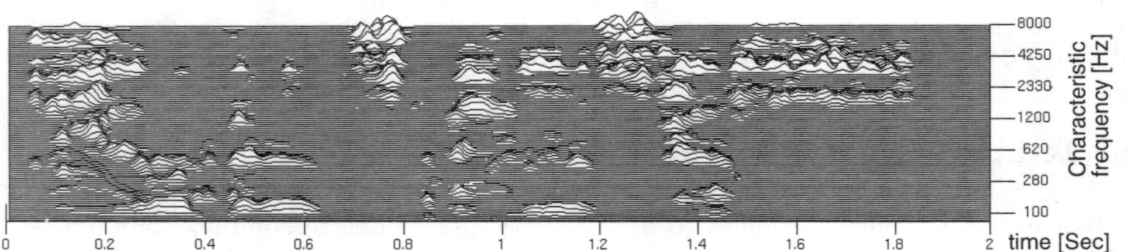

b) LIN.II-Output pattern

Figure 5: Output patterns of LIN.I and LIN.II for the spoken (german) word /Einundzwanzig/

In our simulations, the sample rate of the auditory nerve response patterns is reduced to ≈ 200 samples/sec at the output of LIN.I. Generally, it is possible to simulate the model with a higher resolution, but this is computationally expensive because of the complicated calculations in the LIN.II filter stage. The sample rate reduction is also based on the physiological observation that phase-locking deteriorates significantly in the response of central auditory neurons, which encode only averaged outputs (Shamma [2]), such as shown in Fig.5. The results of the inhibitory filter processes depend on the spectral content and sound intensity of speech stimuli and allow the segmentation of the LIN.II output.

4   Classification by means of an Artificial Neural Network

The third stage of our model for speech processing and recognition is a structured multi-layer formal neural network realized as a modification of the Hypermap Architecture (Brückner et al. [3]). Unlike the Hypermap Architecture, which was introduced by Kohonen in [5], we suggest a structure with an arbitrary number of levels in the input vector with each level containing the transformed input data (Fig.6). In [3] we defined the modification of the Hypermap Architecture. There we described the learning of context-dependent data. The context is generated from the input data. With our modification it is also possible to learn time-dependent data in form of time sequences. Each part of a time sequence is related to the corresponding level in the input vector which forms a time hierarchy. The learning process consists of one step for each level in the hierarchy. The recognition of continuous speech signals is performed by a sequentiation process. Each detected segment is related to a level of the network hierarchy where recognition is done. The initial segment of a speech component is related to level one.

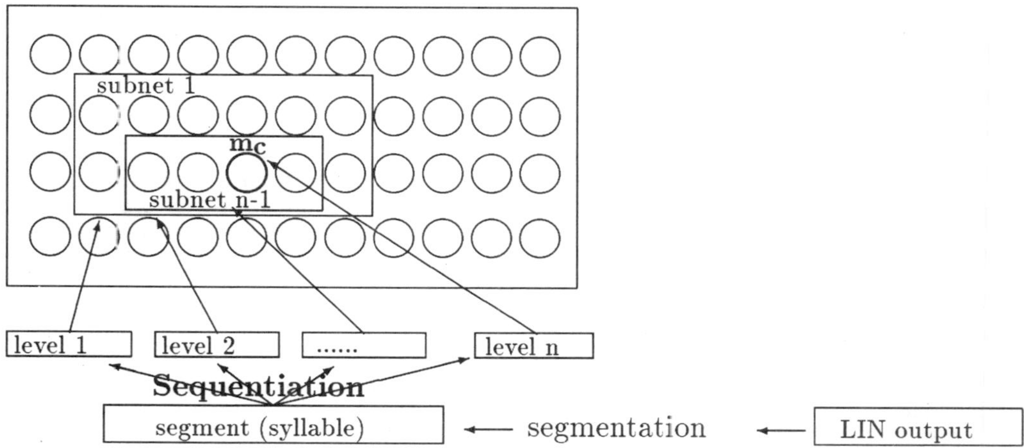

Figure 6: Structure of the modified Hypermap Architecture for speech recognition. The speech evoked LIN output is transformed into segments by a segmentation process. The input vector consists of a concatenation of these segments for one speech component, e.g. a word. The different levels of the input vector are trained and form a hierarchy of encapsulated subsets which define different generalized stages of classification.

The learning algorithm is described in detail in [3] and has the following steps:

- Find a first level with a subset S_j of nodes with an error under a given threshold of that level. The sizes of the thresholds should be decreased according to the order of the levels to obtain encapsulated subsets S_j.

- Find the best match $\mathbf{m}_c$ for all nodes in the subset and adapt the weights accordingly.

- Test for a priori knowledge, i.e. in one level is a significant higher error in comparison with the other levels of this input vector, then an adaptive learning algorithm saves these trained states [3].

Classification is achieved by finding the best matching node for each level of the hierarchy and by determining the square mean error of matching. To protect the algorithm from initial disordering the a priori knowledge learning step should start after a given time t_0.

In our experiments with speech we obtained segment sequences derived from a segmentation process. These segments represent whole syllables or parts of syllables like phonemes. In this sense the whole time sequence represents one complete speech component, i.e. a word or a part of a sentence. The algorithm handles different numbers of segments in the input vector.

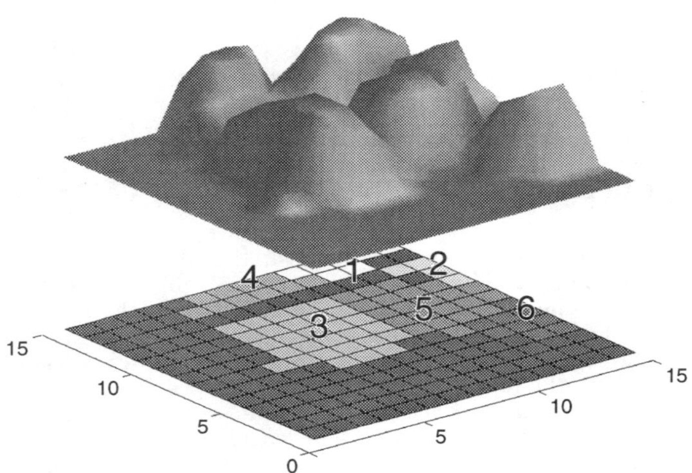

Figure 7: The global error surface (4. level) after learning of 6 german words in form of sequences of segments is shown. The six words are the numbers 21, 32, 43, 54, 56 and 64 in this order. The network topology forms a single cluster for the initial segments of these words and within this cluster subclusters on the lower levels for the segments followed.

5 Discussion

First of all the digitized speech signals are preprocessed and converted into neural excitation patterns by an implementation of a cochlear model (Kates [4]). Subsequently the model of a lateral inhibitory network with a highpass filter behaviour highlights spectral edges of these patterns and suppresses all other activities. The edges, considered as significant features of the stimuli, are particularly stable with respect to sound level variations, despite of the limited dynamic range of the auditory nerve fibres. Consequently, the discontinuities in the complex overall response texture are largely preserved after the LIN filter process (Shamma [2]). The segmentation process following is a filter algorithm indicating the segments' boundaries. This algorithm is independent of the Hypermap Architecture. The trained Hypermap Network is then able to classify speech components from continuous speech signals spoken by different subjects (Fig.7). Taking into account the previous studies with conventional self-organizing maps, our presently available data reveal an improved classification [3]. However, there were some problems with "artefacts" in the training set, e.g., words with an unusual accentuation disordered the achieved classification.

With the new a priori knowledge learning algorithm we can solve this problem. First investigations confirm the expected results, thus we can go on optimizing parameters of the algorithm.

Acknowledgement

This work was supported by LSA grant 851A/0023.

References

[1] B. Brückner and W. Zander, "Neurobiological modeling and structured neural networks", *Proc. Inter. Conf. Artificial Neural Networks*, Amsterdam, Sept. 13-16, 1993, pp. 43-46.

[2] S. Shamma, "Spatial and Temporal Processing in Central Auditory Networks", *C. Koch and I. Segev (eds.): Methods in Neuronal Modeling*, The MIT Press, Cambridge, Massachusetts, pp. 247-289, 1989.

[3] B. Brückner, T. Wesarg and C. Blumenstein, "Improvements of the modified Hypermap Architecture for Speech Recognition", *Proc. Inter. Conf. Neural Networks*, Perth, Australia, Nov.22-Dec.1, 1995, vol. 5, pp. 2891-2895.

[4] J.M. Kates, "A time-domain digital cochlear model", *IEEE Transactions on Signal Processing*, vol. 39, no. 12, pp. 2573-2592, December 1991.

[5] Teuvo Kohonen, "The hypermap architecture", In: T. Kohonen, K. Mäkisara, O. Simula, and J. Kangas, editors, *Artificial Neural Networks*, pp. 1357–1360, Helsinki, 1991. Elsevier Science Publishers.

An Efficient Linguistic Decoder For Continuous Cantonese Word Recognition

K.K. Shin and J.C.H. Poon

Department of Electronic Engineering, The Hong Kong Polytechnic University
Hung Hom, Kowloon, Hong Kong
Tel:(852)7666217;E-mail:ENJPOON@hkpucc.polyu.edu.hk

Abstract

In this paper, a linguistic decoder converts continuous Cantonese phonetic string into word sequence is presented. This acoustic decoder is based on Time-Delay Neural Network which generates the phonetic sequence with both likelihood and duration information to the linguistic decoder. The decoders are implemented to perform the continuous Cantonese key-word detection task. The Cantonese words are decoded hierarchically by a multi-level method to reduce the computation labour.

1   Introduction

A system for recognition of continuous speech usually consists of an acoustic decoder and a linguistic decoder as shown in Figure 1. The acoustic processor uses signal processing and pattern recognition techniques to generate the phonetic information from the input speech signal. Insertion, deletion and substitution errors are introduced in the phonetic sequence due to the imperfect classification. The linguistic decoder utilizes the information provided by the acoustic decoder, together with the phonetic, phonological, and the lexical knowledge, etc, to convert the noisy phonetic string to standard orthography. In our experiment, five Cantonese words /fa/, /fat/, /sa/, /sak/ and /se/ are recorded by one male native speaker. The set of phonemes extracted includes fricatives /f, s/, vowels /a, e/ and plosives /k, t/ for these words.

2   Acoustic Decoder

Time-Delay Neural Network (TDNN) [1] has been proved as a superior method for phoneme recognition because it handles the temporal structure of speech. In our work, TDNN is used as the acoustic front-end to analyse the spectral information within a 64 ms window of input speech. The spectral information is extracted by 64 points FFT computed on the Hamming windowed 10 kHz digitized speech. The Cantonese phonemes are spotted by shifting the TDNN across time, and the sequence of these phonemes will be formulated as a word.

The TDNN used in the experiments consists of three layers. The first 32 neurons of the input layers are copies of the input vector. The hidden layer consists of 10 neurons of which the activation level at time t depends on the activations of the neurons of the input layer at time t, t-1, t-2 (input layer has a delay of 2). The output layer has 6 neurons for classification. Activations of the output neurons depend on the activations of the neurons of hidden layer at time t, t-1,..., t-4 (hidden layer has a delay of 4). The network is trained by backpropagation through time [2]. In backpropagation, the weights of network are adjusted so as to minimize the network's error over the training set by gradient descent. The training set consists of a set of phoneme samples.

Figure 2 shows the activation pattern of the TDNN as it scans across the Cantonese word /fat/. The TDNN provides framewise phoneme classification where each phoneme may spend across several frames. The output activations demonstrate that the TDNN can detect the dynamic characteristic of speech, such as the syllabic onset /f/ and the syllabic coda /t/, and also detect the static vowel /a/. The overlapping and transition of output

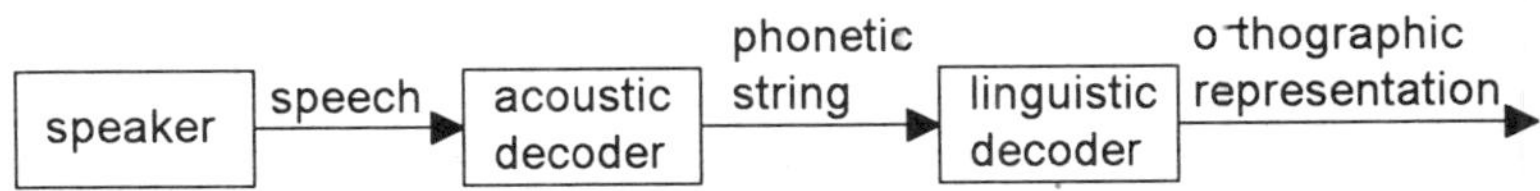

Figure 1. Block diagram of a typical continuous speech recognition system

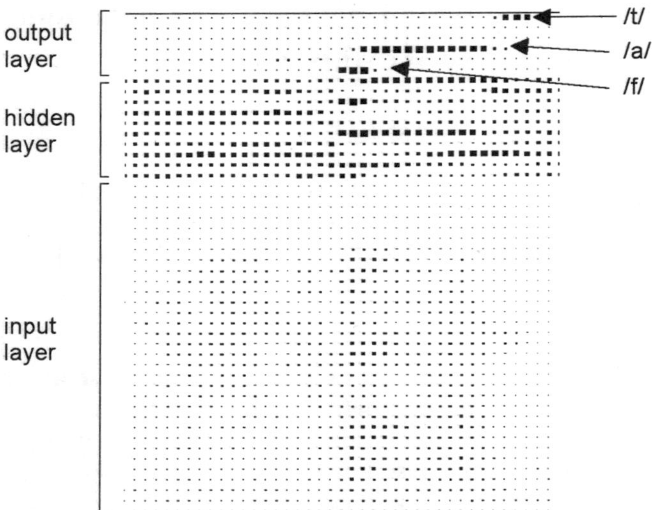

Figure 2. TDNN activation pattern for /fat/

activation from one phoneme to another indicate the coarticulation between phonemes can be modelled by the TDNN by appropriate supervised training method.

3 Linguistic Decoder

A Cantonese word consists of one syllable arranged in the form

$$(O)N(C),$$

where O is a consonant class in the syllabic onset, N is the vowel class in the syllabic nucleus, and C is a consonant class in the syllabic coda. The parentheses represent optional occurrence of phoneme. Hence, in this abstract level, the Cantonese dictionary only consists of four elements, N, NC, ON and ONC, when each word is rewriten using the class names O, N and C. The dictionary can be modelled by the state diagram presented in Figure 3. In our experiment, $O = \{/f/, /s/\}$, $N = \{/a/, /e/\}$ and $C = \{/k/, /t/\}$,and a phoneme which belongs to given class is more liable to be misrecognized as a phoneme in the same class than as a phoneme in another class. The linguistic decoder performs the decoding in two levels. In the first level of decoding which we called the class level decoding, for a given string of framewise output from the acoustic decoder up to time τ, $\mathbf{y} = y_1 y_2 \cdots y_\tau$, a sequence of words represented by their class names

$$\gamma = \gamma_1 \gamma_2 \cdots \gamma_M, \quad \gamma_i \in \{N, NC, ON, ONC\} \text{ and } i = 1, \cdots, M \tag{1}$$

is segmented out by considering the maximum metric values of the path through the class state diagram (Figure 3). Then in the second level of classification called the phoneme level decoding, the exact word w_i is decoded for each γ_i by another ongoing search through the phonetic state dragram or graph.

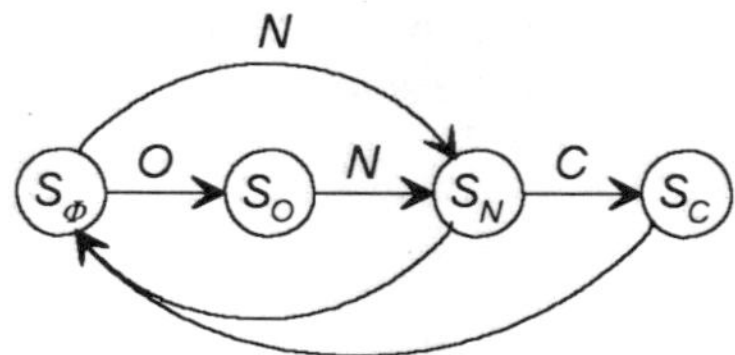

Figure 3. State diagram represents the phonetic entry for a sequence of Cantonese words. $S_\emptyset$ is starting state for a new word. The label above a branch indicates the phoneme generated when that transition is made

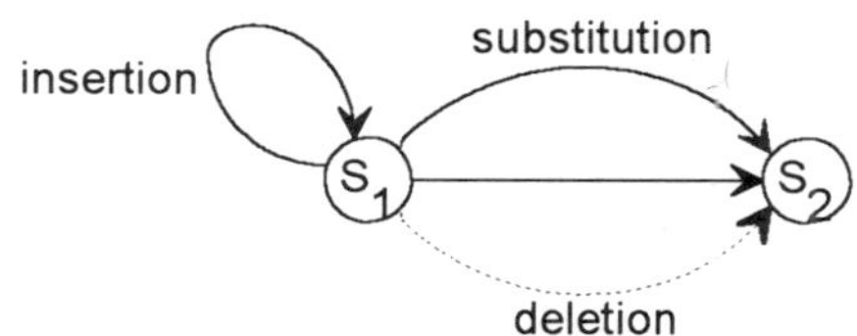

Figure 4. Model incorporates insertion, substitution and deletion errors

Due to imperfect classification, insertion, deletion and substitution errors are introduced in the phonetic sequence, any of these possible types of errors can be accommodated by incorporating variations into the state diagram as shown in Figure 4 [3]. In Figure 4, the transition from S_1 to itself produces an insertion error, the transition from S_1 to S_2 produces a subsitution error and the null transition from S_1 to S_2 produces a deletion error. The performance statistics of the probability of misrecogniting a phoneme, probability of omitting a phoneme, probability of inserting a phoneme could be associated with the paths in the model. Due to the framewise phoneme classification provided by TDNN and the partition scheme described below are adopted in our system, the deletion and insertion errors will be replaced by subsitution error. Therefore, only the substitution path is needed to incorporate into the model in Figure 3.

The TDNN provides framewise phoneme classification, while the linguistic decoder reconstructs the words from the sequence of phonemes. The maximum posteriori probabilities of a phoneme class at a given time frame can be approximated by the output activations of the neural network. A class likelihood would be given by averaging the outputs over time.

3.1 Partition Method

As the TDNN scans the input speech across time, framewise phoneme classification are given continuously. For the sequence of framewise phonemes **y**, we define the partition S^n of the sequence into n segment as the following set of ordered pairs of integers from 1 to τ that

$$S^n = \{(\tau_0 + 1, \tau_1), (\tau_1 + 1, \tau_2), \cdots, (\tau_{n-1} + 1, \tau_n)\}, \tag{2}$$

where

$$0 = \tau_0 \leq \tau_1 < \tau_2 < \cdots < \tau_{n-1} < \tau_n = \tau.$$

Each segment $(\tau_i + 1, \tau_{i+1}) \in S^n$, for $0 \leq i \leq n - 1$, is labelled by a phoneme class symbol $g_{\tau_i+1,\tau_{i+1}}$ based on the likelihood of phoneme substring $y_{\tau_i+1} y_{\tau_i+2} \cdots y_{\tau_{i+1}}$. Therefore, the sequence of spotted phoneme is converted to a sequence of class transitions represented by $\mathbf{g}_n = g_{1,\tau_1} g_{\tau_1+1,\tau_2} \cdots g_{\tau_{n-1}+1,\tau_n}$. Let the set of all possible partitions of **y** be

$$\Psi_\tau = \{\mathbf{g}_n | n = 1, \cdots, \tau\}. \tag{3}$$

For example, $\Psi_3 = \{g_{1,3}, g_{1,1}g_{2,3}, g_{1,2}g_{3,3}, g_{1,1}g_{2,2}g_{3,3}\}$. If one more phoneme $y_{\tau+1}$ is spotted as the TDNN advanced in time. The new set of class transition sequences can be evaluated by

$$\Psi_{\tau+1} = \Psi_0 \oplus g_{1,\tau+1} \cup \Psi_1 \oplus g_{2,\tau+1} \cup \cdots \cup \Psi_\tau \oplus g_{\tau+1,\tau+1}$$

$$\Psi_{\tau+1} = \bigcup_{i=0}^{\tau} \Psi_i \oplus g_{i+1,\tau+1}, \tag{4}$$

where $\oplus$ is the concatenation operator which concatenated the new label $g_{i+1,\tau+1}$ to the end of all the sequence $\mathbf{g} \in \Psi_i$. Figure 5 illustrates an example of the operation.

There are a total of $2^{\tau-1}$ possible partitions for a sequence of τ frames long, and the possible partitions will grow exponentially as phonemes are spotted continuously by the TDNN. Actually, only the set of partitions which will constitute a legal path with metric value greater than a chosen threshold are retained. The number of legal partitions which produce transitions to a node in the class state diagram is usually small.

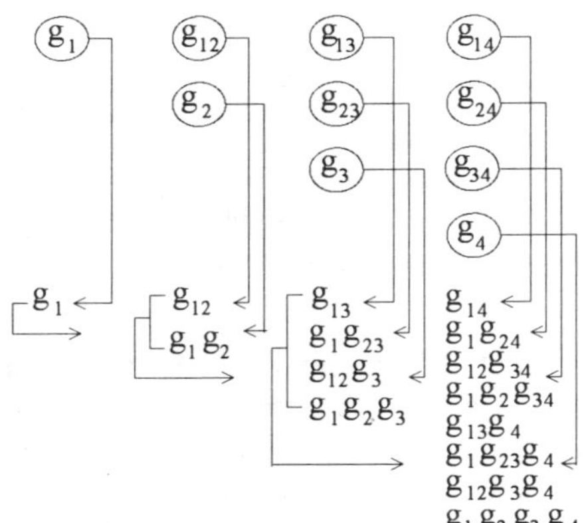

Figure 5. The Construction of sequences of class states

3.2 Class level Decoding

For a given partition, a value of metric $G_i(k)$ is associated with each node S_i at depth k into the class state diagram. This value is a function of the paths that can be traversed in reaching S_i from the starting node S_Φ. The measure employed for an arbitary node i at depth k is given by

$$G_i(k) = \max_{j} \{G_j(k-1) + h_k + d_{k-1}\},\tag{5}$$

where $G(0) = 0$, h_k depends on the type of hypothesis made in traversing from node S_j to node S_i, that is, a match or subsitution. h_k is given by

$$h_k = \log p(g_k) - B_g,\tag{6}$$

where B_g is a constant bias term to provide normalization with respect to the depth into the searching path. B_g is subtracted k times regardless of the path taken to provide fair comparison among paths of different depth. $p(g_k)$ is the likelihood of hypothesizing class element g_k in traversing from node S_j to node S_i. Subscript k refers to the position of class within the partition. And d_{k-1} is a value depends on the duration of the previous hypothesized class. A vowel of shorter duration in Cantonese word will imply there is a following syllabic coda. Hence, a larger d_{k-1} should be added to increase the metric value in searching for a syllabic coda in the decoding process.

After the first level decoding, a given string of phonemes up to time τ, $\mathbf{y} = y_1 y_2 \cdots y_\tau$, is converted to L sequences of word class,

$$\gamma^l = \gamma^l_1 \gamma^l_2 \cdots \gamma^l_{M_l}, \quad l = 1, \cdots, L\tag{7}$$

where M_l is the number of words in the sequence γ^l. A metric value $\mathbf{G}(\gamma^l)$ is associated with each sequence where

$$\mathbf{G}(\gamma^l) = G_{f_l}(K_l).\tag{8}$$

f_l and K_l are the final node and the depth of the path that reachs in the class state diagram at the end of the input partition sequence.

3.3 Phoneme Level Decoding

For each γ^l_i in the sequence γ^l, we decode the word consists of J phonemes , $w^l_i = x^l_{i,1} \cdots x^l_{i,J}$ ($x^l_{i,j}$, for $j = 1, \cdots, J$, are the phonemes constitute that word), by an ongoing search through another phonetic graph describing the dictionary to which γ^l_i belongs. Figure 6 shows the phonetic graphs for words with two and three phonemes in

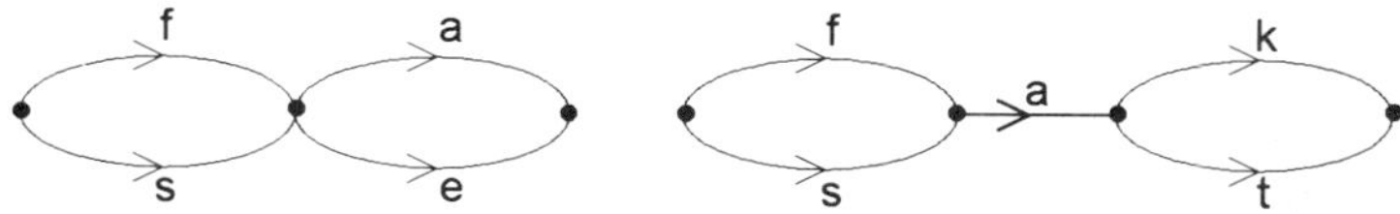

Figure 6. Phonetic graphs for words /fa/, /sa/, /se/, /fat/ and /sak/

our experiment. The path with maximum metric value is determined by evaluating the following expression recursively,

$$W_s(j) = \max_t \{ W_t(j-1) + \log p(x_j) - B_w \}, \tag{9}$$

where $W(0) = 0$, B_w is a constant bias value for normalization, $p(x_j)$ is the likelihood of hypothesizing phoneme x_j in traversing from node S_t to node S_s in the phonetic graph. J refers to the position of phoneme within the word. The metric value for the word w_i^l is given by

$$\mathbf{W}(w_i^l) = W_f(J). \tag{10}$$

f is the index of the final node of the optimum path.

The decoding is finished by determining the word sequence $\mathbf{w} = w_1^{l'} w_2^{l'} \cdots w_{M_{l'}}^{l'}$ in which

$$l' = \arg\max_l \{ \mathbf{G}(\gamma^l) + \sum_{i=1}^{M_l} (\mathbf{W}(w_i^l) - B_T) \}. \tag{11}$$

where B_T is a constant term for normalization with respect to the number of words in a sequence. Table 1 shows the performance of the recognition system. The accuracy of phoneme recognition is calculated by the intergration of the network's output over the chosen segement containing that phoneme. A phoneme is treated as correct when the integrated activation of the correct output neuron is more than 0.5.

4   Conclusion

In this paper, a linguistic decoder using Time-Delay Neural Network (TDNN) as the acoustic front-end is described. The neural network is trained by phoneme level supervision to recognize all the phonemes which will compose all the words in Cantonese dictionary. The phoneme level training can be coarse. While the fine-tune training is used to improve the system performance for a specific task (limited in vocabulary). The linguistic decoder uses partition method on the sequence of phoneme spotted by TDNN to reduce the types of errors to subsitution error only. Two level linguistic decoding is employed to reduce the computation labour. Indeed, each class of phoneme (syllabic onset, syllabic nucleus or syllablic coda) can be further sub-divided into sub-classes to handle larger vocabulary. More levels of decoding can be added such that the range of searching is narrowed down at each level. Moreover, different linguistic constrains can be added at each level to increase the accuracy.

TABLE 1. Experimental results

	phoneme accuracy						word accuracy
	/f/	/s/	/a/	/e/	/k/	/t/	
/fa/	88%	-	100%	-	-	-	96%
/fat/	60%	-	100%	-	-	100%	98%
/sa/	-	98%	100%	-	-	-	100%
/sak/	-	99%	99%	-	99%	-	97%
/se/	-	96%	-	100%	-	-	100%

Reference

[1]   Alexander Waibel, Toshiyuki Hanazawa, Geoffrey Hinton Kiyohiro Shikano and Kevin J. Lang, "Phoneme Recognition Using Time-Delay Neural Networks", IEEE Trans. on ASSP, vol. 37, pp. 328-339, 1989.

[2]   P.J. Werbos, "Backpropagation Through Time: What It Does and How to Do It", Proceedings of IEEE, vol. 78, Oct., 1990.

[3]   Ralph Alter, "Utilization of Contextual Constraints in Automatic Speech Recognition", IEEE Trans. on Audio and Electroacoustics, vol. 16, March, 1968.

[4]   C.C. Tappert, N. Rex Dixon, and A.S. Rabinowitz, "Application of Sequential Decoding for Converting Phonetic to Graphic Representation in Automatic Recognition of Continuous Speech (ARCS)", IEEE Trans. on Audio and Electroacoustics, vol. 21, June, 1973.

An On-line Learning Algorithm for Blind Equalization

Howard Hua Yang[†], Eng Siong Chng[‡]

† Lab. for Inf. Rep., FRP, RIKEN
2-1 Hirosawa, Wako-Shi, Saitama 351-01, JAPAN
e-mail: hhy@koala.riken.go.jp

‡ Inst. of Systems Science
National Univ. of S'pore
SINGAPORE 119597
e-mail: eschng@iss.nus.sg

Abstract— **An on-line algorithm for blind equalization of an FIR channel is proposed by minimizing the mutual information of the output. The algorithm is closely related to the blind separation algorithm based on independent component analysis. It is assumed that the channel impulse responses are unknown and the channel may be non-minimum phase. The algorithm is implemented on a linear neural network in which the weight matrix is updated by the proposed algorithm. The simulation results are used to demonstrate the effectiveness of the algorithm.**

1 Introduction

Blind system identification and equalization are important in the areas such as data transmission, seismic deconvolution, and image de-blurring[6]. Some new developments in these areas are reviewed in [7] and [8] where two new methods for blind system identification and equalization are proposed. These methods are batch type algorithms and require matrix decompositions in the implementations. In addition, the system identification and equalization processes are two pipeline operations in these algorithms. The equalization can only be started after the channel is identified.

Although the blind source separation seems to be an area different from the blind identification and equalization, in fact they are closely related. Recently, several blind separation algorithms have been proposed and analyzed [3, 4, 2, 1]. These algorithms can be applied for blind equalization by formulating the equalization problem appropriately. The application of blind separation algorithms leads to some on-line algorithms which carries the equalization directly without the channel identification process.

2 Channel Model and Problem

Consider the following time invariant channel defined in [7]:

$$x(t) = \sum_{kT \le t} s(k)h(t - kT) + n(t) \tag{1}$$

where $\{s(k)\}$ is an input sequence, T the symbol interval, $n(\cdot)$ the additive noise, and $h(\cdot)$ the channel impulse response function. The problem of the blind identification and equalization is to identify the impulse response function and recover the input sequence.

The model (1) becomes the following multi-channel FIR system when the sampling rate is M times faster than the baud rate:

$$x_m(k) = \sum_{l=0}^{L} h_m(l)s(k - l) + n_m(k), \quad k = 1, \cdots, N, \tag{2}$$
$$m = 1, \cdots, M,$$

where $x_m(k)$ is the output of the m-th channel, $h_m(l)$ the impulse response of the m-th channel, $s(k)$ the common input to M channels, L the maximum order of these M channels, N the data length, and $n_m(k)$ a complex zero mean Gaussian noise.

A blind identification algorithm is given in [7] based on the second order statistics of the oversampled observations. The singular value decomposition (SVD) of the estimated data covariance matrix is used in this algorithm. Another blind identification algorithm is proposed in [8] by solving a linear equation which is derived by exploiting every channel output pair. The latter algorithm generally performs better than the former one and imposes a much weaker condition on the input sequence. Generally, both algorithms can achieve equalization within few hundreds baud intervals. However, both algorithms are batch type and require extensive matrix computations. The SVD is needed in [7] to decompose the data covariance matrix and a large matrix whose size depends on the data size is constructed to form the linear equations in [8]. Some difficulties may arise in the implementation of the algorithms due to these matrix computations.

In this paper, a new on-line algorithm is proposed for the blind equalization problem based on an algorithm for blind source separation. The new algorithm only requires matrix summations/multiplications to update the weight matrix for a linear neural network.

3   Blind Equalization Algorithm Based on ICA

The independent component analysis (ICA) formulated in [5] is a general framework for developing blind separation algorithms. A linear mixture model is

$$\mathbf{x}(t) = \boldsymbol{H}\mathbf{s}(t)$$

where $\boldsymbol{H} \in \boldsymbol{R}^{n \times n}$ is an unknown non-singular mixing matrix, n the number of sources, $\mathbf{s}(t) = [s^1(t), \cdots, s^n(t)]^T$ the vector of sources and $\mathbf{x}(t) = [x^1(t), \cdots, x^n(t)]^T$ the vector of mixtures.

To recover the original sources from the mixtures, we use the linear transform $\mathbf{y}(t) = \boldsymbol{W}\mathbf{x}(t)$. The following learning algorithm (LA) is used to update the weight matrix $\boldsymbol{W}$:

$$\frac{d\boldsymbol{W}}{dt} = \eta(t)\{\boldsymbol{I} - \mathbf{f}(\boldsymbol{y})\boldsymbol{y}^T\}\boldsymbol{W} \tag{3}$$

where $\mathbf{f}(\boldsymbol{y}) = (f(y^1), \cdots, f(y^n))^T$. This algorithm is derived in [2] by minimizing the mutual information of the outputs using natural gradient descent algorithm. There are many extensions[1] of this algorithm and several choices for the function $f(\cdot)$ as well. In this paper, we choose the simplest function $f(y) = y^3$ among all options.

To apply the above algorithm to the blind equalization problem, we write the system (2) in a vector form:

$$\boldsymbol{x}_k = \boldsymbol{H}_1\boldsymbol{s}_k + \boldsymbol{n}_k \tag{4}$$

where $\boldsymbol{x}_k = (x_1(k), \cdots, x_M(k))^T$, $\mathbf{s}_k = (s(k-L), s(k-L+1), \cdots, s(k))^T$, $\boldsymbol{n}_k = (n_1(k), \cdots, n_M(k))^T$, $\boldsymbol{H}_1 = [\,\mathbf{h}_L \mathbf{h}_{L-1} \cdots \mathbf{h}_0\,]$, $\mathbf{h}_l = (h_1(l), \cdots, h_M(l))^T$, $l = 0, 1, \cdots, L$.

Define an $m \times (m + L)$ block matrix $\boldsymbol{H}_m$:

$$\boldsymbol{H}_m = \begin{bmatrix} \mathbf{h}_L & \mathbf{h}_{L-1} & \cdots & \cdots & \mathbf{h}_0 & 0 & \cdots & 0 \\ 0 & \mathbf{h}_L & \mathbf{h}_{L-1} & \cdots & \cdots & \mathbf{h}_0 & \cdots & 0 \\ \cdots & \cdots & \cdots & \cdots & \cdots & \cdots & \cdots & \cdots \\ 0 & \cdots & 0 & \mathbf{h}_L & \mathbf{h}_{L-1} & \cdots & \cdots & \mathbf{h}_0 \end{bmatrix}$$

and each block in $\boldsymbol{H}_m$ is an $M \times 1$ vector.

Stacking m observation vectors $\boldsymbol{x}_1, \cdots, \boldsymbol{x}_m$, we form a joint observation vector. From (4), we have

$$\boldsymbol{u}_1 = \begin{bmatrix} \boldsymbol{x}_1 \\ \vdots \\ \boldsymbol{x}_m \end{bmatrix} = \boldsymbol{H}_m \begin{bmatrix} s(1-L) \\ \vdots \\ s(m) \end{bmatrix} + \begin{bmatrix} \boldsymbol{n}_1 \\ \vdots \\ \boldsymbol{n}_m \end{bmatrix} \tag{5}$$

The next joint observation vector $\boldsymbol{u}_2$ is formed by removing $\boldsymbol{x}_1$ in $\boldsymbol{u}_1$ and appending $\boldsymbol{x}_m$ to $\boldsymbol{u}_1$. Generally, we stack m observation vectors $\boldsymbol{x}_k, \cdots, \boldsymbol{x}_{m+k-1}$ and obtain the k-th joint observation vector $\boldsymbol{u}_k$

$$\boldsymbol{u}_k = \begin{bmatrix} \boldsymbol{x}_k \\ \vdots \\ \boldsymbol{x}_{m+k-1} \end{bmatrix} = \boldsymbol{H}_m \begin{bmatrix} s(k-L) \\ \vdots \\ s(m+k-1) \end{bmatrix} + \begin{bmatrix} \boldsymbol{n}_k \\ \vdots \\ \boldsymbol{n}_{m+k-1} \end{bmatrix}. \tag{6}$$

Note $\boldsymbol{H}_m$ is of $mM \times (m + L)$. In this paper, we consider the blind equalization of the system (2) only for $M = 2$. For the system (1), we only consider the case in which the sampling rate is two times faster than the baud rate. Given $M = 2$, if we choose $m = L$, then $\boldsymbol{H}_m$ becomes a square matrix.

We treat the system (6) as a mixture model and apply the algorithm (3) to update the weight matrix W and recover the source vector by transforming the joint observation vector in the system (6). Since the elements of H_m are unknown, we can not compute its inverse exactly. However, we can use the blind separation algorithm such as (3) to obtain a scaled and permuted inverse DPH_m^{-1} where D is a diagonal matrix with non-zero diagonal elements and P is a permutation matrix. With this scaled and permuted inverse matrix, we achieve the blind separation. We call this algorithm blind equalization by blind separation (BEBS). Denote

$$\underline{s}_k = (s(k-L), \cdots, s(L+k-1))^T.$$

The structure of the equalization system is illustrated in Figure 1.

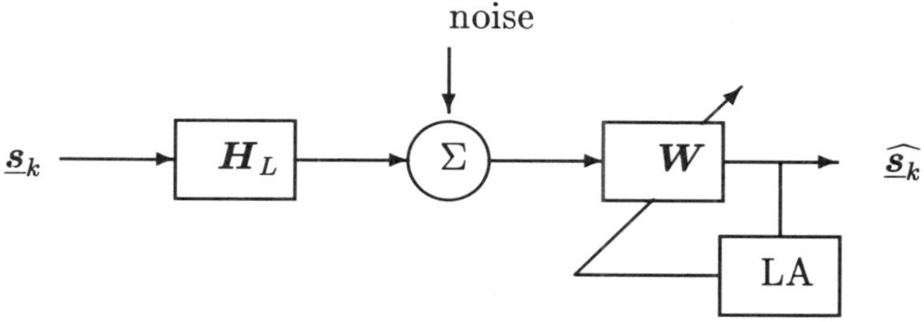

Figure 1: A block diagram of the equalization system when $m = L$

4 Simulation

Let T be the baud interval. Assume that the duration of an FIR channel is 12T and the sampling rate is twice faster than the baud rate. The fractional samples of the FIR channel output is the output of a multi-channel FIR system with the following 2-D vector impulse response:

$$h = \begin{bmatrix} h_1 \\ h_2 \end{bmatrix} \text{ where}$$

$h_1 = [-0.0013 \ -0.0837 \ 0.0138 \ 0.3132 \ 0.5167 \ 0.3874 \ 0.0843 \ -0.0703 \ -0.0196 \ 0.0414 \ 0.0098 \ -0.0279]$
and
$h_2 = [0.0368 \ -0.0514 \ -0.0675 \ 0.1520 \ 0.4494 \ 0.4931 \ 0.2351 \ -0.0241 \ -0.0604 \ 0.0216 \ 0.0343 \ -0.0156]$.

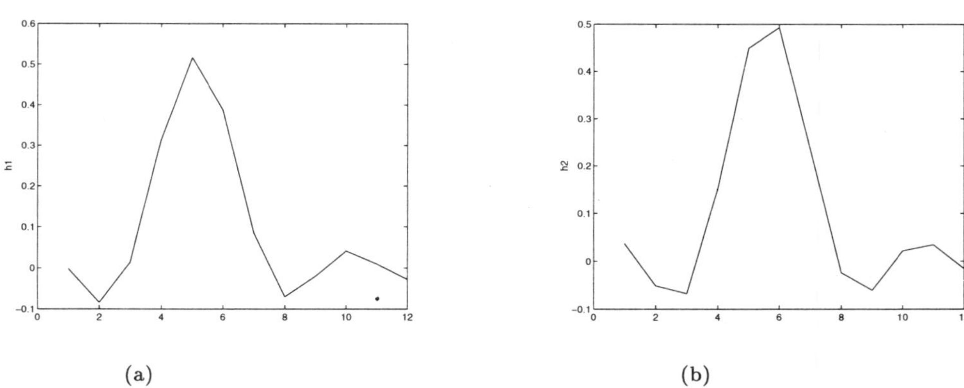

(a)   (b)

Figure 2: The impulse responses of the two FIR channels with the common input.

The impulse responses of the two channels are plotted in Figure 2. The same set of tap values are also used in [7] with a different setting. We test the BEBS algorithm to equalize the above channel. The source symbols are drawn from an iid binary sequence. We choose $M = 2$ and $m = L$ in the BEBS. Assume that the noise in the observation is a Gaussian noise with zero mean and variance σ^2.

The simulation result in Figure 3 is used as a benchmark for comparison. It is obtained by using the algorithm in [8] to estimate the channel responses first, then use the following equation to estimate the source vector in (6) for equalization:

$$(\hat{s}(k - L), \cdots, \hat{s}(m + k - 1))^T = (\widehat{\boldsymbol{H}}_m)^{-1}\boldsymbol{u}_k$$

where $\widehat{\boldsymbol{H}}_m$ is defined from the estimated channel responses in the same way as $\boldsymbol{H}_m$ is defined. We call this algorithm a least-squares blind equalization (LSBE).

The simulation results obtained by the LSBE and BEBS algorithms are shown in Figure 3-4 respectively. In each test, 2000 source symbols are used to equalize the channel. After the equalization, 20000 source symbols are transmitted to estimate the bit-error-rate for each algorithm. When $\sigma = 0.0005$, the bit-error-rate for the BEBS algorithm is 0.025% while bit-error-rate for the LSBE is 29%. Therefore, the BEBS algorithm performs better than the LSBE algorithm when sampling rate is two times faster than the baud rate.

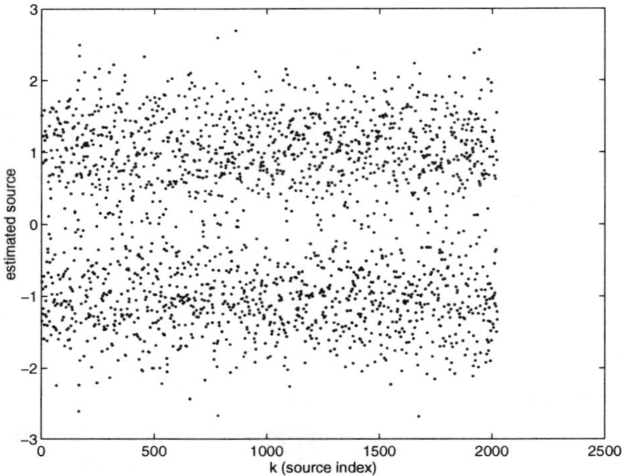

Figure 3: The equalization achieved by the LSBE algorithm when $M = 2$.

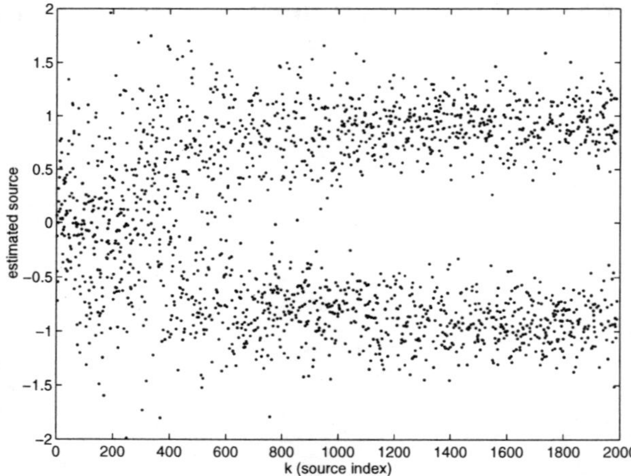

Figure 4: The equalization achieved by the blind separation algorithm when $M = 2$.

5   Conclusion

The on-line blind separation algorithm is applied for the equalization of an FIR channel with fractional sampling or a multi-channel system driven by a single input. When the sampling rate is two times the baud rate, the blind separation algorithm achieves the equalization with much better quality than the least-squares blind equalization algorithm.

References

[1] S. Amari, A. Cichocki, and H. H. Yang. Recurrent neural networks for blind separation of sources. In *Proceedings 1995 International Symposium on Nonlinear Theory and Applications*, volume I, pages 37–42, December 1995.

[2] S. Amari, A. Cichocki, and H. H. Yang. A new learning algorithm for blind signal separation. In *Advances in Neural Information Processing Systems, 8, eds. David S. Touretzky, Michael C. Mozer and Michael E. Hasselmo, MIT Press: Cambridge, MA. (to appear)*, 1996.

[3] A. J. Bell and T. J. Sejnowski. An information-maximisation approach to blind separation and blind deconvolution. *Neural Computation*, 7:1129–1159, 1995.

[4] J.-F. Cardoso and Beate Laheld. Equivariant adaptive source separation. *To appear in IEEE Trans. on Signal Processing*, 1996.

[5] P. Comon. Independent component analysis, a new concept? *Signal Processing*, 36:287–314, 1994.

[6] S. Haykin. *Blind Deconvolution*. Prentice-Hall, Inc., 1994.

[7] L. Tong, G. Xu, and T. Kailath. Blind Identification and Equalization Based on Second-Order Statistics: A Time Domain Approach . *IEEE Trans. on Information Theory*, 40(2):340–349, March 1994.

[8] G. Xu, H. Liu, L. Tong, and T. Kailath. A least-squares approach to blind channel identification. *IEEE Trans. on Signal Processing*, 43(12):2982–2993, December 1995.

Adaptive local Radial Basis Function network for nonstationary channel equalisation problem

Eng-Siong Chng [†][1], Howard Hua Yang [‡], Herbert Wiklicky[‡]

[†] *Institute of Systems Science, National University of Singapore, Singapore 11957. Email : eschng@iss.nus.sg*
[‡] *Brain Information Processing Group, Frontier Research Programme, RIKEN. 2-1 Hirosawa, Wako-shi, Saitama 351-01, JAPAN.*

Abstract— **The computational requirement to implement the optimal Bayesian symbol-decision equaliser using RBF network [1] can be very high as the full RBF Bayesian solution usually requires a large number of centres. To reduce the implementation complexity, we propose to use a subset number of the full RBF network's centres to generate a subset equaliser. The centres to be selected for the subset equaliser are those that have their Euclidean distance close to the equaliser's current input vector. Our results show that the number of centres can be greatly reduced without significant degradation in classification performance.**

1   Introduction

The transmission of digital signal across a communication channel is subjected to noise and inter symbol interference (ISI). At the receiver, these effects must be compensated by an equaliser to achieve reliable data communications [1, 2, 3]. The model used to describe a communication channel is a finite impulse response (FIR) filter with a transfer function $H(z) = \sum_{i=0}^{l-1} a(i)z^{-i}$ where $a(i)$ are the channel impulse response coefficients and and l is the channel's memory length[1, 2]. When transmit signals $s(k)$ are passed through the channel, noise and ISI are introduced into the transmit sequence. The signal $r(k)$ observed at the receiver is

$$r(k) = \hat{r}(k) + n(k) = \sum_{i=0}^{l-1} s(k-i)a(i) + n(k), \tag{1}$$

the corrupted signal of $s(k)$ received by the equaliser at sampled instant time k, $\hat{r}(k)$ is the noise-free received signal, $n(k)$ is the additive Gaussian white noise with variance σ_n^2. The input to the equaliser is a vector of noisy received signal

$$\mathbf{r}(k) = [\hat{r}(k), \cdots, \hat{r}(k-m+1)]^T + [n(k), \cdots, n(k-m+1)]^T \tag{2}$$

where the vector $\mathbf{c} = [\hat{r}(k), \cdots, \hat{r}(k-m+1)]^T$ is called a channel state. Fig. 1 illustrates this channel equalisation problem. To simplify the analysis, we will assume $s(k)$ to be from a binary source with values $I = \{\pm 1\}$. The results derived for the binary transmit symbols case can be generalized to more complicated transmit signal set without any difficulty.

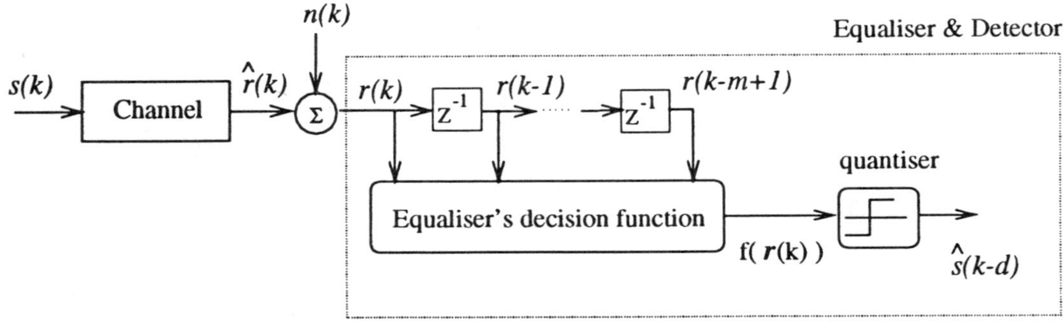

Figure 1: Model of the channel equalisation problem.

The task of the equaliser is to reconstruct the transmitted symbol $s(k-d)$ with the minimum probability P_E of mis-classification. The integers m and d are known as the feedforward and delay order respectively.

---

[1]formely in Lab. for ABS, Frontier Research Programme, RIKEN.

In communication literature [1, 2, 3], the classification performance is usually expressed in terms of the bit error rate (BER), i.e. BER $= \log_{10} P_E$, versus the operating signal to noise ratio (SNR). The SNR is defined as

$$\text{SNR} = 10\log_{10}\frac{E[\hat{r}^2(k)]}{E[n^2(k)]} = 10\log_{10}\frac{\sigma_s^2(\sum_{i=0}^{i=l-1} a(i)^2)}{\sigma_n^2} = 10\log_{10}\frac{\sum_{i=0}^{i=l-1} a(i)^2}{\sigma_n^2} \tag{3}$$

where the variable $\sigma_s^2 = 1$ is the transmit symbol variance and σ_n^2 is the noise variance.

The estimated value of $s(k-d)$ is

$$\hat{s}(k-d) = \text{sgn}(f_b(\mathbf{r}(k))) \tag{4}$$

where $f_b(\mathbf{r}(k))$ is the Bayesian decision function and is described by the following equation [1]

$$f_b(\mathbf{r}(k)) = \sum_{\mathbf{c}_j \in C_d^{(+)}} \exp(-\|\mathbf{r}(k) - \mathbf{c}_j\|^2/(2\sigma_n^2)) - \sum_{\mathbf{c}_k \in C_d^{(-)}} \exp(-\|\mathbf{r}(k) - \mathbf{c}_k\|^2/(2\sigma_n^2)). \tag{5}$$

The sets $C_d^{(+)}$ and $C_d^{(-)}$ are the sets of channel states associated with the value of the transmit symbol $s(k-d)$, i.e. $C_d^{(+)} = \left\{ \mathbf{c} \mid s(k-d) = +1 \right\}$, $C_d^{(-)} = \left\{ \mathbf{c} \mid s(k-d) = -1 \right\}$ and $C_d = C_d^{(+)} \cup C_d^{(-)}$, where the subscript d denotes the equaliser's delay order. A channel state is generated by

$$\mathbf{c} = \mathbf{F}\mathbf{s} \tag{6}$$

where the matrix $\mathbf{F} \in R^{m \times (m+l-1)}$ is

$$\mathbf{F} = \begin{bmatrix} a(0) & a(1) & \ldots & a(l-1) & 0 & .. & \ldots & \ldots & \ldots & 0 \\ 0 & a(0) & a(1) & \ldots & a(l-1) & 0 & \ldots & \ldots & \ldots & 0 \\ \vdots & \vdots & \vdots & \ldots & \ldots & \ldots & \ldots & \ldots & \ldots & 0 \\ 0 & \ldots & \ldots & \ldots & \ldots & \ldots & a(0) & a(1) & \ldots & a(l-1) \end{bmatrix} \tag{7}$$

and $\mathbf{s} = [s_1, \cdots, s_{m+l-1}]^T \in I^{m+l-1}$. There are $N_c = 2^{m+l-1}$ combinations of transmit sequence $\mathbf{s}$ and therefore there be N_c corresponding channel state $\mathbf{c}$

From Eq. 5, it is obvious that $f_b(.)$ has the same functional form as the RBF model with Gaussian function [1, 4], i.e., $f_{\text{rbf}}(\mathbf{r}) = \sum_{i=1}^{N} w_i\phi(\|\mathbf{r} - \mathbf{c}_i\|^2/(2\sigma_n^2))$, where N is the number of centres, w_i are the feedforward weights, $\phi(.)$ is a nonlinear function, $\mathbf{c}_i$ are the centres of the RBF model, and $2\sigma_n^2$ is a constant. The Gaussian RBF network is therefore ideal to model the optimal Bayesian equaliser [1].

2   Selecting subset RBF model

From the previous section, it was shown that the number of centres $N_c = 2^{m+l-1}$ used in the Bayesian RBF equaliser grew exponentially with respect to the number of input parameters and channel memory length. In the case when the channel is nonstationary, the values of all the channel states must be re-calculated before the decision function can be evaluated.

For large N_c, the implementation complexity of the full Bayesian RBF solution is therefore very high. To reduce the computational requirement, we propose to use a subset RBF network to approximate the full Bayesian decision function's response. The idea is to create a subset network whose task is only to approximate the full equaliser's response for the current input vector $\mathbf{r}(k)$ value [5]. To accomplish this, we need only to use the centres which are near, in Euclidean distance sense, to $\mathbf{r}(k)$ location. The reason of this approach is based on the assumption that a local approximation of the decision function response using centres within distance ϵ of $\mathbf{r}(k)$ is very similar to that of the full Bayesian RBF response when ϵ is sufficiently large.

More formally, we define the centres U_d to be included into the subset RBF equaliser as those centres that satisfy

$$U_d = B(\mathbf{r}, \epsilon) \cap C_d \tag{8}$$

where $\mathbf{r} = \mathbf{r}(k)$, $B(\mathbf{r}, \epsilon)$ is a neighborhood function set defined by

$$B(\mathbf{r}, \epsilon) = \{\mathbf{x} \mid \max|x_i - r_i| \leq \epsilon\}, \quad i = 1, \ldots, m. \tag{9}$$

We assume that ϵ is chosen large enough such that $U \neq \{\emptyset\}$. We define U' as the complementary set of U, i.e. $C_d = U \cup U'$. To prove that a local approximation of the decision function will yield a very similar response to that of the full Bayesian model's response, we examine the decision function's response for the case when the additive Gaussian noise goes to zero, i.e. $\sigma_e \to 0$. In the following sections, we will drop the indices d and (k) from the symbols when its meanings is clear from the context.

Let $f_U(.)$ denote the decision function (like in Eq. 5) formed with centres from U, and $f_{U'}(.)$ denote the decision function formed with centres from U'. The response of the two decision functions are related to $f_b(.)$ (Eq. 5) by

$$f_b(\mathbf{r}) \;=\; f_U(\mathbf{r}) + f_{U'}(\mathbf{r}). \tag{10}$$

When $\sigma_n \to 0$, the response of $f_U(\mathbf{r}) \to f_b(\mathbf{r})$ as the response of $f_{U'}(\mathbf{r})$ converges to zero very quickly. This is because the response of $f_{U'}(\mathbf{r})$ is based on the summation of $\exp(-\|\mathbf{r} - \mathbf{c}_j\|^2/(2\sigma_n^2))$ for $\mathbf{c}_j \in U'$. As the centres in U' are much further away from $\mathbf{r}$ than are the centres in U, the response of $f_{U'}(\mathbf{r})$ is much smaller than that of $f_U(\mathbf{r})$ at high SNR. The above analysis however does not provide us with numerical values for ϵ and σ_e which limit the actual approximation error between $f_b(.)$ and $f_U(.)$ to be sufficiently small for our purpose. In this paper, we will use computer simulations to study the effects of ϵ on the performance of the subset equaliser, and reserve the theoretical analysis on the approximation problem for future work.

2.1 Fast implementation to find local centres

The problem of finding the set U is not trivial. A simple implementation of re-calculating all the centres and then evaluating Eq. 8 involves very high computation complexity. In this paper, we propose a novel method of finding U by finding T the set of transmit sequence $\mathbf{s} \in I^{m+l-1}$ which can realise U. The above statement means $U = \mathbf{F}(T)$ where $\mathbf{F}$ is defined in Eq. 7, and therefore

$$T = \mathbf{F}^{-1}(U) = \left\{ \mathbf{s} \;\middle|\; \mathbf{c} := \mathbf{F}\mathbf{s} \in B(\mathbf{r}, \epsilon) \right\} \subseteq I^{m+l-1}. \tag{11}$$

Introducing the time notation into T, we have $T(k)$ to denote the set of $\mathbf{s}$ which can generate channel states satisfying the neighbourhood $B(\mathbf{r}(k), \epsilon)$, i.e.

$$T(k) = \left\{ \mathbf{s}(k) \;\middle|\; \mathbf{F}\mathbf{s}(k) \in B(\mathbf{r}(k), \epsilon) \right\}. \tag{12}$$

By using the fact that $T(k)$ is derived from $T(k-1)$, we can reduce the complexity of the search algorithm considerably. For the initial case, we can set $T(0)$ to be the set all possible transmit sequence. Before introducing the search algorithm, we first define the following notations: $\mathbf{s}' = [s_1, \cdots, s_l] \in I^l$, $h_j(.)$ is a function operating on a vector to return the first j elements of the vector, e.g., $h_{l-1}([s_1, s_2, \ldots, s_l]) = [s_1, s_2, \ldots, s_{l-1}]$. We also define the function $g(\mathbf{s}') = \sum_{i=1}^{l} a(i-1)s_i = \hat{r}$ to describe the ISI introduced by the channel and the inverse image of the function $g(.)$ of a closed, real interval $[\alpha, \beta]$, namely the set $g^{-1}([\alpha, \beta])$ of vectors $\mathbf{s}'$ which satisfy $\alpha \le g(\mathbf{s}') \le \beta$. The details of the algorithm to find $T(k)$ is listed in Table 1.

From $T(k)$, we can generate U to implement the subset equaliser's decision function. If the value of ϵ is small, the number of selected centres in U will be small, and therefore the resultant subset equaliser's complexity will also be small. However, if ϵ is too small, the above algorithm to select the centres may fail, i.e. no centres are found for the ϵ value. We call such a situation an exception in the search. In this case, re-tries must be carried out with larger values of ϵ. In our simulations, we have consistently found that $\epsilon \ge 4\sigma_n$ is sufficient to reduce the number of exceptions to acceptable levels and that the number of centres found can be as small as 5% to 10% of the original number of centres at high SNR.

2.2 Complexity requirement

The computational complexity to implement the full Bayesian RBF equaliser for nonstationary channel consists of two parts, namely the re-calculation of the channel state values and the evaluation of the decision function. To efficiently generate the channel states, a lookup table A1 which records the $N_l = 2^l$ distinct values of $\hat{r}$ and associated $\mathbf{s}'$ coefficients is created. The channel states are then computed by using the lookup table. Computational requirements for these tasks are tabulated in Table 2.

As a comparison, the computational complexity of the subset equaliser is listed in Table 3. As in the full RBF equaliser's case, the lookup table A1 is also generated. In addition, an additional lookup table,

Table A2, which records the sorted order of $\hat{r}$ and the associated s' is generated. Table A2 is used in the operation of $g^{-1}([r(k)-\epsilon, r(k)+\epsilon])$. In the evaluation of channel states and decision function for a subset equaliser, only $\hat{N}_c < N_c$ number of channel states is used. The symbol $\hat{N}_c$ denotes the expected number of centres used for the subset equaliser. In the case when $\hat{N}_c \ll N_c$, the additional processing used to find the subset channel states will be much less than the computational complexity of implementing the subset equaliser's decision function.

3 Simulation results

Simulations were conducted to compare the BER performance of the full RBF Bayesian equaliser and the subset equaliser. The channel used was

$$H_1(z) \;\; = \;\; -0.21 - 0.50z^{-1} + 0.72z^{-2} + 0.36z^{-3} + 0.21z^{-4}. \tag{13}$$

The equaliser's parameters were $m = 4$ and $d = 4$. In this case, the full RBF equaliser had 256 centres. For the experiment, ϵ was set to $4\sigma_n$, and the channel was assumed to be correctly identified.

To compare the classification performance, the simulations were conducted to count the number of mis-classifications which occured for the transmission of 2×10^6 signal data for different SNR values. The results depicted in Table. 5 show that the subset RBF equaliser has similar classification performance to that of the full Bayesian equaliser for various ranges of SNR.

Simulations were also conducted to examine the effects of ϵ on the average number of centres used in the subset equaliser and the number of exception occurrences for various SNR values. In the experiment, these two parameters were measured by simulating the transmission of 1×10^5 signal data across the channel and evaluating the occurrences of these two events. The results in Fig. 2 show the average number of centres used in the subset equaliser. The horizontal axis of the figure shows the value of ϵ with respect to the noise standard deviation σ_n, and the vertical axis indicates the average number of centres used in the subset equaliser. Each line on the graph represents a different SNR operating value. The results show that at high SNR operating condition, the subset equaliser can be formed with very few number of centres without many exceptions. For example, at SNR=12dB and $\epsilon = 4\sigma_n$ (Fig 2) the average number of centres used to implement the subset model was $\hat{N}_c = 16$ out of the full model which had 256 centres. Fig. 3 illustrates the number of exceptions that occured during the simulations for the transmission of 1×10^5 data symbols. The results show that when ϵ is set to values greater than $4\sigma_n$, the number of exceptions which occurs becomes very small.

Table 4 compares the computational requirement between the full RBF Bayesian equaliser and the subset equaliser. The results clearly show that the implementation complexity of the subset equaliser is much lower than that of the full RBF equaliser.

Notations : N_c denotes the total number of centers in C and is equals to 2^{m+l-1}. N_l denotes the total number of $\hat{r}$ and is equals to 2^l. $\hat{N}_c$ denotes the expected number of centres used in the subset model.

4 Conclusions

In this paper, we have discussed a method to reduce the implementation complexity of the RBF equaliser by using only centres within a local vicinity of the current input. By adopting such an approach, the realized subset equaliser has much less centres than the full model, and hence a much reduced implementation requirement. For the case when the channel equalisation problem is non-stationary, such a method allows for a practical implementation of the equalisation problem. Our simulation results have also indicated that the performance of the subset RBF equaliser is very similar to that of the full Bayesian RBF equalisers.

Acknowledgment : We would like to thank Prof. Andrzej Cichocki for his comments on the paper and Dr Su Xiao Yan for proof-reading the paper.

References

[1] S.CHEN, B.MULGREW, and P.M.GRANT, "A clustering technique for digital communications channel equalization using radial basis function networks", *IEEE Trans. Neural Networks*, vol. 4, no. 4, pp. 570–579, 1993.

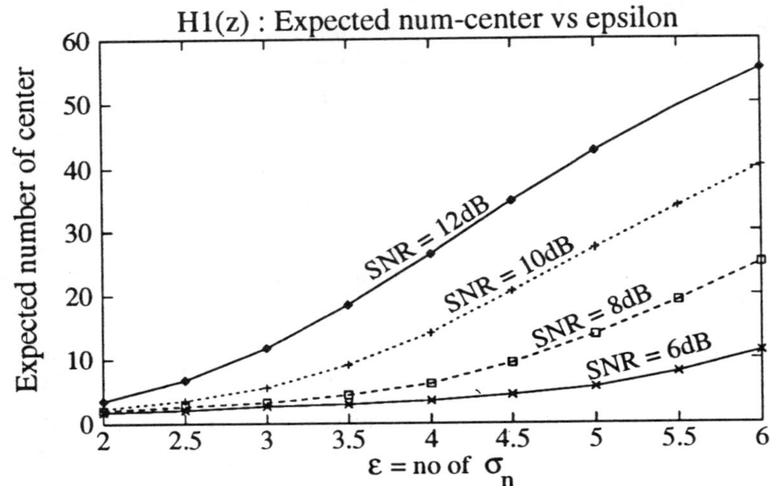

Figure 2: Channel $H_1(z)$: (a) Average number of centres vs ϵ value.

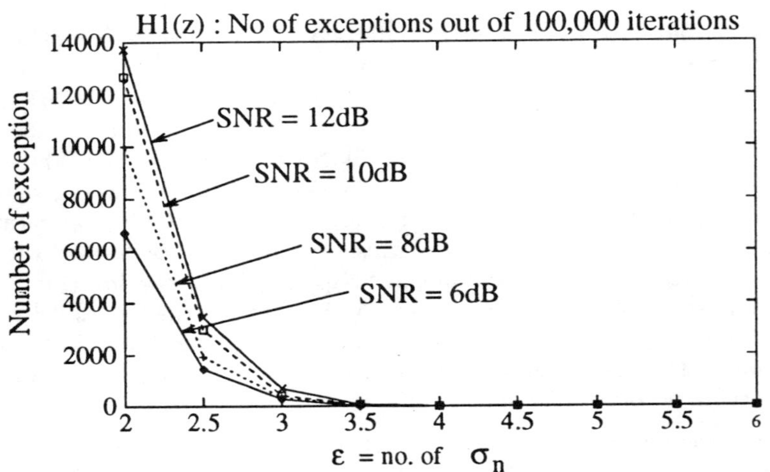

Figure 3: Channel $H_1(z)$: Number of exceptions vs ϵ value.

[2] S.U.H.QURESHI, "Adaptive equalization", *Proc. IEEE*, vol. 73, no. 9, pp. 1349–1387, 1985.

[3] J.G.PROAKIS, *Digital Communications, (2nd edition)*. McGraw-Hill Book Company, 1989.

[4] M.J.D.POWELL, "Radial basis functions for multivariable interpolation: a review", *Algorithms for Approximation*, pp. 143–167, J.C.MASON and M.G.COX (Eds), Oxford, 1987.

[5] E.S.CHNG, H.YANG, and W.SKARBEK, "Reduced complexity implementation of Bayesian equaliser using local RBF network for channel equalisation problem", *Electronics Letters*, vol. 32, no. 1, pp. 17–19, 1996.

Fast algorithm to find $T(k)$.

$T(k) = \{\};$

for $\{s(k-1) \in T(k-1)\}$
begin
$\quad s'(k) = [s,\ h_{l-1}(s(k-1))]$
$\quad\quad$ if $s'(k) \in g^{-1}([r(k) - \varepsilon, r(k) + \epsilon])$
$\quad\quad\quad T(k) = T(k) \cup [s,\ h_{m+l-2}(s(k-1))]$
end

Table 1: Algorithm for fast evaluation of $T(k)$ from $T(k-1)$.

Computational complexity for Full RBF Bayesian equaliser		
1) Create Lookup Table A1	$N_l \times l$	multiplication
2) Re-calculate Channel States	$N_c \times m$	lookups
3) Evaluate decision function	N_c	exp(.)
	$N_c \times m$	multiplications
	$N_c \times m + N_c$	additions.

Table 2: Computational complexity requirement to implement the Full Bayesian equaliser.

Computational complexity for Subset RBF Bayesian equaliser		
1a) Create Lookup Table A1	$N_l \times l$	multiplications
1b) Create Lookup Table A2	$N_l \log N_l$	comparisons
1c) Find $T(k)$	$\hat{N}_c \times 2$	lookups
	$2(\hat{N}_c \times 2)$	comparisons
2) Re-calculate Channel States	$\hat{N}_c \times m$	lookup
3) Evaluate decision function	$\hat{N}_c$	exp(.)
	$\hat{N}_c \times m$	multiply
	$\hat{N}_c \times m + N_c$	additions.

Table 3: Computational complexity requirement to implement the Full Bayesian equaliser.

Example : Computational complexity to implement full and subset RBF equaliser			
Tasks	Full RBF Equaliser	Subset RBF Equaliser	operations
1a) Create Lookup Table A1	160	160	multiplications
1b) Create Lookup Table A2	-	43	comparisons
1c) Find $T(k)$	-	32	lookups
	-	64	comparisons
2) Re-calculate Channel States	1024	64	lookups
3) Evaluate decision function	256	16	exps
	1024	64	multiplies
	1280	60	additions.

Table 4: Computational complexity requirement to implement the Full Bayesian equaliser and subset equaliser using $m = 4$ for channel $H(z)$.

Equaliser Type	SNR				
	6dB	8dB	10dB	12dB	14dB
Full RBF Eq.	-1.411	-1.837	-2.426	-3.535	-4.638
Subset RBF Eq.	-1.419	-1.838	-2.404	-3.484	-4.545

Table 5: BER performance of the full Bayesian equaliser and subset equaliser for channel $H_1(z)$.

An EM Algorithm for Asynchronous Input/Output Hidden Markov Models

Samy Bengio†, Yoshua Bengio‡
† INRS-Télécommunications,
16, Place du Commerce, Ile-des-Soeurs, Qc, H3E 1H6, CANADA
‡ Dept. IRO, Université de Montréal,
Montréal, Qc, H3C 3J7, CANADA

Abstract— In learning tasks in which input sequences are mapped to output sequences, it is often the case that the input and output sequences are not synchronous. For example, in speech recognition, acoustic sequences are longer than phoneme sequences. Input/Output Hidden Markov Models have already been proposed to represent the distribution of an output sequence given an input sequence of the same length. We extend here this model to the case of asynchronous sequences, and show an Expectation-Maximization algorithm for training such models.

1   Introduction

Supervised learning algorithms for sequential data minimize a training criterion that depends on pairs of input and output sequences. It is often assumed that input and output sequences are synchronized, i.e., that each input sequence has the same length as the corresponding output sequence. For instance, recurrent networks [Rumelhart et al., 1986] can be used to map input sequences to output sequences, for example minimizing at each time step the squared difference between the actual output and the desired output. Another example is a recently proposed recurrent mixture of experts connectionist architecture which has an interpretation as a probabilistic model, called *Input/Output Hidden Markov Model* (IOHMM) [Bengio and Frasconi, 1996, Bengio and Frasconi, 1995]. This model represents the distribution of an output sequence when given an input sequence of the same length, using a hidden state variable and a Markovian independence assumption, as in *Hidden Markov Models* (HMMs) [Rabiner, 1989], in order to simplify the distribution. IOHMMs are a form of probabilistic transducers [Pereira et al., 1994, Singer, 1996], with input and output variables which can be discrete as well as continuous-valued.

However, in many sequential problems where one tries to map an input sequence to an output sequence, the length of the input and output sequences may not be equal. Input and output sequences could behave at different time scales. For example, in a speech recognition problem where one wants to map an acoustic signal to a phoneme sequence, each phoneme approximately corresponds to a subsequence of the acoustic signal, therefore the input acoustic sequence is generally longer than the output phoneme sequence, and the alignment between inputs and outputs is often not available.

In comparison with HMMs, emission and transition probabilities in IOHMMs vary with time as a function of an input sequence. Unlike HMMs, IOHMMs with discrete outputs are discriminant models. Furthermore, the transition probabilities and emission probabilities are generally better matched, which reduces a problem observed in speech recognition HMMs: because outputs are in a much higher dimensional space than transitions in HMMs, the dynamic range of transition probabilities is much less than that of emission probabilities. Therefore the choice between different paths (during recognition) is mostly influenced by emission rather than transition probabilities.

In this paper, we present an extension of IOHMMs to the asynchronous case. We first present the probabilistic model, then derive an exact Expectation-Maximization (EM) algorithm for training asynchronous IOHMMs. For complex distributions (e.g., using artificial neural networks to represent transition and emission distributions), a Generalized EM algorithm or gradient ascent in likelihood can be used. Finally, a recognition algorithm similar to the Viterbi algorithm is presented, to map given input sequences to likely output sequences.

2   The Model

Let us note x_1^T for an input sequence $x_1, x_2, \ldots, x_T$, and similarly y_1^S for an output sequence $y_1, y_2, \ldots, y_S$. In this paper we consider the case in which the output sequences are shorter than the input sequences. The more general case is a straightforward extension of this model (using "empty" transitions that do not "take" any time) and will be discussed elsewhere. As in HMMs and IOHMMs, we introduce a discrete *hidden state* variable, q_t, which will allow us to simplify the distribution $P(y_1^S | x_1^T)$ by using Markovian independence assumptions. The state sequence q_1^T is taken to be synchronous with the input sequence x_1^T.

In order to produce output sequences shorter than input sequences, *states may sometimes not emit an output symbol*, but instead would "emit" a null symbol ϵ. Therefore, there exist many sequences of states corresponding to the same output sequence, and a given sequence of states can correspond to output sequences of different lengths.

When conceived as a generative model of the output (given the input), an asynchronous IOHMM works as follows. At time $t = 0$, an initial state q_0 is chosen according to the distribution $P(q_0)$, and the length of the output sequence s is initialized to 0. At other time steps $t > 0$, a state q_t is first picked according to the *transition distribution* $P(q_t|q_{t-1}, x_t)$, using the state at the previous time step q_{t-1} and the current input x_t. A decision is then taken as to wether or not an output y_s will be produced at time t or not, according to the *emit-or-not distribution*. In the positive case, An output y_s is then produced according to the *emission distribution* $P(y_s|q_t, x_t)$. The length of the output sequence is increased from $s-1$ to s, and the sth output y_s is emitted with probability $P(y_s|q_t, x_t)$. The parameters of the model are thus the initial state probabilities, $\pi(i) = P(q_0 = i)$, and the parameters of the emit-or-not, emission and transition conditional distribution models, $P(emit-or-not|q_t, x_t)$, $P(y_s|q_t, x_t)$ and $P(q_t|q_{t-1}, x_t)$. Since the input and output sequences are of different lengths, we will introduce another hidden variable, τ_t, specifically to represent the alignment between inputs and outputs, with $\tau_t = s$ meaning that s outputs have been emitted at time t.

Let us first formalize the independence assumptions and the form of the conditional distribution represented by the model. The conditional probability $P(y_1^S|x_1^T)$ can be written as a sum of terms $P(y_1^S, q_0^T, \tau_1^T|x_1^T)$ over all possible state sequences q_0^T such that the number of emitting states in each of these sequences is S (the length of the output sequence)

$$P(y_1^S|x_1^T) = \sum_{q_0^T, \tau_T = S} P(y_1^S, q_0^T, \tau_1^T|x_1^T) \tag{1}$$

All S outputs must have been emitted by time T, so $\tau_T = S$. The hidden state q_t takes discrete values in a finite set. Each of the terms $P(y_1^S, q_0^T, \tau_1^T|x_1^T)$ corresponds to a particular sequence of states, and a corresponding alignment.

We summarize in table 1 the notation we have introduced and define additional notation used in this paper.

Table 1: Notation used in the paper

- $S =$ size of the output sequence.
- $T =$ size of the input sequence.
- $N =$ number of states in the IOHMM.
- $a(i, j, t) =$ output of the module that computes $P(q_t = i|q_{t-1} = j, x_t)$
- $b(i, l, t) =$ output of the module that computes $P(y_s = l|q_t = i, x_t, \tau_t = s, \tau_{t-1} = s - 1)$, the probability to emit the symbol l at time t in state i given that state i emits at time t.
- $\epsilon(i, t) =$ output of the module that computes $P(\tau_t = s|\tau_{t-1} = s, q_t = i)$, the probability not to emit at time t in state i.
- $\pi(i) = P(q_0 = i)$, initial probability of state i.
- $z_{i,t} = 1$ if $q_t = i$; $z_{i,t} = 0$ otherwise. These indicator variables give the state sequence.
- $m_{s,t} = 1$ if the system emits the sth output at time t, $m_{s,t} = 0$ otherwise. These indicator variables give the input/output alignment.
- $\epsilon_{i,t} = 1$ means that state i did not emit at time t.
- $\tau_t = s$ means that the first s first outputs have been emitted at time t.
- $\sigma_{t,k} = 1$ if the tth input symbol is k, $\sigma_{t,k} = 0$ otherwise.
- $\gamma_{s,k} = 1$ if the sth output symbol is k, $\gamma_{s,k} = 0$ otherwise.
- $pred(i)$ is the set of all the predecessors states of state i.
- $succ(i)$ is the set of all the successors states of state i.

The Markovian conditional independence assumptions in this model mean that the state variable q_t summarizes sufficiently the past of the sequence, so

$$P(q_t|q_1^{t-1}, x_1^t) = P(q_t|q_{t-1}, x_t) \tag{2}$$

and

$$P(y_s|q_1^t, x_1^t) = P(y_s|q_t, x_t). \tag{3}$$

These assumptions are analogous to the Markovian independence assumptions used in HMMs and are essentially the same as in synchronous IOHMMs. Based on these two assumptions, the conditional probability can be efficiently represented and computed recursively, using an intermediate variable

$$\alpha(i, s, t) \stackrel{\text{def}}{=} P(q_t = i, \tau_t = s, y_1^s|x_1^t). \tag{4}$$

The conditional probability of an output sequence, can be expressed in terms of this variable:

$$L \overset{\text{def}}{=} P(y_1^S | x_1^T) = \sum_{i \in F} \alpha(i, S, T) \tag{5}$$

where F is a set of final states. These α's can be computed recursively in a way that is analogous to the forward pass of the Baum-Welsh algorithm for HMMs:

$$\alpha(i, s, t) = b(i, y_s, t)(1 - (\epsilon(i, t))) \sum_{j \in pred(i)} a(i, j, t) \alpha(j, s-1, t-1)$$

$$+\epsilon(i, t) \sum_{j \in pred(i)} a(i, j, t) \alpha(j, s, t-1) \tag{6}$$

where $a(i, j, t) = P(q_t=i | q_{t-1}=j, x_t)$, $b(i, y_s, t) = P(y_s | q_t=i, x_t, \tau_t=s, \tau_{t-1}=s - 1)$, $\epsilon(i, t) = P(\tau_t=s | \tau_{t-1}=s, q_t=i, x_t)$ and $pred(i)$ is the set of states with an outgoing transition to state i. The derivation of this recursion using the independence assumptions can be found in [Bengio and Bengio, 1996].

3   An EM Algorithm for Asynchronous IOHMMs

The learning algorithm we propose is based on the maximum likelihood principle, i.e., here, maximizing the conditional likelihood of the training data. The algorithm could be generalized to one for maximizing the likelihood of the parameters given the data, by taking into account priors on those parameters. Let the training data, D, be a set of P input/output sequences independently sampled from the same distribution. Let T_p and S_p be the lengths of the pth input and output sequence respectively:

$$D \overset{\text{def}}{=} \{(x_1^{T_p}(p), y_1^{S_p}(p)); p=1 \ldots P\} \tag{7}$$

Let Θ be the set of all the parameters of the model. Because each sequence is sampled independently. we can write the likelihood function as follows, omitting sequence indexes to simplify:

$$L(\Theta; D) = \prod_{p=1}^{P} P(y_1^{S_p} | x_1^{T_p}; \Theta) \tag{8}$$

According to the maximum likelihood principle, the optimal parameters Θ are obtained when $L(\Theta; D)$ is maximized. We will show here how an iterative optimization to a local maximum can be achieved using the Expectation-Maximization (EM) algorithm.

EM is an iterative procedure for maximum likelihood estimation, originally formalized in [Dempster et al., 1977]. Each iteration is composed of two steps: an estimation step and a maximization step. The basic idea is to introduce an additional variable, q, which, if it were known, would greatly simplify the optimization problem. This additional variable is known as the missing or hidden data. A joint model of q with the observed variables must be set up. The set D_c which includes the data set D and values of the variable q for each of the examples, is known as the *complete data set*. Correspondingly, $L_c(\Theta; D_c)$ is referred as the *complete data likelihood*. Since q is not observed, L_c is a random variable and cannot be maximized directly. The EM algorithm is based on averaging $\log L_c(\Theta; D_c)$ over the distribution of q, given the known data D and the previous value of the parameters $\hat{\Theta}$. This expected log likelihood is called the auxiliary function:

$$Q(\Theta; \hat{\Theta}) = E_q \left[\log L_c(\Theta; D_c) | D, \hat{\Theta} \right] \tag{9}$$

In short, for each EM iteration, one first computes Q (E-step), then updates Θ such that it maximizes Q (M-step).

To apply EM to asynchronous IOHMMs, we need to choose hidden variables such that the knowledge of these variables would simplify the learning problem. Let q be a hidden variable representing the hidden state of the Markov model (such that $q_t = i$ means the system is in state i at time t). Knowledge of the state sequence q_1^T would make the estimation of parameters trivial (simple counting would suffice). Because states sometimes emit and sometime do not, we introduce an additional hidden variable, τ. representing the alignment between inputs (and states) and outputs, such that $\tau_t = s$ implies that s outputs have been emitted at time t.

Here, the *complete data* can be written as follows:

$$D_c \overset{\text{def}}{=} \{(x_1^{T_p}(p), y_1^{S_p}(p), q_1^{T_p}(p), \tau_1^{T_p}(p)); p=1 \ldots P\} \tag{10}$$

The corresponding complete data likelihood is (again dropping (p) indices):

$$L_c(\Theta; D_c) = \prod_{p=1}^{P} P(y_1^{S_p}, q_1^{T_p}, \tau_1^{T_p} | x_1^{T_p}; \Theta) \tag{11}$$

Let $z_{i,t}$ be an indicator variable such that $z_{i,t} = 1$ if $q_t = i$, and $z_{i,t} = 0$ otherwise. Let $m_{s,t}$ be an indicator variable such that $m_{s,t} = 1$ if the sth output is emitted at time t, and $m_{s,t} = 0$ otherwise.

Let $\epsilon_{i,t} = 1$ if state i do not emit at time t, and $\epsilon_{i,t} = 0$ otherwise. Using these indicator variables and factorizing the likelihood equation, we obtain:

$$L_c(\Theta; D_c) = \prod_{p=1}^{P}\prod_{t=1}^{T_p}\prod_{i=1}^{N}\left(\prod_{s=1}^{S_p} P(y_s|q_t{=}i, x_t, \tau_t{=}s, \tau_{t-1}{=}s{-}1)^{z_{i,t}m_{s,t}(1-\epsilon_{i,t})}\right) \cdot$$

$$\left(\prod_{s=1}^{S_p} P(\tau{=}s|q_t{=}i, x_t, \tau_{t-1}{=}s{-}1)^{z_{i,t}m_{s,t}(1-\epsilon_{i,t})}\right) \cdot$$

$$\left(\prod_{s=1}^{S_p} P(\tau{=}s|q_t{=}i, x_t, \tau_{t-1}{=}s)^{z_{i,t}m_{s,t}\epsilon_{i,t}}\right) \cdot \left(\prod_{j=1}^{N} P(q_t{=}i|q_{t-1}{=}j, x_t)^{z_{i,t}z_{j,t-1}}\right) \quad (12)$$

Taking the logarithm we obtain the following expression for the complete data log likelihood:

$$\log L_c(\Theta; D_c) = \sum_{p=1}^{P}\sum_{t=1}^{T_p}\sum_{i=1}^{N}\left(\sum_{s=1}^{S_p} z_{i,t}m_{s,t}(1-\epsilon_{i,t})\log P(y_s|q_t{=}i, x_t, \tau_t{=}s, \tau_{t-1}{=}s{-}1)\right) +$$

$$\left(\sum_{s=1}^{S_p} z_{i,t}m_{s,t}(1-\epsilon_{i,t})\log P(\tau_t{=}s|q_t{=}i, x_t, \tau_{t-1}{=}s{-}1)\right) +$$

$$\left(\sum_{s=1}^{S_p} z_{i,t}m_{s,t}\epsilon_{i,t}\log P(\tau_t{=}s|q_t{=}i, x_t, \tau_{t-1}{=}s)\right) + \left(\sum_{j=1}^{N} z_{i,t}z_{j\,t-1}\log P(q_t{=}i|q_{t-1}{=}j, x_t)\right) \quad (13)$$

3.1 The Estimation Step

Let us define the auxiliary function $Q(\Theta; \hat{\Theta})$ as the expected value of $\log L_c(\Theta; D_c)$ with respect to the hidden variables q and τ, given the data D and the previous set of parameters $\hat{\Theta}$:

$$Q(\Theta; \hat{\Theta}) = E_{q,\tau}\left[\log L_c(\Theta; D_c)|D, \hat{\Theta}\right] \quad (14)$$

$$Q(\Theta; \hat{\Theta}) = \sum_{p=1}^{P}\sum_{t=1}^{T_p}\sum_{i=1}^{N}\left(\sum_{s=1}^{S_p} \hat{g}_{i,s,t}\log P(y_s|q_t{=}i, x_t, \tau_t{=}s, \tau_{t-1}{=}s{-}1)\right) +$$

$$\left(\sum_{s=1}^{S_p} \hat{g}_{i,s,t}\log P(\tau_t{=}s|q_t{=}i, x_t, \tau_{t-1}{=}s{-}1)\right) +$$

$$\left(\sum_{s=1}^{S_p} \hat{f}_{i,s,t}\log P(\tau_t{=}s|q_t{=}i, x_t, \tau_{t-1}{=}s)\right) + \left(\sum_{j=1}^{N} \hat{h}_{i,j,t}\log P(q_t{=}i|q_{t-1}{=}j, x_t)\right) \quad (15)$$

where, by definition,

$$\hat{g}_{i,s,t} \stackrel{\text{def}}{=} E_{q,\tau}[q_t{=}i, \tau_t{=}s|\tau_{t-1}{=}s{-}1, x_1^T, y_1^S; \Theta] \quad (16)$$

$$\hat{f}_{i,s,t} \stackrel{\text{def}}{=} E_{q,\tau}[q_t{=}i, \tau_t{=}s|\tau_{t-1}{=}s, x_1^T, y_1^S; \Theta] \quad (17)$$

and

$$\hat{h}_{i,j,t} \stackrel{\text{def}}{=} E_q[q_t{=}i, q_{t-1}{=}j|x_1^T, y_1^S; \Theta] \quad (18)$$

The $\hat{\ }$ on $\hat{f}$, $\hat{g}$ and $\hat{h}$ denote that these expectations are computed using the previous value of the parameters, $\hat{\Theta}$. In order to compute $\hat{f}_{i,s,t}$, $\hat{g}_{i,s,t}$ and $\hat{h}_{i,j,t}$, we will use the already defined $\alpha(i,s,t)$ (equations 4 and 6), and introduce a new variable, $\beta(i,s,t)$, borrowing the notation from the HMM and IOHMM literature:

$$\beta(i,s,t) \stackrel{\text{def}}{=} P(y_{s+1}^S|q_t{=}i, \tau_t{=}s, x_{t+1}^T) \quad (19)$$

Like α, β can be computed recursively, but going backwards in time:

$$\beta(i,s,t) = \sum_{j\in succ(i)} a(j,i,t+1)b(j,y_{s+1},t+1)(1-\epsilon(i,t+1))\beta(j,s+1,t+1)$$

$$+ \sum_{j\in succ(i)} a(j,i,t+1)\epsilon(j,t+1)\beta(j,s,t+1) \quad (20)$$

where $pred(i)$ is the set of predecessor states of state i and $succ(i)$ is the set of successor states of state i, $a(j,i,t)$ is the conditional transition probability from state i to state j at time t, $b(i,y_s,t)$ is the conditional probability to emit the sth output at time t in state i given that this state emits at time t, and $\epsilon(i,t)$ is the probability not to emit at time t in state i. The proof of correctness of this recursion (using the Markovian independence assumptions) is given in [Bengio and Bengio, 1996].

Let $\alpha^0(i,s,t)$ be the part of $\alpha(i,s,t)$ computed when state i emits at time t:

$$\alpha^0(i,s,t) \;=\; b(i,y_s,t)(1-\epsilon(i,t))\cdot \sum_{j\in pred(i)} a(i,j,t)\,\alpha(j,s-1,t-1) \tag{21}$$

Similarly, $\alpha^1(i,s,t)$ is the part of $\alpha(i,s,t)$ computed when state i does not emit at time t:

$$\alpha^1(i,s,t) \;=\; \epsilon(i,t)\cdot \sum_{j\in pred(i)} a(i,j,t)\,\alpha(j,s,t-1) \tag{22}$$

We can now express $g_{i,s,t}$, $f_{i,s,t}$ and $h_{i,j,t}$ in terms of $\alpha^0(i,s,t)$, $\alpha^1(i,s,t)$ and $\beta(i,s,t)$ (see derivations in [Bengio and Bengio, 1996]):

$$h_{i,j,t} \;=\; \frac{a(i,j,t)}{L}\cdot \left(\begin{array}{c} \displaystyle\sum_{s=1}^{S}\alpha(j,s-1,t-1)b(i,y_s,t)(1-\epsilon(i,t))\beta(i,s,t) \\[2mm] \displaystyle+\sum_{s=0}^{S}\alpha(j,s,t-1)\epsilon(i,t)\beta(i,s,t) \end{array} \right) \tag{23}$$

$$g_{i,s,t} \;=\; \frac{\alpha^0(i,s,t)\beta(i,s,t)}{L} \tag{24}$$

and

$$f_{i,s,t} \;=\; \frac{\alpha^1(i,s,t)\beta(i,s,t)}{L} \tag{25}$$

3.2 The Maximization Step

After each estimation step, one has to maximize $Q(\Theta;\hat{\Theta})$. If the conditional probability distributions (for transitions as well as emissions) have a simple enough form (e.g. multinomial, generalized linear models, or mixtures of these) then one can maximize analytically Q, i.e., solve

$$\frac{\partial Q(\Theta;\hat{\Theta})}{\partial \Theta} = 0 \tag{26}$$

for Θ. Otherwise, if for instance conditional probabilities are implemented using non-linear systems (such as a neural network), then maximization of Q cannot be done in one step. In this case, we can apply a Generalized EM (GEM) algorithm, that simply requires an increase in Q at each optimization step, for example using gradient ascent in Q, or directly perform gradient ascent in $L(\Theta;D)$.

3.3 Multinomial Distributions

We describe here the maximization procedure for multinomial conditional probabilities (for transitions and emissions), i.e., which can be implemented as lookup tables. This applies to problems with discrete inputs and outputs. Let M_i be the number of input symbols, M_o the number of output classes, $\sigma_{t,k}=1$ when the tth input symbol is k, and $\sigma_{t,k}=0$ otherwise. Also, let $\gamma_{s,k}=1$ when the sth output symbol is k, and $\gamma_{s,k}=0$ otherwise.

For transition probabilities, let $w_{i,j,k}=P(q_t=i|q_{t-1}=j,x_{k,t}=1)$. The solution of equation (26) for $w_{i,j,k}$, with the constraints that transition probabilities must sum to 1, yields the following reestimation formula:

$$w_{i,j,k} = \frac{\displaystyle\sum_{t=1}^{T}\sigma_{t,k}\hat{h}_{i,j,t}}{\displaystyle\sum_{l=1}^{N}\sum_{t=1}^{T}\sigma_{t,k}\hat{h}_{l,j,t}} \tag{27}$$

For emission probabilities, let $\omega_{i,l,k}=P(y=l|q_t=i,x_{k,t}=1)$, with the constraint $\omega_{i,\epsilon,k}+\sum_{l\neq\epsilon}\omega_{i,l,k}=1$, then the reestimation formulae are the following:

$$\omega_{i,l,k} = \frac{\displaystyle\sum_{t=1}^{T}\sum_{s=1}^{S}\sigma_{t,k}\gamma_{s,l}\hat{g}_{i,s,t}}{\displaystyle\sum_{m=1}^{M_o}\sum_{t=1}^{T}\sum_{s=1}^{S}\sigma_{t,k}\gamma_{s,m}\hat{g}_{i,s,t}} \tag{28}$$

For emit-or-not probabilities, let $\psi_{i,0,k} = P(\tau_t=s|\tau_{t-1}=s-1, q_t=i, x_{k,t}=1)$ and $\psi_{i,1,k} = P(\tau_t=s|\tau_{t-1}=s, q_t=i, x_{k,t}=1)$, with the constraint that $\psi_{i,0,k} + \psi_{i,1,k} = 1$.

$$\psi_{i,0,k} = \frac{\sum_{t=1}^{T}\sum_{s=1}^{S}\sigma_{t,k}(1-\epsilon_{i,t})\hat{g}_{i,s,t}}{\sum_{t=1}^{T}\sum_{s=1}^{S}\sigma_{t,k}(\hat{g}_{i,s,t} + \hat{f}_{i,s,t})} \tag{29}$$

$$\psi_{i,1,k} = \frac{\sum_{t=1}^{T}\sum_{s=1}^{S}\sigma_{t,k}\epsilon_{i,t}\hat{f}_{i,s,t}}{\sum_{t=1}^{T}\sum_{s=1}^{S}\sigma_{t,k}(\hat{g}_{i,s,t} + \hat{f}_{i,s,t})} \tag{30}$$

3.4 Neural Networks or Other Complex Distributions

In the more general case where one cannot maximize analytically Q, we can compute the gradient for each parameter and apply gradient ascent in Q, yielding a GEM algorithm (or alternatively, directly maximize L by gradient ascent). For transition probability models $a(j,i,t) = P(q_t=j|q_{t-1}=i, x_t; w_i)$ for state i, with parameters w_i, the gradient of Q with respect to w_i is

$$\frac{\partial Q(\Theta;\hat{\Theta})}{\partial w_i} = \sum_{t=1}^{T}\sum_{j \in succ(i)}\left(\frac{\hat{h}_{j,i,t}}{a(j,i,t)}\frac{\partial a(j,i,t)}{\partial w_i}\right) \tag{31}$$

where $\frac{\partial a(j,i,t)}{\partial u_i}$ can be computed by back-propagation.

Similarly, for emission probability models $b(i,y_s,t) = P(y_s|q_t=i, x_t, \tau_t=s, \tau_{t-1}=s-1; \omega_i)$ with parameters ω_i, the gradient is

$$\frac{\partial Q(\Theta;\hat{\Theta})}{\partial \omega_i} = \sum_{t=1}^{T}\sum_{s=1}^{S}\left(\frac{\hat{g}_{i,s,t}}{b(i,y_s,t)}\frac{\partial b(i,y_s,t)}{\partial \omega_i}\right) \tag{32}$$

where, again, $\frac{\partial b(i,y_s,t)}{\partial \omega_i}$ can be computed by back-propagation.

Finally, for emit-or-not probability models $\epsilon(i,t) = P(\tau_t=s|q_t=i, x_t, \tau_{t-1}=s; \psi_i)$ with parameters ψ_i, the gradient is

$$\frac{\partial Q(\Theta;\hat{\Theta})}{\partial \psi_i} = \sum_{t=1}^{T}\sum_{s=1}^{S}\left(\frac{\hat{f}_{i,s,t}}{\epsilon(i,t)}\frac{\partial \epsilon(i,t)}{\partial \psi_i}\right) + \sum_{t=1}^{T}\sum_{s=1}^{S}\left(\frac{\hat{g}_{i,s,t}}{(1-\epsilon(i,t))}\frac{\partial (1-\epsilon(i,t))}{\partial \psi_i}\right) \tag{33}$$

Table 2: Overview of the learning algorithm for asynchronous IOHMMs

1. Estimation Step: **for each** training sequence (x_1^T, y_1^S) **do**

   (a) **for each state** $j \leftarrow 1\ldots n$ **do**
   - compute $a(i,j,t)$, $b(j,y_s,t)$ and $\epsilon(j,t)$ according to the chosen distribution models.

   (b) **for each state** $i \leftarrow 1\ldots n$ **do**
   - compute $\alpha_{i,s,t}$, $\beta_{i,s,t}$, and L using the current value of the parameters $\hat{\Theta}$ (equations 6, 5 and 20).
   - compute the posterior probabilities $\hat{h}_{i,j,t}$, $\hat{g}_{i,s,t}$ and $\hat{f}_{i,s,t}$ (equations 24, 23 and 25).

2. Maximization Step: **for each state** $j \leftarrow 1\ldots n$ **do**

   (a) Adjust the transition probability parameters of state j using reestimation formulae such as equation 27 (or gradient ascent for non-linear modules, equation 31).

   (b) Adjust the emission probability parameters of state j using reestimation formulae such as equation 28 (or gradient ascent for non-linear modules, equation 32).

   (c) Adjust the emit-or-not probability parameters of state j using reestimation formulae such as equations 29 and 30 (or gradient ascent for non-linear modules, equation 33).

4   A Recognition Algorithm for Asynchronous IOHMMs

Given a trained asynchronous IOHMM, we want to recognize new sequences, i.e., given an input sequence, choose an output sequence according to the model. Ideally, we would like to pick the output sequence that is most likely, given the input sequence. However, this would require an exponential number of computations (with respect to sequence length). Instead, like in the Viterbi algorithm for HMMs, we will consider the complete data model, and look for the joint values of states and outputs that is most likely. Thanks to a dynamic programming recurrence, we can compute the most likely state and output sequence in time that is proportional to the sequence length times the number of transitions (even though the number of such sequences is exponential in the sequence length).

Let us define $V(i, t)$ as the probability of the best state and output subsequence ending up in state i at time t:

$$V(i, t) = \max_{s, y_1^s, q_1^{t-1}} P(y_1^s, q_1^{t-1}, q_t = i, \tau_t = s | x_1^t) \tag{34}$$

where the maximum is taken over all possible lengths s of output sequences y_1^s. This variable can be computed recursively by dynamic programming (the derivation is given in [Bengio and Bengio, 1996]):

$$V(i, t) = \max(\epsilon(i, t), (1 - \epsilon(i, t) \max_l b(i, l, t))) \max_j (a(i, j, t) V(j, t-1)) \tag{35}$$

At the end of the sequence, the best final state i^* which maximizes $V(i, T)$ is picked within the set of final states F. If the argmax in the above recurrence is kept, than the best predecessor j and best output (y_s or the empty symbol ϵ) for each (i, t) can be used to trace back the optimal state and output sequence from i^*, like in the Viterbi algorithm.

5   Conclusion

We have presented a novel model and training algorithm for representing conditional distributions of output sequences given input sequences of a different length. The distribution is simplified by introducing hidden variables for the state and the alignment of inputs and outputs, similarly to HMMs. The output sequence distribution is decomposed into conditional emission distributions for individual outputs (given a state and an input at time t) and conditional transition distributions (given a previous state and an input at time t). This is an extension of the already proposed IOHMMs [Bengio and Frasconi, 1996, Bengio and Frasconi, 1995] that allows input and output sequences to be asynchronous.

The parameters of the model can be estimated with an EM or GEM algorithm (depending on the form of the emission and transition distributions). Both the E-step and the M-step can be performed in time at worst proportional to the product of the lengths of the input and output sequences, times the number of transitions. A recognition algorithm similar to the Viterbi algorithm for HMMs has also been presented, which takes in the worse case time proportional to the length of the input sequence times the number of transitions.

In practice (especially when the number of states is large), both training and recognition can be sped up by using search algorithms (such as beam search) in the space of state sequences.

References

[Bengio and Bengio, 1996] Bengio, Y. and Bengio, S. (1996). Training asynchronous input/output hidden markov models. Technical Report #1013, Département d'Informatique et de Recherche Opérationnelle, Université de Montréal, Montréal (QC) Canada.

[Bengio and Frasconi, 1995] Bengio, Y. and Frasconi, P. (1995). An input/output HMM architecture. In Tesauro, G., Touretzky, D., and Leen, T., editors, *Advances in Neural Information Processing Systems 7*, pages 427–434. MIT Press, Cambridge, MA.

[Bengio and Frasconi, 1996] Bengio, Y. and Frasconi, P. (1996). Input/Output HMMs for sequence processing. *to appear in IEEE Transactions on Neural Networks*.

[Dempster et al., 1977] Dempster, A. P., Laird, N. M., and Rubin, D. B. (1977). Maximum-likelihood from incomplete data via the EM algorithm. *Journal of Royal Statistical Society B*, 39:1–38.

[Pereira et al., 1994] Pereira, F., Riley, M., and Sproat, R. (1994). Weighted rational transductions and their application to human language processing. In *ARPA Natural Language Processing Workshop*.

[Rabiner, 1989] Rabiner, L. R. (1989). A tutorial on hidden Markov models and selected applications in speech recognition. *Proceedings of the IEEE*, 77(2):257–286.

[Rumelhart et al., 1986] Rumelhart, D., Hinton, G., and Williams, R. (1986). Learning internal representations by error propagation. In Rumelhart, D. and McClelland, J., editors, *Parallel Distributed Processing*, volume 1, chapter 8, pages 318–362. MIT Press, Cambridge.

[Singer, 1996] Singer, Y. (1996). Adaptive mixtures of probabilistic transducers. In Mozer, M., Touretzky, D., and Perrone, M., editors, *Advances in Neural Information Processing Systems 8*. MIT Press, Cambridge, MA.

Speech and Signal Processing

(Poster Presentation)

FEATURE EXTRACTION OF BRAINSTEM AUDITORY EVOKED POTENTIAL SIGNALS BASED ON WAVELET TRANSFORM

Yuying Yang   Xizhi Shi

National Key Laboratory for Vibration, Shock & Noise
Shanghai Jiao Tong University
1954 Hua Shan Road, Shanghai 200030, P.R.China
E - mail: xzshi@sjtu.edu.cn

ABSTRACT

In this paper, we propose a feature extraction method based on the wavelet representation of BAEP signals. We have adopted symmetrical wavelet here and demonstrated that not only conventional features but also some new efficient feature can be obtained in wavelet transform domain. Thirty samples divided into three types according to their pathology are analysed.
KEY WORDS: Wavelet transform   Brainstem auditory evoked potential   Feature extraction

INTRODUCTION

Evoked Potential(EP) is the potential generated by the brain as a result of some external stimulus. Physicians have used evoked potentials as a clinical index to diagnose conditions such as brain lesions. The typical method of measuring evoked potentials is to attach AgAgCl electrodes at specific locations and get the data. Visual, auditory and somatosensory stimuli are used for evoked potentials research. Brainstem Auditory Evoked Potential(BAEP) is a kind of EP caused by auditory stimulus, attaching AgAgCl electrodes outside of brainstem. Due to the low SNR of data in this type of research, the stimuli are repeated a large number of times. The assumption is that repeating the stimuli will cause uncorrelated realizations of the noise and will not cause the signal or evoked potential to change. If the signal and the noise are additive, i.e. $d(t) = s(t) + n(t)$, and the signal is purely deterministic, then averaging is an appropriate signal processing technique for evoked potentials research[1].

The field of EP has intrigued researchers in signal processing for many decades. Many techniques of signal processing have been formulated to diagnose conditions of some organ lesions from EP signals, and they are mostly limited in time domain by extracting latent periods, periods between peaks and amplitudes of peaks as features. But the problem is that when signal is abnormal, it is difficult for us to recognize exactly every peak.

In this paper, we propose wavelet transform method applied to feature extraction of BAEP signals, since it can provides simultaneous information on time and frequency localization of the signal. All thirty samples used here are of guinea - pigs', measured by Hospital of the Five Sense Organs attached to Shanghai Medical University. They are divided into three types according to pathology, i.e. normal, conductibility deaf and irritability deaf. The stimuli are sharp click with 55dB sound intensity at a rate of three times per second. Every sample is obtained by averaging thirty recorded samples to improve the SNR.

WAVELET TRANSFORM

We have adopted the symmetrical wavelet proposed by Mallat in 1989. There are two reasons why we use it: First, it has good frequency domain localization property; Second, the places of peaks remain as places of peaks in symmetry wavelet representation, which make it appropriate for peak detection[2]. Since the theory was presented in the reference quoted[3], extensive analysis is not necessary here. In the following, we shall only sketch out the method. The wavelet representation can be realized by means of pyramidal algorithm which is expressed as the following equations:

$$\begin{cases} A_{2^j} f(n) = \sum_{k=-\infty}^{k=\infty} \widetilde{h}(2n-k) A_{2^{j+1}} f(k) \\ D_{2^j} f(n) = \sum_{k=-\infty}^{k=\infty} \widetilde{g}(2n-k) A_{2^{j+1}} f(k), n \in Z \end{cases}$$

Where h is a low - pass filter, g is a high - pass filter, h and g are called quadrature mirror filters. $A_{2^j} f$ is called a discrete approximation of $f(x)$ at the resolution 2^j and $D_{2^j} f$ is called a discrete detail signal at the resolution 2^j. If we define the discrete original signal as $A_{2^0} f(n)$ $0 \le n \le N$, then $A_{2^0} f(n)$ can be decomposed as $\left(A_{2^J} f, \left(D_{2^j} f \right)_{0 < j \le J} \right)$. This set of discrete signals is called an orthogonal wavelet representation. However, it is difficult to give a precise interpretation of the model in terms of a frequency decomposition because of the overlap of the frequency channels. The impulse response and transfer function of filter H and G used here are shown in Fig. 1.

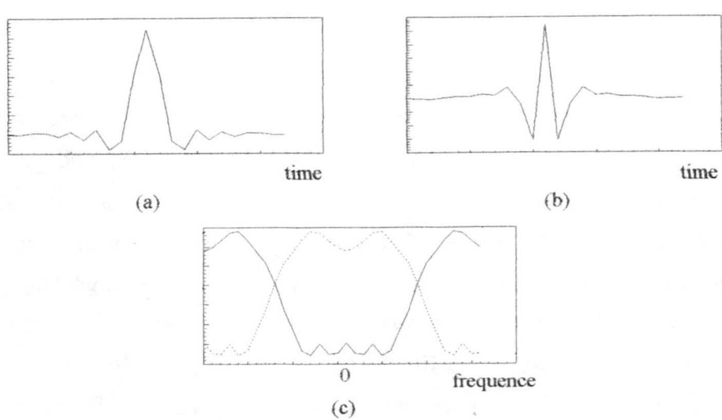

Fig. 1   (a)Impulse response of the filter H   (b)Impulse response of the filter G
(c)Transfer function of filter H and G

RESULTS AND DISCUSSION

Because the frequency band of the BAEP signals is very narrow, we choose 2^1 and 2^2 as the characteristic scales, that is to say we represent the signals at resolution 2^1 and 2^2 only. Fig. 2 to Fig.4 shows separately the original signal and its wavelet representation of normal, conductibility deaf and irritability deaf BAEP signal. We discuss wavelet representation of BAEP signals focusing attention on the following two respects: One is that whether we can still obtain conventional features; The other is that whether we can extract some new features from it that we can not get just from time domain.

1. Among conventional features, latent periods and periods between peaks are of most importance. Observing approximate signals at resolution 2^1 in Fig. 2 to Fig. 4, which are obtained by means of original signals passing through a low - pass filter and have no relative high frequency components any more , we can find   peaks

usually used to diagnose easily. Because the places of maximums remain as places of maximums in symmetrical wavelet representation, we can obtain latent periods and periods between peaks by detecting places of maximums. Amplitudes of peaks in wavelet representation only have relative meaning at each resolution, so it is still a question that whether the ratios of amplitudes are efficient for diagnosis. $\vec{C} = \begin{bmatrix} c_1 c_2 c_3 c_4 c_5 \end{bmatrix}^T$ represents the feature vector, where element c_1 is the latent period of the first peak, elements $c_2 \sim c_5$ are periods between the first five peaks. Define distance between signal and mean normal signals as:

$$d(n,m) = \sqrt{\sum_{i=1}^{5} \left[c_i(n,m) - \overline{c}_i \right]^2}$$

Where n represents the type of signal such as 1 for normal, 2 for conductibility deaf and 3 for irritability deaf; m represents the serial number of signal, $m = 1,10$; $\overline{C} = \begin{bmatrix} \overline{c}_1 \overline{c}_2 \overline{c}_3 \overline{c}_4 \overline{c}_5 \end{bmatrix}^T$ is the mean feature vector of normal signals, which can be obtained by:

$$\overline{c}_i = \tfrac{1}{10} \sum_{m=1}^{10} c_i(1,m) \quad i = 1,5 .$$

Histograms of distance are indicated in Fig.5, from which we can find there different classificatory centers obviously.

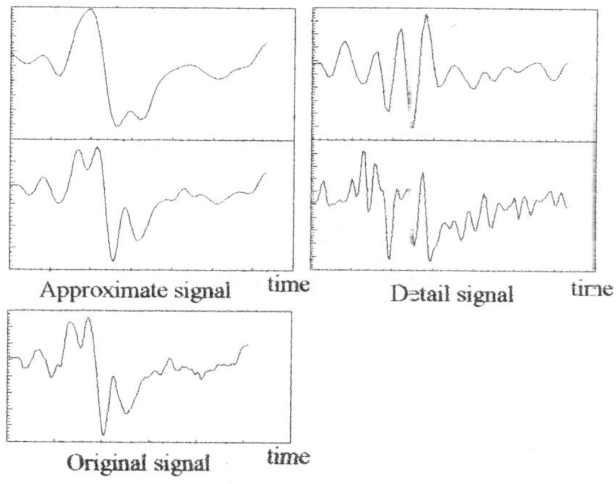

Fig. 2   Normal BAEP Signal

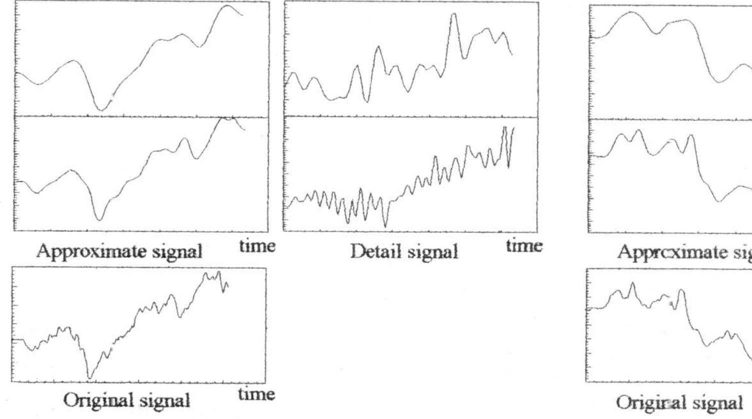

Fig. 3   Conductibility deaf BAEP Signal

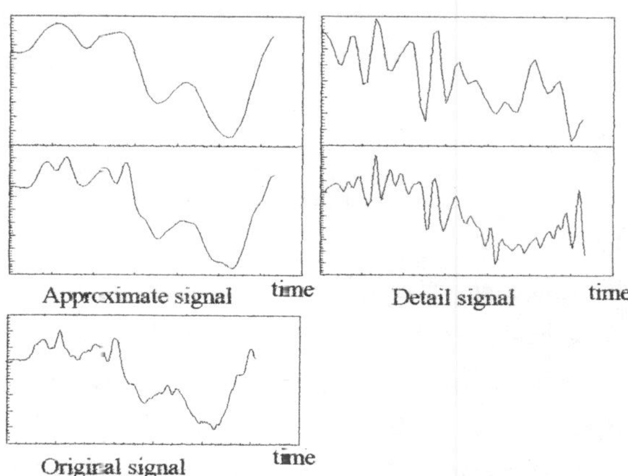

Fig. 4   Irritability deaf BAEP Signal

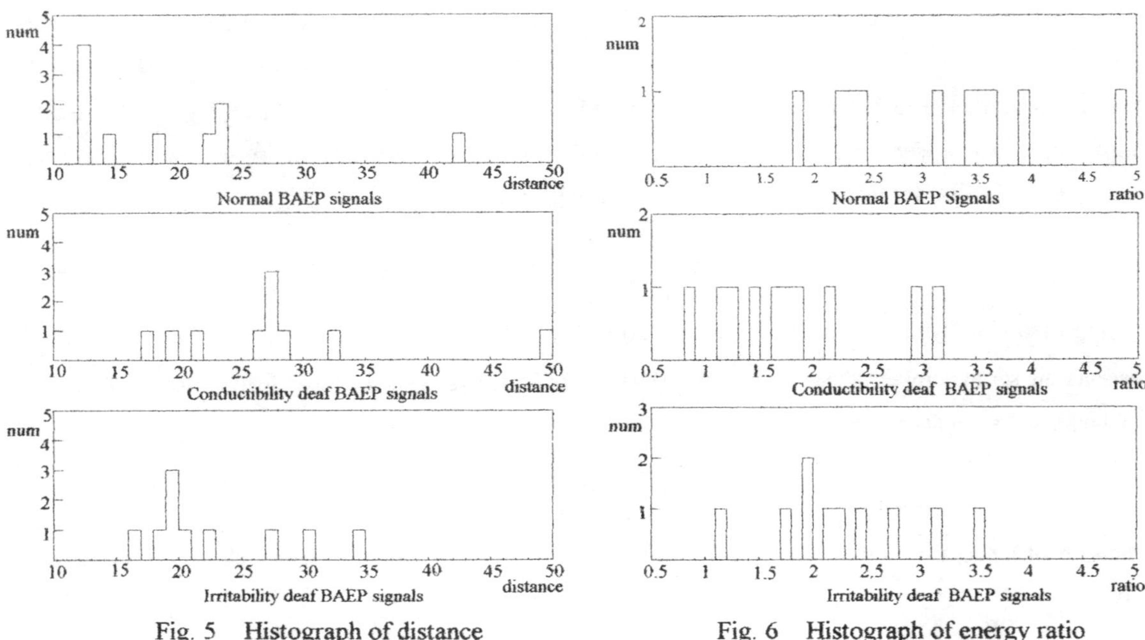

Fig. 5   Histograph of distance   Fig. 6   Histograph of energy ratio

2. Observing original BAEP signals, we have found that there are more small peaks on abnormal signals than those on normal signals. That leads us to think if there is some interesting information in those small peaks and how can we extract it? Detail signals at resolution 2^1 represent these small peaks exactly. Considering the relative meaning of amplitudes in wavelet representation, we extract the ratio of energy of detail signal at resolution 2^1 and that at resolution 2^2 as a new feature. Is it efficient? Let's see Fig. 6, a distribution graph of the ratio. We can find that the ratio distribution of conductibility deaf or irritability deaf are to the left of the ratio distribution of normal signals. This phenomenon demonstrates that more high frequency components are contained in abnormal signals than in normal signals, whose meaning on pathology needs further explorations.

CONCLUSION

The wavelet transform is an efficient tool in analysing BAEP signals. We have demonstrated that some new efficient feature can be extracted by means of it. Not only how to extract more efficient features in the wavelet representation of BAEP signal still remains to be explored by connecting their meanings on pathology, but also further quantitative method needs to develop for evaluating the extracted features.

REFERENCE

[1] Jorge I. Au, "Evoked Potentials Research", IEEE Engineering in Medicine and Biology, pp.67~68, March 1992.

[2] He Lingsong, "Theory and Techniques of Time - Frequency Signal Analysis on Instruments Breakdown Diagnosis", Ph. D Thesis, Huazhong Univ. of Sci. and Tech., P.R.China, June 1993.

[3] Stephane G. Mallat, "A Theory for Multiresolution Signal Decomposition: The Wavelet Representation", IEEE Trans. on Pattern Analysis and Machine Intelligence, Vol. 11, No. 7, pp. 674 ~ 693, July 1989.

[4] E. A. Bartnik, K. J. Blinowska and P.J. Durka, "Single Evoked Potential Reconstruction by means of Wavelet Transform", Biological Cybernetics, Vol. 67, pp. 175~181, 1992.

Application of Recurrent Neural Network to Identification of Defect Depth with Impulsive Sound

Manabu Kotani† and Haruya Matsumoto‡
† Faculty of Engineering, Kobe University
Kobe, Japan
‡ Osaka Institute of Technology
Osaka, Japan

Abstract— In recent years, several studies have been done for the acoustic diagnosis with an impulsive sound. The traditional diagnostic methods make use of monitoring changes in specific frequencies. However, it is difficult to detect the small defects with these methods. We, here, examine a method to identify the defect depth with highly accuracy. We propose to apply neural networks to the diagnostic method. As the result, we obtain over 90% discrimination accuracy with neural networks. This suggests that the neural network is effective for the identification of defect depth with the impulsive sound.

1 Introduction

An acoustic diagnosis with an impulsive sound is usually used to detect defects in mechanical structure, wheels on a train and so on[1][2]. Since the impulsive sound varies with time, it is generally difficult to process the signal and to detect the defects automatically.

Human auditory sensing or the monitoring of changes in the specific frequencies has been used to detect the defects as the condition surveillance technique. Sugiyama et al.[1] have studied to evaluate the quality of maskmelons by the monitoring of the peak frequencies. It, however, is difficult to detect the small defects with these methods, and Haran et al.[2] have studied to apply the pattern recognition technique for the inspection of the railroad wheels.

We examine to apply the pattern recognition techniques used in the speech recognition for the identification of the defect depth. The applied model is the neural network which is to imitate the superior processing performance in human brain and has a good performance for the pattern recognition[3][4]. We have already shown the effectiveness of the multi-layered neural network for the identification of defect depth with the impulsive sound[5]. However, since the impulsive sound is the time series data, it is considered that the recurrent neural network is more proper to the diagnostic method. The purpose of this paper is to evaluate the performance of the recurrent neural networks for the identification of the defect depth.

2 Signal Processing Method

In this section, we describe the outline of the signal processing methods, that is, Euclidean distance measure and the recurrent neural network.

2.1 Euclidean distance measure

Euclidean distance measure is such that the distance, D_i, between vectors of $\vec{x}$ and $\vec{m}_i$ is defined as Eq. (1).

$$D_i = \sqrt{(\vec{x} - \vec{m}_i)(\vec{x} - \vec{m}_i)'} \tag{1}$$

where $\vec{x}$ is the test data, $\vec{m}_i$ is the mean vector of the training data for the i-th experimental condition and $(\vec{x} - \vec{m}_i)'$ means the transposition of $(\vec{x} - \vec{m}_i)$.

The mean vector, $\vec{m}_i$, is calculated from the training data every defect depth. The procedure for the calculation of the discrimination accuracy with the Euclidean distance measure is as follows:

1. Calculate the mean vectors for each experimental condition from the training data.

2. Calculate the Euclidean distance measures, D_i, between the test data $\vec{x}$ and the mean vector $\vec{m}_i$ at each condition.

3. Select the condition for which the minimum distance is obtained.

4. Confirm whether the selected condition corresponds to the experimental condition of the input pattern.

2.2 Recurrent neural network

There are some models of the recurrent neural network[6][7][8][9]. We, here, examine to apply the recurrent neural network proposed by Elman[7] because of its easy handling and the reduction of the learning time. Figure 1 shows the structure of the network.

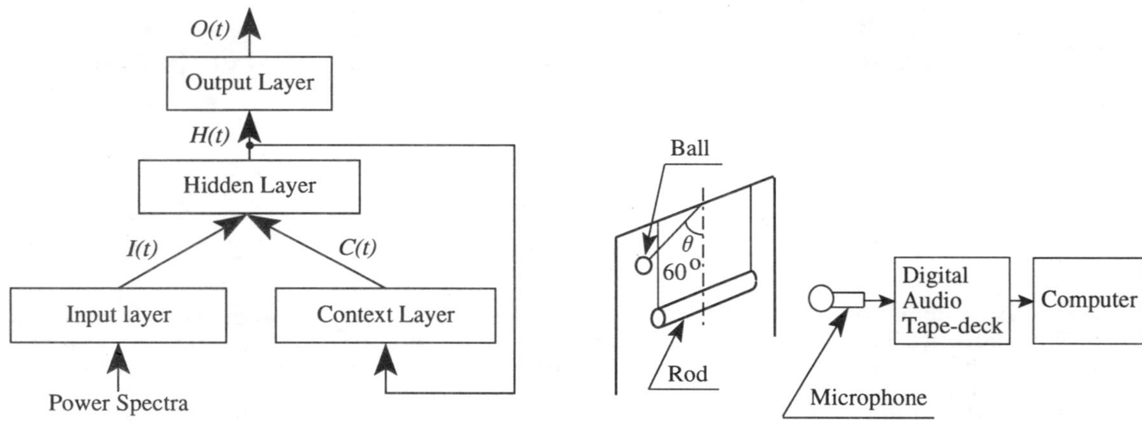

Figure 1: Model of recurrent neural network   Figure 2: Experimental schematic diagram

The input signals to the network, $I(t)$, and the signals of the context units, $C(t)$, are weighted and fed to the hidden units. The signals of the context units are the previous signals of the hidden units, that is, $C(t) = H(t - 1)$. The output signals of the hidden units, $H(t)$, are weighted and fed to the output units. The activation functions in the hidden and output units are the sigmoid functions defined as the Eq. (2). The input units are the linear ones as Eq. (3).

$$f(x_j) = \frac{1}{1 + \exp[-x_j]} \tag{2}$$

$$f(x_j) = x_j \tag{3}$$

where

$$x_j = \sum_i w_{ji} o_i + \theta_j \tag{4}$$

The x_j is the input pattern to the j-th unit, w_{ji} is the weight on the connection from i-th unit in the lower layer to the j-th unit in the upper layer, o_i is the output pattern of the i-th unit, θ_j is the threshold of the j-th unit.

The learning algorithm for weights and thresholds is the error back-propagation method[10]. The object function, E, is defined as Eq. (5).

$$E = \frac{1}{2} \sum_p \sum_j (t_{pj} - o_{pj})^2 \tag{5}$$

where t_{pj} and o_{pj} are the target pattern and the output pattern for the p-th input pattern and the j-th output unit, respectively.

The weight updating rule[10] is as follows:

$$\Delta w_{ji}(t + 1) = \eta \delta_j o_i + \alpha \Delta w_{ji}(t) \tag{6}$$

where $\Delta w_{ji}(t + 1)$ is the change to be made to the weight w_{ji}, δ_j is the back propagated error, o_i is the output signal of the i-th unit, and η, α are constants.

The procedure for the calculation of the discrimination accuracy with the neural network is as follows:

1. Learn weights and biases in the network with the training data.

2. Input the test data to the network after the learning.

3. Select the output unit having the maximum value among the output units.

4. Confirm whether the selected output unit corresponds to the experimental condition of the input pattern.

3   Experiments

Figure 2 shows the experimental schematic diagram. We use three brass rods of 200 mm in a length and 10 mm in a diameter. The rod is hanged by the thin metal wire of about 300 mm length. The ball made of stainless steel is hanged down about 300 mm and shocks at the center of the rod.

A microphone is placed at a distance about 500 mm from the rod, and picks up the acoustic signal. The signals from the microphone are recorded in the digital audio tape-deck at 48 kHz sampling frequency. The recorded data are fed to the computer.

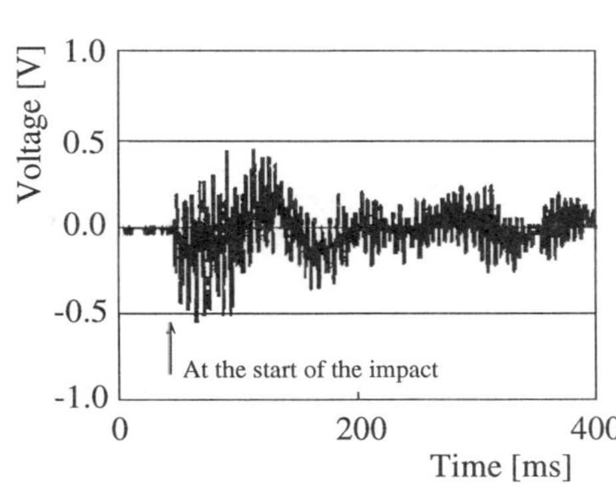

Figure 3: Example of impulsive sound

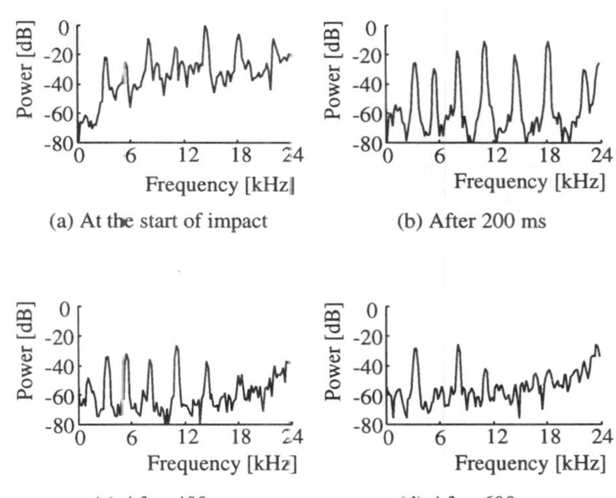

Figure 4: Example of logarithmic power spectra

Table 1: Discrimination result with recurrent neural network

Input Pattern	Discrimination Result [mm]					
	0	1	2	4	7	10
0 mm	23	2	0	1	0	1
1 mm	2	24	0	1	0	0
2 mm	0	1	22	3	0	1
4 mm	0	1	1	25	0	0
7 mm	0	1	0	0	26	0
10 mm	0	0	0	0	0	27

Table 2: Discrimination result with Euclidean distance measure

Input Pattern	Discrimination Result [mm]					
	0	1	2	4	7	10
0 mm	18	0	1	2	6	0
1 mm	0	19	5	0	3	0
2 mm	0	0	19	7	1	0
4 mm	0	0	4	19	4	0
7 mm	0	0	1	2	22	2
10 mm	0	0	1	0	3	23

The acoustic data are recorded from the start of the impact and the number of impacts is eighteen every defect and rod. Defects of 2 mm in a diameter are artificially processed in the center of rods and these depths are 0, 1, 2, 4, 7 and 10 mm.

Figure 3 shows an example of the recorded impulsive sound. The amplitude of the sound decays with time.

The FFT computation is carried out every 5.3 ms over Hanning-windowed frames with the width of 5.0 ms and logarithmic power spectra are calculated at every frame. Though the FFT computation is carried out over all recorded data, it is supposed that there are some frames having the insignificant information about the defect depth. Figure 4 shows an example of logarithmic power spectra. There are no distinct features in the power spectra at the start of the impact or after 600 ms. We, however, are able to observe features after 200 ms or 400 ms. It, therefore, is important to select the most appropriate information to be fed to the discrimination method. We use eight frames from the 10-th frame to the 17-th frame based on our previous result[5]. These data are normalized from 0.1 to 0.9, and are divided into halves as the training data and the test data. So, the numbers of training and test data are 162.

4 Simulation and Results

We, here, examine the performance of the recurrent neural network for the identification of the defect depth. The input patterns for the network are logarithmic power spectra and the number of input units is 128. The number of output units is 6 and each output unit corresponds to the defect depth, that is, none of defect, 1 mm, 2 mm and so on. The number of hidden units is 10. When the input pattern is fed to the network, the target pattern is set to "1" for the only corresponding unit to the input pattern and the others are set to "0". The learning parameters are $\alpha = 0.1, \eta = 0.1$ and the leaning iteration is 2000. Table 1 shows that the discrimination result, that is, how the test pattern discriminates with the neural network. The number of input pattern is 27 every defect. For example, 23 input patterns for the defect depth being 0 mm are discriminated as "0 mm", 2 patterns as "1 mm", 1 pattern as "4 mm" and 1 pattern as "0 mm". After all, 23 patterns of "0 mm" are accurately discriminated among 27 patterns and 4 patterns are inaccurately discriminated. The discrimination accuracy with the recurrent neural network is about 90.7 % (= 147/162).

On the other hand, we examine the performance of the Euclidean distance measure. The Euclidean distance measure is modified as Eq. (7).

$$D = \sum_p D_i(p) \tag{7}$$

where $D_i(p)$ is the same as the D_i in Eq. (1) and p is the frame number. Table 2 shows the discrimination result with the Euclidean distance measure. We obtain the 74.1 % ($= 120/162$) discrimination accuracy with the Euclidean distance measure. These results show that the recurrent neural network is superior to the Euclidean distance measure.

By the way, our previous result[5] shows that the discrimination accuracy with the three-layered neural networks is about 99 % higher than that with the recurrent neural network. While the number of weights in the recurrent neural network is 1,356, the number of weights in the three-layered neural network is 10,316. We can make the structure of the network small in the case of the recurrent neural network. On the other hand, it is generally supposed that the networks with too many weights have the problem for the learning time and the discrimination time.

5   Conclusion

We have described the attempt to apply the recurrent neural network to the signal processing for the impulsive sound. The results show that the discrimination accuracy with the recurrent neural network is over 90%. The result shows that the performance of the recurrent neural network is superior to that of the traditional pattern recognition technique based on the Euclidean distance measure.

The discrimination accuracy, however, is inferior to that with three-layered neural network. Since the approach with the recurrent neural network has the advantage of the compact structure, we would examine to apply the fully-connected recurrent networks to obtain the better discrimination accuracy.

References

[1] J. Sugiyama and S. Usui: Nondestructive Quality Evaluation of Maskmelons by Acoustic Impulse Response, *Transaction of the Society of Instrument and Control Engineers*, vol. 26, no. 4, pp.367-374, 1990

[2] S. Haran and R. D. Finch: Application of an Automated Package of Pattern Recognition Techniques to Acoustic Signature Inspection of Railroad Wheels, *Journal of Acoustical Society of America*, vol. 85, no. 1, pp.440-449, 1989

[3] R. P. Lippmann: Review of Neural Network for Speech Recognition , *Neural Computation*, vol. 1, no. 1, pp.1-38, MIT Press, 1989

[4] A. Waibel, T. Hanazawa, G. Hinton, K. Sikano and K. J. Lang: Phoneme Recognition Using Time-Delay Neural Network, *IEEE Transaction on Acoustics, Speech and Signal Processing*, vol. 37, no. 3, pp.328-339, 1989

[5] M. Kotani, H. Matsumoto and T. Kanagawa: Evaluation Method of Defect Depth with Acoustic Impulse Signal, *Proc. of International Conference on Electronic Measurement & Instruments*, pp.17-21, 1992

[6] M. I. Jordan: Serial Order: A Parallel Distributed Processing Approach, *ICS Report*, no. 8604, pp.270-280, 1986

[7] J. L. Elman: Finding Structure in Time, *CRL Technical Report*, no. 8801, 1988

[8] F. J. Pineda: Dynamics and Architecture for Neural Computation, *Journal of Complexity*, vol. 4, 1988

[9] R. J. Williams and D. Zipser: A Learning Algorithms for Continually Running Fully Recurrent Neural Networks, *Neural Computation*, vol. 1, pp.270-280, 1989

[10] D. E. Rumelhart, G. E. Hinton and R. J. Williams: Learning Internal Representations by Error Propagation, *Parallel Distributed Processing: Explorations in the Microstructure of Cognition*, MIT Press, vol. I, pp.318-362, 1986

Visual Processing

(Oral Presentation)

Learning Probability Models and Algorithms for Vision

A.L. Yuille and S.C. Zhu*
Smith-Kettlewell Eye Research Institute
2232 Webster Street, San Francisco, CA 94115
yuille@skeri.ski.org
* Current address: Department of Applied Sciences, Harvard University, Cambridge, MA 02139.

Abstract— **It is theoretically attractive to formulate vision problems in terms of Bayesian probability theory using maximum a posteriori (MAP) estimation. This presupposes that we know the probability distributions and have fast algorithms for calcuating the estimators. This paper describes theories for unsupervised learning of both the algorithms and the probability distributions.**

1   Introduction

It is attractive to formulate vision as perceptual inference using Bayesian probability theory (for a recent review, see [5]). In particular, work on pattern theory [3] and [7] has advocated the idea of "analysis through synthesis". In this approach the visual system uses statistical knowledge about the structure of the world in order to make the best estimate of the viewed scene.

For this approach to succeed, however, it is critically important to develop general theories for learning both prior knowledge about the world and fast algorithms for making the best interpretation (once the prior knowledge has been learnt).

In this paper we describe theories for learning both prior knowledge and algorithms. In both cases the learning is unsupervised and no teacher is required.

In addition, we prove theoretical results linking the learning of prior knowledge to the Helmholtz machine [1], the Ying Yang machine [12] and work by Saul et al. on belief networks [9].

2   Unsupervised Learning of Algorithms

For a specific visual task we let S represent the properties of the world that we wish to extract and let I be the visual input. The goal of a Bayesian theory is to find an estimate, $S^*(I)$, of the world properties as a function of the input I. The criteria commonly used is to pick the S that maximizes the *a posteriori* probability of the input $P_{post}(S|I)$, given by $P_{post}(S|I) = P_l(I|S)P_{prior}(S)/P(I)$, where $P_l(I|S)$ and $P_{prior}(S)$ are the likelikood function and the prior probability respectively. Formally, this means $S^*(I) = \arg\max_S P_{post}(S|I)$ and is called the MAP estimator.

Computing the MAP estimator, however, is often very difficult. Algorithms for computing it, such as a simulated annealing, are often very slow [2]. But we can think of the MAP estimator as being a *non-linear filter*, $S^*(.)$, applied to the image. So finding the MAP estimator is equivalent to learning this function.

We assume that the function $S^*(I)$ can be approximated by a feedforward network with one layer of hidden units, provided the weights can be chosen appropriately . Theoretical results will guarantee this if we have enough hidden units [4]. We express the output of the network as $S = f(I;\omega)$, where ω represents the weights. The learning task is to determine the set of weights ω^* so that the network closely approximates $S^*(I)$.

It is quite likely that other neural network architectures, such as Radial Basis Functions [8], might be better suited to learning the maximum a posterior estimates. But, for simplicity, we will restrict ourselves to multi-level feedforward perceptrons.

To determine the correct weights we train the system over a representative set of inputs $\{I^\mu : \mu\epsilon\Lambda\}$. We pick ω^* to maximize the energy function $E[\omega,\Lambda] = \sum_{\mu\epsilon\Lambda} \log P_{post}(f(I^\mu;\omega)|I^\mu)$. In the limit as $|\Lambda|$ tends to infinity this energy function becomes:

$$E[\omega] = \sum_I P(I) \log P_{post}(f(I;\omega)|I). \tag{1}$$

Provided the class of input-output functions of our network includes $S^*(I)$, it is clear that $E[\omega]$ will be maximized by ω^* such that $f(I;\omega^*) = S^*(I)$ (recall that $S^*(I) = \arg\max_S P_{post}(S|I)$ and $P(I) \geq 0, \forall I$). If the class of functions is not representative enough we will still obtain the best approximation to the $S^*(I)$ within the class, under the assumption that the training process is capable of finding the optimal ω. We propose using stochastic training which, as recent results have shown [6], is resistant to local minima in the energy function. Observe that if P_{post} is specified by a Gibbs distribution, $P_{post} = (1/Z)e^{-E_{post}}$, then our criteria is equivalent to minimizing the expected value of the corresponding energy E_{post}.

In short, our approach involves using a regular backpropagation algorithm but with the standard error function being replaced by the function $C(\omega) = -\log P_{post}(f(I;\omega)|I)$.

For concreteness, suppose we want to learn a MAP estimator for a one-dimensional variant of the problem studied in [2]. This can be expressed as a Gibbs distribution with energy function:

$$E_{post}[S] = \sum_i \{(S_i - I_i)^2 + G(S_{i+1} - S_i)\}, \tag{2}$$

where $G(.)$ is a function which encourages neighbouring sites to have similar values S_i and S_{i+1}, but does not severely penalize configurations for which S_i and S_{i+1} are very different. This prevents the system from smoothing across sharp discontinuities in the input.

For this problem, our criteria would reduce to an energy function:

$$C(\omega) = \sum_i (f_i(I, \omega) - I_i)^2 + G(f_{i+1}(I, \omega) - f_i(I, \omega)). \tag{3}$$

Observe that the first term is the standard cost function for training an auto-associative neural network. The second term, however, imposes the prior assumptions on the data.

Such a system was successfully trained on artificial data [10].

We should emphasise that this approach is very general and applies in principle to learning any MAP estimator. Moreover, the approach is also unsupervised *provided the posterior distributions can be estimated.* Recent results, which we describe in the next section, show that this is possible for certain important problems.

3   Unsupervised Learning of the Probability Distributions

The methods described in the previous section, would be of little use if the posterior probability models were unknown. Fortunately, however, recent work [13], [14] shows that it is practical to learn these distributions using a minimax entropy principle, first proposed by Zhu, Wu and Mumford[15]. This method currently applies to learning the prior distributions.

This approach assumes that we have a filterbank of linear and non-linear filters, $\{f^\alpha : \alpha \in A\}$, which we can apply to the input data $\{I^\mu : \mu \in \Lambda\}$.

For any subset $\{f^\alpha : \alpha \in B\}$ of the filterbank we apply each filter to the image and measure the histograms of their responses $\{H^\alpha : \alpha \in B\}$. We then derive an estimate $P_B(I)$ by using the maximum entropy principle subject to the constraint that the marginal distribution of the estimated distribution with respect to each filter must agree with the empirically measured histogram. The learned $P_B(I)$ is of the form of Gibbs distributions with potentials built on the filters responses instead of cliques as used in the Markov random field models.

This gives us a set of maximum entropy distributions $\{P_B(I) : B \subset A\}$ which approximate $P(I)$. The similarity between $P(I)$ and any of the estimated distributions $P_B(I)$ is defined to be the Kullback-Leibler divergence:

$$KL(P(I), P_B(I)) = \sum_I P(I) \log \frac{P(I)}{P_B(I)}. \tag{4}$$

The following theorem shows that we can estimate which maximum entropy distribution is closest to the true distribution $P(I)$ *without* knowing $P(I)$. The theorem states:

Theorem 1. *If $P_B(I)$ is a maximum entropy distribution obtained using the constraints that the same histograms of the filters $\{f^\alpha : \alpha \in B\}$ are equal to the observed histograms, then the Kullback Leibler distance between $P(I)$ and $P_B(I)$ is equal to the difference between the entropies of the two distributions.*

Proof.   The result follows from the observation that, for maximum entropy distributions, we have $\sum_I P(I) \log P_B(I) = \sum_I P_B(I) \log P_B(I)$.

The theorem implies that to find the maximum entropy distribution which is most similar to $P(I)$, we merely have to find the distribution with *minimum entropy.* This approach therefore satisfies a minimax entropy principle. Zhu and his collaborators [13], [14] suggest a greedy algorithm for finding the best set of filter B and for its associated distribution $P_B(I)$.

To verify the minimax entropy distributions learned from the observed data, Zhu , Wu, and Mumford sample the distributions by MCMC simulation, and the synthesized images have similar appearances with the observed ones[13], [14]. Interestingly, the distribution learned from natural images is similar to, but with interesting differences from, the Geman and Geman distribution [2] used for image segmentation and which was assumed by Smirnakis and Yuille [10].

4   Relations to the Helmholtz and Ying Yang Machines

The approach for unsupervised learning of the probability distributions has some similarities to recent work on the Helmholtz and the Ying-Yang machine [1], [12], [9]. These approaches use similarity distances to estimate approximate distributions and they are completely in spirit with the pattern theory approach to vision. To our knowledge, however, their particular ideas have not been applied to vision problems with real grey-scale data.

We can, however, prove a theorem which shows that there are strong connections between the minimum maximum entropy approach and the techniques used in [1], [9] which rely on approximating a distribution by a factorized distribution.

Theorem 2 *Applying the maximal entropy principle to estimate a distribution using the contraint that the means of the marginal distributions are known yields the (factorized) mean field distribution.*

Proof. This is a direct application of the maximum entropy principle.

Thus we can derive the factorized (or mean field) distribution (which appears in both [1], [9]) by apply the maximum entropy principle with the constraint that the means of the marginal distributions are known. This work, therefore, is related to minimax entropy where the filters are specified in advance and cannot be choosen. We might speculate that allowing filters to be adaptively choosen, as in the minimum maximum entropy approach, might yield improved results. It should be emphasized that these Helmholtz machines also include other parameters, corresponding to network weights, which are not present in the minimax entropy approach. Understanding the role of these constraints is a subject of current research [11].

5   Conclusion

This paper describes approaches for learning probabiity models and algorithms using unsupervised learning. Both methods have been tested individually on the problem of image segmentation, and our current work combines the two [11]. In addition, we are extending the work to other vision problems and exploring relations to the Helmholtz [1], [9]and Ying-Yang [12] machines.

Acknowledgements   Support was provided by NSF Grant IRI 92-23676 and ARPA/ONR Contract N00014-95-1-1022.

References

[1] P. Dayan, G. Hinton, R. Neal and R. Zemel. "The Helmholtz machine". *Neural Computation*, 7, pp 889-904. 1995.

[2] S. Geman and D. Geman. "Stochastic relaxation, Gibbs distributions and the Bayesian restoration of images". *IEEE Trans. on Pattern Analysis and Machine Intelligence.* PAMI-6(7), pp 721-741. 1984.

[3] U. Grenander, Y. Chow, and D.M. Keenan. *Hands: A Pattern Theroetic Study of Biological Shapes.* New York: Springer-Verlag. 1991.

[4] K. Hornik, S. Stinchocombe and H. White. "Multilayer feed-forward networks are universal approximators". *Neural Networks* 4, pp 251-257. 1991.

[5] D. Knill and W. Richards. (Eds). **Bayesian Approaches to Perception.** Cambridge University Press. 1996.

[6] T.K. Leen and J.E. Moody. "Weight Space Probability Densities in Stochastic Learning". *NIPS 5.* pp 451-458. 1993.

[7] D.B. Mumford. "Pattern Theory: a unifying perspective". *First European Conference on Mathematics.* 1993.

[8] T. Poggio and F. Girosi. "Networks for approximation and learning". *Proc. of IEEE,* vol. 78, pp 1481-1497. 1990.

[9] L.K. Saul, T. Jaakkola and M.I. Jordan. "Mean Field Theory for Sigmoid Belief Networks". *Journal of Artificial Intelligence Research.* 4, pp 61-76. 1996.

[10] S.M. Smirnakis and A.L. Yuille. "Neural Implementation of Bayesian Vision Theories by Unsupervised Learning". In *Proceedings on Computation and Neural Systems.* Monterey, California. 1994.

[11] S.M. Smirnakis, A.L. Yuille, and S. C. Zhu. In preparation. 1996.

[12] Lei Xu. "Bayesian-Kullback Coupled YING-YANG Machines: Unified Learnings and New Results on Vector Quantization". *Proc. 1995 Intl. Conf. on Neural Information Processing.* ICONIP95. pp977-988, 1995.

[13] S.C. Zhu and D.B. Mumford. "Learning Generic Prior Models for Natural Images". Harvard Robotics Laboratory Technical Report No. 95-3. 1995.

[14] S.C. Zhu, Y.N. Wu and D.B. Mumford. "FRAME (Filters, Random Fields, and Minimax Entropy): Towards a unified theory for texture modelling". *Proc. Int. Conf. on Comp. Vision and Patt. Recog.* San Francisco, CA. 1996.

[15] S.C. Zhu, Y.N. Wu and D.B. Mumford. "Minimax Entropy Principle and Texture Modeling", (sumbitted to *Neural Computation*)

A neural network method for correcting the color shifts due to the illuminant changes

Yoshifumi Arai   Shigeki Nakauchi   Shiro Usui

Dept. of Information & Computer Sciences, Toyohashi University of Technology
1-1, Tempaku-cho, Toyohasi, 441, Japan
email : usui@bpel.tutics.tut.ac.jp

Abstract— **The digital color images can be easily edited and corrected by using the color desktop publishing (DTP) software on computer system. However, the problem of the color shifts of the recorded image due to the illuminant changes still remains because conventional color management system of color DTP is typically calibrated only for one illuminant (e.g. daylight illuminant D50). In this paper, we propose a new correction method for color shifts of the recorded images using estimated spectral reflectance by a neural network. The proposed method is compared to White-Point Mapping and principal components method for the evaluation of an accuracy. Our evaluation results show that the proposed method can realize a sufficient accuracy as compared with the others.**

1   Introduction

Illuminant affects the observed and recorded colors of object, that is, colors tend to be reddish or greenish under incandescent or fluorescent lighting. These color shifts due to the illuminant changes in the image would be unacceptable as the natural colors.

In recent years, the color desktop publishing (DTP) system is, in general, used for creating the document or editing the digital images for personal and/or professional use. The digital camera also can be used to take an image for such uses. However the problem of the color shifts due to the illuminant changes will occur when the image is recorded under some other illuminant since the color DTP system is typically calibrated for only one illuminant such as daylight illuminant D50. Thus, it is required to perform a correction of the color shifts prior to printing the image so that it makes a color matching to the image recorded under daylight illuminant.

This paper presents a new correction method of the color shift due to the illuminant changes using the transformation from CMY value to spectral reflectance by a neural network. Two conventional methods for correcting the color shift will be reviewed. Then a new color correction method will be compared to these conventional color correction methods.

2   Color correction methods

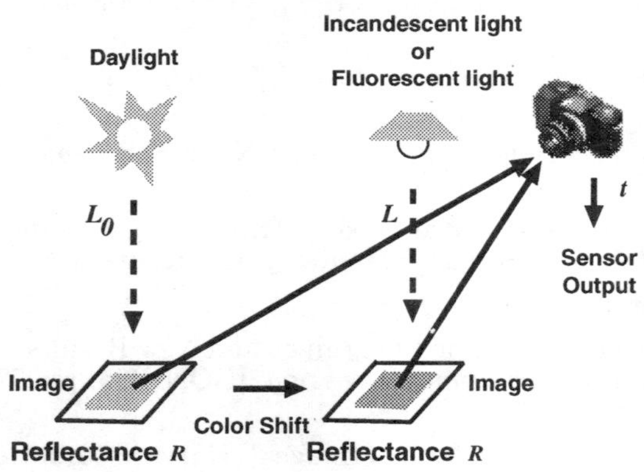

Figure 1: Color shifts of recorded image due to the illuminant changes

The problem of the color shifts due to the illuminant changes shown in Figure 1 involves estimation of the image under daylight illuminant from the image recorded under other possible illuminant. White-point mapping (WPM) is a sort of method for this correction which matches the white point of the image under recording and daylight illuminant. This mehtod would produce significant correction errors in each colors except for the vicinity of the white point. To correct each color in image exactly, it is required to estimate the spectral reflectance from three sensor outputs under recording illuminant. However, estimating the spectral reflectance is mathematically difficult task because the spectral reflectance have larger dimension than the sensor outputs. Vrhel and Trussell [1] have proposed the principal components method based on the approximation of the spectral reflectances of each color in image under recording illuminant using a finite-dimensional linear model with a small number of principal components. Here, we will describe these two methods and our method for correction of the color shifts due to the illuminant changes.

2.1   White-point mapping method

WPM method is used in conventional video system, digital color imaging system and other recording systems because the reproduction of the reference white is important for perceptual reasons. Typically, in video system, the reference white is used to calibrate the system such that three sensor outputs under recording illuminant are equal to the outputs under daylight illuminant.

We use the spectral reflectance of a paper of a dye-sublimation printer as the reference white. We consider the spectral reflectance sampled at N wavelengths from 400nm to 700nm. A sampling width is 10nm which implies $N = 31$.

Three sensor outputs under certain illumination L can be calculated as $t = M^T L R$. Where, Matrix M^T and R represent the spectral sensitivity of sensors and the spectral reflectance, respectively. $N \times N$ diagonal Matrix L describes the spectral distribution of the illuminant.

WPM can be described as follows : if C_{wpm} is a three-element vector produced from viewing R under daylight illuminant L_0, then t can be matched to C_{wpm} by multiplying the correction matrix D

$$C_{wpm} = Dt \tag{1}$$

D is derived from

$$DM^T L R_w = M^T L_0 R_w \tag{2}$$

Diagonal matrix L_0 indicates the spectral distribution of the daylight illuminant. R_w is the spectral reflectance of the reference white. In this paper, we use CIE (*Commision Internationale de l'Eclairage*) color-matching function as spectral sensitivity of sensors; three sensor outputs are tristimulus values.

2.2 Principal components method

2.2.1 Approximation of the spectral reflectance by small number of principal components

It has been shown that a linear combination of k principal component vectors μ_i $(i = 1\cdot,\cdot,\cdot,k)$ gives good approximation of the spectral reflectance as follows :

$$\tilde{R}_j = \bar{R} + \sum_{i=1}^{k} \psi_{ij} \mu_i \tag{3}$$

Where, j is the number of samples, $\bar{R}$ is a mean vector and ψ_{ij} is the principal component associated with i-th principal component vector μ_i, defined as :

$$\psi_{ij} = \mu_i^T \hat{R}_j, \quad \hat{R} = R - \bar{R} \tag{4}$$

It is well known that principal component vectors can minimize the mean square error between original and approximated spectral reflectance (For details on principal component analysis (PCA) see references [6]).

There are several reports on PCA of spectral reflectance. Cohen and Maloney[2, 3] analyzed the spectral reflectance of the Munsell color chips using PCA and suggested that the spectral reflectance can be represented with sufficient accuracy using a small number of principal components. Several researchers [4, 5] have proposed color constancy models based on the computational study of the human color perception. These models stand on an assumption that the spectral reflectance can be approximated by a linear combination of small number of principal components. On the basis of this assumption, Vrhel and Trussell used a finite-dimensional linear model defined by Eq. (3) to correct the color shift due to the illuminant changes.

2.2.2 Analysis of the spectral reflectance by principal component analysis

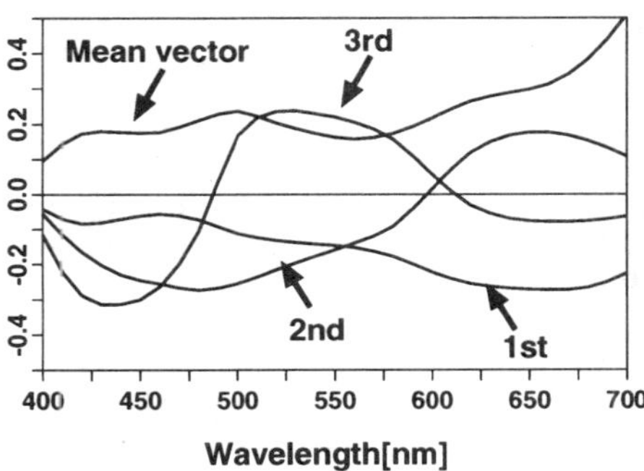

Figure 2: Principal component and mean vectors of the color chips reproduced by a dye-sublimation printer

Here, we analyzed the spectral reflectance of printed color chips by PCA in order to obtain the principal component vectors. We printed 1331 color chips by dye-sublimation printer with changing CMY value from 0% to 100% at 10% steps. For PCA of the spectral reflectance, we chose 216 color chips by changing CMY value from 0% to 100% at 20% steps from the printed 1331 color chips. Figure 2 shows the first three principal component vectors and mean vector $\bar{R}$ for a dye-sublimation printer. To confirm that we can realize the approximation accuracy the same as Vrhel et al. by Eq. (3) using those principal component vectors, we calculated the cumulative proportion of the first three principal component vectors. This cumulative proportion is 97.17%. Thus, it is certain that we can obtain almost the same accuracy as Vrhel et al., that is, their cumulative proportions of five different printers were 92.94% to 99.31%(100 to 512 data were used).

2.2.3   Color correction by principal components method

The tristimulus value t_{pca} can be calculated by using the principal vectors $\mu = [\mu_1, \mu_2, \mu_3]^T$ obtained as described in the above section, which is :

$$t_{pca} = M^T L\mu\psi + M^T L\bar{R} = M^T L\mu\psi + m_t \tag{5}$$

Where, $m_t = M^T L\bar{R}$ is a matrix of the tristimulus value for a mean vector. Then, the principal component $\psi = [\psi_1, \psi_2, \psi_3]^T$ is defined as :

$$\psi = (M^T L\mu)^{-1} [t_{pca} - m_t] \tag{6}$$

By using the finite-dimensional linear model defined by Eq. (3), the tristimulus value C_{vrh} under daylight illuminant corrected by principal components method is :

$$C_{vrh} = M^T L_0\mu[M^T L\mu]^{-1} [t_{pca} - m_t] + m_c \tag{7}$$

For details of this correction method, refer to the article of Vrhel and Trussll [1].

2.3   Color correction method using a neural network

2.3.1   Transformation from CMY value to spectral reflectance by a neural network

First, we determined the structure of the neural network for transforming CMY value to spectral reflectance. An optimal number of units in hidden layer was examined by evaluating the square error of that transformation. For training data set, we used the same 216 data sets as the PCA. The neural network with 13 to 20 hidden units was trained sufficiently, and then evaluated using 1115 unknown data sets except for the training data sets. Figure 3 shows the square error versus number of hidden units. We can see that the square error was minimized when 18 units of hidden layer were used. A structure of the neural network is shown in Figure 4. A number of input and output units corresponds to C, M, and Y values and a number of points of the spectral reflectance ($N = 31$).

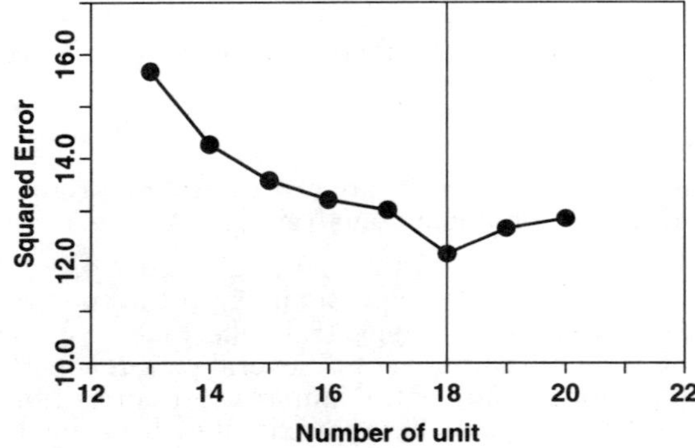

Figure 3: Number of hidden units vs. square error. This shows that the optimal number of hidden units is 18 because the square error for 1115 data sets is minimum.

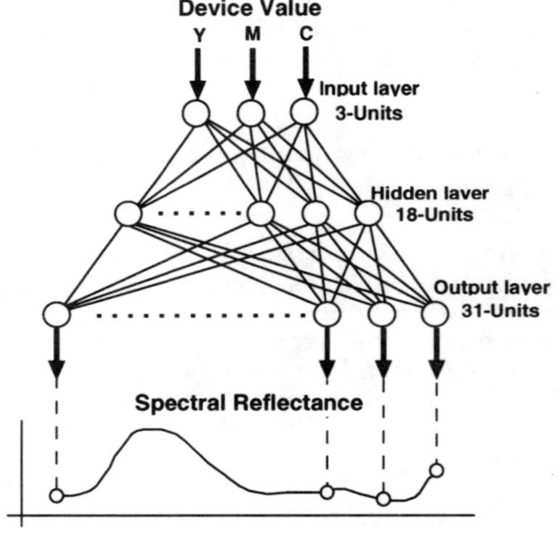

Figure 4: A structure of the neural network. It makes a transformation from color separation value CMY to spectral reflectance.

2.3.2   Method of color correction using a neural network

We can estimate the spectral reflectance using a neural network as shown in Figure 4. When the estimated spectral reflectance is represented as the nonlinear function of C,M and Y, $R(C, M, Y)$, the tristimulus value t_{NN} under the recording illuminant L is calculated from

$$t_{NN} = M^T LR(C, M, Y) \tag{8}$$

Where $R(C, M, Y)$ is updated by the optimization process shown in Figure 5. In this process, CMY value is adjusted so that the square norm between original tristimulus value t and the calculated tristimulus value t_{NN} is minimized using nonlinear optimization method.

The tristimulus value C_{prop} corrected by the proposed method is defined as :

$$C_{prop} = M^T L_0 R_d(C, M, Y) \tag{9}$$

$R_d(C, M, Y)$ corresponds to the determined spectral reflectance by this optimization process.

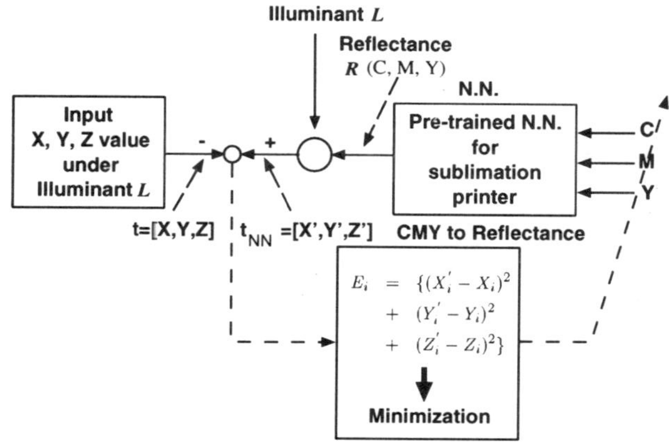

Figure 5: Color correction method using a neural network. The spectral reflectance is updated by nonlinear optimization process.

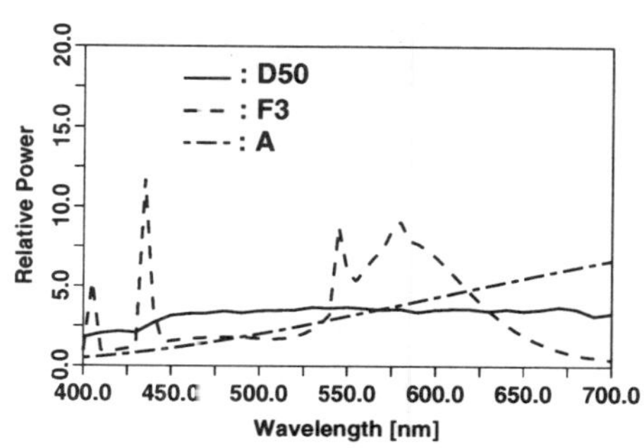

Figure 6: Spectral distribution of the illuminants. For daylight, incandescent light, and fluorescent light, D50, A, and F3 illuminants were used.

3 Evaluation of the color correction accuracy for each method and discussions

3.1 Evaluation of the color correction accuracy for each method

125 color chips were selected from 1115 unknown data (described in section 2.3.1) such that they equally include the chips with many kinds of hue, chroma, and lightness. For evaluation of each color correction method, we calculate the tristimulus values C_{wpm}, C_{vrh}, and C_{prop} of the color chips for two cases: a fluorescent F3 illuminant and an incandescent A illuminant. These are compared to the tristimulus values obtained for actual spectral reflectances under daylight illuminant D50. Figure 6 indicates the spectral distribution of each illuminant are regulated by CIE. The distributions are normalized to the same total energy. Figure 7 and 8 show accuracy of each method for F3 and A illuminant respectively. The upper side of each figure indicates that the errors of color correction are plotted on a*-b* plane of CIE L*a*b* uniform color space. Symbol • is the actual tristimulus value under D50 illuminant. The thin lines correspond to the color differences between estimated and actual tristimulus values. The lower side shows the histograms of these color differences for each method. Vertical lines in this figure represent the mean color differences.

These results shows that WPM can correct the reference white perfectly but produces significant errors in the other colors under either F3 or A illuminant. The mean and maximum color difference for both illuminants are considerably large : $\Delta E_{mean} = 11.204$, $\Delta E_{max} = 25\,324$ under F3 illuminant and $\Delta E_{mean} = 9.7286$, $\Delta E_{max} = 20.768$ under A illuminant, respectively. On the contrary, the principal components method performed a correction with relatively small errors not only for the reference white but also for chromatic colors. The mean and maximum color difference for both illuminants are also relatively small : $\Delta E_{mean} = 3.8705$, $\Delta E_{max} = 17.709$ under F3 illuminant and $\Delta E_{mean} = 3.8296$, $\Delta E_{max} = 15.386$ under A illuminant, respectively. Furthermore, the proposed method can perform better correction than the principal components method, that is, $\Delta E_{mean} = 1.7076$, $\Delta E_{max} = 12.716$ under F3 illuminant and $\Delta E_{mean} = 1.4607$, $\Delta E_{max} = 11.679$ under A illuminant. This evaluation results of a proposed method indicates that the color correction errors would not be visually noticeable.

3.2 Discussions

We described a new method for a correction of the color shifts due to the illuminant changes using three layered neural network. An accuracy of color correction obtained by the proposed method fairly improved as compared with principal components method. We consider that this is because the estimation accuracy of the spectral reflectance by neural network is better than that by finite-dimensional linear model. To examine how well a neural network can approximate the spectral reflectance, we compared the estimation accuracy of a neural network with finite-dimensional linear model with three and four principal components vectors. In this evaluation, 1115 spectral reflectance data were used. The mean square error between original and estimated spectral reflectance were calculated by :

$$MSE = \frac{1}{NM} \sum_{i=1}^{M} \sum_{j=1}^{N} \{R_i(\lambda_j) - \tilde{R}_i(\lambda_j)\} \tag{10}$$

$$M \quad : \quad number\ of\ spectral\ reflectance(M = 1115)$$

Where $R_i(\lambda_j)$ and $\tilde{R}_i(\lambda_j)$ correspond to the original and the estimated spectral reflectance respectively. MSE of each model are specified in Table 3.2. A finite-dimensional linear model can not realize approx-

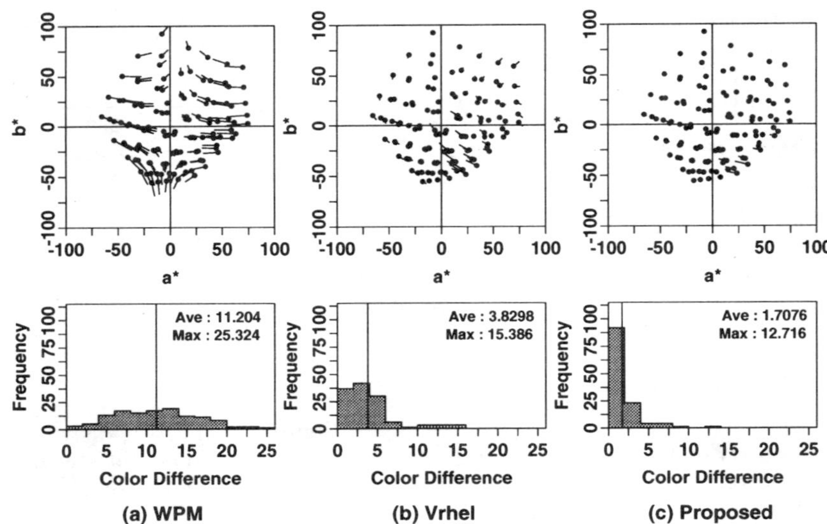

Figure 7: Accuracy of each correction method for the color shift due to the F3 illuminant.

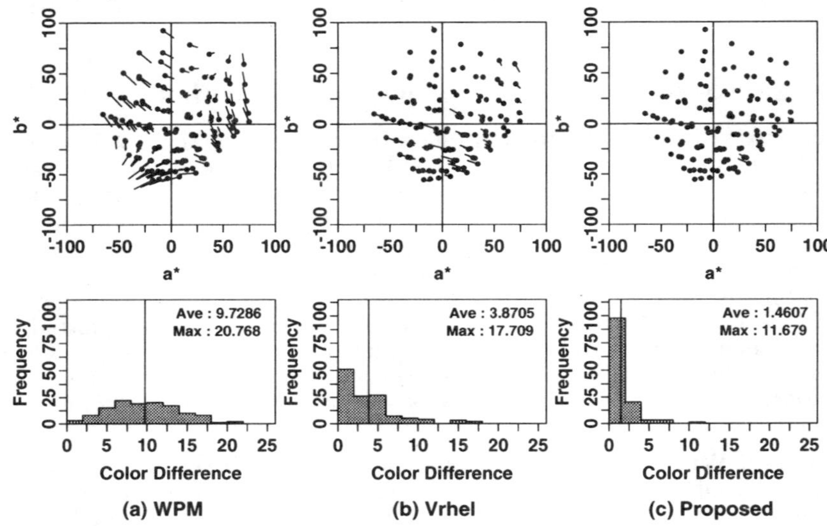

Figure 8: Accuracy of each correction method for the color shift due to the A illuminant.

imation accuracy better than a neural network even if four principal components are used. This suggests that 1115 spectral reflectance data have a nonlinearity that can not be represented by ones. Figure 9 demonstrates chromatic changes of Cyan, Magenta, and Yellow ink according to the increase of transfer density of ink. Symbol ● indicates each colors with changing transfer density from 0% to 100% at 10% steps. We can see that such nonlinearity appears in the saturation of a transfer density for Cyan and Magenta ink. To quantify chromaticity of an approximation errors for individual spectral reflectances, color difference plots on $a^* - b^*$ plane were produced and are shown in Figure 10. Each row of this figure

Table 1: Comparison of the estimation accuracy of the finite linear model with three and four principal components and the neural network model.

Method	3-terms	4-terms	N.N.
MSE	0.00123	0.000691	0.000364

represents the lightness L^*; $L^* : 20 - 25$, $L^* : 40 - 45$ and $L^* : 60 - 65$ respectively. That is, upper row indicates $a^* - b^*$ planes for darker colors. A size of the symbol ■ corresponds to the color difference. In 3-terms approximation, we can see that large approximation errors are equally distributed on $L^* : 20 - 25$ plane and when it is brighter (on $L^* : 40 - 45$ or $L^* : 60 - 65$), they appear only in highly saturated colors. This suggests that the dark colors imply a nonlinearity more than bright ones. Furthermore, from the result of 4-terms approximation, large approximation errors occurred only in dark saturated colors. We found out that those correspond to the colors with the saturation of the transfer density for Cyan and Magenta ink as shown in Figure 9. This means that it can not adequately describe such nonlinearity even though the finite-dimensional linear model with four principal components is used. In contrast, a neural network can considerably well describe such nonlinearity although a few large errors remain in dark saturated colors. We thus consider that the proposed method can realize the color correction with fairly well accuracy as compared with the principal components method because of the approximation accuracy of the spectral reflectance using a neural network.

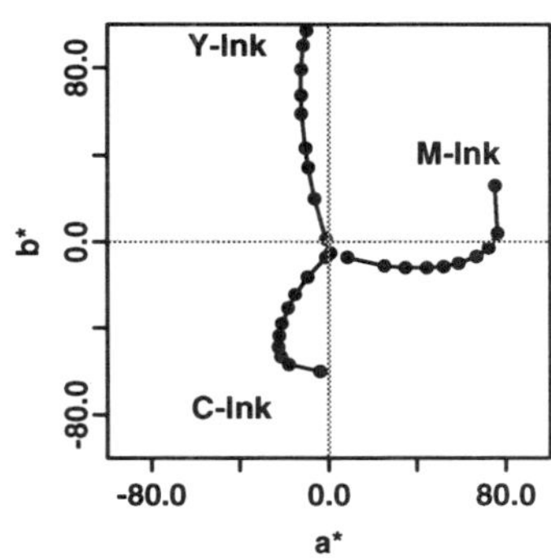

Figure 9: Chromatic changes of Cyan, Magenta, and Yellow ink according to the increase of density

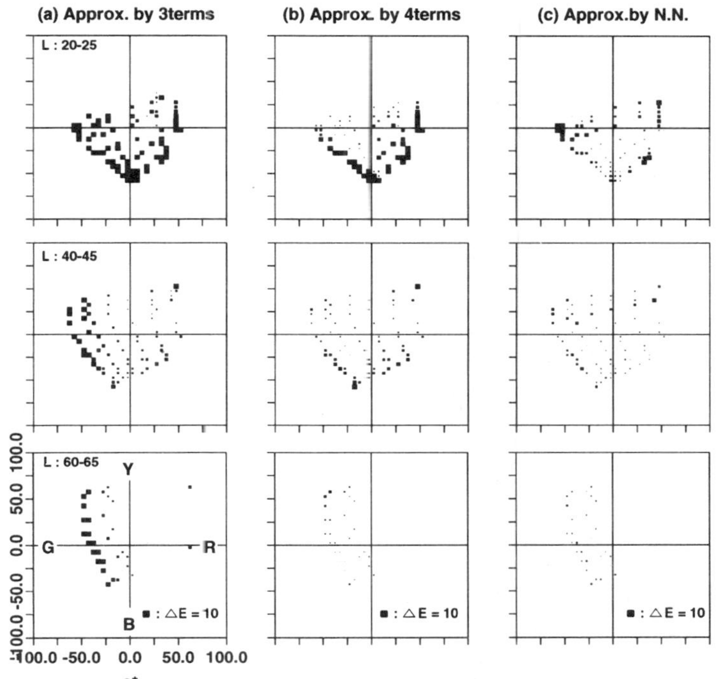

Figure 10: Comparison of the approximation accuracy between a linear model with a small number of principal components and a neural network.

4   Conclusions

A new method of color correction using an approximation of the spectral reflectance by a neural network was described and compared to the standard method of the white-point mapping and principal components method. These methods were tested on spectral reflectance of color chip reproduced by a dye-sublimation printer under F3 and A illuminant. We found out that the proposed method produced color errors less noticeable than white-point mapping method and principal components method. That is, the mean and the maximum color difference was $\Delta E_{mean} = 1.7076$, $\Delta E_{max} = 12.716$ under F3 illuminant and $\Delta E_{mean} = 1.4607$, $\Delta E_{max} = 11.679$ under A illuminant, respectively.

A proposed method still have some problem. Particularly, we must have to know the spectral distribution of an illuminant for correcting the color shifts. Recently, it has been shown that either the spectral reflectance or the spectral distribution of an illuminant can be estimated simultaneously based on a computational study of the human color vision [7]. We would need to adopt such method for estimation of an illuminant.

References

[1] M.J.Vrhel, H.J.Trussell, "Color Correction using Principal Components", *Color Research and Application*, Vol.17, No.5, pp. 328-338, October 1992.

[2] J.Cohen, "Dependency of the Spectral Reflectance Curves of the Munsell Color Chips", *Psychonomic Sci.*, vol.1, pp.369-370, 1964.

[3] L.T.Maloney, "Computational Approaches to Color Constancy", *Tech. Rep. 1985-01*, Applied Psychological Laboratory, Dept. of Psychology, Stanford University, 1985.

[4] L.T.Maloney and B.A.Wandell, "Color Constancy: a Method for Recovering Surface Spectral Reflectance", *J. Opt. Soc. Am.*, vol.A, No.3, pp.29-33, 1986.

[5] R.Gershon and A.D.Jepson, "The Computation of Color Constant Descriptors in Chromatic Images", *Color Research and Application*, vol.14, No.6, pp.325-334, 1989.

[6] E.Oja, *Subspace Methods of Pattern Recognition*: John Wiley & Sons 1983.

[7] K.Takebe,S.Nakauchi and S.Usui : "A Computational Model for Color Constancy by Separating Reflectance and Illuminant Edges within a Scene", *Neural Networks* (in printing), 1996.

A Stereo Matching Network and Its Biological Implications

Tomoya Tsukahara†, Yuzo Hirai‡
† Doctoral Program in Engineering University of Tsukuba
1-1-1 Ten-nodai, Tsukuba Ibaraki 305, Japan
e-mail: tomo@viplab.is.tsukuba.ac.jp
‡ Institute of Information Sciences and Electronics University of Tsukuba
1-1-1 Ten-no dai, Tsukuba Ibaraki 305, Japan
e-mail: hirai@is.tsukuba.ac.jp

Abstract— In this paper a stereo matching network which can reconstruct curved surfaces portrayed in random-dot stereograms is proposed. To discover surfaces from random-dot stereograms, cooperation between neighboring epipolar lines is essential because monocular regions along sharp depth edges will disturb correct matching. In this paper, the ordering constraint used in Hirai and Fukushima network[1] has been extended to the forbidden cone to incorporate that cooperation. There is only inhibitory interaction between a matching element at the vertex of the forbidden cone and every element in the upper and the lower parts of the cone. A series of simulation studies shows that the present network can locate curved surfaces successfully. It is also shown that the network can reproduce some of the response properties of *tuned excitatory, tuned inhibitory, far* and *near* neurons found in primate visual cortices.

1   Introduction

Since mid-1970s, many stereo matching algorithms [1]–[5] have been proposed. Most of the algorithms showed good performance in finding planar surfaces from random-dot stereograms[6], but not for curved surfaces with large curvatures. Pollard et al. showed that PMF algorithm[5] could recover sloping surfaces and jagged surfaces from random-dot stereograms. In their algorithm the forbidden cone which was derived from psychological data on *binocular fusion*[7] was used to implement smoothness constraint. Smoothness constraint has widely been used in stereo matching algorithms[2][4][5] because it works well for certain types of transparent surfaces[4][8]. It has been expressed by excitatory interaction between neighboring matching elements with disparities satisfying predetermined smoothness. Smoothness is specified by the disparity gradient limit of the forbidden cone. The performance of these algorithms clearly depends on the magnitude of the limit. The larger the limit becomes, the weaker the disambiguating power becomes[5][9]. In the PMF algorithm, the disparity gradient limit was set to 1.0 which came from the data on binocular fusion[7]. It should be noted, however, that the binocular fusion and the binocular stereopsis are closely related but different phenomena[10]. As we will demonstrate below, we can perceive 3-D surfaces which contain disparity gradients greater than 1.0.

Ordering constraint is another effective constraint which has been used in[1][3]. Hirai and Fukushima implemented the constraint only by inhibitory interaction between matching elements which violated that constraint. The two-dimensional inhibitory field derived from the constraint corresponds to disparity gradient greater than or equal to 2.0. It was shown that the performance was independent of the curvature of a surface because there was no excitatory interaction that would limit the detectable curvature. On the other hand, since the inhibitory interaction is confined to a single binocular field defined by a pair of epipolar lines, the performance will deteriorate when monocular dots exist.

The effect of monocular dots can be avoided by taking into account the fact that correlation of depths between neighboring epipolar lines is high when surface is locally smooth. This is just the smoothness constraint, but it is implemented in an *implicit* form in this paper. The inhibitory field of ordering constraint is extended to three-dimensional inhibitory volume. The volume is like the forbidden cone, but the disparity gradient limit is set to 2.0 along the horizontal axis and is set to 1.0 along the vertical axis. There is only inhibitory interaction between a matching element at the vertex of the cone and every element in the upper and the lower parts of the cone.

Recent neurophysiological data have shown that in primate visual cortices, there are four types of disparity sensitive neurons[11][12]. They are *tuned excitatory, tuned inhibitory, far* and *near* neurons. It is shown that only inhibitory interaction can reproduce similar disparity tuning curves of tuned excitatory neurons. The fact that the disparity tuning curves of tuned inhibitory, far and near neurons can also be reproduced by the inhibitory interaction implemented by forbidden cone is also shown.

The structure of this paper is as follows. In Section 2, after definitions of symbols describing the network are introduced, the original Hirai-Fukushima network is briefly described and it is extended to incorporate the forbidden cone. In Section 3, the performance of the network is shown by a series of simulation studies. The performance is compared to the performance of Marr and Poggio's first algorithm. In Section 4, biological implications of the present network is discussed. Section 5 concludes this paper.

2 Structure of the Network

2.1 Definitions of symbols

Let a pair of random-dot stereograms be defined by $L^{n \times m}$ and $R^{n \times m}$ as shown in Figure 1. $L^{n \times m}$ represents an image on the left of an $n \times m$ array and $R^{n \times m}$ represents a one on the right. Each image consists of dots denoted by l_i^k and r_j^k on k-th epipolar lines, where $i, j = 1, 2, ..., m$ and $k = 1, 2, ..., n$. A pair of k-th epipolar lines construct the k-th disparity field, denoted by B^k. In the following discussion each element, $b_{i,j}^k$, is assumed to be a processing element activated by taking logical AND or minimum of the inputs, l_i^k and r_j^k, from respective eyes. Each element represents a possible binocular correspondence and is called a *matching element* in this work.

Here, we define relative disparity and relative distance between two matching elements in a disparity field B^k. Let us consider two matching elements, $b_{i,j}^k$ and $b_{p,q}^k$, as illustrated in Figure 1. The relative disparity, d, is the difference between the two disparities and is defined by

$$d = |(q - p) - (j - i)| \ . \tag{1}$$

The relative distance, D, is the horizontal distance between the positions of the two elements projected on to zero disparity plane and is defined by

$$D = |\frac{p + q}{2} - \frac{i + j}{2}| \ . \tag{2}$$

The relative disparity and the relative distance defined above can be considered as coordinate transformation of disparity field. The new coordinates of a matching element $b_{i,j}^k$ in a disparity field B^k are represented by a set of three axes x, y and z. The x represents the horizontal axis and the y represents the vertical axis in a cyclopean image plane, and the z represents the depth axis corresponding to disparity. They are all defined as follows:

$$\begin{cases} x = \frac{i+j}{2} \\ y = k \\ z = \frac{j-i}{2} . \end{cases} \tag{3}$$

The x and the y axis are defined as to take the dimension of a cyclopean image, which is the same as the dimensions of input images. The z axis is defined as to take a negative value when the position of an object is closer than the fixation point and as to take a positive value when the position is farther than it. According to this transformation, the disparity d and the distance D between two points, $P_0(x_0, y, z_0)$ and $P(x, y, z)$, are defined by

$$d \ = \ 2|z - z_0|, \text{ and} \tag{4}$$

$$D \ = \ |x - x_0|. \tag{5}$$

2.2 Hirai–Fukushima network

Hirai and Fukushima[1] employed (a)*uniqueness* and (b)*ordering* constraint which can be stated as follows:

(a) A stimulus feature in one eye should be matched to no more than one feature in the other eye.

(b) *Horizontal* order of stimuli in each eye has to be preserved in the resultant match in a disparity field.

These constraints can be expressed by a disparity gradient which is defined by d/D. From Eq.(1) and Eq.(2), the uniqueness constraint is violated by two matching elements when they satisfy $d/D = 2$. The ordering constraint is violated when $d/D > 2$. From Eq.(4) and Eq.(5), the two-dimensional region where the uniqueness and the ordering constraints are violated against b_{x_0,z_0}^y is expressed as follows:

$$|z - z_0| \ge |x - x_0| \tag{6}$$

where both b_{x_0,z_0}^y and $b_{x,z}^y$ are in the same y-th disparity field.

In Hirai-Fukushima network, the uniqueness and the ordering constraints are implemented by inhibitory interaction between a matching element b_{x_0,z_0}^y and every element in the region defined by Eq. (6). The model worked well when a surface was smooth and the number of stimuli in each pair of epipolar lines was identical. If there is a sharp depth edge, however, a monocular region will appear and it will disturb correct matching in binocular region.

2.3 The present network

In order to avoid the effect of monocular regions and to obtain correct correspondence, most algorithms have employed the smoothness constraint which implies that a surface is locally smooth in the vertical y-direction in 3-D space as well as in the horizontal x-direction. The performance of such algorithm depends on both the spatial properties of the excitatory interaction and the dot-density of input images. But human vision can tolerate large variations in the spatial properties of input images. The purpose of this paper is to propose a stereo matching network which can tolerate these variations.

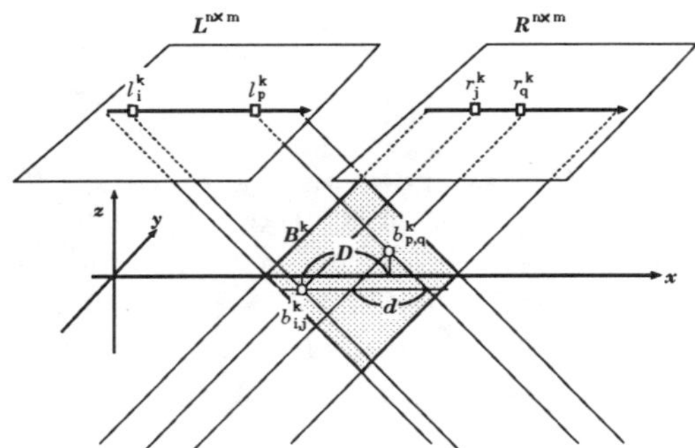

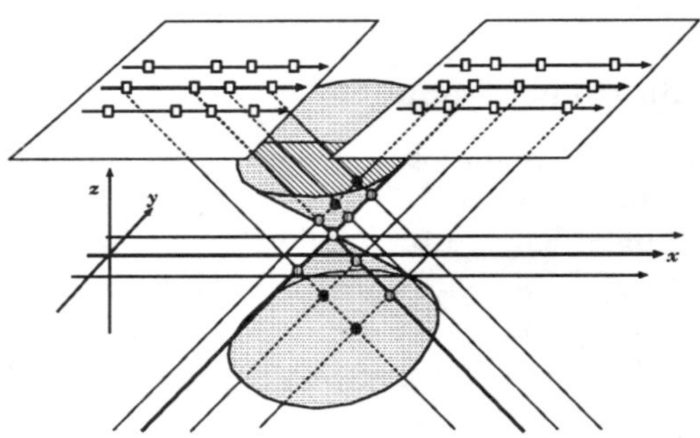

Figure 1: Definitions of input image planes($L^{n \times m}$ and $R^{n \times m}$), disparity field(B^k), relative distance(D) and relative disparity(d) between two matching elements. See text.

Figure 2: Forbidden cone for a matching element denoted by an open circle. The boundary of the cone is delineated by the disparity gradient 2.0 in the x–z plane, and 1.0 in the y–z plane. The triangular section marked by hatching, which goes through the vertex of the cone and is parallel to x-z plane, represents the uniqueness and the ordering constraints used in Hirai and Fukushima (1978). Matching elements violating the uniqueness constraint are denoted by shaded small circles, and those violating the ordering constraint are denoted by filled small circles.

As discussed in the previous section, the disparity gradient greater than or equal to 2.0 violates the uniqueness and the ordering constraints. According to the Burt and Julesz's data on binocular fusion[7], the fusional limit was isotropically distributed, that is to say, the magnitude of horizontal disparity gradient limit was similar to the vertical one. Therefore, if the disparity gradient limit defined for horizontal disparity can be extend to include vertical one, the uniqueness and the ordering constraints can naturally be extended to incorporate vertical interaction as well as interaction in a single disparity field.

The disparity gradient between a matching element $b^y_{x,z}$ and another matching element $b^\eta_{\xi,\zeta}$ is defined by

$$\frac{d}{D} = \frac{2|\zeta - z|}{\sqrt{(\xi - x)^2 + (\eta - y)^2}} \quad,$$

The region where $\frac{d}{D} \geq 2$ holds is described by

$$(\zeta - z)^2 \geq (\xi - x)^2 + (\eta - y)^2 \quad. \tag{7}$$

This region consists of two cones and is called *forbidden cone.*

However, isotropic disparity gradient limit did not provide satisfactory results. From the definition of disparity field given by Eq.(3), the fact that the density of matching elements in the horizontal direction is larger than that in the vertical direction by the factor of 2 can be seen. By taking into account this difference, we introduce an anisotropic forbidden cone whose diameter in y direction is two times larger than that in x direction. Therefore, the disparity gradient in y direction becomes 1, and Eq.(7) becomes

$$(\zeta - z)^2 \geq (\xi - x)^2 + (\frac{\eta - y}{2})^2 \quad. \tag{8}$$

The anisotropic forbidden cone is illustrated in Figure 2.

The present network uses the forbidden cone to define the extent of inhibitory interaction as opposed to the other algorithms[4][5]. The behavior of the present network is described by the following nonlinear differential equations:

$$\tau \frac{db^y_{x,z}(t)}{dt} = -b^y_{x,z}(t) + e^y_{x,z} + \sum_{\xi,\eta,\zeta \in V^y_{x,z}} w_{x,y,z,\xi,\eta,\zeta} \cdot \varphi(b^\eta_{\xi,\zeta}(t)), \tag{9}$$

where τ is the time constant and was set to 1.0. It does not affect the performance, but a converge time is longer as the value of τ is greater. The output function $\varphi()$ is an analog threshold function defined by

$$\varphi(u) = \left\{ \begin{array}{ll} u & \text{if } u > 0 \\ 0 & \text{otherwise.} \end{array} \right.$$

Binocular input to the element $b^y_{x,z}$ is represented by $e^y_{x,z}$. It takes a value 1 when both l^y_{x-z} and r^y_{x+z} are black pixels, otherwise it takes a value 0. The $w_{x,y,z,\xi,\eta,\zeta}$ represents an inhibitory weight from the element $b^\eta_{\xi,\zeta}$ to $b^y_{x,z}$. Inhibitory input comes from every element in the anisotropic forbidden cone, $V^y_{x,z}$.

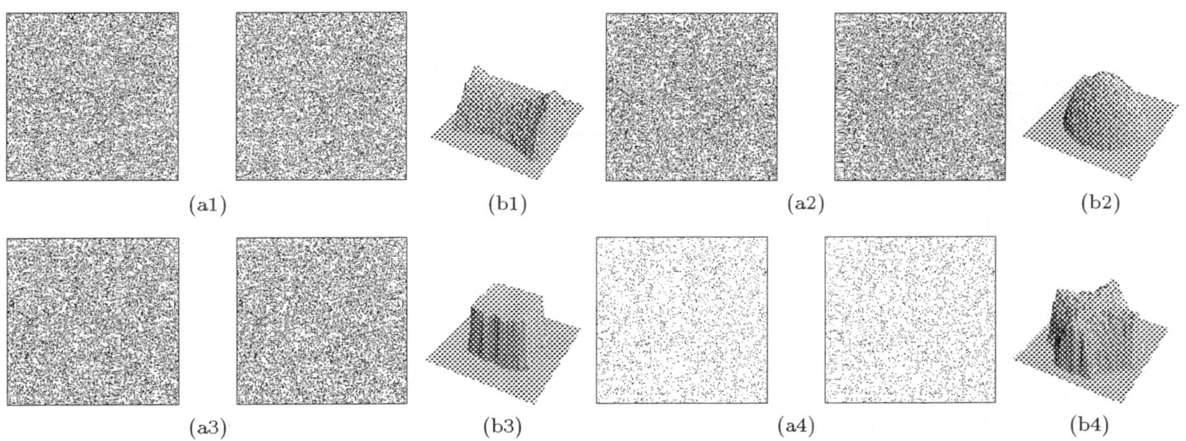

(a1)   (b1)   (a2)   (b2)

(a3)   (b3)   (a4)   (b4)

Figure 3: (a)Random-dot stereograms used in this study, and (b) the reconstructed surfaces obtaind by our network. Each stereogram is composed of 256 × 256 pixels and the dot-density is 20% except the one shown in (a4) where it is 5%. The maximum disparity is 12 pixels in every stereogram. When the dot-density is 20%, there are about 2.4 monocular dots under the highest peak on average.

The strength of inhibitory weight is defined by

$$
w_{x,y,z,\xi,\eta,\zeta} = \left\{ \begin{array}{ll} W(\frac{2}{3})^{|\eta - y|} & \text{if } b_{\xi,\zeta}^{\eta} \in V_{x,z}^{y} \\ 0 & \text{otherwise.} \end{array} \right. \tag{10}
$$

In order to permit the Panum's limit case in which uniqueness constraint is violated, the value of W must be less than 1.0. Another condition is that an incorrectly matched element must continuously be suppressed by correctly matched elements after the network converged to an equilibrium state. So that the strength of the inhibition must not be less than 0.5. In all simulation studies described below, the strength W was set to 0.6. The fraction $\frac{2}{3}$ was chosen experimentally. The inhibitory strength decreases as the distance between epipolar lines increases. This comes from the fact that when a surface is locally smooth, the correlation of depths between epipolar lines will decrease as the distance increases.

The inhibitory interaction in the vertical direction was limited to $|y - y'| \leq 10$ epipolar lines. In order to avoid the calculation of vain matching, the horizontal disparity was limited to $|z| \leq 18$.

3   Performance of the Network

Random-dot stereograms used in this study and the reconstructed surfaces by the present network are shown in Figure 3(a1) to (a4) and in Figure (b1) to (b4), respectively.

In Figure 3(b1), the performance of the network for a reconstructed saddle surface is shown. More than 97% correct matching could be found in this case. Most of the failures in finding correct matching were confined to the narrow regions running along the two sharp depth edges. Hirai-Fukushima network could find only 47.5% correct matching in this case. The improvement of the performance is evident.

It should be noted, however, that the network will not converge to the final state at one time because local minima produced by monocular dots will trap the behavior of the network. When it comes to a local minimum, however, the responses of correctly matched elements become equal to the magnitudes of their inputs. On the contrary, the responses of incorrectly matched elements, which will be mutually inhibited through forbidden cones, become less than their inputs. Therefore, incorrectly matched responses can be identified and ignored. By resetting the initial conditions for incorrect elements to zero and setting the initial conditions for correct elements to 1, and by running the network again, it will be settled to another local minimum whose energy might be smaller than the previous one because the correct elements will uncover other correct elements which were previously inactivated by the incorrect ones. The results were obtained by repeating this procedure.

Figures (a2) and (b2) show another example, a semispherical surface. In this case, there are only a few monocular dots and 99.5% correct matching could be found. The maximum gradient of the surface was 2.8. Figures (a3) and (b3) show an example of square, planar surface. In this case, although there are sharp depth edges surrounding the periphery of the square, over 90% correct matching could be found. Figure (a4) and (b4) show an example of crossed semicylindrical surface. Although the dot-density was changed to 5% in this case, the present network found more than 98% correct matching without changing network parameters.

The performance of the present network is compared with Marr-Poggio algorithm[2] as listed in Table 1. The parameters of their algorithm were adjusted to attain maximum performance in every case.

Table 1: Performance of the present network and Marr-Poggio algorithm.

		(a1)† saddle	(a2) semisphere	(a3) square	(a4) crossed cylinders
Present network	correct	97.2%	99.5%	90.8%	98.3%
	incorrect	0.2%	0.0%	1.3%	0.1%
	unmatch	2.6%	0.5%	7.9%	1.6%
Marr–Poggio algorithm	correct	92.3%	87.2%	98.2%	82.8%
	incorrect	2.3%	3.6%	1.6%	0.8%
	unmatch	5.4%	9.2%	0.2%	16.4%

$\dagger$: These symbols indicate the stereograms shown in Figure 3.

As seen in the table, in all cases except *square*, the performance of the present network is better than Marr-Poggio algorithm. In the case of square, the present network could not find correct matching along sharp depth edges surrounding the square. This can be seen in the relatively high percentage of unmatching. It should be noted, however, that in all cases, the percentages of incorrect matching of the present network is smaller than Marr-Poggio algorithm.

4 Biological implication

Recent neurophysiological studies have found that there are four types of binocular neurons in primate visual cortices[12]: *tuned excitatory, tuned inhibitory, far* and *near* neurons. A tuned excitatory neuron responds to a narrow range of disparities with activation and reveals a sharp disparity tuning characteristic. On the contrary, a tuned inhibitory neuron responds to a narrow range of disparities around zero disparity with inhibition. A far neuron responds with activation to a wide range of disparities in the far side of fixation and with inhibition in the near side. A near neuron responds in an opposite way to the far neuron.

Since these response characteristics were investigated by using narrow bar stimuli, we simulated the response characteristics of our network using a binocular pair of long bar stimuli. The width of each stimulus was set to 7 pixels, the length to 256 pixels, and the disparity was set to zero.

The situation of this simulation is different from the neurophysiological experiments described in[12] in two respects. (1) In the neurophysiological experiments, moving bar stimuli were used, but stationary stimuli were used in our case. To mimic moving stimulus which will go out of the receptive field soon, we only take into account of the first part of the response evoked by a stationary stimulus. (2) Disparity tuning curves of single neurons were obtained by changing stimulus disparity, but they were obtained by the responses of matching elements with different disparities in our case. Tuning curves obtained by both methods may be equivalent. Since stimulus disparity, z_s, was fixed to zero in this simulation, the relative disparity between the stimulus and a matching element, which is defined by $z_s - z = -z$, should be taken as the disparity used in neurophysiological experiment. In this case and in the following, disparity tuning curves are plotted along this relative disparity.

The time courses of the responses of four matching elements, $b_{x_0,-2}^{y_0}$, $b_{x_0,0}^{y_0}$, $b_{x_0,2}^{y_0}$ and $b_{x_0,4}^{y_0}$, are shown in Figure 4(a). To examine the detail of the time course, the time constant was set to 60 in this case. To mimic moving stimuli, only the first fifty time steps of numerical calculation are considered as shown in the figure. During this time interval, the responses of matching elements selective to near zero disparities are suppressed by the 40-th iteration. The disparity tuning curve shown in Figure 4(b) is obtained by time-averaging the individual responses of the matching elements. The shape of the disparity tuning curve has similarity to the neurophysiological one obtained from *tuned zero* excitatory neurons. Since our network has no excitatory interaction, the neurophysiologically obtained tuning curves may not provide direct evidence for the existence of excitatory interaction.

For each matching element there are two cones defined by Eq.(10): one opens toward the direction of nearer disparities($\zeta < z$), and the other one opens toward the opposite direction($\zeta > z$). Let us call them near-cone and far-cone, respectively. Here we assume that there are two (excitatory or inhibitory) interneurons for each matching element: one gathers activities in the near-cone and the other one in the far-cone. Time-averaged responses of these interneurons are calculated in the same way as tuned excitatory neurons. The disparity tuning of the responses of interneurons gathering activities in their *far*-cones is shown in Figure 4(c). It is very similar to the *far* neurons reported in Figure 8 of[12]. The responses of *near*-cones is the mirror image of *far*-cones and is also very similar to the *near* neurons.

These tuning curves were obtained by a stimulus with zero disparity. By changing the stimulus disparity, tuning curves will shift to the far or near side according to the stimulus disparity, so that Figure 4(b) would become *tuned far* and *tuned near* excitatory neurons, and tuning curves of far (Figure 4(c)) and near neurons will shift to the far or near side. On the other hand, all far and near neurons reported in[12] have tuning curves whose midpoints are at or near zero disparity. They suggested, however, that tuning curves of tuned far and tuned near neurons could possibly reflect incomplete summation in far and near neurons. Many far and near neurons with midpoints at nonzero disparities have been found in MST [13].

Disparity tuning curves for *tuned inhibitory* neurons may be obtained by combining the responses of the two interneurons at the same position. Since all of tuned inhibitory neurons investigated so far have

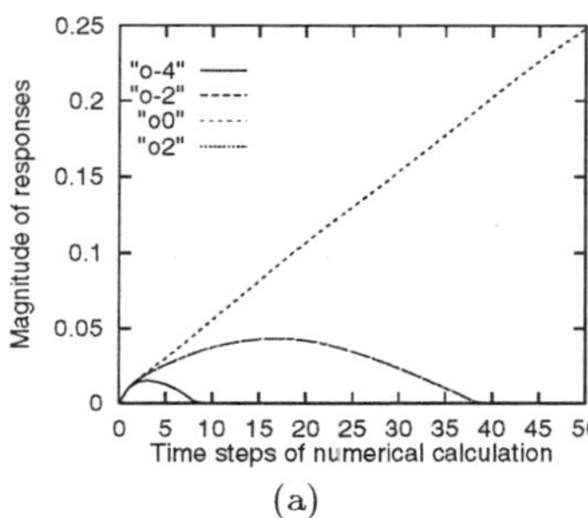 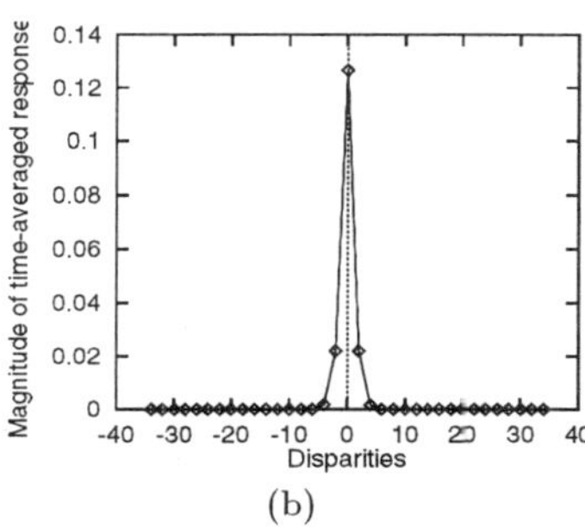 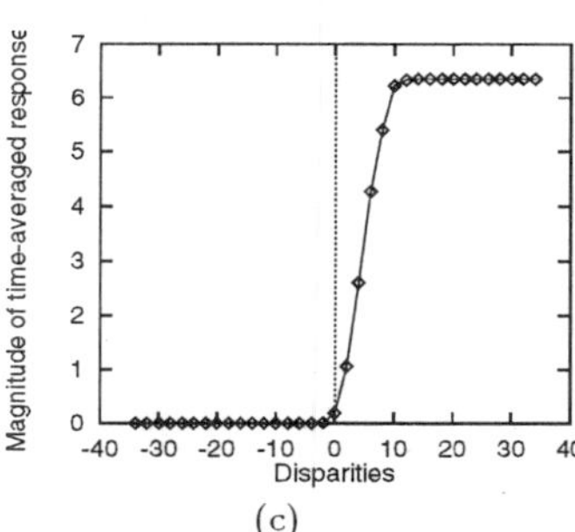

(a) (b) (c)

Figure 4: Simulation result for *tuned excitatory* neurons and *far* neurons. (a) Time courses of the responses of four matching elements, $b^{y_0}_{x_0,-2}$, $b^{y_0}_{x_0,0}$, $b^{y_0}_{x_0,2}$ and $b^{y_0}_{x_0,4}$. They are indicated by using relative disparities as o2, o0, o-2 and o-4, respectively. Since the responses of o2 and o-2 are identical, they are merged into a single line. (b) Disparity tuning curve obtained by time-averaging the responses of matching elements with different disparities. Horizontal axis is represented by relative disparities. (c) Disparity tuning curve of *far*-cones. Definition of the horizontal axis is the same as in (b).

tuning curves whose maximal inhibition occurs at or near zero disparity, this type of neurons may not contribute to *tuned far* and *tuned near* excitatory neurons. It is not clear, however, whether far, near and tuned inhibitory neurons have excitatory or inhibitory effects in disparity detection and how they interact with tuned excitatory neurons.

5 Conclusion

In this paper a stereo matching network is proposed and is applied to a variety of random-dot stereograms. The results of simulation studies have shown that in most cases, the network can find curved surfaces portrayed in stereograms more accurately than the previously proposed algorithms. The network exploits anisotropic forbidden cone to disambiguate possible binocular correspondences. It is shown that the network can reproduce some of the response properties of binocular neurons found in primate visual cortices.

Although we show that the forbidden cone has great disambiguating power, we do not intend to exclude the smoothness constraint. We will include it in combination with the forbidden cone. We will compare the performance in a future publication to the other smoothness constraint algorithms using various types of random-dot stereograms including transparent stereograms, ambiguous ones, and dynamic ones. We will also apply the network to real world scenes by incorporating feature extraction networks.

References

[1] Y. Hirai and K. Fukushima, "An inference upon the neural network finding binocular correspondence," *Biological Cybernetics*, **31**, pp.209–217, 1978.

[2] D. Marr and T. Poggio, "A cooperative computation of stereo disparity," *Science*, **194**, pp.283–287, 1976.

[3] H. H. Baker and T. O. Binford, "Depth from edge and intensity based stereo," *Proceedings of 7th International Joint Conference on Artificial Intelligence*, 631–636, 1981.

[4] K. Prazdny, "Detection of binocular disparities," *Biological Cybernetics*, **52**, pp.93–99, 1985.

[5] S. B. Pollard *et al.* "PMF: A stereo correspondence algorithm using a disparity gradient limit," *Perception*, **14**, pp.449–470, 1985.

[6] B. Julesz, *Foundations of Cyclopean Perception.*, Chicago: University of Chicago Press, pp.203ff, 1971.

[7] P. Burt and B. Julesz, "A disparity gradient limit for binocular fusion," *Science*, **208**, pp.615–617, 1980.

[8] S. B. Pollard and J. P. Frisby "Transparency and the uniqueness constraint in human and computer stereo vision," *Nature*, vol.347, pp.553–536, 1990.

[9] J. P. Frisby and S. B. Pollard, "Computational issues in solving the stereo correspondence problem. In computational models of visual processing," Landy, M. S. and Movshon, J. A. eds., *The MIT Press*, 1991.

[10] K. N. Ogle, "On the limits of stereoscopic vision," *Journal of Experimental Psychology*, Vol.44, No.4, pp.253–259, 1952.

[11] G. F. Poggio *et al*, "Responses of neurons in visual cortex (V1 and V2) of the alert macaque to dynamic random-dot stereograms," *Vision Research*, **25**, pp.397–406, 1985.

[12] G. F. Poggio *et al*, "Stereoscopic mechanisms in monkey visual cortex: Binocular correlation and disparity selectivity," *The Journal of Neuroscience*, vol.8, pp.4531–4550, 1988.

[13] J. P. Roy *et al*, "Disparity sensitivity of neurons in monkey extrastriate area MST," *The Journal of Neuroscience*, vol.12, pp.2478–2492, 1992.

Pattern Recognition and Image Processing

(Oral Presentation)

A Neural Network for Recognizing Rotated Patterns and Estimating Their Rotation Angle

Minoru Fukumi and Norio Akamatsu

University of Tokushima, Faculty of Engineering
2-1, Minami-josanjima, Tokushima 770 Japan,
E-mail: fukumi@is.tokushima-u.ac.jp

Abstract— This paper considers a rotation invariant neural pattern recognition system, which can recognize rotated patterns and estimate their rotation angle. It consists of a preprocessing network to detect edge features of input patterns and a trainable multilayered network. The multilayered network has two output layers, which are a part to recognize an input pattern and a part to estimate its rotation angle. The hidden layer is commonly used by both parts. As a result, it can deal with rotation-sensitive and -insensitive information. It is shown that, by means of computer simulations on a coin recognition problem, the system is able to recognize rotated patterns and estimate their rotation angle.

1   Introduction

Artificial neural networks have been a focus of active research for the last decade, owing to those effectiveness for many problems, pattern recognition, optimization, control, and so forth. Many neural network systems insensitive to different kinds of transformation have now been presented [3]–[15]. However, there is still no useful system insensitive to translation, rotation, and scale. It seems that there have been a few systems imitating the visual system of brain. Elucidation of brain function is important to model it, and also in engineering applications.

It is suggested that, in order to perform invariance to translation and scale, the brain individually normalizes them [1],[2]. For example, the human visual system catches a visual target in its fovea by using the saccadic and the smooth pursuit movements in order to perform the translational invariance. Neural pattern recognition systems based on such a point have been proposed [13]–[15]. Furthermore, it was reported that the scale invariance is achieved by properly using channels with different sizes [16]. The system with such a principle has been presented [5],[14].

With regard to the rotational invariance, it is well known that the human sometimes causes the *mental rotation* to recognize a rotated form [17]. Consideration on the rotational invariance, including this phenomenon, has never been a satisfying level. It seems to be possible to construct a neural network system invariant to translation, scale, and rotation by using a single network. However, it can result in a large system [7],[9]. As those invariance may be individually performed in our brains, it would be important to normalize them separately. Since systems insensitive to translation and scale, which are similar to the saccadic movement, have been presented [13]–[15], we examine a method to perform a normalization for rotation, which is to estimate a rotation angle.

Authors have presented rotation invariant neural pattern recognition systems [18]–[20]. They are effective for a rotated pattern recognition problem. However, they do not have the ability to estimate the rotation angle of an input pattern. Systems which possess it have been already presented [8],[21]. As those systems use a kind of pattern matching method, it is not clear whether they are effective for gray scale images, and they are time-consuming to check out every number of rotation angle to select one.

This paper presents a neural network which can be invariant to rotation of input patterns and estimate their rotation angle. Finally, it is shown that, by means of computer simulations on a coin recognition problem, the system is effective to recognize rotated patterns and estimate their rotation angle compared with conventional systems.

2   A Rotation Invariant Neural Network

A rotation invariant neural network presented in this paper is shown in Fig. 1. It consists of a feature extraction network as a preprocessor and a trainable multilayered network. The preprocessor detects edge features of an input pattern to activate a set of orientation specificity (selectivity) cells according to edge direction included in it. This activity pattern with a 3-dimensional structure is an input pattern into the multilayered network. This pattern, however, is not rotationally invariant. The invariance is accomplished in the multilayered

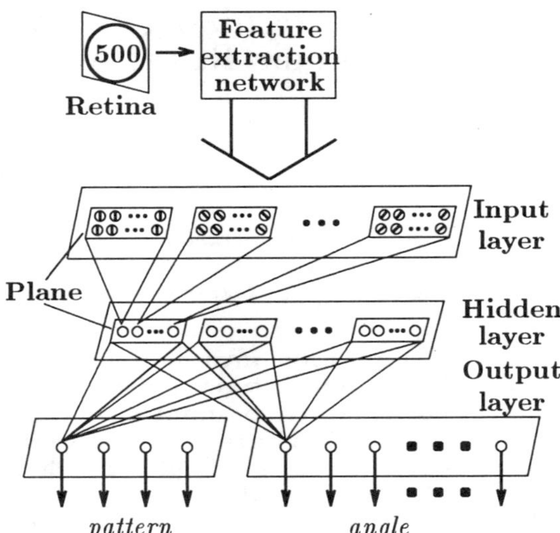

Fig. 1: A neural network to recognize a rotated pattern and to estimate its rotation angle. A hidden layer is used by two different parts in common, although it can be divided into two networks.

network.

As shown in Fig. 1, it is a 3-layered network, in which the input pattern is the edge features from the preprocessor. The network includes in its output layer two different parts, a pattern recognition and a rotation angle estimation parts. Its hidden layer is used in common by both. In learning, different teacher signals are given to the parts, while their trainings simultaneously proceed. In other word, it can gain both the properties sensitive and insensitive to rotation after learning.

2.1 Preprocessing Network

The preprocessor is shown in Fig. 2. It consists of an edge detection layer and a 3-dimensional structure of the orientation specificity cells (OSCs), which is described as an OSC-layer on the same level in Fig. 2.

A square labeled "EN" indicates the edge detection network. Each EN takes an area of a pattern on the retina to compute edge intensity and direction. Then, it produces the directions with high intensity to activate the cells in the OSC-layer. In Fig. 2, a radial and a circumference directions refer to a horizontal and a vertical directions in the edge detection layer and each plane of the OSC-layer, respectively.

In the OSC-layer, the OSCs are arranged in order. The OSC-layer consists of many planes, which include the cells with the same specificity as many as the EN in the edge detection layer. Each cell gets a signal only from the corresponding EN. The number of planes is the same as the division number of the circumference of the pattern on the retina.

Each EN produces the edge directions of the predefined number to activate the cells with specificity near those. In this paper, the Sobel operator with size of 3×3 is used to detect edges. As a result, the preprocessor can produce a rough edge feature of the pattern.

2.2 The multilayered Network

The multilayered network with sigmoid type neuron units is trained by the improved BP to produce desired outputs [18]–[20]. It is trained under restraint in order to achieve a rotational invariance. Also, it has in an output layer two different parts : one can recognize patterns and the other can estimate a rotation angle of patterns.

When an input pattern is rotated, an edge feature to be activated is translated and rotated in the OSC-layer according to a rotation angle. Suppose that the circumference of the retina is divided into 8 segments and a standard pattern is given to the retina to produce the edge feature. Next, if the same pattern except rotated by 45° is given, then this edge feature is translated one on plane and on position in the plane, respectively. Therefore, in order to reach rotational invariance, the training algorithm requires a restriction to be invariant to them which vary according to a rotation angle.

The network has three layers, an input, a hidden, and an output layers. The hidden layer also

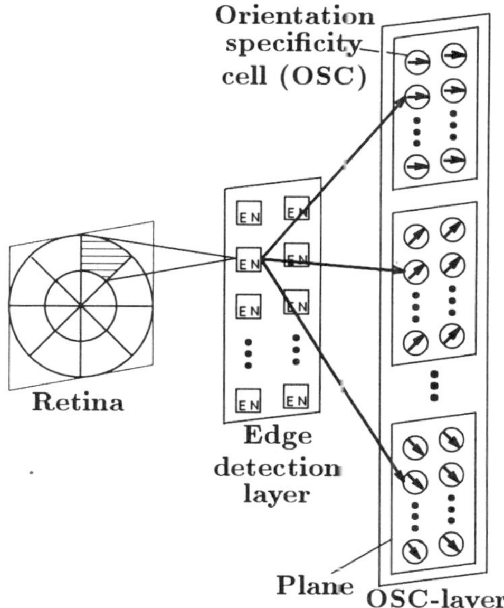

Fig. 2: Feature extraction network. It produces an edge feature to activate the OSCs in the OSC-layer.

consists of the planes, which include sigmoid neuron units as many as the division number of the circumference of the retina. The neuron units in each plane have the same weights, but their receptive fields are different. Neuron units in another plane have different weights. Let weights of the ith plane be $W_{i,k,m}, m = 1 \sim N_{TH}, k = 1 \sim N_R$, where N_{TH} and N_R are the number of segments in the circumference and the radius of the retina, respectively. The input layer (OSC-layer) consists of N_{TH} planes, each of which includes an activity pattern made up of N_R (subscript k) $\times N_{TH}$ (subscript m) OSCs. Let an activity pattern in the input layer be $S_{jj,k,mm}, mm = 1 \sim N_{TH}, k = 1 \sim N_R, jj = 1 \sim N_{TH}$, where jj indicates the jjth plane in the input layer.

Then, the net input values $\mathrm{Net}(L), L = 1 \sim N_{TH}$ to neuron units of the ith plane in the hidden layer are computed as

$$\mathrm{Net}(L) = \sum_{k=1}^{N_R} \sum_{m=1}^{N_{TH}} W_{i,k,m} \times S_{L,k,m+(L-1)}$$

Accordingly, the weights $W_{i,k,m}$ connect between the first plane in the input layer and the first neuron unit of the ith plane in the hidden layer. The second neuron unit with same weights $W_{i,k,m}$ gets inputs from the second plane in the input layer, and the receptive field are translated one to the subscript m. The same procedure is done for the others. The translation to plane and the subscript m correspond to rotation and translation of the edge feature by rotation of the input pattern, respectively. In the point of view, this is different from the traditional methods [3][4][8].

The quantity of weight change $\Delta W_{i,k,m}$ is given as an average over N_{TH} neuron units in the ith plane as follows:

$$\Delta W_{i,k,m} = \sum_{L=1}^{N_{TH}} (\Delta W_{i,k,m})_L / N_{TH},$$

where L is an index of units.

2.2.1 Pattern Recognition Part

In Fig.1, the part which produces *pattern* is to recognize an input pattern. Weights $W_{n,i}$ from a unit in the ith plane to the nth neuron in the part are also restrained to be the same as the others in the ith. The number of weights which each unit in the output layer has, therefore, is the same as the number of planes in the hidden layer. The net input to the nth output unit is computed as

$$\mathrm{Net}(n) = \sum_{i=1}^{N_S} \sum_{j=1}^{N_{TH}} W_{n,i} \times O_{i,j}$$

where $O_{i,j}$ is the output value of the jth unit in the ith plane, and N_S is the number of the planes in the hidden layer. The quantity of weight change is given as an average over N_{TH}

neuron units in the ith plane:

$$\Delta W_{n,i} = \sum_{L=1}^{N_{TH}} (\Delta W_{n,i})_L / N_{TH},$$

where L is an index of units. This is similar to that in the hidden layer.

By using the above training algorithm, a rotational invariance can be achieved in the multilayered network. Presenting a pattern to the retina causes responses from the pattern recognition part. It is clear that those will be unchanged by rotation of the pattern on the retina. Rotation of the pattern by $360°/N_{TH}$ causes an interchange of the role of the units in each planes in making their responses, but since they are all weighted equally and summed by the output units, the output response is unchanged by such a rotation.

2.2.2 Angle Estimation Part

In Fig.1, the part which produces *angle* is to estimate a rotation angle of an input pattern. In this part, rotation of the input pattern causes an interchange of the role of output units unlike the pattern recognition part. This can be achieved by having all the output units had the same weights $W_{i,j}$, where the subscripts i and j refer to an plane in the hidden layer and an unit in the ith plane, respectively. The net input to the nth output unit is computed as

$$\mathrm{Net}(n) = \sum_{i=1}^{N_S} \sum_{j=1}^{N_{TH}} W_{i,j} \times O_{i,j+(n-1)}$$

where $O_{i,j+(n-1)}$ is the output value of the $(j+n-1)$th unit in the ith plane. Therefore, a receptive field of the next output unit is translated one in the ith plane. In training, the weights of all the output units are restrained to be the same. The quantity of the weight change is given by

$$\Delta W_{i,j} = \sum_{n=1}^{N_{TH}} (\Delta W_{i,j})_n / N_{TH},$$

averaged over the output units. The desired signal is 1 for the unit related to a pattern with a standard direction and 0's for the others.

By using such a structure, rotation of the pattern causes an interchange of the role of the units in each planes in making their responses and, as a result, causes an interchanges of the output units, producing 1 and 0's. This structure enables the system to estimate the rotation angle of input patterns.

3   Simulation Results

Computer simulations for a coin image recognition are done to show the effectiveness of the system. In coin recognition, a preprocessing procedure takes out only the coin image from each original image with 256 gray levels by an image scanner in a real coin classifying machine to make an image with 40×40 pixels. A 500 won coin in South Korea and a 500 yen coin in Japan used in the simulations have the same shape and size, the similar weight and color, and the similar pattern structure [18]. A part of the 50 randomly rotated coin images per class is used to train the system and the rest is used as test samples to compute recognition accuracy. The number of edge features used is three in each circular division taken by the "EN". There is little change of the accuracy in three to six edges per circular division. The number of hidden planes in the system, N_S is 10. The number of division of the circumference in the retina, N_{TH} is 18. In this case, the angular resolution or rotational invariance is 20 degree. The results are best in $N_{TH} = 18 \sim 24$.

Recognition accuracy of pattern recognition and rotation angle estimation by two measures is shown in Table 1. It becomes better with increase of training samples. The "MAX" and the "clear" in the Tables represent measures to evaluate accuracy of pattern recognitions and rotation angle estimations. The "MAX" means the results only by considering the maximum output value in the output layer. The "clear" means the results by considering

$$\text{It is a clear result, if } (O_{\mathrm{maximum}} - O_{\mathrm{second\ maximum}}) > \theta,$$

where "O" is a value of an output unit in the networks and θ is a threshold value. In our simulations, $\theta = 0.4$.

Since the coin images used in the simulations have gray scale values, we could not get a 100 % recognition and angle estimation accuracy by using the small number of training sample. Accuracy of the pattern recognition is better than that of the angle estimation.

For reference, the other conventional method is examined for the coin recognition problem. This is illustrated in Fig. 3, which consists of a feature extraction network and a three-layered

	Our system			Conventinal		
No. of samples	1	5	10	1	5	10
Pattern recognition						
MAX (%)	87.8	97.8	99.4	53.1	85.6	90.0
clear (%)	46.9	80.0	87.5	0.0	0.0	1.3
Angle estimation						
MAX (%)	28.1	81.7	91.9	28.1	65.6	77.5
clear (%)	0.0	14.4	33.1	0.0	0.0	1.3

Table 1: Accuracy of pattern recognition and rotation angle estimation using varying number of training samples. N_{TH}=18, N_R=7, and N_S=10.

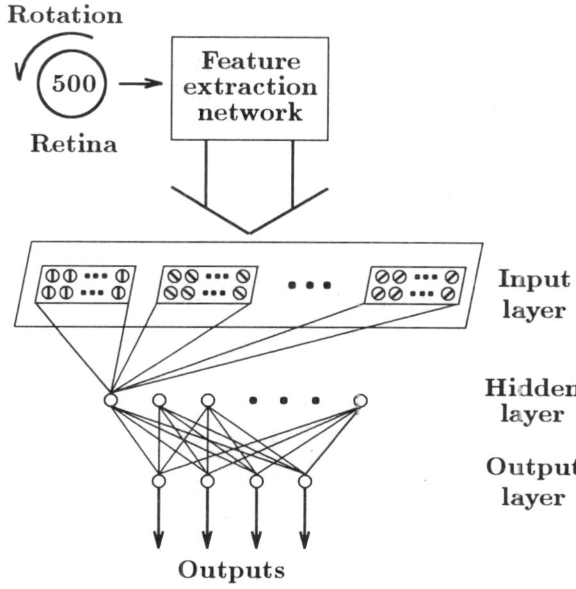

Fig. 3: A conventinal rotation invariant system.

network. The feature extraction network is the same as that shown in Fig. 2. Hidden units in the three-layered network receive inputs from every units in the input layer. The number of hidden units is 20. It has four output units for the coin recognition. Patterns with a standard orientation are used for its training. In recognition, a pattern is rotated by degrees on the retina, producing the outputs. Then, the output values for a rotated pattern and its angle information must be preserved to detect the maximum output value. After the rotations by every degree, the maximum output value is selected with its rotation angle. The unit which produced the maximum indicates its class and the angle information of the maximum output shows its rotation angle [8][21].

The results are shown in Table 1. In the measure "clear", their accuracy becomes nearly zero even for the pattern recognition. Our method gives the better results than those results. These results show that the network presented in this paper can be applied to the other practical applications.

Though the pattern recognition system can be applied to the other image recognition problems, it is not supposed to recognize deformed patterns. In order to overcome this problem, we would need many training samples or a structure as the neocognitron [4]. Further improvements for the system are necessary to have it come to near the human performance. One method to do this is to use two networks and their interaction, considering the information type theory [22].

4   Conclusion

This paper presents the rotation invariant neural network system which can estimate a rotation angle. In the coin image recognition, the results of better recognition accuracy and good rotation angle estimation are given by using our system. The results of rotation angle estimation in the system are about 90 % accuracy by using more than ten training samples. The rotation invariant neural network give a new approach for rotation angle estimation.

The hidden layer in the system could be divided into two networks, each of which uses as its output layer different parts, namely, the pattern recognition part and the angle estimation part. The results of this system is slightly worse than the system presented in this paper.

References

[1] M.Iriki et al. : *Physiology*, Bunkodo (1986) (in Japanese)

[2] K.Yazawa et al. : *Brain and AI : Thinking Machines*, Gakken (1992) (in Japanese)

[3] D.E.Rumelhart et al. : *Parallel Distributed Processing*, 1 and 2, The MIT Press, Cambridge, MA (1986)

[4] K.Fukushima, S.Miyake, and T.Ito : "Neocognitron : a neural network model for a mechanism of visual pattern recognition", *IEEE Trans. Syst., Man, Cybern.*, vol.13, pp.826-834 (1983)

[5] T.Nagano and M.Ishikawa : "A neural network for size-invariant feature extraction", in *Proc. Int. Neural Network Conf.*, vol.1, p.103 (1990)

[6] B.Widrow, R.G.Winter, and R.A.Baxter : "Layered Neural Nets for Pattern Recognition", *IEEE Trans. Acoust, Speech & Signal Process.*, vol.36, no.7, pp.1109-1118 (1988)

[7] M.B.Reid, L.Spirkovska and E.Ochoa : "Rapid training of higher-order neural networks for invariant pattern recognition", in *Proc. of Int. Joint Conf. on Neural Networks*, vol.1, pp.689-692 (1989)

[8] S.Araya, k.Suzaki, and H.Asho : "A neural network for learning and recognizing rotated patterns", *Trans. IEE Japan*, vol.111, no.5, pp.202-208 (1991) (in Japanese)

[9] V.Cruz, G.Cristobal, T.Michaux and S.Barquin : "Invariant image recognition using a multi network neural model", in *Proc. of Int. Joint Conf. on Neural Networks*, vol.2, pp.17-21 (1989)

[10] S.Lee and Y.Choi : "Robust recognition of handwritten numerals based on dual cooperative networks", in *Proc. of Int. Joint Conf. on Neural Networks*, vol.3, pp.760-767 (1992)

[11] M.W.Koch, M.W.Roberts and S.W.Aiken : "A vision architecture for scale, translation and rotation invariance", in *Proc. of Int. Joint Conf. on Neural Networks*, vol.2, pp.393-396 (1990)

[12] G.A.Carpenter and S.Grossberg : "The ART of adaptive pattern recognition by a self-organizing neural network", *IEEE Computer*, vol.21, no.3, pp.77-88 (1988)

[13] K.Imai, K.Gouhara, and Y.Uchikawa : "Pattern extraction and recognition for noisy images using the three-layered BP model", in *Proc. of Int. Joint Conf. on Neural Networks*, vol.1, pp.262-267 (1991)

[14] M.Teranishi, M.Fukumi, and S.Omatu : "Pattern recognition system by neural networks ", in *Proc. of the 34-th ISCIE Conf.*, p.105 (1990) (in Japanese)

[15] G.A.Carpenter, S.Grossberg, and G.W.Lesher : "A what- and where- neural network for invariant image preprocessing", in *proc. Int. Joint Conf. on Neural Networks*, vol.3, pp.303-308 (1992)

[16] A.Pantle and R.Sekuler : "Size-detecting mechanisms in human vision", *Science*, vol.162, pp.1146-1148 (1968)

[17] R.N.Shepard and J.Metzler : "Mental rotation of three-dimensional objects", *Science*, vol.171, pp.701-703 (1971)

[18] M.Fukumi, S.Omatu, F.Takeda, and T.Kosaka : "Rotation-invariant neural pattern recognition system with application to coin recognition", *IEEE Trans. Neural Networks*, vol.2, no.3, pp.272-279 (1992)

[19] M.Fukumi, S.Omatu, F.Takeda, and T.Kosaka : "Rotation invariant neural network with an edge detection network", *Trans. IEE Japan*, vol.112-C, no.8, pp.457-464 (1992) (in Japanese)

[20] M.Fukumi, S.Omatu, F.Takeda, and T.Kosaka : "Rotation invariant neural pattern recognition systems with application to coin recognition", *J. SICE Japan*, vol. 33, no.2, pp.151-165 (1994) (in Japanese)

[21] S.D.You and G.E.Ford : "Network model for invariant object recognition and rotation angle estimation", in *Proc. Int. Joint Conf. on Neural Networks*, vol.3, pp.2145-2148 (1993)

[22] Y.Takano: "Perception of rotated forms : A theory of information types", *Cognitive Psychology*, vol.21, pp.1-59 (1989)

Remote Sensing: Land Use Classification using Neural Gas

Georg S. Ruppert†, Mathias Schardt†, Gerd Balzuweit‡
†Institute for Image Processing, Joanneum Research, Graz, Austria
‡Institute for Information Processing, University of Leipzig, Germany

Abstract— **A hybrid classifier consisting of a Neural Gas quantization process of the entire image and a majority labeling process of the resulting codebook using the ground truth is shown. Besides equal performance to Maximum Likelihood – the most widely used classifier in Remote Sensing – the presented classifier provides a quality measure of the ground truth, a desired feature in practical applications.**

1 Introduction

Land use classification of Satellite Images is a complex problem with many research areas involved. There exists a broad range of publications covering this application ranging from threshold methods to various highly complex classification methods like Neural Networks specially designed and adapted, see for example in [1, 2, 3, 8, 9, 10, 11]. Many publication that concentrate on comparisons of classification methods show superior methods for different statistical data requirements, however, land use classification are characterized by small training areas and unknown distribution of classes in the entire dataset. The authors believe that many existing papers overemphasize the total true error rate approximation, while neglecting similar important areas like comprehensibility, effort, expert knowledge involved, cost. We introduce our hybrid method based on the Neural Gas [6, 7] vector quantization followed by class assignment which, we believe, is a step in the direction of automating the data analysis process. User interaction and necessary knowledge is decreased and the classification performance is up to methods like Multilayer Perceptrons or Maximum Likelihood both widely used among the Remote Sensing community.

2 Neural Gas Theory

Vector quantization is a method to reduce the dimensionality in data space. Such a method defines a set of vectors called codebook. The aim of such a procedure is to filter important features to unite a subset of the dataset in one representation vector. Each vector in the original dataset can be represent by a codebook vector. Martinetz developed an neural structure called Neural Gas [6, 7] for vector quantization. His method is similar to Kohonen's Self-Organizing Map [4]. The Neural Gas algorithm is an un-supervised competition learning scheme. The basic idea is to define a neighborhood inside the neurons (codebook vectors) in each learning step. Then a neurons learn with an intensity defined by the neighborhood rank. The neighborhood width shrinks during the learning phase. For N neurons w_j with $j = 1, ..., N$, one learning step is given in the following flowchart:

(1) present an input signal (a vector of the dataset) v

(2) calculate the distance $\|v - w_j\|$ and sort the neurons $(w_{i_0}, w_{i_1}, w_{i_2}, ..., w_{i_{N-1}})$ in ascending order so that w_{i_0} is the nearest neighbor to the input signal v, w_{i_1} the second nearest neighbor etc.

(3) define the neighborhood rank $k_i(v, w)$ so that $k_i = 0$ for w_{i_0}, $k_i = 1$ for w_{i_1}, ..., $k_i = N - 1$ for $w_{i_{N-1}}$.

(4) learning step: $\Delta w_i = \varepsilon h_\sigma \left(k_i(v, w) \right) \left(v - w_i \right) \qquad i = 1, ..., N$,
with $h_\sigma \left(k_i(v, w) \right) = e^{-k_i(v,w)/\sigma}$.

$\varepsilon \in [0, 1]$ define the learning rate and σ the neighborhood width. Both parameters are decreased during the learning phase. In the last learning steps only the winner w_{i_0} learns.

In the contrary to Kohonen's SOM algorithm the dynamics of this method are gaseous. The neurons behave like gas molecules in the input space. So Martinez called the method Neural Gas. This model is not limited by a given topological structure like Kohonen's SOM. In our case, better results can be expected with Neural Gas than with SOM, because better quantization results can be achieved with Neural Gas as it can be seen in the example in Fig. 1. The major drawback of Neural Gas is its inefficiency, because of the mathematics involved and the fact that the Neural Gas should be cooled down very slowly for good quantization.

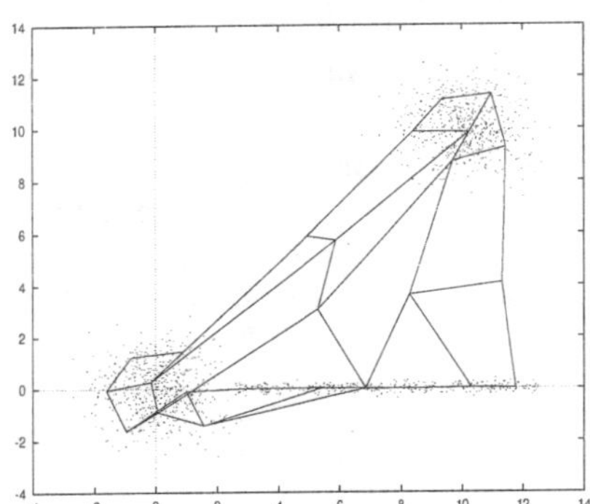 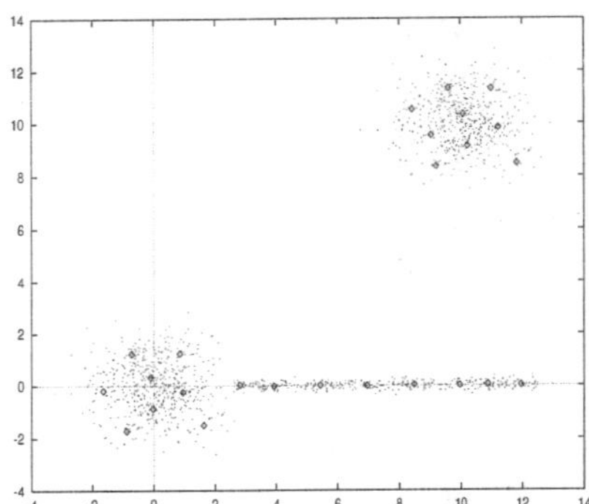

Figure 1: Left: Quantization by SOM, line intersections denote codebook vectors, lines denote neighborhood relations. Right: Quantization by Neural Gas, codebook vectors are shown as squares.

3 Error Measurements

The classification error in Remote Sensing application is generally measured by calculating the confusion matrix (or error matrix) of a random sample of pixels. Ideally this sample will be an independent set of test data, it is clearly not acceptable to use the training data for the calculation of the confusion matrix. However, because of the cost involved in acquiring ground truth, it is desirable to use the entire ground truth as training data. One way around this is n-fold cross validation (CV), well described in [12].

In [5] R. M. Lark describes various probability and conditional probability estimates calculated from the confusion matrix. These estimates provide the calculation user with a deeper understanding with the classification error and its consequences. The columns of the confusion matrix corresponds to true class (tc) and the rows to assigned class (ac), a_{ij} is therefore the confusion matrix element row i column j.

- P1. The probability that the class a randomly selected pixel is assigned to is correct.

$$P1 = p(tc = ac) = \frac{\sum_{i=1}^{n} a_{ii}}{\sum_{i=1}^{n} \sum_{j=1}^{n} a_{ij}} \tag{1}$$

- P2(x). The probability that the class x a randomly selected pixel is assigned to is correct.

$$P2(x) = p(ac = tc | tc = x) = \frac{a_{xx}}{\sum_{j=1}^{n} a_{xj}} \tag{2}$$

- P3(x). The probability that a randomly selected pixel belonging to true class x is correctly assigned.

$$P3(x) = p(tc = ac | ac = x) = \frac{a_{xx}}{\sum_{i=1}^{n} a_{ix}} \tag{3}$$

- P4(x, y). The probability that a randomly selected pixel that has been allocated to class x belongs to true class y.

$$P4(x, y) = p(tc = y | ac = x) = \frac{a_{xy}}{\sum_{j=1}^{n} a_{xj}} \tag{4}$$

- P5(x, y). The probability that a randomly selected pixel that belongs to true class y is allocated to class x.

$$P5(x, y) = p(tc = x | ac = y) = \frac{a_{xy}}{\sum_{i=1}^{n} a_{iy}} \tag{5}$$

Furthermore, estimates of the apriori probability – the distribution of the true classes – and the aposteriori probability – the distribution of the allocated classes – may be calculated.

- P6(x). Apriori probability.

$$P6(x) = p(tc = x) = \frac{\sum_{i=1}^{n} a_{ix}}{\sum_{i=1}^{n} \sum_{j=1}^{n} a_{ij}} \tag{6}$$

- P7(x). Aposteriori probability.

$$P7(x) = p(ac = x) = \frac{\sum_{i=1}^{n} a_{xi}}{\sum_{i=1}^{r} \sum_{j=1}^{n} a_{ij}} \tag{7}$$

The quality of these two estimates depends on the quality cf the ground truth, of course.

4　The Classifier

The classifier is called "Neural Gas classifier" because Neural Gas is used to carry out the Quantization of the entire image not just the training areas as commonly done. Therefore, the remaining training steps can use a codebook which models the apriori probabilities cf the entire image.

To carry out classification using this codebook one has to label the codebook vectors with the correct class they represent. This is done by the following algorithm:

1. Initialize $w_i.class\_count[k] = 0$ for i=1,...,NrOfNeurons, k=1,...,NrOfClasses

2. For all training pixels v_j belonging to class c_k do

   (a) Find the winner w_i for v_j
   (b) Update class statistics: $w_i.class\_count[k] + +$

3. For all neurons w_i do

   (a) Find k with maximum $w_i.class\_count[k]$
   (b) If there is no unique maximum use random number generator to choose k from tie classes
   (c) Label neuron w_i with class c_k

Classification now is a simple find winner operation for all pixels of the image.

An additional feature of the Neural Gas classifier is a quality measure of the training areas can be calculated. Training set and entire image are individually mapped to the codebook and the resulting distributions can be compared. After normalization the mean square errcr is suggested as a measure.

There are constraints to be considered when using the Neural Gas classifier. The codebook size is a compromise between performance, size of training areas in pixel, and computation power available. Quantization will of course improve as the codebook size increases. However, the number of training pixel and the computation power impose upper limits on the codebook size. When running our test on a 50MHz SUN SuperSPARC^R Workstation we reached the computation limit first.

The main advantage of the Neural Gas classifier is that it requires much less user interaction than other classifiers, especially Maximum Likelihood or Multilayer Perceptrons.

5　Performance Evaluation

For performance evaluation the same Landsat TM image – see Fig. 2 – was used as Bischof at al.[1, 2] did in their series of papers on performance analysis of Multilayer Perceptron Networks and Maximum Likelihood. In these papers about 3000 pixel were chosen for training with no further details given. The learned classifier was then verified with the remaining pixels. Unfortunately, the original training areas were unavailable and new training areas had to be chosen. This fact must be considered when comparing Bischof's with our classifier results. Furthermore one has to take into account that there was no preprocessing of the data carried out in contrast to Bischof who used coarse coding with the Multilayer Perceptron. His results were 84.7% for Maximum Likelihood and 85.9% for a 91 Input 5 Hidden 4 Output – Multilayer Perceptron.

For the quantization with Neural Gas, the entire Landsat image ($512 * 512$) was used. In the following table the distribution of the classes is given:

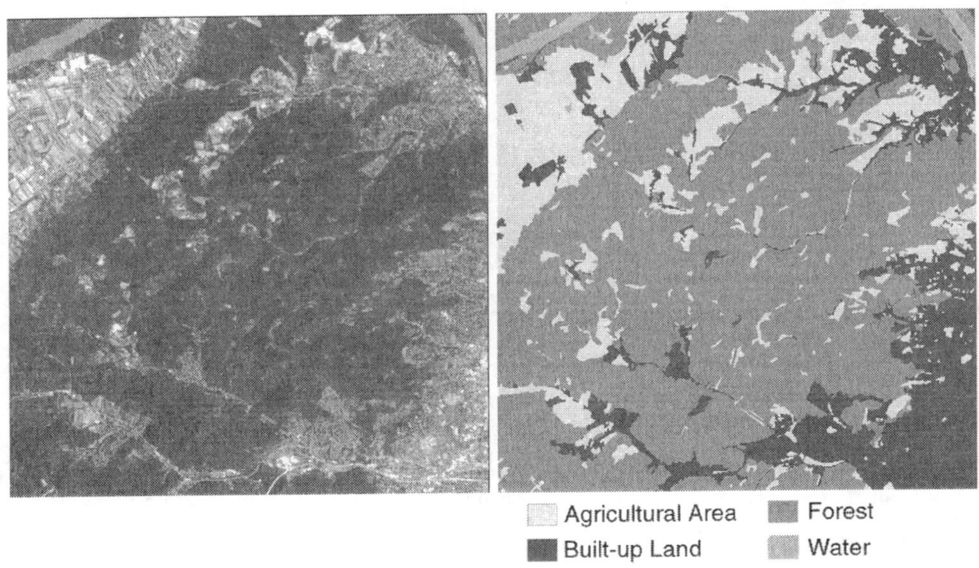

Figure 2: Left: Original Image, Right: Ground Truth

agricultural area	built-up land	forest	water
48611	48824	161610	2583
18.54%	18.62%	61.65%	0.99%

After some initial trails with several human expert chosen training areas which resulted in significantly different confusion matrices, we decided to use about 3000 randomly chosen pixels for training. For this purpose a mask image with uniformly distributed random noise was generated. The labeling and learning verification was carried out using this training set.

Classifier generalization was verified with the remaining pixels. The results of classifiers with three different codebook sizes are shown in the tables 1.

agricultural area	built-up land	forest	water
28512	5611	5344	13
8750	36830	4645	308
11340	6374	151366	329
9	9	255	1933
agricultural area	built-up land	forest	water
29573	5934	6578	13
8461	36605	4046	386
10564	6269	150778	131
13	16	208	2053
agricultural area	built-up land	forest	water
29192	5750	5984	15
8454	37032	4534	250
10907	5885	150245	111
58	157	847	2207

Table 1: Confusion matrix with codebook sizes 200; 300, 400

For classification the codebook with the size 400 was used. In the following table the dump of Lark's probability estimates are given. The columns are true class, the rows assigned class. Class name are like in the tables above.

P1: 0.836

P2: 0.713 0.737 0.899 0.675

```
P4:
0.713 0.140 0.146 0.000
0.168 0.737 0.090 0.005
0.065 0.035 0.899 0.001
0.018 0.048 0.259 0.675


P3: 0.601 0.758 0.930 0.854

P5:
0.601 0.118 0.037 0.006
0.174 0.758 0.028 0.097
0.224 0.121 0.930 0.043
0.001 0.003 0.005 0.854


P6:  0.186 0.187 0.618 0.010

P7:  0.156 0.192 0.639 0.012
```

In Fig. 3 Bischof's Multilayer Perceptron results (without additional smoozing) can be visually compared to the ones achieved by the Neural Gas classifier.

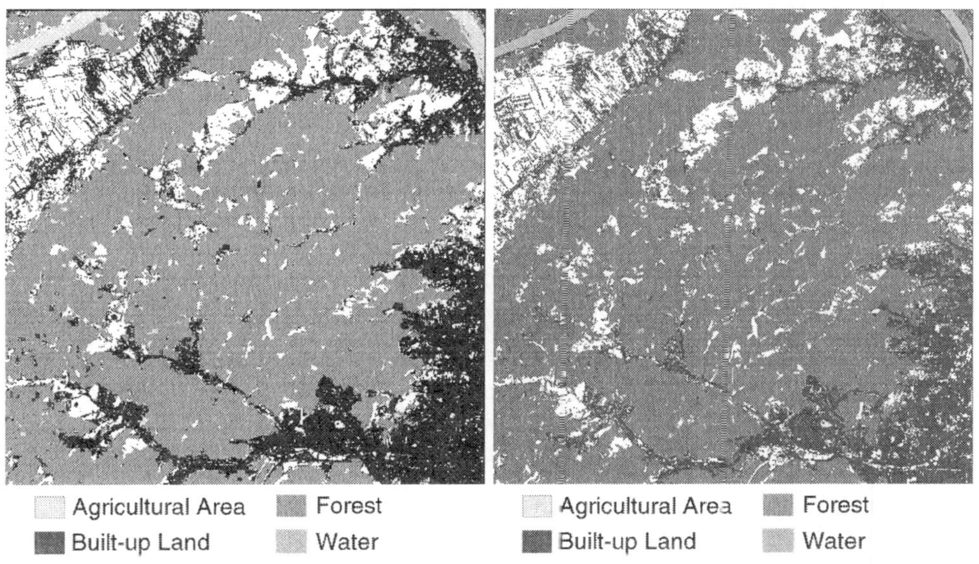

Figure 3: Left: Multilayer Perceptron Result, Right: Neural Gas Result

To sum up we could show a good performance of 83.6% without any kind of preprocessing or optimization. Additionally the distribution of the assigned classes (see P7 above) is quite close to the truth class distribution (see P6 above), even the small class "water" is well represented.

6   Conclusion

A basic approach for a new classifier suited to remote sensing applications was described. Its performance turned out very well. A quality measure of the ground truth is calculated during the training process. Further work is needed for the optimization of the codebook size which should be done automatically. Future performance comparisons will include k-nn Nearest Neighbor, Multilayer Perceptrons, LVQ, and statistical Classifiers.

7   Acknowledgement

The authors want to express their gratitude to Horst Bischof from the Institute for Automation, Vienna University of Technology, Austria, who made his Landsat TM dataset, various classification results, and the visual ground truth available to us.

References

[1] H. Bischof, R. Bartl, A. J. Pinz, W. Schneider. *AI-Methods For Remote Sensing: Neural Networks and Knowledge-Based Vision* Proceedings of the 11th EARSeL Symposium, 1991.

[2] H. Bischof, W. Schneider, and A. J. Pinz. *Multispectral Classification of Landsat-Images Using Neural Networks* IEEE Transactions on Geoscience and Remote Sensing, Vol 30, No. 3, May 1992.

[3] M. Keil, M. Schardt, A. Schurek, and R. Winter. *Forest Mapping using Satellite Imagery. The Regensburg map sheet 1:200.000 as example.* ISPRS Journal of Photogrammetry and Remote Sensing, Heft 45 (1990) S. 33-46, Amsterdam, 1990.

[4] T. Kohonen. *Self-Organization and Associative Memory.* Springer, Berlin, 1984.

[5] R. M. Lark. *Components of accuracy of maps with special reference to discriminant analysis on remote sensing data.* Int. J. Remote Sensing, 1995, Vol. 16, No. 8, 1461-1480.

[6] Thomas Martinetz. *Selbstorganisierende neuronale Netzwerkmodelle zur Bewegungssteuerung.* Gesellschaft für Informatik e.V., 1992.

[7] Thomas Martinetz, Stanislav G. Berkovich, and Klaus J. Schulten. *"Neural-Gas" Network for Vector Quantization and its Application to Time-Series Prediction.* IEEE Transactions on Neural Networks, Vol. 4, No. 4, July 93.

[8] M. Schardt. *Forest Classification with TM Data in the Area of Freiburg, Federal Republic of Germany.* Proceedings of a Workshop on "Earthnet Pilot Project on Landsat Thematic Mapper Applications", S. 251-259, Frascati, 1989.

[9] M. Schardt. *Verwendbarkeit von Thematic Mapper Daten zur Klassifizierung von Baumarten und natürlichen Altersklassen.* DLR-Forschungsprojekt, (DLR_FB 90-44), Oberpfaffenhofen, 1990.

[10] M. Schardt, H. Kenneweg, and H. Sagischewski. *Forest Stand Characteristics to be Applied to Monitoring Lingering Disasters by Satellite Remote Sensing and GIS.* Proceedings of the Symposium "Inventory and Management Techniques in the Context of Catastrophic Events", State College, Pennsylvania, June 21-24.

[11] M. Schardt, K. Martin, and M. Keil. *Mapping of Biotic Damages Using Satellite Data.* Proceedings of the Symposium "Inventory and Management Techniques in the Context of Catastrophic Events", State College, Pennsylvania, June 21-24.

[12] Sholom M. Weiss, Casimir A. Kulikowski. *Computer Systems That Learn.* Morgan Kaufmann Publishers, Inc. San Francisco, California, 1991.

3D Object Recognition by Coupling Mixtures of Autoencoders and Dynamic Matching

Toshifumi Fujita, Satoshi Suzuki, Hiroshi Ando

ATR Human Information Processing Research Laboratories
2-2 Hikaridai, Seika-cho, Soraku-gun, Kyoto 619-02, Japan
E-mail:tfujita@hip.atr.co.jp, ando@hip.atr.co.jp

***Abstract*— This paper proposes a 3D object recognition scheme that consists of a mixture of nonlinear autoencoders and an alignment system. In this scheme, the autoencoders and the alignment system are effectively combined so that the scheme can dynamically recognize a novel view that suffers from image transformations. We demonstrate through computer experiments that the proposed scheme can learn to recognize various gray-level images of 3D objects while tolerating image transformations.**

1   Introduction

A fundamental problem on 3D object recognition is how to achieve invariant object recognition despite image variations caused by a viewpoint change as well as image transformations and nonrigid distortion. Recently, view-based schemes for 3D object recognition have been proposed which achieve view invariance without constructing elaborate 3D models [Poggio & Edelman, 1990; Murase & Nayar, 1995; Suzuki & Ando, 1993, 1995]. Our approach is based on an unsupervised learning scheme that classifies 2D views using a mixture of autoencoders [Suzuki & Ando, 1993, 1995]. The simulations using synthetic 3D wireframe objects demonstrated that the scheme can effectively learn to recognize 3D objects from their 2D features. Nonetheless, the generalization ability of the autoencoders is still limited, i.e., the scheme may suffer from various image transformations, such as shift, rotation and scaling. It is impractical to train the networks with all kinds of input transformations. Thus it seems more useful and practical to combine a direct matching mechanism for recognizing trained patterns with a dynamic matching mechanism for recognizing novel transformed patterns.

The human visual system seems to use similar multiple recognition strategies. Psychological studies have shown that although object recognition time is usually very short, when an input pattern deviates significantly from the training patterns it requires an extended time to recognize an object [Edelman & Bülthoff, 1992]. In such a case, the human visual system may use top-down information to guide the recognition of objects [Cavanagh, 1991]. It is thus reasonable to believe that the neural recognition system may effectively combine a fast direct matching strategy with a fine dynamic matching strategy.

This paper proposes an object recognition scheme that consists of a mixture of nonlinear autoencoders and an alignment system. We demonstrate that the scheme can learn to recognize gray-level images of 3D objects without providing an object identity to the system. The paper also proposes an effective coupling of the autoencoders and the alignment system for dynamic recognition of 3D objects. We consider the encoding network of an autoencoder as a bottom-up process and the decoding network as a top-down process. The scheme iterates between the bottom-up and top-down processes until the generated view aligns with the input view. The computer experiments demonstrate that the proposed matching scheme can identify a novel view through gradually transforming the input image.

2   The Network Model

This section describes a network model for classifying 2D views into 3D objects. Fig.1 illustrates the overall scheme for 3D object recognition. We assume that the region of a 3D object is segmented in the image beforehand. The 2D projected image of the 3D object is first filtered by a smoothing function, such as Gaussian function or Gabor function. The filtered image is then sampled at grid points, each of which has a receptive field on the image. The image on the grid is then fed into a set of modules which consist of five-layer auto-associative networks or autoencoders. Each autoencoder is trained to compress the image nonlinearly and recover the image for one of the objects. The training can be done with no explicit object identity provided to the networks. After training the networks, the classifier identifies the input image as an object by selecting a module that best recovers the image. If the image is distorted or transformed, the position of each receptive field changes iteratively until the sampled image is aligned to the reconstructed image that the autoencoder generates, as illustrated in Fig.1. The following sub-sections describe the unsupervised learning scheme proposed by Suzuki and Ando (1995) and the alignment method in more detail.

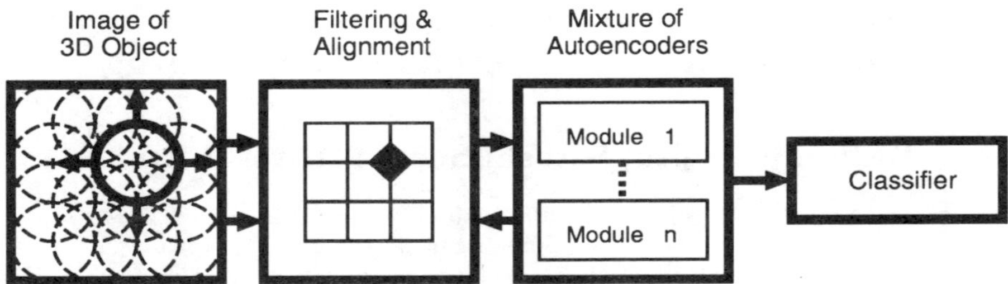

Fig.1: The overall scheme. Each module is a five layer auto-associative network.

2.1 A Mixture of Nonlinear Autoencoders

In order to identify an object, the proposed scheme exploits an auto-associative network or autoencoder. An auto-associative network finds an identity mapping through a bottleneck in the hidden layer. The network, thus, compress the input into a low dimensional representation by eliminating redundancy. If we use a five-layer perceptron network, the network can perform nonlinear dimensionality reduction, which is a nonlinear analogue to the principal component analysis (Oja, 1991; DeMers & Cottrell, 1993).

The scheme consists of a mixture of five-layer autoencoders. In the case where the inputs are the projected views of a rigid object, the minimum dimension that constrains the input variation is *the degree of freedom* of the rigid object, which is six in the most general case, three for rotation and three for translation. Thus a single module can compress the views of an object into a representation whose dimension is its degree of freedom. The proposed scheme categorizes each view of 3D objects into its object class through selecting an appropriate module.

The model selects a module whose output best fits the input. Specifically, we assume a classifier whose output vector is given by the softmax function of negative squared difference between the input and the output of the modules, i.e.,

$$f_k = \frac{\exp\left[-\|I - R_k\|^2\right]}{\sum_i \exp\left[-\|I - R_i\|^2\right]},\tag{1}$$

where I and R_k denote the input and the output of the k th module, respectively. Therefore, if only one of the modules has an output that best matches the input, then the output value of the corresponding unit in the classifier becomes nearly one and the output values of the other units become nearly zero. For training the network with unsupervised learning, we maximize the following objective function:

$$\ln \frac{\sum_k \exp\left[-\alpha\,\|I - R_k\|^2\right]}{\sum_k \exp\left[-\|I - R_k\|^2\right]},\quad (\alpha > 1),\tag{2}$$

where $\alpha(> 1)$ denotes a constant. This function forces the output of at least one module to fit the input, and it also forces the rest of modules to increase the error between the input and the output. Since it is difficult for a single module to learn more than one object, we expect that the network will eventually converge to the state where each module identifies only one object.

2.2 The Alignment Method

The recognition performance of the proposed scheme would be affected by image transformations and distortions, such as position shift, scaling, image rotation or any nonrigid deformation. More specifically, after training the networks, an autoencoder can reconstruct the input image if the image contains no noise, but if the input image is distorted, the reconstructed image may become significantly different from the input image. The underlying idea of the dynamic matching scheme is that the system allows each grid point or receptive field to move around on the image in order to resample the image for the input to the networks (Ando,1995; Fujita et al,1995). The goal is thus to find a resampled image that best matches the reconstructed image that the network generates.

Finding the best matched image, however, is ill-posed because each grid point can move to any image point that has the same brightness. One way to obtain a unique solution is to regularize the problem by imposing an additional constraint (Poggio et al. 1985). Our particular choice is a smoothness constraint which only allows a smooth topological distortion of the grids. We thus minimize the following cost function which is a combination of the term that describes the difference between the resampled image I and the reconstructed image R and the term that describes the grid distortion:

$$\sum_{i,j} \left[I\left(dx_{i,j}, dy_{i,j}\right) - R\left(I\right) \right]^2$$

$$+ \lambda \sum_{i,j} [(dx_{i+1,j} - dx_{i,j})^2 + (dx_{i,j+1} - dx_{i,j})^2 + (dy_{i+1,j} - dy_{i,j})^2 + (dy_{i,j+1} - dy_{i,j})^2], \tag{3}$$

where $(dx_{i,j}, dy_{i,j})$ denotes a displacement vector at the grid point (i, j), which we estimate. λ is a constant that determines a tradeoff between the two terms. We could use the steepest descent method for minimizing this cost function. Note that during the minimization, the network weights are fixed and the error is back-propagated through the network, because R also depends on $(dx_{i,j}, dy_{i,j})$. Therefore, the proposed scheme estimates an object view and transforms the input image at the same time through iterating between the view generation and the view alignment.

3 Computer Experiments

We implemented the proposed network model to evaluate its performance on real images of 3D objects. The 3D objects that we used for experiments are three objects shown in Fig.2. Each object was placed on a motorized turntable and different views of the objects were taken by a camera at every one degree of rotation. We thus obtained 360 images for each object. Each image has 512×480 pixels with 8 bit gray-scale values. We normalized intensities of the images for all objects by roughly setting the background intensity to 0.4 and the brightest portions to 1.6.

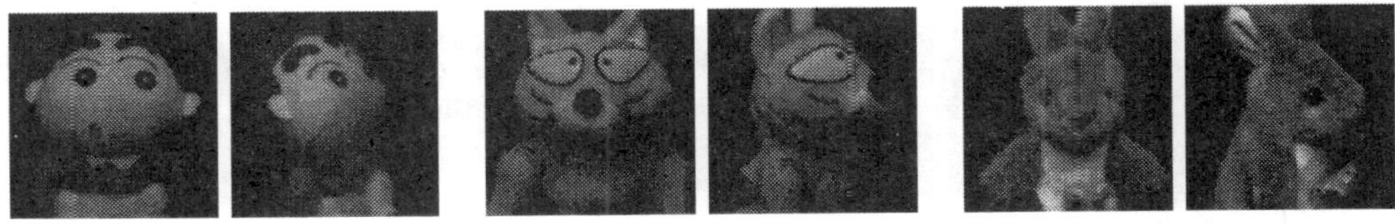

Fig.2: Three objects used in the experiments: Object A (left), B (middle), and C (right).

3.1 Basic Properties of the Autoencoders

This section examines basic properties of each module using supervised learning. For initial filtering and sampling, each image was quantized into a 32×30 image by averaging the brightness within each quantized cell. The input dimension of the networks is thus 960. 10 units were used in the second and fourth layers. The number of units in the third layer of the autoencoders should be set equal to the degree of freedom, which is one in our experiments. However, we used two units instead because it is not possible to represent the periodic nature of rotation in just one dimension. To train each autoencoder, the squared difference between the input and the output images of an object was minimized. At each iteration step, a view of the object was randomly selected from the entire views.

Fig.3 shows four sets of examples of the input images and the recovered images for Object B. The recovered views are significantly similar to the input views, indicating that each autoencoder can successfully compress and recover different views of an object. In fact, as shown in Fig.4 (a) and (b), the reconstruction error between the input and the output images for two modules is nearly zero for only one of the three objects. (The reconstruction error is defined as a root mean squared error per pixel between the input and the output images.) The results indicate that the classifier can correctly identify each image as an object by selecting a module that has the minimum reconstruction error

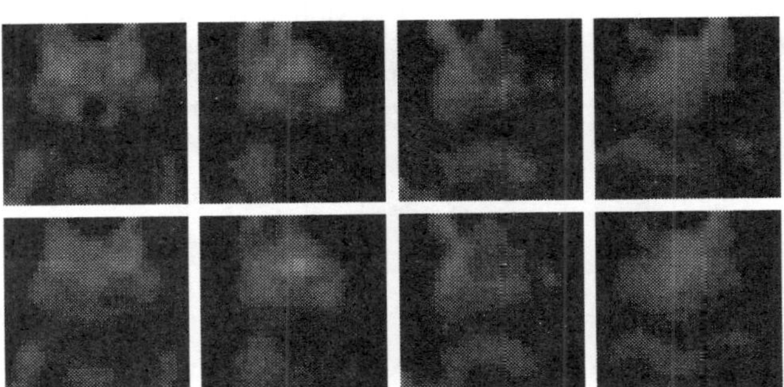

Fig.3: Examples of the input view (top) and its recovered view (bottom) of Object B.

To examine generalization performance of the model, we trained the networks with a sparse set of views, i.e. views are sampled only at 30 or 45 degree intervals. Fig.4 (c) shows the reconstruction error of Object B plotted over the entire view range after training the networks. Comparison between figures (c) and (b) indicates that even when only 8 views with 45 degree intervals are used for training the network, the reconstruction error is smaller than the error of other objects for almost entire view range, which leads to correct classification of the objects. The results suggest that the network exhibits a satisfactory capability of generalization.

(a)   (b)   (c)

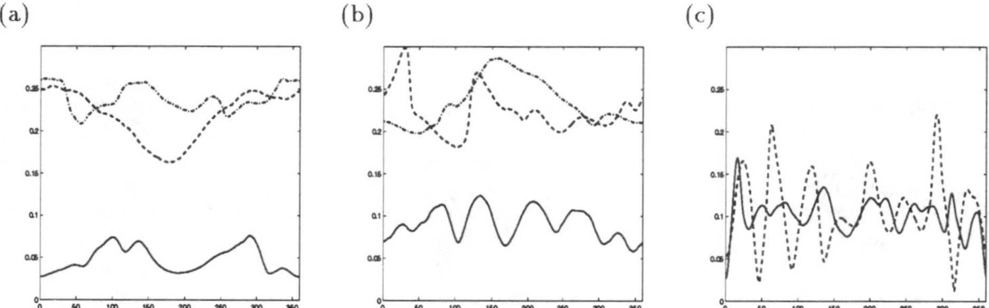

Fig.4: The reconstruction error of two modules as a function of the view direction. The solid curves in (a) and (b) indicate Object A and B, respectively. Other curves indicate other objects. (c) The reconstruction error of Object B when the training views are sampled at 30 (the solid curve) or 45 (the dash curve) degree intervals.

One of the effective properties of an autoencoder is its ability of associative recall (Kohonen,1987). The input image can be contaminated by noise, or a part of the object may be occluded by other objects in the image. We demonstrate how the autoencoder can reconstruct the original images for such noisy inputs. Fig.5 (a) shows a case where a part of the image is masked. After learning the entire views, the autoencoder can effectively reproduce the reconstructed pattern, the information of the missing portion can be estimated. Fig.5 (b) demonstrates that the original image can also be recovered when the input image is superimposed with a white noise.

(a)   (b)

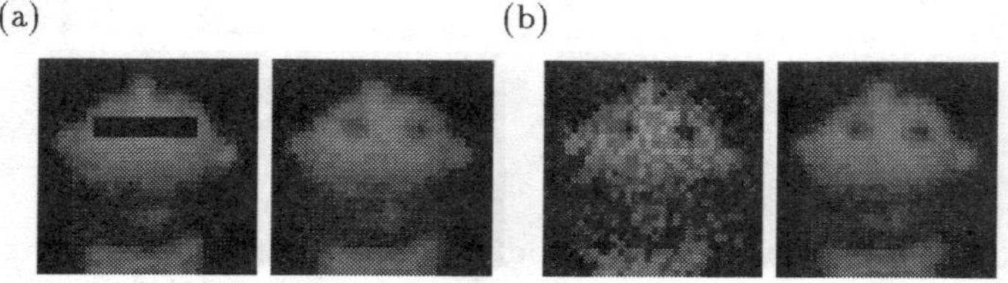

Fig.5: Demonstration of auto-associative reconstruction in the case of the masked input pattern (a) and the noisy input pattern (b).

3.2 Unsupervised Learning

This section describes the experimental results using the unsupervised learning scheme described in section 2.1 We used the same three objects used in the previous experiments, but object labels were not provided to the networks. 16×15 quantized images of the three objects were used for training the model which consists of three modules. The steepest ascent method was used for maximizing the objective function (2), but more efficient methods, such as the conjugate gradient method, can also be used. During the training, objects were randomly selected among the three and their views were also randomly selected. The constant α in the objective function (2) was set to 200. The classifier selects a network that produces minimum error between the output and the input. Fig.6 illustrates the output values of the classifier plotted over the entire view direction after the training, showing that the model effectively classified the views into their original object except for the profile of Object C. The reason for this misclassification is that the profile of Object C happens to be very similar to that of Object B. We confirmed this by computing the squared difference between the images of Object B and C.

(a)   (b)   (c)

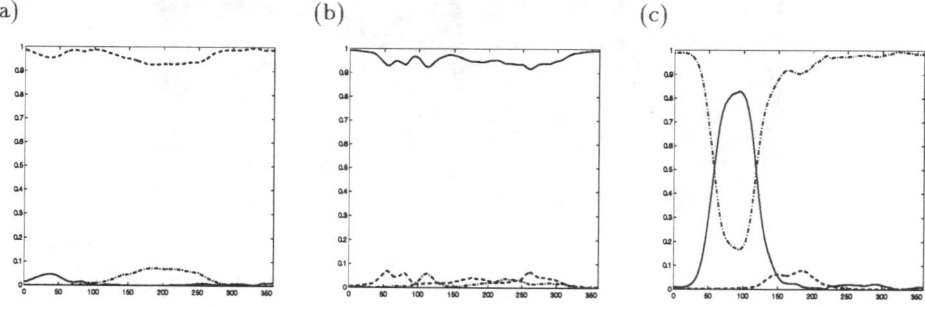

Fig.6: The classifier outputs for the images of Object A (a), B (b) and C (c). The solid, dash and dash-dot curves indicate the units corresponding to Module 1, 2 and 3, respectively.

3.3 Alignment Experiments

This section describes the experiments using the alignment method. The image was blurred by Gaussian filter whose standard deviation was 4.0 pixels. Fig.7 (a) shows an image of Object B sampled at 16×15 grid points. The image was then shifted rightward and downward by one grid point ($=16$ pixels in the original image) each as shown in Fig.7 (b). After training a network with the original 360 images, the shifted image was used as an input, and the relaxation based on the objective function (3) was performed. The parameter λ was set to 0.005. Fig.8 (a) shows the reconstruction error as a function of the number of iterations. Initially the error is so large that the shifted image of Object B is misclassified as Object C (whose error is indicated by the upper line), but in the first 50 iterations, the error dropped rapidly and approached to the original position. Fig.7 (d) shows the alignment result without using the error back-propagation through the network, i.e. R in the objective function (3) was fixed to the recostructed image of the shifted image. A curve in Fig.8 (b) shows the outputs of the two hidden units in the third layer for the entire view range. The figure shows that although the hidden representation of the shifted image is largely separated from the original point, the point moved close to the original point by the alignment relaxation. The alignment without using the network, on the other hand, did not change its position much. The results demonstrate that the proposed alignment relaxation is effective when the image is shifted. Fig.9 shows that the same alignment method can also tolerate rotation in the image.

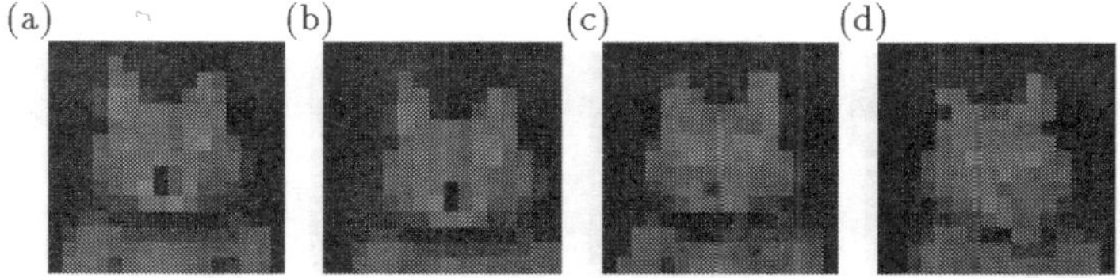

Fig.7: (a) The original sampled image. (b) The shifted image used for the input. (c) The image after alignment. (d) The image after alignment using a fixed reconstructed image.

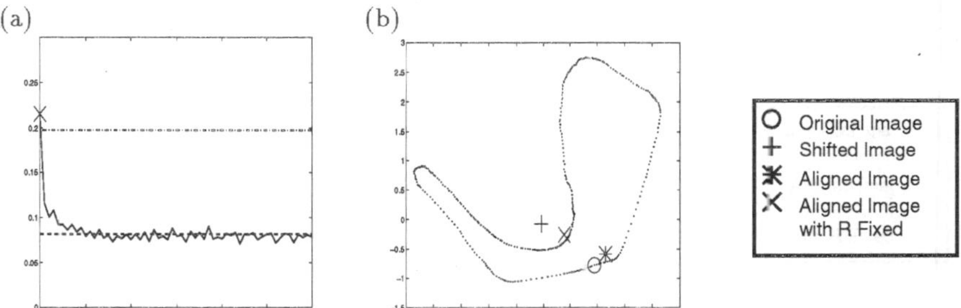

Fig.8: (a) The reconstruction error of the shifted image as a function of the number of iterations. The lower line shows the error of the original image. The upper line shows the error of the shifted image using the Object C module. (b) Outputs of the third-layer units.

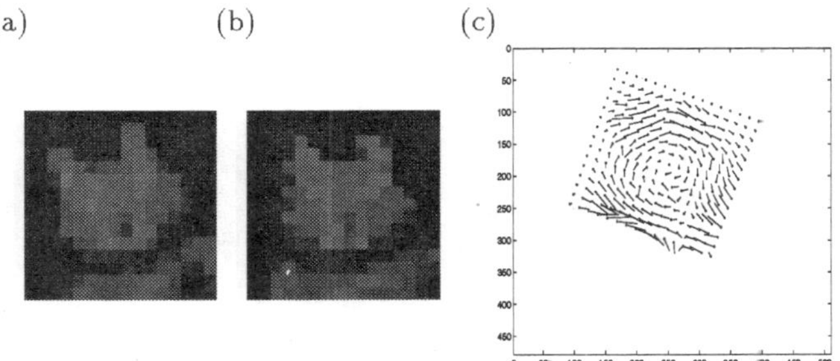

Fig.9: (a) The rotated image. (b) The image after alignment. (c) The displacement vector field computed by the alignment relaxation.

4 Conclusions

We have proposed a 3D object recognition scheme that effectively combines a mixture of nonlinear autoencoders and an alignment system for dynamically recognizing a novel view that suffers from image transformations. The experiments demonstrated that the proposed scheme can learn to recognize various gray-level images of 3D objects and show a flexible alignment for shifted and rotated images. We are currently conducting experiments using other transformations, such as non-rigid deformation and scaling.

Acknowledgements
We would like to thank Mitsuo Kawato for continuous encouragement on this research.

References

[1] Ando,H. (1995). 3D object recognition using bidirectional modular networks. *Proceedings of the Second Asian Conference on Computer Vision.* II 451-455.

[2] Cavanagh,P. (1991). What's up in top-down processing? In Gorea,A. (eds.), *Representations of vision: Trends and tacit assumptions in vision ressearch,* 295-304, Cambridge University Press, Cambridge.

[3] DeMers,D. and Cottrell,G. (1993). Non-linear dimensionality reduction. In Hanson,S.J., Cowan,J. D. & Giles,C.L., (eds), *Advances in Neural Information Processing Systems 5.* Morgan Kaufmann Publishers, San Mateo, CA. 580-587.

[4] Edelman,S and Bülthoff,H.H. (1992). Orientation dependence in the recognition of familiar and novel views of three-dimensional objects. *Vision Research,* **32**(12), 2385-2400.

[5] Fujita,T., Suzuki,S. and Ando, H. (1995). A network model that recognizes 3D objects: Alignment based on regularization principle. *Techinical Report of IEICE, NC95-61, 95-102 (in Japanese).*

[6] Kohonen,T. (1988). *Self-organization and associative memory.* 2nd ed. Springer-Verlag.

[7] Murase,H. and Nayer,S.K. (1995). Visual learning and recogniton of 3-D objects from appearance. *International Journal of Computer Vision,* **14**, 5-24.

[8] Oja,E. (1991). Data compression, feature extraction, and autoassociation in feedforward neural networks. In Kohonen,K. et al. (eds), *Artificial Neural Networks.* Elsevier Science publishers B.V., North-Holland.

[9] Poggio,T. and Edelman,S.(1990). A network that learns to recognize three-dimensional objects. *Nature,* 343,263

[10] Poggio,T. Torre,V. and Koch,C. (1985). Computational vision and regularization theory. *Nature,* 317,314-319.

[11] Suzuki,S. and Ando,H. (1993). Recognition and classification of 3D objects using a modular learning network. *Techinical Report of IEICE, NC93-62, 59-66 (in Japanese).*

[12] Suzuki,S. and Ando,H. (1995). Unsupervised classification of 3D objects from 2D views. In Tesauro,G., Touretzky,D. and Leen,T. (eds), *Advances in Neural Information Processing Systems 7.* The MIT Press, Cambridge, MA., 949-956.

Better Korean Grapheme Recognition by Expanding The Input Subimage Areas

Jin-Soo Lee[*], Oh-Jun kwon and Sung-Yang Bang

Department of Computer Science and Engineering
Pohang University of Science and Technology
Pohang, 790-784 Korea
[*]E-mail : ljsin@blackhol.postech.ac.kr

Abstract

This paper presents an idea how a graphemes can be better recognized by expanding the subimage area which contains the grapheme's image. The recognition of the graphemes is required when we take an approach in which we recognize a given input by first identifying its character type and then recognizing its constituent graphemes. The problem of this approach is that the other graphemes' strokes show up in the image area of a grapheme which we try to recognize. These line segments behave like noises and make the training of the neural network difficult. We solved the problem by expanding the input image area.

1   Introduction

Hanguel, Korean characters, is characterized by its large number of characters and its two dimensional composition of three graphemes called the first sound(consonant), the middle sound(vowel) and the optional last sound(consonant). The number of the graphemes which belong to the first sound is 19, that to the middle sound is 21 and that to the last sound is 27. The two dimensional composition of these graphemes makes it possible to generate, under some restrictions in the composition process, a total of 11,172 characters. But only 2,350 of them are regarded to be enough for daily use and given the two byte computer codes[6]. Since it is not easy to recognize a large number of different characters such as Hanguel, it is preferred to first recognize the constituent graphemes and then recognize the input character by combining them[1-4]. The number of graphemes for each sound is far less than that of characters as mentioned above and therefore the classification task becomes exceedingly easy when we approach the Korean character recognition problem this way. Especially such an approach is effective when we use neural networks since we can use smaller neural networks in stead of one big network. When we work for a large character set, we usually need a network with a large number of output nodes and the the number of the output nodes greatly affects the total size of the network. This is the approach we took. Now the problem is how to find the places of the constituent graphemes of the input so that we can recognize them.

Korean characters can be classified into the six types of composition as shown in Fig. 1. The Korean vowels are usually classified into three types, namely a horizontal, a vertical and a composite vowel. The type of the middle sound, namely the vowel type, and the option of the last sound determines which of the six types the character belongs to. The relative positions of the constituent graphemes in a character are fairly fixed depending on its type although minor shifts of individual graphemes after exist. Therefore it is possible to roughly locate the 3constituent graphemes once we determine the character type.

However it is not easy at all to accurately segment these subimages from the input image because of the following reasons. First, the position of each grapheme is not fixed and changes slightly from time to time depending on what graphemes come to the other sound places. Even the shape of a grapheme may vary for the sake of forming a good-looking and balanced shape of the entire character. Secondly the constituent graphemes in a character are not completely separated[1)] and sometimes even

---

1) Two graphemes are said to be separated when they can be covered by two different and unoverlapping rectangles.

touching each others as seen in Fig. 2. Thirdly, these phenomena exist not only among the characters of the same font but also among the same characters of the same font but of different sizes and among the same characters of different fonts. These factors make it not straightforward to recognize the printed Korean characters of multi-font and multi-size.

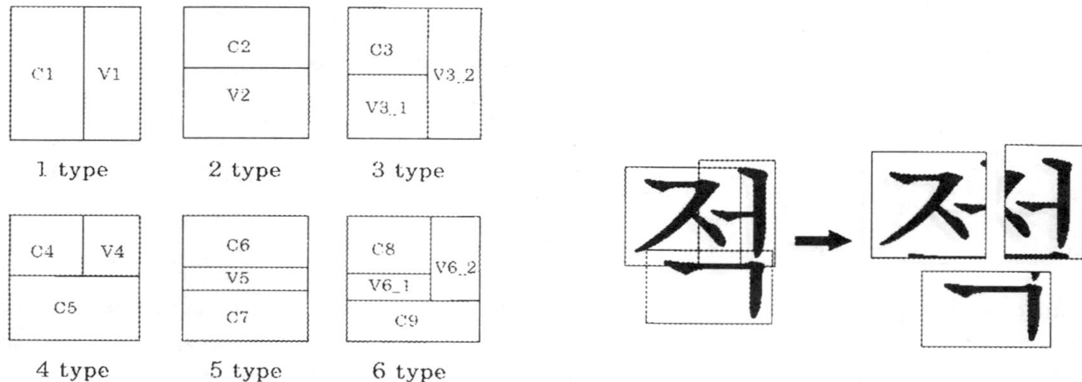

Fig. 1   The six types of Korean characters   Fig. 2   An example of subimage segmentation

The latter group, after the type classification, segment the subimages from the input image which area the constituent graphemes and use them as the inputs for the corresponding grapheme recognition neural networks. Hereafter we will use a subimage or a subimage area in order to denote the rectangle portion in the original input image which covers the subject grapheme's strokes. Our concern here is how to segment the right subimage area in each case.

It is usually not possible for a subimage to cover only the interested grapheme and exclude all other grapheme's strokes as depicted in Fig.2. Fortunately, thanks to the property of neural networks that they are in general robust to noise, we can tolerate this fact to a certain extent. One study reported a fairly nice recognition rate of 98% for a single font case[2]. However in the case of multi-font the recognition rate goes below 98% for most fonts and below 95% for a specific font[1]. It seems that resulted mainly because the portions of the other graphemes' strokes which appear inside a subimage become such an influential noise that it is difficult to train the corresponding neural network.

2   Overall structure of the system

The overall structure of our system is as depicted in Fig. 3. The architecture of the neural networks is the same as previously proposed[1]. It should be noticed that we use 18 modular networks : 1 type classifier and 17 grapheme classifiers. The system works as follows. The input image is first normalized to the size of 40×40 binary pixels and then the input features are extracted without any further preprocessing. Simple mesh feature is used as the input since it not only well represents positional information but also supports some shift invariance[5].

First this input feature is fed to the network which identifies the character type among the six. Once the type is determined, we segment the subimages for the constituent graphemes of the character type. The locations of all subimages are prefixed except for those for horizontal vowels, We will describe their segmentation method later. The number of all subimages for the six character types is 17. The number of the subimages for one type varies from 2 to 4 as seen in Fig. 1. Therefore there are 17 neural networks each of which was trained to recognize the graphemes in a subimage. We again extract the mesh feature from each subimage and use it as the input to the corresponding neural network. By combining the constituent graphemes thus identified we can easily identify the input character.

All the neural networks used here are MLP with one hidden layer[7]. We used the back-propagation algorithm with epsilon errors to train the networks in order to speed up the training and enhance the generalization[8].

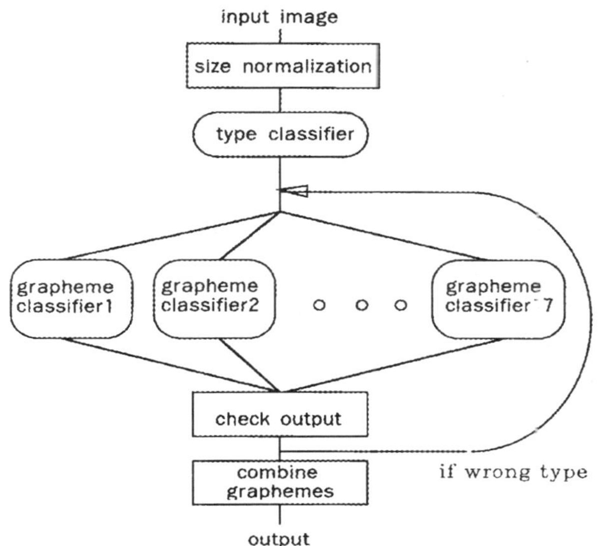

Fig. 3   Overall structure of our system

3   Improved grapheme recognition method

The kind of the noises which we handle here are actually the line segments of the other graphemes which are included in a subimage and hence probably should not be called noise. But we will some-times call them noise. Since we do not mention other regular noises here at all, there will be no con-fusion. In fact these line segments are a major cause for misrecognition of graphemes. The portion of these noises sometimes, especially for vowel graphemes, becomes larger than that of the useful infor-mation.

These noises have the following property. They appear in the same places and in the same shapes if we have the same character of the same font. In other words they appear exactly the same way in the test data as in the training data. However the problem is that these line segments lose their regul-arity and sometimes become real noises through distortion and with the help of other regular noises. We solved the problem by expanding the subimages to the extent that we can disambiguate these line segments with additional information. A simple example may help to understand our idea. The three images in Fig. 4(a) a look alike. Our task here is to recognize the horizontal vowel. The problem is whether the vertical line segment is a part of the vowel or a line segment of the other grapheme. It becomes clear suddenly and easily once we are given the larger pictures as shown in Fig. 4(b). The first and the third are a stroke by itself and a part of the grapheme ' ㅜ ' while the second is the upper line segment of the grapheme ' 人 '. The expanded images are extremely helpful for human to recognize the graphemes. We guess that the same is true for a neural network to learn.

Of course the input sizes becomes larger and hence the grapheme recognition networks become more complex if we expand the subimage areas. However we can show that we do not lose much but gain a lot by so doing. Fig. 5 shows the learning curves of the vowel grapheme recognition networks with the original subimage area sizes and with the new subimage area sizes. The graph indicates that the training of the new networks was easier and faster in spite of the larger input sizes. The original networks learned faster in the beginning, but they slowed down later and had difficulty in further converging after 0.04 of MSE. On the other hand the new networks could converge under 0.009 of MSE.

Next we will explain how to expand the subimage areas in further detail. First we review the orig-inal subimage areas used by the previous work[1] for the comparison. Here the subimage areas corres-ponding only to the vowel graphemes are given in Fig. 6(a) and explained because of the space limit-ation and their importance. They tried to minimize the subimage areas so that all necessary information is included but the line segments which belong to other grapheme's strokes are minimized. In such a case, however, some line segments become extremely ambiguous as mentioned above. This problem becomes worse in the case of the vowel graphemes and when the number of different fonts increases.

It was reported that 65% of the errors come from the incorrect recognition of the vowel graphemes.

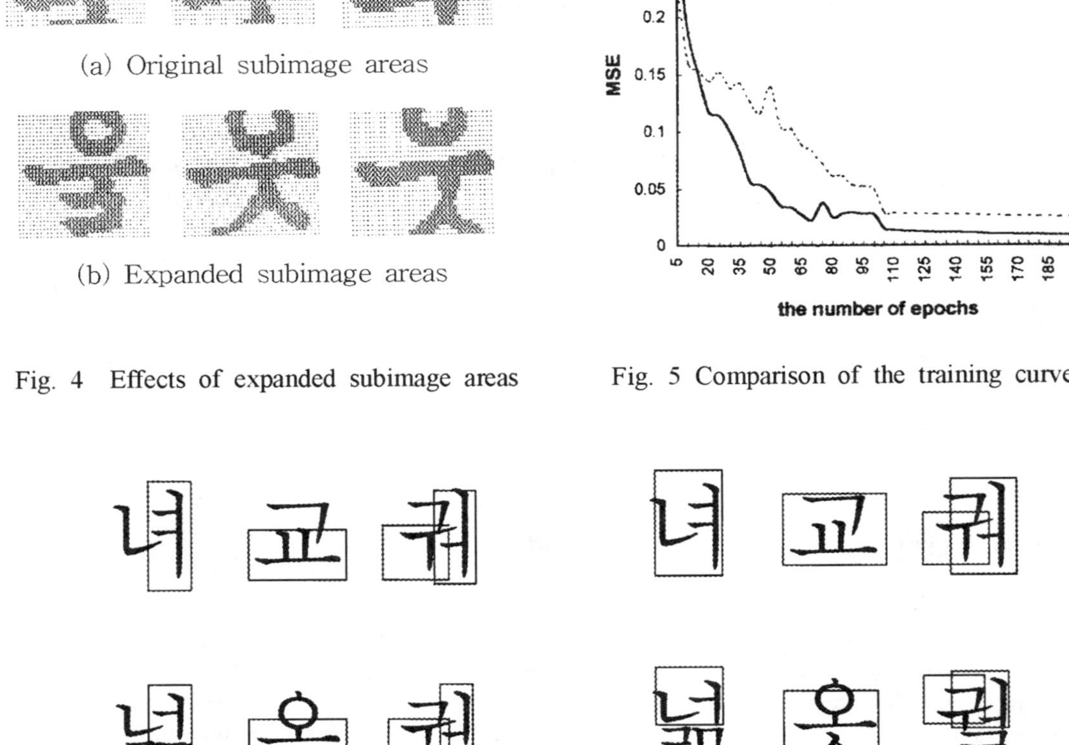

(a) Original subimage areas

(b) Expanded subimage areas

Fig. 4 Effects of expanded subimage areas

Fig. 5 Comparison of the training curves

(a) Original subimage areas

(b) Expanded subimage areas

Fig. 6 Expansion of the subimage areas for vowel graphemes

Next we show the expanded subimage areas adopted by us in Fib. 6(b). As seen in the figure we expanded the subimage areas but only to the extent that we can disambiguate the line segments. For example in case of type 4 the last sound information is usually not necessary and therefore not included. Further, in case of type 3, the vertical vowel information is not necessary to identify the vertical vowel and therefore excluded from the subimage area. However if there exist those line segments like these of the first sounds of all types, which become noises when we try to recognize the vowel graphemes, we include the entire strokes in the new subimages. By so doing we can avoid mistaking those line segments as the part of the vowel graphemes as explained earlier.

4   Evaluation and Analysis

Our system was implemented in C for UNIX on a workstation of HP 735. The tests used the first 1,405 characters according the order of the use frequency[6]. We used the two different fonts which we call 'Myungjo' and 'Gothic'. More specifically we used these fonts generated by a popular word processor called 'Hanguel' used on a IBM PC.

The test data were prepared in the following way. First we printed out the necessary character images by a 300 dpi laser printer on regular A4 print papers and then obtained their binary images by using a 300 dpi scanner. all the character images were segmented and normalized to 80×80 pixel images. We made up 9 different sets of the 1405 character images for each font. Each of these 9 sets corresponds to a specific character size. This means we prepared 9 different character sizes for each fonts. These character sizes were chosen between 10 point and 20 point. Among these nine data sets we used seven sets to train the networks and the other two sets to test the performance. Among these two sets one is of a small character size and the other of a large character size.

The printed character images were in a relatively good condition. However in case of Gothic font of 12 point or smaller there were cases where two close line were often put together.

The result of the test is shown in Table 1. We succeeded in obtaining recognition rate of higher then 99.5% for both fonts. This was made possible by reducing in a large number the errors which had occurred in the previous work. We list the errors of the grapheme recognition by the previous method as well as our method in Table 2. We could almost completely recognize 'ㅗ', 'ㅜ' and 'ㅡ' of type 5 and 'ㅓ', 'ㅕ', 'ㅏ', 'ㅑ' and 'ㅣ' of type 4 which were major problems to the previous method. By using the new method we could improve the performance for the vowel recognition alone by 73% and hence the performance for all grapheme recognition by 63%.

Table. 1 Recognition rates by type

fonts	type 1	type 2	type 3	type 4	type 5	type 6	average
Gothic	99.44%	100.00%	100.00%	99.29%	99.55%	100.00%	99.50%
Myongjo	100.00%	99.04%	100.00%	100.00%	99.55%	100.00%	99.80%
average	99.72%	99.52%	100.00%	99.65%	99.55%	100.00%	99.65%

Table. 2 Error lists of the grapheme recognition
(Each number indicates the frequencies of the error)

graphemes	Original method	Our method
consonant errors	ㄹ -> ㅌ (2) ㅉ -> ㅈ (1)	ㄹ -> ㅌ (2) ㅉ -> ㅈ (1)
vowel errors	ㅓ -> ㅕ (2), ㅑ -> ㅏ (1) ㅓ -> ㅐ (2), ㅐ -> ㅣ (1) ㅜ -> ㅡ (2), ㅠ -> ㅡ (1) ㅡ -> ㅗ (2), ㅡ -> ㅜ (3) ㅟ -> ㅝ (1)	ㅑ -> ㅏ (1), ㅠ -> ㅡ (1) ㅡ -> ㅜ (2)

5   Conclusion

This study presented a recognition system which can obtain a high recognition rate as well as a high reliability for the printed characters of multi-font and multi-size by exploiting the properties of Korean characters.

We took an approach which uses neural networks for type classification and grapheme recognition. We first determine the character type and segment the subimages for the constituent graphemes. Then we use the subimages as the input to the corresponding grapheme recognizer.

The main problem of this approach is that a part of the other graphemes' strokes are included in the subimage of the current grapheme. They not only make the training of the network difficult, but also cause recognition errors. We solved this problem by expanding the original subimage areas so that we can tell which strokes they are a part of. These expanded subimages actually make the network training easier and help obtain a high recognition rate.

Finally we confirmed through experiments that our idea improved the overall recognition rate significantly.

Acknowledgement--This study was supported in part by Korea Telecom under the contract 95-55 and by Korea Science Foundation under grant 92-21-00-05 and by SERI under the contract 94-32.

REFERENCE

[1] S.B.Cho, J.O.Kwon and J.H.Kim, NETeye:A Neural Network System for Recognizing Multi-font /Multi-size Hangul(Korean Script) Documents, in *Proc. 1st Int. Conf. on Document Analysis and Recognition,* 812-820. (1991)

[2] S.B.Cho and J.H.Kim, Recognition of Large-set printed Hangul(Korean Script) by Two-stage Back-propagation Neural Classifier, in *Pattern Recognition,* Vol.25, No.11, 1353-1360 (1992).

[3] S.J.Jang, S.M.Kang, H.G.Kim, W.S.Rho and D.J.Kim, A Study on Hanguel Character Recognition using GRNN, in *Journal of the Korea Institute of Electro- nics and Telematics,* **31-B**(1), 81-87 (1994)(in Korean).

[4] J.I.Doh, A Study on the Letter Segmentation of Hangul Characters for Printed Hangul Character Recognition, in *Proc. Korea Information Science Society,* **17**(2), 175-178 (1990)(in Korean).

[5] S.S.Kim, S.I.Chien, Improving Generalization and Noise Cancelling with the Partially Connected Recurrent Neural Network, in Proc. Int Joint Conf. on Neural Networks, Vol.1, Beijing, China, 166-171 (1992).

[6] K.S.Lee, K.S.Lee, A basic study on the output code system of the Hangeul, in *Proc. The fourth Hanguel and Korean Language Information Processing Confer- ence,* 285-291 (1992)(in Korean)

[7] D.E.Rumelhart, and J.L.McClelland, eds., *Parallel Dist- ributed Processing* : Explorations in the Microstructure of Cognition, **1**. Cambridge, MA : MIT Press (1989).

[8] Y.H.Yu, R.F.Simmons, Descending Epsilon in Back- Propagation : A Technique for Better Gener- ation. in *Proc. IEEE IJCNN,* **III**, 167-172 (1990).

Contour Classification by a Hopfield-Amari Network

Alan M. N. Fu†, Hong Yan‡

†Department of Electrical Engineering, University of Sydney
NSW 2006, Australia
‡Department of Electrical Engineering, University of Sydney
NSW 2006, Australia

***Abstract*—** **In this paper, a type of Hopfield-Amari neural network is built based on a so-called curve bent function for recognition of planar shapes (contours). The experimental results demonstrate that the proposed system is powerful and reliable in solving the shape recognition problems.**

1 Introduction

The Hopfield neural network is widely used to solve pattern recognition problems[1-3]. However, it is not known in advance how long the Hopfield network related to a practical application it will take to arrive at a stable state, and also it is not known whether the stable state is a global one or not.

Another Hopfield-type network is the Hopfield-Amari network, which is a synchronous update recurrent associative memory network. The statistical dynamics of the network has been studied by many researchers (for example, Amari and Maginu[4], Amit[5], Nishimori and Ozaki[6], Patrick and Zagrebnov[7-8], Zagrebnov and Chvyrov[9], and Fu[10]).

An essential dynamical feature of the Hopfield-Amari network is that it always converges to a stable state within about 40 iterations [11]. This property enables us to solve pattern recognition and shape analysis problems from its dynamic process directly[12].

In this paper, the Hopfield-Amari network designed by using the properties of a function called *curve bent function* (CBF) is proposed for classifying planar shapes. In Section 2, we present the CBF and define the features of a planar shape. The structure of Hopfield-Amari network is given in Section 3. The experimental results and conclusion are presented in Section 4.

2 The Properties of CBF and Features of a Planar Shape

A contour is a boundary of an object represented by a binary image:

$$I(x, y) = \begin{cases} 1 & \text{if } (x, y) \in object \\ 0 & \text{otherwise.} \end{cases} \tag{1}$$

The points on a contour can be traced and labeled counter clockwise from an arbitrary starting point, and represented by the array: $\Omega = \{S_k, \ k = 0, 1, \ldots, M-1\}$, where M is the total number of points. A contour is a closed planar curve, thus Ω can be considered as a periodic function with a period M.

A portion of a contour, composed of 2J+1 points $S_i, \ldots, S_{i+2J}$, is denoted by D_i, where J is a positive number called *supported length or step length*.

Suppose a line segment $S_{i+J}H_i$ is drawn perpendicular to S_iS_{i+2J}, and H_i is the intersecting point of $S_{i+J}H_i$ and S_iS_{i+2J}.

Definition 1 If there exists a positive number $k > 0$ such that
$\cos \angle S_{i-l}S_{i-l+J}H_{i-l} \leq \cos \angle S_iS_{i+J}H_i \geq \cos \angle S_{i+l}S_{i+J+l}H_{i+l}$, for $l = 0, 1, \ldots, k$, then $\angle S_iS_{i+J}H_i$ is referred to a curve bent angle (CBA) of D_i. It is satisfactory to set k=5 ~ 10.

Definition 2 For a given J, if there is no more than one CBA which is lay in D_i, then D_i is known as a simple curve segment (SCS), and the J is referred to a suitable step length.

Definition 3 For a given suitable step length J, the type coefficient of D_i is defined as

$$r_i = 2I(c_{ix}, c_{iy}) - 1 \tag{2}$$

where I(x,y) is given by (1), (c_{ix}, c_{iy}) is the coordinate of the centroid c_i of line segment S_iS_{i+2J}.

If $r_i = 1$, then the curve $\widetilde{S_iS_{i+2J}}$ is convex, otherwise it is concave.

A complete description of a contour can be generated by a function known as *Curve Bent Function*(CBF) which is given below.

Definition 4 A CBF is defined on contour Ω given by

$$G(S_i) = a_i \cos(\angle S_iS_{i+J}H_i), \ S_i \in \Omega \tag{3}$$

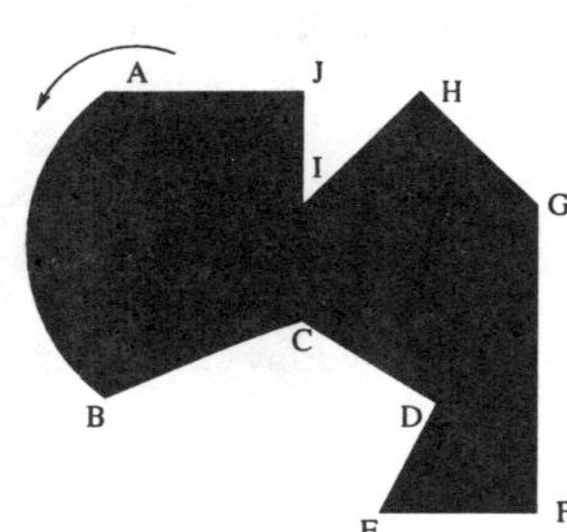
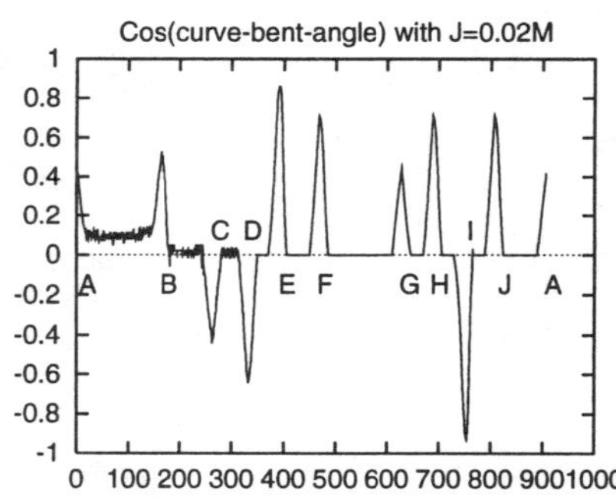

Figure 1: Shape 1 and it's description

Table 1: Degrees of angles of Shape 1

Angles and degrees	J=0.02M	J=0.03M	J=0.05M	J=0.08M
$\angle$A:	128.19°	125.05°	120.51°	114.39°
$\angle$B:	116.61°	114.34°	107.82°	97.51°
$\angle$C: 128° (outer)	-127.32°	-126.28	-124.27°	-121.9°
$\angle$D: 93° (outer)	-100.01°	-98.98°	-98.24°	-105.34°
$\angle$E: 63° (inner)	60.7o	60.55°	61.7°	58.77°
$\angle$F: 90° (inner)	90°	90°	90°	90°
$\angle$G: 132° (inner)	126.87°	126.87°	126.87°	N/A
$\angle$H: 90° (inner)	90°	90°	90°	90.92°
$\angle$I: 45° (outer)	-44.33°	-41.47°	-41.67°	-97.66°
$\angle$J: 90° (inner)	90°	90°	90°	90.14°

where

$$a_i = \begin{cases} 2I(H_i^x, H_i^y) - 1 & \text{if } ((\rho(S_i, H_i) < \rho(S_i, S_{i+2J})) \cap (\rho(S_{i+2J}, H_i) < \rho(S_i, S_{i+2J}))) \\ 1 - 2I(H_i^x, H_i^y) & \text{otherwise.} \end{cases} \tag{4}$$

(H_i^x, H_i^y) is the coordinate of H_i, and the operator $\cap$ in "$X \cap Y$" means both X and Y hold.

Shape 1 and its descriptions, $G(S)$, obtained by CBF with the supported length J=0.02M are shown in Figure 1. The absolute value of $G(S)$ measures the magnitude of a CBA, while its sign indicates whether the CBA is an inner or outer angle. The actual magnitudes of angles of Shape 1 are shown in the first column of Table 1. Note that the "angles" with vertexes A and B are not exact angles, and their actual magnitudes are not available. The other columns of the table show the degrees of angles of the shape evaluated by CBF with J=0.02M, 0.03M, 0.05M and 0.08M, respectively. When J=0.08M, the information of $\angle$G is not available. So the supported length J can not be larger than 0.08M, and its suitable value is 0.02M to 0.05M. In our experiment J is 0.02M.

In order to yield a set of reliable dominant points of Ω by $G(S)$, the two procedures of pre-processing of G(S) below are applied.

- Most angles having values close to 180° are spurious. We have to remove these angles in the pre-processing stage by a thresholding-filter, that is

$$G(S_i) = \begin{cases} G(S_i) & \text{if } |G(S_i)| > c_t \\ 0 & \text{otherwise}, \end{cases} \tag{5}$$

  where c_t is a threshold value, and it is chosen to be 0.3 in our experiments.

- To ensure that no more than one angle exists in each SCS, supposing m angles: $A_{i_1}, A_{i_2}, \ldots, A_{i_m}$ lie on D_i, then we define

$$|G(S_{i_1})| = 1/m \sum_{j=1}^{m} |G(S_{i_j})| \tag{6}$$

and

$$|G(S_{i_j})| = 0, \quad j = 2, \ldots, m. \tag{7}$$

After the above pre-processing we now achieve an approximate representation of Ω, a curve-polygon (CPG)[1] having L corners at which each angle is smaller than 145°. Thus, the problem of contour recognition is reduced to the classification of CPG. A CPG can be characterized by three distributive and three concentrated features which are given below.

---

[1] Two edges of a corner may be line segments or one or both of them are SCS. This is different with an ordinary polygon.

(1) Distributive features.

   (i) The kth corner cosine of CPG is defined as

$$u_1(k) = |G(\hat{S}_k)|\tag{8}$$

  (ii) The kth centroid-corner cosine of CPG is defined as

$$u_2(k) = \cos\left(\angle O\hat{S}_k\hat{S}_{k+1}\right)\tag{9}$$

     where O is the centroid of the shape.

  (iii) The relative cosine between kth and jth corners of CPG is defined as

$$u_3(kj) = \cos\left(\angle \hat{S}_k O\hat{S}_j\right)\tag{10}$$

(2) Concentrated features.

   (i) The kth corner coefficient of CPG is defined as

$$v_1(k) = \hat{r}_k\tag{11}$$

     where the $\hat{r}_k$ is the type coefficient of $\hat{D}_k$ given by (2), and $\hat{D}_k$ is the curve segment composed of $S_{k_l}, \ldots, S_{k_l+2J}$ and S_{k_l} is the same as $\hat{S}_k$.

  (ii) The kth corner left coefficient of CPG is defined as

$$v_2(k) = 2I(\hat{x}_{kk-1}, \hat{y}_{kk-1}) - 1\tag{12}$$

     where $(\hat{x}_{kk-1}, \hat{y}_{kk-1})$ is the coordinate of the centroid of $\hat{S}_k\hat{S}_{k-1}$.

  (iii) The kth corner right coefficient of CPG is defined as

$$v_3(k) = 2I(\hat{x}_{kk+1}, \hat{y}_{kk+1}) - 1\tag{13}$$

     where $(\hat{x}_{kk+1}, \hat{y}_{kk+1})$ is the coordinate of the centroid of line segment $\hat{S}_k\hat{S}_{k+1}$.

3   Neural Network and Matching Procedures

Let n_s and n_m represent the numbers of elements (i.e. *vertexes*) of sample and model shapes' CPG, respectively. For a given model shape and sample shape, a two-dimensional Hopfield-Amari network with $n_s n_m$ neurons related to the two shapes can be constructed. In general, the columns of network correspond to the elements of the model shape, and the rows correspond to the elements of the sample shape. In order to determine the interconnection weights of the network, we consider its energy function defined as[12]:

$$E(t) = -\frac{1}{2}\sum_{i=1}^{n_s}\sum_{k=1}^{n_m}\sum_{j=1}^{n_s}\sum_{l=1}^{n_m} w_{ikjl}V_{ik}(t)V_{jl}(t)\,,\tag{14}$$

where $V_{ik}(t)$ is a state variable which converges to 1 if the ith element in the sample shape matches the kth element in the model shape; otherwise, it converges to -1. w_{ikjl} is the interconnection weight given by

$$w_{ikjl} = \frac{1}{n_m n_s}\left\{\sum_{p=1}^{2} d_1[f_p(i, k) + f_p(j, l)] + d_2 f_3(ij, kl)\right\}\tag{15}$$

where $f_p(\;)\;(p = 1, 2, 3)$ are goodness functions defined as

$$f_p(x, y) = \begin{cases} 1 & \text{if } (\rho(u_p^s(x), u_p^m(y)) < d) \cap (z_1(x, y) = 1)\,, \; p = 1, 2 \\ -1 & \text{otherwise}\,, \end{cases}\tag{16}$$

$$f_3(ij, kl) = \begin{cases} 1 & \text{if } (\rho(u_3^s(ij), u_3^m(kl)) < d) \cap (z_2(ij, kl) = 1) \\ -1 & \text{otherwise}\,, \end{cases}\tag{17}$$

where

$$z_1(x, y) = \begin{cases} 1 & \text{if } \cap_{q=1}^3 (v_q^s(x) = v_q^m(y)) \\ -1 & \text{otherwise}\,, \end{cases}\tag{18}$$

$$z_2(ij, kl) = \begin{cases} 1 & \text{if } \cap_{q=1}^3 (v_q^s(i) + v_q^s(j) = v_q^m(k) + v_q^m(l)) \\ -1 & \text{otherwise}\,, \end{cases}\tag{19}$$

superscripts "m" and "s" denote that the features are extracted from the model and sample shapes, respectively; the operator "$\cap$" in $X \cap Y$ means that both X and Y hold, and $\cap_{q=1}^3 X_q$ means all X_q, ($q = 1, 2, 3$) are true; $d > 0$ is a threshold value; d_1 and d_2 are weight coefficients which satisfy

$$4d_1 + d_2 = 1\,.\tag{20}$$

The condition (20) ensures that $w_{ikjl} = \frac{1}{n_s n_m}$ when the ith element of sample matches the kth element of model, and the jth element of sample matches the lth element of model, respectively.

Neuron activity updates are governed by

$$V_{ik}(t+1) = \text{Sign}\left(\sum_{j=1}^{n_s}\sum_{l=1}^{n_m} w_{ikjl} V_{jl}(t)\right), \tag{21}$$

where

$$\text{Sign}(x) = \begin{cases} 1 & \text{if } x > 0 \\ -1 & \text{otherwise}. \end{cases} \tag{22}$$

The compatibility measure w_{ikjl} can be rewritten as

$$w_{ikjl} = \frac{V_{ik}^0 V_{jl}^0}{n_m n_s} + w_{ikjl} - \frac{V_{ik}^0 V_{jl}^0}{n_m n_s} \tag{23}$$

where $V_{ik}^0 = 1$ or -1, and the $n_s n_m$-dimensional vector $\mathbf{V}^0 = (V_{11}^0, \ldots, V_{n_s n_m}^0)^T$ denote the target memory stored in the network that we intend to retrieve.

The stable state of the network reflect the similarity between the model and sample shapes. The degree of similarity between two shapes called the matching rate denoted by R can be defined as

$$R = \frac{\sum_{i=1}^{n_s} \text{row}_i + \sum_{j=1}^{n_m} \text{col}_j}{n_s + n_m}, \tag{24}$$

where $\text{row}_i = \max\{\frac{V_{ij}+1}{2} : j = 1, \ldots, n_m\}$ and $\text{col}_j = \max\{\frac{V_{ij}+1}{2} : i = 1, \ldots, n_s\}$. Obviously, $0 \leq R \leq 1$.

The achievement of a reliable and accurate matching result, that is, a high matching rate when the sample and model are from a same class, and low matching rate otherwise, depends on identifying appropriate thresholds for transforming element features of model and sample CPG into the neural network weights. This problem is solved through an optimization process using a set of training shapes which is composed of i_m shapes from the same class as the model and i_d other shapes from different classes. The process consists of the following steps:

1. Initialize the neuron activities, setting all neurons to 1 (i.e. in excited state).
2. Set weight coefficients d_1 and d_2.
3. Set initial threshold d.
4. Perform Steps 5 to 7 $n_t = i_m + i_d$ times, using the network to compare the model with each one of the training shapes.
5. Create a 2D Hopfield-Amari network of size n_m by n_s.
6. Determine goodness functions (Equation (16) and (17)) and calculate w_{ikjl} (Equation (15)).
7. Synchronously update the neuron activities (Equation (21)) through 40 iterations.
8. Calculate matching rate R. (For the optimization process, n_t values are calculated, R_{m_i}, $i = 1, \ldots, i_m$ and R_{d_k}, $k = 1, \ldots, i_d$, for shapes in same class as model and in different classes respectively).
9. Update parameters.
   (a) If all $R_{m_i} \sim 1$ and all $R_{d_k} \sim 0$ go to Step 10. (b) If all $R_{m_i} \sim 1$ and $R_{d_k} \sim 1$ decrease d, and goto Step 4. (c) If most $R_{m_i} \sim 0$ and all $R_{d_k} \sim 0$ increase d, and goto Step 4. (d) If it is not successful after (a) to (c), then goto Step 2.
10. Stop.

After this process, a set of estimated thresholds (i.e. d_1, d_2 and d) can be defined for the model. A test shape is compared to the model by calculating the feature values for its elements, constructing a network using the optimized thresholds and evaluating the matching rate. This corresponds to **Steps 6** to **8** in the optimization process, and is carried out for each model in turn.

4   Experimental Results and Conclusion

In our experiments, for each given model the training shapes are composed of 6 shapes, 3 of which are in the same class as the model, while the rest are selected from different classes. We select $d_1 = d_2 = 0.2$, then the optimal threshold d is 0.08 after the optimization process. Note that for different selection of d_1 and d_2, the corresponding optimal threshold d may be different in general. The shapes shown in Fig. 3 are used to test the efficacy of the scheme. The results are shown in Tables 2. A test shape is considered to be in the same class as a model when their matching rate is larger than certain critical value $\bar{R}$. If $\bar{R}=0.8$, then the experimental results suggest that samples 21 to 25, 1 to 5, 8 to 15 and 18 to 20 belong to the classes as models A, B, C and D, respectively. While the rest of samples do not belong to one of the four categories of models. This conclusion is in agreement with the actual distribution of the shapes in Fig. 3. Our system is effective and reliable to classify planar shapes which are composed of several SCS.

Table 2: Matching rates between models and samples.

	Model A	Model B	Model C	Model D
Sample 1	.00	1.0	.12	.11
Sample 2	.00	1.0	.12	.11
Sample 3	.00	1.0	.00	.11
Sample 4	.00	.86	.00	.11
Sample 5	.00	.86	.12	.11
Sample 6	.13	.00	.11	.00
Sample 7	.13	.00	.11	.00
Sample 8	.24	.12	1.0	.19
Sample 9	.24	.12	1.0	.10
Sample 10	.24	.12	1.0	.10
Sample 11	..24	.12	1.0	.10
Sample 12	.24	.12	1.0	.19
Sample 13	.24	.12	1.0	.19
Sample 14	.24	.12	1.0	.19
Sample 15	.24	.12	1.0	.19
Sample 16	.00	.00	.00	.00
Sample 17	.00	.00	.00	.00
Sample 18	.00	.11	.19	1.0
Sample 19	.00	.11	.19	1.0
Sample 20	.00	.11	.19	1.0
Sample 21	1.0	.00	.24	.00
Sample 22	1.0	.00	.24	.00
Sample 23	.86	.00	.24	.00
Sample 24	.86	.00	.24	.00
Sample 25	.86	.00	.24	.00

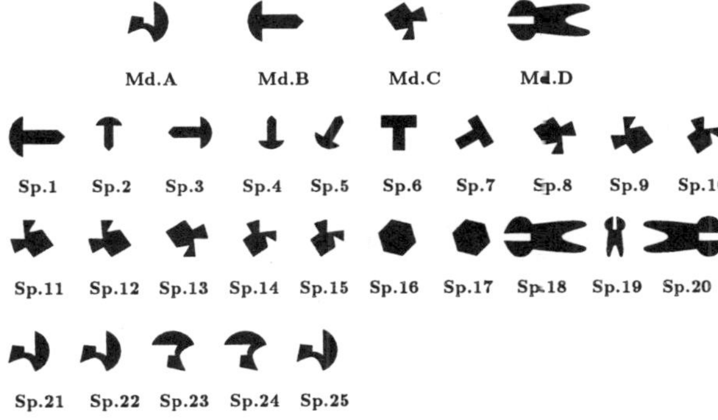

Fig.2. Shapes used in our experiments.

References

[1] J. J. Hopfield and D. W. Tank, ""Neural" computation of decisions in optimization problems," *Biol. Cybern.* **52** 141-152, 1985.

[2] W. C. Lin, H. Y. Liao, C. K. Tsao and T. Lingutla, "A hierarchical multiple-view approach to three-dimensional object recognition," *IEEE Trans. Neural Networks* **2** (1) 84-92, 1991.

[3] H. Y. Liao, J. S. Huang and S. T. Huang, "Stroke-based handwritten chinese character recognition using neural networks," *Pattern Recogn. Lett.*, **14** 833-840, 1993.

[4] S. Amari and K. Maginu, "Statistical neurodynamics of associative memory," *Neural Networks* Vol. **1**, 63-73, 1988.

[5] D. J. Amit, *Modeling brain function*, Cambridge: Cambridge University press, 1989.

[6] H. Nishimori and T. Ozaki, "Retrieval dynamics of associative memory of the Hopfield type," *J. Phys. A: Math. Gen.*, No. **26**, 859-871, 1993.

[7] A. E. Patrick and V. A. Zagrebnov , " On the parallel dynamics for the Little-Hopfield model," *J. S. Phys.*, No. **63**(1/2), 59-71, 1991a.

[8] A. E. Patrick and V. A. Zagrebnov, "A probabilistic approach to parallel dynamics for the Little-Hopfield model," *J. Phys. A: Math. Gen.*, **24**, 3413-3426, 1991b.

[9] V. A. Zagrebnov and A. S. Chvyrov, "The Little-Hopfield model: Recurrence relations for retrieval-pattern errors," *Sov. Phys.-JETP*, **68**, 153-157, 1989.

[10] A. M. N. Fu, "Statistical analysis of an autoassociative memory network," *Neural Computation*, Vol. **6**, No. **5**, 837-841, 1994.

[11] A. M. N. Fu and H. Yan, "The distributive properties of main overlap and noise terms in autoassociative memory network," *Neural Networks*, Vol. 8, No. **3**, 405-410, 1995.

[12] A. M. N. Fu, H. Yan and M. G. Suters, "Flexible pattern matching using a Hopfield-Amari neural network," *Optical Engineering*, Vol. 34, No. **8**, 2467-2474, 1995.

Deformation Theory of the Dynamic Link Architecture

Toru AONISHI, Koji KURATA
Department of Biophysical Engineering, Faculty of Engineering Science, Osaka University
1-3, Machikaneyama-cho, Toyonaka, Osaka 560, Japan
aonishi@bpe.es.osaka-u.ac.jp

Abstract— Dynamic link is a topographic mapping formed between template image and data image. The mapping is continuous, but tends to link two points sharing similar local features, and so, can be deformed to some extent. To analyze this deformation mathematically, we reduce the model equation to a phase equation of reaction-diffusion type.

1 Introduction

Pattern recognition invariant against deformation or transformation can be performed with the dynamic link architecture, which has been proposed by von der Malsburg[1]. The dynamic links specify a flexible matching between a template pattern and a data pattern, where local features in the data pattern have to be matched with their counterparts in the template pattern. The dynamic link architecture is based on the models of self-organizing topographic map and has a week tendency to link two points sharing similar features. Since the self-organizing map has a characteristic of *elastic nets*, the map tends to conserve an identical relation repulling disturbances. So, the map is continuous, but tends to link two points sharing similar local features, and so, can be deformed to some extent.

The dynamic links are applied to some engineering examples [3][4] efficiently, but have not yet been analyzed mathematically. We propose a mathematically tractable model based on the local excitation system. We reduce the model equation to a phase equation of reaction-diffusion type which gives us a mathematical understanding on the principle of the flexible matching process.

We can classify the dynamic link architecture into two types. One is the high-dimensional representation(von der Malsbulg[1] [2]), in which the map is expressed by synaptic weight distribution on the product space of the two image spaces. The other is the low-dimensional representation corresponding directly to the graph matching (von der Malsbulg[3], E. Bienenstock[4]). The map is, in this case, expressed by the reference vectors like in Kohonen map [5]. Our theory bridges the gap between these two types.

2 Model description

Figure (1.a) shows the schematic diagram of the model. The problem we are considering here is how to build a flexible matching between a one-dimensional data image and a one-dimensional template image. Input patterns are feature vector functions defined on F_1 and F_2. Here, we simply take $F_1 = F_2 = \mathbf{R}$ to avoid boundary effects. This assumption does not lose the generality, since the theory can be applied to the models with boundary conditions. These feature vectors are defined as $I_1(r_1), r_1 \in F_1$ and $I_2(r_2), r_2 \in F_2$. I_1 and I_2 are equal up to a certain deformed topographic transformation. The system has to match local features in the data image with their counterparts in the template image, thus produce a topographic mapping from F_1 to F_2. The map is expressed by synaptic weight distribution $w(r_1, r_2)$ on $F_1 \times F_2$.

The model equation is

$$\frac{\partial}{\partial t} w(r_1, r_2, t) = -w + K f(w) + \varepsilon^2 s(r_1, r_2), \tag{1}$$

$$K f(w) = \int_{-\infty}^{\infty} \int_{-\infty}^{\infty} dr_1' dr_2' k(r_1', r_2') f\left(w(r_1 - r_1', r_2 - r_2')\right),$$

where $|\varepsilon| << 1$ and $s(r_1, r_2)$ is a local similarity between $I_1(r_1)$ and $I_2(r_2)$

$$s(r_1, r_2) = v(I_1(r_1), I_2(r_2)). \tag{2}$$

This equation consists of two parts. The first part $-\frac{\partial}{\partial t} w - w + K f(w)$ is a self-organizing part, which tends to conserve topology. The second part $\varepsilon^2 s$ is a perturbation term, which tends to link two points assigned similar features in I_1 and I_2.

3 Self-organizing part

Let us begin with considering about the self-organizing part

$$\frac{\partial}{\partial t} w(r_1, r_2, t) = -w + K f(w). \tag{3}$$

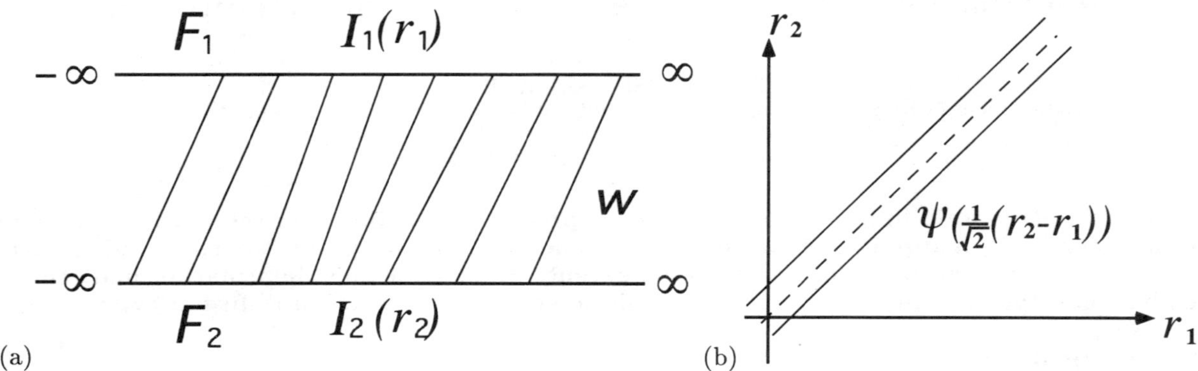

Figure 1: (a)Schematic diagram of our model. I_1 and I_2 are equal up to a certain deformed topographic transformation. The system has to produce a topographic mapping from F_1 to F_2. The mapping is expressed by synaptic weight distribution $w(r_1, r_2)$ on $F_1 \times F_2$. (b)Schematic diagram of a topographic mapping (an equilibrium solution). This solution is a mountain chain on a diagonal line.

The integration kernel k in the linear operator K(Eq. (1)) is 2-dimensional isotropic Mexican hat type and f is a sigmoidal function with $f'(x) > 0$ (monotonous increasing function).

If all parameters are set appropriately, we can make this dynamics have a following equilibrium solution:

$$w(r_1, r_2, t) = \psi\left(\frac{1}{\sqrt{2}}(r_2 - r_1)\right).$$

This solution is a mountain chain on a diagonal line as shown in Figure(1.b) . Figure(2.b) shows an example of $\psi(x)$ obtained by a computer simulation. If $r_1 \in F_1$ is fixed, w is a function in the domain F_2. Then, we can define a topographic mapping as:

$$w: \quad F_1 \to F_2$$
$$r_1 \to r_2|\text{maximum point of } w.$$

By easy mathematical treatments, this system is put in another coordinate system

$$\begin{pmatrix} x \\ y \end{pmatrix} = \begin{pmatrix} 1/\sqrt{2} & 1/\sqrt{2} \\ 1/\sqrt{2} & -1/\sqrt{2} \end{pmatrix} \begin{pmatrix} r_1 \\ r_2 \end{pmatrix}. \tag{4}$$

Rewriting in this coordinates, we obtain

$$\frac{\partial}{\partial t} w(x, y, t) = -w + Kf(w), \tag{5}$$

$$Kf(w) = \int_{-\infty}^{\infty} \int_{-\infty}^{\infty} dx'dy'k(x', y')f\left(w(x - x', y - y')\right),$$

where kernel k is not changed by the transformation of coordinate because of its isotropy. The equilibrium solution is rewritten as:

$$w(x, y, t) = \psi(y). \tag{6}$$

Figure(2.a) shows an example of the equilibrium solution obtained by a numerical calculation of Eq. (5).

Eq. (5) is invariant under the spatial shift along y-axis. Therefore, $\psi(y+\theta)$ is also an equilibrium solution in any $\theta, |\theta| < \infty$. The θ stands for the *phase* of this solution. If we define $\psi(0)$ as a maximum value, θ represents the center of the receptive field, which can be considered as the reference vector, for example, in Kohonen map[5].

Substituting $w(x, y, t) = \psi(y + \theta) + \varepsilon u(y, t)$ into Eq. (5), and linearizing around $\varepsilon = 0$, we obtain the following operator

$$L_\theta = -1 + K_y(f'(\psi(y + \theta)) \cdot), \tag{7}$$

$$K_y u(x, y) = \int_{-\infty}^{\infty} \int_{-\infty}^{\infty} dx'dy'k(x', y')u(x, y - y').$$

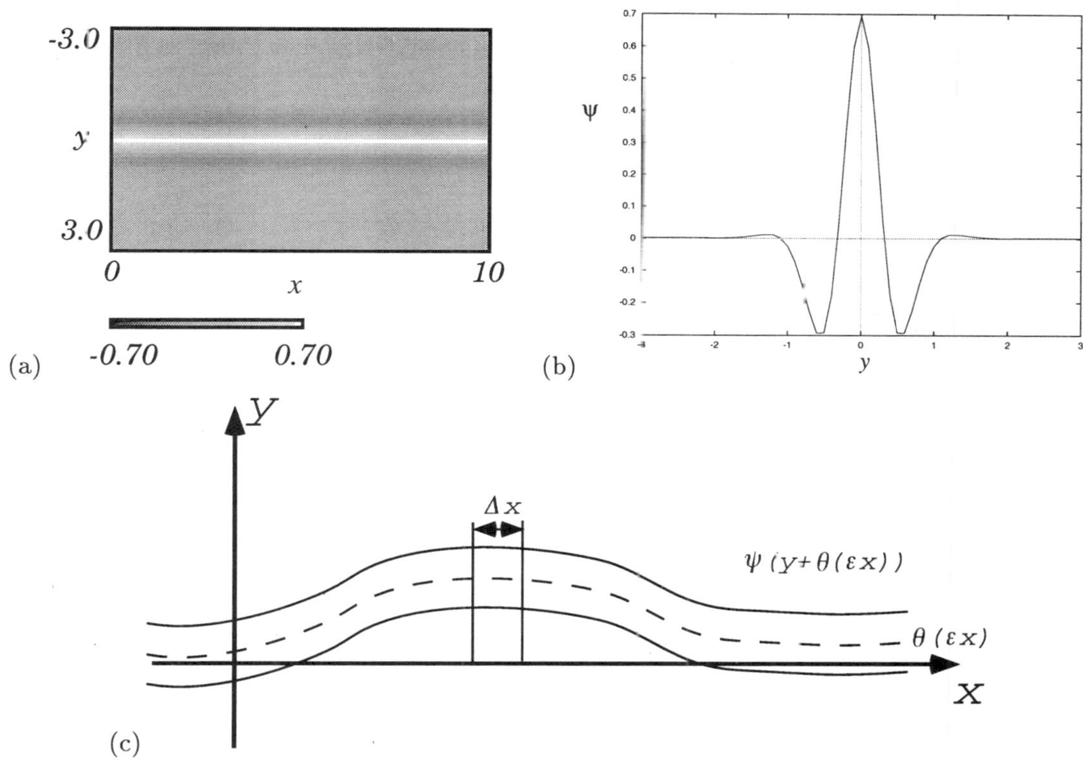

Figure 2: (a) Rotated equilibrium solution obtained by a computer simulation. (b) One-dimensional cross section of the equilibrium solution (b). (c) Schematic diagram of a deformed solution by the perturbation. We can regard that this solution does not vary along x axis within a small region.

All the eigen-values of L_θ are non-positive since the equilibrium solution $\psi(y+\theta)$ is stable. However, 0 is its eigen-value with eigen-function $\psi'(y+\theta)$ because $-\psi + Kf(\psi) = 0$. This eigen-function corresponds to a perturbation of spatially shifting, because $\psi(y+\theta+\varepsilon) \doteq \psi(y+\theta) + \varepsilon\psi'(y+\theta)$. We assume there exist no other eigen-functions for eigen-value 0, that is,

$$\ker L_\theta = \mathrm{span}\{\psi'(y+\theta)\}. \tag{8}$$

Thus, this assumption is equivalent to the wave form stability of $\psi(y+\theta)$.

Here, we consider Hilbert space $H = \{u : \mathbf{R} \to \mathbf{R} | \langle u, u \rangle < \infty\}$. The inner product is defined as:

$$\langle u_1(y), u_2(y)\rangle \equiv \int_{-\infty}^{\infty} dy u_1(y) u_2(y). \tag{9}$$

We can explicitly obtain the adjoint operator of L_θ

$$L_\theta^* = -1 + f'(\psi(y+\theta))K_y, \tag{10}$$

as far as k is even w.r.t y. we can obtain the kernel function of L_θ^*

$$\ker L_\theta^* = \mathrm{span}\{f'(\psi(y+\theta))\psi'(y+\theta)\}. \tag{11}$$

4   Perturbation

Here, we consider the perturbed model

$$\frac{\partial}{\partial t}w(x,y,t) = -w + Kf(w) + \varepsilon^2 s(x,y), \tag{12}$$

where the local similarity in Eq. (2) is transformed into $s(x,y)$ by Eq. (4). Since ε is very small, the self-organizing part is weakly affected by the image data. The equilibrium solution Eq. (6) is gently deformed by the effect of the perturbation. We assume that the deformed solution can be expressed by

$$w(x,y,t) = \psi(y + \theta(\xi,\tau)) + \varepsilon u_1(\xi,y,\tau) + \varepsilon^2 u_2(\xi,y,\tau), \tag{13}$$

where $\xi = \varepsilon x$, $\tau = \varepsilon^2 t$. ξ is slowly varying space variable and τ denotes slowly varying time. We can regard that this solution does not vary along x axis within a small region as shown in Figure(2.c).

From this assumption, we can derive the following equations

$$0 = -\psi + K_y f(\psi) + \varepsilon L_\theta u_1 + \varepsilon^2 \left(L_\theta u_2 - m_2 \right), \tag{14}$$

$$
\begin{aligned}
m_2 \;=\; & \psi'(y+\theta)\frac{\partial\theta}{\partial\tau} \\
& - \frac{1}{2}G_1(y+\theta)\left(\frac{\partial\theta}{\partial\xi}\right)^2 - \frac{1}{2}G_2(y+\theta)\frac{\partial^2\theta}{\partial\xi^2} \\
& - \frac{1}{2}K_y f''(\psi(y+\theta))u_1{}^2 - s(x,y),
\end{aligned}
$$

$$G_1(y) = \int_{-\infty}^{\infty}\int_{-\infty}^{\infty} dx'dy' k(x',y')x'^2 \left(f'(\psi(y-y'))\psi''(y-y') + f''(\psi(y-y'))\psi'(y-y')^2 \right),$$

$$G_2(y) = \int_{-\infty}^{\infty}\int_{-\infty}^{\infty} dx'dy' k(x',y')x'^2 f'(\psi(y-y'))\psi'(y-y').$$

Here we can not neglect the $O(\varepsilon^2)$ term since the order of the perturbation is $O(\varepsilon^2)$. The coefficient of ε^0 satisfies 0 from the equilibrium condition. Therefore Eq. (14) can be reduced as follow:

$$0 = L_\theta u_1 + \varepsilon \left(L_\theta u_2 - m_2 \right). \tag{15}$$

Since $L_\theta u_1 = O(\varepsilon)$, $\varepsilon << 1$, we get u_1 in the following form:

$$u_1 = a\psi'(y+\theta) + \varepsilon \overline{u}_1. \tag{16}$$

where a is an arbitrary constant. Substituting this into Eq. (15), we obtain

$$L_\theta \overline{u}_1 + L_\theta u_2 - m_2 = 0. \tag{17}$$

Taking the inner product (9) between $f'(\psi(y+\theta))\psi'(y+\theta)$ and Eq. (17), we obtain

$$\langle f'(\psi(y+\theta))\psi'(y+\theta), m_2\rangle = 0. \tag{18}$$

Since $k(x,y)$ is the even function, we can expect that $\psi(y)$ is also the even function. Thus $\psi'(y)$ and $f'(\psi(y))\psi'(y)$ are the odd functions, $G_1(y)$ is the even function and $G_2(y)$ is the odd function.

Eliminating some terms by the inner product, the equation of reaction-diffusion is derived as follows:

$$c\frac{\partial\theta(\xi,\tau)}{\partial\tau} = \frac{d}{2}\frac{\partial^2\theta(\xi,\tau)}{\partial\xi^2} + \frac{\partial}{\partial\theta}\langle f(\psi(y+\theta)), s(\xi/\varepsilon, y)\rangle, \tag{19}$$

where

$$c = \langle f'(\psi(y))\psi'(y), \psi'(y)\rangle, \qquad d = \langle f'(\psi(y))\psi'(y), G_2(y)\rangle.$$

Since there exist no degree of freedom for u_1 and u_2, we can uniquely determine θ. Thus, we have reduced the model equation to the phase equation.

The first term of the right hand side is the diffusion term, which tends to conserve the spatial continuity of θ. As previously discussed, θ is the center of the receptive field. The second term of the right hand side is the reaction term, which tends to give us θ with the maximal covariance between $f(\psi(y+\theta))$ and $s(x,y)$. s is large at points where I_1 and I_2 have similar local features. Thus we can interpret that the reaction term contributes to linking two points sharing similar local features. Clearly, this phase equation corresponds to the low-dimensional representation of the dynamic link architecture, that is, the graph matching.

5   Parameters

We used a following convolution kernel

$$k(x,y) = \frac{1}{\sigma_1^2}\exp(-\frac{x^2+y^2}{2\sigma_1^2}) - \frac{1}{\sigma_2^2}\exp(-\frac{x^2+y^2}{2\sigma_2^2}),$$

and the sigmoidal function

$$f(x) = \frac{1}{1+\exp(-\beta(x-h))},$$

where $\sigma_1 = 0.25$, $\sigma_2 = 0.33$, $\beta = 10$ and $h = 0.36$. In following simulations, we set $\varepsilon = 0.2$.

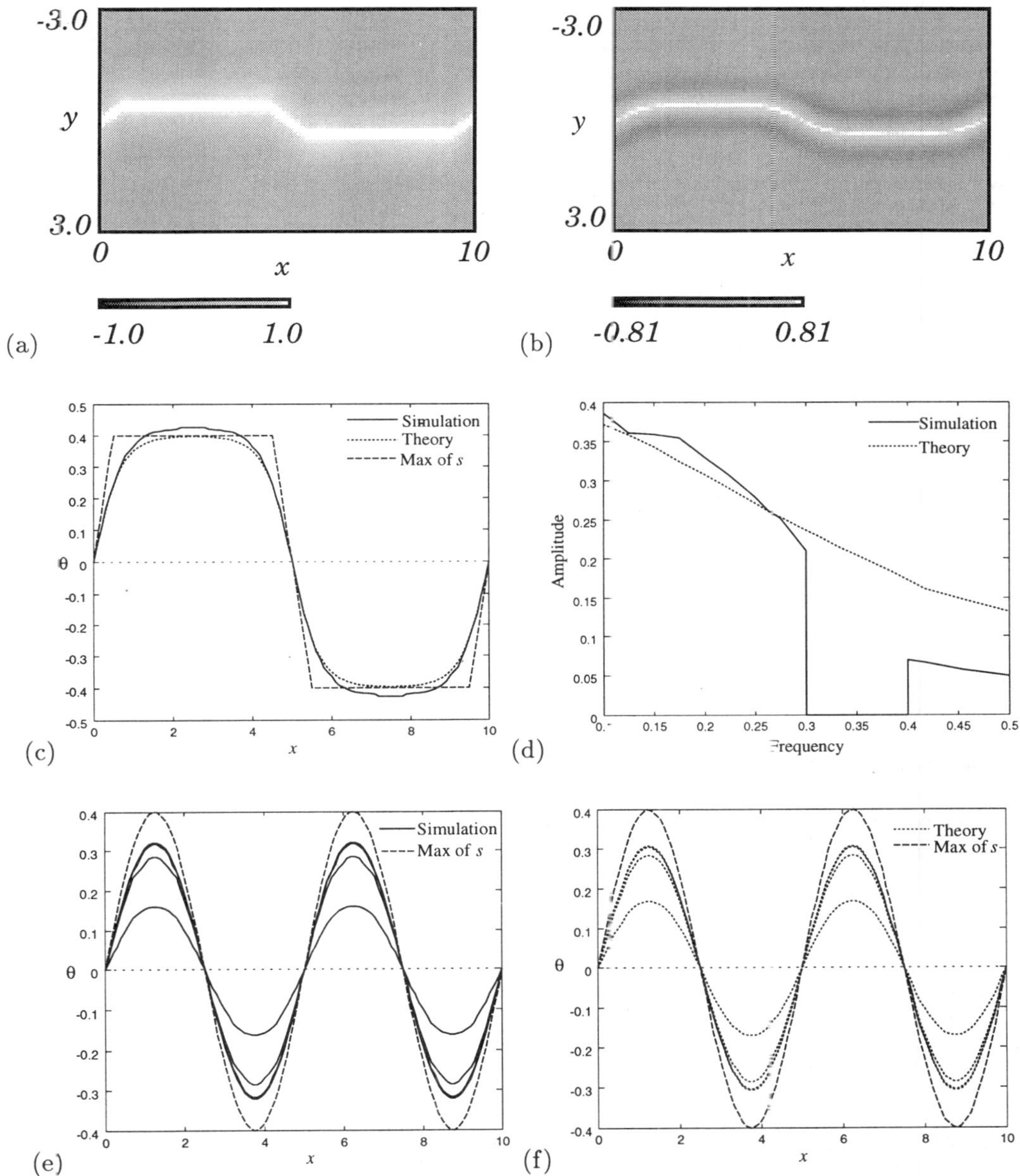

Figure 3: (a) Example of $s(x, y)$. (b) Deformed equilibrium solution by the perturbation with local similarity function shown in (a). (c) Ridge of $s(x, y)$ and that of deformed equilibrium solution (b), together with a theoretical curve by Eq. (19). (d) Frequency responses to sinusoidal ridge of $s(x, y)$(the amplitude is 0.4). (e)(f) Time dependent behavior of θ. Time intervals between two curves correspond to 5.6 in τ. $d = 0.019453$, $c = 5.034132$.

6   Computer simulation

In numerical simulations, we used a periodic boundary condition. We made artificial local similarity $s(x, y)$ shown in Figure(3.a). Beginning with the $\psi(y)$ (Figure(2.a)), we solved the model equation (12) numerically for the estimation of the deformation. In following simulations, $d = 0.019453$ and $c = 5.034132$. Figure(3.b) shows the deformed equilibrium solution by the perturbation with the local similarity in Figure(3.a). In Figure(3.c) we show $\theta(x)$, the ridge of the deformed equilibrium solution (3.b), together with a theoretical curve by Eq. (19).

We also investigate frequency responses of the system. Let the similarity be a function with a sinusoidal ridge. The amplitude of the curve is fixed to 0.4. Figure(3.d) shows the amplitude of the solution wave versus various frequencies of input wave. The dotted curve in the same figure indicates the theory from the phase equation (19). According to Figure(3.d) the theory is in good agreement with the results from simulations at $f < 0.3$, but at $f > 0.3$ our theory fails. The solutions (which initially have the continuous ridge) at $0.3 < f < 0.4$ break into the blobs, thus our theory is no more valid. The solutions at $f > 4.0$ keep the continuous ridge, but the assumption that the solution slowly vary along x axis is not satisfied any more.

Figure(3.e)(3.f) shows a time dependent behavior of θ. Our theory gives a good description of the simulation data in the time scale.

7   Conclusion

In this paper we proposed a mathematically tractable dynamic link architecture. Dynamic link is a topographic mapping formed between template image and data image. The mapping is continuous, but tends to link two points sharing similar local features, and so, can be deformed to some extent. To analyze this deformation mathematically, we derived a phase equation of reaction-diffusion type from the model equation. We showed that the theory is in good agreement with a behavior of the system using computer simulations.

We can classify the dynamic link architecture into two types. One is the high-dimensional representation. Eq. (1) corresponds to this type since the map is expressed by synaptic weight distribution on the product space of the two image spaces. The other is the low-dimensional representation. Eq. (19) corresponds to this type because the reaction-diffusion equation is equivalent to the graph matching model. Our theory bridges the gap between these two types and gives us a mathematical understanding on the principle of the flexible matching process.

Acknowledgment

This work was partly supported by Grants-in-Aid for Scientific Research on Priority Areas (2) No. 07252219, Grants-in-Aid for Encouragement of Young Scientist No. 2871 and JSPS Research Fellowships for Young Scientists.

References

[1] W. K. Konen and Chr. von der Malsburg, " Learning to Generalize from Single Examples in the Dynamic Link Architecture", *Neural Computation*, **5**, pp. 719-735, 1993.

[2] W. K. Konen, T. Maurer, and Chr. von der Malsburg, "A Fast Dynamic Link Matching Algorithm for Invariant Pattern Recognition", *Neural Networks*, **7**[6/7], pp. 1019–1030, 1994.

[3] J. Buhmann, J. Lange, Chr. von der Malsburg, J. C. Vorbruggen, R. P. Wurtz, and W. Konen," Distortion Invariant Object Recognition in the Dynamic Link Architecture", *IEEE Tran. on Computer*, **3**, pp. 300–311, 1993.

[4] E. Bienenstock and R. Doursat, "A Shape-recognition model using dynamical links", *Network*, **5**, pp. 241–258, 1994.

[5] T. Kohonen, "Self-organized formation of topologically correct feature maps", Biol. Cybern., **43**, pp. 59–69, 1982.

How to train an unknown 2 D camera movement system to generate time-optimal saccades*

Volker Zahn, Rolf Eckmiller

Dept. of Computer Science VI (Neuroinformatik), University of Bonn
Römerstr. 164, D-53117 Bonn, F.R. Germany
Tel.: ++49-228-550-364, FAX: +−49-228-550-425
e-mail: zahn@nero.uni-bonn.de

Abstract— For active vision purposes, a 2 D camera movement system with unknown dynamics was trained to generate saccade-like point-to-point movements (PTP). Initially 1,000 time-optimal 2 D reference movements with bang-bang type torque profiles, covering the working range of ±30 deg, were acquired by feeding both actuators with maximum torque steps for acceleration with randomly selected duration. The required corresponding deceleration durations were experimentally determined. Subsequently a multi-layer perceptron (MLP) was trained by supervised learning to assign appropriate acceleration and deceleration times for reaching any desired 2 D goal from any initial position. Following about 10^6 simulated reference movements the open-loop system was expanded by the MLP as neural controller. Real time tests of this 2 D camera movement system with goal positions within ±30 deg yielded saccade-like time-optimal PTP's with maximum velocities well above 800 deg/sec and average position errors less than 0.5 deg.

1 Introduction

Intelligent active vision systems based on flexible camera movement control are increasingly competing with the primate visual system [1] in the combined task of object location (where) versus object recognition (what). A special technical challenge is the generation of saccade-like camera movements without explicit knowledge of the system dynamics.

In principle, there are two ways of implementing a time-optimal controller. An open-loop control can reach time optimality by calculating an optimal torque profile and applying it to the real system [2]. A closed-loop control uses a phase state feedback [3, 4].

From Pontrjagin's Maximum Principle [5] for linear systems it follows, that time-optimal control (TOC) essentially is bang-bang control: the system is driven with maximum positive or negative torque. For a linear 2nd-order system, only two intervals of constant maximum torque with one sign-switching point are required for TOC. The control profile is uniquely defined by acceleration time t_1 and deceleration time t_2 [6]. Thus a time-optimal open-loop controller has to allocate these times for any desired point-to-point movement (PTP).

2 Control Concept and Training

We describe a successful approach of training an unknown 2 D camera movement system to perform time-optimal PTP's with the help of a multi-layer perceptron (MLP). Our camera movement system with two perpendicular axes allows to rotate a light-weight camera horizontally (x-direction) and vertically (y-direction). Our linear 2nd-order system approach disregards non-linearities and higher order flexibilities [7, 8].

Specifically, random bang-bang movements were initially generated by accelerating both actuators over randomly chosen durations t_{x1}, t_{y1} and subsequently measuring the required durations t_{x2}, t_{y2} for deceleration to zero velocity. All data of these reference movements were acquired and used to train a MLP to approximate the mapping of start/goal points to acceleration/deceleration times. Following the off-line training with 10^6 reference movement repetitions, the MLP was integrated into the open-loop controller (Fig. 1).

Simulations of the entire control system (Fig. 1), replacing the real system by numerical solutions of differential equations, were used to test the controller and to develop both MLP topology and training procedure [9]. To map the start/goal positions of a desired PTP movement to acceleration/deceleration

*supported by Federal Ministry for Education, Science, Research and Technology (BMBF) under grant "Electronic Eye"

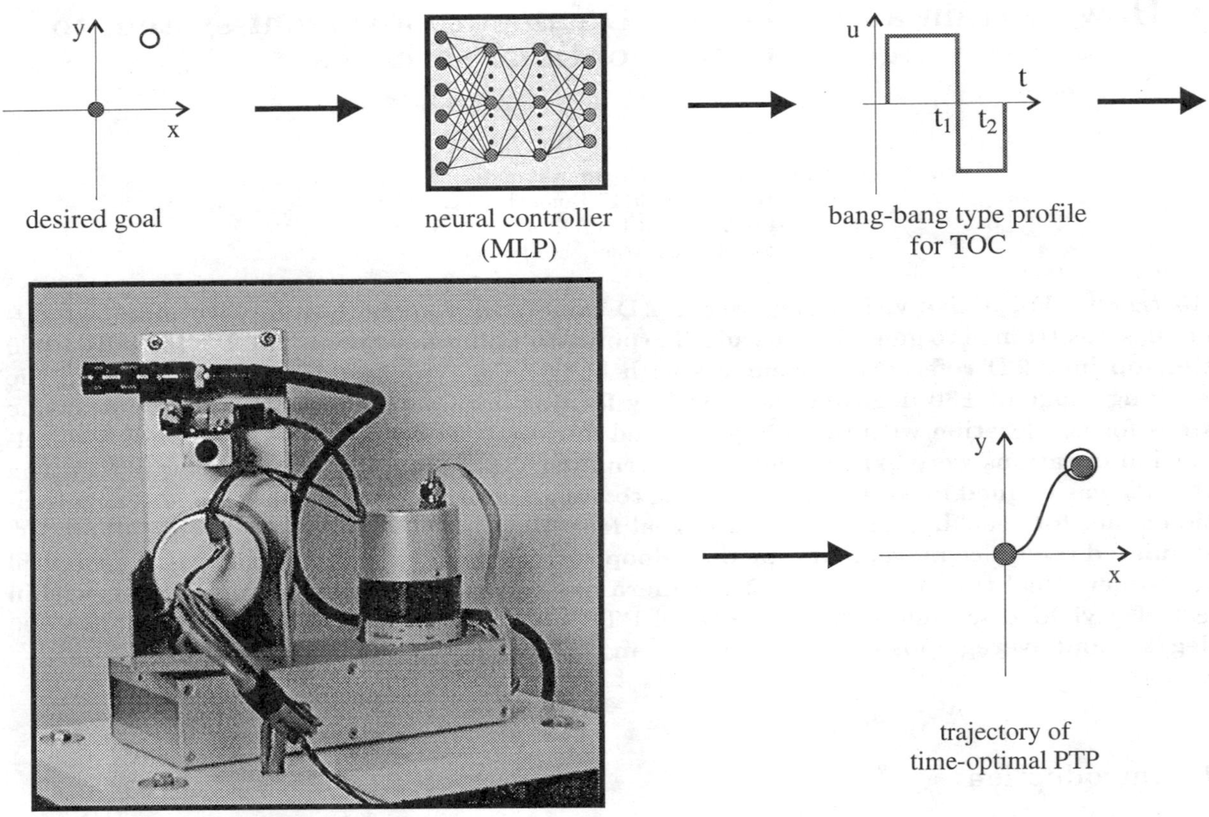

Figure 1: Open-loop control: MLP generates acceleration/deceleration times based on start and goal positions; the derived torque profile for time-optimal control (TOC) is applied to the real system to achieve a PTP movement.

times (Fig. 2B) we used a 4-layer MLP trained by the backpropagation algorithm with momentum term and decaying learning rate in single step learning.

The acceleration times were chosen so as to keep the camera moving system within the working range and to guarantee a uniform statistical distribution of movement amplitudes and start positions. This discrete system with a control frequency of $5\,kHz$ cannot guarantee deceleration to zero velocity. Therefore a combination of ϵ-criterion and sign-change-criterion for the stop-velocity was used to end the reference movements. This yielded a uniform statistical distribution of stop-velocities about zero for use as additional input to the MLP. This way, a data set from 1,000 reference movements by the 2 D camera movement system for subsequent training of the neural network was established in about 10 minutes.

The MLP with two hidden layer (25 neurons each, activation function: *tan hyp*) received three inputs (start-position, end-position, and stop-velocity of PTP) and two outputs (acceleration and deceleration time) per axis. Following a period of about 10^6 learning steps, the desired approximation was already sufficient, but could be improved marginally in following learning steps (Fig. 2A). This off-line training of the MLP took about 4 hours using a SUN Sparc-20 for 10^7 steps of learning.

3   Real Time Tests

The velocity and position diagrams (Fig. 3) demonstrate the real-time behavior of the 2 D camera movement system under open-loop control with the MLP for a typical PTP movement. The y-axis responds to the constant accelerating torque with a nearly linear velocity ramp (the slight curvature reflects the presence of small friction), whereas the y-position response exhibits a nearly parabolic time course in agreement with a linear 2nd-order system. The response to the subsequent decelerating torque is roughly similar. The x-axis behavior shows additional effects: the flexibility of the transmission of the motor torque causes temporary oscillations, which are gradually dampened by friction. Thus the x-axis move-

A)

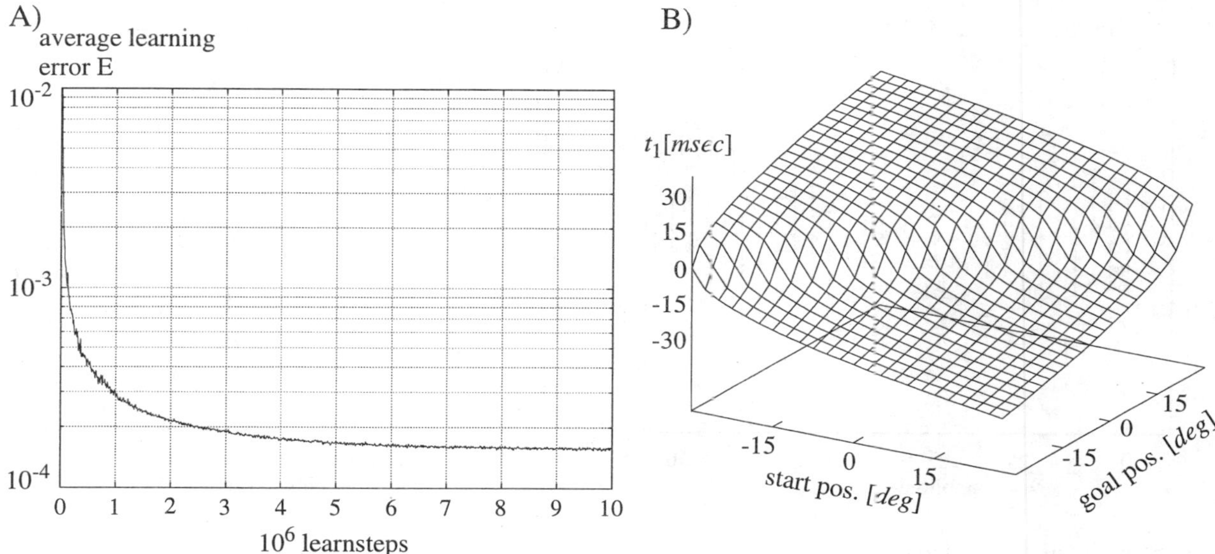

Figure 2: Learning profile and resulting acceleration time for TOC: A) development of the average error of acceleration and deceleration times during MLP training with reference movements. B) acceleration time t_1 as function of start/goal position following MLP training (neg. times = acc. with neg. torque).

ment can only be loosely approximated by a linear 2nd-order system.

The positioning accuracy was tested with 10,000 newly selected random PTP movements (Fig. 4) The positioning error of the open-loop control system depends on the amplitude of the PTP movement. The average error of x-axis movements up to 50 *deg* remains less than 0.5 *deg*; the error deviation is less than 1 *deg*. For small movements up to 15 *deg* even the maximum positioning error is less than 0.5 *deg*. The error diagram of the y-axis (Fig. 4) shows similar results with the exception of a slight tendency to undershoot. Thus a set of two subsequent time-optimal movements, which is typical for rapid eye movement in primates for fixation, can guarantee an overall positioning error of less than 0.5 *deg*.

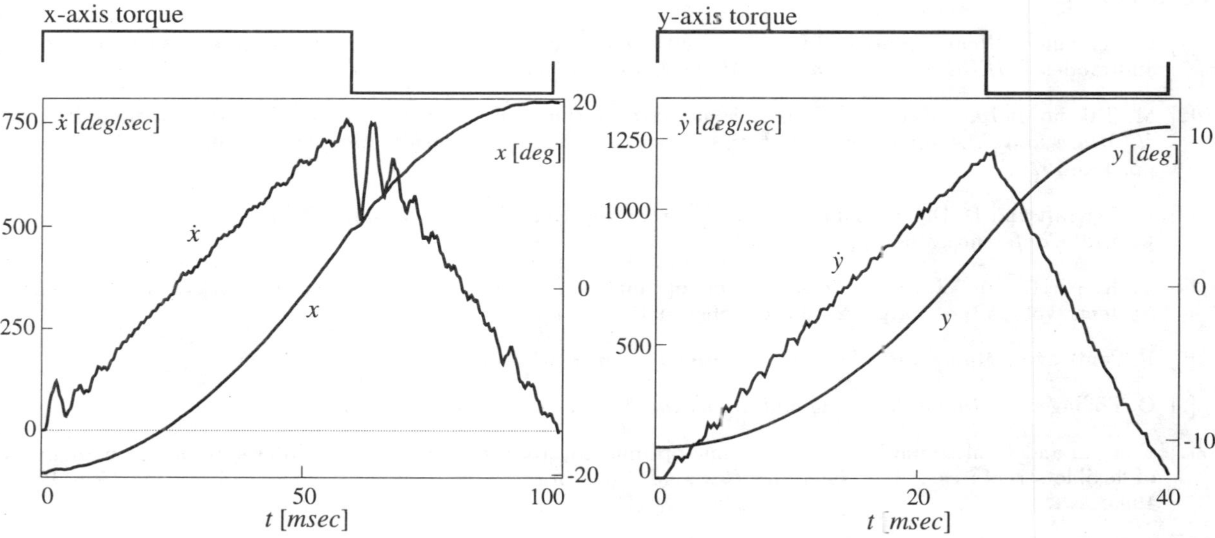

Figure 3: Dynamic behavior of the real system under bang-bang control: velocities $\dot{x}$, $\dot{y}$ and positions x, y as functions of time t during a typical time-optimal PTP movement.

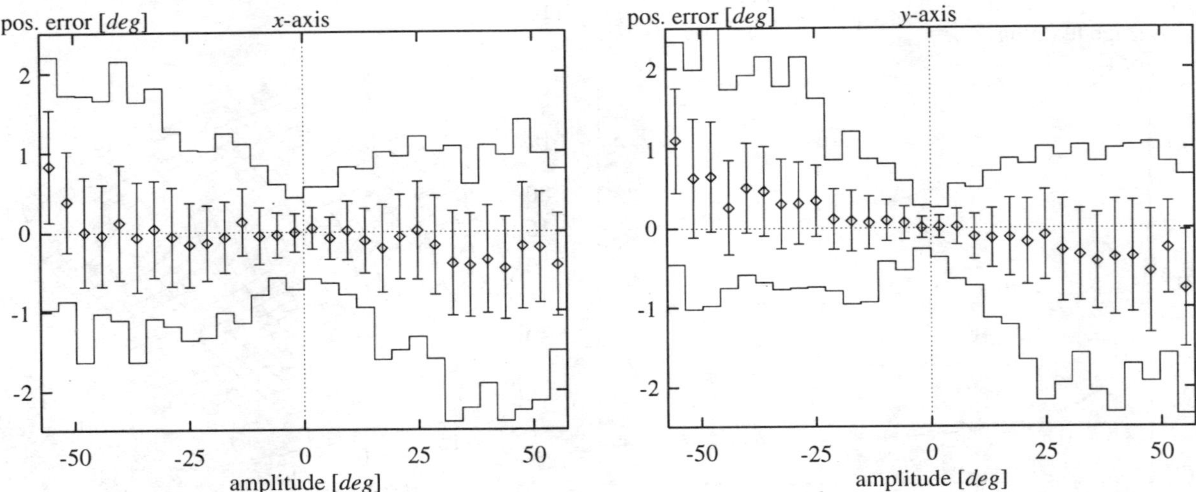

Figure 4: Positive (undershoot) and negative (overshoot) positioning error of PTP movements as mean values with standard deviation and maximum values as function of movement amplitude and direction.

4   Discussion and Conclusions

An unknown 2 D camera movement system was trained to function as open-loop system with a MLP neural controller and subsequently trained to perform time-optimal PTP movements. The implemented open-loop was stable and yielded a positioning error less than 0.5 *deg*. No model or prior knowledge of the system's differential equations was used. Due to the adaptive character, our control system is also in principle capable of adapting to parameter variations (mass, friction, etc.) by learning of the neural controller.

Further studies reducing the positioning error and considering various flexibilities as well as developing a stable on-line adaptation of the neural controller are in progress. Additionally, a stable neural feedback controller will be included into the system to combine quick saccadic movements with pursuit movements.

In summary, we developed an adaptive control system, which is able to perform time-optimal saccade-like 2 D camera movements without prior knowledge about system dynamics.

References

[1] R. Eckmiller, "Neural control of foveal pursuit versus saccadic eye movements in primates – single-unit data and models," *IEEE Transactions on SMC*, vol. 13, pp. 980–989, September 1983.

[2] M. Takano and G. Matsuno. "Research on learning time optimal control of PTP motion of robot arms," *H. Miura und S. Arimoto (ed.), Robotics Research: The Fifth International Symposium*, MIT Press, 1990, pp. 185–192.

[3] L. G. Kraft und D. Dietz. "Time-optimal control using CMAC neural networks," *Proc. of the 1994 American Control Conference*, 1994, pp. 2943–2944.

[4] T. R. Niesler and J. J. d. Plessis, "Time-optimal control by means of neural networks," *IEEE Control Systems*, vol. 15, no. 10, pp. 23–33, October 1995.

[5] L. Pontrjagin, *Mathematische Theorie optimaler Prozesse*. München: Oldenbourg, 1967.

[6] O. Föllinger, *Optimale Regelung und Steuerung*. München: Oldenbourg, 1994.

[7] F. Y. Li and P. M. Bainum, "Analytic time-optimal control synthesis of a 4th-Order system and maneuvers of flexible structures", *Astrodynamics 1993, Advances in the Astronautical Sciences*, vol. 85, pp. 1925–1944, 1993

[8] L. Y. Pao, "Characteristics of the time-optimal control of flexible structures with damping," *Proc. 3rd IEEE Conf. on Control and Applications 1994*, 1994, pp. 1299–1304.

[9] V. Zahn, "Zeitoptimale Steuerung eines Kameraführungssystems mit neuronalen Netzen," *Masters Thesis*, University of Bonn, January 1996.

Handwritten Digit Recognition with a Neocognitron Using Different Thresholds in Learning and Recognition

H.Shouno, K.Nagahara, K.Fukushima, M.Okada
Dept. of Biophysical Engineering Faculty of Engineering Science, Osaka University,
1-3, Machikaneyama, Toyonaka Osaka, Japan

Abstract— **The ability of the neocognitron to recognize patterns is influenced by the selectivity of feature extracting cells in the networks. This selectivity can be controlled by the threshold of the cells. In the previous work, use of different thresholds for feature extracting cells in the learning and recognition was proposed: The thresholds in the recognition phase are set low enough to maintain the generalization ability. The thresholds in the learning phase, however, are set high to generate a sufficient number feature-extracting cells. We verify this method using large hand-written character database. Using this method, we obtained a recognition rate of 97.4 % for handwritten digits in the ETL-1 database.**

1   Introduction

The purpose of this paper is to demonstrate that the neural network called neocognitron can robustly recognize a large set of patterns encountered in the real world.

We showed previously that the use of different thresholds in learning and recognition phases produces a good recognition ability of the neocognitron [1]. It was tested, however, using a simple and small database. So we test performance of the neocognitron with dual thresholds using a large database, ETL-1. The ETL-1 database is a handwritten character database, and contains varieties of handwritten digits written freely by 1,400 persons.

2   Network Architecture in this Experiment

Figure 1 shows that the neocognitron used in this experiment. The initial stage of the network, U_0 is the input layer consisting of a two dimensional array of receptor cells. Each of the succeeding stages has a layer of 'S-cells' followed by a layer of 'C-cells' Thus, layers of S-cells and C-cells are arranged alternately. U_{Sl} and U_{Cl} are the S-cell layer and C-cell layer of the lth layer. S-cells are feature extracting cells. C-cells are put into the network to allow for positional error in the features extracted by the S-cells. In the hierarchical network of the neocognitron, feature extraction by the S-cells and a blurring operation by the C-cells are repeated. During this process, local features extracted in lower stages are gradually integrated to more global features.

Layer U_{S1} consists of edge extracting S-cells. The S-cells extract line components using edge feature extracted in U_{S1}. Layer $U_{S2'}$, which is in a detouring path between layers U_{S2} and U_{S3}, consists of bend

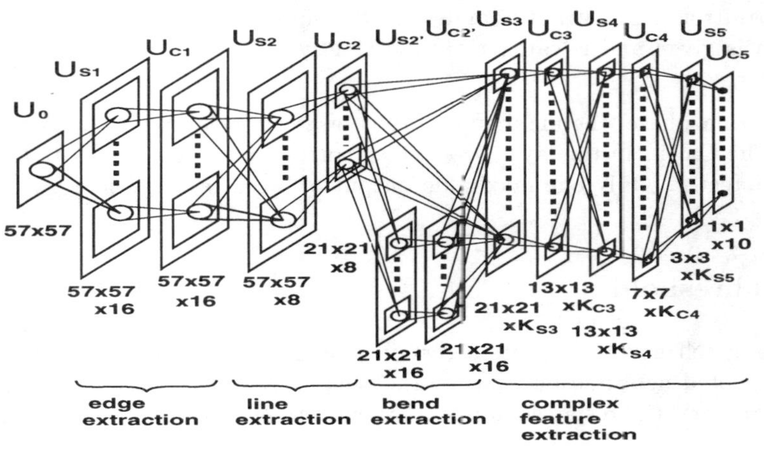

Figure 1: Network architecture of the Neocognitron used in the experiment

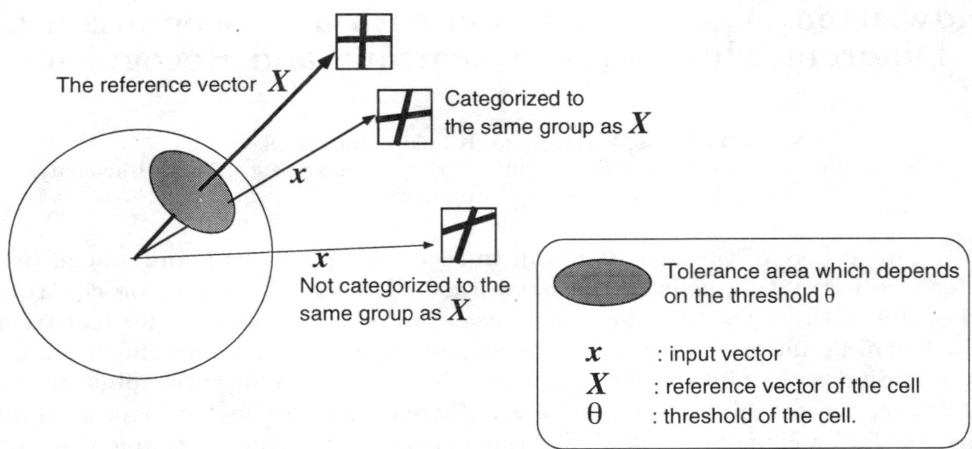

Figure 2: Relation between the threshold of a feature extracting cell and the tolerance for deformation

detecting cells. The input connection of these S-cells are fixed and determined before the training of the succeeding layers. Layer U_{S3} receives input connections from U_{S2} and $U_{S2'}$.

2.1 Unsupervised Learning of the Feature Extracting Cells

The S-cells in layers U_{S3}, U_{S4}, U_{S5} have variable input connections which are modified through unsupervised learning with a kind of winner-take-all process. After the learning process is completed, they are able to extract features from the input pattern. The features to be extracted by these S-cells are automatically determined during learning process. Learning is performed from lower to higher stages. After the training of a stage have been completely finished, the training of the succeeding stage begins.

In principle, the method of unsupervised learning is the same as the one used in the conventional neocognitron [2], [3]. Seed cells are selected with a type of winner-take-all rule. Among the cells that have receptive fields in the same vicinity, only the one responding which responds most strongly is selected as the seed cell. Each input connection of the seed cell is reinforced by the amount proportional to the intensity of the response of the cell from which the connection comes. The other cells in the cell-plane automatically have their input connections reinforced in the same way as the seed cell.

2.2 The Highest Stage, U_{S5} and U_{C5} Layers

S-cells in the U_{S3}, and U_{S4} layers are trained using training patterns only. In U_{S5}, however, the S-cells are trained by the information of not only the training patterns but also the category label put onto the each training patterns. The plural number of cell plane for one category is usually created in U_{S5}, because the neocognitron learns varieties of deformed training patterns. We adopt the method that when a training pattern is given and is categorized incorrectly, new S-cell plane is created to categorize the training pattern correctly.

During the recognition phase, the maximum output of S-cell in layer U_{S5} determines the final result of the recognition. The C-cells in the layer U_{C5}, which correspond to the 10 digits to be recognized, works like a maximum detector. Only one maximum output of S-cell in the whole U_{S5} layer can transmit its output to U_{C5}.

3 Effect of Threshold

A feature extracting cell usually accepts a certain amount of deformation in the shape of the feature. The amount of accepted deformation, that is, the selectivity of the cell depend on the threshold of the cell. In the neocognitron, the response of a feature extracting S-cell can be represented by

$$u = \gamma\lambda\psi\left[\frac{(\boldsymbol{X},\boldsymbol{x})}{||\boldsymbol{X}||\cdot||\boldsymbol{x}||} - \frac{\theta}{\lambda}\right], \tag{1}$$

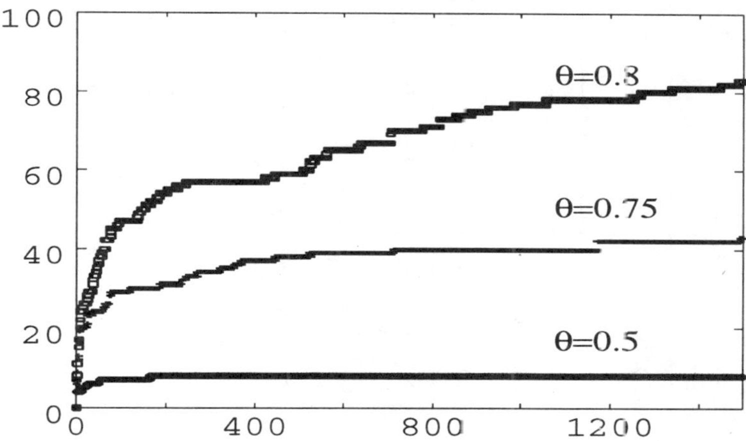

Figure 3: Number of S-cell planes vs. the number of training patterns.

where

$$\psi[x] = \max(x, 0), \tag{2}$$
$$0 < \theta < 1, \tag{3}$$

and γ is a positive constant [1]. In Eq. (1), x represent the input vector to an S-cell. The responses of C-cells of the preceding stage are arranged in an array using a vector notation x. X is the reference vector of the S-cell, or the vector sum of all the training vectors used to train this particular S-cell. As can be seen from Eq. (1), (X, x) denotes an inner product of the test vector x and the reference vector X normalized by their norms [3]. We can interpret normalized inner products $\frac{(X, x)}{||X|| \cdot ||x||}$ as a measure of similarity between the reference vector and the input vector. The S-cell responds only when the similarity between test vector x and the reference vector X, is larger than the threshold θ/λ. Figure 2 shows this situation. The cell responds only when the test vector x falls into the hatched circular region (tolerance area) surrounding the reference vector X. The size of tolerance area depends on threshold. A cell with a lower threshold θ/λ accepts larger deformation in test patterns, while a cell with a higher threshold θ/λ responds only to lesser deformed test patterns [1].

If the threshold is too high, the tolerance area becomes small. So, even if the input feature x is deformed slightly from the learning feature X, the S-cell does not classify it as the learned one. If the threshold is too low, however, tolerance area becomes large. In this case, the important information will be lost in succeeding stages [1]. Tanigawa et al. showed that the recognition rate of the neocognitron becomes better if different thresholds are used in the learning and the recognition [1].

4   Learning Method

4.1   Calculating Inhibitory Variable Connection

In the conventional learning method [2] [3], λ in Eq.(1) is given by $\lambda = \frac{||X||}{\sum_n ||x^{(n)}||}$, where $x^{(n)}$ is the nth training vector of a S-cell, and $X = \sum_n x^{(n)}$ [3]. In general, $\lambda \leq 1$. If λ takes a smaller value, the effective threshold θ/λ becomes larger. If the threshold is too high during the learning phase, cell planes are generated more than necessary [1]. Generation of a large number of cell planes increases computational cost seriously. So we change the method of the reinforcement of inhibitory variable connections so as to always keep $\lambda = 1$ [4] [5].

4.2   Threshold in Learning Phase

In the learning phase, we need to determine the threshold parameter θ to an appropriate value. If training vector does not fall into the tolerance area of any S-cells, no S-cell responds and then new S-cell plane is generated. Therefore, the higher threshold in the learning phase, the larger becomes the number of S-cell planes created, and the larger becomes the network size.

Figure 4: Example patterns in the ETL-1 database

In order to know the relation between the threshold parameters θ and the generation of S-cell planes, we observed how the number of S-cell plane in the layer U_{S3} changes with the threshold parameter. Figure 3 shows the result. The abscissa is the training pattern number, and the ordinate is the number of S-cell planes.

The increasing of the number of S-cell planes saturates. For example, when we set $\theta = 0.75$, the curve almost saturates around 1,000 patterns. If we set θ higher than 0.75, the curve is not saturate at the point that 1,000 training patterns are given to the network. If we use lower θ, say 0.5, the curve is saturate before the 1000 patterns are given.

When we have 1,000 patterns to train the network, what θ is effective? If we set θ of U_{S3} higher than 0.75, the S-cell planes does not saturate. It is inferred that the vector space would not be covered with tolerance areas with 1,000 training patterns. Probably some reference vectors are crowded at some directions where training vectors are concentrated. It is not so effective to generate many reference vectors crowdly.

When the number of training patterns is limited to 1,000. From these data, we think it is better to set θ as 0.75 or lower. Too low θ, however, is not effective, because 1,000 training patterns are not used effective.

5   Results

We use 1,000 patterns to train the network. These patterns are randomly sampled from the ETL-1 database. Figure 4 shows examples of patterns in the ETL-1 database. We also prepared a validation set of randomly sampled 1,000 patterns, which does overlap with the training set.

Let θ of the lth stage in learning phase be θ_l^L, and let *theta* of the l the stage in recognition phase be θ_l^R. Reinforcement is performed from lower to higher stages. When the lth S-cell layer is to be trained, the threshold parameter is set to θ_l^L. The threshold parameter in lower stages up to the $(l-1)$ are set to $\theta_1^R, \cdots, \theta_{l-1}^R$.

We measured the recognition rate for many different combinations of the threshold values. During the learning phase, 1,000 training patterns were given 5 times for the training of each layer. We searched the best combination of thresholds, which produces the maximum recognition rate for the validation pattern set.

When we tuned threshold parameters to $\{\theta_3^L, \theta_3^R, \theta_4^L, \theta_4^R, \theta_5^L, \theta_5^R\} = \{0.75, 0.68, 0.65, 0.53, 0.77, 0.5\}$, the recognition rate for the validation patterns was 97.5 % and for the training patterns was 100.0 %.

After finding these parameters, we also tested performance for novel patterns ,which does not overlap training patterns and validation patterns in the ETL-1 database. We used 3,000 novel patterns randomly sampled and obtained a recognition rate of 97.4 %.

Incidentally, LeCun et al. [6] showed that a large size back-propagation network trained to recognize digit patterns. Some part of structure of their network resembles that of the neocognitron. They use a zip code database provided by U.S.Postal, and the misclassification rate of their network was 0.14 % on for the training set, and 5.0 % for a novel test set.

Acknowledgments

This research was supported in part by Grant-in-Aid #07408005 and #08279226 for Scientific Research from the Ministry of Education, Science, Sports and Culture of Japan; and by a grant for Frontier Research Projects in Telecommunications from the Ministry of Posts and Telecommunications of Japan.

References

[1] K.Fukushima M.Tanigawa. Use of different threshold in learning and recognition. *Neurocomputing*, to appear, 1996.

[2] K.Fukushima. Neocognitron: A hierarchical neural network capable of visual pattern recognition. *Neural Networks*, 1(2):119–130, 1988.

[3] K.Fukushima. Analysis of the process of visual pattern recognition by the neocognitron. *Neural Networks*, 2(6):413–420, 1989.

[4] K.Fukushima. Analysis of the process of visual pattern recognition by the neocognitron. *Neural Networks*, the first annual INNS Meeting(Boston, Sep. 6–10, 1988), 1988.

[5] M.Ohno M.Okada K.Fukushima. Neocognitron learned by backpropagation. *SYSTEMS and COMPUTERS in JAPAN*, 26(5):19–28, 1995.

[6] Y.LeCun B.Boser J.S.Denker D.Henderson R.E.Howard W.Hubbard L.D.Jackel. Backpropagation applied to handwritten zip code recognition. *Neural comutation*, 1(4):541–551, 1989.

Study on High Performance OCR system implemented by Hybrid Neural Networks

Youshou WU, Xiaoqing DING, Mingsheng ZHAO, Hong GUO and Fangxia GUO
OCR R&D Group, Image Processing Division
Department of Electronic Engineering, Tsinghua University
Beijing 100084, China
E-mail: deewys@tsinghua.edu.cn

Abstract

A project of high performance bilingual Chinese-English character recognition system using hybrid neural network modules is briefly addressed in this paper. The mixed Chinese and English character strings in the input printed document images are detected and separated from each other first, and then pass to their respective OCR sub-systems to recognize. The Chinese OCR sub-system is a well designed unbalanced hierarchical tree structure with its functional parts working in a cooperative way according to their functions, and a comprehensive recognition technique has also been adopted for improving robustness of the system. Simulations show that the whole system is of reasonable size, easy to learn and satisfactory performances.

1   Introduction

OCR techniques have had great progress in China in the past decade. Some systems for printed Chinese character as well as for on-line hand-written Chinese character recognition have been developed and commercialized. They provide powerful tools for inputting Chinese characters automatically into computers which is very crucial for OA and Chinese information processing. However, there exist some problems, both theoretical and practical, which are very interesting and important for us to study. For examples: most of existed OCR systems are implemented by traditional method. Can it be constructed by the usage of ANN with reasonable architecture, easy to train and with better performance? Besides, there are more and more English or western words in Chinese printed materials, such as THE PC WORLD (Chinese Magazine), etc. nowadays. The correctness of word segmentation is a serious problem affecting the recognition rate of the system. Furthermore, owing to the fact that OCR systems now become more popular in daily use, and the quality of materials to recognize are covered a quite various range, how to increase the correct recognition rate of poor quality documents becomes an important problem in daily life.

According to the situation mentioned above, we try to development a high performance Bilingual Chinese-English Character recognition system using Neural Networks. Some of the key techniques related to the ANN recognition, such as feature selection and extraction, clustering, individual character recognizing networks, robustness of the system, and even the strategy of the system design, etc. , have been investigated first, and then simulation of the Bilingual Chinese-English character recognition system conducted to test the correctness of the design. Some experimental results will be reported briefly in this paper.

2   System Overview

The theory and method of neural networks have been rapidly developed since 1980's. They imitate information processing in human brain based on studying the operation principle of human cranial nerve system. Therefore, it is very suitable for solving pattern recognition problems.

The application of neural networks for character recognition is so far mostly concentrated on that of relatively small number of category sets, but not large number of categories as Chinese character set. The main difficulties are those for requiring huge network size with complex structure, and very difficult to train. A kind of reasonable network structure and efficient training algorithm are needed when we attempt to use neural networks for such a special huge pattern recognition problem.

Aiming at the goal mentioned above, we have tried to construct a hybrid neural networks which suit for printed bilingual Chinese-English character recognition. We not only adopt the strategy of implementing traditional Chinese character recognition system, but also consider properties of many kinds of neural networks. This work is an extension of former results in our OCR lab.

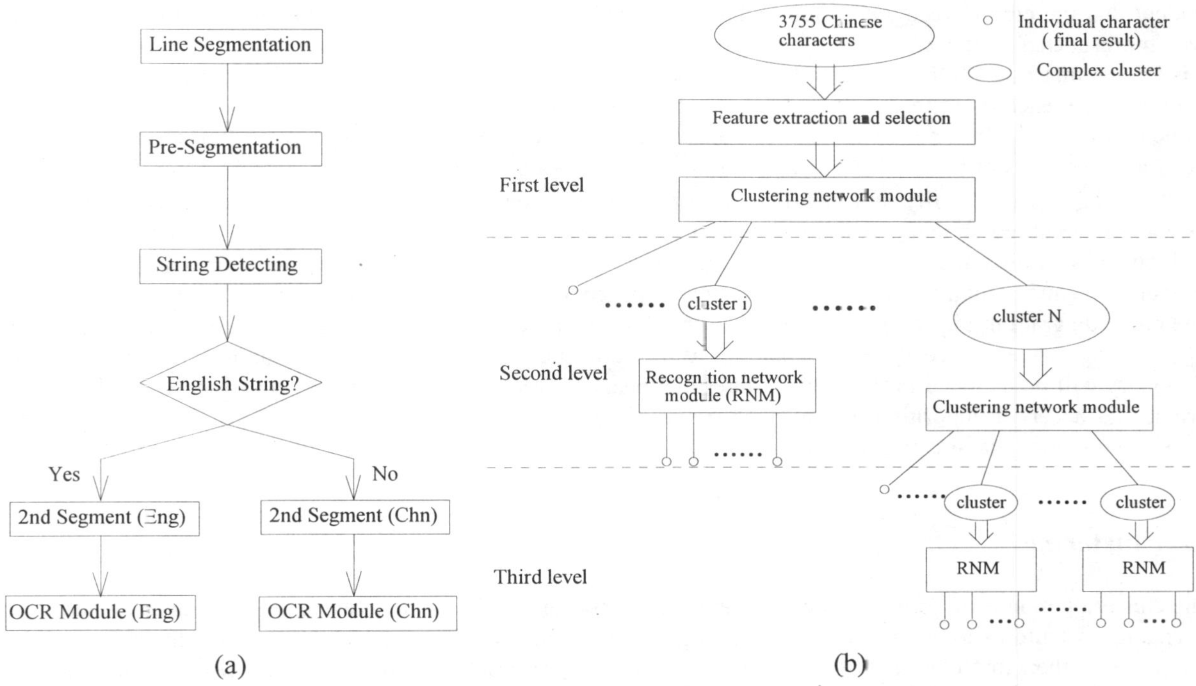

Fig. 1. (a) Flow chart of the TSA algorithm; (b) Diagram for the architecture of the hybrid neural networks for printed Chinese character recognition system

The proposed Bilingual OCR system consists of four main subsystems, namely: the pre-processing and segmentation sub-system, the English and Chinese characters recognition subsystems and the supplementary sub-system. Here, only the English-Chinese character segmentation block and the Chinese OCR sub-system are shown in Fig. 1 for simplicity. Both Chinese and English characters are assumed to be printed in the same papers of the document to be recognized. They should be separated and formed an English and Chinese characters string by segmentation first and then recognized by their respective OCRs as shown in Fig. 1(a).

The Chinese character recognition sub-system is a multi-stage unbalanced tree structure. Owing to the fact that the structure of Chinese characters is very complex and has so many fonts and sizes, it is difficult to determine the number of stages of the classification tree theoretically. However, it seems that a three-stage configuration is quite enough in our system for Chinese recognition in our case.

In the clustering module, similar Chinese characters in the Chinese character set are grouped into a cluster. By proper choice of the features for clustering, there are many very small clusters, each of which consists only one character category. So the output of which can be used as the final recognition result. But some of clusters have several tens of character categories. These clusters have to be clustered once more as shown in the figure in order to simplify the fine recognition networks.

The recognition stage of the system is relatively simple because the number of characters in every cluster to be recognized is very few after clustering. Three kinds of neural networks include the modified RBF network, RBF network[8] and the BP network are used in this stage to get final recognition results. A modified training algorithm (OHLO algorithm)[6] has been proposed to speed up the training process of a conventional BP network. .

The clustering and recognition modules stated above will be working in a cooperative way in order to reduced the accumulative errors which is a serious problem in recognition system with hierarchical structure. Furthermore, a Comprehensive Recognition Method (CRM is short) [7] will also be used to improve the robustness of the system.

3 Segmentation of English and Chinese Characters Mixed in a Document

Word segmentation is not only a serious problem in connected cursive handwritten character recognition, but also important in printed character recognition, especially in bilingual document recognition.

There are more and more English words in printed Chinese materials, especially in technical documents. Because different features and recognition methods are required for English and Chinese characters recognition, it is evident that the correct recognition rate will be seriously reduced if one cannot separate them from each other, even more, such a system cannot be used at all.

It is known that English letters are similar to some components (radical) of Chinese characters, but they may be different from each other in widths and heights; besides, English letters also have different fonts, sizes, and are prone to touch with one another sometimes. Moreover; there are many left-right separable Chinese characters, i. e. a character consists of two radicals located parallelly in the left and right positions of the character (e. g. 北,兆, 儿,八,叭,小,非,加,叫,叩,川), and look like an English word made of two letters. These phenomena will produce wrong segmentations so that certain Chinese radicals will mixed in the English word strings. In order to solve this problem, a so-called the Twice-Segment Algorithm (TSA is short) and a Connected-Domain-Based (CDB) segmentation and recognition technique had been proposed to improve the recognition rate.

The block diagram in Fig. 1(a) shows that both the English and Chinese word strings will pass to their respective OCR modules to recognize after segmentation. At this moment, it is important to point out that a special "radical" dictionary will be included in the English letter dictionary for recognizing the radical mixed in the English word string, and a certain algorithm will also be provided to combine the radicals to form the Chinese character. Experiments show that the proposed techniques will improve the performance of the system to a certain extent.

4   Clustering

The clustering module used in our system is an efficient coarse classification network. It is to reduce the large set of characters patterns to many small subsets according to certain similarity measures. Similar characters will be mapped into the same cluster, thus the further recognition processing will be simplified. If a character is very unlike all the others, it will be mapped into a cluster in which there is only one character category. In such case, the character to be recognized is already identified and can be output as the recognition result as shown in Fig. 1(b) by the small circles.

The clustering network is an improvement version of neural network which based on the RBF network and its training algorithm [8]. The network has the similar structure and configuration as RBF network with one hidden layer and one output layer. The hidden layer is composed of Gaussian activation function neurons, which produce Gaussian kernel function on the incoming inputs. The output layer is composed of linear nodes which is simply a weighted linear summation of the outputs of the hidden layer nodes. The main difference between the proposed clustering network and the RBF network is that the mechanism of self-organization is incorporated in the learning algorithm of the modified network. The self-organizing learning can effectively control of automatic recruitment of hidden neurons during the training phase according to the requirement. This network generates of an arbitrary mapping over the input space by synthesizing a number of individual hidden Gaussian units, and thus has the main characteristic of very suitable for non-Gaussian distributed pattern clustering problems.

The problem of input character's features is very crucial for clustering. Three kinds of conventional features[1] are generally performed well, which are Micro Structure Feature (MSF), Peripheral Feature (PF) and Peripheral+Stroke Density Feature (P+PDF). MSF feature is effective for broken characters and the PF feature performs well for merged characters.

Recently, we have developed a new kind of features based on the wavelet analysis. The research results show that the proposed wavelet features work well for clustering. This may be mainly attributed to its excellent time-frequency resolution. It can be found that main features of Chinese characters, such as information of long horizontal strokes, long vertical strokes, terminal nodes of strokes, horizontal edges and vertical edges, are embodied in the specific wavelet coefficients. Even more, the wavelet features are not sensitive to noise. The recently experiments show that this features contain relatively overall characteristic of Chinese characters and a certain extent of robust properties on noise non-sensitive and distortion invariant.

Another point should be noticed that Principal Component Analysis (PCA) technique [9] has been used in our system for features selection before them inputted to the clustering network. This technique can extract the most effective set of features and abandon redundant ones in the meanwhile. So the performance of clustering is promoted by the decreased non-effective features and the dimension of input feature vector.

5   Fine Recognition

The fine recognition module is used to classify clusters with relatively small pattern categories, such as the clusters generated by clustering network mentioned above and English alphabetic set, in order to obtain the final recognition result of individual character pattern.

The output clusters with more than one pattern categories have two characteristics: The one is that there are a few number of pattern categories in each cluster; The other is that patterns in a cluster are similar to each other. So a small scale neural network is sufficient for fine recognition of a cluster according to the first characteristic. Some common used neural network models, such as BP net, RBF net and modified RBF net, are adopted in our system. The second characteristic of the recognition cluster arises difficulty for achieving high correct classification rate, because the patterns are close to each other in the feature space. We solve this difficulty in two aspects. First, we use feature analysis technique of PCA [9] to get effective features. Second, comprehensive recognition method (CRM)[7], which makes decision by the results of more than one kinds of trained network classifiers, is used to achieve robust recognition results. The CRM technique control the working network classifier and its specific input features based on the quality of recognized character, pattern categories contained in a cluster, the similarity of patterns in a cluster and the confidence of recognition results.

In this recognition module, features take more affection on the performance of the classifier. Sufficient information must be contained in the feature vector of the character in order to get good separability among all the patterns in a cluster. The PCA technique is also used for selecting effective features as recognition network inputs. It is proved that this technique is useful for features selection.

In general, clusters with equal or more than 15 pattern categories are first clustered by the modified RBF network mentioned in the previous Section. Any cluster or sub-cluster with less than 15 pattern categories is classified by RBF or BP net controlled by CRM technique. BP nets are trained by a new fast training algorithm, called the OHLO algorithm [6], which yields an acceleration of about one order of magnitude compared to the classical BP algorithm. Thus, it provides us with more convenient to implement the recognition system.

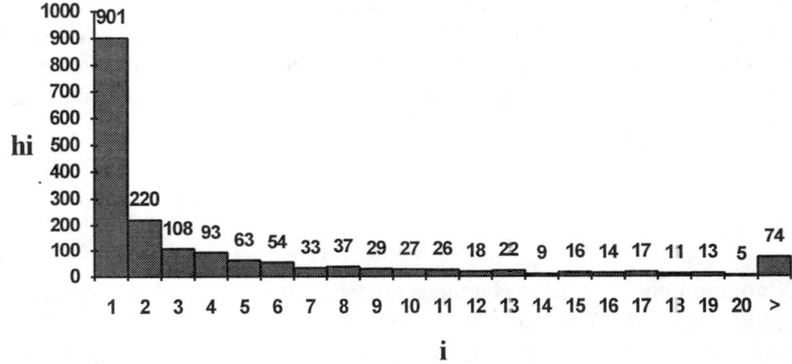

Fig. 2. Histogram for number of clusters vs. contained pattern categories

6   Experimental Results

In order to illustrate the performance of the strategy of our hybrid neural network bilingual character recognition system, several experiments and tests have been conducted. The preliminary tests show that this system has achieved promise results and has considerable extent to improve its performance.

Two data bases, printed Chinese and printed English character data bases are used for training propose in our experiments. The Chinese character set consists of 3755 characters, each of which has three different fonts and four different sizes. To increase variety of the training samples in addition to several fonts and sizes, two different quality of character images are include in this data base. Hence the total amount of training samples is 90,120. All are normalized as 64*64 dotted binary image. The English data base contains with lowercase and uppercase 26 alphabet of commonly used Times Roman font. Each character has 50 different samples which is normalized as 64*48 dotted binary image. The test samples are collected from the daily used Chinese printed newspapers, magazines and books. They are total of about 110,000 characters. Most of them are Chinese characters.

Fig. 2 is the histogram of clustering result for 3755 Chinese characters by 90,120 training samples. Where the horizontal coordinate i represents the number of Chinese characters' categories in a cluster. The vertical coordinate h_i represents number of clusters with i kinds of categories. Total number of clusters are $\sum_k h_k = 1790$, i.e., 90,120 characters are clustered into 1790 subsets. From the Fig. 2, we can find that about 76 percents of clusters have pattern categories less than 6 and about 50 percents of clusters have only individual characters. This means that by use of the clustering block mentioned above, the Chinese character set can be divided into 1790 subsets, among which there are 901 single category subsets (i.e. i=1). In these subsets, there is only one pattern category in a subset and thus it can be identified, no further processing is necessary for these characters. Therefore, this clustering module reduce the complexity of the system very well. The tested experimental results show that the correct clustering rate is superior to 99% for the testing samples.

The whole recognition system has also been tested to evaluate its performances. The recognition result has shown that the correct recognition rate is about 98%. Tests on the system with CRM control and without CRM control are also conducted. The correct recognition rates are 98.63% and 97.62% respectively when the CRM technique is involved and not involved.

7   Conclusion Remarks

In this paper, we have briefly introduced the strategy of a hybrid neural networks system for high performance bilingual Chinese and English character recognition. The system has many kinds of functional neural network modules which form a huge harmonic network with the structure of an unbalanced hierarchical tree working in a cooperative way. TSA algorithm is employed for isolating Chinese and English characters mixed in the same document. A modified RBF net with self-organizing learning is used for clustering large scale Chinese character categories into many small clusters with a few character pattern categories. Three kinds of the small scale neural networks with the CRM control are adopted for robust fine recognition. The proposed wavelet features and the adopted PCA feature analysis technique are demonstrated to be effective for the character recognition propose. The preliminary experimental tests show that this system has achieved promise results.

The further improvements are attempted to promote the robustness of the system by optimizing each module in the system. And we are adopting the strategy of this system for hand-printed Chinese character recognition now. Some crucial problems, such as distortion invariant recognition network, effective features extraction and selection and etc., are focused in studying.

References

[1] Youshou Wu and Xiaoqing Ding, "Chinese character recognition — principles, methods and implementation". Higher education publishing house, Beijing, 1992. (In Chinese)

[2] Y. S. Wu, et al., "A new clustering method for Chinese character recognition using ANN", Chinese Journal of Electronics. Vol. 2, No. 3, 1993, pp. 1-8.

[3] X. F. Huang, Y. S. Wu, "A constrained approach to multi-font Chinese character recognition", IEEE Trans. PAMI, Vol. 15, No. 8, 1993, pp. 838-843.

[4] T. F. Togawa, et al., "Receptive field neural network with shift tolerant capability for Kanji Recognition", Proc. IJCNN'91, Singapore.

[5] A. Iwata, et al, "A large scale neural network — CombNet-II", Proc. IJCNN'91, Seattle, II, p.932.

[6] Mingsheng Zhao, Youshou Wu and Xiaoqing Ding, "Speeding up the training process by optimizing hidden layers' outputs", Intl. Journal of Neurocomputing , Vol. 10, 1996, pp. 1-12.

[7] H. Guo, et al., "Realization of a high-performance bilingual Chinese-English OCR system", Proc. of 3rd ICDAR, 1995, pp. 978-981.

[8] M. T. Masavi, et al., "On the training of radial basis function classifiers", Neural networks, Vol. 5, 1992, pp. 595-603.

[9] Sami Bannour and M. R. Azimi-Sadjadi, "Principal component extraction using recursive least squares learning", IEEE Trans. Neural Networks, Vol. 6, No. 2, 1995, pp. 457-469.

Pattern Recognition and Image Processing

(Poster Presentation)

An Analog Neural Network For Gabor-type Image Filtering

Bertram E. Shi

Department of Electrical and Electronic Engineering
Hong Kong University of Science and Technology
Clear Water Bay, Kowloon, HONG KONG
email: eebert@ee.ust.hk

Abstract- **This report describes a circuit architecture and CMOS circuit components implementing a cellular neural network (CNN) which filters an input image with two convolution kernels similar to odd and even phase Gabor filters. The Gabor filter is a preprocessing stage used in several different types of computer vision and image processing algorithms. One of its primary drawbacks is that it is computationally intensive on a digital computer. Implemented in analog VLSI using the circuits described here, a CNN could decrease both the time and the power required to perform the filtering.**

1 Introduction

Gabor filters are used as preprocessing stages for different tasks in computer vision and image processing, such as stereo vision[1][2], texture segmentation[3], face recognition[4] and image motion analysis[5][6]. Initial evidence indicates that approaches based upon Gabor filtering can outperform previously developed approaches[7]. Unfortunately, Gabor filter preprocessing stages are computationally intensive on a serial digital computer.

A cellular neural network (CNN) which can filter images with convolution kernels similar to those of the Gabor filter is described in [8]. Below, we describe an analog circuit architecture which implements this cellular neural network and is robust in the presence of random component variations. We also describe CMOS circuit elements which can be used to build the architecture in analog VLSI and show by simulation that the resulting circuit can implement the filters described. An analog VLSI implementation of this architecture will be able to compute the outputs of the filters faster and with less power consumption than a digital implementation of the convolution.

2 Cellular neural networks for Gabor-type filtering

The Cellular Neural Network (CNN)[9][10][11] is a neural network architecture consisting of an array of neurons, called "cells". To filter a one dimensional image $u(n)$, $n \in \{1, ..., N\}$, we use a linear array of N cells. Suppose each cell has two states $v_e(n)$ and $v_o(n)$ whose evolution over time is given by

$$\frac{\partial}{\partial t} v_e(n) = (\cos \omega_o) v_e(n-1) - (\sin \omega_o) v_o(n-1) - (2 + \lambda^2) v_e(n) \tag{1}$$

$$+ (\cos \omega_o) v_e(n+1) + (\sin \omega_o) v_o(n+1) + \lambda^2 u(n)$$

$$\frac{\partial}{\partial t} v_o(n) = (\cos \omega_o) v_o(n-1) + (\sin \omega_o) v_e(n-1) - (2 + \lambda^2) v_o(n) \tag{2}$$

$$+ (\cos \omega_o) v_o(n+1) - (\sin \omega_o) v_e(n+1)$$

where $\lambda > 0$ and $\omega_o \in [0, 2\pi]$. This CNN is stable with a unique equilibrium point. The steady state values of $v_e(n)$ and $v_o(n)$ are the input $u(n)$ convolved with convolution kernels approximately equal to

$$g_e(n) = \frac{\lambda}{2} e^{-\lambda |n|} \cos(\omega_o n) \quad \text{and} \quad g_o(n) = \frac{\lambda}{2} e^{-\lambda |n|} \sin(\omega_o n) . \tag{3}$$

We refer to $g_e(n)$ as the even convolution kernel since it is an even function of n and $g_o(n)$ as the odd convolution kernel. See Figure 5(a) and Figure 5(b). The convolution kernels of a Gabor filter are similar to (3), except that the modulating function $e^{-\lambda |x|}$ is replaced by a Gaussian function. This CNN can be extended to filter two dimensional images as well.

In an analog circuit implementation of this CNN, each state variable corresponds to the voltage across a capacitor. Writing KCL at each node, one can verify that any of the three circuits in Figure 1 implements this CNN. In selecting which architecture to implement, we examined the effects of random variations in the component values on the output. Using the technique described in [12], we can find analytical expressions for the sensitivities of each implementation[13]. The sensitivity is defined to be the noise power in the output due to spatially varying

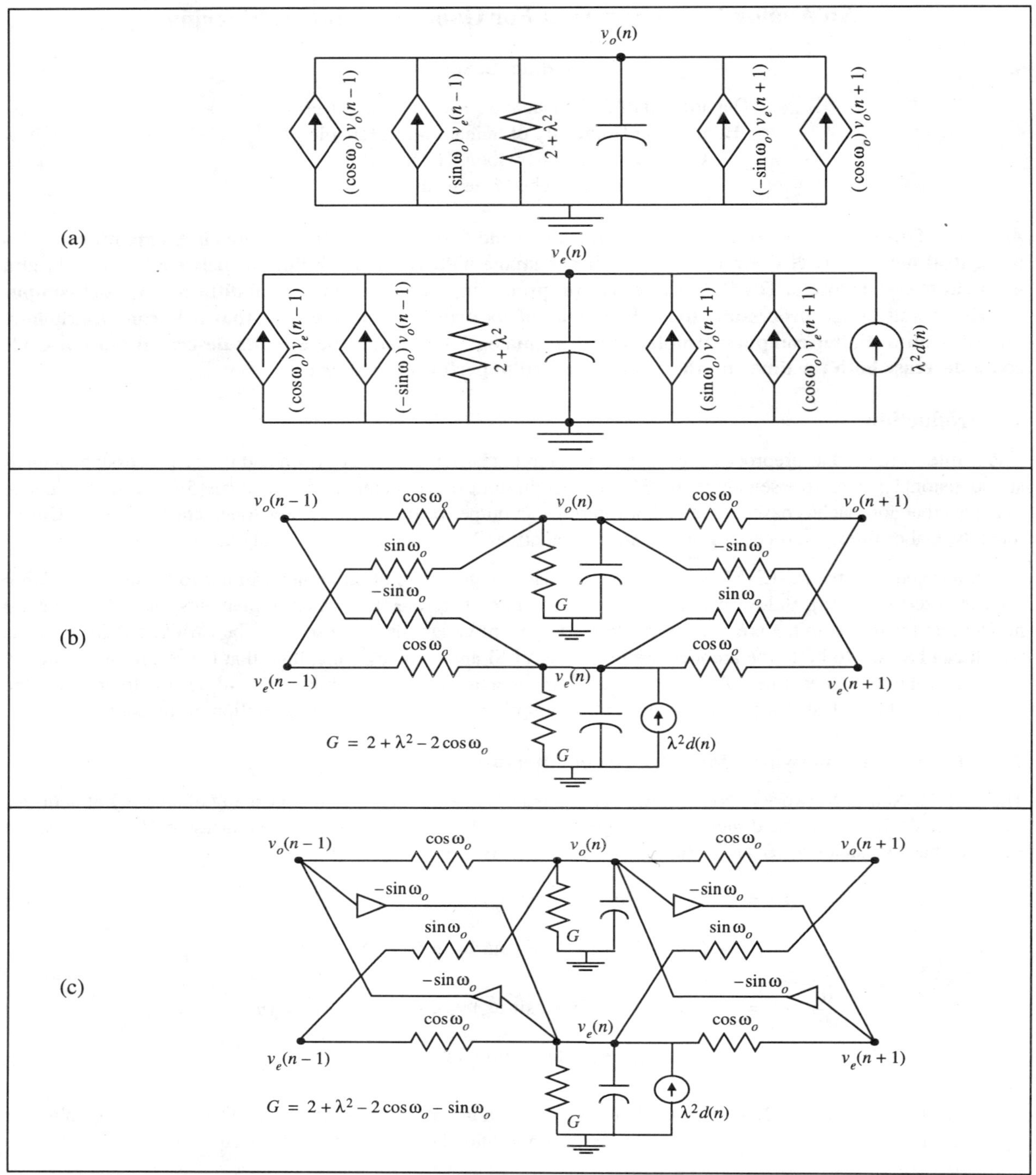

Figure 1: Three circuit architectures which implement the CNN described in the text. Resistor labels denote conductances. (a) An OTA implementation. (b) A resistor implementation. (c) A mixed OTA/resistor implementation. The triangular blocks denote transconductance amplifiers labelled by their gains.

component mismatch normalized by the power in the ideal output and the variance of the percentage component mismatch.

Figure 2 plots the sensitivities for $\lambda = 0.3$ and varying ω_o. For a wide range of ω_o, the implementation in Figure 1(c) is the most robust. Although not shown here, as λ decreases the effect of component mismatch increases for all implementations and for all values of ω_o. Intuitively, the smaller λ^2 the wider the convolution kernel and the less stable the CNN. If λ^2 is negative, then the CNN is unstable. The less stable the CNN, the greater the effect of mismatches.

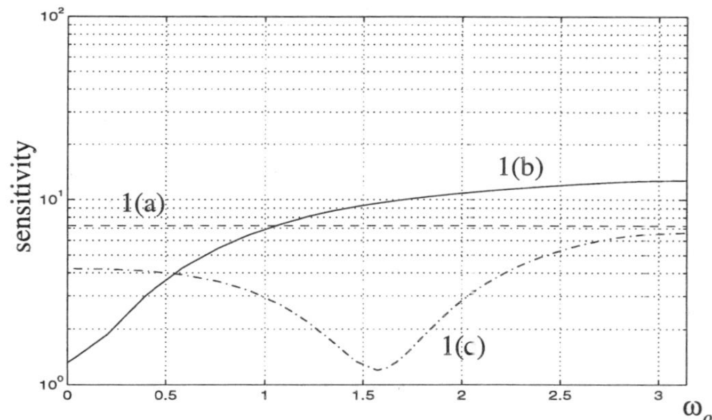

Figure 2: The sensitivity of the implementation in Figure 1 to spatially varying component mismatches. The sensitivity is defined to be the noise power due to mismatch normalized by the ideal output power and the variance of the mismatch.

3 CMOS Building Blocks

This section describes CMOS transistor circuits which implement the transconductance amplifiers and resistors in Figure 1(c). It is not necessary to implement the capacitors explicitly. Since the equilibrium point of the CNN is unique, the parasitic capacitances of the circuit are sufficient to ensure the circuit operates correctly.

3.1 Transconductance amplifier

The transconductance amplifiers can be implemented using the circuit shown in Figure 3(a). For $V_{in} \approx V_{GND}$, the output current is approximately $I_{out} = \sqrt{\beta_n I_{SS}} V_{in}$ where $\beta_n = \mu_n C_{ox} (W/L)$ and (W/L) is the ratio between the width and length of the transistors in the differential pair. The transistors in the current mirrors are assumed to be matched. Using cascoded current mirrors decreases static errors such as offsets caused by the finite output impedance of the MOS transistors in saturation.

3.2 Resistors

Since the convolution kernels implemented are modulated sine and cosine functions, the nodal voltages $v_e(n)$ and $v_o(n)$ can be both positive and negative with respect to the ground potential. The resistors in the circuit must be floating and exhibit good linearity and invariance to common mode offsets for voltages around the ground potential. Several different types of resistor circuits are described in [14]. However, these typically require bias circuitry implemented at each cell. Since for image processing tasks, we are interested in maximizing the number of pixels processed, eliminating the need for bias circuitry at each cell will decrease its area and in turn increase the number of cells implementable within a given area.

A resistor circuit which satisfies the requirements above is shown in Figure 3(b). This circuit is essentially a CMOS transmission gate with adjustable gate voltages. The gate voltages for all resistors of a given value are supplied by a single global bias circuit. In the following, we assume that all voltages are referenced to V_{GND} where $V_{SS} < V_{GND} < V_{DD}$. In addition, we assume that the bulk potential is V_{SS} for NMOS transistors and V_{DD} for PMOS transistors.

The drain currents in the conduction region $(V_{Pp} < V_D, V_S < V_{Pn})$ for M_n and M_p are [15]

$$I_{Dn} = n_n \beta_n \left(V_{Pn} - \frac{V_D + V_S}{2} \right)(V_D - V_S) \text{ and } I_{Dp} = -n_p \beta_p \left(V_{Pp} - \frac{V_D + V_S}{2} \right)(V_D - V_S) \tag{4}$$

where $\beta_n = \mu_n C_{ox} \left(\dfrac{W}{L} \right)_n$ and $\beta_p = \mu_p C_{ox} \left(\dfrac{W}{L} \right)_p$. The pinch-off voltages (V_{Pn} and V_{Pp}) and slope factors (n_n and n_p) are nonlinear functions of the gate voltages (V_{Gn} and V_{G_p}) and the process parameters. The total current

$$I = (n_n \beta_n V_{Pn} - n_p \beta_p V_{Pp})(V_D - V_S) + \left(\frac{n_p \beta_p - n_n \beta_n}{2} \right)(V_D^2 - V_S^2) \tag{5}$$

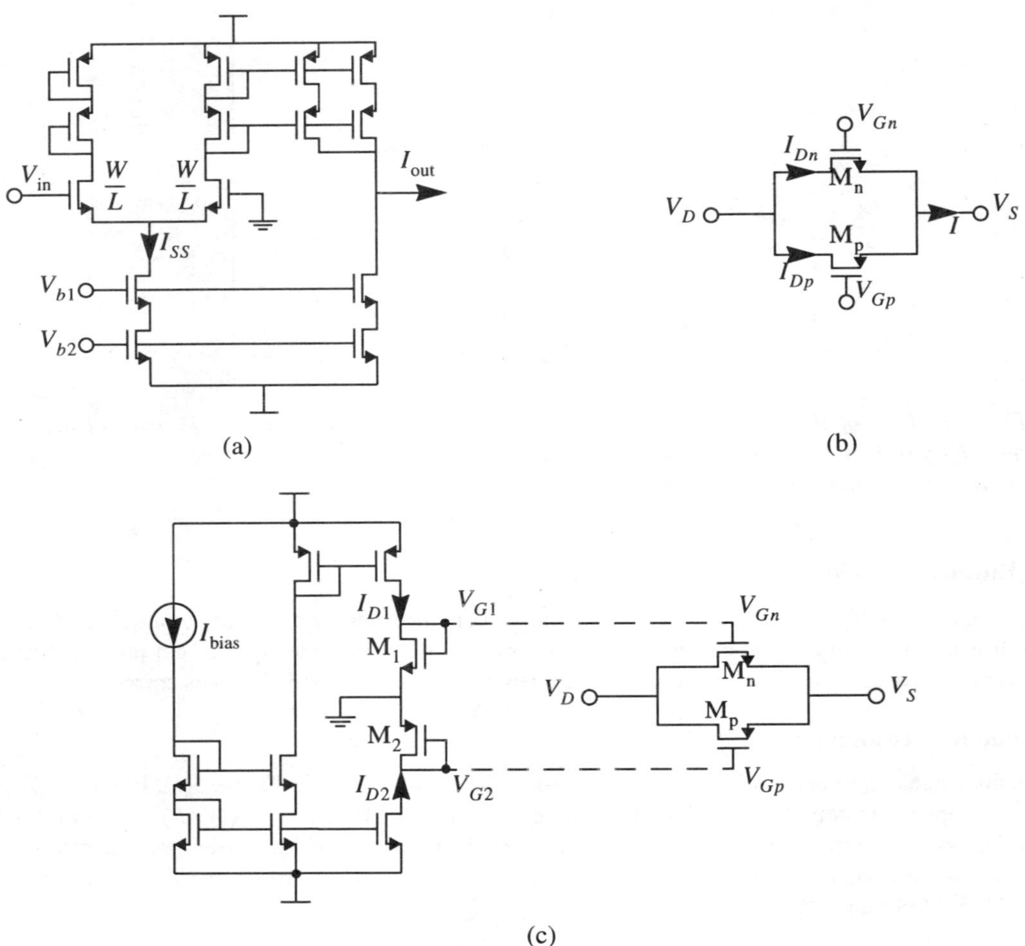

(a)

(b)

(c)

Figure 3: (a) A CMOS circuit for implementing the OTAs. (b) A CMOS circuit for implementing floating resistors. (c) The bias circuit which generates the gate voltages in the CMOS resistor is shown on the left. The gate bias voltages V_{G1} and V_{G2} are distributed to each resistor designed with the same value.

consists of a component which is linear in $(V_D - V_S)$ plus a nonlinear component. Assuming that $n_n \approx n_p \approx 1$, the nonlinear component can be cancelled by choosing the transistor sizing such that $\beta_p = \mu_p C_{ox} (W/L)_p = \mu_n C_{ox} (W/L)_n = \beta_n$, resulting in a linear resistor with conductance

$$G = n_n \beta_n V_{Pn} - n_p \beta_p V_{Pp}. \tag{6}$$

The bias circuit shown in Figure 3(c) supplies the gate voltages. The transistors M_1 and M_n are matched, as are M_2 and M_p. The remaining transistors are current mirrors which set $I_{D1} = -I_{D2} = I_{BIAS}$. Since M_1 operates in saturation,

$$I_{D1} = \frac{n_1 \beta_n}{2} (V_{P1})^2 = I_{BIAS}. \tag{7}$$

Since the gate voltages of M_1 and M_n are the same and the transistors are matched, $V_{P1} = V_{Pn}$ and $n_1 = n_n$. Solving for V_{P1} in (7), we obtain $n_n \beta_n V_{Pn} = \sqrt{2 n_n \beta_n I_{BIAS}}$. Similarly, $n_p \beta_p V_{Pp} = -\sqrt{2 n_p \beta_p I_{BIAS}}$. Combining these results with (6), we obtain

$$G = \sqrt{2 n_n \beta_n I_{BIAS}} + \sqrt{2 n_p \beta_p I_{BIAS}} \approx \sqrt{8 \beta_n I_{BIAS}}. \tag{8}$$

Figure 4 shows simulated v-i characteristic of the resistor circuit for a common mode voltage $(V_D + V_S)/2 = 0$ as well as plots of the current versus the common mode voltage for fixed differential voltages. For this circuit,

$V_{DD} = -V_{SS} = 5\text{V}$ and $I_{\text{bias}} = 20\mu\text{A}$. The circuits were simulated in Hspice using BSIM models where $\mu_n C_{\text{ox}} \approx 4.5\times10^{-5}$ and $\mu_p C_{\text{ox}} \approx 1.7\times10^{-5}$. With transistor sizing $(W/L)_n = 7/12$ and $(W/L)_p = 14/8$, the estimated conductance is $G = 6.7\times10^{-5}$. The conductance obtained in simulation is approximately 6.4×10^{-5}.

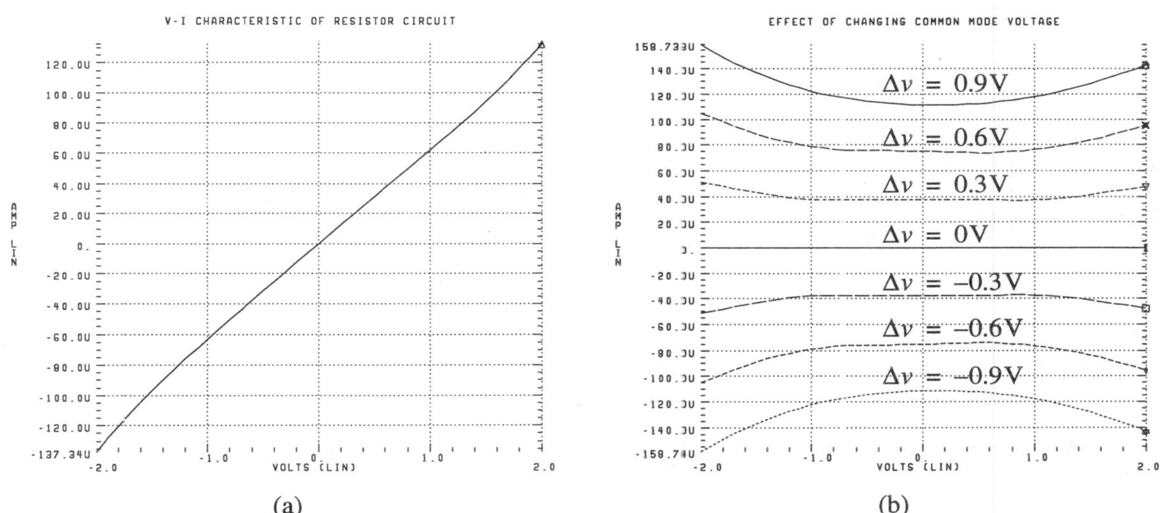

Figure 4: (a) The v-i characteristic of the resistor circuit for a common mode voltage of 0V. (b) The current through the resistor circuit for fixed differential voltages Δv plotted as a function of the common mode voltage.

Figure 5 compares the ideal convolution kernels as well as the convolution kernels resulting from the transistor level HSpice simulations of the circuit implementation described here. The ideal and simulated kernels agree quite closely. The signal to noise ratio is 25dB. The majority of the error appears to be caused by mismatch in the parameters λ and ω_o of the ideal and the simulated circuits.

4 Conclusion

We have described an analog circuit architecture and CMOS circuit building blocks which implement a cellular neural network designed to filter and image with two convolution kernels similar to even and odd Gabor functions. Based upon simulation results, the circuit successfully implements odd and even Gabor-type filters. We are currently fabricating a test chip based upon the circuit described here. This chip implements a 13 cell one dimensional Gabor filtering CNN in a 2μm CMOS n-well process. Future work includes fabricating chips with larger numbers of cells, two dimensional arrays and chips which integrate photosensors along with the Gabor filtering circuits to acquire and process images simultaneously.

References

[1] T. Sanger, "Stereo disparity computation using Gabor filters,", *Biological Cybernetics,* vol. 59, no. 6, pp. 405-18, 1988.

[2] C. Chang and S. Chatterjee, "Ranging through Gabor logons - A consistent, hierarchical approach", *IEEE Transactions on Neural Networks*, vol. 4, pp. 827-43, Sept. 1993.

[3] M. Porat and Y. Y. Zeevi, "Localized texture processing in vision: Analysis and synthesis in Gaborian space", *IEEE Transactions on Biomedical Engineering*, vol. 36, pp. 115-29, Jan. 1989.

[4] N. Petkov, P. Kruizinga, and T. Lourens, "Biologically motivated approach to face recognition", in *New Trends in Neural Computation, International Workshop in Artificial Neural Networks*, pp. 68--77, 1993.

[5] D. J. Fleet, *Measurement of Image Velocity*, Boston. MA: Kluwer Academic Publishers, 1992.

[6] D. J. Heeger, "Model for the extraction of image flow," *J. Optical Society of America A*, vol. 4, pp. 1455-1471, Aug. 1987.

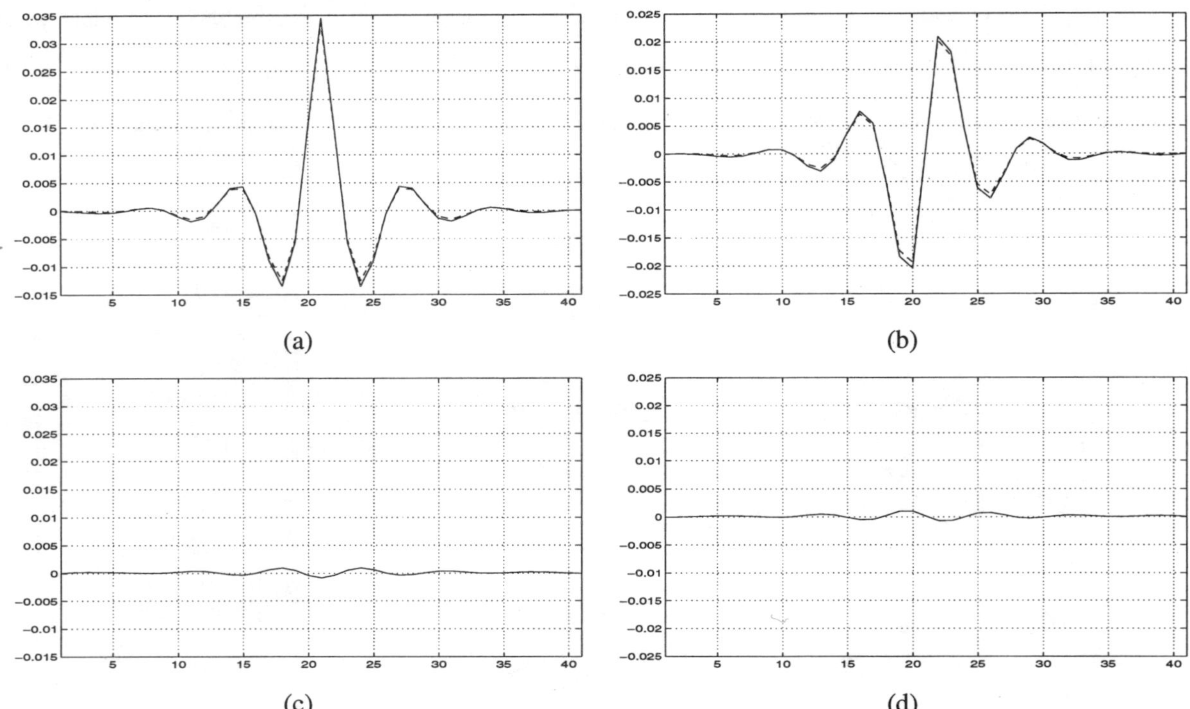

(a)   (b)

(c)   (d)

Figure 5: (a) The ideal and simulated impulse response of the even CNN filter for $\lambda^2 = 0.08$ and $\omega_o = 0.94$. The dotted line shows the ideal response. The solid line shows the response obtained from transistor level simulations of the circuits described here. (b) The ideal and simulated impulse responses of the odd CNN filter. (c) The error between the ideal and simulated impulse responses of the even filter. (d) The error between the ideal and simulated impulse responses of the odd filter. To aid in comparison, the errors are plotted on the same scale as the impulse responses.

[7] J. Barron, D. S. Fleet, S. S. Beauchemin, and T. A. Burkitt, "Performance of optical flow techniques," in *Proc. of CVPR*, (Champaign, IL), pp. 236-242, IEEE, 1992.

[8] B. E. Shi, "Gabor-type image filtering with cellular neural networks," *Proceedings of the 1996 IEEE International Symposium on Circuits and Systems*, to appear.

[9] L. O. Chua and L. Yang, "Cellular Neural Networks: Theory," *IEEE Transactions on Circuits and Systems*, vol. 35, pp. 1257-1272, Oct. 1988.

[10] L. O. Chua and L. Yang, "Cellular Neural Networks: Applications," *IEEE Transactions on Circuits and Systems*, vol. 35, pp. 1273-1290, Oct. 1988.

[11] L. O. Chua and T. Roska, "The CNN paradigm," *IEEE Transactions on Circuits and Systems - I: Fundamental Theory and Applications*, vol. 40, pp. 147-156, Mar. 1993.

[12] B.E. Shi, T. Roska and L.O. Chua, "Random parameter variation in analog VLSI neural networks for linear image filtering", *Proceedings of IEEE International Conference on Neural Networks*, Vol. 3, p. 1917-1922, 1994.

[13] K. F. Hui and B. E. Shi, "Robustness of CNN Implementations for Gabor-type Filtering," submitted to *Asia Pacific Conference on Circuits and Systems*, IEEE, 1996.

[14] M. Ismail and T. Fiez, ed., *Analog VLSI Signal and Information Processing*, McGraw-Hill, Inc., Singapore, 1994.

[15] C. C. Enz, F. Krummenacher, and E. A. Vittoz, "An analytical MOS transistor model valid in all regions of operation and dedicated to low-voltage and low-current applications," *Analog Integrated Circuits and Signal Processing*, vol.8, no.1 (July 1995) p83-114.

Radar Target Identification Using Wavelet Transform of Range Profiles

Qun Zhao[*], Zheng Bao[**] and Huisheng Chi[*]

* National Lab of Machine Perception and Center for Information Science
Peking University, Beijing 100871, P.R.China
** Institute of Electronics Engineering, Xidian University, 710071, Xi'an, P.R.China
Email: zhao@cis.pku.edu.cn

Abstract   A wavelet based representation of radar targets using pre-transformed range profiles is presented in this paper for the purpose of radar target identification (RTID). In [1], a neural network based RTID scheme had been proposed, using high resolution range profiles. The target-specific information useful for RTID is investigated, which is contained in the representation of multiresolution scales of wavelet transform of the range profiles. A nearest-neighbor classifier is employed for comparison of classification performance between the original profiles and the wavelet based representations.

1. Introduction

Both theoretical and empirical studies indicate that analytical representation suitable for target identification can be based upon the concept of scattering centers which dominate the radar cross-section (RCS) of a target. The range sorted echo from each cell of a three-dimensional target, making up of a range profile, consists of the phasor sum of the signals received from all scattering centers contained in the range cell, weighted by their respective amplitude and phase.

In [1], a radial basis function network (RBFN) was utilized by us to perform the task of RTID, using two kinds of transformed high-resolution range profiles. The range profiles contain target-specific information relevant to the identity of the target, such as the number of strong scattering centers and their relative positions. Altes proposed a representation [2] of impulse response of a target , that is,

$$x(t) = \sum_{m=1}^{M} \sum_{n=-N}^{N} x_{nm} \delta^{(n)}(t - \tau_m) \tag{1}$$

The significance of Eq.(1) extends beyond the principle of approximating a target impulse response by a weighted sum of integrated and differentiated impulse functions, and is directly related to the geometry of the target. Based on this model, Jouny [3] gave a description of a ultra-wideband radar target using wavelet expansion techniques and found that it provided significant insight into the mechanism of scattering from radar targets and contributed to the identification of geometrical features of unknown targets. It was shown in [3] that wavelet decomposition helps discriminating between scatters whose response increases with frequency and those whose response decreases with frequency, and besides, the proposed scatterer identification method does not require a priori knowledge of the number of scattering centers located along the target.

In this paper, we will investigate the problem of RTID using wavelet expansion of range profiles obtained by a high-resolution radar (HRR). Wavelets are better suited to analyze signals with high frequency components of short periods or transient signals. From this point of view, the wavelet expansion of range profiles could contain target-specific information. In section 2, a nonlinear transform of the range profiles is performed . Then a dyadic wavelet representation of the transformed range profiles is given in section 3. Experiment results are presented in section 4.

2. Pre-transform

The proposed representation is based on the derivative or differentiation of the range profiles with respect to the time or range, transformed by a single-tuned nonlinear function. In the discrete case, this transformation is defined as follows:

$$g(n) = f(x(n+1) - x(n)) \tag{2}$$

where $x(n)$ represents a range profile, with $n=0,...,N-1$, and N is the length of the range profile. The nonlinear function f can have various forms, in this paper the anti-tangent or anti-sinusoid angle function is utilized. The expression of Eq.(2), called curvature description of a range profile, has the property of rotation and translation invariance for a planar closed boundary.

The expression of Eq.(2) eliminates the component of DC and bounds the differentiation of the range profiles within the extent $\left[-\frac{\pi}{2}, \frac{\pi}{2}\right]$. In this sense, the strong scattering centers will be observed at locations where the differentiation magnitude between two successive points exceeds $\pi/2$ radians. These abrupt changes will form so called feature points which are very useful for reliable classification.

3. Wavelet Based Representation

Singularities and irregular structures often carry the most important information in range profiles. By decomposing signals into elementary building blocks that are well localized in both space and frequency domains, the wavelet transform can detect and characterize the local regularity of signals.

Let φ be a smoothing function, and using a wavelet which is the first derivative of φ ,that is

$$\psi(t) = \frac{d\varphi(t)}{dt} \tag{3}$$

then the irregular structure of a signal g can be detected. The dyadic wavelet transform of g with respect to this wavelet is defined as

$$W_j g(t) = g * \psi_j(t)$$
$$= 2^j \frac{d}{dt}(g * \varphi_j)(t)$$
$$= 2^j \frac{d}{dt} g(t) * \varphi_j(t) \tag{4}$$

It is shown that the wavelet transform of g, with respect to a wavelet as the first derivative of a smoothing function, will be proportional to the curvature of g, smoothed by the smoothing function.

The wavelet transform of the pre-transformed range profiles $g(k)$, which are discrete time sequences, is essentially a multiresolution characterization of $g(k)$. Wavelet decomposition of a signal $g(k)$ of length N, can be represented by a set of detailed signals that are associated with the high frequency components of $g(k)$ and a final coarse approximation. In this paper, this set of detailed signals of multiresolution scales will be used respectively for the task of RTID , and the results of which are to be compared with that acquired using the original range profiles directly.

4. Experimental Results

The data set used in our experiment consists of the Ku-band radar range profiles of models of three aircraft, the B52, Q6 and Q7. These models were placed on a rotating platform in a microwave anechoic chamber, with azimuth changed from $0°$ to $30°$ and constant elevation (approximately $5°$). The three targets have similar sizes, and each range profile has 64 range bins with a resolution of approximately 50mm. There are 50 range profiles for each target, among which 10 profiles uniformly distributed along the azimuth within the range of $0°$ to $30°$ are selected from each class as templates, and the rest are used as testing samples.

The methods dealing with stability and shift-invariance of the range profiles has been proposed by us in [1]. The main idea of this paper is to investigate the target-specific information contained in the wavelet expansions of multiresolution scales of the range profiles after nonlinearly pre-transformed by Eq.(2). We suppose that all the profiles have been processed to be position aligned.

Huang and Lippmann had shown in their paper that feedforward neural network classifiers and nearest-neighbor (NN) classifies have comparable performances. Therefore the NN classifiers are used in this paper. The nearest-neighbor classification error rate is counted to indicate how well the wavelet-based representation of different   scales preserve or contain target-specific information.

Since the classification error by using the wavelet representation of multiresolution levels depends on the classification error by employing the original range profiles, a normalized ratio is proposed in this paper, i.e.,

$$NR_e = \frac{1 + P_e(resolution - level)}{1 + P_e(original - profile)} \qquad (5)$$

where $P_e(resolution - level)$ indicates the rate of classification error at a certain resolution level, and $P_e(original - profile)$ is the rate of error using the original profiles. The value of NR_e is within the range of (0.5, 2.0). When $NR_e = 1.0$, it means that the representation at this resolution level has the same performance in terms of classification accuracy as the original range profiles for the NN classifier. If $NR_e < 1.0$, then the representation has a better performance.

Orthogonality is an important element of wavelet analysis. Orthonormal expansion basis is smooth and smooth functions have a rapidly decaying Fourier representation which enhances the frequency resolution of wavelet analysis. However, with consideration of compromise between the classification performance and the orthogonality of the wavelet, redundant wavelet transform is sometimes preferable for it can provide more information necessary for patter classification or RTID. In this paper, both non-orthogonal wavelet[4] and orthogonal wavelet [5]   are employed. Since the length of $g(k)$ is 64, it can be decomposed into 6 scales. During the experiment, the representation of the first five levels 1,2,3,4 and 5 are used for comparison, indicating how much target-specific information is carried in each level respectively. The multiresolution representation of the first five scales of a range profile are illustrated in Figure 1. It is shown that the representation on higher levels using the orthogonal wavelet (Fig.1-b) attenuates more rapidly than that employing non-orthogonal wavelet(Fig.1-a). However, target-specific information is contained in these different scales.

Table 1   NN classification error rate using
dyadic non-orthogonal wavelet transform

	B52	*Q6*	*Q7*
level 1	0.938	1.000	1.023
level 2	0.958	1.000	1.023
level 3	0.938	1.098	0.930
level 4	0.930	1.122	0.930
level 5	0.896	1.195	0.977

Table 2   NN classification error rate using
dyadic orthogonal wavelet transform

	B52	*Q6*	*Q7*
level 1	0.938	1.000	1.023
level 2	0.979	1.000	1.047
level 3	0.958	1.049	1.000
level 4	0.833	0.976	0.977
level 5	0.896	1.000	1.023

The classification result of the three targets counted by Eq.(5) is illustrated in Table 1 and Table 2, using the two kinds of wavelets respectively.

In Table 1 and Table 2, the classification performance by using the non-orthogonal wavelet representation is generally comparable to that by employing the orthogonal wavelet representation. However, the result is better on resolution levels 3 and 4, implying that it may contain more target-specific information on these two levels than on other levels. Besides, the performance on all scales for B52 is better since the NR_e is less than 1.0, while for Q6 and Q7, the performance is worse (except for level 3 and level 4).

On the other hand, the combination of results of multiclasifiers is more reliable than that of some a single classifier. Therefore, our next step is decision combination using the results of multiresolution representations.

5. Conclusions

A wavelet based representation of radar targets using nonlinearly pre-transformed range profiles is presented in this paper for the purpose of RTID. A nearest-neighbor classifier is employed for comparison of classification performance between the original profiles and the wavelet based representations. The experimental results show that the target-specific information useful for RTID is, to a certain degree, contained in the multiresolution scales of wavelet transform of the range profiles.

6. References

[1]   Q.Zhao and Z.Bao, "Radar target recognition using a radial basis function neural network", *Neural Networks,* Vol.9 (To be published).

[2]   R.A.Altes, "Sonar for generalized target description and its similarity to animal echolocation systems," *J. Acoust. Soc. Am*, **59**, 1 (1975), 97-105.

[3]   I.Jouny, "Description and classification of ultra-wideband radar targets using wavelets," *Digital Signal Processing,* **3** (1993), 78-88.

[4]   S.Mallat and W.L.Hwang, "Singularity detection and processing with wavelets," *IEEE Tran. on Information Theory*, **38**, 2 (1992), 617-643.

[5]   S.G.Malat, "A theory for multiresolution signal decomposition: the wavelet representation," *IEEE Tran. on Pattern Analysis and Machine Intelligence*, **11**, 7 (1989), 674-69

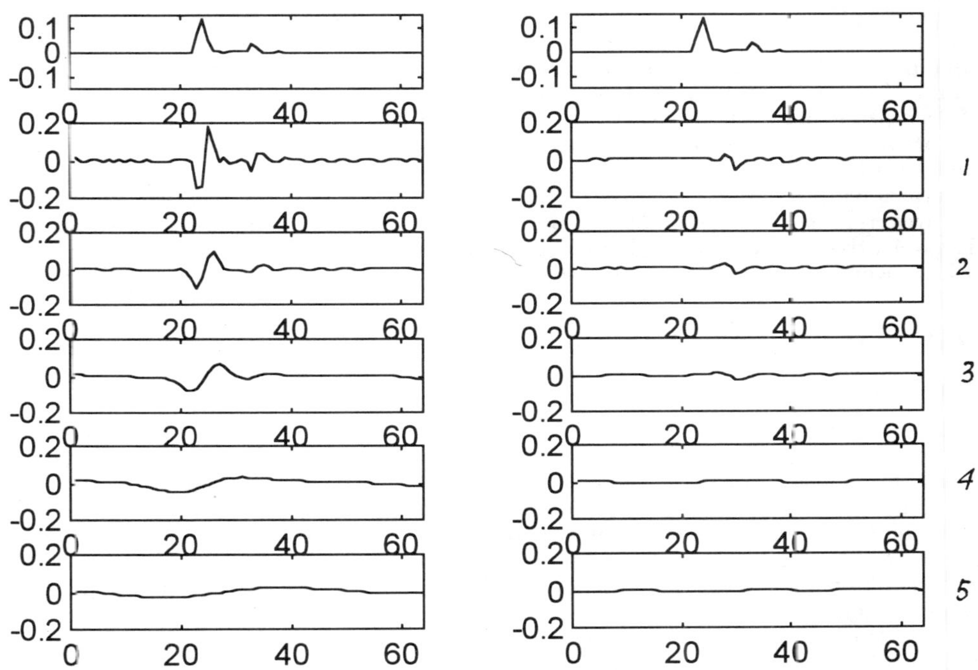

(a). expansion using non-orthogonal wavelet   (b). expansion using orthogonal wavelet

Figure 1. The wavelet based representation of a range profile at levels 1,2,3,4 and 5.

Using a modified Hypermap for analyzing moving scenes

C. Blumenstein†, B. Brückner†, R. Mecke‡, T. Wesarg†, C. Schauer†
‡Institute of Process Measurements Technology and Electronics, University of Magdeburg, Germany
†Informatics, Federal Institute for Neurobiology
P.O.Box 1860, 39008 Magdeburg, Germany
e-mail: brueckner@ifn-magdeburg.de

Abstract— This paper deals with the use of the Modified Hypermap Architecture for classification of object-specific MAD features.
By means of simple methods of image processing it is possible to improve the feature extraction preprocessing of the neural network task and therefore of the accuracy of pixelbased blockmatching functions. This improvement in motion estimation is necessary, because it isn't possible to get a significant classification of object-specific MAD features.
The performance capability and suitability of the Modified Hypermap Architecture for the problems of classification and its use as an associative memory is shown for selected two-dimensional measuring situations.

1   Introduction

The importance of analyzing moving scenes within the wide area of digital image processing is increasingly high. Particularly, methods of motion estimation are increasing in their practical importance. The employment of neural structures to solve the problems of determination of complex object displacements in undistorted and distorted environments is an innovative way.
Kohonen's self-organizing maps [1] are very powerful networks allowing the projection of a set of n-dimensional vectors onto a two-dimensional array of processing units. The main part of the paper deals with an implementation of the Modified Hypermap Architecture (MHA) [2, 3, 4] for classification of object features in a moving scene.
The trained features, represented by the object-specific MAD, are used as an associative memory. The recall from this associative memory is usable for recognition of the two-dimensional object-specific MAD features for an improvement of motion estimation.

2   Problem description and modeling

The starting point of investigation is the system model shown in Figure 1.

In a first step the subsystem 2 realizes the well-known block matching method by comparison of consecutive image pairs [5]. The Mean Absolute Difference (MAD) is used as a similarity criterion. The principle and mathematical description of the block matching procedure is explained in more detail in [6]. Traditional matching algorithms perform a MAD minimum search for displacement detection. There are some problems for motion determination in the case of image acquisition in distorted environments (e.g. overlapping movements in one block, textured foreground or background or noise) and, if high spatial resolution is required. Particularly in the region of the MAD minimum it can cause wrong measurements. Additionally the emergence of that multiple similar minima can prevent the unique correspondence between the object movement and the coordinates of location. Here methods of improvement of motion estimation must be integrated (subsystem 3 in Fig. 1). First attempts of postprocessing the object-specific MAD features by application of an artificial neural network are described in [7].

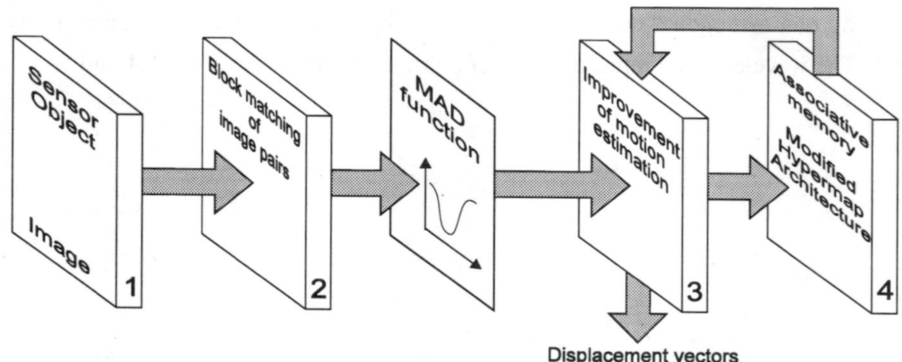

Figure 1: System model for motion analysis with a neural network based structure

Artificial input functions have been used as training data, especially, the objects pyramid, cuboid, apex and stump (Fig.2). These function are obtained from the block matching algorithm which is explained in [7].

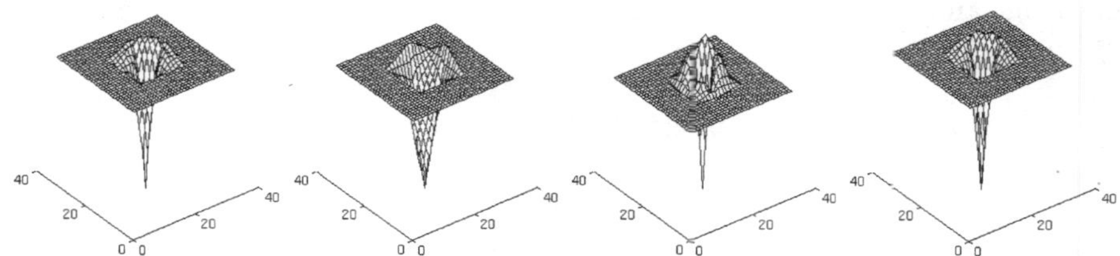

Figure 2: Artificial object-specific MAD for training: pyramid, cuboid, apex, stump

One image of the moving scene is divided into several subimages and their object-specific MAD features are calculated. The hypermap network is trained with the object-specific MAD features which represent the related artificial objects in the best way. After training, the network receives a continuous input of object-specific MAD features from subsystem 2 and should be able to recognize the typical object-specific MAD features of our trained artificial objects.

3   Classification by means of an Artificial Neural Network

Subsystem 4 was used as an associative memory of trained object-specific MAD features. This subsystem is a structured multi-layer formal neural network realized as a modification of the Hypermap Architecture (Brückner et al. [3]). Unlike the Hypermap Architecture, which was introduced by Kohonen in [2], we suggest a structure of an arbitrary number of levels in the input vector with each level containing the transformed input data (Fig.3). In [3] we defined the modification of the Hypermap Architecture. There we described the learning of context-dependent data. The context is generated from the input data. With our modification it is possible to learn features of different classes in priority, which represent the context of the input data. Each part of a feature class is related to the corresponding level in the input vector which forms a hierarchy. The learning process consists of one step for each level in the hierarchy.

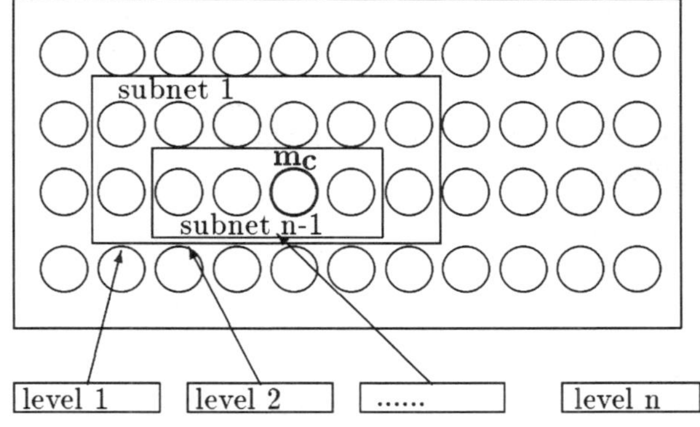

Figure 3: Structure of the Modified Hypermap Architecture. The input vector consists of a concatenation of segments. Each segment contains input data for one feature class and thus for one level in the hierarchy. The different levels of the input vector are trained and form a hierarchy of encapsulated subsets which define different generalized stages of classification.

4   The learning algorithm

Let the input vector of one level l_j be $\mathbf{x}_{l_j}$ and one processing unit $\mathbf{m}_{i,l_j}$ then, in a first phase, one has to find a first level with a subset S_j of nodes for which

$$\|\mathbf{x}_{l_j} - \mathbf{m}_{i,l_j}\| \leq \delta_j, \tag{1}$$

with δ_j being the threshold of that level. Then it is necessary to find the best match $\mathbf{m}_c$ for all nodes in the subset and to adapt the weights accordingly.

The learning algorithm of the new Modified Hypermap Architecture depends now on the a priori knowledge. The a priori knowledge is defined by the mean error

$$\sigma = \frac{1}{n}\sum_{j=1}^{n}\|\mathbf{x}_{l_j} - \mathbf{m}_{c,l_j}\| \tag{2}$$

If the difference $\|\mathbf{x}_{l_j} - \mathbf{m}_{c,l_j}\| - \sigma$ is greater than a given ϵ for one or more levels l_j, than we have a node with a priori knowledge and the affiliated levels in the input vector represent no regular data for training (i.e. artefacts, see discussion below).

$$\mathbf{m}_{c,l_j}(t+1) = \mathbf{m}_{c,l_j}(t) + \alpha'(l_j)\alpha(t)[\mathbf{x}_{l_j}(t) - \mathbf{m}_{c,l_j}(t)], \tag{3}$$

where

$$c = arg\min_{i}\{\|\mathbf{x}_{l_j} - \mathbf{m}_{i,l_j}\|\}, \tag{4}$$

$$\alpha'(l_j) = e^{-\|l_i - l_j\|} \tag{5}$$

and

$$\alpha(t) = c_0 e^{-D(t)}, \; D(t) \; distance \; function \tag{6}$$

The sizes of the thresholds δ_j should be decreased according to the the levels to obtain encapsulated subsets S_j.

If a priori knowledge has been detected then (3) is modified by (7)

$$\mathbf{m}_{c,l_j}(t+1) = \mathbf{m}_{c,l_j}(t) + \alpha''(l_j)\alpha'(l_j)\alpha(t)[\mathbf{x}_{l_j}(t) - \mathbf{m}_{c,l_j}(t)], \tag{7}$$

where

$$\alpha''(l_j) = e^{-\|\mathbf{x}_{l_j} - \mathbf{m}_{c,l_j}\| - \sigma} \tag{8}$$

for all these levels l_j (for $t > t_0$).

Classification is achieved by finding the best matching node for each level of the hierarchy and by determining the square mean error of matching. To protect the algorithm from initial disordering the a priori knowledge learning step should start after a given time t_0.

5   Results

In our experiments the MHA network was trained with data which represent features of typical objects in images of a moving scene. These features were extracted from a block matching algorithm, the so called object-specific MAD features. First the network was trained with one level in the input vector, i.e. the conventional SOM algorithm was used. In these experiments the network was not able to distinguish between similar object-specific MAD features, e.g. between pyramid and stump. New features were obtained by a conventional image processing task. Because the object-specific MAD is an image whose pixels next to the border are sometimes noisy, we define a region as a centered circle and exclude this region from the object-specific MAD. The input vector included now 2 levels, the first level is the whole object-specific MAD and the second the circled subimage.

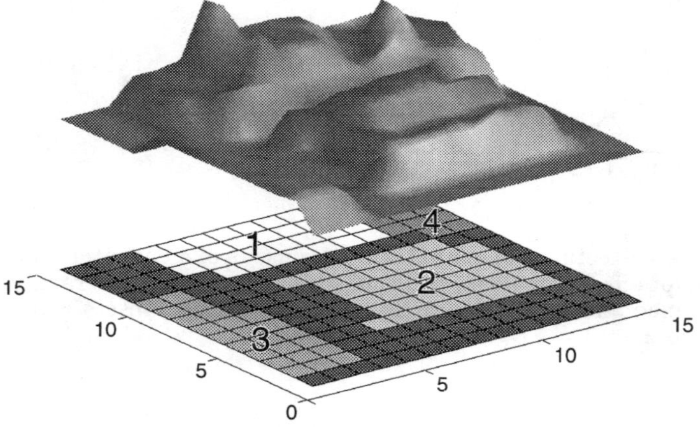

Figure 4: Global error surface of the second layer after classification of the object-specific MAD features of 4 artificial objects (1-pyramid, 2-cuboid, 3-apex, 4-stump)

After training the network can distinguish all object-specific MAD features of our typical artificial objects in the second layer (Fig.4). In the first layer we still found a common cluster for similar objects. In this way the network is able to solve both tasks, to find similarities between objects and to classify the objects.

Because we utilize in our tests the image processing system KHOROS, we prepared the algorithm of the Modified Hypermap Architecture to run as a KHOROS module. In this way it is possible to combine customary image processing algorithms with our network.

The next step of our work will be the recognition of objects with an advanced complexity. In all cases the features of the objects, to be detected, are extracted from the block matching process. Because the Modified Hypermap Architecture is able to handle with more complex featured data, we expect, that the described system is also usable for analyzing moving scenes of real objects. The construction of an associative memory with object-specific MAD features of real objects in a high quantity which can be used for the calculation of displacement vectors in motion estimation is a further step of our investigation.

Acknowledgement

This work was supported by LSA grant 1441B/0083.

References

[1] T. Kohonen. The self-organizing map. *Proceedings of the IEEE*, 78(9):1464–1480, 1990.

[2] Teuvo Kohonen. The hypermap architecture. In T. Kohonen, K. Mäkisara, O. Simula, and J. Kangas, editors, *Artificial Neural Networks*, pages 1357–1360, Helsinki, 1991. Elsevier Science Publishers.

[3] Bernd Brückner, Marcella Franz, and Andreas Richter. A modified hypermap architecture ... In Aleksander and Taylor [14], pages 1167–1170.

[4] B.Brückner, T.Wesarg, and C.Blumenstein. Improvements of the modified hypermap architecture for speech recognition. In *Proc. Inter. Conf. Neural Networks*, volume 5, pages 2891–2895, Perth, Australia, 1995.

[5] H.-G.Musmann, P.Pirsch, and H.-J.Grallert. Advances in picture coding. *Proceedings of the IEEE*, 73(4):523–530, 1985.

[6] O.Schnelting, B.Michaelis, and R.Mecke. Motion estimation with artificial neural networks by utilisation of a-priori information. In *International Scientific Colloquium*, volume 2, pages 83–90, Ilmenau, Germany, 1994.

[7] O.Schnelting, B.Michaelis, and R.Mecke. Artificial neural networks for motion estimation. In *ICANNGA*, pages 136–139, Ales, France, 1995.

[8] B. Brückner and W. Zander. Neurobiological modelling and structured neural networks. In S. Gielen and B. Kappen, editors, *ICANN'93*, pages 43–46, London, 1993. Springer Verlag.

[9] Bernd Brückner and Wiebke Zander. Classification of speech using a modified hypermap architecture. In I. Aleksander and J. Taylor, editors, *Proceedings of the WCNN'93*, volume III, pages 75–78, Hillsdale, 1993. Lawrence Earlbaum Associates.

[10] W. Zander, B. Brückner, T. Behnisch, and T. Wesarg. Modeling biologically relevant temporal patterns. In M. Marinaro and P. G. Morasso, editors, *ICANN'94*, pages 98–101, London, 1994. Springer Verlag.

[11] Teuvo Kohonen. What generalizations of the self-organizing map make sense? In M. Marinaro and P. G. Morasso, editors, *ICANN'94*, pages 292–297, London, 1994. Springer Verlag.

[12] T.Kohonen. *Self-Organization and Associative Memory*. Springer-Verlag, New York, 1988.

[13] H. Ritter, T. Martinetz, and K. Schulten. *Neuronale Netze*. Addison-Wesley, Bonn, 1990.

[14] I. Aleksander and J. Taylor, editors. *Artificial Neural Networks,2*, Amsterdam, 1992. Elsevier Science Publishers.

Robust Face Image Retrieval by Fuzzy Gated Neuronal Architecture *

V.Chandrasekaran† and Zhi-Qiang Liu‡
Department of Computer Science
University of Melbourne,
Carlton, Victoria-3053, Australia
e-mail: †vc@cs.mu.oz.au, ‡zliu@cs.mu.oz.au

Abstract— Conventional systems require precise location of important facial image fragments such as eyes and nose to perform necessary transformations such as rotation and normalization on the probe image for the purpose of invariant feature extraction, and face image recognition/retrieval. In addition, there exists a certain amount of ambiguity and impreciseness associated with the feature extraction process, thus making the recognition task difficult. In this paper, an approach that is robust to localization errors is presented for face image retrieval using novel gated neuronal architectures. The proposed system is capable of quickly adapting to additions and deletions to the database without increasing the computational burden. A database containing 140 poor resolution images is used for testing the system for its performance over a range of spatial errors in locating the eyes and nose during feature extraction.

1   Introduction

Machine recognition of faces has been an active area of research in view of its potential applications ranging from a simple mug shot matching to surveillance via video images. The remarkable ability with which humans recognize faces is yet to be matched by any machine recognition system. The task of face recognition undoubtedly poses several challenges to various disciplines such as image processing, pattern recognition, computer vision, expert systems and neural networks. Such a task involves segmentation of human faces from the background, extraction of useful features from the face region for learning the underlying qualities and structure of individual person's face, and identification and matching [1]. In this paper, we are considering retrieval of facial images from the database for electronic line-up and/or browsing.

Given a probe image, the common approach has been to locate the eyes, nose and mouth first [2-8] and then extract features from each of these regions and also from the part of facial image encompassing these important facial image segments. To obtain features that are independent of rotation, scaling and translation etc., certain affine transforms are usually carried out prior to feature extraction. These normalization procedures require sufficiently accurate location of the facial parts such as eyes, nose, and mouth. Any spatial location errors will certainly result in inaccurate feature vectors and the recognition process becomes susceptible to such changes. It is often difficult to find an automated system to precisely locate the eyes (say at their centers) and the nose (say at its tip) in view of different pose, lighting and other special conditions (such as spectacles) that may be encountered in real life. Therefore, there exists a certain amount of ambiguity and impreciseness associated with the feature extraction process that requires precise locations of important image fragments as a starting point. In this paper, a novel approach that is robust to such localization errors is presented for face image retrieval. Also the proposed system is capable of quickly adapting to additions and deletions to the database which have often resulted in computationally expensive training/searching task in the existing systems.

2   Face Image Retrieval System

The face image retrieval system proposed in this paper is shown in Fig. 1. The first stage of operation is to grab the locations of the centers of right and left eyes and the tip of the nose manually. The second stage carries out affine transformations to normalize and grab the image part that is considered useful. The third stage performs the image decomposition into a time-sequence of image frames from which seven types of temporal features of the statistical type are extracted. These are then used in the fourth stage for training the fuzzy gated neural networks. There are seven such networks operate in parallel and provide their decisions to the final stage for face image retrieval.

3   Image Preprocessing

3.1   Face Database

Facial image data is obtained from the Archive - SunSITE Northern Europe located at the Department of Computing, Imperial College, London, U.K via anonymous ftp to host:sunsite.doc.ic.ac.uk [155.198.1.40].

---

*This work is supported by Australian Research Council large grants.

These files are in postscript format and converted to preferred PBM ascii by unix xv tool. There are nearly 3900 images available of which 140 images are acquired for testing. 97 of these images are reserved for training and testing for image retrieval under imprecise location of eyes and nose. The rest of the images are retained for false acceptance rate testing.

3.2 Identification and Extraction of Important Image Fragments

As is evident, the important image fragments that characterize a face are the area bounding the eyes, nose and mouth. In order to extract features that are invariant to scaling and head tilt, centers of the eyes and the tip of the nose are manually located first. Let the pixel locations be (xl, yl) for left eye, (xr, yr) for right eye and (xn, yn) for the tip of the nose. The image is then rotated clockwise by an angle $\theta = \arctan(\frac{xl-xr}{yr-yl})$ with (xn, yn) as its center. Such a rotation brings the centers of the eyes horizontal and will compensate for any tilt in the head posture. The center to center distance between the eyes and the perpendicular distance to the tip of the nose from the line joining the eye centers are then normalized to become 40 and 30 pixels respectively. Then an image area of the size 64×64 pixels from the above normalized part is extracted with its origin placed at $(\hat{xr} - 24, \hat{yr} - 24)$. $(\hat{xr}, \hat{yr})$ refers to the right eye location after rotation by angle θ.

3.3 Convolution by Fractional Derivative Mask

The above normalized image is processed further by convolving it with a derivative mask. This mask is designed based on the principles of fractional differentiation operator illustrated in [17]. The elements of the mask are computed at the derivative index 1.0 on a 5×5 mask. The main objective of this convolution is to compute an aggregated multi-directional derivative value at each pixel in the image. This convolution characterizes the underlying morphological structure of the face thus facilitating the extraction of discriminating features. Such a characterization stems from the fact that the binary edge contours of the image obtained either by a maxima or a minima criterion reflect the underlying structure of the object. A number of examples of edge contour maps are shown in [16,17].

4 Feature Extraction by Sparse Decomposition

The ultimate goal in any recognition system is to extract notable and useful features from which a description, interpretation and understanding of the source or scene characteristics by the machine can be accomplished at ease. Such features from the source must provide sufficient discriminatory power during the classification task.

4.1 Sparse Decomposition by Gated Neuronal Array

The task of feature extraction is accomplished by sparse decomposition of the face images using a gated neuronal array. In the paper [11], it is demonstrated that an image can be decomposed into a time-sequence of image frames by controlling the neuronal gates via a time-varying spatial grating function. From the above sequence of images, statistical information such as entropy, mean, second and third order invariant moments can be extracted. These temporal features code the structural aspect of the facial image effectively. The discriminating quality of such features were assessed in [16] on a set of range image data for 3-D objects and found to be useful. The general architecture of the feature extraction network is shown in Fig. 2. The gates are controlled by a function whose spatial grating frequency parameter is reduced to zero from a chosen maximum value (4 Hz) over a time period T (39 in this paper).

4.2 Statistical Features

The sparse decomposed images of the selected patches appear at the output side of the second layer of the gated neuronal array. From these decomposed time sequence of images, mean, entropy, two second and three third order invariant moments are extracted. At any instant of time, we can obtain at the output a 7-D feature vector whose elements are the ordered set of mean(t), entropy(t), $\phi_1(t)$, $\phi_2(t)$, $\phi_3(t)$, $\phi_4(t)$ and $\phi_5(t)$ [18] for all $t = 0, \cdots, 39$. One can use these 7-D feature vectors as they arrive in sequence over the time period T to collect evidence on various class hypotheses. Alternatively, the entire feature data can be treated as a $\{7 * 40\}$ vector. In this paper, 40-D feature vectors of each type are used in parallel as input to classifier networks.

5 Fuzzy Gated Neuronal Architecture for Pattern Recognition

In the paper [9], a novel Fuzzy Gated Neuronal Architecture(FGNA) is proposed and demonstrated on a 3-D object recognition problem. FGNA eliminates the need for *training the synaptic weights to a set of nodes* so as to represent the cluster centroids. The output of a Fuzzy Gated Neuron(FGN) is a set of discrete time-varying class membership grades which when combined properly provides an overall class membership grades that are close to the class probability densities. These are then used for class label prediction.

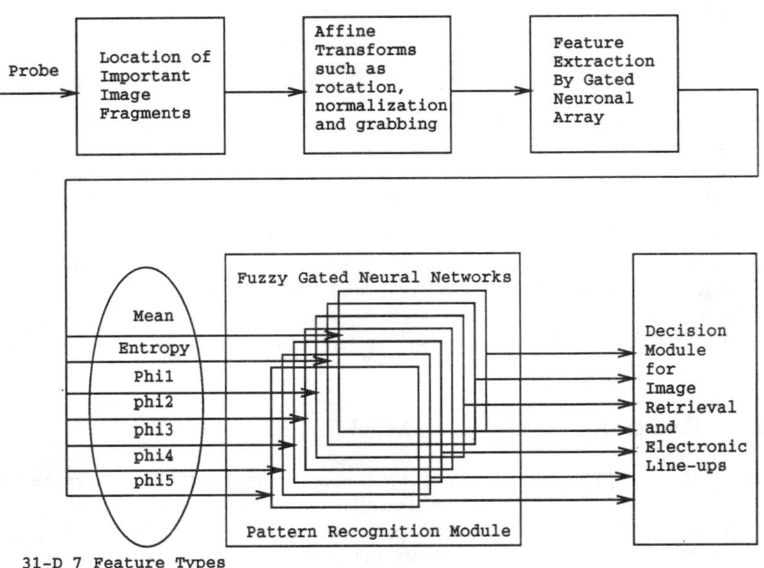

Figure 1: Face Image Retrieval System

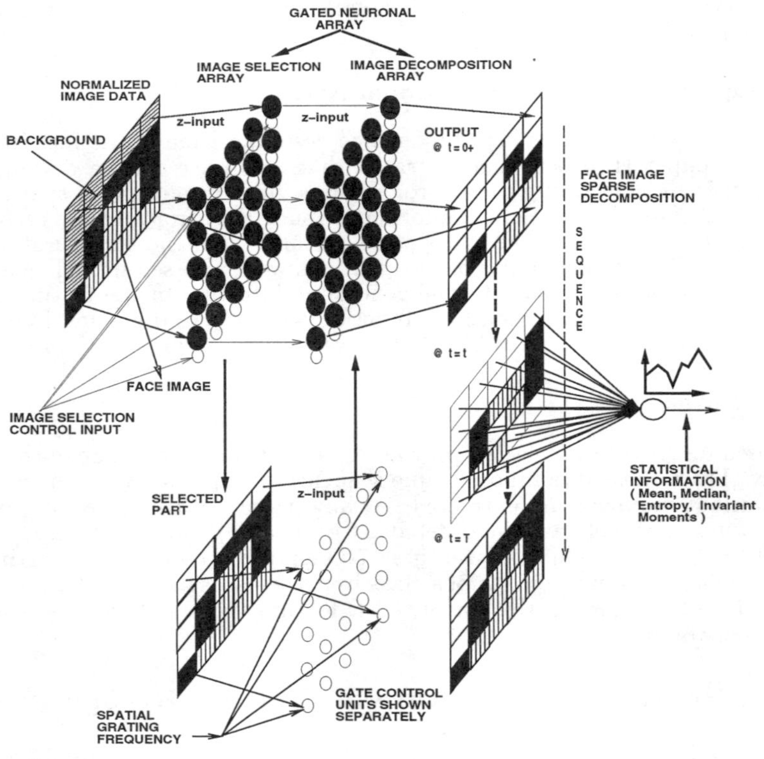

Figure 2: Feature Extraction by Gated Neuronal Array

5.1 Fuzzy Gated Neuronal Architecture

The general organization of the FGNA is shown in Figure 3. The FGNA is adapted for pattern classification with input, gate control and output functions exactly as described in [9]. For want of space, these are not repeated here.

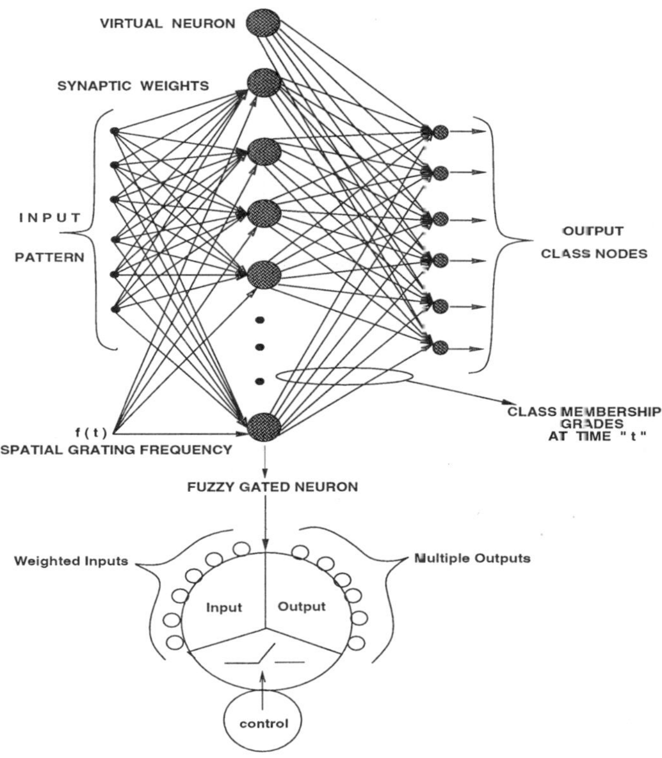

Figure 3: Fuzzy Gated Neuronal Architecture for Pattern Recognition

The novelty of FGNA lies in two aspects; i) selective competition among neurons and ii) time-indexed rectangular class membership grades selected by a time-sequence of winning nodes when the spatial grating frequency is varied from its maximum to zero in discrete time interval T. Instead of fuzzifying the cluster boundaries for classification, the FGNA utilizes all possible combinations of the decision planes between the nodes to generate overlapping decision regions. Such regions are formed by deterministically selecting a set of nodes for competition by introducing an eligibility criterion and then varying the set criterion over discrete time steps to obtain a sequence of winning nodes. The evidence available at each winning instance is then combined using various strategies for accurate class label prediction. This combination approach is similar to the defuzzifying procedure in fuzzy clustering-based classification.

When no neuron is selected for some input samples at any chosen frequency, then a *virtual* node is assigned to provide the fuzzy class membership grades to output class nodes. The above virtual node concept facilitates an easy representation of the class probability distributions within the feature space partitions where no competition occurs at any discrete spatial grating frequency.

5.2 Weight Selection

The major advantage of FGNA is that it does not require weights based on any clustering or rigid feature space partitioning strategy. The only requirement is that the weights should be stratified and contained within the convex hull of the input space [16]. Based on the feature extraction process described earlier, the training patterns are obtained from the set of mug shot face images. From these training patterns, the weights can be directly selected. There are two approaches by which one can select the weights from the training data set. These are i) random picking and ii) bi-section search. A bi-section approach will guarantee the weights uniformly spread in the input space but computationally expensive. On the other hand, the random picking of weights from the data set is extremely quick but may not be stratified. In [9,16], it is demonstrated that the random picking performs equally well.

5.3 Class Membership Grade Table Generation

For a set of frequencies $[f(0), f(1), \cdots, f(T)]$, FGNA generates a time-sequence of winning nodes for every input pattern. Each winning node k at any $f(t)$ is associated with a set of class frequency counts

$[n_{k1}(t), n_{k2}(t), \cdots, n_{kC}(t)]$. The total number of training patterns of all classes associated with a winning node k is equal to $\sum_{i=1}^{C} n_{ki}(t)$. From the above, class membership grades can be computed by taking ratio of $n_{ki}(t)$ to $\sum_{i=1}^{C} n_{ki}(t)$. These grades can be stored as connections to the class nodes at the output of FGNA for a suitable combination and class label prediction.

Common Steps

- Present a probe image.
- Locate the right and left eye centers.
- Locate the tip of the nose.
- Place a 3×3 window at each of the above locations.
- Select a triple $(xr, yr), (xl, yl), (xn, yn)$ based one pixel from each window.
- Normalize and grab the part of the face image for the above.
- Extract seven types of feature vectors from the above grabbed image by sparse decomposition technique using gated neuronal array.

Training Mode:

- Carry out Common Steps as above.
- Generate a time-sequence of winning nodes in each of the FGNA for each input pattern.
- Repeat the process for all 729 combinations of right, left and nose locations.
- Generate Time-Node frequency table for the input class.
- Repeat the above process for all classes and their associated input images.

Run Mode:

- Carry out Common Steps as above.
- Generate a time-sequence of winning nodes in FGNA for each input pattern.
- Predict the class label in FGNA for each of the 729 combinations.
- Hypothesize and retrieve the face images based on the above 729 predictions on each of the seven FGNA networks.

6   Experimental Set-up

In order to test the system for spatial errors, a table of spatial deviations within ± 2 pixels is created by a pseudo-random number generation and these deviations are added to the training parameters of eye and nose locations. These are then used to evaluate the robustness of the image retrieval system.

7   Results

The following simulations are carried out to test the face image retrieval system.

On Training Images:

- As a first step, 97 images are tested for zero spatial location errors. The face image retrieval is 100% accurate.
- Based on the perturbed locations, a set of face images are retrieved and lined up. If the original image is picked in the line-up, then the system performance is considered satisfactory. Based on this criterion, the accuracy of face image retrieval system is found to be 98%. The false rejection rate 2% is due to a ratio of 1/729 between seen and unseen feature vectors generation.

On Test Images

Based on a preset confidence level, the system is found to be capable of retrieving images that are similar. However, the decision strategy is found to be inadequate to reject the new input as "unseen". This is still being investigated at present.

8   Conclusions

In this paper, we have proposed a novel architecture for face image retrieval system capable of accommodating spatial location errors introduced either by a human operator or by an automated localizer. The architecture provides a novel approach to feature extraction and pattern recognition in contrast to conventional systems. In addition, the training time required to set up FGNA is minimal. The system is capable of quickly adapting to the changes in the image database as it would normally happen in any image retrieval system. The proposed system will be integrated with an automated eye and nose locator system being developed in our laboratory at a later date. The system needs to be tested for its generalization capability to identify the person(s) over a range of conditions. The present database is not suitable for this purpose as it contains only one mug shot person.

9 References

[1] Rama Chellappa, Charles L. Wilson and Saad Sirohey, "Human and Machine Recognition of Faces: A Survey", Proceedings of IEEE, vol.83, No.5, pp 704–740, May 1995.

[2] Hans Peter Graf, Tshuan Chen, Eric Petajan and Eric Cosatto, "Locating Faces and Facial Parts", Proceedings of the International Workshop on Automatic Face- and Gesture-Recognition, pp 41–46, Zurich, 1995.

[3] R.Herpers, H.Kattner, H.Rodaux and G.Sommer, "GAZE: An Attentive Processing Strategy to Detect and Analyze the Prominent Facial Regions, Proceedings of the International Workshop on Automatic Face- and Gesture-Recognition, pp 214–220, Zurich, 1995.

[4] I.A.Rybak, A.V.Golovan, V.I.Gusakova, N.A.Shevtsova and L.N.Podladchikova, "A Neural Network System for Active Visual Perception and Recognition", Proceedings of Neural Networks World, vol.4, pp. 245–250, 1991.

[5] Advait Mogre, Robert McLaren, James Keller and Raghuram Krishnapuram, "Uncertainty Management for Rule-Based Systems with Applications to Image Analysis", IEEE Transactions on Systems, Man, and Cybernetics, vol.24, No.3, pp 470–481, March 1994.

[6] Baback Moghaddam and Alex Pentland, "Maximum Likelihood of Detection of Faces and Hands", Proceedings of the International Workshop on Automatic Face- and Gesture-Recognition, pp 122–128, Zurich, 1995.

[7] Nathan Intrator, Daniel Reisfeld and Yehezkel Yeshurun, "Extraction of Facial Features for Recognition using Neural Networks", Proceedings of the International Workshop on Automatic Face- and Gesture-Recognition, pp 260–265, Zurich, 1995.

[8] Jiang Kang Wu and Arcot Desai Narasimhalu, "Identifying Faces Using Multiple Retrievals", IEEE Multimedia, pp 27–38, 1994.

[9] V.Chandrasekaran, Zhi-Qiang Liu and M.Palaniswami, "Fuzzy Gated Neuronal Architecture for Pattern Recognition", Proceedings of the IEEE International Conference on Neural Networks(ICNN), vol.4 of 6, pp 1622–1627, Nov.27–Dec 1, 1995.

[10] V.Chandrasekaran, M.Palaniswami and Terri M.Caelli, 'Pattern Recognition by Topology Free Spatio-Temporal Feature Map", Proceedings of the IEEE International Conference on Systems, Man,and Cybernetics, Vancouver, British Columbia, Canada, vol 2 of 5, pp 1136–1141. Oct22-25, 1995.

[11] V.Chandrasekaran, M.Palaniswami and Terri M.Caelli, "Temporal Feature Extraction by Sparse Decomposition of Range Images using Gated Neurons", Proceedings of the IEEE World Congress on Computational Intelligence, Orlando, Florida, USA, Jun26-Jul2 1994, pp 4033-4037, 1994.

[12] V.Chandrasekaran, M.Palaniswami and Terri M.Caelli, "Spatio-Temporal Feature Maps using Gated Neuronal Architecture", IEEE Transactions on Neural Networks, vol.6, No.5, pp 1119-1131, September 1995.

[13] V.Chandrasekaran, M.Palaniswami and Terri M.Caelli, "Range Image Segmentation by Dynamic Neural Network Architecture", Pattern Recognition, vol.28, No.4, 1995.

[14] V.Chandrasekaran, M.Palaniswami and Terri M.Caelli, "Performance Evaluation of Spatio-Temporal Feature Maps with Gated Neuronal Architecture", Proceedings of INNS World Congress on Neural Networks(WCNN), Oregon, USA, pp IV-112-118, July 1993.

[15] Richard Hoffman and Anil K.Jain, "Sparse Decompositions for Exploratory Pattern Analysis", IEEE Transactions on Pattern Analysis and Machine Intelligence, vol.PAMI-9, pp 551–560, July 1987.

[16] V.Chandrasekaran, "Gated Neural Networks for Three Dimensional Object Recognition Systems", PhD Thesis, Department of Electrical and Electronic Engineering, The University of Melbourne, June 1995.

[17] V.Chandrasekaran, M.Palaniswami and Terry M.Caelli, "Range Image Segmentation by Dynamic Neural Network Architecture", Pattern Recognition Journal (in press).

[18] Anil K.Jain, "Fundamentals of Digital Image Processing", Prentice Hall International Editions, Thomas Kailath(Ed.), 1989.

A Computational Model for The Extraction of Really Moving Objects From The Entire Retinal Image Flow

Ken-ichiro Miura, Takashi Nagano

College of engineering, Hosei University
3-7-2, Kajino-cho Koganei, Tokyo, JAPAN
e-mail nagano@nagano.is.hosei.ac.jp

Abstract —— **In this paper, a general computational model is proposed that can extract the local velocity vectors caused only by really moving objects from widely spread retinal image flows caused by observer's movement. First, the property of the retinal image flow field caused by really moving objects and the observer's movement is analyzed. Then a new computational model is constructed based on the property. In the proposed model, the local velocity vectors of really moving objects are extracted by using signals related to self-motion. The extraction of image flows of really moving objects corresponds to the detection of positions and local velocity vectors of really moving objects.**

1 Introduction

It is well known that, in the primate cerebral cortex, the signals induced by a moving visual stimulus are mainly processed on the pathway from LGN to area 7a in the parietal cortex via areas V1, MT and MST. Each cell in V1 and MT has a local receptive field and detect a local motion information of a moving image on the retina [1]. In other words, these cells compute a kind of image flow field of a moving retinal image. There are many cells in MST and 7a which have large receptive fields. Each of them responds selectively to a specific image flow pattern detected by many cells in V1 and MT [2]. Generally, an image flow pattern is induced all over the retina when an observer moves. So, it is thought that these cells in MST and 7a play an important role in the estimation of self-motion. Accordingly, the information processing pathway is thought to be related to various motion perceptual phenomena induced by image flow. The perceptual phenomena can be divided into two classes: the perception of the motion of really moving objects and that of self-motion. So far, some computational and neural network models for the perceptual phenomena have been proposed [3]-[6]. However, in all of the models, extreme cases were assumed, that is, either only objects in the surroundings or only an observer moved. That is, it was assumed in the models for object motion detection that an observer did not move. On the other hand, it was assumed in the self-motion detection model that only an observer moved. However, in most cases in the real world, both objects and an observer move simultaneously. Therefore, we have to take the case into account in order to explain general motion perceptual phenomena.

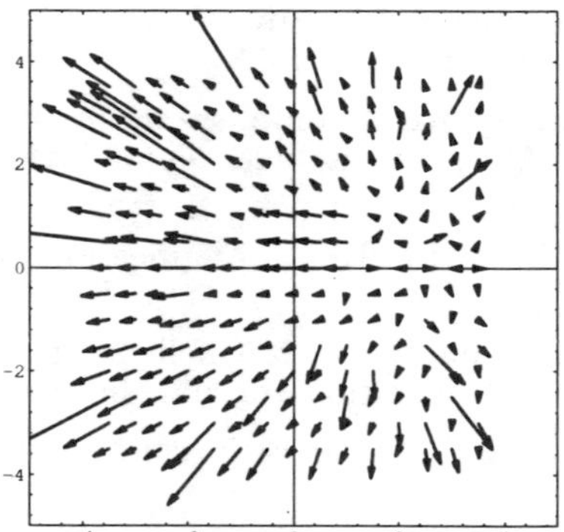

Figure1: An example of image flow on the retina when both a body and objects existing in the visual space move. Each arrow shows the local velocity vectors detected at each position on the retinal image.

In this paper, we propose a computational model that explains the perception of object motion in more general case where an observer may also move. Especially, we study about the mechanism of the detection of positions and velocity vectors of really moving objects. Generally, a self-motion causes "image flow" at all the positions on the retina of an observer when the observer moves around (Figure1). The image flow field caused by self-motion can be regarded as a kind of "noise" for the computational system to detect velocity vectors and positions of really moving objects. In most cases, image flow informations at most positions will be "noise" since a really moving object usually occupies a small region in the retina. In spite of the fact, we can detect the positions and velocity vectors of really moving objects. Therefore, it can be thought that there is an earlier computational process in our visual system that extract the local velocity vectors caused only by really moving objects than the computational process of velocity vectors of the objects are computed after the extraction process. Since the model of the later computational process was already proposed by us [6][7], we propose here a computational model that can extract the image flows caused only by really moving objects. There are some physiological findings suggesting that many cells in MST and 7a receive signals from the nervous system other than the visual system [8][9]. Therefore, we construct a model that can extract the local velocity vectors of really moving objects using such signals. The extraction by the proposed model corresponds to the detection of positions and local velocity vectors of really moving objects.

We first examine characteristics of the image flow field caused by both really moving objects and self-motion in section2. Then we propose in section3 a general computational model for the extraction of local velocity vectors caused only by a really moving objects based on the characteristics.

2 Retinal image flow field

First, the retinal image flow field caused by both object motion and self-motion is analyzed geometrically. The coordinate system used in the following analysis is shown in Figure 2. For simplicity, the projection to the retina is approximated by the projection to a plane. A standard equation is shown which represent the relation between the velocity vector of point p: $^T(x_0,y_0,z_0)$ on the eye-centric coordinate system $x_e\text{-}y_e\text{-}z_e$ and the velocity vector of retinal point P which is the projected point of p on the retina [10].

$$\begin{pmatrix} dX_0/dt \\ dY_0/dt \end{pmatrix} = \begin{pmatrix} f/z_0 & 0 & -(f \cdot x_0)/z_0^2 \\ 0 & f/z_0 & -(f \cdot y_0)/z_0^2 \end{pmatrix} \begin{pmatrix} v_x \\ v_y \\ v_z \end{pmatrix} \tag{1}$$

, where X_0 and Y_0 denote the position of point P on the retinal coordinate system $X\text{-}Y$, dX_0/dt and dY_0/dt

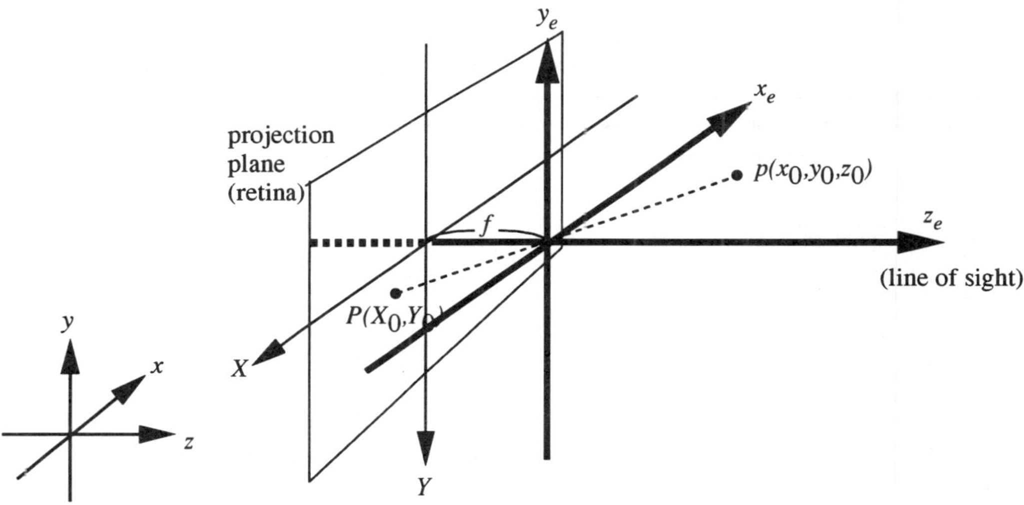

Figure2: Three coordinate systems used in the analysis of retinal image flow field. *x-y-z* system shows a fixed coordinate system in the environment. $x_e\text{-}y_e\text{-}z_e$ and *X-Y* systems show an eye-centric coordinate system and retinal image coordinate system respectively. In the eye-centric coordinate system, z_e corresponds the line of sight. $x_e\text{-}y_e\text{-}z_e$ and *X-Y* systems moves with self-motion in the fixed coordinate system *x-y-z*.

represent the velocity vector components of P, f denotes the focal length of the eye lens and is assumed to be constant, and $^{T}(v_x, v_y, v_z)$ denotes the velocity vector of p on the eye-centric coordinate system. It is given by the composition of the velocity vector of the really motion of p and those of eye and body movements as is described by equation (2).

$$\begin{pmatrix} v_x \\ v_y \\ v_z \end{pmatrix} = \begin{pmatrix} v_{p,x} \\ v_{p,y} \\ v_{p,z} \end{pmatrix} + \left\{ -\begin{pmatrix} v_{b,x} \\ v_{b,y} \\ v_{b,z} \end{pmatrix} - \begin{pmatrix} \omega_{e,x} \\ \omega_{e,y} \\ \omega_{e,z} \end{pmatrix} \times \begin{pmatrix} x_0 \\ y_0 \\ z_0 \end{pmatrix} \right\} \tag{2}$$

, where $^{T}(v_{p,x}, v_{p,y}, v_{p,z})$ shows the velocity vector of the real motion of p on the fixed coordinate system in the environment x-y-z, and $^{T}(v_{b,x}, v_{b,y}, v_{b,z})$ and $^{T}(\omega_{e,x}, \omega_{e,y}, \omega_{e,z})$ show the translation velocity vector component of an eye caused by body motion and the rotation velocity vector component caused by eye movement on the fixed coordinate system in the environment respectively. Therefore, the retinal image flow field caused by both really moving objects and self-motion is given by the following equation.

$$V(X,Y) = V_p(X,Y) + V_{eb}(X,Y) \tag{3}$$

,where $V(X,Y)$ shows the image velocity vector at retinal position (X, Y), and $V_p(X, Y)$ and $V_{eb}(X, Y)$ denote those caused by objects and self-motion (eye and body movements) respectively. The equation means that an image flow field is given by the simple summation of those caused by really moving objects and self-motion.

3 Computational model

A computational model for the extraction of the local velocity vectors of really moving objects is proposed based on the analysis in section 2. As shown in equation(3), a whole image flow field is divided into two terms related to real motion of objects and self-motion respectively. Therefore, the image flow field caused by really moving is given by the following equation.

$$V_p(X,Y) = V(X,Y) - V_{eb}(X,Y) \tag{4}$$

A computational model for the extraction based on equation(4) is schematically shown in Figure3. The model is constructed with three modules:(A), (B) and (C). Module(A) computes the image flow field of a moving image on the retina. In module(B), the predicted retinal image flow field caused only by eye and body movements is computed with self-motion signals obtained from nervous system other than the visual system. In module(C), the comparison the image flow field computed in module(A) with the predicted retinal image flow field computed in the module (B) is performed in order to extract only the image flow

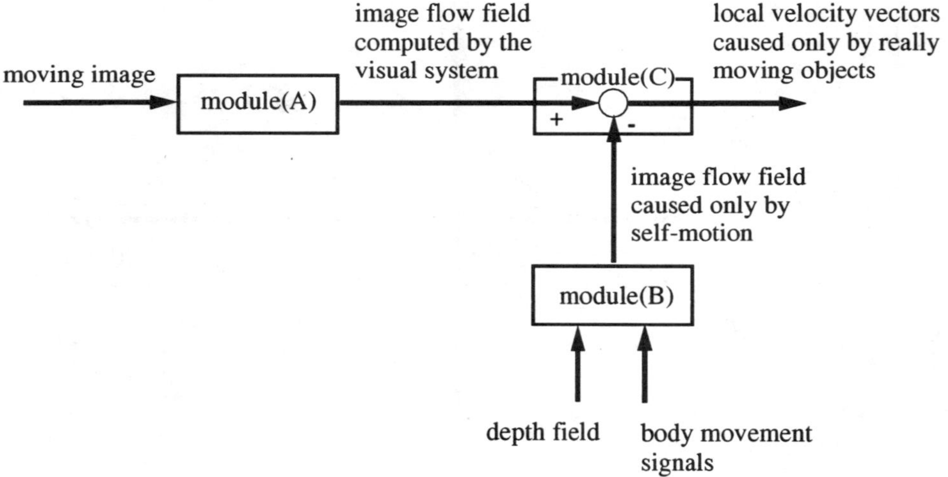

Figure3: Schematic diagram of the proposed computational model. The model is composed of three modules: (A), (B) and (C). Module(A) computes a retinal image flow field. Module(B) predicts the image flow field on the retina which caused by self-motion. Module(C) compare the image flow field computed in module(A) with that of module(B) and outputs the local velocity vector of really moving objects.

field caused by really moving objects.

So far, some computational models for the detection of image flow in module(A) were proposed [11]-[13]. For example, Heeger proposed the model that can extract almost correct image flow field with immediate computation [12]. So, we assume here that the nervous system can accurately compute the retinal image flow field of a moving image on the retina which is obtained by equation(1) and (2).

We explain the computation in module(B), that is, the way of computation of the predicted retinal image flow field caused only by eye and body movements. It can be derived from equation(1) and (2) that the predicted retinal image flow field is given by the following equation.

$$\mathbf{V}_{eb}(X,Y) = \begin{pmatrix} -f/z(X,Y) & 0 & X/z(X,Y) \\ 0 & -f/z(X,Y) & Y/z(X,Y) \end{pmatrix} \begin{pmatrix} v_{bx} \\ v_{by} \\ v_{bz} \end{pmatrix}$$

$$+ \begin{pmatrix} X \cdot Y/f & -(f+X^2/f) & Y \\ (f+Y^2/f) & -X \cdot Y/f & -X \end{pmatrix} \begin{pmatrix} \omega_{ex} \\ \omega_{ey} \\ \omega_{ez} \end{pmatrix} \tag{5}$$

,where $z(X,Y)$ shows the depth of the point projected at retinal position (X, Y) for a fixed line of sight, and $^T(v_{bx}, v_{by}, v_{bz})$ and $^T(\omega_{ex}, \omega_{ey}, \omega_{ez})$ are the translation component of an eye caused by body movement and the rotation component caused by eye movement respectively. These self-motion components are assumed to be given by the efference copy of motor command signals and signals from the vestibular system, etc.. $z(X,Y)$ can be computed by using the method with the mechanism of stereo vision shown in Figure4 [14]. We assume here that $z(X,Y)$ can be given accurately by the actual nervous system. Therefore, module(B) can compute the image flow field in which all the objects involved in a moving image are regarded as stationary objects. It is assumed that computations in module(A) and module(B) are performed in parallel.

Module(C) preforms the computation shown by equation(4). That is, the local velocity vectors caused by really moving objects is extracted in the module since the local velocity vectors of stationary objects caused by self-motion are all cancelled. Accordingly, the positions and local velocity vectors of really moving objects are given simultaneously by outputs of the module.

4 Discussion

When we move our eyes voluntary in stationary surroundings, we feel our surroundings stationary in spite that there are retinal image flows according to eye movements. However, if an eye is moved passively, for example

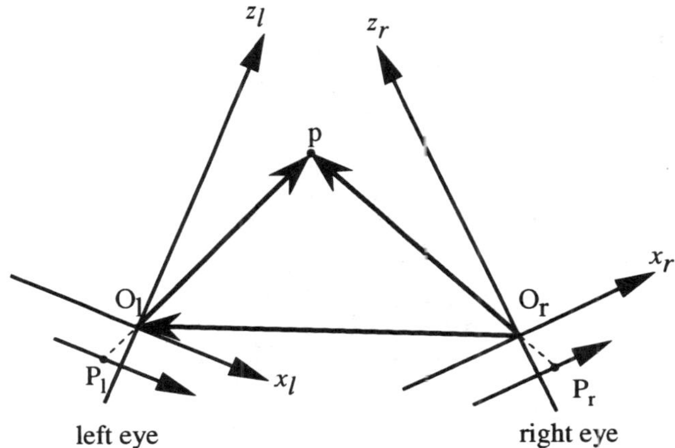

Figure4: Schematic diagram of the mechanism of stereo vision. x_e-z_e and x_r-z_r systems show left and right eye-centric coordinate systems respectively. O_r and O_l show center of eye lens of left and right eyes respectively. p shows a point in the environment and P_l and P_r show the projected points of p on the left and the right retinas respectively. Using the geometrical relations illustrated in the figure, the absolute depth value corresponding to each location on the both retinas can be computed (Horn, 1986).

with a finger, we feel that our surroundings move. Holst [15] and Mackey [16] proposed hypotheses for the perceptual difference independently. They said in the common part of their hypotheses that our perceptual system has a mechanism to decide that our surroundings move or not with the efference copy of voluntary oculomotor command signals. In other words, this means that the local velocity vectors caused by really moving objects are computed with the efference copy of oculomotor command signals. In our computational model, local velocity vectors caused by really moving objects are assumed to be extracted based on the difference between the image flow field computed by the visual system and the predicted retinal image flow field derived from self-motion information. That is, local velocity vectors caused by really moving objects are computed with self-motion information. Therefore it can be thought that the computational model is an development of their hypothesis. In the computational model, the information of self-motion is extended to more general body movement signals which include not only the efference copy of oculomotor command signals but also motor commands of entire body movement and vestibular signals etc.. There is a finding that supports their hypotheses [8]. According to the finding, some cells in the parietal cortex respond to a moving visual stimulus but are inhibited by the efference copy of the voluntary oculomotor command that causes the same retinal image motion. The cells have not be found yet which show the response like that to more general self-motion signals other than eye movement. However, it can be thought that body and eye movement is always kept under observation in the cortex because it is known that vestibular signals are projected to the cortex and that motor command signals of a body are generated in the cortex. Therefore, it may be thought that a computational process similar to the model exists in the brain.

It is generally known that some special image flow patterns can cause self-motion perception even when an observer does not move actually. For example, image flow patterns induced all over the retina frequently tend to cause self-motion perception [17]. An example of the flow fields is shown in Figure5. This means that flow fields are not necessarily interpreted as the ones caused by really moving objects in the brain in spite that there are no signals of any actual body movements. Therefore, we have to improve the computational model in order to be consistent even with these special perceptual phenomena. The improvement is made by modifying module(B). That is, $^T(v_{bx}, v_{by}, v_{bz})$ and $^T(\omega_{ex}, \omega_{ey}, \omega_{ez})$ are assumed to be given by not only the efferent copy of eye and body motor command signals and vestibular signals but also the self-motion information obtained by the visual motion processing system. The modification will make the model to be more consistent with human visual motion perception.

We assume that the method based on the stereo vision is used in the computation of depth field in our model. The method has the problem called "correspondence problem" which is known to be difficult to solve. There are some cases that the pairs of corresponding points between both eyes can not be found accurately because of aperture and occlusion. Therefore, the method may be insufficient for the estimation of depth. However, monocular cues can also be used to estimate a depth field. For example, a human being can perceive the 3-D structure of a visual scene only with the information of "shading". This fact suggests that there are some independent computational modules for depth estimation other than the module based on the binocular cue in the actual nervous system. It can be thought that the accurate depth of a visual scene is given by the composition of the outputs of the modules that compute the depth field of the image given to the retina from each cue.

In the proposed model, all the parameters are assumed to be given accurately. However, the parameters are not thought to be computed exactly in the actual nervous system. So, we will consider the problem and

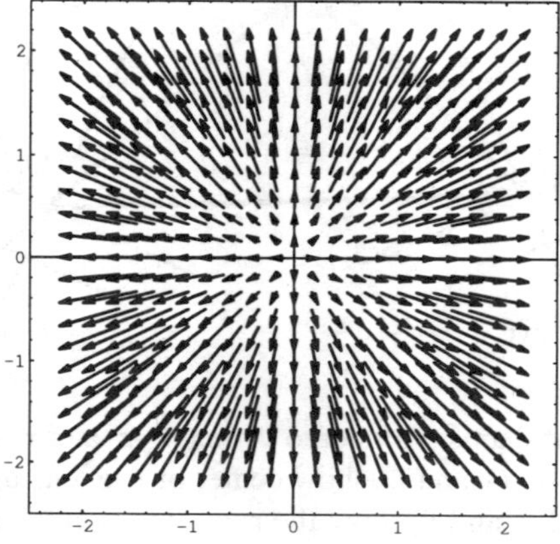

Figure5: An example of image flow patterns which cause the perception of self-motion.

construct a neural network implementation based on the proposed computational model in our successive study.

5 Conclusion

In this paper we propose a general computational model that can extract local velocity vectors caused only by really moving objects. The proposed model can detect positions and local velocity vectors of really moving objects simultaneously. It may be natural to assume the existence of the computational process in the actual nervous system.

Acknowledgment

This research was supported by Grant-in Aid #5267105 for Scientific Research on Priority Areas on "Higher-Order Brain Functions", the ministry of Education, Science, and Culture of Japan.

References

[1] J.H.R.Maunsell, D.C.VanEssen, "Functional properties of neurons in middle temporal visual area of the macaque monkey.I.Selectivity for stimulus direction, speed and orientation", *J.Neurophysiol.*, vol.49, pp. 1127-1147, 1983

[2] H.Saito, M.Yukie, K.Tanaka, K.Hikosaka, Y.Fukuda, E.Iwai, "Integration of direction signals of image motion in the superior temporal sulcus of the macaque monkey", *J.Neuroscience*, vol. 6, no. 1, pp. 145-157, 1986

[3] J.A.Perrone, "Model for the computation of self-motion in biological systems", *J. Opt. Soc. Am. A*, vol. 9, no. 2, pp. 177-194, 1992

[4] J.A.Perrone, L.S.Stone, "A model of self-motion estimation within primate extrastriate visual cortex", *Vision Res.*, vol. 34, no. 21, pp. 2917-2938, 1994

[5] S.J.Nowlan, T.J.Sejnowski, "Filter selection model for motion segmentation and velocity integration", *J. Opt. Soc. Am. A*, vol. 11, no. 12, pp. 3177-3200, 1994

[6] K.Miura, T.Nagano, "Biologically plausible neural network for motion detection", *Neural processing Letters*, vol. 2, no. 5, pp. 4-8, 1995

[7] K.Miura, T.Nagano, "A neural network model for motion detection of moving objects", *Proc. of the 5th Tohwa University International symposium*, Fukuoka, Oct., pp. 139, 1995

[8] H.Sakata, "The role of the parietal association areas in spatial vision", *Advances in neurological sciences*, vol. 27, no. 5, pp 809-821, 1983 (in japanese)

[9] W.T.Newsome , R.H.Wurtz, H.Komatsu, "Relation of cortical areas MT and MST to pursuit eye movements. II. Differentiation of retinal from extraretinal inputs", *J. Neurophysiol.*, vol. 60, no. 2, pp. 605-620, 1988

[10] H.C.Longuet-Higgins, K.Prazdny, "The interpretation of retinal moving images", *Proc. of the R. Soc.Lond. B*, vol. 208, pp. 385-397, 1980

[11] B.K.P.Horn, B.G.Schunck, "Determining optical flow", *Artificial Intelligence*, vol. 17, pp. 185-203, 1981

[12] D.J.Heeger, "Model for the extraction of image flow", *J. Opt. Soc. Am. A*, vol. 4, no. 8, pp. 1455-1471, 1987

[13] N.M.Grazywacz, A.L.Yuille, "A model for the estimate of local image velocity by cells in the visual cortex", *Proc. of the R. Soc.Lond. B*, vol. 239, pp. 129-161, 1990

[14] B.K.P.Horn *Robot Vision.* MIT Press, 1986

[15] E.Holst, "Relations between the central nervous system and the peripheral organs", *Br. J. Animal Behavior*, vol. 2, pp. 89-94, 1954

[16] D.M.Mackay, "Visual stability and voluntary eye movements", In: R.Jung (eds.) *Handbook of Sensory Physiology vol.VII/3A*, Springer, Berlin Heidelberg NewYork, pp. 307-331, 1973

[17] J.Dichigans, T.Brandt, "Visual-vestibular interaction". In: R.Held, et al. (eds.) *Handbook of Sensory Physiology vol.8.*, Springer, Berlin Heidelberg NewYork, pp.755-804, 1978

Hybrid Architecture for Image Understanding by Mutual Evaluation of Symbol and Pattern processing

Yoshiyuki Mitsumori,* Daisuke Saeki,† Yoshinori Tsuji,* Takashi Omori*‡

*Graduate School of Bio-Applications & Systems Engineering, Tokyo University of Agriculture & Technology.
Nakamachi 2-24-16, Koganei, Tokyo 184, Japan
†Nohmi Bosai Limited
Nakamachi 2-24-16, Koganei, Tokyo 184, Japan
‡PRESTO, JRDC,
Honmachi 4-1-8, Kawaguchi 332, Japan.

***Abstract*— A symbol processing and a pattern processing are basic paradigms of intelligent system implementation. Though they have been studied separately, their integration is an essential factor for a realization of the higher level intelligent system. In this paper, we propose a design concept of a hybrid image understanding system. It is a hybrid of a symbol processing system and an image processing system that are connected by a symbol-pattern mutual transformation mechanism. There, a mutual evaluation of the symbol processing and the pattern processing plays an important role. We have implemented it by the Neocognitron and examined its ability by a simple image and a real image.**

1   Introduction

Symbolic processing and Pattern processing are central field of conventional intelligent system study. They have developed independent fields of the Artificial Intelligence and the Pattern Recognition. Though each of them is powerful enough, it is also recognized widely that their integration is necessary for the development of more powerful intelligent system.

It is obvious that human has an ability to integrate a language processing and a visual pattern processing. In our visual scene understanding, we can infer from local recognition result, and can confirm the inference result in a visual imagery. Though both of them are results of the symbol and pattern integration, detailed mechanism of the interaction in not clear yet.

In this paper, we propose a method of hybrid image understanding system. In the system, each of the two heterogeneous systems, the symbol and pattern systems, evaluates their processing results each other to realize a robust image understanding. A key feature of the system is a mutual transformation of the symbol and image representations. We used the Neocognitron for the transformation mechanism. Computer simulation results on model and real images show a effectiveness of the method.

2   Image Understanding System

2.1   Hybrid Image Processing

A basic hypothesis on a realization of the image understanding is a necessity of a bi-directional combination of the pattern recognition that classifies objects in an image and the symbolic inference that estimates a situation by the recognition result and a knowledge on the world. The image recognition technique is not almighly on variety of image condition. We need a parameter tuning for the robust image recognition depending on objects and conditions. It requires a evaluation of initial recognition result by apriori knowledges. In the symbolic inference from the recognition result, we often get multiple situation candidates. We must verify them in the image level to select correct one. We suppose that the interaction between the pattern recognition and the symbolic processing is implemented by a symbol-pattern bi-directional transformation and a cross evaluation of each processing result.

We have reported a case study of image understanding system that use the image recognition/recollection neural network Neocognitron [1]. In the system, a image processing system and a symbolic processing system are located in parallel, and the Neocognitron realize their interaction as the transformation system. But we could not construct general image understanding system because of a lack of a designing guideline for the symbol-pattern interaction.

In this paper, we propose a designing guideline for the symbol–pattern mutual evaluation system, and show a case study of the hybrid image understanding system.

2.2   Image Processing – Transformation – Fuzzy Inference

Fig.1 shows basic structure of the image understanding system. It has an image processing module (IPM), a symbol processing module (SPM), and a imege-symbol bi-directional transformation module (BTM). We adopt the Neocognitron and the Prolog language system as the trnsformation and the symbolic modules[2][3]. The IPM preprocesses an input analogue image to a binary line image, and evaluates a SPM inference result at the image level. The BTM transform the objects in image style and its symbolic representation bi-directionaly. The function make use of the Neocognitron's object recognition and image recollection function to obtain consistent symbolic representation and image segmentation. The SPM use Fuzzy inference to estimate a situation of the image scene. As the Fuzzy is an extension of logic processing, we call it a "symbolic" in this paper. Each module has different knowledge. The SPM uses symbolically represented knowledge, and make inference by a symbolic data manipulation. The BTM uses knowledge that is embedded in neural connections of the Neocognitron.

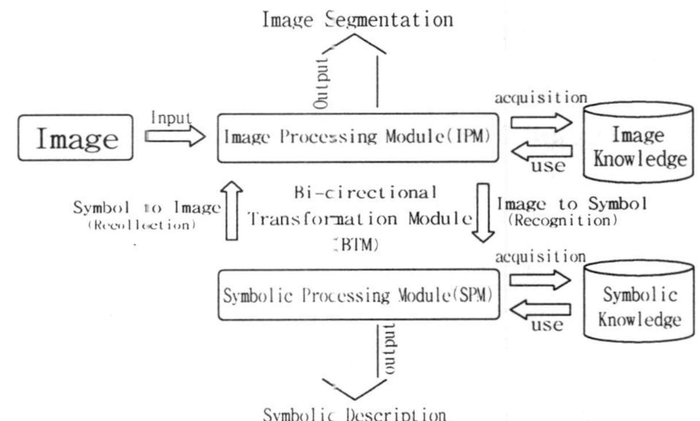

Figure 1: Basic structure of the hybrid image understanding system

2.3 Mutual Evaluation of Symbol and Image Processing

The main feature of our system is the mutual evaluation of the recognition and inference by largely different processing systems of the symbol and pattern. In the SPM for example, the Prolog system can't evaluate its multiple answers. The inference results from the recognition results are re-projected to the IPM, and are evaluated on the image. The BTM transforms a symbolic scene representation into a image, and the recognized objects are eliminated from the input image. A remainder of the elimination shows a correctness of the object recognition in the SPM.

Oppositely, it is possible to evaluate an image processing result by a "goodness" of the symbolic inference. An image preprocessing for an image understanding should be evaluated by a change of the quality of understanding with it. For example, we must evaluate a threshold value for the image binarization by an appropriateness of the Neocognitron recognition result and the inference.

Both of these cases obtain its evaluation by transforming its representation between the symbol style and the image style. As they have largely different representation and processing characteristics, it is not so much a case that both of them fall into processing difficulty at the same time. So far as the bi-directional transformation is possible, we can expect the hybrid system to have a robustness that is superior to each of its elements. The discussion will not be limited to the symbol and pattern hybrid, but also apply to more general cases of hetero-information integration.

2.4 Process of Image Understanding

Fig.2 shows a detail of the system behavior. Each of the IPM, BTM and SPM has its own processings.

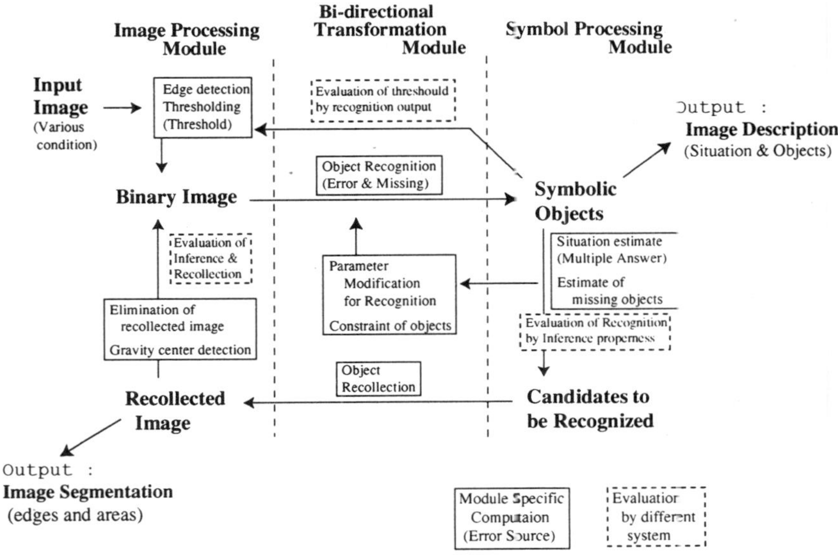

Figure 2: Detail of the understanding process

Image Processing Module

A. Preprocessing The IPM generates a binary image for the BTM input by an edge extraction and thresholding from an input image. (_Threshold_)

B. Object elimination The IPM eliminates the recollected object image from the BTM input image to avoid its re-recognition.

C. Position acquisition The IPM calculates a gravity center of the recollected image as its position.

Bi-directional Transformation Module

D. Recognition The BTM recognizes objects from the binary image, and describes them by symbolic representation. (Error and missing of the recognition)

E. Recollection The BTM extracts set of edges that belong to each of the symbolically represented objects. (Error of the recollection)

F. Parameter control The recognition and the recollection process are many to one transformation. The Neocognitron requires some parameter tuning to properly transform them. It affects on a recognition strictness, and changes the recognition result.

Symbolic Processing Module

G. Inference The SPM infers a situation that the scene belongs to. The situation designates objects that should be found in the scene. From the knowledge and the recognition output value of the Neocognitron, the SPM decides which objects to be evaluated in the image level. (Multiple interpretable situation)

The underlined items are factors of the erroneous recognition and understanding. We can imagine some mutual evaluating methods for them.

- **Threshold value evaluation by the recognition output**
  The recollected image from a recognized object decides an image area that the objerct occupies. We can find a best threshold value in the area by monitoring the Neocognitron output for each object.
- **Evaluation of the recognition correctness by the symbolic inference**
  The SPM compares the Neocognitron output with the situation knowledge. Un-plausible recognition results are put into the image recollection and confirmation process. The Neocognitron parameters are changed to find objects that are expected to be in the scene but not.
- **Inference evaluation by edge image difference**
  The recollected edges of an object are eliminated in the input binary image, and an amount of remaining edges in the area is measured. The remainder is much if the symbolic input for the recollection is mistaken.

As the result, the system repeats the information transformation between the object symbol and its image level representation. It continues until all the recognition and image segmentation becomes consistent, or no improvement is obtained with the processing. The final outputs of the system are a description of the scene in the symbol style and the segmented image areas.

2.5   Fuzzy Inference

The BTM recognition result take a continuous value between zero and one depending on an amount of object deformation. So, conventional binary value based inference methods are not available on it. We use a fuzzy logic based inference for it.

Table 1: Symbolic knowledge in Fuzzy style

	situation A	situation B
object1	def 0.9	def 0.1
object2	def 0.9	def 0.1
object3	def 0.9	def 0.9
object4	def 0.1	deg 0.9
object5	def 0.1	def 0.9

Table 1 shows an example of fuzzy knowledge representation. A situation "A" contains objects 1,2 and 3 with high probability, and objects 4 and 5 with low probability. Equations (1) and (2) are used to compare the knowledge and the recognition results from the BTM. Here, R_e is the output of the recognition, K_n is the value of the knowledge element, m is a number of learned objects, and n is a situation number.

$$Sum_n = \sum_{k=1}^{m} |Re_k - Kn_k| \tag{1}$$

$$\mu_n = 1 - \frac{1}{1 + exp(-Sum_n)} \tag{2}$$

The value μ_n takes value one when the recognition results exactly match to the knowledge, and becomes to zero when they are different. A situation that has largest μ_n is adopted for a candidate of the scene interpretation. Use of the fuzzy inference enables the situation estimation with ambiguous or erroneous recognition results. We can obtain those objects that may have been miss-recognized, and infer its correct recognition condidate.

Table 2 shows a miss-recognition case of object-3 to object-4. We can easily estimate miss-recognized outputs and expected objects by comparing the Neocognitron outputs and the knowledge description. The information is send to the BTM and IPM to transform into image and to evaluate them.

Table 2: Evaluation of the recognition results.

	situation A		
	Re	Kn	Re-Kn
object1	0.9	0.9	0.0
object2	0.9	0.9	0.0
object3	0.0	0.9	-0.9
object4	0.8	0.1	0.7
object5	0.0	0.1	-0.1

3 Computer Simulation

3.1 Simulation System Implementation

Fig.3 shows a structure of the simulation system. The system is composed of the three modules in Fig.2, and a system manager that controls behavior of them. Each module is an independent computing processes, and communicates each other through the system manager.

3.2 Simulation on a model image

We used simple model images in Fig.4 for a basic evaluation of our system. At first, the Neocognitron learned the five objects in Fig.4(a) for the object recognition and the image recollection. The symbol knowledge in Fig.4(b) is given to the SPM in advance. Fig.4(c) is an input image for the understanding.

At first, the Neocognitron failed to recognition a circle for a square. The situation-D was obtained as a result of the symbolic inference. Next, the Neocognitron recollects images of the recognized parts to evaluate the SPM result(Fig.5(a)). Only the common feature of the circle and square are recollected in the image. The recollected edges are subtracted from the binary image (Fig.5(b)). The corner edges of the circle remain. From the amount of the remainder, we can judge that the recognition "square" is mistaken. The area is recognized again. This time, the Neocognitron is controlled not to recognize the square, and its feature extraction parameters are changed to extract other features of the image.

As a result of the re-recognition, the circle is recognized correctly, and the situation-B is obtained as an answer from symbolic inference. Its recollected image has small difference from the input image(Fig.5(c)), and the situation-B is confirmed as a final result of the recognition-inference-recollection iteration.

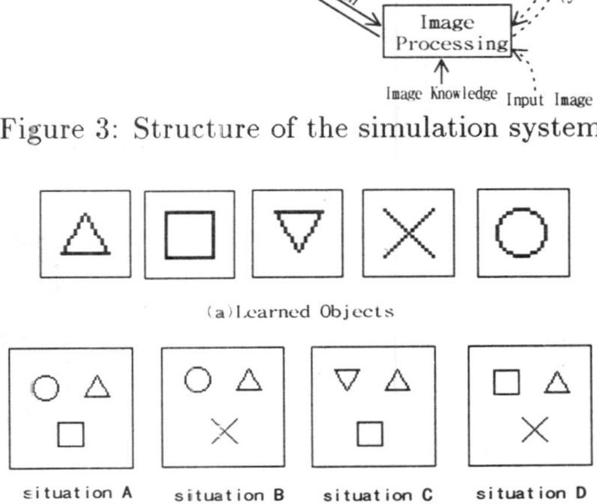

Figure 3: Structure of the simulation system

Figure 4: Model image for the simple simulation

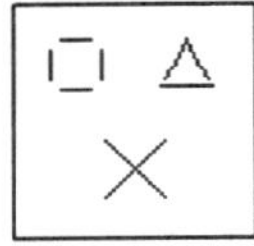
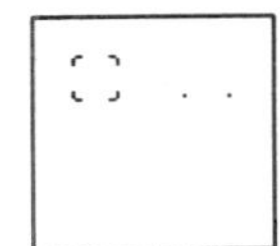
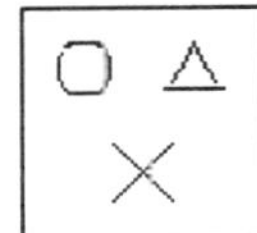

Figure 5: Evaluation of recognition and inference in image representation.

3.3   Simulation on a real image

As is same as the model image case, we made the BTM learn the eight objects in Fig.6(a), and gave the knowledge in Fig.6(b) to the SPM.

At first, the image thresholding parameter in the IPM is changed by the evaluation of the BTM output(Fig.7). In this example, we adopted a middle threshold value because the output value of the Neocognitron is biggest with it.

Left part of Fig.8 shows a result of the first recognition. The Neocognitron recognized a real object "ashtray" as both of an "ashtray" and a "dish". This is because the competition of output layer in the Neocognitron is weaken to obtain robust recognition. Next, the input scene is inferred as a situation "resting table" from the symbolic knowledge. Because the "dish" doesn't match to the symbolic knowledge and shares the same position with the "ashtray", we can judge the recognition "dish" to be mistaken. Therefore, the parameter in the IPM and the BTM corresponding to the "dish" area is changed, and the object is re-recognized. Then, only the "ashtray" is recognized, and a consistent recognition and inference result is obtained.

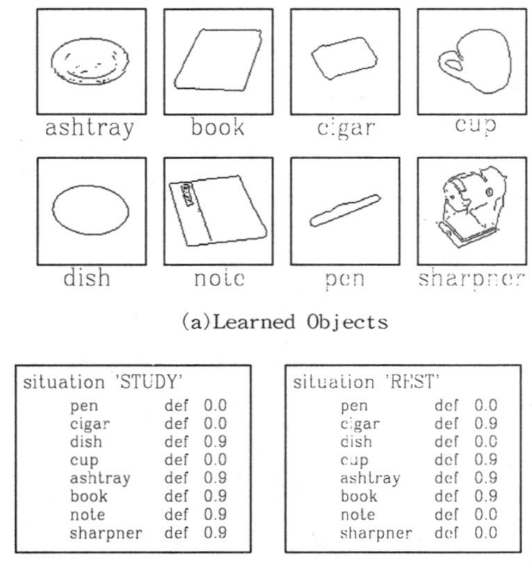

(a)Learned Objects

(b)Symbolic Knowledge

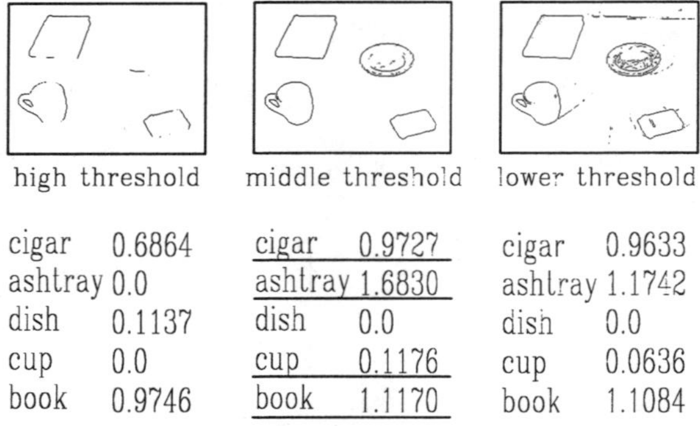

(c)Input Image

Figure 6: Real image for the understanding

	high threshold	middle threshold	lower threshold
cigar	0.6864	0.9727	0.9633
ashtray	0.0	1.6830	1.1742
dish	0.1137	0.0	0.0
cup	0.0	0.1176	0.0636
book	0.9746	1.1170	1.1084

Figure 7: Thresholding of the continuous valued image

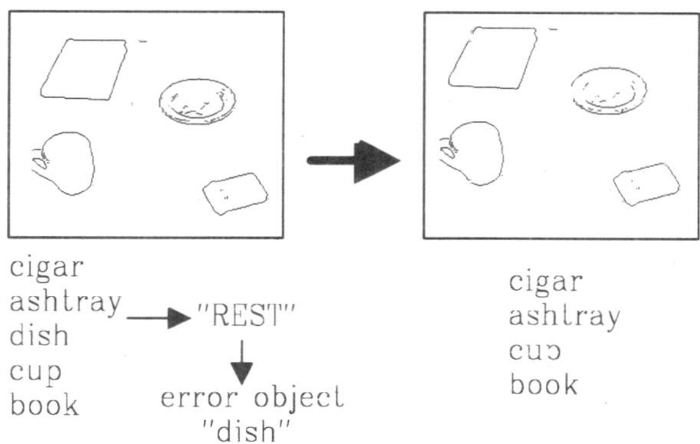

Figure 8: Result of real image understanding

4 Discussion

4.1 Problem on the Symbol-Pattern Bi-directional Transformation

The main problem of our system is an incompleteness of the Neocognitron image recollection. A recollected image from a symbol often has lack of corner edges, and has unnecessary edges. It leads to an incorrect evaluation in the IPM. As the image and symbol bi-directional transformation is the most important factor of our system, its atable function is necessary. We need an improvement of the Neocognitron or a development of new recognition-recollection model for the BTM function.

4.2 Problem in the real image understanding

In the simulation, we normalized size of the objects in the image. But in a real world image, each object is located in different distance and has different size. The assumption doesn't apply. Though the Neocognitron recognition is robust for the size and deformation in some amount, it is not almighty. We need some systematic way for the object size invariance.

In the IPM, we used the subtraction of the recollected edges and counted its remainder for the image level evaluation. It doesn't work well for a noisy and low quality image. We need more sophisticated method for the image level evaluation.

5 Conclusion

We have proposed the design concept of hybrid image understanding that use mutual evaluation of the symbol and pattern processing. Computer simulations showed effectiveness of the method. Currently, not all the possible mutual evaluation methods are implemented yet. We have to improve it, and more automatic understanding on various objects is necessary.

References

[1] Nishi M, Ohzeki K, Sakurai N, Omori T. : An Architecture for Image Understanding by Symbol and Pattern Integration, Proc. of International Conference on Artificial Neural Networks 94,268/271,1994

[2] K.Fukushima, S.Miyake : "Neocognitron": a new algorithm for pattern recognition tolerant of deformations and shifts in position, Pattern Recognition, 15, 6, pp455-469 (1982)

[3] K.Fukushima : "A neural network model for selective attention in visual pattern recognition",Biol. Cybernetics, 55[1], pp.5-15(Oct. 1986)

Fuzzy Neural Network for Radar Target Identification

Chunling Yang, Guosui Liu, Yunhong Wang

Teaching and Research Section 412

Department of Electronic Engineering

Nanjing University of Science and Technology

Nanjing, Jiangsu, China, 210094

ABSTRACT   Three kinds of Fuzzy Neural Network (FNN) are discussed in this paper. The comparison between Fuzzy Neural Network and traditional BP Network for Radar Target Identification is made. From the computer simulations, we obtain some attractive results.

1 INTRODUCTION

BP Neural Network has been used in Radar Target Identification in recent years[1-2]. It has high classification rate, but requires long training time and cannot classify fuzzy sample. In this article, we discuss Fuzzy Neural Network which combines the Fuzzy System with Neural Network. The Fuzzy Neural Network can classify the Fuzzy sample.

2 ALGORITHM OF FUZZY NEURAL NETWORK

The follow figure shows the graph of Fuzzy Neural Network.

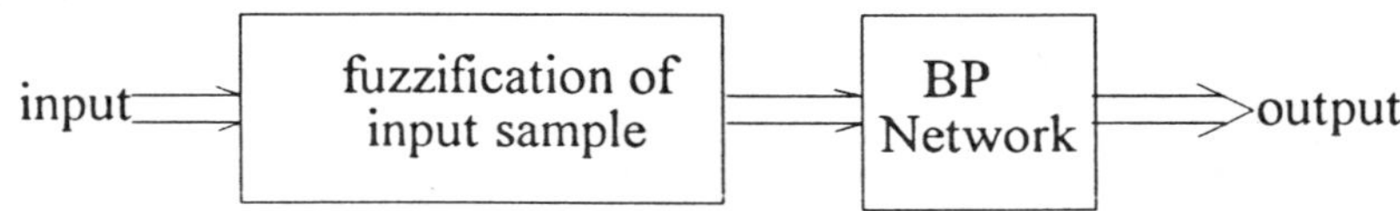

Fig. the graph of Fuzzy Neural Network

In the Fuzzy Neural Network, we use π-function to fuzzify the input sample, and the Neural Network is BP network which consists of three layers: input layer, nonlinear hidden layer and output layer. During the training, the desired output of the network is membership value of the sample.

1. The Fuzzification of the input sample[3].

We fuzzify the input samples with π-function, which is given by the following formula.

$$\pi(r,c,\lambda) = \begin{cases} 2\cdot(1-\dfrac{\|r-c\|}{\lambda})^2 & \dfrac{\lambda}{2} \le \|r-c\| \le \lambda \\[2ex] 1-2\cdot(\dfrac{\|r-c\|}{\lambda})^2 & 0 \le \|r-c\| \le \dfrac{\lambda}{2} \\[2ex] 0 & else \end{cases} \tag{1}$$

Where: $r \in R^n$, R^n expresses the n-dimensional space, $\lambda > 0$ is the radius of R^n, c is the center.

Every characteristic space is divided into three fuzzy dim-spaces: low space, medium space, high space. $f_{j\,max}$ and $f_{j\,min}$ express the upper limit and the lower limit of the characteristic f_j, then c and λ of the low space, medium space and high space are given by the following formulas.

$$\begin{cases} \lambda_m(f_j) = 0.5\cdot(f_{j\,max} - f_{j\,min}) \\ c_m(f_j) = f_{j\,min} + \lambda_m(f_j) \end{cases} \tag{2}$$

$$\begin{cases} \lambda_l(f_j) = \dfrac{c_m(f_j) - f_{j\,min}}{f_d} \\[2ex] c_l(f_j) = c_m(f_j) - 0.5\cdot\lambda_l(f_j) \end{cases} \tag{3}$$

$$\begin{cases} \lambda_h(f_j) = \dfrac{f_{j\,max} - c_m(f_j)}{f_d} \\[2ex] c_h(f_j) = c_m(f_j) + 0.5\cdot\lambda_h(f_j) \end{cases} \tag{4}$$

Here, f_d is used to control the overlapping degree of the close spaces, generally $f_d \in [0.5, 1.0]$.

Now we can use the π-function to calculate the membership values of the f_j in the low, medium and high space. So a n-dimensional input feature vector can be expressed as a $3n$-dimensional feature vector.

2. Choosing the desired output

The n-dimensional vectors $\mathbf{O}_k$ and $\mathbf{V}_k$ are the average vector and the variance vector of the kth cluster. The distance between the sample $\mathbf{F}_i$ and the kth cluster is given by formula(5)[3]:

$$z_{ik} = \sqrt{\sum_{j=1}^{n} \left[\frac{f_{ij} - o_{kj}}{v_{kj}} \right]^2} \qquad\qquad k = 1,2,\cdots,l \qquad\qquad (5)$$

f_{ij} is the *jth* characteristic value of sample $\mathbf{F}_i$.

The membership value of $\mathbf{F}_i$ in the *kth* cluster is given by the following formula[3]:

$$\mu_k(\mathbf{F}_i) = \frac{1}{1 + \left(\dfrac{z_{ik}}{f_g}\right)^{f_e}} \qquad\qquad (6)$$

Where: f_e and f_g are used to control the fuzzy degree of the cluster.

Formula (6) shows that the larger is the distance between the sample $\mathbf{F}_i$ and the *kth* cluster, the smaller is the membership value. When the distance is "0" , the membership value is the biggest: "1" .

The membership value which is given by the formula(6) can reflect the real feature of the sample. Sometimes, the membership values of some fuzzy samples in more than two clusters are big, so we use the following formula to modify them.

$$\mu'_{(k)}(\mathbf{F}_i) = 0.5\cdot(\mu_k(\mathbf{F}_i) + \mu_k) \qquad\qquad (7)$$

Where:

$$\mu_k = \begin{cases} 1 & F_i \in kth \quad cluster \\ 0 & F_i \notin kth \quad cluster \end{cases}$$

3   COMPUTER SIMULATIONS

We use the Doppler signals collected by surveillance radar as our database. The targets needed to be classified are man, bicycle and truck which are identified by three kinds of Fuzzy Neural Network and BP Network.

The three kinds of Fuzzy Neural Network are:

1. Fuzzy desired output BP Network (FOBP). In this Network, the desired output is the membership value of the sample, and the input vector is not fuzzified.

2. Fuzzy Input and desired output BP Network (FIOBP). The desired output is the membership value of the sample, and the input vector is fuzzified.

3. Fuzzy Input BP Network (FIBP). The desired output is "0" or "1" and the input vector is fuzzified.

In our experiments, the hidden units and output units of all the Neural Networks are respectively 6 and 3.

The results by Fuzzy Neural Networks and BP Network are presented in table1.

From table1, it is evident that FOBP Network has higher classification rate than the other three kinds of Network, and FOBP Network has faster convergence.

4 CONCLUSION

From the theory and the experimental results,we have the following conclusion:

First, FOBP Network has higher classification rate and faster convergence. It is because that the membership value of the sample is regarded as the desired output is more reasonable.

On the other hand, the classification rate for bicycle using FOBP Network and FIOBP Network is higher than using BP Network.

Last, when the input sample is expressed by value feature vector, using the Fuzzy Neural Network whose input vector is not fuzzified, we can obtain better results. The reason is that the fuzzification of the input vector can lose some characteristics of the sample.

table1 results by BP Network and FBP Networks

Network	Iteration number	classification rate(%)			
		Man	Bicycle	Truck	Average
BP	1286	87.98	73.33	90.68	83.99
FOBP	204	99.45	81.67	86.44	89.19
FIOBP	180	96.72	80.00	80.51	85.74
FIBP	7761	84.15	73.33	89.83	82.44

REFERENCES

[1].R.P.Gorman,T.J.Seimowski, " *Learned classification of sonar Targets using a Massively Parallel Network*" ,IEEE Trans. on ASSP,Vol.36 No.5, July1988.

[2].C.C.Piazza, " *Modified Backward Error Propagation for Tactical Target recognition* " , AD-A202666,1988.

[3].Falong Luo, yanda Li, *Neural Network and Signal Processing*, Publishing house of Electronic Industry, 1993, PRC.

Classifying Facial Emotions by Backpropagation Neural Networks with Fuzzy Inputs

J Zhao & G Kearney
University of Greenwich, Wellington St. Woolwich, London SE18 6PF
J.Zhao@gre.ac.uk

Abstract

The classification of emotional expressions by Backpropagation neural networks with fuzzy inputs is described. A success rate of 100% over training data and of up to 83.3% success rate over testing data has been achieved for six primary emotions: happiness, surprise, sadness, fear, anger and disgust. Face data in the form of 10 hand measurements made on 94 well-validated full-face photographs provided the input data. These measures had previously been shown to discriminate between emotions (Pilowsky & Katsikitis, 1993).

Introduction

The automatic recognition of human emotional expressions is becoming a frontier interest in the computer and communications industry. Automated verification or recognition of face identity must succeed regardless of the emotion displayed, whereas face emotion recognition rests on the assumption that there exists a commonality in the display and recognition of at least happiness, surprise, sadness, fear, anger and disgust - the so-called "Universal" or "Primary" emotions (Ekman & Friesen,1971; Ekman, Sorenson & Friesen, 1969), which transcends the individual. As man-computer interfaces take on human characteristics (Kaiser & Wehrle, 1994); Morishima, Okade, & Harashima, 1991), the need for automated coding of facial expressions becomes desirable, since the trend is to video the user and mediate system responses via a screened face with voice and appropriate affect. The determination of the user's emotional expression, if it reflects the prevailing emotive state, can indicate the fate of his motives (Sloman, 1986). The use of models of the face in video-phone telecommunications and other fields requiring synthesised emotional expressions (Chang 1990, Welsh 1991, Mizuno et al, 1991) and the appeal of the face as a complex multi-signalled image, auger well for continued research in the field.

Review of the Relevant literature

It has been shown that it is feasible to use mathematical models of the face for coding and indexing face databases (Turk & Pentland, 1990). These models are often based on face-feature locations, shape information and measures based on these, which can be characterised as a vector of distances between feature points on the face. These can considerably reduce retrieval time. The measurements used in indexing identity are different and more static than those used to define emotion. Normalisation is usually carried out in emotion face vectors in order to make processing robust to differing types of face size. Techniques are continually evolving for the automatic measuring of these face features and distances (Hasegawa & Shimizu, 1992). In any multi-poser project based on comparison of such measures from photographs, it is essential to standardise camera features and poser feature such as distance and orientation to the camera and rotations of the head.

A few classificatory studies on face emotion using neural network technology have been published. Ushida, Takagi and Yamaguchi (1993) use top-level bi-directional associative memories to promote a singular classification - one of happy, sad or anger thereby inhibiting fuzziness induced by lower level Kohonen-type image instants classification. Zhao, Kearney & Soper (1995) achieved a success rate of 100% on training data and up to 87% on test data using separate cascade-correlation networks to classify the six primary emotions and a separate net to resolve ambiguities. The face representation used in this 1995 study consisted of normalised change in 10 of the 12 Pilowsky measures (Figure 1 left). This latter net alone achieved a rate of 75% with its classification into the six primary emotions. Kobayashi and Hara (1993) reported a success rate of up to 91.2% for the six categories with feed-forward back-propagation architecture trained on both face shape and position data from 30 subjects.

Measuring Faces

The reduction of a face to 10 2-D distances results in a loss of 3-dimensional and contour information as well as brightness, colour, wetness and softness information, and emergent qualities such as intensity, sincerity, intent and probably many others. It is doubtful whether the alternative use of intensity images encompass all such qualities in their illumination intensity measures anyway. It is however, prudent to keep in mind that such a reduction to 10 distances is gross reductionism. There are gains too, in using these instead of an image. Solheim, Payne and Castain(1992) remind one that if using pictures or images, one has to worry about whether the net is not learning unintended discriminations from the background or from demographic, illumination or personal characteristics or from differing orientation to the camera.

The expertise was provided by the commercial availability of a large set of well-validated poses in the form of projector transparencies (Pictures of Facial Affect, Ekman,1976: The Consulting Psychologists Press) photographed with the best technology of the time portraying 14 subjects posing the six primary emotions and also neutral expressions. The measurements were made by hand when each image was projected onto an acetate transparent film which was co-extensive with the 200x200 mm screen of a Osram Diastar 200 viewer. The required landmarks were made in ink on the sheet and their inter-distances were later measured. Pre-processing of these measures before input to the net is directed to quantifying change and correcting for differing size of face (see Figure 1 right). This consists of normalisation of the changes between them and the same measures on the neutral face of the same person. Following from this, the change-distribution for each of the 10 measures was separately processed to produce its average and standard deviation from the mean. Thereafter each distance on each face was mapped into one of the following signed intervals: 0.125, 0.5, 1.0, 2.0, 3.0, 4.0, 5.0 and 6.0 standard deviations from the average. If a distance is below the mean, the sign will be negative. For example, given a pre-processed value x, if x > (mean - 0.125 × standard deviation) and x < mean, the it is coded as - 0.125 for the distribution of that face measure. One may understand these intervals as representing degrees of movement of the face features which often is correlated with intensity of emotion, e.g. the widening of the eye in startled surprise.

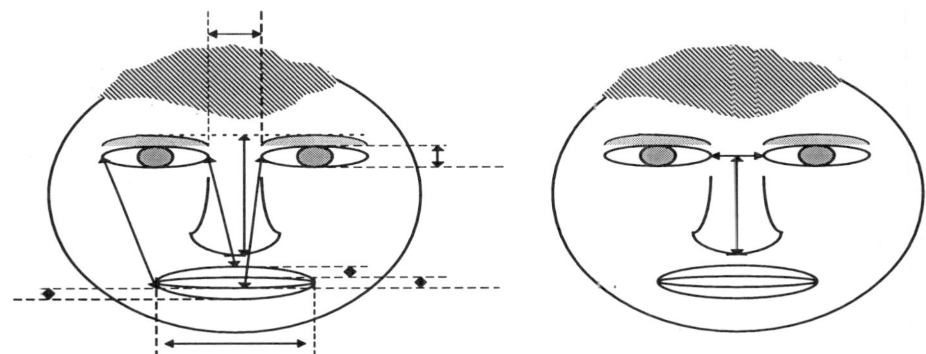

Figure 1: The Ten Pilowsky Measures (left) and the Two Measures (right) for Normalisation

Training and Testing Data

In order to train a Backpropagation neural network, we need to present inputs and outputs. In our case, the inputs for each training are the ten mappings as described in above section; while the output is the associated emotion. Each emotion is coded as three digit binary numbers, for example, the binary string "0 0 1" is used to represent the emotion "happy". Table 1 shows the complete binary codings for the six emotions and their abbreviations that will be used in later sections.

Binary String	Emotion	Abbreviation
0 0 1	happy	ha
0 1 0	surprised	su
0 1 1	sad	sa
1 0 0	afraid	af
1 0 1	angry	an
1 1 0	disgusted	ds
0 0 0	unknown	un
1 1 1	unknown	un

Table 1: Emotion Codings and Abbreviations

There are 94 patterns available of which 24 patterns (4 from each emotion) were randomly selected for testing and the rest for training.

Results and Discussion

Two kinds of simulations were conducted, in which three layer networks were used. In all simulations, a learning rate of 0.25 was used. The first one is to test whether the representation of face features has the ability to discriminate the emotions. In this case, we trained a neural network (10x10x3) over the whole data set (i.e. 94 patterns) and obtained 100% correct training rate. We repeated training the network several times with different initialisations, and the network was always successfully trained. This shows that the representation described above has the ability to discriminate the emotions. In this case, the error threshold was set to 0.4, i.e. any output from a node is greater than 0.6 was considered as 1. We also tried to train several nets over the raw data, however we could not achieve a 100% correct training rate.

The second kind of simulation was used to test the generalisation ability of a network. In this case, several neural networks with different number of hidden nodes were trained and tested. For each architecture, we trained three times with different thresholds and tested. We started to train a network with four hidden nodes. However, the training processes have shown that a three layer network with less than ten hidden nodes cannot be successfully trained. The testing results from successfully trained networks (with 10, 12, 14, 16 and 18 hidden nodes) are shown in Figures 2 and 3. In these simulations, error thresholds were set to 0.4, 0.2 and 0.05. For each threshold, the network was trained three times. In testing the threshold was always set to 0.4. All training and testing were performed on a Pentium 90 machine and it took less than 3 minutes (about 650 epochs) to train the largest net, a net with 18 hidden nodes.

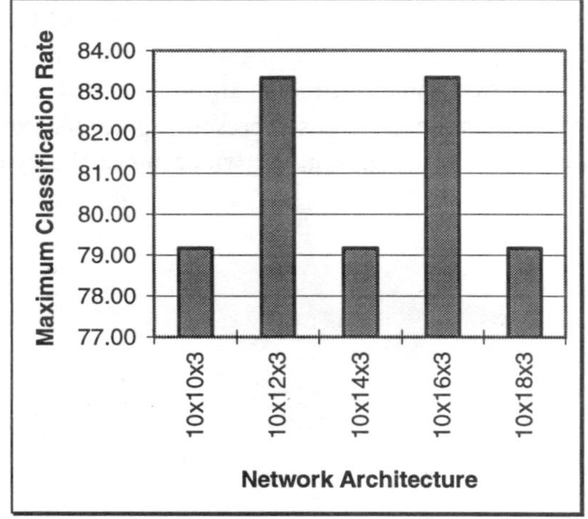
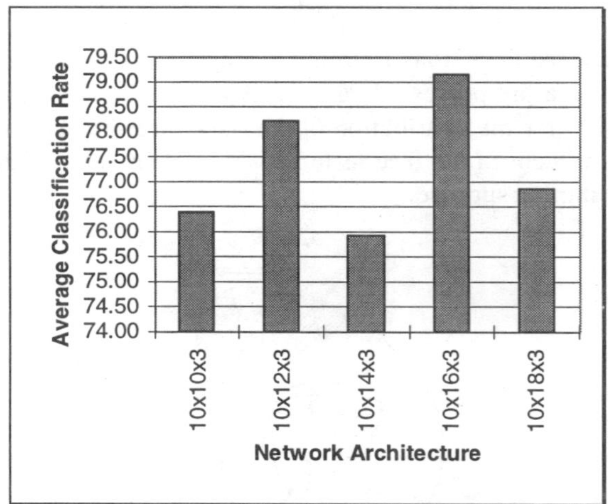

Figure 2: Classification Rate of the Trained Networks

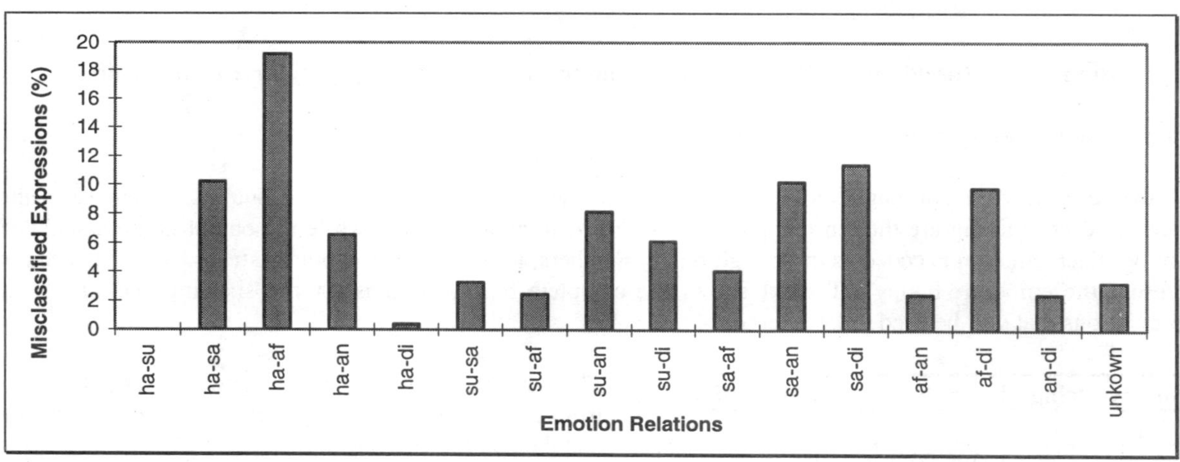

Figure 3: Misclassified Emotions

It can be seen from Figure 2 that the highest classification rate was found in the networks with 12 and 16 hidden nodes. In terms of average classification rate, the network with 16 hidden nodes did the best. Figure 3 shows the misclassification propositions in emotion relations. One can see that there was not any emotion "happy" classified as a "surprised" and vice versa. The result in Figure 3 also shows that the most confused emotions are "happy" and "afraid". The cause of such confusion is still unknown in terms of measurements. However, this provides a start point to refine the measurements and improve the classification performance.

Conclusions and Future Work

We have shown that it is possible to use the Backpropagation networks to discriminate between the six emotions with a good success rate. Pre-processing the data in the way described appears to have been helpful. Using the fuzzy data, we have successfully trained a network over 94 patterns to classify the six emotions with 100% correct training rate, while a Backpropagation network could not be trained successfully with the raw data. Our study has also shown that neural networks can be used to alert one to a possible weakness in the representation.

The immediate concern is to investigate why the happy and afraid emotions are not well discriminated. In the course of this work, we may enlarge the set of distances to be measured, thereby we hope to derive a foolproof representation for more emotions. As the reviewers pointed out, apart from the classes used we can also have one class for neutral face and one class for unknown in any future investigation. Finally, the authors would like to thank the reviewers for their effort and useful comments.

References

Chang, SC, Harashima H & Takete T (1990). 3-dimensional model based description and synthesis of facial expressions. Trans. Inst. Electr. Infor. Comm. Eng. 1270-1280.

Ekman, P. & Friesen, W. (1969). Constants across cultures in the face and emotion. J. Personal and social psychology, 17, 124-129.

Ekman, P., Sorenson, E. & Friesen, W. (1971). Pan-cultural elements in facial displays of emotion. Science, 164, 86-88.

Hasegawa, H. & Shimizu, E. (1992). Person recognition system using face information. Robot: 85, 60-69. Japan.

Kaiser, S. & Wehrle, T. (1994). Emotion research and AI: some theoretical and technical issues. Geneva Studies in Emotion and Communication.

Kobayashi, H. & Hara, F.(1993a) The recognition of basic facial expressions by neural network. In Transactions of the Society of Instrument and Control Engineers. 29, 1, 112-118.

Kobayashi H., & Hara, F. (1993b). Dynamic recognition of basic facial expressions by discrete-time recurrent neural network. In Proceedings of 1993 International Joint Conference on Neural Networks, part 1, 1, 155-158.

Mizuno, T., So, T., Minami, T. & Nakemuro, O. (1991). Model based coding for facial images on feature points and isodensity maps. Journal of Institute of Television Engineers of Japan, 45: 2, 216-224.

Pilowsky, I. & Katsikitis, M. (1993). The classification of facial emotions: a computer-based taxonomic approach. Journal of Affective Disorders, 30, 61-71.

Morishima, S., Okade, S., & Harashima, H. (1991). A facial motion synthesis for intelligent man-machine interface. Systems and Computers in Japan, 22, 5 50-59., U.S.A.

Solheim, I., Payne, T. L. & Castain, R. (1992). The potential for using backpropagation neural networks for facial verification systems. Simulation 58:5, 306-310.

Sloman, A. (1986). Motives, mechanisms and emotions. University of Sussex Cognitive Science Research Reports, no. CSRP 062. School of Social Studies, Falmer, Brighton, BN1 9QN, U.K.

Turk, M. & Pentland, A. (1990). Face processing: models for recognition. Proceedings of the SPIE- The International Society for Optical Engineering, 1192,1,22-32.

Ushida, H., Tagaki, T., & Yamaguchi, T. (1993). Conceptual fuzzy sets application to facial expression recognition using associative memory system. In Stan Gielen and Bert Kappen, (Eds.), Proceedings of the International Conference on Artificial Neural Networks, Amsterdam, Netherlands, 13-16th September. Springer-Verlag, London.

Welsh, WJ (1991). Model based coding of video-phone images, Electronics & Communication Engineering Journal. Feb. England.

Zhao, J. Kearney, G. & Soper, A. (1995). Classifying expressions by cascade-correlation neural network. Neural Computing & Applications; 3:113-124. Springer-Verlag, London Ltd.

Evolutionary Cellular Automata
for Emergent Image Features

Jiming Liu   H. J. Zhou   Y. Y. Tang

Department of Computing Studies
Hong Kong Baptist University
224 Waterloo Road, Kowloon, Hong Kong
E-mail: *jiming@comp.hkbu.edu.hk*

Abstract— **This paper introduces a new class of evolutionary cellular automata (ECA) in which organisms react to the local stimuli encountered in two-dimensional discrete environments, resulting in either asexual reproduction, random movement, or death due to aging. Such behaviors of reproduction and diffusion through external selection, when employed as a model of evolutionary computation in image processing, can readily manifest both interesting fixed-point properties and robust behaviors capable of adapting to a dynamic environment. The paper demonstrates the applications of ECA in image processing with two illustrative examples where the emergent behavior of the cellular adaptation enables the simultaneous detection of salient features, in their broader sense, from a single image frame as well as the active following of the found features from a sequence of motion image frames.**

1   Introduction

The study of Cellular Automata (CA), which drew upon Von Neumann's early work [3], is concerned mainly with the emergent behaviors in a lattice of finite automata where cells react locally according to a set of cellular rules [2]. Several CA models have been proposed and experimentally studied in recent years. As a typical example of the CA studies, Shanahan [5] has investigated a class of evolutionary automata in which a population of organisms evolves in a microworld of square grid locations. The characteristics of Shanahan's evolutionary automata consist in that a sequence of states in the microworld can be non-deterministically generated by repeatedly executing four local procedures, namely, deaths, moves, meals and births. Sipper [6] has presented a non-uniform CA class that evolves not only in state space but also in rule space, by allowing rules to be updated every time the cell is unsuccessful. Tamayo and Hartman [7] have applied cellular automata to model reaction-diffusion systems from which interesting space-time patterns reminiscent of chemical turbulence, solitons and self-excited oscillations can be constructed and observed.

The goal of our work is to develop a new Evolutionary Cellular Automata (ECA) model with a focus on emerging important features from image environments rather than merely producing complex structures. The proposed ECA model exhibits common cellular behavior characteristics (i.e., locality, parallelism etc.), however, with the following unique features; namely: (1) in our evolutionary model, the automata operate in a grey-scale digital image and hence inanimate stimuli are present in the cellular environment, (2) the mutation rate changes in our automata, resulting from the interaction with and within the environment, and (3) the emergent behaviors of our automata are marked and interpreted directly in relation to the given environment, whereas in the existing cellular automata studies [5], they are assessed based on the size of organism population.

The motivations behind our research are two-fold. First, it serves a case study to demonstrate the power of Artificial Life approach to solving real engineering problems, besides being a synthetic methodology to reverse-engineer and thus understand life-like systems. Second, it emphasizes on a bottom-up, discentralized, and distributed approach to image processing and relies on local "processes" whose behaviors are both easy to define and natural for parallel implementation.

2   Asexual Reproduction Based Evolutionary Cellular Automata (ECA)

The class of Cellular Automata proposed in this paper is termed Asexual Reproduction Based Evolutionary Cellular Automata (ECA). The evolutionary nature of the proposed automata is manifested from the way in which the generations of organisms are reproduced and selected. This class of CA operates in rectangular lattices that correspond to the digitized images of natural scenes.

2.1   A Description of Two-Dimensional ECA

In the proposed ECA, an image is represented into a two-dimensional rectangular gird lattice where each of the 8-connected grids represents an image pixel. The grid also signifies a possible location for an organism to inhibit, either temporarily or permanently. During the course of evolution, each of the organisms in the lattice environment demonstrates three important behaviors; namely, asexual reproduction, random movement, and death. These behaviors can be triggered by the external stimuli present in the environment. Here, the lattice locations at which triggering conditions are checked and corresponding cellular behaviors are applied constitute the *genotypes* of the organisms. As a result of the cellular evolution, certain patterns, i.e., the *phenotypes* of the organisms, will emerge that in turn characterize the features in the cellular environment.

Definition 2.1 *Let the grey-scale value at a location (i,j) be $I(i,j)$. Thus, the triggering conditions for the behaviors of an organism at (i,j) are determined by the density distribution of all the pixels in its neighboring region whose grey-scale values are close to $I(i,j)$. Specifically, the density distribution is computed as follows:*

$$D^r_{I(i,j)} = \sum_{s=-r}^{r} \sum_{t=-r}^{r} \left\{ s^0 t^0 \mid \; \| \; I(i+s, j+t) - I(i,j) \mid \; < \delta \right\} \tag{1}$$

where D is the sum of the pixels belonging to a r-radius region, satisfying the condition that the difference between their grey-scale values and the value at (i,j) is less than a pre-selected positive constant, δ.

Definition 2.2 *Let $\lambda = [u, v]$ where $u \leq v$. A class of organisms is said to be λ-sensitive if and only if they react to the environment in the following manner:*

1. *the organisms asexually reproduce their offsprings whenever the density distribution, as defined in Eq. 1, falls into the λ interval, i.e., $D^r_{I(i,j)} \in \lambda$.*

2. *the organisms randomly move to their adjacent locations whenever this density distribution falls outside the λ interval, i.e., $D^r_{I(i,j)} \notin \lambda$.*

In our present experimentation, an organism is coded in such a way that it always checks its neighboring environments, i.e., small circles, and selects its behavior, according to the concentration of an particular region elements.

Taking a border-tracing organism as an example, if an organism of border-sensitive class reaches a border location, then it will *permanently* inhabit at the border and proceed to reproduce both within its immediate neighboring region and inside a large region. Here, it is assumed that the reproduced offsprings will inherit all the characteristics of the parent organisms except their ages.

2.2 Mutation for Selection

The aforementioned asexual reproduction and diffusion scheme is analogous to one of the recombination operations commonly used in Generic Algorithm, namely, mutation. Schuster [4] has provided an example of molecular evolution in the test tube to provide a simple system for the study of evolutionary phenomena and discussed the application of the principle of variation and selection to design novel biopolymers with predetermined functions. From a point of view of evolutionary computation, our method essentially utilizes certain sensitive locations, as a selection screening constraint, where desired properties are encoded in an array of spatial positions. Organisms that have high fitness are selected while organisms that have low fitness gradually disperse and vanish in space and time due to aging. *Note that here the fitness of an organism is signified and computed based on the deviation of its current location from the sensitive areas. In other words, the closer is an organism to a sensitive location, the higher fitness will the organism have.*

Let us now revisit the previous border-tracing organism example. At a certain discrete time, if an organism is selected at the border, a cloud of *mutants* is generated and diffused within a certain region which delimits the spectrum of mutants of varying spatial deviations (error rates). Some of the generated mutants will be more fitted than others as they are spatially closer to the border and hence are more likely to be selected in the image environment. The spectrum of mutants will determine the domain of fitness distribution in the mutants. For those that have high error rates (i.e., far from the mutating cells) and are not selected will embark on a sequence of mutations, i.e., spatial displacements. This in turn will further increase the error rates. As a result, some of them will get selected since the increase on the error rate will also extend the domain of fitness distribution. Others may exceed a certain number of mutations (and critical error rates) and then vanish. This number is, in our case, programmed into the organisms in the form of life-span parameters.

2.3 The Dynamics of ECA

In what follows, let us examine the dynamics of ECA ecosystem in terms of how the population of organisms will change in discrete space and time. First of all, we observe that at a discrete time k, the number of organisms get selected can be calculated as follows:

$$R_k = \sum_{i=1}^{\Delta} \psi_k^{k-i} \tag{2}$$

where Δ denotes the age of the organisms, and ψ_k^{k-i} denotes all the organisms that were reproduced at time $k - i$ and got selected at time k.

Based on the above definition, we can further derive the equation for computing the organisms that vanish at time k, as follows:

$$D_k = \alpha R_{k-\Delta} - \sum_{i=k-\Delta+1}^{k} \psi_i^{k-\Delta} \quad . \tag{3}$$

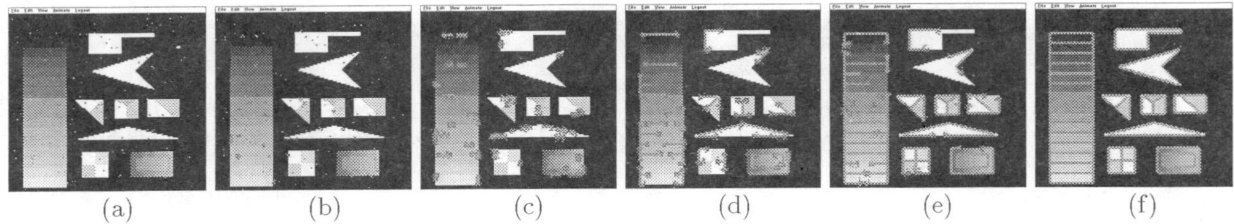

Figure 1: The emergence of edges from a digital image based on ECA computation model. Note that the triggering condition for the behaviors of an organism is computed from the 8-connected neighbors of the organism. (a) presents the original input image, (b)–(e) give the intermediate steps of phenotype evolution, and (e) presents the final permanent organisms in the image whose configuration identifies the salient edges information from the image.

where $R_{k-\Delta}$ is computed by Eq. 2, and α denotes the number of offsprings asexually generated by a single reproducing organism. The first term of this equation indicates all the organisms reproduced at time $k - \Delta$. The second term indicates how many of them get selected during a period from time $k - \Delta$ till time k. In other words, this equation expresses that the organisms will vanish at time k if they exceed their life-span.

From Eqs. 2 and 3, we know the entire population of organisms at time k. The equation reads:

$$U_k = U_0 + \sum_{j=1}^{k}(\alpha R_j) - \sum_{j=\Delta}^{k} D_j \tag{4}$$

where U_0 denotes the number organisms initially distributed over the two-dimensional lattice.

Substituting R_j and D_j with Eqs. 2 and 3, respectively, we have:

$$U_k = U_0 + \alpha \sum_{j=1}^{k}\sum_{n=1}^{\Delta} \psi_j^{j-n} - \sum_{j=\Delta}^{k}(\alpha \sum_{n=1}^{\Delta} \psi_{j-\Delta}^{j-\Delta-n} - \sum_{n=j-\Delta+1}^{j} \psi_n^{j-\Delta}) \tag{5}$$

It can readily be noted that the growth rate of the organism population is *positive* if the following is satisfied:

$$\alpha R_k - D_k > 0 \tag{6}$$

Based on Eqs. 2 and 3, we can rewrite the above condition as follows:

$$\alpha R_k > \alpha R_{k-\Delta} - \sum_{i=k-\Delta+1}^{k} \psi_i^{k-\Delta} \tag{7}$$

3 Emerging Image Features with ECA

With conventional techniques for image feature identification, grid template-like look-up tables are used to detect the direction of tracing from the current pixel to one of its neighbors [1]. The disadvantages of this approach are (1) that all the possible situations must be manually enumerated and stored, and (2) that the complexity of computing a closed border for a region depends on the complexity of the regions. In our ECA approach to image processing, new computational "organisms" can be reproduced and diffused in both the immediate adjacent regions and the nearby regions, and thus maintain the chance for the reproduced organisms to encounter new sensitive locations (or segments of the border), simultaneously.

3.1 Experimental Results

Experiment 1: Shape Edge Searching Figure 1(a) presents a 150×150 256-grey-scale digital image, which was used as the grid lattice for our ECA. Initially, a group of 400 edge sensitive organisms were randomly distributed in the lattice. Since this was a relatively small number of organisms, the majority of them will not immediately be selected by the external features, but rather after a few random movements as illustrated in Figure 1(b).

In this experiment, the life-expectancy of the organisms was set to 5. In other worlds, if an organism remains unselected during the interaction with the environment for more than 5 discrete time steps, it will vanish from the lattice environment. Recall that a λ-sensitive class of organisms in our grey-scale image environment asexually reproduce offsprings if the triggering condition of certain density-distribution satisfying the λ interval. In the present experiments, we have set: $\lambda = [2, 6]$, $r = 1$, and $\delta = 45$. In other words, an organism will get selected if the density distribution of its immediate neighboring pixels, whose grey-scale values are not deviated from that at the current location by 45, falls into the specific interval of $[2, 6]$.

Figure 2 presents the dynamics curves of the population, showing the rates of (1) the entire population change, (2) selection based on mutation, and (3) death due to aging, respectively. It can be observed that the growth rate decreases drastically after the selected organism curve and the organism death curve

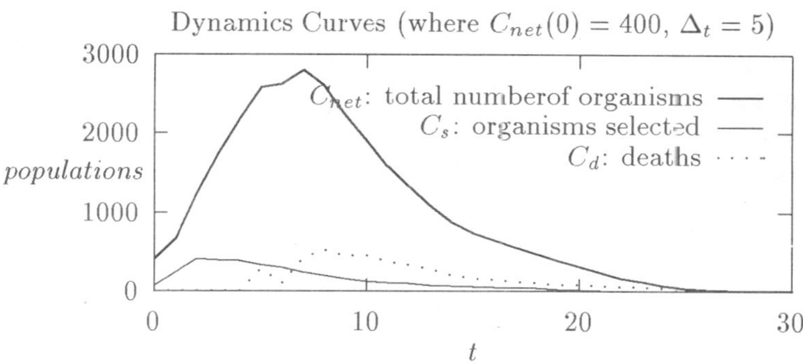

Figure 2: The dynamics curves showing (1) the total number of organisms existing in the lattice, (2) the number of selected fit organisms in space and time, and (3) the decay rate of the organisms.

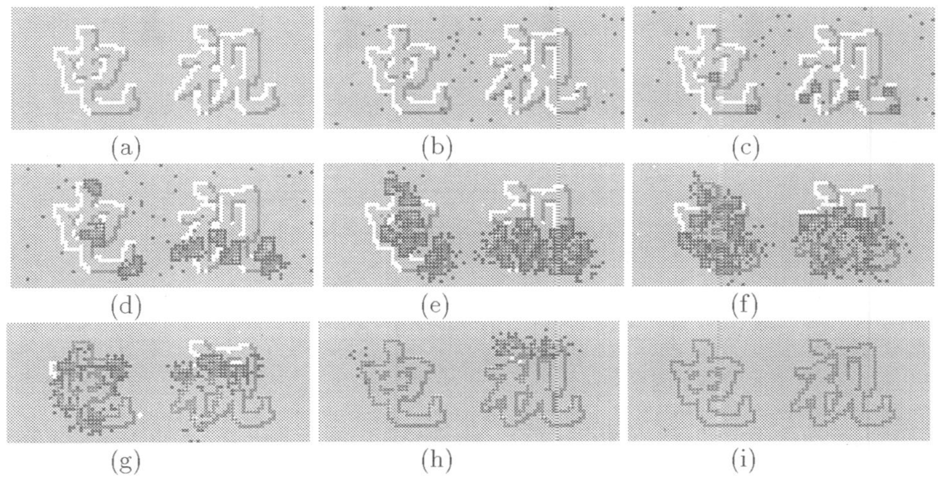

Figure 3: Character border finding with ECA, where $\lambda = [1, 10]$ and $r = 2$ (refer to the text).

intersect. The growth rate switches from positive to negative when the death rate is the highest. *These experimental findings are consistent with our previously derived dynamics results, as given in Eqs. 4–6.*

Experiment 2: Character Border Searching Figures 3(a)−(i) present the evolution of organisms, belonging to particular λ-sensitive ECA class, in a digital image. The fixed-point emergent phenotype of the evolution, as shown in Figure 3(i), gives the external borders of two simplied Chinese characters. It can be noted from the figure that the border features of the image were emerged gradually as a result of mutation for selection. In this experiment, the neighboring region, from which the triggering condition was verified, was composed of two consecutive layers from the current location of the organism. Or, in other words, the radius of the triggering region, r, was equal to 2. The λ value was set to $[1 - 10]$ in the triggering condition. Other parameters such as age and initial population size were exactly the same as those in the previous shape border searching experiment.

4 Adaptation of ECA in Dynamic Environments

This section is concerned with how to modify our ECA in such a way that the organisms are capable of following previously found features in a sequence of digital image frames. This task represents one of the important image processing problems, namely, motion tracking. Figure 4 (left) presents an overlaid view of multiple digital image frames, each of which gives the location of an object at a certain discrete time.

4.1 Rule Evolution in ECA

Recall that in Section 2.1, the reaction scheme for ECA in a static digital image environment defines that within a given triggering region, an organism will decide how to behave, depending on whether the organism is fit with respect to the stimuli presented. Once an organism is fit and selected, it starts to undergo an asexual reproduction and aging cycle. In the case of dynamic environments, we modify the previous scheme by adding a new behavior called `rule_learning` such that an organism can learn conditional movements based on its previously experienced successful motions.

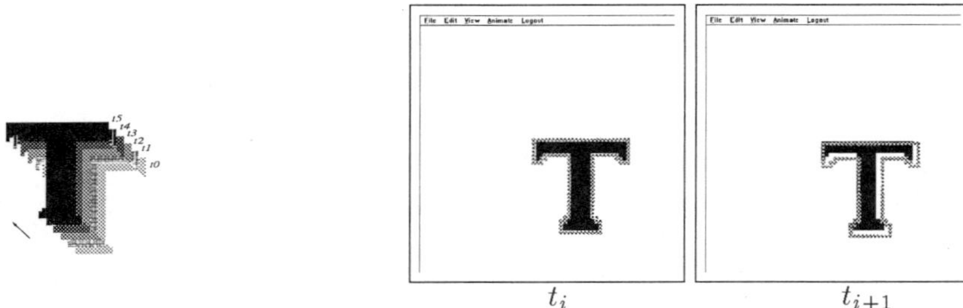

Figure 4: An example of moving dynamic environment where a T-shape object moves in discrete space and time. Assume that organisms have been selected in the T-shape environment at time t_i. At time t_{i+1}, the T-shape object moves to a new location, resulting in previously high-fitness organisms to become lower-fitness.

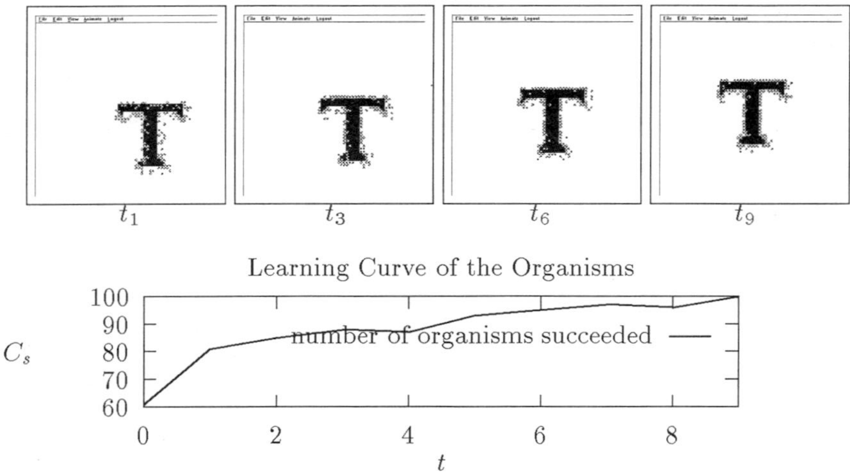

Figure 5: The snapshots of the organisms and their learning curve. After the target has been moved, some of the cells will attempt to move towards the target based on their *learned rules*, while others will make a randomized movement, during which new biased-movement rules will be acquired. As shown in the learning curve, the number of organisms succeeded in following the image features increases, gradually.

In other words, suppose that at a specific time, the image features have been identified in a manner that was described in the static-environment case. After an interval of time, the image features move to new locations. Subsequently, some of the previously selected organisms will no longer be selected in this environment, as illustrated in Figure 4 (right). When such an instance occurs, the low-fitness organisms randomly move to their adjacent locations. This will in turn enable some of those organisms to be selected again in the new environment. Of most significant is that the modified ECA will enable the newly selected organisms *to acquire a biased movement behavior that is triggerable if the previously seen stimuli are found again.*

4.2 Experimental Results

Figure 5 presents the experimental results concerning the adaptation of the organisms in the dynamic environment in which a T-shape object moves in time, as shown in Figure 4. In such a dynamic environment, the organisms that were previously selected will again try to adjust their error rates in order to *maximize* their fitness in the new environment (i.e., local fitness optimization). This is demonstrated in the target following behavior presented in Figure 5.

5 Discussion and Conclusion

With respect to the first experiment as mentioned in the preceding section, we further investigated the effect of initial population size on the dynamics of the evolution. In Figure 6(a), the dynamics of the ECA with 400 initial organisms and 5 step life-span is presented. It can readily be noted that the areas under the three curves are much the same (in a qualitative sense), and that the curve under higher initial population size converges faster.

Apart from the initial population size, the second factor that is of interest is the life-span of the organisms. In our experimental results as shown above, the maximum life-expectancy was set to 5. Our further experiments showed that if the life-expectancy increased, mutations to higher error rates would be more likely to occur. This is equivalent to say that increasing the error rate extends the domain of fitness

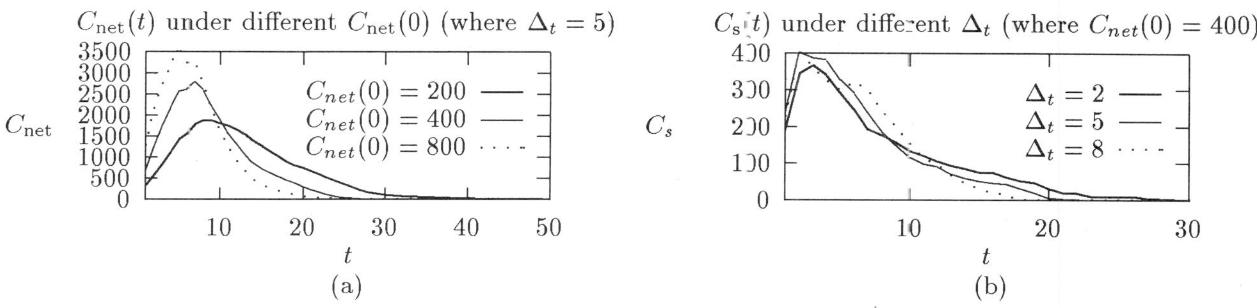

Figure 6: (a) The dynamics of ECA in the case of shape-edge-searching experiment, under three different initial population sizes, where $C_{net}(t)$ curve shows the total number of organisms existing in the lattice. (b) The effect of different life-span values on the dynamics of feature emergence, where $C_s(t)$ curve shows the total number of organisms being selected during their interaction with the environment.

distribution As a result, more organisms will get selected. This phenomenon can readily be observed from Figure 6(b), i.e., the slight differences among the population curves of mutating organisms with three different life-spans, respectively.

In this paper, we have described a class of cellular automata, ECA, with a focus on the behaviors of organisms emergent from local cellular interaction with an environment. The repository of the local cellular behaviors consists of asexual reproduction, random movement, and death, each of which is triggered and hence determined by the stimuli of the environment. We experimentally examined the evolution of ECA in digital image environments. As it was shown in our experiments, when the internal λ parameters were tuned to particular values, interesting phenotype of the organisms can readily be observed which corresponded to the locations of particular features in the images.

While relying on distributed processors, our approach makes parallel implementation possible. Each organism is a self-organizing agent that evolves while interacting with the environment and its neighbors. Such a self-organizing agent is also capable of *active* searching for features based on the learned knowledge.

Last but not the least are the λ parameter that determines the goodness of the final search results, and the region size from which triggering conditions are checked. For the set of the results presented here, these parameters were adjusted manually. However, it has been our current goal of research to implement an automatic adjustment mechanism for determining λ and triggering condition region size (i.e., amount of stimuli). At present, we are examining the effectiveness of adjusting these parameters in *multi-class ECA* based on some global diversity and complexity criteria, e.g., the relative population size of each class to globally govern the change of parameters at the level of individual organisms.

References

[1] Y. Liow. A contour trancing algorithm that presevers common boundaries between regions. *CVGIP - Image Understanding*, 53(3):313–321, 1991.

[2] Marek W. Lugowski. Computational metabolism: Towards biological geometries for computing. In *Artificial Life: Proceedings of an Interdisciplinary Workshop on the Synthesis and Simulation of Living Systems, Los Alamos, New Mexico*, pages 341–368, Redwood City, CA, 1988. Addison-Wesley Publishing Company, Inc.

[3] J. Von Neumann. *Theory of Self-Reprodcing Automata*. University of Illinois Press, Urbana, IL, 1966.

[4] P. Schuster. Extended molecular evolutionary biology: Artificial life bridging the gap between chemistry and biology. In Christopher G. Langton, editor, *Artificial Life: An Overview*, pages 39–60. The MIT Press, Cambridge, MA, 1995.

[5] Murray Shanahan. Evolutionary automata. In Rodney A. Brooks and Pattie Maes, editors, *Artificial Life IV: Proceedings of the Fourth International Workshop on the Synthesis and Simulation of Living Systems*. pages 387–393. The MIT Press, Cambridge, MA, 1994.

[6] Moshe Sipper. Non-uniform cellular automata: Evolution in rule space and formation of complex structures. In Rodney A. Brooks and Pattie Maes, editors, *Artificial Life IV: Proceedings of the Fourth International Workshop on the Synthesis and Simulation of Living Systems*, pages 394–399. The MIT Press, Cambridge, MA, 1994.

[7] Pablo Tamayo and Hyman Hartman. Cellular automata, reaction-diffusion systems and the origin of life. In *Artificial Life: Proceedings of an Interdisciplinary Workshop on the Synthesis and Simulation of Living Systems, Los Alamos, New Mexico*, pages 105–124, Redwood City, CA, 1988. Addison-Wesley Publishing Company, Inc.

Handwritten Character Recognition using a New Dynamic Forward-Propagation Neural Network and Fourier Descriptors

Ian P. Morns[†] & Satnam S. Dlay

Department of Electrical & Electronic Engineering
University of Newcastle upon Tyne
NE1 7RU. United Kingdom
E-mail i.p.morns@newcastle.ac.uk - s.s.dlay@newcastle.ac.uk

† Ian Morns is supported by an EPSRC grant

Abstract - **A new neural network, called the "Dynamic Supervised Forward-Propagation Network", is presented for recognition tasks. The network is based upon the Counterpropagation Network but trains using a supervised learning algorithm and incremental training. In addition it allows unsupervised dynamic growth of the middle layer allowing unknown subclasses to be learnt. The performance of the network, in classifying handwritten numerals presented as fourier descriptors, is compared with the performance of other neural networks: the Back Propagation Network and the Counterpropagation Network. The new network shows an increase in classification accuracy over the Back Propagation Network along with a 436 times decrease in the number of pattern presentations required for training. A considerably higher accuracy is obtained than that for the Counterpropagation network.**

1 Introduction

Many studies have used fourier descriptors and Back Propagation Networks (BPN) for classification tasks. Fourier descriptors were used in [1] to recognise handwritten numerals. The resulting vectors were classified by classical vector matching techniques. Although a high accuracy was obtained, this method requires that all subclasses (i.e. different handwriting styles for a given character) are identified manually for each input data class. In [2], fourier descriptors and a Back Propagation Network were used to classify tools, wave descriptors and Back Propagation Networks were used to classify handwritten characters in [3] and in [4] the BPN was used to classify printed characters. The BPN used in the previous three cases is a complicated network with three [2] or two [3,4] trained weight layers. It uses a slow training algorithm which takes many epochs. In addition the BPN [3] failed to overcome the problem of different handwriting styles, with only a single style being acceptable for certain characters in the training and test data. The Counterpropagation Network will learn in very few epochs but its unsupervised learning algorithm does not give a high classification accuracy.

A new type of neural network for recognition tasks is presented in this paper. The network, called the "Dynamic Supervised Forward-Propagation Network" (DSFPN), is based upon the forward only version of the Counterpropagation Network (CPN) [5]. Unlike the CPN, the DSFPN is trained using a supervised algorithm which gives a better classification accuracy than the CPN but still trains quicker than the BPN. The middle layer of the DSFPN can grow dynamically during training, allowing it to learn subclasses in the training data in an unsupervised manner.

To test the classification performance of the network, handwritten numerals presented as fourier descriptors are used.

2 Edge Following and Fourier Descriptors (pre-processor)

Before examples of handwritten characters can be presented to the neural network, they must first be converted into files of fourier descriptors. This is performed in three stages: the scanning of handwritten characters, boundary tracing of handwritten characters and the calculation of fourier descriptors.

Numerals are handwritten on paper and then converted into two-colour bitmap form on a personal computer using a bench scanner. The image of each character is stored as a separate file with the first letter of that file indicating the character represented. The bitmap names are then used as the supervising information for training and testing. The stored files are fed, in random order, into a pre-processor program which takes a boundary trace and then calculates fourier descriptors for each character.

2.1 Edge following

The edge following routine produces an ordered list of border points. The list is re-ordered with the top point taken as the starting point. This reduces the intra-class phase difference in the fourier coefficients calculated later.

2.2 Fourier descriptors

Once a boundary image is obtained then fourier descriptors are found as in [1]. This involves finding the discrete fourier coefficients a[k] and b[k] for $0 \leq k \leq L\text{-}1$, where L is the total number of boundary points found, by applying equations (1) and (2).

$$a[k] = \frac{1}{L} \sum_{m=1}^{L} x[m] e^{-jk(2\pi/L)m} \tag{1}$$

$$b[k] = \frac{1}{L} \sum_{m=1}^{L} y[m] e^{-jk(2\pi/L)m} \tag{2}$$

where x[m] and y[m] are the x and y co-ordinates respectively of the mth boundary point. The values for k=0 are discarded as they only contain information about the position of the image. The coefficients for high values of k describe high frequency features in the image but do not contain much information about the overall shape of the character. For this reason only 10 values representing $1 \leq k \leq 5$ are used. Tests show that increasing the number of coefficients used beyond this point does not improve accuracy but does slow down training.

The moduli of the complex coefficients, |a[k]| and |b[k]| are used in the input data, giving an input vector

$$\mathbf{i} = [|a[1]|, |b[1]|, \ldots, |a[5]|, |b[5]|]^{T} \tag{3}$$

(Note, bold type indicates a vector). This is then normalised to compensate for image scaling. To spread the input-data more evenly over the input space, mean and standard deviation vectors are found over the whole set of test and training data. The jth component of input vector $\mathbf{i}_p$ is calculated as in equation (4).

$$i_{pj} = \left(i_{poj} - \bar{i}_{oj}\right)\left(\alpha\left(\frac{1}{\sigma_{noj}} - 1\right) + 1\right) \tag{4}$$

where i_{poj} is the jth component of the original vector for pattern p, $\bar{i}_{oj}$ is the mean of the jth components of the original vectors and σ_{noj} is the corresponding standard deviation. α linearly controls the degree of standard deviation compensation. If $\alpha = 0$ there is no compensation for variations of standard deviation from one vector dimension to the other whilst, if $\alpha = 1$ the standard deviation of all dimensions will be forced to equal 1 giving full standard deviation compensation. For values of α between 0 and 1 the amount of compensation changes linearly. In the data used later a value of $\alpha = 0.5$ is used throughout.

Although this data matched most numbers well it largely failed to distinguish 6's and 9's. This is because the moduli of the complex coefficients are invariant for reflections parallel to the y or x axis or rotations of 180°. To counter this the argument of coefficient b[1] is also included in the input data in order to indicate such transformations. To match the scale of the angle better to that of the rest of the vector it is multiplied by a constant β before inclusion in the input data. A value of $\beta=2$ was found to give the best results and is used in later tests.

As the DSFPN, like the CPN, requires its input data to be normalised all input vectors are normalised to a magnitude of 1 before being used. These normalised vectors of fourier descriptors are stored together in either training or test data files. For analytical purposes, the filename of the bitmap which produced the descriptors is stored along with each input vector.

3   The Neural Network

The DSFPN, shown in figure 1 below, is based upon the forward only CPN without any training connections to the output layer [5]. The supervised training algorithm and the dynamic growth which have been developed are described in two later subsections.

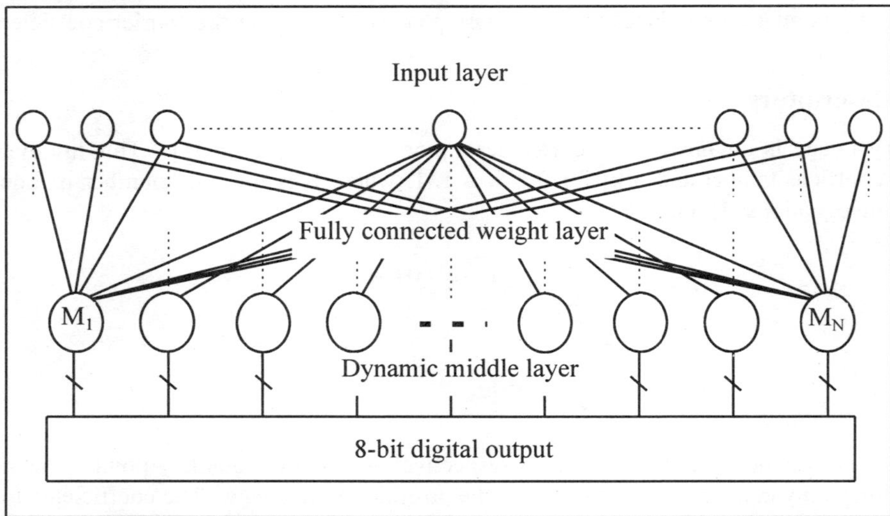

The DSFPN - Figure 1

3.1   Architecture

The DSFPN has three layers: an input layer which is the same size as the input vector, a hidden middle layer, which starts with no neurons but has fully connected neurons added to it during training, and an output layer. As the output layer of the DSFPN plays no part in classification, this layer can be in any form appropriate to the specific problem to be solved. In the case of character recognition the output layer has 8 neurons which allows the output of the network to be in ASCII form. For example if middle neuron M_1 is to represent '0', then the input weight vector $\mathbf{x}_1$ will equal the normalised fourier descriptor vector for a typical example of the letter '0', $\mathbf{i}_0$, and the output vector $\mathbf{y}_1$ will equal $(0,0,1,1,0,0,0,0)^T$, which is the binary form of 48, the ASCII code for '0'.

3.2   Operation

When an input vector $\mathbf{i}_p$ is applied at the input layer the activation of middle layer neuron n is given as

$$A_n = \mathbf{i}_p \cdot \mathbf{x}_n \tag{5}$$

(for $1 \leq n \leq N$, where N is the total number of hidden layer neurons). As both input vector and weight vector are normalised, the activation A_n is always between 1 and -1 and represents how closely the input vector matches the weight vector. A competition is held between each hidden neuron and the one with the greatest activation is the winner. The output is 1 from the winning neuron and 0 from all other neurons. The activation of the output layer is

$$\mathbf{o}_p = \mathbf{y}_w \tag{6}$$

where w is the number of the winning neuron. The output of the network is then simply the activation of the output layer $\mathbf{o}_p$.

3.3   Supervised training

Unlike the CPN, the DSFPN uses a supervised training algorithm. This allows the new network to be trained on data divided into known classification categories, such as handwritten characters. The supervised training process is described in this subsection.

During training an input vector $\mathbf{i}_p$ is applied to the neural network and two middle layer neurons are found. The 'winning' neuron M_w, with input-weight vector $\mathbf{x}_w$, is the neuron with the highest activation and the 'best' correct neuron M_B, with input-weight vector $\mathbf{x}_B$, is the neuron with the highest activation out of those that give the correct output. Training then proceeds as follows:

If M_B cannot be found, then there is no neuron existing to classify the current input pattern. In this case a new neuron is created with input-weight vector $x_N = i_p$, where N is the new total number of hidden neurons. Output vector y_N is set to the ASCII code of pattern p.

If the winning neuron M_w and the best neuron M_B are the same neuron, the input pattern i_p has been classified correctly. The weight vector x_w is updated using equation (7) This has the effect of moving the winning weight vector towards the input vector.

$$x_w = x_w + (x_w - i_p). \rho_+ \tag{7}$$

The parameter ρ_+: $0 \le \rho_+ \le 1$ is a training rate.
If the winning neuron and the best neuron are not the same then the input has been classified incorrectly. In this case there is a probability that a new middle layer neuron will be created to represent the current pattern; this process is described in subsection 3.4. If no new neuron is created then equations (8) and (9) are applied which have the effect of moving x_B closer to the input vector i_p and x_w further away from it.

$$x_B = x_B + (x_B - i_p). \rho_+ \tag{8}$$

$$x_w = x_w - (x_w - i_p). \rho_- \tag{9}$$

where ρ_-: $0 \le \rho_- \le 1$ is a training rate.
After (9) is applied the vector, x_w must be re-normalised as (9) will cause de-normalisation. This problem does not occur with (7) and (8) as they 'pull' the weight vectors towards the normalised input vector, which has the effect of correcting any variation in magnitude. On the other hand (9) 'pushes' the weight vector away from the input vector hence increasing any error in the weight-vector magnitude.

3.4 Dynamic middle layer

The dynamic growth of the middle layer allows the network to learn subclasses of the main classification groups by producing new neurons for new subclasses in an unsupervised manner; this is helpful for handwriting recognition as it allows characters written in different styles to be learnt. A new neuron may be added during training if an incorrect classification is given by the middle layer. To prevent the middle layer growing uncontrollably, new neurons are only introduced on a probabilistic bases, where the probability P of a new neuron being created is given by

$$P = \begin{cases} P_g & if \quad (11) \quad is \quad true \\ P_g + P_l & if \quad (11) \quad is \quad false \end{cases} \tag{10}$$

where:

$$x_B . i_p > x_B . x_w \tag{11}$$

$$P_l = (x_B . x_w - x_B . i_p). \frac{P_0}{2} . \left(1 - \frac{N^2}{R^2 + N^2}\right) \tag{12}$$

$$P_g = (x_w . i_p - x_B . i_p). \frac{P_1}{2} . \left(1 - \frac{N^2}{R^2 + N^2}\right) \tag{13}$$

where N is the current number of neurons in the middle layer, P_0 and P_1 are the maximum probability of a new neuron being created and R is the number of neurons that will exist when the maximum probability will fall by half. P_0, P_1 and R are network parameters. When a new neuron is created, N is increased by 1, the new input weight vector x_N is set to i_p and the new output weight vector y_N is set to the binary ASCII code of the letter represented by i_p. Testing inequality (11) allows for a greater probability of a new neuron being set if the winning-neuron weight-vector lies between that of the best neuron and the input vector.

The right-hand set of brackets in (12) and (13) limit the probability of creating a new neuron as the total number of neurons increase.

3.5　Training strategy

Training is continued until the percentage of correct classifications during one epoch reaches a pre-set training limit. After this the network is tested on a set of unseen test data to evaluate its performance. Incremental step training [6] is used to train the DSFPN.

4　Experimental Procedure

A set of 800 patterns is used containing 80 examples of each numeral '0'-'9'. Fourier descriptors for each pattern are calculated as described above. These are then shuffled into a random order. The resulting descriptors are split into two files, one containing 300 training samples and the other 500 test samples. This data is then used to train and test a DSFPN as well as a Back Propagation Network and a forward only Counterpropagation Network in order to compare classification accuracies and training times.

Due to the time required for training, an optimum set-up for the BPN is difficult to find and the one used here represents the best of several configurations tried. The network has three layers: an input layer of 11 neurons, a middle layer of 10 neurons and an output layer of 10 neurons. The training rate is 0.3 and a logarithmic-sigmoidal transfer function is used for both layers. After every 100 training epochs the recognition performance of the network is tested on the training set and training stops when the classification accuracy reaches a pre-set level called the training limit. Each output neuron of the BPN represents one of the possible pattern classifications. A '0.8' in the jth position with all other positions containing '0.2' indicates the data represents the number j. During testing the neuron producing the highest output is judged to be the winner.

The output data presented to the CPN is a 10-dimensional vector. A '1' in the jth position with all other positions containing '0' indicates the data represents the number j. A middle layer size of 50 neurons is chosen allowing more than one neuron to represent each output classification. All weights are randomised before each test run. For each training epoch a mean square error is calculated for the output layer and training stops when this value changes by less than 1×10^{-8} from one epoch to the next. During testing the output with the largest value indicates the network classification.

5　Results

Table 1 below shows the results of tests on the DSFPN. Different values of P_0 and P_1 have been used for each set of tests. The first two lines of the table shows the mean and standard error for 50 different tests and the other lines show mean and standard error for 100 tests.

Network: DSFPN, α=0.5, β=2, R=50, ρ_+=0.5, ρ_-=0.5, incremental step size=30, training limit=98%.					
P_0 and P_1	Size of middle layer after training	Training presentations	Training time (seconds)	Accuracy on training data %	Accuracy on test data %
0.2	19.34±0.11	68878±4538	20.80±1.26	99.17±0.05	97.75±0.03
0.5	19.78±0.13	28170±1689	8.53±0.50	99.24±0.06	97.73±0.04
1	20.01±0.16	15097±869	4.80±0.26	99.19±0.05	97.81±0.05
2	20.85±0.16	8558±455	2.93±0.15	99.24±0.05	97.69±0.06
5	21.97±0.17	3856±134	1.47±0.05	99.36±0.05	97.73±0.06
10	23.05±0.17	2762±89	1.07±0.03	99.40±0.05	97.68±0.07
15	23.83±0.15	2477±69	1.00±0.02	99.36±0.05	97.69±0.07
20	24.51±0.17	2282±48	0.96±0.02	99.35±0.06	97.62±0.08

Mean results of tests on DSFPN - Table 1

Note that although the training limit is set to 98%, the network often trains above this value. Increasing the training limit does not give any improvement in the test-data accuracy. The results show a slight decrease in test data accuracy as the probability of creating new neurons increases but this is accompanied, as might be expected, by a large decrease in training times. Also, as would be expected, the number of middle layer neurons produced increases as the likelihood of creating new neurons increases. These properties can be made use of by choosing a high value for P_0 and P_1 during the optimisation phase of creating a network. Many different network and input data configurations can then be tested in a short time due to the low number of training presentations required. Once optimisation is complete P_0 and P_1 can be decreased so as to achieve the highest possible classification accuracy from the network.

Table 2 below shows results taken from a forward only Counterpropagation network using the same data as in table 1 above. So the results can be compared with those in table 1 the mean results and the standard errors for the network are given in the last line of the table.

Network: forward only CPN, size 11x50x10, training rates=0.5,trained until mean square error change$<10^{-8}$			
Training Presentations	Training time (sec)	Accuracy on training data %	Accuracy on test data %
3900	1.92	91	89.2
4200	2.08	94.67	91.8
4200	2.09	95.33	93
mean: 4100±100	2.03±0.06	93.66±1.35	91.33±1.12

Results of tests on forward only CPN - Table 2

Although these networks train quickly the accuracy never approaches that of the DSFPN in table 1.

Table 3 shows the results of training and testing a BPN using the same data as in table 1.

Network: BPN, training rate 0.3, size 11x10x10, training limit=100%			
Training Presentations	Training time (sec)	Accuracy on training data %	Accuracy on test data %
3 450 000	2524	100	97.2
12 000 000	8756	90.67 (failed to reach target)	86.8
840 000	612	100	96
10 020 000	7459	100	97
mean: $(6.58±2.65)x10^6$	4838±1946	97.67±2.33	94.25±2.50

Results of tests on BPN - Table 3

(On one test training was abandoned after $12x10^6$ presentations as the network showed no tendency to train further.) These results show that as well as producing a classification accuracy lower than the DSFPN, the BPN also takes considerably longer to train. On average the best DSFPN, with P_0 and P_1 set to 1, trained in 436 times less presentations than the BPN.

6 Conclusions

A new network has been presented which performs the numeric character recognition task at least as well as the popular Back Propagation Network but is a simpler and trains using far less pattern presentations. The results show the average reduction to be a factor of 436. The results also show that the modifications of the forward only CPN algorithm producing the DSFPN give a considerable improvement in accuracy.

Further work on the network algorithm and the form of the input data should improve the network accuracy still further.

References

[1] M. Shridhar and A. Badreldin, "High accuracy character recognition algorithm using fourier and topological descriptors", Pattern Recognition, Vol. 17, No. 5, pp. 515-524, 1984.

[2] Hongbong Kim and Kwanghee Nam, "Object Recognition of One-DOF Tools by a Back-Propagation Neural Net", IEEE Transactions on Neural Networks, Vol. 6, No. 2, pp. 484-487, March 1995.

[3] Patrick Wunsch and Andrew F. Laine, "Wave descriptors for multiresolution recognition of handprinted characters", Pattern Recognition, Vol. 28, No. 8, pp. 1237-1249, 1995.

[4] Hadar I. Avi-Itzhak, Thanh A. Diep and Harry Garland, "High accuracy optical character recognition using neural networks with centroid dithering", IEEE Transactions on Pattern Analysis and Machine Intelligence, Vol. 17, No. 2, pp. 218-224, February 1995

[5] Robert Hecht-Nielsen, "Counterpropagation networks", Applied Optics, Vol. 26, No.23, pp. 4979-4983, December 1987.

[6] P. J. Wyard and C. Nightingale, "Grammar recognition by a single layer higher order neural net", BT Technology Journal, Vol. 10, No. 3, pp. 77-96, July 1992.

Isolated Digit Recognition Using a NeuralTree

Shesha Shah

Department of Electrical Engineering,
Indian Institute of Science, Bangalore - 560 012   INDIA.
e-mail : shesha@expertix.ee.iisc.ernet.in

Abstract— Classification Trees and Neural Networks are two popular approaches to Pattern Recognition problems. Both these approaches are combined in *NeuralTree* which uses a Multi-layer Perceptron (MLP) at each decision node of binary classification tree to extract non-linear features. NeuralTree exploits the power of tree classification using appropriate local features obtained by trained Neural Networks at internal nodes. This approach has been successfully applied to recognize hand-written isolated digits. The proposed method achieves significant decrease in error-rate compared to other classical methods and the size of NeuralTree classifier is also small compared to that of Classification and Regression Tree (CART).

1   Introduction

Binary Trees offer a multistage decision making procedure by breaking a complex procedure into simpler decisions, hoping that the final solution obtained would resemble the desired solution. In general, Tree classifiers have many advantages over other non-parametric methods. They offer an efficient classification method which is easy to understand and which can generalize well.

In a Decision tree each non-leaf node is associated with a decision rule of the form $f_i(X) < \theta_i$, also known as split rule, which decides whether a given pattern X will go to the left or right subtree. Each terminal node is having class label C_j associated with it - which says that all the patterns X landing in that node are from class C_j (See Fig.1). Power of the classification tree approach lies in the fact that appropriate features can be selected at different nodes. It does context sensitive feature subset selection which tackles High-dimensionality problem without losing any information.

1.1   Classification using Tree

Given a sample of pattern vectors and corresponding class labels, classification tree is constructed by determining split rules in top-down fashion. Here the issues are :

1. Selection of appropriate splitting rule for each decision node.

2. Determination of appropriate terminal nodes.

We select the splitting rule which maximizes splitting criterion that measures goodness of a split. There are many criteria proposed in literature [2] and it is observed that performance of tree does not vary

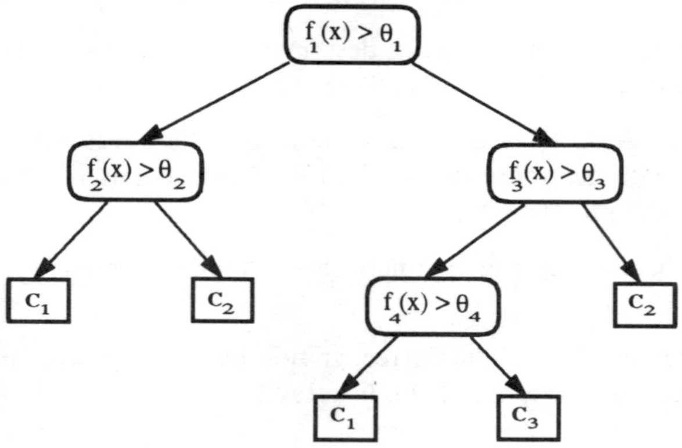

Figure 1: Binary Classification Tree

significantly over wide range of splitting criteria. The family from which the splitting rule is selected has a very significant effect on the performance of classification tree. We have used MLP for non-linear feature extraction at each decision node which expands power of classification tree and provides structured approach to Neural Network classifier design.

2   CART methodology

In CART a decision rule is associated with a tree by specifying splitting rule at non-terminal nodes and class at terminal nodes. Two phases of CART construction are : Tree growing and Tree pruning.

2.1   Tree growing

At every node i, let X_i represent set of all patterns landing at that node and $\{q_j\}$ be set of all possible splitting rules. Associate a figure of merit to each splitting rule which is denoted by $F_{ij} = F(X_i, q_j)$. So, the problem is to find the splitting rule which maximize the F_{ij}. Repeat this process recursively to find splitting rule until the nodes are pure (or nearly pure based on some splitting criteria). If all patterns falling at a node are of the same class then it is a pure node. In our implementation we have used Gini impurity decrement at each node as splitting criterion.

Let,

$$
\begin{array}{ll}
N & : \text{total number of training samples,} \\
N(t) & : \text{number of training samples landed at node } t, \\
N_j(t) & : \text{number of training samples of class } j \text{ landed at node } t, \text{ and} \\
M & : \text{total number of classes.}
\end{array}
$$

Define,
$P(t) = N(t)/N$, $P_L(t) = P(t_L)/P(t) = N(t_L)/N(t)$, $P_R(t) = P(t_R)/P(t) = N(t_R)/N(t)$ and $P(j|t) = N_j(t)/N(t)$ where,

$$
\begin{array}{ll}
t_L & : \text{Left child of node } t, \\
t_R & : \text{Right child of node } t, \\
P(t) & : \text{Estimated probability of randomly selected training samples landing in } t, \\
P(t_L) & : \text{Estimated probability of randomly selected training samples landing in } t_L, \\
P(t_R) & : \text{Estimated probability of randomly selected training samples landing in } t_R, \\
P(j|t) & : \text{Estimated probability of randomly selected training samples of class } j \text{ landing in } t.
\end{array}
$$

Using Gini impurity, defined as $i(t) = -\sum_j P(j|t) \ln P(j|t)$, as impurity function now define decrease in node impurity as,

$$\triangle I(f, \theta, t) = i(t) - i(t_L).P_L(t) - i(t_R).P_R(t)$$

The best feature f^* and θ^* at node t is obtained by,

$$\triangle I(f^*, \theta^*, t) = max_{f \in F, \theta} \triangle I(f, \theta, t)$$

In CART, $f(.)$ is linear function and using exhaustive search their optimal values can be obtained.

2.2   Tree pruning

To avoid problem of overfitting tree pruning is used. There are many methods given in [2, 3] for pruning to obtain better estimate of error rate.

3   Classification using a NeuralTree

For multi-class classification the idea of our training algorithm is to partition classes into two 'good' groups through each decision node and hence a good overall split. Training is carried out recursively by growing a tree based on Gini impurity decrement with an MLP at each internal node. That is, this problem involves two optimization problems. Inner optimization is to minimize LMS error in MLP training to find good split and outer optimization is a heuristic or exhaustive search to minimize Gini imputity criteria over pairs of aggregate classes.

3.1 Algorithm for training MLP as decision rule

Let, t : Decision node and $C = \{\ w_1, .. , w_M\ \}$: set of M classes at node t.

1. Select an initial partition C_L and C_R of C.

2. Train MLP at t to separate C_L and C_R. i.e. learn $f(.)$ and θ such that for each training sample X at t, X goes to t_R if $f(X) > \theta$ otherwise to t_L, where $f(.)$ is over all input output function of MLP. Compute $\triangle I_0$ Gini impurity decrement.

3. For $m = 1,..,M$ form $C_L(m)$ and $C_R(m)$ from C_L and C_R by changing class w_m. i.e.
    If class $w_m \in C_L$ then $C_L(m) = C_L - \{\ w_m\ \}$ and $C_R(m) = C_R + \{\ w_m\ \}$
    else $C_R(m) = C_R - \{\ w_m\ \}$ and $C_L(m) = C_L + \{\ w_m\ \}$
   Train MLP for each $C_L(m)$ and $C_R(m)$ and compute corresponding $\triangle I_m$.

4. Let, $\triangle I_m^* = max_{1 \le m \le M} \triangle I_m$
    If $\triangle I_m^* \le \triangle I_0$ then exit
    else assign $C_L \leftarrow C_L\ (m^*)$, $C_R \leftarrow C_R\ (m^*)$ and goto 2.

Above steps are carried out at each internal node in NeuralTree. It is observed during experiments that the overall performance of the classification tree is not very sensitive to choice of initial class partition. Instead of Gini impurity some other splitting criteria can be used. We can also use some other method, like RBF, instead of MLP.

4   Experimental results

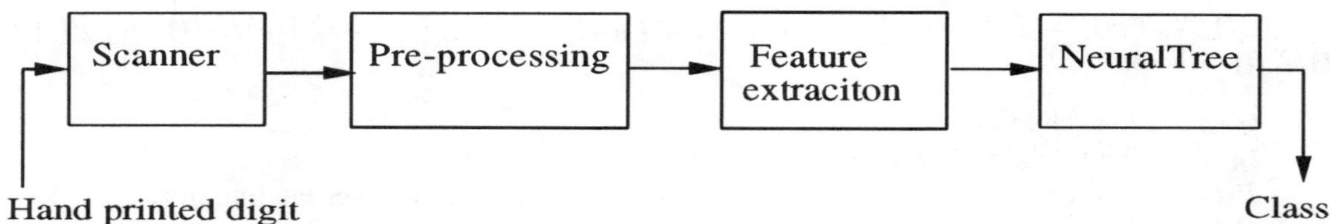

Figure 2: Block Diagram

4.1 Feature Extraction

16 Real valued features were extracted by taking "ON" pixel's projections on nearest diagonal, vertical and horizontal line as shown in the Fig 3. So, counting this way input vector dimension is reduced from 32x24=768 binary values to 16 real values. With this method of feature extraction, NeuralTree recognition becomes translation, rotation (upto $\pm\ 20^o$) and scale invariant. In following discussion all references to input pattern refers to new 16 dimensional vector.

4.2 Training NeuralTree for Digit Recognition

Training is carried out as explained in Section 3.1 on standard database from Recognition Equipment Incorporation, USA, 1990 for Hand-printed Digits on training set consisting of 200 training pattern of

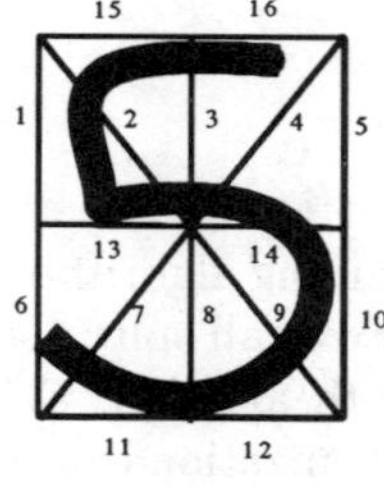

Figure 3: Feature extraction

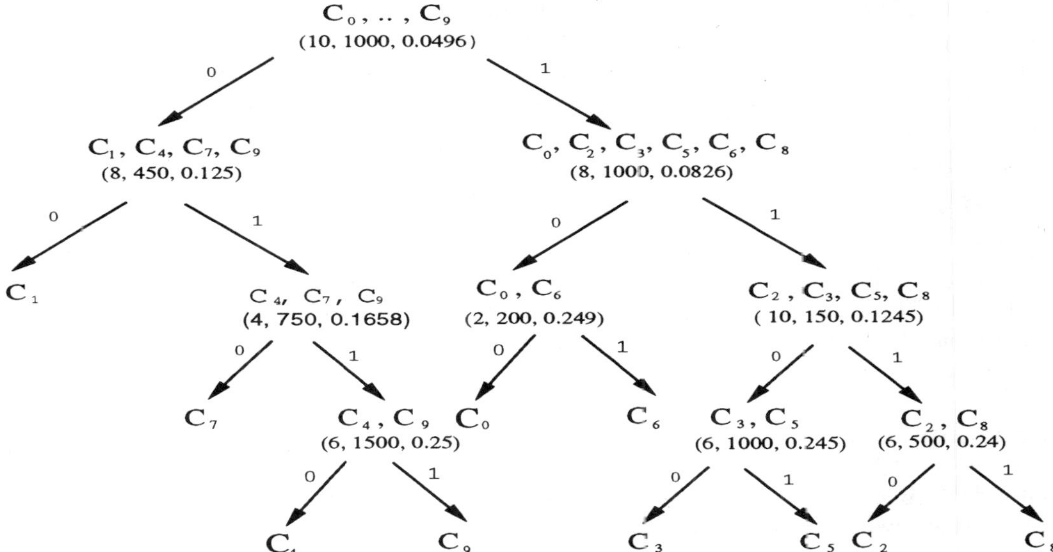

Figure 4: Final NeuralTree for Digit Recognition. At each decision node we show the subset of classes at that node. We also show the parameters of MLP (hidden nodes, trn epochs gini impurity decrement)

each digit. 100 test patterns of each digit were used to check generalization. Final NeuralTree obtained for 0 to 9 digit recognition is as shown Fig 4.

All nets used at internal nodes in the above tree are 2-layered MLP with 16 input nodes and 1 output node with hidden nodes as given in Fig 4. The BP parameters were set to $\eta=0.6$ (learning rate) and $\alpha=0.3$ (momentum). It required approximately 10^9 multiplications to train and testing requires maximum 680 multiplications.

In our simulation for Digit Recognition for multiclass classification at every internal node we treated it as 2 class classification problem. Also, we did not prune final NeuralTree by comparing 2-class classification versus multiclass classification at each internal node.

4.3 Comparison

Classifier	% Accuracy		Comments
	Training	Testing	
NeuralTree	99.5	92.0	Final NeuralTree is shown in Fig. 4.
3-layered MLP	95.0	88.0	Network architecture has 16-10-32-10 nodes and training took 1000 epochs.
K-NN	-	87.0	K=3 gives the best results.
CART	98.5	81.5	No pruning with 239 nodes and depth 16 tree.
	97.0	82.0	Pruned tree has 187 nodes and depth 14.
OC1	98.7	84.7	No pruning with 137 nodes and depth 16 tree.
	94.5	86.0	Pruned tree has 42 nodes and depth 11.

Table 1: Comparison of Different Digit Recognizers

For comparison various classifiers like, single 3-layered MLP, K-NN, CART and OC1 were tried. The first few steps till feature extraction (see Fig 2) are same in all classifiers. In our training of 3-layered MLP, for each input desired output is a unit verctor i.e. if pattern X is from class k then desired output is e_k. Various achitectures with 16 inputs and 10 outputs and with 10-15 nodes in first hidden layer and 25-30 nodes in second hidden layer were tried with BP. The best results obtained is shown in Table 1. CART and OC1 classifiers were trained using Murthy's OC1 software on same training set. For K-NN we used Euclidian distance as measure of similarity and for K=3 it gives maximum accuracy. The results of comparison are summarized in Table 1.

NeuralTree approach performs better than other methods. The training time required NeuralTree is also less than that of single 3-ayered MLP as 2-layered MLP at internal nodes of NeuralTree are much smaller and can be parallely trained.

We have not tried any pruning techniques or different learning algorithms for training NeuralTree. NeuralTree can be pruned by comparing performance of MLP for 2 classes versus multiclass classification at each internal node. Training time as well can be improved using Conjugate Gradient or Quasi-Newton method.

5   Conclusion

Hand-printed Digit Recognizer is successfully implemented using a NeuralTree. The method proposed for Feature Extraction gives Translation and Scale invariance. It also offers dimensionality reduction. The NeuralTree also offers Rotation (upto $\pm 20^o$) invariace for Hand-printed Digit Recognition. NeuralTree distinguishes itself from other standard classification trees in two ways : it extracts local and non-linear features at each decision node using small MLPs. It is a more powerful method with lower error rates and fewer nodes and training time is less compared to a 3-layered MLP. This approach is more suitable for problems where input space can be sub-divided and can be learned separately.

Acknowledgement

I thank Sant and Sanmukh for going through my work and give me suggestions. I would also like to thank Dr P S Sastry and Dr M Narasimha Murthy for discussions and comments on earlier version. And thanks a ton to Krishna for help in LaTeXing this paper.

References

[1] D E Rumelhart and J L McClelland, (eds.) *Parallel and Distributed Processing Vol – 1*, MIT Bradford Press, 1986.

[2] L Brieman, J H Friedman, A Ghnene and J Stone, *Classification and Regression Trees* ,Wadworth International Group,1984.

[3] Glfand Saul and Geo Heng, "Classification Trees with Neural Network Feature Extraction," *IEEE trans. NN*, Vol. 5, pp 923 - 953, 1992.

[4] S Murthy, S Kasif, S Salzberg and R Beigel, "OC1: Randomized induction of oblique decision tree," *AAAI*, Vol 8, pp 322-327, 1993.

A New Approach for Contour Extraction from Handwritten Zip Code by Using Adaptive Double Threshold Binarization

Itaru Nagayama, Tomio Takara

Faculty of Engineering, University of the Ryukyus,
Nishihara, Okinawa 903-01, Japan
nagayama@ie.u-ryukyu.ac.jp

Abstract **A new method for contour extraction from handwritten zip code is presented. Our computational basis is based on a double threshold binarization and neural network approach. The method we propose is simple in its nature and avoids the computational complexity belonging to conventional filtering methods. The proposed method is applied to the processing of contour extraction for handwritten zip code obtained from postal materials. The experimental results indicate that the proposed method has good performance and it is an effective method in comparison with conventional operator based methods.**

1 Introduction

An automatic zip code recognition system for Japanese postal materials is one of the most important systems in industrial distribution and circulation. Of course, the problem of handwritten character recognition remains an extremely important subject due to the great variability in handwriting styles, handwriting devices, and so on. On the other hand, contours are significant features for handwritten character recognition, because they are robust features that are relatively insensitive to character variability. In order to extract contours, Laplacian operator, Sobel operator and other edge extraction operators are used. Otherwise, edge detective approaches under logical procedure are used[1]-[3][5]. But those methods need some computational complexity. The purpose of this paper is to describe a new method for contour extraction from handwritten zip code and some experimental results on its performance. The proposed method is based on double threshold binarization and neural network approach.

2 Japanese Zip Code Database

The Institute for Post and Telecommunication Policy(IFTP) in Japan fabricated a Japanese zip code database named IPTP-CD-ROM1. The database consists of about 12000 images written by four different writing devices. Half of them include specified frame for writing area. And another half of them do not include specified frame, because the frame is printed with drop-out color and eliminated by drop-out color scanner. A 3-dimensional view of the image consists three numerals is shown in Fig.1. An image in the database is a 256 leveled gray image on area 30mm width × 15mm height. It is quantized in 16 dots per mm and the grid size of an image is 480 × 240. The x-coordinate is defined as width ranging from 0 to 480 counted from left to right. Also y-coordinate is defined as height ranging from 0 to 240 counted from top to bottom.

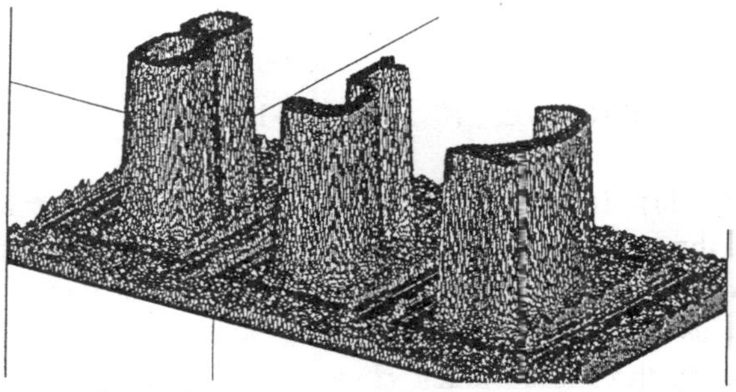

Figure 1   3-dimensional view of Japanese zip code images.

3 Double Threshold Binarization

Figure 2 indicates schematic procedure of the double threshold binarization. In general, a gray scale image has the density inclination about its figures. Also the density of noise is smaller than figures. The double threshold binarization is composed of following steps.

step1: Binarization of gray image. Two binary images A and B are obtained by thresholding with α and β, respectively. Denote that $\alpha < \beta$. Hence, a binary image B thresholded with β has fewer remaining pixels than a binary image A thresholded with α when $\alpha < \beta$.

step2: XOR operation between A and B. Exclusive OR calculation of each pixel between two binary images A and B is executed. Since B is smaller than A, pixels belonging near edge of image A are extracted as contour. A lower threshold α leads to elimination of noisy bits in the image, also leads to binary image of numerals. Otherwise, higher threshold β leads to somewhat small binary image of numerals. These two images are XOR operated between each corresponding pixel. Then, extracted contour will consist of edge pixels of binary images thresholded with α.

Computation of the above method is simple and light. Thus, contour extraction with proposed method is simpler than conventional detective method or operator based method as like Laplacian, Sobel, etc⋯.

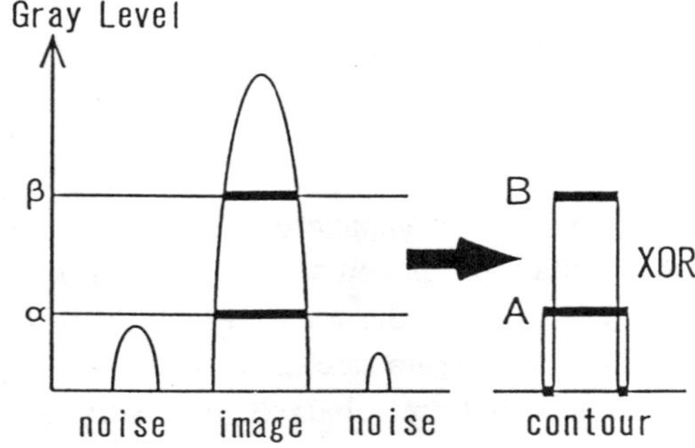

Figure 2   Double Threshold Binarization.

4 Decision of Threshold Values by Neural Network

It is very important for proposed method to adjust and to decide two thresholding values α and β. The quality of each image will cause significant influence on the result of proposed method, because of the variability of each image. In this section, neural network based threshold decision is discussed. In this approach, a gray level histogram is used as an input data to neural network to obtain two threshold values α and β [4]. To achieve above purpose, it is necessary to make the neural network learn the relationship between a histogram and threshold values that give a properly extracted contour. In the learning phase, 100 images are selected as test data and train the neural network by presenting a histogram and its desirable threshold values for each image. The network is three-layered network with N units in the input, middle and output layers. The input data to the network is a histogram of a 64 gray-leveled image. The histogram h(i) is normalized within 0<h(i)<1. Suppose that the pixel value of an original image ranges within 0,⋯,N-1. Let H(s) to be the number of pixels whose value is s. Thus, the normalized histogram h(s) is

$$h(s)=H(s)/L, \quad (0 \leqq s \leqq N\text{-}1) \tag{1}$$

where $L = \max\{H(0),H(1),\cdots,H(N\text{-}1)\}$. In this situation, the input layer of the network accepts normalized histogram as an input data and the output layer produces a set of output signals. A set of output signals consists of binary values that whose components are 0 or 1. The teacher signal at the unit which indicates desired threshold should be set as 1, and that at other units as 0. Hence, two units in the output layer should be set as 1 corresponding to threshold values α and β. The network is trained by using conventional back-propagation with momentum term. The weight updating are performed 20,000 iterations and adapted after each iteration.

Two desired threshold values for each test image are determined by visually suitable result via trial-and-error processing of contour extraction with proposed method. The neural network is trained by presenting a pair of input and output signals, those of a normalized histogram and its desired threshold values. Training iterations are updated under the back-propagation and connection weights are adapted after each training trial[6]. After the training, new 100 images are selected from the database as test data for extracting contour. The extracting process is performed by proposed method using two threshold values α and β determined by neural network.

5 Experimental Results

5.1 Contour Extraction

In general, performance evaluation of image processing is not easy, since evaluating criterion is not always clear. However, it is relatively easy to evaluate the extracting contour results from the quality of the resultant contour patterns which can be observed visually. The results of evaluating the performance of four schemes are shown in Fig.3. Extracted contours from original images by using Laplacian operator, Sobel operator and proposed method are shown together. Each figure consists of four different images written with ball-point pen, ink pen, felt-tipped pen and Japanese brush pen. Our observation indicates that extracted contour by proposed method is visually suitable as well as other methods, without Laplacian operator. Laplacian operator shows noisy performance even for the images within the same set. Thus, it need to apply somewhat smoothing process.

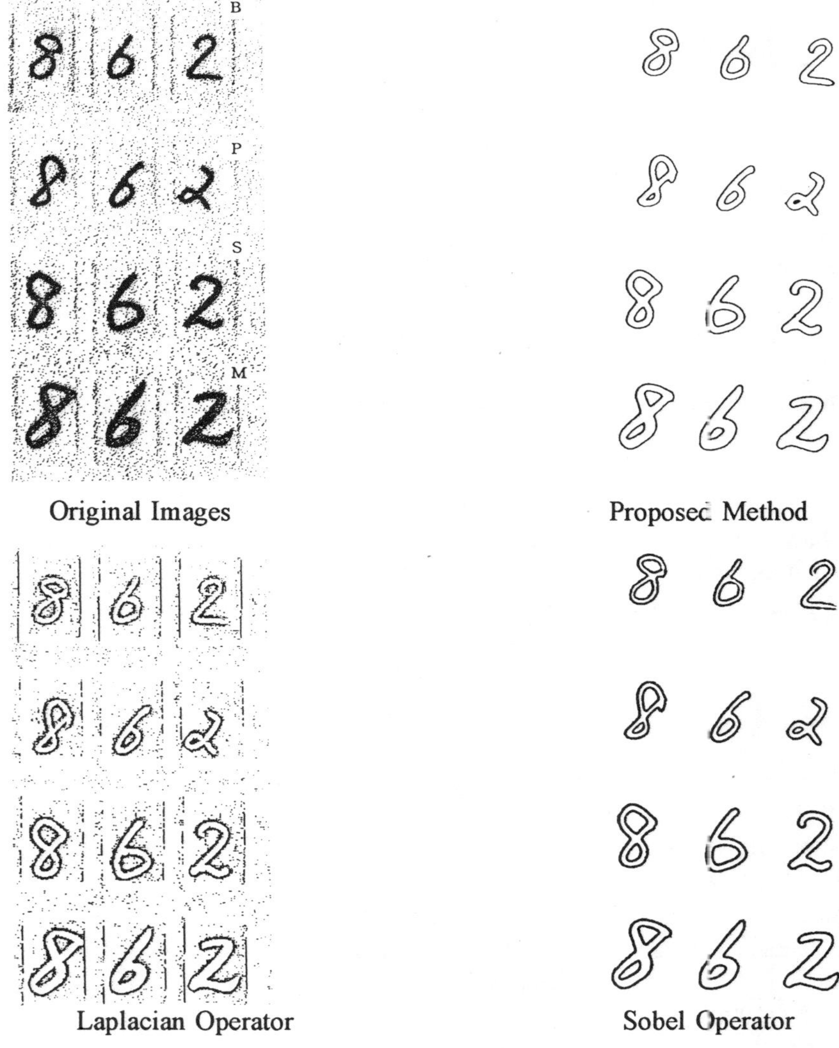

Figure 3   Extracted Contour

5.2 Processing Time

The comparison of the processing speed of the different four schemes including proposed method is described in this section. Processing performance for original images is evaluated, using Laplacian operator, Sobel operator, Roberts operator and proposed method. In testing for new Japanese zip code images, each of them is 256 gray scaled and 480 × 240 pixels, are used. For the proposed method, threshold values α and β for each test image are decided by trained neural network in advance. Figure 4 indicates processing performance for above four methods. The result show that the proposed method has preferred property compared to others.

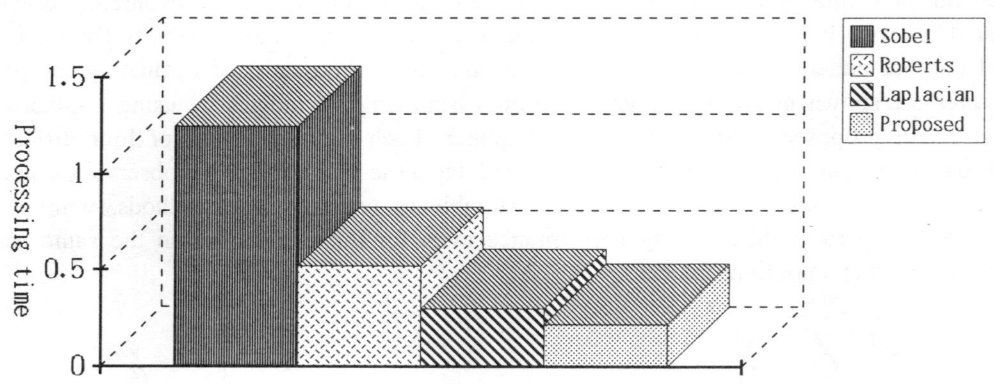

Figure 4   Processing Time(sec.)

6 Conclusion

In this paper we focus on basic preprocessing stage within whole recognition system. We propose a new contour extraction method named adaptive double threshold binarization. Generally speaking, contours are significant features for handwritten character recognition, because they are robust features that are relatively insensitive to character variability. Extracting contours, Laplacian operator, Sobel operator and other operators are used. Otherwise, edge detective approaches under logical procedure are used. But those methods need some computational complexity. The purpose of this paper is to describe a new method for contour extraction from handwritten zip code and some experimental results on its performance. The method is capable of producing a visually appropriate contour from handwritten zip code images. Two proper threshold values are decided by using neural network according to the quality of each image. Availability of this method is indicated by applying it to handwritten postal code images obtained from postal matters. As a result, we show that the proposed method can produce desirable contour with good performance.

References

[1] J.R.FRAM, E.S.Deutsch,"On the Quantitative Evaluation of Edge Detection Schemes and Their Comparison with Human Performance," *IEEE Trans .Computer.*, vol.C-24, No.6, pp.616-628,1975.

[2] J.Canny,"A Computational Approach to Edge Detection," *IEEE Trans.Pattern Analysis and Machine Intelligence*,vol.PAMI-8.No.6, pp.679-698,1986.

[3] H.Tamura, Introduction to Image Processing by Computer, Soken-Syuppan,1985.

[4] N.Babaguchi,K.Yamada,K.Kise,K.Tezuka,"An Experimental Consideration on Image Binarization by Connectionist Model," *IEICE Trans.Information and Systems, D-II*, vol.J73, No.8, pp.1281-1287,(1990).

[5] R.O.Duda, P.E.Hart, Pattern Classification and Scene Analysis, John Wiley & Sons, 1973.

[6] R.P.Lippman,"Pattern Classification using Neural Network," *IEEE Comm.*,pp.47-64,Nov.1989.

Recurrent Networks, Automata and Dynamics

(Oral Presentation)

Analog Computing in Physical Systems

Hava T. Siegelmann
Faculty of Industrial Engineering and Management
Technion, Haifa 32000, Israel
iehava@ie.technion.ac.il

Shmuel Fishman
Department of Physics
Technion, Haifa 32000, Israel
fishman@physics.technion.ac.il

Abstract

This work is aimed to gain an enlarged and deeper understanding of the computation processes possible in natural and artificial systems. We introduce an interface between dynamical systems and computational models. The theory that is developed encompasses discrete and continuous analog computation by means of difference and differential equations, respectively. Our complexity theory for continuous time systems is very natural and requires no external clocks or synchronizing elements.

As opposed to previous models we do not apply some nature principles to the Turing model but rather start from realizable and possibly chaotic dynamical systems and interpret their evolution as generalized computation. By applying the basic computational terms such as, halting, computation under resource constraints, nondeterministic and stochastic behavior to dynamical systems, a general, continuous-time computational theory is introduced. The new theory is indeed different from the classical one: in some ways it seems stronger but it still has natural limits of decidability.

1   Introduction

In the field of analog computation each result of an experimentalist in a laboratory and each dynamical behavior in nature are captured as computational processes. Blum, Shub and Smale were the first to insist on a computational model, in which — unlike classical computational models — the operations are done on the values irrespectively of their radix two representation [BSS89]. Siegelmann and Sontag suggested another model based on real-valued neural networks [SS94]; their model assumes continuity in the flow, a requirement which was not enforced in the model of Blum et al. Both models allow computational capabilities which surpass those of the classical digital computer [Sie95]. In this paper we introduce another model; as opposed to the previous two models it assumes continuous time update.

In the theory of computation, efficiency is estimated by the number of discrete computational steps as a function of the input precision. In continuous systems the efficiency of computation seems ill-defined in standard theories. In particular, assume we wish to describe computation by system modeled by a differential equation

$$\frac{d\mathbf{x}}{dt} = \mathbf{F}(\mathbf{x}(t)) \ .$$

If $\mathbf{F}$ is multiplied by a constant a it may look that the computation time changes. We propose the following resolution of this problem: the systems that we focus on (most typical systems existing) have characteristic time scales, to be defined later. Multiplying $\mathbf{F}$ by a constant is equivalent to changing the time units that measure the evolution. It will not affect the trajectory of the system in phase space and therefore the nature of computation. It will however determine the speed this trajectory is traversed.

In this paper we consider various dynamical systems as models of computation and study the consequences in detail. We focus on *dissipative systems* only; there, the phase space volume decreases in time. As a consequence, dissipative systems typically are characterized by the presence and the nature of attractors. We interpret reaching the attractors or some points on the attractors as finishing the computation. Note that the attractors may be either strange and regular and the boundaries between the basins are either smooth or fractal [MGOY85]. (The boundaries may be fractal even if the attractors are regular [HOG88].) In spite of this variety, the computation and computation times in dynamical systems will be defined in unified, natural, and unambiguous mathematical terms.

After creating a natural bridge between the theory of dynamical systems and the field of computational complexity, we draw a clear correspondence between the various dynamical behaviors (and expected attractors) and the level of computational hardness. Our main results are:

- Definition of computation by dynamical systems.

- Definition of computation time that applies to both discrete and continuous time.

- Complete analysis of the continuous-time Hopfield network.

- For systems with regular attractors the computation is deterministic and most often in P.

- If the attractors are chaotic but isolated, polynomial time is not sufficient to trace an attractor. Here, exponential deterministic time is needed. However, we can naturally define nondeterministic computation in this case and these systems typically are in NP. In this case P $\subset$ NP (they are different).

- If the attractors are chaotic and intermingled we can define probabilistic computation. We conjecture that in this case the computation PP (Probabilistic Polynomial) of our model is stronger than NP.

- Chaotic systems which exhibit crisis (or chaotic intermittency) demonstrate natural undecidable computation.

2   Definition of Computation and Computation Time

A computing device maps an input into an output; the internal evolution, or its trace by observers, is regarded as the computation. Here, we take the view that a computing device can be characterized by the function it computes and by its associated computation time; *we ignore the particular evolution path it takes.* This view allows the development of a general theory of computation for dynamical systems. For us, the initial condition corresponds to the input and the system evolves until approaching an attractor. The possible outcome of the computation can be:

(1) Flow to a stable fixed point.
(2) Flow to a stable periodic orbit.
(3) Flow to union of fixed points and orbits connecting them.
(4) Flow to an isolated strange attractor.
(5) Flow to a strange attractor with points of the basin of attraction of another attractor arbitrarily close to it or to intermittent attractors.
(6) Flow on a repelling nonwandering set (including also boundaries).

(7) Flow to infinity.

In (5) the computation, if deterministic, will never end. Case (6) may occur only if the initial condition is on a particular set of measure zero. We suggest that the class of computation associated with a dynamical system can be characterized by the features of the nonwandering sets; thus creating a possible bridge between computation complexity and the theory of dynamical systems.

The actual convergence to an attractor takes an infinite time. We thus do not require complete convergence but rather define that the calculation is completed when an ε-vicinity of the attractor is approached and the system is confined there. Note that the ϵ-vicinity may contain several attractors that can be resolved only for smaller values of ϵ. Thus, as the resolution is refined more results are found.

To comply with the finiteness of input and output (for computability) and the decision of ending a computation, *the computation in a dynamical system is defined relatively to a grid*. The spacing of the grid is of the order of the precision in the initial conditions, unless otherwise is explicitly specified. The connection between the precision in the dynamical evolution and the number of bits in the input is given by the log ratio; that is, for grid spacing of size ϵ the number of "input bits" is $|\log \epsilon|$. Having defined a grid, the computation time indeed increases with the precision.

For continuous dynamical systems, defined by differential equations, there are several alternatives to associate computation time. Our definition will be introduced with the help of the stroboscopic map. The computation time, defined in terms of the number of steps, is $n_c = t_c/\tau$, where t_c is the convergence time to the ε-vicinity of the nonwandering set and τ is the step of the map. The step τ should be chosen much smaller than the characteristic time so that to preserve the general dynamical features of the system.

We next define the characteristic time scale for most typical dissipative systems: Assume first that the stable nonwandering set is a fixed point x^*, one can linearize

$$\frac{d\mathbf{x}}{dt} = \mathbf{F}(\mathbf{x}(t))$$

around this point, to obtain

$$\dot{\delta\mathbf{x}} = M \ \delta\mathbf{x} \tag{2.1}$$

where $\delta\mathbf{x} = \mathbf{x} - \mathbf{x}^*$ and M is the *stability matrix* defined by

$$M_{ij} = \frac{\partial F_i}{\partial x_j}\big|_{\mathbf{x}=\mathbf{x}^*} \ . \tag{2.2}$$

The eigenvalues of the stability matrix are called the Lyapunov exponents. Let us denote the eigenvalues of M by λ_i (the fixed point is assumed to be stable, hence all λ_i are negative). The rate of convergence is determined by the largest of them, that will be denoted by $\lambda_1 = -\lambda$. In the vicinity of the fixed point $|\mathbf{x}(t) - \mathbf{x}^*| \sim e^{-\lambda t}$. The distance from the fixed point decreases by a factor of e in each time interval of $1/\lambda$. So $1/\lambda$ is a natural characteristic time scale for convergence. Since the time spent near a fixed point dominates the elapsed time (unless the initial point is very close to the boundaries), we can choose $1/\lambda$ as the formal characteristic time of the computation and in discretizing the continuous equation we have to take $\tau << \frac{1}{\lambda}$. Note that the characteristic time $\frac{1}{\lambda}$ depends only on the nature of the fixed point and not on any detail of the physical system. Obviously the numerical value of λ depends on the units used to measure time. The change of the time scale is equivalent to the multiplication of $\mathbf{F}$ by a scalar constant. Such a characteristic time scale will be found any time exponential convergence to a nonwandering set takes place. This set may be a fixed point, a periodic orbit or even a strange attractor. If the attractor is a fixed point the time scale is calculated via the stability matrix M at the point. All real parts of the eigenvalues are negative; the largest of them is chosen.

Having this time scale, we can calculate the computation time of dynamical systems. The *convergence time* t_c is what it takes for the trajectory to flow from the initial point to the point where it terminates. It consists of three contributions. t_ε is the contribution from the vicinity of the attractor in the linear regime where (2.1) is justified. t_B is the contribution from the flow in the vicinity of the boundary, if the initial condition is in its vicinity. Finally, t_f is the contribution from the flow not in these two regions. The convergence time is therefore

$$t_c = t_\varepsilon + t_f + t_B \tag{2.3}$$

The convergence time t_c is shorter than the total period required for the computation. One also has to verify that the computation has indeed ended. The *total computation time*, t_t is thus the sum of the convergence time t_c and the *verification time t_v*:

$$t_t = t_c + t_v . \tag{2.4}$$

The time t_v is polynomial in $\log \epsilon$ in the case of a regular attractor, but it dominates the total computation time for chaotic systems.

Comment: It may happen that one of the eigenvalues of the stability matrix (2.2) vanishes for the attractor and then the convergence is not exponential any more. This case is not typical and will not be considered in the present work.

3 Systems with a Lyapunov Functional

We next calculate explicit bounds on the computation time for simple systems for which a Lyapunov or energy functional satisfying

$$\frac{dE(\mathbf{x}(t))}{dt} < 0 \tag{3.1}$$

or

$$E(\mathbf{x}_{n+1}) - E(\mathbf{x}_n) < 0 \tag{3.2}$$

can be defined. We obtain $t_v = O(\log^2 \epsilon)$; $t_\varepsilon = \frac{1}{\lambda}|ln\frac{\varepsilon}{\delta}|$ where $\lambda_1 = -\lambda$ is the largest Lyapunov exponent; and $t_B \sim \frac{1}{\tilde{\lambda}}|ln\eta|$ where $\tilde{\lambda}$ is the largest Lyapunov exponent of the corresponding fixed point on the boundary and the initial point is assumed to be in a narrow region of width $\eta < \varepsilon$ in the vicinity of the basin boundary. We also find that $t_f < \frac{\Delta E}{v_\delta}$ where v_δ is the rate of change of energy at a point x_δ in the linear regime. For lack of space we only state the results: that for a gradient flow v_δ is the value of $|\mathbf{F}(\mathbf{x}_\delta)|^2$ and in the case of Hopfield neural network $v_\delta = cB_W|\mathbf{F}(\mathbf{x}_\delta)|^2$ where B_W and c are constants.

Although for sufficiently small τ the stroboscopic map is a good approximation of the continuous system, in course of the dynamics these two systems will usually flow apart due to the accumulation of differences. We prove that in the particular case of systems with a Lyapunov functional the discrete maps and the corresponding continuous equations describe an equivalent computation in the limit $\tau \to 0$ (both have the same attractors and the same basins). The existence of the Lyapunov functional is a sufficient, though not necessary condition for the equality of continuous and discrete time systems.

4 Computation for Chaotic Systems

Often the stable nonwandering sets are chaotic strange attractors. The behavior of a chaotic system can be very rich, exhibiting structures on all scales. Our results for chaotic attractors include:

1. We start with isolated strange attractors. If one has to determine the location of the attractor within the precision ϵ, there is a profound difference between regular and strange attractors. In the first case the computation is polynomial while it may require exponentially long time in the second case.

2. Next, we are going to consider the question "Is a given point $\mathbf{x}$ approaching a typical isolated attractor Φ ?" The attractor is specified by one of its fixed points. We prove that this problem is in NP in our model and conclude that: In the case of isolated chaotic attractors P $\subset$ NP, while for regular attractors P=NP.

3. For chaotic systems there is also the possibility of intermingled — rather than isolated — attractors. In this case in any δ-vicinity of an attractor there are points belonging to the basin of attraction of another attractor. In this case a deterministic computation will never converge. Yet, probabilistic convergence is still well defined.

4. Although our analog computation model is strong, it has its own clear limits. A strong undecidability takes place when "crisis," namely a sudden change in the structure of the attractor with the change of a parameter p, occurs [Ott93]. One type of crisis is boundary crisis, where at $p = p_c$ the attractor touches its basin boundary, as in the case of the Ikeda map [Ott93, GORY87]. Another type of crisis is "attractor merging crisis," where strange attractors merge when the parameter p is varied [Ott93].

References

[BSS89]   L. Blum, M. Shub, and S. Smale. On a theory of computation and complexity over the real numbers: Np completeness, recursive functions, and universal machines. *Bull. A.M.S.*, 21:1–46, 1989.

[GORY87]   C. Grebogi, E. Ott, F. Romeiras, and J.A. Yorke. Critical exponents for crisis-induced intermittency. *Phys. Review A*, 36:5365–5380, 1987.

[HOG88]   G. H. Hsu, E. Ott, and C. Grebogi. Strange saddles and the dimensions of their invariant manifolds. *Physics Letters*, 127(4):199–204, February 1988.

[MGOY85] S. W. McDonald, C. Grebogi, E. Ott, and J. A. Yorke. Fractal basin boundaires. *Physica*, 17D:125–153, 1985.

[Ott93]   E Ott. *Chaos in Dynamical Systems*. Cambridge University Press, Cambridge, 1993.

[Sie95]   H. T. Siegelmann. Computation beyond the turing limit. *SCIENCE*, 268(5210):545–548, April, 28 1995.

[SS94]   H. T. Siegelmann and E. D. Sontag. Analog computation via neural networks. *Theoretical Computer Science*, 131, 1994. 331-360.

A Cascade Neural Network Model
with Nonlinear Poles and Zeros

Andrew D. Back[1,2] and Ah Chung Tsoi[1]

[1]Department of Electrical and Computer Engineering, University of Queensland
Brisbane, Qld 4072. Australia

[2]Frontier Research Program RIKEN, Institute of Physical and Chemical Research
Hirosawa 2-1, Saitama 351-01, Wako-Schi, Japan.
{back,act}@elec.uq.edu.au

Abstract— **In this paper we propose a novel nonlinear model which is an extension of the usual cascade model structure to one which permits nonlinear mappings of the poles and zeros.**

1   Introduction

Linear models for time series prediction, system identification and control, are widely used in many different fields. For many physical processes however, the underlying physics of the problem may demand that a nonlinear model is required to obtain an accurate approximation of the systems behaviour. Consequently, there is much interest in novel nonlinear models, in particular, neural network approaches [1, 5, 8, 10, 14, 15].

In previous work, linear ARMA (autoregressive moving average) models have been extended to the nonlinear case resulting in NARMA and NARX models [4]. These model structures are defined as

$$
\begin{aligned}
y(t) &= \tfrac{B(q)}{A(q)}u(t) + \tfrac{C(q)}{A(q)}e(t) &\quad \text{ARMAX} \\
y(t) &= F\left(\tfrac{B(q)}{A(q)}u(t) + \tfrac{C(q)}{A(q)}e(t)\right) &\quad \text{NARMAX}
\end{aligned}
\tag{1}
$$

where $u(t)$ is the input and $e(t)$ is a disturbance term usually treated as a sequence of independent random variables [9], or as zero for deterministic models. The nonlinear function $F(\cdot)$ has been recently modelled using a multilayer perceptron. The backpropagation algorithm then allows for $F(\cdot)$ to be adjusted on-line using measured data.

Other recent approaches have been proposed which employ a multilayer perceptron as the basic model structure. These models have been constructed by using *global* feedback, where connections exist from the output of the model to the input [8, 10, 15]. Feedback from within the model to the input has also been considered [5]. Recently, models have also been proposed which allow a *local* feedback where linear filters, which may be recursive, are placed in line with the usual MLP weights.

These models have been studied quite extensively, with some understanding being obtained of their computational and representational capabilities [2, 6]. In this paper, we propose a new nonlinear model, based on drawing together approaches from linear systems theory and neural networks.

2   A Nonlinear Pole-Zero Cascade Model

In this paper, we wish to propose a new modelling approach. We do not claim that this is this has never been considered before, as the idea does seem quite simple, however we are not aware of where or when others may have considered the approach. The model we propose has arisen out of our interest in developing a rapprochement between linear signal processing and control techniques and recent neural network approaches.

The proposed nonlinear model is defined as

$$
y(t) = \frac{\prod_{i=1}^{n}(q - \tilde{z}_{ri})\prod_{j=1}^{m}(q - \tilde{z}_{cj})(q - \tilde{z}_{ci}^{*})}{\prod_{i=1}^{n}(q - \tilde{p}_{ri})\prod_{j=1}^{m}(q - \tilde{p}_{cj})(q - \tilde{p}_{ci}^{*})}x(t)
\tag{2}
$$

$$
\begin{aligned}
\tilde{z}_{ri} &= f_{ri}\left(z_{ri}; g(x)\right) \tag{3} \\
\tilde{z}_{cj} &= f_{ci}\left(z_{cj}; g(x)\right) \tag{4} \\
\tilde{p}_{ri} &= f_{ri}\left(p_{ri}; g(x)\right) \tag{5} \\
\tilde{p}_{cj} &= f_{ci}\left(p_{cj}; g(x)\right) \tag{6}
\end{aligned}
$$

As a notational convenience, we will use λ to generically represent any of $\{z_{ri}, z_{ci}, p_{ri}, p_{ci}\}$ where appropriate. Hence, we have

$$
\begin{aligned}
f\left(\lambda; g(x)\right) &= z_{k}^{L}(t) \tag{7} \\
z_{k}^{l}(t) &= h\left(\hat{x}_{k}^{l}(t)\right) \tag{8} \\
\hat{x}_{k}^{l}(t) &= \begin{cases} \sum_{i=1}^{N_{l}} w_{ij}^{l} z_{j}^{l-1}(t) & l = 2, ..., L \\ w_{i1}^{l}\lambda + w_{i2}^{l}g(x) & l = 1 \end{cases} \tag{9}
\end{aligned}
$$

where $h(\cdot)$ is a sigmoid function, $\{w_{ij}^l\}$ are the weights and $\{\hat{x}_k^l(t)\}$ are the states of the neurons.

This model can be considered as a *nonlinear cascade structure*. The usual cascade filter structure is extended to allow for poles and zeros which are obtained as the output of nonlinear functions. The nonlinear functions $f_i(\cdot;\cdot)$ are formed by using multilayer perceptrons, consequently, it is possible to adapt the model on-line using the backpropagation algorithm [11]. The aim of the model is to allow for an otherwise linear cascade structure, to have its pole/zero positions be dependent on a function of the incoming signal $x(t)$. $g(x)$ can be fixed by the user or it is easily seen, may be some other adaptive model, linear or nonlinear. We do not go into detail with this area in the paper, due to lack of space.

In practice, although λ may be complex, two real MLPs may be used to process the signals. Thus, the actual model which may be used would be of the form

$$\tilde{\lambda} = f(\lambda; g(x)) \tag{10}$$

It can be observed that this model is similar to the TAR (Threshold Autoregressive) model proposed by Tong [12]. In this case however, we allow for a *continuous* variation of the model, rather than switching between models depending on the input signal. The TAR model however, can be derived as a special case of the proposed architecture.

This model differs quite substantially from the previous dynamic neural network models. While the NARMAX models have a nonlinear component following a linear component, there are a number of important differences:

1. The nonlinear functions operate on the pole/zero positions directly, rather than the output signal from a linear model.

2. The proposed model is constructed as a cascade structure, comprising of only 1st and/or 2nd order sections. This allows the nonlinear functions to process the pole/zero positions of an existing, or underlying, linear model, thus causing a readily determined change in the instantaneous frequency response of the structure.

3. A nonlinear function or MLP can be used for every pole and zero. Alternatively, it is possible to introduce a *hybrid linear-nonlinear* model by using nonlinear functions only on some of the poles or zeros. For example, just on the poles. In this case, the model would have a linear MA part and a nonlinear AR section. Another approach would be to generalize the usual linear model to allowing nonlinear poles and zeros, Thus, we may have a model of the form:

$$y(t) = \frac{\prod_{i=1}^{n}(q - v_{ri}) \prod_{j=1}^{m}(q - v_{cj})(q - v_{ci}^*)}{\prod_{i=1}^{n}(q - s_{ri}) \prod_{j=1}^{m}(q - s_{cj})(q - s_{ci}^*)} \frac{\prod_{i=1}^{n}(q - \tilde{z}_{ri}) \prod_{j=1}^{m}(q - \tilde{z}_{cj})(q - \tilde{z}_{ci}^*)}{\prod_{i=1}^{n}(q - \tilde{p}_{ri}) \prod_{j=1}^{m}(q - \tilde{p}_{cj})(q - \tilde{p}_{ci}^*)} x(t) \tag{11}$$

where $\{v_i, s_i\}$ are the linear zeros and poles respectively, and $\{\tilde{z}_i, \tilde{p}_i\}$ are as defined before.

4. The nonlinear functions used for the complex poles and zeros can be complex, however this is not necessary. The model designer can choose whether this possibility is required or not, allowing interaction between the pole/zero angle and radius.

Since the nonlinear model allows for a change in the poles and zeros at each instant of time, it is also possible to view it in terms of a *time-varying linear model*.

In the next section we derive a learning algorithm for the proposed model, using the well known backpropagation algorithm.

3   A Learning Algorithm

The derivation follows closely, the usual backpropagation algorithm [11].

Let the instantaneous output error between the model and the desired output[1] be

$$J(t;\theta) = \frac{1}{2} e_k^2(t) \tag{12}$$

$$= \frac{1}{2}(d(t) - y(t))^2 \tag{13}$$

where $d(t)$ is the desired output at time t. The weights are updated according to

$$\Delta w_{ik}^l(t) = \eta \delta_k^l(t) w_{ik}^l z_i^{l-1}(t) \qquad\qquad l = 1, ..., L$$
$$\delta_k^l(t) = \begin{cases} e_k(t) h'(\hat{x}_k^l(t)) & l = L \\ h'(\hat{x}_k^l(t)) \sum_{p=1}^{N_{l+1}} \delta_p^{l+1}(t) w_{kp}^{l+1} & 1 \le l \le L-1 \end{cases} \tag{14}$$

where $h(\cdot)$ is the usual sigmoid function, typically given as $\tanh(\cdot)$, $\delta_k^l(t)$ term is the usual backpropagated error [11] and

$$z_1^0(t) = \lambda \tag{15}$$

$$z_2^0(t) = g(x) \tag{16}$$

---

[1] We only consider a SISO (single-input single-output) model in this paper, though an extension to MIMO (multiple-input multiple-output) models can be readily implemented.

4 Stability

It is important to consider the stability properties of a model so that the model can be adapted on-line or parametrized without becoming unstable. This is considered below.

4.1 Linear models

A linear FIR model with constant coefficients and bounded input signal, will produce a bounded output and is therefore stable. However, maintaining stability of linear recursive models such as the IIR filter, is a well known problem. During adaptation, if one of the poles of the characteristic equation $(A(q^{-1}) = 0)$ moves outside the unit circle, the filter becomes unstable. A number of methods exist to overcome these stability problems in IIR filters.

For low order systems, the test $\sum_i |a_i| < 1$ will indicate whether a filter is stable. The problem with this method is that it is too restrictive, since clearly it will give false indications of instability. The modified Schur-Cohn test [13] indicates the presence of unstable poles without the restrictions above. However, the polynomial still needs to be factorized to project the unstable roots back inside the unit circle. Performing this operation does not guarantee convergence to the desired parameter values, neither is there a proof that the projection will only be needed finitely many times [7].

4.2 Nonlinear Cascade Model

The issue of stability for the proposed model may be tackled in a number of ways. Since the roots of the polynomials change at every time instant, it is clear that computing the stability of such a model could seemingly require a large computational effort. Even if we did do this however, it may be unnecessary, since it is evident that the model could go unstable for a brief period of time before returning to stable operation, without any problems. Aspects of such self-stabilization type properties have been considered in the literature in various forms before [3].

It is possible to see that, in the same manner as for the linear model, if the poles, as determined by the nonlinear function outputs, are *continuously* outside the unit circle for some sufficient period of time, then the model will be unstable.

Since the nonlinear functions are already operating on the poles and zeros directly, a much simpler approach is to simply use the nonlinear mappings to guarantee stability. Hence we have the following stability condition:

Property 4.1 *A nonlinear model with characteristic equation given by*

$$A(q) = q^{-(n+2m)} \prod_{i=1}^{n} (q - \tilde{\lambda}_{ri}) \prod_{j=1}^{m} (q - \tilde{\lambda}_{cj})(q - \tilde{\lambda}_{ci}^{*}) \tag{17}$$

$$\tilde{\lambda}_{ri} = f_{ri}(\lambda_{ri}; x)$$

$$\tilde{\lambda}_{ci} = f_{ci}(\lambda_{ci}; x)$$

where $\{\tilde{\lambda}_{ci}\}$, $\{\tilde{\lambda}_{ci}\}$ are outputs of the corresponding nonlinear functions $\{f_{ri}(\cdot; \cdot)\}$, $\{f_{ci}(\cdot; \cdot)\}$, with inputs $\{\lambda_{ri}\}$ or $\{\lambda_{ci}\}$ and x which are real roots, complex roots and the input signal to the model respectively; is stable, having bounded output, provided

$$max[f_{ri}(\lambda_{ri}; x)] \leq 1.0 \forall \lambda_{ri}, x \tag{18}$$

$$max[f_{ci}(\lambda_{ci}; x)] \leq 1.0 \forall \lambda_{ci}, x \tag{19}$$

where

$$f_{ri}(\lambda_{ri}; x) = 1.0$$

$$f_{ci}(\lambda_{ci}; x) = 1.0$$

is the usual marginal stability condition.

Consequently, the model is made stable by simply ensuring the nonlinear functions as produced by the MLPs, are restricted to $\mathcal{R}^2 \rightarrow \mathcal{R}^1 : [0, 1]$. The problem of instability that is normally present with linear IIR filters does not arise in the same way with the model presented here.

5 Examples

5.1 Example 1

To give an indication of the type of modelling behaviour that is possible with the proposed structure, we consider a straightforward example.

Let us begin with an underlying linear model described by

$$H_l(q) = \frac{(q - z)(q - z^*)}{(q - p)(q - p^*)} \tag{20}$$

where $z = 0.7 + \jmath 0.6$, $p = 0.95 + \jmath 0.15$. Now introduce the nonlinear model

$$H_n(q) = \frac{(q - \tilde{z})(q - \tilde{z}^*)}{(q - \tilde{p})(q - \tilde{p}^*)} \tag{21}$$

where $\tilde{z} = f(z; g(x))$, $\tilde{p} = f(p; g(x))$. Note that a different $f(\cdot; \cdot)$ could be used for the poles and zeros, but for simplification, we consider them as the same in this case.

We have

$$\begin{aligned}
z &= x_z + \jmath y_z \\
&= r_z e^{\jmath \omega_z} \tag{22} \\
p &= x_p + \jmath y_p \\
&= r_p e^{\jmath \omega_p} \tag{23}
\end{aligned}$$

and

$$\begin{aligned}
\tilde{z} &= \tilde{r}_z e^{\jmath \tilde{\omega}_z} \tag{24} \\
\tilde{p} &= \tilde{p}_z e^{\jmath \tilde{\omega}_p} \tag{25}
\end{aligned}$$

Therefore, we will define $f(\cdot; \cdot)$ by the following.

$$\tilde{r} = \left[c_2 \left((r - c_1)^2 + c_0 \right) + c_3 \right] g(x) \tag{26}$$

where the same nonlinear mapping is used for the radii of the zeros and poles. We select $c_0 = 0.1$, $c_1 = 0.35$, $c_2 = 1.5$, $c_3 = 0.3$. The resulting nonlinear mapping is shown in Fig. 1.

Now, we could introduce a similar mapping for the pole/zero angles $\{\omega_p, \omega_z\}$, however in order to simplify this experiment, we will not use a nonlinear function for the pole/zero angles. Thus.

$$\tilde{\omega} = \omega \tag{27}$$

Finally, since we would like the model to vary nonlinearly with the input signal magnitude we choose

$$g(x) = |x| \tag{28}$$

The pole-zero plot for the linear system and the resulting nonlinear system are shown in Fig. 2. As a means of indicating a time domain response of the model, a white gaussian input signal of zero mean and unit variance was input to the linear and nonlinear models. The resulting outputs are shown in Fig 3. It can be observed that the nonlinear mapping produces a substantially different model than the linear case. The resulting output signal from the nonlinear model departs significantly from gaussianity.

To indicate the time-varying nature of the model, the coefficients of the equivalent linear model $H_n(q)$ are shown in Fig. 4. The equivalent linear model is given by

$$H_n(q) = \frac{b_0(x;t) + b_1(x;t)q^{-1} + b_2(x;t)q^{-2}}{1.0 + a_1(x;t)q^{-1} + a_2(x;t)q^{-2}} \tag{29}$$

where $\{a, b\}$ are obtained by multiplying out the instantaneous $\{\tilde{z}, \tilde{p}\}$ values at each time step.

5.2 Example 2

For the second experiment, we considered exactly the same arrangement as for Experiment 1, however in this case, we introduce nonlinear mappings on the pole-zero angles ω. Here, instead of (27), we use

$$\tilde{\omega} = \left[c_2 \left((\omega - c_1)^2 + c_0 \right) + c_3 \right] g(x) \tag{30}$$

with $c_0 = 0.1$, $c_1 = 0.35$, $c_2 = 1.5$, $c_3 = 0.3$, which is exactly the same nonlinear mapping used for the radii.

The pol-zero plot for the nonlinear model produced for an input variable $x(t)$ ranging in magnitude from 0 to 1, is shown in Fig. 5. The response of the nonlinear model to a white gaussian input signal is shown in Fig. 5(b). As before, it is evident that the model is highly nonlinear. The time-varying coefficients of the a linear model, equivalent instantaneously with the nonlinear model, are shown in Fig. 6.

6 Conclusions

In this paper we have proposed a class of nonlinear model which we term a nonlinear cascade structure. The model introduces nonlinear mappings on each of the pole-zero positions in a cascade form model. Consequently, we have shown that a more general linear-nonlinear hybrid sturcture can be derived. The model can be adapted on-line using a form of the usual backpropagation algorithm. The stability of this class of network was examined and it was shown that by ensuring simple bounds are maintained on the MLPs, the model will remain stable. Consequently, no stability checking is required as the poles cannot move outside the unit circle. This is a significant advantage over linear IIR filters which have well-known instability problems. The proposed nonlinear model can has an equivalent linear model form with time-varying coefficients. Experiments were conducted which gave an indication of the highly nonlinear behaviour of.

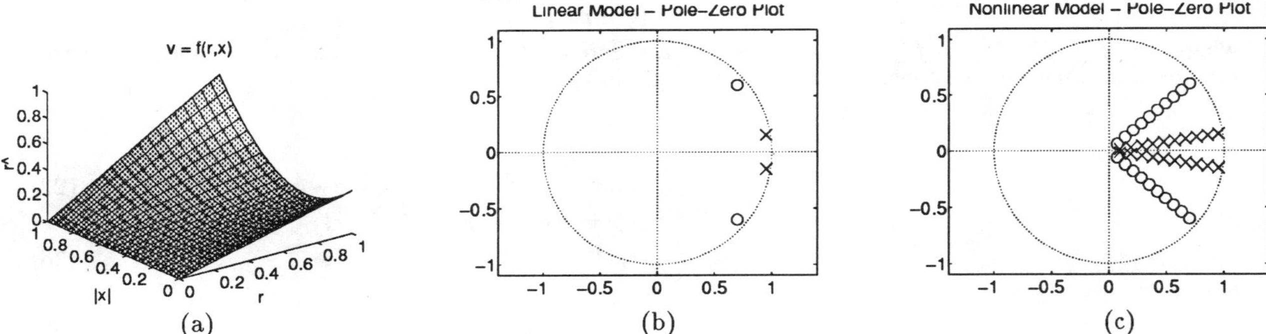

Figure 1: Experiment 1. (a) Nonlinear mapping $f(\lambda; |x|)$ used. (b) Pole zero plot of linear system. (c) In order to see the variation of pole-zero positions with input magnitude, the poles and zeros are plotted while varying $|x|$ from 0 to 1.

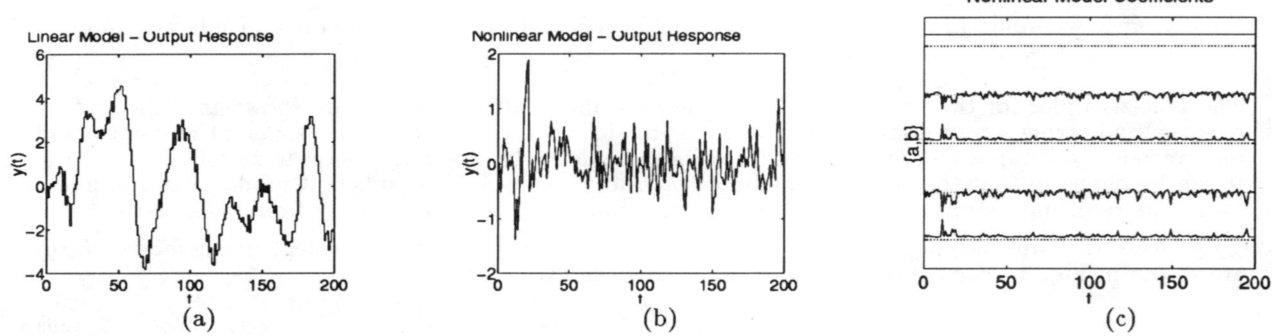

Figure 2: Experiment 1. Output response from (a) the linear model, and (b) the nonlinear model due to a white gaussian input signal. (c) This plot shows the time-varying nature of the equivalent linear coefficients from the nonlinear model.

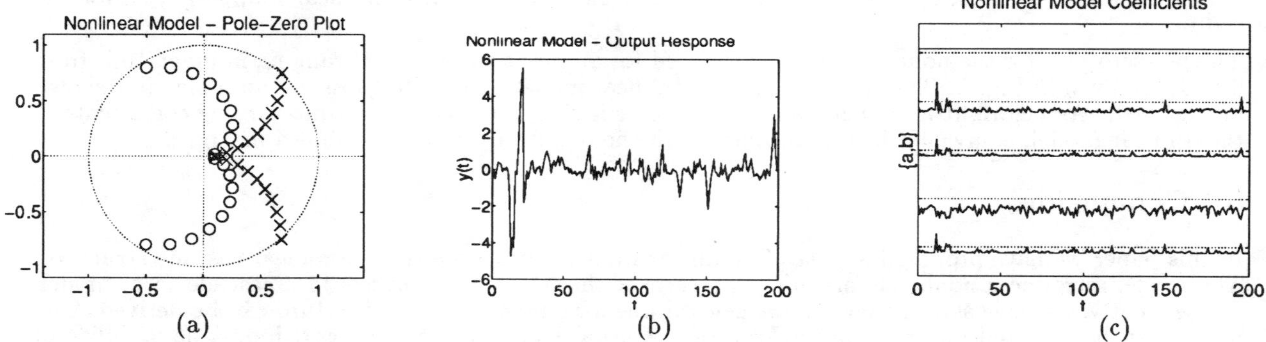

Figure 3: Experiment 2. (a) Pole zero plot of nonlinear linear system. The poles and zeros are plotted while varying $|x|$ from 0 to 1. (b) Output response from the nonlinear model considered due to a white gaussian input signal. (c) The variation over time of the coefficients in the equivalent linear model of the nonlinear model.

Acknowledgements

The first author gratefully acknowledges support from the Australian Research Council and the Frontier Research Program RIKEN. The second author acknowledges partial support from the Australian Research Council.

References

[1] A.D. Back and A.C. Tsoi. FIR and IIR synapses, a new neural network architecture for time series modelling. *Neural Computation*, 3(3):375–385, 1991.

[2] A.D. Back and A.C. Tsoi. Nonlinear system identification using multilayer perceptrons with locally recurrent synaptic structure. In J. Aa. Sorenson S.Y. Kung, F. Fallside and C.A. Kamm, editors, *Proc. of the 1992 IEEE Workshop Neural Networks for Signal Processing 2 (NNSP92)*, pages 444–453, Piscataway, NJ, 1992. IEEE Press.

[3] A.D. Back and A.C. Tsoi. Stabilisation properties of multilayer feedforward networks with time-delay synapses. In I. Aleksander and J. Taylor, editors, *Artificial Neural Networks 1*, volume 2, pages 1113–1116, Helsinki, 1992. Elsevier Science Publishers B.V. (North Holland).

[4] S.A. Billings. Identifiation of nonlinear systems - a survey. *Proc. IEE*, Pt. D(127):272–285, 1980.

[5] J.L. Elman. Finding structure in time. *Cognitive Science*, 14:179–211 1990.

[6] P. Frasconi. Computational capabilities of local-feedback recurrent networks. In *NIPS Workshop on Neural Networks for Signal Processing*, 1994.

[7] C.R. Johnson. Adaptive IIR filtering: Current results and open issues. *IEEE Trans. Inform. Theory*, 30(2):237–250, 1984.

[8] M.I. Jordan. Supervised learning and systems with excess degrees of freedom. Technical Report 88-27, Massachusetts Institute of Technology, COINS, 1988.

[9] L. Ljung and T. Soderstrom. *Theory and Practice of Recursive Identification*. The MIT Press, Cambridge, MA, 1983.

[10] A.J. Robinson. *Dynamic Error Propagation Networks*. PhD thesis, Cambridge University Engineering Department, 1989.

[11] D.E. Rumelhart, G.E. Hinton, and R.J. Williams. Learning internal representations by error propagation. In D.E. Rumelhart, J.L. McClelland, and the PDP Research Group, editors, *Parallel Distributed Processing, Vol. 1. Foundations*, pages 318–362, Cambridge, MA, 1986. The MIT Press.

[12] H. Tong. *Threshold Autoregressive Models*. Springer-Verlag, 1983.

[13] S.A. Tretter. *Introduction to Discrete-Time Signal Processing*. Wiley, New York, 1976.

[14] E.A. Wan. Temporal backpropagation for FIR neural networks. In *Proc. Int. Joint Conf. Neural Networks, San Diego*, volume I, pages 575–580. IEEE Press, 1990.

[15] R.J. Williams and D. Zipser. A learning algorithm for continually running fully recurrent neural networks. *Neural Computation*, 1:270–280, 1989.

Network response time for a general class of WTA

Peter K.S. Tam[1], John P.F. Sum[2], C.S. Leung[2] and L.W. Chan[2]

[1] Dept. of Electronic Engg., Hong Kong Polytechnic University, Hung Hom, Kowloon.
[2] Dept. of Computer Science and Engg., Chinese University of Hong Kong, Shatin, N.T., Hong Kong
enptam@hkpucc.polyu.edu.hk;pfsum,csleung,lwchan@cs.cuhk.hk

Abstract— **In [1] we proposed a simple circuit of Winner-Take-All neural network and derived an analytical equation for its network response time [2]. In this paper, we explore this analytical equation for a more general class of winner-take-all circuits. We show that this equation for network response time is indeed an upper bound for a general class of WTA.**

1   Introduction

Since the beginning of neural network research, the Winner-Take-All (WTA) network has played a very important role in the design of most of the unsupervised learning neural networks [3] such as competitive learning and Hamming network. Lippman first proposed a discrete-time algorithm called Maxnet to realize the Hamming network [4]. Recently, Dempsey and McVey designed an alternative one called peak detector neural network (PDNN) based on the Hopfield network topology [7], and provided a hardware implementation for it [6]. Seiler and Nossek [8] independently proposed an inputless WTA cellular neural network based on Chua's CNN [9].

Amongst most of the models, their dynamical equations are governed by many parameters and so the design of such networks are complicated. Only a few of them provided analysis on the network response time [6]. In accordance with these difficulties, we proposed in [1] a simple analog circuit for WTA with its dynamical equation being governed by just one parameter. Therefore, the design of the network is relatively simple and the analysis on the network response time becomes feasible.

In [2], an analytic equation for a simple WTA circuit is derived, under mild assumptions. Intensive computer simulation confirms that the derived equation is a close approximation to the true network response time. In this paper, we further demonstrate that this analytic equation for network response time is indeed an upper bound on a more general class of WTA networks.

This paper is organized into six sections. The next section will introduce the model proposed in [1] and the general WTA model. Then some properties governing the derivation of the analytical equation for network response time will be stated in section three. Section four presents the derivation of this analytical equation. Section five will present those simulation results and confirms that the analytical equation can be treated as an upper bound for the general WTA model. The conclusion is presented in section six.

2   Network Model

We consider an N-neurons fully connected inputless WTA neural network. For the ith neuron, $i = 1, \ldots, N$, the state potential (state variable) and the output of the neuron are denoted by $v_i(t)$ and h_i respectively, where h_i is a piecewise linear function of v_i, i.e.

$$h_i = h(v_i) = \begin{cases} 1 & \text{if } v_i > 1 \\ v_i & \text{if } 0 \leq v_i \leq 1 \\ 0 & \text{if } v_i < 0. \end{cases} \tag{1}$$

Simple WTA model — In our proposed model [1], the output of each neuron is connected to all the other neurons and itself, in the same way as *Maxnet*. The connection is excitatory if the output is self-fedback. It is inhibitory when the connection is interneuron. The network dynamics can be described as follows:

$$\frac{dv_i(t)}{dt} = h(v_i(t)) - \epsilon \sum_{k=1}^{N} h(v_k(t)), \tag{2}$$

for all $i = 1, \ldots N$ and $\frac{1}{2} < \epsilon < 1$. The condition on ϵ is used to assure that $\frac{dv_i}{dt} < 0$ if the ith neuron is not the winning neuron for all time and $\frac{dv_{\pi_N}}{dt} > 0$ when non-winning neurons have reached zero [1].

General model — For some models such as Seiler-Nossek [8], a decay term $-v_i(t)$ is usually involved in the dynamical equation:

$$\frac{dv_i(t)}{dt} = -\beta v_i(t) + h(v_i(t)) - \epsilon \sum_{k=1}^{N} h(v_k(t)), \tag{3}$$

where $0 < \beta$. In this case, even the winner, its state potential will also decay to zero as $t \to \infty$. This general WTA model has been proposed for a long time. However, the bound on its response time has not been studied.

3 Properties of Simple WTA model

For the ease of discussion, it is assumed that the initial state potentials can be arranged in a strictly ascending order, i.e. $v_{\pi_1}(0) < v_{\pi_2}(0) < \ldots < v_{\pi_N}(0)$, for a suitable index set $\{\pi_1, \ldots, \pi_N\}$. Now, let us present some properties of the simple WTA model (2) which are useful for the later discussion. The proofs are omitted here but they can be found in [1].

Theorem 1 *If, $v_{\pi_1}(0) < v_{\pi_2}(0) < \ldots < v_{\pi_N}(0)$, then $v_{\pi_1}(t) < v_{\pi_2}(t) < \ldots < v_{\pi_N}(t)$, for all $t > 0$.*

Theorem 2 *If $v_{\pi_1}(0) < v_{\pi_2}(0) < \ldots < v_{\pi_N}(0)$, then there exists $T_1 < \infty$, such that $0 = v_{\pi_1}(T_1) < v_{\pi_2}(T_1) < \ldots < v_{\pi_N}(T_1)$.*

Theorem 3 *If $v_{\pi_1}(0) < v_{\pi_2}(0) < \ldots < v_{\pi_N}(0)$, then there exists $T_1 < \infty$, such that $0^+ = h_{\pi_1}(T_1) < h_{\pi_2}(T_1) < \ldots < h_{\pi_N}(T_1)$.*

Theorem 4 *If $v_{\pi_1}(0) < v_{\pi_2}(0) < \ldots < v_{\pi_N}(0)$, then there exists $0 < T_1 < T_2 < \ldots < T_{N-1} < \infty$ such that*

$$h_{\pi_i}(t) = 0 \ \ \forall t \geq T_i.$$

Theorem 5 *If $v_{\pi_1}(0) < v_{\pi_2}(0) < \ldots < v_{\pi_N}(0)$, then there exists $T_N < \infty$ such that $\forall \, t > T_N$,*

$$h_i(t) = \begin{cases} 1 & \textit{if } i = \pi_N \\ 0 & \textit{if } i \neq \pi_N, \end{cases}$$

where $i = 1, 2, \ldots, N$.

4 Network Response Time of the Simple WTA Model

We can proceed to see what will happen immediately after T_1. Once $t \geq T_1$ of Theorems 2–4,

$$h_{\pi_1}(t) = 0, \quad \frac{dh_{\pi_1}(t)}{dt} = 0$$

and

$$\begin{bmatrix} \dot{h}_{\pi_2}(t) \\ \dot{h}_{\pi_3}(t) \\ \ldots \\ \dot{h}_{\pi_N}(t) \end{bmatrix} = \begin{bmatrix} 1-\epsilon & -\epsilon & \ldots & -\epsilon \\ -\epsilon & 1-\epsilon & \ldots & -\epsilon \\ \ldots & \ldots & \ldots & \ldots \\ -\epsilon & -\epsilon & \ldots & 1-\epsilon \end{bmatrix} \begin{bmatrix} h_{\pi_2}(t) \\ h_{\pi_3}(t) \\ \ldots \\ h_{\pi_N}(t) \end{bmatrix}.$$

The output dynamic is now governed by an $N-1$ dimension first order differential equation. Let us denote

$$\hat{h}_N(t) = (h_{\pi_1}(t), h_{\pi_2}(t), \ldots, h_{\pi_N}(t))'$$

for all $0 < t < T_1$ and

$$\hat{h}_{N-1}(t) = (h_{\pi_2}(t), \ldots, h_{\pi_N}(t))',$$

when t is just greater than T_1, where $'$ denotes transpose. Note that π_N is the index of the neuron for which the initial state potential is the largest. Therefore, when $0 < t < T_1$,

$$\frac{d}{dt}\hat{h}_N(t) = A_N \hat{h}_N(t) \tag{4}$$

and when t is just greater than T_1,

$$\frac{d}{dt}\hat{h}_{N-1}(t) = A_{N-1}\hat{h}_{N-1}(t), \tag{5}$$

where

$$A_k = \begin{bmatrix} 1-\epsilon & -\epsilon & \ldots & -\epsilon \\ -\epsilon & 1-\epsilon & \ldots & -\epsilon \\ \ldots & \ldots & \ldots & \ldots \\ -\epsilon & -\epsilon & \ldots & 1-\epsilon \end{bmatrix}_{k \times k},$$

for $k = N-1, N$. Just after $t = T_1$, the network dynamical equation may be changed from (4) to (5) which represents a reduced-dimension system. Hence T_1 can be evaluated using the technique of eigenvalue-eigenvector analysis on A_N[1]. For all $t \in \{s \geq 0 | 0 < h_{\pi_i}(s) < 1, i = 1, 2 \ldots, N\}$,

$$h_{\pi_i}(t) = e^{(1-N\epsilon)t}\left[\frac{\sum_{k=1}^{N} v_{\pi_k}(0)}{N}\right] + e^t\left[v_{\pi_i}(0) - \frac{\sum_{k=1}^{N} v_{\pi_k}(0)}{N}\right] \tag{6}$$

for all $i = 1, 2, \ldots, N$. Obviously, the output of the π_1 neuron will be the first one reaching zero since $h_{\pi_i} < h_{\pi_j}$ if $i < j$. Hence, T_1 can be evaluated by setting $h_{\pi_1}(t) = 0$.

$$T_1 = -\frac{1}{N\epsilon} \log \left[\frac{\frac{\sum_{k=1}^{N} v_{\pi_k}(0)}{N} - v_{\pi_1}(0))}{\frac{\sum_{k=1}^{N} v_{\pi_k}(0)}{N}} \right]. \tag{7}$$

Substituting T_1 into Equation (6), we can readily show that

$$h_{\pi_i}(T_1) = \left[\frac{\frac{\sum_{k=1}^{N} v_{\pi_k}(0)}{N} - v_{\pi_1}(0))}{\frac{\sum_{k=1}^{N} v_{\pi_k}(0)}{N}} \right]^{\frac{-1}{N\epsilon}} (v_{\pi_i}(0) - v_{\pi_1}(0)),$$

for all $i = 2, 3, \ldots, N$. Note that h_{π_N} may reach 1 within the time period $0 < t < T_1$. However, extensive simulations indicated that the case when v_{π_N} reaches one earlier than $v_{\pi_{N-1}}$ reaches zero is scarce. So we can make the following assumption.

Assumption 1 *The π_N^{th} neuron reaches one later than the π_{N-1}^{th} neuron reaching zero.*

Using the above assumption and Equation (6), we can readily deduce that

$$T_2 - T_1 = -\frac{1}{(N-1)\epsilon} \log \left[\frac{\sum_{k=2}^{N}(v_{\pi_k}(0) - v_{\pi_2}(0))}{\sum_{k=2}^{N}(v_{\pi_k}(0) - v_{\pi_1}(0))} \right], \tag{8}$$

$$T_3 - T_2 = -\frac{1}{(N-2)\epsilon} \log \left[\frac{\sum_{k=3}^{N}(v_{\pi_k}(0) - v_{\pi_3}(0))}{\sum_{k=3}^{N}(v_{\pi_k}(0) - v_{\pi_2}(0))} \right] \tag{9}$$

$$\cdots$$

and

$$T_{N-1} - T_{N-2} = -\frac{1}{2\epsilon} \log \left[\frac{\sum_{k=N-1}^{N}(v_{\pi_k}(0) - v_{\pi_{N-1}}(0))}{\sum_{k=N-1}^{N}(v_{\pi_k}(0) - v_{\pi_{N-2}}(0))} \right]. \tag{10}$$

Hence, the network response time $T_{rt} = T_{N-1}$, can be written explicitly as follows:

$$T_{rt} = \sum_{j=2}^{N-1} \frac{1}{j\epsilon} \log \left[\frac{\sum_{k=N+1-j}^{N}(v_{\pi_k}(0) - v_{\pi_{N-j}}(0))}{\sum_{k=N+1-j}^{N}(v_{\pi_k}(0) - v_{\pi_{N+1-j}}(0))} \right]$$

$$+ \frac{1}{N\epsilon} \log \left[\frac{\sum_{k=1}^{N} v_{\pi_k}(0)}{\sum_{k=1}^{N}(v_{\pi_k}(0) - v_{\pi_1}(0))} \right]. \tag{11}$$

It is interesting to note that the network response time is dependent solely on ϵ and the initial conditions of the neurons only.

5   Simulation Verification

Equation (11) indicates that the network response time relies on two factors: the initial conditions of the neurons' state potentials and the parameter ϵ for a fixed size of the network. But, it may be queried about the consistency of Equation (11) and the actual network response time because an assumption has been made prior to the derivation. In [2], we have demonstrated that Equation (11) is indeed a close approximation to the actual network response time. The results are listed here in the first two columns of Table 1. For the cases when $\beta > 0$, they are depicted from the third column to the sixth column.

For each specified pair of ϵ and β, the computer simulates the Equation (3) for $N = \{20, 24, 28, \ldots, 100\}$ and get 21 sampled network response times for such (ϵ, β). Then we repeat this run for additional 49 times with different initial conditions. Therefore, for each (ϵ, β), we collect altogether 21×50, i.e. 1050, sampled network response times. The average of these 1050 samples constitutes one entry listed on the table[1] Figure 1 shows the simulation results. The two solid lines correspond to the network response time of the simple WTA model while the four dash lines correspond to the network response time of the general WTA circuit.

In accordance with Table 1 and Figure 1, it is found that the simulated network response times of the general WTA model are well below to that of the simple model and also the response time evaluated by the analytical equation (11). Furthermore, it is also found that the decreasing trends of those response time curves (dash lines) are the same. We therefore suggest that the analytical equation (11) derived for the simple WTA model can be treated as an upper bound for those general WTAs.

---

[1] For the details of obtaining the first column, please refer to [2].

ϵ	$\beta = 0$ (eva.)	$\beta = 0$	$\beta = 0.05$	$\beta = 0.10$	$\beta = 0.15$	$\beta = 0.20$
0.6	2.5521	2.4870	2.4374	2.3084	2.1795	2.0508
0.7	2.1875	2.1263	2.0838	1.9734	1.8628	1.7522
0.8	1.9141	1.8559	1.7849	1.6898	1.5948	1.4999
0.9	1.7014	1.6454	1.5605	1.4773	1.4134	1.3106

Table 1: The network response time of WTA with different decay values β. The system is described as follows: $\frac{dv_i(t)}{dt} = -\beta v_i(t) + h(v_i(t)) - \epsilon \sum_{k=1}^{N} h(v_k(t))$. The first column corresponds to the case when $\beta = 0$ and the results are evaluated using the analytic equation. The second to the sixth column correspond to the results obtained from intensive computer simulation.

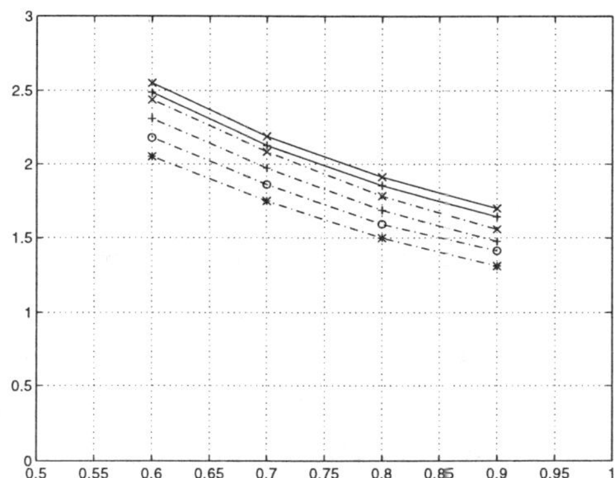

Figure 1: The average response time of the network for different values of ϵ and different values of β. The horizontal axis corresponds to the value of ϵ while the vertical axis corresponds to the response time. Solid lines are the cases when $\beta = 0$: solid-x is the evaluated and solid-+ is the actual. Dot-dash lines correspond to the cases when $\beta > 0$: $\beta = 0.05$ (dot-dash-x), $\beta = 0.10$ (dot-dash-+), $\beta = 0.15$ (dot-dash-o) and $\beta = 0.20$ (dot-dash-*).

6 Conclusion

In summary, we have reviewed a simple WTA model proposed in [1] and some of its properties. An analytical equation for its response time is presented – Equation (11). In accordance with extensive computer simulations, it is demonstrated that this equation can be treated as an upper bound for a more general class of WTA models. Hence, it can be treated as a cue for the design of those general WTA models.

References

[1] J. Sum and P. Tam, Design and analysis of a simple circuit for Winner-Take-All neural network, *submitted to IEEE Transaction on Circuit and System, Part I.*

[2] J. Sum and P. Tam, Network response time of a simple circuit for WTA, *submitted to IEEE Transaction on Circuit and System, Part I.*

[3] Y. Pao, *Adaptive Pattern Recognition and Neural Networks.* Addison-Wesley, 1989.

[4] R. Lippman, An introduction to computing with neural nets, *IEEE ASSP Magazine*, Vol. 4, pp.4-22, 1987.

[5] J. Lazzaro et.al., Winner-Take-All network of $O(N)$ complexity, *NIPS'89.* pp.703-711, 1989.

[6] G.L. Dempsey and E.S. McVey, Circuit implementation of a peak detector neural network, *IEEE Transactions on Circuits and Systems-II*, Vol.40, No.9, September, pp.585-591, 1993.

[7] J.J. Hopfield, Neurons with graded response have collective computational properties like those of two-state neurons. *Proceedings of National Academy of Sciences*, Vol.81, pp.3088-3092, 1984.

[8] G. Seiler and J. Nossek, Winner-Take-All cellular neural networks, *IEEE Transactions on Circuits and Systems-II*, Vol.40, No.3, March, pp.184-190, 1993.

[9] L. Chua and L. Yang, Cellular neural networks: theory, *IEEE Transactions on Circuits and Systems*, Vol.35, No.10, October, pp.1257-1272, 1988.

[10] A. Yuille and N. Grzywacz, A Winner-Take-All mechanism based on presynaptic inhibition feedback, *Neural Computation*, 1, 334-347, 1989.

An Artificial Chaotic Neural Network
For Image Feature Extraction

Harold Szu, Charles Hsu, Marie Erie, Michael Weeks
Center for Advanced Computer Studies, University of Southwestern Louisiana, Lafayette, LA
P. O. Box 44330, Lafayette, LA 70504, hszu@cacs.usl.edu

Abstract

We present a neuron model with a simple processor element, which is capable of generating chaos and can realize a synaptic Hebbian learning in the framework of artificial neural networks (ANN). The model is a variant of classical McCulloch-Pitts neurons. Thus, this model has been demonstrated with the bifurcation cascade toward chaos in the Feigenbaum sense. Furthermore, we have numerically investigated a large set of such neuron models. The neural images illustrate the iterative neurodynamics. The fixed-point attractor dynamics, based on the Hebbian learning rule of the synaptic weight matrix among all chaotic neurons, has generated a mean field of the iteration feedback baseline from other neurons. It reveals a spatially coherent neural image as the information content. To achieve an exponentially fast pattern recognition inherited from the iterative mapping chaos, designs of electronic implementation of chaotic ANN chip are desired. A modified N-shaped function, named as a piece-wise linear (PWL) N-shaped function, is designed and implemented by a voltage CMOS circuit, and a VLSI chip with two chaotic neurons was fabricated through MOSIS program. The chaotic behavior is analyzed and verified by Lyapunov exponents. The measurement diagnoses of the chip are demonstrated.

I. Introduction

This paper summarizes the biological and physical perspectives of neural network chaos for the purpose of efficient spatiotemporal information processing. Two major novel results are (i) class of a one-dimensional time-discrete analog neuron mapping model is demonstrated in an iterative fashion, without assuming replenishment delay, in order to exhibit Feigenbaum-like bifurcation cascades to chaos; (ii) the equilibrium ensemble of such a large set of chaotic neural networks (CNN) is insured because each neuron's input-output mapping baseline is changed according to a fixed-point Hebbian learning dynamics under the surrounding influence averaged over all other neurons. In Section II, the biological motivation of current trends of CNN's is succinctly itemized. The chaotic neural model is presented, and the feedback baseline function is given and compared to the role in the Feigunbaum logistic function. In Section III, the potential applications and the reasons for investigating artificial neural network (ANN) chaos are discussed. The simulation results of neural images are shown and demonstrated. In Section IV, the modified PWL N-shaped function to drive chaos is implemented by a VLSI chip. The SPICE simulations are used to demonstrate the chaotic behavior of the neuron. The CMOS circuit was fabricated using 2μ technology through MOSIS program. The chip measurement is included to illustrate the chaotic behavior of the proposed neuron model.

II. Theory of a Chaotic Neural Network

McCulloch-Pitts neuron [1], a classical model to which Caianiello introduced a refractory feature [2], is widely applied to construct an artificial neural network. The description of

McCulloch-Pitts neuron is shown in equation(1). In equation (1.b), a sigmoid function is used instead of a step function in McCulloh-Pitts model.

$$U_i(t_{n+1}) = \sum_{j \neq i}^{N} W_{ij}(t_n)V_j(t_n) \tag{1.a}$$

$$V_i(t_{n+1}) = \sigma(U_i(t_{n+1})) = \frac{1}{1 + e^{-U_i(t_{n+1})/\varepsilon}} \tag{1.b}$$

$$W_{ij}(t_n) = X_i(t_n)X_i(t_n) = (2V_i(t_n) - 1)(2V_j(t_n) - 1) \tag{2}$$

W_{ij} is the weight matrix which uses the bipolar Hebbian learning rule for the synaptic weights and accounts for excitation ($W_{ij} > 0$) and inhabitation ($W_{ij} < 0$). U_i is the input of the i-th neuron, and V_i is the output of the i-th neuron. t_n is at the discrete time, t_n. N is the number of neurons, and X_i is the biploar output of the i-th neuron. σ is the transfer function, and ε is a scale factor.

The transfer function in equation(1.b) can be replaced to be a sigmoid N-shaped function augmented with feedback so as to introduce the desired chaotic features into network. This modification is motivated by the observation by Matsumoto, *et al* [3] of chaos in electrophysiological experiments with squid axons. The breakdown in the experimentally observed transfer function can be modeled in a variety of ways, among which Aihara, *et al* [4,5] reproduce the physiological property of refractory delay. A simple model by Szu *et al* [6,7] employed as instantaneous mapping. The sigmoid N-shaped mapping function with a downslope is expressed in equation(3), and the graphic sigmoid N-shaped function is shown in Fig.1.

$$V_i(t_{n+1}) = \sigma_N(U_i(t_{n+1})) = \begin{cases} \dfrac{1}{1 + e^{-(U+0.5)/0.3}} & x < -0.5 \\ -0.5U + 0.25 & -0.5 \leq x < 0.5 \\ \dfrac{1}{1 + e^{-(U-0.5)/0.3}} - 1 & 0.5 \leq x \end{cases} \tag{3}$$

The downslope of σ_N for $-0.5 < U < 0.5$ provides the non-linearity of a chaotic map. Counter to the behavior of standard sigmoidal logic, more input will result in less output if the net firing rate falls within the domain of the downslope. This chaotic behavior may explain the phenomenon that external drug effects cause inhibition of certain firing channels. The σ_N map is consistent with the observations by Aihara and Matsumoto with respect to the input-output response of squid axons. In addition, this CNN model (equation 1-3) theoretically possesses the features of a Feigenbaum-like instantaneous quadratic map [8]. In the Feigunbaum logistic function, $V_n = f(U_n) = 4\lambda U_n (1-U_n)$ with λ-knob constant, describes, for example, the population of shrimps and fish under a constant food reserve λ. The bifurcation of Feigunbaum's logistic function in space of λ is shown in Fig.2. Recursive feedback with unit slope, $U_{n+1} = V_n$ gives equation(4).

$$k_n U_{n+1} = f(U_n) = 4\lambda U_n (1-U_n), \qquad K_n = 1 \text{ for all } n \tag{4}$$

Theorem: Assume a CNN model, (Eq.1-3), using sigmoid N-shaped mapping and Hebbian learning. Then a coupled set of logistic bifurcation maps follows with a time dependent slope,

$$K_n U_{n+1} = F(U_n) \tag{5}$$

where $F(U)$ is a bipolar version of $\sigma_N(U)$ and is shown in Fig.1.b.

Proof: From the bi-linear Hebbian learning rule (Eq. 2), the total net output (Eq. 1) follows:

$$U_i(t_{n+1}) = F_i(t_n) S_i(t_n) \tag{6}$$

where $S_i(t_n) \equiv \sum_{j \neq i}^{N} F_j(t_n) V_j(t_n)$ and $F_i(t_n) = 2\sigma_N(U_i(t_n)) - 1$ (substituting Eq.3 into Eq.2).

Suppressing index i, and representing t_n as subscript n with $F(U_n) \equiv F(t_n)$, the net output (Eq.6) is:

$$U_{n+1} = F(U_n)\, S_n \qquad ; \text{or} \qquad \frac{1}{S_n} U_{n+1} = F(U_n) \tag{7}$$

Define $K_n = 1/S_n$ to obtain equation 5: $K_n U_{n+1} = F(U_n)$.

$F(U)$ serves a role analogous to the logistic map $f(U)$ above with the exception that $F(U)$ must eventually saturate as the input increases, as dictated by sigmoidal logic. $S_i(t_n)$ represents the surrounding medium's contribution to the update of unit i. The feedback slope is K_n (cf. Eq. 4 & 5), and the lines drawn through Fig.3.b,c,d are exemplary feedback. This recursive feedback is due to output firing rates eventually returning to the neuron from the changing surrounding medium. For simplicity, only one single neuron is considered; the bifurcation spectrum of σ_N in space of K_n is displayed in Fig.3.a. Fig.3.b,c,d shows the behavior of σ_N with different K_ns. Although K_n is a complex function of a given unit's surrounding CNN state at the time t_n, we nonetheless expect that the formalism presented here should generate a bifurcation cascade toward chaos, characteristic of the logistic map $f(U)$. Indeed, the simulation discussed below seems to support this expectation.

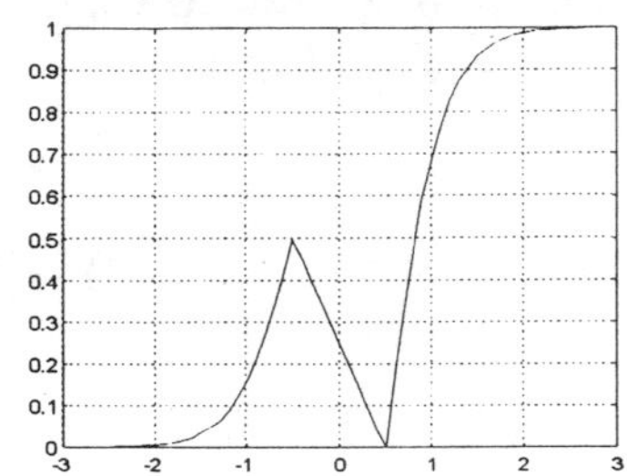

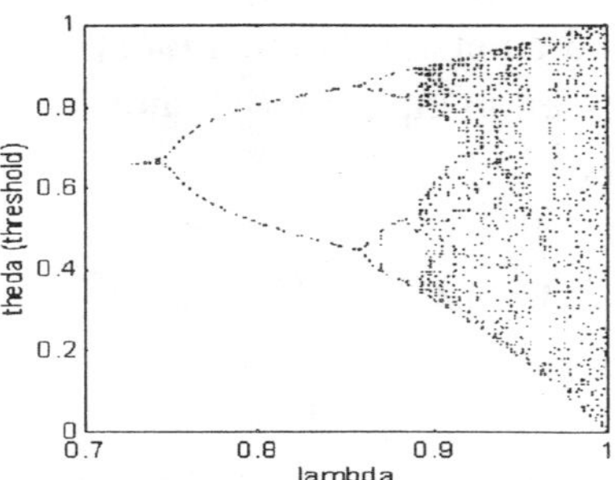

Fig.1.a   Uni-polar $\sigma_N(U)$ function   Fig.1.b Bipolar $\sigma_N(U)$ function   Fig.2 Bifurcation spectrum of Eq.4

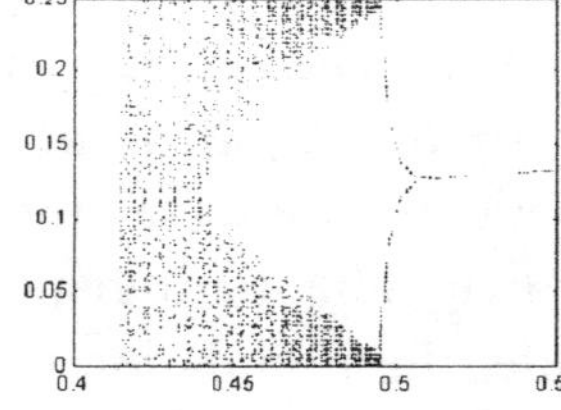

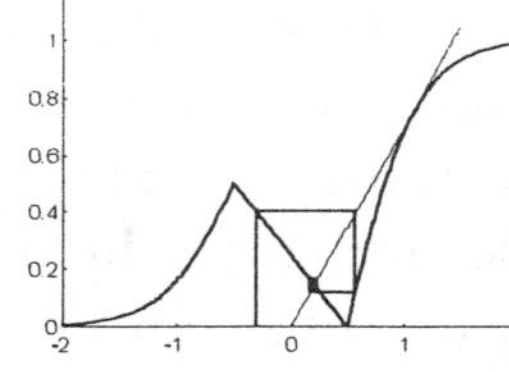

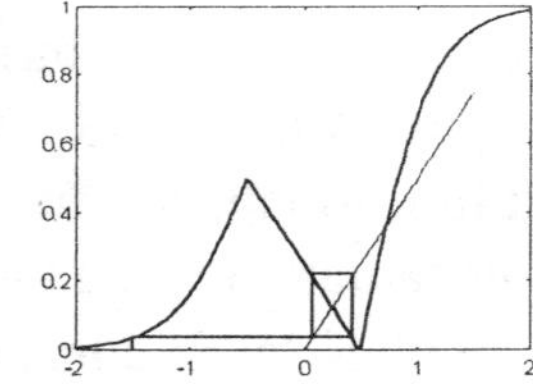

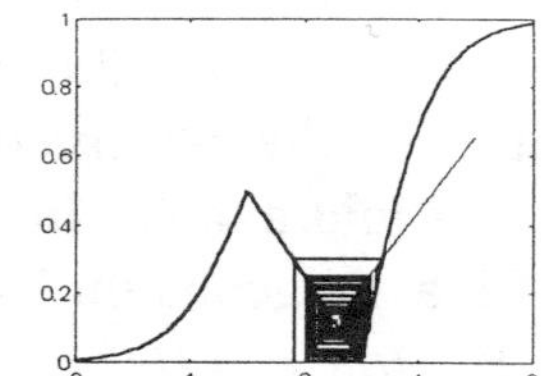

a. Bifurcation spectrum   **b**. convergent when $K_n>.5$ **c**. oscillation when $K_n=.5$ **d**. chaotic when $K_n<.5$

Fig.3

III. Simulations and Results

The behavior of a neural network composed of 27x36 fully connected N-shaped sigmoidal neurons governed by Hebbian learning is illustrated by image processing. We study the perception habituation. Simulation steps are given as follows:

1. Initiation of Bipolar Memory: Substitution of image **I** (row 1, column 1 in Fig.4) into Eq.2:

$$W_i = (x(\mathbf{I})_i\, x(\mathbf{I})_j - \delta_{ij}\, x(\mathbf{I})_i\, x(\mathbf{I})_j) \equiv [x(\mathbf{I})_i\, x(\mathbf{I})_j] = W_{ij}^{t=1} \tag{8.a}$$

2. N-shaped sigmoidal output of unipolar image (row 1, column 2 in Fig.4):

$$V_i^{t=1} = \sigma_N(U_i^{t=1})$$ (8.b)

3. Updated U_i^{t+1} by Hebbian learning algorithm in Eq. 2:

$$U_i^{t+1} = X_i^t \sum_{j \neq i}^{N} (2X_j^t - 1)X_j^t$$ (8.c)

4. N-shaped sigmoidal output of image (top left 3rd in Fig.4):

$$V_i^t = \sigma_N(U_i^t)$$ (8.d)

Repeat the above processes 3 and 4, fifteen iterations plus the original image are displayed in Fig.4. From the result of the simulation, it can be observed that (1) the image is bifurcated and oscillates and (2) the output values of neurons are roughly among 0,0.25 and 1. When we take a close look at the sigmoid N-shaped function, two attractors (0 and 1) of the iteration feedback baseline function in Eq.8.c can be observed and are shown in Fig.5. In addition, we discover that if U = 0, V = σ_N(U) = σ_N(0) = 0.25 from Fig.5. Chaos behavior of two linear functions has been shown in [9]. The convergence of the intersection of the baseline function and the sigmoid N-shaped function σ_N is illustrated as follows. The three results can be summarized : (1) if |n| = |b|, the system is oscillated; (2) if |n| < |b|, the system is convergent; (3) if |n| > |b|, the system is divergent which could produce chaos. (n and b are the slopes of the negative segment of σ_N function, and the baseline function respectively.) The characteristics of the three attractors can help to extract the images.

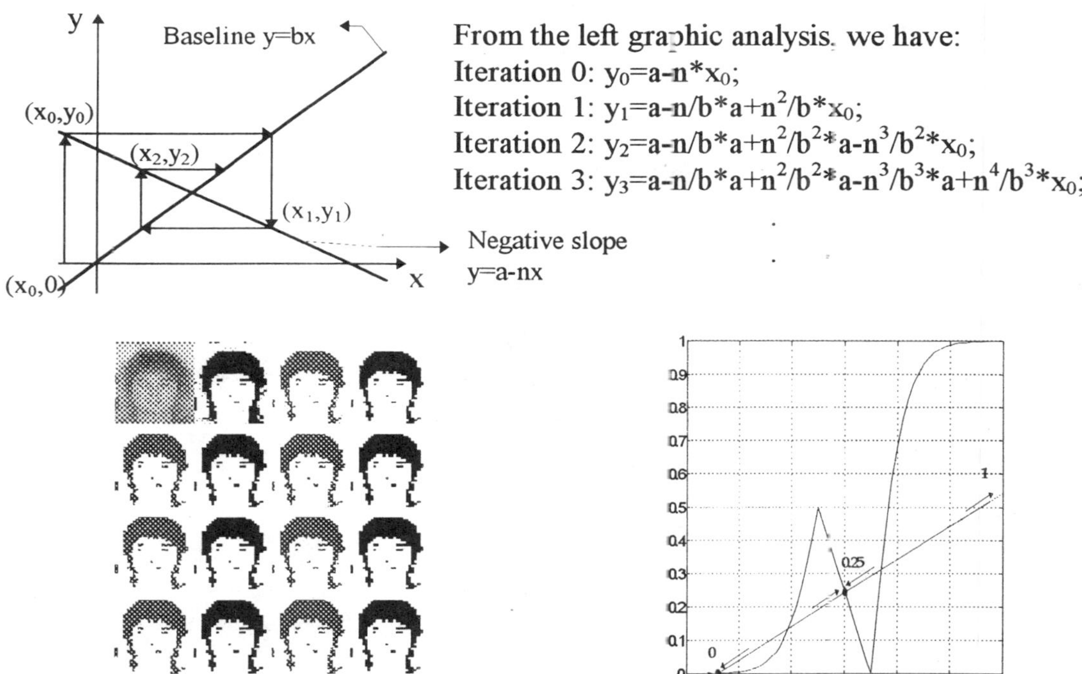

Fig.4 15 iterations plus the original image   Fig.5. The characteristic of the three attractors in σ_N

IV. Hardware Implementation

The chaotic neural network can be implemented by CMOS voltage/current mode circuits. [10, 11] In this section, the CMOS voltage mode of the neural model with the PWL N-shaped function is represented by the block diagram of Fig.6. V_n in Fig.7 is the control voltage for changing a of the PWL N-shaped function. V_c, and V_a in Fig. 7 are the control voltages to change the parameters a and c of the *baseline* function in Fig.6. The circuit is easily implemented in CMOS technology. A possible integration is shown in Fig. 7. In our circuit realization, parameter a of the *baseline* function is fixed at value one. Parameter c, which represents external inputs to the neuron from the other neurons, can be easily varied by the voltage V_c. V_n is the control voltage for the parameter a. a is realized as a ratio of resistances of a variable resistor and a passive resistor connected in series. SPICE simulations of phase diagrams for some chosen cases are shown in Fig.8. The voltage-mode CMOS chaotic neuron was fabricated in a VLSI chip through MOSIS program. The whole layout of chip is shown in Fig.10. The VLSI chip with two chaotic neurons was fabricated by using 2μ technology through MOSIS program. Two measurements of the chaotic chip are shown in Fig.9.

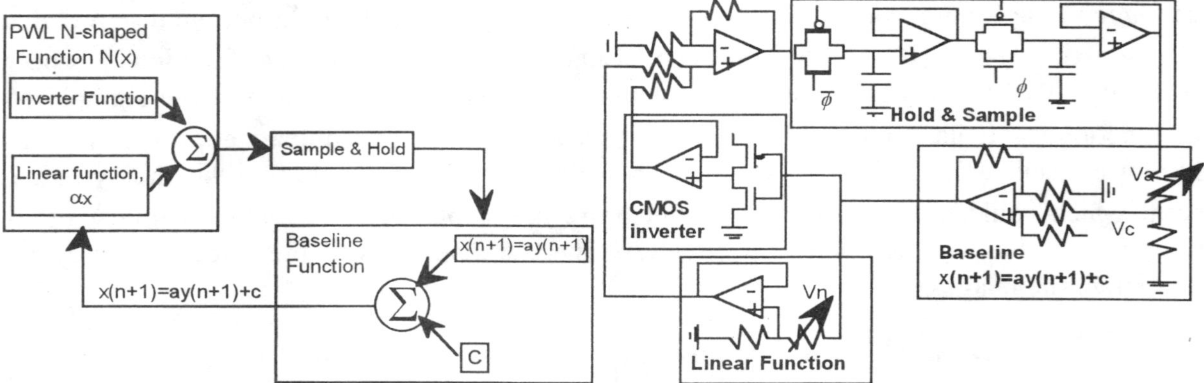

Fig.6 Conceptual Block diagram of one chaotic neuron   Fig.7 Circuit realization of one chaotic neuron, where V_a, V_n, V_c are controlled voltages.

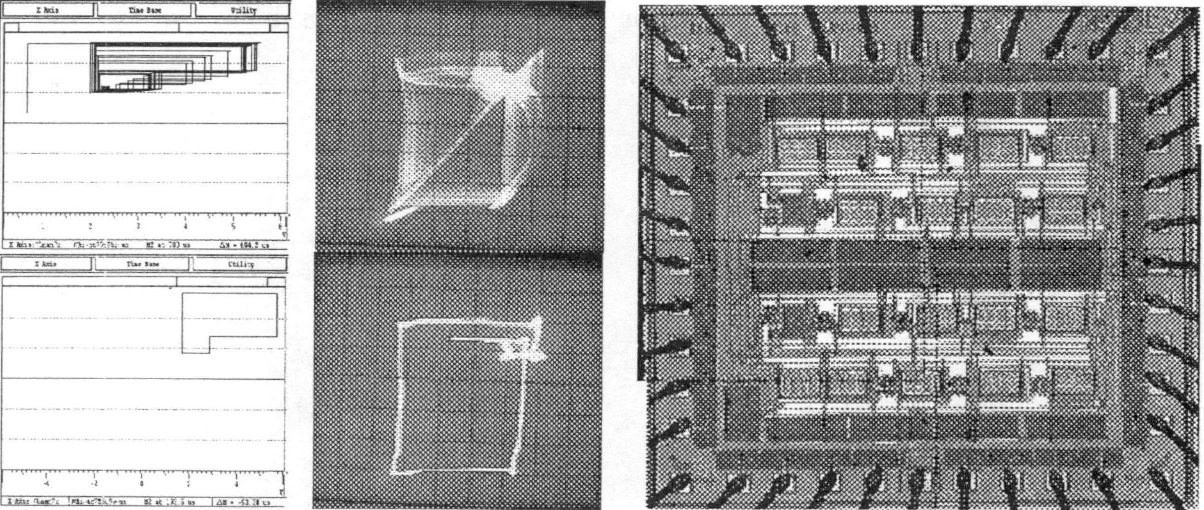

Fig.8. SPICE simulations   Fig.9 Chip measurements   Fig.10 Physical Chip layout

V. Conclusion

Collective interaction of nonlinear dynamics can yield an emergent reduction in the dimensionality or degrees of freedom among individual chaos--the locking or quenching in a collective chaos. The characteristic of three attractors of the sigmoid function, σ_N, can be applied into the feature extraction of image processing. The baseline iteration function in Eq.8.c is given and the diagnoses of the chaotic behavior are analyzed in Section II and the simulation is given in Section III. The collective artificial neurons with the σ_N function may response to the external drug effects. Noise phenomena can produce a de-locking of the "coherence" effect of collective chaos--the switch-off of the collective chaos. The latter will be reported elsewhere. We have introduced the (artificial) neural images as the graphical output of collective behaviors. Indeed, these figures have supported that goal of reduced dimensionality in the collective chaos. The chaotic behavior of the neuron model is simulated numerically, and the chaotic behavior of the neuron circuit is verified by SPICE simulation. The VLSI chip with two chaotic neurons was fabricated through MOSIS program. The measurements of the chip correspond to the theoretical expectations. Further work is planned to demonstrate technology applications based on the emergent collective property of neural chaos, such as real time chaos information processing, and control of chaotic dynamics using chaos neurochips.

VI. Reference

[1]. W.S. McCulloch, W.H. Pitts, " *Bull. Math. Biophys.* 5, (1943), pp. 115.

[2]. E.R. Caianiello, "Outline of a Theory of Thought-Process and Thinking Machines," *J. Theor. Biol.*, 2, 1961, pp. 204-235.

[3]. T. Matsumoto, L. O. Chua, and M. Komuro, " The Double Scroll,*" IEEE Transactions on Circuits and Systems*, Vol. CAS-32, No. 8, August 1985, pp. 798-818

[4]. K. Aihara, T. Takbe, M.Toyoda, "Chaotic Neural Networks," *Phys. Lett. A,* Vol. 144, No. 6,7, March 1990, pp. 333-340.

[5]. N. Kanou, Y. Horio, K. Aihara, S. Nakamura, "A Current-Mode Circuit of a Chaotic Neuron Model," *Proc. of the 35th Midwest Symposium on Circuits and Systems,* Washington, DC, Aug. 1992, pp. 1530-1533.

[6]. H. Szu, G. Rogers," Single Neuron Chaos," IJCNN-92 Baltimore,Vol. III,pp.103-108. H. Szu, G. Rogers,"Generalized McCullouch-Pitts Neuron Model with Threshold Dynamics,"IJCNN-92 Baltimore,Vol. III,pp.535-540 (June 7-11,1992).

[7]. H. Szu, B. Telfer, G.Rogers, D. Gobovic, C. Hsu, M. Zaghloul, W. Freeman, "Spationtemporal Chaos Information Processing in Neural Networks-Electronic Implementation," World Conference of Neural Network, Oregon, pp719-734, July 1993

[8]. D.R. Hofstadter, "Metamagical Themas: Questing for the Essence of Mind and Pattern," Chapter 16 ("Mathematical Chaos and Strange Attractors"), Basic Books: NY, 1985, pp364-395

[9]. Charles C. Hsu, "Chaotic Neural Network Model and VLSI implementation", Dissertation of Doctor of Science, Electrical Engineering and Computer Science Department, The George Washington University, Washington D.C..

[10]. A. Rodriguez-Vazquez, J.L. Huertas, A. Rueda, B. Perez-Verdu, L.O. Chua, "Chaos from Switched-Capacitor Circuits: Discrete Maps," *Proceeding of the IEEE*, Vol. 75, No. 8, August 1987, pp. 1090-1106.

[11]. Charles C. Hsu, Desa Gobovic, Mona Zaghloul, and Harold Szu, "Chaotic Neuron Models and Their VLSI Circuit Implementations", accepted by IEEE transaction on Neural Network, #TNN2376.

Chaotic-Classified Properties and Application in Cryptography of Hopfield Neural Network under Overstorage

Donghui Guo[1,2], L.M.Cheng[1], L.L.Cheng[1],
Zhenxiang Chen[2], Ruitang Liu[2], Boxi Wu[2]

[1] *Department of Electronic Engineering, City University of Hong Kong, Hong Kong.*
E-mail: eedhguo@plink.cityu.edu.hk Fax: (852)2788-7791 Tel: (852)2788-9897
[2] *Department of Physics, Xiamen University, Xiamen 361005, P.R.China.*
E-mail: rtliu@xmu.edu.cn Fax: (86)592-2181673 Tel: (86)592-2182459

Abstract

In this paper, some chaotic-classified properties of Hopfield Neural Network (HNN) under over-storage were presented and analyzed by computer simulations. With the synaptic matrix or stored patterns of HNN being changed, the convergent domains of every stored patterns will vary chaotically and drastically. By mean of concealing the stored patterns with elements of their chaotic convergent domains to eliminate the statistic probabilities of plaintext characters, the chaotic-classified properties of HNN can be used for data encryption with great security.

1   Introduction

In the last few years, some spin-glass models of neural network which can show the properties of associative memory have attracted popular attentions of many scientists[1-3]. Such as the Hopfield model[1] which is one of most typical and wide influence network, it regards recalling memories as a dynamic course of the dynamic network's system and stores memory patterns on system stable attractors. The dynamics of the network's system can be investigated by using statistical mechanics, because it is possible to define an energy of the network which obeys detailed balance. And, the storage capacity of associative memories of the network is one of the most perfect results which can be derived by the methods of statistical physics[2,3]. However, if the number of stored patterns exceeds the maximal storage capacity of associative memory, attractors of the network's system will become irregular and can not attract messages in minimal Hamming-Distance way but chaotically. In this paper, we will mainly describe some special properties of the chaotic-attractive phenomena in the overstorage neural network, and find an application of them into cryptography.

2   The Principle of Chaotic Attraction

In general, neural networks can be traced back to the McCulloch-Pitts Neuron Model[4] and Hebb Learning Ruller[5]. For the simplest case, we consider a network of N neurons, in which each neuron is a non-linear threshold unit with two states (0,1) and all of the neurons are totally interconnected. In the course of the network's system evolution, the next state of each neuron depends on current states of other neurons in following way:

$$S_i(t+1) = f(\sum_{j=0}^{N-1} T_{ij}S_j - \theta_i) \qquad i = 0, \cdots, N-1. \tag{1}$$

where T_{ij} is the synaptic strength of neuron i receiving information from neuron j, θ_i is the threshold value of neuron i, and the nonlinear function $f(\cdot)$ is a sigma function: $f(x) = \sigma(x) = \{ \begin{array}{ll} 1, & x \geq 0 \\ 0, & x < 0 \end{array}$.

In the neural network of Hopfield Model[1], the value of neuron threshold is defined as: $\theta_i = 0$; and synaptic matrix was made up of stored patterns S^μ as follow:

$$W_{ij} = \left\{ \begin{array}{ll} \sum_{\mu=0}^{P-1}(2S_i^\mu - 1)(2S_j^\mu - 1), & i \neq j \\ 0, & i = j \end{array} \right. \qquad i,j = 0, \cdots, N-1. \tag{2}$$

where $S^\mu \in \{0,1\}^N$, $\mu = 0, \cdots, P-1$. In order to be implemented easily in silicon or optic devices, clipped model of the neural network is the most interesting subject in our research. Its synaptic matrix is defined as:

$$T_{ii} = 1 \qquad and \qquad T_{ij} = \phi(W_{ij}) = \left\{ \begin{array}{ll} 1, & W_{ij} > 0 \\ 0, & W_{ij} = 0 \\ -1, & W_{ij} < 0 \end{array} \right. \tag{3}$$

With system energy (or Liapunov function) of neural network defined by Hopfield as follow:

$$E = -\frac{1}{2} \sum_{i,j} T_{ij} S_i S_j \tag{4}$$

for the symmetric matrix T, it is easy to prove that: the system energy is monotone decreasing in system evolution[1]. Since the system energy is bounded, the network's system must converges to a stable state from any initial state. We called the stable state as a attractor of system. That the stable states of system attract messages in minimal Hamming Distance way is generally referred as associating memories of neural network.

If the ratio of P/N of the neural network is small enough, the system can store all patterns at the local minima of energy space and show perfectly the function of associative memory. Based on the results of the methods of statistical physics[2,3], the maximum associative memory capacity of the system is no more than $0.15N$(i.e. $P/N < 0.15$). And, if the number of patterns in Eq.2 is more than the maximum capacity of associative memory, the patterns will not be stored at the states of local minima of the system energy space, or the patterns are still stored at the states of local minima of the system energy but attract the messages chaotically instead of in minimal Hamming Distance way.

Where, we were more interested in the later case of above phenomena and called it as chaotic-classified attraction in the neural network under overstorage. After having investigated the overstorage neural network by computer simulations, we can give out some properties of chaotic-classified attraction in the next section.

3   Chaotic-Classified Properties

As known from Eq.1, any pattern S^m wished to be stored as the state of local minimal energy for attracting messages should firstly obey the following stable condition:

$$S_i^m = \begin{cases} 1, & \sum_{j=0}^{N-1} T_{ij} S_j^m \geq 0 \\ 0, & \sum_{j=0}^{N-1} T_{ij} S_j^m < 0 \end{cases} \qquad i = 0, \cdots, N-1 \tag{5}$$

Then, the stability and the convergent property of stored patterns depend on the distribution of $\{-1, 0, 1\}$ in the clipped synaptic matrix T_{ij}.

In N-dimension state space of system, it is known to have 2^N pieces of message states. The number of the states which are of N_0 inactive neuron ($S_i = 0$) or of $N - N_0$ active neuron ($S_i = 1$) is $C_N^{N_0}$. And, the states that the number of active neuron or inactive is about $\frac{N}{2}$ are in the majority. According to the view-points of statistical probability method for the Eq.5, to obtain more attractors and larger convergent domain of each attractors, the synaptic matrix T_{ij} should be built up as that the number of "1" is equal to the number " -1" in each line and each row.

In order to test the above ideas, we choose $P = 8$ pieces of the stored patterns of $N = 8$ as: $S^0 = 11111000$, $S^1 = 11110001$, $S^2 = 11100011$, $S^3 = 11000111$, $S^4 = 10001111$, $S^5 = 00011111$, $S^6 = 00111110$, $S^7 = 01111100$. The required synaptic matrix T_{ij} can be built by Eq.2 and Eq.3 as follow:

$$T = \begin{pmatrix} 1 & 1 & 0 & -1 & -1 & -1 & 0 & 1 \\ 1 & 1 & 1 & 0 & -1 & -1 & -1 & 0 \\ 0 & 1 & 1 & 1 & 0 & -1 & -1 & -1 \\ -1 & 0 & 1 & 1 & 1 & 0 & -1 & -1 \\ -1 & -1 & 0 & 1 & 1 & 1 & 0 & -1 \\ -1 & -1 & -1 & 0 & 1 & 1 & 1 & 0 \\ 0 & -1 & -1 & -1 & 0 & 1 & 1 & 1 \\ 1 & 0 & -1 & -1 & -1 & 0 & 1 & 1 \end{pmatrix} \tag{6}$$

With the message states all over the 8-dimension state space being put into the network for Eq.1 iterating by computer simulation, the 8 pieces of stored patterns are all on the points of local minima of the system energy, and each pattern can attract $k = 20$ pieces of messages such as listed in *Tab.*1. As known from every convergent domains of stored patterns S^μ in any columns of *Tab.*1, we can found following property:

Property 1: *The relation of any messages in the same convergent domain to the attractor is irregular and chaotic instead of in minimal Hamming Distance. Furthermore, the "1" and "0" in the convergent domain of every attractors are of same probabilities.*

Table 1: The chaotic-classified table of $N = 8$ neural network with the synaptic matrix T of $Eq.6$.

S^μ	11111000	11110001	11100011	11000111	10001111	00011111	00111110	01111100
	$\xi^{0\nu}$	$\xi^{1\nu}$	$\xi^{2\nu}$	$\xi^{3\nu}$	$\xi^{4\nu}$	$\xi^{5\nu}$	$\xi^{6\nu}$	$\xi^{7\nu}$
	00100000	01000000	01000001	00000001	00000010	00000100	00001000	00010000
	00110001	01010001	01001001	00100011	00000101	00001010	00010100	00101000
	01010000	01100001	01100011	01000011	00000111	00001101	00011001	00101001
	01010010	01100010	01101011	01000101	00001011	00001110	00011010	00110010
	01100100	01110011	10000000	01100111	00010011	00010101	00011100	00110100
	01101000	10100000	10010001	10000010	00100101	00010110	00101010	00111000
	01110000	10100100	10100001	10000011	00100111	00011011	00101100	00111001
	01110010	10110001	10100010	10000101	01000110	00011111	00110110	01010100
A^μ	01110101	10110101	10110011	10001001	01001111	00100110	00111011	01011000
	01111001	11001000	11000001	10010010	01010111	00101111	00111101	01101100
	10101000	11010000	11000010	10010011	10000110	00110111	00111110	01101101
	10110000	11011001	11000100	10100111	10001010	01001010	01001100	01110110
	10111001	11100000	11001001	10101011	10001101	01001110	01011101	01111010
	11011000	11100100	11010011	11000110	10001111	01011011	01011110	01111100
	11011010	11101001	11010101	11000111	10010111	01011111	01101110	01111101
	11101100	11101010	11100011	11001011	10011011	10001100	01111111	10011000
	11110100	11110001	11100101	11001101	10101101	10011101	10010100	10111010
	11111000	11110010	11100110	11010110	10101111	10011110	10011100	10111100
	11111010	11110101	11101011	11010111	11001110	10101110	10110110	11011100
	11111101	11111011	11110111	11101111	11011111	10111111	10111110	11111110

Besides the example of $N = 8$, the large scale networks (such as $N = 10$, $N = 12$, $N = 16$, and etc.) also had been simulated by computer, and the same properties of these networks had also been obtained.

According to the system energy defined in Eq.4, the state energy distribution of neural network or the convergent domains of every attractors will vary with any stored patterns or any elements of the synaptic matrix being changed. For example, if a random permutation H such as $(0, 1, 2, 3, 4, 5, 6, 7) \rightarrow (4, 7, 2, 1, 6, 0, 3, 5)$ is given for changing the stored patterns S^μ or the synaptic matrix T, the new synaptic matrix $\hat{T}$ can be given in following way:

$$\hat{T}_{ij} = \phi[\sum_{\mu=0}^{P-1}(2\hat{S}_i^\mu - 1)(2\hat{S}_j^\mu - 1)] = \phi[\sum_{\mu=0}^{P-1}(2HS_i^\mu - 1)(2HS_j^\mu - 1)]$$

$$= HT\tilde{H} = \begin{pmatrix} 1 & -1 & 0 & -1 & 0 & -1 & 1 & 1 \\ -1 & 1 & -1 & 0 & 1 & 1 & -1 & 0 \\ 0 & -1 & 1 & 1 & -1 & 0 & 1 & -1 \\ -1 & 0 & 1 & 1 & -1 & 1 & 0 & -1 \\ 0 & 1 & -1 & -1 & 1 & 0 & -1 & 1 \\ -1 & 1 & 0 & 1 & 0 & 1 & -1 & -1 \\ 1 & -1 & 1 & 0 & -1 & -1 & 1 & 0 \\ 1 & 0 & -1 & -1 & 1 & -1 & 0 & 1 \end{pmatrix} \qquad (7)$$

where $\tilde{H}$ is the transposed matrix of H. With exhaustively searching over the 8-dimension state space in Eq.1, the new 8 pieces of stored patterns $\hat{S}^\mu = HS^\mu$ are also all on the points of local minima of the system energy, and each one can attract $k = 20$ pieces of new messages such as listed in $Tab.2$. As known from Tab.1 and Tab.2, the messages "00100000", "01110000" and "11111101" are all belong to the same convergent domain of the pattern $S^0 = (11111000)$ of the network with T. However, in the network's system of synaptic matrix $\hat{T}$, the message "00100000", "0111000" and "11111101" are attracted to the patterns of $\hat{S}^0 = (10110110)$, $\hat{S}^1 = (01110110)$ and $\hat{S}^3 = (01011101)$, respectively. So that, a property of the chaotic-classified attraction can be given as in *Property 2*.

Property 2: *If the random permutation H is kept in secret, it is too difficult to determine whether the messages (such as "00100000", "0111000" and "11111101") are belong to same convergent domain, or which attractors the messages will converge to.*

At the same time, if the convergent domains of attractors S^μ in the network's system of synaptic matrix T are indicated as $A^\mu\{A^\mu|\xi^{\mu\nu}\}$ (where $\xi^{\mu\nu}$ is any element in the convergent domains A^μ), and

Table 2: The chaotic-classified table of $N = 8$ neural network with the synaptic matrix $\hat{T}$ of $Eq.7$.

$\hat{S}^\mu$	10110110	01110110	01111100	01011101	11001101	11001011	10101011	10110011
	$\hat{\xi}^{0\nu}$	$\hat{\xi}^{1\nu}$	$\hat{\xi}^{2\nu}$	$\hat{\xi}^{3\nu}$	$\hat{\xi}^{4\nu}$	$\hat{\xi}^{5\nu}$	$\hat{\xi}^{6\nu}$	$\hat{\xi}^{7\nu}$
	00010010	00010000	00000100	00001100	00001000	00000001	00000011	00000010
	00011010	00010110	00010101	00001110	00001101	00001011	00000111	00010011
	00100000	00100100	00011100	00011101	00011001	00101001	00101011	00100011
	00100110	00100101	00101100	00011111	01000001	01000011	00101111	00101010
	00110001	00110100	00111101	01000000	01001001	01101011	10000000	00111011
	00110010	00110101	01000110	01000101	01001010	10000101	10000011	10000110
	00110111	00111000	01010000	01001100	01001111	10001000	10000111	10010010
	00111010	00111110	01010100	01001110	01011011	10001001	10001010	10010111
$\hat{A}^\mu$	01100010	01010010	01010111	01010001	01100001	10001111	10010001	10100000
	01110011	01100110	01011110	01011000	01101001	10011000	10011011	10100010
	10010110	01100111	01100100	01011101	10001100	10011001	10100001	10100111
	10011110	01110000	01101110	01011111	10011101	10101101	10101000	10101110
	10100100	01110110	01110101	01101000	11000101	11000001	10101011	10110001
	10110000	01110111	01111000	01101101	11001000	11000111	10101111	10110011
	10110101	01111010	01111100	01111001	11001101	11001010	10111001	10111010
	10110110	10010100	01111111	11000100	11001110	11001011	11000010	10111111
	10111110	10111100	11010000	11010101	11011001	11011010	11010011	11100000
	11100110	11010110	11010100	11011100	11011111	11011011	11100011	11100010
	11110010	11110100	11111000	11101100	11100101	11101001	11101010	11110001
	11110111	11111110	11111100	11111101	11101101	11101111	11111011	11110011

anyone message such as $\hat{\xi}^{\mu\nu} = H\xi^{\mu\nu}$ is put into the network's system of synaptic matrix $\hat{T}$ as initial state $S(0)$, the evolution of the system can be given as follow:

$$
\begin{aligned}
S(\infty) = \{\cdots\cdots\} = S_i(1) \;&=\; \sigma[\sum_{j=0}^{N-1} \hat{T}_{ij} S_j(0)] \\
&=\; \sigma[\sum_{j=0}^{N-1} \hat{T}_{ij} H\xi_j^{\mu\nu}] \\
&=\; \sigma[\sum_{j=0}^{N-1} HT_{ij}\tilde{H}H\xi_j^{\mu\nu}] \\
&=\; H\sigma[\sum_{j=0}^{N-1} T_{ij}\xi_j^{\mu\nu}] \\
&=\; HS_i(1) \Longrightarrow HS(\infty) = HS^\mu = \hat{S}^\mu \qquad (8)
\end{aligned}
$$

where $\{\cdots\cdots\}$ is referred as the course of system's iteration; where $i, j = 0, \cdots, N-1$; $\mu = 0, \cdots, P-1$; $\nu = 0, \cdots, \Lambda\text{-}1$. The above equation of system evolution means that: the state HS^μ must be an attractor $\hat{S}^\mu$ of the network with the synaptic matrix $\hat{T} = HT\tilde{H}$, and any message $\hat{\xi}\mu\nu = H\xi^{\mu\nu}$ must be attracted to and just only be attracted to the convergent domains $\hat{A}^\mu\{\hat{A}^\mu|\hat{\xi}^{\mu\nu}\}$ of the attractor $\hat{S}^\mu = HS^\mu$. However, it is still too difficult to determine which message in the convergent domains A^μ (such as A^0) of T network is correspond to the message (Such as "10010110" in Tab.2) in $\hat{A}^0$ of $\hat{T}$ network, if the random permutation H is kept in secret. So that, an other property of the chaotic-classified attraction can be concluded as in *Property 3*.

Property 3: *Even if all the elements in the convergent domains $\hat{A}^\mu$ and in the convergent domains A^μ are known, it is difficult to calculate the permutation matrix H.*

Based on the above properties, we can find a possible application of the clipped Hopfield neural network in cryptography. In the next section, the details of the new cryptographic scheme will be given out.

4   Application in Cryptography

Based on the *Property 1*, every stored pattern stored in the clipped HNN is of a set of elements which have no obviously relations between each other. So that, the method concealing the stored patterns with any one element in their chaotic convergent domains can be used to eliminate the statistic probabilities of plaintext characters. And, if the random permutation H and a random substitution M are kept in secret, the special chaotic-classified properties of neural network described in the previous section can be applied in cryptography with great security in following schemes:

Encryption

1. Choose stored patterns S^μ to establish an available synaptic matrix T (such as T in the Eq.6 of $N = 8$), which can meet the above statistic rule of that the number of "1" should be equal to the number " -1" in each line and each row.

2. Random key-in a few parameters as a secret key to give out a random permutation matrix H and a random substitution matrix M, then produce the new stored patterns $\hat{S}^\mu$ and the new synaptic matrix $\hat{T}$ (such as Eq.7).

3. Search all messages in state space, and build up the table of chaotic attractive domains $\hat{A}^\mu$.

4. Use the random substitution matrix M to encoding the plaintext Y into $Y_x\{Y_x|\hat{S}^\mu\}$ with the new stored patterns S^μ.

5. The new patterns S^μ are random substituted by any element $\hat{\xi}^{\mu\nu}$ in their convergent domain. Then, the plaintext Y is encrypted to ciphertext $X\{X|\hat{\xi}^{\mu\nu}\}$

For example: With a neural network of $N = 8$ applied in the encryption scheme, we can choose $P = 8$ pieces of stored patterns: $S^0 = 11111000$, $S^1 = 11110001$, $S^2 = 11100011$, $S^3 = 11000111$, $S^4 = 10001111$, $S^5 = 00011111$, $S^6 = 00111110$, $S^7 = 01111100$; and give out the synaptic matrix T as in E.6. Afterwards, we can random key-in a secret key to produce a permutation matrix H and a substitution matrix M. If the random permutation matrix H is give as $(0, 1, 2, 3, 4, 5, 6, 7) \rightarrow (4, 7, 2, 1, 6, 0, 3, 5)$), $P = 8$ pieces of new patterns (i.e., $\hat{S}^0 = 10110110$, $\hat{S}^1 = 01110110$, $\hat{S}^2 = 01111100$, $\hat{S}^3 = 01011101$, $\hat{S}^4 = 11001101$, $\hat{S}^5 = 11001011$, $\hat{S}^6 = 10101011$, and $\hat{S}^7 = 10110011$) and the new synaptic matrix $\hat{T}$ can be obtained to search for a chaotic-classified table (such as Tab.2). Moreover, any plaintext can be encoded into block code for every 3-bit, such as:

$$000 \rightarrow 0, \quad 001 \rightarrow 1, \quad 010 \rightarrow 2, \quad 011 \rightarrow 3, \quad 100 \rightarrow 4, \quad 101 \rightarrow 5, \quad 110 \rightarrow 6, \quad 111 \rightarrow 7.$$

And, the substitution matrix M is given out for the random substitution of the numbers 0, 1, 2, 3, 4, 5, 6 and 7 with $\hat{S}^5$, $\hat{S}^2$, $\hat{S}^1$, $\hat{S}^0$, $\hat{S}^7$ $\hat{S}^4$, $\hat{S}^3$ and $\hat{S}^6$, respectively. Then, such as a plaintext of 3-bit "101", it can be encrypted as follow:

$$101 \rightarrow 5 \qquad \xrightarrow{\text{Substitution(M)}} \qquad \hat{S}^4\,(11001101) \qquad \xrightarrow{\text{Concealment }(\hat{A}^\mu)} \qquad 01101001$$

$$\text{Plaintext } Y \qquad\qquad \text{Attractor } \hat{S}^\mu \qquad\qquad \text{Ciphertext } X\,(\hat{\xi}^{\mu\nu})$$

where the ciphertext "01101001" is random chosen from the convergent domain $\hat{A}^4$ of pattern $S^4(11001101)$. Such as one ASCII characters "F''" in plaintext, it maybe encrypted the message of "WJP''" in the ciphertext.

Decryption

1. Key-in the secret key to get the same permutation H and substitution M.

2. According to the stored patterns S^μ and the synaptic matrix T, to give out the new patterns $\hat{S}^\mu$ and the synaptic matrix $\hat{T}$ with the permutation matrix H.

3. Put the ciphertext $X\{X|\hat{\xi}^{\mu\nu}\}$ into the Equation (1) for iterating, and $Y_x\{Y_x|\hat{S}^\mu\}$ is given out.

4. With the substitution matrix M, decode $Y_x\{Y_x|\hat{S}^\mu\}$ into plaintext Y.

For example: if a ciphertext such as "01101001" is received, we can have the same permutation H and substitution M with the same secret key, and give out the same stored patterns $\hat{S}^\mu$ and the same synaptic matrix $\hat{T}$. With the ciphertext put into the network as the initial state $S(0) = 01101001$, then the plaintext can be obtained as following process:

$$S(\infty) \quad = \quad \{\cdots\cdots\} \quad = S_i(1) = \sigma[\sum_{j=0}^{N-1} \hat{T}_{ij} S_i(0)], \quad i = 0, \cdots, N-1.$$

$$\underset{\Longrightarrow}{\overset{\text{Convergence}}{\quad}} \quad \hat{S}^4 \ (11001101) \quad\quad Y_x$$

$$\underset{\Longrightarrow}{\overset{\text{Substitution(M)}}{\quad}} \quad 5 \rightarrow 101 \quad\quad \text{Plaintext}$$

Where, we just gave out the example of $N = 8$ network, the large scale networks (such as $N = 10, N = 12, N = 16$, and etc.) being of the same chaotic-classified properties can also be used in the cryptographic scheme. Even though the commercial available chip of neural network is only of a small scale of neurons (such as MD1220, $N = 8$)[6] at present, it also can be use for build up a cryptographic scheme of great security. Let us consider a network of scale N being used in the above cryptographic scheme, there are $N!$ kinds of random permutation H and $P!$ kinds of substitutions M for being chosen as the secret key. So that, if we make up a network of $N = 16$ with two pieces of MD1220 for the cryptographic scheme, the assemblage of secret keys is too large for opponent to determine which secret key is used in the encryption scheme.

Additionally, the essentiality of this cryptographic scheme is that the stored patterns S^μ are concealed in their chaotic convergent domains to low the statistic probabilities of ASCII characters in plaintexts. The number k of message states in the chaotic convergent domains is the key parameter which the security of this cryptographic scheme depends on. The more k is, the more security the cryptographic scheme is. For example, if there are $10,000$ ASCII characters "F" in one document, the message of "WJP" will appear in the ciphertext no more than one times, because: $k^3 = 20^3 \simeq 10^4$. So that it is also impossible to uncover the ciphertext based on the statistic probabilities.

5 Conclusion

Neural network made up of simple nonlinear neurons is a complex dynamic system, of which many nonlinear dynamic properties have not been understood, although some associative dynamic properties of neural network can be perfectly derived by the methods of statistical physics. In this paper, we just investigated several special nonlinear dynamic properties (i.e. chaotic-classified properties) of the clipped HNN under overstorage by computer simulation. Fortunately, the chaotic-classified properties of the overstorage network are very suitable for application in data encryption. Since that, in the modern cryptology[7], to setup a high security cryptosystem, scientists always devote themselves to find those algrithms which just only depend on a few parameters being changed to give out the large scale pseudo-random stream, or depend on the complexity of NP-complete problem. And, the chaotic-classified properties of HNN can be considered as the complexity of NP-complete problem, especially that, only few elements in neuron synaptic matrix being changed, the distribution of system energy will vary drastically and chaotically.

Acknowledgments:

Dr. Guo acknowledged the financial support of this work by the Strategic Grant Committee of City University of Hong Kong and partly by the Advance School Doctor Discipline Special Research Foundation through Grant: No.9438409.

Reference:

[1] J.J.Hopfield, *Proc. Natl. Acad. Sci. USA*, Vol.79, 1982, p.2554-2558.

[2] D.J.Amit, et al., *Phys. Rev.A*, Vol.32(2), 1985, p.1007.

[3] R.J.McEliece, et al., *IEEE Trans. Inform. Theory*, Vol.IT-33, No.4, 1987, pp.461-482.

[4] W.S.McCulloc, et al., *Bull. Math. Biophys.*, Vol.5, 1943, pp.115-133.

[5] D.O.Hebb, *The Organization of Behavior*. New York: Wiley, 1949.

[6] *Micro Devices MD1220 Neural Bit Slice Data Sheet*, March 1990.

[7] G.Brassard, *Modern Cryptology*, Spriger-Verlay, 1988.

On the Relatively Simple Statistical Mechanics of Neural-Network Acceptors

M.F.J. Drossaers,* Computer Science Department, University of Twente,
P.O Box 217, 7500 AE Enschede, The Netherlands. Email: mdrssrs@cs.utwente.nl

Abstract— **We define a neural network for sequence recognition, or simulation of abstract automata. This network can simulate any finite-state acceptor. We also define an energy function and show that the network minimizes its energy. Then we show how to derive a free-energy function, which has only boundary minima, and an expression of the average overlap for the network. These derivations are simpler than the analysis of the attractor network, from which the techniques for analysis have been adapted. This simplicity is intimately connected to the network's design as a neural-network acceptor.**

1 Introduction

There are numerous proposals of neural networks for sequence recognition or simulation of abstract automata that lack a thorough analysis of the proposed model; see for instance [4][8][12]. On the other hand, attractor neural networks allow for a rigorous analysis, but they seldom deal with the simulation of abstract automata. Usually they are confined to the storage and retrieval of activity patterns and sequences of activity patterns, see e.g. [10][2][9]. The few proposals of attractor nets for sequence recognition were rather restricted [1], or computationally too weak for simulation of finite-state acceptors [10]. General drawbacks of attractor nets are, among others, that their analysis is complex, even more so in the case of temporal sequences, see [11], and that they are slow: a single transition takes several updates per neuron, which is inefficient in applications.

In this paper we define a stochastic neural network for the simulation of abstract automata. This network is fast and has been proven to be computationally equivalent to the finite-state acceptor (FSA) [6]. For this network we show how to derive a free-energy function. This derivation is more simple than the derivation of a free-energy function for an attractor network that stores and retrieves sequences of activity patterns.

2 Definition of the Network

The stochastic neural network for sequence recognition that is defined in this section is called a neural-network acceptor (NNA). The generic architecture of the NNA is shown in figure 1. The definition of

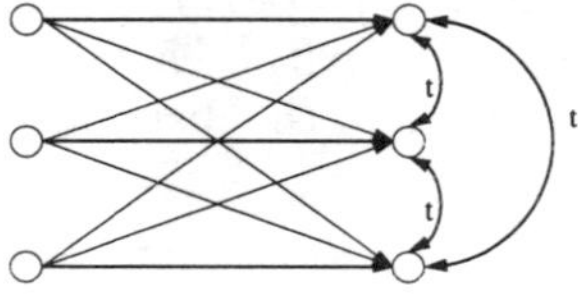

Figure 1: *A schema of the architecture of the NNA. The three leftmost circles represent an input network. The rightmost circles represent a recognition network. The left-to-right arrows represent input synapses, and the arched arrows represent temporal synapses.*

the NNA starts at the neurons. A *formal neuron* is a state variable $S \in \{0, 1\}$. $S = 1$ denotes neural activity. Neurons assume either state with a probability that will be defined below. A *neural network state* is a set $\{S_i \mid i = 1, \ldots, N\}$ of neurons. This is written as $\{S\}$. A specific network state is a *activity pattern* $\{\xi_i^\mu \mid i = 1, \ldots, N\}$, written as $\{\xi^\mu\}$, where $\mu = 1, \ldots, p$. Instead of ξ also the Greek character ζ may be used. A bit ξ in an activity pattern is a random variable with probability distribution $\Pr(\xi) = a\delta(\xi - 1) + (1 - a)\delta(\xi)$, where δ is the Dirac delta and $a \in [0, 1]$ is the *activity level*.

The overlap of a network state, by default of the recognition network, at time n with pattern $\{\xi^\mu\}$ is measured by the *overlap parameter* $m^\mu(n)$, we have $m^\mu(n) = \frac{1}{N} \sum_{i=1}^{aN} \xi_i^\mu S_i(n)$. The *largest overlap*

*The author wishes to express his gratitude to the Parlevink project, Computer Science Department, University of Twente for providing the facilities needed to write this article.

is $m(n) = \max\{m^\mu(n) \mid \mu = 1, \ldots, p\}$. The *noise correction factor* is a real number $m \in [0, 1]$. It measures the effect of the stochastic neural dynamics on the overlap: division by m yields the overlap for deterministic neural dynamics. A definiens for m will be obtained in section 5.

In the NNA the synaptic coefficients are obtained by an Adaline learning process; see e.g. [5]. Let $\{\xi^1\}, \ldots, \{\xi^p\}$ be p linear independent activity patterns. J^{temp} is the $(N \times N)$ *matrix of synaptic coefficients of the temporal synapses*, with components defined by infinite, but convergent, recursion as follows.

$$J_{ij}^{temp}(0) = 0, \qquad J_{ij}^{temp}(k) = J_{ij}^{temp}(k-1) + \sum_{\mu=1}^{p} \Delta J_{ij}^{temp,\mu}(k-1),$$

$$\Delta J_{ij}^{temp,\mu}(k-1) = \frac{\rho}{1 + \left(J_{ij}^{temp}(k-1)\right)^2} \left(\lambda^{temp}\xi_i^{\mu+1} - \sum_{l=1}^{N} J_{il}^{temp}(k-1)\xi_l^\mu\right) \xi_j^\mu,$$

where $k \in \mathbb{N}^+$ signifies temporal order. If pattern index $\mu = p$ then take $\mu + 1$ equal to 1. The learning rate ρ is a small constant, $\lambda^{temp} \in \mathbb{R}^+$ is the relative strength of the temporal synapses. J^{ext} is the $(N \times N)$ *matrix of synaptic coefficients of the external input synapses*. Let $\{\xi^1\}, \ldots, \{\xi^p\}$ and $\{\zeta^1\}, \ldots, \{\zeta^p\}$ denote two collections of p linearly independent activity patterns. Then the components of J^{ext} are defined by a similar iterative process as defined above, but with superscript 'ext' substituted for 'temp', ξ_i^μ for $\xi_i^{\mu+1}$, and ζ_i^μ for ξ_i^μ. Synaptic coefficients may also be called synapses. The storage capacity $\alpha_c = \frac{p_{max}}{N}$ of the network is $\alpha_c = 1$; see e.g. [5]. The required linear independence of the activity patterns involved is no problem for the NNA, since the patterns are pseudo-orthogonal, see section 3. A Hebbian storage prescription; see e.g. [3], cannot be used in this network because of strong fluctuations in the input due to pattern correlations at finite N. These fluctuations are summed along with the input and thus grow beyond the control of the network's threshold.

Network states produce neural input via the synapses. Given are network states $\{S(t)\}$ and $\{S'(t)\}$. The *external input* on neuron i at time $n + 1$ is $h_i^{ext}(n+1) = \sum_{j=1}^{N} J_{ij}^{ext} S_j'(n)$, where n enumerates discrete unit periods of time. The *temporal input* on neuron i at time $n + 1$ is $h_i^{temp}(n+1) = \sum_{j=1}^{N} J_{ij}^{temp} S_j(n)$. The *total neuronal input* on neuron i at time n is $h_i(n) = h_i^{ext}(n) + h_i^{temp}(n)$.

The *threshold* at time n is $U(n) = (\lambda^{ext} - \frac{1}{2}\lambda^{temp})m + \lambda^{temp}m(n-1)$, where $\lambda^{ext} \in \mathbb{R}^+$. $U(n)$ is a multilevel threshold controlled by the maximum overlap $m(n-1)$. The threshold is a substitute for inhibitory input, generated by the input network and the recognition network. This threshold has the advantage over inhibitory input not to restrict the number of activity patterns that can be simultaneously present as a complex network state. This allows the network to evaluate in parallel all different temporal sequences that the input sequence supports. A drawback is the appearance in its expression of nonlocal forms of information: the noise correction factor and the maximum overlap. We will show below that neural input satisfies an expression containing m.

For the input network virtual input based on an activity pattern $\{\zeta^\mu\}$ is provided. The *virtual input* on neuron i at time n is $h_i'(n) = (\lambda^{ext} + \lambda^{temp})\zeta_i^\mu m$, where m is the noise correction factor, and $\{\zeta^\mu\}$ is an activity pattern. When no input is present, it is assumed that $\{\zeta^\mu\} = \{\zeta^0\} = \{0\}$. For this network also a *virtual threshold* is used: $U' = (\lambda^{ext} + \frac{1}{2}\lambda^{temp})m$.

The *NNA* is defined by its architecture, its synaptic interactions, and its neural dynamics. The *architecture* of the NNA consists of two networks, see figure 1. The recognition network consists of neurons $S_1, \ldots, S_N$, the input network consists of $S_1', \ldots, S_N'$. J^{ext} defines the effect of the neurons of the input network on the neurons of the recognition network. J^{temp} defines the temporal, or delayed, interaction between the neurons in the recognition network. The neural dynamics are defined by the *neural firing probabilities*. For the recognition network the firing probability is $\Pr(S_i = 1) = (1 + \exp[-(h_i - U)/T])^{-1}$, $\Pr(S_i = 0) = 1 - \Pr(S_i = 1)$. The firing probabilities for the input network are the same, but with the virtual input and the virtual threshold substituted for the regular input and threshold. We always choose $p\lambda^{temp} < \lambda^{ext}$, where p is the number of activity patterns that are used to form the temporal synapses. From this constraint follows that in the limit $T \to 0$ precisely those neurons that receive both excitatory temporal and external input become active.

The NNA is assumed to be consistent. For the limit $N \to \infty$ this is articulated as follows. $\langle S_i \rangle = \frac{1}{2}\left(1 + \tanh\left[\frac{1}{2}(h_i - U)/\right]\right)$, and $\langle S_i' \rangle = \frac{1}{2}\left(1 + \tanh\left[\frac{1}{2}(h_i' - U')/T\right]\right)$, are assumed to produce $h_i = \sum_{j=1}^{N} J_{ij}^{ext} \langle S_j' \rangle + \sum_{j=1}^{N} J_{ij}^{temp} \langle S_j \rangle$. Concerning the timing of the input patterns $\{\zeta^1\} \ldots \{\zeta^p\}$ it is assumed that virtual input at consecutive unit time periods depends on consecutive activity patterns. The NNA operates under synchronous dynamics. In each unit time period all $2N$ neurons adjust their state to the received input.

3   The Energy Function

An energy function will be defined below for the recognition network. In spite of the fact that it has asymmetric synaptic matrices, we will show that the network minimizes the energy function to a finite minimum. This can be shown because the energy minimization process is restricted to a single unit time period. Each unit time period the network receives input from a new input pattern $\{\zeta^\mu\}$, which defines a new minimization process. This is unlike the energy minimization process in an attractor network which, due to the fact that its time evolution depends only on the network itself, ranges over multiple unit time periods. In this paper, the general strategy with respect to analysis of the NNA is to generalize over subsequent input patterns and to evaluate the recognition network's behavior in response to this generalized input.

We restrict the discussion to NNAs that might simulate FSAs, because these are the only NNAs we are interested in. So, the number of activity patterns p remains finite as $N \to \infty$ in analysis. We also assume that $a = c/N$, where c is a constant, denoting the average number of 1-bits in each activity pattern. The constant c depends on the information requirement in simulating a given FSA. We have that $a \to 0$ as $N \to \infty$ but $aN = c$. A consequence is that any two activity patterns $\{\xi^\mu\}$ and $\{\xi^\nu\}$ are pseudo-orthogonal. That is, if $\mu \neq \nu$ then $\Pr\left(\sum_i \xi_i^\mu \xi_i^\nu > 0\right) \to 0$ as $N \to \infty$. In this section it is also assumed that $T = 0$.

The *energy function* for the NNA is

$$
E(n) \;=\; - \sum_{i=1,j=1}^{N} J_{ij}^{ext} S_i(n) S_j'(n-1) \;-\; \sum_{i=1,j=1}^{N} J_{ij}^{temp} S_i(n) S_j(n-1) + U \sum_{i=1}^{N} S_i(n).
$$

This will also be written as $E(n) = - \sum_{i=1}^{N} h_i(n) S_i(n) + U \sum_{i=1}^{N} S_i(n)$.

Neural input is based on neural states a unit period of time earlier and, therefore, stable for the duration of a unit period of time. It is not affected by neural state changes in the same unit period of time; all neural interaction is concentrated in the transition from one unit period of time to another. Since the neurons do not interact within one unit period of time, the energy associated with such a period is just the sum of the energies of the individual neurons. Consequently, if a neuron lowers its energy, the energy of the whole system is lowered. This will be shown to hold. Let S_i denote the state of neuron i in the recognition network before it adapts its state to the received input, and let $\widetilde{S}_i$ denote it after adaptation. $\widetilde{E}$ is the energy of the recognition network computed using $\widetilde{S}_i$. Let $\Delta S_i = \widetilde{S}_i - S_i$ and $\Delta E = \widetilde{E} - E$. Then, $\Delta S_i \neq 0$ implies $\Delta E < 0$ as follows. If S_i changes state, $\Delta E = - \left[\widetilde{h}_i \widetilde{S}_i - U \widetilde{S}_i \right] + [h_i S_i - U S_i]$. Within one unit period of time the input is stable, $\widetilde{h}_i = h_i$, so $\Delta E = -\Delta S_i (h_i - U)$, which implies that $\Delta E < 0$ in case $\Delta S_i \neq 0$.

When all the neurons have assumed a state that is in agreement with the total input they receive, $\Delta E = 0$ and consequently the network state designates an energy minimum. The energy minima are finite. That is, in the limit of $N \to \infty$, $E(\{S\}) > -\infty$. This is a consequence of the fact that the energy as an infinite sum over sites has a finite support: there is a finite number of patterns with each a finite number of 1-bits. Moreover, by the learning algorithm all the synapses are finite. Hence the energy is always finite.

4   The Free-Energy Function and the Average Overlap

The construction of a free-energy function is simplified by the fact that the NNA is not equipped with stabilizing synapses: the construction does not require the Gaussian integral trick and the saddle point method; see [2]. Furthermore, the use of the Adaline learning algorithm assures that there is no cross-talk between correlated activity patterns. Therefore, the replica method is not required. The fact that p remains finite as $N \to \infty$ has as a favorable consequence that the free-energy and related quantities are self-averaging. For the remainder of this paper we assume that $T \in \mathbb{R}^+$.

The *Boltzmann-Gibbs distribution*: $\Pr(\{S\}) = \frac{1}{Z} \exp(-E\{S\}/T)$, which equals $\prod_{i=1}^{N} \Pr(S_i)$, and where $Z = \sum_{\{S\}} \exp(-E\{S\}/T)$, is used to derive average properties of the NNA. In the standard attractor network, average quantities are computed by differentiation of the moment generating function Z. In case of computation of the average overlap we have there $\langle m^\mu \rangle = \frac{T}{NZ} \frac{\partial Z}{\partial h^\mu}\big|_{h^\mu=0}$, where $Z = \sum_{\{S\}} \exp[-\frac{1}{T}(E - N\sum_{\mu=1}^p h^\mu m^\mu)]$. In fact, h^μ is the attractor network analogue of the total input of the NNA which is not uniform, and therefore written as h_i^μ. Clearly, it is not an auxiliary variable that can be set to zero after differentiation of Z in the computation of an average. But not setting h_i^μ to zero after differentiation of Z leads to awkward results, unless the input can be rewritten as if the quantity to be averaged is appended to it. This is the key to the derivation of the free-energy function.

The overlap is proportional to the inner product of a network state and an activity pattern. A least requirement is therefore to show that the input can be written as an expression of such an inner product. The temporal input per pattern is $h_i^{temp,\mu} = \sum_{j=1}^N J_{ij}^{temp} S_j \xi_j^{\mu-1}$, the external input per pattern is $h_i^{ext,\mu} = \sum_{j=1}^N J_{ij}^{ext} S_j' \zeta_j^\mu$ From the pseudo-orthogonality of the activity pattern follows that $\sum_{\mu=1}^p h_i^{temp,\mu} \to h_i^{temp}$, $\sum_{\mu=1}^p h_i^{ext,\mu} \to h_i^{ext}$, and consequently that $\sum_{\mu=1}^p h_i^\mu \to h_i$, as $N \to \infty$.

Theorem 4.1 In the limit $N \to \infty$, the energy of the NNA,

$$E = -\sum_{i=1}^N h_i S_i + U \sum_{i=1}^N S_i, \quad \text{equals} \quad E = -\sum_{\mu=1}^p \sum_{i=1}^N h_i^\mu \xi_i^\mu S_i + U \sum_{i=1}^N S_i.$$

Proof: It is useful to reiterate at this point that the sum over neurons has only a finite support. Applying the principles above we have that, in the limit $N \to \infty$

$$E = -\sum_{\mu=1}^p \sum_{i=1}^N \sum_{j=1}^N J_{ij}^{ext} S_j' \zeta_j^\mu S_i - \sum_{\mu=1}^p \sum_{i=1}^N \sum_{j=1}^N J_{ij}^{temp} S_j \xi_j^{\mu-1} S_i + U \sum_{i=1}^N S_i.$$

For every j such that $\zeta_j^\mu = 1$, a fraction $\lambda^{ext} \xi_i^\mu S_j'/c$ is added to the external input on neuron i. This follows from the orthogonality of the patterns in the limit $N \to \infty$. Under this condition the learning algorithm produces equal size, nonzero synapses. Therefore we can write

$$E = -\frac{\lambda^{ext}}{c} \sum_{\mu=1}^p \sum_{i=1}^N \sum_{j=1}^N \xi_i^\mu \zeta_j^\mu S_j' S_i - \frac{\lambda^{temp}}{c} \sum_{\mu=1}^p \sum_{i=1}^N \sum_{j=1}^N \xi_i^\mu \xi_j^{\mu-1} S_j S_i + U \sum_{i=1}^N S_i, \quad \text{giving}$$

$$E = -\sum_{\mu=1}^p \sum_{i=1}^N h_i^{ext,\mu} \xi_i^\mu S_i - \sum_{\mu=1}^p \sum_{i=1}^N h_i^{temp,\mu} \xi_i^\mu S_i + U \sum_{i=1}^N S_i \ (\text{with } \xi_i^\mu = (\xi_i^\mu)^2),$$

from which the theorem follows. □

Now the free-energy function can be derived. This and subsequent theorems have more or less standard proofs which are, therefore, omitted.

Theorem 4.2 In the limit $N \to \infty$, the free-energy per neuron can be derived from Z to be

$$f(\beta,h) = -\frac{1}{\beta N} \sum_{i=1}^N \ln\left(1 + \exp\left[\beta\left(\mathbf{h}_i \boldsymbol{\xi}_i - U\right)\right]\right), \quad \text{where} \quad \mathbf{h}_i = \left(h_i^1, \ldots, h_i^p\right)^T, \boldsymbol{\xi}_i = \left(\xi_i^1, \ldots, \xi_i^p\right)^T,$$

$h = (\mathbf{h}_1, \ldots, \mathbf{h}_N)$, and $\beta = 1/T$. □

The proof for theorem 4.2 uses theorem 4.1 to rewrite the energy in Z and performs the trace from which $f(\beta,h)$ follows. The free-energy does not blow-up nor is it zero, as becomes clear from the next theorem.

Theorem 4.3 The free-energy per neuron is self-averaging. This is written as

$$f(\beta,h) = -\left\langle\left\langle \frac{1}{\beta} \ln\left(1 + \exp\left[\beta\left(\mathbf{h}\boldsymbol{\xi} - U\right)\right]\right)\right\rangle\right\rangle.$$

□

The free energy is self-averaging because ξ_i^μ and h_i^μ have a finite number of realizations at each site i. The h_i^μ can be rewritten as $h_i^\mu = \left(\lambda^{ext} m^{\mu'} + \lambda^{temp} m^{\mu-1}\right) \xi_i^\mu$, see theorem 4.1, where $m^{\mu'}$ is the overlap in the input network. This can be applied to the current, noisy case using the consistency assumption, yielding $h_i^\mu = \left(\lambda^{ext} \langle m^{\mu'} \rangle + \lambda^{temp} \langle m^{\mu-1} \rangle\right) \xi_i^\mu$, which has a finite number of realizations at every site.

The self-averaged free-energy function of a NNA has a finite boundary minimum. This follows immediately from the facts that the exp and ln functions are monotonously increasing, $1/\beta \in \mathbb{R}^+$, and h_i^μ is finite.

Theorem 4.4 In the limit $N \to \infty$, the average overlap $\langle m^\mu \rangle$ can be computed from the free-energy per neuron, theorem 4.2, to be

$$\langle m^\mu \rangle = \frac{1}{2c} \sum_{i=1}^{N} \xi_i^\mu \left(1 + \tanh\left[\tfrac{1}{2}\beta \left(h_i \boldsymbol{\xi}_i - U \right) \right] \right).$$

$\square$

The proof of this theorem employs the identity $\langle m^\mu \rangle = -\frac{1}{a} \sum_{i=1}^{N} \frac{\partial f(\beta,h)}{\partial h_i^\mu}$ which comes from $\langle m^\nu \rangle = \sum_S m^\nu\{S\} \Pr(\{S\}) = \frac{1}{\beta c} \sum_{i=1}^{N} \frac{\partial \ln Z}{\partial h_i^\nu}$, and $f(\beta,h) = -\frac{1}{\beta N} \ln Z$.

Theorem 4.5 The average overlap is self-averaging. This is written as

$$\langle m^\mu \rangle = \left\langle\!\!\left\langle \frac{1}{2a} \xi^\mu \left(1 + \tanh\left[\tfrac{1}{2}\beta \left(\boldsymbol{h}\boldsymbol{\xi} - U \right) \right] \right) \right\rangle\!\!\right\rangle.$$

$\square$

The proof of this theorem is similar to the proof of theorem 4.3.

5   Average Size of the Overlap Parameter

From the learning algorithm we know that $\lambda^{temp}\xi_i^\mu = \sum_{j=1}^{N} J_{ij}^{temp}\xi_j^{\mu-1}$. We call $\lambda^{temp}\xi_i^\mu$ a temporal image of $\{\xi^{\mu-1}\}$. In a similar fashion we have an external input image $\lambda^{ext}\xi_i^\mu$. From theorem 4.5 we know that in the limit $N \to \infty$: $h_i^{temp,\mu} = \lambda^{temp} \langle m^{\mu-1} \rangle \xi_i^\mu$. With the definition of the noise correction factor we can write this as $h_i^{temp,\mu} = m\lambda^{temp}m^{\mu-1}\xi_i^\mu$, where $m^{\mu-1}$ describes a noiseless situation. If we take $m^{\mu-1} = 1$ we see that $h_i^{temp,\mu} = m\lambda^{temp}\xi_i^\mu$; that is, the noise correction is part of the temporal input. To the external input a similar line of reasoning applies.

Theorem 5.1 Let $T > 0$. Assume the limit of $N \to \infty$. The size of the overlap is the solution of

$$m \text{ in: } m = \tfrac{1}{2}\left(1 + \tanh\left[\tfrac{1}{4}m\lambda^{temp}/T \right] \right) \text{ in case of two input sources,} \tag{1}$$

$$\text{of } m_{ext} \text{ in: } m_{ext} = \tfrac{1}{2}\left(1 + \tanh\left[-\tfrac{1}{4}m\lambda^{temp}/T \right] \right) \text{ in case of only external input, and} \tag{2}$$

$$\text{of } m_{temp} \text{ in: } m_{temp} = \tfrac{1}{2}\left(1 + \tanh\left[-\tfrac{1}{4}m\left(2\lambda^{ext} - \lambda^{temp}/T \right) \right] \right) \text{ in case of only temporal input.} \tag{3}$$

These solutions are the same for any number of patterns in a mixture state.

Proof: Assume that the vectors of neuronal inputs, or input images are

$$\boldsymbol{h}_i^{ext} = m(\underbrace{\lambda^{ext}\xi_i^1, \ldots, \overbrace{\lambda^{ext}\xi_i^{k+1-n}, \ldots, \lambda^{ext}\xi_i^k}^{n}}_{k}, \underbrace{0, \ldots, 0}_{p-k})^T, \text{ and}$$

$$\boldsymbol{h}_i^{temp} = m(\underbrace{0, \ldots, 0}_{k-n}, \underbrace{\overbrace{\lambda^{temp}\xi_i^{k+1-n}, \ldots, \lambda^{temp}\xi_i^k}^{n}, \ldots, \lambda^{temp}\xi_i^{k+l-n}}_{l}, \underbrace{0, \ldots, 0}_{p-(l+k-n)})^T.$$

These input vectors are substituted in the expression of the average overlap, giving:

$$m_{k+l-n} = \frac{1}{2a(k+l-n)} \left\langle\!\!\left\langle \sum_{\nu=1}^{k+l-n} \xi^\nu \left(1 + \tanh\left[\tfrac{1}{2}\beta \left(\lambda^{ext}m \sum_{\nu=1}^{k} \xi^\nu + \lambda^{temp}m \sum_{\nu=k+1-n}^{k+l-n} \xi^\nu - U \right) \right] \right) \right\rangle\!\!\right\rangle.$$

Because $S_i \in \{0,1\}$ the size of the overlap is independent of the number of patterns participating in a mixture state. This fact is used to split the expression for the average overlap into three subexpressions according to the input the neurons receive. The expression for the two input images case is

$$m_n = \frac{1}{2an} \langle\!\langle z_n \left(1 + \tanh\left[\tfrac{1}{2}\beta \left(m\lambda^{ext}z_n + m\lambda^{temp}z_n - U \right) \right] \right) \rangle\!\rangle \quad \text{where} \quad z_n = \sum_{\nu=k+1-n}^{k} \xi^\nu.$$

The probability that a bit in z_n has value 1 equals an. The threshold in the arguments of the tanh functions is high because temporal input is present. So, computing the expected value of z_n and subtracting

U leads to equation 1, but with m_n instead of m at the left-hand side of the equation. By the consistency assumption, in case of both external and temporal input the size of the overlap, or in this analysis the noise correction factor, should be reproduced by the total input. Therefore we substitute m_n by m and thus obtain equation 1, which is the definiens of the noise correction factor. The consistency assumption does not apply in case of a single source of input, so to obtain equations (2) and (3), m_{k-n} and m_{l-n} are replaced by the pattern independent m_{ext} and m_{temp} respectively, after averaging out the z variables and subtracting U. □

The graphs in figure 2 show that the robustness of the NNA is very good, much better than the robustness of the standard attractor network. For increasing noise levels, the performance of the network degrades gracefully. The NNA defined in this article is an improvement relative to an earlier version which was

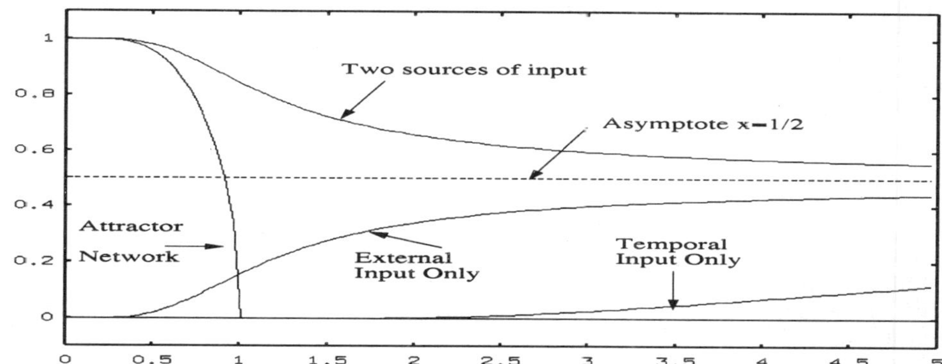

Figure 2: *Graphs of the numerical solutions of equations (1), (2), (3), and a comparable equation for an attractor network: $m = \tanh[\beta m]$, as a function of the noise (x-axis). $\lambda^{temp} = 4$ and $\lambda^{ext} = 20$.*

defined and analyzed in [7]. The main difference was in the firing probability: $\Pr(S_i = 1) = (1 + \exp[-(h_i/T - U)])^{-1}$. Although it was well motivated, the network turned out to break down under noise fairly soon, and abruptly.

6 Conclusions

We defined a stochastic neural network for sequence recognition. This neural network can simulate any FSA. Although the network has only asymmetric synaptic matrices an energy function was defined for the network, and it was proven that the network minimizes its energy to a finite minimum as a response to external input. The network was also analyzed by statistical mechanics means. A free-energy function was obtained along with an expression of the average overlap. This analysis was relatively simple. The resulting equations of the average overlaps show that the NNA is extremely robust, much more than the attractor network under comparable parameter choices.

References

[1] D.J. Amit. *Proceedings of the National Academy of Sciences, USA*, 85:2141–2145, 1988.

[2] D.J. Amit. *Modeling Brain Function*. Cambridge University Press, Cambridge, USA, 1989.

[3] J. Buhmann et al. *Physical Review A*, 39(5):2689–2692, 1989.

[4] A. Cleeremans et al. *Neural Computation*, 1(3):372–381, 1989.

[5] E. Domany et al. *Models of Neural Networks*. Springer, Berlin, Germany, 2nd ed., 1992.

[6] M.F.J. Drossaers. In *Proceedings of COLING '92*, pages 113–119, 1992.

[7] M.F.J. Drossaers. In *Proceedings of ICANN '93*, pages 396–399. Springer, Berlin, Germany, 1993.

[8] C. L. Giles et al. *Neural Networks*, 8(9):1359–1365, 1995

[9] A. Herz et al. *Biological Cybernetics*, 60:457–467, 1989.

[10] D. Kleinfeld. *Proceedings of the National Academy of Sciences, USA*, 83:9469–9473, 1986.

[11] Z. Li and A.V.M. Herz. In *Proceedings of Sitges XI*, pages 287–302. Springer, Berlin, Germany, 1990.

[12] F. van der Velde. *Connection Science*, 7(24):247–280, 1995.

A Simplified Architecture for Nonlinear Recurrent Neural Filter

Jianting CAO and Andrzej CICHOCKI
Laboratory for Artificial Brain Systems, FRP,
The Institute of Physical and Chemical Research (RIKEN)
2-1 Hirosawa, Wako-shi, Saitama 351-01, JAPAN
E-mail: cao@negi.riken.go.jp and cia@kamo.riken.go.jp

Abstract— **In this paper, we present a simplified architecture for recurrent neural network. Instead of using several subnetworks which are connected in parallel, we can employ only one recurrent network with scaling adjustable gain M. Due to this gain factor, the range of output is expanded from $y(t) \in [-1, 1]$ to $y(t) \in [-M, M]$. Furthermore, the estimation accuracy of the proposed architecture is better than that of the standard recurrent neural network. By extensive computer simulations, we compared the performance of the proposed architecture with parallel neural network which consists of many subnetworks.**

1 Introduction

The artificial neural networks are applied to various fields of engineering and science due to their remarkable learning capability [1],[2]. Several approaches and algorithms in the identification and control of unknown nonlinear dynamical systems have been proposed [3]-[7]. As parallel neural networks in the field of adaptive signal processing, the Parallel Multilayer Neural Digital Filter (PMNDF) and Parallel Recurrent Neural Digital Filter (PRNDF) have been proposed [8],[9]. With the aid of parallel processing using some subnetworks, the computational burden associated with parameter estimation can be reduced considerably.

The purpose of this paper is to present a simplified architecture for nonlinear adaptive filter using recurrent neural network. The simplified architecture can be considered as a standard recurrent network with an amplifier, so that it is possible to estimate the nonlinear system whose amplitude of output exceeds the range of [-1,1]. Also, instead of using several subnetworks which are connected in parallel, we can employ only one recurrent network for adaptive signal processing. Furthermore, simulation results are presented to illustrate the effectiveness and performance of the proposed method.

2 Parallel Recurrent Neural Filter

Consider the following unknown nonlinear discrete-time system expressed by

$$d(t) = f(\boldsymbol{a}, \boldsymbol{b}, d(t-1), \cdots, d(t-m), x(t), \cdots, x(t-n)), \tag{1}$$

where $x(t)$ and $d(t)$ are the input and output signals, respectively, $f(\cdot)$ is an unknown nonlinear function, $\boldsymbol{a}$ and $\boldsymbol{b}$ are the vectors of parameters, respectively, m and n denote the maximum time delay.

To estimate the unknown nonlinear system, the M recurrent subnetworks can be connected in parallel to build up the parallel recurrent neural digital filter (PRNDF) [9]. The architecture of PRNDF is shown in Fig. 1.

For the neural filter of Fig. 1, the input-output relation can be expressed as

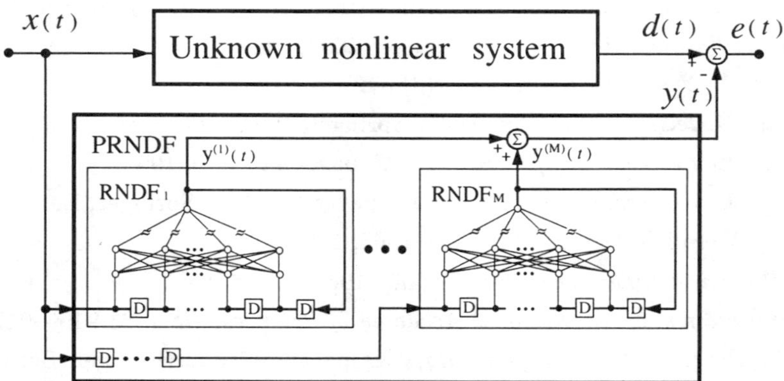

Fig. 1 Configuration of parallel recurrent neural digital filter (PRNDF).

$$
\begin{aligned}
y(t) &= \sum_{i=1}^{M} y^{(i)}(t) \\
&= \sum_{i=1}^{M} F^{(i)}(\boldsymbol{w}^{(i)}(t), y^{(i)}(t-1), \cdots, y^{(i)}(t-m_i), x^{(i)}(t-(n_i+1)(i-1)), \cdots, x^{(i)}(t-in_i)), \quad (2)
\end{aligned}
$$

where $y(t)$ denotes the estimate of the desired value $d(t)$, $y^{(i)}(t)$ is output of ith subnetwork ($i = 1, 2, \cdots, M$), M is the number of partitions, $\boldsymbol{w}^{(i)}(t)$ is the vector of weights, $x^{(i)}(t-(n_i+1)(i-1))$ is the input in ith subnetwork, m_i, n_i denote the time delay, and $F^{(i)}(\cdot)$ are nonlinear functions.

In the ith subnetwork, let $y_{l-1,k}^{(i)}$ be the output of the kth neuron in layer $l-1$ ($l = 1, 2, \cdots, L$), $w_{l,j,k}^{(i)}$ be the weight which connects the kth neuron in layer $l-1$ to the jth neuron in layer l, N_l be the number of neurons in layer l, then the output of the jth neuron in layer l is expressed as

$$
y_{l,j}^{(i)}(t) = \Psi^{(i)}\left(\sum_{k=0}^{N_{l-1}} w_{l,j,k}^{(i)}(t) y_{l-1,k}^{(i)}(t) \right), \tag{3}
$$

where $w_{l,j,0}^{(i)}$ is the bias weight, $y_{l,0}^{(i)} = 1$ and function $\Psi^{(i)}(\cdot)$ is a sigmoidal nonlinearity in the form of a hyperbolic tangent.

To obtain the optimal values of the weights of the PRNDF the total error $e(t) = d(t) - \sum_{i=1}^{M} y^{(i)}(t)$ is used in each subnetwork for training the weights. The performance index J can be given by

$$
J = \frac{1}{2}(d(t) - y(t))^2 = \frac{1}{2}\left(d(t) - \sum_{i=1}^{M} y^{(i)}(t)\right)^2 \tag{4}
$$

The updating equation of the ith subnetwork can be derived as

$$
w_{l,j,k}^{(i)}(t+1) = w_{l,j,k}^{(i)}(t) - \eta[d(t) - \sum_{i=1}^{M} y^{(i)}(t)]\frac{\partial y^{(i)}(t)}{\partial w_{l,j,k}^{(i)}}, \tag{5}
$$

where $\eta > 0$ is the fixed learning rate, the initial condition of partial derivatives is

$$
\frac{\partial y^{(i)}(t)}{\partial w_{l,j,k}^{(i)}} = 0, \quad t \le 0. \tag{6}
$$

In Ref. [9], several examples that illustrate the use of above learning algorithm are also presented.

3   Simplified Architecture for PRNDF

In Fig. 1, let the input signal enter each subnetwork directly without delay, and all of the subnetworks are also assumed to be with identical structure. Upon above condition, Eq. (2) can be derived as

$$
y(t) = My^{(i)}(t). \tag{7}
$$

The total error becomes $e(t) = d(t) - My^{(i)}(t) = M[d(t)/M - y^{(i)}(t)]$. In this case, instead of using M subnetworks we can employ only one recurrent network. Also the updating algorithm in Eq. (5) can be expressed by

$$
w_{l,j,k}^{(i)}(t+1) = w_{l,j,k}^{(i)}(t) - \eta[d(t) - My^{(i)}(t)]\frac{\partial y^{(i)}(t)}{\partial w_{l,j,k}^{(i)}}, \quad \eta > 0. \tag{8}
$$

The simplified architecture associated with Eq. (7) is shown in Fig. 2. When $i = 1$ and $M = 1$, the architecture in Fig. 2 is identical to the network with output feedback (Model IV) that proposed by Narendra and Parthasarathy [10]. In the case of $M > 1$, the simplified architecture also can be considered as such network with the amplifiers gain M. This architecture make it possible to estimate the nonlinear system whose amplitude of output exceeds the range of [-1,1].

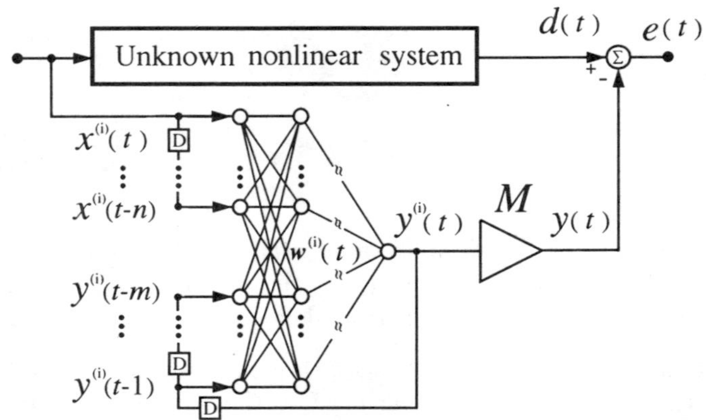

Fig. 2 Simplified architecture for PRNDF.

4 Computer simulations

In this section, we perform three examples on the simplified architecture for recurrent neural network presented in preceding section. In each experiment, only a 3-layer recurrent neural network was used, the number of neurons in input, hidden and output layers are 2, 2, and 1, respectively, it symbol as $N^3_{2,2,1}$. A Comparative study is made using preceding method [9],[10].

Example 1 :

We first use the one of the examples given in Ref. [10]. The nonlinear dynamic system is given by

$$\begin{aligned} d(t) \quad = \quad & 0.3d(t-1) + 0.6d(t-2) + 0.6\sin(\pi x(t-1)) \\ & + 0.3\sin(3\pi x(t-1)) + 0.1\sin(5\pi x(t-1)). \end{aligned} \tag{9}$$

The input signal is as follows.

$$x(t) = \sin(2\pi t/250). \tag{10}$$

In Ref. [10], the series-parallel model governed by the difference equation $y(t) = 0.3y(t-1) + 0.6y(t-2) + N[x(t-1)]$ was used. The multilayer neural network belonged to the class $N^4_{1,20,10,1}$.

A comparison between the estimate $y(t)$ and the desired value $d(t)$ and their difference $e(t)$ are shown in Fig. 3. In Fig. 3, a very simple recurrent neural network $N^3_{2,2,1}$ was used. With the aid of amplifier, it is possible for the output of the network $y(t)$ could be adjusted the output of nonlinear system $d(t)$ whose amplitude exceeds the range [-1,1]. In this example, the gain is given as $M = 12$ ($M > 6$ is necessary), the learning rate $\eta = 0.25$, the weights were updated at on-line.

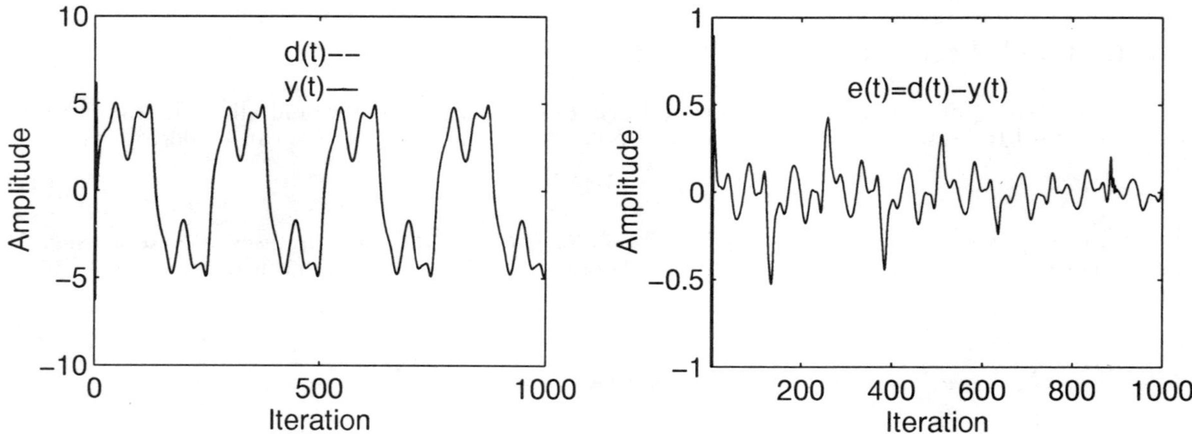

Fig. 3 Comparison of $y(t)$ and $d(t)$, the error signal $e(t)$.

As can be seen from Fig. 3, the output signal $y(t)$ approximates the target signal $d(t)$ very well. Also the computational complexity of network $N^3_{2,2,1}$ is lower than that of using network $N^4_{1,20,10,1}$ in [10].

Example 2 :

Next, we use the another example given in Ref. [10]. The nonlinear dynamic system is given by

$$d(t) = \frac{d(t-1)d(t-2)d(t-3)x(t-2)[d(t-3)-1]+x(t-1)}{1+d^2(t-3)+d^2(t-2)}.$$
(11)

The following input signal is used.

$$x(t) = \sin(2\pi t/250), \qquad\qquad t \le 500$$
(12)
$$x(t) = 0.8\sin(2\pi t/250)+0.2\sin(2\pi t/25), \quad t > 500.$$
(13)

In Ref. [10], the model IV was used. The recurrent neural network belonging to the class $N^4_{1,20,10,1}$ is used to estimate nonlinear system.

A Comparison of results for different value of gain are shown in Fig. 4. In Fig. 4(a), recurrent neural network $N^3_{2,2,1}$ was used. The gain $M = 1$, in fact, it is a standard recurrent neural network whose architecture is same as the the model IV [10]. In Fig. 4(b), also recurrent neural network $N^3_{2,2,1}$ was used. The gain of amplifier $M = 20$, the learning rate $\eta = 0.25$, the weights were updated at on-line.

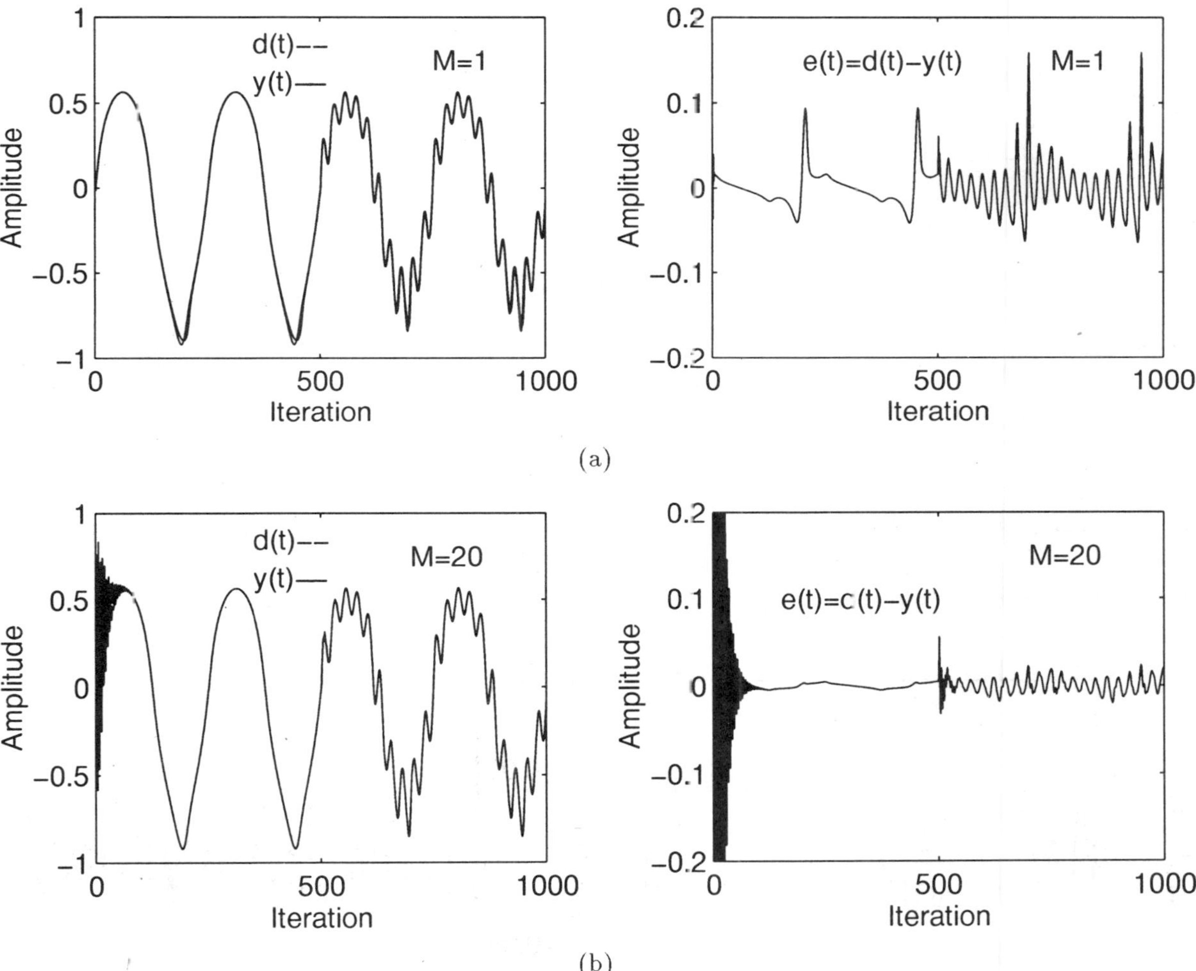

Fig. 4 Comparison of results for different value of gain.

It is clear from the results that the estimation accuracy of the proposed architecture is better than that of standard recurrent neural network. Also, they have better performance than the model IV [10] both in respect to the accuracy and in the computational complexity.

Example 3 :

Furthermore, we use the example of NARMAX (nonlinear autoregressive moving average with an exogenous signal) model in Ref. [9]. The NARMAX system is expressed by

$$
\begin{aligned}
d(t) \;=\; & a_0 + \sum_{i=1}^{n_a} a_i d(t-i) + \sum_{i=1}^{n_b} b_i x(t-i) \\
& + \sum_{i=1}^{n_a} \sum_{j=1}^{n_b} c_{ij} d(t-i) x(t-j) \\
& + \sum_{i=1}^{n_a} \sum_{j=1}^{n_b} f_{ij} d(t-i) x^2(t-j) + \cdots .
\end{aligned}
\tag{14}
$$

The following parameters associate with NARMAX model are used for simulation.

$$
a_0 = 0.17,
\tag{15}
$$

$$
\sum_{i=1}^{2} a_i d(t-i) = 0.88 d(t-1) - 0.54 d(t-2),
\tag{16}
$$

$$
\sum_{i=1}^{2} b_i x(t-i) = -0.16 x(t-1) + 0.84 x(t-2),
\tag{17}
$$

$$
\begin{aligned}
\sum_{i=1}^{2} \sum_{j=1}^{2} c_{ij} d(t-i) x(t-j) \;=\; & 0.78 d(t-1) x(t-1) - 0.52 d(t-1) x(t-2) \\
& + 0.19 d(t-2) x(t-1) - 0.71 d(t-2) x(t-2),
\end{aligned}
\tag{18}
$$

$$
\begin{aligned}
\sum_{i=1}^{2} \sum_{j=1}^{2} f_{ij} d(t-i) x^2(t-j) \;=\; & 1.32 d(t-1) x^2(t-1) - 0.59 d(t-1) x^2(t-2) \\
& - 2.81 d(t-2) x^2(t-1) + 1.15 d(t-2) x^2(t-2).
\end{aligned}
\tag{19}
$$

The input signal $x(t)$ is given by

$$
x(t) = 0.34 \cos(0.11t - 10) - 0.03 \cos(0.09t + 25) - 0.52 \cos(0.02t + 80).
\tag{20}
$$

A Comparison of results for PRNDF and its simplified architecture are shown in Fig. 5. In Fig. 5(a), 4 recurrent subnetworks $N^3_{2,2,1}$ connected in parallel but with corresponding delays (see Fig. 1) were used. In Fig. 5(b), only one recurrent neural network $N^3_{2,2,1}$ was used. The gain of amplifier $M = 4$.

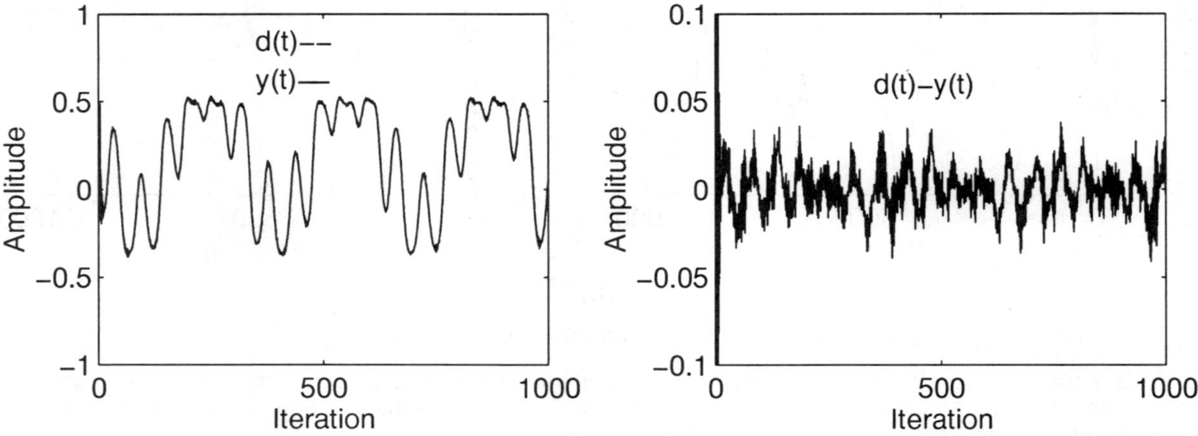

(a)Results for 4 subnetworks connected in parallel according to Fig. 1

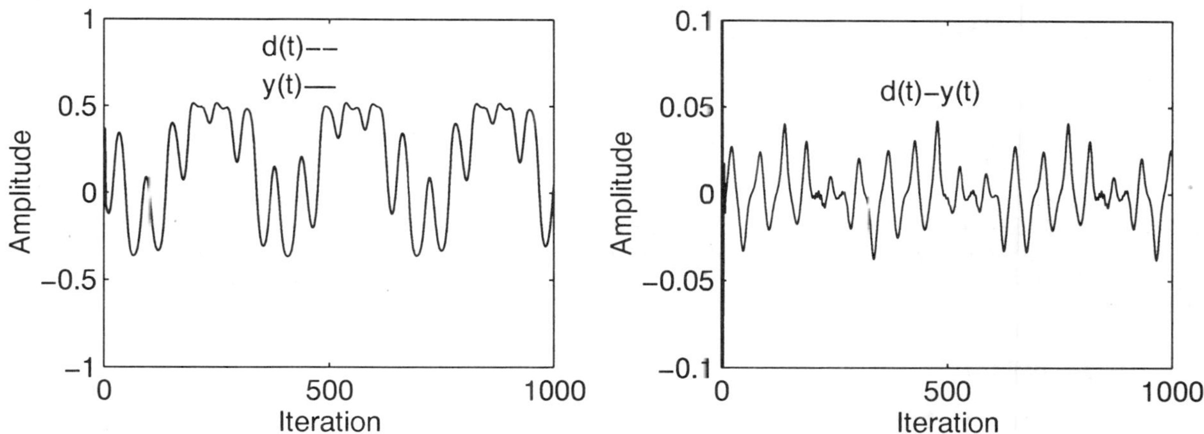

(b)Results for one network with gain $M = 4$ according to Fig. 2

Fig. 5 Comparison of results for PRNDF and its simplified architecture.

As can be seen from Fig. 5, in both case, the output signal $y(t)$ approximates the desired signal $d(t)$ very well.

5   Conclusion

A simplified architecture for recurrent neural network has been proposed. Instead of using M subnetworks which are connected in parallel, we can use only one recurrent network for adaptive signal processing. The main feature of our approach is to use nonlinear output neurons with adjustable gain factor what considerably decreases complexity of neural network models. Also with the aid of this architecture, the range of output is expanded from $y(t) \in [-1, 1]$ to $y(t) \in [-M, M]$. Furthermore, the estimation accuracy of the proposed architecture is better than that of the standard recurrent neural network. The proposed architecture is especially suitable for nonlinear systems where real-time processing is essential, due to very low complexity and high speed of learning.

References

[1] A. Cichocki and R. Unbehauen : "Neural Networks for Optimization and Signal Processing", Wiley, New York, 1993.

[2] S. Haykin : "Neural Networks ", Macmillan, Englewood Cliffs, NJ, 1994.

[3] R. J. Williams and D. Zipser : "A learning algorithm for continually running fully recurrent neural networks", *Neural Computation*, 1, pp.270-280, 1989.

[4] R. S. Scalerro and N. Tepedelenlioglu : "A fast new algorithm for training feedforward neural networks", *IEEE Trans. Signal Processing*, **40**, 1, pp.202-210, Jan. 1992.

[5] Y. Iiguni, H. Sakai and H. Tokumaru : "A real-time learning algorithm for a multilayered neural network based on the extended Kalman filter", *IEEE Trans. Signal Processing*, **40**, 4, pp.959-966, Apr. 1992.

[6] S. W. Piche : "Steepest descent algorithms for neural network controllers and filters", *IEEE Trans. Neural Networks*, 5, 2, pp.198-212, Mar. 1994.

[7] S. Tan, J. Hao and J. Vandewalle : "Efficient identification of RBF neural net models for nonlinear discrete-time multivariable dynamical systems", *Neurocomputing*, 9, pp.11-25, Nov. 1995.

[8] J. Cao and T. Yahagi : "Nonlinear adaptive digital filters using parallel neural networks", *Procs. Inter. Conf. Neural Networks*, Australia, Nov.27-Dec.1, 1995, pp.850-853.

[9] J. Cao and T. Yahagi: "Parallel nonlinear adaptive digital filters using recurrent neural networks", *The Trans. of the Institute of Electronics, Information and Communication Engineers A*, **J79 − A**, 4, pp.868-877, April 1996.

[10] K. S. Narendra and K. Parthasarathy : "Identification and control of dynamical systems using neural networks", *IEEE Trans. Neural Networks*, **1**, 1, pp.4-27, March 1990.

Stability analysis of Real-Time Recurrent Learning

K. C. Sio, C. K. Lee
Department of Electronic Engineering, The Hong Kong Polytechnic University,
Hong Kong

Abstract— **The real-time recurrent learning commonly used in recurrent neural networks is studied and analyzed. It is shown that there exists a possibility of instability during the real-time learning. Illustrations have been given to show its implication and possible solutions.**

1   Introduction

Neural networks have been widely used in various applications in control systems as well as pattern recognition. Among the simplest, single-layer (or multi-layer) recurrent neural networks are common tools in the identification of nonlinear time series and plant response. As introduced in [1–2], the error backpropagation method used in training multi-layer feedforward neural networks may be extended to train recurrent networks. The backpropagation rules are applied throughout a window of time and error gradients are calculated similar to the calculations in feedforward networks. However, as shown in later sections, there exists implicit possibility of instability during real-time learning. This instability may be avoided by adding a regularization coefficient in the updating rules.

This paper consists of 4 sections: A brief background of recurrent neural network learning is introduced in the first section (this section). In section 2, the error gradients and updating rules in real-time recurrent learning are outlined and analyzed. Regularization is then introduced in section 3. Illustrations and results are shown in section 4 and a.conclusion is drawn in the last section.

2   Real-Time Recurrent Learning

The recurrent learning rules to be studied in this paper are derived from [2], commonly known as the Real-Time Recurrent Learning (RTRL). The advantages of using this learning rules may include its small memory usage and simplicity in gradient calculations. Consider a single-layer recurrent neural network as in Fig. 1, the inputs to the neurons may be written as:

$$z_k(t) = \begin{cases} x_k(t) & \text{if} \quad k \in I \\ y_k(t) & \text{if} \quad k \in U \end{cases} \tag{1}$$

where $\mathbf{x}(t)$ denotes the m-tuple of external input signals and I is the corresponding set of indices, $\mathbf{y}(t)$ denotes the n-tuple of feedback outputs and U is the corresponding set of indices. Let the weighted-sums at the neurons be:

$$s_k(t) = \sum_{l \in U \cup I} w_{kl} z_l(t) \tag{2}$$

and the neuron outputs be:

$$y_k(t+1) = f_k(s_k(t)) \tag{3}$$

where $f_k(\cdot)$ is the neuron activation function.

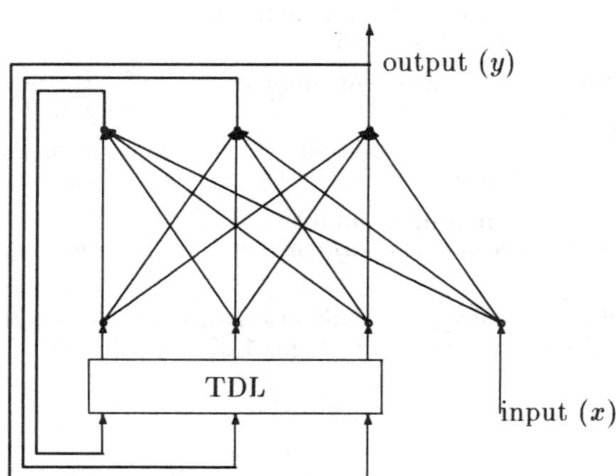

Figure 1: Architecture of a real-time recurrent network (TDL stands for Tapped-Delay-Line)

Similar to the error backpropagation method in feedforward networks (e.g., in [3–4]), the instantaneous sum-squared error (SSE) of the recurrent network can be written as:

$$E(t) = \frac{1}{2} \sum_{k \in U} (e_k(t))^2 \tag{4}$$

and the total error over the whole trajectory (over the window of time considered) can be written as:

$$E_{\text{total}} = \sum_{t=t_{\text{start}}}^{t_{\text{stop}}} E(t). \tag{5}$$

The weight coefficients can then be updated in opposite to the gradient direction:

$$\Delta w_{ij} = \sum_{t=t_{\text{start}}}^{t_{\text{stop}}} \Delta w_{ij}(t) = \sum_{t=t_{\text{start}}}^{t_{\text{stop}}} -\alpha \frac{\partial E(t)}{\partial w_{ij}} \tag{6}$$

where α is the learning rate.

The gradients with respect to the weight coefficients are then:

$$\frac{\partial y_k(t+1)}{\partial w_{ij}} = f'_k(s_k(t)) \left[\sum_{l \in U} w_{kl} \frac{\partial y_l(t)}{\partial w_{ij}} + \delta_{ik} z_j(t) \right] \tag{7}$$

with

$$\frac{\partial y_k(t_{\text{start}})}{\partial w_{ij}} = 0. \tag{8}$$

The derivation of this real-time recurrent learning rules is a straight-forward extension of the backpropagation method. However, as shown in equation (7), each gradient depends on the weighted-sum of the previous gradients and this recursion may lead to instability.

Assuming that only one of the gradients $(\frac{\partial y_k(t)}{\partial w_{ij}})$ with respect to the weight w_{ij}, is non-zero. According to RTRL, the gradient in the next time interval becomes:

$$\frac{\partial y_k(t+1)}{\partial w_{ij}} = f'_k(s_k(t)) \left[\sum_{l \in U} w_{kl} \frac{\partial y_l(t)}{\partial w_{ij}} + \delta_{ik} z_j(t) \right] \tag{9}$$

$$= f'_k(s_k(t)) \left[w_{kk} \frac{\partial y_k(t)}{\partial w_{ij}} + \delta_{ik} z_j(t) \right] \tag{10}$$

$$= f'_k(s_k(t)) w_{kk} \frac{\partial y_k(t)}{\partial w_{ij}} \quad \text{for } i \neq k \tag{11}$$

In other words, if the product $f'_k(s_k(t)) w_{kk}$ is greater than 1 at any instant during the epoch, instability might occur, however rare.

3 Regularization

To avoid the aforementioned instability condition, a regularization coefficient may be added to the gradient equation. The gradient may be modified as:

$$\frac{\partial y_k(t+1)}{\partial w_{ij}} = f'_k(s_k(t)) \left[\lambda \sum_{l \in U} w_{kl} \frac{\partial y_l(t)}{\partial w_{ij}} + (1-\lambda) \delta_{ik} z_j(t) \right]. \tag{12}$$

The regularization coefficient λ may be varied in different time intervals. For example, the coefficient may be calculated as:

$$\lambda = \frac{1}{N \max_{k,l \in U}(w_{kl})} \tag{13}$$

where N is the size of the time window (or the number of data sets to be considered). This regularization method reduces recurrent relationship and, on the other hand, reinforces the influence of the neuron inputs.

4 Illustrations and examples

Consider a simple problem involving a single layer recurrent neural network, with a 2-1 structure as shown in Fig. 2. A ramp signal is to be learned by this simple network. To simplify the calculations, let the training sequence be [0.6 0.5 0.4 0.3] and the bias terms in the neurons are ignored. The optimal weight coefficients would then be calculated as:

$$0.4 = f(0.6w_1 + 0.5w_2)$$
$$0.3 = f(0.5w_1 + 0.4w_2)$$

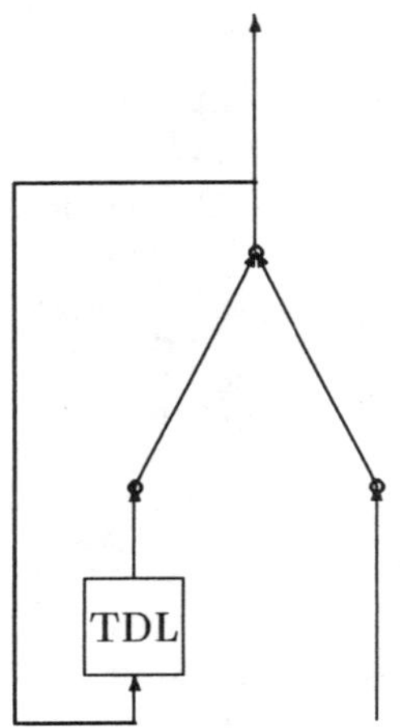

Figure 2: A simple recurrent neural network

$$f^{-1}\left(\begin{bmatrix} 0.4 \\ 0.3 \end{bmatrix}\right) = \begin{bmatrix} 0.6 & 0.5 \\ 0.5 & 0.4 \end{bmatrix}\begin{bmatrix} w_1 \\ w_2 \end{bmatrix}$$

$$\begin{bmatrix} w_1 \\ w_2 \end{bmatrix} = \begin{bmatrix} -26.1463 \\ 30.5646 \end{bmatrix}$$

From the previous sections, the output gradient with respect to the weight coefficient w_1 may be written as:

$$\frac{\partial y(0)}{\partial w_1} = 0$$

$$\frac{\partial y(1)}{\partial w_1} = f'(s(0))\left[x(0) + w_2\frac{\partial y(0)}{\partial w_1}\right]$$

$$= f'(s(0))x(0)$$

$$\frac{\partial y(2)}{\partial w_1} = f'(s(1))\left[x(1) + w_2\frac{\partial y(1)}{\partial w_1}\right]$$

$$\vdots$$

$$\frac{\partial y(k+1)}{\partial w_1} = f'(s(k))\left[x(k) + w_2\frac{\partial y(k)}{\partial w_1}\right]$$

The output gradient with respect to w_2 can be derived similarly. The weight coefficient w_2 in the recurrent connection is comparatively large and the product $f'(s(k))w_2$ is likely to be greater than 1. If the above network is trained with these gradients, the network is likely to undergo instability. Consequently, the gradients $\frac{\partial y(k)}{\partial w_i}$ would be amplified exponentially regardless of the learning rate.

To show the possibility of instability, the aforementioned problem in an epoch may be analyzed. The weight coefficient w_2 is fixed to be the ideal value 30.5646 and bias term is ignored. A random value is chosen to be the initial value of the weight coefficient w_1 and RTRL is performed.

Since there are only two sets of data in the data sets (i.e., the window of calculation is 2), the gradient with respect to w_1 becomes:

$$\frac{\partial y(0)}{\partial w_1} = 0$$

$$\frac{\partial y(1)}{\partial w_1} = f'(s(0)) \times 0.6$$

$$\frac{\partial y(2)}{\partial w_1} = f'(s(1))\left[0.5 + 30.5646\frac{\partial y(1)}{\partial w_1}\right]$$

The gradient in the last equation is amplified to w_2-times of its previous value (ignoring the attenuation by the term $f'(\cdot)$) and if the window of time is larger (it is common practice to employ a large data set), the amplification would be more serious. If, however, regularization is applied to the above equations, the gradient becomes:

$$\frac{\partial y(0)}{\partial w_1} = 0$$

$$\frac{\partial y(1)}{\partial w_1} = f'(s(0)) \times (1 - \lambda) \times 0.6$$

$$\frac{\partial y(2)}{\partial w_1} = f'(s(1)) \left[(1 - \lambda) \times 0.5 + 30.5646\lambda \frac{\partial y(1)}{\partial w_1} \right]$$

The unstable amplification term may be reduced by choosing an appropriate regularization coefficient. In this case, a value smaller than w_2^{-1} would be more than enough.

This simple example shows that when the weight coefficients (especially the recurrent coefficients) are large, instability would occur during real-time recurrent learning. Networks involving more connection and neurons would require far more complicated analysis but the possibility of instability is undeniable.

5 Conclusion

This paper presents a primitive analysis on the stability of real-time recurrent learning algorithm. An illustration is given to show the possibility of unstably growing error gradients. Though an in-depth stochastic analysis is not provided in the paper (the gradient amplification effect is influenced by the change in any single weight coefficient), a hypothetical regularization term is introduced to avoid this ill-effect. As further studies, stochastic analysis of this unstability condition may be performed and optimal value of regularization coefficient may be derived.

Acknowledgement

The authors would like to show their gratitude to the Croucher Foundation for providing the funds for this project.

References

[1] Paul J. Werbos, "Backpropagation Through Time: What It Does and How to Do It," *Proceedings of the IEEE*, vol. 78, no. 10, pp. 1550-1560, October 1990.

[2] Ronald J. Williams, "A Learning Algorithm for Continually Running Fully Recurrent Neural Networks," *Neural Computation*, vol. 1, pp. 270-280, 1989.

[3] Bernard Widrow and Michael A. Lehr, "30 Years of Adaptive Neural Networks: Perceptron, Madaline, and Backpropagation," *Proceedings of the IEEE*, vol. 78, no. 9, pp. 1415-1442, September 1990.

[4] Simon Haykin, "Neural Networks: A Comprehensive Foundation," *Macmillan*, 1994.

A Chaos Association Model
with
a Time-Dependent Periodic Activation Function

Tsuyoshi TANAKA and Masahiro NAKAGAWA

Department of Electrical Engineering, Faculty of Engineering, Nagaoka University of Technology, Kamitomioka 1603-1, Nagaoka, Niigata 940-21, Japan

e-mail: tanaka@pelican.nagaokaut.ac.jp
e-mail: masanaka@voscc.nagaokaut.ac.jp

Abstract   In this paper we shall propose an autoassociation model with a parameter controlled periodic activation function.   In practice the activation function will be controlled between a monotonous periodic function and a nonmonotonous one to achieve a high memory capacity avoiding an unfavourable trapping at a spurious state.   The presently proposed model involves a chaotic dynamics in itself and realises a chaotic wandering mode as well as an autoassociation mode.   In practice, as a result of the computer simulation, one sees that the complete association can be realised up to the loading rate $L/N \sim 0.5$ even for the searching mode.

§1. Introduction

Several associative models have been extensively put forward hitherto on the basis of the autocorrelation dynamics with monotonous activation functions.[1-7]   In such models the monotonous dynamics has been considered to be important to assure the monotonic decreasing of the objective function, or the energy.   In spite of this characteristics, it is also well known that the system may be trapped at a spurious state corresponding to a certain local minimum. In practice the memory capacity of the autocorrelation associative model, or the number of completely associated pattern vectors, is estimated as $\sim 0.15N$ at most for the autocorrelation learning model.

In contrast to the above-mentioned monotonous activation functions, the neurodynamics with nonmonotonous mappings have been recently proposed by several authors,[8,9] who have found that the nonmonotonous mapping in a neuron dynamics possesses a certain advantage of the memory capacity superior than the conventional association models with such a monotonous mapping as the signum function, $\mathrm{sgn}(x)$ for the abbreviation.   This finding was explained as a result of an orthogonalisation process of the apparent synaptic weight matrix as a first approximation through the nonmonotonous dynamics.[9]   Later Shiino and Fukai have analysed the memory capacity for a somewhat simplified nonmonotonous activation function with the continuous time in a differential framework, and have concluded that the complete association can be realised for the loading rate $L/N \sim 0.38$ with the critical overlap 0.57.[10]

Very recently, in contrast to the previously reported monotonous chaotic models,[11-15] the present author proposed a novel neuron model with a periodic activation function to construct an association model with chaotic dynamics with the discrete time model.[16-21] Therein the memory capacity was found to be increased up to $L/N \sim 0.4$ beyond the previously proposed monotonous dynamic models with the discrete time. This fact may be explained qualitatively as a result of the relaxation of the monotonous decreasing condition of the energy, which may prevent the system from an escaping from an unfavourable local minimum.

From the above-mentioned viewpoints, we shall propose a novel dynamic retrieval model with a time-dependent activation function which will be controlled continuously from a monotonous increasing periodic function to a decreasing one via nonmonotonous ones. Such a time-dependent periodic mapping is found to possess a capability to escape from an unfavourable spurious metastable state as a result of such a nonmonotonous property of the mapping as well as the resultant chaotic behaviour of the neurons. In the next section some theoretical preliminaries will be given to construct a periodic chaos dynamics. Then some computational results will be provided in §3 to present an ability for the memory retrieval. Finally a few concluding remarks will be addressed in §4 to elucidate the effect of the chaos in the present neurodynamics.

§3. Theory

The present neuro-dynamics with the discrete time and the continuous information is defined by the conventional steepest descent algorithm, i.e.

$$\sigma_i(t+1) = k \bullet \sigma_i(t) - (1-k) \bullet \left(\frac{\partial E}{\partial s^\dagger_i} \right)(t) \quad , \tag{1}$$

where k is a memory constant ranging over $(0,1)$, the neuron output s_i and the internal state have to be related in terms of

$$s_i = f(\sigma_i) + \chi(t) \bullet \theta_i \quad , \tag{2}$$

where $f(\bullet)$ is the activation function, $\chi(t)$ is a time decreasing function as will be defined later, and the objective function to be minimised, or the energy of the system, E may be put into

$$E = -\frac{1}{2} \sum_{i=1}^{N} \sum_{j=1}^{N} w_{ij} s^\dagger_i s_j \quad . \tag{3}$$

The weighting matrix w_{ij} can be defined as

$$w_{ij} = \sum_{r=1}^{L} e^{(r)}_i e^{\dagger(r)}_j \quad , \tag{4}$$

where the embedded vectors $e^{(r)}_i$ and the conjugate ones $e^{\dagger(r)}_j$ are orthogonal each other as follows,

$$\sum_{i=1}^{N} e^{(r)}{}_{i} e^{\dagger(s)}{}_{j} = \delta_{rs} \quad , \tag{5}$$

Noting that the conjugate vector $s^{\dagger}{}_{i}$ can be related to s_{i} in terms of

$$s_{i}{}^{\dagger} = \sum_{r=1}^{L}\sum_{j=1}^{N} e^{\dagger(r)}{}_{i} e^{\dagger(r)}{}_{j} s_{j} \quad , \qquad s_{i} = \sum_{r=1}^{L}\sum_{j=1}^{N} e^{(r)}{}_{i} e^{(r)}{}_{j} s^{\dagger}{}_{j} \quad , \tag{6}$$

the dynamics of the present system can be reduced to

$$\sigma_{i}(t+1) = k \bullet \sigma_{i}(t) + (1-k) \bullet \sum_{j=1}^{N} w_{ij} s_{j}(t) \quad . \tag{7}$$

Here it should be borne in mind that the present model leads to the continuous time model as $k \to 1$, whereas it reads the discrete time model as $k \to 0$.

The period $\tau(t)$ and the symmetric parameter $d(t)$ are to be controlled as the system is driven from a chaotic state into an association point in the following manner.

$$\tau(t) = \begin{cases} \left\{ \dfrac{1}{1-d(t)+c} - \dfrac{1}{1+c} \right\} + \tau(0) & (\tau < \tau_{max}) \\[2mm] \tau_{max} & (\tau \geq \tau_{max} \gg 1) \end{cases} \qquad (0<c \ll 1) \quad , \tag{8}$$

$$d(t) = \begin{cases} \dfrac{t}{T_{d}} & (t \leq T_{d}) \\[2mm] 1 & (t > T_{d}) \end{cases} \quad , \tag{9}$$

$$\chi(t+1) = \chi(t) - \kappa \bullet \chi(t) \bullet (1-\chi(t)) \qquad \left(\chi(0) = 1-\varepsilon \ \left(0<\varepsilon \ll 1 \right) \right) \quad . \tag{10}$$

Assuming that an asynchronous updating holds, the time dependence of the energy function under an asynchronous mode can be derived as

$$E(t+1) - E(t) = -\frac{1}{2} \sum_{i=1}^{N}\sum_{j=1}^{N} w_{ij} \left\{ s^{\dagger}{}_{i}(t+1) s_{j}(t+1) - s^{\dagger}{}_{i}(t) s_{j}(t) \right\}$$

$$= -\sum_{j \neq k}^{N} w_{kj} s_{j}(t) \bullet (s^{\dagger}{}_{k}(t+1) - s^{\dagger}{}_{k}(t)) - \frac{1}{2} w_{kk} \left\{ s^{\dagger}{}_{k}(t+1) s_{k}(t+1) - s^{\dagger}{}_{k}(t) s_{k}(t) \right\} \quad . \tag{11}$$

$$= -\frac{1}{(1-k)} (\sigma_{k}(t+1) - k \bullet \sigma_{k}(t)) \bullet (s^{\dagger}{}_{k}(t+1) - s^{\dagger}{}_{k}(t)) \quad (\text{if } w_{kk}=0)$$

Especially the discrete time model is assumed as argued below, the above equation reads

$$E(t+1) - E(t) = -\sigma_{k}(t+1) \bullet (s^{\dagger}{}_{k}(t+1) - s^{\dagger}{}_{k}(t)) \quad . \tag{12}$$

On the other hand, for the continuous time model as $k = 1-\varepsilon$ $(0<\varepsilon \ll 1)$, the time dependence of the energy leads to

$$E(t+1) - E(t) = = -\frac{1}{\varepsilon} (\sigma_{k}(t+1) - \sigma_{k}(t)) \bullet (s^{\dagger}{}_{k}(t+1) - s^{\dagger}{}_{k}(t)) \quad . \tag{13}$$

Hence, in any event, the energy has a tendency to decrease and to increase for $d=0$ and $d=1$, respectively. In our model the piecewise linear periodic activation function is assumed to be controlled in terms of a couple of the parameters, $d(t)$ and $\tau(t)$, as depicted in Fig.1. That is, the symmetry and the periodicity of the activation function can be controlled by the symmetric parameter $d(t)$ and the period $\tau(t)$, respectively. The dependence of the activation function on $d(t)$ is shown in Fig.2(a)-(c).

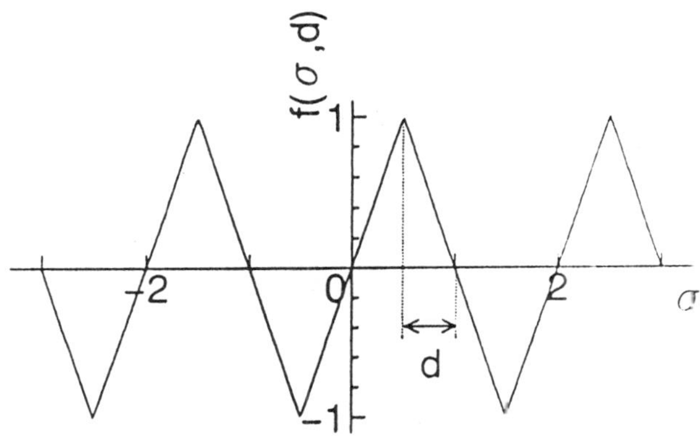

Fig.1 Piecewise linear periodic activation function.

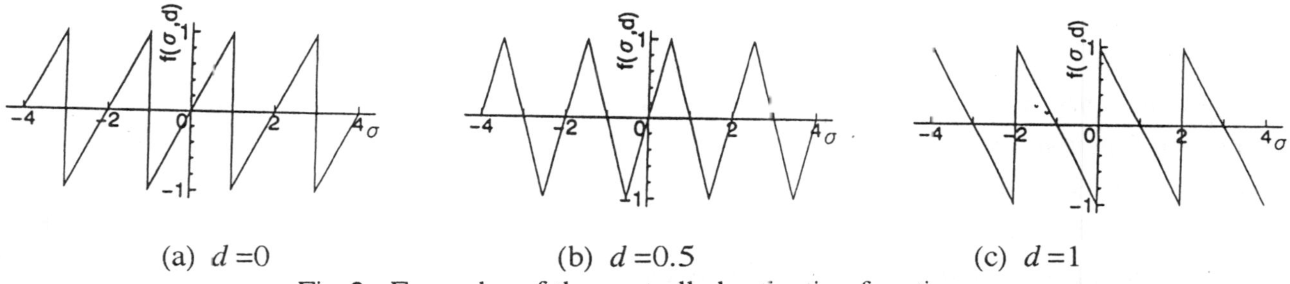

(a) $d=0$ (b) $d=0.5$ (c) $d=1$

Fig.2 Examples of the controlled activation function

The overlaps can be defined in terms of

$$o^{(r)}(t)=\sum_{i=1}^{N} e^{\dagger(r)}{}_i s_i(t) \qquad (1 \leq r \leq L) \tag{14}$$

§3. Results

Let us present first the time dependences of the overlaps $o^{(r)}(t)$, energy $E(t)$ in Figs.3 (a) and (b), respectively, for $N=50$, $L=10$, and $\kappa=0.5$.

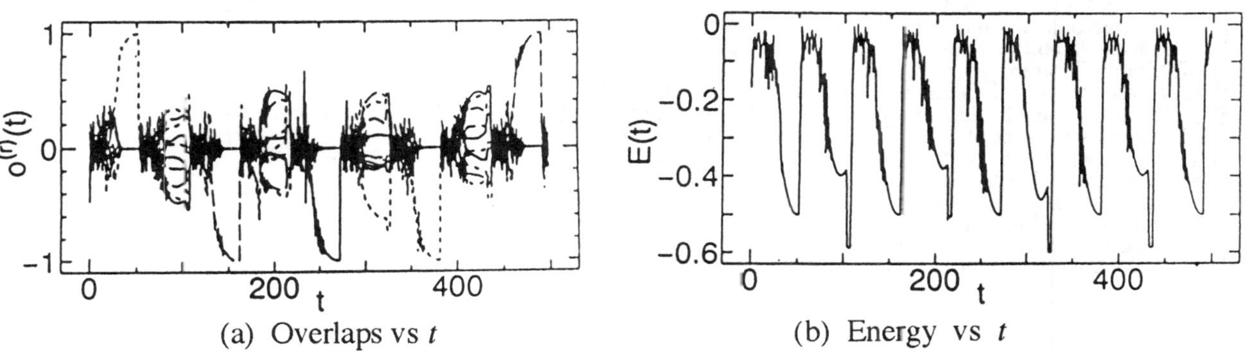

(a) Overlaps vs t (b) Energy vs t

Fig.3 An example of the autoassociation process.

Next let us present the association characteristics with respect to the loading rate L/N in Fig.4. Here the success rate was evaluated for 50 trials with different embedding random patterns and initial state, and N and T_{max} were set to 50 and 5000, respectively. The initial Hamming distance H_d was set to 5 therein. For comparison we have presented, in Fig.4(b), the loading characteristics for the associatron with the conventional activation function such that

$$s_i(t) = \text{sgn}\big(\sigma_i(t)\big) . \tag{15}$$

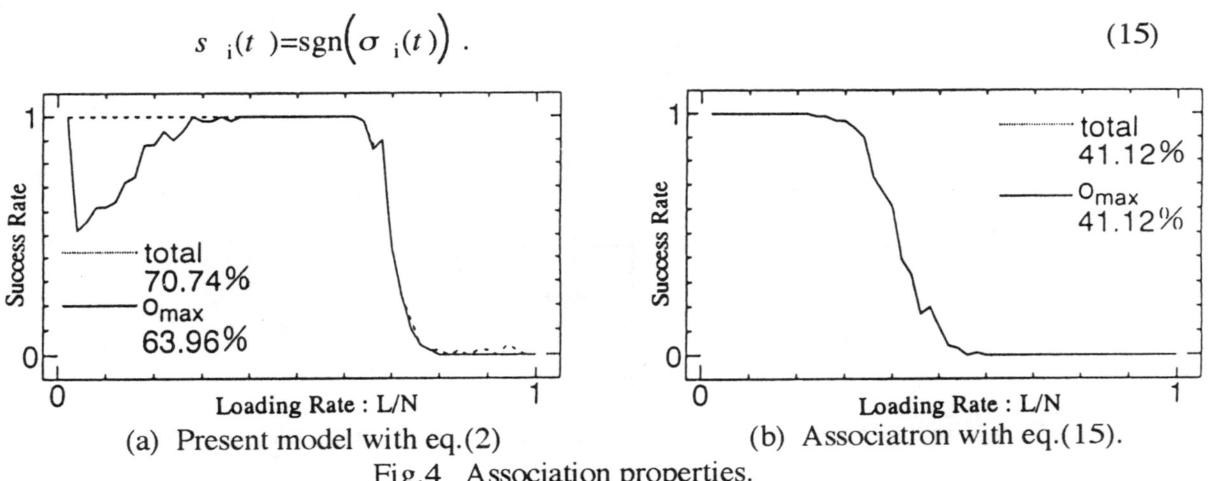

(a) Present model with eq.(2)   (b) Associatron with eq.(15).

Fig.4   Association properties.

§4.   Conclusions

In this work, we have proposed a chaos neural network model with a time-dependent periodic activation function, and found a remarkable promotion of the memory retrieval rate as a parameter controlled chaotic dynamics in comparison with the conventional association model as seen in the associatron. In practice one has confirmed that the memory rate becomes 2~3 times larger than the conventional association model. In addition it has been found that the present system can achieve a complete association through the transient chaotic state up to $L/N \sim 0.5$ without any information for the embedded patterns. This finding remarkably implies an application to the memory searching model.

References
1)   J.A.Anderson: Math. Biosci.**14**(1972)197.
2)   T.Kohonen: IEEE Trans.**C-21**(1972)353.
3)   K.Nakano: IEEE Trans. **SMC-2**(1972)380.
4)   S.Amari: Biol. Cybern.**26**(1977)175.
5)   D.J.Amit, H.Gutfreund, and H. Sompolinsky:Phys. Rev. Lett.**55** (1985)1530.
6)   E. Gardner: J. Phys. **A19**(1986)L1047.
7)   R.J. McEliece, R.J. Posner, E.R. Rodemich and S.S. Venkatesh: IEEE Trans. on Information Theory, **IT-33**(1987)461.
8)   M.Morita :Neural Networks **6**(1993)115.
9)   Hiro-F.Yanai and S.Amari: Proc. of ICNN'93, San Francisco (1993)1385.
10) M. Shiino and T. Fukai: J. Phys. Math. Gen. **26**(1993)L831.
11) M.Inoue and A.Nagayoshi: Phys.Lett.**A158**(1991)373.
12) H. Kakeya and T. Kindo: J. J. N. N. S. **1**(1994)20[in Japanese].
13) K.Aihara, T.Numajiri, G.Matsumoto, and M.Kotani: Phys. Lett. **A116**(1986)313.
14) K.Nakamura and M.Nakagawa:J. Phys. Soc. of Jpn.**62**(1993)2942.
15) T. Kasahara and M. Nakagawa: IEICE Trans. on Fundamentals **J78-A**(1995)114[in Japanese].
16) M.Nakagawa: Proc. of ICONIP'94,Seoul, **1**(1994)609.
17) M.Nakagawa: Proc. of ICDC'94,Tokyo, **2**(1995)603.
18) M. Nakagawa: J. Phys.Soc. Jpn.**64**(1995)1023.
19) T. Kasahara and M. Nakagawa: J. Phys. Soc. Jpn.**64**(1995)4964.
20) M. Nakagawa:IEICE Trans. on Fundamentals **E78-A** (1995)412.
21) M. Nakagawa: J. Phys.Soc.Jpn.**64**(1995)3112.
22) M. Nakagawa: Proc. of ICNN'95, Australia(1995)3028.

EXPERIMENTAL STUDIES OF RECURRENT NETWORKS
FOR LEARNING REGULAR GRAMMARS

Li. H. Chen and Poy B. Tan
School of Electrical and Electronic Engineering
Nanyang Technological University, Nanyang Avenue,
Singapore 639798, Republic of Singapore.
Phone : +65-799-1207   Fax : +65-791-2687
E-mail : elhchen@ntuix.ntu.ac.sg, ea1814168@ntuvax.ntu.ac.sg

ABSTRACT

Experimental study of two existing second order recurrent neural network models for learning regular grammars is reported. Structural and algorithmic differences between the two models are analysed using a generalised recurrent network topology. Two benchmark problems : Tomita and Reber Grammars have been used to explore the behaviour of the two models. State transition diagrams and numerical results are shown to provide insights to virtues and drawbacks of both approaches. Comparisons are made based on training speed and generalisation accuracy. This justified the existing approaches and therefore lays foundations for the development of new models for fulfilling more complicated tasks.

1.   INTRODUCTION

Learning to infer grammatical rules from a finite set of example strings is commonly referred as grammatical inference [3]. Recently, much effort has been made using connectionist architectures to model the language inference engine. Notably, the earlier work of Elman [4] and Servan-Schreiber etc. [5] employed Simple Recurrent Networks as a predictive machine to deduce the next in-coming symbols. Pollack [6] later used a backpropagation-based methodology to compactly represent variable-size structures present in languages.

In recent years, many research papers have been found investigating various types of recurrent networks for inferring regular grammars and context-free grammars [1], [7], [8], [9], [10], [11]. Of particular interest here is the analog second-order network proposed by Giles et al in [1], [10], [11] for regular grammars inference. This topology is commonly referred to as Neural Network Finite State Automata (NNFSA). Under formal language theory [12], a particular regular grammar has a one-to-one correspondence with an ideal finite state automata (FSA) M. The ultimate objective of regular grammar learning is then to extract a set of discrete grammatical rules governing the state transitions in M. Using NNFSA, an extra step for rules extraction is necessary after training is completed. This is due to the analog nature of its output signals. The entire setup involving NNFSA is shown in Figure 1.

The most common approach for rules extraction in neural networks is to divide the state space into uniform, disjoint partitions as mentioned in [1], [10]. However, NNFSA does not consider how the neural network formulates the discriminant function to identify individual states. In this case, when the extracted grammatical rules are applied to perform classification of longer strings, error may occur due to imprecision in state quantization. An alternative model based on NNFSA proposed by Zeng et al [2] function by discretizing the analog states into binary states before feedback. We call this model a Discrete Neural Network Finite State Automata (DNNFSA). The central idea of the approach is to integrate rule-extraction into training, eliminating the need and problems of the postprocessing.

The purpose of this study is to obtain a deep understanding of the behaviour of the two models for learning regular grammars by testing their strength on solving the two benchmark problems. This gives us more insights into the capability of the models, which in turn may provide us the foundations needed for future development.

In the next section, a generalized topology will be introduced to highlight the structural and algorithmic discrepancies between NNFSA and DNNFSA. Subsequently, we present simulation results obtained by training and testing these two models on the Tomita grammars as well as the more complex Reber grammar. State transition diagrams and numerical results are shown to provide insights to the pros and cons of both approaches.

We end this paper by emphasizing the significant points of this investigation accompanied by a brief conclusion.

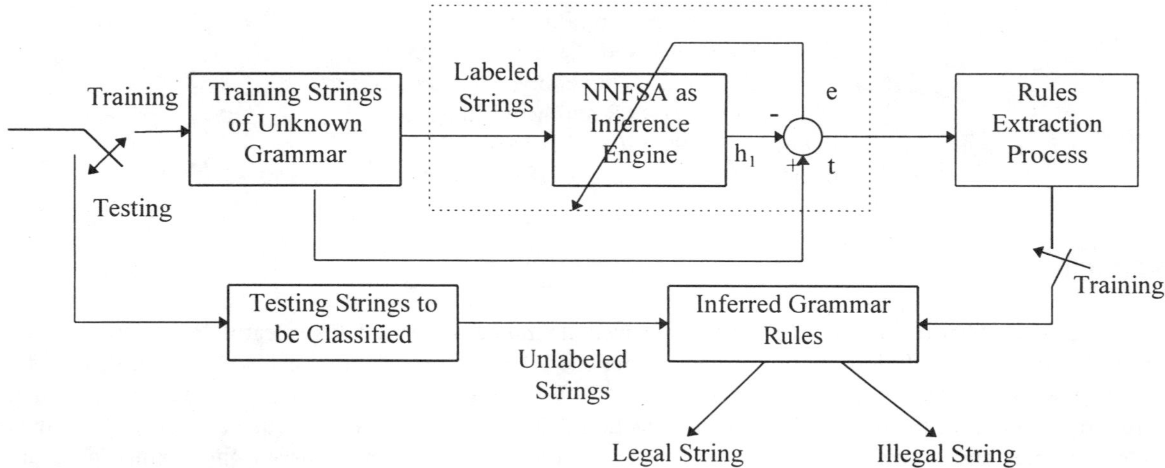

Figure 1   Overall picture of regular grammar learning using NNFSA

2.   ARCHITECTURE & LEARNING ALGORITHM FOR NNFSA & DNNFSA

The generalized network architecture for NNFSA and DNNFSA is a second-order variant of the fully connected recurrent network first used by Williams and Zipser [13]. Figure 2 shows the arrangement of the neurons and the associated variables. The following equations specify the forward propagation for both NNFSA and DNNFSA:

$$h_i^{t+1} = f(\sum_j \sum_k W_{ijk} S_j^t I_k^t) \quad \forall i = 1 \text{ to } N \tag{1}$$

$$S_i^{t+1} = g(h_i^{t+1}) \quad \forall i = 1 \text{ to } N \tag{2}$$

I_k^t refers to the kth element of the input vector. W_{ijk} denotes the weight link from unit j in layer 1 to unit i in layer 2 for the kth input element. h_i^t and S_i^t represent the ith activation and output values at time-step t respectively (i=1 denotes the neuron which has a target value). N is the total number of hidden neurons in layer 2. f is the sigmoid function for both NNFSA and DNNFSA. However, g is the identity function i.e. g(x)=x for NNFSA. While for the case of DNNFSA, g is the threshold function with bias at 0.5. Equations (1) and (2) totally specify the state transition relationship.

The objective function is defined as:

$$E = \tfrac{1}{2}\sum_{p=1}^{P} e_p^2 = \tfrac{1}{2}\sum_{p=1}^{P} (T_p - h_1^L)^2 \tag{3}$$

where P is the total number of training strings used in the training set. h_1^L is the value of h_1^t when the end of individual string is reached. System starts accepting inputs at t=1. T_p is the teacher signal provided at the end of each string. For NNFSA, an application of Real Time Recurrent Learning [13] to calculate the forward sensitivity variables results in following relationships:

$$\Delta W_{ijk} = -\eta \frac{\partial e_p}{\partial W_{ijk}} = -\eta \frac{\partial e_p}{\partial h_1^L} \frac{\partial h_1^L}{\partial W_{ijk}} = \eta(T_p - h_1^L) \frac{\partial h_1^L}{\partial W_{ijk}} \tag{4}$$

$$\frac{\partial h_m^{t+1}}{\partial W_{ijk}} = f' \cdot (\sum_d W_{mdk'} \frac{\partial h_d^{t+1}}{\partial W_{ijk}} + \delta_{im}\delta_{kk'} S_j^t) \tag{5}$$

δ_{ij} is the Kronecker delta for index i and j. We are using a localist one-hot encoding for the input symbols. Therefore, this results in only a single summation term for d = 1 to N and k' signifies the only non-zero element in input vector $\mathbf{I}^t$.

For DNNFSA, equation (4) and (5) hold except that all $\dfrac{\partial(\cdot)}{\partial W_{ijk}}$ terms are replaced by $\dfrac{\tilde{\partial}(\cdot)}{\partial W_{ijk}}$ which called the "pseudo-gradient" terms [2]. This change is necessary to reflect that equation (5) is now an approximation since we cannot use the slope of the threshold function in (5), instead we have to replaced it with the slope of the sigmoid.

Therefore, in DNNFSA the feedback vector is of binary nature in contrary to analog values in NNFSA. During adaptation, NNFSA used equation (5) while DNNFSA actually employ an approximated version of (5). The justification of the use of the pseudo-gradient can be found in [2].

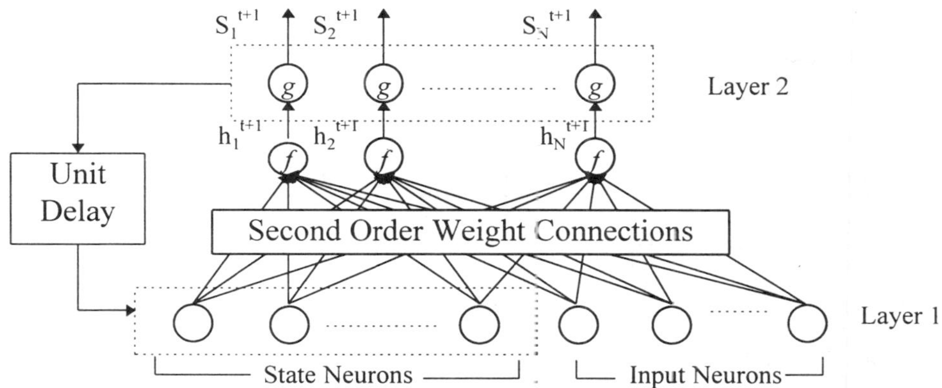

Figure 2. The generalized architecture for NNFSA and DNNFSA.

3.   SIMULATION RESULTS AND DISCUSSIONS

Two sets of experiment have been carried out using both NNFSA and DNNFSA models to learn a subset of Tomita grammars and the Reber grammar. The simulations on Tomita grammars aimed to provide a preliminary investigation on the effectiveness of NNFSA and DNNFSA in learning simple regular grammars. Efficiency of training phase and the generalization performances are the two major metrics of interest. Subsequently, we would like to determine how both approaches scale up as the number of input symbols increases. We used the Reber grammar for this purpose, which contains 7 input symbols compared to 2 in the Tomita grammars.

Initial network weights are randomly set to between -1.0 and 1.0. We represented a binary 'high' by 0.8 and 'low' by 0.2 in DNNFSA. At t = 1, the internal states vector $\mathbf{S}^0$ are initialized with $S_1^0 = 0.8$ and $S_1^0 = 0.2$ for i = 2 to N. At the end of each string's presentation, we reset the $\mathbf{S}^t$ vector to $\mathbf{S}^0$. T_p is assigned a target of 1.0 for legal strings and 0.0 for illegal strings.

The stopping criteria for NNFSA and DNNFSA differed slightly. For DNNFSA, we claimed that a trial converges if :
  (1) all training strings are correctly classified based on the binary value of S_1^L
  (2) accumulative error E fells below a pre-selected value.
Whereas for NNFSA, we check the follow conditions for convergence
  (1) individual error e_p for each of training strings has an absolute value, which must be less than a preselected value ε
  (2) accumulative error E fells below a pre-selected value.
  (3) During testing, strings are classified as legal if $S_1^L >= 0.50$ and illegal otherwise.

For all the trials for training the 4 Tomita grammars: #1, #4, #5 and #7, the number of hidden neurons N is arbitrarily chosen to be 4 or 5. We considered a trial failure if training did not converged within 1000 epochs. The training set comprised all strings up to length L_{train}, with no repetitions. The testing set contained all strings up to length L_{test}, but excluding those strings in the training set. P_{train} and P_{test} refer to the number of training and testing strings used respectively. The training and testing sets were identical for both NNFSA and DNNFSA.

The results obtained from training the four Tomita grammars are presented in Table 1. Ten trials are carried out for each grammar. Table 1 shows the training epochs and convergence rate together with the generalization performances.

Table 1. Training and testing results for Tomita grammars

Tomita Grammar Expt.	Training Sets		Testing Sets		NNFSA ($\varepsilon = 0.2$)		DNNFSA	
					Training	Testing	Training	Testing
	L_{train}	P_{train}	L_{test}	P_{test}	Ave. Epochs	%Correct	Ave. Epochs	%Correct
1	5	62	9	960	30.2	100.0	24.2	100.0
4	8	510	10	1536	55.3	100.0	25.6	100.0
5	8	510	10	1536	119.8	100.0	93.8	100.0
7	8	510	10	1536	292.0#	99.6#	371.3*	99.1*

Notes :
Total 8 trials did not converge. * Total 7 trials did not converge.

From the Table 1, the results suggested that Tomita #1, Tomita #4 and Tomita #5 can be learnt very well by both NNFSA and DNNFSA. However, Tomita #7 appeared to be difficult for both models. In terms of training speed, we find that DNNFSA converged faster for the first 3 grammars but NNFSA managed to find a solution faster in Tomita #7. Since we used $\varepsilon = 0.2$ in NNFSA and the corresponding value in DNNFSA = 0.5 (due to using g=threshold biased at 0.5), a concrete, unprejudiced conclusion cannot be made unless both figures are close to each other. This point will be further investigated for Reber grammar. Both trained models are on par with respect to generalization performance with NNFSA having a slight edge in the difficult Tomita #7 grammar.

To confirm that both NNFSA and DNNFSA had learnt the underlying grammars, we provide the state transition diagrams for the FSA learnt in Tomita #4 and Tomita #7 grammars. In Figure 3a, we show the ideal FSA for Tomita #4 grammar, which accepts strings not containing "000" as substring. This is compared against the inferred FSA extracted from a particular DNNFSA and NNFSA trial. The FSAs are shown in Figure 3b and 3c respectively. Dark rings represent accepting states while light rings indicate non-accepting states. A string is classified as legal if it terminated on one of the accepting states. 'XXXX' represents the internal binary state of the FSA learnt by the neural network.

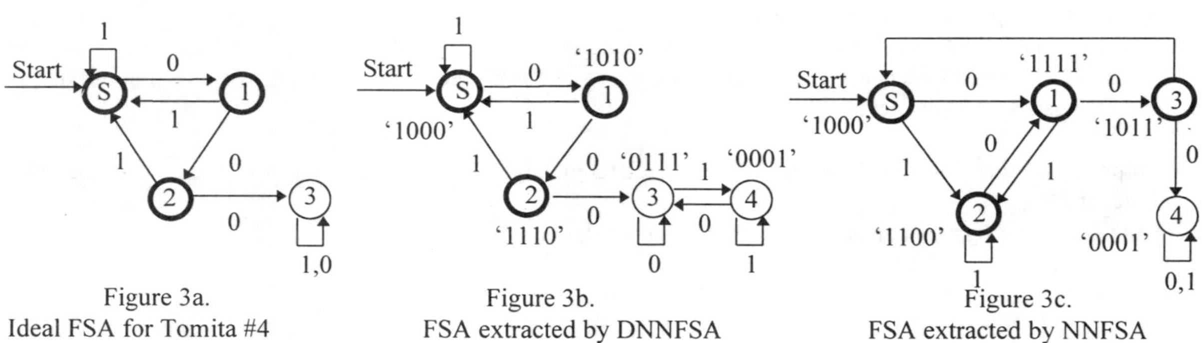

Figure 3a.	Figure 3b.	Figure 3c.
Ideal FSA for Tomita #4	FSA extracted by DNNFSA	FSA extracted by NNFSA

A check on the FSAs depicted in Figure 3b. and 3c. confirm that both DNNFSA and NNFSA learnt the underlying rules effectively. In fact, both FSAs will reduce the ideal FSA in Figure 3a. by applying standard Moore's Minimization algorithm [12].

On the other hand, both type of networks appeared to have difficulty in trying to mimic the Tomita #7 grammar. This particular grammar accepts strings with (0*1*0*1*). Only 2 out of 10 trials for NNFSA managed to converge with N = 4, while only 3 trials were successfully trained for DNNFSA. The level of difficulty for this grammar is clearly higher compared to the other 3 grammars. By using more hidden neurons in the network or including longer strings in training, we might be able to obtain better results. This exercise was not actively pursued as our intent here is to demonstrate the capabilities of DNNFSA and NNFSA. The state transition diagrams extracted from trained DNNFSA and NNFSA networks are depicted in Figure 4a. and 4b. respectively. Both FSAs have 7 internal states, they are almost equivalent operationally except for a slight difference in representation of the 'trap' state. In DNNFSA, state 2 is designated for that purpose whereas in NNFSA, state 2 and 4 are used.

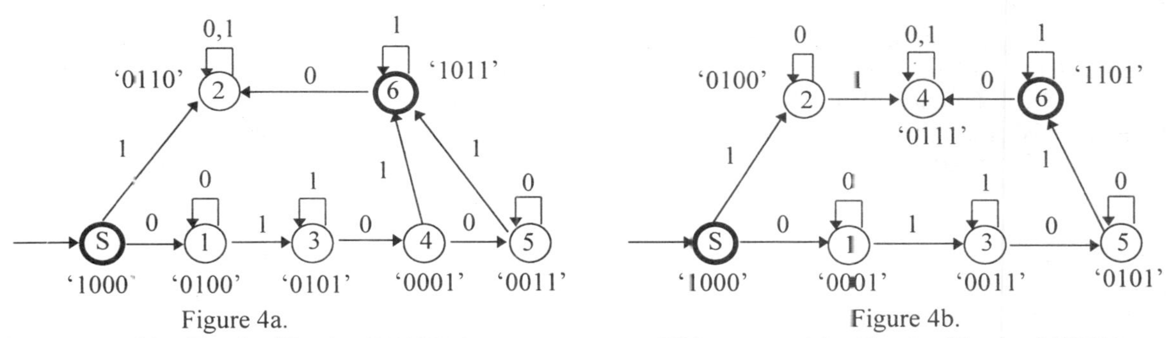

<table>
<tr><td>Figure 4a.</td><td>Figure 4b.</td></tr>
<tr><td>FSA extracted for Tomita #7 using DNNFSA</td><td>FSA extracted for Tomita #7 using NNFSA</td></tr>
</table>

The results from Tomita grammars act as a preliminary examination of the viability of both NNFSA and DNNFSA for inferring regular grammars. However, the simplicity of the grammars prevented us from observing any noticeable difference in their respective virtues. We propose a set of more complex regular grammar first introduced by Reber [15]. Particularly, we are also interested to know how both approaches scale up when the number of symbols increases substantially. In this case, we would have to infer from a limited, given set of training strings permitted by the environment. This is more akin to practical situations where the training set forms only a small part of the set containing all possible strings. The training and testing sets were mutually exclusive collections of 500 randomly selected, non-repeated strings from pre-defined maximum fixed length L_{train} = 15 and L_{test} = 36 respectively. Number of hidden units N was set to 7 for all simulations performed. Earlier we mentioned the effect of ε when using NNFSA, here we provide whole range of simulation results corresponding to different ε values. Five independent trials are run for each architectural settings. The results are summarized in Table 2.

Table 2. Training and testing results for Reber grammar

Experiment	Network	Training		Testing
Number @	Architecture	Convergence Rate	Ave. Epochs	%Correct
1	NNFSA (ε=0.1)	5/5	339.0	95.6
2	NNFSA (ε=0.2)	5/5	197.2	95.4
3	NNFSA (ε=0.3)	5/5	146.6	93.4
4	NNFSA (ε=0.4)	5/5	70.6	94.1
5	NNFSA (ε=0.5)	5/5	77.0	97.0
6	DNNFSA	5/5	302.2	94.1

From Table 2, we confirm our earlier proposition that the selection of ε value has a notable effect on the outcome of the simulations. Generally, as the output tolerance ε increases, NNFSA converged faster. Comparing the readings (in @5) for the case of NNFSA (ε=0.5) against DNNFSA, we observed a 4.5 times speedup in training time. This comparison indicated strongly that NNFSA has a better convergence quality than DNNFSA given identical error tolerance. This point was further reinforced by observations of many plateaus in the error surface landscape during DNNFSA training. This can be attributable to the use of "pseudo" gradient descent RTRL rather than the "true" gradient descent in NNFSA.

Quality of generalization did not suffer due to relaxation of ε, and in fact NNFSA (ε=0.5) is about 3% better than DNNFSA. Overall, the generalization properties for both models are comparable. Another objective in this experiment is to examine the NNFSA and DNNFSA's usefulness as the number of input symbols becomes big. Both structures showed promising recognition rates ($\geq$93%) even when the training set constitutes only a minute ratio of the entire possible strings ($500/\sum_{i=1}^{1} to 15} 7^i \approx 9.03 \times 10^{-11}$).

4.   CONCLUSION

In this paper, we explored the behaviour of two existing recurrent network models for learning regular grammars. Our independent experiments have not only confirmed that both models are plausible approaches for deducing underlying grammar rules. The results derived from the set of experiments also helped to analyse individual features of the two models.

Given identical final error tolerance values, NNFSA appeared clearly to converge faster during training. The inferior convergence property in DNNFSA is due to the use of 'pseudo-gradient descent'. However DNNFSA does show the capability of formulating isolated points in activation space to represent internal states of a FSA in training. This effectively eliminates the need for a post training rule extraction process in NNFSA. NNFSA and DNNFSA also demonstrated high recognition rate even for the much more sophisticated Reber grammar. The quality of generalisation as a whole is comparable between the two models.

From the above analyses, we envisage a combination of NNFSA and DNNFSA should be able to give a better solution to regular grammar inference tasks. This leads to the development of a new adaptively discretizing model which will be described in another paper.

REFERENCES

[1]   Giles, C. L., Chen D., Miller, C. B., Chen, H. H., Sun, G. Z. and Lee, Y. C., "Second-Order Recurrent Neural Networks for Grammatical Inference", in Proceedings of International Joint Conference on Neural Networks, July 1991, Vol. 2, pp273-281.

[2]   Zeng, Z., Goodman, R. M. and Smyth, P., "Learning Finite State Machines with Self-Clustering Recurrent Networks", Neural Computation, Vol. 5, No. 6, pp977-990, 1993.

[3]   Fu, K. S., "Syntactic Pattern Recognition and Applications", Englewood Cliffs, New Jersey, Prentice Hall, 1982.

[4]   Elman, J. L., "Finding Structure in Time", Cognitive Science, Vol. 14, pp179-211, 1990.

[5]   Servan-Schreiber, D., Cleeremans, A. and McClelland, J. L., "Learning Sequential Structure in Simple Recurrent Networks", in Advances in Neural Information Processing Systems 1, pp643-652, 1989.

[6]   Pollack, J. B., "Recursive Distributed Representations", Artificial Intelligence, 46, pp77-105, 1990.

[7]   Das, S., Giles, C. L. and Sun, G.-Z., "Learning Context-Free Grammars : Capabilities and Limitations of a Recurrent Neural Network with an External Memory Stack", in Proceedings of the Fourteenth Annual Conference of the Cognitive Science Society, pp791-795, 1992.

[8]   Das, S., Giles, C. L. and Sun G.-Z., "Using Prior Knowledge in a NNPDA to Learn Context-Free Languages", in Advances in Neural Information Processing Systems 5, S. J. Hanson, J. D. Cowan and C. L. Giles (eds.), pp65-72, 1993.

[9]   Giles, C. L., Sun, G. Z., Chen, H. H., Lee, Y. C. and Chen, D., "Higher Order Recurrent Neural Networks and Grammatical Inference", in Advances in Neural Information Processing Systems 2, D. S. Touretzky (ed.), pp380-387, 1990.

[10]   Giles, C. L., Miller, C. B., Chen, D., Chen, H. H., Sun, G. Z. and Lee, Y. C., "Learning and Extracting Finite State Automata with Second-Order Recurrent Neural Networks", Neural Computation, 4, pp395-405, 1992.

[11]   Giles, C. L., Miller, C. B., Chen, D., Sun, G. Z., Chen, H. H. and Lee, Y. C., "Extracting and Learning an Unknown Grammar with Recurrent Neural Networks", in Advances in Neural Information Processing Systems 4, J. E. Moody, S. J. Hanson, R. P. Lippmann (eds.), pp317-324, 1992.

[12]   Carroll, J. and Long, D., "Theory of Finite Automata - with an Introduction to Formal Languages", Prentice Hall, 1989.

[13]   Williams, R. J. and Zipser, D., "A Learning Algorithm for Continually Running Fully Recurrent Neural Networks", Neural Computation, Vol. 1, No. 2, pp270-280, 1989.

[14]   Tomita, M., "Dynamic Construction of Finite-State Automata from Examples Using Hill-Climbing", in Proceedings of the Fourth Annual Cognitive Science Conference, pp105, 1982.

[15]   Reber, A. S., "Implicit Learning of Artificial Grammar", Journal of Verbal Learning and Verbal Behavior, 5, pp855-863, 1962.

Cooccurrence Links: Analogical Inference with an Oscillatory Neural Network

Tokiko Yamanoue

Kyushu Institute of Technology
1-1,Sensui-cho,Kitakyushu,Japan 804
tokiko@comp.kyutech.ac.jp

Abstract— Analogical inference seems to be a good starting point to bridge the gap between "symbolic" and "pattern" processing, since it can be understood as structured mapping or unification between predicate arguments, while it can also be considered as pattern matching between previously acquired facts. In this paper, we model predicates and unification by extending the oscillatory neural network solution to the binding problem, and numerically examine if such a system can perform analogical inference.

1 Introduction

In order to model human intelligence, several ideas have been proposed to incorporate "symbolic" with "pattern" information processing. Some try to start from "pattern" [5], some from "symbols" [1] and others choose hybrids [7]. Another possibility is to start from a task that can be understood from both sides: Analogical inference seems to be a good candidate of such a task, since it can be understood as structured mapping (or unification) between predicate arguments [6], while it can also be considered as pattern matching between previously acquired facts.

Neural network implementation of predicates and unifications seems to be a good candidate to implement such analogical inference. However, among such studies [1, 4, 5, 8, 9], analogical inference has not been investigated. Miikkulainen's system[5] is based on similarity of sentences and cannot realize structured mapping. Touretzky et al.'s system[8] can bind only one variable at a time and is not satisfactory to realize structured mapping. Shastri et al.'s, Lange et al.'s and the authour's systems[1, 4, 9] employ oscillatory neural networks (ONN) and realize unification as synchronization. Among them, Lange et al.'s system[4] labels each object by individual frequency, leading to difficulty in flexible identification necessary for analogical identification. Shatri et al.'s and the authour's systems[1, 9] are more suited for our purpose in that they label objects by phase, enabling flexible identification. In this paper, we encode predicates and unifications in a method similar to [1, 9] and examine if such a system can perform analogical inference. Note that while Shastri et al.'s system[1] is designed to mimic rigorous predicate calculus with given rules, we design our system so that it can perform analogical inference which is more like dynamic creation of rules from a dataset of facts. In this way, we do not have to imagine that pre-installed predicates themselves correspond to complex symbols, but rather expect that symbols evolve as structures realized as repeated synchronized evocation of pre-installed predicates.

To be more precise with our idea, let us briefly summarize the so called binding-problem [2]. Non-oscillatory neural networks suffer this binding-problem in that they require complex architecture to express multiple objects like "a red square and a green circle". Binding-problem is easily solved in ONNs, as the unit "RED" synchronized with the unit "SQUARE", and the unit "GREEN" synchronized with the unit "CIRCLE" (Figure 1A). Hence, ONNs are capable of handling attributes, or unary predicates by using synchronization as unification.

Can we extend this scheme to realize multi-place predicates and simply express "P(a,b)" as "P_argument1" synchronized with "a", and "P_argument2" synchronized with "b" (Figure 1B)? This scheme turns out to be problematic in that it cannot handle cooccurrences, i.e. a dataset {P(a,b), P(c,d)} and its fillers-swapped dataset {P(a,d), P(c,b)} can not be distinguished. This is a crucial problem when trying to extract rules from a dataset of facts. Shastri et al.[1] deals with such multiple-instantiation problem using complex "switch" mechanism [3]. However, their architecture is unsatisfactory for our purpose, since each switch has to be precisely constructed to suite the given rules, leading to difficulty in dynamic formation of rules. In this paper, we present a much simpler solution which enables a flexible organization and usage of previously acquired data.

In the following sections, we describe our scheme to realize predicate descriptions and numerically examine if the system can perform appropriate analogical inferences, given a set of facts.

2 Basic Structure of our ONN

2.1 Implementation of Cooccurrences

In order to properly encode cooccurrences, we employ the following scheme: The effect of synchronization interaction between a predicate_argument and its filler object is made proportional to the extent that the

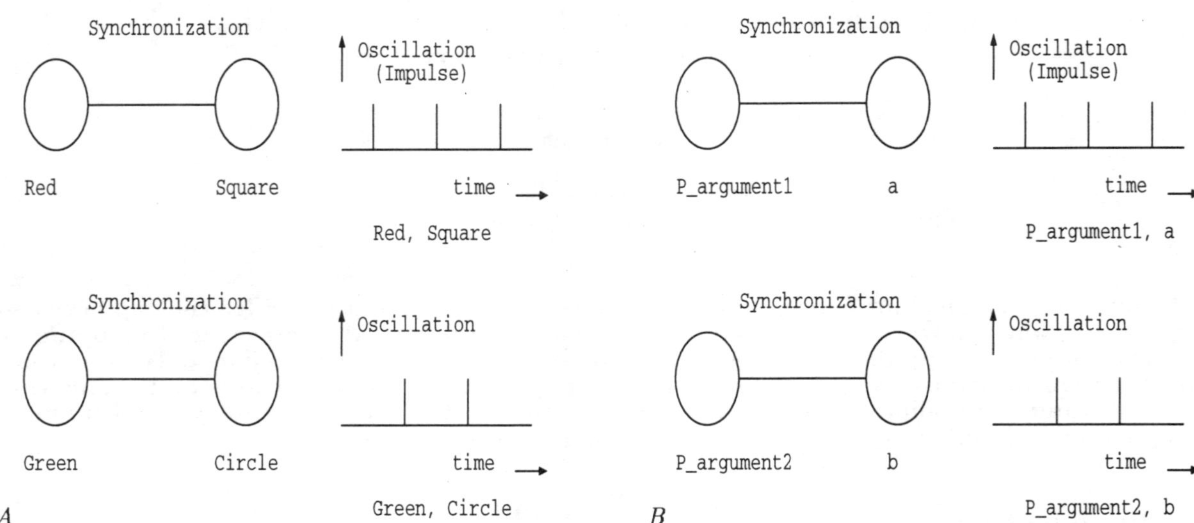

Figure 1: Unification in Oscillatory Neural Networks. *A*: An ONN solution to the "binding problem" concerning unary predicates, coding "a green circle and a red square". *B*: A simple (still unsatisfactory) extension of *A* to code a multi-place predicate, P(a,b).

remaining part of the predicate is properly bound to express that data.

For example, to install a datum P(a,b) regarding a predicate P, the coefficient of synchronization interaction between the unit "P_argument1" and the unit "a" is made proportional to a measure of synchronization between "P_argument2" and "b", (and vice versa). To describe it more generally, our synchronization interaction between a pair of oscillators is affected by the synchrony between another pair. This kind of synchronization interaction will be called *cooccurrence link*, hereafter. Also, notations P_1 for P_argument1, and P_2 for P_argument2 etc. will be used. Detailed equation of motion to realize this idea will be given in subsection 2.3.

In such a system, correct reproduction of cooccurrence can be expected: When the system is fed with the question "P(a,?)" by forced synchronization between "P_1" and "a", it can answer "P(a,b)", even when there are other data like "P(c,d)" (Figure 2A)[1]. Another point is that another synchronization state, namely, synchronization among a,c,P_1 and that among b,d,P_2, is also possible. Such a state can be a source of an analogical mapping between data, "P(a,b)" and "P(c,d)".

Note that when there are multiple data with fillers partially matched, as in {P(a,b),P(a,c)}, an additional method to combine synchronization measures has to be considered. For example, for the above dataset , coefficient of P_1 - a interaction can be either addition, maximum, ..etc. of synchrony between P_2-b and of P_2-c. In order to avoid additional complexity, we will leave this issue for future studies and simply exclude this kind of data here.

2.2 Multiple Instantiations of a predicate

To this extent, the system cannot simultaneously evoke multiple instantiations of a predicate like {P(a,b),P(c,d)}. However, this kind of evocation is necessary to produce certain kind of inference (e.g. reflective rules). One solution to this problem is to consider that there are multiple copies of predicate units and induce desynchronization between these copies. Weak noise is also necessary for symmetry breaking. Note that these copies ARE copies and they all have the same interaction structure with other units. In other words, for two copies systems, dataset {P(a,b),P(c,d)} is installed as {P1(a,b),P2(a,b),P1(c,d), P2(c,d)}(Figure 2B).

Note that if we do not use copies and merely code individual instances separately, like {P1(a,b), P2(c,d)}, analogical mappings as described in the previous subsection can no more be expected. Even if we added synchronization links among predicate units in order to obtain analogical mappings, the problem of cooccurrences appears again in that each argument of one instance can be synchronized to arguments of separate instances: e.g. in dataset {P1(a,b), P2(c,d),P3(e,f)}, P1_1 can be synchronized to P2_1 even when P1_2 is synchronized to P3_2.

---

[1] Another way to model a question is to use a dummy oscillator related to '?'. Complex questions like {?X—P(a,?X) ∧ P(?X,c)} can be installed in this way.

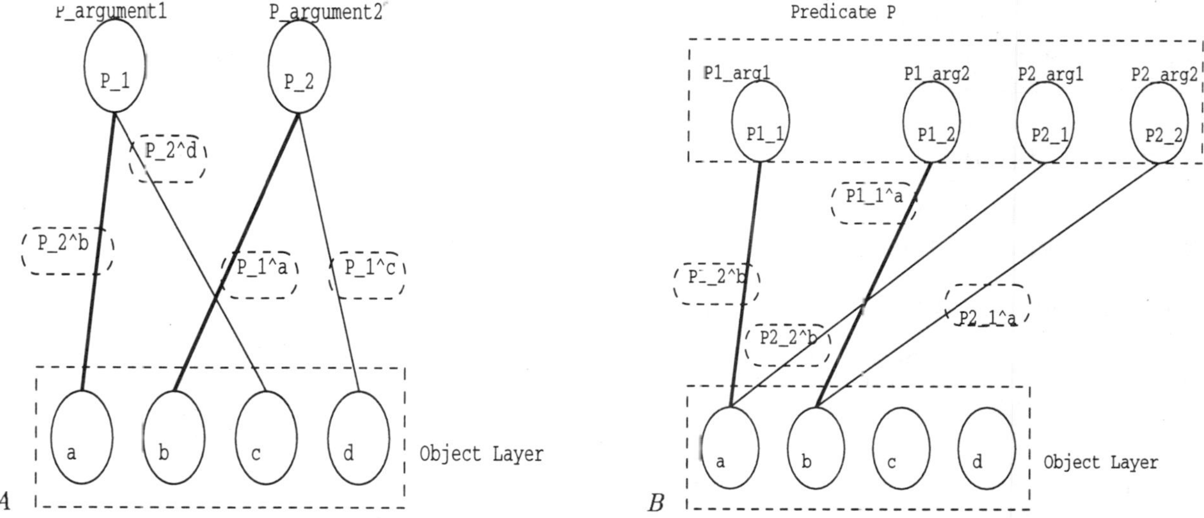

Figure 2: A modified scheme to code a multi-place predicate. *A*: Cooccurrence links to code cooc-currences in data P(a,b) and P(c,d). Dashed square represents a layer in which all units are linked by desynchronization interaction. Links accompanied by dashed ellipses represent cooccurrence-links; strings in those ellipses in the form "X$\hat{Y}$" denote that the synchronization interaction between the linked units gets stronger as the units X and Y synchronize. *B*: Multiple copies of a predicate. P(a,b) is installed as {P1(a,b),P2(a,b)}.

2.3 Equation of Motion

Actual equation of motion for the i-th unit oscillator is the following: (For simplicity, only binary predi-cates are considered here.)

$$\frac{d}{dt}x_i = -x_i + vS(-y_i + a_i + I_i) + Rr_i(t)$$

$$\frac{d}{dt}y_i = -y_i + x_i$$

,where

$$S(x) = 1/(1 + e^{-(x-0.2)/0.05})$$

$$I_i = \sum_j c_s p_{ij} x_j / p_i - n_{ij} x_j / n_i$$

Parameter a_i contributes to the amplitude of oscillation. I_i corresponds to the interactin term. In order to realize cooccurrence link, p_{ij}, the synchronization interaction coefficient, is also a variable with

$$\frac{d}{dt}p_{ij} = c_p(-p_{ij} + C_{kl})$$

$$C_{kl} = r_{kl} \ (if \ r_{kl} > 0), \quad = 0(otherwise)$$

$$r_{kl} = (x_k - X_k, y_k - Y_k)(x_l - X_l, y_l - Y_l^T)$$

$$\frac{d}{dt}X_i = c_x(-X_i + x_i)$$

$$\frac{d}{dt}Y_i = c_y(-Y_i + x_i)$$

,where the units k and l consists an instantiation of a binary predicate, together with the units i and j. e.g. Considering P(a,b), units i, j, k and l can be related to P_1, a, P_2 and b, respectively. C_{kl} is used as a rough estimation of synchrony between units k and l. Note that synchronization interaction is nonzero only between an "object" unit and an "argument" unit, since we only input facts and no rules. For forced synchronization used to code questions, we employ C_{kk} instead of C_{kl}, where k is the bound predicate_argument in the question. Also, this link has to be enhanced by a factor $c_s q$. Initial condition is (10., 0.) for all (x_i, y_i)s and 0. for all other dynamical variables. Small random sequence ($r\ i(t)$) of uniform distribution [0.,1.] is added for symmetry breaking

The magnitude of desynchronization interaction between units i and j is a constant, with

$n_{ij} = c_{do}$(among all "object" units), c_{dc}(among copies of one predicate arguments) and c_{dp}(among all predicate arguments).

p_i and n_i correspond to the sum of p_{ij}s and n_{ij}s , respectively. All interactions are symmetric, namely, $p_{ij}=pji$ and $n_{ij}=n_{ji}$.

3 Analogical Inference with the System

3.1 Dynamic Extraction of Prototypes

It was numerically examined if such a system can perform simple analogical inference, given a dataset of facts. For example, consider a dataset A: {P(a,b),P(b,c),Q(a,c),P(d,e),P(e,f)}, which is the union of $A1$:{P(a,b),P(b,c),Q(a,c)} and $A2$:{P(d,e),P(e,f)}, with the former being the extension of the latter under an identification, {a $\Rightarrow$ d, b $\Rightarrow$ e, c $\Rightarrow$ f }. Accordingly, when one's prior knowledge is dataset A and the question is "Q(d,?)", a popular answer will be "Q(d,f)", using this identification structure as analogy; dataset $A1$ is considered as a prototype (a model) and $A2$ (plus the question) is properly mapped to this prototype, using the analogical identification. In a way, our system behaves in a similar manner: synchronization in our ONN can be related to analogical identification structure.

To be more precise, when this dataset is installed as an ONN in the way described in section 2 with two predicate copies [2], and the question "Q(d,?)" is added to the system as forced synchronization between the units "Q1_1" and "d", this ONN segments into three phase segments like {a, d, P1_1, Q⋆_1}, {b, e, P1_2, P2_1} and {c, f, P2_2, Q⋆_2} (Q⋆ stands for both Q1 and Q2)(Figure 3A). This result can be interpreted as the evocation of dataset {P1(a,b),P2(b,c), Q⋆(a,c)} (i.e. the prototype or the model), with the identification {a $\Rightarrow$ d, b $\Rightarrow$ e, c $\Rightarrow$ f}, resembling human analogy process: [3] synchronization between objects can be interpreted as analogical mapping, and that between object and predicate_argument can be thought of as unification or evocation of certain data.

This result can be related to a major part of analogical inference, namely, extraction of the model(prototype) related to the question from prior knowledge (given dataset), and the mapping between the model and the question. In particular, it chose an "appropriate" model considering a larger context compared to a trivial model like {Q(a,b)} leading to an answer Q(d,b). To make the understanding easier, one may identify the predicate P as 'Father-of', and Q as 'Grandfather-of': The system correctly grasped the structure, while a more trivial analogy can lead to misunderstanding that someone's grandfather is everybody's.

In order to further examine the effect of cooccurrence links, a filler-swapped dataset of A, dataset A_{sw}: {P(a,c),Q(a,c),P(b,e),P(e,b),P(d,f)}, was considered. If it were not for the cooccurrence links, A_sw and A result in the same ONN and thereby produces the same state. In our system, the same question "Q(d,?)" applied to A_sw results in two phase segments like {a,b,d,P⋆_1,Q⋆_1} and {c,e,f,P⋆_2,Q⋆_2}. In other words, rule "P(x,y) $\rightarrow$ Q(x,y)" is extracted this time, regarding the subset {P(a,c),Q(a,c)}. (Reflecting the symmetry of b and e, another, essentially similar result with b and e swapped exists.) The result suggests that a filler swapped dataset can result in different synchronization structure, properly reflecting cooccurrence links. Also, it chose the largest possible context for a model again.

A_{sw} has another prototypical (systematic) subset, {P(b,e),P(e,b)}. In fact, when another question "P(f,?)" is installed, this subset is evoked as prototype; the resultant phase segments are {a, P2_1, Q⋆_1},{c, P2_2, Q⋆_2} and {b, d, e, f, P1_⋆}, when this question was installed to P1. Although the former two segments are still related to {P(a,c),Q(a,c)}, the focus of question, P1, is included in the last segment which can be related to {P(b,e),P(e,b)} matched with {P(d,f),P(f,?)}. The result suggests that given a different question, the system can properly extract another prototype from the same dataset.

Another point is that in this case, there are multiple data regarding predicate P which is under question. Although there are many candidates to map the question "P(f,?)", the system can select the one that leads to the largest mapping structure. In order to further examine this issue, we have considered another dataset B: {P(a,b),Q(a,c),P(b,c),P(d,e),Q(d,f)} and applied the question, "P(e,?)". The system ends up in similar segment structure as in dataset A, confirming the above observation. Note that such formation of prototype structure (i.e. evocation of the model) has not been included in many analogy tasks which are essentially mapping tasks between a given model and the question [6].

Experiments with datasets A, A_{sw} and B suggest that models are extracted in a very flexible way and that each extracted model is appropriate in that it corresponds to the largest possible context regarding that question within that dataset. Such dynamic structure of coherent predicates may be regarded as establishment of a new "distributed" predicate based on initially defined unit predicates.

---

[2] One will observe from the results that predicate copies can segment or merge depending on the data structure, suggesting that the number of copies are not so critical to the system.

[3] Reflecting the symmetry in the equation, another (essentially the same) result with P1 and P2 swapped exists, but no other basin was observed.

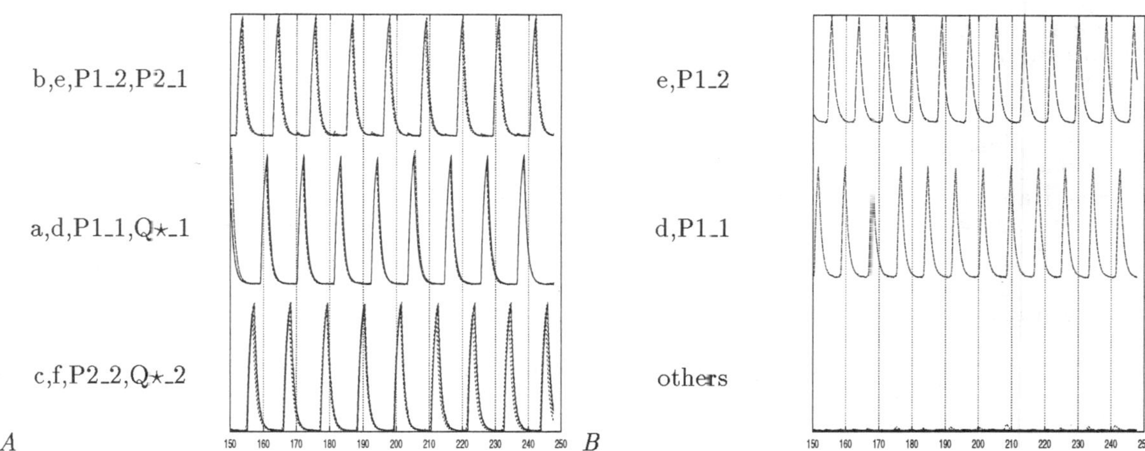

Figure 3: Time (horizontal) vs. x-coordinates (vertical) of individual units coding dataset $\{P(a,b),P(b,c),Q(a,c),P(d,e),P(e,f)\}$. A: Analogy mode, question "Q(d,?)". Parameters.. $c_s=1.,c_{do}=1.12,c_{dc}=1.4,c_{dp}=.7$ $a_i=1.$ $c_{sq}=2c_s$. B: Reproduction mode, question "P(d,?)". Parameters $c_s=.5,c_{do}=1.92,c_{dc}=2.4,c_{dp}=1.2$ $a_i=1.$(all "objects" and P1), 0.(others), $c_{sq}=4c_s$. For both cases, $v=10.,c_p=0.02,c_x=c_y=0.002.$, R=0.5

So far, the actual answer to the question "Q(d,?)" is still ambiguous, in that "?" is unified to both "c" and "f". We will consider this issue in the next subsection.

3.2 Amplitude Control: Reproduction of cooccurrence and the extraction of actual answer

There exists a different parameter region that gives correct reproduction of existent data, instead of analogical inference (Figure 3B). In order to avoid the evocation of other data as in analogical inference, the "amplitude" parameter, a_i can be controlled. The coefficient of forced synchronization to drive the question, c_{sq}, also had to be controlled to get an answer, but a straightforward procedure to "increase c_{sq} while there is no answer" was sufficient to get an appropriate magnitude.

Such control of amplitude parameter can also provide a simple means to obtain the "actual answer" for the analogy. The idea is to evoke the prototype alone and subtract it from the analogical identification structure. For example, when dataset A added with the question "Q(d,?)" produces the synchronized segments like $\{Q\star\_1, a, d\}$ and $\{Q\star\_2, c, f\}$, another question, "Q(a,?)" with the object "d" suppressed on its amplitude parameter, can evoke the prototype alone. Subtracting the prototype from the analogy segment gives the answer.

Same parameter region works for dataset A_{sw} also. In this case, question "Q(d,?)" produces larger synchronized segments like $\{Q\star\_1, a, b, d\}$ and $\{Q\star\_2, c, e, f\}$, but we can ask the question "Q1(a,?) and Q2(b,?)", where we get the segments $\{a, b, P\star\_1, Q\star\_1\}$ and $\{c, e, P\star\_2, Q\star\_2\}$. Subtracting these segments gives us the answer, Q(d,f).

3.3 More complex inference

So far, we have only considered the tasks in which evocation of single prototype was sufficient to provide an answer. This corresponds to extracting and using only one inference rule. One can think of a more complex task by combining prototypes or rules, like combining "$P(x,y) \rightarrow Q(x,y)$" and "$Q(x,y) \rightarrow R(x,y)$" to produce "$P(x,y) \rightarrow R(x,y)$". Regarding this issue, dataset B:$\{P(a,b),Q(a,b),Q(c,d),R(c,d),P(e,f)\}$ was examined with the question "R(e,?)". The system could merge the two prototypes, $\{P(a,b),Q(a,b)\}$ and $\{Q(c,d),R(c,d)\}$, and gave the segments, $\{a, c, e, P\star\_1, Q\star\_1, R\star\_1\}$ and $\{b, d, f, P\star\_2, Q\star\_2, R\star\_2\}$.

When there are competing prototypes for one question, a sensible system would produce a more plausible answer. Regarding this issue, another dataset C:$\{P(a,b),Q(a,b),P(c,d),Q(c,d),P(e,f),Q(f,e),P(g,h),P(i,g)\}$ was examined. When the question "Q(g,?)" is considered, this dataset can evoke two competing types of prototypes, $\{P(X,Y),Q(X,Y)\}$ resulting in the answer Q(g,h), and $\{P(X,Y),Q(Y,X)\}$ resulting in the answer Q(g,i). In our system, the more frequent prototype is always active, although the less frequent one can also appear. Interestingly, in free evocation without question, the more frequent prototype takes over and the less frequent one never appears.

In the present system, negation can be installed to binary predicates by using desynchronization for cooccurrence links. In this way, the issue of inconsistency can be considered. As for this topic we already have some results with ONNs without cooccurrence-links, i.e. limited to the unary predicates; in [9], we have argued that an ONN can deal with inconsistent knowledge base with a reasonable starategy, at least for unary predicates. Whether or not the result of unary predicates can be extended to binary predicates is left for future studies.

In a complex database, evocation of relevant knowledge should also be studied. Again, we have some results for this issue also with respect to the unary predicates [10]; e.g. we have argued that a similar ONN can activate the units which are more interconnected with the externally activated units and leave the other units inactive. The extension of such result to cooccurrence-links has to be further studied.

4 Conclusion

Our system's performance seems to be promising in that not only can it establish appropriate mappings between a model and a question, it can find out an appropriate model depending on the question and the given dataset. Such dynamical evocation of prototypes may lead to more complex predicates as we humans conceive, or even complex symbolic structures like schema and script.

Studies on wider class of predicates and further examination on more complex inference has to be made.

References

[1] V.Ajjanagadde and L. Shastri, "Efficient inference with multi-place predicates and variables in a connectionist system", *Proc. 11th Cognitive Science Society Conference*, 1989, pp. 396-403.

[2] Ch. von der Malsburg and W.Schneider, "A Neural Cooktail-Party Processor", *Biological Cybernetics*, vol. 54, pp.29-40, 1986.

[3] D. R. Mani and L. Shastri, "Reflexive reasoning with multiple instantiation in a connectionist reasoning system with a type hierarchy", *Connection Science*, vol. 5(3,4), pp.205-242, 1993.

[4] T.E.Lange, J.J.Vidal and M.G.Dyer, *Artificial Neural Oscillators for Inferencing*, TR UCLA-AI-89-11, 1989.

[5] R. Miikkulainen, *Subsymbolic Natural Language Processing.* MIT press, 1993.

[6] M. Mitchell, *Analogy-Making as perception.* MIT press, 1993.

[7] R. Sun, "Beyond Associative Memories: Logics and Variables in Connectionist Models", *Information Sciences*, vol. 70, pp. 49-73, 1993.

[8] D. S. Touretzky and G. E. Hinton, "A Distributed Connectionist Production System", *Cognitive Science* vol. 12(3), pp. 331-392, 1988.

[9] T. Yamanoue, "Phasal Segmentation of Oscillatory Neural Networks: A Graph Theoretical Classification and Application to Information Processing", *Proc. Second International Computer Science Conference*, Hong Kong, Dec. 13-16, 1992, pp. 474-480.

[10] T. Yamanoue, "Effect of complexity in an oscillatory neural network: Relation to human-like reasoning", *International Journal of Fuzzy Sets and Systems*, In press.

Recurrent Neural Networks for Digital Sequential Circuits

Hiroshi NINOMIYA and Hideki ASAI

Department of Systems Engineering, Faculty of Engineering, Shizuoka University
3-5-1, Johoku, Hamamatsu, 432, Japan
Telephone: +81-53-478-1237, Telefax: +81-53-475-1764, e-mail: hideasai@eng.shizuoka.ac.jp

Abstract—In this paper we propose a novel three-layer binary recurrent neural networks(3LBRNN) for training digital sequential circuits(finite state machines). The input and output layers of the 3LBRNN are composed of latch neurons, and the hidden layer is constructed by perceptron models. The unique feature of the proposed network is that it enables to form any digital sequential circuit—previous work has shown that the simple digital sequential circuits such as shift register and asynchronous binary counter can be realized by Hopfield neural networks. Boolean-like training algorithm(BLTA)[5] is extended to the 3LBRNN for training digital sequential circuits. Consequently we show that any digital sequential circuit can be implemented by using the 3LBRNN with the latch neurons. Finally, the behavior of proposed networks is demonstrated through the computer simulations.

I. INTRODUCTION

Learning of temporal sequences is a very important and interesting problem in neural networks. A number of networks have been proposed for this purpose(*e.g.*[1]-[3]), where recurrent neural networks have been demonstrated to have the ability to learn chaotic time series and to learn finite-state automata(digital sequential circuits). Most of the training algorithms have been based on the gradient descent techniques. Typically, an extremely high number of iterations become necessary to possibly obtain desirable outputs.

On the other hand, for binary-to-binary spatial mappings, attempts have been made at improving convergence speed[4][5]. In [4] the geometrical learning algorithm called expand-and-truncate learning(ETL) has been proposed to train a three layer binary feedforward neural network(3LBFNN). In [5] a new training algorithm, which is called the Boolean-like training algorithm(BLTA), has been presented to implement binary-to-binary spatial mappings utilizing a four-layer binary feedforward neural network(4LBFNN). The principal difference between the BLTA and standard digital logic design(digital circuit building) method is that the 4LBFNN is realized using analog hardware whereas digital circuit building results are implemented by digital hardware. Therefore, the BLTA has the capability to add new relations as well as to forget or correct old or undesired relations without changing the previously constructed network, while digital circuit building dose not possess this capability as well as the training algorithm based on gradient descent techniques[6].

Recently, as an application to temporal information processing, we have proposed the procedure to design some logic circuits and latch circuits with global convergence using Hopfield neural networks[7][8]. Furthermore, we have constructed simple digital sequential circuits such as the shift register and the asynchronous binary counter composed of the logic and latch circuits in the same way as the construction of the conventional digital sequential circuits. However, these circuits have been based on Hopfield neural networks, in which finding the adequate energy functions to determine synaptic weights is a difficult planning problem.

In this paper we propose a novel three-layer binary recurrent neural networks(3LBRNN) for training digital sequential circuits(finite state machine). The input and output layers of the 3LBRNN are composed of latch neurons, and the hidden layer is constructed by perceptron models. Furthermore, the BLTA is applied to the 3LBRNN for training digital sequential circuits. Consequently, we show that any digital sequential circuit which has the capability to train the new state transition into the existing network without changing the previously constructed network, can be implemented, using the 3LBRNN. Finally, proposed networks are demonstrated through the computer simulations.

II. NETWORK ARCHITECTURE

2.1. 3-layer binary recurrent neural networks

The 3LBRNN is illustrated in Fig.1, where the layers from input to output are referred to in this paper as the master, hidden and slave layers, respectively. The connections between the i-th neuron of the master layer and the j th neuron of the hidden layer are defined as $W_1(i, j)$. The connections between the i-th neuron of the hidden layer and the j th neuron of the slave layer are $W_2(i, j)$. The connection strengths utilized in the architecture assume one of three possible values -1, 0 and $+1$. The master and slave layers are composed of D-latch neurons, and the hidden layer is constructed by perceptron models.

That is to say, 3LBRNN proposed here is master/slave synchronous neural networks. The perceptron model that constructs the hidden layer is described by

$$U = \sum_{i=1}^{m} W_i X_i - \theta,$$
$$V = f_H(U) \tag{1}$$

where, X_i and $W_i (i = 1 \cdots m)$ represent inputs and connection strengths, respectively. θ denotes a threshold and V denotes the output of a neuron which is modeled by

$$V = f_H(U) = \begin{array}{ll} 0 & \text{if } U < 0, \\ 1 & \text{if } U \geq 0. \end{array} \tag{2}$$

D-latch neuron is designed in the next subsection.

2.2. Design of D-latch neuron

Here, we discuss the way how to design a D-latch neuron, which has the global convergence property, in order to construct the master and slave layers. Here, global convergence property means that the energy function of D-latch is monotonically decreasing and D-latch neuron always operates correctly for the continuous time series input according to the characteristic table.

The output logic function of D-latch is defined as

$$Q^{n+1} = (1 - C) \cdot Q^n + C \cdot D \tag{3}$$

where $\overline{C} = 1 - C$ and Q^{n+1}, Q^n, C, D denote the next and the present statuses, the clock and input signals, respectively. (3) is formulated as the optimization problem of the following objective function,

$$\min |(1 - C) \cdot Q^n + C \cdot D - Q^{n+1}|. \tag{4}$$

The objective function (4) can be reduced to the simple function as

$$\min |-C \cdot Q + C \cdot D|. \tag{5}$$

Namely, the objective function for D-latch permits the following assumption[7]

$$Q^n = Q^{n+1} = Q. \tag{6}$$

The constraint function is defined as

$$\min |Q(1 - Q)| \tag{7}$$

in order that the output Q may settle down to the binary values of '0' or '1'. From (5) and (7), the energy function for D-latch circuit is given by

$$E = -\frac{1}{2}(2 - C)Q^2 - \{C \cdot D - 1\}Q \tag{8}$$

which is illustrated in Fig.2. From Fig.2, we can confirm that D-latch neuron operates correctly even if the initial value of Q is given by the output Q which is stabilized during the previous clock cycle.

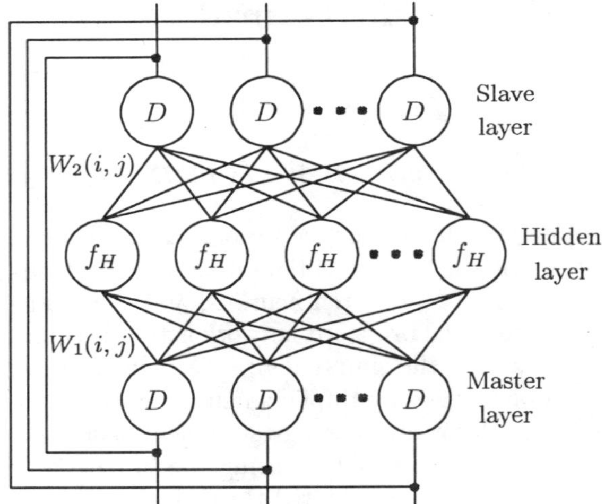

Fig.1. The three-layer binary recurrent neural network.

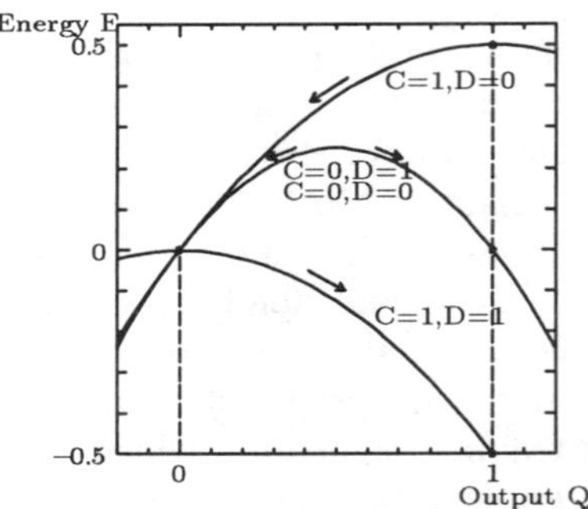

Fig.2. Energy function(D are digital values).

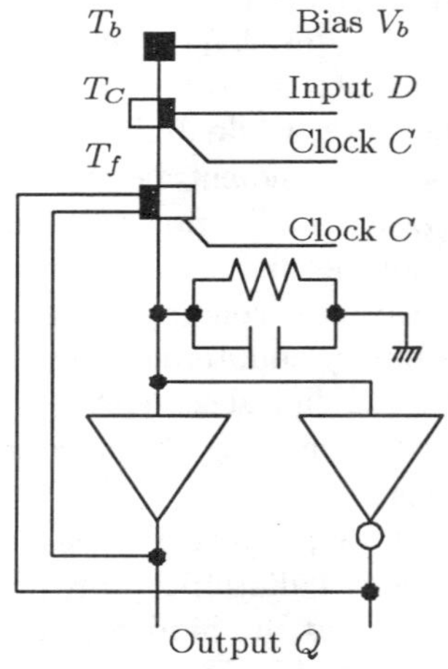

Fig.3. D-latch neuron.

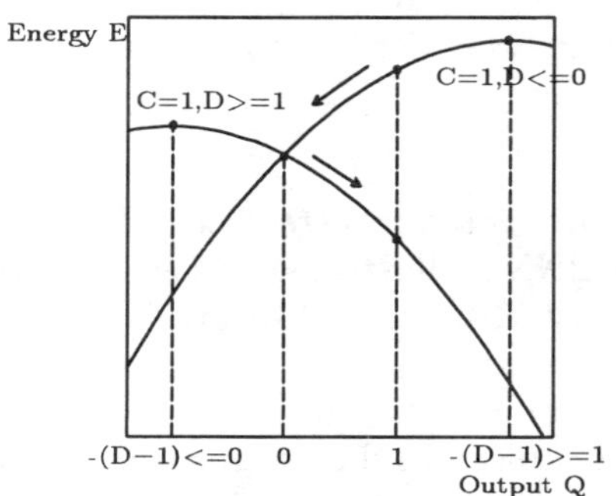

Fig.4. Energy function(D are integer values).

By comparing (8) with the energy function of Hopfield network, D-latch neuron is designed as shown in Fig.3 and the parameters in Fig.3 can be determined as follows,

$$T_f = 2 - C, \quad T_C = C, \quad T_b = 1, \quad V_b = -1 \tag{9}$$

Here, T_C and T_f are realized by the nonlinear resistances whose values are changed by the clock C.

In Fig.2, we show that D-latch neuron has the global convergence property when the input signal D is binary values, namely '0' or '1'. In the 3LBRNN, the inputs of D-latch neuron of slave layer may be integers because of the construction of the 3LBRNN. Therefore, we also show that D-latch neuron has the global convergence property for the integer inputs. The energy function of D-latch neuron for the integer input D is illustrated in Fig.4. From Fig.4, we can confirm the following facts,

$$\text{if} \quad D \le 0 \quad \text{then} \quad Q = 0, \tag{10}$$
$$\text{if} \quad D \ge 1 \quad \text{then} \quad Q = 1. \tag{11}$$

Consequently D-latch neuron with integer input D has the global convergence property.

The transfer function of D-latch neuron is modeled by the sigmoid function,

$$V = f_S(U) = \frac{1}{2}\left\{1 + \tanh(U/\mu)\right\}. \tag{12}$$

The slave layer is composed of D-latch neurons with the transfer function(12). On the other hand, the master layer is constructed by D-latch neurons with the transfer function given by

$$V = f_M(U) = \tanh(U/\mu). \tag{13}$$

Therefore, using the following equation,

$$f_S(U) = (f_M(U) + 1)/2, \tag{14}$$

the parameters of (9) are rewritten by

$$T_f = 1 - C/2, \quad T_C = C, \quad T_b = C, \quad V_b = -1/2, \tag{15}$$

for D-latch neuron of the master layer.

TABLE I. The state transition table of Fig.5.

Q_1^n	Q_2^n	x	Q_1^{n+1}	Q_2^{n+1}	z
0	0	0	1	0	0
0	0	1	0	1	0
0	1	0	0	0	0
0	1	1	0	0	0
1	0	0	1	0	0
1	0	1	1	1	0
1	1	0	0	0	0
1	1	1	0	0	1

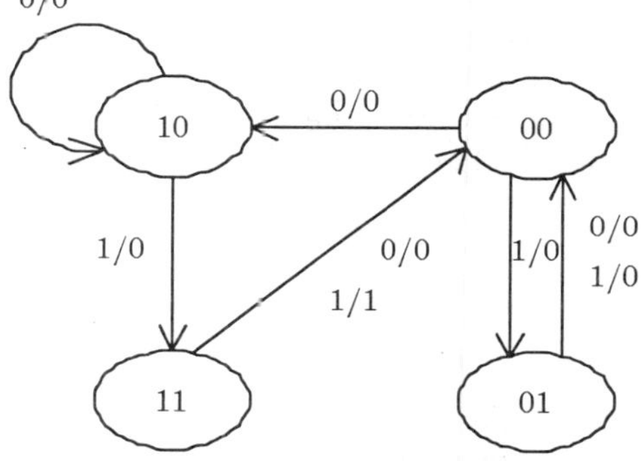

Fig.5. The state transition diagram

III. Design of Sequential Circuits with D-latch Neurons and BLTA

We are now in a position to discuss the way how to design the sequential circuits using the 3LBRNN with the BLTA, where D-latch neurons are used to implement the sequential circuits. We give a specific example of a sequential circuit.

3.1. Default Configuration

We begin the presentation of the training algorithm by first considering the initial(default) configuration of the neural networks. The master and slave layers are constructed by D-latch neurons with transfer function (13) and ones with transfer function (12), respectively. The neurons of the hidden layer utilize the characteristics of (2). The 3LBRNN is initially implemented with m master layer neurons, h hidden layer neurons and s slave layer neurons. The thresholds of the initiating hidden layer neurons are taken to be

$$\theta_H(i) = m \qquad \forall i = 1, \cdots, h.$$

The initial values of the interconnections are

$$W_1(i, j) = -1 \qquad \forall i, j,$$
$$W_2(i, j) = 0 \qquad \forall i, j.$$

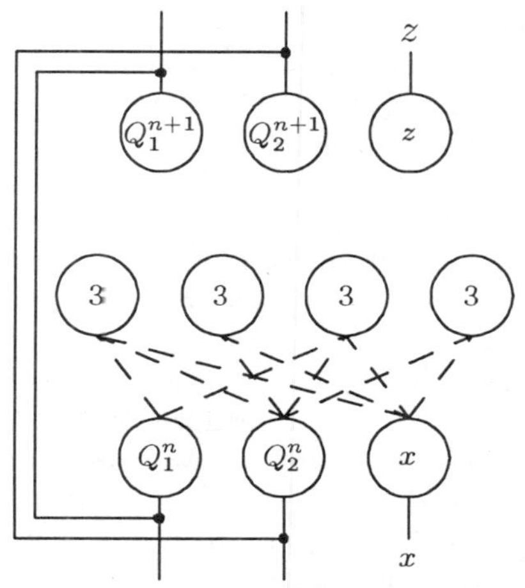

Fig.6. Default 3LBRNN.

3.2. Design of next state decoder by BLTA

The default assumptions made in the above subsection are applied to a problem of a state transition diagram as shown in Fig.5, where x/z denotes input x and output z. The state transition table of Fig.5 is illustrated in TABLE I. The default neural network is shown in Fig.6, including neurons which represent the input x and the output z. As shown in Fig.6, the present statuses and input x are allotted for the master layer neurons, and the next statuses and output z are assigned to the slave layer neurons. The perceptron model of the neuron with the threshold $\theta = 1$ is utilized to realize the input x. The characteristic of this neuron is

$$V = f(x) = \begin{array}{ll} -1 & \text{if } x < 0, \\ 1 & \text{if } x \geq 0. \end{array} \qquad (16)$$

The output neuron z is realized by D-latch neuron with the transfer function of (12). Further, in Fig.6, solid lines show connections with positive weight, $+1$, and dotted lines denote connections with negative weight, -1. Connections of zero strength are omitted from the figure. The value of a neuron's threshold θ of hidden layer is depicted by placing it inside of the neuron. We number the neurons of each layer $1, 2, \cdots$, counting from the lefthand side of the network.

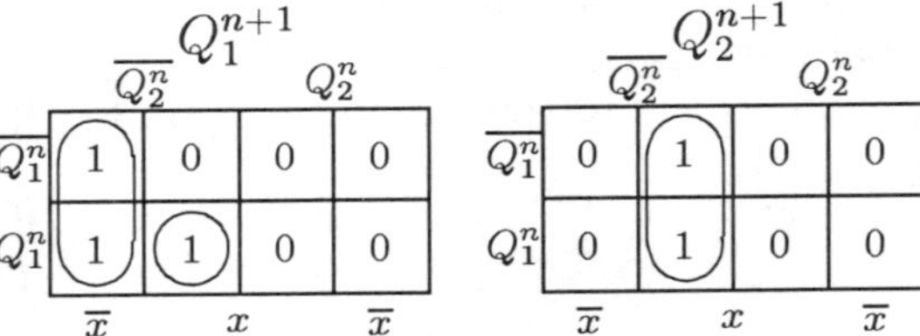

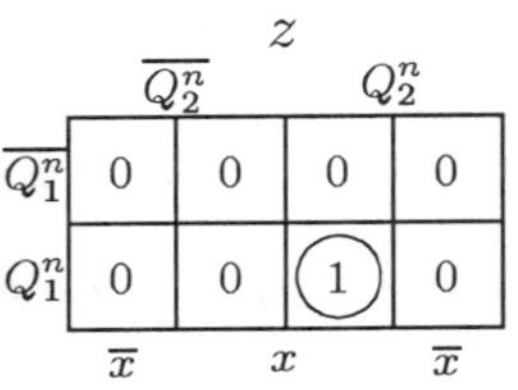

Fig.7. Karnaugh map.

The Karnaugh map is subsequently used as aids to help visualize the operation of the training algorithm. The Karnaugh map of TABLE I is shown in Fig.7. In the case of logic reduction of the function on the Karnaugh map, the BLTA is based on the following rule, "no element can appear in more than one grouping". Performing a logic reduction under the above rule, we obtain the following equations,

$$Q_1^{n+1} = Q_1^n \cdot \overline{Q_2^n} \cdot x + \overline{Q_2^n} \cdot \overline{x}, \qquad (17)$$

$$Q_2^{n+1} = \overline{Q_2^n} \cdot x, \qquad (18)$$

$$z = Q_1^n \cdot Q_2^n \cdot x. \qquad (19)$$

The BLTA requires N hidden neurons to assimilate N-minterm logic functions. Therefore, this example requires 4 hidden neurons. Furthermore, the above rule imposes no change in the minimum number of minterms(and hence hidden layer neurons) required to implement the function, compared with the ordinary logic reduction.

First of all, we begin the implementation of (17) of slave layer neuron '1'. The first minterm of function Q_1^{n+1} is $Q_1^n \cdot \overline{Q_2^n} \cdot x$. We begin with the leftmost hidden layer neuron '1'. The implementation of this minterm will require that the default connection weights of -1, between the master layer and the hidden layer neuron '1', are changed to ones of $+1$ from all the master layer neurons i which correspond to the noncomplemented literals of the given minterm. In this case this means $W_1(1, 1) = +1$ and $W_1(3, 1) = +1$, since the literals Q_1^n and x of the minterm $Q_1^n \cdot \overline{Q_2^n} \cdot x$ are uncomplemented. The connection $W_1(2, 1)$ is already equal to -1 by the defaults of subsection 3.1. Next, we must establish the appropriate connections to the slave layer. Therefore, to produce a $+1$ at the slave layer, we need only connect the output of hidden layer neuron '1' to the slave layer neuron. This results in the creation of the hidden layer to slave layer connection $W_2(1, 1) = +1$. This completes the implementation of the first minterm of function Q_1^{n+1}. Further, The second minterm, $\overline{Q_2^n} \cdot \overline{x}$, is implemented using the hidden layer neuron '2'. This minterm is produced by logic reduction of minterms $\overline{Q_1^n} \cdot \overline{Q_2^n} \cdot \overline{x}$ and $Q_1^n \cdot \overline{Q_2^n} \cdot \overline{x}$. The minterm $\overline{Q_1^n} \cdot \overline{Q_2^n} \cdot \overline{x}$ differs only by one bit from the minterm $Q_1^n \cdot \overline{Q_2^n} \cdot \overline{x}$. The implementation of this group, $\overline{Q_2^n} \cdot \overline{x}$, is accomplished by eliminating (zeroing) the interconnection from the master layer neuron corresponding to the differing bit (i.e., the differing literal Q_1^n is obtained from master layer neuron '1') and the hidden layer neuron '2'. Therefore, $W_1(1, 2)$ is set to 0. In conjunction with the zeroing of a connection to a hidden layer neuron '2', we must also reduce the threshold of hidden layer neuron '2' by 1. These result in $W_1(1, 2) = 0$, $W_1(2, 2) = -1$, $W_1(3, 2) = -1$, $W_2(2, 1) = +1$ and $\theta(2) = 3 - 1 = 2$.

Second, function (18) of the slave layer neuron '2' is implemented. The minterm of this function is $\overline{Q_2^n} \cdot x$ which is obtained by logic reduction of minterms $\overline{Q_1^n} \cdot \overline{Q_2^n} \cdot x$ and $Q_1^n \cdot \overline{Q_2^n} \cdot x$. Therefore, in a similar way of minterm $\overline{Q_2^n} \cdot \overline{x}$, $\overline{Q_2^n} \cdot x$ is trained to the hidden neuron '3'. As a result, the connection strengths and threshold are $W_1(1, 3) = 0$, $W_1(2, 3) = -1$, $W_1(3, 3) = +1$, $W_2(3, 2) = +1$ and $\theta(3) = 3 - 1 = 2$.

Finally, the minterm $Q_1^n \cdot Q_2^n \cdot x$ of function (19) is implemented, where the hidden layer neuron '4' is utilized. The connection weights are $W_1(1,4) = +1$, $W_1(2,4) = +1$, $W_1(3,4) = +1$ and $W_2(4,3) = +1$. Consequently, the completed neural network is depicted in Fig.8.

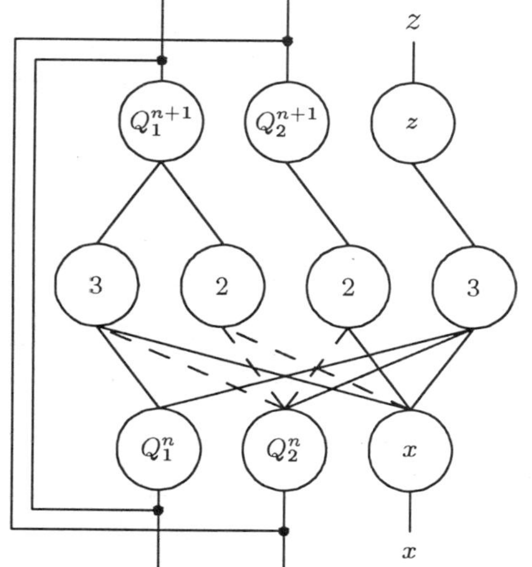

Fig.8. The completed 3LBRNN.

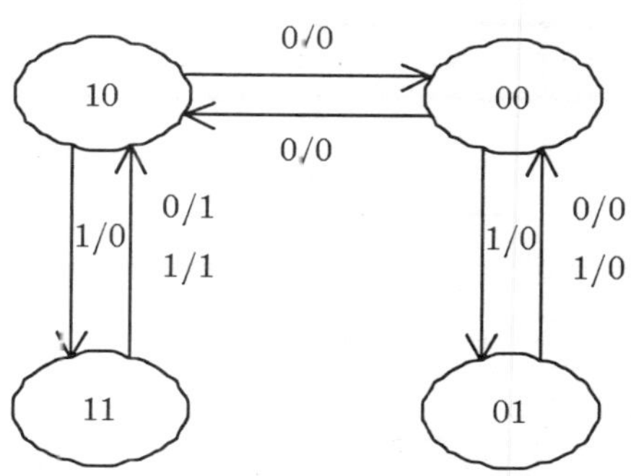

Fig.9. The state transition diagram.

TABLE II. The state transition table of Fig.9.

Q_1^n	Q_2^n	x	Q_1^{n+1}	Q_2^{n+1}	z
0	0	0	1	0	0
0	0	1	0	1	0
0	1	0	0	0	0
0	1	1	0	0	0
1	0	0	0	0	0
1	0	1	1	1	0
1	1	0	1	0	1
1	1	1	1	0	1

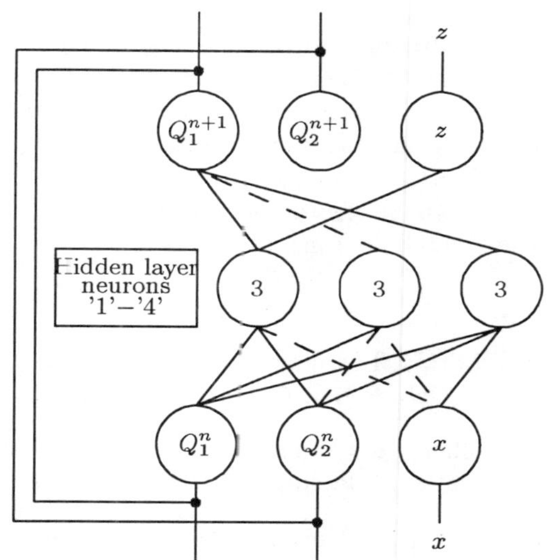

Fig.10. The completed 3LBRNN.

Let us next consider an example in which new state transitions(memories) can be added to an existing network implementation and how incorrect, undesired, or outdated state transitions can be forgotten(suppressed), preserving the previously stored state transition. The BLTA is also utilized to implement the new state transition of Fig.9 which is changed from the state transition of Fig.5. The state transition table of Fig.9 is illustrated in TABLE II. In TABLE II, the underlined states are added and forgotten states. We show in Fig.10 the 3LBRNN, in which the training of the new state transition into the existing network without changing the previously constructed network is completed by adding three hidden layer neurons, where D-latch neurons are used to implement the digital sequential circuits.

IV. SIMULATION RESULTS

We demonstrate the 3LBRNNs proposed here through the numerical analysis. Simulation results of Fig.8 and Fig.10 are illustrated in Fig.11 and Fig.12, respectively. As shown in Fig.11 and Fig.12, we can confirm that each 3LBRNN with latch neurons correctly operates according to each state transition diagram. Both clock periods of Fig.11 and Fig.12 are 100[ns].

V. CONCLUSION

In this paper we have proposed a novel three-layer binary recurrent neural networks(3LBRNN) for training digital sequential circuits(finite state machine). Using the BLTA to train the 3LBRNN and D-latch

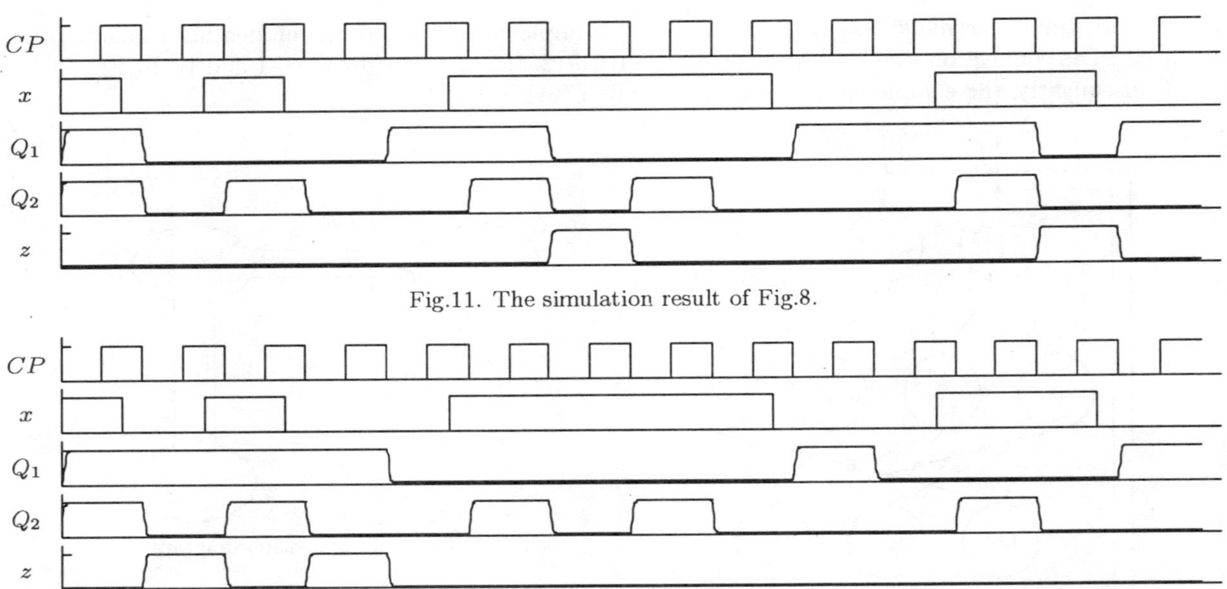

Fig.11. The simulation result of Fig.8.

Fig.12. The simulation result of Fig.10.

neurons, any digital sequential circuit, which has the capability to train the new state transition into the existing network without changing the previously constructed network, has been implemented. Finally, proposed networks have been demonstrated through the computer simulations. We have confirmed that each 3LBRNN has correctly operated according to each state transition diagram.

In the future we are going to implement with the analog hardware. In [10], we have already implemented the D-latch neuron on the breadboard. Therefore, 3LBRNN is going to be easily constructed by using the D-latch neurons.

REFERENCES

[1] Sato, M.: "A Learning Algorithm to Teach Spatiotemporal Patterns to Recurrent Neural Networks" ,*Biol. Cybernetics*, **62**, pp.259-263, 1990.

[2] Zeng, Zheng, Goodman, Rodney M. and Smyth, Padhraic: "Discrete Recurrent Neural Networks for Grammatical Inference" ,*IEEE Trans. Neural Networks*, **vol.5**, no.2, pp.320-330, March, 1994.

[3] Nishigaki, M.: "Universal Digital Sequential Circuit Using Programmable Wavelet Array and Its Application" , *Proc. NOLTA'95*, **vol.2 of 2**, pp. 1041-1044(1995).

[4] Kim, Jung H. and Park, Sung-Kwon: "The Geometrical Learning of Binary Neural Networks" ,*IEEE Trans. Neural Networks*, **vol.6**, no.1, pp.237-247, January, 1995.

[5] Gray, Donald L. and Michel, Anthony N.: "A Training Algorithm for Binary Feedforward Neural Networks" ,*IEEE Trans. Neural Networks*, **vol.3**, no.2, pp.320-330, March, 1992.

[6] Yamauchi, K. and Ishii, N. : "An incremental learning method with recalling interfered patterns" ,*Proc. of IEEE/ICNN*, pp.3159-3164, Nov, 1995.

[7] Ninomiya, H. and Asai, H.: "Design and Simulation of Neural Network Digital Sequential Circuits" , *IEICE Trans. Fundamentals.*, **vol.E77-A**, no.6, pp. 968-976(June 1994).

[8] Ninomiya, H. and Asai, H.: "Neural Networks for Digital Sequential Circuits" , *IEICE Trans. Fundamentals.*, **vol.E77-A**, no.12, pp. 2112-2115(Dec. 1994).

[9] Tank, D.W. and Hopfield, J.J.: "Simple 'Neural' Optimization Networks: An A/D Converter, Signal Decision Circuit, and a Linear Programming Circuit" ,*IEEE Trans. Circuit & Syst.*, **CAS-33**, 5, pp.533-541, May, 1986.

[10] Egawa, K., Kamio, T., Ninomiya, H. and Asai, H.: "Implementation of Neural Network Digital Circuits" , *Tech. Rep. of IEICE*, **NLP94-111**, pp.57-64, March, 1995.

GLOBAL STABILITY ANALYSIS FOR THE
ASYMMERTRIC CONTINUOUS TIME HOPFIELD NETWORK

Xiaofeng Liao   and   *Juebang Yu*
(Dept. of Optoelectronic Technology, UEST. of China, Chengdu, 610054, PR China)

Abstract   In this paper, a positively definite Lyapunov-function for nonlinear continuous time Hopfield network is constructed. Its global stability property is discussed in detail. Our approach is different from those described in [1-13] and is suitable for stability investigation of general neural networks.

I . Introduction

The collective computational capabilities of neural networks, such as optimization and associative memory, rely on the dynamic behaviors of the neural networks. The qualitative analysis of the neural networks helps us to understand the dynamics of the neural networks. When Hopfield investigated stability for continuous-time neural networks[12], he constructed an energy function (Lyapunov function) to discuss their asymptotic stability property. But his approach requires a network constrain of having symmetric connection weight matrix. However, the symmetry assumption is not reasonable for some neural networks such as the Master/Slave net[10] and recurrent networks. In fact. this assumption is not essential for the stability of the neural networks. The simulation results on the Master/Slave network show that the asymmetric synaptic connection offers more potential for the neural networks. The dynamics of the asymmetric neural networks are more complex than symmetric ones. Stable, unstable [3], oscillatory and chaotic behavior [1] may appear in the dynamics of asymmetric networks.

In the design of a stable neural network, some constraints are imposed on the connection matrix and other system parameters to control its dynamics. The sufficient conditions for asymptotic stability of asymmetric Hopfield network have been derived by using matrix perturbation theory and the Gershgorin's Theorem in [2], In [4], based on the Maxwell Minimum Heating Theorem and the stability criteria of continuous autonomous dynamic networks, the sufficient conditons for the stability of asymmetric Hopfied network are obtained, the results are the same as [2]. In [3], the qualitative theory of large scale interconnected dynamical systems are applied to investigate neural networks of the asymmetric Hopfield type, and criteria for the exponential stability, asymptotic stability and instability of an equilibrium are established. In [5], some asymptotically stable outputs can be attained as the network is driven by prescribed inputs, the approach consists of decomposing the interconnection matrix and using the deremainder control technique. The linearization method for the ordinary differential equation is used in [6-7] to find a series of constraint under Ostrowaki's and Brauer's theorems. Another stability criteria is given in [8] for a contractive mapping.

It is well known that zero solution stability definitions is local in the Lyapunoy Sense. However, in practical problems, we will investigate system's global stability for any initial values.

The above mentioned literature does not touch upon global stability for neural networks. In this paper, we introduce an infinity positively definite Lyapunov function and discussed global stability for continuous-time Hopfield network in detail. A series of sufficient conditions for global stability of asymmetric Hopfield networks are given. As compared to the previous results, the constraints on the connection matrix given in this paper are more meticulous than those given in [2-10]. It is believed that our approach is suitable for stability property investigation of general neural networks.

II . Continuous-Time Hopfield Neural Network Model

The Hopfield neural network can be realized by an analog circuit which is described by[12]

$$\dot{x} = -a_i x_i + \sum_{j=1}^{n} W_{ij} G_j(x_j) + I_i, i = 1, 2, \cdots, n \tag{1}$$

Where $G_i(0) = 0$, and the origin $X = (x_1, x_2, \cdots, x_n)^T = (0, 0, \cdots, 0)^T = \mathbf{0}$ is an isolated equilibrium for eq(1). Under well-known assumptions[15], for any given $X = (x_1^0, x_2^0, \cdots, x_n^0)^T \in R^{n \times 1}$ and for a specific allowable external input $\bar{I} = [\bar{I}_1, \bar{I}_2, \cdots, \bar{I}_n] \in R^{n \times 1}$ the system (1) will have a unique solution.

III . The Global Stability Analysis for Hopfield Network

In this section, we will give the sufficient conditions of global stability of an equilibrium point $X = \mathbf{0}$ for system (1). We define first the following function:

$$\varphi_i(x_i) = \begin{cases} \alpha_i, & if\ x_i \geqslant 0 \\ -\beta_i, & if\ x_i < 0 \end{cases} \tag{2}$$

Where $\alpha_i > 0, \beta_i > 0, i = 1, 2, \cdots, n$, we will have

Theorem 1. Let $\overline{I}_i = 0$, and there exist functions $\varphi_i(x_i)$, $i = 1, 2, \cdots, n$, such that if $x_j \neq 0$, and

$$(\overline{W}_{jj}G_j(x_j) - a_jx_j)\varphi_j(x_j) + \sum_{\substack{i=1 \\ i \neq j}}^{n} \varphi_i(x_i)\overline{W}_{ij}G_j(x_j) < 0 \tag{3}$$

Then an equilibrium point $X = \mathbf{0}$ of neural networks system (1) is globally stable.

Before Theorem 1 is proved, we first point out the following fact. If we fix $x_j = x_j^0 \neq 0$ and let the other x_i vary, $i = 1, 2, \cdots, j-1, j+1, \cdots, n$, the summation:

$$\sum_{\substack{i=1 \\ i \neq j}}^{n} \varphi_i(x_i)\overline{W}_{ij}G_j(x_j) + (\overline{W}_{jj}G_j(x_j) - a_jx_j)\varphi_j(x_j)$$

has obviously at most $2(n\text{-}1)$ different negative values. Then since $\varphi_i(x_i)$ can only take α_i or $-\beta_i$ no matter what value $x_i (i \neq j)$ take. Therefore there exist positive function $k_j(x_j^0)$ such that

$$\sum_{\substack{i=1 \\ i \neq j}}^{n} \varphi_i(x_i^0)\overline{W}_{ij}G_j(x_j^0) + (\overline{W}_{jj}G_j(x_j^0) - a_jx_j^0)\varphi_j(x_j^0) \leqslant -k_j(x_j^0) < 0 \tag{4}$$

Proof: We construct the following Lyapunov function

$$V(X) = V(x_1, x_2, \cdots, x_n) = \varphi_1(x_1)x_1 + \varphi_2(x_2)x_2 + \cdots + \varphi_n(x_n)x_n \tag{5}$$

By (2), if $x_i \neq 0$ then $\varphi_i(x_i)x_i > 0$ and $V(X)$ is infinity positively definite function in $x_1, x_2, \cdots, x_n$. It is obvious that $V(X)$ is continuously function in $x_1, x_2, \cdots, x_n$. We consider any nonzero solution for system (1)

$$X(t; X^0, t_0) \qquad [X(t_0; X^0, t_0) = X^0 \neq 0]$$

we prove first

$$V[X(t; X^0, t_0)] < V(X^0) \qquad if\ t > t_0 \tag{6}$$

since by eq(1)

$$\frac{dx_i}{dt}\Big|_{t=t_0} = (\overline{W}_{jj}G_j(x_j) - a_jx_j) + \sum_{\substack{i=1 \\ i \neq j}}^{n} \overline{W}_{ij}G_j(x_j^0) \triangleq l_i, i = 1, 2, \cdots, n$$

By limit definition

$$\lim_{t \to t_0} \frac{x_i(t; X^0, t_0) - x_i^0}{t - t_0} = l_i$$

Hence for any $\varepsilon > 0$, there exist $\delta > 0$, if $t_0 < t \leqslant t_0 + \delta$, then

$$l_i - \varepsilon < \frac{x_i(t; X^0, t_0) - x_i^0}{t - t_0} = l_i + \varepsilon$$

Thus

$$x_i(t; X^0, t_0) < x_i^0 + (l_i + \varepsilon)(t - t_0) \tag{7}$$

$$x_i(t; X^0, t_0) > x_i^0 + (l_i - \varepsilon)(t - t_0) \tag{8}$$

If $x_i(t; X^0, t_0) > 0$, then $\varphi_i[x_i(t; X^0, t_0)] = \alpha_i > 0$. By (11), we have

$$\varphi_i[x_i(t; X^0, t_0)]x_i(t; X^0, t_0) < \varphi_i[x_i(t; X^0, t_0)]x_i^0 + (l_i + \varepsilon)(t - t_0)\varphi_i[x_i(t; X^0, t_0)]$$

If $x_i(t; X^0, t_0) < 0$, then $\varphi_i[x_i(t; X^0, t_0)] = -\beta_i < 0$. By (12), we have

$$\varphi_i[x_i(t; X^0, t_0)]x_i(t; X^0, t_0) < \varphi_i[x_i(t; X^0, t_0)]x_i^0 + (l_i - \varepsilon)(t - t_0)\varphi_i[x_i(t; X^0, t_0)]$$

Hence, the above two inequity can write $(\varepsilon_i = \pm\varepsilon)$

$$\varphi_i[x_i(t; X^0, t_0)]x_i(t; X^0, t_0) < \varphi_i[x_i(t; X^0, t_0)]x_i^0 + (l_i + \varepsilon_i)(t - t_0)\varphi_i[x_i(t; X^0, t_0)]$$

As a result

$$V[X(t; X^0, t_0)] < \sum_{i=1}^{n} \varphi_i[x_i(t; X^0, t_0)]x_i^0 + (t - t_0)\sum_{i=1}^{n} \varphi_i[x_i(t; X^0, t_0)](l_i + \varepsilon_i)$$

Note $x_i(t; X^0, t_0)$ is a continuously function in t, therefore, if $x_i^0 \neq 0$, then $x_i(t; X^0, t_0) \neq 0$ in neighorhood of t_0. Now we choose δ, such that when $t_0 \leqslant t \leqslant t_0 + \delta$, sign of every nonzero components x_j^0 hold identical to components $x_j(t; X^0, t_0)$. i.e.

$$\varphi_j(x_j(t; X^0, t_0)) = \varphi_j(x_j^0)$$

Thus

$$\sum_{i=1}^{n} \varphi_i[x_i(t; X^0, t_0)]l_i = \sum_{i=1}^{n} \varphi_i[x_i(t; X^0, t_0)] \cdot \left[(\overline{W}_{ii}G_i(x_i^0) - a_ix_i^0) + \sum_{\substack{j=1 \\ j \neq i}}^{n} \overline{W}_{ij}G_j(x_j^0)\right]$$

$$= \sum_{j=1}^{n} \{\varphi_i(x_j^0)(\overline{W}_{jj}G_j(x_j^0) - a_j x_j^0) + \sum_{i \neq j} \varphi_i[x_j(t;X^0,t_0)\overline{W}_{ij}G_j(x_j^0)]\}$$

$$\leq \sum_{j} \{- k_j(x_j^0)\}$$

(Here summation is on j for all $x_j^0 \neq 0$) . Therefore

$$V[X(t;X^0,t_0)] < \sum_{i=1}^{n} \varphi_i(x_i^0)x_i^0 + (t - t_0)\{- \sum_{j} - k_j(x_j^0) + \sum_{i=1}^{n} \varphi_i[x_j(t;X^0,t_0)]\varepsilon_i\}$$

Because $k_j(x_j^0) > 0$ and ε_i may be chosen sufficiently small, $\varphi_i[x_i(t;X^0,t_0)]$ is bounded ($i = 1,2,\cdots,n$) . Hence we choose ε_i such that

$$- \sum_{j} k_j(x_j^0) + \sum_{i=1}^{n} \varphi_i[x_i(t;X^0,t_0)]\varepsilon_i < 0$$

Therefore, there exist T , such that

$$V[X(t;X^0,t_0)] < V(X^0), t_0 < t \leq T$$

We will prove that formula (8) is tenable for $t > t_0$ as follows. If formala (8) is untenable, then there exist $t_2 > t_0$, such that

$$V[X(t;X^0,t_0)] < V(X^0), if \ t_0 < t \leq t_2$$
$$V[X(t_2;X^0,t_0)] = V(X^0)$$

Because $V[X(t;X^0,t_0)]$ is a continuously function in t . Thus there exist $t_1 \in (t_0,t_2)$, such that $V[X(t;X^0,t_0)]$ on $[t_0,t_2]$ have

$$V[X(t;X^0,t_0)] \qquad t_0 < t < t_2$$

We assume

$$X' = X(t_1;X^0,t_0), \qquad X(t;X',t_0) = X(t;X^0,t_1)$$

as stated above

$$V[X(t;X^0,t_0)] = V[X(t;X',t_1)] < V(X'), \qquad t_1 < t \leq t_1 + \delta$$

This is contradictory with minimal value $V[X(t;X^0,t_0)]$. Therefore formula (12) is tenable.

Let

$$\lambda_1 = \min(\alpha_i,\beta_i), \lambda_2 = \max(\alpha_i,\beta_i)$$

Since $V[X(t;X^0,t_0)](t \geq \tau)$ is a monotonic decreasing function on t , it is obvious that $(3)'$ s trivial solution $X = 0$ is stable. This is because

$$|X(t;X^0,t_0)| \leq \frac{1}{\lambda_1}V[X(t_0;X^0,t_0)] \leq \frac{1}{\lambda_1}V[X(t;X^0,t_0)] \leq \sqrt{n}\,\frac{\lambda_2}{\lambda_1}|X^0| \leq \varepsilon \qquad (t \geq t_0)$$

We take

$$|X^0| \leq \delta(\varepsilon) = (\lambda_1\varepsilon)/(\lambda_2\sqrt{n})$$

then one may conclude that solution $X(t;X^0,t_0)$ for $t \geq t_0$ is bounded, and

$$\lim V[X(t,X^0,t_0)] = V_0 \geq 0$$

exists.

Because the solutions of Eq(1) have a nonempty ω-limit set, there exist an ω-limit trajectory $X_0(t)$, and for every fixed t , we may find a monotonic increasing divergent sequence $\{t_k\}$ such that

$$\lim X(t_k;X^0,t_0) = X_0(t)$$

and

$$\lim V[X(t_k;X^0,t_0) = V[X_0(t)]$$

Hence, for all t

$$V[X_0(t_0)] = V_0$$

we obtain $X_0(t) = 0$ and $V_0 = 0$. on the other hand, since function $V[X(t;X^0,t_0)]$ along every nontrivial solution is strictly monotonic decreasing, we obtained directly

$$\lim X(t;X^0,t_0) = 0$$

i. e. system (1) is globally stable. $\qquad\qquad\qquad\qquad\qquad\qquad\qquad\qquad\qquad\qquad\qquad\qquad\square$

Theorem 2. Let $\overline{I}_i = 0$, then for $x_j \neq 0$, we have

$$x_j(\overline{W}_{jj}G_j(x_j) - a_j x_j) < 0, \quad j = 1,2,\cdots,n,$$

and there exists constant $\alpha > 0$ such that

$$\left|\frac{\overline{W}_{ij}G_j(x_j)}{\overline{W}_{jj}G_j(x_j) - a_j x_j}\right| \leq \frac{\alpha^{j-i}}{n}, \qquad i,j = 1,2,\cdots,n, i \neq j$$

Then equilibrium point $X = 0$ of system (1) is globally stable.

Proof: The result follows directly from theorem 1. $\qquad\square$

Ⅳ. Stability Criteria for Hopfield Neural Network by Using First Approximation

If the origin $X = (0,0,0,\cdots,0)$ is not an equilibrium point of systems (1), we assume that $X^* = (x_i^*)$ $\in R^{n\times 1}$ is an equilibrium point of system (1). Then system (1) can be expanded into Taylor series at $X=X^*$:

$$\dot{X} = LX + R(X) \tag{9}$$

Where $X = (x_1,\cdots,x_n)^T$, $L = (l_{ij})_{n\times n}$, and

$$l_{ij} = \begin{cases} \overline{W}_{ii}G_i'(x_i^*) - a_i, & i = j \\ \overline{W}_{ij}G_j'(x_j^*), & i \neq j \end{cases} \quad \text{and} \quad \lim_{|X|\to 0} \frac{\|R(X)\|}{\|X\|} = 0 \tag{10}$$

By [16] if we know that all eigenvalues of matrix L in system (9) have negative real parts, asymptotic stability of system (1) are obtained. Hence we have the following Theorem:

Theorem 3. Suppose

$$a_j > \overline{W}_{jj}G_j'(x_j^*), \qquad j = 1,2,\cdots,n$$

and there exist $\alpha_j > 0, \beta_j > 0, j = 1,2,\cdots,n$, such that the following inequilities are satisfied:

$$\alpha_j(\overline{W}_{jj}G_j'(x_j^*) - a_j) + \sum_{\substack{i=1 \\ i\neq j}}^{n} \varphi_i(x_i)\overline{W}_{ij}G_j'(x_j^*) < 0 \tag{11}$$

$$- \beta_j(\overline{W}_{jj}G_j'(x_j^*) - a_j) + \sum_{\substack{i=1 \\ i\neq j}}^{n} \varphi_i(x_i)\overline{W}_{ij}G_j'(x_j^*) > 0, j = 1,\cdots,n \tag{12}$$

Then eigenvalues of matrix L have negative real parts. Hence system (1) is asymptotically stable.

Theorem 4: If matrix satisfied

$$a_j > \overline{W}_{jj}G_j'(x_j^*), j = 1,2,\cdots,n$$

and let

$$\alpha = \max_{j=2,\cdots,n}\left\{ \max_{i=1,\cdots,n-1} \left| \frac{n\overline{W}_{ij}G_j'(x_j^*)}{\overline{W}_{jj}G_j'(x_j^*) - a_j} \right|^{\frac{1}{j-i}} \right\}, j > i$$

$$\frac{1}{\beta} = \max_{i=1,\cdots,n-1}\left\{ \max_{j=2,\cdots,n} \left| \frac{n\overline{W}_{ij}G_j'(x_j^*)}{\overline{W}_{jj}G_j'(x_j^*) - a_j} \right|^{\frac{i}{j-i}} \right\}, i > j$$

and, $\beta \geq \alpha > 0$. Then eigenvalues of matrix L have negative real parts.

Ⅴ. Conclusion

In this paper, by introducing an infinity positively definite function and surmount symmetric connection matrix conditions, the global stability property for continuous time Hopfield networks are discussed in detail. Our approach is different from literature [1—13] and is suitable for stability investigation of general neural networks as well. The sufficient conditions for stability of asymmetric Hopfield network have been obtained by using the lineraization method for the ordinary differential equation.

Reference

[1]   Cohn, M, A and Grossberg, S. IEEE Trans on Syst. Man Cybern, Vol 13, No. 5, pp. 815-826, 1983

[2]   A. Guez et al. IEEE Trans on Syst Man Cybern, 1988, **18**, pp. 80-87

[3]   A. N. Michel *et al*, IEEE Trans, CAS, Vol 36, No. 2, pp. 229-243, 1989

[4]   Jianping Xu, Juebang Yu. Proc. CAS-NN' 89, Guangzhou, pp. 15, 1989

[5]   Huanglin Zeng, Juebang Yu, Proc of China 1991 International Conference on Circuits and Systems, Shenzhen, pp. 268-270, 1991

[6]   Xiaofeng Liao, Juebang Yu. Journal of UEST, Vol 23, No. 6, pp. 163-168, 1994

[7]   Xiaofeng Liao, Wenquan Mu, Juebang Yu. ICCNSP' 95, Nanjing, China, pp. 238-241, 1995

[8]   Kelly, D. G. IEEE Trans on Bio. Engineering, Vol 37, No. 3, March, 1990

[9]   Hirsch, M. W. Neural Networks, Vol 1 pp. 331-349, 1989

[10]   Lapedes, *A adm* Farber, R. Physica **22D** pp. 247-259, 1986

[11]   J. H. Li, *et al*, IEEE Trans on CAS, Vol 35, No. 8, pp. 976-986, 1989

[12]   J. J. Hopfield, Proc Nat Acad Sci USA, 1984, **81**, pp. 3088-3092

[13]   E. Noldus, *et al*, Int J. Systems SCI, Vol. 1, No. 1, 19-31, 1994

[14]   S. Grossberg, Neural Networks, Vol. 1, pp. 17-61, 1988

[15]   A. N. Miller and A. N. Michel Ordinary Differential Equations, Academic Press, 1982

[16]   J. K. Hale, Ordinary Differential Equations, Academic Press, 1982

[17]   Mauro Fort *et al*, IEEE Trans on CAS, Vol. 41, No. 7, 491-494, 1994

Stability Conditions for Nonlinear Continuous Random Neural Networks[1]

Xin Sheng Zhang

Institute of Mathematics, Shantou University
Shantou 515063, P.R.China
Department of Computer Science, The Chinese University of Hong Kong
Shatin, N.T., Hong Kong

Abstract—In this paper, one kind of nonlinear continuous random neural networks with asymmetric connection weights are discussed. This neural networks can be considered as the recurrent neural network perturbed by random noise. Some sufficient conditions for a given network to have a globally asymptotically stability equilibrium distribution for arbitrary input are derived. We also give one example to show that the globally asymptotically stability of this neural networks is greatly dependent on the random noises.

1 Introduction

The stability of dynamics of neural network has been extensively studied by many authors. In [2], Cohen and Grossberg described a general principle for assessing the stability of a certain class of neural networks, which is described by the following system of coupled nonlinear differential equations:

$$\frac{du_i}{dt} = a_i(u_i)\left[b_i(u_i) - \sum_{j=1}^{N} c_{i,j}\phi_j(u_j)\right], \quad i = 1, 2, \cdots, N.$$

The results of Cohen and Grossberg require that the synaptic weights of the network be "symmetric", i.e $c_{i,j} = c_{j,i}$. Recently in [5], Kiyotoshi Matsuska dealt with the following type of neural network which he called a nonlinear continuous neural network with asymmetric connection weights. The dynamics of the network are represented by

$$\begin{cases} \tau\frac{dx_i(t)}{dt} = -x_i(t) + \sum_j \bar{w}_{ij}y_j(t) + s_i \\ y_i(t) = \bar{g}_i(x_i(t)) \end{cases} \tag{1}$$

$$i = 1, 2, \cdots, n$$

where $x_i(t)$ is the variable that represent a state of unit neurons i at time $t(i = 1, 2, \cdots, n)$, s_i a constant input fromm the outside of the network, and $y_i(t)$ an output at time t, $\bar{w}_{ij}$ is the strength of connection from unit j to unit i, which can be asymmetric. τ is a time constant governing the rate of change of each unit's state. Matsuoka obtained some stability conditions for these neural networks.

In reality, however, the neural network model is always affected by random noises when we apply this model to solve problems. So, when we deal with the stability of dynamics of neural network, we should determine whether the neural network model, perturbed by random noises is stable or not. That is to say, we should deal with the following type of neural networks, the dynamics of which are represented by

$$\begin{cases} \tau dx_i(t) = (-x_i(t) + \sum_j \bar{w}_{ij}y_j(t) + s_i)dt + dz_i(t) \\ y_i(t) = \bar{g}_i(x_i(t)) \end{cases} \tag{2}$$

where $z_i(t), 1 \leq j \leq n$ are some kind of random noise. We call system (2) as nonlinear continuous random neural networks with asymmetric connection weights. In this paper, some stability conditions are obtained for these neural networks. In particular, when the random noise is white noise our conditions are the same as K.Matsuoka's. We also give one example to show the Matsuoka's conditions are not valid if the noise is not white noise. This means that stability of system (2) is greatly dependent on the random noise.

---

[1]The author would like to thank Dr. L. Xu for his hospitality and financial supports.
Research supported in part by the Natural Science Foundation of Gauangdong Province.

2   Stability and stability conditions

In this section we will give the proper definition of stability for system (2) and some stability condition for system (2) will be derived.

In the following discussion we assume that output function $\bar{g}_i$ satisfies

(i) $\bar{g}_i$ is a strictly monotone increasing function,

(ii) $\bar{g}_i$ is continuously differentiable

(iii) $0 < \bar{g}_i' \leq \sup_z g_i'(z) = r_i < \infty$

where $\bar{g}_i'$ represents first-order derivative of $\bar{g}_i$

(iv) $\bar{g}_i$ in bounded (i.e., $\sup_z |\bar{g}_i(z)| < \infty$)

Remark: The widely used sigmoid-shaped function $g_i(z) = \frac{1}{1+\exp(-cz)}$ has these properties, where c is a positive constant. Without lose of generality, r will be assumed to be unity. Putting $w_{ij} = \bar{w}_{ij} r_j$ and $g_i(z) = \bar{g}_i(z)/r_i$, we can rewrite (2) as

$$dx_i(t) = (-x_i(t) + \sum_j w_{ij} g_i(x_j(t)) + s_i)dt + dz_i(t) \tag{3}$$

Then (iii) reads

(iii)' $0 < g_i'(z) \leq \sup_z g_i'(z) = 1$.

Expressing (3) in vector-matrix notation, we have

$$dX(t) = (-X(t) + Wg(X(t)) + S)dt + dZ(t) \tag{4}$$

where $X(t) = (x_1(t), \cdots, x_n(t))^T$, $S = (s_1, \cdots, s_n)^T$, $W = (w_{ij})$, $g(x) = (g_1(x_1), \cdots, g_n(x_n))^T$, and $Z(t) = (z_1(t), \cdots, z_m(t))^T$.

When $Z(t)$ is White noise or Levy noise, it is well known that system (4) is a Markov process on R^n. Let $P_x(t, dy)$ be the transition probability i.e. $P_x(t, B) = P(X_t \in B | X_0 = x)$. It represents the probability of systems (4) transfer to set B at time t from initial state x, $P_x(t, y)$ denote the density function of $P_x(t, dy)$, $P_x(t, y)$ is called the transition function of Markov process $X(t)$. With each transition function $P_x(t, y)$ can be associated two families of operators, the first is defined on functions and the second on measures

$$T_t f(x) = \int P_x(t, y) f(y) dy,$$

$$S_t \mu(A) = \int_A \int_\mu (dx) P_x(t, y) dy.$$

It is easy to check that T_t and S_t are semigroup on $C^2(R^n)$ and $M(R^n)$ respectively, where $C^2(R^n)$ represents the family of twice continuously differentiable function bounded and continuous with its derivatives, and $M(R^n)$ is the family of some kinds of measures on R^n. A probability distribution μ on R^n is called equilibrium distribution of system (4), if it satisfies:

$$S_t \mu = \mu.$$

In order to state our main results, we need to introduce the following definition.

Definition: System (4) is called absolutely stable. If it has an unique equilibrium distribution μ, and for any initial distribution ν, we have $\|P_\nu(t, \cdot) - \mu(\cdot)\| \to 0$ as $t \to \infty$. Where $\| \cdot \|$ represents total variation of signal measure and $P_\nu(t, \cdot) = \int P_x(t, \cdot)\nu(dx)$. For system (4), we have

Theorem 1. Suppose $Z(t)$ is d-dimensional white noise. If

$$\lambda_{max}\{(W + W^T)/2\} < 1,$$

then the network (4) is absolutely stable. Where $\lambda_{max}(\cdot)$ represent the maximum eigenvalue of symmetric matrix.

As discussion in [5], we also have

Corollary 1. If one of the following conditions is satisfies.

(a) $\frac{1}{2}(\sum_{i,j}(w_{ij}+w_{ji})^2)^{\frac{1}{2}} < 1$;

(b) $\max_i\{w_{ii}+\sum_{j\neq i}(|w_{ij}+w_{ji}|/2\} < 1$;

(c) there exists $P = \text{diag}\{p_1, \cdots, p_n\}$ $(p_i > 0)$,

  such that $\lambda_{max}\{PWP^{-1}+P^{-1}W^TP)/2\} < 1$;

(d) there exists matrix P,

  such that $\frac{1}{2}(\sum_{i,j}(p_iw_{ij}/p_j+p_jw_{ji}/p_i)^2)^{\frac{1}{2}} < 1$;

(e) there exists matrix P,

  such that $\max_i\{w_{ii}+\sum_{ji}|p_iw_{ij}/p_j+p_jw_{ji}/p_i|/2\} < 1$.

Then the network (4) is absolutely stable.

But, if the random noise $Z(t)$ is other kind of stochastic process the above conditions is not valid to guarantee the stability of system (4). For example, we assume $Z(t)$ is composed Poisson process, i.e. $Z(t)$ is a homogeneous process with independent increments on R^n, which has the characteristic function

$$E \exp\{i(\alpha, Z(t))\} = \exp\left\{t\int_{R^n}(e^{i(\alpha,x)}-1)\Pi(dx)\right\},$$

where Π is a finite measure on R^n. In the following discussion, we will assume Π is a probability measure on R^n. Denote the time of the first jump of the process $Z(t)$ by τ_1 and its value by η_1, the time of the second jump by $\tau_1+\tau_2$ and its value by η_2, the time of kth jump by $\tau_1+\tau_2+\cdots+\tau_k$ and its value by η_k, etc. Then the pairs of random variables $\{(\tau_k,\eta_k),\ k=1,2,\cdots\}$ are independent and equally distributed, moreover,

$$P(\tau_1 > t,\ \eta_1 \in A) = e^{-t}\Pi(A), \quad \forall t > 0, \quad A \in \mathcal{E}(R^n).$$

Let T_t and L be the transition semigroup and infinitesimal operator of $X(t)$, respectively. If we assume $\int_{|x|>1}\ln|x|\ \Pi(dx) = \infty$, then we can prove that $T_tf(x) \to 0$ as $t \to \infty$ for all $f \in C^2(R^n)$. Therefore, $X(t)$ has no invariant probability distribution. By the definition , we know that system (4) is unstable.

3 Discussion.

We have discussed the stable problem of system (4). On one hand, when the random noise $Z(t)$ is white noise, we prove that system (4) has an unique equilibrium distribution if Matsuoka's conditions are met. Moreover, the system (4) will be converged to this equilibrium distribution from any initial distribution. As we point out in the introduction, the system (4) can be considered as the system (1) perturbed by random noises. Our results show Matsaoka's results are still correct even if the system (1) perturbed by random noise, i.e., the stability of system (1) is not affected when system (1) is perturbed by white noise. But in here, we have to deal with stochastic nonlinear differential equations. The combination of stochasticity and nonlinearity makes the subject more difficult to handle. On the other hand, if system (1) is perturbed by other random noise, for example, composed Poisson process, the Matsaoka's conditions are not valid to guarantee the stability of system (4). This means the system (1) is not stability perturbed by any kind of random noises. The stable problem of the system (1) perturbed by more general random noise is still open. It seems to be more difficult to solve this problem completely at present.

4 Appendix

The Proof of Theorem 1 By putting $\tilde{g}(x) = g(x) - g(0)$ and $\tilde{S} = Wg(0) + S$. We can rewrite (4) as

$$dX(t) = (-X(t) + W\tilde{g}(x(t)) + \tilde{S})dt + dZ(t) \tag{5}$$

Note that $\tilde{g}$ satisfies (i)—(iv) of section 2. Hence, we can assume that $g(0) = 0$.

Applying one-term Taylor expansion to $Wg(x)$, we have

$$Wg(x) = \int_0^1 WJ(\theta x)x d\theta$$

where

$$J(\theta x) = \begin{pmatrix} \frac{\partial g_1}{\partial x_1}(\theta x) & & \\ & \ddots & \\ & & \frac{\partial g_n}{\partial x_n}(\theta x) \end{pmatrix}$$

Therefor

$$x^T Wg(x) = \int_0^1 x^T WJ(\theta x)x d\theta$$

Note that

$$x^T J(\theta x)x = x^T \left[\frac{1}{2}(WJ(\theta x) + (WJ(\theta x))^T) \right] x$$

By (iii) of section 2, $\sup_x |\frac{\partial g_i}{\partial x_i}(x)| \leq 1$.

Therefore

$$x^T WJ(\theta x)x \leq x^T \lambda_{max} \left\{ \frac{1}{2}(W + W^T) \right\} x,$$

where $\lambda_{max}\{\cdot\}$ represents the maximum eigenvalue of symmetric matrix $\{\cdot\}$.

Let L be the infinitesimal operator of semigroup T_t. Then:

$$Lf(x) = \frac{1}{2}\sum_{i=1}^n \frac{\partial^2 f(x)}{\partial x_i^2} + \sum_{i=1}^n \left(-x_i + \sum_j w_{ij}g_j(x) \right) \frac{\partial f(x)}{\partial x_i}$$

Set $f(x) = |x|^2$, we have

$$Lf(x) = 1 + x^T(-x + Wg(x)) \leq 1 - |x|^2(1 - 1/2\lambda_{max}(W + W^T)) < 0$$

provide $|x|^2$ big enough.

By the theory on diffusion process, we know that $X(t)$ has a unique invariant probability measure and $X(t)$ is ergodic. If we set $\mathcal{F}_t = \sigma(X(u): \ u \geq t)$, $\mathcal{T} = \cap_{t>0}\mathcal{F}_t$, then for any B of $\mathcal{T}$, $P_x(B) = 0$ holds for all x or $P_x(B) = 1$ holds for all x. Using the above fact, we can prove: for any probability measure ν

$$\lim_{t \to \infty} \sup_{A \in \mathcal{F}_t} |P_\nu(A \cap B) - P_\nu(A)P_\nu(B)| = 0 \tag{6}$$

Our result can be proved by applying Jordan-Hahn decomposition theorem to singed measure and (6).

References

[1] S.Amari, Mathematical foundations of neurocomputing,Proceedings of the IEEE 78(1990), 1443-1463.

[2] M. A. Cohen and S. Grossberg, Absolute stability of global pattern formation and parallel memory storage by competitive neural networks, IEEE Transactions on Systems, Man, and Cybernetics bf SMC-13(1983), 815-826.

[3] R. Z. Haśminskii, Stochastic stability of differential equations. Sijthoff & Noordhoff 1980.

[4] J. J Hopfield, Neural Networks and physical system with emergent Collective computertational abilities. Proc. Natl. Acad. Sci., U. S. A., Vol.79,(1984) 2554-2558.

[5] Kiyotoshi Matsuska, Stability Conditions for Nonlinear Continuous Neural Networks with Asymmetric Connection Weights Neural Networks Vol.5 (1992), 495—500.

Recurrent Networks, Automata and Dynamics

(Poster Presentation)

Usefulness of Edge of Chaos State for Synchronous Response of Receptor Cell Syncytium

Hirofumi Funakubo,Yoshiki Kashimori, and Takeshi Kambara
Department of Applied Physics and Chemistry,
The University of Electro-Communications,Chofu,Tokyo,182,Japan
E-mail funakubo@nerve.pc.uec.ac.jp

Abstract— We studied the dependence of response characteristics of the syncytium on the collective gating dynamics, which are periodic, chaotic, and edge of chaos states. The correlation between two cells in a syncytium system changes noticeably depending on what kind of collective gating state the receptor cell syncytium is in. The response property of edge of chaos state to external stimuli is and synchronous, while the response property of periodic state and of chaotic state is not synchronous.

1 Introduction

Many receptor cell in some sensory system such as visual, auditory, and gustatory systems [1, 2] have a syncytium structure in which cells are interconnectioned through gap junctions. It is not yet clear what kind of role the syncytium structure plays on the receptor systems. In the previous paper [3], we investigated effects of intercellular coupling through the gap junctions on dynamics of ion channel gating and the coupling between the ion channels and the membrane potential of cells in a receptor cell syncytium. This is because a response of receptor cells to stimuli is produced by a change in membrane potential of the cells which is induced by ionic current through ion channels in the cell membrane. It has been shown [3] that there exist three kinds of dynamics of collective ion channel gating which are periodic,chaodtic, and edge of chaos states. Which dynamic state appears depends mainly on the gating property of a single ion channel described by a reasonable mapping function.

In the present paper, we investigate how the response characteristics changes depending on the dynamical state of the syncytium. First, we study on an ability of the syncytium to propagate a stimulus applied to one receptor cell through the system. Second, we investigate an ability of the syncytium to synchronize the responses to two stimuli applized to simultaneously to two receptor cells. We consider a possibility that the syncytium extracts, based on the synchronization, only meaningful signal from noisy stimuli applied simultaneously to many receptor cells in the syncytium. We consider also whether the chaotic fluctuation of membrane potentials is useful for very weak stimuli to be detected by stochastic resonance [4].

2 Model of Single Ion Channel

It has been consider in many models of ion channels that the gating of channels is stochastic , that is, whether the gate of a channel is opened or closed depends on random process. However, recently it has been shown based on analysis of variation of charge distribution in single ion channels [5] that the transient change associating with the ion channel gating arises from the deterministic conformation change of the channels. Liebovitch and Toth [6] analysed the fluctuation of ionic current through channels based on both a stochastic gating model and a deterministic one and showed that it is highly possible for channel gating to be a chaotic process.

Therefore, we adopt a deterministic gating model which is an extension of the mapping model given by Liebovitch and Toth. The quantity Z(t+1) representing a state of channel gating at a time (t+1) is given by Z(t) at a previous time t according to the mapping function,

$$Z(t+1) = \begin{cases} a_1(2d_1 - Z(t))Z(t) & ; \ 0 \leq Z(t) < d_1 \\ \frac{d_2 - Z(t)}{d_2 - d_1} & ; \ d_1 \leq Z(t) < d_2 \\ a_2(Z(t) - 1)(Z(t) - 2d_2 + 1) + 1 & ; \ d_2 < Z(t) \leq 1 \end{cases} \tag{1}$$

where a_i and d_i (i=1,2) are constant parameters. The gate is closed for $0 \leq Z(t) < d_1$ and opened for $d_2 < Z(t) \leq 1$. The mapping function is shown in Fig.1.

The gating dynamics of single ion channel includes periodic and chaotic oscillations. The branching diagram of gating dynamics produced by the mapping function (1) is shown in Fig.2 , where the branching parameter is a_1 in the case of $a_2 = a_1$.

3 Model of Receptor Cell Syncytium

In order to study the effect of intercellular coupling of ion channel gating through the gap junction , we present a model of the receptor cell syncytium as shown in Fig.3. Each receptor cell includes pNa^+ channels and qK^+ channels in its apical membrane. N receptor cells are arrayed linearly and the two adjacent cells are interconnectioned through gap junctions in which Na^+ and K^+ ion pass smoothly.

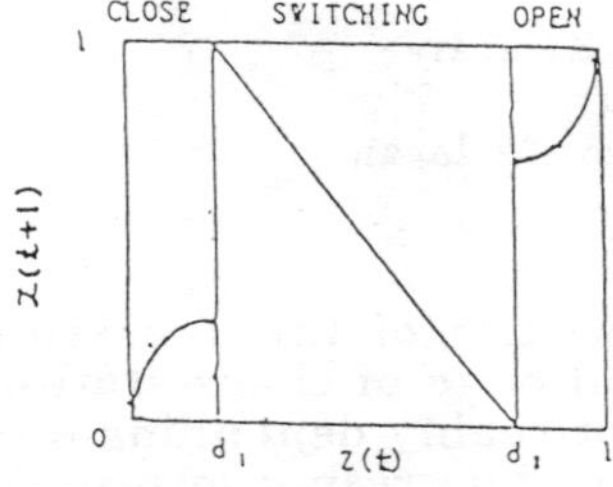

Fig. 1 The mapping function describing the gating process of single ion channel.

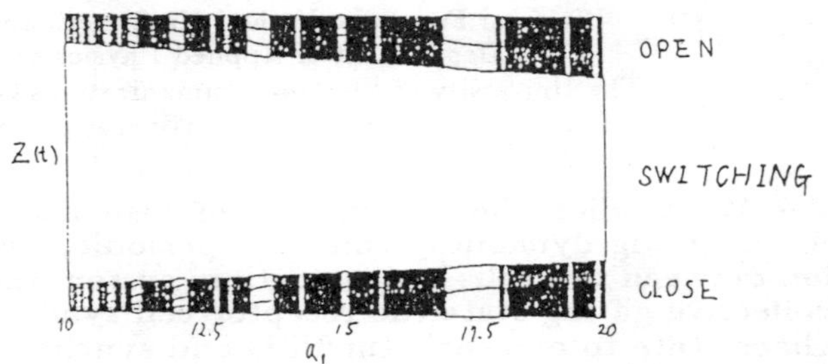

Fig.2 The branching diagram of gating dynamics of single ion channel. The branching parameter is a_1 . The parameter value used are $a_1 = a_2, d_1 = 0.1, d_2 = 0.9$

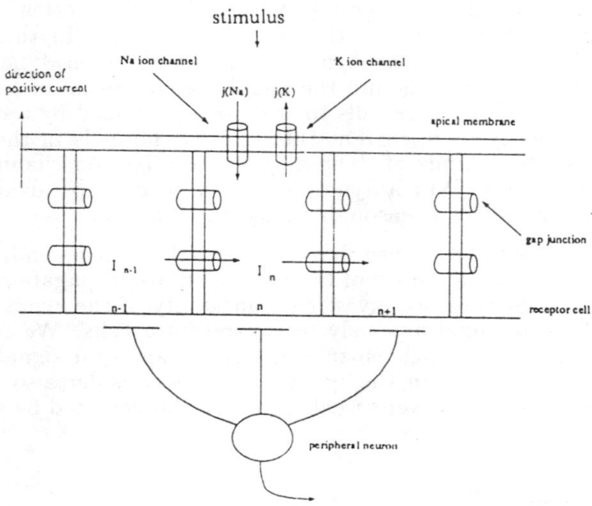

Fig.3 A model of receptor cell syncytium with peripheral neuron. Each receptor cell incledes pNa channels and qK channels in its membrane. The two adjacent cells are connected electrically through gap junctions in their basolateral membrane.

We consider the relations of gating quantities Z with the electric potential difference V across the apical membrane. The relations are derived from the conservation law of electric current in each cell which is described as

$$C\frac{dV_n}{dt} + J_n(Na) + J_n(K) = I_{n-1} + I_n \tag{2}$$

where V_n is the membrane potential of nth cell, $J_n(X)(X = Na, K)$ the current through the X channels in the nth cell apical membrane, C the membrane capacitance, and I_n the electric current from nth cell to (n+1)th cell through gap junctions. The channel currents are given by

$$J_n(Na) = g_{Na} \sum_{k=1}^{p} x_{n,k}(V_n - E_{Na}) \tag{3}$$

$$J_n(K) = g_K \sum_{k=1}^{q} y_{n,k}(V_n - E_K) \tag{4}$$

where $x_{n,k}$ and $y_{n,k}$ are the gating quantities for Na^+ channels and K^+ channels respectively, their temporal variation is given by Eq.1, gx is the electric conductance of a X channel and E_X is the equilibrium potential for X ions and p and q are the numbers of Na^+ and K^+ channels in a single cell, respectively. The electric current I_n is represented with the membrane potential V_n as

$$I_n = \frac{V_n - V_{n+1}}{r} \tag{5}$$

where r is the resistivity of gap junctions.

Eq.(2) is reasonably approximated by using the Euler method as

$$V_n(t+1) = V_n(t) - \sigma_{Na} \sum_{k=1}^{p} x_{n,k}(V_n(t) - E_{Na}) \tag{6}$$

$$-\sigma_K \sum_{k=1}^{q} y_{n,k}(V_n(t) - E_K) + \lambda\{V_{n+1}(t) + V_{n-1}(t) - 2V_n(t)\}$$

where $\sigma_{Na} = g_{Na}\Delta t/C, \sigma_K = g_K \Delta t/C$ and $\lambda = \Delta t/(rC)$.

Since we consider that the Na^+ and K^+ channels are voltage-dependent, we introduce the relation of channel gating function for the cells with the membrane potential V_n , which is given through the voltage dependence of the branching parameter a_i ,

$$a_i(t+1) = a_{i0} + \epsilon \tanh[\frac{F\{V_n(t) - E_n\}}{2RT}], (i = 1, 2) \tag{7}$$

where E_n is the resting potential corresponding to the value of V_n in the steady state ($I_n = I_{n-1}, J_{Na} + J_K = 0, dV_n/dt = 0$), F is a_{i0} is the value for the resting state and + for i=1, - for i-2.

In order to investigate the mechanism of stochastic resonance (SR) in the receptor cell syncytium, we consider a peripheral neuron innervating each cell, as seen in Fig. 3. The outputs of receptor cells converge on the peripheral neuron. Then, the membrane potential is determined by

$$C_p \frac{dV_p}{dt} = g_{Na}(V_p - V_{Na}) - g_K(V_p - V_K) + g_{Cl}(V_{pn} - V_{Cl}) + w \sum_{n=1}^{10}[1 + \exp(-\frac{V_n - V_{th}}{B})]^{-1} \tag{8}$$

where C_p is the capacitance of membrane of the neuron, g_{Na} and g_K are the conductances of active Na^+ and K^+ channels, respectively, g_L is the conductance of leak channel(Cl^- channel), and V_X is the equilibrium potential of ion X(X=Na^+, K^+, Cl^-). The last term of Eq.(9) means the postsynaptic current which is injected by the neural transmitter release from the presynaptic membrane of receptor cells. The magnitude of the current is nearly proportional to the amount of released transmitter which is determined by the membrane potential of receptor cell. It seems reasonable that the amount is proportional to a sigmoid function of V_p. In Eq.(9) , w is the strength of synaptic connection, V_{th} the threshold values, and B the parameter determining the rising of the sigmoid curve.

4 Dynamical Property of Ion Channel Gating and Membrane Potential

In the previous paper [3, 7], we calculated the dynamics of periodic, chaotic, and the edge of chaos state. For the convenience, we briefly summarize the dynamical properties of these states. The periodic state for a=11.25 is shown in Fig.4a, where all of the ion channels makes spatially synchronous and temporary periodic gating. The membrane potentials also oscillate periodically. Because the gating of an isolated single channel for $a_0 = 11.25$ is chaotic, the synchronous collective gating is produced by the interchannel interaction through the membrane potential. The chaotic state ($a_0 = 16.5$) is shown in Fig.4b, where the gating of any channels is chaotic. The membrane potentials also fluctuate chaotically. The edge of chaos state for $a_0 = 12.3$ is shown in Fig.4c, where the regions in which the gating is spatially synchronous and temporary periodic propagate into the surrounding. The bursts of the potential oscillation appear in one cell and propagate into the neighboring cells.

In order to investigate the qualitative properties of the three kinds of the dynamical states, we calculated the autocorrelation function [8] of gating qualities, $x_{m,k}$, defined by

$$C_G(\tau) = \sum_{m=1}^{10} \sum_{k=1}^{p} \{\langle x_{m,k}(t)x_{m,k}(t+\tau)\rangle - \langle x_{m,k}(t)\rangle^2\} \tag{9}$$

$$\langle f(t)\rangle \equiv \lim_{T\to\infty} \frac{1}{T} \int_0^T f(t)dt \tag{10}$$

Figure 5 shows three kinds of autocorrelation function $C_G(\tau)$ for three collective channel gating. When the collective dynamics is periodic, $C_G(\tau)$ is periodic and does not decrease with increase of the correlation time τ, as seen in Fig. 5a. When the collective dynamics is chaotic, $C_G(\tau)$ decreases exponentially as seen in Fig.5b. When the dynamics is an edge of chaos state,$C_G(\tau)$ also decreases, but the time constant of the decay is larger than that in the chaotic state, as seen in Fig. 5c. It is seen in these results that the edge of chaos state corresponds to the state between periodic and chaotic states, that is, a weak chaotic state. The autocorrelation function of the membrane potentials, V_i, shows also similar dependences on the collective gating dynamics.

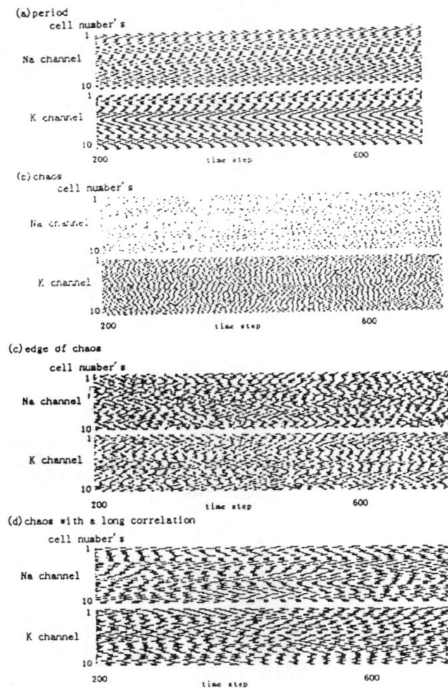

Fig.4 The three kinds of dynamical states for collective ion channel gating (a)Periodic state ($a_0 = 11.25$),(b) Chaotic state($a_0 = 16.5$), (c) Edge of chaos state ($a_0 = 12.3$) and (d) Chaos with a long range correlation ($a_0 = 10.65$).Each diagram shows the temporal variations of gating quantities ($x_{m,k}, y_{n,k}$) for n=1-10,k=1-5,where the black points means opened gates. The parameter values used are p=q=5,n=10,$\lambda = 0.2, \sigma = 0.07$, and $\epsilon = 0.1$.

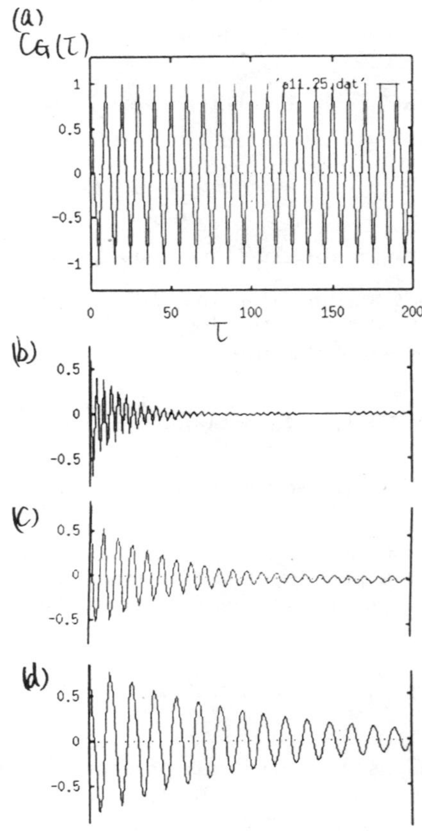

Fig.5 Three kinds of autocorrelation function $C_G(\tau)$ for collective ion channel gating state. (a) for the periodic state ($a_0 = 11.25$), (b) for chaos state ($a_0 = 16.5$), (c) for the edge of chaos state ($a_0 = 12.3$), and (d) for chaos with a long range correlation ($a_0 = 10.65$).

5 Dependence of Response Characteristics of the Syncytium on the Collective Dynamics

In order to consider what kinds of benefit the receptor cells gain by making a syncytium structure, we calculated the response properties of syncytium structure to single sinusoidal stimulus and two sinusoidal stimuli.

5.1 Response properties under single cell stimulation

We consider how a single stimulus received by a receptor cell propagates into the surrounding cells in a syncytium. The correlation between membrane potentials in the cell stimulated and in the other cell changes noticeable depending on what kinds of collective state the receptor syncytium is in. The correlation between gating of ion channels also has a similar tendency. We calculated the relative correlation function of membrane potentials defined by

$$\Delta C_V(m,n;\tau) = \int_0^\infty V_m(t+\tau)V_n(t)dt - \int_0^\infty V_m^0(t+\tau)V_n^0(t)dt \ . \tag{11}$$

Here, $V_m(t)$ is the relevant quantity in the case where the sinusoidal electric current is injected into the mth cell, while $V_m^0(t)$ is for the case where the current is not injected.

In order to investigate dependence of the ability to propagate a signal on the collective dynamical state of syncytium, Furthermore, we calculated the crosscorrelation for the four types of states shown in Fig.4 and 5. We show the calculated results of $\Delta C_V(5,n,\tau)$ (n=6-8). When the collective dynamics is periodic, $\Delta C_V(5,n;\tau)$ is very small as seen in Fig.6a. When the collective dynamics is chaotic, $\Delta C_V(5,n,\tau)$ is very small as seen in Fig. 6b. When the collective dynamics is in the edge of chaos, $\Delta C_V(5,n,\tau)$ is larger than those for the periodic and chaos states as seen in Fig 6. It is seen from these results that when the receptor cell syncytium is in the edge of chaos state, the stimulus injected in 5th cell propagates efficiently into the surrounding cells. Therefore, the response of edge of chaos state to the external stimulus is more synchronous than that of the periodic and chaotic states.

We classified the dynamical states of syncytium into the three types, periodic, chaotic, and edge of chaos based on the properties of autocorrelation function $C_G(\tau)$ and of relative correlation $\Delta C_V(m, n; \tau)$. We consider how the type depends on the branching parameter a_0 for the gating dynamics. Fig.7 shows the maximum Lyapunov exponent λ_{max} as a function of a_0. The dynamical states corresponding to every values of a_0 are classified into the three types according to the response property. In the regions of a_0 in which λ_{max} is negative, the response property is quite similar to that of the system with $a_0 = 11.25$, that is, the property belongs to the periodic type. The regions of a_0 in which λ_{max} is positive, are divided into two classes, EC-zone and C-zone, as shown in Fig 7. The values of $C_G(\tau)$ and $\Delta C_V(5, n; \tau)$ were calculated for the system with $a_0 = 10.65$, which is in EC-zone. The results are shown in Figs.5d and 6d. The gating dynamics (Fig.5d) and the response propagation (Fig.6d) are qualitatively equivalent to those (Figs.5c and 6c) for $a_0 = 12.3$, respectively. The gating dynamics and the response propagation in the systems with a_0 within C-zone are qualitatively equevalent to those (Figs.5b and 6b) for $a_0 = 16.5$, that is, the response for C-zone belongs to the chaotic type.

5.2　Response properties under double cell stimulation

In order to consider what kind of benefit the receptor cells gain by making a syncytium structure , we study how two stimuli received by two different cells in a syncytium influence each other [3].

The correlation between gating of ion channels in the two cells stimulated simultaneously changes noticeably depending on what kinds of collective gating state the receptor cell syncytium is in. The Correlation between membrane potentials also has a similar tendency. We calculated the relative correlation function of gating quantity $x_{n,k}$ defined by

$$\Delta C_G(m, n; \tau) = \int_0^\infty x_{m,k}(t + \tau) x_{n,l}(t) dt - \int_0^\infty x_{m,k}^{(0)}(t + \tau) x_{n,l}^{(0)}(t) dt, \tag{12}$$

Here, $x_{m,k}(t)$ is the relevant quantity in the case where the sinusoidal electric current is injected into the m and nth cells simultaneously, while $x_{m,k}^{(0)}(t)(x_{n,l}^{(0)}(t))$ is for the case where the current is injected into only mth(nth) cell.

We show the calculated results of $\Delta C_G(5, 8; \tau)$ in Fig.8. When the collective gating dynamics is periodic, $\Delta C_G(5, 8; \tau)$ is almost zero as seen in Fig.8a. This means that there is no interference between the changes of channel gating in the two cells induced by the current injection. When the collective gating dynamics is chaotic, the interference is not zero, but very small and not synchronous as seen in Fig.8b. When the collective gating dynamics is in the edge of chaos state, the interference is noticeable and synchronously as seen in Fig.8c. The interference between the potential variations shows also similar dependences on the collective gating dynamics.

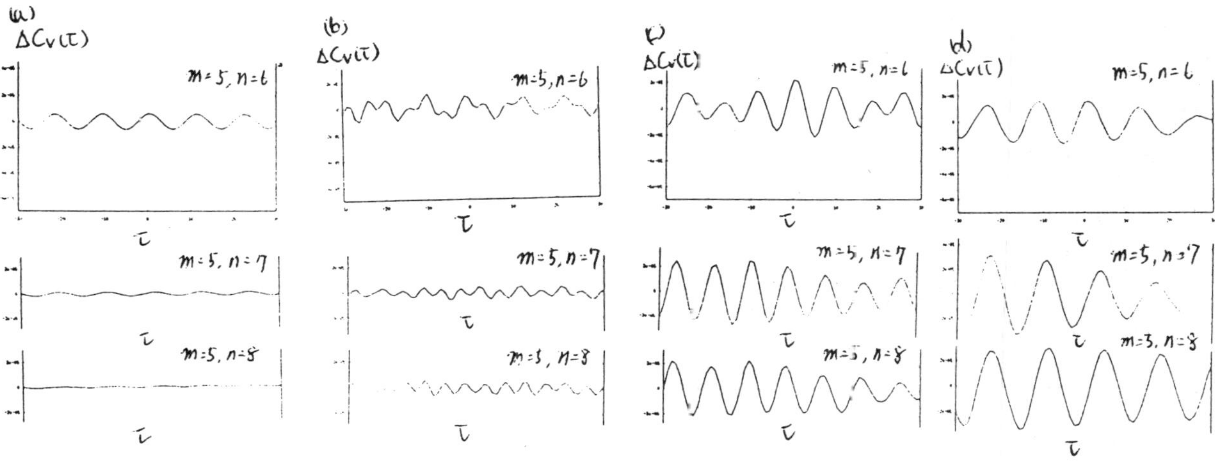

Fig.6 The correlation $\Delta C_V(5, n; \tau)$, $(n = 6 - 8)$ between membrane potentials in a single cell stimulated and those in the other cell n. The value of parameters relevant to the syncytium system are the same as those used in Fig.4. The input current is sinusoidal wave nad injected into 5th cell. The state of collective gating dynamics before stimulation is (a) periodic, (b) chaotic, (c) edge of chaos and (d) chaos with a long range correlation.

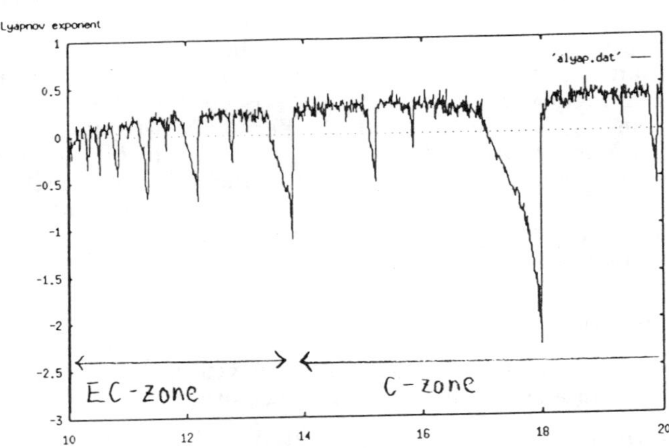

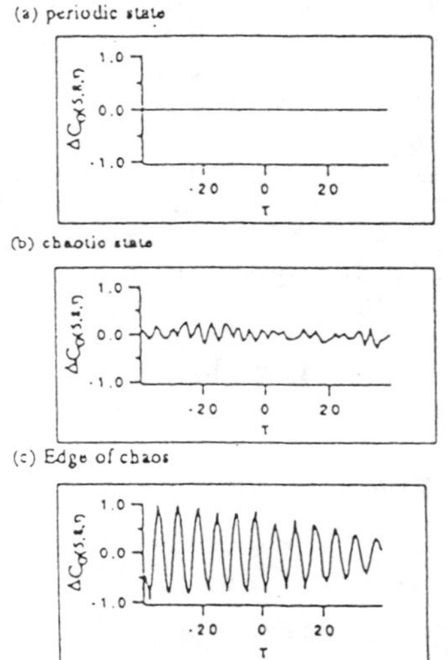

Fig.7 The maximum lyapunov exponent λ_{max} diagram in the receptor cell syncytium. The branching parameter is $a_0(= a_{10}, a_{20})$ in Eq.(7). EC and C zone are useful to classify the dependence of response property on value of a_0 .

Fig.8 The relative correlation $\Delta C_G(m, n; \tau)$ between gating ion channels in the two cells (m,n) stimulated simultaneously. The value of parameters used are the same as those used in Fig.4. The input current wave is sinusoidal and injected into m=5th and n=8th cells. The state of collective gating dynamics before stimulation is (a) periodic, (b) chaotic and (c) edge of chaos.

6   Discussion

We have shown that the edge of chaos state has larger synchronous response than those of periodic and chaotic states. If the input signals include a large noise, the synchronous response obtained in the edge of chaos state may play a significant role in the collective reception of noisy signals. Since the meaningful signal components of noisy inputs to the two cells are common between the two cells, the synchronous intensification may occur only for the meaningful signal component and the noise component is cancelled due to the interference. We will calculate the response of receptor cell syncytium to noisy signals.

Furthermore, when the input signal is too weak as to be detected by the receptor cell, the burst fluctuation of the membrane potential in the edge of chaos state may play an important role in the detection of the input signal. It is likely that the sensitivity of external input is enhanced by stochastic resonance (SR) mechanism. We will calculate the response of a peripheral neuron and show that the syncytium system makes use of SR in the edge of chaos state for the weak stimuli.

References

[1] E.A.Schwartz, "Electrical properties of the rod syncytium in the retina of the turtle," *J.Physiol.(Lond)*,vol.257,pp379-406,1976.

[2] V.F.Holland et.al., "Morphology of fungiform papillae in cannine lingual epathelium: Location of intercellular junctions in the epithelium," *J.Comp.Neural*,vol.279.pp.13-27,1989.

[3] Y.Kashimori,et al., "Effect of intercellular coupling through gap junctions on dynamics of ion channel gating - a role of edge of chaos state on response characteristics ." *Proc.Int.Conf.on Neural Information Processing (Iconip'95)*, vol.1,pp.19-22,1995.

[4] K.Wiesenfeld and F.Moss, "Stochastic resonance and the benefits of noise:from ice ages to crayfish and squids." *Nature* 373,pp.33-36,1995.

[5] Y.H.Mika and Y.Palti, "Charge displacements in a single potassium ion channel macromolecule during gating," *Biophys.J*,vol.67,pp.1455-1463,1994.

[6] L.S.Liebovich and T.I.Toth, "A model of ion channel kinetics using deterministic chaotic rather than stochastic process," *J.Theory.Biol.*,vol.148,pp.243-267,1991.

[7] Y.Kashimori et al. "Spatiotemporal gating pattern pf ion channel assembly and its role on cell functions," *Proc.of Information Processing Symposium of Japan Electric Society (in Japanese)*,IP-95-17,pp37-46,1995.

[8] H.Nishimura and T.Shinchi, "Fractal Analysis of One-dimensional Cellular Automata as Time-series Vectors" *Transaction of Information Processing Society of Japan(in Japanese)*,vol.36,No.4,pp.787-796,1995.

Binary State Machines for Arithmetic Operations on Pulse-Coded Signals

D Gorse †

† Department of Computer Science, University College
London, UK
D.Gorse@cs.ucl.ac.uk

Abstract- **Novel constructions are presented which allow the spike-based computation of various arithmetic functions. These constructions, which are binary I/O stochastic automata with an internal counter state, are able to give faithful reproductions of the desired function whenever the output would fall into the range [0,1], and automatic clipping to 0 or 1 otherwise. It is demonstrated how such arithmetic modules can be used to provide an output transform function for pulse-processing digital neural networks; many other applications within the field of stochastic neural computing are possible.**

1 Introduction

Implementing neural computing techniques in dedicated hardware has many advantages - hardware-based networks would be expected to be faster and cheaper, as well as providing self-contained, physically robust solutions for application areas where it is not feasible to install a PC/workstation running neural network software. Analog implementaion has many attractions (such as asynchronousness and lack of quantisation effects) but also some significant disadvantages - analog signals are especially susceptible to noise and interference, and analog weights are frequently unable to represent adaptive parameters sufficiently accurately to allow on-chip learning. Digital implementation can solve some of these problems, but introduces new ones in that digital arithmetic (required for example for the formation of a linear weighted sum of neural inputs) is area- and power-hungry. Recently a number of hardware-implementable neural network models have been introduced which aim to solve these latter problems by replacing conventional arithmetic procedures by operations, using only simple gate arrays, on pulse-stream representations of weights and activations [1-4]. These networks may be entirely digital [1-3], or use hybrid analog/digital techniques [4]. All are underpinned by the ideas of 'stochastic' (pulse-stream) computing first discussed in the 1960s by Gaines [5] and others. In stochastic computing signals are represented by probabilities encoded in random pulse streams, a value $x \in [0,1]$ being substituted by a measured value $\hat{x}$ which is the proportion on '1' ('on') signals counted in an R-bit stream:

$$\hat{x} = \frac{1}{R} \sum_{r=1}^{R} a(r) \quad \text{where} \quad \text{Prob}(a(r) = 1) = x, \quad r=1..R$$

Classical stochastic computing [5] substitutes the multiplication of two values x_1, x_2 by bitwise AND

$$\hat{y} = \frac{1}{R} \sum_{r=1}^{R} a_1(r)a_2(r) \approx x_1 x_2$$

(where $\text{Prob}(a_i(r) = 1) = x_i$) and addition by bitwise OR

$$\hat{y} = \frac{1}{R} \sum_{r=1}^{R} a_1(r) + a_2(r) - a_1(r)a_2(r) \approx x_1 + x_2 - x_1 x_2$$

AND operations are entirely adequate for multiplying probabilities, but OR is a poor approximation to addition. Purely digital approaches [1-4] which represent synaptic weights and neuron states by probabilities find it difficult to adequately accomplish a 'squashed weighted sum of inputs' using classical stochastic computing techiques - it is especially hard to get a steep, threshold-like response (which in conventional neural computing would correspond to weights of large magnitude) given that the stochastic weights are restricted to the range [0,1]. pRAM networks [6], which do not attempt to form a linear weighted sum of their inputs, are one solution to the problem of getting sharply-defined responses from pulse-mode neural networks. However the pRAM-256 chip [6] is optimised to use only one learning algorithm, a nonlinear version of the A_{RP} reinforcement procedure. A set of techniques will be described below which, by supplementing gate arrays with digital counters, allow very accurate approximations to a range of arithmetic operations to be performed using pulse stream computation, and which may significantly widen the range of network functions implementable by this type of digital hardware.

2 Stochastic automata for approximating arithmetic operations on pulse trains

All the modules to be described below are implementable using a combination of simple logic gates and digital counters with depth (representing the maximum number of '1's stored) N. N determines the accuracy with which the relevant arithmetic operation is accomplished. It will be seen that relatively small values of N allow very accurate implementations of saturating arithmetic functions ('saturating' in this context meaning performing an *automatic* clipping to 0 or 1 whenever the value produced by the computation would be outside the range [0,1] representable by a pulse-stream transmitted probability).

2.1 Addition

The desired function is defined, for $x_1, x_2 \in [0,1]$, by

$$\mathrm{Sum}(x_1, x_2) = \begin{cases} x_1 + x_2 & \text{if } x_1 + x_2 \leq 1 \\ 1 & \text{otherwise} \end{cases}$$

This is to be implemented using pulse-stream representations of x_1 and x_2, binary signals a_1 and a_2 such that $\mathrm{Prob}(a_i = 1) = x_i$, to give a stream of output pulses b such that $\mathrm{Prob}(b = 1) = \mathrm{Sum}(x_1, x_2)$. The summation module is constructed as a binary I/O stochastic automaton with inputs a_1, a_2, internal state S (equal to counter value $n \in \{0,1,..,N\}$), and output b. The state transition table governing its operation is given below

$a_1(r)$	$a_2(r)$	$S(r-1)$	$S(r)$	$b(r)$
0	0	n	$\max\{0,n-1\}$	0
0	1	n	n	1
1	0	n	n	1
1	1	n	$\min\{N,n+1\}$	1

where r = 1..R (the length of the spike train used to compute the output $y = \langle b \rangle \approx \mathrm{Sum}(x_1, x_2)$) and the initial state (counter value) S(0) is set to zero. Figure 1a shows the result (averaging over pulse streams of length R = 5000) of adding 0.25 to $x \in [0,1]$, for counter depths N = 0, 1, 50. N = 50 gives an accurate approximation to the saturating addition function Sum(x,0.25) whilst N = 0 (equivalent to the OR function used to add signals in classical stochastic computing) is a much poorer approximation to this function. Figure 1b shows the effect of counter depth N on the computation of Sum(x,1-x), for which the desired output is 1 for all $x \in [0,1]$.

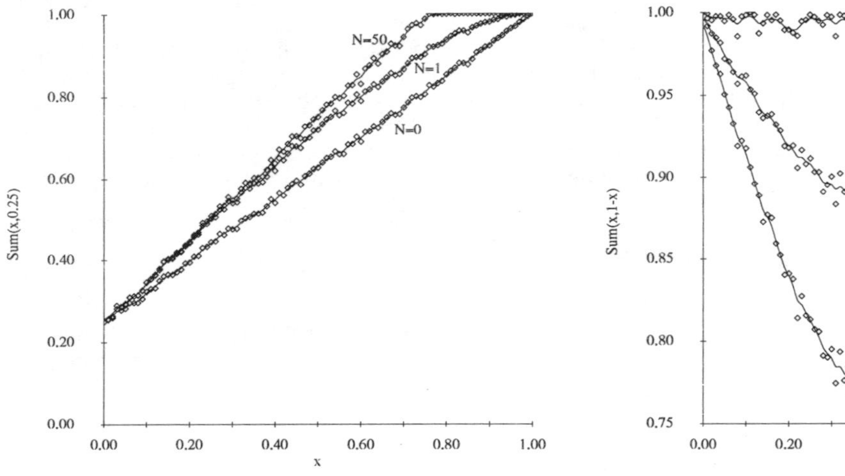

Figure 1a   **Figure 1b**

2.2 Subtraction

The saturating subtraction function is defined by

$$\mathrm{Sub}(x_1, x_2) = \begin{cases} x_1 - x_2 & \text{if } x_2 \leq x_1 \\ 0 & \text{otherwise} \end{cases}$$

and is implemented by a module with the state transition table

$a_1(r)$	$a_2(r)$	$S(r-1)$	$S(r)$	$b(r)$
0	0	n	n	0
0	1	n	$\min\{N,n+1\}$	0
1	0	0	0	1
1	0	n	n-1	0
1	1	n	n	0

Figure 2a shows approximations (R = 5000) to Sub(x,0.25) for N = 0, 1, 50; Figure 2a shows the result of subtracting x from itself (the function Sub(x,x), which should ideally give 0 for all $x \in [0,1]$) for the same range of counter depths.

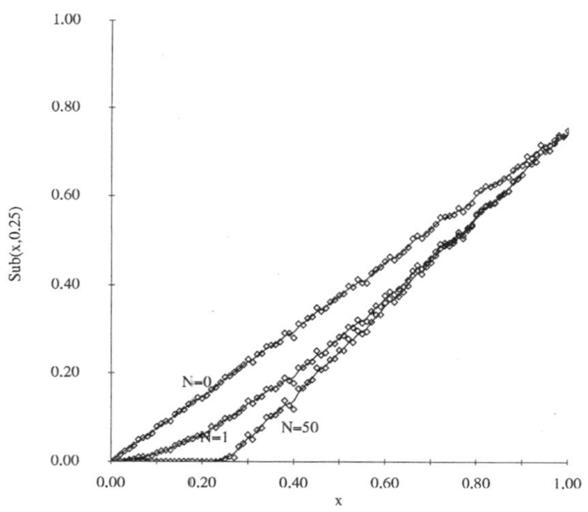

Figure 2a

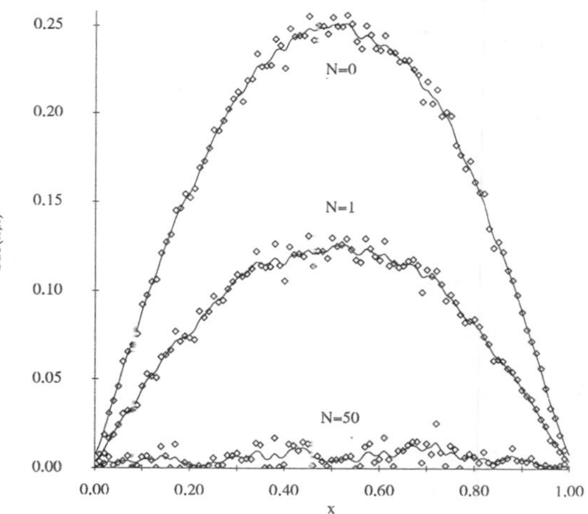

Figure 2b

2.3 Division

Saturating division, defined for $x_1, x_2 \in [0,1]$ by

$$Div(x_1, x_2) = \begin{cases} 0 & \text{if } x_1 = x_2 = 0 \\ x_1/x_2 & \text{if } x_2 > x_1 \\ 1 & \text{otherwise} \end{cases}$$

is a slightly more complex procedure, but can be accomplished using the Sum module of section 2.1. The implementation of Div is based in part on the work of Gaines [5]. Gaines defined the "division error" in x_1/x_2 as $e = yx_2 - x_1$ (since if $e = 0$, $y = x_1/x_2$) and aimed to set up a recurrent circuit implementing $\dot{y} = -\alpha e = -\alpha(yx_2 - x_1)$. It was noted in [5] that this cannot be done exactly; in the present case it is implemented approximately by first discretising (operating on individual pulses) to give (setting $\alpha = 1$ for simplicity) $b(r) = b(r-1)(1 - a_2(r)) + a_1(r)$ and then replacing the '+' by the Sum operation. $y = Div(x_1, x_2)$ is then obtained by averaging the steady state spike output of the recurrent circuit of Figure 3a. Because a fixed point must be reached before y can be computed, it is necessary to discard a certain number R_{trans} of spikes emitted during the initial transient period. In Figure 3a, which illustrates the result of computing (a) $y = Div(x,0.25)$ ($= 4x$ for $x \leq 0.25$, 1 otherwise) and (b) $y = Div(0.25,x)$ ($= 1/4x$ for $x \geq 0.25$, 1 otherwise) R_{trans} is set to 1000, the averaging period R to 5000, and the depth of the Sum module counter, N, to 50.

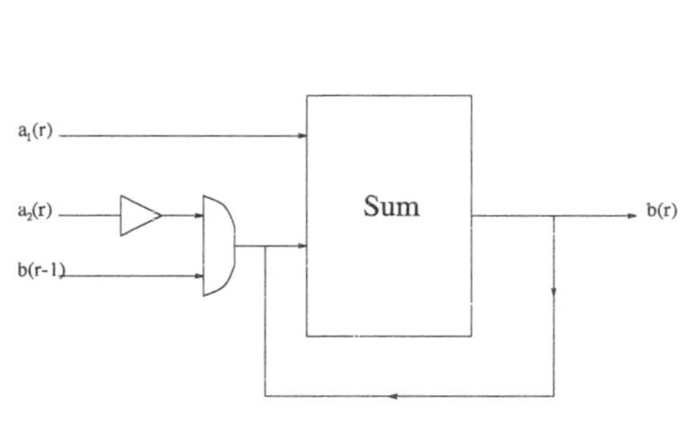

Figure 3a

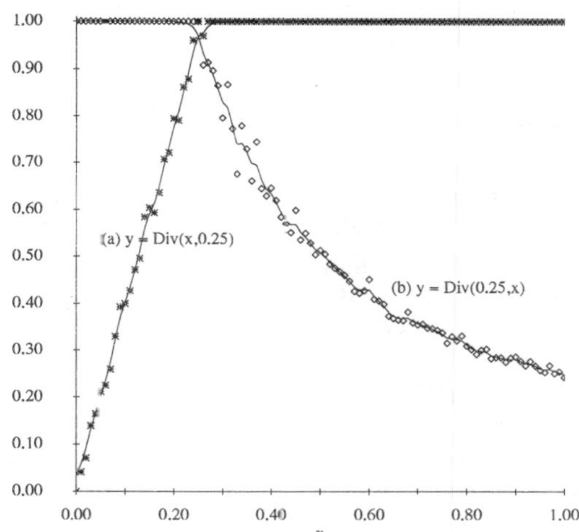

Figure 3a

2.4 Application - an output transform function for pulse-coded digital neural networks

In this final section it will be shown how a combination of Div and Sub modules can be used to construct a parametrised 'squashing' function which compresses the mean value x carried by an output neural pulse stream in such a way as to provide enhanced discrimination within a threshold region. This transform function is defined for a, b, x ∈ [0,1] by

$$
\text{Ramp}(a, b, x) = \begin{cases} 0 & \text{if } x < a(1-b) \\ (x-a(1-b))/b & \text{if } a(1-b) \le x \le a(1-b) + b \\ 1 & \text{if } x > a(1-b) + b \end{cases} = \text{Div(\ Sub}(x, a(1-b)), b\ )
$$

The Ramp module has two internal state counters, associated with the Sub and Div submodules, and because of the feedback structure of the Div circuit (Figure 3a) requires a 'running in' period during which R_{trans} output spikes are discarded. The parameters a and b (also carried by spike trains) determine the position of the threshold region (beginning at x = a(1-b)) and its steepness (gradient 1/b). Figure 4a shows the effect of varying the steepness (gain) parameter b, for a fixed a = 0.5; Figure 4b shows, for a fixed b = 0.5, the effect of varying a.

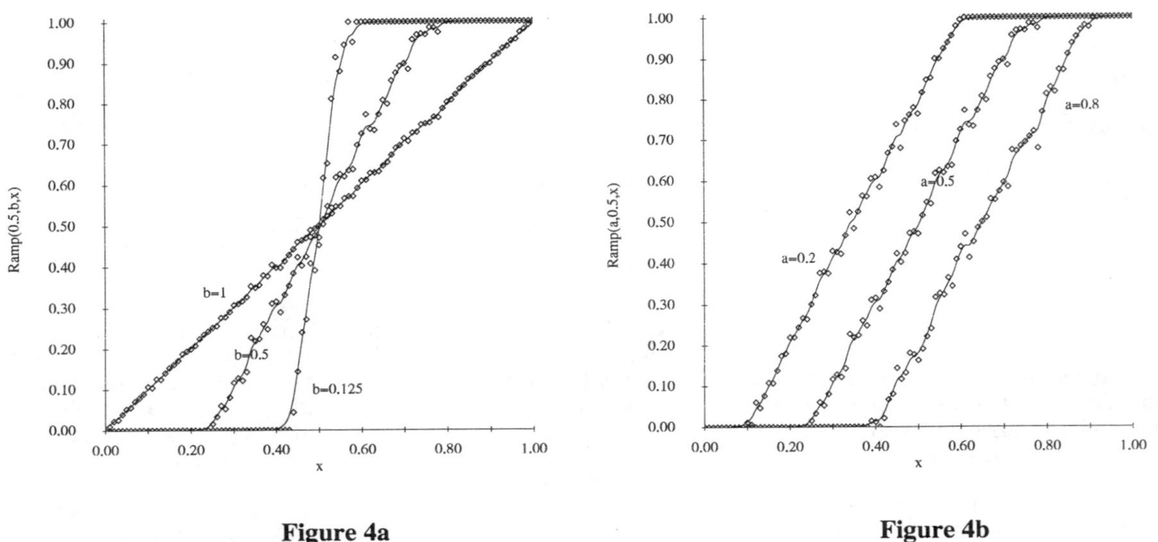

Figure 4a   **Figure 4b**

For neural network applications the Ramp function would be most useful if the parameters a and b were adaptive; this could be accomplished using the continuous value stochastic reinforcement rule of [7], for example.

References

[1]   Y.-C. Kim and M. A. Shanblatt, "Random noise effects in pulse-mode digital multilayer neural networks", *IEEE Trans. on Neural Networks*, vol. 6(1), pp. 220-229, January 1995.

[2]   S. Oteki, A. Hashimoto, T. Foruta, S. Motomura, T. Watanabe, D. G. Stork and H. Eguchi, "A digital neural network VLSI with on-chip learning using stochastic pulse encodiing", *Proc. Inter. Conf. Neural Information Processing*, Nagoya, October 17-20, 1993, pp. 3039-3045.

[3]   J. Shawe-Taylor, P. Jeavons and M. Van Daalen, "Probabilistic bit stream neural chip: theory", *Connection Science*, vol. 3(3), pp. 317-328, 1991.

[4]   A. Hamilton, A. F. Murray, D. J. Baxter, S. Churcher, H. M. Reekie and L. Tarassenko, "Integrated pulse stream neural networks: results, issues and pointers", *IEEE Trans. on Neural Networks*, vol. 3(3), pp. 385-393, May 1992.

[5]   B. R. Gaines, "Stochastic computing systems", in *Advances in Information Systems Science*, ed. J. T. Tou, Plenum Press, 1969, pp. 37-172.

[6]   T. G. Clarkson, C. K. Ng, D. Gorse and J. G. Taylor, "Learning probabilistic RAM nets using VLSI structures", *IEEE Trans. on Computers*, vol. 41(12), pp. 1552-1561, December 1992.

[7]   D. Gorse, D. A. Romano-Critchley and J. G. Taylor, "A pulse-based reinforcement algorithm for learning continuous functions", *Neurocomputing* (to appear).

A Back Propagation Model
with
Periodic Chaos Neurons

Hiroshi MAEDA and Masahiro NAKAGAWA

Department of Electrical Engineering, Faculty of Engineering, Nagaoka University of Technology, Kamitomioka 1603-1, Nagaoka, Niigata 940-21, Japan

e-mail: maeda@pelican.nagaokaut.ac.jp
e-mail: masanaka@voscc.nagaokaut.ac.jp

Abstract   In this paper we report a back propagation scheme with a periodic chaos neuron model.   In contrast to the conventional model,   each neuron in the network may involve the chaotic behaviour in the learning process.   In practice one may confirm that there exists a close relation between the learning process and the chaotic dynamics, and that chaotic dynamics promotes the learning speed with a certain success rate as seen in the conventional nonchaotic models.   The parameter related to the chaos will be controlled to drive the system from a chaos to a nonchaos through the learning process to assure the high success rate.

§1. Introduction

Since the proposal of the error back propagation learning by Rumelhart[1], a number of modifications have been put forward to revise the learning ability, e.g. learning speed, success rate[2-6].   Although the stochastic model may promotes the success rate for the learning,   the learning speed might be depressed at the expense of the high success rate.   On the other hand, the deterministic algorithm may encounter an unfavourable trapping at a local minimum.

Form the other respect, some chaotic dynamics have been applied to the combinatorial optimization problems as seen in the Travelling Salesman Problems by Kasahara and Nakagawa[7].   In addition the present authors have proposed a chaos learning model with chaos neurons[8] and clarified that the involved chaotic noise is available to enhance the learning speed as a result of the contraction of the parameter space to be searched during the learning process. Very recently a few types of chaos neuron models with periodic activation functions have been proposed to be applied to the optimization problems or the autoassociation model[9-15].   Therein it has been found that the nonmonotonous dynamics due to the periodic activation function plays an important role to avoid the trapping at local minima.   This is considered as a result of certain relaxation of the restriction of the monotonic decreasing of the energy which is to be supported by the monotonous increasing activation function in the conventional models.   Therefore the nonmonotonous dynamics may also play a novel contribution in the learning model.

     From the above-mentioned aspect, we shall propose a chaos back propagation model with the sinusoidal activation function.   In the next section the back propagation algorithm will be reviewed in brief.   In §3 some numerical results will be given so as to present the capability of the presently proposed model.   Finally §4 is devoted to note some remarkable conclusions as well as the discussions.

§2. Theory

     First of all let us we shall write down the dynamic equations for the chaos neurons in the *sth* layer as follows,

$$y_{pi}^{(s)}(n+1) = \sum_{j=1}^{N} w_{ij}^{(s)}(n)\, x_{pj}^{(s-1)}(n) + \Theta_i^{(s)}(n) \qquad , \tag{1}$$

$$x_{pi}^{(s)}(n+1) = f\,(\,y_{pi}^{(s)}(n+1)\,) = \sin\left(\frac{\pi}{2}\; \frac{y_{pi}^{(s)}(n+1)}{\tau(n)} \right) \qquad , \tag{2}$$

where $y_{pi}^{(s)}(n)$ and $x_{pi}^{(s)}(n)$ are the internal state and the output state of the *ith* neuron in the *sth* layer corresponding to the *pth* training epoch.   Here it has to be noted that $\tau(n)$ in eq.(2) is introduced to control the contribution of the chaotic noise during the learning process.   In practice the periodic $\tau(n)$ is assumed to be controlled as[11]

$$\tau(n+1) = \tau(n) + \kappa\,\tau(n)\,(\,1 - \tau(n)\,) \qquad (0<\kappa\le 1)\ . \tag{3}$$

Then the periodicity changes from $\varepsilon(0)$ $(<<1)$ to 1 as the time goes on.   Then system will be driven from a chaotic state to a nonchaotic one during the learning process as found in the previous works[9-13].

     Now the updating schemes are defined by

$$\Delta w_{ij}^{(s)}(n+1) = \nu\,\tau(n)\frac{1}{P}\sum_{p=1}^{-} \delta_{pi}^{(s)}(n)\, x_{pj}^{(s-1)}(n) + \mu\,\Delta w_{ij}^{(s)}(n) \quad , \tag{4}$$

$$\Delta\Theta_i^{(s)}(n+1) = \nu\,\tau(n)\frac{1}{P}\sum_{p=1}^{-} \delta_{pi}^{(s)}(n) + \mu\,\Delta\Theta_i^{(s)}(n) \quad , \tag{5}$$

where ν and μ are the learning coefficient and the acceleration constants, respectively, which are set to certain positive numbers, and the $\delta_{pi}^{(s)}(n)$ are defined as

$$\delta_{pi}^{(S)}(n) = (\,t_{pi} - x_{pi}^{(S)}(n)\,)\, f'(\,y_{pi}^{(S)}(n)\,) \qquad\qquad s\in\text{Output Layer} \quad , \tag{6}$$

$$\delta_{pi}^{(S-1)}(n) = f'(\,y_{pi}^{(S-1)}(n)\,)\sum_{k=1}^{N^{(S)}} \delta_{pk}^{(S)}(n)\, w_{kj}(n) \qquad\qquad s\notin\text{Output Layer} \quad . \tag{7}$$

Therefore our scheme is essentially based on the conventional error back propagation model with a certain acceleration term proportional to μ apart from the fact such that the presently introduced activation function is a sinusoidal one instead of the monotonous sigmoid.

§3. Simulation Results

     In this section we shall present a couple of examples applied to the learning problems as XOR as well as the 7 points problem (7PP) as shown in Tables I and II .

Table I (XOR)

X	Y	Z
0	0	0
0	1	1
1	0	1
1	1	0

Table II (7PP)

X	Y	Z
0	0	0
0	1	1
1	0	1
1	1	0
0.5	0.5	1
0.25	0.75	0
0.75	0.25	0

The constructions of the system are depicted in Figs. 1 and 2, respectively.

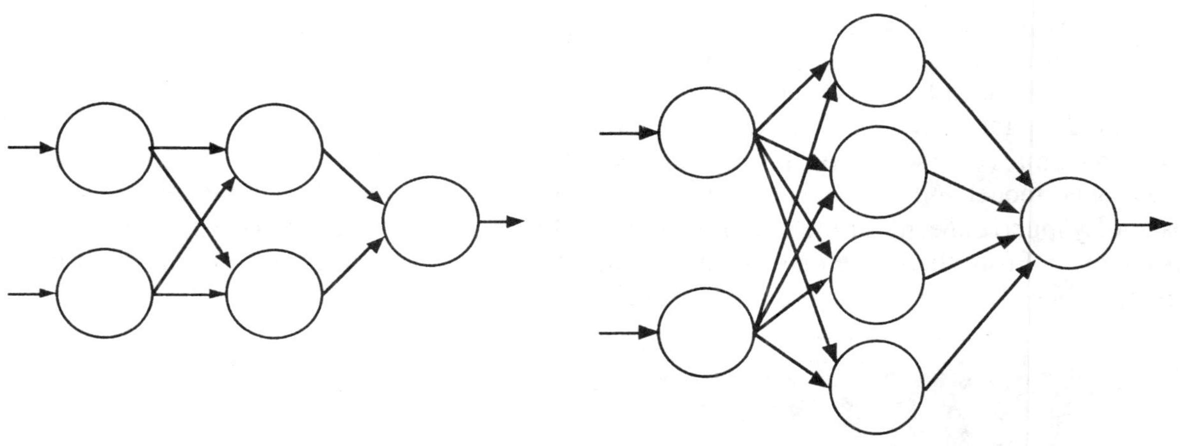

Fig.1   XOR (2-2-1)   Fig.2   7PP (2-4-1)

The corresponding learning curves are shown in Figs. 3 and 4, respectively.

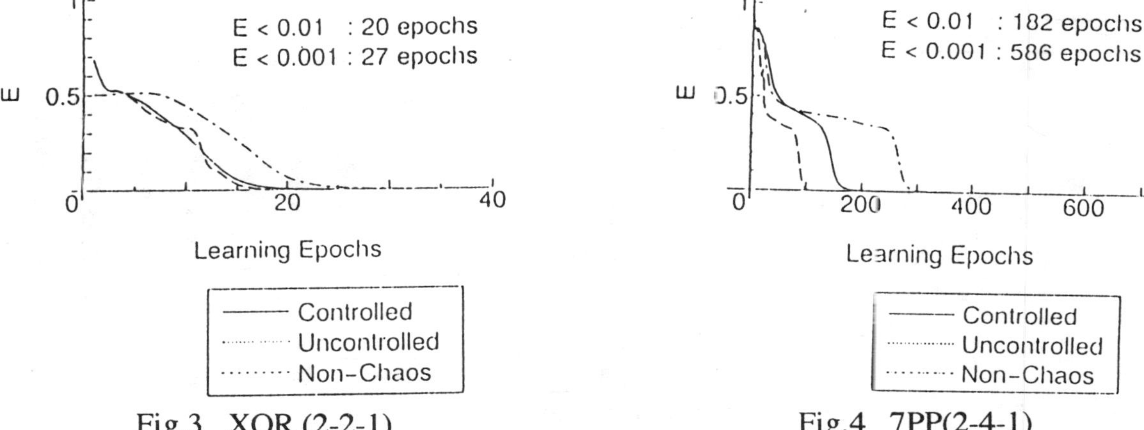

Fig.3   XOR (2-2-1)   Fig.4   7PP(2-4-1)

From these results, one may confirm that the present model achieve a relatively high speed learning in comparison with the previous non-chaotic model[1].   In Tables III and IV, one summarizes the performance of the present chaotic model.

Table III **XOR**

Model	Average Epochs	Success Rate
nonChaos NN	37.5	100%
periodic Chaos NN	36.3	100%

Table IV **7PP**

Model	Average Epochs	Success Rate
nonChaos NN	3117.8	92%
periodic Chaos NN	78.1	100%

§4. Concluding remarks

In this work we have proposed a chaos learning model for the multilayered neural networks and applied it to the error back propagation problems, and found that the periodic chaos neuron model with a sinusoidal activation function seems to be available for the learning model with multilayered neural networks.   In fact, from the Lyapunov analysis[16] one could confirm that the chaotic dynamics substantially results in the advantage of the present model beyond the conventional model and other related learning models.   An example of the time dependence of the transient Lyapunov spectra of the output neuron for XOR and 7PP the are shown in Figs. 5 and 6, respectively.   From these one may conclude that the chaotic dynamics plays an important role for the remarkable advantage of the presently proposed leaning model.

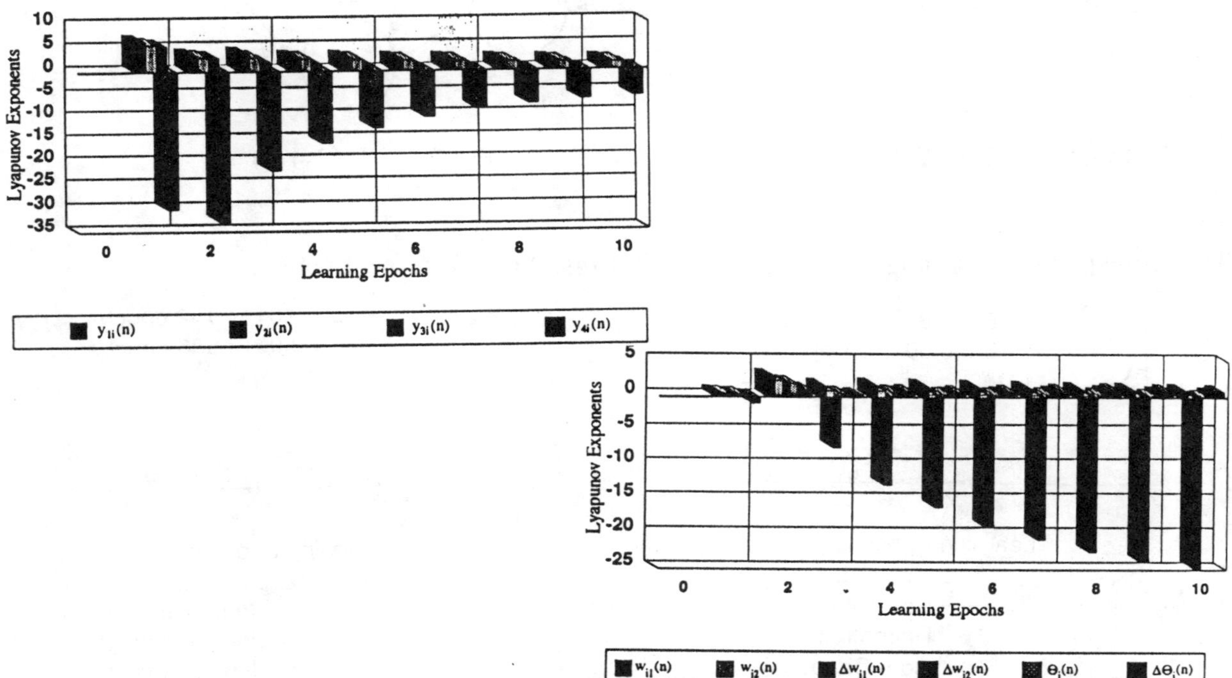

Fig.5 Lyapunov spectrum (XOR)

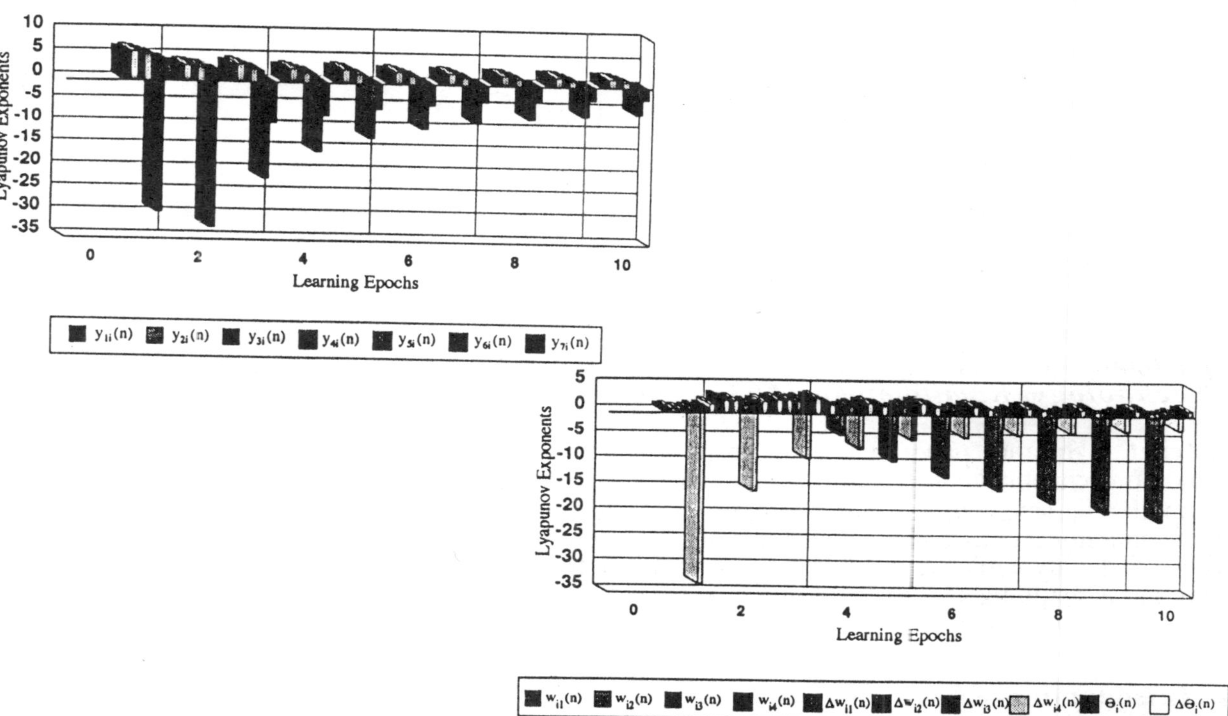

Fig.6 Lyapunov spectrum (7PP)

As a future problem it seems to be worthwhile to generalize the present model to involve an autonomous control of the periodicity $\tau(n)$.

References

[1]   D. E. Rumelhart, J. L. McClelland and the PDP Research Group : *Parallel Distributed Processing* , MIT Press(1986).

[2]   S. Geman and C. Hwang : Journal of Control and Optimization, **24**(1986)1031.

[3]   S. Kirkpatrick et al. : IBM Thomas J. Watson Research Center Report(1982).

[4]   N. Baba : Neural Networks,**2**(1989)367.

[5]   J. Matyas : Automation and Remote Control, **26**(1965).246.

[6]   F. J. Solis and J. B. Wets :   Mathematics of Operations Research, **6**(1981)19.

[7]   T. Kasahara and M. Nakagawa: IEICE Trans. on Fundamentals J**78**-A,No.2(1995)114.

[8]   H. Maeda and M. Nakagawa : IEICE Technical Report NC95-3(1995)17.

[9]   M.Nakagawa: Proc. of ICONIP'94,Seoul, **1**(1994)609.

[10] M.Nakagawa: Proc. of ICDC'94,Tokyo, **2**(1995)603.

[11] M. Nakagawa: J. Phys.Soc. Jpn.**64**(1995)1023.

[12] T. Kasahara and M. Nakagawa: J. Phys. Soc. Jpn.**64**(1995)4964.

[13] M. Nakagawa:IEICE Trans. on Fundamentals **E78-A** (1995)412.

[14] M. Nakagawa: J. Phys.Soc.Jpn.**64**(1995)3112.

[15] M. Nakagawa: Proc. of ICNN'95, Australia(1995)3028.

[16] K. Nakamura and M. Nakagawa: J. Phys. Soc. Jpn. **62**(1993)2942.

An Autonomous Control
of
Periodic Chaos Neural Network

Masahiro NAKAGAWA
E-mail : masanaka@voscc.nagaokaut.ac.jp

***Department of Electrical Engineering, Faculty of Engineering, Nagaoka University
of Technology, Kamitomioka 1603-1, Nagaoka, Niigata 940-21,* Japan**

Abstract   In this paper we shall propose a simple chaos neural network model applied to autonomous chaotic wandering and the autoassociation models. The present artificial neuron model is properly characterized in terms of a sinusoidal activation function to involve a chaotic dynamics as well as an autonomous control of the period. It is elucidated that the present neural network has an ability of the dynamic memory retrievals beyond the conventional chaotic model with such a monotonous mapping as a sigmoid function.

§1. Introduction

A variety of associative models have been extensively put forward hitherto on the basis of the autocorrelation dynamics.[1-7]   Since the foundations of the retrieval model by Anderson,[1] Kohonen,[2] and Nakano,[3]   some works related to such an association model of the inter-connected neurons with an autocorrelation matrix have been proposed to date by Amari,[4] Amit *et al.*[5] and Gardner.[6]   So far it has been known that the memory capacity of the autocorrelation associative model, or the number of completely associated pattern vectors, is estimated as $\sim 0.15N$ at most for the autocorrelation learning model.   If one increases the memory loading rate further, which is defined by (Number of embedded patterns)/(Number of neurons)=L/N, the system can achieve no longer a complete association even for an infinitesimally small amount of error involved in an initial vector.[7]

From another aspect concerned with chaotic dynamics, some applications of the chaotic neural networks have been investigated recently by Inoue and Nagayoshi,[8] Aihara *et al.*,[9] Nakamura and Nakagawa.[10]   In practice, however, the chaotic dynamic association has been found to be accompanied with the problem such that the complete association of the embedded patterns becomes rather troublesome if we increase L/N up to ~ 0.05 .[10,11]   Recently Kasahara and Nakagawa have applied the monotonous chaotic dynamics to such a combinatorial optimization problem as the Travelling Salesman Problem (TSP).[12]   Therein chaotic behaviour has been found to play an important role to obtain an optimal solution and to realise the dynamic memory retrievals.

In contrast to the above-mentioned models with monotonous activation functions, the neurodynamics with a nonmonotonous mapping have been recently proposed by Morita,[13] Yanai and Amari.[14] They have found that the nonmonotonous mapping in a neuron dynamics possesses a certain advantage of the memory capacity superior than the conventional association models with such a monotonous mapping as the signum function, $\mathrm{sgn}(x)$ for the abbreviation.   This is considered as a result of an orthogonalisation process of the apparent synaptic weight matrix as a first approximation through the nonmonotonous dynamics.[14]   That is, they claimed   that   a nonmonotonous neuron dynamics involves in itself an approximate one-step orthogonalising process.   Later Shiino and Fukai have analysed the memory capacity for a somewhat simplified nonmonotonous activation function with the continuous time in a differential framework, and have concluded that the complete association can be realised for the loading rate $L/N \sim 0.38$ with the critical overlap 0.57.[15]   Very recently the present author proposed a novel neuron model with a periodic activation function to construct an association model with chaotic dynamics with the discrete time model.[16-19]   Therein the memory capacity was found to be increased up to $L/N \sim 0.4$ beyond the previously proposed monotonous dynamic model with the discrete time.   More recently such a chaotic dynamics was involved in the previously formulated synergetic neural network[20] to construct a chaos synergetic neural network model.[21,22]   Therein it has been concluded that the chaos synergetic neuro-dynamics assures the complete association of the analogue pattern vectors up to $L/N = 1$ with $N \to \infty$.   In the previously proposed model with a periodic activation function, however, the period related to the chaotic dynamics has been externally controlled to drive the system from a chaotic state to a nonchaotic one for simplicity.   That is, the scheme of controlling chaos was assumed to be independent of the objective chaotic system.

From the above-mentioned aspects, in the present paper, let us propose a simple dynamic retrieval model with an autonomous parameter control instead of the previously investigated external control.[16-19,21,22]   In practice a sinusoidal mapping will be introduced as an artificial activation function in similar manner to the previous works concerned with the autoassociation model.[16-19,21,22]   Such a periodic mapping is found to possess a capability to escape from an unfavourable spurious metastable state as a result of such a nonmonotonous property of the mapping as well as the resultant chaotic behaviour of the neurons. In addition the presently proposed chaotic dynamics will be found to promote the memory capacity of the neural network towards $L/N \to 1$. In the next section some theoretical preliminaries will be reviewed in brief to construct an autonomously controlled chaos dynamics.   Then some computational results will be given in §3 to show an ability for the memory retrieval.   Finally a few concluding remarks will be addressed in §4 to elucidate the effect of the chaos in the present neurodynamics.

§2.Theory

We shall define some dynamic rules to construct an autonomous chaotic neural network below. For this purpose let us define first the internal state and the corresponding output of the i th neuron as σ_i and s_i, respectively, which have to be related to each other in terms of the following sinusoidal mapping which results in a chaotic dynamics as was confirmed in the previous works.[16,17]

$$s_i = f(\sigma_i) = \sin\left(\frac{\sigma_i}{\tau}\right) + \chi(\tau)\,\theta_i \qquad . \tag{1}$$

where $\chi(\tau)$ is the monotonous decreasing function with respect to the period τ such as $1-\tau^2$, θ_i is an input vector for the autoassociation process. The Lyapunov function of the dynamical system with N neuron system may be defined by

$$E = -\frac{1}{2}\sum_{i=1}^{N}\sum_{j=1}^{N} w_{ij} s^{\dagger}_i s_j + \frac{1}{2}\sum_{i=1}^{N} \lambda_i (s^{\dagger}_i \sigma_i + s_i \sigma^{\dagger}_i) \qquad , \tag{2}$$

where w_{ij} is the autocorrelation memory matrix or the interconnection strengths between the neurons and assumed to be symmetric, *i.e.* $w_{ij} = w_{ji}$, below, $\dagger$ represents the covariant component as will be mentioned in detail later, λ_i $(1 \leq i \leq N)$, which will be also determined later to assure a complete association at a fixed point, are the coupling constants between σ_i and s_i. In the orthogonal autocorrelation learning model, w_{ij} may be simply defined by

$$w_{ij} = \sum_{r=1}^{L} e^{(r)}_i e^{\dagger(r)}_j \qquad , \tag{3}$$

where L is the number of the embedded patterns and $e^{(r)}_i$ $(=\pm 1)$ is the r th embedded pattern. Now the covariant vector $e^{\dagger(r)}_i$ is defined as the generalised inverse matrix corresponding to $e^{(r)}_i$

such that

$$\sum_{i=1}^{N} e^{\dagger(r)}{}_{i}\, e^{(r')}{}_{i} = \delta_{rr'}$$ (4)

One has to note here the following reciprocal relations between s_i and $s^{\dagger}_i$,

$$s^{\dagger}{}_{i} = \sum_{r=1}^{L}\sum_{j=1}^{N} e^{\dagger(r)}{}_{i}\, e^{\dagger(r)}{}_{j}\, s_{j} \quad , \quad s_{i} = \sum_{r=1}^{L}\sum_{j=1}^{N} e^{(r)}{}_{i}\, e^{(r)}{}_{j}\, s^{\dagger}{}_{j} \quad .$$ (5)

It should be borne in mind that the similar conjugate relations hold between σ_i and $\sigma^{\dagger}_i$.

Now let us define the dynamics of the present system below.   The time-dependent Ginzburg-Landau (TDGL) equation of the internal state σ_i may be given by

$$\frac{D\sigma_{i}}{Dt} = -\frac{\partial E}{\partial s^{\dagger}{}_{i}} \quad ,$$ (6)

where the operator, $D\bullet/Dt$,   may regarded as   the time difference operator (for the discrete time model) or the time differential operator (for the continuous time model).   In the above dynamic equations, the constant λ_i is concerned with the relaxation time of the i th neuron.   Substituting eq.(2) into eq.(6a), one readily has

$$\frac{D\sigma_{i}(t)}{Dt} = -\lambda_{i}\,\sigma_{i}(t) + \sum_{j=1}^{N} w_{ij} s_{j}(t) \quad .$$ (7)

If we resort on the discrete time model under consideration, the difference operator may be replaced as follows,

$$\frac{D\sigma_{i}(t)}{Dt} = \frac{\sigma_{i}(t+h) - \sigma_{i}(t)}{h} \quad ,$$ (8)

where h is the division interval for the time t .   For a continuous time model one may assume $h \rightarrow 0$. If we assume that $s_i(t) = e^{(r)}{}_i$ in a steady state with the rth pattern noting that $\left| e^{(r)}{}_i \right| = 1$, λ_i have to be put into

$$\lambda_{i} = 2/\pi \qquad (1 \leq i \leq N) \quad .$$ (9)

Consequently our dynamic equation (6) reads

$$\sigma_{i}(t+h) = \left(1 - \frac{2}{\pi} h\right)\sigma_{i}(t) + h \sum_{j=1}^{N} w_{ij} s_{j}(t) \quad ,$$ (10)

in the discrete time model under consideration.   It should be borne in mind here that $s_i(t)$ and $\sigma_i(t)$ have to be related each other in terms of eq.(1), and that τ is assumed to be controlled to 1 at a retrieval point, or a fixed point corresponding to a basin in the phase space spanned in terms of the coordinates s_i $(1 \leq i \leq N)$.   It should be noted again that the present model leads to the continuous time model if $h \rightarrow 0$.

Now we shall define the dynamics of the period τ to complete the autonomous dynamic memory retrieval framework defined in terms of eqs.(1) and (10).   As was previously reported,[15-18] the dynamics of τ is to be closely related to the chaotic behaviour of the neuron.   Therefore τ has to be even smaller than 1 so as to involve the chaos dynamics.[16-19]   On the other hand, in order to accomplish a complete association such that $s_i = e^{(s)}_i$ $(1 \leq s \leq L)$, τ must be controlled towards 1 near a complete retrieval point, where a unique overlap will take +1 or -1 whereas all the others must completely vanish to 0. According to this respect, we shall control autonomously τ in the following manner,

$$\tau(t+h) = \varphi\left(\tau(t) + h \cdot \kappa \cdot o(t) \cdot \left(1 + (E(t) - E_0)\right)\right) \, , \tag{11}$$

where κ $(0 < \kappa < 1)$ is a constant concerned with the relaxation time of $\tau(t)$ dynamics, $o(t)$ is an overlap to be chosen for the dynamic mode, i.e. for a searching mode or for an association one as will be defined later, and $\varphi(x)$ is defined by

$$\varphi(x) = \begin{cases} 1 & |x| > 1 \\ |x| & |x| \leq 1 \end{cases} . \tag{12}$$

The optimal value of E, E_0, with $s(t) = e^{(s)}_i$ $(1 \leq s \leq L)$ at an association point, can be readily derived as $E_0 = 1/2$. Depending on the searching model and the autoassociation model, the overlap to be utilised as a control parameter, $o(t)$, in eq.(12) may be put into

$$o(t) = \underset{1 \leq r \leq L}{\text{Max}} \left\{ \varphi\left(\mu^{(r)}(t)\right) \right\} \quad : \quad \text{Searching Model} , \tag{13a}$$

and

$$o(t) = \varphi\left(\mu^{(s)}(t)\right) \quad : \quad \text{Autoassociation Model with Target } s , \tag{13b}$$

respectively; here $\mu^{(r)}$ is defined by

$$\mu^{(r)} = \sum_{i=1}^{N} e^{\dagger}_i s_i . \tag{13c}$$

Then $\tau(t)$ has to be initialized by setting to ε, or a sufficiently small number or the machine epsilon, so as to induce a chaotic dynamics [16-19] as follows,

$$\text{if } t = 0 \vee \left\| \frac{\sigma(t+h) - \sigma(t)}{h} \right\| < \varepsilon \quad \text{then } \tau(t) = \varepsilon \, . \tag{14}$$

This is considered to be a rule such that the system is to be involved into a chaotic state as an initial state once an association has been achieved,[16-19] which can be determined from the following criteria.

$$\text{if } \underset{1 \leq i \leq N}{\text{Max}} \left\{ \frac{\left| \sigma_i(t+h) - \sigma_i(t) \right|}{h} \right\} < \varepsilon \wedge \left| \underset{1 \leq r \leq L}{\text{Max}} \left\{ o^{(r)}(t) \right\} - 1 \right| < \varepsilon \rightarrow \begin{array}{l} \text{success of the memory} \\ \text{retrieval at time } t . \end{array} , \tag{15}$$

where the overlap with the rth pattern, $o^{(r)}(t)$, can be defined by

$$o^{(r)}(t) = \sum_{i=1}^{N} e^{\dagger(r)}_i \, \text{sgn}\left(s_i(t)\right) ; \tag{16}$$

here $\text{sgn}(s_i(t))$ $(1 \leq i \leq N)$ are regarded as the output pattern of the network. Thus the memory search is accompanied with the transition from chaotic $(\tau(t) \ll 1)$ state to non-chaotic $(\tau(t) \sim 1)$ one.

§3. Results

In this section let us show the association properties of the presently proposed autonomous association model, and compare them with the monotonous dynamic system.

Herein we shall present a few examples of the dynamic behaviour of our model in a chaotic search mode with eq.(13a) (Fig.1(a)) and an autoassociation mode with eq.(13b) (Fig.1(b)).   Here h, κ and ε are set to 1, 0.5 and 10^{-16}, respectively, below if not mentioned. The initial state $s_i(0)$ $(1 \leq i \leq N)$ was also set to a random pattern which are different from the embedded pattern. The embedded pattern vectors were randomly picked up from 2^N patterns, and put into

$$e^{(r)}_i = \text{sgn}(z^{(r)}_i) \qquad (1 \leq r \leq L,\ 1 \leq i \leq N)\ , \tag{17}$$

where $z^{(r)}_i$ $(1 \leq i \leq N,\ 1 \leq r \leq L)$ are the pseudo-random numbers between -1 and +1 with zero-mean value. Of course the each vector $e^{(r)}_i$ is chosen to be linearly independent of each other in order to assure the existence of the conjugate vector $e^{T(r)}_i$, *i.e.* the generalized inverse matrix.   The time-dependent overlaps $o^{(r)}(t)$ $(1 \leq r \leq L)$ are presented in Figs.1(a)and(b) for $N = 20$ and L/N =0.4 and 0.8, respectively.   Complete associations of the embedded patterns are realised in Figs.1(a) and (b) after the transient chaotic states close to the state with $\tau = \varepsilon$ $(\ll 1)$ defined by eq.(14).   These results substantially imply that the memory search can be achieved after a transient chaotic state in similar manner as found in the previous works,[16-19] and that there may exist a certain upper limitation of the number of the embedded patterns to be completely retrieved. Then let us examine the dynamic memory retrieval capability of the present neural network.   Here N was set to 50 somewhat larger than the previous case.   The dynamic memory retrieval process was evaluated during $t = 0 \sim 5000$ $(= T_{\max})$.   In Fig.2 the association rate was defined in terms of the successful rate for 50 trials with different initial input states.   From this result, one finds that the memory capacity L/N may be promoted beyond ~ 0.4 in the searching mode(Fig.2(a)).   In fact one may confirm that the $\sim 100\%$ success rate even for $L/N \sim 0.7$ in the autoassociation mode in the case of the initial directional cosine 0.8 with a target vector(Fig.2(b)).

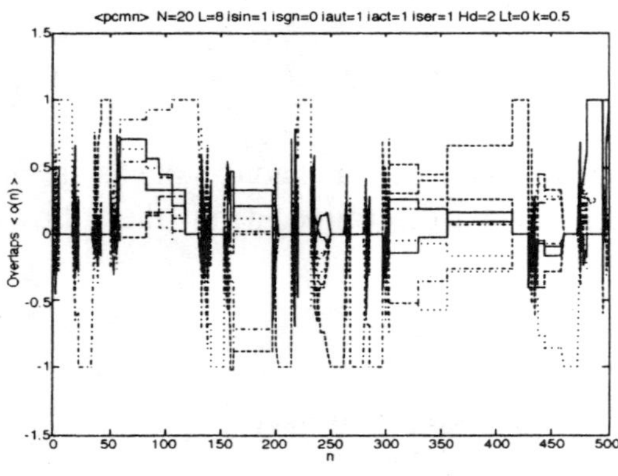 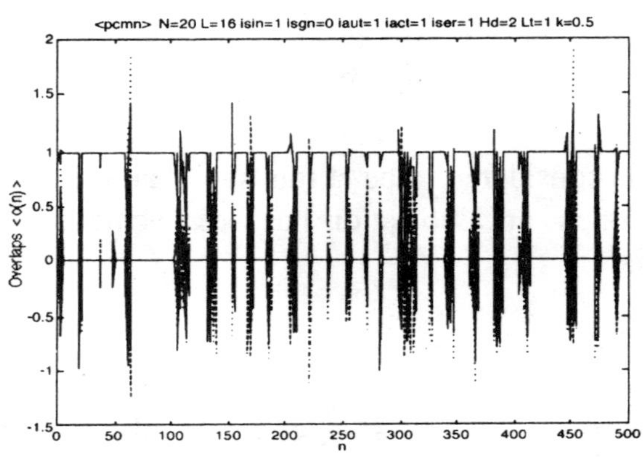

(a) $L/N = 0.4$ $\theta_i = 0$ (b) $L/N = 0.8$ $\theta_i \neq 0$

Fig.1   Examples of time dependence of the overlaps. Here $N = 20$.

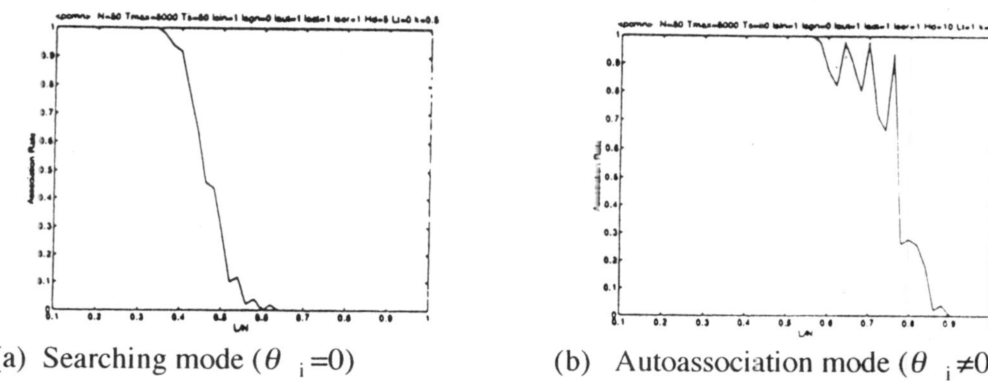

(a) Searching mode ($\theta_i = 0$)   (b) Autoassociation mode ($\theta_i \neq 0$)

Fig.2   Success rate vs loading rate. Here N =50 and T_{max}=5000.

§4. Concluding remarks

In this paper we have proposed a simple chaotic memory retrieval model with an autonomously controlled period of the sinusoidal activation function which relates the internal state σ_i to the output s_i. While such a periodic mapping does no longer assure the monotonous decreasing of the energy, it may prevent the system from an unfavourable trapping at a spurious state as was previously noted.[6-19] In practice the dynamic memory retrieval characteristics of such a periodic chaos neural network with a certain autonomous period control has been found to be considerably improved in comparison with the conventional chaos neural networks with such monotonous mapping as a sigmoid function.[10,11]   In addition the total memory capacity of the presently proposed autoassociation model, was found to be promoted up to 4-5 times larger than the monotonous model as the associatron with $s_i = \mathrm{sgn}(\sigma_i)$. From these findings, one may conclude that the analogue periodic mapping which involves a chaotic behaviour has apparently a certain advantage beyond the previously proposed monotonous mapping or the nonmonotonous one.   In addition it is also found that a considerably high association rate can be achieved as a result of the autonomous control of the chaotic dynamics.

References

1) J.A.Anderson: Math. Biosci.**14**(1972)197.
2) T.Kohonen: IEEE Trans.**C-21**(1972)353.
3) K.Nakano: IEEE Trans. **SMC**-2(1972)380.
4) S.Amari: Biol. Cybern.**26**(1977)175.
5) D.J.Amit, H.Gutfreund, and H. Sompolinsky:Phys. Rev. Lett.**55** (1985)1530.
6) E. Gardner: J. Phys. **A19**(1986)L1047.
7) R.J. McEliece, R.J. Posner, E.R. Rodemich and S.S. Venkatesh: IEEE Trans. on Information Theory, **IT-33**(1987)461.
8) M.Inoue and A.Nagayoshi: Phys.Lett.**A158**(1991)373.
9) H. Kakeya and T. Kindo: J. J. N. N. S. **1**(1994)20[in Japanese].
10) K.Aihara, T.Numajiri, G.Matsumoto, and M.Kotani: Phys. Lett. **A116**(1986)313.
11) K.Nakamura and M.Nakagawa:J. Phys. Soc. of Jpn.**62**(1993)2942.
12) T. Kasahara and M. Nakagawa: IEICE Trans. on Fundamentals **J78-A**(1995)114[in Japanese].
13) M.Morita :Neural Networks **6**(1993)115.
14) Hiro-F.Yanai and S.Amari: Proc. of ICNN'93, San Francisco (1993)1385.
15) M. Shiino and T. Fukai: J. Phys. Math. Gen. **26**(1993)L831.
16) M.Nakagawa: Proc. of ICONIP'94,Seoul, **1**(1994)609.
17) M.Nakagawa: Proc. of ICDC'94,Tokyo, **2**(1995)603.
18) M. Nakagawa: J. Phys.Soc. Jpn.**64**(1995)1023.
19) T. Kasahara and M. Nakagawa: J. Phys. Soc. Jpn.**64**(1995)4964.
20) M. Nakagawa:IEICE Trans. on Fundamentals **E78-A** (1995)412.
21) M. Nakagawa: J. Phys.Soc.Jpn.**64**(1995)3112.
22) M. Nakagawa: Proc. of ICNN'95, Australia(1995)3028.
23) T. Tanaka and M. Nakagawa: J. Phys. Soc. Jpn.(1995, to be submitted).
24) K. Maeda and M. Nakagawa: J. Phys. Soc. Jpn.(1995, in preparation).

Associative Memory

(Oral Presentation)

Equivalence and differences in recall and storage dynamics of associative memory

Hiro-Fumi Yanai

Department of Information and Communication Engineering
Faculty of Engineering, Tamagawa University
Machida, Tokyo 194, Japan
E-mail: yanai@eng.tamagawa.ac.jp

Abstract— I introduce two-stage-dynamics neuron, and discuss the relationship between recall and storage dynamics of associative memory. In conventional studies of neural nets, recall and storage dynamics have been treated separately. But recent studies on two-stage neuron revealed their close relationship. I discuss equivalence and differences of those dynamics that might be interesting to be noted from experimental as well as theoretical points of view. Although this paper focuses on associative memory, the kind of equivalence as is shown here could also be seen in other types of neural nets.

1 Recall and storage dynamics

Neural nets process information by dynamically updating states of neurons as well as modifying weights of synapses. I shall call those two phases of dynamics as recall and storage dynamics, respectively. Recall is often called retrieval, and storage dynamics is usually called learning. For studies of various aspects of recall dynamics see [2, 3, 5, 6, 8, 9, 10, 11, 12, 13, 14, 15], and for the combined discussions of recall and storage dynamics see [1, 4, 7].

1.1 Fundamental models

The simplest model of recall dynamics is

$$x_i(t + 1) = \text{sgn}\left(\sum_{j=1}^{n} w_{ij}x_j\right),\tag{1}$$

where $x_i(t) = \pm 1$ is the output of the ith neuron at discrete time t, w_{ij} is the weight of synapse which connects jth and ith neurons, and $\text{sgn}(u) = 1(u > 0)$ and $-1(u \leq 0)$. In matrix form, Eq. (1) is

$$x_{t+1} = \text{sgn}\left(W x_t\right),\tag{2}$$

where x_t is a column vector whose ith component is $x_i(t)$, and W, called synaptic weight matrix, is a $n \times n$ matrix whose (i, j) component is w_{ij}.

Widely analyzed type of synaptic weight matrix is correlation one. In the case of auto-associative memory, given m column vectors $\boldsymbol{\xi}^1, \boldsymbol{\xi}^2, \ldots, \boldsymbol{\xi}^m$ to be stored (I call these vectors *embedded vectors*), synaptic weight is given by

$$w_{ij}^c = \frac{1}{n}\sum_{\mu=1}^{m}\xi_i^\mu\xi_j^\mu.\tag{3}$$

By defining the $n \times n$ matrix $S = (\boldsymbol{\xi}^1, \boldsymbol{\xi}^2, \ldots, \boldsymbol{\xi}^m)$, the above synaptic weight is expressed as matrix form

$$W^c = \frac{1}{n}SS'\tag{4}$$

$$= \frac{1}{n}\sum_{\mu=1}^{m}\boldsymbol{\xi}^\mu(\xi^\mu)',\tag{5}$$

where $'$ denotes transposition. The matrix W^c is the auto-correlation matrix.

The above correlation-type synapses are obtained by the storage dynamics of

$$W(s + 1) = (1 - \gamma)W(s) + \beta \xi^{\mu(s)}(\xi^{\mu(s)})', \tag{6}$$

where $\mu(s) \in \{1, 2, \ldots, m\}$, and γ and β are positive constants. Apart from fluctuations, if conditions are appropriate, the matrix $W(s)$ converges to W^c [1].

Dynamics of Eq. (1) with correlation-type synapses (cross-correlation as well as auto-correlation) are reviewed and analyzed in [3].

1.2   Generalized models

In [4] Caianiello has made a unified treatment on the generalized model of the above two phases of dynamics, where they are described by *neuronal equation* and *mnemonic equation*, respectively. The neuronal equation has the form

$$x_{t+1} = \mathrm{sgn}\left(\sum_{k=0}^{\infty} W^{(k)} x_{t-k}\right). \tag{7}$$

The mnemonic equation is an extension of the correlation synapse for multiple delays. By adding threshold and external force terms, the neuronal equation includes most models that have ever been analyzed as associative memories.

Another direction of generalizing recall dynamics is the *two-stage model*.

$$\begin{cases} u_t = W x_t, \\ \tilde{u}_t = F(u_t, W), \\ x_{t+1} = \mathrm{sgn}(\tilde{u}_t), \end{cases} \tag{8}$$

where $F(u, W)$ is, in general, a nonlinear function of u and W.

Models of storage dynamics other than correlation type include *pseudoinverse-matrix-type* [1, 7] and *perceptron-type*. For the case of auto-associative memory, pseudoinverse-matrix-type storage dynamics is

$$W(s + 1) = (1 - \gamma)W(s) + \beta \left[\xi^{\mu(s)} - W(s)\xi^{\mu(s)}\right] (\xi^{\mu(s)})', \tag{9}$$

which converges to the orthogonal-projection matrix ·

$$P = SS^+, \tag{10}$$

where S^+ is the pseudoinverse of S, and is expressed as $S^+ = (S'S)^{-1}S'$. By these synaptic weights the neural net can store linearly independent vectors as fixed points of the recall dynamics of Eq. (1). Perceptron-type storage dynamics is

$$W(s + 1) = (1 - \gamma)W(s) + \beta \left[\xi^{\mu(s)} - \mathrm{sgn}(W(s)\xi^{\mu(s)})\right] (\xi^{\mu(s)})', \tag{11}$$

by which the net can store linearly separable vectors.

2   Recall dynamics of associative memory

When the embedded vectors are random, recall dynamics of associative memory are characterized by *capacity* and *basin of attraction*. Capacity is the largest number of embedded vectors that can be stably stored as fixed points (auto-association) or sequences (sequence-association). There are two definitions of capacity, *absolute capacity* and *relative capacity* [2]. Allowing no error, we have absolute capacity, and allowing errors, we have relative capacity[1]. For example, auto- and sequence-associative memory with correlation-type synapses (and no selfcouplings, i.e. $w_{ii} = 0$) have the absolute capacity of $n/(2\log n)$ with the number of neurons n tending to infinity. For finite n, the absolute capacity is monotonically decreasing with n.

The relative capacity of the above auto-associative memory is well known to be *near* $0.15n$, exact value being still unclear. For sequence-associative memory, it is quite close to the corresponding value $0.27n$ of layered net [5].

---

[1]The relative capacity is defined by the phase diagram of the equilibrium states without ambiguity.

The basin of attraction of an embedded vector is the domain of state space $\{-1, 1\}^n$ which is attracted to (absolute case) or attracted close to (relative case) the embedded vector by the recall dynamics. To discuss the property, let me define *distance* and *overlap*. Distance of the output state x_t from the embedded vector ξ in concern is

$$d_t = \frac{1}{2n} \sum_{i=1}^{n} |\xi_i - x_i(t)|, \tag{12}$$

and the overlap is the direction cosine of x_t and ξ

$$l_t = \frac{1}{n} \sum_{i=1}^{n} \xi_i x_i(t), \tag{13}$$

$$= 1 - 2d_t \tag{14}$$

When the number of embedded vectors is less than the absolute capacity, that is $m = \kappa n / (2 \log n)$ with $\kappa < 1$, for initial distance satisfying $d_0 < (1 - \sqrt{\kappa})/2$, the embedded vector in concern is perfectly recalled by one step, i.e. $d_1 = 0$. In this case the radius of basin of attraction is $(1 - \sqrt{\kappa})/2$. When the number of embedded vectors is larger, recall dynamics is characterized by the *loading rate* $r = m/n$. The phase diagram for correlation-type sequence-associative memory can be seen in [5]. The phase diagram for correlation-type auto-associative memory is qualitatively the same according to the theory with several approximations [2, 3, 14].

3 Relationship between two-stage model and pseudoinverse matrix

3.1 Their correspondence

Two-stage neuron model of Eq. (8) is an extension of the discrete non-monotonic neuron model proposed in [8][2]. For the case of correlation-type auto-associative memory without selfcouplings, recall dynamics in the regime of absolute capacity are studied for various choices of the function F in Eq. (8) [11, 12]. A good choice of the function F is

$$F(u, W) = u + W_0^c f(u) \tag{15}$$

with

$$f(u) = -au + (2a - 1)\mathrm{sgn}(u), \quad a > 0, \tag{16}$$

where $W_0^c = W^c - \frac{m}{n} I$ (I is a unit matrix). With the above function, the absolute capacity is, independently of a,

$$\frac{n}{\sqrt{2 \log n}}. \tag{17}$$

And the relative capacity is greater than $0.3n$.

The simplest form of Eq. (16) is the linear function obtained by putting $a = 1/2$. To write down the recall dynamics of Eq. (8) explicitly for $a = 1/2$, we have

$$x_{t+1} = \mathrm{sgn}\left[\left(I - \frac{1}{2}W_0^c\right) W_0^c x_t\right]. \tag{18}$$

In fact, the matrix $(I - \frac{1}{2}W_0^c)W_0^c$ corresponds to the first-degree approximation of the orthogonal-projection matrix P that realizes error-less autoassociation. That is, since the von Neumann expansion of the pseudoinverse S^+ of S is[3]

$$S^+ = \frac{\alpha}{n} \sum_{k=0}^{\infty} \left(I - \frac{\alpha}{n} S' S\right)^k S', \tag{19}$$

the corresponding orthogonal-projection matrix P is

$$P = SS^+$$

$$= \sum_{k=0}^{\infty} (I - \alpha W^c)^k \alpha W^c. \tag{20}$$

---

[2] For theoretical analyses of continuous non-monotonic models, see [10, 15]

[3] Convergence of the series, Eq. (19), is guaranteed if $0 < \alpha < 2/\lambda$ is satisfied, where λ is the maximum eigenvalue of $(1/n)S'S$.

The first two terms of the expansion is

$$\sum_{k=0}^{1}(I - \alpha W^c)^k \alpha W^c = 2\alpha \left(I - \frac{\alpha}{2}W^c\right)W^c. \tag{21}$$

This proves the correspondence.

If we focus on the linear two-stage model, since we know the correspondence between recall and storage dynamics through Eq. (20), it is straightforward to extend the linear two-stage model to higher-degree ones which better approximate the storage dynamics that yield P. Let me define a linear two-stage model of degree τ as

$$\text{Stage 1} \quad : \quad \boldsymbol{u}_t = W^c \boldsymbol{x}_t, \tag{22}$$

$$\text{Stage 2} \quad : \quad \tilde{\boldsymbol{u}}_t^{(\tau)} = \sum_{k=0}^{\tau}(I - \alpha W^c)^k \alpha \boldsymbol{u}_t, \tag{23}$$

$$\text{Output stage} \quad : \quad \boldsymbol{x}_{t+1} = \text{sgn}\left(\tilde{\boldsymbol{u}}_t^{(\tau)}\right), \tag{24}$$

where t is the time. Stages 1, 2 and output stage are applied cyclically. Initial condition is given by $\boldsymbol{x}_0$ and $\boldsymbol{u}_t$ is calculated (This is the stage 1), and according to Eq. (23) $\boldsymbol{u}_1^{(\tau)}$ is calculated (This is the stage 2), then $\boldsymbol{u}_1^{(\tau)}$ is substituted into Eq. (24) (This is the output stage), that determines $\boldsymbol{x}_1$. In this way, the output state vectors $\boldsymbol{x}_t (t = 2, 3, \ldots)$ are determined. Stage 2 dynamics, Eq. (23), can be realized by recurrent rules which are plausible as neural net models. One example is

$$\tilde{\boldsymbol{u}}_t^{(k+1)} = \tilde{\boldsymbol{u}}_t^{(k)} + (I - \alpha W^c)(\tilde{\boldsymbol{u}}_t^{(k)} - \tilde{\boldsymbol{u}}_t^{(k-1)}) \quad \text{with} \quad \tilde{\boldsymbol{u}}_t^{(0)} = \alpha W^c \boldsymbol{x}_t \text{ and } \tilde{\boldsymbol{u}}_t^{(-1)} = 0, \tag{25}$$

and another is

$$\begin{cases} \boldsymbol{v}_t^{(k+1)} = (I - \alpha W^c)\boldsymbol{v}_t^{(k)} \\ \tilde{\boldsymbol{u}}_t^{(k+1)} = \tilde{\boldsymbol{u}}_t^{(k)} + \boldsymbol{v}_t^{(k+1)} \end{cases} \quad \text{with} \quad \boldsymbol{v}_t^{(0)} = \alpha \boldsymbol{u}_t \text{ and } \tilde{\boldsymbol{u}}_t^{(0)} = 0. \tag{26}$$

Equivalence of recall and storage dynamics is exact when $\tau \to \infty$. That is, the two-stage dynamics with correlation matrix is equivalent to the conventional (threshold) dynamics with pseudoinverse matrix. Thus the two-stage model with $\tau \to \infty$ is fully understood by the analysis of pseudoinverse matrix associative memories, e.g. Kohonen [7] and Kanter & Sompolinsky [6].

3.2 Examples from numerical simulations

Some numerically simulated results for recall of a memory vector from noisy initial conditions are presented in Figures 1 and 2. In the simulations the output stage is slightly modified to demonstrate interesting properties of the model. That is, the selfcoupling term is added as

$$\boldsymbol{x}_{t+1} = \text{sgn}\left(\tilde{\boldsymbol{u}}_t^{(\tau)} + \text{selfcoupling } \boldsymbol{x}_t\right). \tag{27}$$

According to [6], if the every diagonal elements of the orthogonal projection matrix are set to zero, the basin of attraction of memory is enlarged (compare two figures in Figure 1). In the present model, since we are concerned with the orthogonal projection matrix only implicitly, we cannot manipulate those diagonal elements directly. To achieve the equivalent situation, the selfcoupling term helps — if we put selfcoupling $= -r = -m/n$, the present model is equivalent to the orthogonal projection matrix model with zero diagonal elements. But note that, in the exact sense, the equivalence here is in a statistical sense, where the fluctuation is of the order $1/\sqrt{n}$.

Next I show an interesting behavior in the recall dynamics that is specific to the two-stage-model.

The dynamics of the stage 2 is written using W^c in order to be compatible with Eq. (20). But what happens if we replace W^c with W_0^c as is often done in the studies of associative memory?[4] The result is shown in Figure 2. The model discriminates the memory vector itself and noisy vectors (The exactness of the discrimination differs depending on the various parameters involved, e.g. r, τ, α). This might be an important property as a subsystem of an autonomous memory system.

---

[4] If the dynamics is simple and described by Eq. (2), there is no essential difference by the replacement.

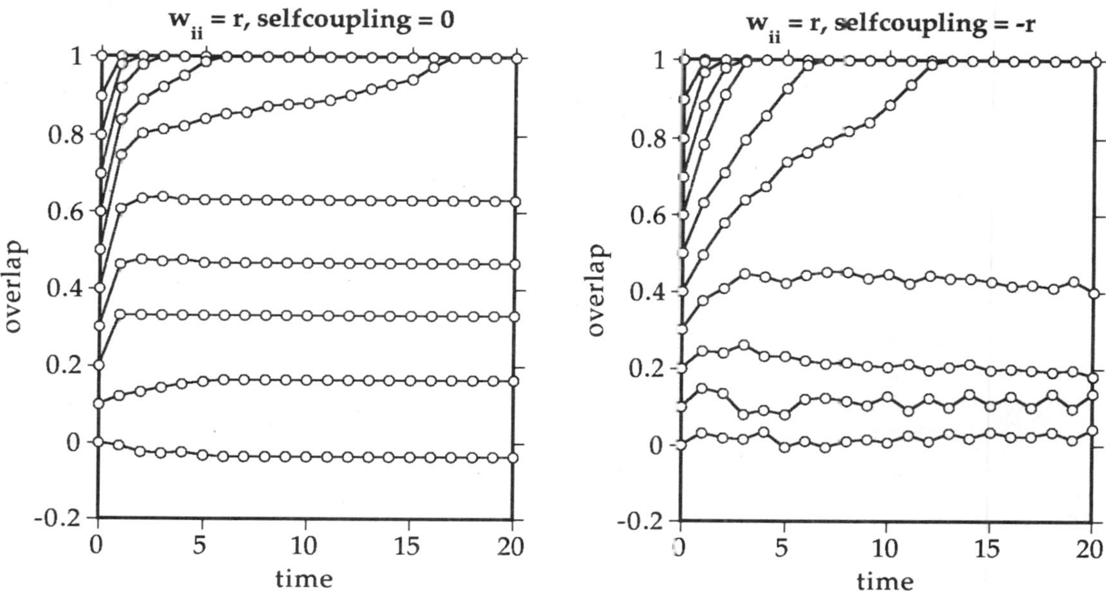

Figure 1: Numerically simulated recall processes of associative memory with two-stage-neurons. $n = 500, r = 0.3, \tau = 5, \alpha = 0.5$. w_{ii} represents the diagonal elements of the correlation matrix, so that $w_{ii} = r$ means that W^c is used. Left: corresponds to fundamental orthogonal projection matrix model. Right: corresponds to orthogonal projection matrix model with zero diagonal elements.

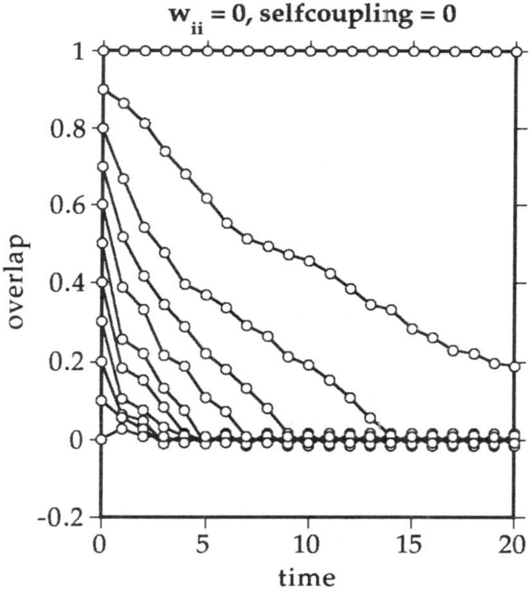

Figure 2: Effect of using W_0^c instead of W^c for associative memory with two-stage-neurons. $n = 500, r = 0.3, \tau = 5, \alpha = 0.5$.

4   Interesting differences — a summary

Finally I summarize interesting differences between two-stage model and pseudoinverse-matrix model.

- Since the matrix involved in two-stage model is correlation one, addition and removal of vectors are easily manipulated by a simple procedure.

- Although two-stage neurons are more complex than threshold neurons, the entire net could be less complex than the net of threshold neurons with pseudoinverse or similar types of synapses. This is because, in general, the number of synapses in a neural net with n neurons is $O(n^2)$.

- Pseudoinverse-type associative memory is more sensitive than correlation-type to noise in storage processes. In two-stage model the sensitivity could be adjusted by choosing suitable degree τ.

- By replacing W^c in Eq. (22) and (23) with W_0^c, and taking τ large enough, the associative memory performs as a "match detector". That is, if the initial condition is one of the embedded vectors itself, the state of the net remain unchanged, but if it is noisy, the state goes far away from it converging to the state that is correlated to neither of embedded vectors.

References

[1] Amari, S. (1977): Neural theory of association and concept-formation, *Biological Cybernetics*, **26**, 175–185

[2] Amari, S. and Maginu, K. (1988): Statistical neurodynamics of associative memory, *Neural Networks*, **1**, 63–73

[3] Amari, S. and Yanai, H.-F. (1993): Statistical neurodynamics of various types of associative nets, *Associative Neural Memories — Theory and Implementation*, M. H. Hassoun ed. , Oxford University Press: New York

[4] Caianiello, E. (1961): Outline of a theory of thought-processes and thinking machines, *J. Theoret. Biol.*, **2**, 204–235

[5] Domany, E., Kinzel, W. and Meir, R. (1989): Layered neural networks, *J. Phys. A: Math. Gen.*, **22**, 2081–2102

[6] Kanter, I. and Sompolinsky, H. (1987): Associative recall of memory without errors, *Phys. Rev. A*, **35**, 380–392

[7] Kohonen, T. (1989): Self-Organization and Associative Memory, Springer-Verlag

[8] Morita, M. (1993): Associative memory with nonmonotone dynamics, *Neural Networks*, **6**, 115–126

[9] Okada, M. (1995): A hierarchy of macrodynamical equations for associative memory, *Neural Networks*, **8**, 833–838

[10] Shiino, M. and Fukai, T. (1993): Self-consistent signal-to-noise analysis of the statistical behavior of analog neural networks and enhancement of the storage capacity, *Physical Review E*, **48**, 867–897

[11] Yanai, H.-F. and Amari, S. (1993): A theory on a neural net with non-monotone neurons, *Proceedings of 1993 IEEE Conference on Neural Networks*, 1385–1390

[12] Yanai, H.-F. and Amari, S. (1996): Auto-associative memory with two-stage dynamics of non-monotonic neurons, *IEEE Trans. Neural Networks*, **7**, Issue 3, in press

[13] Yanai, H.-F. and Sawada, Y. (1990): Integrator neurons for analogue neural networks, *IEEE Trans. on Circuits and Systems*, 37, 854–856

[14] Yanai, H.-F., Sawada, Y. and Yoshizawa, S. (1991): Dynamics of an auto-associative neural network model with arbitrary connectivity and noise in the threshold, *Network: Computation in Neural Systems*, **2**, 295–314

[15] Yoshizawa, S., Morita, M. and Amari, S. (1993): Capacity of associative memory using a nonmonotonic neuron model, *Neural Networks*, **6**, 167–176

Retrieval of Patterns from Hopfield Network
Using Prior Knowledge

Hyoungsoo Yoon*

Physics Department, University of California, Santa Cruz
Santa Cruz, CA 95064, USA
email: hyoung@galaxy.postech.ac.kr

Abstract— In the associative memory neural networks, stored patterns are retrieved with
the aid of two information sources; one in the synaptic efficacies and the other in the triggering input pattern. In the traditional approach, the latter merely gives the starting point
of the computation. In this paper, we present a systematic way of utilizing the information
present in inputs in the Hopfield model, through the Bayesian method. In simple cases
considered here, the information is given in terms of the relative uncertainty of the input
with respect to the retrieving pattern. In such cases, it has been found that the retrieval
capability of the network is greatly improved.

1   Introduction

An attractor neural network is a statistical mechanical system of stochastic neurons whose Hamiltonian
is designed such that local (free) energy minima may correspond to stored patterns. The information
is generally stored in the synaptic couplings between pairs of neurons by some learning algorithms. In
particular, the Hopfield model with the Ising-like Hamiltonian [1]

$$H = -\frac{1}{2} \sum_{i \neq j} J_{ij} S_i S_j \tag{1}$$

for N binary neurons $\{S_i = \pm 1\}$, uses *Hebbian rules* to store p patterns, $\{\xi_i^\mu\}$, in the synaptic couplings $\{J_{ij}\}$. That is,

$$J_{ij} = \frac{1}{N} \sum_{\mu=1}^{p} \xi_i^\mu \xi_j^\mu \qquad \text{for} \quad i \neq j \tag{2}$$

and 0 otherwise. It has been shown that as long as p/N is smaller than a certain number $\alpha_c \approx 0.138$ the
stored patterns are indeed located close to local minima [2]. Then one retrieves the stored patterns by
finding these local minima through a thermal relaxation process.

Attractor neural networks invariably use two information sources; the input pattern and the synaptic
couplings of the network. The computation (i.e., retrieval of memories) performed by a network can be
viewed as an amplification of the information contained in the input by the network. Even though the
information contents of the network has been studied extensively over the years, relatively little attention
has been paid to the study of the input. Especially, the importance of the input in terms of the amount
of the information provided to the network has been mostly overlooked. In most cases studied so far, the
input pattern is simply assumed to have a macroscopic overlap m^0 with one of the stored patterns.

In this paper we consider a situation in which some extra information regarding the "closeness" of the input
to the retrieving pattern is available. In such a case we can improve the retrievability of the network by
maximally utilizing the information provided. In the simplest case considered in this work, the information
is given in terms of the relative uncertainty of the input pattern with respect to the retrieving (desired) one.
We will develop a systematic way of utilizing such information within the framework of the equilibrium
statistical mechanics, and apply it to the Hopfield model.

2   The Model

The Hopfield model uses Glauber dynamics with the usual spin-Hamiltonian given by Eq. (1). The network
is fully connected and the couplings are given by Hebbian rules, Eq. (2). The distribution of the stored

---

*Present Address: Basic Science Research Institute, Postech, Pohang, Korea 790–784

patterns ξ_i^μ is assumed to be unbiased in this paper, that is,

$$P(\xi_i^\mu) = \frac{1}{2}\delta(\xi_i^\mu + 1) + \frac{1}{2}\delta(\xi_i^\mu - 1) \tag{3}$$

where $\delta(x) \equiv \delta_{x0}$ is the symbol for Kronecker delta.

The initial pattern $\{S_i^0\}$, given as a starting point of the dynamics, is usually assumed to have a non-zero overlap m^0 with one and only one of the learned patterns, which we label as the first $\{\xi_i^1\}$ throughout this paper, that is,

$$\frac{1}{N}\sum_i^N \xi_i^\mu S_i^0 = m^0 \qquad \text{for} \quad \mu = 1 \tag{4}$$

and 0 otherwise. Roughly speaking, m^0 is a measure of the *average* discrepancy between the corresponding bits in the input and in the target. If we assume that the contribution to m^0 from each bit is uniform in statistical sense, S_i^0's can be regarded as random variables with the conditional probability

$$P(S_i^0|\xi_i^1) = \frac{1 + m^0}{2}\delta(S_i^0 - \xi_i^1) + \frac{1 - m^0}{2}\delta(S_i^0 + \xi_i^1) \tag{5}$$

Then the initial overlap parameter m^0 can be written as $\langle \xi_i^1 S_i^0 \rangle_{P(S_i^0|\xi_i^1)}$. m^0 varies from 1 for absolute certainty of $\{S_i^0\}$ being $\{\xi_i^1\}$, in which case it is not necessary to use the network since the answer is already known, to 0 for complete randomness of $\{S_i^0\}$ regardless of $\{\xi_i^1\}$, in which case it is highly unlikely that the desired memory will ever be retrieved out of many stored patterns. We will not consider negative values of m^0.

We describe next how to incorporate such information present in input into the equilibrium statistical mechanics approach, which has proven to be indispensable in many areas of neural network studies [3]. Let us suppose, for the moment, that the conditional probability of ξ_i^1 given the value of S_i^0, $P(\xi_i^1|S_i^0)$, is known somehow. Then, given this information, it should be clear that one does not have to "search" the whole phase space for the local minimum which corresponds to ξ_i^1. Rather, a small volume around $\{S_i^0\}$ will be the most important part to be searched. Therefore we perform our phase space integration (*partition function*), which is usually taken over the whole phase space, only over this volume. More specifically, the trace $\text{Tr}_{S_i} \equiv \sum_{S_i=\pm 1}$ is taken with the weight $W(S_i) = P(\xi_i^1 = S_i|S_i^0)$, that is,

$$Z = \underset{\{S_i\}}{\text{Tr}} \prod_i W(S_i)e^{-\beta H(\{S_i\})} \tag{6}$$

where β^{-1} indicates the level of "thermal" noise. We will calculate Z to obtain the thermodynamic properties of the system as in the conventional approach [2], but there will be some differences in the procedure. Most importantly, we are only interested in finding the single solution $\{\xi_i^1\}$, which is the answer to the given question $\{S_i^0\}$. This will be explained in more detail in the next section. Incidentally, the quenched average over the input variables $\{S_i^0\}$ as well as over the memories $\{\xi_i^\mu\}$ should be taken in this formalism. Average over quenched inputs to find the typical behavior of the system is a common practice in the studies of feedforward neural networks [4].

Now we can calculate $P(\xi_i^1|S_i^0)$ from the *presumed* prior knowledge $P(S_i^0|\xi_i^1)$ and $P(\xi_i^1)$ using Bayes' rule.

$$P(\xi_i^1|S_i^0) \propto P(S_i^0|\xi_i^1)P(\xi_i^1) \tag{7}$$

From the normalization condition, we can easily obtain

$$P(\xi_i^1|S_i^0) = \frac{1 + m^0}{2}\delta(\xi_i^1 - S_i^0) + \frac{1 - m^0}{2}\delta(\xi_i^1 + S_i^0) \tag{8}$$

The apparent similarity of this equation to Eq. (5) is due to our choice of the priors concerning ξ_i's and due to some restrictions in our model. In the more general cases considered in [5], this is not the case.

From Eq. (8), $W(S_i)$ becomes

$$W(S_i) = e^{hS_i^0 S_i} \tag{9}$$

where

$$h = \frac{1}{2}\ln\left(\frac{1+m^0}{1-m^0}\right) \tag{10}$$

Hence restricting the phase space around S_i^0 in calculating Z is equivalent to applying a magnetic field h/β in the "direction" of the input pattern S_i^0 [6]. Note that when the temperature β^{-1} is zero, the system is equivalent to the one with no magnetic field. Hence the information in the input plays no role in this case. When β^{-1} is very large, however, the performance of the conventional system deteriorates rapidly and beyond a certain noise level ($\beta_c^{-1} \lesssim 1$) it stops working as a memory. But our model is saved from this total disaster because we do not throw away our initial information in the triggering input, which becomes the sole source of the information concerning the desired pattern in this limit. This is a very reasonable model of the memory retrieving process from associative memory systems.

3 Retrieval of Desired Memory

Since the purpose of this paper is to illustrate the new formalism, we will only consider the finite storage case in this paper. That is, we will take the thermodynamic limit ($N \to \infty$) with the number of patterns p fixed. In this limit, the partition function Z is easily integrated to give the free energy

$$f = \frac{\vec{m}^2}{2} - \frac{1}{\beta}\langle\!\langle \ln[2\cosh(\beta\vec{m}\cdot\vec{\xi_i} - hS^0)]\rangle\!\rangle_{\vec{\xi},S^0} \tag{11}$$

and the order parameter

$$\vec{m} = \langle\!\langle \vec{\xi}\tanh(\beta\vec{m}\cdot\vec{\xi} + hS^0)\rangle\!\rangle_{\vec{\xi},S^0} \tag{12}$$

where the indices from $\vec{\xi_i}$ and S_i^0 have been dropped since the problem has been reduced to the effective single-site problem.

Since we are only interested in the retrieval of the first pattern, we will only consider solutions of the type $\vec{m} = (m, 0, 0, \cdots, 0)$. For such solutions, Eq. (12) becomes, after the quenched average,

$$m = \frac{1+m^0}{2}\tanh(\beta m + h) + \frac{1-m^0}{2}\tanh(\beta m - h) \tag{13}$$

This equation can be easily solved by graphical methods, and we present the results next. First, since we are insisting on the uniqueness of this solution for each input, we must ensure that its overlap with all the stored patterns other than $\{\xi_i^1\}$ be zero. The solution has been obtained with this constraint and the critical line is plotted in Fig. 1. Unique solutions exist only in the right-hand side region of the curve. In the region left to the curve, the desired memory may not be retrieved due either to lack of initial information or to presence of many local minima. Note that solutions exist even when $\beta^{-1} > 1$ as long as m^0 is non-zero, unlike in the conventional approach.

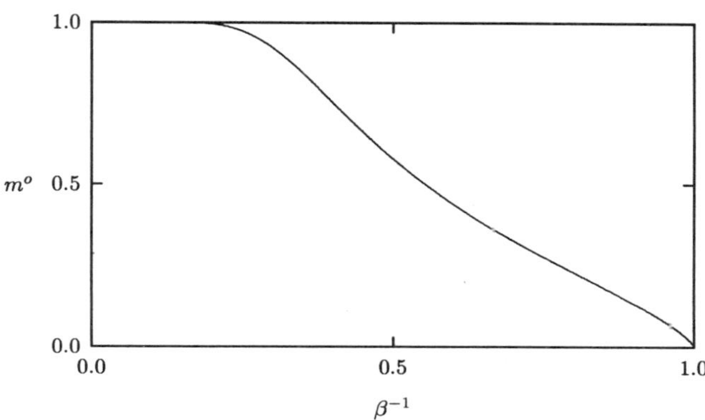

Figure 1: The curve shows the minimum m^0 at fixed β^{-1} to obtain a solution. Or alternatively, the curve can be viewed as minimum β^{-1} at given m^0.

The final overlap parameter, m, is plotted against m^0 in Fig. 2 for various values of β^{-1}. As shown in the figure, m is a monotonically increasing function of m^0. Note that lower β^{-1} generally means a better solution (bigger m), if it exists, for a given m^0. We can, therefore, find an optimal solution for a given m^0 by lowering the temperature until the critical line is reached, which was shown in Fig. 1. This is shown in Fig. 3 for various values of m^0. Note that m starts to increase rapidly around $\beta^{-1} = 1$ when we lower the temperature. The optimal m for a given m^0 is plotted in Fig. 4. Note that this curve consists of the terminal points of the curves shown in Fig. 2.

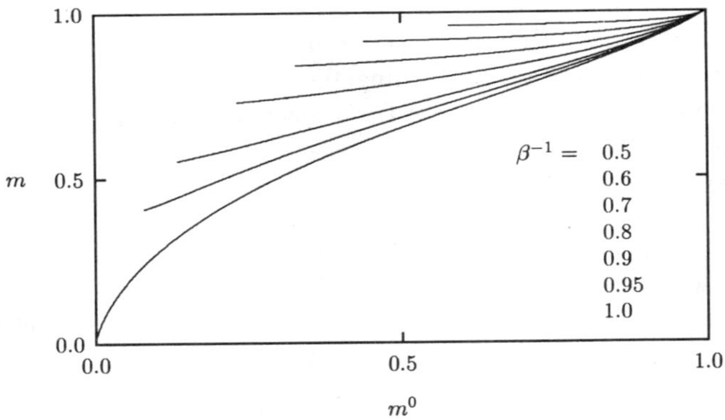

Figure 2: m vs. m^0 for fixed values of β^{-1}. As indicated in the figure, the curves correspond, from the top, to $\beta^{-1} = 0.5$, 0.6, 0.7, 0.8, 0.9, 0.95, and 1.0. Note that the curves for $\beta^{-1} < 1.0$ terminate at the critical line of Fig. 1.

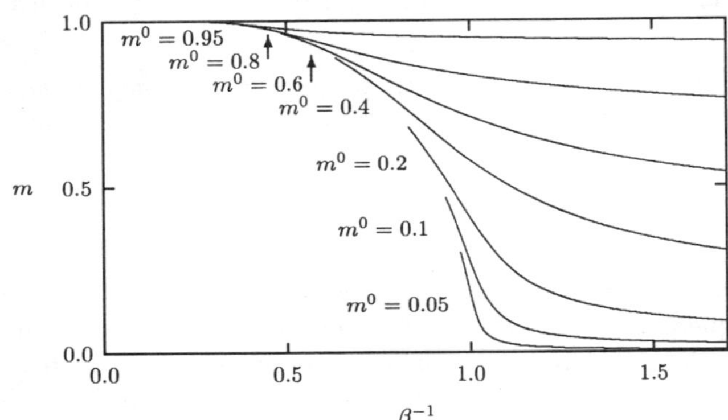

Figure 3: m vs. β^{-1} for various values of m^0 from 0.05 to 0.95, as indicated in the figure. Note that, when $\beta^{-1} \gtrsim 1$, m is around its initial value, m^0. m eventually vanishes at high temperature.

Since if one starts from non-zero m^0 at a sufficiently high temperature he can get $m > m^0$ by lowering the temperature, he can eventually reach $m = 1$ by iterating this process. This can be viewed as a simulated annealing. One example is shown in Fig. 4 starting from $m^0 = 0.1$. As shown in the figure, m reaches very close to 1 after only three iterations. Hence we can conclude that, in the finite storage case, any *non-zero* m^0 can help retrieve the *complete* pattern through this method.

4   Conclusion

In attractor neural networks such as the Hopfield model, stored patterns are retrieved as fixed points in some stochastic dynamics. The dynamics uses not only the structure of the network via the synaptic connections but also the initial pattern which is assumed to be close enough to the desired pattern. In most models of associative memory, the latter information merely gives the starting point of the dynamics and fades away as the system relaxes to one of the stored patterns. One exception to this scheme has been studied by Engel et al. [6], who showed that retrieval properties are improved when the triggering pattern persists in the form of magnetic fields. We have proposed a more systematic way of utilizing

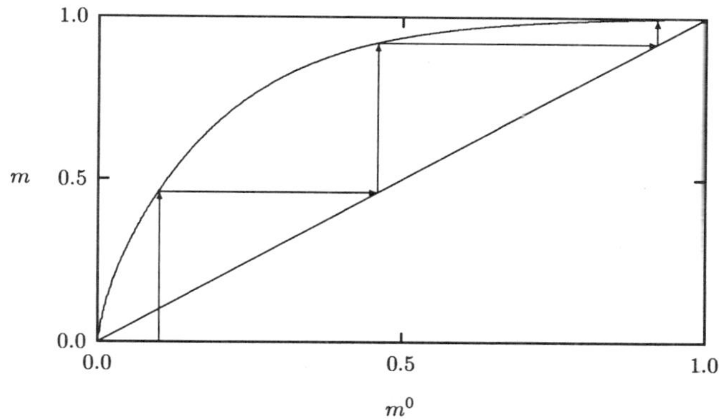

Figure 4: The curve indicates the maximal m for a given m^0, which is obtained by lowering β^{-1} until it reaches the critical value. This process can be repeated to obtain m which is arbitrarily close to 1. The upward arrows indicate three such iterations.

the information contained in the initial cue using the Bayesian method. When, for instance, an image of a stored pattern is shown to a network through a semi-transparent filter, the information regarding its transmission coefficient can be used to increase the retrieval capability of the network.

We have restricted ourselves in this paper to the simplest case of uniform uncertainty across the input pattern. There are, however, many different types of inputs where the noise level or the uncertainty varies from one part of the pattern to another as in the case where a partially hidden pattern is used to trigger the corresponding memory. It is also conceivable that the uncertainty depends on whether ξ_i^1 (or S_i^0) is 1 or -1 such as in the case of black and white photos taken through a lens on which random patterns are drawn with black colors [5].

Acknowledgment

This work was partly supported by NSF Grant DMR-9419362.

References

[1] J. J. Hopfield. Neural networks and physical systems with emergent collective computational abilities. *Proc. Natl. Acad. Sci. USA*, 79:2554–2558, 1982.

[2] Daniel J. Amit, Hanoch Gutfreund, and H. Sompolinsky. Statistical mechanics of neural networks near saturation. *Annals of Physics*, 173:30–67, 1987.

[3] Jong-Hoon Oh, Chulan Kwon, and Sungzoon Cho, editors. *Neural Networks: The Statistical Mechanics Perspective*, volume 1 of *Progress in Neural Processing*. World Scientific, 1995.

[4] H. S. Seung, H. Sompolinsky, and N. Tishby. Statistical mechanics of learning from examples. *Physical Review A*, 45:6056, 1992.

[5] Hyoungsoo Yoon. Retrieval of memories from Hopfield model: A Bayesian approach. Postech Technical Report BS-96-03, January 1996.

[6] A. Engel, H. Englisch, and A. Schütte. Improved retrieval in neural networks with external fields. *Europhysics Letters*, 8(4):393–397, 1989.

Q-state Associative Memory Rules and Comparisons

Aregahegn Negatu †, Arun Jagota ‡
† Department of Mathematical Sciences, University of Memphis
Memphis, TN, 38152 USA
‡ Department of Computer Science, University of North Texas
Denton, TX, 76203, USA

Abstract— In this paper, we extend several storage rules for the binary Hopfield associative memory to store Q-state vectors, for $Q \geq 2$. These include the Hopfield outerproduct rule, its true Hebbian variant, and the Willshaw rule. These rules are compared with the Q-state Hopfield-clique rule, developed earlier, on training sets consisting of k random Q-state vectors of length n, for different k, Q and n. When between $0.16n$ and $0.50n$ random patterns are stored in the network, our experimental results are as follows. On stability alone, the Hopfield-clique rule works best; the Willshaw rule second-best for Q not too small; the True Hebb rule third-best; and the outerproduct rule poorest except when $Q = 2$. Intuitive explanations of these results are given. On recall of non-spurious states, the Hopfield-clique rule works best; the True Hebb rule second-best; the Willshaw rule third-best; and the outerproduct rule poorest. All rules work poorly at $Q = 2$. Theoretical analysis of stability in the Q-state Willshaw rule is conducted. Numerical calculations from this analysis agree closely with the experimental results, and also provide estimates of average-case stability capacity.

1   Introduction

The Hopfield neural network [5] is a popular model of associative memory with an attractor dynamics that minimizes an energy function. Memories are attempted to be stored as local minima of the energy function, by setting the weights and thresholds appropriately. A stored memory may subsequently be retrieved by dynamical rules that decrease energy. Because there are many memories one may wish to store, and only one set of weights and thresholds on which they are somehow to be recorded, there is no way, in general, to avoid weight and threshold adjustments required to store a particular memory from destructively interfering with weight and threshold adjustments required to store other memories. The amount and nature of interference depends, however, on the particular storage rule. This has led to a great deal of research on trying to find storage rules for the Hopfield model that minimize the amount of undesirable interference (see [4]). What are the undesirable effects of interference? There are two. First, after storage, not all patterns we wish to store may become a stable state. Second, after storage, new *spurious* stable states, states that do not correspond to any stored pattern, may develop.

The capacity of the Hopfield model and variants has been extensively studied [11, 1, 10, 8, 3, 2]. Despite the fact that the capacity is fundamentally limited no matter what storage rule is used [1], this model continues to remain popular for a variety of reasons [4]. Due to its simplicity, the model lends itself to specialized hardware implementations—digital, analog, optical, or hybrid. The model has interesting connections to spin models and statistical physics. The model exhibits autonomous convergence from arbitrary initial states, correcting errors in the process. In some situations, when the model is not asked to retrieve a presented memory in its entirety, it works well in practice [6].

It is clearly useful, hence, to evaluate different storage rules for the Hopfield model, in terms of the number of patterns that are made unstable and the number of spurious memories that get created. Whereas many storage rules have been proposed in the past, comparisons among them on the same training sets have been fewer. Storage rules for Q-state vectors are less common, and comparisons among them even rarer.

Q-state vectors arise naturally in certain real-world applications: in dictionary storage, and in storing grayscale images, to name two. This has led some researchers to propose extensions of the Hopfield model to the Q-state case [12, 9, 7]. Rieger [12] extended the binary Hopfield model to Q-states, by using Q-state neurons. He showed that the stable storage capacity, for random Q-state vectors of length n, dropped to $\Theta(n)/Q^2$. Kohring [9] modified Rieger's Q-state model and improved the stable storage capacity to $\Theta(n)/\log_2 Q$. Kohring's modification involved recoding a Q-state vector of length n, using $\log_2 Q$ bits for each component value (0 through $Q - 1$), and creating $\log_2 Q$ independent attractor networks, to process the bits. This scheme uses $N = n \times \log_2 Q$ neurons overall, and $\log_2 Q \times n^2$ weights.

Our Q-state model in the current paper employs a unary recoding of a Q-state vector, i.e. one which uses Q bits for each component value. Thus our scheme uses $N = n \times Q$ neurons overall. Our choice of this recoding is motivated by the fact that, though it uses more neurons than that of Kohring, it guarantees stable storage to arbitrary collections of Q-state vectors when used in conjunction with the Hopfield-clique storage rule [7].

In our Q-state model, we present Q-state extensions of several well known storage rules for the binary Hopfield model: the outerproduct rule, its true Hebbian variant, and the Willshaw rule. These rules are chosen because they are local, simple, realizable in hardware, and easy to extend to the Q-state case. These rules are compared with the Q-state Hopfield-clique rule, developed earlier, on training sets consisting of k random Q-state vectors of length n, for different k, Q and n.

When between $0.16n$ and $0.50n$ random patterns are stored in the network, our experimental results are as follows. On stability alone, the Hopfield-clique rule works best; the Willshaw rule second-best for Q not too small; the True Hebb rule third-best; and the outerproduct rule poorest except when $Q = 2$. Intuitive explanations of these results are given. Theoretical analysis of stability in the Q-state Willshaw rule is conducted. On recall of non-spurious states, the Hopfield-clique rule works best; the True Hebb rule second-best; the Willshaw rule third-best; and the outerproduct rule poorest. All rules work poorly at $Q = 2$. For $Q = 2$, all Q-state rules are shown to work better than their binary versions.

2   The Hopfield Model and Storing Binary Vectors

The Hopfield network [5] consists of n neurons interconnected pairwise by weights w_{ij}. Neuron i has a state $S_i \in \{0, 1\}$ and an external threshold Θ_i. With a symmetric weight matrix (i.e., with $w_{ij} = w_{ji}$) with nonnegative diagonals, a rule that updates the states S_i of the network one at a time according to

$$S_i(t+1) := \begin{cases} 1 & \text{if } \sum_{j=1,\dots,n} w_{ij} S_j(t) \geq \Theta_i \\ 0 & \text{otherwise} \end{cases} \tag{1}$$

minimizes the energy function $E = -1/2 \sum_{ij} w_{ij} S_i S_j + \sum_i \Theta_i S_i$ thereby guaranteeing eventual convergence to a state, called a *stable state*, at a local minimum of the energy function E [5]. A state $S \in \{0, 1\}^n$ is at a *local minimum* of E if the energy of every state T which is at Hamming distance one from S is no lower than that of S.

We first describe the storage rules in their usual binary versions. All rules described below attempt to store a given collection of binary $(0/1)$ vectors of length n in a Hopfield network composed of n neurons. A neuron is indexed as i where $i \in \{1, \dots, n\}$.

The Outerproduct Rule. All thresholds Θ_i equal 0. Initially, $w_{ij} := 0$ for all i, j. A sequence $X^1, \dots, X^p$ of vectors $X^i \in \{0, 1\}^n$ is stored by presenting each vector sequentially as follows. To store X^μ, for all $i \neq j$:

$$w_{ij}(t+1) := w_{ij}(t) + \begin{cases} 1/n & \text{if } X_i^\mu = X_j^\mu \\ -1/n & \text{otherwise} \end{cases} \tag{2}$$

The True Hebbian Variant. In (2), a weight is increased even when both neurons connected to it are not firing. The true Hebb rule increases the value of a weight only when both neurons are firing. This gives us the following variant of (2), in which w_{ij} and Θ_i are again 0 initially. To store X^μ, for all $i \neq j$:

$$w_{ij}(t+1) := w_{ij}(t) + \begin{cases} 1/n & \text{if } X_i^\mu = X_j^\mu = 1 \\ 0 & \text{if } X_i^\mu = X_j^\mu = 0 \\ -1/n & \text{otherwise} \end{cases} \tag{3}$$

The Willshaw Rule. The Willshaw rule [14] is a simple variant of the binary outerproduct and true Hebb rules. Like the binary outerproduct and true Hebb rules, initially, $w_{ij} := 0$ for all i, j. A sequence $X^1, \dots, X^p$ of vectors $X^i \in \{0, 1\}^n$ is stored by presenting each vector sequentially as follows. To store X^μ, for all $i \neq j$:

$$w_{ij}(t+1) := \begin{cases} 1 & \text{if } X_i^\mu = X_j^\mu = 1 \\ w_{ij}(t) & \text{otherwise} \end{cases} \tag{4}$$

Notice that the thresholds Θ_i of the neurons i have not yet been specified. The binary Willshaw rule was shown to have a large capacity, but provided that the patterns were sufficiently sparse, [11] (also see [4, p. 51]), and the neuron thresholds were chosen appropriately. In this paper, every binary vector in our training set, which will arise from a recoded Q-state vector, will contain exactly m ones, for some m.

We will choose the threshold of every neuron as $\Theta_i := m - 1$ for all i. This choice of threshold will guarantee that the one-bits in the presented pattern are stable (see Section 5). A similar choice, in an analogous situation, is in [11].

The Hopfield-clique Rule. The Hopfield-clique rule for binary vectors [7] is similar to the Willshaw rule for binary vectors. The self-weights w_{ii} equal zero for all i. The rule differs in that, initially, $\Theta_i := N$ for all i and that $w_{ij} := \rho$ for all $i \neq j$. Here ρ is a scalar parameter whose value is less than $-N$. A sequence $X^1, \dots, X^p$ of vectors $X^\mu \in \{0, 1\}^n$ is stored by presenting each vector sequentially as follows. To store X^μ, for all $i \neq j$:

$$w_{ij}(t+1) \; := \; \left\{ \begin{array}{ll} 1 & \text{if } X_i^\mu = X_j^\mu = 1 \\ w_{ij}(t) & \text{otherwise} \end{array} \right. \tag{5}$$

and for all i:

$$\Theta_i(t+1) \; := \; \left\{ \begin{array}{ll} -1 & \text{if } X_i^\mu = 1 \\ \Theta_i(t) & \text{otherwise} \end{array} \right. \tag{6}$$

where (6) is needed only to eliminate neurons with zero-weights to all others as singleton spurious memories. This rule is called the Hopfield-clique rule because of its connection with cliques in graphs, a connection that we do not explain here.

3   Storing Q-state Vectors

For positive integer $Q \geq 2$, a Q-state vector of length n is an n-tuple $(x_1, \ldots, x_n)$ where $x_i \in \{0, 1, \ldots, Q-1\}$. We store Q-state vectors by first recoding them as binary vectors, in a manner described below, and storing the binary vectors via the storage rules described in the previous section. We call the resulting storage rules the Q-state versions of the binary rules.

The recoding process is as follows. Let $X_q = (x_1, \ldots, x_n)$ denote a Q-state vector of length n. X_q is recoded as a binary vector of $Q \times n$ bits. Each component x_i of X_Q is represented by a block B_i of Q bits, exactly one bit in B_i is set to one—the bit whose position equals $x_i + 1$. For example, the 4-state vector (1,2,3) is recoded as the binary vector 010000100001.

Notice that under this recoding, all binary vectors contain exactly n ones. Since each such vector is of length $N = n \times Q$, this recoding, for fixed N, becomes sparser as Q increases. This sparseness is exploited by several of our Q-state storage rules. As noted in Section 2.3, the fact that all recoded vectors contain the same number of ones also permits us to set the threshold for the Willshaw rule optimally.

This method of storing Q-state vectors was originally motivated by the following result: in any collection whatsoever of Q-state vectors of length n stored via our recoding using the Hopfield-clique rule, all vectors are stable after storage [7]. This result says in particular that any collection of binary (2-state) vectors of length n can be stored stably in a Hopfield network employing $2n$ neurons by storing the recoded vectors via the Hopfield-clique rule. By contrast, it is well known that there are collections of three binary vectors of length n that cannot be stored stably in any Hopfield network of n neurons, regardless of the storage rule used [3].

4   Experiments

This section describes experiments of two kinds: ones involving stability and ones involving recall. Our training sets comprised of k random Q-state vectors of length n, for different k, Q and n. In all the experiments, we fixed $N = Q \times n$ to 120 and varied k and Q.

4.1   Stable Storage Tests

The first set of experiments was designed to address the following question: what percentage of the k stored vectors are stable, as functions of the storage rule, the number of states Q, and the number of stored patterns k? Table 1 reports the results.

Table 1: k random Q-state vectors of length N/Q were stored, where $N = 120$. Percentage of these vectors that were stable, as a function of the storage rule, and of Q, are reported. Each entry is the average of five independent trials.

Q	2	6	10	20	24	30	40	60
		k=5						
Outerproduct	100%	0%	0%	0%	0%	0%	0%	0 %
True Hebb	0%	0%	12%	68%	76%	80%	88%	92%
Willshaw	92%	100%	100%	100%	100%	100%	100%	84%
		k=10						
Outerproduct	72%	0%	0%	0%	0%	0%	0%	0%
True Hebb	0%	0%	0%	16%	50%	66%	80%	82%
Willshaw	2%	100%	100%	100%	100%	100%	100%	66%
		k=15						
Outerproduct	32%	0%	0%	0%	0%	0%	0%	0%
True Hebb	0%	0%	0%	4%	22.7%	34.7%	74.7%	82.7%
Willshaw	0%	100%	100%	100%	100%	100%	97.3%	64 %

These results are summarized as follows:

- The Q-state outerproduct rule performed very poorly, except at $Q = 2$, ranking last.
- The Q-state True Hebb rule ranked third, performing significantly better than the outerproduct rule, at large Q. The performance of the True Hebb rule improved monotonically with Q.
- The Q-state Willshaw rule ranked second, performing much better than the True Hebb rule for Q in the middle, between 6 and 40. Interestingly, the performance of the Willshaw rule peaked in this middle range and dropped at $Q = 60$, where it was overtaken by the True Willshaw rule.
- The Q-state Hopfield-clique rule performed the best.

These results are intuitively explained as follows. Let r denote the number of weights w_{ij} whose values change during presentation of a single vector X^μ, divided by the total number of weights in the network. Assume that the number of neurons in the network is fixed at $N = n \times Q$, where n is the length of a Q-state vector. The Q-state outerproduct rule does not exploit the sparseness present in the recoded vectors for large Q. Regardless of the value of Q, r equals 1. The Q-state True Hebbian variant exploits the sparseness to some degree. Upon presentation of a binary recoded vector X^μ, this rule does not change the value of any weight w_{ij} with $X_i^\mu = X_j^\mu = 0$. Thus $r = (\binom{n}{2} + (Q - 1) \times n^2)/\binom{N}{2}$, which decreases as Q increases.

The Q-state Willshaw rule exploits the sparseness the most. For this rule, $r \leq \binom{n}{2}/\binom{N}{2}$ which decreases rapidly as Q increases. This reasoning seems to indicate that the Willshaw rule's performance should improve monotonically as Q increases. That this does not happen, as reported in Table 1, is explained as follows. Upon presentation of a binary recoded vector X^μ, all the one-valued bits in X^μ are stable, as noted in Section 2.3 (also see Proposition 1 in Section 5). Each of the zero-valued bits in X^μ is unstable, however, with some probability p calculated in the appendix (recall that the presented vectors are random). This effect competes with the sparseness one. As Q increases, though r decreases, the number of zero-valued bits in X^μ increases and, eventually, even the probability p of instability of any one such bit increases, thereby increasing the probability of X^μ becoming unstable. Eventually the second effect overtakes the first one, as it did for us at $Q = 60$.

The Q-state Hopfield-clique rule exploits the sparseness to the same degree as the Willshaw rule, and has the same upper bound on r. This rule, furthermore, was designed explicitly to guarantee stability to an arbitrary collection of Q-state vectors.

4.2 Spurious Tests

Stable storage results reveal only one aspect of the effectiveness of an associative memory model. The Q-state Hopfield-clique rule, for example, has the perfect stability property. This by itself is of limited use if a large number of spurious memories are present as well.

This section compares the various Q-state rules on the frequency of recall of a non-spurious stable state from a random initial state. Table 2 presents the results. Binary recodings of the same set of k random Q-state vectors were stored in different networks, one per storage rule. After storage, the same recall process, using asynchronous updates [5], was used on all the networks. The output of the network was checked against the Q-state vectors given for storage.

Table 2: k random Q-state vectors were stored. Five hundred random Q-state vectors were used as test vectors, and the network used in retrieval mode. Each entry records the percentage x of the five hundred tests in which some stored vector was retrieved. Note that $100 - x$ is the percentage of tests in which some spurious memory was retrieved.

Q	2	6	10	20	30	40	60
		k=10					
Outerproduct	0%	0%	0%	0%	0%	0%	0%
True Hebb	0%	0%	0%	14.4%	24%	29.2%	16.4%
Willshaw	0%	2%	2%	2%	2.4%	3.4%	14%
Hopfield-clique	2%	92.5%	97.6%	100%	100%	100%	100%
		k=20					
Outerproduct	0%	0%	0%	0%	0%	0%	0%
True Hebb	0%	0%	0%	0%	17%	23.6%	31.2%
Willshaw	0%	4%	4%	4%	4.8%	6.2%	20.4%
Hopfield-clique	4%	42.4%	85.2%	99.8%	100%	100%	100%
		k=30					
Outerproduct	0%	0%	0%	0%	0%	0%	0%
True Hebb	0%	0%	0%	0%	7.2%	31.6%	45.6%
Willshaw	0%	5.4%	6%	6%	7%	7.2%	24.2%
Hopfield-clique	6%	13.2%	73.2%	99.8%	100%	100%	100%

The results are summarized as follows:

- The Q-state outerproduct rule worked the poorest, retrieving some spurious memory every time.

- The Q-state Willshaw rule worked moderately better, with performance improving with increase in Q. Interestingly, the performance improved with increase in k, across all Q.

- The Q-state True Hebb rule worked moderately better than the Willshaw rule, with performance improving with increase in Q also. Like the Willshaw rule, its performance improved with increase in k, but only at $Q = 60$.

- The Q-state Hopfield-clique rule worked the best. Just like the others, its performance improved with increase in Q. It performed perfectly for $Q \geq 30$.

A qualitative explanation of the broad trends in these results is probably similar to that of the stability results of the previous section. The following argument provides some additional insight into some of the particularly interesting results. For $n = 2$, which occurs at $Q = 60$ in our case, the Hopfield-clique rule provably not only guarantees stable storage but also the non-existence of any spurious memories [7]. This explains the excellent performance in Table 2 of the Hopfield-clique rule, at $Q = 60$. From the analysis in Section 5, one may infer that the Q-state Willshaw rule does not provide such a guarantee. Indeed, if any two Q-state vectors of length 2 share one component with the same value, then a spurious memory develops when the Q-state Willshaw rule is employed for storage. Since in a sequence of presented random Q-state vectors, this event is likely to occur often, several spurious memories are expected to form at $Q = 60$, for the Willshaw rule, explaining why it performs poorly in this case even though the Hopfield-clique rule performs excellently. This argument can probably be adapted to explain why the Hopfield-clique rule performs well for all $Q \geq 20$ in our experiments where as the Willshaw rule does not.

5   Stable Storage Analysis of the Q-state Willshaw Rule

In this section, we analyze the stable storability of Q-state vectors of length n stored via the Q-state Willshaw rule. Our analysis is somewhat similar to that of Palm's [11], who analyzed the stable storage properties of the Willshaw model on the presentation of random binary vectors of length n, each containing exactly k ones. The main difference arises from the fact that our vectors are binary recodings of random Q-state vectors, and though they all contain exactly N/Q ones, they are not the same as random vectors with exactly N/Q ones. In particular, what happens is that though in both cases the one-bits of a presented vector are stable when $\Theta_i := N/Q - 1$, the stability situations of the zero-bits differ. When binary recodings of Q-state vectors are presented, no zero-bit in a presented vector has weights of value 1 with *all* the one-bits in the vector. This is not in general true when arbitrary binary vectors with exactly N/Q ones are presented. Finally, the analysis in [11] is asymptotic without being exact; ours is exact without leading to a closed-form expression.

The necessary and sufficient condition for stability in the Q-state Willshaw rule, refered to in the previous paragraph, is formally described as follows.

Proposition 1 *Let $\mathcal{X} = \langle X^1, \ldots, X^p \rangle$ denote an arbitrary sequence of Q-state vectors of length n stored via the Q-state Willshaw rule, after binary recoding. Let X^μ denote one of these vectors. Then X^μ remains stable after storage of $\mathcal{X}$ if and only if, for every $i \in \{1, \ldots, n\}$, and for every $q : X_i^\mu \neq q$, there exists $j \neq i \in \{1, \ldots, n\}$ such that there does not exist $\gamma \neq \mu$ with $X_j^\gamma = X_j^\mu$ and $X_i^\gamma = q$.*

The proof is omitted. Proposition 1 implies that, for any presented vector X^μ, all one-valued bits in its binary recoding x^μ are stable after storage of $\mathcal{X}$. A zero-valued bit in x^μ is stable if and only if it satisfies the condition of Proposition 1.

The main result, which gives the expected number of unstable bits in a presented vector X^μ when the vectors in the sequence $\mathcal{X}$ are random ones, is as follows.

Proposition 2 *Let k Q-state vectors $X^1, \ldots, X^k$ of length n be sampled randomly with replacement and stored via the Q-state Willshaw rule. Then, for any $\mu \in \{1, \ldots, k\}$, the probability that X^μ is unstable after all vectors are stored is less than or equal to the expected number of bits of X^μ which are unstable, which is*

$$(Q-1) \times n \times (1 - \sum_{m=1}^{n-1} (-1)^{m+1} \binom{n-1}{m} (\frac{(Q-1) \times Q^{n-1} + (Q-1)^m \times Q^{n-m-1}}{Q^n})^{k-1} \qquad (7)$$

The proof is omitted. Table 3 reports numerical values of (7) for different values of Q. The expected number of unstable bits is large at small values of Q, decreases a lot at medium values of Q, and increases somewhat at larger values of Q. These results are consistent with those of Section 4.1 associated with Table 1 and, indeed, serve as an explanation of them.

Table 4 reports simulation experiments on networks, under the same conditions as in Table 3. We see that these results are in close agreement with those of Table 3, except for medium values of Q where there are some discrepancies. The results of Table 4 and Table 3 were arrived at independently, by different authors, without cross-communication during the process.

Table 3: Numerical results on Proposition 2: the expected number of unstable bits in any given stored Q-state vector, that is, an upper bound on the probability that the stored vector is unstable. The number of neurons N is fixed to 120, as in Table 1. The number of states Q is varied, as is k, the number of random Q-state vectors to be stored according to the Q-state Willshaw rule.

k \ Q	2	4	6	10	20	30	40	60
40	59.9	19.9	0.9	0.02	0.008	0.03	0.13	1.27
80	60	77.0	20.0	0.75	0.08	0.14	0.4	2.56
160	60	89.9	81.9	13.5	0.81	0.72	1.28	5.1

Table 4: Simulation experiments on networks, under the same conditions as in Table 4.

k \ Q	2	4	6	10	20	30	40	60
40	59.9	20.3	1.6	1.0	1.0	1.0	1.05	1.67
80	60	76.6	20.0	1.54	1.1	1.03	1.2	2.77
160	60	90.0	81.85	13.8	1.55	1.42	1.87	5.05

6 Conclusions

This paper has introduced several natural Q-state extensions of local storage rules for the binary Hopfield model, all employing a unary recoding of Q-state vectors to binary ones. One of them, the Hopfield-clique rule, guarantees stable storage to arbitrary collections of presented Q-state vectors. Empirically, it has been shown to work well for large Q, better than others evaluated, on recall of non-spurious memories when initialized to random Q-state vectors. The popular outerproduct rule does not work well at all in its Q-state extension, except when Q is very small. The Willshaw rule works well at medium values of Q, but not as well as the Hopfield-clique rule. Finally, though the model employs binary neurons, we call it a Q-state memory model to emphasize that it is designed for storing Q-state vectors.

Further work to consider includes the following. What happens if we employ a *binary* recoding of Q-state vectors to binary ones, i.e. one that represents a Q-value with $\log_2 Q$ bits, for all our storage rules? Clearly, the stability and non-spurious properties of the rules that work well in their unary versions are expected to degrade. The question is by how much?

References

[1] Y.S. Abu-Mostafa and J.S. Jacques. Information capacity of the Hopfield model. *IEEE Transactions on Information Theory*, 31(4):461–464, July 1985.

[2] S. Amari. Characteristics of sparsely encoded associative memory. *Neural Networks*, 2(6):451–457, 1989.

[3] A. Dembo. On the capacity of associative memories with linear threshold functions. *IEEE Transactions on Information Theory*, 35(4):709–720, 1989.

[4] J. Hertz, A. Krogh, and R.G. Palmer. *Introduction to the Theory of Neural Computation*. Addison-Wesley, 1991.

[5] J.J. Hopfield. Neural networks and physical systems with emergent collective computational abilities. *Proceedings of the National Academy of Sciences, USA*, 79, 1982.

[6] A. Jagota. Applying a Hopfield-style network to degraded text recognition. In *International Joint Conference on Neural Networks*, volume 1, pages 27–32, New York, 1990. San Diego, July, IEEE.

[7] A. Jagota. A Hopfield-style network with a graph-theoretic characterization. *Journal of Artificial Neural Networks*, 1(1):145–166, 1994.

[8] J.D. Keeler. Capacity for patterns and sequences in Kanerva's SDM as compared to other associative memory models. Technical report, Research Institute for Advanced Computer Science: RIACS TR 87.29, NASA Ames Research Center, 1987.

[9] G.A. Kohring. On the problems of neural networks with multi-state neurons. *Journal De Physique I*, 2:1549–1552, August 1992.

[10] R.J. McEliece, E.C. Posner, E.R. Rodemich, and S.S. Venkatesh. The capacity of the Hopfield associative memory. *IEEE Transactions on Information Theory*, 33:461–482, 1987.

[11] G. Palm. On associative memory. *Biological Cybernetics*, 36:19–31, 1980.

[12] H. Rieger. Storing an extensive number of grey-toned patterns in a neural network using multi-state neurons. *Journal of Physics A*, 23:L1273–L1280, 1990.

[13] J. Spencer. Random graphs ii. In J. Spencer, editor, *Ten Lectures on the Probabilistic Method*, chapter 7, pages 51–56. Society for Industrial and Applied Mathematics, Philadelphia, Pennsylvania, 1987.

[14] D.J. Willshaw, O.P. Buneman, and H.C. Longuet-Higgins. Non-holographic associative memory. *Nature*, 222, 1969.

Pipeline Redundancy Implementation of the Theorem of Fault Tolerance Associative Memory

Pirawat Watanapongse[†‡], Harold H. Szu[†], Chidchanok Lursinsap[§]

† Center for Advanced Computer Studies
The University of Southwestern Louisiana
Lafayette, LA 70504, USA
E-mail: hszu@cacs.usl.edu.

‡ Department of Computer Engineering, Faculty of Engineering
Kasetsart University
Bangkaen, Bangkok 10903, THAILAND
E-mail: pw@cpe.ku.ac.th.

§ Department of Mathematics, Faculty of Science
Chulalongkorn University
Patumwan, Bangkok 10330, THAILAND
E-mail: lchidcha@netserv.chula.ac.th.

Abstract— Two issues in Associative Memory systems are investigated: We try to make the systems themselves inherently noise-tolerant by first investigate the use of *Eigenmemory System* as an auto-associative memory and extend it for the case of hetero-associative memory. We found it to have the maximum memory capacity and angular fault tolerance. Then, we identify the computation "hot spot" in the inner product operation of the neurons themselves. Therefore we propose a parallel pipelined implementation of the modified inner product algorithm in the fashion of Triple Modular Redundancy, realizable in hardware. We call it *Vote-Sum-Crosscheck(VSC)* algorithm.

1   Introduction

Artificial Neural Networks units commonly used today are almost all based on the classical McCulloch-Pitts model[1, 2] defined by Equations (1)-(3)

$$v_i = \sigma(u_i - \theta_i) \tag{1}$$

$$\sigma(u_i) = \frac{1}{1 + \exp(-u_i)} \tag{2}$$

$$u_i = \sum_j w_{ij} v_j \tag{3}$$

v_i is the output signal of neuron i

$\sigma(u_i)$ is nonlinear sigmoid activation function[2, 3]

u_i is the net input which is the weighted sum of output signals v_j of other neurons j.

θ_i is threshold/bias value— depending on the sign—of neuron i which can be thought of as providing point-wise or local fault tolerance as oppose to distributed fault tolerance that will be discussed within this paper in term of w_{ij}.

w_{ij} are weights, or connection strengths, between neuron i and all other neurons j, usually excluding itself, that are connected to it.

To build an efficient Neural Networks Classifier, maximum memory capacity as well as inherent tolerance against "misclassification" are desirable properties. Eigenstate Associative Memory, or *Eigenmemory system(EM)*, possesses both characteristics. It is defined as the memory, or weights matrix, consists of c orthonormal *eigenvector, or feature axes* representing c distinct "features" or classes of the inputs. Such system can be summarized by Equations (4)-(8)

$$[M_i] = |e_i >< e_i| \tag{4}$$

$$< e_i|e_j > = \delta_{ij} = \begin{cases} 1 & \text{if } i = j \\ 0 & \text{if } i \neq j \end{cases} \tag{5}$$

$$m_{ii} = 0 \tag{6}$$

$$[\text{EM}] \;=\; \sum_{i=1}^{c} [M_i] \tag{7}$$

$$[\text{EM}] \cdot e_i \;=\; \lambda_i \cdot e_i \tag{8}$$

$[M_i]$ is a memory, or weight matrix, of feature i

e_i and e_j are an eigenvectors representing features i and j, respectively

$| >< |$ is Dirac's bracket notation denotes outer-product operation

$< | >$ is Dirac's bracket notation denotes inner-product operation

δ_{ij} is the Kronecker Delta function

m_{ii} are all diagonal terms in matrix M_i

$[\text{EM}]$ is an eigenstate matrix: the super-imposition of all c $[M]$ weight matrices computed from Equation (4) and (6)

λ_i is the ith eigenvalue of the matrix $[\text{EM}]$ which relates to the depth of energy landscape

Being a real, symmetric auto-associative memory matrix, orthogonality between all eigenvectors in $[\text{EM}]$ are guaranteed[4]. Furthermore, memory capacity of the Eigenmemory is 100% (i.e., the number of features stored are equal to the number of bits used) compare to approximately 15% when using randomly generated pseudo-orthonormal vectors as in Hopfield Networks[5, 6].

2 Angular Fault Tolerance Associative Memory

Eigenmemory "recalls" by projecting incoming input onto feature axis. Thus, each input vector u can be viewed as consist of 2 components:

$$u \;=\; u_{\|i} + u_{\perp i} \;=\; u_{\|i} + \sum_{i \neq j} u_{\|j} \tag{9}$$

u is an input vector

$u_{\|i}$ and $u_{\|j}$ are vector components of u that parallel to feature axis i and j, respectively

$u_{\perp i}$ is the vector component of u that is perpendicular to feature axis i

By discarding the perpendicular term in Equation (9), we "polarize" the input vector into the direction of the feature, thus providing fault tolerance by means of angular error-correction[7]. Still, condition analogy to old expression "someone's trash is the other's jewel" can occur in the sense that, if input vector is angularly so far apart from the desired axis, then the perpendicular term—which is equivalent to the parallel term on other undesired axes—will outweigh the parallel term, producing incorrect output. In other word, according to Equation (9), the only time misclassification can occur is when input vector is more parallel to undesirable feature axis than the desirable one. For example, input vector u supposes to be in class i but somehow has $u_{\|j} > u_{\|i}$, then Eigenmemory will answer input vector u as belonging to feature j; the wrong answer. However, Eigenmemory system provides the maximum fault tolerance in those condition, as stated in Theorem 1:

Theorem 1 *Eigenmemory system achieves maximum degree of fault tolerance, which is 50% for scalar fault tolerance, or 45 degree in term of angular fault tolerance*

Proof By defining degree of fault tolerance $= \|u_\perp\|/\|u\|$, error will occur when $\|u_\||\| \leq \|u_\perp\|$, thus the degree of fault tolerance of Eigenmemory is 50% or translate into angular fault tolerance of 45 degree, which is the maximum for orthonormal system. Figure 1 illustrates both the concept of polarization and maximum fault tolerance by means of geometrical interpretation.

To bring the advantage of Eigenmemory into the hetero-associative memory, we try to derive weight matrix W in terms of $[\text{EM}]$

$$[W] \;=\; \sum_{i=1}^{p} |v_i >< u_i| \;=\; \sum_{i=1}^{p} I|v_i >< u_i|I \;=\; \sum_{k=1}^{c}\sum_{j=1}^{c}\sum_{i=1}^{p} |e_j >< e_j|v_i >< u_i|e_k >< e_k|$$

$$=\; \sum_{k}\sum_{j}\sum_{i=1}^{p} |e_j >< v_{\|j}|u_{\|k} >< e_k| \tag{10}$$

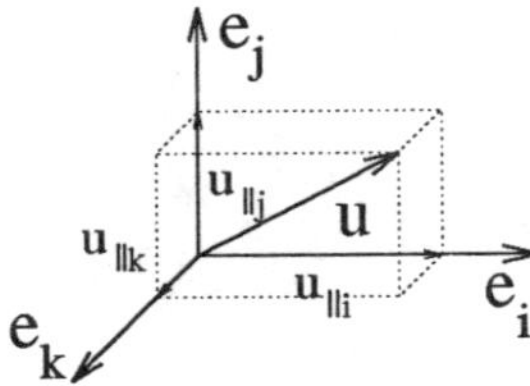

Figure 1: Data Hyperspace of the Eigenmemory with 3 eigenvectors, capable of classifying 3 "features". Notice that the component $u_{\parallel i}$ is the longest among all axis projections. If input vector u in fact belongs to axis (or feature) j, however, this Eigenmemory will give the wrong answer.

[W] is the hetero-associative memory matrix
v^i is the memorized response (or output) for pattern i
u^i is the stimulus (or input) for pattern i
e_j and e_k are eigenvectors associate with feature j and k, respectively
I is an identity matrix

3   Parallel Pipeline Fault Tolerance Computation

From Equation (3) and (10), it is quite clear that the heaviest calculations for those NN units centers around the inner product between weight matrix and inputs vectors. It also points out that this would be the most likely place where fault due to miscalculation will occur. Now let us, for a moment, take a look at scalar multiplication. Normally, there is no fault-tolerance aspect built-in to such operation. For example, let variables a and b equal to 9 and 6, respectively, and c is a result of the multiplication.

$$
\begin{aligned}
a \cdot b &= c \\
9 \cdot 6 &= 54
\end{aligned}
\tag{11}
$$

However, scalar value can be expressed as *additive vector*. For the sake of clarity, we will limit the number of elements of vector to 3, although any odd number of elements can be used. Therefore, a and b become $(a_1 + a_2 + a_3)$ and $(b_1 + b_2 + b_3)$, respectively. Together with Distributive Law, the Equation (11) now looks very much like the outer product between 2 additive vectors, forming a resulting *additive matrix*

$$
a \cdot b =
\begin{pmatrix} a_1 \\ + \\ a_2 \\ + \\ a_3 \end{pmatrix} \cdot (b_1 + b_2 + b_3) =
\begin{pmatrix} 3 \\ + \\ 3 \\ + \\ 3 \end{pmatrix} \cdot (2+2+2) =
\begin{pmatrix} 6 & + & 6 & + & 6 \\ + & & + & & + \\ 6 & + & 6 & + & 6 \\ + & & + & & + \\ 6 & + & 6 & + & 6 \end{pmatrix}
\tag{12}
$$

$$
= (18+18+18) = 54
$$

Notice that the different between plus symbols $+$ and $+$ represents 2 distinct views of how to apply the distribute law: as sum-of-column or sum-of-row.

Equation (12) can be further generalized to compute more than 1 pair of scalar numbers at the same time. Let a, b, c, and d be 4 scalar variables with value of 9, 6, 3, and 3, respectively. With the scalar expansion, the expression $a \cdot b + c \cdot d = 9 \cdot 6 + 3 \cdot 3$ is equal to

$$
\begin{pmatrix} 3 & 1 \\ + & + \\ 3 & 1 \\ + & + \\ 3 & 1 \end{pmatrix} \cdot
\begin{pmatrix} 2 & + & 2 & + & 2 \\ 1 & + & 1 & + & 1 \end{pmatrix} =
\begin{pmatrix}
(3\cdot2+1\cdot1) & + & (3\cdot2+1\cdot1) & + & (3\cdot2+1\cdot1) \\
+ & & + & & + \\
(3\cdot2+1\cdot1) & + & (3\cdot2+1\cdot1) & + & (3\cdot2+1\cdot1) \\
+ & & + & & + \\
(3\cdot2+1\cdot1) & + & (3\cdot2+1\cdot1) & + & (3\cdot2+1\cdot1)
\end{pmatrix}
\tag{13}
$$

The similarity between Equation (13) and (3) is inescapable, thus the following equation:

$$h = \begin{pmatrix} \sum \frac{w}{n}\frac{u}{n} & + \underbrace{\cdots}_{n-2} + & \sum \frac{w}{n}\frac{u}{n} \\ + & & + \\ \vdots & \ddots & \vdots \\ + & & + \\ \sum \frac{w}{n}\frac{u}{n} & + \underbrace{\cdots}_{n-2} + & \sum \frac{w}{n}\frac{u}{n} \end{pmatrix} \tag{14}$$

where n is the number of elements in the additive vector that will represent the original scalar values. By split the initial scalar values into n independent elements, we exploit the full potential of pipelined, parallel processing aspect of the inner-product units currently in common use.

From Equation (14), we can then use the most simple technique of checking the row-sum against column-sum of the matrix to verify the integrity of the computation, or employ various types of fault-tolerance inner-product units, such as *REcomputing with Triplication With Voting (RETVW)* method[8] to increase fault-tolerance.

4   Fault Tolerance Through Redundancy

In order to achieve fault tolerance, some form of redundancy must be presented, whether it be additional hardware (hardware redundancy), additional codes (software redundancy), extra data (information redundancy), multiple execution of code on the same hardware (time redundancy), or the combination of the above.

Of all the techniques that provide fault tolerance, *triple modular redundancy(TMR)* or voting method, is one of the most popular due to its relative ease of understanding and implementation. However, TMR suffers from the possibility that the majority of the results might be wrong, the condition not rare enough for some critical computation.

We propose a new technique that would improve the error detection capability of the TMR method even further without prohibitively large investment in additional hardwares and computation time, since we use the combination of both redundant hardware and computation to achieve that effect. We call this new technique *Vote-Sum-Crosscheck(VSC)* algorithm.

5   Vote-Sum-Crosscheck Algorithm

The algorithm for the proposed VSC method is as follows:

1. divide each input data into 3 identical partial inputs

2. perform dot-product on partial inputs

3. perform voting method among partial results from (2). if successful, go to (3a). if not, go to (1)

 (a) multiply voting result from (3) by three.

4. perform summation on partial results from (2)

5. if result from (3a) and (4) agree, stop. if not, go to (1)

The block diagram of the pipelined inner product unit is shown in Figure 2. The reason that this technique can achieve better fault tolerance compare to voting method is that by dividing input data into 3 identical *partial inputs*, we in essence provide additional information inherent to the data itself by form of recoding, and those additional data can be used in aid of reconstruction of the original data.

Table 1 list all possible cases of errors that can occur in 3-way voting method. First column shows the partial results with appropriate error attached. Second column shows the result of voting method applied to those partial outputs. Third column shows the result, with accumulated errors, *if* the voting method alone is to be used and the voting result is simply multiplied by 3. Fourth column shows the result if we simply sum up all the partial results with their associated errors. Last column show the cases in which

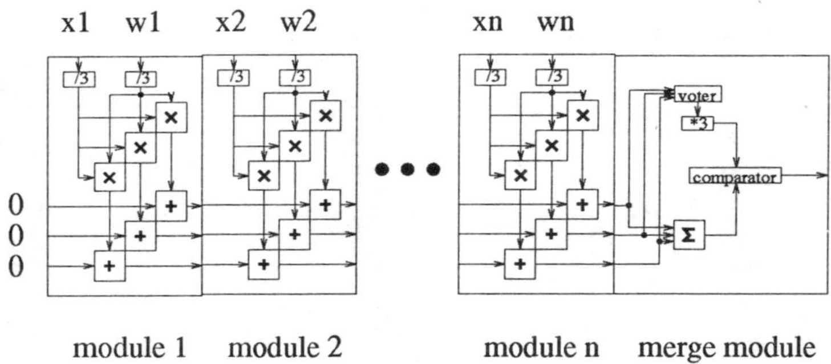

Figure 2: Block diagram of the VSC pipelined inner product unit

result from voting and summation methods are in agreement. Notice that Table 1 does not take into consideration the fact that the probability of having error in one or more partial results is small, and thus each row in the table should not be interpreted as happening equally frequently. It is clear that there is only 2 chances in 27 possible cases that the cross-check between the voting and summation method still let the incorrect result slip through, as oppose to 14 in 27 cases and 20 in 27 cases when using the voting or summation method alone, respectively.

6   Error Performance Analysis

As stated in previous section and in Table 1, our algorithm is proven to be better than using TMR method alone. However, that prove is limited only for the case of the 3-values systems—correct result x, error result $x + \delta$, and error result $x - \delta$. Therefore, we extend the proof to cover the general case for situation where the output value—correct value plus error— of each computation units are not known, stronger prove must be supplied to guarantee that our algorithm will not let the error through. First, we

Lemma 1 *3-way VSC algorithm consists of 3 partial computation units will yield the result if and only if partial results from* all *3 partial computation units are identical*

Proof Let x be correct partial result, ε_1 be the majority error, ε_2 be the minority error

In order to pass the voting process, there must be at least 2 partial results that carry ε_1. To pass VSC algorithm, the final result obtained from both voting and summation process must agree, thus

$$\begin{aligned}
\text{result from voting process} \quad &= \quad \text{result from summation process} \\
3(x + \varepsilon_1) \quad &= \quad (x + \varepsilon_1) + (x + \varepsilon_1) + (x + \varepsilon_2) \\
\varepsilon_1 \quad &= \quad \varepsilon_2
\end{aligned}$$

If $\varepsilon=0$ —there is no error—then the result from the algorithm will be correct. If not, the algorithm will yield incorrect result plus 3ε, as shown in column 4 and 5 of Table 1. Provided that such possibility is extremely remote, the possibility of letting error result slip through is negligible.

7   Conclusion

Associative Memories, by design, are already distributed parallel processing systems that behave like a voting committee in a sense that individual errors are masked out by the collective effort of the rest of the system. By using Eigenmemory which implies orthogonality, we make sure that those committee members do not have a hidden agenda (i.e., favor towards particular feature). We also strengthen each neuron against miscalculation by replacing inner product computation with our *Vote-Sum-Crosscheck* algorithm. Although demonstrated with 3-way units for clarity, it can be derived for all odd-number partial units.

References

[1] W. S. McCulloch and W. Pitts, "A Logical Calculus of the Ideas Immanent in Nervous Activity," *Bulletin of Mathematical Biophysics*, vol. 5, pp. 115–133, 1943.

multiplication partial results			vote	result by vote	result by sum	cross-check agree?
$x-\delta$	$x-\delta$	$x-\delta$	$x-\delta$	$3x-3\delta$	$3x-3\delta$	yes ($\times$)
$x-\delta$	$x-\delta$	x	$x-\delta$	$3x-3\delta$	$3x-2\delta$	
$x-\delta$	$x-\delta$	$x+\delta$	$x-\delta$	$3x-3\delta$	$3x-\delta$	
$x-\delta$	x	$x-\delta$	$x-\delta$	$3x-3\delta$	$3x-2\delta$	
$x-\delta$	x	x	x	$3x$	$3x-\delta$	
$x-\delta$	x	$x+\delta$	No Majority	—	$3x$	
$x-\delta$	$x+\delta$	$x-\delta$	$x-\delta$	$3x-3\delta$	$3x-\delta$	
$x-\delta$	$x+\delta$	x	No Majority	—	$3x$	
$x-\delta$	$x+\delta$	$x+\delta$	$x+\delta$	$3x+3\delta$	$3x-\delta$	
x	$x-\delta$	$x-\delta$	$x-\delta$	$3x-3\delta$	$3x-2\delta$	
x	$x-\delta$	x	x	$3x$	$3x-\delta$	
x	$x-\delta$	$x+\delta$	No Majority	—	$3x$	
x	x	$x-\delta$	x	$3x$	$3x-\delta$	
x	x	x	x	$3x$	$3x$	yes ($\surd$)
x	x	$x+\delta$	x	$3x$	$3x+\delta$	
x	$x+\delta$	$x-\delta$	No Majority	$3x$	$3x$	
x	$x+\delta$	x	x	$3x$	$3x+\delta$	
x	$x+\delta$	$x+\delta$	$x+\delta$	$3x+3\delta$	$3x+2\delta$	
$x+\delta$	$x-\delta$	$x-\delta$	$x-\delta$	$3x-3\delta$	$3x-\delta$	
$x+\delta$	$x-\delta$	x	No Majority	—	$3x$	
$x+\delta$	$x-\delta$	$x+\delta$	$x+\delta$	$3x+3\delta$	$3x+\delta$	
$x+\delta$	x	$x-\delta$	No Majority	—	$3x$	
$x+\delta$	x	x	x	$3x$	$3x+\delta$	
$x+\delta$	x	$x+\delta$	$x+\delta$	$3x+3\delta$	$3x+2\delta$	
$x+\delta$	$x+\delta$	$x-\delta$	$x+\delta$	$3x+3\delta$	$3x+\delta$	
$x+\delta$	$x+\delta$	x	$x+\delta$	$3x+3\delta$	$3x+2\delta$	
$x+\delta$	$x+\delta$	$x+\delta$	$x+\delta$	$3x+3\delta$	$3x+3\delta$	yes ($\times$)

Table 1: Exhaustive State Space Analysis of fault tolerance for cases with exactly 3 possible error values for each partial computation units $\{\delta, 0, -\delta\}$. x and $3x$ are expected output of the partial units(column 1) and result after voting process(column 3), respectively.

[2] J. Hertz, A. Krogh, and R. G. Palmer, *Introduction to the Theory of Neural Computation*, vol. 1 of *Santa Fe Institute Lecture Note Series*. Reading, Massachusetts: Addison-Wesley Publishing Company, 1991.

[3] S. Haykin, *Neural Networks: A Comprehensive Foundation*. Los Alamitos, California: IEEE Computer Society Press, 1994.

[4] H. H. Szu, "Three layers of vector outer product neural networks for optical pattern recognition," in *Optical Hybrid Computing* (H. H. Szu, ed.), vol. 634 of *Advanced Optical Technologies Series*, pp. 312–330, SPIE, 1986.

[5] H. H. Szu and J. Tan, "Can Associative Memory Recognize Characters?," in *U.S. Postal Service Advanced Technology Conference*, vol. 2, pp. 1003–1017, 1988.

[6] J. J. Hopfield, "Neural networks and physical systems with emergent collective computational abilities," in *Proceedings of the National Academy of Science*, vol. 79, pp. 2554–2558, The National Academy of Science, 1982.

[7] K. Scheff and H. H. Szu, "Gram-schmidt orthogonalization neural networks for optical character recognition," *Journal of Neural Network Computing*, vol. 2, pp. 5–13, winter 1990.

[8] Y.-M. Hsu, V. Piuri, and E. E. Swartzlander, Jr., "Efficient time redundancy for error correcting inner-product units and convolvers," in *1995 Proceedings of the IEEE International Workshop on Defect and Fault Tolerance in VLSI Systems (DFT'95)—Lafayette, Louisiana*, pp. 198–206, 1995.

Learning Rules of Neural Networks using Time Difference Simultaneous Perturbation

Yutaka Maeda and Yakichi Kanata

Kansai University, Faculty of Engineering,

Department of Electrical Engineering

3-3-35, Yamate-cho, Suita, Osaka 564 JAPAN

maedayut@kansai-u.ac.jp

ABSTRACT

Learning scheme is very important in neural networks to take advantage of their flexibility. Usually, the backpropagation method is widely used as a learning rule of neural networks. The backpropagation needs so-called error back propagation to update weights.

In this paper, we propose learning rules using time difference simultaneous perturbation. The learning rules need only one forward operation of networks. Thus, without complicated calculation of gradient of an error function, these can update the all weights. Therefore, application of this learning rule to many problems is very easy. Moreover, the learning rules are easy to realize as a neural network circuit as well.

1   Introduction

Learning ability is one of our great expectations to neural networks (NNs). When we make use of this ability, learning scheme is imperative. Usually, the backpropagation method (BP) is widely used as a learning rule of NNs. Moreover, it is well-known that the BP is a gradient method. The BP calculates the first differential coefficient of an error function with respect to weights in a network. Then, so-called the error-back-propagation has an important role. This gives the first differential coefficient analytically.

On the other hand, the finite difference gives an estimated value of the first differential coefficient by the difference approximation. There is no need to do the error-back-propagation. We use two values of the error function; one is a value when we added a small perturbation to a certain weight, the other is a value without the perturbation. Using the difference approximation, viz., dividing a difference of these two values by a magnitude of the perturbation, we can obtain an estimation of the first differential coefficient with respect to the weight. Repeating this procedure for all weights, we can modify the weights of the NN[1]. This technique has a crucial disadvantage. If the NN is large, the number of the weights is large. This means that we have to repeat that procedure so often to update all weights[1].

The simultaneous perturbation (SP) technique overcomes this problem. Instead adding the perturbation to all weights one by one, we add the perturbations to all weights simultaneously. Magnitude of the perturbation is different for different weight. Then we can obtain estimated values of the first differential coefficients with respect to all weights as same as the finite difference. In this technique, only two values of the error function are required to obtain modifying quantities corresponding to all weights, even if the NN is large.

The SP method was proposed by J. C. Spall[2,3,4]. Independently, the author proposed the identical scheme of learning rule of NNs[5,6]. J. Alespector et al. also reported the same learning rule[7]. Furthermore, some applications of this learning rule are reported[5,8,9,10]. The author also fabricated an NN circuit using this learning rule and showed a viability of this learning rule[6].

However, the SP technique uses two values of the error function under the same condition except existence or non-existence of the perturbation. In some applications, e.g. on-line control of dynamical systems like chemical process or robot manipulator, it is difficult to obtain these two values under a quite same condition, because the state of the plant is changing constantly. We need new method to solve this issue.

From this point of view, we have proposed a time difference simultaneous perturbation technique[11]. We have a comparison of this method for an optimization problem[11]. This technique utilize a difference of two values of the error function; a value at a time and one at the previous time. At the same time, we add perturbations to all weights every iteration. We apply the SP using these two values of the error function and the perturbations. In this sense, we are employing the SP technique and the difference of the values of the error function between a time and the previous time.

In Chapter 2, we introduce the time difference simultaneous perturbation learning rule and examine a property of the rule. In Chapter 3, some numerical examples are shown to know an ability of the learning rule.

2 Time difference simultaneous perturbation

Now, we consider a NN with n weights including thresholds. Then, $w_t \in \Re^n$ denotes the weight vector at t-th iteration.

$$w_{t+1} = w_t - \alpha \Delta w_t + c_t S_t \tag{1}$$

$$\Delta w_{t,i} = \begin{cases} \Delta w_{\max} & \text{if } \dfrac{J(w_t) - J(w_{t-1})}{\left(c_{t-1,i} S_{t-1,i}\right)} > \Delta w_{\max} \\[2ex] -\Delta w_{\max} & \text{if } \dfrac{J(w_t) - J(w_{t-1})}{\left(c_{t-1,i} S_{t-1,i}\right)} < -\Delta w_{\max} \\[2ex] \dfrac{J(w_t) - J(w_{t-1})}{\left(c_{t-1,i} S_{t-1,i}\right)} & \text{if else} \end{cases} \tag{2}$$

where, $\Delta w_{t,i}$ denotes the i-th component of the vector Δw_t. α is a positive coefficient. $\Delta w_{\max}$ restricts maximum quantity of modification. S_t is a diagonal sign matrix. $s_{t-1,i}$ represents the i-i component of the matrix S_t. These components are +1 or -1 and the other components of the matrix are all zero. Furthermore, $E(s_{t-1,i})=0$ and $E(s_{t-1,i} s_{t-1,j})=0(i \neq j)$. $c_{t-1,i} (>0)$, which is a component of the vector c_t, denotes a magnitude of the perturbation. These are generated randomly on $[c_{\min} \quad c_{\max}]$. By means of the term $c_t S_t$, random perturbation $+c_{t,i}$ or $-c_{t,i}$ are added to all weights. The perturbations are different in a different weight.

In (1), the vector Δw_t means an estimated gradient vector derived from the second procedure (2). Perturbations are added to all weights simultaneously by the third term of (1). Since expectation of the sign matrix is zero, the weight w_t is updated only by the second term in the sense of expectation.

In (2), a difference of the values of the function at time t and time $(t-1)$ is divided by the magnitude of the perturbation. This gives an estimated gradient. However, $J(w_t)$ includes an effect of Δw_{t-1}. When we expand $J(w_t)$ at w_{t-1}, there exists w_m such that

$$J(w_t) = J(w_{t-1}) - \left(\alpha \Delta w_{t-1} - c_{t-1} S_{t-1}\right)^T J'(w_{t-1})$$
$$+ \left(\alpha \Delta w_{t-1} - c_{t-1} S_{t-1}\right)^T J''(w_m)\left(\alpha \Delta w_{t-1} - c_{t-1} S_{t-1}\right) \tag{3}$$

```
begin
    •Measure a value of the error function J(w_t).
    •Subtract the value J(w_t) from the previous value of J(w_{t-1}).
      (* Obtain time difference of the error function *)
      for i:=1 to n do
        begin
          •Multiply the time difference by αs_{t-1,i}/c_{t-1,i}
            (* αΔw_{t,i} *)
          •Generate new sign randomly. (* s_{t,i} *)
          •Generate new perturbation randomly. (* c_{t,i} *)
          •Add the perturbation to αΔw_{t,i}. (* αΔw_{t,i} +c_{t,i}s_{t,i} *)
          •Update the parameter.
        end;
    •Renew the iteration (* t =t +1 *)
end.
```

Figure 1 Procedure of the learning rule.

Therefore, since $s_{t-1,i}=\pm1$, we have

$$\Delta w_{t,i} = \frac{J(w_t) - J(w_{t-1})}{c_{t-1,i}} s_{t-1,i} = \frac{\left(\alpha\Delta w_{t-1} + c_{t-1}S_{t-1}\right)^T J'(w_{t-1})}{c_{t-1,i}} s_{t-1,i}$$

$$+ \frac{\left(\alpha\Delta w_{t-1} + c_{t-1}S_{t-1}\right)^T J''(w_m)\left(\alpha\Delta w_{t-1} + c_{t-1}S_{t-1}\right)}{c_{t-1,i}} s_{t-1,i}$$

$$= \frac{\left(\alpha\Delta w_{t-1,1} + c_{t-1,1}s_{t-1,1}\right)}{c_{t-1,i}} s_{t-1,i} J_1'(w_{t-1})$$

$$+\cdots+ \frac{\left(\alpha\Delta w_{t-1,i} + c_{t-1,i}s_{t-1,i}\right)}{c_{t-1,i}} s_{t-1,i} J_i'(w_{t-1})$$

$$+\cdots+ \frac{\left(\alpha\Delta w_{t-1,n} + c_{t-1,n}s_{t-1,n}\right)}{c_{t-1,i}} s_{t-1,i} J_n'(w_{t-1})$$

$$+ \frac{\left(\alpha\Delta w_{t-1} + c_{t-1}S_{t-1}\right)^T J''(w_m)\left(\alpha\Delta w_{t-1} + c_{t-1}S_{t-1}\right)}{c_{t-1,i}} s_{t-1,i}$$

$$(4)$$

where, $J_i'(w_{t-1}) = \partial J(w_{t-1}) \Big/ \partial w_{t-1,i}$. Since $\mathrm{E}(s_{t-1,i}\, s_{t-1,j})=0$ for different i and j, taking expectation of (4) yields

$$E\left(\Delta w_{t,i}\right) = J_i'(w_{t-1}) \tag{5}$$

That is, the modifying vector Δw_t is the gradient of the function in the sense of the expectation. In other words, we can find this procedure a stochastic gradient method as same as the SP method.

The previous learning rule utilized only one estimated gradient of the error function via time difference. However, this estimated value would contain too much noise, compared with these via the finite difference or the ordinary SP technique. This will result slow convergence. Thus, we have to deliberate improving this point. Averaging these estimated values decreases this noise effect. However, since one merit of the learning rule is that the rule requires only one observation unlike the SP learning rule, if we average these based on observations of the error function at a same weight, this ruins the advantage.

Thus, we average past several estimated gradient of the error function. We need only one observation for every iteration in this scheme as well. We can reduce the noise effect without losing the advantage of our new learning rule. The learning rule is described as the following equations (6) and (7).

$$\Delta w_{t,i} = \begin{cases} \Delta w_{\max} & \text{if } \Delta a_t > \Delta w_{\max} \\ -\Delta w_{\max} & \text{if } \Delta a_t < -\Delta w_{\max} \\ \Delta a_t & \text{if else} \end{cases} \tag{6}$$

$$\Delta a_t = \sum_{k=t}^{t-\lambda+1} \frac{J(w_k) - J(w_{k-1})}{\left(c_{k-1,i}s_{k-1,i}\right)} \tag{7}$$

λ denotes a number of averaging. Instead Eq.(2), we can use Eqs.(6) and (7) with averaging.

Table 1 Convergence rate and average epoch

	Convergence rate(%)	Average epoch
Learning rule by SP[6](α=0.8,c=0.2. see [6])	66.0	9492
Learning rule by Time Difference Simultaneous Perturbation	2.0	42860
Learning rule by Time Difference Simultaneous Perturbation with five averaging (λ=5)	52.0	57566
Learning rule by Time Difference Simultaneous Perturbation with ten averaging (λ=10)	64.0	53460

3   Examples

In order to confirm a feasibility of the learning rules, we use these learning rules of NNs to the exclusive OR problem.

The exclusive OR problem is a kind of benchmark to know an ability of learning rules. NN used here is three layer feedforward network with two neurons in the hidden layer. The activation function of the neurons is sigmoid function except the input layer. The input layer is linear.

Table 1 shows results of simulations of the proposed learning rules for the exclusive OR problem.

Convergence rate in this table means rate of trials in which the error function arrived at the value 0.1 or less. Trial number is 50 times. Initial values of all weights and thresholds of the NN were generated randomly on [-1.0 1.0].

In these simulations, α is 0.005. The maximum of modification for weights Δw_{max} is 0.1. c_{min}=0.0001, c_{max}=0.001, that is, $0.0001 \leq c_{t,i} \leq 0.001$. These values were determined empirically. The weights in the network were updated every sample set. Since the exclusive OR comprises four patterns, we accumulated modifying

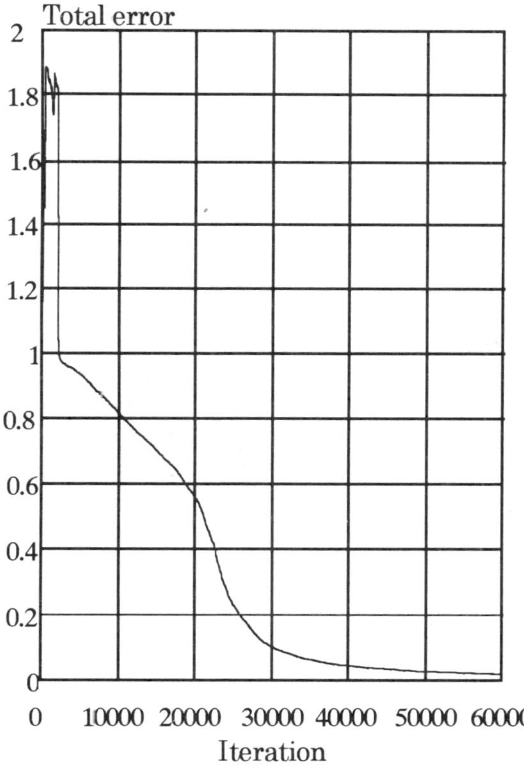

Figure 2 Time difference simultaneous perturbation learning rule with five averaging.

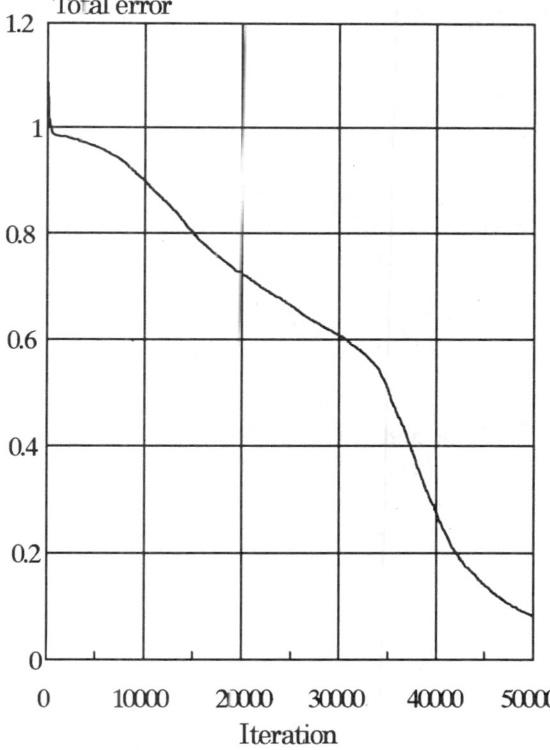

Figure 3 Time difference simultaneous perturbation learning rule with ten averaging.

quantities for these four patterns, then we updated the weights. These presentation of four patterns is referred to as epoch.

If the value of the total error function arrived at 0.1 or less, we found this trial successful. Moreover, if epoch was greater than 100,000, we stopped the trial.

Figure 2 shows a change of the total error function for this problem by the time difference simultaneous perturbation learning rule with five averaging. Figure 3 shows a similar result with ten averaging. The total error decreases as iteration increases. The network using the time difference simultaneous perturbation learning rule learns the exclusive OR relation.

If the averaging number increases, noise effect included in each estimation of the first differential coefficient of the error function decreases. Thus, this would avoids reckless modification of weights.

Compared with the ordinary SP learning rule or the BP method, convergence speed of this learning rule is slow. As we described before, perturbations are superimposed on the modifying quantities of weights all the time. This is compulsory to obtain the estimated first differential coefficient at the next iteration. At the same time, this disturbs the exact modification of the weights at the iteration. Adjusting the coefficients α, c_{max} and c_{min} , we can control them.

4   Conclusion

In this paper, we proposed the learning rules of NNs using the time difference simultaneous perturbation. This learning rules require only once forward operation of a network to obtain modifying quantities corresponding to all weights in the network. Numerical results of the learning rules for the exclusive OR problem were shown. These types of learning rules are very simple in their realization. Therefore, we can expect applications of the rules in many fields.

References

[1] Y.Maeda, H.Yamashita and Y.Kanata: 'Learning rules for multilayer neural networks using difference approximation', *Proceedings of IJCNN Singapore*, **1**, 1991, pp.628-633

[2] J.C.Spall:'A stochastic approximation technique for generating maximum likelihood parameter estimates', Proc. of the 1987 American Control Conference, 1987, pp.1161-1167

[3] J.C.Spall:'A stochastic approximation algorithm for large-dimensional systems in the Kiefer-Wolfowitz setting', *Proc. of the 27th IEEE Conference on Decision and Control*, 1988, pp.1544-1548

[4] J.C.Spall:'Multivariable stochastic approximation using a simultaneous perturbation gradient approximation', *IEEE Trans.*, **AC-37**, 1992, pp.332-341

[5] Y.Maeda and Y.Kanata:'Learning rules for recurrent neural networks using perturbation and their application to neuro-control', *Trans. of the Institute of Electrical Engineers of Japan*, **113-C**, 1993, pp.402-408 (in Japanese)

[6] Y.Maeda, H.Hirano and Y.Kanata:'A learning rule of neural networks via simultaneous perturbation and its hardware implementation', *Neural Networks*, **8**, 1995, pp.251-259

[7] J.Alspector, R.Meir, B.Yuhas, A.Jayakumar and D.Lippe:'A parallel gradient descent method for learning in analog VLSI neural networks', in S.J.Hanson, J.D.Cowan and C.Lee(eds.), *Advances in neural information processing systems 5*, 1993, pp.836-844, San Mateo, CA, Morgan Kaufmann Publisher

[8] J.C.Spall and J.A.Cristion:'Nonlinear adaptive control using neural networks : Estimation with a smoothed form of simultaneous perturbation gradient approximation', *Statistica Sinica*, **4**, 1994, pp.1-27

[9] J.C.Spall and D.C.Chin:'A model-free approach to optimal signal light timing for system-wide traffic control', *Proc. of the 1994 IEEE Conference on Decision and Control*, 1994, pp.1868-1875

[10] Y.Maeda and Y.Kanata:'A learning rule of neural networks for neuro-controller', Proc. of the 1995 World Congress of Neural Networks, 2, 1995, pp.II-402-II-405

[11] Y.Maeda: 'Time Difference Simultaneous Perturbation Method', Electronics Letters, to be published

Associative Memory

(Poster Presentation)

Combinative Implementation of Associative Memory

Zhou Jing-Zhou

Electronic engineering dept.
Shenzhen University
Shenzhen   China

Abstract

Both bidirectional associative memory and binary valued, feedforward topology associative memory are discussed. The fatal limitation is their inability to encode a large number of pattern pairs. Combining the advantages of these two types of associative memory, a new mechanism is advanced in this paper. Through performing a number of simple operations on the binary valued basic elements provided by the mechanism, a high storage capacity of the associative memory can be achieved and these operations can be performed in a massively parallel way.

Key words: associative memory, fault tolerance, storage capacity, matrix

1. Introduction

A neural network is a parallel, distributed information processing structure consisting of processing elements interconnected together with unidirectional channels called connections [1]. Until now, there have been a variety of neural network coming up for simulating   human information processing. The majority of these neural networks can be thought of as dynamical systems. Though they are globally stable, they don't guarantee to map all inputs into the desired outputs. The primary limitations include their inability to encode a large number of patterns.

For example, for a bidirectional associative memory (BAM), pattern pair associations are encoded in its matrix W by summing the outer products of the m pattern pairs using the equation

$$W = \sum_{K=1}^{M} A_K^T B_K$$

where each $A_K \in \{-1,+1\}^n$ and $B_k \in \{-1,+1\}^p$.

For the following five pattern pairs $(A_1\ B_1)$, (A_2,B_2), (A_3,B_3), (A_4,B_4), and (A_5,B_5)

$$
\begin{array}{llll}
A_1=(\ \ 1 \quad -1 \quad 1\ \ ) & & & B_1=(\ -1 \quad 1 \quad 1 \quad -1\ \ ) \\
A_2=(\ \ 1 \quad -1 \quad -1\ \ ) & & & B_2=(\ \ 1 \quad -1 \quad -1 \quad 1\ \ ) \\
A_3=(\ \ 1 \quad 1 \quad 1\ \ ) & & & B_3=(\ \ 1 \quad 1 \quad 1 \quad 1\ \ ) \\
A_4=(\ \ 1 \quad 1 \quad -1\ \ ) & & & B_4=(\ \ 1 \quad 1 \quad -1 \quad -1\ \ ) \\
A_5=(\ -1 \quad 1 \quad -1\ \ ) & & & B_5=(\ \ 1 \quad -1 \quad -1 \quad -1\ \ )
\end{array}
$$

we have

$$W = \sum_{k=1}^{5} A_k^T B_k = \begin{pmatrix} 1 & 3 & 1 & 1 \\ 3 & 1 & -1 & -1 \\ -3 & 3 & 5 & 1 \end{pmatrix}$$

During recall process, we want to test the recall of the vector $A_1=(\ 1 \quad -1 \quad 1)$ using the equations

$$b_j(t+1) = \begin{cases} 1 & if \ \ y_j > 0 \\ b_j(t) & if \ \ y_j = 0 \\ -1 & if \ \ y_j < 0 \end{cases}$$

where

$$y_j = \sum_{i=1}^{n} a_i(t) w_{ij}$$

$$a_i(t+1) = \begin{cases} 1 & if \quad x_i > 0 \\ a_i(t) & if \quad x_i = 0 \\ -1 & if \quad x_i < 0 \end{cases}$$

where

$$x_i = \sum_{j=1}^{p} b_j(t)w_{ji}$$

we get:

$$A_1W = (\text{-5 5 7 3}) \Rightarrow threshold \Rightarrow (\text{-1 1 1 1}) = B_1{}'$$
$$B_1{}'W^T = (\text{4 -4 12}) \Rightarrow threshold \Rightarrow (\text{1 -1 1}) = A_1$$

and so on forever.

The BAM stabilized in a state with A=(1 -1 1) B=(-1 1 1 1) which doesn't represent the desired situation in which the recalled pattern should be B_1=(-1 1 1 -1).

Another type of associative memory (AM) has the same kind problem. An example given by Palm [2] which has already been quoted by the author [3]verified that even three pattern pairs $(A_k, B_k),k=1,2,3$,each $A_k \in \{0,1\}^n$ and $B_k \in \{0\ 1\}^p$, cannot correctly recalled.

$$A_1 =(\text{1 1 0 0 0})\ B_1=(\text{0 1 0 1 0})$$
$$A_2 =(\text{1 0 1 0 0})\ B_2=(\text{0 1 0 0 1})$$
$$A_3 \ =(\text{0 1 1 0 0})\ B_3=(\text{1 0 1 0 0})$$

After encoding these pattern pairs in a matrix, we get

	1		1	1
1	1	1	1	
1	1	1		1

Suppose A_3 is given as an input, during recall process, we have

$$1\ 1\ 1\ 1\ 0$$
$$1\ 1\ 1\ 0\ 1$$
$$\overline{\hspace{4cm}}$$
$$2\ 2\ 2\ 1\ 1$$

Binarising the result on threshold $\theta=2$ leads to the following output pattern which doesn't agree with the correct response pattern B_3.

$$1\ 1\ 1\ 0\ 0$$

In order to solve the problems discussed above, a combinative method is introduced in this paper.

2. Combinative mechanism

For BAM, the matrix W is obtained by summing the outer products of the stored pattern pairs using the equation

$$W = \sum_{k=1}^{m} A_k{}^T B_k \qquad (1)$$

Each pattern pair distributes over its corresponding outer product. The summation of these outer products makes all of the pattern pairs get involved in the matrix W. During recall process, as the equation

$$y_j = \sum_{i=1}^{n} a_i(t)w_{ij}$$

is used, each w_{ij} has a tendency to make the summation have a desired sign (either positive or negative). But when more pattern pairs are encoded, the sign of the summation may gradually change to the opposite direction.

In AM, the binary valued pattern pairs are encoded. These values are either 1 or 0. During recall process, the elements of the intermediate result which will correspond to the 1's in the finally recalled pattern are expected to have the maximum values. Then binarise them on the threshold of the maximum value in order to filter other patterns. But in encoding process, when a newer 1 superimposes atop an older 1, the result doesn't explicitly reflect this fact. This procedure may end up with errors for a later recall process.

To solve these problems, in this paper a mechanism which combines the advantages of the two types of associative memory into a single scheme is presented.

2.1 Encoding

This time the binary valued pattern pairs, where $A_k \in \{0,1\}^n$, $B_k \in \{0,1\}^p$, are encoded in the associative memory matrix W. For each element of the matrix, instead of using the following encoding equation

$$w_{ij} = \sum_{k=1}^{m} a_i^k b_j^k$$

a binary string is formed which consists of the bit information of the stored patterns. That is, rather than performing the normal mathematic summation, the formation of the binary string is gradually formed by connecting the bit information of the pattern to be encoded with that of whatever has already been stored. The length of the binary string is decided by the number of the encoded patterns. For the purpose of forming the binary string for each element of the matrix W, we change the sign $\sum$ into $\sum_{con}$. Thus, instead of equation (1), we have:

$$W = \sum_{con\,k=1}^{m} A_k^T B_k \qquad (2)$$

or in its point-wise form

$$w_{ij} = \sum_{con\,k=1}^{m} a_i^k b_j^k$$

For example, using equation (2) we will encode the two pattern pairs (A_1, B_1) and (A_2, B_2) in W as follows:

$$A_1 = (\,1\ 0\ 1\,) \qquad B_1 = (\,1\ 0\ 0\ 1\,)$$
$$A_2 = (\,1\ 1\ 0\,) \qquad B_2 = (\,0\ 1\ 0\ 1\,)$$

$$A_1^T B_1 = \begin{pmatrix} 1 \\ 0 \\ 1 \end{pmatrix} (1\ 0\ 0\ 1) = \begin{pmatrix} 1 & 0 & 0 & 1 \\ 0 & 0 & 0 & 0 \\ 1 & 0 & 0 & 1 \end{pmatrix}$$

$$A_2^T B_2 = \begin{pmatrix} 1 \\ 1 \\ 0 \end{pmatrix} (0\ 1\ 0\ 1) = \begin{pmatrix} 0 & 1 & 0 & 1 \\ 0 & 1 & 0 & 1 \\ 0 & 0 & 0 & 0 \end{pmatrix}$$

$$W = \sum_{con\,k=1}^{2} A_K^T B_k = \begin{pmatrix} 10 & 01 & 00 & 11 \\ 00 & 01 & 00 & 01 \\ 10 & 00 & 00 & 10 \end{pmatrix}$$

2.2 Recalling

Normally, the following procedure is required.

1. Determine the rows in W according to the positions of 1's in the input pattern.
2. For each element of the output pattern, perform logic AND operations as follows

$$y_j = w_{1j}{}^{\wedge}w_{2j}{}^{\wedge}\ldots{}^{\wedge}w_{rj}$$

where 1,2,... ,r are the rows in W determined by step, j=1,...,m is the length of the output pattern.

3. Apply the following threshold function to each Y_j, where the threshold θ is determined by the rightmost 1 of y_j's.

$$b_j = \begin{cases} 0 & \quad if \quad y_j < \theta \\ 1 & \quad if \quad y_j = \theta \\ (further\ operations) & \quad if \quad y_j > \theta \end{cases}$$

In case $y_j > \theta$, the following procedure is needed.

1. Apply logic NOT operation to each element of the input pattern.
2. Determine the rows in W according to the positions of 1's in the pattern resulting from step 1.
3. For each row obtained from step 2, apply logic NOT operations to each element of it.
4. Execute logic AND operations on y_j and each $\bar{w}_{ij}$, which result from step 3, we have

$$y_j' = y_j \wedge \bar{w}_{1j} \wedge \bar{w}_{2j} \wedge \cdots, \wedge \bar{w}_{sj}$$

where j=1,...,m, 1,2,...,s are the rows in W determined by step 2.

5. By now, y_j' is guaranteed to have either all 0's or only one 1 at a fixed position of it and in latter case a threshold θ is formed. Apply the following threshold function to y_j^1

$$b_j^1 = \begin{cases} 0 & if \quad y_j' < \theta \\ 1 & if \quad y_j' = \theta \end{cases}$$

a correct pattern can be recalled.

Example:

Taking the pattern pairs given in section 1 as $A_k \in \{0,1\}^n$, $B_k \in \{0,1\}^p$, for an input pattern $A_1 = (1 \quad 0 \quad 1 \quad)$, we will recall the corresponding output pattern B_1, which we failed to do in section 1, by going through the following procedure:

ENCODING:

$$W = \sum_{con \; k=1}^{5} A_k^t B_k = \begin{pmatrix} 01110 & 01101 & 00101 & 00110 \\ 11100 & 01100 & 00100 & 00100 \\ 00100 & 00101 & 00101 & 00100 \end{pmatrix}$$

RECALL:

For $A_1 = (1 \; 0 \; 1)$, we will deal with the elements in the first and third rows of the matrix by applying logic AND operations to them:

$$y_1 = W_{11} \wedge W_{31} = (0\;1\;1\;1\;0) \wedge (0\;0\;1\;0\;0) = 0\;0\;1\;0\;0$$
$$y_2 = W_{12} \wedge W_{32} = (0\;1\;1\;0\;1) \wedge (0\;0\;1\;0\;1) = 0\;0\;1\;0\;1$$
$$y_3 = W_{13} \wedge W_{33} = (0\;0\;1\;0\;1) \wedge (0\;0\;1\;0\;1) = 0\;0\;1\;0\;1$$
$$y_4 = W_{14} \wedge W_{34} = (0\;0\;1\;1\;0) \wedge (0\;0\;1\;0\;0) = 0\;0\;1\;0\;0$$

The threshold $\theta = 00001$. As $y_j > \theta$, the further operations are needed, Apply logic NOT operation to A_1, we have $\overline{A_1} = (0 \quad 1 \quad 0)$.

Apply logic NOT operations to the second row of W, we get

$$\overline{W_{21}} = (0 \quad 0 \quad 0 \quad 1 \quad 1) \qquad\qquad \overline{W_{22}} = (1 \quad 0 \quad 0 \quad 1 \quad 1)$$
$$\overline{W_{23}} = (1 \quad 1 \quad 0 \quad 1 \quad 1) \qquad\qquad \overline{W_{24}} = (1 \quad 1 \quad 0 \quad 1 \quad 1)$$

Execute logic AND operations on y_j and $\overline{W_{2j}}$, we have

$$y_1' = y_1 \wedge \overline{W_{21}} = (0 \quad 0 \quad 1 \quad 0 \quad 0) \wedge (0 \quad 0 \quad 0 \quad 1 \quad 1) = 0 \quad 0 \quad 0 \quad 0 \quad 0$$
$$y_2' = y_2 \wedge \overline{W_{22}} = (0 \quad 0 \quad 1 \quad 0 \quad 1) \wedge (1 \quad 0 \quad 0 \quad 1 \quad 1) = 0 \quad 0 \quad 0 \quad 0 \quad 1$$
$$y_3' = y_3 \wedge \overline{W_{23}} = (0 \quad 0 \quad 1 \quad 0 \quad 1) \wedge (1 \quad 1 \quad 0 \quad 1 \quad 1) = 0 \quad 0 \quad 0 \quad 0 \quad 1$$
$$y_4' = y_4 \wedge \overline{W_{24}} = (0 \quad 0 \quad 1 \quad 0 \quad 0) \wedge (1 \quad 1 \quad 0 \quad 1 \quad 1) = 0 \quad 0 \quad 0 \quad 0 \quad 0$$

So far, we have the threshold $\theta = 1$. Apply the threshold function to $y_j (j=1,\ldots,4)$, we have

$$0\;1\;1\;0$$

which is the desired pattern B_1.

3.   Fault tolerance

As the stored patterns are distributed over the matrix W, this mechanism is fault tolerant.

For example, for the example given in last section, if we take the $A_3' = (0\;1\;1)$, rather than $A_3 = (1\;1\;1)$, as input, to recall the desired pattern, we have

$$y_1 = w_{21} \wedge w_{31} = (1\;1\;1\;0\;0) \wedge (0\;0\;1\;0\;0) = 0\;0\;1\;0\;0$$
$$y_2 = w_{22} \wedge w_{32} = (0\;1\;1\;0\;0) \wedge (0\;0\;1\;0\;1) = 0\;0\;1\;0\;0$$
$$y_3 = w_{23} \wedge w_{33} = (0\;0\;1\;0\;0) \wedge (0\;0\;1\;0\;1) = 0\;0\;1\;0\;0$$
$$y_4 = w_{24} \wedge w_{34} = (0\;0\;1\;0\;0) \wedge (0\;0\;1\;0\;0) = 0\;0\;1\;0\;0$$

Hence $\theta = 100$. Execute the threshold function to $y_i (i=1,\ldots,4)$, we get

$$b_1 = b_2 = b_3 = b_4 = 1$$

So the result is $(1\;1\;1\;1)$ which is the desired pattern B_3.

4.   Capacity

It is guaranteed by the mechanism presented in this paper that a large number of the pattern pairs can be stored in the matrix and then can be correctly recalled later. We define the storage capacity of the matrix as the maximum number of the pattern pairs that can be stored in it. The total number Z of the stored pattern pairs can be

$$Z = (2^n - 1)$$

where n is the length of the input pattern. As the output patterns are distributed over the matrix according to the positions of 1's in the input pattern (or vice versa), the total number C of the output patterns to be encoded would be

$$C = (2^n - 1)\, np$$

where p is the probability of being 1 in a input pattern.

5.   Conclusions

The encoding scheme introduced in this paper makes the recall process extremely explainable by hand. That means that the whole procedure is controllable. As a large number of identical processing elements are provided by this method, the operations executed on them can be performed in a massively parallel way. Applications of this kind of associative memory, which involve a way of transforming one string of symbols into another, are widespread. However, it should be admitted that the major advantage, that is, the gain of such a high storage capacity, has to be paid for in terms of a large number of parallel logic operations.

REFERENCES

[1] P.K.Simpson, Artificial Neural Systems, Pergamon Press, Inc., 1990
[2] G.Palm, Neural Assemblies, Springer-Verlag, 1982.
[3] J.Z.Zhou, "Densely Coded Matrix Model of Associative Memory", Hildesheimer Informatik-Berichte, 22/95, 1995.

A Memory Neural Network and Its Functions[*]

Jinwen Ma

Institute of Mathematics

Shantou University, Guangdong, China

jwma@mailserv.stu.edu.cn

Abstract

A memory neural network—simplex memory neural network—is proposed to describe the mechanisms of pattern memory in the brain. It is constructed to memorize any binary pattern with content-addressable memory function. Under Hebbian learning rule, this biological network has some important functions in accord with the learning and memory behaviors of the brain.

1 Introduction

A fundamental question about understanding the memory mechanisms of the brain is "where and how the information is memorized in the brain". This question has not been structurally solved yet. By physiological anatomy, it is clear that the brain is made up of neurons(neural cells), which can be only in the excited state 1 or the quiescent state 0 as being expressed in a MP model[1]. Then we generally consider that any piece of information memorized in the brain is a binary code. A (binary) pattern is a binary code to express the form (the binary picture) of any thing like a letter, a face, etc. We also consider that a pattern as a basic unit of information can be retrieved or recognized on a time in the brain. According to the functions of memory of the brain, we can divide the memory about a pattern into two categories: pattern memory and associative memory. By pattern memory, we mean to memorize a pattern directly and to obtain the ability of recognizing and retrieving it. By associative memory, we mean to memorize the relations between two patterns in order to associate (retrieve) a pattern from the other one. Pattern memory is the prime kind of memory which is the base of associative memory and intelligence. We wonder how a pattern can be memorized for a long term and where it is. Psychological experiments show that the memory is stored in the brain by groups individually, and the memorizing or learning behaviors on a group is simply reading it repeatedly. In this way, a pattern (as one group of information) is itself probably memorized individually in a local place —a number of neurons—in the brain. This set of neurons, in fact, form a local neural network. Hence we suppose that a pattern is itself memorized in a unique local neural network of the brain which we call a simplex memory neural network. More concretely, the supposal means that a memorized pattern is itself memorized in its simplex memory neural network(hereafter referred to as SMNN) for pattern memory and a SMNN has relations to other neural networks for associative memory.

As we expect, the SMNN of a pattern U should have the two basic functions: (1) CAM (Content-Addressable Memory) function: (i) when the input pattern to the SMNN is U or the pattern nearby U(in a certain neighborhood of U), the SMNN will be excited, i.e.,the state of the network is U. So the pattern U is retrieved. (ii) When the input pattern is very different from U, the network will not be excited, i.e. the state of the network is $O = (0, 0, \cdots, 0)$ so that every neuron of the network is in the quiescent state, which means U is not retrieved. (2) AM (Associative Memory) function: When the SMNN is excited, the only memorized pattern U is retrieved. Then the network will associate to the related neural networks to retrieve their memorized patterns. And in the contrary case, another neural network may associate the SMNN in the same way.

The purpose of this paper is to construct a model of SMNNs. As to associative memory, there are many researches approaching to it. It can be done by means of associative matrix or

---

[*]This work is supported by China Tianyuan Funds under Project 1937015.

other methods. Since the structures for associative memory are built between two networks, we will not consider AM functions of the SMNN for simplicity here. Then the architecture of a SMNN will be established only by the CAM function.

2 The Mathematical Model of SMNN

In this section, a model of SMNN is constructed mathematically. Firstly, Let N be a neural network of n pair-wised connected neurons, then N is uniquely defined by (W,θ) where W is an $n \times n$ zero-diagonal matrix, with element w_{ij} denotes the weight from neuron j to neuron i; θ is a vector of dimension n, where component θ_i denotes the threshold of neuron i.

Every neuron here can be in one of two possible states, either 1 or 0. The state of neuron i at time t is denoted by $s_i(t)$. The state of the neural network at time t is the vector $S(t) = (s_1(t), s_2(t), \cdots, s_n(t))^T$.

The state of neuron i at time $(t+1)$ is computed by

$$s_i(t+1) = Sgn(H_i(t)) = \begin{cases} 1 & \text{if } H_i(t) \geq 0, \\ 0 & \text{otherwise.} \end{cases} \tag{1}$$

where

$$H_i(t) = \sum_{j=1}^{n} w_{ij} s_j(t) - \theta_i \tag{2}$$

The next state of the network, i.e., $S(t+1)$, is computed from the current state by performing the evaluation eqn.(1) at any neuron of the network. The mode of operation is synchronous. When the symmetric condition is satisfied, i.e., $w_{ij} = w_{ji}$ for any pair $(i,j)(i \neq j)$, the network is certainly a Hopfield network of the synchronous operation mode[2].

The state $S(t)$ is called stable iif

$$S(t) = Sgn(WS(t) - \theta), \tag{3}$$

i.e., the state of the network is not changing as a result of computation.

As a dynamic system, this kind of networks may have CAM function as Hopfield networks. The network starts in an initial state and runs with each neuron synchronously reevaluating itself. The network enters a stable state which constitutes a stored pattern in the memory.

According to CAM function of the networks, we introduce a mathematical definition of the SMNN of a pattern $U = (u_1, u_2, \cdots, u_n)^T$ as follows.

Given $X = (x_1, x_2, \cdots, x_n)^T$ as a n-dim input pattern. We define

$$d(X, U) = \sum_{i=1}^{n} |x_i - u_i| \tag{4}$$

as the Hamming distance between X and U.

DEFINITION 1 Define the t-neighborhood of U over the binary n-dim space $\{0,1\}^n$ as following:

$$R_t(U) = \{X : d(X,U) \leq t, X \in \{0,1\}^n\}. \tag{5}$$

DEFINITION 2 As to a fixed pattern U, if a network (W, θ) of n neurons satisfies:

$$E(X) = \begin{cases} U & \text{if } X \in R_t(U), \\ O & \text{otherwise.} \end{cases} \tag{6}$$

where $E(X)$ is the stable state of the network (if it exists) when the network starts in the initial state X. Then the network is called a SMNN of the pattern U with error-correcting capacity t $(t \geq 0)$.

From *DEFINITION 2*, the performances of a SMNN can be understood in this way. Firstly the initial state X is inputted to the network. If the network operates at last to the stable state U, we think the network is excited, and the pattern U is retrieved, or U is perceived. If the stable state of the network at last is O, which means the network is in the quiescent state, we think the pattern U isn't retrieved. By the definition of $R_t(U)$, the SMNN certainly has CAM function.

As to a fixed pattern, if the required error-correcting capacity t satisfies:

$$0 \leq t < (\frac{1}{2}d(U) - 1). \quad (d(U) = \sum_{i=1}^{n} u_i) \tag{7}$$

where $d(U)$ is the Hamming weight of U, a symmetric SMNN of U with error-correcting capacity t (like a Hopfield network) can be constructed by

$$w_{ij} = \begin{cases} 1 & u_i + u_j = 2, i \neq j, \\ -1 & u_i + u_j = 1, i \neq j, \\ 0 & u_i + u_j = 0, i \neq j, \\ 0 & i = j. \end{cases} \tag{8}$$

$$\theta_i = d(U) - (t+1) \tag{9}$$

for all $i, j = 1, 2, \cdots, n$.

$THEOREM\ 1$ For any fixed pattern U, if $d(U) > 0$, and $0 \leq t < \frac{1}{2}d(U) - 1$,the network (W, θ) constructed by eqn.(8),(9), is a SMNN of U with error-correcting capacity t.

The proof is given in [3].

3   The Biological Functions of SMNN

Now we consider the SMNN as a biological neural network. Then the weight w_{ij} is considered as the efficiency of the synapse from neuron j to neuron i. Firstly, some biological meanings and supposals on the network are given as follows.

As being expressed in the mathematical model, the neurons are not permitted to fire(excite) at any random time but rather that they are synchronized such that they can only fire at some integral multiple of the refractory period of the neuron(The supposal was suggested by Little in [4]).

We suppose that the learning process is just the modification process of synapses. In fact, threshold values of neurons make no contributions to the learning results. We can further suppose that all neurons of the network have the same positive threshold value, i.e., $\theta_1 = \theta_2 = \cdots\cdots = \theta_n = \theta > 0$. According to Hebbian Learning supposal[5], we use the following formulas as Hebbian learning rule for the plastic synapse.

In a period, the state of neuron i is $x_i \in \{0, 1\}$, and the state of neuron j is $x_j \in \{0, 1\}$, ,then an incremental synapse efficiency(weight) $\triangle w_{ij}$ is obtained to w_{ij}. $\triangle w_{ij}$ is computed by

$$\triangle w_{ij} = \begin{cases} +\alpha & \text{if } x_i = x_j = 1, \\ -\alpha & \text{if } x_i + x_j = 1, \\ 0 & \text{if } x_i = x_j = 0. \end{cases} \tag{10}$$

where $\alpha > 0$.

We suppose that the synapse is in the plastic or stable form, corresponding to short-term or long-term memory respectively. When the synapse is plastic, the efficiency of it can be modified by the learning rule eqn.(10), or the absolute value of it attenuates to zero(forgetting). When the synapse is stable, the efficiency of it $w_{ij} = \pm E(E > 0)$, where E is the saturation value which has two implications: (1) When the absolute value of the plastic synapse efficiency increases up to E, the plastic synapse transforms into the stable one; (2) The stable synapse efficiency $\pm E$ can not be changed by further learning or forgetting. In the supposal, when $w_{ij} = +E$, the long term synapse is excitatory; and when $w_{ij} = -E$, the long term synapse is inhibitory. We further suppose that $E = 1$ for E certainly can be chosen as the unit of weight.

By the above facts and supposals, given a neural network of n neurons with all plastic synapses (W_0, θ), let it learn the simplex pattern $U \in \{0, 1\}^n$, i.e., repeatedly input U to the network and make the network to be in the state of U for a certain time (period). As the learning process continues properly, the synapse efficiencies of the network will come up to the stable values :

$$\widehat{w}_{ij} = \begin{cases} 1 & u_i + u_j = 2, i \neq j, \\ -1 & u_i + u_j = 1, i \neq j, \\ 0 & u_i + u_j = 0, i \neq j, \\ 0 & i = j. \end{cases} \tag{11}$$

According to *THEOREM 1*, the network $(\widehat{W}, \theta)$ is a SMNN of U, with the error-correcting capacity $t = d(U) - \theta - 1$.

So we have showed that the SMNN given by eqn.(8).(9), may be constructed in the brain by repeatedly learning the specified pattern U with Hebbian learning rule from any network of plastic synapses. Hence there may be biological SMNNs in the brain.

As required, the SMNN certainly has the function of CAM. We further discuss the two biological functions with the SMNN.

A. The error correcting property

According to *THEOREM 1*, the threshold value θ, error correcting capacity t and $d(U)$ satisfy that

$$t = d(U) - \theta - 1 \tag{12}$$

So when θ is stable(fixed), the error correcting capacity t is directly proportional to $d(U)$. As $d(U)$ increases, the error correcting capacity increases too. In fact, as $d(U)$ (supposing that $d(U) \leq \frac{n}{2}$. If $d(U) > \frac{n}{2}$, we memorize the dual pattern $\overline{U} = (1 - u_1, 1 - u_2, \cdots, 1 - u_n)$ instead of U, which is a common phenomenon in memorizing patterns or figures by the brain) becomes greater, the pattern becomes more complex, so it contains more information with which the greater capacity of error correcting is obtained. Thus the relation eqn.(12) conforms to the memory behaviors of the brain.

B. The effects of fluctuation of the threshold value

As we suppose above, the threshold values are stable and don't affect the learning results. In fact, the stability is relative. The threshold value may fluctuate under certain conditions. When there appears exciting (inhibiting) on a local field of the brain, this may cause that each neuron of the SMNN is easily excited (inhibited), which means the threshold value is decreased(increased) to a lower(higher) value. According to eqn.(12), when the threshold value of the network is decreased, i.e., the excitatory level is increased, the error correcting capacity is increased so that the retrieval of the pattern becomes easy. Alternatively, when the threshold value of the network is increased, i.e., the inhibitory level is increased, the error correcting capacity is decreased so that the retrieval of the pattern becomes difficult. This function seems reasonable.

4   Conclusion

We have proposed a model of SMNN to describe the mechanism of pattern memory in the brain. The SMNN is defined to memorize only a simplex pattern with CAM function. Then a mathematical model of SMNN is constructed for any pattern. Under some physiological supposals(these seem reasonable), the mathematical model can be formed by repeatedly learning the pattern U with Hebbian learning rules from any neural network of plastic synapses. Hence there may be biological SMNNs in the brain. From the discussion, we have showed that the SMNN as a biological neural network has some important functions in accord with the memory behaviors of the brain.

As a whole, the model of SMNN is significant to recognizing the memory architecture of the brain. Certainly we need further psychological experiments to verify it.

References

[1] W.S., McCulloch, & W. Pitts, "A logical calculus of the ideas imminent in nervous activity," *Bulletin of Mathematical Biophysics*, vol.5, pp.115-133, 1942.

[2] J.J. Hopfield, "Neural networks and physical systems with emergent collective computational abilities," *Proceeding of the National Academy Sciences, USA*, vol.79, pp.2245-2558, 1982.

[3] J. Ma, "Simplex memory neural networks," submitted to *Neural Networks*, 1995.

[4] W.A. Little, "The existence of persistent states in the brain," *Mathematical Biosciences*, vol.19, pp.101-120, 1974.

[5] D. Hebb, *The organization of behaviour*, New York: Wiley, 1949

Optimization

(Oral Presentation)

Testing Neural Net Algorithms on General Compressible Data

Arun K. Jagota †, Kenneth W. Regan ‡
† Department of Computer Sciences, University of North Texas, email: jagota@cs.unt.edu
Denton, TX, 76203, USA
‡ Department of Computer Science, State University of New York at Buffalo
Buffalo, NY, USA

***Abstract*— This paper advocates that a "realistic" evaluation of a algorithm should include tests not only on "random" data, but also on *compressible* data. We evaluate a suite of nine neural-net heuristics for the MAX CLIQUE problem on both uniformly-random and compressible data, using a time-bounded analogue q of the *Solomonoff-Levin universal distribution* m for the latter. The Maximum Clique problem is NP-hard to solve approximately in the worst-case; however it is easy to approximate within a factor of 2 on "random" graphs. Three of the neural net algorithms, while nearly competitive with the other six on random data, are observed to work poorly under q, for graphs with 100 and 400 vertices. These results indicate that the compressible distribution q discriminates the performance of various algorithms better than does random data. We suspect that a theoretical result of Li and Vitanyi, namely that the distribution m asymptotically draws out worst-case behavior in an algorithm, shows up as a practical phenomenon. Our experimental results so far do not strongly support (or refute) this; however they do provide clear indications of at least a weaker phenonemon, namely that the compressible distribution q draws out poor behavior on the simpler heuristics, whereas the uniform distribution does not.**

1   Introduction

Most algorithm testing is done either on "random" instances of the problem at hand, or on a relatively narrow range of instances tied to a particular application. Our first purpose is to point out that "random" instances are not necessarily *realistic* instances. Our second purpose is to shed more light on the possibility of doing scientific testing in ways that retain both realism and generality over many applications. This paper reports our results on work-to-date that neural-net heuristics behave markedly differently on "random" data versus data drawn from distributions that attempt to reflect how instances arise in practice. A full current version of our work is available by e-mail to the first author.

Our point of departure is the common-sense position that real-world instances are *not* "random." The usual meaning of "random" is (1) that the instance is drawn from the uniform distribution on the space of all possible instances. For example, a "random" n-vertex undirected simple graph is obtained by flipping a coin for each pair (i,j) $(1 \leq i < j \leq n)$ to see whether edge (i,j) is present in the graph. (Note that the underlying sample space will have many isomorphic copies of the same graph.) Information theory provides a second perspective: (2) a random instance is one that is *incompressible*; i.e., one whose standard encoding to a solving algorithm cannot be replaced by an appreciably shorter string encoding. These two meanings mostly align for our purposes, since (by a standard counting argument) the vast majority of strings cannot be appreciably compressed. Thus a "random" string from (1) will, with high probability, be one of the strings in (2). For example, while some special n-vertex graphs such as the n-cycle can be compressed to $O(\log n)$ bits under fairly general "smart encoding" schemes, the standard encoding length of $N = (n^2 - n)/2$ bits cannot be improved for the vast majority of graphs.

Note that (2) does not pre-suppose a distribution or an instance space. Instead, it leads to one, called the *Solomonoff-Levin distribution* m. The basic idea of m is that if a graph (or any string) g_1 is compressible to K bits while g_2 cannot be compressed below N bits, then g_1 is 2^{N-K} times as likely to occur as g_2. The two main scientific ideas behind m, which have recently been expounded at length in articles and a book by Li and Vitanyi [14, 15, 17], are:

1. Compressible inputs occur much more frequently than "random" ones.

2. In the absence of any specific knowledge about the distribution of inputs to a computational problem, one should assume that they come from m.

The latter statement is justified by a theorem that for every computable distribution d on strings, there is a constant C depending only on d such that for all strings x, $m(x) \geq d(x)/C$. That is, m makes all strings at least as likely, within the constant factor C, as d did. The former expresses that real-world data sets usually have a much shorter specification than the number of data points entered or generated. For instance, graphs having specific regularities tend to present themselves to be solved more frequently than do "scattershot" graphs. For both reasons, m is also called the *universal prior distribution*.

The major rub is that m itself is not a computable distribution; indeed, there is no computable way to sample according to m, or even to estimate $m(x)$ within a constant factor—all attempts will undershoot $m(x)$ on many x. However, we *can* attempt to sample in ways intended to preserve many of the important properties of m. Whereas m is based on a universal programming system for all computation, we define a distribution q based on a programming system that is universal only for those computations that can be done in time $n \cdot (\log n)^{O(1)}$, which is called *quasi-linear* time. Li and Vitanyi themselves suggested polynomial-time sampling, but times above n^2 are not really efficient in practice. Quasi-linear time includes many important computational primitives, including sorting and FFT, that are not known to be computable in strictly-linear time. Our $\mathbf{q}$ assigns higher weight to size-N structures that can be (compressed and) decompressed in time that is quasi-linear as a function of N (not of K). Scientifically, the relevance of $\mathbf{q}$ amounts to asserting that real-world instances have regularities that can be efficiently perceived and produced. In our actual sampling, we made some further compromises described and justified below.

The main spur to our work was the following theoretical result of Li and Vitanyi [17]:

> **Theorem.** The average-case running time under $\mathbf{m}$ of any terminating algorithm is within a constant factor of its *worst*-case running time over all inputs of a given size.

With essentially the same proof, we show in our full report that the same statement can be made about optimization performance: any algorithm with instances drawn according to $\mathbf{m}$ fares nearly as poorly as it does on the worst instances. The proof idea is mainly that "the worst instance of size n" is a $(\log(n)+\text{const})$-sized description of itself, and so gets high weight under $\mathbf{m}$—hurting the $\mathbf{m}$-average more than "the best instance" helps it. Miltersen [18] shows that, subject to something like P $\neq$ NP, no polynomial-time computable distribution can be "malign" to the same degree as $\mathbf{m}$. Hence $\mathbf{q}$ itself is not so malign; note also that the above description does not give a $qlin(n)$ time way to decompress itself. Despite this and the way the proof of the Li-Vitanyi result borders on a triviality, we suspect that the above is the iceberg's tip of a phenomenon that compressible instances as they arise in the real world really tend to be harder than "random ones." The particular phenomenon we test is:

> **Test Question.** Is the performance of heuristic algorithms for problems markedly poorer under $\mathbf{q}$ than under uniform distribution?

The particular computational problem we study is the MAX CLIQUE problem: given an undirected graph G, compute $\omega(G)$, which stands for the maximum size of a clique in G—and furthermore, find a clique of that size. This is a well-known NP-hard problem. We study it for several reasons:

1. Many important computational problems can be efficiently transformed into cases of the MAX CLIQUE problem.

2. Clique problems are well-suited to neural nets. There is a wide variety of heuristics that can be tested.

3. A great deal is known about the theory of cliques in graphs, especially under uniform distributions. This theory acts as a scientific control on our experiments.

For a practically-minded treatment of the first point see [10], while the second is borne out by the algorithms described below. We discuss the third point now. The main theoretical results about cliques in random graphs are:

> **Theorems.** With very high probability, an n-vertex graph selected under uniform distribution will have maximum clique size about $2 \log_2 n$, and will also have no maximal cliques of size less than $\log_2 n$ at all.

Indeed, according to *Matula's Theorem* [19, p. 76], $\omega(G)$ clusters into two adjacent integer values near $2 \log n$. Since any halfwitted algorithm can be expected at least to output a maximal clique, the second clause says that all algorithms come within a factor of 2 of optimum on random graphs. Karp [13] suggested that all polynomial-time algorithms eventually fall down to that factor of 2 on random graphs as n gets large. Practical tests on random graphs up to several thousand vertices do much better than a factor of 2 and often come within 10%; see [4, 19] and our own results under $\mathbf{u}$ below.

Now we argue that in "real-world" clique instances G, the critical size of $\omega(G)$ that one needs to know about is more like n/C or $n^{1/2}$, *not* so low as $\log n$ or $2 \log n$. The standard transformation from an m-clause, n-variable instance ϕ of 3SAT to an equivalent instance of MAX CLIQUE produces a graph G_ϕ of $3m + 2n$ vertices that has a clique of size $n + m$ iff ϕ is satisfiable. Common transformations from other combinatorial optimization problems also have target clique sizes in the n^ϵ-to-$\Omega(n)$ range. This higher range also figures into the celebrated non-approximability results of Arora et al. [1] and later refinements. These results produce graphs G such that in the "yes" case, G has a clique of size n^e, while in the "no" case, G has no clique of size n^{e-d}, where $e > d > 0$ are fixed constants. It is now known that d can be larger than $e/3$, with the conclusion that (unless NP = P) $\omega(G)$ cannot be approximated within a factor of $\omega(G)^{1/3}$, let alone a factor of 2, in the worst case [2]. The graphs in all these results have only $O(n) = O(N^{1/2})$ non-edges ($6m + n$ non-edges in the first) and hence are compressible to $O(N^{1/2})$ size. These facts led us to do our actual testing on the "slice" of $\mathbf{q}$ afforded by graphs decompressed from seeds of sizes in some interval around $N^{1/2}$.

Thus the MAX CLIQUE problem gives a sharp distinction between "random" and "real-world" instances. This distinction applies also to *pseudo*random instances, insofar as the pseudorandom generators (PSRGs) that produce them are intended to replicate all properties of uniform distribution that are subject to feasible statistical tests. Note that graphs G produced by a PSRG are compressible, since they are described by the relatively short seed string s used and the number i such that the ith iteration of the PSRG on s produced G. However, such PSRG graphs may still be only a tiny fraction of those produced by a *universal* decompressor, such as the programming system on which $\mathbf{q}$ is based. This distinction seems borne out by our statistics below; the q-graphs had much larger clique sizes than the "random" graphs produced by the standard UNIX PSRG. Note also that we are not claiming that all compressible instances are hard, but only that "general compressible data," where "general" refers to a universal distribution such as $\mathbf{m}$ or $\mathbf{q}$, is harder on average than random data.

Still, this distinction does not say anything about the behavior of heuristic algorithms on these respective kinds of instances. However, the above theory gives us a good control benchmark for a positive answer to our above **Test Question**.

Benchmark. We consider a heuristic algorithm A to perform "markedly poorer" under $\mathbf{q}$ than under $\mathbf{u}$ if its average performance ratio $\omega(G)/A(G)$ under $\mathbf{q}$ falls below the factor-of-2 guarantee under $\mathbf{u}$.

In test cases where one cannot compute $\omega(G)$ exactly, and one is testing a suite of algorithms of varying strengths, one can use the stronger algorithms A' to control the weaker ones, by using $A'(G)/A(G)$ instead as the term for G in the average computed for $\mathbf{q}$. This is a "conservative" pragmatic choice and cannot produce a "false positive" result. Using an exact clique solving, branch and bound algorithm of D. Johnson and others at AT&T Bell Labs [5], we were able to compute $\omega(G)$ for all the 100-vertex graphs we generated, but on 17 of the fifty 400-vertex graphs (all with larger clique sizes), this algorithm did not halt within at least two day's computing time per graph (on one graph, it ran for two weeks without termination). Note also that by Matula's Theorem above, we were able to simply use $2\log_2 n$ in place of $\omega(G)$ for all the graphs G generated under $\mathbf{u}$, with a clear conscience. (Matula's closed form is inaccurate for small-order graphs when p is close to zero or one. In this case, we were still able to obtain a sharp estimate on the maximum clique size by numerically computing directly from the distribution of the expected number of k-cliques in a p-random graph.)

Our *results* for the suite of nine neural algorithms that we tested are summarized in Tables 1 and 2 below. Tables of results on the individual q-graphs are available in the full report. There were three positive answers, but the other six heuristics performed just as well under $\mathbf{q}$ as under $\mathbf{u}$. Hence our best conclusion about whether the Li-Vitanyi principle sits atop a real practical phenomenon is "maybe: needs more testing on larger graphs."

Our results do support the conclusion that $\mathbf{q}$ discriminated the quality of the heuristics better than $\mathbf{u}$ did. Or stated a little differently, they do support the conclusion that the distribution $\mathbf{q}$ draws out poor behavior on certain heuristics—the simpler ones—as measured by the fact that these simple heuristics perform much poorer on $\mathbf{q}$ than on $\mathbf{u}$.

It is useful to note that our approach is not limited to performance on optimization problems—it is equally applicable to *learning* problems, which are the main focus of much current mainstream neural network research. Our general position is:

If one has tested an algorithm on random data and it performs well, one should also test it on compressible data. One may find that the good results on random data do not transfer over to compressible data. This may give a better indication of how the algorithm will perform on real data than the results on random data alone.

Section 2 describes the q-sampler; this description facilitates independent implementation. to be implemented in practice. Section 3 describes the neural algorithms in some detail; this section has independent interest. Section 4 gives more detail of the methodology of our experiments. Section 5 discusses the results and conclusions further.

2 The q(x) Sampler

We use a functional programming notation $\mathcal{L}$ due to Y. Gurevich and S. Shelah [6] which captures all programs which run in *nearly linear time*. Programs written in this formalism take a binary string y as input and perform a sequence of transformations, using operations described below, to generate a new string x. This formalism contains operations that contract strings and others that expand strings, so that the length of the resulting x can be quite different from that of the starting string y.

The G-S formalism [6] provides eight basic string operations. Our description assumes that the shown occurrences of substrings meeting the 'if' conditions are leftmost in x, and for $R2$, $R3$, and E, that the "parameter strings" $u, v, \ldots$ all have the same length. The operations are

$R0_{u,y}(x)$: If $x = ur$ then yr, else x.

$R1_{u,y}(x)$: If $x = tur$ then tyr, else x.

$R2_{u,v,y,z}(x)$: If $x = sutvr$ then $sytzr$, else x.

$R3_{u,v,w,y,z}(x)$: If $x = sut_1vt_2wr$ with $|t_1| = |t_2|$ then sut_1yt_2zr, else x.

$E_{u,v}(x)$: Simultaneously replace every 0 in x with u and every 1 with v.

$C_{u,v}(x)$: If $x = E_{u,v}(y)$ for some y then y, else x.

$A_u(x)$: Add a tail of $|x| \log |x|$-many copies of u to x.

$D_u(x)$: Delete the maximal tail of u's in x.

There are two constructors: functional composition, and "iterated replacements" of the form $(\vec{R})^*(x)$, where $\vec{R}$ is a composition of any number of $R0 \ldots R3$ functions, and $\vec{R}$ is applied $|x|$-many times.

Our heuristic analogue **q** uses the G-S formalism in the following way. We take a seed string $z \in \{0,1\}^m$ as input and decode this string into a pair (P, y), where P is a program in the G-S formalism and y a binary string. We then run program P on string y as input, to output the string x. We repeat this process on random strings $z \in \{0,1\}^m$ and keep only those strings x for which $n >> m$, in particular $n \geq m^2$. Such strings x are highly compressible under the G-S formalism. The G-S formalism is universal for nearly linear time computations [6] in the sense that any function computable on a random access machine in nearly linear time is computable by a program in this formalism and vice-versa. This is the justification for us to regard **q** as an efficiently computable analog of **m**.

The main practical reason for using $\mathcal{L}$ is its simplicity and ease of implementability. Also, while the expansion operations E and A always apply, the contraction operations C and D most often have no effect. Hence $\mathcal{L}$ has a bias toward expansion which is not unnatural, and which reduces the sampling time. Indeed, we were surprised to find that no fewer than one out of every six randomly chosen seeds expanded out to a large enough graph.

3   The Neural Network Algorithms

All neural network algorithms evaluated in this paper are based on the Hopfield model [8, 9], and are described in detail in [11]. Here we describe them only briefly, without explaining their neural network implementation in much detail. It is worth noting that all these algorithms arise as manifestations of essentially a single meta-algorithm: one that minimizes the usual *energy function* in the Hopfield model [8, 9].

3.1   Discrete Algorithms

Steepest Descent. Steepest Descent (SD) is a discrete serial-update neural network heuristic that minimizes energy in greedy fashion. In each time step, the unit to switch decreases energy by the maximum amount. We use the notation $SD(V_0)$ to denote that Steepest Descent starts initially from some subset $V_0 \subseteq V$ of vertices. SD iteratively transforms V_0 into a maximal clique C, terminating efficiently within $2n$ iterations [11]. Let V_i denote the vertex-set in iteration i and assume that it is not a maximal clique. SD emulates the following heuristic in iteration i:

If V_i is not a clique then
   a vertex with minimum degree in the induced subgraph $G[V_i]$ is removed from V_i
else if V_i is a clique then
    a vertex in $V \setminus V_i$ adjacent to every vertex in V_i is added to V_i.

Ties are broken lexicographically.

ρ-annealing. ρ-annealing is another discrete serial-update neural network heuristic, which works by carrying out annealing while minimizing energy. More precisely, a certain parameter of the network, called ρ, is varied while the network minimizes energy by steepest descent. This is analogous to varying the temperature T in simulated annealing. We omit the precise description of ρ-annealing here, for which the reader is refered to [11]. An intuitive description is as follows.

1. Start with small ρ and with the initial state $V_0 := V$.

2. Run $SD(V_0)$ with this value of ρ to transform V_0 into U.

3. Increase ρ, set $V_0 := U$, and go to step 2.

The algorithm is terminated when ρ becomes sufficiently large. It turns out that when ρ is small, the set U retrieved in step 2 is not required to be a clique; however as ρ is increased, certain constraints get ever tighter, ultimately forcing U to be a clique. In other words, like simulated annealing, this algorithm starts with loose constraints—allowing an unbiased exploration of the search space—and progressively tightens them until the final solution U forms a clique. A precise characterization of the behavior of this algorithm is in [11].

Stochastic Steepest Descent. Stochastic Steepest Descent (SSD) is a randomized variant of SD. The deterministic moves of SD are replaced by energy-minimizing moves that favor the steepest direction, but probabilistically. More precisely,

The unit to switch is picked with probability proportional to the amount of energy its switch would decrease. (The probability is zero if the switch would keep the energy same or increase it.)

The algorithm is motivated by the desire to randomize the choice of unit to switch, which allows one to use repeated runs of the algorithm to boost the size of the clique found, while not totally relinquishing the greedy heuristic emulated by SD, which often works well (see Tables 1 and 2, and [11]).

Let $SSD(V_0, i)$ denote i runs of SSD on a given graph, with V_0 as the initial state (vertex set) in each run. (Note that the initial state is the same in each run.) The largest clique found in a run is the output of the algorithm. One run of SSD terminates within $2n$ unit-switches (iterations) [11], which keeps one run as efficient as SD.

3.2 Continuous Algorithms

The description of the continuous algorithms assumes familiarity with the continuous Hopfield model [9].

Continuous Hopfield Dynamics.   This algorithm, called the continuous Hopfield dynamics (CHD) [9, 7], is described by a system of n coupled nonlinear differential equations, presented here in discretized form:

$$S(t+1) := S(t) + \gamma(-S(t) + \bar{g}_\lambda(WS(t) + I)) \tag{1}$$

Here $S_i \in [0, 1]$ is the state of the ith neuron, I_i the external bias of the ith neuron, W the $n \times n$ symmetric weight matrix, $g_\lambda(x) = \frac{1}{1 + e^{-\lambda x}}$ a sigmoid with gain λ, $\bar{g}(\bar{x})$ notational shorthand for $(g(x_i))$, and γ the Euler step size. The continuous-time version of (1) minimizes an energy function during its evolution [9], into which the MAX-CLIQUE problem can be encoded [11]. With sufficiently large λ and sufficiently small γ, if (1) is started from any initial state $S(0) \in [0, 1]^n$ and iterated sufficiently-many times, it provably terminates at a fixed point S from which a maximal clique of the encoded graph can be recovered [11].

For a discussion of the significance of CHD from the point of view of neural implementation and optimization applications, see [9, 7, 11]. CHD is especially interesting because it may be viewed as the essential special case of the algorithm presented next—a continuous optimization method developed only recently, but one that is already beginning to make its mark on optimization as it occurs in practice.

Mean Field Annealing. The second continuous heuristic, called *Mean Field Annealing* (MFA) [3, 20], may be described as a generalization of CHD in which the sigmoidal gain λ is varied during the evolution of (1). This is done by employing an annealing schedule, a sequence $\{\lambda_i, \mu_i\}$ of k elements, where λ_i is the value of the sigmoidal gain and μ_i the number of times (1) is to be iterated with the sigmoidal gain set at λ_i. Usually λ_i is a monotonically increasing function of i. The detailed algorithm is as follows.

```
S := S(0)
for i := 1 to k do
    for j := 1 to μ_i do
        S := S + γ(-S + ḡ_λ_i(WS + I)
```

With sufficiently small γ and sufficiently large μ_i, S converges to a fixed point at each value of i [9, 7]. Additionally, with sufficiently large k, and with λ_i growing sufficiently slowly with i, MFA is known to deterministically approximate simulated annealing during its evolution [3, 7], while being more efficient.

4 Experimental Methodology

All experiments on the neural network algorithms and their evaluation on $u(n)$ and $q(x)$ were performed on a SUN SparcStation I.

Details of the Test Graphs. Experiments were performed on 100-vertex graphs and on 400-vertex graphs. The bitstrings of the 100-vertex graphs had length 4950, and those of the 400-vertex graphs had length 79,800. For $n = 100$ and $n = 400$, three sets of fifty n-vertex graphs were generated. One set was drawn from the uniform distribution with $p = 0.5$, and one with $p = 0.9$. All seed strings were generated using the standard UNIX pseudorandom number generator, and recorded to make the experiments repeatable.

The third set was generated using seed strings of lengths 65..85 for the fifty 100-vertex graphs and eleven of the 400-vertex graphs, and 270..285 for thirty-nine of the 400-vertex graphs. When we compiled the 100-vertex set we found that eleven seeds expanded to strings of length greater than $79,800$. Rather than truncate them to length 4950, we decided to discard them from the 100-vertex sample but include them into the 400-vertex sample. For hardware reasons we also set a limit of 700,000 on the number of bits produced at any stage of the decoding, and discarded those seeds which broke it from the 400-vertex sample. We believe that these practical decisions did not bias our results in any significant way. Nevertheless, it should be mentioned that at our seed sizes, the effects were dominated by the two operations that expand strings; the four operations that alter bits in strings had only limited (though perhaps sometimes significant) effect. It took about 12 hours of computing time to assemble this set.

The long strings of 0s and 1s were truncated to length 4950 or 79,800 and formed into an adjacency matrix for the graph in the order (1,2), (1,3), (2,3), (1,4),... of edges. Over three-fourths of these strings were generated by $\mathcal{L}$-programs whose final instruction was "Add a tail of $|x|$-many copies of u to x," where u was fairly long, and so ended with many repetitions of u. We do not have an intuitive idea of the extent to which this yielded repeated patterns in the graph. The average density of the fifty 100-vertex graphs was about 0.47, with a large variance. Four of these graphs were nearly empty, while there was one occurrence of the complete graph on 100 vertices.

Nine heuristics were tested on each of the six sets, giving 2700 runs in all. For each 400-vertex graph, it took about two hours to run all nine. The MFA heuristic was by far the slowest of the lot.

Sample Sizes. Each set of test graphs contained fifty graphs. It is reasonable to ask if this sample size is adequate. For graphs drawn from $\mathbf{u}_p(n)$, several arguments lead to the conclusion that a sample size of fifty graphs is more than adequate for our purposes. First, the expected size of the maximum clique in a graph drawn from $\mathbf{u}_p(n)$ has a sharp threshold [19] and the range of sizes of maximal cliques in such graphs is also quite narrow. Thus, any maximal-clique finding algorithm, for example most of the ones in the current paper, is guaranteed to find a clique in a narrow range. This argument is buffeted by experimental results reported in [11], which give the distribution of clique sizes found in fifty graphs drawn from $\mathbf{u}_p(400)$, $p = 0.5, 0.9$, which turns out to have a very small variance.

For graphs drawn from $\mathbf{q}(x)$, however, it was not clear a priori what an adequate sample size should be. We decided to start with a sample size of fifty. On this sample size, the results reported in Tables 1 and 2 (see Section 6 for their presentation and analysis) displayed certain trends so clearly and consistently that we felt confident that our observations were sound and would remain basically unchanged on larger sample sizes.

Evaluating Performance. The main hurdle in analyzing the results is that there is no easy way of calculating the size of the largest clique in a graph. We could have used some exponential-time algorithm to find the exact answer, but this would have been quite time-consuming on the 2700 runs. Therefore, instead of comparing the *absolute* performance of these algorithms on $\mathbf{u}(n)$ versus those on $\mathbf{q}(x)$, we decided to compare their *relative* performances, in particular how well or poorly certain algorithms performed relative to others, on $\mathbf{u}(n)$ versus $\mathbf{q}(x)$.

Parameter Settings of the Continuous Algorithms. The continuous algorithms—CHD and MFA— use certain free parameters whose values needed to be set. The values that we used are described below to make the experiments independently repeatable. One needs to refer to [11] in order to understand some of the parameters.

CHD was operated at $\rho = -10n$, $\lambda = 1$, $\gamma = 0.1$, $I_i = |\rho|/4$ for all i, and with the number of iterations of (1) fixed in advance to n. The initial state to CHD was set to $S(0) := (0.5 + \delta)^n$, where δ was a random value in $[-0.05, 0.05]$. The settings are the same as in [11], and are motivated there.

MFA was operated with the same settings for ρ, λ, γ, I, and the initial state $S(0)$ as was CHD, and with the following geometric annealing schedule:

$$T_i = a_{i-1}T_{i-1}; T_1 = \frac{2}{6}n|\rho|$$

where $a_i = 0.9$ for $i \leq 4$ and $a_i = 0.5$ for $i > 4$. Here $T_i = 1/\lambda_i$. The settings are essentially the same as in [11], and are motivated there. Experimental results in [11] also reveal that CHD and MFA continue to work well on the graphs tested in [11], on parameter settings in a reasonably large neighborhood of those described above.

5 Experimental Results

Table 1 gives the size of the clique retrieved by each of the nine algorithms on random graphs. Table 2 gives the performance ratio of the nine algorithms, relative to the best one, on random graphs and on graphs sampled from $\mathbf{q}(x)$, respectively.

$SD(\emptyset)$ is the steepest descent algorithm whose initial state is the empty set. It emulates the naive heuristic:

> Start from the empty set and extend it, by adding, in each step, one suitable vertex selected lexico-graphically, until it forms a maximal clique.

$SSD(\emptyset,1)$ is a randomized version of $SD(\emptyset)$ in which the vertex to be added is selected randomly, from the feasible choices, instead of in lexicographic fashion. $SD(V)$ is the steepest descent algorithm whose initial state is the entire vertex set V. It turns out that $SD(V)$ emulates the following algorithm [11]:

```
S := V
while S is not a clique do
        Pick a vertex v ∈ S with minimum degree in S
        Delete v from S
```

```
endwhile
while S is not a maximal clique do
      Pick the lexicographically first vertex v ∉ S adjacent to every vertex in S
      Add v to S
endwhile
```

$SD(V, 1)$ is a randomized version of $SD(V)$ in which the vertex to be deleted in an iteration of the first loop is picked with probability proportional to $S - \text{degree}_S(v)$ (the smaller the degree, the higher the probability), and the vertex to be added in an iteration of the second loop is picked at random from the feasible choices. $SSD(\emptyset,n)$ and $SSD(V,n)$ are multiple restart versions of $SSD(\emptyset,1)$ and $SSD(V,1)$ respectively—the largest clique found in the n runs is output.

From Table 2, the following observations can be made, regarding performance of the nine algorithms on graphs drawn from $\mathbf{q}$

- $SD(\emptyset)$ works the poorest. $SSD(\emptyset,1)$ and $SSD(V,1)$ work moderately better but remain significantly poorer than the best algorithms. Thus, randomization alone helps but not as much as one might expect.

- $SD(V)$ works much better than $SD(\emptyset)$ and nearly as well as the best algorithms. Thus replacing the initial state of $SD(\emptyset)$ by V, which makes the SD algorithm greedier, improves the performance much more dramatically than by randomizing $SD(\emptyset)$ alone. Randomizing $SD(V)$, to get $SSD(V,1)$, in fact worsens the performance significantly.

- The ρ-annealing algorithm consistently works just slightly better than $SD(V)$.

- The multiple restart algorithms—$SSD(\emptyset,n)$ and $SSD(V,n)$—work the best, with $SSD(V,n)$ working just very slightly better. This shows that the real benefit of randomization is that it allows multiple restarts, which boosts performance immensely.

- The continuous algorithm CHD works moderately poorer than the continuous algorithm MFA, which was anticipated, but also works discernably poorer than the discrete algorithm $SD(V)$, which was not anticipated.

These observations hold for both the 100- and 400-vertex graphs—if anything, the effects are more pronounced in the latter case.

From these results we may cluster the algorithms into four groups, using the relative performance ratio as the measure. In order of decreasing performance, the clusters are:

1. $SSD(V,n)$, $SSD(\emptyset,n)$, ρ-annealing, MFA, and $SD(V)$.

2. CHD.

3. $SSD(V,1)$ and $SSD(\emptyset,1)$.

4. $SD(\emptyset)$.

Notice that graphs drawn from $\mathbf{q}(x)$ have much larger clique sizes on average than graphs drawn from $\mathbf{u}_{1/2}(n)$. This, as discussed in previous sections, is to be expected. Notice, from Table 2, that the relative performance ratio of $SD(\emptyset)$ on graphs drawn from $\mathbf{q}(100)$ is 2.42, which worsens markedly, to 7.56, on graphs drawn from $\mathbf{q}(400)$. By contrast, $SD(\emptyset)$ has much better performance ratios on graphs drawn from $\mathbf{u}_p(100)$, $p = 0.5, 0.9$, which remain unchanged on graphs drawn from $\mathbf{u}_p(400)$, $p = 0.5, 0.9$. It is also interesting to note

References

[1] S. Arora, C. Lund, R. Motwani, M. Sudan, and M. Szegedy. Proof verification and hardness of approximation problems. In *The Proceedings of the 33rd Annual IEEE Symposium on Foundations of Computer Science*, page to appear, 1992.

[2] M. Bellare, O. Goldreich, and M. Sudan. Free bits, PCPs, and non-approximability—towards tight results. In *Proceedings of the Thirty-Sixth Symposium on Foundations of Computer Science*, pages 422–431, 1995.

[3] G. Bilbro, R. Mann, T.K. Miller, W.E. Snyder, D.E. Van den Bout, and M. White. Optimization by mean field annealing. In D.S. Touretzky, editor, *Advances in Neural Information Processing Systems*, volume 1, pages 91–98, San Mateo, 1989. (Denver 1988). Morgan Kaufmann.

[4] B. Bollobás and P. Erdős. Cliques in random graphs. *Proc. Camb. Phil. Soc.*, 80:419–427, 1976.

[5] D.S. Johnson. An Implementation of the "Semi-Exhaustive Greedy Independent Set Algorithm of Matula and Johri". Benchmark Algorithm for the Second Dimacs Challenge: Cliques, Coloring, and Satisfiability. 1983.

[6] Y. Gurevich and S. Shelah. Nearly linear time. In *Proceedings, Logic at Botik*, Lecture Notes in Computer Science No. 363, pages 108–118. Springer-Verlag, 1989.

[7] J. Hertz, A. Krogh, and R.G. Palmer. *Introduction to the Theory of Neural Computation*. Addison-Wesley, 1991.

[8] J.J. Hopfield. Neural networks and physical systems with emergent collective c omputational abilities. *Proceedings of the National Academy of Sciences, USA*, 79, 1982.

[9] J.J. Hopfield. Neurons with graded responses have collective computational properties like those of two-state neurons. *Proceedings of the National Academy of Sciences, USA*, 81, 1984.

[10] A. Jagota. Optimization by reduction to maximum clique. In *International Conference on Neural Networks*, pages 1526–1531, New York, March 1993. San Francisco, IEEE.

[11] A. Jagota. Approximating maximum clique in a hopfield-style network. *IEEE Transactions on Neural Networks*, 6(3):724–735, 1995.

[12] A. Jagota, L. Sanchis, and R. Ganesan. Approximating maximum clique using neural network and related heuristics. In D.S. Johnson and M. Trick, editors, *DIMACS Series: Second DIMACS Challenge*, page To Appear. AMS, January 1995. Proceedings of the Second DIMACS Challenge: Cliques, Coloring, and Satisfiability.

[13] R.M. Karp. The probabilistic analysis of some combinatorial search algorit hms. In J.F. Traub, editor, *Algorithms and Complexity: New Directions and Recent Results*, pages 1–19. Academic Press, New York, 1976.

[14] M. Li and P.M.B. Vitanyi. Kolmogorov complexity and its applications. In J. vanLeeuwen, editor, *Handbook of Theoretical Computer Science*, pages 187–254. Elsevier and MIT Press, Amsterdam/New York, 1990.

[15] M. Li and P. Vitanyi. Learning simple concepts under simple distributions. *SIAM Journal on Computing*, 20:911–935, 1991.

[16] M. Li and P. Vitányi. Philosophical issues in Kolmogorov complexity. In *Proceedings of the Nineteenth International Conference on Automata, Logic, and Programming*, volume 623 of *Lecture Notes in Computer Science*. Springer-Verlag, 1992.

[17] M. Li and P.M.B. Vitanyi. Average case complexity under the universal distribution equals worst-case complexity. *Information Processing Letters*, 42:145–149, May 1992.

[18] P. Miltersen. The complexity of malign ensembles. In *The Proceedings of the 6th Annual IEEE Conference on Structure in Complexity Theory*, pages 164–171, 1991.

[19] E.M. Palmer. *Graphical evolution*. Wiley, New York, 1985. Matula's theorem on page 76.

[20] C. Peterson and B. Söderberg. A new method for mapping optimization problems onto neural netw orks. *International Journal of Neural Systems*, 1:3–22, 1989.

Table 1: Average performance on p-random graphs. This table is excerpted from Table I in [11].

n	p	SD($\emptyset$)	SD(V)	ρ-A	SSD($\emptyset,1$)	SSD($V,1$)	SSD($\emptyset,n$)	SSD(V,n)	CHD	MFA
100	0.5	6.34	7.98	8.06	6.48	6.42	8.36	8.60	7.44	8.50
100	0.9	23.86	28.16	28.34	23.40	24.82	27.60	28.76	27.92	30.02
400	0.5	8.30	9.88	10.34	8.44	8.24	10.80	11.04	9.16	10.36
400	0.9	36.12	43.80	44.58	35.84	36.82	41.86	43.20	43.24	49.94

Table 2: Average performance ratio SSD(V,n)(G)/A(G) on all graphs. The numbers for the q graphs are obtained by averaging over the performance ratios, not by taking the performance ratio of the average.

Source	SD($\emptyset$)	SD(V)	ρ-A	SSD($\emptyset,1$)	SSD($V,1$)	SSD($\emptyset,1$)	SSD(V,n)	CHD	MFA
q(100)	2.42	1.10	1.09	1.79	1.60	1.03	—	1.31	1.10
$\mathcal{G}_{.5}$(100)	1.35	1.08	1.07	1.37	1.32	1.02	—	1.15	1.01
$\mathcal{G}_{.9}$(100)	1.20	1.02	1.01	1.23	1.15	1.04	—	1.03	0.96
q(400)	7.56	1.09	1.03	2.64	2.19	1.02	—	1.24	1.05
$\mathcal{G}_{.5}$(400)	1.33	1.12	1.07	1.31	1.33	1.02	—	1.21	1.02
$\mathcal{G}_{.9}$(400)	1.19	0.99	0.97	1.21	1.17	1.03	—	1.00	0.87

A Binary Neural Network Approach for Max Cut Problems

Nobuo Funabiki, Seishi Nishikawa, and Shigeto Tajima
Department of Information and Computer Sciences, Osaka University
1-3 Machikaneyama, Toyonaka, Osaka 560, Japan
funabiki@ics.es.osaka-u.ac.jp

Abstract
The max cut problem of a graph $G(V, E)$ is to find a partition of V into two disjoint subsets such that the sum of weights of cut edges in E is maximized. This paper presents a binary neural network for this NP-complete problem, which is suitable for the hardware implementation on digital circuits. The shaking term is newly introduced in order to drastically improve the performance. The simulation results in weighted complete graphs and unweighted random graphs with up to 1000 vertices show that the binary neural network provides the satisfactory solution quality as compared to the latest algorithm.

Introduction
Let $G(V, E)$ be a undirected graph with a vertex set V and a edge set E where each edge is given a weight. The max cut problem of a graph $G(V, E)$ is to find a partition of V into two disjoint vertex sets such that the cut size, i.e., the sum of weights of cut edges in E, is maximized. A cut edge has two endpoints in different vertex sets. The max cut problem is known to be NP-complete for arbitrary graphs including unweighted graphs [1], although it can be solved in polynomial time for some classes such as planar graphs [2] and circulant graphs [3]. The max cut problem has been studied in several applications including VLSI design and statistical physics [4][5].

A number of papers have been reported for the max cut problem [2]-[8][16]. Delorme et al. presented the eigenvalue upper bound on the maximum cut size, and proved to be computable with an arbitrary precision in polynomial time [6]. They showed the performance of the bound in a variety of graph examples [7]. Poljak et al. proposed the upper bound approach via a relaxation of the discrete problem to a continuos convex problem [8].

As a polynomial time approximation algorithm, the neural network has been studied in many combinatorial optimization problems. Among variations such as the continuos Hopfield neural network [9], the mean field annealing [10], and the Boltzmann machine [16], the binary neural network has been shown to be an effective method for NP-complete graph problems [11]-[13]. In addition, it is much suitable for the hardware implementation on digital circuits [14]. This paper presents a binary neural network for the max cut problem. A shaking term is newly introduced in the motion equation in order to drastically improve the solution quality. The performance is evaluated through extensive simulations where it is compared with the results of the latest algorithm by Poljak [8].

Binary Neural Network for Max Cut Problem
The binary neural network (BNN) is composed of N binary neurons for the N-vertex graph problem. The output V_i of the ith neuron is updated from the input U_i by [15]:
If $U_i > 0$ then $V_i = 1$ else $V_i = 0$. (1)
The "zero output ($V_i = 0$)" represents the partition of vertex #i into the first vertex set, and the "one output ($V_i = 1$)" does the partition into the second set. Fig. 1 illustrates a max cut problem for a 4-vertex graph, and the neural network representation corresponding to the optimum solution. The white square represents the zero output and the black square does the one output.

The energy function $E(V_1,...,V_N)$ represents the cost function to be minimized in the problem, which is the sum of weights of edges inside each partition:

$$E = \frac{A}{2}\sum_{i=1}^{N} \sum_{\substack{j=1 \\ j \neq i}}^{N} e_{ij}((1-V_i)(1-V_j)+V_iV_j) \tag{2}$$

where A is a coefficient, and e_{ij} is the weight of the edge between vertex #i and vertex #j.

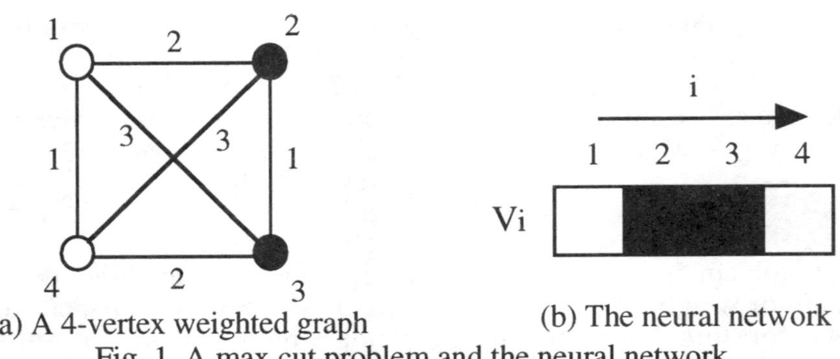

(a) A 4-vertex weighted graph   (b) The neural network

Fig. 1 A max cut problem and the neural network

As the driving force of the minimization, the motion equation is derived by the partial derivative of the energy function and the shaking term which is newly introduced in this paper:

$$\frac{dU_i}{dt} = -\frac{\partial E}{\partial V_i} + (\text{shaking term}) = A\sum_{\substack{j=1\\j\neq i}}^{N} e_{ij}(1\text{-}2V_j) + B(t)(1\text{-}2V_i). \tag{3}$$

where $B(t)$ is a coefficient determined by the iteration step t. The shaking term tries to reverse the output state of the neuron. With the gradient descent approach of the A-term, the B-term encourages the state of the neural network to escape from the local minimum and to reach the better solution by "shaking" it. $B(t)$ is an "annealed" square function so that the shaking effect is gradually decreasing. Note that the local minimum convergence of the binary neural network without the shaking term has been proved [11]. As shown in Fig. 2, the length of "on" period $T(t)$ is shortened gradually as the computation is advanced:
$S=Tmax/T_0$,

If $kS\leq t<(k+1)S$ then $T(t)=T_0\text{-}k\text{-}1$ for $k=0,...,T_0\text{-}1$, else $T(t)=0$,
If $(t \bmod T_0)<T(t)$ then $B(t)=B_0$ else $B(t)=0$. $\tag{4}$
where Tmax is the maximum number of iteration steps, T_0 is the constant period, and B_0 is the constant amplitude of the square function.

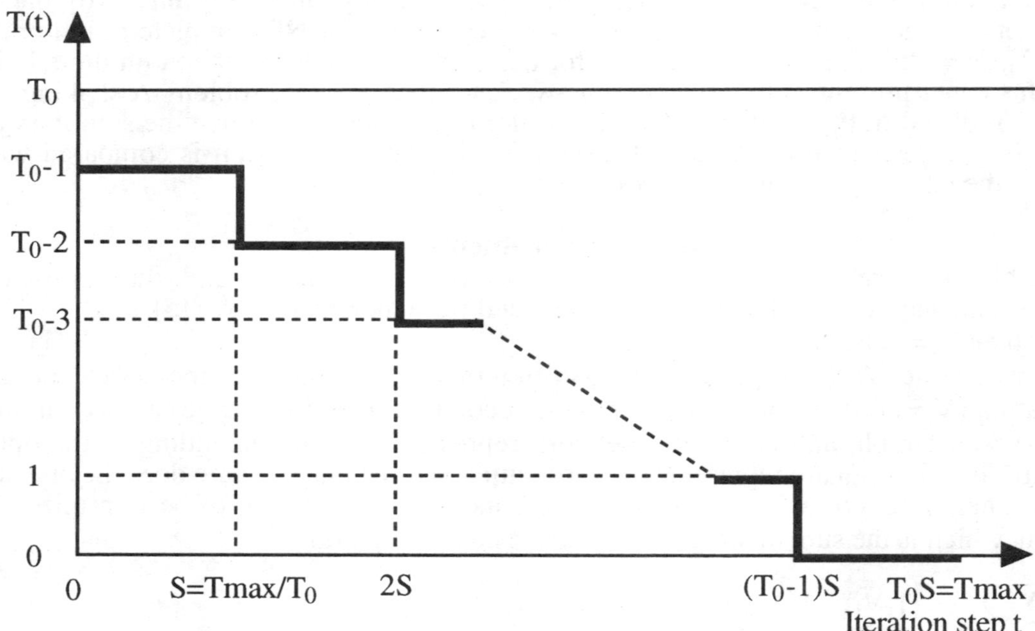

Fig. 2 The change of "on" period in the shaking term

The motion equation is solved by the first order Euler method on the synchronous parallel computation. It sometimes causes the oscillation of neuron states where several neurons repeat the same states simultaneously. In order to avoid this undesirable situation, the initial states of neuron inputs are randomized between $-U_{in}/2$ and $U_{in}/2$, where U_{in} is the expected sum of weights of edges incident to one vertex:

$$U_{in} = \frac{2}{N} \sum_{i=1}^{N-1} \sum_{j=i+1}^{N} e_{ij} \qquad (5)$$

In the initial state, the number of vertices in each vertex set is almost equal so that as many as edges are cut there.

The following is the synchronous parallel algorithm for the max cut problem. The set of parameters have been empirically selected through simulations.

1) Set $t=0$, $A=1$, $T_0=10$, and $Tmax=5N$.
2) Calculate U_{in} by (5), $B_0=U_{in}/10$, and $B(t)$ for $t=0,...,Tmax$ by (4).
3) Initialize U_i for $i=1,...,N$ with uniformly randomized numbers between $-U_{in}/2$ and $U_{in}/2$, and initialize $V_i=1$ if $U_i>0$, $V_i=0$ otherwise.
4) Compute the motion equation for $i=1,...,N$ based on the first Euler method:

$$U_i = U_i + A \sum_{\substack{j=1 \\ j \neq i}}^{N} e_{ij}(1-2V_j) + B(t)(1-2V_i).$$

5) Check the termination: if $((V_i=0 \ \& \ \left(\sum_{\substack{j=1 \\ j \neq i}}^{N} e_{ij}(1-2V_j) \right) \leq 0)$ or $(V_i=1 \ \& \ \left(\sum_{\substack{j=1 \\ j \neq i}}^{N} e_{ij}(1-2V_j) \right) \geq 0)$ for

$i=1,...,N)$ or $(t=Tmax)$ then terminate the procedure, else go to 6).
6) Update V_i by the binary neuron model:
If $U_i>0$ then $V_i=1$ else $V_i=0$.
7) Increment t by 1: $t=t+1$. Go to 4).

The first condition for the termination check in 5) is introduced to stop the iteration only when the neural network cannot improve the solution quality. It aims to hasten the iterative computation while keeping the solution quality.

Simulations and Discussion
The binary neural network is simulated through both randomly weighted complete graphs, where each weight e_{ij} is uniformly randomized between 1 and 100, and unweighted random graphs with 50% edge density and with each weight $e_{ij}=1$. First, the effects of the shaking term is evaluated. Table 1 shows the best results of the neural network among 10 simulation runs with a variety of B_0 in 5 weighted complete graphs (upper 5 rows) and 3 unweighted random graphs (lower 3 rows). Each run is executed from different initial states of the neural network. Note that the performance of the binary neural network has sometimes depended on the initial state selection [11]-[13]. Table 1 depicts that the shaking term can drastically improve the solution quality, where the underline indicates the best solution in each graph. From them, $B_0=U_{in}/10$ is the most reasonable choice, which is used for the simulations in Table 2. Fig. 3 illustrates the change of cut sizes with the iteration steps for the 100-vertex weighted complete graph. The larger amplitude of the shaking term requires longer computation time, although it can provide a better solution.
Then, the performance of the binary neural network is compared with the existing algorithm. For this comparison, the results by Poljak et al. [8] are adopted, because they show the cut sizes for randomly weighted complete graphs and unweighted random graphs with different numbers of vertices in their paper. Table 2 shows the cut sizes known by two algorithms for 8 weighted complete graphs (left columns) and 5 unweighted random graphs (right columns) with up to 1000 vertices, where the cut sizes by Poljak are taken from their paper [8]. Note that we use the same weight distribution and the same edge density to generate the simulated graphs as Poljak et al. Table 2 depicts that our binary neural network provides the satisfactory performance as compared to the latest algorithm both in weighted complete graphs and unweighted random graphs. In addition, our binary neural network can be implemented on

a digital parallel machine with a maximum of N processors [14], while Poljak's algorithm is sequential.

Conclusion

This paper presents a binary neural network for the max cut problem which is generally NP-complete. The newly introduced shaking term in the motion equation can drastically improve the solution quality. The simulation results in weighted complete graphs and unweighted random graphs show that our binary neural network provides the satisfactory performance as compared to the latest algorithm. Although the shaking term prolongs the computation time, the binary neural network can be implemented on a digital parallel machine with a maximum of N processors.

Table 1 Simulation results with different shaking terms

Graph	Bo=0	Bo=Uin/5	Bo=Uin/10	Bo=Uin/20	Bo=Uin/30
N=100	135573	<u>136502</u>	136263	136118	135857
N=200	530820	<u>534635</u>	534584	534574	533571
N=300	1182365	1189493	<u>1190886</u>	1189019	1188185
N=400	2093571	2102210	<u>2103345</u>	2102320	2101174
N=500	3257342	3270152	<u>3273826</u>	3272575	3270286
N=100	1426	1429	<u>1430</u>	1426	1426
N=250	8454	8538	8541	<u>8544</u>	8495
N=500	33147	<u>33367</u>	33364	33326	33301

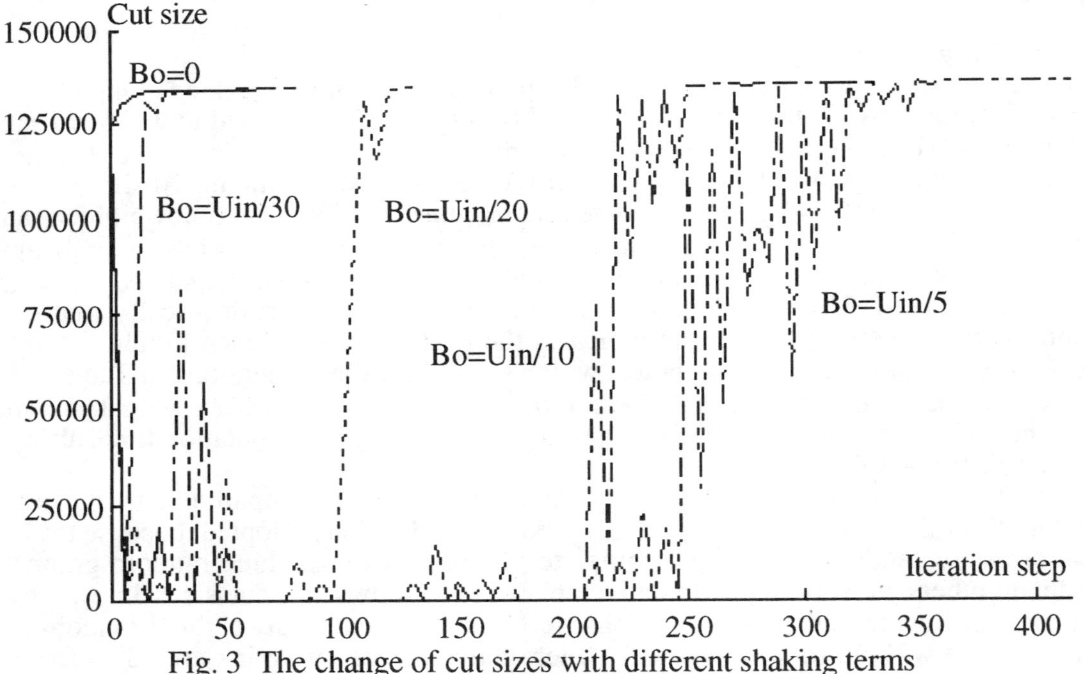

Fig. 3 The change of cut sizes with different shaking terms

Table 2 Performance comparisons of two algorithms

Graph	Poljak	BNN	Graph	Poljak	BNN
N=100	133858	136263	N=100	1430	1430
N=200	527069	534584	N=250	8535	8541
N=300	1171149	1190886	N=500	33242	33364
N=400	2069083	2103345	N=750	74117	74152
N=500	3215025	3273826	N=1000	130871	130964
N=600	4609261	4699396			
N=800	8143208	8323976			
N=1000	12703570	12961119			

References

[1] M. R. Garey and D. S. Johnson, *Computers and intractability*, Freeman, San Francisco, 1979.

[2] G. I. Orlova and Y. G. Dorfman, "Finding the maximum cut in a graph," Eng. Cybern., vol. 10, pp. 502-506, 1972.

[3] S. Poljak and D. Turzik, "Max-cut in circulant graphs," Discrete Math., vol. 108, pp. 379-392, 1992.

[4] C.-P. Hsu, "Minimum-via topological routing," IEEE Trans. CAD/ICAS, vol. CAD-2,. no. 4, pp. 235-246, Oct. 1983.

[5] F. Barahona, M. Grötschel, M. Jünger, and G. Reinelt, "An application of combinatorial optimization to statistical physics and circuit layout design," Oper. Res., vol. 36, no. 3, pp. 493-513, May 1988.

[6] C. Delorme and S. Poljak, "Laplacian eigenvalues and the maximum cut problem," Math. Program., vol. 62, pp. 557-574, 1993.

[7] C. Delorme and S. Poljak, "The performance of an eigenvalue bound on the max-cut problem in some classes of graphs," Discrete Math., vol. 111, pp. 145-156, 1993.

[8] S. Poljak and F. Rendl, "Node and edge relaxations of the max-cut problem," Computing, vol. 52, pp. 123-137, 1994.

[9] J. J. Hopfield and D. W. Tank, "Neural computation of decisions in optimization problems," Biological Cybernetics, vol. 52, pp. 141-152, 1985.

[10] C. Peterson and J. R. Anderson, "Neural networks and NP-complete optimization problems; a performance study on the graph bisection problem," Complex Systems, vol. 2, pp. 59-89, 1988.

[11] Y. Takefuji, *Neural network parallel computing*, Kluwer Academic Publishers, 1992.

[12] N. Funabiki, Y. Takefuji, and K. C. Lee, "A neural network model for finding a near-maximum clique," J. Paral. Dist. Comput., vol. 14, no. 3, pp. 340-344, March 1992.

[13] N. Funabiki, Y. Takefuji, K. C. Lee, and Y. B. Cho, "A neural network parallel algorithm for clique vertex-partition problems," Int. J. Elect., vol. 72, no. 3, pp. 357-372, March 1992.

[14] T. Kurokawa and H. Yamashita, "Bus connected neural network hardware system," Electronics Letters, vol. 30, no. 12, pp. 979-980, June 1994.

[15] W. S. McCulloch and W. H. Pitts, "A logical calculus of the ideas immanent in nervous activity," Bulletin of Mathematical Biophysics, 5, pp. 115-133, 1943.

[16] J. H. M. Korst and E. H. L. Aarts, "Combinatorial optimization on a Boltzmann machine," J. Paral. Dist. Comput., vol. 6, pp. 331-357, 1989.

An Improved Neural Net Algorithm
for the Hypergraph Vertex Cover Problem

Dmitri Kaznachey†, Arun Jagota‡
† St. Jude Chidren's Research Hospital/ University of Memphis
Memphis, TN 38152, USA
‡ Dept. of Computer Sciences, University of North Texas
Denton, TX 76203, USA

Abstract— The *hypergraph vertex cover problem* (HVC) is an NP-hard problem on hypergraphs
with numerous theoretical and practical applications. There has been much work on solving graph optimization problems using neural networks; however almost none on solving
hypergraph problems. In previous recent work we designed and evaluated a Hopfield-type
network for approximately solving the HVC problem. Approximation performance was
experimentally determined on random hypergraphs, as well as on some structured hypergraphs, by comparing it to a well known greedy algorithm. The greedy algorithm found
somewhat better solutions. The neural network algorithm was, however, significantly faster
on random hypergraphs of edge-cardinality up to three.

In this paper we present an improved mapping of the HVC onto a Hopfield network, which
also leads to an improved dynamical algorithm. We experimentally compare the performance of this algorithm to that of our previous algorithm, and to a more efficient implementation of the greedy algorithm than our previous one. The new neural net algorithm finds
significantly better solutions than the previous neural net algorithm and of the same quality
as those found by the greedy algorithm. The efficient version of the greedy algorithm runs
faster on random hypergraphs. We also evaluate our new algorithm on certain hypergraphs
that are provably hard for the greedy algorithm, and on a large randomized variant of this
class of hypergraphs. The new neural net algorithm finds much better solutions on these
hypergraphs than does G_2.

1   The Hypergraph Vertex Cover Problem

The *Hypergraph vertex cover problem* (HVC) is an NP-hard optimization problem on hypergraphs, and
generalizes the well-known vertex cover problem (VC) on graphs [1]. The HVC, also known as the *hitting
set problem* [1], is described as follows. Let $H = (V, E)$ be a hypergraph with vertex-set $V = \{v_1, ..., v_n\}$
and edge-set $E = \{e_1, ..., e_m\}$ with $e_i \subseteq V$. A *vertex cover* in H is a subset C of the vertices that
covers all the (hyper) edges in H, i.e. for all $e_i \in E$, $e_i \cap C \neq \emptyset$. HVC is the problem of finding the
minimum-cardinality vertex cover in a given hypergraph. When, for all i, $|e_i|$ equals 2, the hypergraph
is a graph and the problem reduces to the *vertex cover problem* (VC).

The Hopfield neural network [6] represents an attractive computational paradigm for solving optimization problems because it minimizes an energy function in a manner that is plausible to implement in
parallel, distributed, or autonomous hardware (possibly special-purpose). There has been much work on
heuristically solving difficult graph optimization problems with neural networks [5, chp. 4] [12]. However,
there has been almost no work on solving *hyper*graph optimization problems. Hypergraph problems—
though less familiar than their graph versions—often retain their theoretical and practical applications
in a generalized setting. Furthermore, they pose interesting challenges to neural networks because they
involve structures higher-order than those of graphs.

Most previous neural net work on HVC is on its special case VC [2, 12, 13, 11, 7, 8]. In [7, 8] a neural
network model for the HVC problem was also proposed. This model employed a neuron for every edge of
the hypergraph. This is quite inefficient, because hypergraphs can have upto exponentially-many edges
in terms of the number of nodes. This model did, however, provide a worst-case performance guarantee,
though no experiments were conducted to determine how well it worked in practice.

A problem closely related to HVC is the *Set Cover Problem* (SC) [1], defined as follows. Unlike the
vertex cover, a set cover in a hypergraph is a subset E' of edges that covers all the vertices, i.e. for all
$v \in V$ there exists an edge $e \in E'$ so that $v \in e$. SC is the problem of finding the minimum-cardinality
set cover in a given hypergraph. A neural network algorithm was designed and extensively evaluated
for the SC problem by Grossman [3]. Earlier, a Boltzmann Machine algorithm for the SC problem was
proposed in [14] but no experimental results reported. The SC problem can be easily reduced to the HVC
problem. However, the reduction involves some intricacies—for example the HVC instance produced is
much larger than the original SC instance—making direct comparisons with the approaches of [3, 14] and
with experimental results of [3] infeasible.

In recently reported work [9] we mapped HVC to a Hopfield-type neural network in such a way that
each vertex of the hypergraph is represented by one neuron. This mapping is thus significantly more
efficient than the one in [7]. In results reported in [9] this approach found solutions somewhat poorer on
average than a greedy algorithm while running significantly faster (on the same computer, under the same

conditions). In this paper we present an improvement to this mapping which retains the compactness of the previous one. The resulting algorithm finds significantly better solutions than our previous neural net algorithm, while retaining its time superiority over the greedy algorithm.

Let $HVC(H)$ denote the size of the minimum vertex cover in a hypergraph H. The greedy algorithm that we have chosen to compare against is guaranteed to find a vertex cover no larger than $O(\log \Delta(H)) \times HVC(H)$ in every hypergraph H [10]. Here $\Delta(H)$ denotes the maximum degree of a vertex in H, where the degree of a vertex v in a hypergraph is defined as the number of edges that v is contained in. In one sense this is the best known theoretical performance guarantee for the HVC problem. This greedy algorithm, which we call G_2, was independently discovered by Johnson and Lovasz, as noted in [10].

G_2 sequentially puts vertices in the vertex cover in greedy fashion. Whenever a vertex v is added to the cover C, all edges containing v are deleted (i.e., noted as being covered by v). The algorithm terminates when no edges remain, i.e. when all edges have been covered. The formal description is as follows.

ALGORITHM G_2 (*Input:* Hypergraph, *Output:* Vertex cover)
1. $C := \oslash$
2. **while** $E \neq \oslash$
3.   [Pick a vertex v of maximum degree in H]
4. $H := H\backslash\{v\}$ [delete v and edges containing v]
5. $C := C \cup \{v\}$
6. **return** C.

Our efficient implementation of this algorithm involves an array of vertices and a doubly-linked list holding one node for each edge. Each element in an array holds two fields: the degree of a vertex, and a pointer to a doubly-linked list. Each node representing an edge has as many fields as there are vertices in this edge. Each field is divided into two subfields: the first subfield contains the vertex number and the second subfield contains left and right pointers to the linked list of that vertex. In the implementation of G_2 at each step we first find the vertex of a maximum degree, and then follow the doubly-linked list to remove all edges the vertex is contained in. The time complexity of this implementation is $O(km + n^2)$ for hypergraphs containing hyperedges of cardinality at most k, which is significantly better than our previous implementation based on the incidence matrix, which was $O(mn^2)$ [9]. The new implementation requires very slightly more memory though, $\Theta(km + n)$ versus $\Theta(km)$.

Much of our experimental work in this paper is on a restricted class of hypergraphs called k-cardinality hypergraphs in which no hyper-edge has cardinality more than k. There is another greedy algorithm, that we call MM, which is guaranteed to find a vertex cover no larger than $k \times HVC(H)$ in any hypergraph H. This algorithm generalizes a well-known greedy algorithm for VC with a performance guarantee of two, described in [1] and attributed to F. Gavril. For sufficiently small k, the algorithm MM gives a better theoretical performance guarantee than G_2. However, in practice we found that MM works considerably poorer than both G_2 and our previous neural network algorithm, even on 3-cardinality random hypergraphs [9]. Therefore, in the current paper, we have eliminated MM from consideration.

2   The Improved Neural Net Algorithm

We begin this section with the improved mapping of the HVC problem onto an energy function for a Hopfield network. First we present the mapping and then briefly explain how it improves upon the one in [9]. Represent hypergraph H by an incidence matrix $A = (a_{ij})$ in which a_{ij} is 1 if vertex j is in the edge i, and 0 otherwise. Describe any subset C of the vertices by a vector $S_c \in \{0, 1\}^n$ in which S_i equals 1 if the vertex i is in C and 0 otherwise. Then our goal is to minimize $\sum_{i=1}^{n} S_i$ subject to constraints $\sum_{i=1}^{n} a_{ei}S_i \geq 1$ for each edge $e = 1, ..., m$. Then the following energy function may be formulated:

$$E = \alpha \sum_{i=1}^{n} S_i + \beta \sum_{e=1}^{m}(d_e - \sum_{i=1}^{n} a_{ei}S_i)^2 \tag{1}$$

The second term in (1) represents the quadratic constraints and is minimized when the number of vertices covering an edge $\sum_{i=1}^{n} a_{ei}S_i$ equals d_e. The energy function (1) differs from the energy function in [9] in that, in the latter, $d_e = d$ for all e (i.e., there was a single scalar parameter d). The role of d was to control the average number of vertices covering an edge e. A small d would bias the network in trying to seek a solution in which this average was low (hence, hopefully, a small vertex cover). However, if the d was too small, this could lead to an infeasible solution (perhaps a small cover, but with not all edges covered). This suggested a binary search algorithm in [9] for finding a "good" d, which worked reasonably well in practice. In (1), we replace d by a vector (d_e). This allows each edge to be covered by a possibly different number of vertices without considering that as a soft violation. Although this allows us to represent the coverage constraints more accurately, the cost we pay is that the algorithm for choosing a "good" (d_e) vector becomes more complicated. When there was a single scalar parameter d we could resort to binary search. Now finding a good (d_e) vector involves solving a multivariate optimization problem.

Given a hypergraph $H(V, E)$, the Hopfield net is constructed of n units with the weights w_{ij} and biases

I_i derived from (1).

$$w_{ij} = -2\beta \sum_{e=1}^{m} a_{ei}a_{ej}; \; I_i = 2\beta \sum_{e=1}^{m} d_e a_{ei} - \alpha; \tag{2}$$

Notice that the biases I_i in (2) embody the heuristic to include into the set cover vertices with larger degrees, while the weights w_{ij} capture the number of edges both vertices i and j are contained in, thus being biased against including both i and j in the vertex cover if this number is high. Both of these heuristics are also implicitly in G_2.

We will use *serial update dynamics* to find the stable states. In serial updates exactly one unit i is picked and updated according to the asynchronous updates rule of Hopfield [6]. *Steepest descent* is an instance of serial-update dynamics in which a unit i whose switch reduces the energy maximally is picked to switch; see [7], [8]. In our implementation of the steepest descent ties are broken by picking the smallest-numbered neuron whose switch reduces the energy maximally.

The algorithm below implements a heuristic search for a "good" vector (d_e) using which we hope to retrieve a network stable state that constitutes a small vertex cover.

ALGORITHM HNDE (*Input*: hypergraph H, *Output*: vertex cover)
1. $d_e := 1$ for all e;
2. $\langle$ Map H into HN with $\alpha = 2.0, \beta = 1.0 \rangle$;
3. $S := (0)$; $pnc := 0$;
4. **repeat**
5. $S' := \langle$ Apply steepest descent dynamics from initial state S until convergence $\rangle$;
6.   **for all** edges e
7. $ds_e := \langle$ number of vertices in S' covering $e \rangle$;
8.   **if** (S' is NOT a vertex cover) **then**
9.   **for all** $e : d_e < ds_e$
10. $d_e := ds_e$;
11.   **if** (no such e exists) **then**
12.   **for all** $e : ds_e = 0$
13. $d_e := d_e + 1$;
14.   **if** (S' is a vertex cover) **then**
15.   **for all** $e : d_e > ds_e$
16. $d_e := ds_e$;
17. $\langle$ Remap H into HN with same α, β but with new (d_e) $\rangle$
18. $nc := \langle$ number of on-vertices in $S' \rangle$;
19.   **if** ($nc, pnc \leq \frac{n}{2}$ OR $nc, pnc > \frac{n}{2}$) **then**
20. $S := S'$;
21.   **else**
22.   **if** ($nc \leq \frac{n}{2}$)
23. $S := (0)$;
24.   **else**
25. $S := (1)$;
26. $pnc := nc$;
27. **until** no d_e changed in this iteration of the repeat-until loop;
28. **return** S

In step 1, all d_e's are initialized to 1, to try to find a solution in which every edge is covered by exactly one vertex. When this fails, which is quite likely, the individual d_e's are increased as shown steps 9–13. In particular, the d_e's whose values are less than the associated ds_e's—the actual number of vertices in the found S' covering edge e—are *increased* to their associated ds_e's. Similarly, when S' is a set cover, the d_e's whose values are larger than their associated ds_e's are *decreased* to the ds_e's.

3   Experimental Results

We evaluated HNDE and G_2 on random 3-cardinality hypergraphs as well as on some structured hypergraphs. Table 1 presents the results on the random hypergraphs. These hypergraphs were the same as those evaluated in [9], facilitating comparisons with our previous algorithm HscN-D and with G_2. From Table 1 we see that our improved algorithm HNDE finds significantly smaller vertex covers than our previous algorithm HscN-D on medium-density 3-cardinality hypergraphs. HNDE finds vertex covers of almost the same size as those found by G_2 across all densities. G_2 runs faster than both neural net algorithms, especially on dense hypergraphs.

Table 2 presents the experimental results on structured hypergraphs arising from the *instructor hiring problem* (IHP), explained below. Simply put, the IHP involves selecting a smallest subset of the applicants for an unspecified number of instructor positions so that all courses are covered. Each applicant is required to provide a list of courses that he or she can teach. The IHP problem reduces to the HVC problem as

Table 1: Experimental results on hypergraphs of varying density. Each row represents results averaged over ten random hypergraphs. The column labeled n gives the number of vertices. The column labeled **density** gives the number of edges divided by the number of vertices in a hypergraph, averaged over the hypergraphs in the corresponding row. The column HND/G_2 ($HNDE/G_2$) gives the ratios of the vertex cover sizes and running times of HscN-D to G_2 (HNDE to G_2). Running times of all algorithms are reported on the same computer.

Test hypergraphs		Vertex cover size					Running time	
n	density	HND	G_2	HND/G_2	HNDE	$HNDE/G_2$	HND/G_2	$HNDE/G_2$
50	0.45	10.5	10.8	0.97	10.7	0.99	2.35	1.24
100	0.53	23.4	23.1	1.01	23.1	1.00	1.52	1.14
200	0.56	47.9	46.7	1.03	46.7	1.00	1.25	1.07
50	5.00	35.4	28.6	1.24	29.6	1.03	3.40	2.85
100	4.97	70.5	56.0	1.26	58.8	1.05	2.25	2.03
200	5.07	144.2	112.0	1.29	116.8	1.04	1.65	1.54
50	49.40	45.0	41.7	1.08	42.7	1.02	6.66	17.89
100	50.34	91.5	83.1	1.10	84.2	1.01	6.35	17.94
200	50.28	182.1	164.7	1.11	167.6	1.02	4.60	13.70

follows. The vertices of the hypergraph are the applicants; the edges of the hypergraph are the courses. A vertex cover is a subset of the applicants that can cover all courses. For further details the reader is referred to [9]. Structure comes into hypergraphs arising from the IHP problem because candidates may apply for different kinds of positions (e.g. junior or senior), and certain kinds of candidates are only required to include certain kinds of courses in their course lists. Somewhat interestingly, we found that

Table 2: Experimental results on hypergraphs arising from the IHP problem. In all cases, the hypergraph had 50 vertices (applicants) and 23 edges (courses). The parameter α denotes the ratio of junior to senior applicants, β the number of courses in each applicant's course list, and γ the minimum percentage of graduate courses in the course list of a senior applicant.

Instance parameters			vertex cover size			Running time		
α	β	γ	HNDE	HscN-D	G_2	HNDE	HscN-D	G_2
3/7	4	75	7.3	8.6	7.4	0.0	0.7	0.0
1	4	75	7.4	7.3	7.4	0.0	0.9	0.0
7/3	4	75	7.7	7.4	7.6	0.0	1.0	0.0
3/7	5	80	6.3	6.9	6.2	0.0	0.7	0.0
1	5	80	6.4	5.9	6.2	0.0	0.8	0.0
7/3	5	80	6.8	6.7	6.7	0.0	1.0	0.0
3/7	6	67	5.7	5.6	5.5	0.0	0.7	0.0
1	6	67	5.7	5.3	5.5	0.0	0.9	0.0
7/3	6	67	5.9	5.7	5.6	0.0	1.0	0.0

in previously reported experiments on the same IHP instances [9] HscN-D not only found very slightly larger vertex covers than G_2 but also ran consistently slower. Here we find that HNDE finds vertex covers that are very slightly larger than G_2 (and about the same on average as HscN-D) but runs as fast as the efficient implementation of G_2. More experimentation is clearly needed, on larger instances of the IHP problem.

4   Hard Hypergraphs for G_2

On random hypergraphs and on hypergraphs arising from the IHP problem we have seen that the HNDE algorithm retrieves roughly the same size solutions as does G_2. However, on dense random hypergraphs G_2 finds a solution much faster. Knowing that G_2 is a greedy algorithm, can we construct some large class of hypergraphs on which G_2 works poorly and HNDE better? This section describes one such class of hypergraphs, and evaluates the performance of G_2 and HNDE on them.

First we describe a *deterministic* version of this class of hypergraphs, defined as follows. Let an r-edge denote a hyperedge of cardinality r. First define $\mathcal{H}_1^l = (V_1, E_1)$ as a family of hypergraphs whose set of vertices V_1 is partitioned into two sets L and R_1 with $|L| = |R_1| = l$ and whose set of edges E_1 comprises of 2-edges (l, r_1) in which every vertex from L is connected to a unique vertex in R_1.

Then define families of hypergraphs $\mathcal{H}_k^l = (V_k, E_k)$ inductively as follows:

$$V_k = V_{k-1} \cup R_k \text{ with } |R_k| = |R_{k-1}| - j_k, \text{ where } j_k \geq 2$$
$$E_k = E_{k-1} \cup \{(r_1, r_2, ..., r_{k-1}, r_k)|r_i \in R_i \text{ for } 1 \leq i \leq k\}$$

where $(r_1, r_2, \ldots, r_k)$ denotes a k-edge.

We now show that the families $\mathcal{H}_k^l$ of hypergraphs are hard for G_2. It is easy to see that, for fixed l, the size of a minimum vertex cover in all hypergraphs in the family $\mathcal{H}_k^l$ is the same, namely l. The set L or the set R_1, for example, is a vertex cover. Let $G_2(\mathcal{H}_k^l)$ denote the size of a vertex cover that G_2 finds on any hypergraph in $\mathcal{H}_k^l$. Our result is that

Proposition 1 *On any hypergraph in $\mathcal{H}_k^l$, $G_2(\mathcal{H}_k^l) = |R_1| + |R_2| + |R_3| + \ldots + |R_k|$.*

Proof. The proof involves showing that, with any hypergraph in $\mathcal{H}_k^l$ as input, G_2 first deletes all vertices in R_k, then all vertices in R_{k-1} and so on until only the vertices in $R_1 \cup L$ are left. After this point, G_2 deletes exactly l appropriately chosen vertices from $R_1 \cup L$. The result will then follow since the set of deleted vertices constitutes the found vertex cover.

Before we proceed, the following notation is useful. In a hypergraph from the family $\mathcal{H}_k^l$, for any subset $S \subseteq V$ containing vertices of equal degree (in V), let $d_k(S)$ denote this degree.

The proof hinges on the following claim. Let $P(k)$ denote the proposition: *In any hypergraph in $\mathcal{H}_k^l$ $d_k(R_k) > \max_{1 \leq j < k}\{d_k(R_j)\}$.* We use induction on k to prove $P(k)$ for all $k \geq 2$.

Base case. This is $k = 2$, and is easily proven since $d_2(R_2) = l$ and $d_2(R_1) \leq l - 2 + 1$.

Inductive step. We assume that $P(k)$ is true for some $k \geq 2$. Consider $k + 1$, namely the assertion that $P(k+1)$ is true for any hypergraph in $\mathcal{H}_{k+1}^l$. Let $\epsilon_m = \prod_{j=1}^m |R_j|$ denote the total number of m-edges in a hypergraph in $\mathcal{H}_p^l$, for $p \geq m$. Note that, for $1 \leq j \leq k$: $d_{k+1}(R_j) = \epsilon_{k+1}/|R_j| + d_k(R_j)$. Since, by the inductive assumption, $d_k(R_k) > \max_{1 \leq j < k}\{d_k(R_j)\}$ and since $\epsilon_{k+1}/|R_k| > \max_{1 \leq j < k}\{\epsilon_{k+1}/|R_j|\}$ by our choice of $|R_k|$ we have that $d_{k+1}(R_k) > \max_{1 \leq j < k}\{d_{k+1}(R_j)\}$. Therefore it remains to compare $d_{k+1}(R_k)$ with $d_{k+1}(R_{k+1})$. Noting that $d_{k+1}(R_{k+1}) = \epsilon_{k+1}/|R_{k+1}| = \epsilon_k$ and that $d_{k+1}(R_k) = \epsilon_{k+1}/|R_k| + \epsilon_k/|R_k| = (|R_{k+1}|+1)\epsilon_k/|R_k|$ gives $\frac{d_{k+1}(R_{k+1})}{d_{k+1}(R_k)} = \frac{|R_k|}{|R_{k+1}|+1} > 1$ since $j_{k+1} \geq 2$, which completes the proof.

At this point we have proven that $P(k)$ is true for all k. What remains involves just mirroring this inductive proof. More precisely, let a hypergraph in $\mathcal{H}_k^l$ be input to G_2. Since the vertices in R_k have largest degree, these vertices are first deleted one by one. At this point, the remaining hypergraph is one in H_{k-1}^l. Now since the vertices in R_{k-1} have largest degree, these vertices are deleted from the hypergraph. And so on, until only the vertices in $R_1 \cup L$ are left. After this point l appropriate vertices are deleted from $R_1 \cup L$. $\square$

Proposition 1 implies

Corollary 1 *When all $j_m \geq 2$, $2 \leq m \leq k$ are constants, then $G_2(\mathcal{H}_k^l) = \Theta(k \times l)$.*

namely, that G_2 finds a vertex cover that is a factor of order of k larger than the smallest one.

Though, as we have seen, G_2 provably performs poorly on $\mathcal{H}_k^l$ and, as we show below, HNDE empirically performs better, the families $\mathcal{H}_k^l$ have very specialized structure, containing only a small number of hypergraphs (in fact, just one graph, upto isomorphism, for each pair of l and k). It is useful, therefore, to consider the following *randomized* generalization of $\mathcal{H}_k^l$, that we call $\mathcal{R}_k^l(p)$, where $p \in [0, 1]$, and compare the performance of G_2 versus HNDE on this randomized family. This randomized family $\mathcal{R}_k^l(p)$ is defined as follows. The definition is identical to that of $\mathcal{H}_k^l$ except that, when the edge-set E_k is constructed from E_{k-1}, instead of adding *all* k-tuples $(r_1, r_2, \ldots, r_k)$, each such tuple is added, independently of all others, with probability p. Clearly $\mathcal{H}_k^l = \mathcal{R}_k^l(1)$. For $p < 1$, though we clearly cannot give a deterministic guarantee that G_2 always performs sub-optimally on hypergraphs from $\mathcal{H}_k^l$, we expect that, for p not arbitrarily small, on average, G_2 will work poorly. Though we think a theoretical probabilistic result of this kind is not difficult to obtain, we do not present one here. Instead, here we present an empirical evaluation of G_2.

Finally, though we have seen that G_2 obtains the same size vertex cover on every hypergraph in $\mathcal{H}_k^l$, HNDE does not. This is because HNDE employs steepest descent which breaks ties lexicographically, and is hence sensitive to the labels of the vertices in the hypergraph. (Indeed in our experiments, different hypergraphs in $\mathcal{H}_k^l$, i.e. different orderings of vertices, gave quite different results.) For this reason, for each triplet of $\langle l, k, p \rangle$ evaluated, we generated several hypergraphs in $\mathcal{R}_k^l(p)$ by rearranging the vertices randomly, and reported the average performance of HNDE on them. Table 3 reports the experimental results. The results reported in Table 3 permit the following observations. HNDE always finds, on average, a much smaller vertex cover than does G_2. For $p = 1.0$, note that the average reported for G_2 is the same as the number calculable from Proposition 1. HNDE also runs slightly faster than G_2 in almost all cases. Using the well-known notion from random graph theory that if a result holds with high probability on a random graph then it holds deterministically on almost every graph, we may infer the following. From Table 3, for p values close to one-half, HNDE outperforms G_2 by a large amount on almost every graph in the family $\mathcal{R}_k^l(p)$. A theoretical version of this empirical result is the topic of future work for us.

Table 3: Experimental results on hypergraphs in $\mathcal{R}_k^l$. In all cases $l = 15$, and $j_m = 2$ for all $2 \leq m \leq k$. Each row reports results averaged over ten hypergraphs.

$\mathcal{R}_k^l(p)$ hypergraphs				Vertex cover size		Running time	
k	p	$\lvert V \rvert$	$\lvert E \rvert$	HNDE	G_2	HNDE	G_2
3	1.0	54	2355	28	39	0.7	0.8
4	1.0	63	21660	28	48	9.1	10.8
5	1.0	70	156795	28	55	86.2	100.6
3	0.75	54	1775.1	22.8	35.1	0.6	0.6
4	0.65	63	14041.7	24.1	43.0	5.9	7.0
5	0.55	70	86349.3	22.8	51.1	47.7	55.8
3	0.45	54	1079.8	20.2	28.1	0.3	0.4
4	0.35	63	7595.5	24.1	37.3	3.2	3.8
5	0.25	70	39404.6	21.1	43.7	21.7	25.0

5 Conclusions

We have presented an improved mapping of the hypergraph vertex cover problem onto a neural network, which also leads to a more intricate dynamical algorithm. Our new algorithm consistently finds smaller vertex covers—i.e., better solutions—than its older version and roughly the same size covers, on average, as those found by the greedy algorithm G_2. Our algorithm runs slower, however, than G_2 on random hypergraphs. We have also presented two families of hypergraphs that are "hard" for G_2. One is provably hard and the other, a larger class, is hard in a probabilistic sense. In experiments on these hypergraphs, our neural net algorithm always outperforms G_2 on average, finding near-optimal solutions.

References

[1] Garey M.R. & Johnson D.S. *Computers and Intractability: A Guide to the theory of NP-Completeness*. Freeman, New York, 1979.

[2] Goldbeer G.H., Lipscomb J., & Luby M. On the computational complexity of finding stable state vectors in connectionist models (Hopfield nets). TR, Dept of Comp Sci U of Toronto, 1988.

[3] Grossman T. A Neural Computation Approach to the Set Covering Problem. Submitted to *Neural Information Processing Systems Conference*, 1995.

[4] Grossman T. & Wool A. Computational Experience with Approximation Algorithms for the Set Covering Problem. Unpublished Report, 1995.

[5] Hertz, K., Krogh A., & Palmer R. *Introduction to the Theory of Neural Computation*. Addison-Wesley.

[6] Hopfield J.J. Neural Networks and Physical Systems with Emergent Collective Computational Abilities. In *Proc National Academy of Sciences*, volume 79, 1982.

[7] Jagota A. Optimization by Reduction to Maximum Clique. In *International Conference on Neural Networks*, pages 1526-1531, New York, March 1993.

[8] Jagota A. Optimization by a Hopfield-style Network. In *Optimality in Artificial and Biological Networks*, D.S. Levine, W. Elsberry (Eds), Lawrence Erlbaum, 1994. To appear.

[9] Kaznachey D. & Jagota A. Approximating Minimum Set Cover in a Hopfield-style Network, in *Proc of Second Joint Conference on Information Sciences*, pages 358-361, Wrightsville Beach, NC, 1995. Expanded version submitted to full conference proceedings.

[10] Motwani R. Lecture notes on approximation algorithms. TR, Dept of Comp Sci, Stanford U, 1992. Available from author.

[11] Peng Y., Reggia J., and T. Li. A Connectionist Model to Vertex Covering Problems. *International Journal of Neural Systems*, pages 43–56, vol. 3, no. 1, 1992.

[12] Ramanujam J. & Sadayappan. Optimization by neural networks. In *IEEE International Conference on Neural Networks*, volume 2, pages 325-332, New York, 1988.

[13] Shrivastava Y., Dasgupta S., & Reddy S.M. Neural network solutions to a graph theoretic problem. In *Proc of IEEE International Symposium on Circuits and Systems*, pages 2528-2531, New York, 1990, IEEE.

[14] Zissimopoulos V., Paschos V. & Pekergin F. On the Approximation of NP-Complete Problems by Using the Boltzmann Machine Method: The Cases of Some Covering and Packing Problems. *IEEE Transactions on Computers*, vol. 40, no. 12, 1991.

Numerical Soap Film for the Steiner Tree Problem

Cheng-Yuan Liou and Quan-Ming Chang

Department of Computer Science and Information Engineering,
National Taiwan University, Taipei, Taiwan, R.O.C.
Tel: 8862-3625336 ext 515, Fax: 8862-3628167, Email: cyliou@csie.ntu.edu.tw.

Abstract — **A neural-based approach to solve the Steiner minimal tree problem is presented. The Steiner minimal tree is a tree of shortest possible length with the given vertices and some extra points. It has applications in computer networks, VLSI design, and so on. We devise a mesh model to solve this problem. The mesh is composed of many units what called snakes. It is controlled by an energy function and we will minimize it using Hopfield network. Some experimental results show that our mesh model is promising to solve the Steiner minimal tree problem, which has been shown to be NP-complete.**

1   Introduction

Given a set of points $\mathcal{A} = \{a_1, a_2, ..., a_t\}$, a minimal spanning tree is a tree having these points as its vertices and having minimal length, e.g., the sum the lengths of all its lines is as small as possible. If an extra vertex set $\mathcal{S} = \{s_1, s_2, ..., s_k\}$ can be added during constructing the tree, the length of the tree may be reduced. Those points in set $\mathcal{S}$ are called Steiner points, and the shortest possible tree is called Steiner minimal tree (SMT). It is well known that in an SMT no two deges can meet at an angle less than $120°$ [5]. Consequently, every Steiner point is incident to three edges, and the number of Steiner points is at most $t - 2$.

The Steiner minimal tree problem has a long history of nearly three centuries. It has been shown to be NP-complete [4]. Thus, even for a small number of vertices, the number of possible solutions is too large to solve it using exhaustive search. In general, there are two types of schemes to solve this problem — optimal solution algorithm and heuristic algorithm. A comprehensive survey of Steiner problems has been given by Hwang and Richards [6].

However, using neural network to solve the Steiner problems is not yet investigated. Until recently, an energy-minimizing based solution to the SMT problem has been proposed by Jayadeva [7]. The initial curve he presents will self-organize to form a different local minimal tree. Minimal number of Steiner points needs to be made a priori. Although the model he presents can escape from local minima, it may trap into another local minima. In [11, 15], another type of problem what called constrained Steiner tree problem is discussed. The Steiner points are limited in the given set of vertices $\mathcal{A}$.

In this paper, we propose a neural network approach to solve the Steiner problems. Our idea is motivated from the soap film experiments [3, p391]. Owing to the action of surface tension, a film of liquid is in stable equilibrium only if its area is a minimum. At the same time, a Steiner tree is formed. We devise a mesh model which can simulate the behavior of the soap film. The mesh model is composed of many units what called "snakes" [9], and is controlled by an energy function. We will minimize it use the Hopfield network. When the energy is minimized, the SMT is formed automatically. No assumption about the number of Steiner points or the topology of the tree needs to made a priori. Kahng [8] presents an "analog" approach which shrinks a bubble to construct the rectilinear Steiner tree. However, his approach does not include the mechanics of bubble actually. Also, he is concerned with the *rectilinear* SMT problem, while we are devoted to the *Euclidean* SMT problem.

2   The snake model

In this section, we will investigate the snake model which forms the element of our mesh. The original type of snake is modifed such that it can be implemented using neural network, and is suitable for our purpose.

The snake model proposed by Kass et al. [9] is an active contour model which can provide a unified account of a number of visual problems, including detection of edges, motion tracking, and image matching. A snake is an energy-minimizing spline guided by internal stretching and bending forces, and influenced by image forces that pull it toward interesting features such as lines and edges. If we represent the position of a snake parametrically by $\mathbf{V}(s) = (x(s), y(s))$, we can write its energy function as

$$E^{*}_{snake} = \int_{0}^{1} [E_{int}(\mathbf{V}(s)) + E_{image}(\mathbf{V}(s)) + E_{con}(\mathbf{V}(s))]ds \tag{1}$$

where E_{int} represents the internal energy of the splin due to bending and stretching, E_{image} is the energy function derived from the image forces and E_{con} is the energy function due to the external constraint forces. The internal spline energy can be written as

$$E_{int} = (\alpha(s) \mid \mathbf{V}_{s}(s) \mid^{2} + \beta(s) \mid \mathbf{V}_{ss} \mid^{2})/2 \tag{2}$$

The above equation contains a first-order term which will have larger value if the distance between two neighboring points is longer, and a second-order term which will be larger where the curve is bending rapidly. Therefore, when we minimize the energy, the first-order term cause the snake to behave like a string (i.e. resisting stretching), and the second-order term causes the snake to behave like a rod (i.e. resist bending). Adjusting the weights $\alpha(s)$ and $\beta(s)$ controls the relative importance of the two terms.

In eqn(1), the image energy E_{image} sources from salient features such as lines and edges. The external constraint energy E_{con} can provide a repulsion force controllable by the user. These two types of energy are not used in our model.

The original snake model has many drawbacks such as relatively unstable numerical behavior, slow speed of convergence and difficulty to handle discontinuities. Many methods have been proposed to solve these problems. Basing the idea presented in [13, 14], we devise a Hopfield type energy function for the snake model. How it can be extended to form the mesh is shown in next section.

The internal energy E_{int} in eqn(1) is used only in our approach, and it will be discretized. Thus, the energy function for the snake model can be written as

$$E^{'}_{snake} = \sum_{i=1}^{n} \alpha_{i} \mid \mathbf{V}_{i} - \mathbf{V}_{i-1} \mid^{2} + \beta_{i} \mid \mathbf{V}_{i-1} - 2\mathbf{V}_{i} + \mathbf{V}_{i+1} \mid^{2} \tag{3}$$

where n is number of points of the snake, and $\mathbf{V}_{i} = (x_{i}, y_{i})$ is the position of point i. Note that this snake will shrink to one point since there is no image force and external constraint imposed upon it. To find the minimum of eqn(3), a two-dimensional Hopfield network is used. The network consists of $n * m$ mutually interconnected neurons, where n is the number snake points and m is the number of neighbors around each point (Figure 1). The energy function is computed at $\mathbf{V}_{i}$ and each of its neighbors. The location having the smallest value of the energy function is chosen as the new positon of $\mathbf{V}_{i}$. Let $\mathbf{V}_{i,p}$ denote the position of the neighbors around point i ($\mathbf{V}_{i} = \mathbf{V}_{i,5}$), and $v_{i,p}$ denote the binary state of the (i,p)th neuron (1 for firing and 0 for resting). Then, the Hopfield type energy function for eqn(3) is

$$E_{snake} = \sum_{i=1}^{n} \{ w_{1}[(\sum_{p=1}^{m} x_{i,p}v_{i,p} - \sum_{p=1}^{m} x_{i-1,p}v_{i-1,p})^{2} + (\sum_{p=1}^{m} y_{i,p}v_{i,p} - \sum_{p=1}^{m} y_{i-1,p}v_{i-1,p})^{2}]$$

$$+ w_{2}[(1 - \sum_{p=1}^{m} v_{i,p})^{2}] + w_{3}\sum_{p=1}^{m} v_{i,p}(1 - v_{i,p})\} \tag{4}$$

where the second term is included to imply that only one point can be selected from the neighboring points $(i,1), (i,2), ..., (i,m)$ for each i. The last term is called self-connection eliminating term, which

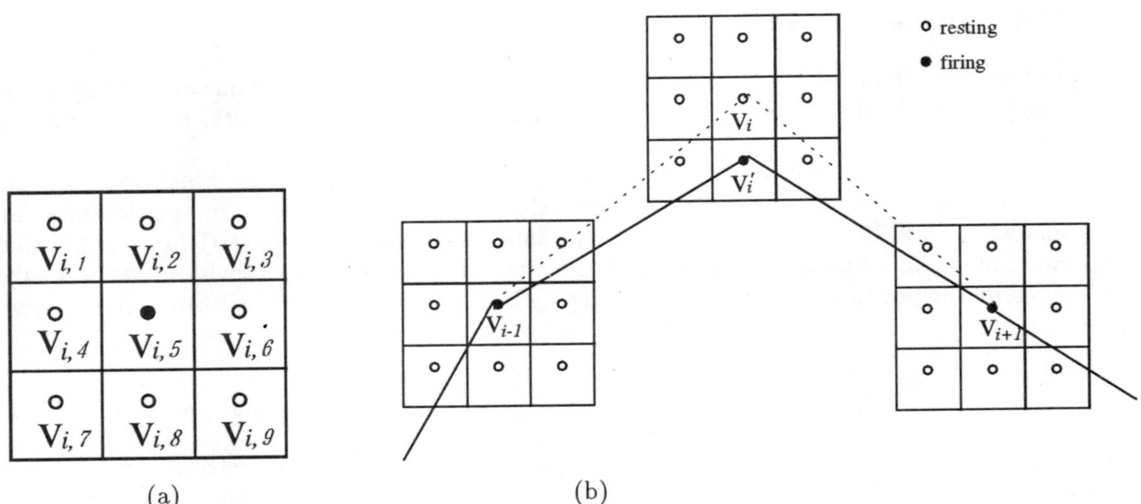

Figure 1: (a) Each snake point has eight neighbors around it ($\mathbf{V}_i = \mathbf{V}_{i,5}$). Thus, $m = 9$ in our case (including itself). (b) The energy function (3) is computed at $\mathbf{V}_i$ and each of its neighbors. The location $\mathbf{V}_i'$ which has the smallest value is selected as the new position of $\mathbf{V}_i$. The dotted line in the figure is the original curve and the thick line is the new curve.

will be clear in next section. It will constrain the states of neurons to be a binary number, too. The constants w_1, w_2 and w_3 are used to weight the three terms. Note that α_i in eqn(3) is regarded as constant for every i and is absorbed into w_1. Also, the second term in eqn(3) is discarded for our purpose in emulating the soap film. This is because a soap film can not withstand bending or shearing forces. The normal surface tension is the only internal force which can be emulated by the first term of (3).

3   The mesh model for emulating the soap film

In this section, we show how the snake model presented in previous section can be formed into a meshed type, and how the Hopfield network works.

A mesh is composed of finite number of nonoverlapping polygonal elements. Each element in the mesh is considered as a snake, with 4 nodes in it (Figure 2). Thus, if there are $row * col$ nodes in the mesh, we will have $Sn = (row - 1) * (col - 1)$ snakes. Note that each element in the mesh is not limited to having 4 nodes. As we can see in Figure 2, every boundary node (excluding the corner nodes) is shared by two snakes, and every internal node is shared by four snakes. There are four forces imposing upon each internal node, and they will keep balance at the beginning. However, the boundary nodes (including the corner nodes) are not in steady states initially. The mesh will shrink to one point if there is no constraint imposed upon it. How it can be used to solve the Steiner minimal tree problem is shown in next section.

Then, we can define the energy function of the mesh as

$$E_{mesh} = \sum_{s=1}^{Sn} E_{snake(s)} \tag{5}$$

where Sn is the total number of snakes in the mesh and $E_{snake(s)}$ is defined in eqn(4).

The Liapunov function of a two-dimensional Hopfield network has the form as:

$$E_{Hopfield} = -\frac{1}{2} \sum_{i=1}^{N} \sum_{p=1}^{m} \sum_{j=1}^{N} \sum_{q=1}^{m} W_{i,p;j,q} v_{i,p} v_{j,q} - \sum_{i=1}^{N} \sum_{p=1}^{m} I_{i,p} v_{i,p} \tag{6}$$

where N is the number of nodes of the mesh. Rearranging equation(5) and comparing it with equation(6) we have:

$$W_{i,p;j,q} = (T_1(i,j) + T_2(i,j)) * (x_{i,p} x_{j,q} + y_{i,p} y_{j,q}) + T_3(i,j) \tag{7}$$

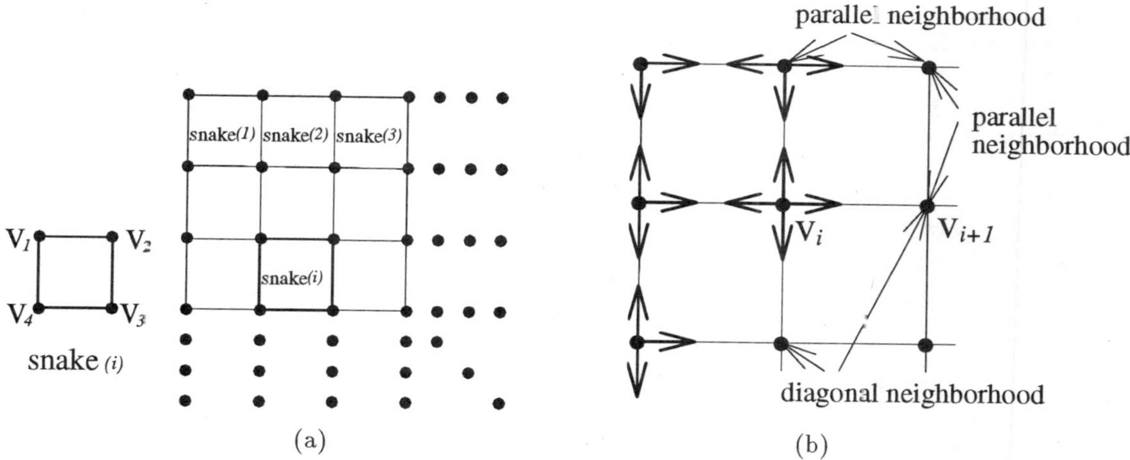

Figure 2: (a) The mesh is composed of many snakes. Each snake has four nodes in it. (b) The internal nodes in the mesh are drived by four forces. At the beginning, it will keep balance. However, the boundary nodes are not in steady states. Consequently, the mesh will shrink to one point.

where
$$T_1(i,j) = \sum_{k=1}^{N}[-2w_1\phi_1(i,k)(2 - B(i)B(k))(2 - \delta_{p,q})]\delta_{i,j}$$

$$T_2(i,j) = 4w_1\phi_1(i,j)[2 - B(i)B(k)]$$

$$T_3(i,j) = \sum_{k=1}^{N}[(-2w_2(2 - \delta_{p,q}) + 2w_3\delta_{p,q})\phi_2(i,k)]\delta_{i,j}$$

and
$$I_{i,p} = \sum_{k=1}^{N}(2w_2 - w_3)\phi_2(i,k)$$

respectively, where $\delta_{i,j}$ is the Kronecker delta function. $\phi_1(i,j)$, $\phi_2(i,j)$ and $B(i)$ are defined as:

$$\phi_1(i,j) = \begin{cases} 1 & \text{, if } i \text{ and } j \text{ are parallel neighborhood (Figure 2(b)).} \\ 0 & \text{, otherwise} \end{cases}$$

$$\phi_2(i,j) = \begin{cases} 1 & \text{, if } i \text{ and } j \text{ are diagonal neighborhood (Figure 2(b)).} \\ 0 & \text{, otherwise} \end{cases}$$

$$B(i) = \begin{cases} 1 & \text{, if } i \text{ is boundary or corner node.} \\ 0 & \text{, otherwise} \end{cases}$$

Note that the including of self-connection eliminating terms in eqn(4) may change the diagonal elements of the interconnention matrix W, and then change the stability of the network. Following the proof in [2] and Matsuda's approach [10], we can derive the conditions of convergence to a stable state and a valid solution. The selections of w_1, w_2 and w_3 are according to these conditions.

A neuron (i,p) in the network receives weighted input $W_{i,p;j,q}$ from each neuron (j,q) and a bias input $I_{i,p}$. The total input, $net_{i,p}$, of the (i,p)th neuron is computed as

$$net_{i,p} = \sum_{j=1}^{N}\sum_{q=1}^{m} W_{i,p;j,q}v_{j\,q} + I_{i,p} \tag{8}$$

Then the (i,p)th neuron is updated as follows:
$$v_{i,p} = \begin{cases} 1 & \text{,if } net_{i,p} \geq 0 \\ 0 & \text{,if } net_{i,p} < 0 \end{cases}$$

The rule described above for updating the neuron is applied in an asynchronous fashion. This means that for a given time, only a single neuron (which is selected randomly) is allowed to update its output. The iterative algorithm is shown below.

```
/*The pseudo code for the generatoin of the mesh*/
Procedure
do        /* loop to update the mesh */
          initialize the matrix W and I used in eqn(8);
          Moved = 0;
          do            /* loop to update the network until it converges in this epoch*/
              Changed = 0;
              UpdateCount = 0;
              do      /* loop to move nodes to new position among the neighboring points */
                  randomly select a node from the mesh for updating;
                  update the position of this selected node;
                  if its state changes ,Changed = 1 and Moved = 1;
                  UpdateCount+ = 1;
              until UpdateCount = N;          /* N is the number of the nodes of the mesh */
          until Changed = 0;
until Moved = 0;
```

4   Solving The Steiner Minimal Tree Problem

Suppose that we want to find the Steiner minimal tree of four vertices set shown in Figure 3. At the beginning, each vertex catches the nearest node of the mesh and then fixes the node. When eqn(5) is minimized, the mesh will shrink unless some nodes are catched. As we can see in Figure 3(b), the corner nodes are fixed but others are not. When the minimum of the energy function is reached, the Steiner tree is formed (Figure 3(e)). Other tests with different number of vertices are shown in Figure 4.

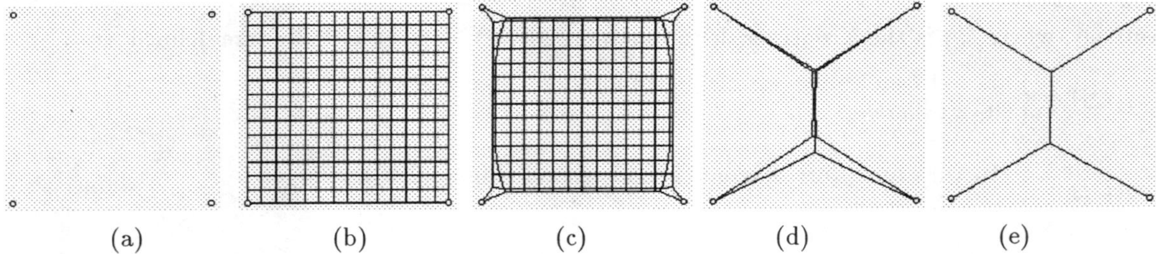

   (a)   (b)   (c)   (d)   (e)

Figure 3: (a) The Steiner minimal tree for the four vertices will be formed. (b) Initially, each vertex will catch the nearest node of the mesh and fix it. (c) The mesh will shrink except for those nodes which are catched. (d) The intermediate configuration. (e) The Steiner minimal tree for the four vertices is formed by the mesh.

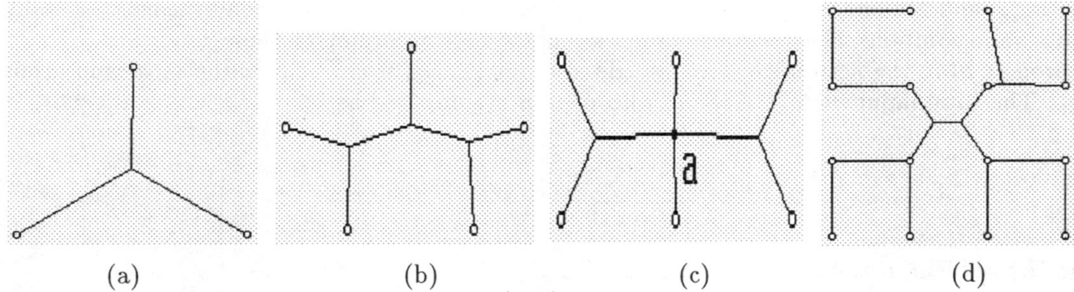

   (a)   (b)   (c)   (d)

Figure 4: Several tests with different number of vertices.

The vertex a in Figure 4(c) is a steiner point and has degree of four. The vertex a should be splitted into two nodes. However, the nodes of our mesh is not dense enough to resolve the tree length. Another way to conquer this problem is that the original set of vertices can be separated automaticly into many subsets. Then, each subset is solved individually by a separate mesh.

The mesh model is employed to find the solutions for the set of example obtained from the literature [12]. Table 1 contains the performance of the mesh model and of the well-known heuristic algorithm for the SMT [1].

Ex.	Mesh	Heuristic	Ex.	Mesh	Hsuristic	Ex.	Mesh	Hsuristic
1	1.72522	1.66440*	17	1.64279	1.64279	33	2.34309	2.22953
2	1.50050*	1.50050*	18	4.08557	3.85130	34	2.16454	2.13813
3	2.07767*	2.07767*	19	1.76156	1.72225	35	1.36447	1.35545
4	2.13879*	2.13879*	20	1.05752	1.03962*	36	0.89119	0.87891*
5	2.04424	2.04405*	21	1.87556	1.81818	37	0.77002	0.76603
6	2.20364	2.22239*	22	0.50339	0.50329*	38	1.43501	1.43501
7	2.26468	2.20529	23	0.51967	0.51303*	39	1.43125*	1.43125*
8	2.17784	2.17779*	24	0.25494	0.25282*	40	1.46284	1.41803
9	1.62917	1.58783	25	0.20109	0.19897*	41	1.99260	1.97672
10	1.64085	1.64728	26	0.12456	0.12534*	42	1.33087	1.31535
11	1.33007	1.27411*	27	1.18156	1.17817*	43	2.38740	2.36719
12	1.71984	1.64853	28	0.20442*	0.20442*	44	2.20311	2.19744
13	1.28871	1.27338	29	1.46598*	1.46598*	45	1.96164	1.93584
14	2.25469	2.20492*	30	1.07091	1.03323	46	1.39783	1.42209
15	1.23253	1.23041*	31	2.52183	2.34009			
16	1.16678*	1.16678*	32	2.95600	2.85677			

Table 1: The solutions found by the mesh model and the heuristic algorithm. Symbol * means that the solution is the optimal solution.

References

[1] J. E. Beasley, A heuristic for Euclidean and rectilinear Steiner problems. *Euro. J. Oper. Res.*, **58**: 284–292, (1992).

[2] J. Bruck, On the convergence properties of the Hopfield model. *Proc. IEEE*, **78**(10):1579–1585 (1990).

[3] R. Courant and H. Robbins, *What Is Mathematics ?* Oxford Univ. Press, New York (1941).

[4] M. R. Garey, R. L. Graham and D.S.Johnson, The complexity of computing Steiner minimal trees. *SIAM J. Appl. Math.*, **32**: 835 –859 (1977).

[5] E. N. Gilbert and H. O. Pollak, Steiner minimal trees. *SIAM J. Allp. Math.*, **16**: 1–29 (1968).

[6] F. K. Hwang and D. S. Richards, Steiner tree problems. *Networks*, **22**: 55–89 (1992).

[7] B. B. Jayadeva, A neural network for the Steiner minimal tree problem. *Biol. Cybern.*, **70**: 485–494 (1994).

[8] A. B. Kahng, A Steiner tree construction for VLSI routing. *Int. Joint Conf. on Neural Network*, part I:133–139 (1993).

[9] M. Kass, A. Witkin and D. Terzopoulos, Snakes: active contour models. *Proc. of IEEE Conf. on Computer Vision*,pp. 259–268 (1987).

[10] S. Matsuda, The stability of the solution in Hopfield neural network. *IJCNN'93*, pp. 1524–1527 (1993).

[11] C. Pornavalai, G. Chakraborty and N. Shiratori, Neural networks for solving constrained Steiner tree problem. *ICNN'95*, pp. 1867–1870 (1995).

[12] J. Soukup & W. F. Chow, Set of test problems for minimal length connection networks, *ACM/SIGMAP Newsletter*, (15):48–51, (1973).

[13] C. T. Tsai, Y. N. Sun and P. C. Chung, Minimising the energy of active contour model using a Hopfield network. *IEE Proceedings-E*, **140**(6): 297–303 (1993).

[14] D. J. Williams and M. Shah, A fast algorithm for active contours and curvature estimation. *CVGIP: Image Understanding*, **55**(1): 14–26 (1992).

[15] J. Zhongqi, S. Huaying and G. H. Ming, Using neural network to solve Steiner tree problem. *IEEE TENCON'93*, pp. 807–810 (1993).

New Results on The Hybrid of Lagrange and Transformation Approaches For Combinatorial Optimization

Jiong Ruan[1,2] and Lei Xu[1]
1. Department of Computer Science and Engineering
The Chinese University of Hong Kong
Shatin, N. T., Hong Kong
2. Department of Mathematics, Fudan University
Shanghai, 200433, China

Abstract

A theorem on convergence of the Hybrid of Lagrange and Transformation approaches for the constrained optimization has been proved, which can also guide us to choose the barrier functions and their controlling parameters. Moreover, an improved family of U-type shape barrier functions has been proposed.

1   Introduction

Recently, using neural networks to solve combinatorial optimization problems has been one of the main interest in neural network research. In 1985, Hopfield and Tank proposed to use neural networks for combinatorial optimization. Following that pioneer work, a lot of efforts have been made. In these research works the existing combinatorial optimization networks share two common features. One is that the Hopfield type networks will finally become a unconstrained analog optimization of a quadratic energy function. The other is that these netwerks transform the constraints into penalty functions, which are weighted by arbitrary external parameters as part of the resulted unconstrained energy function. Because these algorithms are either implemented by Hopfield network or variants, we refer them as Hopfield scheme.

In 1994 one of this paper's authors [2] proposed the Hybrid of Lagrange and Transformation Approaches (Hybrid LT) to solve combinatorial optimization problem. Hybrid LT approach separates the constraints into two parts. One part is the linear-constant-sum constraints, which are treated by Lagrange approach, other part is the binary constraints, which are transformed into penalty or barrier functions.

Hybrid LT scheme has several advantages. First, it can be used for nonquadratic energy functions, while Hopfield scheme applies only to quadratic energy functions. Second, it ensures the linear-constant-sum constraints satisfied exactly without an approximate treatment via penalty functions weighted by the parameters controlled heuristically and externally.

In the paper [3], a new family of barrier functions is proposed to provide the U-type berriers and shown that the role of these barrier functions is equivalent to sigmoid activation in Hopfield-type networks, that is, it attempts to minimize the total leaking energy, and that the role is also equivalent to maximizing the system's entropy or impose the least assumption to the system's configuration.

The paper [1] compares the performance of the Hopfield net and the Hybrid LT by computer simulation in solving the Traveling Salesman Problem (TSP).

There are some open problems remained. An important one is the convergence proof of the novel scheme. The other is how to choose a good barrier function with the U-type shapes.

In this paper we first improve the barrier functions given in [3] into an even better form, and then we proved a theorem on the convergence of this novel scheme [2,3] for the constrained optimization. This convergence theorem applies to many combinatorial optimization problems, including the Traveling Salesman Problem (TSP), the Standard Linear Assignment Problem (SLAP), the Graph K-Partition Problem (GKPP), the Graph Bipartition Problem (GBP). Also this Theorem can guide us choosing suitable parameters in the proposed barrier functions.

2 An Improved Family of Barrier Functions for The Hybrid LT Approach

In this paper we still consider following combinatorial optimization problem [2,3]

$$minE_{cost}(V), V = \{v_{ij};\ i = 1, 2, \cdots, N;\ j = 1, 2, \cdots, M\}. \tag{1}$$

$$C_s^{col} : \sum_{i=1}^{N} v_{ij} = D_j^{col},\ j = 1, 2, \cdots, M; \tag{2}$$

$$C_s^{row} : \sum_{j=1}^{M} v_{ij} = D_i^{row},\ i = 1, 2, \cdots, N; \tag{3}$$

$$C_b : v_{ij} = 1\ or\ v_{ij} = 0\ for\ each\ v_{ij}. \tag{4}$$

with $D_j^{col}, j = 1, 2, \cdots, M$ and $D_i^{row}, i = 1, 2, \cdots, N$ being given constants. TSP with N=M is one of some typical examples

$$E_{cost}(V) = \sum_{x=1}^{N} \sum_{y \neq x} \sum_{i=1}^{N} d_{xy} v_{xi}(v_{y,i+1} + v_{y,i-1}), \tag{5}$$

$$C_s^{col} : \sum_{i=1}^{N} v_{ij} = 1, j = 1, 2, \cdots, M;\ C_s^{row} : \sum_{j=1}^{M} v_{ij} = 1,\ i = 1, 2, \cdots, N. \tag{6}$$

where d_{xy} are known parameters. The Hybrid LT approach with barrier function [2,3] attempts to minimize the following cost function

$$\begin{aligned} E(V) &= E_{cost}(V) + \sum_{j=1}^{M} \lambda_j^{col}[\sum_{i=1}^{N} v_{ij} - D_j^{ccl}] + \sum_{i=1}^{N} \lambda_i^{row}[\sum_{j=1}^{M} v_{ij} - D_i^{row}] \\ &\quad + \beta \sum_{i=1}^{N} \sum_{j=1}^{M} B(v_{ij}), \end{aligned} \tag{7}$$

The first and second are Lagrange terms with Lagrange coefficients $\lambda_i^{row}, \lambda_j^{col}$ for row/column linear constant-sum constraints.

A family of barrier functions given in [3], which generate U shape and $B(0) = 0$, but not enfore $B(1) = 0$ necessarily. Now we improve this family into a better family:

$$B(v_{ij}) = \int_0^{v_{ij}} ln[vR(v)]dv \tag{8}$$

where $R(v)$ satisfies

$$B(0) = 0, B(1) = 0, B(v) \neq 0, v \in (0,1). \tag{9}$$

Some new U-shape barrier functions $B(v)$ are followings:
$-exp[-\frac{1}{v^p(1-v)^q}];\ v^p exp[-\frac{1}{(1-v)^q}];\ (1-v)^q exp[-\frac{1}{v^p}];\ v^p[lnv]^q;\ (1-v)^p[ln(1-v)]^q;$
$[lnv]^p exp[-\frac{1}{(1-v)^q}];\ [ln(1-v)]^p exp[-\frac{1}{v^q}], (p > 0, q > 0).$

From the above barrier functions we can obtain respectively functions $R(v)$ by $R(v) = \frac{exp[B'(v)]}{v}$. We shall discuss the role of these new barrier functions elsewhere.

An example is $R(v) = \frac{cv^{p-1}}{(1-v)^q}$, where choose c such that B(0)=B(1)=0. In this case, $B(v_{ij}) = \int_0^{v_{ij}} ln\frac{cv^p}{(1-v)^q}dv = pv_{ij}lnv_{ij} + q(1 - v_{ij})ln(1 - v_{ij}) + [lnc + q - p]v_{ij}$.

If we choose $c=e^{p-q}$, that is,

$$R(v) = \frac{e^p v^{p-1}}{e^q (1-v)^q}. \tag{10}$$

then we get

$$B(v_{ij}) = \int_0^{v_{ij}} \frac{(ev)^p}{[e(1-v)]^q} dv = pv_{ij}lnv_{ij} + q(1-v_{ij})ln(1-v_{ij}). \tag{11}$$

Notice that here we have $B(0) = B(1) = 0$. When $p \neq q$, $B(v)$ improves the U-shape barrier functions gived [3], where it only enfores $B(0) = 0$. When $p = q$ and $c = 1$, eq.(11) retuns to exactly the barrier function given by eqs. (5), (9) in [3].

Using the iterative scheme given in [2], we further insert the family eq.(8) of barrier function into eq.(7) and solve it by

$$\frac{\partial E(V)}{\partial v_{ij}} = \frac{\partial E_{cost(v)}}{\partial v_{ij}} + \lambda_j^{col} + \lambda_i^{row} + \beta ln(v_{ij}R(v_{ij})). \tag{12}$$

From $\frac{\partial E(V)}{\partial v_{ij}} = 0$, we have that

$$ln(v_{ij}R(v_{ij})) + \frac{1}{\beta}[\frac{\partial E_{cost}(V)}{\partial v_{ij}} + \lambda_j^{col} + \lambda_i^{row}] = 0. \tag{13}$$

$$v_{ij} = \frac{a_i b_j}{R(v_{ij})} exp[-\frac{1}{\beta}(\frac{\partial E_{cost}(V)}{\partial v_{ij}})]. \tag{14}$$

where

$$a_i = exp(-\frac{1}{\beta}\lambda_i^{row}),$$

$$b_j = exp(-\frac{1}{\beta}\lambda_j^{col}).$$

Also from $\sum_{i=1}^{N} v_{ij} = D_j^{col}$ and $\sum_{j=1}^{M} v_{ij} = D_i^{row}$, we can obtain two recursive equations as did in [2]. Specifically, given β and initialize a set of $N \times M$ array of neurons $v_{ij}^{(0)}$ randomly by taking values between [0,1], as well as a set of $N + M$ dummy variables $a_i^{(0)}, b_j^{(0)}$. We start an iterative process by the following recursive equations

$$a_i^{(k+1)} = D_i^{row} / \sum_{j=1}^{M} \frac{b_j^{(k)}}{R(v_{ij}^{(k)})} exp[-\frac{1}{\beta}(\frac{\partial E_{cost}(V)}{\partial v_{ij}})], \tag{15}$$

$$b_j^{(k+1)} = D_j^{col} / \sum_{i=1}^{N} \frac{a_i^{(k)}}{R(v_{ij}^{(k)})} exp[-\frac{1}{\beta}(\frac{\partial E_{cost}(V)}{\partial v_{ij}})], \tag{16}$$

$$v_{ij}^{(k+1)} = \frac{a_i^{(k+1)}b_j^{(k+1)}}{R(v_{ij}^{(k)})} exp[-\frac{1}{\beta}(\frac{\partial E_{cost}(V)}{\partial v_{ij}})]. \tag{17}$$

3 Stability and Convergence of The Hybrid LT Approach

Many constrained optimization problems can be mathematically formulated into the following types:

Type 1. $\frac{\partial^2 E_{cost}(V)}{\partial v_{lj}\partial v_{ij}} = 0, \frac{\partial^2 E_{cost}(V)}{\partial v_{i\nu}\partial v_{ij}} = 0$, for all $i,l = 1,2,\cdots,N; j,\nu = 1,2,\cdots,M$.

Type 2. $\frac{\partial^2 E_{cost}(V)}{\partial v_{ij}^2} \neq 0; \frac{\partial^2 E_{cost}(V)}{\partial v_{ij}\partial v_{i\nu}} = 0(\nu \neq j); \frac{\partial^2 E_{cost}(V)}{\partial v_{ij}\partial v_{lj}}(l \neq i)$, for all $i,l = 1,2,\cdots,N;$ $j,\nu = 1,2,\cdots,M$.

Type 3. $\frac{\partial^2 E_{cost}(V)}{\partial v_{ij}\partial v_{lj}} \neq 0, \frac{\partial^2 E_{cost}(V)}{\partial v_{ij}\partial v_{i\nu}} \neq 0$, for all $i,l = 1,2,\cdots,N; j,\nu = 1,2,\cdots,M$.

For example, TSP, SLAP, GK-PP belong to type 1; GBP belong to type 2; type 3 is general case.

Eqs.(15),(16), (17) define a recurrent optimization network. The analog dynamical equations of the network are given by

$$\frac{da_i}{dt} = \sum_{j=1}^{M} v_{ij} - D_i^{row},$$ (18)

$$\frac{db_j}{dt} = \sum_{i=1}^{N} v_{ij} - D_j^{col},$$ (19)

$$\frac{dv_{ij}}{dt} = -[ln(v_{ij}R(v_{ij})) + \frac{1}{\beta}(\frac{\partial E_{cost}(V)}{\partial v_{ij}})] + ln(a_i) + ln(b_j).$$ (20)

Theorem 1. Solutions of eqs. (18), (19), (20) have a stable limit equilibrium set.

Proof. It is easy to see that E(V) in eq.(7) is a Lyapunov function for motion eqs. (18),(19),(20).

$$\frac{dE(V)}{dt} = \sum_{i=1}^{N}\sum_{j=1}^{M} \frac{\partial E(V)}{\partial v_{ij}}\frac{dv_{ij}}{dt} + \sum_{i=1}^{N} \frac{\partial E(V)}{\partial a_i}\frac{da_i}{dt} + \sum_{j=1}^{M} \frac{\partial E(V)}{\partial b_j}\frac{db_j}{dt}$$

$$= -\beta[\frac{1}{\beta}\frac{\partial E_{cost}(V)}{\partial v_{ij}} + ln(v_{ij}R(v_{ij})) - ln(a_i) - ln(b_j)]^2$$

$$-\frac{\beta}{a_i}(\sum_{j=1}^{M} v_{ij} - D_i^{row})^2 - \frac{\beta}{b_j}(\sum_{i=1}^{N} v_{ij} - D_j^{col})^2 \leq 0.$$

In general E(V) is bounded below, so a_i, b_j, v_{ij} will finally fall in limit equilibrium set of eqs.(18),(19),(20).

In the following Theorem 2 and Theorem 3, we take $R(V) = \frac{e^{p-q}v^{p-1}}{(1-v)^q}, p, q \in (-\infty, +\infty)$, and rewrite eq.(17) by $v_{ij}^{(k+1)} = F(v_{ij}^{(k)}, \cdot)$.

Theorem 2. Given that $\epsilon > 0$ is small enough. For the problem of type 1, if p, q satisfy any one of following conditions:

(1). $q(p-1) > 0, q/(p-1) \leq 1, (p-1)(\frac{1}{\epsilon} - 1) + q < 1/2$;

(2). $q(p-1) > 0, q/(p-1) \geq 1, (p-1) + q(\frac{1}{\epsilon} - 1) < 1/2$;

(3). $q > 0, p-1 < 0, \frac{1}{\epsilon} - 1 \leq \frac{q}{1-p} < \frac{\epsilon}{1-\epsilon}[1 + \frac{1}{2(p-1)}]$;

(4). $q < 0, p-1 > 0, (\frac{1}{\epsilon}-1) - \frac{1}{2(p-1)} < \frac{q}{1-p} \leq 1$, or $q < 0, p-1 > 0, 1 \leq \frac{-q}{p-1} < \frac{\epsilon}{1-\epsilon}[1 + \frac{1}{2(p-1)}]$;

(5). $q = 0, |p-1| < \frac{\epsilon}{2(1-\epsilon)}$ or $p = 1, |q| < \frac{\epsilon}{2(1-\epsilon)}$;

then $v_{ij}^{(k)}$ is converge as $k \to +\infty$;

Proof. The key idea for the proof of convergence given as follows:

If we can choose suitable parameters p, q, β such that $|\frac{\partial F(v, \cdot)}{\partial v}| \leq \eta < 1$, that is,

$$|v_{ij}^{(k+m)} - v_{ij}^{(k)}| \leq |\sum_{r=k+1}^{k+m} [v_{ij}^{(r)} - v_{ij}^{(r-1)}]| \leq \frac{\eta^k}{1-\eta}|v_{ij}^{(1)} - v_{ij}^{(0)}|,$$ (21)

then $v_{ij}^{(k)}$ converges as $k \to +\infty$ by Cauchy convergence criterion. Since our simulation is finite, the neurons can never reach the boundaries 0 and 1. They will only come close to the boundaries, so we have to devise a scheme to choose which neuron should be set to 1 or 0. We let $v_{ij}^{(k)} = 0$ when $v_{ij}^{(k)} < \epsilon$ (e.g, 0.1) and let $v_{ij}^{(k)} = 1$ when $v_{ij}^{(k)} > 1 - \epsilon$ (e.g., 0.9), that is, $v_{ij}^{(k)} \in [\epsilon, 1 - \epsilon]$.

We rewrite (15),(16),(17) using following form:

$$a_i^{(k+1)} = D_i^{row}/\sum_{j=1}^{M} b_j^{(k)}T_{ij}(V^{(k)}),$$ (22)

$$b_j^{(k+1)} = D_j^{col} / \sum_{i=1}^{N} a_i^{(k)} T_{ij}(V^{(k)}), \tag{23}$$

$$v_{ij}^{(k+1)} = a_i^{(k+1)} b_j^{(k+1)} T_{ij}(V^{(k)}), \tag{24}$$

$$T_{ij}(V^{(k)}) = \frac{1}{R(v_{ij}^{(k)})} exp[-\frac{1}{\beta}\frac{\partial E_{cost}(V^{(k)})}{\partial v_{ij}^{(k)}}]. \tag{25}$$

We further get,

$$\frac{\partial T_{ij}(V^{(k)})}{\partial v_{ij}^{(k)}} = T_{ij}(V^{(k)})[-\frac{R'(v_{ij}^{(k)})}{R(v_{ij}^{(k)})} - \frac{1}{\beta}\frac{\partial^2 E_{cost}(V^{(k)})}{\partial^2 v_{ij}^{(k)}}], \tag{26}$$

$$\frac{\partial T_{lj}(V^{(k)})}{\partial v_{ij}^{(k)}} = T_{lj}(V^{(k)})(-\frac{1}{\beta})\frac{\partial^2 E_{cost}(V^{(k)})}{\partial v_{lj}^{(k)}\partial v_{ij}^{(k)}}, (l \neq i), \tag{27}$$

$$\frac{\partial T_{i\nu}(V^{(k)})}{\partial v_{ij}^{(k)}} = T_{i\nu}(V^{(k)})(-\frac{1}{\beta})\frac{\partial^2 E_{cost}(V^{(k)})}{\partial v_{ij}^{(k)}\partial v_{i\nu}^{(k)}}, (\nu \neq j), \tag{28}$$

$$\frac{\partial F(v_{ij}^{(k)},\cdot)}{\partial v_{ij}^{(k)}} = \frac{\partial}{\partial v_{ij}^{(k)}} \frac{D_i^{row} D_j^{col} T_{ij}(V^{(k)})}{[\sum_{\nu=1}^{M} b_\nu^{(k)} T_{i\nu}(V^{(k)})][\sum_{l=1}^{N} a_l^{(k)} T_{lj}(V^{(k)})]}$$

$$= v_{ij}^{(k+1)}[-\frac{R'(v_{ij}^{(k)})}{R(v_{ij}^{(k)})} - \frac{1}{\beta}(\frac{\partial^2 E_{cost}(V^{(k)})}{\partial v_{ij}^{(k)}}) - \frac{\sum_{l=1}^{N} a_l^{(k)} \frac{\partial T_{lj}(V^{(k)})}{\partial v_{ij}^{(k)}}}{\sum_{l=1}^{N} a_l^{(k)} T_{lj}(V^{(k)})}$$

$$-\frac{\sum_{\nu=1}^{M} b_\nu^{(k)} \frac{\partial T_{i\nu}(V^{(k)})}{\partial v_{ij}^{(k)}}}{\sum_{\nu=1}^{M} b_\nu^{(k)} T_{i\nu}(V^{(k)})}]. \tag{29}$$

For type 1, we have that

$$\frac{\partial F(v_{ij}^{(k)},\cdot)}{\partial v_{ij}^{(k)}} = \frac{v_{ij}^{(k+1)}}{T_{ij}(V^{(k)})}[\frac{\partial T_{ij}(v^{(k)})}{\partial v_{ij}^{(k)}}][1 - \frac{a_i^{(k)} T_{ij}(V^{(k)})}{\sum_{l=1}^{N} a_l^{(k)} T_{lj}(V^{(k)})} - \frac{b_j^{(k)} T_{ij}(V^{(k)})}{\sum_{\nu=1}^{M} b_\nu^{(k)} T_{i\nu}(V^{(k)})}], \tag{30}$$

Thus we have,

$$|\frac{\partial F(v_{ij}^{(k)},\cdot)}{\partial v_{ij}^{(k)}}| \leq 2|v_{ij}^{(k+1)}||\frac{R'(v_{ij}^{(k)})}{R(v_{ij}^{(k)})}| \leq 2|\frac{p-1}{v_{ij}^{(k)}} + \frac{q}{1-v_{ij}^{(k)}}|(1-\epsilon) < 1 \tag{31}$$

if we choose p,q such that

$$0 < 2(1-\epsilon)max|\frac{p-1}{v} + \frac{q}{1-v}| \leq \eta < 1. \tag{32}$$

which can be easily varified to be true when p, q satisfy the condition of this theorem. So theorem is proved according to eq.(21).

Let $|\frac{\partial^2 E_{cost}(V^{(k)})}{\partial v_{ij}^{(k)2}}| \leq E_0, D_2 = max[|\frac{\partial^2 E_{cost}(V^{(k)})}{\partial v_{ij}^{(k)}\partial v_{ij}^{(k)}}|, |\frac{\partial^2 E_{cost}(V^{(k)})}{\partial v_{ij}^{(k)}\partial v_{lj}^{(k)}}|, |\frac{\partial^2 E_{cost}(V^{(k)})}{\partial v_{ij}^{(k)}\partial v_{i\nu}^{(k)}}|].$

Theorem 3. (a). For the problem of type 2, $\beta > 4(1-\epsilon)E_0$ and p, q satisfy one of the following conditions:

(1). $q(p-1) > 0, q/(p-1) \leq 1, (p-1)(\frac{1}{\epsilon}-1) + q < 1/4;$

(2). $q(p-1) > 0, q/(p-1) \geq 1, (p-1) + q(\frac{1}{\epsilon}-1) < 1/4;$

(3). $q > 0, p-1 < 0, \frac{1}{\epsilon} - 1 \leq \frac{q}{1-p} < \frac{\epsilon}{1-\epsilon}[1+\frac{1}{4(p-1)}];$

(4). $q < 0, p-1 > 0, (\frac{1}{\epsilon} - 1) - \frac{1}{4(p-1)} < \frac{-q}{1-p} \leq 1$, or $q < 0, p-1 > 0, 1 \leq \frac{-q}{p-1} < \frac{\epsilon}{1-\epsilon}[1 + \frac{1}{4(p-1)}]$;

(5). $q = 0, |p-1| < \frac{\epsilon}{4(1-\epsilon)}$ or $p = 1, |q| < \frac{\epsilon}{4(1-\epsilon)}$;

(b). For the problem of type 3, $\beta > 6D_2(1 - \epsilon)$ and p, q satisfy the condition of Theorem 2, then $v_{ij}^{(k)}$ converge as $k \to +\infty$.

Proof. According to eq.(21), for the problem of type 2, we want to obtain that

$$|\frac{\partial F(v_{ij}^{(k)}, \cdot)}{\partial v_{ij}^{(k)}}| \leq 2(1 - \epsilon)|\frac{R'(v_{ij}^{(k)})}{R(v_{ij}^{(k)})} + \frac{1}{\beta}\frac{\partial^2 E_{cost}(V^{(k)})}{\partial v_{ij}^{(k)} \partial v_{ij}^{(k)}}| \leq \eta < 1. \tag{33}$$

which can be verified to be true if p, q, β satisfy the conditions in this theorem. Similarly, for the problem of type 3, we want to obtain that

$$|\frac{\partial F(v_{ij}^{(k)}, \cdot)}{\partial v_{ij}^{(k)}}| \leq (1 - \epsilon)(|\frac{R'(v_{ij}^{(k)})}{R(v_{ij}^{(k)})}| + \frac{3D_2}{\beta}) \leq \eta < 1. \tag{34}$$

which can be varified to be true if p, q, β satisfy the conditions of this theorem, So Theorem is proved.

Notice that in general E_0, D_2 are finite, for example, $E_0 = 2\sum_{i=1}^{N}\sum_{j=1}^{N}|w_{ij}|$ for GBP. Moreover, if $v_{ij}^{(k)}$ converges v_{ij}^*, then we have that $|v_{ij}^{(k)} - v_{ij}^*| \leq \sum_{r=k+1}^{\infty}|v_{ij}^{(r)} - v_{ij}^{(r-1)}| \leq \frac{\eta^k}{1-\eta}|v_{ij}^{(1)} - v_{ij}^{(0)}|$, by which we can control the rate of convergence.

Notice that for the problem of type 1 we can also choose small β such that eq.(32) to be true. In fact, putting eq.(11) into eq.(7) we have that $\beta B(v_{ij}) = (\beta p)v_{ij}lnv_{ij} + (\beta q)(1 - v_{ij})ln(1 - v_{ij})$. So we can use $(\beta p), (\beta q)$ to replace p,q in eq.(32). For example, in the Case 2 $(q \geq p - 1 > 0)$ of the above proof we can choose small enough β such that $\beta p \leq 1 + \frac{\eta}{4}, \beta q \leq \frac{\eta\epsilon}{4(1-\epsilon)}, \beta \leq \frac{1}{p-q}$, which lets eq. (32) to be true. This also explains why the heuristic criteria in [1] works.

References

[1] Lau, K.M, Chan, S.M & Xu, L(1995), Comparison of the Hopfield Scheme and the Hybrid of Lagrange and Transformation Approaches for Solving the Traveling Salesman Problem, Proc. of Intl IEEE Symposium on Intelligence In Neural And Bioligical Systems, May 29-31, Washington DC, IEEE Computer Society Press, 1995, pp209-218.

[2] Xu, L.(1994), New Neural Networks for analog Combinatorial Optimizations, Proc. of World Congress on Neural Networks, Vol.II, 399-404, June 4-9, 1994, SanDiego, CA.

[3] Xu,L.(1995) On The Hybrid LT Combinatorial Optimization:New U-Shape Barrier, Sigmoid Activation, Least Leaking Energy and Maximum Entropy, Prcceedings of Intl. Conference on Neural Information Processing, Oct.30- Nov.3,1995 Beijing, China. Vol.I. pp309-312.

A dynamical neural network for solving a class of linear complementary problems

Youshen Xia, Junliang Huang

Department of Mathematis
Nanjing University of Posts and Telecommuncation
Nanjing 210003, China

Abstract

This paper presents a dynamical neural network for solving a class of linear complementary problems, and shows that it globally converges an exact solution.The neural network use only simple hardware, and has no requirement for analogue multipliers, in contrast to existing network [1] which need plenty of analogue multipliers.

1   Introduction

Let H be an $n \times n$ positive semidefinite matrix, and $c \in R^n$.The problem of finding $x \in R^n$ satisfying

$$(LCP) \qquad\qquad\qquad x \geqslant 0, \;\; Hx + c \geqslant 0, \;\; x^T(Hx + c) = 0 \qquad\qquad (1)$$

is know as a linear complementary problem (abbreveated to LCP).The LCP has been recognized as a unifying description of a wide class of problems including sets of piecewise linear equations, variational inequalities, fixed point problems and bimatrix equilibrium points.In many applications an in real–time solution of these problems is desired.However a digital computer often cannot comply with the desired computation time, or its use is too expensive.There is one possible approach to solve this problem.It is to employ artifical neural networks on basis of parallel multifeedback circuit since these specialized networks can solve the problems which are computed in execution time which are orders of magnitude fasfer than the most popular algorithms for general purpose digitial computers.Recently, there are many neural networks for solving optimization problems [3–5], and in our paper [1], we presented neural network for solving the LCP, which globally converges an exact solution. But the main disadvantage of the network is the requiement to use relatively expensive analogue multipliers, thus the cost of its hardware implementation is expensive, and the circuit elements is not accurate.This paper presents an improved neural network which not only has advantages of the network [1] but also has no requirement to use an alogue multipliers.

2   Neural Network Model

We first assume that H is symmetric. If H is not symmetric, the problem (1) can be simply reformulated by replacing H with its symmetric component $\hat{H} = \dfrac{1}{2}(H + H^T)$.

For the problem (1), the paper [1] presented a new neural network whose dynamics are governed by

$$\frac{dx}{dt} = -r\{Hx + c + H[x - (x - Hx - c)^+]\} \qquad\qquad (2)$$

where $r = \|(x - Hx - c)^+ - x\|_2^2$, $(x)^+ = [(x_1)^+, \; \cdots, \; (x_n)^+]^T$, and $(x_i)^+ = \max\{0, \; x_i\}$. The network has avoided shortcomings of Cichocki and Unbehauen's network in that it can be completely stable to the exact solutions and there are no parameters to set.Yet, it has plenty of analogue multplivers, and thus the cost of its hardware implementations is expensive.

Now we propose an improved neural network whose state vector x is governed by equations

$$\frac{dx}{dt} = -\{(Hx + c) + H[x - (x - Hx - c)^+]\} \qquad\qquad (3)$$

A simplified network diagram of (3) is shown in Fig.1 where vector c is are the external input, and x is the network output.From Fig.1, we see that the circuit consists of adders (summing amplifiers) and integrators, and there are no analogue mulitipliers.Thus, from hardware implementation point of view, the proposed network in (3) improves the network in (2).

3 Neural Network Theory

In this section, the neural network descirbed by (3) will be proved to be completely stable to the exact solutions.First, we need the following some lemmas.

Lemma 1. Let $R_+^n = \{x = (x_1, \cdots, x_n)^T \in |x_i \geqslant 0, \ i = 1, \cdots, n\}$, then for all $x \in R_+^n$,

$$[x - (x - Hx - c)^+]^T[Hx + c] \geqslant \|x - (x - Hx - c)^+\|_2^2.$$

Proof.See Appendix

Lemma 2. Let $x \in R_+^n$ defined in lemma 1, then $[x - (x - Hx - c)^+]^T(Hx + c) = 0$ if and only if

$$Hx + c \geqslant 0 \ \text{ and } \ x^T(Hx + c) = 0$$

Proof. Let $[x - (x - Hx - c)^+]^T[Hx + c] = 0$ and assume that there exists an i_0 such that $(Hx + c)_{i_0} < 0$.Then, from $(x - Hx - c)_{i_0} > 0$ we have

$$[x - (x - Hx - c)^+]_{i_0}[Hx + c] = [x_{i_0} - (x_{i_0} - (Hx + c)_{i_0})][Hx + c]_{i_0}$$
$$= [(Hx + c)_{i_0}]^2 > 0.$$

Thus this will lead to a contradiction, so $Hx + c \geqslant 0$.

Now we prove that $x^T(Hx + c) = 0$.Assume that $x^T(Hx + c) \neq 0$, then

$$x^T(Hx + c) > 0$$

From lemma 1 we have

$$x = (x - Hx - c)^+$$

and

$$x^T(Hx + c) = [(x - Hx - c)^+]^T[Hx + c],$$

thus

$$[(x - Hx - c)^+]^T[Hx + c] > 0.$$

Then there exist an i_0 such that

$$x_{i_0} > (Hx + c)_{i_0} \ \text{ and } \ (Hx + c)_{i_0} > 0$$

Therefore

$$[x - (x - Hx - c)^+]^T[Hx + c] \geqslant [(Hx + c)_{i_0}]^2 > 0$$

This is also a contradicion, and so $x^T(Hx + c) = 0$.Conversely, it is similar to the above proof.

Lemma 3. Let x^* is an optimal solution to the problem (1), then for all $x \in R_+^n$,

$$(x - x^*)^T g(x) \geqslant \varphi(x) + (x - x^*)^T H(x - x^*) \tag{5}$$

where $\varphi(x) = [x - (x - Hx - c)^+]^T(Hx + c)$, and $g(x) = Hx + c + H[x - (x - Hx - c)^+]$.

Proof.Using $Hx^* + c \geqslant 0$, $c^T x^* = -(x^*)^T Hx^*$, we have

$$(x - x^*)^T g(x) = (x - x^*)^T[Hx + c + H(x - (x - Hx - c)^+)]$$
$$= (x - x^*)^T H(x - x^*) + (x - x^*)^T(Hx^* + c) + [x - (x - Hx - c)^+]^T H(x - x^*)$$
$$= \varphi(x) + (x - x^*)^T H(x - x^*) + (Hx^* + c)^T(x - Hx - c)^+ \geqslant \varphi(x) + (x - x^*)^T H(x - x^*)$$

since $Hx^* + c \geqslant 0$ and $(x - Hx - c)^+ \geqslant 0$.

Now we can establish main result of the proposed network in (3)

Theorem 1. The neural network in (3) is completely stable to exact solutions of the problem (1).

Proof.We first show that equilibrium points of (3) are optimal solutions to the problems (1).Let $\hat{x}$ be an equilibrium point of (3), then $g(\hat{x}) = 0$.From lemma 3 we have

$$\varphi(\hat{x}) + (\hat{x} - x^*)^T H(\hat{x} - x^*) \leqslant (\hat{x} - x^*)^T g(\hat{x}) = 0.$$

thus $\varphi(\hat{x}) = 0$, hence from lemma 2, we know that x is an optimal solution to the problem (1).

Now, it remains to show that the network in (3) is completely stable.Let x^0 be any initial point taken in R_+^n, and let $x(t) = x(t;\ t_0;\ x^0)$ be the solution of the initial value porblem associated with (3).Consider the function $V(x) = \dfrac{1}{2}\|(x - x^*)\|_2^2$, where fixed x^* is an optimal solution to the problems (1).Then from lemma 4 we have

$$\frac{dV(x(t))}{dt} = \frac{dV}{dx} \cdot \frac{dx}{dt} = -(x - x^*)^T g(x) \leqslant -\varphi(x) - (x - x^*)^T H(x - x^*) \leqslant 0$$

since the matrix H is symmetric semidfinite.Thus

$$\|x(t) - x^*\|_2^2 \leqslant \|x^0 - x^*\|_2^2, \ \forall t \geqslant t_0,$$

hence the solution $x(t)$ is bounded.Again, similarly to proof of the paper [2] we can complete the rest of the proof.

4   Simulation Examples

To check the convergence of the proposed network in (3), an example for the problem (1) has been simulated on a computer.The numerical algorithm used a stepsize–variable intergration method.

Example 1. Consider the problem (1) where

$$H = \begin{bmatrix} 2 & 2 & 2 \\ 0 & 2 & 0 \\ 0 & 0 & 1 \end{bmatrix}, \quad c = \begin{bmatrix} -8 \\ -6 \\ -4 \end{bmatrix}$$

Because H is not symmetric, we first replace H with it symmetric component $\hat{H} = \dfrac{1}{2}(H + H^T)$.

We solve the problem using system (3), and the trajectories of x with various initial points in R_+^n is globally convergent.A numerical result on a computer is

$$x \approx (1.99998,\ 2.00001,\ 2.00003)^T$$

which is more approximate with exact solution to the problem

$$x^* = (2,\ 2,\ 2)^T$$

The state trajectories of x with a given initial point $x^\circ = (6,\ 12,\ 21)^T$ is show in Fig.2.

Example 2. Consider the problem (1) where

$$H = \begin{bmatrix} 2 & 1 & -1 & 1 & -2 \\ 1 & 1 & 1 & 1 & 1 \\ -1 & 1 & 5 & 1 & 7 \\ 1 & 1 & 1 & 1 & 1 \\ -2 & 1 & 7 & 1 & 9 \end{bmatrix}, \quad c = \begin{bmatrix} 0 \\ 0 \\ 0 \\ 0 \\ 0 \end{bmatrix}$$

We solve the problem using the system (3).The simulation result of the trajectories of x with a given initial point $x^\circ = (14,\ 21,\ 2,\ 5,\ 10)^T$ are shown in Fig.3.

Reference

(1) Youshen Xia and Junliang Huang, Neural network for solving a class of linear complementary problems, Journal of Southast University, vol.25, no.6, Nov., 1995.

(2) Youshen Xia and Jiasong Wang, Neural network for solving linear programming problems with bounded variables, IEEE Trans.Neural networks, vol.6, no.2, March 1995.

(3) A.Cichocki, R.Unbehauen, Neural networks for computing optimization and signal processing, Teubner Wiley, 1992.

(4) Youshen Xia, A new neural network for solving linear programming problems and its application, IEEE Trans.Neural Networks, vol.7, no.2, March 1996.

(4) Wu Xinyu, Youshen Xia, and Chen Waikai.A high performance neural network for Solving linear and quadratic programming problem IEEE Trans.Neural Network, to appear.

(5) D. G. Luenberger, Introduction to Linear and nonlinear programming. Reading, MA: Addison Wesley, 1973.

Appendix: The proof of lemma 1

Theorem 2. Let $\Omega \subset R^n$ be a closed convex set, and let $P_\Omega(\,\cdot\,)$ be a projection operator on the set Ω. Then for any $v \in \Omega$ but fixed

$$\{u - P_\Omega(u)\}^T \{P_\Omega(u) - v\} \geqslant 0, \quad \forall\, u \in R^n$$

Proof.See [4].

Proof of the lemma 1: From the theorem 2 we obtain by setting $v: = x$ and $u: = x - Hx - c$

$$[x - Hx - c - (x - Hx - c)^+]^T [(x - Hx - c)^+ - x] \geqslant 0,$$

thus

$$[x - (x - Hx - c)^+]^T [(x - Hx - c)^+ - x] - [Hx + c]^T [(x - Hx - c)^+ - x] \geqslant 0$$

hence

$$[x - (x - Hx - c)^+]^T [Hx + c] \geqslant \| x - (x - Hx - c)^+ \|_2^2.$$

This completes the proof the lemma 1.

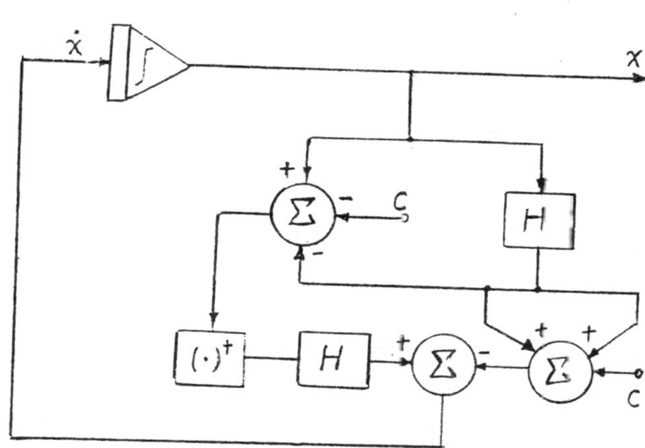

Figure 1

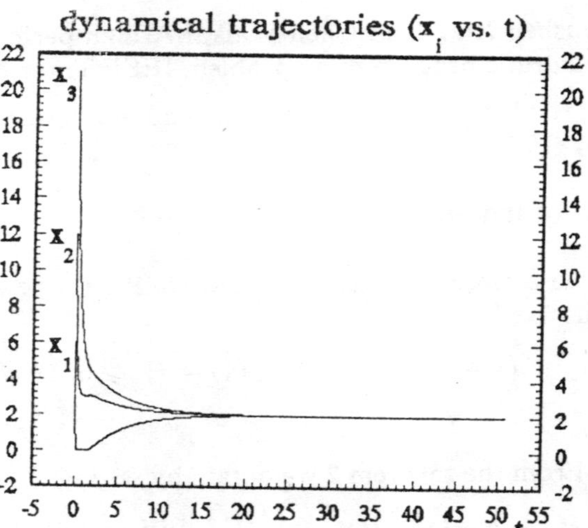

Figure 2

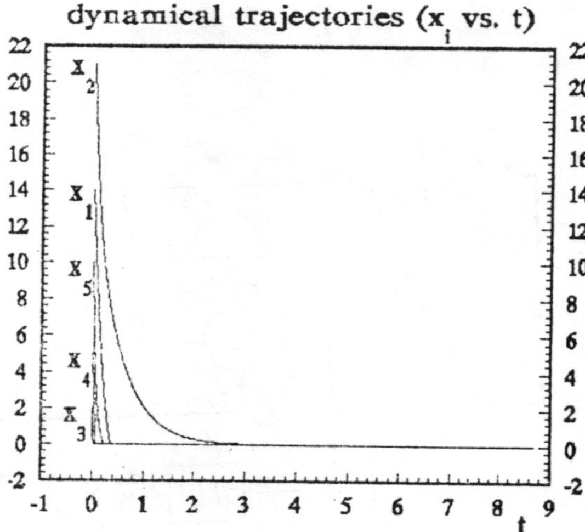

Figure 3

A Recurrent Neural Network for Solving the Assignment Problem Based on Its Dual Formulation

Jun Wang

Department of Mechanical and Automation Engineering
The Chinese University of Hong Kong
Shatin, New Territories, Hong Kong
jwang@mae.cuhk.edu.hk

Abstract— **This paper presents a recurrent neural network, called the dual assignment network, for solving the assignment problem. The dual assignment network, based on the dual assignment problem, has less complex architecture than its predecessor. The dual assignment network is guaranteed to make optimal assignment. The application of the dual assignment network for sorting is discussed. The performance and operating characteristics of the dual assignment network are demonstrated by means of an illustrative example.**

1   Introduction

The assignment problem (also known as the linear assignment problem and matching problem) is concerned with assigning a number of entities to a number of positions and minimizing a linear cost function. The assignment problem is a classical combinatorial optimization problem arising in numerous planning and designing contexts. Various solution procedures for solving the assignment problem have been investigated over decades. Besides the classical methods such as the simplex method and the Hungarian method, many new and improved methods have been developed [1,2]. For time-varying and/or large-scale assignment problems such as weapon-target assignment, the existing algorithms may not be effective and efficient due to the time-varying problem parameters and stringent processing requirement, real-time solution methods are more desirable. Since Hopfield and Tank's seminal work [3], neural networks for solving optimization problems have been a major area in neural network research [e.g., 4-7]. In particular, various neural networks have been developed for solving the assignment problem [8-13].

2   Problem Formulation

2.1   Primal Assignment Problem

The assignment problem can be formulated as the following zero-one integer linear program:

$$\text{minimize} \quad \sum_{i=1}^{n} \sum_{j=1}^{n} c_{ij} x_{ij}, \tag{1}$$

$$\text{subject to} \quad \sum_{i=1}^{n} x_{ij} = 1, \quad j = 1, 2, \ldots, n; \tag{2}$$

$$\sum_{j=1}^{n} x_{ij} = 1, \quad i = 1, 2, \ldots, n; \cdot \tag{3}$$

$$x_{ij} \in \{0, 1\}, \quad i, j = 1, 2, \ldots, n. \tag{4}$$

where c_{ij} and x_{ij} are respectively the cost coefficient and decision variable associated with assigning entity i to position j. In general, a cost coefficient can be positive representing a loss or negative representing a gain. The decision variable is defined such that $x_{ij} = 1$ if and only if entity i is assigned to position j. The objective function to be minimized, eqn. (1), is the total cost for the assignment. Eqn. (2) ensures that exactly one entity is assigned to each position; i.e., each column of x_{ij} has only one decision variable being 1. Eqn. (3) ensures that each entity is assigned to exactly one position; i.e., each row of x_{ij} has only one decision variable being 1. Eqn. (4) is the zero-one integrality constraint on decision variables.

It is well known, from the optimal solution point of view, that the assignment problem is equivalent to a linear programming problem by replacing the zero-one integrality constraints (4) with nonnegativity constraints, due to the total unimodularity property [1,2]:

$$x_{ij} \geq 0, \quad i, j = 1, 2, \ldots, n. \tag{5}$$

The resulting linear program is called the primal assignment problem hereafter. The primal assignment problem contains n^2 decision variables, $2n$ equality constraints, and n^2 nonnegativity constraints.

2.2 Dual Assignment Problem

Since the number of equality constraints is less than the number of decision variables for $n > 2$, it is more desirable to formulate the dual of the primal assignment problem. Based on the primal assignment problem, the dual assignment problem can be formulated as follows:

$$\text{maximize} \qquad \sum_{i=1}^{n}(u_i + v_i) \tag{6}$$

$$\text{subject to} \qquad u_i + v_j \leq c_{ij}, \ i,j = 1,2,\dots,n; \tag{7}$$

where u_i and v_i denote the dual decision variables. According to the Duality Theorem in optimization theory [1,2], the value of the objective function at its maximum is equal to the total cost of the primal assignment problem at its minimum [1,2.

Because a solution to the dual assignment problem does not directly show an assignment, the decoding from the dual optimal solution to the primal optimal solution is needed for solving the assignment problem with dual decision variables. According to the Complementary Slackness Theorem [2]: Given the feasible solutions x_{ij} to the primal assignment problem and u_i and v_i to the dual assignment problem respectively, the solutions are optimal if and only if for $i,j = 1,2,\dots,n$,

1. $x_{ij} = 1$ implies $u_i + v_j = c_{ij}$ and

2. $x_{ij} = 0$ is implied by $u_i + v_j < c_{ij}$.

The Complementary Slackness Theorem can be used to decode the optimal solution to the primal assignment problem from that to the dual assignment problem.

3 Network Description

3.1 Energy Function

Because the dual assignment problem is a linear program, it can be solved by the neural networks proposed for solving linear programming problems in [3-7]. In [6,7], a recurrent neural network called the deterministic annealing network is presented and demonstrated to be capable of solving linear programming problems. The dual assignment network (DAN) is tailored from the deterministic annealing network [8,9].

An energy function based on the dual assignment problem can be formulated as:

$$E_d[t, u(t), v(t)] = \frac{w}{2}\sum_{i=1}^{n}\sum_{j=1}^{n}\{g[u_i(t) + v_j(t) - c_{ij}]\}^2 - \beta\exp(-t/\tau)\sum_{i=1}^{n}[u_i(t) + v_i(t)], \tag{8}$$

where $g(\cdot)$ is a nonnegative and nondecreasing activation function defined as $g(s) = 0$ if $s \leq 0$ and $g(s) > 0$ if $s > 0$.

3.2 Dynamical Equations

Let $du_i(t)/dt = -\partial E_d[t, u(t), v(t)]/\partial u_i$ and $dv_i(t)/dt = -\partial E_d[t, u(t), v(t)]/\partial v_i$, the dynamical equations of the dual assignment network (DAN) are as follows: for $i = 1, 2, \dots, n$;

$$\frac{du_i(t)}{dt} = -w\sum_{j=1}^{n} g[u_i(t) + v_j(t) - c_{ij}] + \beta\exp(-t/\tau), \tag{9}$$

$$\frac{dv_i(t)}{dt} = -w\sum_{j=1}^{n} g[u_j(t) + v_i(t) - c_{ji}] + \beta\exp(-t/\tau). \tag{10}$$

The solution from DAN can be easily decoded into that from PAN by using the Complementary Slackness theorem as follows:

$$x_{ij}(t) = h[u_i(t) + v_j(t) - c_{ij}], \tag{11}$$

where $h(z)$ is the output function defined as $h(z) = 1$ if $z = 0$, or $h(z) = 0$ otherwise.

3.3 Network Architectures

The dual assignment network consists of $2n$ neurons representing $[u_i]$ and $[v_i]$ arranged spatially in two layers. The dynamical equations (9) and (10) of DAN show that there is an inhibitory connections with weight of $-w$ from every pair of $u_i(t)$ and $v_j(t)$ $(i,j = 1,2,\dots,n)$. That is, the number of connections is $2n^2$, n^2 for from $u(t)$ to $v(t)$ and another n^2 from $v(t)$ to $u(t)$. The dynamical equations also show that all the $2n$ neurons share the common decaying external input $\beta\exp(-t/\tau)$. Figure 1 illustrates the architecture of DAN.

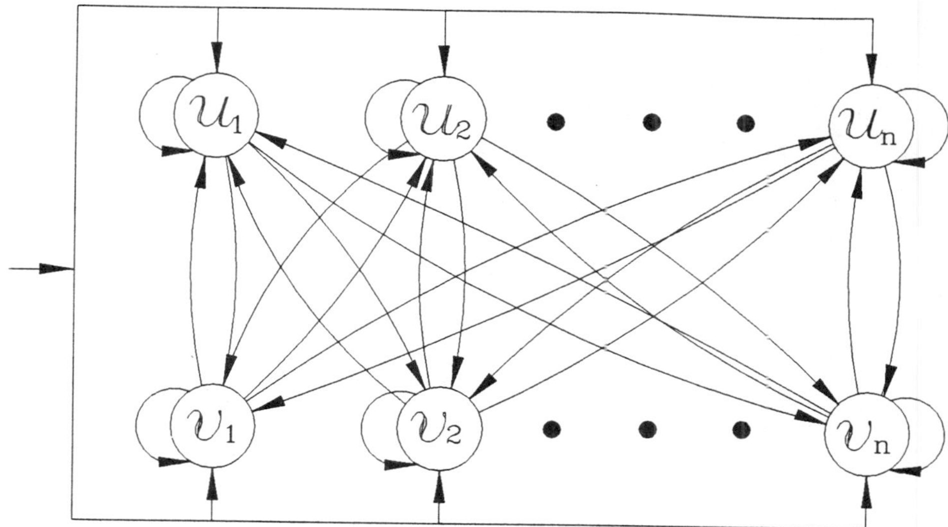

Figure 1: Architecture of the Dual Assignment Network.

3.4 Design Parameters

Because the constraint coefficient matrix in a dual problem is the transpose of that in the primal problem, it is not difficult to see that the nonzero eigenvalues of the connection weight matrix in DAN are either $-nw$ or $-2nw$. Large w can expedite the convergence of DAN as well. The role of β is to balance the effects of constraint satisfaction and objective maximization. It is usually set $\beta \approx wc_{\max}$.

The role of the activation function in DAN is to enforce the inequality constraints (7) and scale the sensitivity of the activation. A good choice is the Heaviside activation function defined as $g[u_{ij}(t)] = \xi u_{ij}(t)$ for $u_{ij}(t) > 0$ and $g[u_{ij}(t)] = 0$ otherwise, where $\xi > 0$ is the slope of the activation function in the positive half-space.

4 Sorting Application

Sorting is a process of arranging items in order, used widely in numerous application areas such as database management, network communication, digital signal processing, and VLSI design. As a fundamental operation in data processing, sorting operations account for over 25 percent of processing time.

In [18], the sorting problem is formulated a primal assignment problem and solved using a single-layer deterministic annealing network (the primal assignment network). The decision variable is defined as that $x_{ij} = 1$ if item i with numerical key r_i is in the j-th position of the sorted list. The cost coefficients of the assignment problem for sorting are defined as $c_{ij} = r_i s_j$ where r_i and s_j denote respectively the numerical key of the i-th item to be sorted and the nonzero weighting parameter for the j-th position in the desired sequence (sorted list).

Consider the sorting problem (Example 1) in [18]: rank a set of 10 items $\{$-1.3, 1.7, 0.5, 2.2, -2.6, 1.5, -0.6, 0.9, -1.2, 1.1$\}$ in an ascending order. Let $s_j = 11 - j$ for $j = 1, 2, \ldots, 10$. Accordingly, the cost coefficient matrix can be defined as follows.

$$[c_{ij}] = \begin{pmatrix}
-13.0 & -11.7 & -10.4 & -9.1 & -7.8 & -6.5 & -5.2 & -3.9 & -2.6 & -1.3 \\
17.0 & 15.3 & 13.6 & 11.9 & 10.2 & 8.5 & 6.8 & 5.1 & 3.4 & 1.7 \\
5.0 & 4.5 & 4.0 & 3.5 & 3.0 & 2.5 & 2.0 & 1.5 & 1.0 & 0.5 \\
22.0 & 19.8 & 17.6 & 15.4 & 13.2 & 11.0 & 8.8 & 6.6 & 4.4 & 2.2 \\
-26.0 & -23.4 & -20.8 & -18.2 & -15.6 & -13.0 & -10.4 & -7.8 & -5.2 & -2.6 \\
15.0 & 13.5 & 12.0 & 10.5 & 9.0 & 7.5 & 6.0 & 4.5 & 3.0 & 1.5 \\
-6.0 & -5.4 & -4.8 & -4.2 & -3.6 & -3.0 & -2.4 & -1.8 & -1.2 & -0.6 \\
9.0 & 8.1 & 7.2 & 6.3 & 5.4 & 4.5 & 3.6 & 2.7 & 1.8 & 0.9 \\
-12.0 & -10.8 & -9.6 & -8.4 & -7.2 & -6.0 & -4.8 & -3.6 & -2.4 & -1.2 \\
11.0 & 9.9 & 8.8 & 7.7 & 6.6 & 5.5 & 4.4 & 3.3 & 2.2 & 1.1
\end{pmatrix} .$$

Let $w = 10^8, \beta = 5w, \tau = 10^{-7}\mu s, u(0) = v(0) = 0$, and the Heaviside activation function be used. The result of the numerical simulation shows that the steady state of the dual assignment network is $u^* = [-10.3590, 7.0418, 2.0478, 7.7890, -22.6886, 6.5418, -5.0089, 4.2475, -9.5090, 5.1475]$ and $v^* = [-3.3114, -1.3410, -0.0911, 0.8089, 0.9522, 0.2525, -0.7475, -2.0418, -3.6418, -5.5890]$. Figure 3 depicts the transient behavior of the activation states of the simulated DAN. It shows that the simulated DAN takes about $0.4\mu s$ (4τ) to converge. Using eqn. (11), the optimal solution to the corresponding primal

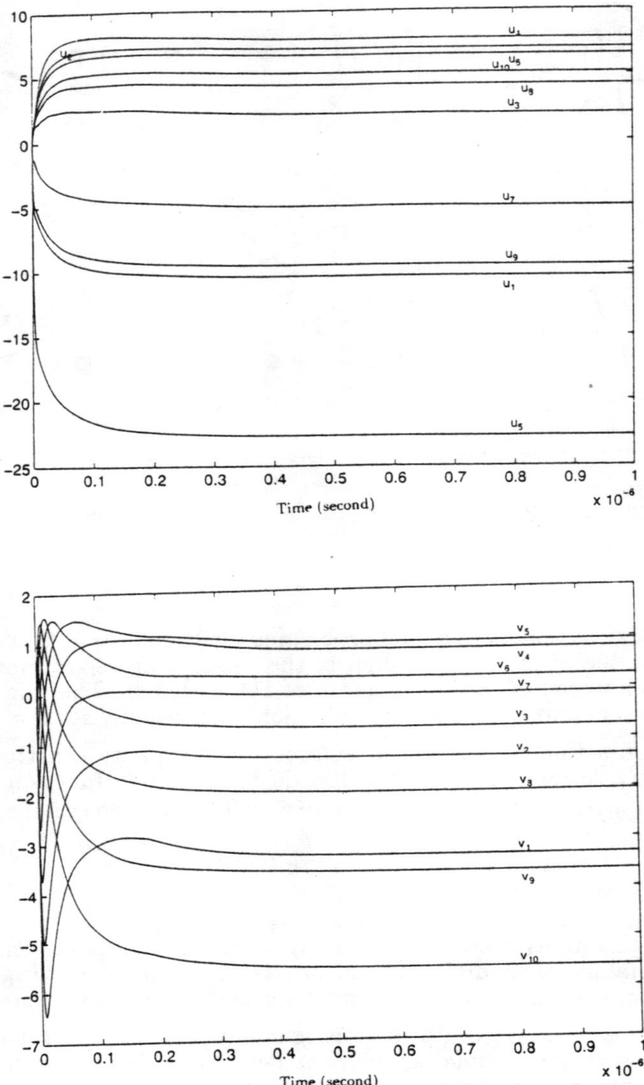

Figure 2: Transient States of the Dual Assignment Network in the Sorting Example.

assignment problem can be easily interpreted as follows:

$$
[x_{ij}^*] = \begin{pmatrix}
0 & 1 & 0 & 0 & 0 & 0 & 0 & 0 & 0 & 0 \\
0 & 0 & 0 & 0 & 0 & 0 & 0 & 0 & 1 & 0 \\
0 & 0 & 0 & 0 & 1 & 0 & 0 & 0 & 0 & 0 \\
0 & 0 & 0 & 0 & 0 & 0 & 0 & 0 & 0 & 1 \\
1 & 0 & 0 & 0 & 0 & 0 & 0 & 0 & 0 & 0 \\
0 & 0 & 0 & 0 & 0 & 0 & 0 & 1 & 0 & 0 \\
0 & 0 & 0 & 1 & 0 & 0 & 0 & 0 & 0 & 0 \\
0 & 0 & 0 & 0 & 0 & 1 & 0 & 0 & 0 & 0 \\
0 & 0 & 1 & 0 & 0 & 0 & 0 & 0 & 0 & 0 \\
0 & 0 & 0 & 0 & 0 & 0 & 1 & 0 & 0 & 0
\end{pmatrix} .
$$

The order representation can be accordingly decoded as a sorted sequence $\{r_5, r_1, r_9, r_7, r_3, r_8, r_{10}, r_6, r_2, r_4\}$; i.e., $\{-2.6, -1.3, -1.2, -0.6, 0.5, 0.9, 1.1, 1.5, 1.7, 2.2\}$. Obviously, the solution from DAN in this sorting example represents a correct order.

5 Concluding Remarks

In this paper, a dual assignment network has been proposed. The dual assignment network has been shown to be capable of making optimal assignments in real time. Compared with the primal assignment network [9,14] which consists of $O(n^2)$ neurons and $O(n^3)$ connections, the dual assignment network is composed of $O(n)$ neurons and $O(n^2)$ connections, thus is more routable in hardware realization. One salient attribute of the dual assignment network is the independence of the connection weight matrix upon specific problems. Specifically, only the external inputs (cost coefficients) are different for a different assignment problem. Furthermore, the dual assignment network can be modulized with a large number of neurons. In a specific application, the unused neurons can be disabled by assigning very large cost coefficients to penalize the selection of the corresponding decision variables. These desirable features facilitate the hardware implementation of the dual assignment network. Since the minimum absolute value of the nonzero eigenvalues of the dual assignment network is directly proportional to the size of the assignment problem, the convergence rate of the dual assignment network to be implemented in hardware ultimately is statistically proportional to the size of the assignment problem. The dual assignment network implemented in a VLSI circuit will serve as co-processors for onboard planning in dynamic decision environments for solving the large-scale assignment problems in real time.

References

[1] M. S. Bazaraa, J. J. Jarvis, and H. D. Sherali, *Linear Programming and Network Flows* (2rd Ed.), New York: John Wiley & Sons, 1990.

[2] D. G. Luenberger, *Linear and Nonlinear Programming* (2rd Ed.), Reading, MA: Addison-Wesley, 1984.

[3] J. J. Hopfield and D. W. Tank, "Neural computation of decisions in optimization problems," *Biological Cybernetics*, vol. 52, pp. 141-152, 1985.

[4] D. W. Tank and J. J. Hopfield, "Simple 'neural optimization networks: an A/D converter, signal decision circuit, and a linear programming circuit," *IEEE Transactions on Circuits and Systems*, vol. 33, no. 5, pp. 533-541, 1986.

[5] M. P. Kennedy and L. O. Chua, "Neural networks for nonlinear programming," *IEEE Transactions on Circuits and Systems*, vol. 35, no. 5, pp. 554-562, 1988

[6] J. Wang, "Analysis and design of a recurrent neural network for linear programming," *IEEE Transactions on Circuits and Systems I: Fundamental Theory and Applications*, vol. 40, no. 9, pp. 613-618, 1993.

[7] J. Wang, "A deterministic annealing neural network for convex programming," *Neural Networks*, vol. 7, no. 4, pp. 629-641, 1994.

[8] S. P. Eberhardt, T. Duad, D. A. Kerns, T. X. Brown, A. P. Thakoor, "Competitive neural architecture for hardware solution to the assignment problem," *Neural Networks*, vol. 4, no. 4, pp. 431-442, 1991.

[9] J. Wang, "Analog neural network for solving the assignment problem," *Electronics Letters*, vol. 28, no. 11, pp. 1047-1050, 1992.

[10] W. J. Wolfe, J. M. MacMillan, G. Brady, R. Mathews, J. A. Rothman, M. D. Orosz, C. Anderson, and G. Alaghband, "Inhibitory grids and the assignment problem," *IEEE Transactions on Neural Networks*, vol. 4, no. 2, pp. 319-331, 1993.

[11] J. J. Kosowsky and A. L. Yuille, "The invisible hand algorithm: Solving the assignment problem with statistical physics," *Neural Networks*, vol. 7, pp. 477-490, 1994.

[12] K. Urahama, "Analog circuit for solving assignment problem," *IEEE Transactions on Circuits and Systems I: Fundamental Theory and Applications*, vol. 40, no. 5, pp. 426-429, 1994.

[13] P.-Y. Ting, and R. A. Iltis, "Diffusion network architectures for implementation of gibbs sampler with applications to the assignment problem," *IEEE Transactions on Neural Networks*, vol. 5, no. 4, pp. 622-638, 1994.

[14] J. Wang, "Analysis and design of an analog sorting network," *IEEE Transactions on Neural Networks*, vol. 5, pp. 962-971, 1995.

Optimization

(Poster Presentation)

Augmented Lagrange-Hopfield Method
for Combinatorial Optimization

S. Z. Li   L. H. Chen
School of Electrical and Electronic Engineering
Nanyang Technological University, Singapore 639798

Abstract—

A method called Augmented Lagrange-Hopfield (ALH) method is presented for solving combinatorial optimization problems. It is a differential system for solving a constrained optimization problem into which the original combinatorial problem is converted. By using the augmented Lagrangian multiplier technique, the ALH method effectively overcomes instabilities of the penalty method (*e.g.* Hopfield network) or the Lagrange multiplier method alone in constrained optimization. We provide experiments on weighted graph matching. The results show that the ALH solution is almost as good as that of stochastic simulated annealing and better than deterministic mean field annealing yet need much less computational effort than simulated annealing.

1   Introduction

Developing neural algorithms for solving combinatorial optimization problems has been one of the main interests in neural network research. An important work in this area is that of Hopfield [8] and Hopfield and Tank [9]. The resulting algorithm correspond to certain highly-interconnected network of non-linear neurons. It is appealing because it offers possibility for analog "silicon implementation". Following that work, many related approaches are also proposed such as the elastic net of Durbin and Willshaw [2] and the mean field annealing of Peterson and Soderberg [13]. They usually have good convergence property compared with Hopfield network and they find sub-optimal solutions with much less expenses than the time consuming stochastic simulated annealing [10, 5]. Relations between these neural algorithms are studied in [17, 22].

Recent studies have found that problems in convergence and stability exist in Hopfield networks [20] and also in elastic net [18]. Those neural algorithms may either not converge to valid solutions or produce solutions which are far from the optimal one. This is not surprising considering that they are instances of the penalty method. In order for the penalty method to converge to a feasible solution, the weighting factors for the penalty terms must be sufficiently large. However, as the penalty terms become stronger, the constraints on the original problem becomes relatively weaker and solution quality is deteriorated. Worse, when the weighting factors are sufficiently large, the problem becomes ill-conditioned and the output oscillates [4]. This is a dilemma in the penalty method.

The Lagrange multiplier technique can be used to overcome the above problems associated with the penalty method [14, 3, 21]. In [19], the Lagrange technique is combined with the Hopfield network. With the use of Lagrange multipliers, the weighting values for the penalty terms can be much smaller than those required by the penalty method. However, the standard Lagrange technique such as used in [19, 21] may have difficulties converging to an optimum because of a so-called zigzagging problem [4].

This paper presents a neural algorithm, called the Augmented Lagrange-Hopfield (ALH) method, for solving combinatorial optimization problems, in particular, the graph matching problem. It is based on the augmented Lagrange multiplier technique [15, 7, 14] for constrained optimization and the Hopfield method [8] for bridging the gap between combinatorial and continuous optimization. In solving the constrained optimization, the ALH method overcomes instabilities associated with the penalty method or Lagrange multiplier method alone. The ALH method not only converges to valid solutions but also good quality solutions in terms of optimized objective values. Experiments on the weighted graph matching problem are shown to compare the ALH with the mean field theoretical annealing (MFA) algorithm [13], the letter having has been shown to give good performance on graph problems [13], and simulated annealing [10]. The results show that the ALH solution is almost as good as that of stochastic simulated annealing and better than deterministic mean field annealing yet needs much less computational effort than simulated annealing.

The rest of the paper is organized as follows: Section 2 describes the ALH method and discusses its relations to the standard penalty the Lagrange methods. Section 3 presents the experiments. Conclusions are given in Section 4.

2   The Augmented Lagrange-Hopfield Method

We convert the original combinatorial problem to a form suitable for continuous computation. A convenient way is to consider it as a label assignment problem. Let $\mathcal{S} = \{1, \ldots, m\}$ be a set of m objects and $\mathcal{L} = \{0, 1, \ldots, M\}$ be a set of $M + 1$ labels. In traveling salesman problem, $i \in \mathcal{S}$ is the order of visit and $I \in \mathcal{L}$ indexes one of the $M + 1 = m$ cities. We use an $M + 1$ position vector $p_i = [p_i(I) \mid I \in \mathcal{L}]$ to represent the state of the assignment for $i \in \mathcal{S}$. The real value $p_i(I) \in [0, 1]$ reflects the strength with which i is assigned label I. The matrix $p = [p_i(I) \mid i \in \mathcal{S}, I \in \mathcal{L}]$ is the state of the assignment. This representation has been used in image analysis for continuous relaxation labeling [16].

With such a representation, a combinatorial problem may be reformulated as the following constrained minimization

$$\min_{p} \quad E(p) \tag{1}$$

$$\text{subject to} \quad C_k(p) = 0 \quad k = 1, \ldots K \tag{2}$$

$$p_i(I) \geq 0 \forall i \in \mathcal{S}, \forall I \in \mathcal{L} \tag{3}$$

where $E(p)$ is the objective energy function, C_k's are some real functions and K is an integer number. The final solution p^* is subject to additional constraints

$$p_i^*(I) = 0 \quad \text{or} \quad 1 \qquad \forall i, I \tag{4}$$

In this paper, we are interested in the following equality constraints

$$C_i(p) = \sum_I p_i(I) - 1 = 0 \qquad \forall i \in \mathcal{S} \tag{5}$$

in which case $K = m$. This is imposed for problems such as graph partition and matching, For traveling salesman problem, it needs further equality constraints as $\sum_i p_i(I) - 1 = 0$ $(\forall I)$. The constraints in (4) are imposed because the final solution p^* must be decisive. In many cases such as graph problems and the TSP, the energy takes the following form:

$$E(p) \;=\; \sum_{i \in \mathcal{S}} \sum_{I \in \mathcal{L}} r_i(I)\, p_i(I) + \sum_{i \in \mathcal{S}} \sum_{I \in \mathcal{L}} \sum_{i' \in \mathcal{S}, i' \neq i} \sum_{I' \in \mathcal{L}} r_{i,i'}(I, I')\, p_i(I)\, p_{i'}(I') \tag{6}$$

$$\tag{7}$$

where $r_i(I)$ and $r_{i,i'}(I, I')$ are unary and binary interaction functions.

Now we describe the ALH method aimed to solve the above constrained minimization problem. First, we introduce internal variables $u_i(I) \in (-\infty, +\infty)$ $(\forall i, I)$ and relate them to $p_i(I)$ via

$$p_i(I) = \psi_T(u_i(I)) \tag{8}$$

where $\psi_T(x)$ is a sigmoid function

$$\psi_T(x) = 1/[1 + e^{-x/T}] \tag{9}$$

controlled by a temperature parameter $T > 0$. With the introduction of the internal u variables, the energy function can be considered as $E(u) = E(p(u))$. This treatment confines $p_i(I)$ to the range $(0, 1)$ to impose the inequality constraints of (3). When $T \to 0^+$, $p_i(I)$ is forced to be 0 or 1 depending on whether $u_i(I)$ is positive or negative, thus imposing the unambiguity constraints of (4).

Next, we use the Lagrange method to impose the equality constraints of (2). Define the following Lagrange function

$$L(p, \gamma) = E(p) + \sum_k \gamma_k C_k(p) \tag{10}$$

where γ_k are called the Lagrange multipliers. It is a function of the $M \times m$ variables of p and the K variables of γ. For p^* to be a local minimum subject to the constraints, it is necessary that (p^*, γ^*) be a stationary point of the Lagrange function:

$$\begin{aligned} \nabla_p L(p^*, \gamma^*) &= 0 \\ \nabla_\gamma L(p^*, \gamma^*) &= 0 \end{aligned} \tag{11}$$

If (p^*, γ^*) is a saddle point for which

$$L(p^*, \gamma) \leq L(p^*, \gamma^*) \leq L(p, \gamma^*) \tag{12}$$

then p^* is a local minimum of $E(p)$ satisfying $C_k(p^*) = 0$, *i.e.* a local solution to the constrained optimization problem [6].

The following dynamic equations, called the basic differential multiplier method [14], can be used to find such a saddle point

$$\frac{dp_i(I)}{dt} = -\frac{\partial L(p, \gamma)}{\partial p_i(I)} \tag{13}$$

$$\frac{d\gamma_k}{dt} = +\frac{\partial L(p, \gamma)}{\partial \gamma_k} \tag{14}$$

It performs energy descent on p but ascent on γ. The convergence of this system is illustrated in [1].

The Lagrangian (10) can be augmented by adding penalty terms $[C_k(p)]^2$, giving an augmented Lagrange function [15, 7]

$$L_\beta(p, \gamma) = E(p) + \sum_k \gamma_k C_k(p) + \frac{\beta}{2} \sum_k [C_k(p)]^2 \tag{15}$$

where $\beta > 0$ is a finite weighting factor. The introduction of the quadratic term $\beta \sum_k [C_k(p)]^2$ with $C_k(p) = 0$ does not alter the location of the saddle point. The quadratic terms in effect stabilize the system.

The dynamic equations for minimizing L_β are

$$\frac{dp_i(I)}{dt} = -\frac{\partial L_\beta(p, \gamma)}{\partial p_i(I)} = -\frac{\partial E(p)}{\partial p_i(I)} - \sum_k \gamma_k \frac{\partial C_k(p)}{\partial p_i(I)} - \beta \sum_k C_k(p) \frac{\partial C_k(p)}{\partial p_i(I)} \tag{16}$$

$$\frac{d\gamma_k}{dt} = +\frac{\partial L(p, \gamma)}{\partial \gamma_k} = +C_k(p) \tag{17}$$

This corresponds to the modified differential multiplier method [14]. Our experiments show that the penalty terms are necessary for damping oscillations and hence helping the convergence of the numerical computation.

In the ALH method, the updating of label assignment is performed on u, rather than on p. With $\partial C_k(p)$ defined in (5), Equ.(16) is replaced by

$$\frac{du_i(I)}{dt} = -\frac{\partial L_\beta(p(u), \gamma)}{\partial p_i(I)} = -\left[q_i(I)/m + \sum_k \gamma_k + \beta \sum_k C_k(p) \right] \tag{18}$$

where $q_i(I) = \frac{\delta E}{\delta p_i(I)}$ is weighted by a factor of $1/m$ to achieve some invariance to m. Because $\frac{\partial p_i(I)}{\partial u_i(I)} = \frac{e^{-u_i(I)/T}}{T(1 + e^{-u_i(I)/T})^2}$ is always positive, $\frac{dp_i(I)}{dt}$ has the same sign as $\frac{du_i(I)}{dt}$.

The corresponding neural network is composed of the $m \times (M + 1)$ $p_i(I)$ neurons, associated with the internal u variables via the sigmoid function circuits, and K γ_k neurons. The dynamics of these neurons are described by the equations (18), (8) and (17).

In numerical computation, the ALH algorithm consists of the following three equations corresponding to (18), (8) and (17):

$$u_i^{(t+1)}(I) \leftarrow u_i^{(t)}(I) - \mu \left\{ q_i^{(t)}(I)/m + \sum_k \gamma_k^{(t)} + \beta \sum_k C_k(p^{(t)}) \right\} \tag{19}$$

$$p_i^{(t+1)}(I) \leftarrow \psi_T(u_i^{(t+1)}(I)) \tag{20}$$

and

$$\gamma_k^{(t+1)} \leftarrow \gamma_k^{(t)} + \beta C_k(p^{(t)}) \tag{21}$$

In the above, μ is a step size factor; and during the update, T may be decreased and β increased to speedup convergence. The updating is performed synchronously in parallel for all i and I. Comparing the ALH algorithm with the mean field theoretical algorithms of Peterson and Soderberg [13], we see that the ALH does not need the normalization operation required by the latter algorithm and thus is more convenient for analog implementation.

3   Experimental Results

In the following experiments, we compare the ALH algorithm with the mean field annealing (MFA) algorithms of Peterson and Soderberg [13]. The comparison is in terms of the solution quality measured by the minimized energy value. The convergence rates of the algorithm are also provided. Results obtained by using the simulated annealing (SA) algorithm of [10] are also included as a reference. The comparison is in terms of (i) the solution quality measured by the optimized objective value, and (ii) the convergence rate measured by the number of required iterations.

The test bed is partial matching of weighted graphs in which the optimal node correspondences between the largest common parts of the two weighted graphs are to be established. Here, a node corresponds to a point in $X - Y$ plane. Two random graphs, each containing $m = M$ nodes, are randomly generated as follows. First, a number of $\lfloor \frac{2}{3}m \rfloor$ nodes, where $\lfloor \cdot \rfloor$ is the "floor" operation, are generated using random numbers uniformly distributed within a box of size 100×100. They are for the first graph. Their counterparts in the other graph are generated by adding Gaussian noise of $N(0, \sigma^2)$ to the x and y coordinates of each of the nodes in the first graph. This gives $\lfloor \frac{2}{3}m \rfloor$ deviated locations of the nodes for the second graph. Then, the rest of the $\lceil \frac{1}{3}m \rceil$ nodes in each of the two graphs are generated independently using random numbers uniformly distributed in the box, which simulates outlier nodes. Between each pair of nodes in a graph is a weight equal to the Euclidean distance between them.

The above steps generate two weighted graphs $\mathcal{G} = (\mathcal{S}, d)$ and $\mathcal{G}' = (\mathcal{L}_0, D)$ where $\mathcal{S} = \{1, \ldots, m\}$ and $\mathcal{L}_0 = \{1, \ldots, M\}$ index the sets of nodes and $d = [d(i, i')]_{i,i' \in \mathcal{S}}$ and $D = [D(I, I')]_{I,I' \in \mathcal{L}_0}$ are the distances between nodes in the first and second graph, respectively. The basis of matching is the weights in d and D which reflect bilateral relations between nodes; unary properties of nodes are not used in the test. We augment $\mathcal{L}_0$ by a special node, called the NULL node and indexed by 0, into $\mathcal{L} = \{0, 1, \ldots, M\}$. The purpose is to cater for the matching of outlier nodes. The matching is to assign a node from $\mathcal{L}$ to each of the nodes in $\mathcal{S}$ so that the energy E is minimized.

From the two weighted graph, the interaction matrix $[r_{i,i'}(I, I')]$ is defined in the following way

$$r_{i,i'}(I, I') = \begin{cases} [d(i, i') - D(I, I')]^2 & \text{if } I' \neq 0 \ \& \ I' \neq 0 \\ r_{20} & \text{otherwise} \end{cases} \tag{22}$$

where $r_{20} > 0$ is a constant. For a pair of non-NULL matches, $i \leftarrow I$ and $i' \leftarrow I'$ where $I, I' \neq 0$, $r_{i,i'}(I, I')$ measures the cost of the pair. When $d(i, i') = D(I, I')$, it is zero, meaning the pair of matches are perfect; otherwise it is $[d(i, i') - D(I, I')]^2 > 0$. In the case where either of I and I' is 0, $r_{i,i'}(I, I')$ takes a prescribed value r_{20}.

Initial labeling is assigned as follows: First, we set $p_i^{(0)}(I) = 1/(M+1) + 0.001 * rnd \ (\forall i, I)$ as the starting point common to all the compared algorithms, where rnd is a random number evenly distributed in $[-1, 1]$. For the ALH, the updated variables are initialized as $u_i^{(0)}(I) = \psi_T^{-1}(p_i^{(0)}(I))$ and $\gamma_i = 0$. For the SA algorithm, we set initial label for i as $I^* = \arg\max_I p_i^{(0)}(I)$.

The parameters for the ALH equations (19) – (21) are set as follows: $\beta = 100$, T decreased from 100000 to 10000 according to $T^{(t+1)} \leftarrow 0.9T^{(t)}$, β increased from 1 to 100 according to $\beta \leftarrow 1.01\beta$, and $\mu = 1000$. The annealing schedule for SA is as $T^{(t+1)} \leftarrow 0.99T^{(t)}$ with the initial temperature set to $T^{(0)} = 10^9 \times m$. (A critical value for $T^{(0)}$ which may be lower than this value can be computed analytically [13] but this is not implemented in this work.)

The schedules for the annealing algorithms are as follows: We implemented two annealing schedules for MFA. In the first schedule which is given in [13], T is decreased according to $T^{(t+1)} \leftarrow 0.99T^{(t)}$; we set the initial temperature as $T^{(0)} = 10^9 \times M \times m$. The second is also in the form $T^{(t+1)} \leftarrow \kappa^{(t+1)}T^{(t)}$ but $\kappa^{(t+1)}$ is chosen on an *ad hoc* basis of trial and error to get the best result, which is $\kappa^{(t+1)} = 0.9$ if $S < 0.9 \ \& \ \kappa^{(t)} \leq 0.9$, 0.95 if $S < 0.95 \ \& \ \kappa^{(t)} \leq 0.95$, or 0.99 otherwise, where $S = \frac{1}{m}\sum_I p_i^2(I)$ is the saturation measure [13]. We refer to these two schedules as MFA-1 and MFA-2, respectively.

The convergence of the continuous algorithms is judged by checking whether $\max_{i,I} |p_i^{(t+1)}(I) - p_i^{(t)}(I)|$ is smaller than $0.01/m^2$. For SA, the computation stops if the desired number of acceptances is not achieved at 100 successive temperatures [10].

Fig.1 shows the results which are the averaged values of 200 runs. The solution quality is illustrated in terms of the minimized energy value as a function of the noise level σ. In terms of the quality, the SA algorithm is the best of all, and the ALH is better than the MFA. For "harder" problems, *e.g.* when $m = M = 20$ and with high σ^2 values, the MFA results produced with the schedule MFA-1 deteriorate

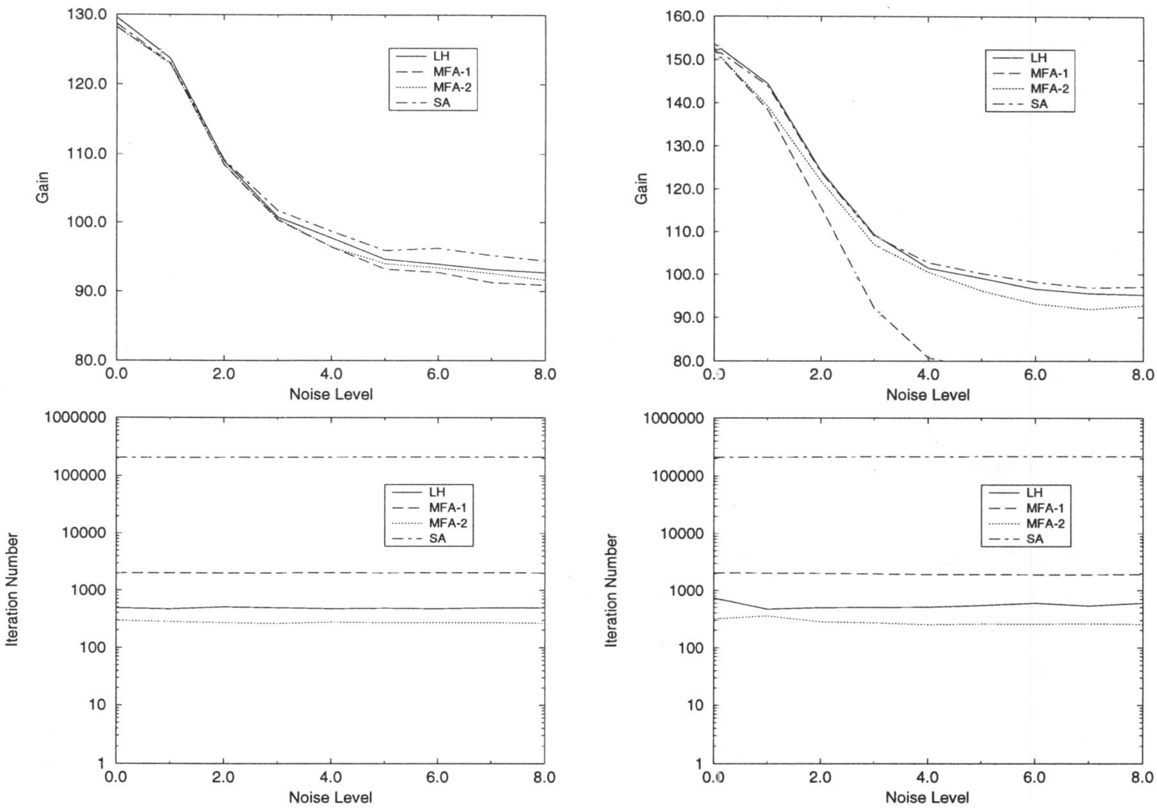

Figure 1: Comparison for problems of size $m = M = 10$ (left) and $m = M = 20$ (right). The horizontal axis is the noise level σ. (Top) The maximized gain $G(p^*) = Const - E(p^*)$ (after divided by a factor of m^2); the higher, the better. (Bottom) The number of iterations; the lower, the better.

quickly as the noise level σ increases. In this case, the algorithm is often trapped to the all-NULL solution, which is a significant local optimum. In comparison, the ALH solution is quite stable and consistent. The computational cost is illustrated in terms of the required number of iterations for convergence as a function of the noise level σ. The ALH has the same order of convergence rate as the MFA. The SA needs several order higher iterations than the deterministic algorithms.

4   Conclusion

The ability of the ALH to find better quality solutions than the penalty method of Hopfield networks while maintaining the convergence is due to the use of the augmented Lagrange technique. Basically, one is converting a combinatorial optimization to a constrained real optimization, and solving the constrained problem using an unconstrained real optimization method. In the penalty method, the objective for the unconstrained optimization is a weighted sum of the original objective function and other terms which penalize the violation of the constraints. To produce valid solutions, the relative weight for the original objective function must be kept relatively small in order to satisfy the constraints; therefore the solutions can deviate significantly from the true minimum of the original objective function, owing to large influence from the penalty terms of constraints.

With the use of Lagrange multipliers as in the augmented Lagrangian, the weighting values for the penalty terms can be much smaller than those required by the penalty method; thus the relative weight for the original objective is increased, which helps yielding a lower objective value. At the same time, the augmented Lagrange method also overcomes the zigzagging problem with the standard Lagrange method and improve the convergence. These advantages of the augmented Lagrangian plus the use of Hopfield method for imposing the inequality and unambiguity constraints have made the success of the ALH method. A recent result shows that the ALH method significantly improves the Hopfield type networks in solving the traveling salesman problem [12]. The ALH has also been used for image restoration and segmentation [11].

References

[1] K. J. Arrow, L. Hurwicz, and H. Uzawa. *Studies in Linear and Nonlinear Programming*. Stanford University Press, 1958.

[2] R. Durbin and D. Willshaw. "An analog approach to the travelling salesman problem using an elastic net method". *Nature*, 326:689–691, 1987.

[3] I. M. Elfadel and A. L. Yuille. "Mean-field phase transitions and correlation functions for gibbs random fields". *Journal of Mathematical Imaging and Vision*, 3:167–186, 1993.

[4] R. Fletcher. *Practical Methods of Optimization*. Wiley, 1987.

[5] S. Geman and D. Geman. "Stochastic relaxation, Gibbs distribution and the Bayesian restoration of images". *IEEE Transactions on Pattern Analysis and Machine Intelligence*, 6(6):721–741, November 1984.

[6] B. S. Gottfried. *Introduction to Optimization Theory*. Prentice-Hall, 1973.

[7] M. R. Hestenes. "Multipler and gradient methods". *Journal of Optimization Theory and Applications*, 4:303–320, 1969.

[8] J. J. Hopfield. "Neurons with graded response have collective computational properties like those of two state neurons". *Proceedings of National Academic Science, USA*, 81:3088–3092, 1984.

[9] J. J. Hopfield and D. W. Tank. " 'Neural' computation of decisions optimization problems". *Biological Cybernetics*, 52:141–152, 1985.

[10] S. Kirkpatrick, C. D. Gellatt, and M. P. Vecchi. "Optimization by simulated annealing". *Science*, 220:671–680, 1983.

[11] S. Z. Li. "A constrained optimization method for bayesian image restoration and segmentation". In *Proceedings of IEEE Computer Society Conference on Computer Vision and Pattern Recognition*, page to appear, San Francisco, CA, June 16-20 1996.

[12] S. Z. Li. "Improving convergence and solution quality of Hopfield-type neural network with augmented Lagrange multipliers". *IEEE Transactions on Neural Networks*, page accepted for publication, 1996.

[13] C. Peterson and B. Soderberg. "A new method for mapping optimization problems onto neural networks". *International Journal of Neural Systems*, 1(1):3–22, 1989.

[14] J. C. Platt and A. H. Barr. "Constrained differential optimization". In *Proceedings of the IEEE 1987 NIPS conference*, 1988.

[15] M. J. D. Powell. "A method of nonlinear constraints in minimization problems". In R. Fletcher, editor, *Optimization*, London, 1969. Academic Press.

[16] A. Rosenfeld, R. Hummel, and S. Zucker. "Scene labeling by relaxation operations". *IEEE Transactions on Systems, Man and Cybernetics*, 6:420–433, June 1976.

[17] P. D. Simic. "Statisrical mechanics as the underlying theory of 'elastic' and 'neural' optimization". *Network*, 1:89–103, 1990.

[18] M. W. Simmen. "Parameter sensitivity of the elastic net approach to the traveling salesman problem". *Neural Computation*, 3(3):363–374, 1991.

[19] E. Wacholder, J. Han, and R. C. Mann. "A neural network algorithm for the multiple traveling salesman problem". *Biological Cybernetics*, 61:11–19, 1989.

[20] G. V. Wilson and G. S. Pawley. "On the stability of the travelling salesman problem algorithm of Hopfield and Tank". *Biological Cybernetics*, 58:63–70, 1988.

[21] L. Xu. "Combinatorial optimization neural nets based on a hybrid of Lagrange and transformation approach". In *Proc. World Congress on Neural Networks, SanDiego*, volume II, pages 399–404, 1994.

[22] A. L. Yullie. "Generalized deformable models, statistical physics and matching problems". *Neural Computation*, 2:1–24, 1990.

Sweeping generalizations of continuous Hopfield and Hopfield-Lagrange networks

Jan van den Berg

Dept. of Computer Science, Faculty of Economics, Erasmus University Rotterdam
P.O. Box 1738, 3000 DR Rotterdam, The Netherlands
Email: berg@cs.few.eur.nl

Abstract— **A far-reaching generalization of the classical continuous Hopfield model is described where almost arbitrary cost functions can be chosen and where, at the same time, certain sets of constraints can directly be incorporated in the neural net. Next, the generalized Hopfield-Lagrange network is analyzed where constraints are (partly) tackled using Lagrange multipliers.**

1 Introduction

Since 1985, it is tried to apply neural networks, especially Hopfield and allied networks, in the field of combinatorial optimization. For an overview, we refer to [6, 1]. In many cases, the problem is, basically, to minimize a certain cost function where, at the same time, a given set of constraints should be fulfilled. Using a classical Hopfield model, the cost function is a quadratic expression in the output of the neurons. Besides, three ways can be distinguished to deal with the constraints. The first and eldest one is the penalty approach, where, usually, quadratic penalty functions are added to the original cost function. In practice, in turns out very difficult to find penalty weights that guarantee both valid and high quality solutions. In a second approach, constraints are directly incorporated in the neural network by choosing appropriate transfer functions in the neurons. Up till now, the applicability of this method is limited to independent, linear constraints. A third way to grapple with the constraints, is combining the neural network with the Lagrange multiplier method.

In this paper, we start generalizing the classical Hopfield model to the so-termed *most general framework of continuous Hopfield models* where both non-quadratic cost functions and constraints of all kind, can be incorporated in the neural network (more elaborated versions of this framework can be found in [1, 2]). Next, the general framework is combined with an approach using Lagrange multipliers yielding the so-termed *generalized Hopfield-Lagrange model*. A corresponding stability theorem is given and furthermore, the general effect of the application of quadratic constraints is discussed.

The 'most general framework' can be interpreted as a sweeping generalization of the original continuous Hopfield model [7] and of statistical mechanical interpretations of this model as has been discussed, e.g., in [6, 8, 9]. The 'Hopfield-Lagrange model' is a sweeping generalization of work that was pioneered in [10, 12]. Quite recently, we came across analyses [13, 14] which show certain similarities to the one presented here (and to the ones given in [1]). However, the precise relationships between all these analyses and still other ones (see, e.g., the references as mentioned in [14] and the references [5, 11] of this paper) are still subject of study.

2 A first generalization of continuous Hopfield networks

In 1984, Hopfield introduced his well-known continuous model [7] having energy

$$E_{\rm c}(V) \;=\; -\tfrac{1}{2}\sum_{i,j} w_{ij}V_iV_j - \sum_i I_iV_i + \sum_i \int_0^{V_i} g^{-1}(v)dv \tag{1}$$

$$=\; \underbrace{}_{E(V)} + \underbrace{}_{E_{\rm h}(V)} . \tag{2}$$

$E(V)$ is the quadratic cost function to be minimized, V_i represents the output value of neuron i, and $E_{\rm h}(V)$ is termed the Hopfield term. $E_{\rm h}$ has a statistical mechanical interpretation [6, 1, 4]. Its general effect is a displacement of the minima of $E(V)$ towards the interior of the state space depending on the value of the current temperature [1]. The motion equations corresponding to (1) are

$$\dot{U}_i = -\frac{\partial E_{\rm c}(V)}{\partial V_i} = \sum_j w_{ij}V_j + I_i - U_i, \tag{3}$$

---

[1] In case of choosing the sigmoid $V_i = 1/(1 + \exp{(\beta U_i)})$ as the transfer function, the part of temperature is acted by $T = 1/\beta$ and the Hopfield term can be written as $E_h(V) = \tfrac{1}{\beta}\sum_i (V_i \ln V_i + (1 - V_i)\ln(1 - V_i))$.

where continuously $V_i = g(U_i)$ should hold. U_i represents the input of neuron i. The following theorem [7] gives conditions for which an equilibrium state eventually will be reached:

Theorem 1 (Hopfield). *If (w_{ij}) is a symmetric matrix and if $\forall i : V_i = g(U_i)$ is a monotone increasing, differentiable function, then E_c is a Lyapunov function for motion equations* (3).

We now first generalize the model by admitting almost *arbitrary cost functions* $-H(V)$, where external inputs I_i are still allowed. At the same time, we transform $E_c(V)$ to $F_1(U, V)$, an expression in both the input and the output value of all neurons.

Theorem 2. *Let $H(V) = H(V_1, V_2, \ldots, V_n)$ be a function for which*

$$\forall i : \int_0^{V_i} h_i(V_1, V_2, \ldots, V_{i-1}, v, V_{i+1}, \ldots, V_n)\mathrm{d}v = H(V). \tag{4}$$

Then any stationary point of the energy function F_1 defined by

$$F_1(U, V) = -H(V) + \sum_i U_i V_i - \sum_i \int_0^{U_i} g(u)\mathrm{d}u \tag{5}$$

coincides with an equilibrium state of the continuous Hopfield neural network defined by

$$\forall i : V_i = g(U_i) \quad \wedge \quad U_i = h_i(V). \tag{6}$$

Proof. F_1 can be derived from (1) by partial integration of $E_h(V)$. Having $V_i = g(U_i)$, we can write

$$\sum_i \int_0^{V_i} g^{-1}(v)\mathrm{d}v = \sum_i \left[g^{-1}(v)v\right]_0^{V_i} - \sum_i \int_{g^{-1}(0)}^{U_i} v\mathrm{d}u = \sum_i U_i V_i - \sum_i \int_0^{U_i} g(u)\mathrm{d}u + c, \tag{7}$$

where $c = -\sum_i \int_{g^{-1}(0)}^0 g(u)\mathrm{d}u$ is an unimportant constant which may be neglected. Replacement of $E(V)$ by $-H(V)$ together with a substitution of (7) in (1) yields (5). Furthermore, by resolving

$$\forall i : \partial F_1/\partial U_i = 0 \ \wedge \ \partial F_1/\partial V_i = 0, \tag{8}$$

the set of equilibrium conditions (6) is found. Thus, the stationary points of F_1 indeed coincide with equilibrium states of the generalized network. $\qquad\square$

3 The most general framework of continuous Hopfield networks

We now generalize the transfer function $V = g(U_i)$ to $V_i = g_i(U) = g_i(U_1, U_2, \ldots, U_n)$. Thus, $g_i(U)$ is a function of *all inputs*. Choosing appropriate functions g_i, various types of constraints can directly be built-in in the neural network (an example is given below). By the generalizations of this and the previous section, the so-termed *most general framework* of continuous Hopfield networks has been created.

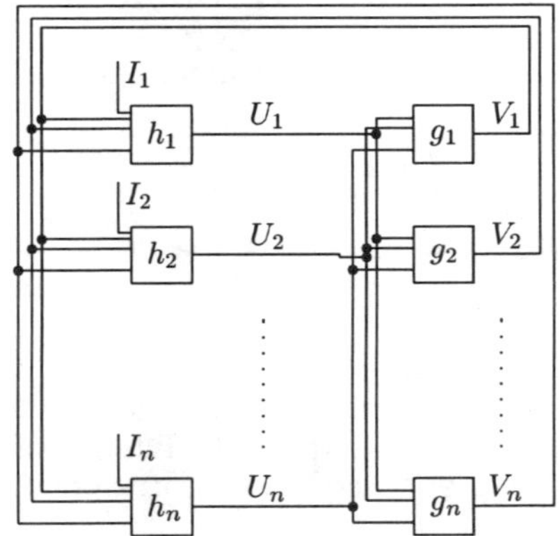

Figure 1: The most general continuous Hopfield network with equilibrium condition: $\forall i : U_i = h_i(V)$ and $V_i = g_i(U)$.

Theorem 3. *Let $G(U) = G(U_1, U_2, \ldots, U_n)$ be a function for which*

$$\forall i : \int_0^{U_i} g_i(U_1, U_2, \ldots, U_{i-1}, u, U_{i+1}, \ldots, U_n) \mathrm{d}u = G(U) \tag{9}$$

and let $H(V) = H(V_1, V_2, \ldots, V_n)$ be defined as in theorem 2, then any stationary point of

$$F_2(U, V) = -H(V) + \sum_i U_i V_i - G(U) \tag{10}$$

coincides with an equilibrium state of the most general continuous Hopfield neural network defined by

$$\forall i : V_i = g_i(U) \quad \wedge \quad U_i = h_i(V) \tag{11}$$

Proof. The set of equilibrium conditions (11) is found in the same way as the set (6) in the proof of the theorem 2. This demonstrates that the stationary points of F_2 indeed coincide with equilibrium states of the most general continuous Hopfield network. $\qquad\square$

Theorem 4. *Suppose that $F_2(U, V)$ is bounded below. Then the following statements hold:*
(a) If, during updating, the Jacobian matrix $J_g = (\partial V_i / \partial U_j)$ first is or becomes and then remains positive definite, then the energy function F_2 is a Lyapunov function for the motion equations

$$\dot{U}_i = h_i(V) - U_i, \text{ where } V_i = g_i(U). \tag{12}$$

(b) If, during updating, the Jacobian matrix $J_h = (\partial U_i / \partial V_j)$ first is or becomes and then remains positive definite, then the energy function F_2 is a Lyapunov function for the motion equations

$$\dot{V}_i = g_i(U) - V_i, \text{ where } U_i = h_i(V). \tag{13}$$

(c) If, during updating, the Jacobian matrices J_g and J_h first are or become and then remain positive definite, then the energy function F_2 is a Lyapunov function for the motion equations

$$\dot{U}_i = h_i(V) - U_i \quad \wedge \quad \dot{V}_i = g_i(U) - V_i. \tag{14}$$

Proof. Assuming that the conditions as mentioned in (c) hold, we obtain

$$\begin{aligned}
\dot{F}_2 &= \sum_i \frac{\partial F_2}{\partial V_i} \dot{V}_i + \sum_i \frac{\partial F_2}{\partial U_i} \dot{U}_i \\
&= \sum_i (-h_i(V) + U_i) \sum_j \frac{\partial V_i}{\partial U_j} \dot{U}_j + \sum_i (V_i - g_i(U)) \sum_j \frac{\partial U_i}{\partial V_j} \dot{V}_j \\
&= -\sum_i \dot{U}_i \sum_j \frac{\partial V_i}{\partial U_j} \dot{U}_j - \sum_i \dot{V}_i \sum_j \frac{\partial U_i}{\partial V_j} \dot{V}_j = -\dot{U}^T J_g \dot{U} - \dot{V}^T J_h \dot{V} \le 0.
\end{aligned} \tag{15}$$

Then, the boundedness of F_2 is sufficient to guarantee stability where at equilibrium $\forall i : \dot{U}_i = \dot{V}_i = 0$ implying the general equilibrium condition

$$\forall i : U_i = h_i(V) \quad \wedge \quad V_i = g_i(U). \tag{16}$$

Using (15), the proofs of (a) and (b) can be done in a similar, straightforward way. $\qquad\square$

From the above given theorem it should be clear that there exist various ways in configuring Hopfield models: one can choose between various updating rules and between various sets of transfer functions (where each set implements a certain group of built-in constraints). Moreover, it is clear that the conditions of the various updating rules guaranteeing stability, differ substantially. In case (a) of theorem 4, stability depends on the transfer functions $g_i(U)$ chosen, while in case (b), it depends on the $h_i(V)$'s and thus, on the concrete cost function $-H(V)$ at hand.

Next to the classical model, a continuous Hopfield network coinciding with a mean field approximation of a stochastic Potts glasses model [9, 1], appears to fit in the most general framework introduced. In both cases, it is possible to derive [1] an explicit expression for $G(U)$ being respectively

$$G^{\mathrm{class}}(U) = \tfrac{1}{\beta} \sum_i \ln(1 + \exp(\beta U_i)) \qquad \text{and} \qquad G^{\mathrm{potts}}(U) = \tfrac{1}{\beta} \ln(\sum_i \exp(\beta U_i)). \tag{17}$$

The corresponding transfer functions equal

$$V_i^{\text{class}} = \frac{1}{1 + \exp(\beta U_i)} \quad \text{and} \quad V_i^{\text{potts}} = \frac{\exp(\beta U_i)}{\sum_l \exp(\beta U_l)}. \tag{18}$$

It is clear that the last type of transfer functions implement the constraint $\sum_i V_i - 1 = 0$. Similarly, 'higher order neural networks' as applied in [5] and [11] in order to solve certain combinatorial optimization problems, are examples of models which suit the general framework. On the other hand, it is relevant to observe that some experimental results using new transfer functions of type $g_i(U)$, show certain restrictions [1, 2]. The difficulties encountered are related to the *statistical mechanical* question whether the concrete continuous network at hand can indeed be considered a mean field approximation of a corresponding stochastic Hopfield network. If so, the energy F_2 approximates the cost function $-H(V)$ on lowering the temperature and so-called mean field annealing (a deterministic approximation of simulated annealing [8, 6]) can be applied. Unfortunately, certain transfer functions appear to destroy this statistical mechanical interpretation. The phenomenon begs for further research efforts.

4   The generalized Hopfield-Lagrange model

Instead of applying penalty terms or trying to directly incorporate the constraints of a given constrained optimization problem in the neural network, they can also be tackled using the well-known technique of Lagrange multipliers. The original Hopfield-Lagrange model [12, 1, 3] is based on this approach where, unlike the U_i's, the value of every multiplier is calculated applying a gradient *ascent* to the corresponding Lagrangian function L. The essential point of the method is the fact that the global stationary points of L coincide with the constrained extrema of the given problem.

Here, we analyze a sweeping generalization of the original Hopfield-Lagrange model. Using this model, part of the constraints can be built-in directly (in the way described in the previous section) and part can be tackled using multipliers. The set of the constraints $C_\alpha = 0$ $(\alpha = 1, \ldots, m)$ is assumed to belong to the last part. Starting point of the analysis is equation (10) extended with multiplier terms. This yields the Lagrangian function

$$L(U, V, \lambda) = -H(V) + \sum_\alpha \lambda_\alpha C_\alpha(V) + \sum_i U_i V_i - G(U). \tag{19}$$

Its stationary points can be calculated by means of the differential equations

$$\dot{U}_i = -\frac{\partial L}{\partial V_i} = \frac{\partial H}{\partial V_i} - \sum_\alpha \lambda_\alpha \frac{\partial C_\alpha}{\partial V_i} - U_i, \tag{20}$$

$$\dot{\lambda}_\alpha = +\frac{\partial L}{\partial \lambda_\alpha} = C_\alpha(V), \tag{21}$$

where $V_i = g_i(U)$. Note that $\forall i : V_i = g_i(U)$ implies that $\forall i : \partial L/\partial U_i = 0$.

Theorem 5. *If the matrix (d_{ij}) defined by*

$$d_{ij} = \sum_k c_{ik} \frac{\partial V_k}{\partial U_j} + \delta_{ij}, \quad where \quad c_{ik} = -\frac{\partial^2 H}{\partial V_i \partial V_k} + \sum_\alpha \lambda_\alpha \frac{\partial^2 C_\alpha}{\partial V_i \partial V_k}, \tag{22}$$

first is or becomes and then remains positive definite, then the energy function[2]

$$E_{\text{kin+pot}} = \sum_i \tfrac{1}{2}\dot{U}_i^2 + \sum_{i,\alpha} \int_0^{U_i} C_\alpha \frac{\partial C_\alpha}{\partial V_i} \, du \tag{23}$$

is a Lyapunov function for the set of motion equations (20) and (21).

Proof. As was pioneered in an analysis of a much simpler model [10] and, next, was pushed on to a certain extent [3], so we join the equations (20) and (21) yielding

$$\ddot{U}_i = -\sum_j c_{ij} \sum_k \frac{\partial V_j}{\partial U_k} \dot{U}_k - \dot{U}_i - \sum_\alpha C_\alpha \frac{\partial C_\alpha}{\partial V_i}. \tag{24}$$

---

[2]Physically, this function represents the sum of kinetic and potential energy of a damped oscillating mass-spring system.

Using this result and taking the time derivative of (23), we obtain

$$
\begin{aligned}
\dot{E}_{\text{kin+pot}} &= \sum_i \dot{U}_i \ddot{U}_i + \sum_{i,\alpha} C_\alpha \frac{\partial C_\alpha}{\partial V_i} \dot{U}_i \\
&= \sum_i \dot{U}_i \left(-\sum_j c_{ij} \sum_k \frac{\partial V_j}{\partial U_k} \dot{U}_k - \dot{U}_i - \sum_\alpha C_\alpha \frac{\partial C_\alpha}{\partial V_i} \right) + \sum_{i,\alpha} C_\alpha \frac{\partial C_\alpha}{\partial V_i} \dot{U}_i \\
&= -\sum_{i,j} \dot{U}_i \sum_k c_{ik} \frac{\partial V_k}{\partial U_j} \dot{U}_j - \sum_i \dot{U}_i^2 = -\sum_{i,j} \dot{U}_i d_{ij} \dot{U}_j \le 0.
\end{aligned}
\tag{25}
$$

Provided $E_{\text{kin+pot}}$ is bounded below (which is expected to hold in view of its definition), its value constantly decreases until finally $\forall i : \dot{U}_i = 0$. From (20) we see that this normally implies that $\forall \alpha : \dot{\lambda}_\alpha = 0$. So, the set of differential equations (20), (21) is convergent. □

It also follows from (20), (21), and $\forall i : V_i = g_i(U)$ that all partial derivatives of $L(U, V, \lambda)$ are zero in the end, meaning that a stationary point of L has been reached and thus a constrained equilibrium state of the neural network.

Inspection of the derivation reveals why the gradient ascent is needed in (21): only if this 'sign flip' is applied the two terms $\sum_i \dot{U}_i \sum_\alpha C_\alpha \partial C_\alpha / \partial V_i$ cancel each other. In order to prove stability in practice, we can try to analyze the complicated matrix (d_{ij}) which in full equals

$$
d_{ij} = \sum_k \left(-\frac{\partial^2 H}{\partial V_i \partial V_k} + \sum_\alpha \lambda_\alpha \frac{\partial^2 C_\alpha}{\partial V_i \partial V_k} \right) \frac{\partial V_k}{\partial U_j} + \delta_{ij}.
\tag{26}
$$

If we confine ourselves to constraints C_α which are linear functions in V, equation (26) reduces to

$$
d_{ij} = -\sum_k \frac{\partial^2 H}{\partial V_i \partial V_k} \frac{\partial V_k}{\partial U_j} + \delta_{ij}.
\tag{27}
$$

If the δ_{ij}-terms dominate, then (d_{ij}) is positive definite and stability is sure. However, it seems impossible to formulate general conditions which guarantee stability since the matrix elements d_{ij} are a function of the derivatives $\partial V_k / \partial U_j$ and thus change dynamically during the update of the differential equations. We should therefore often rely on experimental results.

Alternatively, we can apply *quadratic* constraints having the form

$$
C_\alpha(V) = \tfrac{1}{2} (\sum_{i_\alpha} V_{i_\alpha} - n_\alpha)^2 = 0, \quad \alpha = 1 \cdots m,
\tag{28}
$$

where every n_α equals some constant. Commonly, the constraints relate to only a subset of all V_i. That is why we use the subscript i_α. Using this type of constraints, stability of the Hopfield-Lagrange model can generally be guaranteed [1]. The idea is roughly the following. Suppose that all constraints are tackled by means of quadratic constraints of the given type and suppose too that, in case of fulfillment of these constraints, the differential equations (20) are stable[3]. This implies that instability can only be caused by the non-fulfillment of constraints. From equations (21) and (28) we conclude that – as long as a constraint is not fulfilled – the corresponding multiplier λ_α increases and that, if this situation endures, the multiplier will eventually become positive. By this process, parabolic 'troughs' are created in the energy landscape of L, the minima of which correspond to feasible (i.e., legal) solutions. Eventually, the quadratic terms will dominate and the system will settle down in approximately one of the created (combinations of) troughs. There, as was assumed, the system is stable.

Actually, the quadratic terms $\lambda_\alpha C_\alpha(V)$ go and behave like penalty terms. By the growth of the multiplier values, the weights of these terms increase dynamically. That is why we say that in case of using the quadratic constraints (28), the Hopfield-Lagrange model degenerates to a *dynamic penalty model*.

Finishing this section, we note that the Hopfield-Lagrange model has already proven to be (more and less) successful in applications in the field of combinatorial optimization [10, 1, 3, 12]. The precise results of simulations concerning problems like the 'weighted matching', the 'n-rook' and 'the travelling salesman problem' using merely multipliers as well as using multipliers in combination with the approach of building-in constraints, can be found in [1], some of which results are also reported in [3].

---

[3]Since fulfillment of the quadratic constraints implies that differential equation (20) reduces to equation (3) or, more generally, to equation (12), stability in constrained states can simply be forced by choosing appropriate transfer functions conform the conditions of the corresponding theorems in section 1 and 2.

5   Discussion and outlook

We have introduced the most general framework of continuous Hopfield networks where in principle, both an arbitrary cost function $H(V) = H(V_1, \ldots, V_n)$ and at the same time, arbitrary transfer functions $V_i = g(U) = g(U_1, \ldots, U_n)$ can be chosen. To use the model in practice, certain limitations should be taken into account. The first one relates to the stability of the used set of differential equations, of which several relevant theorems have been given. The second one refers to the behavior of the model as function of the temperature parameter: the transfer function of the neurons should be chosen in such a way that the usual statistical mechanical interpretation is maintained! Although the framework has already proven to possess certain promising qualifications (the results of which we have quoted in the text), the complete capabilities of the framework are not yet clear. More theoretical and practical work is needed to get a full understanding of this.

Furthermore, we have given an analysis of the stability properties of the generalized Hopfield-Lagrange model, where again an arbitrary cost function can be chosen and where, this time, the constraints are (partly) tackled using multipliers. The corresponding theorem yields a matrix which, in case of first becoming and then remaining positive definite, guarantees stability of the model. In practice, the analysis of this dynamic matrix may be tough. Alternatively, one can apply quadratic constraints. Then, stability can generally be guaranteed. Also the Hopfield-Lagrange model has proven to possess promising capabilities, but again their full range is not completely clear yet.

References

[1] J. van den Berg. Neural Relaxation Dynamics, Mathematics and Physics of Recurrent Neural Networks with Applications in the Field of Combinatorial Optimization. *PhD thesis*, Erasmus University Rotterdam, 1996.

[2] J. van den Berg. The most general framework of continuous Hopfield neural networks. To appear in: *Proceedings of the 1966 International Workshop on Neural Networks for Identification, Control, Robotics, and Signal/Image Processing*, NICROSP'96, Venice, IEEE Computer Society Press, 1996.

[3] J. van den Berg and J.C. Bioch. Constrained Optimization with the Hopfield-Lagrange Model. *Proceedings of the 14th IMACS World Congress*, 470–473, Atlanta, GA 30332 USA, 1994.

[4] J. van den Berg and J.C. Bioch. On the (Free) Energy of Hopfield Networks. In *Neural Networks: The Statistical Mechanics Perspective*, Proceedings of the CTP-PBSRI Joint Workshop on Theoretical Physics, eds. J.H. Oh, C. Kwon, S. Cho, 233–244, World Scientific, Singapore, 1995.

[5] B.S. Cooper. Higher Order Neural Networks for Combinatorial Optimisation - Improving the Scaling Properties of the Hopfield Network. *Proceedings of the IEEE International Conference on Neural Networks*, 1855–1860, Perth, Western Australia, 1995.

[6] J. Hertz, A. Krogh, and R.G. Palmer. *Introduction to the Theory of Neural Computation*. Addison-Wesley, 1991.

[7] J.J. Hopfield. Neurons with Graded Responses Have Collective Computational Properties Like Those of Two-State Neurons. *Proceedings of the National Academy of Sciences, USA*, 81, 3088–3092, 1984.

[8] C. Peterson and J.R. Anderson. A Mean Field Theory Learning Algorithm for Neural Networks. *Complex Systems* 1, 995–1019, 1987.

[9] C. Peterson and B. Söderberg. A New Method for Mapping Optimization Problems onto Neural Networks. *International Journal of Neural Systems* 1, 3–22, 1989.

[10] J.C. Platt and A.H. Barr. Constrained Differential Optimization. *Proceedings of the IEEE 1987 NIPS Conference*, 612–621, 1988.

[11] J. Starke, N. Kubota, and T. Fukuda. Combinatorial Optimization with Higher Order Neural Networks - Cost Oriented Competing Processes in Flexible Manufactoring Systems, *Proceedings of the IEEE International Conference on Neural Networks*. 1855–1860, Perth, Western Australia, 1995.

[12] E. Wacholder, J. Han, and R.C. Mann. A Neural Network Algorithm for the Traveling Salesman Problem. *Biological Cybernetics* 61, 11–19, 1989.

[13] L. Xu. Combinatorial Optimization Neural Nets Based on A Hybrid of Lagrange and Transformation Approaches. *Proceedings of the 1994 World Congress on Neural Networks* (WCNN'94), 2, 399–404, San Diego, 1994.

[14] L. Xu. On The Hybrid LT Combinatorial Optimization: New U-Shape Barrier, Sigmoid Activation, Least Leaking Energy and Maximum Entropy. *Proceedings of the 1995 International Conference on Neural Information Processing* (ICONIP'95), 1, 309–312, Beijing, 1995.